HANDBOOK OF

EUROPEAN FINANCIAL MARKETS AND INSTITUTIONS

HANDBOOK OF

EUROPEAN FINANCIAL MARKETS AND INSTITUTIONS

Edited by

XAVIER FREIXAS

PHILIPP HARTMANN

and

COLIN MAYER

OXFORD
UNIVERSITY PRESS

OXFORD
UNIVERSITY PRESS

Great Clarendon Street, Oxford OX2 6DP

Oxford University Press is a department of the University of Oxford.
It furthers the University's objective of excellence in research, scholarship,
and education by publishing worldwide in

Oxford New York

Auckland Cape Town Dar es Salaam Hong Kong Karachi
Kuala Lumpur Madrid Melbourne Mexico City Nairobi
New Delhi Shanghai Taipei Toronto

With offices in

Argentina Austria Brazil Chile Czech Republic France Greece
Guatemala Hungary Italy Japan Poland Portugal Singapore
South Korea Switzerland Thailand Turkey Ukraine Vietnam

Oxford is a registered trade mark of Oxford University Press
in the UK and in certain other countries

Published in the United States
by Oxford University Press Inc., New York

© Oxford University Press 2008

The moral rights of the authors have been asserted
Database right Oxford University Press (maker)

First published 2008

British Library Cataloguing in Publication Data
Data available

Library of Congress Cataloging in Publication Data
Data available

Typeset by SPI Publisher Services, Pondicherry, India
Printed in Great Britain
on acid-free paper by
Antony Rowe Ltd., Chippenham, Wiltshire

ISBN 978–0–19–922995–6

1 3 5 7 9 10 8 6 4 2

FOREWORD

This is a timely and eminently useful collection of articles on the broad topic of financial integration in Europe, which I warmly recommend for careful reading.

It is timely because there is good news and bad news in this field. The good news is that I perceive a growing consensus among economists that, beyond the well-known influence of demographic developments (and of the apparent reluctance of most Europeans to spend more time working), the responsibility for the dismal rate of growth of Europe's potential output lies in the inadequate productivity increases of labour and capital. This is genuinely worrying because the impact of demography will intensify as time goes by. To offset this impact, we shall have to rely more and more on productivity increases. But the consensus goes even a step further. To raise the rate of increase in total factor productivity, Europe should take major steps towards the deregulation of the services industry in general and promote, specifically, the emergence of a well-integrated, liquid, competitive, and innovative financial services industry. This seems to be the lesson we can draw from the US experience: the acceleration of productivity growth in the mid-1990s followed the large-scale deregulation moves of the 1980s. Until this acceleration the rate of growth of productivity had been, to say the least, mediocre.

The bad news is that not much is happening—this is an understatement—in the field of productivity, and progress towards financial integration, while not nil, is far too slow. I shall not dwell on the first topic: the distressing saga of the 'Bolkestein directive' for the internal market on services speaks for itself. But let me make more explicit my second point, by listing three concerns I have.

The first is obviously close to my heart. The four-level approach to the Europe-wide regulatory process has achieved some success. The process has become transparent, and nobody complains about the inadequate consultation of stakeholders. There is also far less grumbling about the poor quality of directives. Most important, the Financial Services Action Plan has been completed, in the sense that the core legislative framework (level 1) is in place and the directives on implementation 'technicalities' (level 2) are well advanced. Finally, the monitoring exercise, to which we attached great importance, has yielded good reports. So far so good; but I am beginning to hear complaints that the process of national transposition (level 3) has in some cases run into trouble. The reasons for this are not yet quite clear (at least not for me). They may have to do with the fact that the national supervisory authorities are far from being a homogeneous lot: their powers vary, and so does their degree of independence from political interference. In my less optimistic moments I also suspect the reappearance of protectionist instincts: they did not prevail at levels 1 and 2, but now, when it comes to implementation at the national level, they try to have the upper hand.

This suspicion is confirmed—and this is my second observation—by a growing number of reports on governments' or national regulators' opposition to cross-border takeovers. In some cases the opposition concerned initiatives taken by non-European corporations—and the argument then was that we needed to nurture European 'champions'. But in many others it has been directed against corporations with headquarters in other EU countries; so the argument has been adapted (if there has been any clear argument at all) by insisting on the need to foster national 'champions'. Several methods have been used to prevent such takeovers: unashamed political pressure on national regulators unwilling to play a protectionist game; arbitrary interpretation of the takeover directive; or even a legislative initiative to amend, with retroactive effect, the national transposition of the directive. Admittedly, not everything is going wrong in this area so crucial for integration. One major— admittedly non-hostile—takeover initiated by a bank located in one large country has not run into opposition by the authorities of another large country. At the same time, the resignation of the head of a national regulatory authority (who had acquired the well-deserved reputation of wanting to protect his banks against foreign takeovers) has been followed by a clear change of attitude of the authority itself. So the jury is still out on the question of whether we are just watching rearguard actions which are doomed to fail with the multiplication of hostile cross-border takeovers, or whether there is a broadly based renaissance of national protectionism.

My third observation concerns the current state of financial integration within the EU. The picture is uneven. By any conceivable measure of integration, the unsecured interbank market has become unquestionably integrated. By most measures, the euro-denominated government debt market can be regarded as having achieved a high degree of integration. Note that these two markets play a major role in the implementation of the single monetary policy, and could also become crucial in ensuring the efficiency of crisis prevention emergency actions. So this is a 'good thing'. There has also been progress, but far less, towards integration in the euro-denominated corporate debt market. But at the other end of the spectrum, integration has barely advanced: in equity markets—partly (but surely not exclusively) because of the sorry state of the post-trading infrastructure—and, most important, in retail banking. And the first of this is—together with start-up financing, venture capital, private equity, and the re-emergence of 'new' stock markets—a privileged vehicle through which Europe can meet the challenge of raising the rate of growth of both labour and capital.

Alexandre Lamfalussy

PREFACE

....

In 2004, the ECB-CFS research network on 'Capital markets and financial integration in Europe' and the *Oxford Review of Economic Policy* joined forces to publish an issue on European Financial Integration (see www.eu-financial-system.org for more information). It contained a series of articles on European policy towards financial integration. The journal issue and the conferences of the network received a lot of attention from policy makers, market participants, and academics. It was clear that there was a need for further serious analysis of financial integration and the development of capital markets to evaluate the principal components of financial systems and to address the policy questions raised in the *Oxford Review* issue and network conferences. This volume attempts to meet that need.

We approached leading academics, market participants, and policy makers throughout the world to contribute to this issue. The purpose was to provide only limited guidance constraining the nature of the studies to a particular format and to allow each of the authors to focus on what they regarded as the most important aspects of the topic on which they were writing. We have attempted to provide as comprehensive a coverage of the financial system as possible though no doubt there will be some areas that could not be fully included.

We are very grateful for the enthusiasm and care with which authors have participated in this project. We believe that the result is a unique analysis of a financial system that sheds important insights on the workings of financial markets, institutions, and regulators. We hope that it will be a significant contribution to the debate on the European financial system, integration, and global capital markets more generally.

We would like to thank Otmar Issing, Lucas Papademos, and Gertrude Tumpel-Gugerell from the ECB Executive Board, Jan-Pieter Krahnen from the Center for Financial Studies, as well as Sarah Caro and Andrew Schuller from Oxford University Press for their support of this project. They have provided much encouragement and advice. Any views expressed should not be associated with the ECB or any other institution with which the editors or authors are affiliated. Finally, we are grateful to Alison Gomm and Sabine Wiedemann for their editorial assistance.

X.F.
P.H.
C.M.

23 December 2006

PREFACE

Contents

PART I FINANCIAL SYSTEMS AND ECONOMIC PERFORMANCE

PART II FINANCIAL SYSTEMS AND THE CORPORATE SECTOR

PART III FINANCIAL INSTITUTIONS

PART IV FINANCIAL MARKETS

PART V FINANCIAL REGULATION AND MACROECONOMIC POLICY

LIST OF FIGURES

List of Tables

List of Contributors

Kpate Adjaouté, HSBC Private Bank (Suisse) SA

Philippe Aghion, Harvard University

Franklin Allen, The Wharton School of Business, University of Pennsylvania

Ronald W. Anderson, London School of Economics

Lieven Baele, Tilburg University

John Berrigan, European Commission

Ulrich Bindseil, European Central Bank

Mike Burkart, Stockholm School of Economics

Michael K. F. Chui, Bank for International Settlements

Luis Correia da Silva, Oxera

Jean-Pierre Danthine, University of Lausanne

E. Philip Davis, Brunel University

François Degeorge, Swiss Institute, University of Lugano

Hans Degryse, Katholieke Universiteit Leuven and Tilburg University

Annalisa Ferrando, European Central Bank

Maciej Firla-Cuchra, Oxera

Julian Franks, London Business School

Xavier Freixas, Universitat Pompeu Fabra

Thomas P. Gehrig, Universität Freiburg

Alberto Giovannini, UNIFORTUNE Asset Management

Charles Goodhart, Financial Markets Group, London School of Economics

Philipp Hartmann, European Central Bank

Florian Heider, European Central Bank

Boris Hofmann, Deutsche Bundesbank

Cornelia Holthausen, European Central Bank

Peter Hördahl, Bank for International Settlements

Tim Jenkinson, Saïd Business School, Oxford University

Sebnem Kalemli-Ozcan, University of Houston

Elizaveta Krylova, European Central Bank

Marco Lo Duca, European Central Bank

Kenneth McKay, London School of Economics

Angela Maddaloni, European Central Bank

Ernst Maug, Universität Mannheim

Colin Mayer, Saïd Business School, Oxford University

Cyril Monnet, European Central Bank

Kjell G. Nyborg, Norwegian School of Economics and Business Administration

Steven Ongena, Tilburg University

Marco Pagano, Università di Napoli Federico II

Fausto Panunzi, University of Bologna

Elias Papaioannou, Dartmouth College

Ray Rees, Universität München

Ailsa Röell, Columbia University

Daniela Russo, European Central Bank

Miguel Segoviano, International Monetary Fund

Bent Sørensen, University of Houston

Bernhard Speyer, Deutsche Bank

Oren Sussman, Saïd Business School, Oxford University

Kostas Tsatsaronis, Bank for International Settlements

Natacha Valla, Banque de France

Ernst-Ludwig von Thadden, Universität Mannheim

Andreas Worms, Deutsche Bundesbank

INTRODUCTION

XAVIER FREIXAS
PHILIPP HARTMANN
COLIN MAYER

This book brings together leading economists and financial experts from around the world to provide a European perspective on developments in financial markets and institutions. Since Walter Bagehot and Joseph Schumpeter, it has been well known that financial systems are critical for economic productivity, growth, and welfare. Europe is a particularly interesting continent to analyse because of its size and importance in the world economy, the recent introduction of the euro—already today one of the world's two key currencies—the historically high degree of fragmentation and diversity of its financial systems, and the pace of integration that has been recently pursued. Last but not least, the long period of slow growth in many European countries raises the issue of how financial sector policies can contribute to the structural reforms necessary to improve Europe's competitiveness and enhance its economic performance in an increasingly global marketplace.

The present volume addresses these issues in detail, covering all the principal components of the financial system and their relationship to the economy at large. In this introductory chapter, we provide a comprehensive overview of the state of the European financial system and of the most important developments in it, including the processes of financial integration and financial development. In particular, we summarize the main findings of the twenty-eight chapters of this book and outline the principal conclusions for economic policy and financial sector reform. In the first two sections we sketch the context to European financial sector reforms and argue that financial economics is a particularly valuable approach for assessing the functioning of capital markets and answering pressing policy questions.

Section 3 provides an overview of the five parts of the book and summarizes each chapter in a few paragraphs. The last section describes lessons for policy. These summarize a selection of the most important policy conclusions of the authors of the chapters and do not necessarily reflect the views of the editors of this volume.

1. POLICY CONTEXT

Financial integration has risen to the top of the European policy agenda. In 1998, the European Commission proposed a Financial Services Action Plan (FSAP) to establish deep and liquid capital markets in Europe and to broaden consumer choice. In 2000, the Lisbon European Council set 2005 as the date by which the Action Plan should be fully implemented. In 2002, the European Central Bank (ECB) set up a research network on 'Capital markets and financial integration in Europe', in collaboration with the Centre for Financial Studies (CFS) in Frankfurt, to improve understanding of the structure and integration of the European financial system (ECB and CFS 2004). In 2005 the European Commission issued a White Paper on 'Financial sector policies (2005–2010)', defining the policy agenda following the FSAP. A year later the Eurosystem proposed sweeping changes to how securities are settled across borders in the euro area and beyond by announcing the development of a public platform—TARGET 2 Securities (Tumpel-Gugerell 2006). The year 2007 sees the introduction of the Markets in Financial Instruments Directive (MiFID), a key piece of legislation for European securities markets.

Integration of financial markets lies at the heart of the FSAP. It is designed to remove the regulatory and market barriers that exist to the cross-border provision of financial services and to encourage the free flow of finance within Europe. The drive for financial integration comes from a belief that financial markets in Europe are too small and fragmented. The introduction of the euro has unquestionably been a major spur to the integration of markets but a series of microeconomic policies relating to market structures, national regulation, and governance arrangements is also required.

Despite the importance that policy makers have attached to financial integration and significant progress in a number of important areas, Alexandre Lamfalussy reckons that in many respects progress is far too slow—and this assessment is shared by many experts in the field. Regulations have been changed, legislatures have enshrined new laws, but resistance to integration remains, leading inter alia to diverse implementation and enforcement at the national level. In the foreword to this volume, Lamfalussy uses the case of cross-border takeovers to illustrate his point that national governments remain inherently resistant to the consequences of integration.

In addition to the important objective of completing financial integration, it is also time to widen the perspective to capture all aspects of the evolution of the European financial system. This has been argued in a contribution by ECB staff to the Helsinki Informal Ecofin meeting of 8–9 September 2006, which is reprinted in this volume as Chapter 4 of Part I. In particular, financial development or modernization may be an even more important process for enhancing the contribution of the financial system to economic welfare. A broad perspective on financial sector reforms that incorporates financial modernization opens up entirely new avenues for European financial policies that can promote productivity and growth.[1] Too narrow a focus on financial integration alone could easily miss some important aspects of European financial system reform.

Sustainable growth is by no means the only goal to which financial policies can contribute. Other goals are price stability, as targeted by monetary policy, and financial stability. The ECB and other central banks increasingly recognize how financial sector developments influence their policies and vice versa. Papademos (2006) illustrates this for monetary policy and financial stability policies, the latter also involving supervisory authorities. For example, various crisis simulation exercises took place in Europe recently, involving not only supervisory authorities and central banks but also national Treasuries. In this context, difficult issues such as the sharing of the burdens of international financial crises in Europe have started to be addressed.

2. IMPORTANCE OF FINANCIAL ECONOMICS

Against this background, the purpose of this book is to use the latest tools of finance and extensive data to analyse the functioning of developed financial systems, notably financial markets and institutions, and how they interact with the macroeconomy. There have been remarkable advances in the economic analysis of financial markets over the last few decades that have greatly strengthened the ability of financial economists to address policy issues and concerns of market participants. This book demonstrates the important contribution that economists armed with the tools of finance can make. In so doing it also illustrates why finance becomes ever more important in policy authorities, be it national Treasuries, central banks, international organizations, or other bodies, and in the internal work of financial and non-financial corporations.

---

[1] While financial integration refers to a process that consolidates previously separate or fragmented geographical markets, financial modernization can be regarded as a process of financial innovation, strengthening institutions and organizational improvements of a financial system that reduce asymmetric information, increase the completeness of markets, extend financial contracts, reduce transaction costs, or increase competition.

Much of the research that has been performed to date has come from a US perspective. While there has been a significant growth in financial economics in Europe, it remains overwhelmingly a North American subject. That means that North American financial markets have received vastly more attention than their European equivalents. This book attempts to redress that balance and to encourage economists on both sides of the Atlantic to consider the issues that face policy makers and practitioners in Europe. Arguably, the returns to be reaped from sound financial analysis and its use in policies and market practices are greater in the European region than in the more 'mature' US environment. This is underlined by the disappointing growth performance of many Western European countries until recently.

As financial markets have become increasingly globalized, it is important that the study of European markets is placed in a world context and many chapters in this book do exactly that. In particular there are frequent references to comparisons and links with other developed financial systems such as the USA.

Two reasons why financial economics has been such a successful discipline are that it has a sound underlying theoretical framework and it is informed by empirical analysis frequently based on large data sets. Relevant theory is based on the principles of efficient capital markets and the pricing of securities according to fundamental theories of valuation. While few people today hold religiously to efficient markets and most recognize the significant deviations from its predictions, it nevertheless provides an important benchmark against which to consider violations. Many of the chapters in this book therefore examine European capital markets from the perspective of the various models of market inefficiencies that derive from imperfect information, incomplete markets, and transaction costs. These are particularly relevant to the study of corporate finance and the way in which financial institutions and financial markets interact with the corporate sector.

3. Summaries of the Contributions

The book is divided into five parts. Part I introduces the basic role and functioning of financial systems, in particular when they are already relatively developed. Part II focuses on how non-financial firms interact with financial systems in Europe. Part III addresses the behaviour of the main financial institutions in Europe. The functioning of the most important financial markets in Europe is reviewed in Part IV. Part V discusses regulatory issues and how monetary policy interacts with financial systems.

3.1. Financial Systems and Economic Performance

The book begins in Part I by considering macroeconomic aspects of finance, in particular how the functioning of financial markets and institutions influences economic performance. It examines the structure of financial systems in different countries around the globe, how financial development stimulates economic growth, how financial integration can be measured in various markets, and how it affects economic welfare. From a policy perspective two chapters try to answer which financial sector reforms could be most effective in stimulating financial development and in which markets further integration would be desirable in Europe.

There are pronounced differences across countries in the structure of their financial systems. Conventionally, these are categorized into market- and bank-oriented financial systems. Bank-oriented systems are supposed to have large and influential banks that provide a substantial proportion of corporate finance while market-oriented systems are dominated by their public equity and bond markets. Germany and Japan are frequently upheld as the classic examples of bank-based systems, while the UK and USA are the most prominent market-oriented systems.

Franklin Allen, Michael Chui, and Angela Maddaloni argue that this conventional distinction is misleading and not borne out by the data. For example, the UK has a large stock market and bank loans but a small bond market while the euro area has a small stock market and large bank loans but also has a large bond market. Allen, Chui, and Maddaloni argue that the different structures of financial systems may have important implications for their stability and in particular for the operation of their housing and mortgage markets and for corporate governance. They also show that institutional investors differ in important ways across the regions considered. One recent change is that central banks, particularly those in Asia, have become significant institutional investors.

The strand of empirical research relating economic growth to financial development, starting with King and Levine (1993) and Rajan and Zingales (1998), has been one of the major advances of financial economics over the past decade. The finding that better functioning financial systems enhance growth has been shown to be robust to many alternative methodologies. It holds for different levels of aggregation (cross-country, industry-level, and country-specific studies), different ways of controlling for simultaneity bias, different measures of growth (for example total factor productivity versus input growth), and a number of measures capturing different aspects of financial system development. Elias Papaioannou's contribution carefully surveys this literature.

He places particular importance on results that apply to industrial countries and are therefore most relevant for Europe. For example, he surveys finance and growth studies using large cross-country panels and controlling for different forms of economic and institutional development. Perhaps most applicable are a few country case studies analysing the effects of banking reforms in France, Italy, and the United States. While the finance and growth literature is concerned with financial development and hardly addresses financial integration, the case studies on the deregulation of geographical bank branching restrictions also illustrate the benefits of integration.

In his chapter, Philippe Aghion presents a novel approach to the finance and growth literature that considers the joint effects of financial and technological development, on the one hand, and financial development and macroeconomic volatility, on the other. The analysis of the interaction between financial and technological development points to a key effect of financial development in the process of international growth convergence: the probability that a country will converge to the frontier growth rate increases with its level of financial development. The joint effects of financial development and macroeconomic volatility indicate that the impact of business cycle fluctuations will be much stronger for lower levels of financial development, as in a recession lower levels of current earnings and lower ability to borrow may force firms to cut down on their R&D investment.

This is related to the Schumpeterian view of economic development. Recessions cleanse economies of inefficient organizations and encourage the redeployment of resources to more productive activities. Aghion's contribution is to point out that 'credit market imperfections may prevent firms from innovating and reorganizing in recessions'. Macroeconomic volatility therefore tends to be more harmful to growth in countries with lower levels of financial development. He also suggests that one of the consequences of this is that countercyclical public sector budget deficits can be growth enhancing and in particular countercyclical public investments are highly growth enhancing at low levels of financial development.

The next chapter turns to the question of which areas of financial development could be best fostered in Western Europe in order to enhance the financial system's contribution to overcoming the extended period of limited growth. For example, measured productivity differentials between Europe and the United States seem to originate particularly from the financial sector and from sectors that are finance dependent. Philipp Hartmann, Florian Heider, Elias Papaioannou, and Marco Lo Duca build on the literature to establish first a comprehensive practical framework for financial sector analyses and policies in which a number of key concepts are defined. Next, they present a selection of indicators describing the development and efficiency of the European financial system along a number of important dimensions. Third, the chapter shows econometric estimates of the extent to which greater financial development and efficiency improve the allocation of productive capital in industrial countries. While in the recent past the research and policy debate in Europe has very much revolved around fostering financial integration, the present chapter puts the main emphasis on financial development or modernization in the sense of the finance and growth literature.

Overall, the results suggest that there is significant room for further modernizing and developing European capital markets. For example, relative to their respective economies continental European capital markets tend to be considerably smaller than US or UK markets. In fact, in the estimations total capital market size comes out as the main financial determinant of the speed with which capital is reallocated from declining to rising industries.

European financial policies may be particularly advisable in fields that are highlighted by the finance and growth literature in general, where the indicators show a low performance for at least some European countries and where the estimations presented suggest a positive impact on capital reallocation. Hartmann et al. find that all three inputs point in the same direction in a number of areas. First, in the area of corporate governance the enforcement possibilities of laws protecting minority shareholders against self-dealing by controlling shareholders or company directors could be improved in many countries. Second, in a few countries the efficiency of legal systems in resolving financial conflicts is quite low. Making them faster and less formal is likely to foster financial development. Third, some structural features of European banking sectors could be improved. For example, a small number of countries still have significant levels of public bank ownership. It could be advisable for those countries to provide evidence that their banking sectors do not suffer from the inefficiencies typically detected in the literature. Also some European countries have by now quite concentrated banking sectors. The potential adverse effects could for example be countered by greater integration, such as the cross-border provision of financial services or a greater external component in the ongoing consolidation process (cross-border bank mergers). Last, some other but less strong results are found concerning the room to improve the information-processing capacity of European stock markets, the strength of creditor rights, and the incentives some aspects of banking regulation and supervision provide, in particular regarding the moral hazard implications of the funding and pricing of deposit insurance schemes.

The authors also highlight two areas in which significantly more research is needed before strong policy conclusions can be drawn. One is the low levels of venture capital financing observed in many European countries (compared to the United States for example), in particular (but not only) at early investment stages. The other concerns the benefits and risks of swiftly developing securitization business. For both these areas important new insights are provided in the chapters by Jenkinson on private equity and by Cuchra on structured finance.

The remaining two chapters of Part I turn to financial integration. Lieven Baele, Annalisa Ferrando, Peter Hördahl, Elizaveta Krylova, and Cyril Monnet set out a framework for evaluating the degree of integration in different European financial markets. They provide extensive evidence on the evolution of financial integration, both before and after the introduction of the euro. Baele et al. cover five main markets in the euro area: money, corporate bond, government bond, retail credit, and equity markets. Results are provided for both established measures of integration and some new ones using price- and news-based as well as quantity-based indicators.

The results differ by market segment. In some cases a substantial degree of integration has been achieved over time and elsewhere it is still quite limited. The greatest degree of integration is observed in the money markets, in particular in the unsecured rather than the repo segment. Baele et al. show that in this market interest rate differentials are now of the same magnitude across as within countries, which is precisely the condition that would be expected of full integration.

There has also been a high degree of integration in the government bond market since the introduction of the euro. Yields have converged and have increasingly been driven by common rather than local risk factors. The European trading platform euro-MTS has attracted a significant share of secondary market trading.[2] However, convergence is not yet complete. There is still evidence of the influence of local risk factors on yield movements, even on sovereign bonds with the same credit rating. Baele et al.'s chapter also documents the degree of integration in the corporate bond market. This fast-growing market is fairly well integrated with country of issuance having little power in explaining corporate bond yield spreads. In addition, there has been a marked increase in cross-border investments with European bond funds increasing their market share appreciably.

It is in relation to retail markets and corporate lending that Baele et al. observe the lowest levels of integration. The only market for which there seems to be an unambiguous trend towards convergence is the one for time deposits. The greatest cross-border interest differentials exist in the market for consumer loans, which is clearly not integrated, though there has been some convergence of mortgage market interest rates. While there has been an increase in the importance of common euro area factors for corporate lending rates, particularly since the introduction of the euro, these rates do not show any convergence, either for short-term loans or for medium- and long-term loans.

Sebnem Kalemli-Ozcan and Bent Sørensen survey the theoretical link that might exist between financial integration and economic welfare. There is a distinction be-tween those economists who view international capital mobility as facilitating the efficient global allocation of savings to their most productive uses and those who believe that capital flows are driven by animal spirits and have little connection with real economic activity. In the former context, financial integration could raise economic growth and welfare through a number of channels including increasing investment to potentially higher levels than domestic savings, reducing the cost of capital via a more efficient allocation of capital, technology transfer, and stimulating domestic financial development.

Kalemli-Ozcan and Sørensen emphasize another channel and that is the risk- shar-ing benefits that come from financial integration. Risk sharing involves smoothing consumption relative to endowments which can be decomposed into smoothing income relative to endowments and consumption relative to income. Kalemli-Ozcan, Sørensen, and Yosha (2001) compare the benefits of risk sharing for the states of the USA and the members of the European Union. They find similar orders of magnitude for the two. Demyanyk and Volosovych (2005) estimate the potential gains from integrating the accession countries into the EU financial system. Unsurprisingly, they record that they are much larger for the accession countries, e.g. 18.5 per cent for Lithuania, than for large countries such as Germany and the UK.

One of the impediments to financial integration is the 'home bias', the holding of an unduly large proportion of investors' securities in domestic as against foreign assets. For example, Sørensen et al. (2007) describe how less home bias is associated with a greater degree of risk sharing. There are several explanations for this which are

---

[2] In 2004 there were serious liquidity problems and extreme volatility on MTS resulting from large trades by Citibank. The full impact of this on the trading platform is yet to be determined.

based on transaction costs, informational problems, sovereign risk, and a desire on the part of investors to hedge currency risk.

3.2. Financial Systems and the Corporate Sector

Part II of the book addresses the important role of financial systems in contributing to efficient corporate decisions. It covers corporate financing in general, a discussion on insolvency laws, takeover legislation and rules, corporate governance, as well as the important area of how start-ups and unlisted firms receive financing in Europe.

In their survey of corporate finance in Europe, François Degeorge and Ernst Maug begin by noting that companies coming to the stock market in Europe tend to be much larger and older than their US counterparts. This might be due to weaker investor protection in Europe, smaller venture capital markets, a lower equity cost of capital in the USA, or overpricing of equity in the USA. In addition, equity issuing techniques are different in the USA with book building being the traditional method for taking companies public in the USA but only relatively recently introduced into Europe.

One of the advantages that it is thought that book building offers is that it provides a mechanism by which issuers can acquire information about the value of their firms. The ability to allocate shares on a discretionary basis may be an important part of the process of encouraging purchasers to reveal such information. However, there is less evidence in Europe than in the USA that book building is part of the information revelation process and it might also be the source of some of the scandals that have afflicted the IPO market over the last few years. The traditional methods of selling shares by auction appear to be cheaper and offer a lower degree of price uncertainty.

One feature of equity markets is the cross-listing of company shares on foreign stock markets. European companies have listed on US markets and US firms on European markets and there has been cross-listing of shares within Europe. Companies that list in the USA are typically fast-growing, high-technology stocks while those listing in Europe tend to be more mature firms that do not grow so fast. One explanation for cross-listings is a bonding hypothesis that companies choose to abide by tougher foreign market governance standards. However, the recent aversion of firms to US markets following Sarbanes–Oxley suggests that there are limitations to this thesis.

Degeorge and Maug point to the continuing diversity in the structure of European firms. The ownership of continental European firms is marked by concentrated shareholding, cross-shareholdings, pyramids, and dual class shares and of UK firms by the absence of these features and dispersed ownership instead. There have been some attempts at evaluating the significance of these differences for performance. For example, Cronqvist and Nilsson (2003) examine the impact of dual class shares, cross-shareholdings, and pyramids in Sweden and record that the control of votes by minority shareholders adversely affects valuations, reducing Tobin's q (the ratio of market to book valuations of companies) by between 6 and 25 per cent . But probably the most significant effects are on corporate governance and takeovers.

The market for corporate control has been one of the most controversial areas of European financial integration. Some recent attempts by EU governments to prevent takeovers by foreign bidders (for example the takeover of Spain's Endesa SA by Germany's E.ON AG and France's Arcelor by Mittal) have reinforced commentators' suspicions that, below the surface, national sentiment remains strong. The controversy about takeovers reflects the fact that they bring about changes in the ownership and control of corporations. These are most pronounced in relation to hostile takeovers where proposed acquisitions are opposed by the management of the target firm.

As Mike Burkart and Fausto Panunzi note, the justification for takeovers is that they bring about improvements in the performance of firms and industries. Economies of scale and scope can be exploited by merging the operations of firms and, in what are termed 'disciplinary takeovers', poor management can be replaced by superior acquiring management. On the basis of this one would expect to observe substantial improvements in corporate performance as a result of acquisitions. In some respects this is borne out by the evidence: there are substantial gains to shareholders of the target firms around the announcement of acquisitions. On the other hand, the post-takeover performance of firms is not always consistent with this.

Furthermore, there are grounds for believing that takeovers can be detrimental as well as beneficial. They may be undertaken for empire-building reasons and give rise to underinvestment in firm-specific human capital. It is not then surprising to discover that some countries are much more supportive of takeover markets than others. Furthermore, the ownership structure of companies in some countries introduces serious impediments to takeovers. Large shareholders may have incentives to trade blocks of shares but not to support tender offers for shares in the market. This is what one appears to observe in practice with active markets in share blocks in some countries at the same time as there is only a modest takeover market.

The European Commission has been attempting to promote the market in corporate control by reducing the existing barriers to takeovers. This has involved circumventing the impediments that exist from takeover restrictions and resistance from holders of large blocks of shares. These attempts have run into strong opposition in some countries and, as Burkart and Panunzi argue, it is questionable whether the elimination of these barriers is necessarily beneficial. Large shareholders play an important role in the governance of some countries' corporate sectors and their replacement by acquiring shareholders will not necessarily improve their corporate performance. As Burkart and Panunzi state, 'the role of takeovers—or large shareholders for that matter—as a disciplining mechanism must ultimately be analysed within the overall governance system'.

The Takeover Directive raises the more general question of harmonization versus diversity in rule setting and legislation. Oren Sussman addresses that in the context of corporate insolvency (bankruptcy) law. He describes the changes introduced by the 2002 new legislation that harmonizes insolvency laws within Europe and notes that the EU's drive to harmonize bankruptcy legislation is governed by the 'real seat' doctrine by which the bankruptcy laws of the member where the debtor has the centre of its main interest prevail. The argument behind harmonization is that the objectives of the free movement of capital between member states 'cannot be achieved to a sufficient degree at national level and action at Community level is therefore justified'.[3]

One of the most controversial areas of financial market reform has concerned corporate governance. A wave of scandals in both the USA and Europe has prompted calls for radical reform. These have been particularly prominent in the USA, and as Ailsa Röell records the scale of reform in the USA has been extensive. In her chapter she reviews the reforms that have occurred in disclosure, audit committees, boards, election to boards, voting on remuneration, private litigation, and institutional voting. Some of the most important pressure for change has come from the emergence of new participants in corporate governance, in particular private equity investors and hedge funds.

Recent developments in corporate governance have been particularly focused on executive pay awards and self-dealing revealed in recent stock option deals. Some argue that the pay awards are justified by shareholder considerations but many are more sceptical and in the USA the legislative agenda has been dominated by a perception that changes need to be made. In Europe, there has been a much more limited response, with a perception that the scale of the problem is not as acute as in the USA with less reliance being placed on high-powered executive compensation schemes. In the UK, which comes closest to the US market practices, there are significant differences in corporate governance rules regarding in particular remuneration and board elections. More generally, there is a greater emphasis on principle- than rule-based corporate governance mechanisms and less reliance placed on litigation through the courts.

The chapter brings out the critical question of whether current reforms will solve the deficiencies of the US market system or leave it in a morass of complex and intrusive regulation that raises the costs of doing business to an unacceptable extent. It also raises the issue of whether the continental European approach of placing less reliance on market than private forms of ownership and control is competitively sustainable. There is concern about inadequate protection of minority investors in continental Europe and the impact that this has on the cost at which firms can raise external capital. The UK system lies somewhere between the US and continental European and to some observers combines some of the merits of both. However, the perceived benefits of different forms of corporate governance change rapidly and are yet to be fully tested.

Sussman argues that there is little evidence to support the proposition that harmonization improves economic efficiency. On the contrary, one of the anticipated effects of improved bankruptcy procedures is an increased level of gearing amongst

---

[3] Council Regulation on Insolvency Proceedings (1346/2000).

EU companies, but Sussman reports exactly the opposite. Instead of harmonization of legislation regarding bankruptcy, Sussman argues for a market solution. 'Since a mechanism for enforcing the contract and settling emerging disputes is an integral part of the contract itself, it makes sense to allow every contract to determine these clauses without state interference and independently of other contracts that the company has signed, and independently of decisions such as location of head office.' In other words, parties to a debt contract should be free to determine where they wish their claims in the event of bankruptcy to be settled.

One of the fastest-growing areas of corporate finance in recent times has been private equity. Tim Jenkinson records that from relative insignificance, European private equity raised about the same amount in 2004 as US private equity. There is a great deal of cross-border flow in private equity both between the ultimate investors and the private equity firms and between private equity firms and the companies in which they are investing. Private equity appears to run counter to the argument that cross-border flows are restricted to public securities markets and are undermined by information problems in relation to private capital. The private equity business appears to have developed institutional mechanisms that allow finance to flow across borders.

There is an important difference in the nature of private equity between Europe and the USA. Whereas in the USA it is largely associated with venture capital for early stage finance, in Europe it is concentrated on management buyouts and takeovers. It is therefore primarily used for restructuring and changes in ownership rather than start-up finance. Consistent with this, Jenkinson reports that while good returns have been earned on buyouts, superior to those in the USA, they have been poor on early-stage investments, and consistently below those in the USA. Capital is therefore flowing where returns are highest but further research is required to establish why early-stage financing is so unattractive in Europe. One explanation is that there is greater expertise available for bridging financial and managerial skills in the USA than in Europe.

3.3. Financial Institutions

The third part of the book (Part III) turns to the different financial institutions active in the European financial system. It starts with the driving forces behind cross-border integration of commercial banking activities. It then looks in turn at asset management, the pension fund industry, insurance and reinsurance industries, and the payment systems.

A crucial issue for the structure of the future European financial system is the extent to which banking is going to be internationalized. Degryse and Ongena identify two major forces that influence the geographical scope of commercial banking: technology and regulation. They first analyse how physical distance and the presence of borders affect bank lending. They then study how advances in information technology and changes in financial regulation have altered these relationships.

Degryse and Ongena come to the conclusion that retail lending in Europe is characterized by both spatial pricing and (regional and/or national) market segmentation. Since the cross-border provision of financial services and direct market entry are hampered by asymmetric information and substantial fixed costs, cross-border bank mergers and acquisitions seem to be the best way to enter a foreign market. They believe that further technical progress and financial liberalizations may not be sufficient to achieve very much more integrated retail loan markets in Europe. Degryse and Ongena highlight the role that active competition policy and accommodating supervisory policies could play in improving European banking. More multilateral or even centralized European banking supervision could be helpful in this regard as well.

One of the fastest growing areas of financial services is asset management. Julian Franks, Colin Mayer, and Luis Correia da Silva record significant differences in the nature of asset management across European countries. At one end, the UK has a large number of small, independent asset management firms. At the other, asset management is largely integrated into financial groups in Germany, in particular in banks and insurance companies. Concentration of ownership is appreciably higher in continental Europe than it is in the UK or USA.

Differences in the structure of asset management firms have influenced the form that regulation has taken. Where asset management firms are part of larger groups their parent firms are able to bail out failing subsidiaries. Capital requirements are less onerous for asset management firms that are part of larger groups than they are for smaller independent firms. In the case of the UK greater emphasis is placed on conduct of business rules and protection through investor compensation schemes than on capital requirements.

The appropriate form of regulation of asset management firms is quite different from other parts of financial services. Capital requirements in banks are primarily associated with prudential regulation and avoidance of systemic risks. Pure asset management firms that do not take positions on their own accounts are less prone to financial failure and the interlinkages between institutions are less pronounced than in the banking sector. As a consequence, financial failure and systemic risks are less relevant to asset management firms than other parts of financial services. Instead, failure is primarily associated with operational risks and fraud. Capital requirements are an expensive form of protection against these risks. Franks, Mayer, and Correia da Silva suggest that insurance (either private or mutual), auditing, and custodianship may provide more cost-effective forms of investor protection.

A crucial driver of the development of European capital markets in the long term is further advances towards funded pension systems and the related expansion of the pension fund industry. Phil Davis first summarizes the main trends in EU pension funds in the context of long-term financial developments. He then discusses extensively the effects further growth of these funds should have on European capital markets, including interrelations with EMU. Finally, he relates continuing ageing in European OECD countries to the sustainability of fiscal policies and the stability of EMU and the European financial system.

Davis concludes that further pension fund growth will benefit the development of capital markets in Europe. It will help complete markets and reduce the cost of capital. It will stimulate the market-based parts of the European financial system and promote further financial integration. At present pension fund growth is extremely uneven in Europe, with countries like Denmark, Finland, Ireland, the Netherlands, and the United Kingdom displaying a relatively large sector and countries like Belgium, France, Germany, Greece, Italy, and Spain as well as many new EU member states having smaller sectors. Given the ageing process in major European countries, Davis warns that insufficient replacement of pay-as-you-go pension systems by capitalized systems will pose significant fiscal, monetary, and financial risks to the European economy.

The following chapter by Ray Rees turns to non-life insurance and reinsurance companies. It explains their economic functions (risk allocation and financial intermediation) and compares their different organizational forms (public and mutual insurance companies as well as insurance syndicates). Moreover, it discusses the optimality of various insurance regulations and summarizes the main policy initiatives at the EU level. The last section of the chapter discusses the *raison d'être* of reinsurance companies and how they can be complemented by the securitization of catastrophe risk in world capital markets.

As regards regulatory policy, Rees highlights the adverse consequences premium and contract condition regulations may have on competition and efficiency. He argues that solvency regulation and guarantee schemes should be sufficient to achieve prudential objectives. The policy principles introduced in the early 1990s at the EU level to promote the Common Market in the services sector actually led to a relaxation of regulations in the countries with particularly restrictive regimes (e.g. Germany and Italy) towards the looser systems of France and the UK. Moreover, Rees illustrates how the European 'Solvency II' programme, which is not expected to replace 'Solvency I' (which came into force in 2004) before 2008 or 2009, is likely to turn the attention of insurance regulators from relatively mechanistic formulae linking insurance type, reserves, premia, and reinsurance to the quality of risk management and managerial controls. Finally, Rees foresees that a further development of catastrophe insurance through capital markets, such as 'catbonds', could change the nature of reinsurance business in major ways.

Part III of the book concludes with a chapter by Xavier Freixas and Cornelia Holthausen about European payment systems. The authors first identify a number of global trends in the payment industry and discuss the most important developments in European large-value and retail payment systems.

Freixas and Holthausen point out that technical progress, better risk management features of net settlement systems, and the move towards real-time gross settlement (RTGS) and hybrid systems have made large-value payments generally safer. Moreover, internationalization of payment systems, as happened for example with EMU, enhances the need for cooperation between the bodies overseeing the systems and national authorities supervising the participating banks.

As regards European large-value systems, the Eurosystem's TARGET has become the most important transmitter of payments as of day 1 of EMU. The private Euro 1 system is the next most important, increasingly specializing in higher numbers of smaller large-value payments. The greater use of TARGET for large and time-critical payments is in line with European financial stability. As of 2007, TARGET is planned to move from a system of interconnected national RTGS to a system with a single shared platform that realizes greater scale economies and delivers more homogeneity at the user ends.

The very successful integration of large-value systems contrasts with the situation for retail payments. The use of diverse means of payments, their lack of acceptability across countries, and the concentration of cross-border payments in the hands of a few market players lead to high prices and also substantial monopoly profits. A regulatory attempt by the European Commission in 2001 to reduce cross-border prices to the ones observed within countries turned out to be a challenge. Modest progress was made by private sector initiatives to introduce pan-European standards for cross-border credit transfers (Credeuro), bank accounts (IBAN), and bank codes (BIC). But overall, the projects to create single EU and euro area payment areas (SPA and SEPA) have met substantial obstacles.

3.4. Financial Markets

After financial intermediaries and institutions we examine financial markets (Part IV). We start with fixed income markets, money markets, and bond markets, and continue with equity markets. The fourth chapter examines the important area of clearing and settlement infrastructures that support the functioning of these markets. European derivatives markets and the structured finance markets are discussed in the fifth and sixth chapters. The last chapter of this part addresses competition between financial centres.

The starting chapter by Philipp Hartmann and Natacha Valla provides a comprehensive discussion of the new euro money markets. It addresses the role of money markets in the financial system, the agents active in them, and the major forms of trading. It reports extensive data on the size of different money market segments and on observed transaction costs, volatilities, and spreads within and across different money market segments. Last, the authors discuss a number of major policy issues, such as the predictability of monetary policy with money market rates, the integration and development of different money markets, as well as money market stability and the lender of last resort in Europe.

Since the start of EMU, euro money markets have grown spectacularly, displaying high liquidity in the major market segments. Recently, the repo market has replaced the unsecured deposit market as the largest market segment. Overnight interest rate swaps have become a central instrument to manage short-term interest rate risk and to take trading positions. On the policy side, Hartmann and Valla argue that most research suggests that ECB monetary policy decisions are equally or more predictable than decisions by the US Federal Reserve or the Bank of England. Money market integration and development still exhibit major divergences across market segments. Whereas the unsecured deposit and most derivative markets are highly integrated, some obstacles remain to the full integration of repo markets. Moreover, the authors find that the integration and development of short-term securities markets, such as commercial paper or certificates of deposits, still leave much to be desired. Further market-led initiatives such as STEP (which stands for Short-Term European Paper) can therefore result in major economic benefits.

Corporate and government bond markets are then discussed in the chapter by Marco Pagano and Elu von Thadden. They first characterize the structure, size, and development of European bond markets in the global context, distinguishing supply and demand factors in their evolution. They then address secondary market trading mechanisms and the relationship between cash and derivatives markets. Finally, the authors briefly describe the sovereign yield convergence in the run-up of EMU and discuss the reasons for the remaining smaller yield differentials since January 1999.

Pagano and von Thadden's analysis suggests that euro area sovereign and corporate bond markets have become increasingly integrated over time and that corporate bond issuance has picked up significantly. The authors argue that investors and issuers have reaped the considerable benefits afforded by greater competition in the underwriting of private bonds and auctioning of public ones, and by the greater liquidity of secondary markets. Still, the persistence of small and variable yield differentials for sovereign debt under EMU indicates that euro area public bonds of similar credit rating are still not perfect substitutes. It can be explained to a large extent by rather small differentials in fundamental risk and not so much by persistent market segmentation. Pagano and von Thadden see the main challenges for European bond markets as being, inter alia, the unbalanced liquidity of the bonds futures with respect to the underlying cash market, the vulnerability of existing trading platforms to manipulation by large players and the integration of clearing and settlement systems.

Kpate Adjaouté and Jean-Pierre Danthine look at the question of how economic and financial integration changes the functioning of European equity markets. They first address changes in the factors that the literature has identified to be important for pricing equities, namely macro- and microeconomic fundamentals as well as risk premia and stochastic discount factors. They then turn to realized returns, asking what they imply for diversification opportunities between countries and sectors.

It turns out that Europe has experienced a significantly lower dispersion of growth rates since the late 1980s/early 1990s. Despite the fact that macroeconomic fundamentals have tended to comove more appreciably, the cost of equity capital has declined, and equity premia have converged, pure pricing changes have been harder to identify. Earlier results suggesting a greater attractiveness of sector diversification as opposed to country diversification are not confirmed by the latest data. What is, however, confirmed is that asset allocation strategies would benefit from more disaggregated approaches, e.g. diversifying across countries and sectors at the same time.

An area often neglected in the academic literature but of immense importance for the integration of European securities markets is clearing and settlement systems. This is discussed by Alberto Giovannini, John Berrigan, and Daniela Russo. They first present a number of stylized facts about these market infrastructures in Europe and then review past attempts to reform them. Giovannini et al. further interpret the need for restructuring the clearing and settlement industry in the context of the strategic objective of European financial integration and answer a few fundamental questions that could be raised against restructuring efforts. Finally, they propose a novel approach to the reform process.

The authors argue that these traditionally ignored post-trading services are at the core of securities markets, because they concern the basic process of exchange between buyers and sellers. For the whole of Europe the market for these services is of about the same size as in the United States. The extent of consolidation is, however, much less advanced in Europe. Five years after the introduction of the euro there were still eighteen European securities settlement systems compared to four in the USA. There is fragmentation across the different steps of the value creation process (trading, clearing, and settlement) and different types of aggregation coexist (vertical 'silos' versus horizontally integrated structures). Moreover, cross-border trades are still several times more expensive to settle than domestic trades.

Private incentives for consolidation are constrained by earlier infrastructure investments, individual benefits from complexity, and attempts to maximize revenue in the transition. Despite a number of initiatives, most of them shying away from direct public sector intervention, Giovannini, Berrigan, and Russo report that the general consensus is that progress in removing barriers to the efficient restructuring of clearing and settlement systems in Europe remains low. The new policy approach they propose is based on the creation of a 'common framework' of market standards, regulations, and laws that would address the barriers identified in the earlier reports by the Giovannini Group. Finally, they argue that a major factor in reforming the European post-trading infrastructure is to create more transparent and standardized pricing structures.

The chapter by Ron Anderson and Kenneth McKay turns to derivatives markets. It starts with a general overview of the growth in derivatives trading worldwide and then describes the main product innovations. Further topics addressed are the organization of derivatives markets, the use of derviatives by end-users, and finally regulatory issues.

Anderson and McKay document the strongest worldwide growth of derivatives markets over the last twenty years, with a prominent role played by European markets (for example in London). They explain the strong European growth with reforms of debt and equity markets, capital flow liberalizations and financial integration, the introduction of the euro, and, in particular, the more successful introduction of electronic trading. Moreover, over-the-counter derivatives trading has outstripped exchange-based trading. The reasons are advances in information technology and the establishment of common standards for documentation and trading practices by global financial institutions. The authors suggest that these factors are nowhere clearer than in credit derivatives trading, which is one of the most important innovations during the last ten years.

The very important area of securitization business for developed financial systems is discussed in the chapter about 'Structured Finance' by Maciej Firla-Cuchra. He first reviews the development of European securitization business, identifying the leading trends at the aggregate level and national differences. Cuchra then discusses salient characteristics of European securitizations, including peculiar transaction types and pricing features, going deeper into mortgage-backed securities, synthetic securitizations, and corporate securitizations. Last, he summarizes the most important explanations for the emergence of securitization given in the literature. Throughout the chapter the author describes the European markets in relation to developments in the United States.

The principal concept behind all structured finance products is the conversion of idiosyncratic assets, real or synthetically created, into tradeable financial securities. The expansion of credit derivatives (as, for example, described in the chapter by Anderson and McKay) has resulted in a fundamental division between 'true sale' (with actual transfer of securities) and 'synthetic' securitizations. According to Cuchra, the European securitization markets are considerably less developed than the US markets, as for example reflected in the fact that the combined volume of European mortgage-backed securities (MBS) and asset-backed securities (ABS) represents under 4 per cent of the US volume. Moreover, the dynamic European developments of the late 1990s and early 2000s have been followed by a significant slowdown. As only a small number of countries, notably the UK but also Italy, Spain, and the Netherlands, constitute almost 90 per cent of the market at present, there seems to be significant room for further growth. The author sees significant legal, regulatory, structural, and tax obstacles to this further growth. This is all the more important as Cuchra reckons that further development of securitization 'can be seen as one of the most critical determinants of future innovation and value creation by the financial industry'.

Peculiar features of the European situation are a high degree of differentiation between similar companies and the low number of deals per originator. European markets are as yet also not as much dominated by mortgage-backed securities as the US markets, potentially related to the absence of large government-sponsored enterprises (GSEs, such as Fannie Mae and Freddie Mac) that are characteristic of the US market and to the legal and regulatory obstacles to constructing large cross-country mortgage portfolios in Europe. Synthetic deals have been highly stimulated by the dominance of European banks in trading risks among each other. The review of the literature provided by Cuchra suggests a considerable amount of confusion about the real drivers of securitization business and whom it benefits. The literature identifies incomplete markets, market segmentation, asymmetric information, as well as managerial and cash flow control as potential sources. But there is little empirical evidence about which of those factors is the most important. Overall, the author points to improvements of pricing models and, in the European context, the elimination of legal and regulatory obstacles as areas where further progress is needed.

The last chapter of Part IV, written by Thomas Gehrig, discusses where financial centres emerge and how they compete with each other. Gehrig first goes through the evidence about the relative importance of different international financial centres and their changes over time in terms of the location of bank branches and stock market cross-listings. Then he summarizes theories that explain the geography of financial centres and discusses the role of financial centres in producing information. The following section describes competition between financial centres as a strategic game involving public authorities and private agents. Gehrig concludes with thoughts about issues for European financial centres.

After substantial growth over previous decades the chapter reports data showing a significant reduction of bank branches from foreign locations in almost all major financial centres. While this reduction was in relative terms not much larger in continental Europe than in other regions, still New York, London, Hong Kong, Singapore, Tokyo, and Zurich remain more important by this measure than financial centres located in the euro area, such as Frankfurt, Paris, Amsterdam, or Brussels. In particular, Gehrig argues that Asian centres like Hong Kong and Singapore were among the winners in relative terms. He is particularly critical of the apparent inability of Frankfurt to capitalize on the introduction of the euro and the ECB to expand its role. The author then describes how cross-listings generate competition between financial centres and how particularly New York attracted them for some time. Nevertheless, London seems to be the only centre that earns larger revenues from foreign stocks than from domestic stocks.

Gehrig explains the geography of financial centres by the interplay of centripetal forces emerging from scale economies and externalities and centrifugal forces emerging from a variety of factors including local information as well as regulatory and political factors. For example, financial centres play the role of information aggregators for a given region. Cross-listing may be helpful to 'import' better accounting standards and better pricing from major centres. Nevertheless, Gehrig reports evidence that the International Accounting Standards (IAS) now introduced in Europe tend to be associated with similar transaction costs in stock trading to US-GAAP. Overall, together with the ongoing consolidation tendencies in stock markets, regulatory issues and accounting standards seem to be of major importance for competition. For Europe, Gehrig suggests policies supporting innovations and new growth firms, reforms of pension systems, regulations, and taxation.

3.5. Financial Regulation and Macroeconomic Policy

The last part of the book (Part V) turns to the most important policy areas relating to the modernization and integration of the European financial system. It starts with discussions of European securities market regulation and banking supervision. The impact of banking regulations on macroeconomic fluctuations and the implications of changes in the financial structure for the transmission of monetary policy are then addressed. The final chapter tackles the relationship between central bank liquidity management procedures and the financial system.

The chapter on securities market regulation in the European Union is authored by Bernhard Speyer. He first outlines the economic rationale for further integration of EU securities markets and then describes the main elements of the Financial Services Action Plan. A separate section is dedicated to the Lamfalussy process introduced to improve and accelerate legislative activity in this area. Speyer provides assessments of both the FSAP and the working of the Lamfalussy procedures. He closes with an outlook for further steps needed in the area of EU securities market regulation.

Speyer concludes that the FSAP has been a catalyst to further securities market integration and its effectiveness has been enhanced by the benefits of the Lamfalussy approach. In particular, the Lamfalussy procedures created the framework for a future pan-European approach to securities market regulation and supervision. Whether the ultimate goal of fully integrated European securities markets can be reached will depend on a strong political will by all policy bodies involved in Europe and by financial institutions and their clients. A number of problems illustrate that all stakeholders have to go much further than they have so far. For example, it was unfortunate that the 'Market in Financial Instruments Directive' (the amendment of the earlier Investment Services Directive) was brought forward very late. It constitutes a type of 'basic law' for securities markets on which many of the other directives passed in the context of the FSAP should have been based. The fact that this did not happen contributed to a number of inconsistencies between the multiple regulatory changes that happened over the last years. Speyer also thinks that the FSAP process would have benefited from the early establishment of a number of fundamental economic principles relating to the efficiency of financial markets and a better consideration of the international context.

Speyer sees some challenges in the effective implementation of the Lamfalussy procedures. A structural feature of it is for example the increasing use of 'soft law' at the level of homogeneous national implementation (level 3). For example, it is very hard for the Committee of European Securities Regulators (CESR)—the level 3 committee for securities market regulation—to set binding rules that all countries have to adhere to. As for the future, Speyer expects securities market regulation to play a less central role in upcoming financial sector reforms, as this area received greater emphasis in the FSAP than other areas. He endorses however the European Commission's view that further progress is needed in terms of the clearing and settlement and investment fund industries. He suggests also that further consideration needs to be given to a Single European Act for securities markets regulation in which a variety of inconsistencies in the current regulatory set-up could be addressed.

Banking supervision is another key issue in the process of European integration. The issues at stake are analysed by Kostas Tsatsaronis in the second chapter of Part V. His contribution offers a comprehensive perspective on banking supervision, first describing the main achievements of the theory of banking risk and regulation, then turning to the current state of affairs in Europe, and concluding by considering future progress.

The first aspect Tsatsaronis analyses is the insight offered by applied theory. As is well known, the justification for prudential regulation is the social cost of bank failures, including the cost of bank failures to depositors, the cost of the severance of bank relationships, and the impact on payment systems. This social cost of bank failures is related to a number of externalities. This chapter carefully documents the externalities identified by recent research on cross-border banking and their effect on financial intermediaries' and supervisors' incentives. Regarding the former, multinational financial intermediaries develop a net of subsidiaries or branches that affect their incentives in the presence of limited liability. Concerning the latter, in a global framework, supervisors have to consider that tougher regulation increases the stability of domestic banking but potentially at the price of rendering it less competitive and making financial activity migrate abroad. Consequently, absence of coordination will lead to suboptimal outcomes as the objective functions of the supervisors differ. This is reinforced by the fact that supervisors' incentives to share information in a global framework may be limited by their own domestic interests.

The second aspect examined is the state of integration of banking supervision. This is a complex issue, as Europe's prudential architecture is based on a set of national structures overlaid by a superstructure of area-wide arrangements Each country retains important regulatory powers, and consequently we witness a whole array of different banking supervisory structures. This is substantiated by the different models chosen to regulate and supervise the financial sector, with a unified regulator in some countries like Norway and the UK and with disjoint regulation of banking, brokerage, and insurance in others. This diversity is corroborated by the diversity of arrangements to deal with crisis situations and the rules that govern the closure of troubled banks.

Confronted with this diversity, European harmonization has developed based on two principles: the principle of mutual recognition of national regulatory competences subject to a minimum harmonization framework, and the principle of the assignment of control to the home country. As cross-border banking and M&A have developed, some of the weaknesses of the present framework have become apparent. So, in order to achieve a more streamlined decision and rule-making process, while maintaining sufficient political control and accountability, a new structure was drawn up in 2003, following the recommendations of the Lamfalussy Group of 'Wise Men'. Four different levels of coordination were established: coordination at the level of principle setting *level 1* includes the legislative bodies in the EU (i.e. the European Parliament, the European Commission, and the Ecofin council of finance ministers) which have the exclusive power to set high-level rules and principles for the entire area. The *level 2* committee also has rule-making powers but these are limited to mainly technical rules within the framework principles set by level 1 organs. The role of *level 3* supervisory committees is to provide technical advice at the Commission's request and to enhance regulatory and supervisory convergence. Finally, *level 4* refers to the application of the supervisory framework at the national level and on the enforcement of EU rules by the Commission.

The third aspect developed in Tsatsaronis's chapter is concerned with the future. The future of European banking supervision has to be built around efficiency concerns, but different types of agents disagree on the costs of different solutions. The proposals range from more conservative ones that preserve the existing structures to the more radical ones, which advocate the creation of a central European supervision or the introduction of the lead supervisor approach. The debate is open and the resulting decision will definitely impact on the structure, competitiveness, and stability of the European banking industry.

The chapter by Charles Goodhart, Boris Hofmann, and Miguel Segoviano considers the relation between macroeconomic stability and financial fragility. It records how financial liberalization has exacerbated the amplitude of economic cycles resulting in periods of boom and bust. The chapter reports some formal evidence supporting the association of financial liberalization with the procyclicality of financial systems. It then considers how the changing nature of the trade cycle through financial liberalization and the internationalization of financial markets led to attempts to coordinate banking supervision across countries, most notably through the Basel Committee on Banking Supervision. The chapter considers the implications of capital adequacy requirements in Basel I and Basel II on macroeconomic stability.

The main conclusion of the chapter is that regulation is inherently procyclical. The reason for this is that prudential regulation bites harder during periods of economic weakness. As a consequence, lending by banks is more heavily constrained by regulation during economic downturns and the amplitude of the cycle is thereby increased. Furthermore, the more accurately the value and relative riskiness of each bank is measured, the greater will be the procyclicality of prudential regulation. Therefore Basel II will be more procyclical than Basel I. The chapter demonstrates that this is likely to be the case on the basis of an extensive simulation analysis.

Boris Hofmann and Andreas Worms survey the transmission mechanisms by which monetary policy affects an economy's output and prices. The chapter describes the influence of interest rates, asset prices, and the credit channel through balance sheets and bank lending. It then considers the way in which financial integration is likely to influence these transmission channels.

The chapter concludes that, through competition and a greater market orientation in financial and banking markets, the efficiency of monetary policy in the euro area should improve. Increased significance of non-bank finance in the form of bond markets implies that transmission via capital market interest rates is likely to become more important. Furthermore the pass-through of policy rates to euro bank lending rates will accelerate. Conversely, the credit channel of monetary transmission should diminish in significance and this will reduce capital market distortions in the monetary transmission process. The chapter also notes that integration should diminish differences across euro area countries in the nature of transmission mechanisms. This will reduce problems created by differential effects of monetary policy in the EMU. However, differences may persist because of variations in institutional arrangements, in particular in relation to mortgage and housing markets.

Ulrich Bindseil and Kjell Nyborg survey the way in which monetary policy is implemented. They consider the operational targets that central banks set in relation to interbank interest rates, the operational framework for controlling the targets, and the day-to-day use of open market operations to control liquidity. They discuss alternative interest rates that can form the basis of operational targets and compare gradualist and exhaustive changes to interest rates, i.e. progressive movements in interest rates over an extended period of time versus full adjustments that render future movements unpredictable. They discuss three instruments for controlling the operational target—standing facilities, open market operations and reserve requirements.

The chapter considers the implication of monetary policy implementation for financial markets. It compares the approaches used by the German Reichsbank in history, in modern times by Norway, the USA, and the ECB for the euro area. It argues that by taking different types of collateral, central banks can influence the relative price of assets in the market. In addition, central bank operations can have markedly different effects on market liquidity. There are two types of techniques that central banks use to influence liquidity—fixed and variable rate tenders. The chapter contrasts fixed and variable rate tenders organized by the ECB and concludes that allocations in tenders can be very different under the two systems. The implication of the chapter is that careful consideration needs to be given to the design of open market operations to ensure that they have desired rather than unintended consequences for financial markets.

4. Policy Implications

The clear message to emerge from the first part of the book is that financial development and financial integration do matter in industrial countries like those of the European Union. Economic performance is positively related to the levels of financial development and integration. In industrial countries they improve productivity through reductions in the cost of capital and improvements in the allocation of capital to investment projects.[4] They enlarge the scope for risk sharing and allow countries with investment opportunities beyond their financial means to expand more rapidly than would otherwise be the case.

The EU's experience with policies for promoting financial integration has been mixed to date. There has been much progress made in money markets and government and corporate bond markets but more limited progress in retail banking and equity markets. There are natural impediments that arise in retail and private equity markets due to problems of imperfect information. These make local proximity

---

[4] In developing countries their contribution to capital deepening may be more important than that to productivity.

important and mean that banks have to establish local branch networks before they can gain access to retail outlets.

This raises a question that is particularly relevant to corporate finance of the extent to which harmonization should be pursued by the EU. There is considerable diversity in patterns of ownership and control of companies across Europe, which has complicated the pursuit of harmonization policies. That has been most strikingly observed in relation to the Takeover Directive but it may well apply to other areas of corporate finance such as bankruptcy law. The question that this raises is where the EU should persist with harmonization and where it should promote the benefits that may come from diversity in and potential competition between financial systems.

The areas where there has been most progress to date have been those where capital market imperfections are least pronounced: debt rather than equity markets, public rather than private securities, wholesale rather than retail, standardized rather than diverse instruments. However, there is also evidence that institutional innovation has allowed integration and modernization to occur where it might not have been expected, for example in relation to private equity. Technology allows market barriers to be reduced and cross-border transactions to occur where previously they were limited. New financial instruments allow for better insurance against certain risks. Facilitating these innovations may be a particularly promising line of development. Imposing uniformity through standardization or harmonization may sometimes limit innovation or be rendered obsolete just when regulation is introduced. Standardization is required in some areas, in particular in relation to clearing and settlement where there are important networking and interconnection benefits. Elsewhere, however, regulation may be better focused on the promotion of markets and innovation through rules relating to disclosure and transparency rather than the structure and conduct of business.

Many conclusions relevant for policy makers and market participants have been reached in the numerous chapters of this book, as illustrated in the extensive summary of the previous section. In order to facilitate identifying them, we close this introductory chapter with a brief list of the most important conclusions oriented towards European financial policies. We group them in four areas.

1. *Improving financial market framework conditions*
   - Large policy programmes, for example the FSAP, would benefit from the prior establishment of a basic economic framework with which each measure can be related to the efficiency and stability of a financial system and its contribution to growth and welfare. Such a framework would also help understanding about how different legislative and regulatory measures interact.
   - Specific aspects of corporate governance could be improved. In particular, in many European countries it is still quite difficult for minority shareholders to protect themselves against self-dealing by controlling shareholders or company directors.

- In a small number of European countries legal systems are formalistic and slow. This hampers financial development, as conflict resolution is slow and payment and credit transactions are discouraged.
- Some structural features of banking sectors may limit the size of capital markets and their contribution to economic growth. For example, the few European countries that still have significant shares of public bank ownership should consider whether their banks perform better than the average recorded in the literature for public banks.
- High degrees of bank concentration, as observed in a number of smaller countries that are more advanced in the financial consolidation process, may have adverse effects on the real economy. These could be countered by further moves towards financial integration, possibly elevating the importance of competition policy in banking and by more accommodating supervisory attitudes towards cross-border bank mergers.
- Continuing the process of focusing insurance regulation and oversight more on solvency rules and guarantee schemes rather than premium and contract regulation is likely to strengthen competition and efficiency in this sector. The path towards Solvency II reforms should be pursued, thereby placing greater emphasis on risk management quality and internal controls in preference to mechanistic regulatory formulae.
- Further reforms of pension systems towards full funding in countries that still have pay-as-you-go systems will stimulate capital market development and are likely to reduce risks to fiscal, monetary, and financial stability.
- Further consideration should be given to the development of a Single European Act for securities market regulation in which a variety of inconsistencies in the current regulatory set-up could be removed. The increased use of 'soft law' in the current Lamfalussy approach easily leads to a proliferation of inconsistent forms of implementation and enforcement mechanisms across countries.
- The further integration of European securities clearing and settlement systems remains of primary importance for efficient European securities and derivatives markets. The development of a common framework of market standards, regulations, and laws addressing the Giovannini barriers and greater price transparency would be very helpful in this regard. The introduction of a single public platform—as currently considered by the Eurosystem under the TARGET 2 Securities project—would be a major step forward.
- The relatively fast introduction of area-wide or interconnected electronic trading platforms for securities and derivatives in Europe (as compared to the USA for example) is to be welcomed and promoted. Further market and policy efforts are however necessary to reduce the vulnerability of these systems to market manipulation. Moreover, liquidity imbalances between cash and derivatives segments in government bond markets need to be addressed.

- The internationalization of large-value payment systems, as is occuring with TARGET and TARGET 2, suggests more cooperation is needed among the authorities that supervise the banks active in these systems.

2. *Developing risk capital markets*

- An area of primary attention needs to be the limited returns and activity of European early-stage venture capital financing markets. This illustrates the difficulties start-ups face in Europe, also limiting the attractiveness of the equity market segments of European financial centres.
- A critical area for the further modernization of European capital markets is the speed and breadth of securitization, including sophisticated structured finance transactions. Legal, regulatory, and tax obstacles to cross-country asset securitizations need to be carefully analysed and where possible removed. In so doing, however, financial stability risks need to be considered as well.
- The least developed and integrated part of the major European capital markets is the market for short-term securities (for example commercial paper and certificates of deposits). Major efforts by both market participants and policy makers to improve short-term funding possibilities for European corporations are warranted.

3. *Integrating retail financial services*

- Retail banking is one of the areas where financial integration has advanced the least, in particular in relation to consumer loan, corporate loan, and mortgage markets. More cross-border consolidation of banking groups seems to be the only realistic avenue at present for making further progress. In order to achieve this, a strong role for competition policies and an accommodating stance by national supervisory authorities is called for.
- In the area of asset management, it may be advisable to make greater use of auditing, custodianship, and protection schemes rather than basing investor protection on prudential capital requirements. This poses challenges for countries in which universal banks or financial conglomerates have integrated most of their asset management business.
- A higher level of compatibility and acceptability across retail payment systems is important. The efforts to create Single Euro and European Payments Areas (SEPA and SPA) are valuable in this respect.

4. *Lessons for macroeconomic policies*

- Research using money market interest rates suggests that ECB monetary policy is at least as predictable as the policies of the US Federal Reserve and the Bank of England.
- Greater competition in euro area financial sectors and an increasing use of market-based instruments accelerate the pass-through of monetary policy decisions. They also increase the importance of the interest rate channel of monetary policy transmission relative to the credit channel. Together with financial integration they make the transmission of monetary policy through the euro area more homogeneous.

- The design of operational frameworks for the implementation of monetary policy by central banks has implications for market liquidity and the pricing of assets in, for example, choosing acceptable types of collateral and forms of liquidity auctions.
- Increasingly precise risk weightings of financial regulations, as implied by the move from Basel I to Basel II, tend to amplify the procyclical effects of regulations.

REFERENCES

CRONQVIST, H., and NILSSON, M. (2003), 'Agency costs of controlling minority shareholders', *Journal of Financial and Quantitative Analysis*, 38, 695-719.

DEMYANYK, Y., and VOLOSOVYCH, V. (2005), 'Macroeconomic asymmetry in the European Union: the difference between new and old members', CEPR Working Paper no. 4847.

EUROPEAN CENTRAL BANK and CENTER FOR FINANCIAL STUDIES (2004), 'Research network on capital markets and financial integration in Europe: results and experiences after two years', Frankfurt, December.

EUROPEAN COMMISSION (2005), 'Financial sector policies (2005-2010)', COM(2005) 629 final, Brussels, 1 December.

KALEMLI-OZCAN, S., SØRENSEN, B. and YOSHA, O. (2001), 'Regional integration, industrial specialization and the asymmetry of shocks across regions', *Journal of International Economics*, 55, 107-37.

KING, R., and LEVINE, R. (2005), 'Finance and growth: Schumpeter might be right', *Quarterly Journal of Economics*, 153(3), 717–38.

LEVINE, R. (2005), 'Finance and growth: theory and evidence', in P. Aghion and S. Durlauf (eds.), *Handbook of Economic Growth*, Amsterdam: North Holland.

PAPADEMOS, L. (2006), 'Price stability, financial stability and efficiency and monetary policy', speech delivered at the third conference of the Monetary Stability Foundation on 'Challenges to the financial system: aging and low growth', Frankfurt, 7 July.

RAJAN, R., and ZINGALES, L. (1998), 'Financial dependence and growth', *American Economic Review*, 88, 559–86.

SØRENSEN, B., WU, Y.-T., YOSHA, O., and ZHU, Y. (2007), 'Home bias and international risk sharing: twin puzzles separated at birth', *Journal of International Money and Finance* 26(4), 587–605.

TUMPEL-GUGERELL, G. (2006), 'TARGET2-Securities: from vision to reality. The Eurosystem's contribution to an integrated securities market', speech delivered at the EU Commission Conference on 'The EU's new regime for clearing and settlement in Europe', Brussels, 30 November.

PART I

FINANCIAL SYSTEMS AND ECONOMIC PERFORMANCE

CHAPTER 1

FINANCIAL STRUCTURE AND CORPORATE GOVERNANCE IN EUROPE, THE USA, AND ASIA

FRANKLIN ALLEN

MICHAEL K. F. CHUI

ANGELA MADDALONI

1. INTRODUCTION

DESPITE the trend of globalization in recent years, the financial structures of different economies and the way in which corporate governance is implemented remain diverse. In this chapter we compare the structure of the euro area with the UK, the

This is based on Allen, Chui, and Maddaloni 2004 but is updated and includes a section on corporate governance. The views expressed here are the personal views of the authors and do not necessarily reflect the views of the Bank for International Settlements or the European Central Bank or the Hong Kong Monetary Authority.

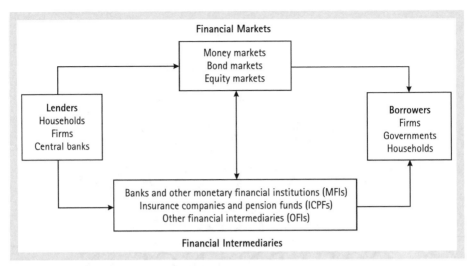

Fig. 1.1. An overview of the financial system

USA, Japan, and, to the extent possible, non-Japan Asia.[1] Figure 1.1 gives an overview of the functioning of a financial system. Lenders of funds are primarily households and firms. As we shall see, they are also increasingly central banks, particularly in Asia. These lenders can supply funds to the ultimate borrowers, who are mainly firms, government, and households, in two ways. The first is through financial markets, which consist of money markets, bond markets, and equity markets. In this chapter we focus mainly on bond and equity markets. The second is through financial intermediaries. These are credit institutions such as banks, and money market funds, insurance companies, and pension funds, and other financial intermediaries such as mutual funds.

Why do financial structure and corporate governance matter? They are important for at least three reasons.

1. efficiency;
2. financial stability;
3. monetary policy transmission channels.

The efficiency properties of a financial system determine how well it does its job of allocating resources. In terms of Figure 1.1 the issue is how effectively funds flow from borrowers to lenders so that everybody's welfare is maximized. A first aspect of this is how the financial system allows risk to be shared and who bears it. A second is the incentives to produce and use information. In particular, is information provided to indicate where resources can be most profitably invested? A third is how effective corporate governance is implemented. What objectives do managers pursue and how does the financial system constrain them? One of the most important determinants of long-run growth is the extent to which new industries are funded; a fourth aspect is

---

[1] This includes China, Hong Kong, India, Indonesia, Korea, Malaysia, the Philippines, Singapore, Taiwan, and Thailand.

how effectively this is done. Finally, there is the issue of how a financial system evolves over time, and the role of law and politics in determining this.

Financial stability is another reason why financial structure is important. Prior to the twentieth century, banking crises, currency crises, and stock market crashes occurred frequently. The Great Crash of 1929 and the Great Depression that followed convinced almost all governments to heavily regulate their financial system to prevent instability. This was successful in that from the end of the Second World War until the collapse of the Bretton Woods System in 1971, there was only one banking crisis in the world. However, stability was achieved only by severely restricting the efficiency properties of the financial system. The financial liberalization aimed at improving efficiency led to the re-emergence of instability. Banking crises, currency crises, asset price bubbles and crashes, contagion, and financial fragility have occurred in emerging and developed countries in recent years. This raises the issue of what exactly is the relationship between financial structure and these phenomena.

Finally, financial structure is important in determining monetary policy transmission channels. The traditional *money view* is that interest rates affect consumption and investment as predicted by neoclassical theories based on perfect capital markets. In this setting institutions do not matter. The *credit view*, on the other hand, stresses that with imperfect capital markets the effects of monetary policy depend on access to finance. How finance is obtained by firms, households, and governments depends critically on the financial structure.

As we will see, there are numerous ways of categorizing financial structure. The one that is most useful in any particular instance will depend on the precise question that is being asked. The first categorization is bank based versus market based. The conventional wisdom is that the euro area and Japan would be bank based systems, while the UK and the USA would be market based. It can be seen from Figure 1.2 that the conventional wisdom is rather simplistic. Figure 1.2 shows a comparison of the long-term financing structure of these economies in 1996 (before the Asian financial crisis) and 2004. The figures are given as a percentage of GDP. Bank loans consist of domestic credit to the private sector. The figures in the stock market column are the total market capitalization. The bond market figures exclude international securities and are divided into public and private sector bonds.

It can be seen from Figure 1.2(a) that in 1996 the euro area had small stock markets but large bank loans and in that sense could be considered as bank based. However, it also had a significant bond market both in terms of public and private sector debt. The UK was significantly different with a large stock market and bank loans but a small bond market, particularly in terms of private sector debt.[2] In some sense it seems to be both market based and bank based. The main features of the US financial structure are a small amount of bank loans, a significant stock market, and a much larger bond market than any of the other areas in relative terms. It is the most market-based economy. Japan has significant amounts of finance in all categories. It

---

[2] The UK used to have a significant corporate bond market but this died during the 1970s when inflation was high. It has not revived in recent years despite the reduction in inflation.

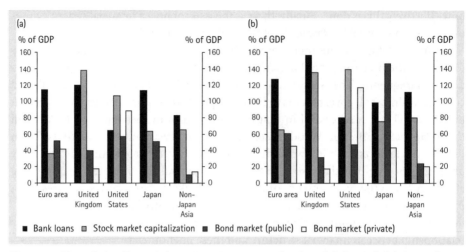

Fig. 1.2. Size of the financial markets by country/region (a) (1996) (b) (2004)

Sources: Bank for International Settlements, CEIC Data Ltd, Central Bank of China (Taiwan), International Financial Statistics, World Economic Outlook, and World Federation of Exchanges

is very much a bank- and market-based economy. Non-Japan Asia is more similar to the UK: Bank loans and the stock market are important but the bond market is not.

Figure 1.2(b) shows the situation in 2004 several years after the Asian crises. It can be seen that the structure is basically the same. The main difference is that Japanese government debt has increased significantly. One interesting feature is that the financial structure in non-Japan Asia has not changed significantly despite the Asian crises.

Figure 1.2 focuses on the claims that are issued by borrowers. Another way of asking whether economies are bank based or market based is to look at household assets. These are shown in Figure 1.3(a). This shows that all the economies are distinctly different. Again, no simple categorization into market based or bank based is possible. Households in the euro area own significantly fewer financial assets than in the other economies, with a total of 194 per cent of GDP compared with 285 per cent, 326 per cent, and 268 per cent for the UK, the USA, and Japan, respectively. In terms of the composition of assets there are also large differences. In the euro area, assets held in banks are the most important; insurance and pension funds are next, with direct holdings of shares after that. One striking thing is that household portfolios in the UK are very similar to those in the euro area with one significant difference: the investment in insurance and pension funds is dramatically higher. This is presumably a result of the difference in public sector pension schemes. In the UK the basic pension from the state is minimal, while in the euro area state pensions are usually generous. However, current pension reforms in continental Europe, which were mainly triggered by population ageing that imposes a large burden on the traditional social security systems, are likely to increase the importance of institutional investors

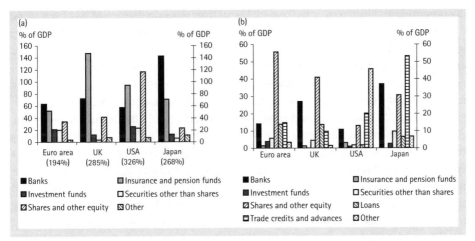

Fig. 1.3. Portfolio allocation (average 1995–2003) (a) Households (b) Non-financial corporations

Sources: ECB, Federal Reserve Board, and Bank of Japan

(pension funds, in particular) in the euro area as well. The USA is an outlier in terms of the direct holdings of shares and other equity. Also, households have relatively little in banks. Meanwhile, Japan is an outlier in terms of the amount of assets held in banks, where households hold much more in this form than households in other countries. They also have significant amounts in insurance and pension funds. This is to a large extent in insurance companies that offer debt-like contracts. Given the small holdings of shares and other equity, the Japanese bear significantly less financial risk than the households in the USA and UK.[3] The USA has somewhat less intermediation than the other economies, although the total amount of intermediation is significant in all economies.

Figure 1.3(b) shows the assets of non-financial corporations. These again underline significant differences across the economies. The euro area and the UK are quite similar except for the amount of shares and other equity held, and the financial investments held in banks. The USA has much less investment than the other countries except for the 'other' category. This includes holdings of other assets, which are not identified in the flow of funds data.[4] Japan is perhaps the most different. It has significantly more assets in banks and more trade credit than other countries.

Much work has already been done on financial structure of countries (see, for example, Allen and Gale 2000a; ECB 2002, 2003a; Hartmann, Maddaloni, and Manganelli 2003; and Baele et al. 2004). Much of this work is concerned with

---

[3] It is an interesting question how Japanese households can bear less risk than US and UK households. Allen and Gale 1997 have argued that this can occur if banks engage in intertemporal smoothing so that the real assets in the economy are different. Another possibility is that in Japan risk is borne through the government. During the 1990s when the Japanese government bailed out several banks by injecting public money, the households' financial risk had been transferred to the government.

[4] In particular, this category also includes the equity holdings of non-financial corporations.

documenting the differences in financial structure. A limited amount has been done on how the significant differences between financial systems manifest themselves in terms of efficiency, stability, and monetary policy transmission channels. These are obviously immense subject areas. In this chapter we wish to focus on two aspects that have received relatively little attention in this literature. The first is a comparison of financial institutions in the different economies, which is considered in Section 2. As Figure 1.2 indicated, intermediaries are important in all of the economies but institutional structure differs significantly across countries. Section 3 considers the real estate and mortgage markets in the different economies. This is a large part of the financial sector but again has not been considered in great depth in the financial structure literature. Since institutional investors play such a large role in the financial sector and real estate is a major part of household wealth, understanding the operation of these parts of the financial system is crucial for analyses of efficiency, stability, and monetary policy transmission channels. In Section 4 we consider the differences in corporate governance in the different regions, which are significantly different. Finally, Section 5 contains concluding remarks.

2. THE ROLE OF INSTITUTIONAL INVESTORS

In the USA, households do hold significant amounts of securities directly. However, even there, the majority of financial assets are held in intermediaries. In all of the other economies considered in Figure 1.3(a) the vast majority of assets are held by financial intermediaries. There have recently been some important contributions to the literature on institutional investors (see, for example, Davis and Steil 2001; Guiso, Halliassos, and Jappelli 2002a, 2002b; and Davis 2003), which have highlighted not only their growing role as financial market participants but also their importance for the efficiency and stability of the financial systems. In this section we divide the institutional investors into three categories, following the standard statistical classification. The first is Monetary Financial Institutions (MFIs), which includes banks, money market funds, and other credit institutions. The second is Insurance Corporations and Pension Funds (ICPFs). The final category is Other Financial Intermediaries (OFIs). The definition of this last category varies across countries but it includes securities and derivatives dealers and mutual funds. In Japan it includes also government intermediaries.[5] In Figure 1.4 we consider the assets of these institutions and in Figure 1.5 we consider the liabilities.

---

[5] These are public financial institutions owned and controlled by the central government whose principal business is financial intermediation. This sector includes the Fiscal Loan Fund and other government financial institutions. The Fiscal Loan Fund supplies funds to institutions covered by the Fiscal Investment and Loans Program. Postal savings and postal life insurance are classified as depository corporations and life insurance, thus they are included in the MFI and ICPF category, respectively (see Bank of Japan 2002).

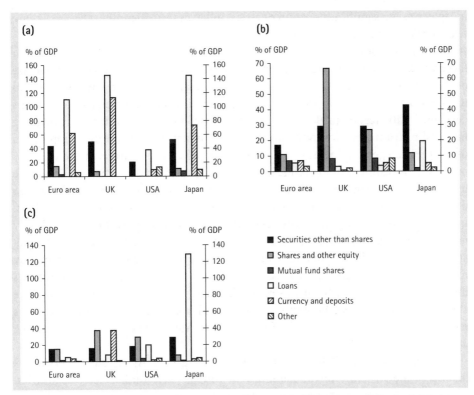

Fig. 1.4. Portfolio allocation (average 1995–2003) (a) Monetary financial institutions (b) Insurance companies and pension funds (c) Other financial intermediaries

Sources: ECB, Federal Reserve Board, and Bank of Japan

Figure 1.4(a) shows the assets of MFIs. Perhaps not surprisingly, given that this category consists mostly of banks, the allocation is similar in all economies. The UK MFIs have somewhat higher currency and deposits than the others, presumably reflecting a larger interbank market. The USA has a much smaller total size of the sector relative to GDP than the other countries. MFIs in the USA also have much smaller holdings of equity and other securities than in other countries. For regulatory reasons, they can only hold equity in special situations such as when a firm goes bankrupt.

The portfolio allocations of insurance companies and pension funds are shown in Figure 1.4(b). These are also fairly similar across countries. As has already been stressed in the discussion of Figure 1.2(a), UK pension funds hold significantly more equities than those in other countries. UK insurance companies also hold significant amounts of shares. Thus, UK ICPFs have significantly more equity exposure than in other countries. The euro area ICPFs have a diverse set of holdings with significant amounts of a number of assets. The USA is unusual in not having many loans while in Japan this is a significant portion of assets. In Japan securities other than shares are relatively large while equity is fairly small.

Figure 1.4(c) shows the allocation of OFIs. As mentioned above, the definition of these varies considerably across countries. A first observation is that the total size of OFIs' portfolios is relatively smaller in the euro area compared with the UK and the USA. At first sight, it seems as though the euro area financial system is less developed with regard to different (new) types of financial institutions providing financial instruments. However, this difference in fact stems from the composition of the OFI category in the euro area and in the UK. In the euro area the majority of OFIs are investment funds, while in the UK securities and derivatives dealers make up the largest share of the sector. Securities and derivatives dealers typically have large deposit and loan positions on both the asset and the liability side of the balance sheet. In the USA, OFIs consist primarily of mutual funds, which invest their funds mainly in shares and in several kinds of fixed income securities (Treasury, agency, municipal, and corporate bonds). US finance companies engaged in lending activity (primarily mortgages and consumer credit) are also included in this category, which explains the large value of loans. In this category the most surprising outlier is Japan. The amount of loans that its OFIs grant is many times larger than in other countries. This reflects the activity of some public financial institutions, which are included in the OFI category.

Figure 1.5 shows the liabilities of financial institutions. As already observed for the assets, the structure of the liabilities of MFIs is fairly similar across countries, as shown in Figure 1.5(a). Again, the size of the currency and deposits in the UK is larger than in the other economies, reflecting presumably interbank activities. Another observation is that US MFIs issue very little in securities compared to the other economies. By contrast, in the euro area, securities issued by MFIs are large and represent the majority of the amount outstanding of corporate bonds. Figure 1.5(b) shows the liabilities of the ICPF sector. Not surprisingly, they are almost totally insurance and pension fund reserves. As previously observed, the weight of the ICPF sector in the UK is significantly higher than in the other economies. Figure 1.5(c) shows the liabilities of OFIs across countries. It can be seen that the liabilities structure also varies considerably. In the euro area and in the USA, the major liability item is mutual fund shares since mutual funds are the biggest institutions in the OFI sector. The liability structure in the UK and in Japan is significantly different, reflecting also the already mentioned institutional differences.

Institutional investors in non-Japan Asia provide an interesting contrast to the euro area, UK, USA, and Japan. As shown in Table 1.1, they have so far played a rather minor role in the financial system in the relatively more developed Asian economies, but have grown strongly over the past few years. This was particularly so in the mutual fund sector. Total net assets under management by mutual funds in Hong Kong rose by almost ten times between 1997 and 2004 to US$832 billion, accounting for more than 54 per cent of total GDP.[6] Strong growth is due to a number of factors. In

---

[6] Figures are reported for Hong Kong, Korea, Malaysia, Singapore, Taiwan, and Thailand due to data availability.

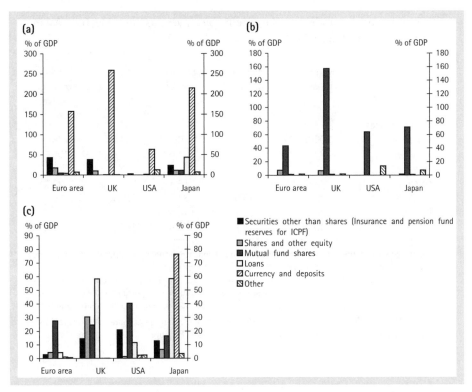

Fig. 1.5. Liabilities (average 1995–2003) (a) Monetary financial institutions (b) Insurance companies and pension funds (c) Other financial intermediaries

Sources: ECB, Federal Reserve Board, and Bank of Japan

Hong Kong and Singapore, initiatives by the regulators to help promote the status of financial centres have attracted overseas funds to invest in the two economies. Between 2000 and 2004, funds sourced from overseas investors have consistently accounted for 60–70 per cent of the asset management sector. As for the rest of Asia, the low returns on equity markets and low interest rate environment over the past few years have induced local retail investors to subscribe to bond funds in search of higher yields. However, this also raised concerns about overall financial stability in these economies as the local bond markets are comparatively illiquid and volatile. For example, the accounting scandal of the SK Group in Korea in 2003 triggered retail investors to redeem more than US$13 billion from the local investment trust companies in a few days (out of assets of more than US$140 billion), severely affecting other asset prices.

Despite the rapid growth in mutual funds, insurance companies, especially life insurers, remain the largest institutional investor in most emerging Asian economies except the two financial centres. This is partly due to the tradition of incorporating some savings components into life policies. Pension funds in non-Japan Asia are mostly under government-sponsored national provident funds. Notable examples are Malaysia and Singapore where the governments direct a fully funded, defined contribution

Table 1.1. Assets under management by investors in selected Asian economies (2004)(% of GDP)

	Mutual funds[a]	Insurance companies	Pension funds[b]	Banks	Foreign exchange reserves
Financial centres					
Hong Kong	208.8	n.a.	9.4	557.0	75.1
Singapore	193.5	42.6	62.9	220.6	105.6
Others					
Korea	26.0	32.4	17.1	105.4	29.2
Malaysia	19.5	19.0	53.7	170.1	56.6
Taiwan	25.3	56.1	n.a.	235.2	79.2
Thailand	10.7	10.1	4.6	116.2	30.5

[a] From the Survey of the Singapore Asset Management Industry, Monetary Authority of Singapore, Investment Company Institute, and Thai Securities and Exchange Commission.

[b] Apart from Thailand, figures include only public pension funds. From 1 July 2005, Taiwan's employers will have to pay 6% of employees' monthly salaries as contributions to portable individual pension accounts. The government estimates that T$150 billion (US$4.8 billion) will be accumulated annually.

Sources: IMF International Financial Statistics, World Economic Outlook, Singaporean Central Provident Board, the Hong Kong Mandatory Provident Fund Authority, and Employees Provident Fund, Malaysia.

system for domestic workers. Consequently, the assets under management by pension funds in these two countries are much larger than the rest of the region. However, as pointed out by Holzmann, MacArthur, and Sin (2000), despite their relatively large asset size, these national mandatory funds have not contributed to a significant development of local capital markets as their assets are required to be invested mainly in government securities. In Hong Kong, the government launched the Mandatory Provident Fund in 2000, which allows citizens to choose their investment plans among a group of approved private investment funds. Including some assets transferred from other privately set-up pension schemes before the launch, the size of total net assets remains relatively small. Also, growth could be slowed by the low incentives for individual employees to voluntarily contribute extra funds to the scheme since there is no capital gains tax there.

How do the differences in financial institutions across economies affect efficiency, financial stability, and monetary policy transmission channels? This is an important question which has received little attention. The relative unimportance of monetary financial institutions in the USA is striking. Some might argue that this is superior in terms of efficiency, stability, and the transmission of monetary policy. Other institutions and direct investment in securities by households may generate a superior allocation of resources. Since the major form of instability has traditionally been banking crises, having fewer funds in banks and other MFIs would appear to be desirable. Finally, if MFIs are less important, monetary policy may be transmitted to the real economy more effectively. However, it is not at all clear that these arguments are correct. For example, it is often suggested that institutions overcome market imperfections so economies like those in the euro zone may be more efficient than the USA. Much more research is needed on these topics.

Box 1.1. Central Banks as Institutional Investors

Traditionally, institutional investors have been thought of as banks, insurance companies, pension funds, and mutual funds. One of the dramatic developments over the past few years is that central banks in Asia (including Japan) have become major institutional investors. They have built up large foreign exchange reserves, with an intention to buffer unpredictable balance-of-payments shocks and to smooth extreme exchange rate volatility. Consequently, aggregate foreign exchange reserves in Asia grew sharply from less than US$1 trillion at end 1999 to US$2.5 trillion (some 70% of the world total) at end May 2004 (Figure 1.6). Since a large part of these reserve assets is held in US Treasury securities, these central banks have become an important player in the US Treasury markets. The holdings of US Treasury securities by non-US official institutions (mostly central banks) reached US$1.2 trillion at end 2004. Assuming 70% of the total was held by Asian central banks, this means that they could hold up to US$840 billion of US Treasury securities.

Does the growing role of central banks as institutional investors matter? It can be argued that it is very significant, in terms of both market efficiency and financial stability. Central banks have different objective functions from private financial institutions. They may care considerably more about financial stability. As a result, they may be willing to hold positions that enhance stability at the cost of efficiency. For example, Japan's enormous holdings of US securities are largely funded by issuing low-yield government securities (Figure 1.7). The Bank of Japan in effect has an enormous carry trade (i.e. borrowing at a low rate in one country to invest at a higher rate in another). When interest rates in Japan rise above those in the USA, private institutions would quickly unwind their positions. However, the Bank of Japan, which is also concerned with overall financial stability, may be willing to unwind this position quite slowly to avoid disruption of the financial markets even though this could be very costly. On the other hand, for those countries where interest paid on domestic debt is higher than that earned on holdings of foreign assets (e.g. from 2002 to 2004 in Korea), it can be argued that the reserve accumulation is inefficient as the cost might outweigh its benefit as a crisis prevention measure (see IMF 2003).

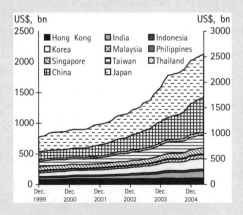

Fig. 1.6. Foreign exchange reserves

Source: CEIC Data Limited

Box 1.1. (continued)

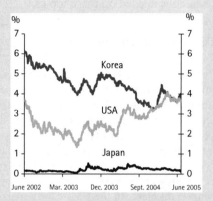

Fig. 1.7. Three-year government bond yields

Source: CEIC Data Limited

The strong demand of Asian central banks for US Treasury securities might also have contributed to the unusually low long-term US bond yields over the past few years. Historical evidence shows that nominal GDP growth in the USA has moved broadly in line with the long-term bond yields (Figure 1.8). However, since the second quarter of 2003, nominal GDP growth has exceeded long-term Treasury yields by some two percentage points. In addition, in contrast to the past experience that longer-term rates rose during an interest rate tightening cycle, they have fallen since the current cycle began in June 2004.

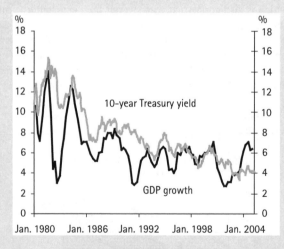

Fig. 1.8. US long-term Treasury yield nominal GDP growth

Sources: US Federal Reserve Board and Bureau of Economic Analysis

The low levels of long-term bond yields pose a risk to financial stability in the sense that a sharp correction, say triggered by the selling of US Treasury notes by the Asian central banks, could roil the global financial markets. Given the increasingly globalized capital markets, a rapid increase in long-term Treasury yields could lead to more widespread increases in other bond yields. Apart from the disruptions to the functioning of the capital markets, for those countries that need to loosen their monetary policy to stimulate growth, a substantial increase in bond yields could reduce the effectiveness of such policy. In addition, in the event of a sharp rise in US Treasury yields, those countries with large holdings of such securities in their reserve portfolio could incur significant mark-to-market losses.

3. THE HOUSING AND MORTGAGE MARKETS

So far we have focused on financial wealth and the allocation across institutions. This is only one component of wealth. Another major component is housing. In this section we will focus on the housing and mortgage markets. As Maclennan, Muellbauer, and Stephens (2000) have stressed, these are very important for efficiency, stability, and the monetary policy transmission process. For example, in many European countries housing costs typically involve a fifth to a quarter of disposable incomes, and housing wealth accounts for over half of household net wealth. In the UK a housing bubble in the late 1980s had a disastrous effect on the economy when it burst in the early 1990s. The predominance of variable rate mortgages in the UK and some other countries means that monetary policy transmission works in a quite different way from in countries such as the USA, where mortgages primarily have long-term fixed rates.

Housing prices are quite volatile and the resulting changes in housing wealth, which is a major part of households' wealth, affect the rest of the economy. Changes in house prices may be caused by a variety of factors that affect both the supply of and the demand for housing. Real house prices tend to track the business cycle. Since the mid-1990s, residential property prices have recorded widely differing rates of increase in real terms across the industrialized countries.

Real house prices in most EU countries have followed long cycles,[7] of amplitude of around ten years, around an upward trend in the last twenty years. Since the mid-1990s, real house prices have risen at an accelerated pace in most EU countries, particularly so in Ireland, the Netherlands, and Spain (see Figure 1.9). Internationally, a rising trend is discernible in the USA as well, where house prices continue to grow, notwithstanding the recession in 2001 and the loss of jobs in 2002–3. Examples of countries where the trend was different are Germany, Japan, and Switzerland. These stand out as countries where real house prices have shown a decline since the mid-1990s, and their current level is not far from where it was in 1970 (see OECD 2004).

---

[7] Throughout the paper, the term EU does not include the ten countries which joined the Union on 1 May 2004 or the two which joined on 1 January 2007.

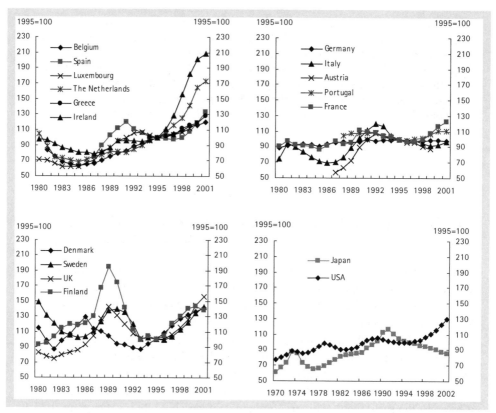

Fig. 1.9. Real house prices in the EU, USA, and Japan

Sources: ECB 2003 and BIS

As for non-Japan Asia, the importance of the housing market for the overall economy was clearly evidenced during the 1997/8 financial crisis. The pre-crisis property market bubbles in many countries have often been cited (e.g. Quigley 2001) as a major cause of the regional financial crisis in 1997/8. Financial liberalization and the strong growth in many countries in the early 1990s attracted large capital inflows, which in turn fuelled a rapid expansion in lending to the private sector for construction projects and mortgage financing. The speculative attacks on the currencies and the sudden capital outflows brought about recessions in these economies and the collapse in their property prices. Pre-1997 data on the real estate sector in non-Japan Asia are scarce, but Figure 1.10 shows that real house prices in Hong Kong and Korea fell sharply in the wake of the crisis. Note that, apart from Korea where government policy helped create a house price boom in 2002 (see below), property prices in most other non-Japan Asian economies remain weak despite the fact that the economies have returned to positive economic growth in 1999.

Several factors have been established by the empirical literature as affecting housing markets. In the EU the affordability of owner-occupied housing has generally remained constant or improved over the long term. In more recent times, however,

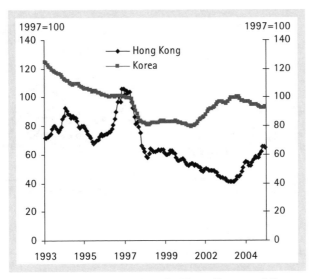

Fig. 1.10. Real house prices in Hong Kong and Korea

Source: CEIC Data Limited

house prices have risen faster than disposable income in a number of countries and the ratio of house prices to income has been at, or close to, its maximum since 1980. At the same time, the low level of interest rates and thus of mortgage rates over the last few years might have partly compensated for the increase in house prices, increasing affordability (see ECB 2003b, 2006).

Both real and nominal mortgage rates in the EU and in the USA fell considerably in the 1990s, after having increased in the 1980s (see Figure 1.11). These developments closely followed developments in other fixed income markets, although some of the variation may have been due to other factors, like changes in regulations and increased competition.

In the long run, demand for housing should depend on the number of households, which is linked to population growth.[8] The growth rate of working age population, and in particular of the 'purchasing' age group—people aged between 30 and 40 years old—is expected to decline in most developed countries. In Europe, however, this decline seems to be partly counterbalanced by the increase, over most recent years, of the number of households, reflecting an increasingly larger number of small households as well as migration flows.

Another microeconomic factor that is of considerable importance is the structure and institutions of credit markets. The advent of financial liberalization, particularly in mortgage markets, has increased the sensitivity of house prices to interest rates, as credit constraints were reduced. During the 1990s, the policy of several

---

[8] Mankiw and Weil 1989 find evidence in the USA that a change in the number of births over time leads to a large change in the demand for housing, which, in turn, could have substantial effects on house prices.

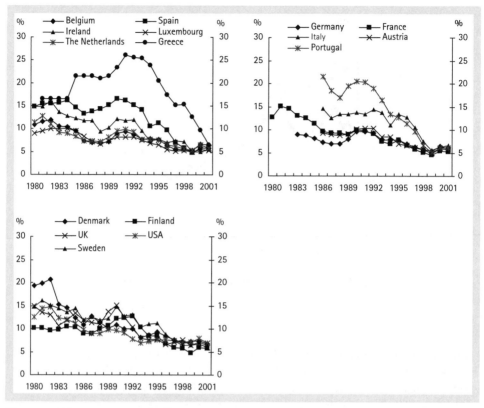

Fig. 1.11. Mortgage rates in EU countries and in the USA

Sources: ECB 2003b and US Federal Housing Finance Board Monthly Interest Rate Survey

EU governments was directed toward favouring owner-occupation, through means of tax exemptions, interest deductibility, and state guarantees for private housing loans which have been restricted to owner-occupied houses (see ECB 2003b). Korea gives another interesting example of government policy directed to the housing market. House prices in Korea began to rise sharply in 2001 after the government announced a series of measures to boost the local housing market that was badly affected by the economic crisis. These included providing greater financial assistance to qualified non-homeowners to purchase their first property through low-interest loans; lowering the acquisition, registration, and capital gains taxes, and liberalizing the trading in contracts for the right to purchase apartments prior to their completion. Against the background of favourable macroeconomic conditions, house prices rose by more than 25 per cent between 2001 and 2003. The Korean government has since introduced counter-measures to stabilize the housing market. Prices slowed initially in late 2002 but have resumed a rising trend again recently, especially in certain areas in Seoul where demand for housing has remained strong.

3.1. Mortgage Markets

Most transactions in the housing market involve a corresponding transaction in the mortgage market. Mortgage markets in the EU largely reflect several deregulation measures which were carried out from the 1980s on (and for some countries even earlier). These measures included, for example, the abolition of interest-rate ceilings, the relaxation both of quantitative credit controls and of contractual restrictions, and the removal of strict barriers to entry into the mortgage market. Public mortgage institutions scaled back the size of their activities and measures were taken to facilitate the securitization of mortgage loans.

Notwithstanding the common effort toward a more integrated mortgage market, housing credit systems in the EU continue to be characterized by different types of mortgage contracts, partly reflecting regulatory differences and partly contracts and conventions established in earlier periods when inflation rates and interest rate variability were very different across EU countries (see, for example, Maclennan, Muellbauer, and Stephens 2000). The relative importance of variable and fixed interest rate contracts and the fees applying to the borrower in case of an early repayment of the mortgage debt are examples of characteristics of the mortgage contracts where large differences are evident across countries.

The degree of mortgage market 'completeness' can be defined as the ability of the mortgage market to serve a broad range of borrowers and to apply lower mortgage interest-rate spreads. A cross-country comparison addressing the issue of mortgage market 'completeness' is available only for a group of eight European countries (see Mercer Oliver Wyman 2003). Among those, Denmark, the Netherlands, and the UK seem to have the most complete mortgage market in terms of the range of products offered and a choice between alternative interest rate adjustment and repayment options.

Two key indicators of mortgage market ability to provide financing are typically the maximum loan-to-value (LTV) ratios and the mortgage repayment terms. Across countries these indicators tend to be correlated with the size of mortgage debt. High LTV ratios allow borrowers to take out more debt, and longer repayment terms are then needed to keep debt-service-to-income ratios affordable.

The fragmented evidence available (especially at the EU level) suggests also that loan-to-value ratios have risen in most countries in recent years, possibly reflecting the greater availability of mortgage products that permit households to better match their income and their debt servicing. There are also exceptions to this trend. In Korea, the financial regulator lowered the guideline for the ceiling on LTV for apartments to 60 per cent from 70–80 per cent in 2002 to curb real estate speculation.

Over the past two decades most industrialized countries have also shown significant changes in the ratio of household mortgage debt over GDP (see Figure 1.12). Among European countries, the Netherlands, Portugal, Germany, and Spain all experienced a rapid accumulation of debt during the 1990s. Significant differences exist across countries which most likely depend on structural features of the mortgage markets.

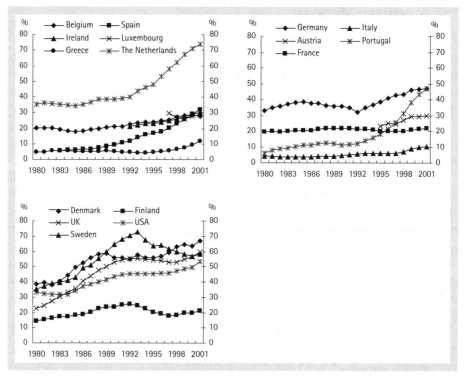

Fig. 1.12. Ratio of nominal mortgage debt over GDP

Source: ECB (2003b) and Federal Reserve Board

An important characteristic of the housing market which has an impact on the mortgage market structure is the extent of owner-occupation. Housing tenancy structures differ considerably across OECD countries (see Table 1.2). Broadly speaking, the share of ownership housing is very high in southern European countries, relatively low in Austria, Germany, and the Netherlands, and in some Nordic countries, and around two-thirds in most other industrialized countries. In part, these differences reflect tax incentives, but they are also supposed to reflect differences in access to mortgage financing, since access to mortgage markets should allow households to achieve homeownership earlier. In practice, however, some of the countries with the highest number of owner-occupied houses—such as Italy and Spain—are also those with the least developed mortgage markets. This suggests that mechanisms like intergenerational transfers and bequests are at work in these countries.

3.2. House Equity Withdrawal

A rise in housing prices is going to affect household consumption if households can effectively spend the extra liquidity on consumption goods (or invest it in financial assets). This can take place essentially in two ways. First, households can refinance

Table 1.2. Mortgage and housing market indicators

	Residential mortgage debt (% of GDP)		Loan-to-value ratios (%)		Typical loan term	Share of owner-occupied housing (%)		
	1992	2002	Typical	Max.	(years)	1980[a]	1990[a]	2002[a]
Austria	—	—	60	80	20–30	52	55	56
Belgium	19.9	27.9	83	100	20	59	67	71
Denmark	63.9	74.3	80	80	30	52	52	51
Finland	37.2	31.8	75	80	15–18	61	67	58
France	21.0	22.8	67	100	15	47	54	55
Germany	38.7	54.0	67	80	25–30	41	39	42
Greece	4.0	13.9	75	80	15	75	76	83
Ireland	20.5	36.5	66	90	20	76	79	77
Italy	6.3	11.4	55	80	15	59	68	80
Japan	25.3	36.8	80	—	25–30	60	61	60
Luxembourg[b]	23.9	17.5	—	80	20–25	60	64	70
The Netherlands	40.0	78.8	90	115	30	42	45	53
Portugal	12.8	49.3	83	90	15	52	67	64
Spain	11.9	32.3	70	100	15	73	78	85
Sweden	37.5	40.4	77	80	<30	58	56	61
United Kingdom	55.5	64.3	69	110	25	58	65	69
United States	45.3	58.0	78	—	30	65	64	68

[a] Approximate dates.
[b] 1994.
Source: OECD 2004.

an existing mortgage loan and take out more debt. Second, when house prices have risen, households can borrow more from the overall credit system when they transact with each other in the housing market, because the collateral value of their assets has risen. The literature refers to the overall result in both cases as 'mortgage equity withdrawal', although the underlying mechanisms are rather different. In most EU countries mortgage equity withdrawal is not common. Since 1985, for example, considering the five largest countries in continental Europe (all in the euro area), households have been net acquirers of mortgage equity every year, though the amount has declined in recent years (as a percentage of disposable income). The only exception is the Netherlands, where the household sector withdrew mortgage equity between 1996 and 2002 coinciding with the boom in the domestic housing market (see Figure 1.13).

Mortgage equity withdrawal is much more common in the UK and US markets, and it has been increasing significantly in the last few years (see Figure 1.14). As outlined above institutional set-ups in housing and mortgage markets are likely to be the main reason behind these developments. Other factors of importance could be low transaction costs and a high rate of homeownership.

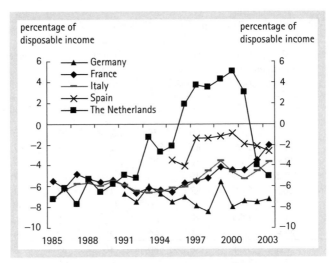

Fig. 1.13. Mortgage equity withdrawal in selected European countries

Note: Mortgage equity withdrawal is calculated as the difference between the net increase in loans for housing and residential investment

Sources: ECB and EU National Central Banks

Survey evidence in the USA and in the UK suggests that the equity value that households extract from the refinancing of their mortgages is mainly used to fund home improvements and to pay down consumer debt.[9]

3.3. Discussion

The importance of housing for household wealth, the effect of boom–bust cycles on financial stability, and the role of mortgage features for the transmission of monetary policy show how crucial it is to consider housing and mortgage markets as a part of financial structure. This is particularly true in Europe where the creation of a single market for financial services has so far had little impact (see Maclennan, Muellbauer, and Stephens 2000). Even within the current European Monetary Union countries there is significant divergence. This seems to be an important difference from other places where the mortgage market is fairly homogeneous within each currency area. As the euro zone expands it will be important to understand the effect of this factor, particularly on monetary policy transmission channels.

Efficiency factors are also important in the housing and mortgage markets as Box 1.2, on the mortgage-backed securities markets in the USA and Europe, illustrates. The size of the market in the USA and scale of the government-sponsored

[9]   See for example Board of Governors of the Federal Reserve System 2004.

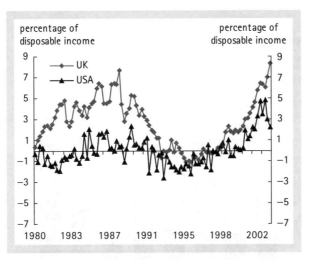

Fig. 1.14. Mortgage equity withdrawal in the UK and the USA

Note: Mortgage equity withdrawal is calculated as the difference between the net increase in loans for housing and residential investment

Sources: Bank of England and Federal Reserve Board

agencies are now so large that issues of stability have also come to the fore. A number of commentators worry that if any of the large agencies were to fail there would be a significant risk of instability.

Box 1.2. The Mortgage-backed Securities Market and the Role of Government-sponsored Agencies

The market for mortgages and for mortgage-related products has increased remarkably in the last few years. It has become the biggest fixed income market in the United States (see Figure 1.15). While in the USA more than half of the stock of mortgages is securitized, the European market for mortgage-related products continues to be very small, albeit with very large rates of growth occurring in the last few years.

This situation reflects the existence of a number of features of the US mortgage market which have encouraged the growth of securitization and reduced the need for mortgage lenders to hold capital. The US mortgage market is currently dominated by mortgage banks, which are typically the originators of the loans. These loans are then sold primarily to the US government-sponsored enterprises. These housing agencies play a pivotal role in the US mortgage market. They buy individual packages of mortgage loans from lending institutions and either hold them on their balance sheet or securitize them, selling them into the secondary mortgage market. There are currently five mortgage agencies in the USA, with different corporate structures: one is fully private (Sallie Mae), one is fully public

Box 1.2. (continued)

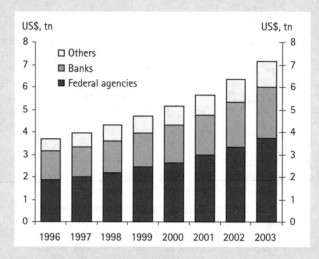

Fig. 1.15. Outstanding home mortgages in the USA

Note: Federal agencies are government-sponsored enterprises and federally related mortgage
pools
Source: Federal Reserve Board

(Ginnie Mae), three have a hybrid statute (Fannie Mae, Freddie Mac, and FHLB).[a] These last three agencies are privately owned, but operate under a charter with an 'implicit' state guarantee and some advantages (taxes, registration fees, disclosure requirements).[b] Fannie Mae and Freddie Mac are the largest among the agencies. They were created in the 1930s and in the 1970s respectively, as part of an effort to increase homeownership and improve liquidity in the residential mortgage market. They enjoy an implicit US government guarantee: there is a belief that, in case of possible failures, the agencies would be bailed out by the US government. In other respects, however, they are conventional shareholder-owned institutions.

[a] Government National Mortgage Association (Ginnie Mae) is a US government-owned corporation within the Department of Housing and Urban Development. Its securities are the only mortgage-backed securities that offer the full faith and credit guaranty of the US government. Student Loan Marketing Association (SLM or Sallie Mae) was created by the US Congress in 1972 as a government-sponsored enterprise (GSE). But privatization began in 1997 and the organization offers a wider range of financial loans. The GSE became a subsidiary of SLM corporation and terminated its ties to the federal government at the end of 2004.

[b] Fannie Mae and Freddie Mac are the only for-profit shareholder-owned companies in the USA that have a special status granted by a specialized federal charter. They are exempt from local and corporate taxes and their securities are treated as government securities under federal securities laws. Moreover, they have access to a Treasury line of credit, as the Secretary of Treasury has discretionary authority to purchase up to $2.25 billion in obligations issued by them.

Fannie Mae and Freddie Mac have two main lines of business. On the one hand they buy and hold mortgages and issue unsecured bonds (in both callable and non-callable form and with various maturities). On the other hand they provide a guarantee on the MBS backed by the pools they have assembled in exchange for a fee. They have been increasing significantly the importance of their first line of business, which is more profitable, especially in the last few years. In addition, they have recently been annually repurchasing about 50 per cent of their newly issued MBS each year.

Among the financial products related to the mortgage market, the mortgage-backed securities (MBS) market has grown particularly strong over the last decade, with an average growth of more than 10 per cent per annum in terms of outstanding amounts. It is currently the largest fixed income sector in the USA, with an outstanding balance significantly larger than the balance of the total Treasury securities market.[c]

As already mentioned, the European market for mortgage-related products is very small. MBS issuance accounts for around 50 per cent of the overall European securitization market, but still represents a small portion of all funding supply for mortgages. Despite significant growth rates in issuance recorded over recent years, the European market for MBS is liquid only in the UK and the Netherlands.[d] In the last few years there were a limited number of cases of securitization of mortgages originated in another country, but they never involved mortgages originated in more than one country.

The main reason why the European MBS market remains small and fragmented is the lack of a harmonized legal framework both concerning features and rules applicable to mortgages and mortgages loans and the securitization of such loans. This is reflected in the great variety of mortgage products across Europe. In addition, mortgage markets are essentially local markets and require in-depth knowledge of the local housing markets, and only a few European banks originate mortgages in more than one EU country.

Some form of common multi-seller platform has emerged at the domestic level, but the private sector has to overcome serious coordination problems when setting up these kinds of platforms.[e]

In non-Japan Asia, the MBS markets were less developed but issuance has taken off in Hong Kong, Korea, Malaysia, and Taiwan in recent years. While the MBS markets in Hong Kong, Malaysia, and to a lesser extent in Korea, are led by government-sponsored agencies (the Hong Kong Mortgage Corporation, Cagamas, and the Korea Housing Finance Corporation), MBS in Taiwan are issued by private banks. In particular, in Taiwan and Malaysia, MBS first appeared in 2004. In Taiwan, four MBS transactions, all originated by commercial banks, were recorded in 2004, totalling around T$20 billion (US$600 million). Separately, Cagamas, 'the Malaysian Fannie Mae', issued its inaugural issuance of MBS of ringgit 1.6 billion (US$420 million) in the same year.

One of the main reasons for these government-sponsored agencies to issue MBS is to enhance banking stability by reducing the risks associated with mortgage lending. For example, in Hong Kong, property-related lending accounted for 55 per cent of total bank

---

[c] The total MBS outstanding are the sum of MBS issued by federal agencies and by other asset-backed securities issuers.

[d] See for example Moody's Investor Service 2004.

[e] Examples of common structures that have emerged at the domestic level are the Promise-Provide platform sponsored by the KfW and the multi-seller securitization of Spanish saving and cooperative banks. On 17 November 2003, the European Financial Mortgage Association project team released a report proposing a new European-based financial institution, the European Mortgage Finance Agency (EMFA).

Box 1.2. continued

lending in 2004. In addition, while mortgage loans in Hong Kong have a typical contractual life of over ten years, the average maturity of funding is mostly less than three months. Thus, Hong Kong banks are exposed to both significant concentration and liquidity risks to mortgage lending.

Given the high ownership ratios in these Asian economies—for example Taiwan has one of the highest ratios in the world at more than 80 per cent—there are abundant suitable assets for generating MBS. However, market sources suggest that a major impediment to the MBS market in these economies is that Asian investors, used to investment instruments with shorter maturities, are often put off by the long legal maturities of MBS.

4. Corporate Governance

In this section we discuss corporate governance in different regions around the world. Broadly speaking, three types of governance system are observed. In the Anglo-Saxon countries such as the USA and UK, shareholder wealth creation is the objective of the governance system. The law is clear that the shareholders are owners of the firm and the managers have a fiduciary (i.e. very strong) duty to the shareholders. In continental European countries such as Germany and France, and Japan, corporate governance is concerned with stakeholders such as workers, suppliers, and so forth as well as shareholders (see e.g. Allen and Gale 2000a; O'Sullivan 2000). In Germany the system of codetermination ensures that in large corporations workers' representatives have half the seats on the supervisory board so the firm is not run exclusively in shareholders' interests. In France and Japan and many other countries it is widely acknowledged that in practice the firm is run in the interests of many stakeholders and not just shareholders (see e.g. Allen 2005). Finally, in non-Japan Asia, family firms predominate and corporate governance is to a large extent concerned with family control (Claessens, Djankov, and Lang 2000).

Despite the wide variety of corporate governance systems, the vast majority of the academic literature on corporate governance has focused on the creation of shareholder value (see e.g. Becht, Bolton, and Röell 2003; Tirole 2006). According to much of this literature what is desirable for shareholder wealth creation is a well-functioning board of directors with sufficient outside directors that it is independent of management, good managerial incentives that align their interests with those of the shareholder, effective protection of minority shareholders, and full transparency, disclosure, and accountability. In stakeholder societies much of the literature that exists is concerned with the role of financial intermediaries and in particular banks. This would be the *Hausbank* system in Germany and the main bank system in Japan (see Allen and Gale 2000a and the references therein). In non-Japan Asia the usual argument is that family firms create the possibility for exploitation of minority shareholders. This means that minority protection of shareholders and transparency, disclosure, and accountability are important.

In recent years, the aftermath of the large corporate bankruptcies that first took place in Asia in the middle and late 1990s and then in the USA and Europe has precipitated a debate about corporate governance. In what follows we will analyse, using recent examples of corporate scandals and financial market instability, the most recurrent sources of market failures linked to these episodes and we will briefly describe the most recent policy reforms addressing these issues.

Recent corporate scandals in the USA, and less significantly in Europe, tended to be characterized by strong conflicts of interest between managers and shareholders and between managers and external intermediaries, primarily auditors and financial intermediaries. Conflicts of interest were significant in the USA, where shareholding is much more dispersed and the use of reward systems which have proved to have perverse incentives (like stock options, for example) is much more significant. In Europe and also in Asia, where the role of banks—both as financing providers and also shareholders—tends to be bigger, problems deriving from ownership concentration have been more severe. In all cases the lack of transparency of publicly disclosed information was pivotal in the building up of unmanageable balance sheet positions.

When there are several shareholders, the monitoring of managers by a small group of owners may not be effective because of a free-rider problem. Everybody gets the benefit from the monitoring but only the small group pays the cost. These 'collective action' problems tend to be more severe when ownership is dispersed, as is especially the case in the USA and in the UK. High dispersion of ownership creates the need for reputational intermediaries, i.e. external monitors that have the task of reviewing the activities of the firm and ensuring that managers act in the interests of shareholders. Unfortunately the recent scandals which were brought to light in the USA—primarily the bankruptcy of Enron and WorldCom—have shown that financial intermediaries can be ineffective and at worst even collude with firms' management, because of the presence of conflicts of interest.

Conflicts of interest may arise in different ways, can involve different actors, and can be the result of certain institutional settings or corporate practices. Perverse incentives seem to have originated from share-based company executives' compensation, in particular in the form of stock options. This form of payment encouraged managers to drive up the stock price of the company (for example, increasing the expected return but also the riskiness of future projects) and then realize large gains through the exercise of their options. At the same time, until very recently, companies in the USA and in Europe were not required to expense employees' stock options in financial statements but only to release the information about the amount outstanding in footnotes. This may have contributed to a misleading picture of the financial situation of companies.

Other sources of conflicts of interest relate to financial intermediaries which can be involved in multiple activities (like underwriting, research, and brokerage activities) with the same company. Similarly, 'reputational intermediaries', like auditing

Table 1.3. Corporate ownership structure in different countries

Country	No. of companies	Largest voting block: median	Second largest voting block: median	Third largest voting block: median
Austria	50	52	2.5	0[a]
Belgium	140	56	6.3	4.7
Germany	372	57	0[a]	0
Spain	193	34.5	8.9	1.8
France	CAC40	20	5.9	3.4
Italy	214	54.5	5	2.7
The Netherlands	137	43.5	7.7	0[a]
Sweden	304	34.9	8.7	4.8
UK	207	9.9	6.6	5.2
USA	0	0	0	0
NYSE	1,309	5.4	0[a]	0[a]
NASDAQ	2,831	8.6	0[a]	0[a]

Note: The table reports the size of the largest, second largest and third largest median voting blocks for non-financial companies listed on an official market. For France, the main stock price index (CAC40) is reported.
[a] No 5% + voting block.
Source: ECGN (European Corporate Governance Network) as detailed in Barca and Becht 2001.

companies and rating agencies, which review and analyse information on the activities of the firm, have proved to be ineffective on occasion. For example, in the case of Enron, the SEC investigation concluded that rating agencies failed to use their powers to investigate the operations of the company: this could have resulted from conflict of interests as well as poor monitoring.

A system which is more common in continental Europe is the stakeholder model where managers' interests tend to be less aligned with the shareholders. In these countries concentrated ownership of shares is more prevalent. Large shareholders have an incentive to monitor the firm and they tend to become closer to managers and to be informed about the activities of the company. In 50 per cent of non-financial listed companies in Belgium, Germany, Italy, and Austria a single blockholder controls more than 50 per cent of voting rights (see Table 1.3). In addition, a particular feature of the European system is the role played by banks which are often also large shareholders. For example, some reports suggest that German banks hold around 10 per cent of national corporate equity. But even without holding equity directly, banks can exert a significant pressure for at least two reasons. First, they are often custodians for customers that are shareholders and as such represent them and vote their shares. For example, in Germany, large commercial banks through proxy voting arrangements often control over a quarter of the votes in major companies. Second, banks are often directly involved in the management of the company.

Ownership concentration, especially when the regulation framework and other protection systems against expropriation of minority shareholders are weak, can become a major corporate governance problem (see Shleifer and Vishny 1997 for the pros and cons of ownership concentration). Through owning a large proportion of the shares, the owners have the power to appoint directors and managers and to make major corporate decisions that normally require the approval of a range of shareholders.

Problems with this setting can arise when advantages deriving from the prominent position of large blockholders outweigh the benefits affecting all shareholders. These advantages could be monetary (for example, exploiting synergies of production) or non-monetary, like enjoying amenities associated with the control of the firm. In the case of Parmalat, for example, majority shareholders exercised considerable power over the management of the firm to the disadvantage of the other shareholders. At the same time, mechanisms like pyramid structures, cross-shareholdings, voting agreements, which are common in Europe as well as in Asia, can undermine market discipline: such corporate structures often imply that the only effective option for minority shareholders is to sell their holdings. Parmalat, for example, was characterized by a strong pyramid structure, with two companies at the top that were exclusively controlled by majority shareholders.

A major source of market failure recorded in the USA and in Europe in the context of the recent corporate scandals was the lack of relevant information being publicly disclosed. For example, following the collapse of Enron, substantial differences in alternative profit measures published by listed companies came to light, in particular between the so-called *pro forma* earnings and the earnings reported to the SEC. Bhattacharya, Daouk, and Welker (2003) try to measure 'earnings opacity' in companies' financial accounts in several countries. In terms of the overall earnings opacity measure, the USA performs better than most other countries, although some differences exist when more detailed measures are taken into account. Nevertheless, big accounting scandals were brought to light primarily in the USA, which seems to imply that more information does not always coincide with more disclosure. In this context, a key issue is represented by the increasing use of financial innovations and the related disclosure requirements. The Parmalat as well as the Enron scandals were characterized by a significant presence of offshore entities or *special purpose vehicles* (SPV) that served the purpose of processing fraudulent transactions. The presence of these instruments can make it very difficult for an investor to comprehend the true financial position of the company.

We now turn to the situation of corporate governance prevailing in emerging Asia before the financial crises. It is often argued that weak corporate governance contributed to the depth of the 1997/8 financial crisis in Asia (Johnson 2000). In the early 1990s when the five crisis-affected economies—Korea, Indonesia, Malaysia, the Philippines, and Thailand—registered strong economic growth, companies borrowed heavily from banks to finance their investment projects, some of which were found to be non-viable ex post. Over-leveraging and overinvestment made them particularly vulnerable to economic shocks. When the crisis started in 1997, many firms could not secure enough liquidity and went bankrupt, which in turn caused severe distress to the financial sector and the economy as a whole.

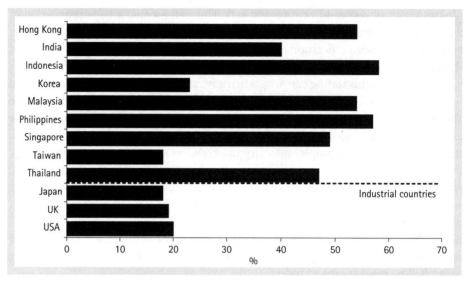

Fig. 1.16. Ownership of ten largest non-financial firms by large shareholders

Source: La Porta et al. 1998

In general, the weak corporate governance system in these economies in the early 1990s was characterized by a series of interrelated problems: concentrated ownership, a high level of diversification of large companies, little or no effective regulation to ensure the controlling shareholders and management treat small investors fairly and equitably, and lack of transparency, disclosure, and accountability.

One prominent feature of corporate governance in the crisis-hit Asian economies was the existence of large controlling shareholders, usually in the form of controlling family owners. Figure 1.16 shows that, apart from Korea and Taiwan, the average (cash flow) ownership stakes of the ten largest non-financial domestic firms by the three largest shareholders in emerging Asian economies were substantially higher than those in the UK and the USA. However, cash flow ownership could underestimate the ultimate controlling stake of major shareholders because of the existence of complex ownership structures of large companies. In Korea, the owners of some large conglomerates or *chaebol* controlled a large number of affiliates through cross-ownerships, effectively exerting much greater influence on important corporate decisions. Thus, when the ownership definition is based on control rights, which takes into account the pyramidal ownership structures, the concentration measures for Korea and Taiwan are increased substantially.[10] Table 1.4 shows that for all non-Japan emerging Asian economies, more than 44 per cent of publicly traded firms in 1996 were controlled by a family (in the sense that it

---

[10] For example, if a family controls 10% of stock of firm A, which in turn holds a 20% stake in firm B, by control rights ownership, the family will be measured as having 10% of the voting rights of firm B, rather than 2% as in cash flow rights.

Table 1.4. Proportion of family-controlled publicly traded companies in East Asia in 1996

Cut-off control rights	20%	30%	40%
Japan	9.7	2.8	0.9
Philippines	44.6	22.1	8.3
Taiwan	48.2	18.4	5.0
Korea	48.4	20.1	3.5
Singapore	55.4	32.6	14.9
Thailand	61.6	54.8	38.9
Hong Kong	66.7	34.4	17.6
Malaysia	67.2	45.6	14.7
Indonesia	71.5	58.7	35.4

Source: Claessens, Djankov, and Lang 1998.

holds at least 20 per cent of the publicly traded stock of that firm). It is interesting to note that even at a much higher cut-off level of 40 per cent, more than one-third of companies were controlled by a family in Indonesia and Thailand.

Indeed, the 1997/8 financial crisis exposed the tendency that some family owners could pursue their self-interest at the expense of minority shareholders, resulting in a high degree of diversification across different businesses and excess borrowing. In Korea, for example, the number of affiliates of the thirty largest chaebols expanded from an average of four companies in 1970 to twenty-two companies, spanning nineteen different industries, in 1996. Very often, the family owners relied on debt, rather than equity, financing to fund the expansion. The limited use of equity financing was in part attributed to the reluctance of the owners to dilute their control over the companies. The weak corporate governance of the banks themselves as well as the cross-ownership of other financial companies also facilitated the easy credit available to the family owners. Consequently, the leverage positions of the corporate sectors of these countries rose sharply in the run up to the crisis (Table 1.5).

Even under concentrated ownership, over-borrowing could not happen easily if the stakeholders and other minority shareholders were kept informed about the financial health of the firm. The proper disclosure of information, however, was hindered by the lack of independent boards of directors and auditors. Given the dominance of bank financing in those countries, banks could fulfil a role in checking on whether the firms are properly run. But banks' monitoring function was hindered by some controlling family shareholders who were reluctant to disclose financial information of the companies so as to protect their control over the firms and other insider benefits. In addition, the existence of relationship banking and weak governance of the banks themselves prior to the crisis meant that banks were not in a position to properly assess the risks. These factors eventually resulted in large-scale bank closures in these countries (Table 1.6).

Table 1.5. Debt-to-equity ratios of the corporate sectors

	Indonesia	Korea	Malaysia	Philippines	Thailand
1990	n.a.	297	40	181	145
1991	n.a.	318	45	149	152
1992	253	325	45	121	138
1993	238	313	42	119	140
1994	215	308	46	102	126
1995	223	306	49	107	140
1996	229	336	71	109	146
1997	307	425	88	149	350

Notes: Debt-to-equity ratio = total liabilities/stockholders' equity.

Source: Asian Development Bank 2001.

4.1. Recent Corporate Governance Reforms in the USA, Europe, and Asia

In the wake of the financial crises in Asia and the recent corporate scandals in the USA and Europe several policy measures were implemented to address the sources of

Table 1.6. Mergers, closures, and state interventions of financial institutions (June 1997 to June 1999)

	Mergers	Closures	State interventions
Indonesia	Four of the seven state commercial banks to be merged into a single commercial bank.	Sixty-four commercial banks.	Twelve commercial banks.
Korea	Nine commercial banks and two merchant banks to create four new commercial banks.	Five commercial banks, seventeen merchant banks, more than 100 other non-bank financial institutions.	Four commercial banks.
Malaysia	fifteen mergers (finance companies and commercial banks).	None.	One merchant bank and three finance companies under central bank control.
Philippines	Four commercial bank mergers.	One commercial bank.	None.
Thailand	Three mergers involving five commercial banks and twelve finance companies.	fifty-six finance companies and one commercial bank.	Six commercial banks and twelve finance companies.

Source: Lindgren et al.1999.

market failures. In the USA, policy measures addressed conflict of interests and lack of disclosure/transparency. Most of these reforms were included in the Sarbanes–Oxley Act and in related changes to the rules required by the SEC for disclosure of information of listed companies. Concerning conflict of interests of financial intermediaries, these new measures require investment banks to adopt operating procedures aimed at separating their research functions from their underwriting business. In terms of disclosure requirements, CEOs and CFOs can be criminally prosecuted when the accounting statements accompanying company reports turn out to be inaccurate.

Several actions were taken also in Europe.[11] In particular, in May 2003 the European Commission adopted the 'Company Law and Corporate Governance Action Plan'. The two guiding principles of this action plan are improving transparency and empowering shareholders. No proposal was made for a European Governance Code and it was recognized that 'in this area soft law instruments such as recommendations, rather than prescriptive detailed legislation' are more appropriate.[12] All in all EU responses—which took the form of several directives to be implemented at the national level—seem to be more inspired by a principle-based regime, emphasizing transparency and self-governance, rather than a rule-based regime.

Proposed measures are aimed at increasing transparency in company accounts, shareholders' rights, and establishing requirements for higher quality of auditors' work. The main regulatory change which took place was the introduction of International Financial Reporting Standards (IFRS) for the financial years starting on or after 1 January 2005. After this date all EU listed companies have to follow these common standards, which aim to increase transparency and comparability of financial statements. The disclosure of information on SPVs and the recognition in income statements of the fair value of stock options and similar forms of employee compensation are also included in these reporting standards. In the USA, the recognition of stock options in a company's financial accounts was also required starting June 2005.

In the aftermath of the Asian crises, the affected countries introduced wide-ranging reform measures to address problems of weak corporate governance. Most of these measures focused on how to improve the protection of the rights of both minority shareholders and creditors.

In terms of the protection of creditors' rights, Korea, Thailand, and Indonesia have amended their bankruptcy-related laws since 1997. Thailand and Indonesia also used informal workouts extensively in corporate restructuring while Korea introduced the Corporate Restructuring Act recently to provide formal legal ground for workouts. Meanwhile, much more work has been done to improve the rights of minority shareholders. For example, in Indonesia, Korea, Malaysia, and Thailand, the authorities strengthened the transparency and disclosure requirements. Now, all four countries require listed companies to submit their audited annual reports within

---

[11] For a review of the policy initiatives in the pipeline see, for example, Maddaloni and Pain 2004.

[12] See 'Future of the company law action plan', speech by Charlie McCreevy, European Commissioner of Internal Market and Services, on the occasion of the Listed Companies and Legislators in Dialogue Conference, Copenhagen, 17 November 2005.

Table 1.7. Corporate governance in Asia

	China	HK	India	Indon.	Korea	Malay.	Phil.	Sing.	Taiwan	Thai.
Must companies report their annual results within two months?	x	x	x	✓	x	✓	x	✓	x	✓
Are class action lawsuits permitted?	s	x	x	x	✓	x	x	x	s	x
Is voting by poll mandatory for resolutions at AGMs?	x	s	x	x	x	x	x	x	s	x
Can minority shareholders easily nominate independent directors?	x	s	x	x	s	s	x	s	s	x
Can shareholders easily remove a director who has been convicted of fraud or other serious corporate crimes?	s	s	x	s	x	s	s	✓	✓	x

Note: s = somewhat.

Source: Asian Corporate Governance Association Corporate Governance Watch 2004.

three months and report information that is sensitive to share prices immediately. In addition, all these countries tightened the conditions for appointing a director and an internal auditor.

While it is generally agreed that corporate governance in post-crisis Asia has improved significantly, there is still room for further changes to move them in the direction of the USA. Table 1.7 shows that many countries in Asia still lack provisions in five major areas of corporate governance.

One key impediment to corporate governance in non-Japan Asia, at least for the less developed economies, is weak enforcement. Nam and Nam (2005) suggest that regulatory bodies, including the securities exchanges and financial regulators, as well as the prosecutors' offices appear to be far less active in enforcing the rules that aim to improve corporate governance. As a result, the effects of many of the reform measures introduced were severely limited.

Another important issue is the extent to which these legal rules matter in practice. Other mechanisms such as competition, reputation, and relationships also have an important role to play. Allen and Gale (2000b), for example, argue that in many cases competition can lead to efficient governance. In the UK, Franks, Mayer, and Rossi (2000) have shown that significant changes in minority shareholder rights had little effect. They argue that trust and reputation played an important role. Allen, Qian, and Qian (2004) find that in China an ineffective legal system and rampant corruption do not prevent very fast growth. They also argue trust and reputation can take the place of legal protections.

In the same vein, many have argued in recent years that good corporate governance can be obtained by listing in a country with good governance laws. Our box for this section casts doubt on the validity of this notion.

The focus on Anglo-Saxon views of corporate governance in the academic literature also leads to a lack of perspective on stakeholder and family systems. Although when evaluated in terms of the Anglo-Saxon norms of creating wealth for shareholders they may do poorly, they may allow greater efficiency overall. For example, Allen and Gale (2000a) and Allen (2005) show that stakeholder governance taking into account a broader range of interests can lead to a Pareto improvement compared to pursuing just shareholders' interests when markets are incomplete and contracts are imperfect. Much more research on the different ways in which corporate governance operates around the world is needed.

Box 1.3. Overseas listing and corporate governance: the case of China Aviation Oil (Singapore) Corporation

---

Over the past few years, more and more Chinese enterprises, especially the state-owned firms, have applied for public listings in major international financial centres such as Hong Kong and Singapore to raise funds. In fact, the initial public offerings by Chinese-related companies have dominated the public listing activity in Hong Kong in recent years (Figure 1.17). Meanwhile, the Chinese authorities hope that the management of Chinese corporations can be improved by being exposed to oversight by international regulators and investors. However, the application for court protection from creditors by China Aviation Oil (Singapore) Corporation Limited (CAO) after losing US$550 million in derivative trading in December 2004 has brought to light broader concerns about the governance of these overseas-listed Chinese companies.[a]

CAO was listed in the Singapore Stock Exchange in December 2001. Its parent company in China—the state-controlled China Aviation Oil Holding Company (CAOHC)—supplies jet fuel for domestic and foreign airlines, accounting for one-third of total consumption in China. CAO began using derivatives in 2003 to help airlines hedge their exposures to volatile oil prices, and the company acted as a back-to-back agent between the airlines and oil derivative traders. However, soon the chief executive of CAO decided to use the company's funds for trading oil derivatives and hoped that would earn the company much higher profits. At first, CAO recorded strong gains in 2003 and share prices rose sharply from SGD 0.3 at end 2002 to a peak of SGD 1.9 in March 2004.

Entering 2004, however, CAO started to incur losses in its derivative dealing by speculating that oil prices would fall. By March 2004, the CEO realized that CAO had incurred a potential loss of US$5.8 million in derivative trading and the potential loss escalated to US$35.8 million in the following quarter. Instead of cutting back the positions, CAO increased its exposures in anticipation of oil prices falling. In October 2004, as crude-oil

---

[a] In February 2004, China Life Insurance acknowledged—after its New York Stock Exchange-listed shares fell sharply—that Chinese government auditors had uncovered widespread irregularities at its parent company.

Box 1.3. (continued)

prices rose to a record high of over US$50 a barrel, the company's debt mounted rapidly. On 29 November 2004, CAO filed for court protection after realizing losses of US$550 million from trading oil derivatives, and was granted by the High Court until 21 January 2005 to work out a restructuring plan and to get the creditors' approval by 17 May.

The event highlights some corporate governance issues. First, corporate governance and enforcement mechanisms are closely linked as they affect the ability of companies to commit to their external investors and other stakeholders. While well-established legal systems and capital markets provide a good platform for good corporate governance, an effective check-and-balance system on the managers should also be in place. Second, an important policy challenge is how to ensure that managers will disclose accounting information to the public on a consistent and timely basis. In the case of CAO, if the management could have stopped taking excessive risks in derivative trading and also if shareholders and regulators had been aware of the losses earlier in the year, the damage could potentially have been reduced to a more manageable level. Third, the risk of investing in overseas-listed state-owned enterprises could be much higher than perceived, as it is not necessarily covered by a state guarantee. CAO resumed trading in 2006 after the Singapore High Court had approved a restructuring plan under which CAOHC, two other companies, and creditors agreed to inject fresh capital into CAO.

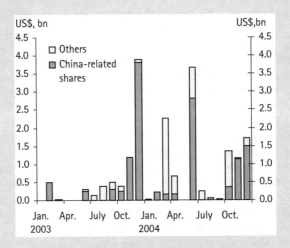

Fig. 1.17. Initial public offerings in Hong Kong

Source: HK Exchange and Clearing Ltd

5. CONCLUDING REMARKS

We have considered the different patterns of institutional ownership in the euro area, the UK, the USA, Japan, and non-Japan Asia. The role of institutions in each country is quite different. In the euro area and Japan the most important institutions are banks and other MFIs. Households put a large amount of their assets in their instruments. In the UK and USA, households are much more exposed to equity fluctuations. In the UK this is through equity held in insurance companies and pension funds while in the USA there is a considerable amount of directly held equity in addition. One interesting development in recent years is that central banks, particularly those in Asia, have become major institutional investors. This is likely to have a significant impact on the US Treasury market and the determination of medium- and long-term interest rates. The difference in objective functions between central banks and private financial institutions is also likely to have important beneficial implications for financial stability.

We also considered differences in the housing and mortgage markets. Since housing is such a major component of wealth in most countries, these are a key part of the financial structure of economies. Housing prices have risen in most countries but at widely different rates. This has led to differences in the rate of equity withdrawal. Possible falls in house prices in countries where large increases have occurred potentially impose a systemic risk. The large differences in the structure of mortgage markets across countries suggest a significant difference in efficiency. The role of MBS in the USA compared to other countries is particularly striking in this regard.

Corporate governance differs significantly around the world. We have suggested that the sole focus on creating value for shareholders may be misplaced, particularly in Europe and Asia. Widespread failures of corporate governance are still not fully understood.

Institutional investors, the housing and mortgage markets, and corporate governance are important components of a financial system. They play a significant role in determining the efficiency, stability, and monetary policy transmission properties of a financial system. One important question concerns whether one financial structure is better than another. To answer this question requires a full understanding of how different financial structures affect efficiency, stability, and monetary policy transmission and how these factors should be traded off. We believe that much more research remains to be done before these issues are fully understood.

REFERENCES

ALLEN, F. (2005), 'Corporate governance in emerging markets', *Oxford Review of Economic Policy*, 21, 164–77.

——— CHUI, M., and MADDALONI, A. (2004), 'Financial systems in Europe, the USA, and Asia', *Oxford Review of Economic Policy*, 20, 490–508.

——— and GALE, D. (1997), 'Financial markets, intermediaries, and intertemporal smoothing', *Journal of Political Economy*, 105, 523–46.

——— ——— (2000a), *Comparing Financial Systems*, Cambridge, Mass: MIT Press.

——— ——— (2000b), 'Corporate governance and competition', in X. Vives (ed.), *Corporate Governance: Theoretical and Empirical Perspectives*, Cambridge: Cambridge University Press, 23–94.

ALLEN, F., QIAN, J., and QIAN, M. (2005), 'Law, finance and economic growth in China', *Journal of Financial Economics*, 77, 57–116.

ASIAN DEVELOPMENT BANK (2001), *Corporate Governance and Finance in East Asia: A Study of Indonesia, Republic of Korea, Malaysia, Philippines, and Thailand*, vol., Manila: Asian Development Bank.

BAELE, L., FERRANDO, A., HÖRDAHL, P., KRYLOVA, E., and MONNET, C. (2004), 'Measuring Financial Integration in the Euro Area', ECB Occasional Paper no. 14.

BANK OF JAPAN (2002), *Guide to Japan's Flow of Funds Accounts*, Research and Statistics Department, Bank of Japan.

BARCA, F., and BECHT, M. (2001), *The Control of Corporate Europe*, Oxford: Oxford University Press.

BECHT, M., BOLTON, P., and RÖELL, A. (2003), 'Corporate governance and control', in G. Constantinides, M. Harris, and R. Stulz (eds.), *Handbook of the Economics of Finance*, Amsterdam: Elsevier-North-Holland, 1–109.

BHATTACHARYA, U., DAOUK, H., and WELKER, M. (2003), 'The world price of earnings opacity', *Accounting Review*, 78, 641–78.

BOARD OF GOVERNORS OF THE FEDERAL RESERVE SYSTEM (2004), 'Monetary policy report to the Congress', February.

CLAESSENS, S., DJANKOV, S., and LANG, L. (1998), 'Who controls East Asian corporations?', World Bank, mimeo.

———— ———— ———— (2000), 'The separation of ownership and control in East Asian corporations', *Journal of Financial Economics*, 58, 81–112.

DAVIS, E. P. (2003), 'Institutional investors, financial market efficiency and financial stability', The Pension Institute, Discussion Paper Pi-0303.

———— and STEIL, B. (2001), *Institutional Investors*, Cambridge, Mass.: MIT Press.

ECB (2002), *Report on Financial Structures*, Frankfurt am Main: European Central Bank.

———— (2003a), 'Recent developments in financial structures in the euro area', *Monthly Bulletin*, October, 39–52.

———— (2003b), *Structural Factors in the EU Housing Market*, Frankfurt am Main: European Central Bank.

———— (2006), 'Assessing house price developments in the euro area', *Monthly Bulletin*, February, 55–70.

FRANKS, J., MAYER, C., and ROSSI, S. (2003), 'Ownership: evolution and regulation', Working Paper, London Business School.

GUISO, L., HALIASSOS, M., and JAPPELLI, T. (2002a), *Stockholding in Europe*, Basingstoke: Palgrave Macmillan Press.

———— ———— ———— (2002b), *Household Portfolios*, Cambridge, Mass.: MIT Press.

HARTMANN, P., MADDALONI, A., and MANGANELLI, S. (2003), 'The euro area financial system: structure, integration and policy initiatives', *Oxford Review of Economic Policy*, 19, 180–213.

HOLZMANN, R., MACARTHUR, I., and SIN, Y. (2000), 'Pension systems in East Asia and the Pacific: challenges and opportunities', World Bank Social Protection Discussion Paper no. 0014, Washington, DC.

IMF (2003), *World Economic Outlook*, chapter II, September, Washington, DC.

———— (2004), *Global Financial Stability Report*, April, Washington, DC.

———— (2005), *Global Financial Stability Report*, April, Washington, DC.

JOHNSON, S. (2000), 'Corporate governance in the Asian financial crisis', *Journal of Financial Economics*, 58, 141–6.

LA PORTA, R., LÓPEZ-DE-SILANES, F., SHLEIFER, A., and VISHNY, R. (1998), 'Law and finance', *Journal of Political Economy*, 106, 1113–55.

LINDGREN, C., BALIÑO, J., ENOCH, C., GULDE, A., QUINTYN, M., and TEO, L. (1999), 'Financial sector crisis and restructuring: lessons from Asia', International Monetary Fund Occasional Paper, no. 188, Washington, DC.

MACLENNAN, D., MUELLBAUER, J., and STEPHENS, M. (2000), 'Asymmetries in housing and financial market institutions and EMU', Nuffield College, Oxford, mimeo.

MADDALONI, A., and PAIN, D. (2004), 'Corporate "excesses" and financial market dynamics', ECB Occasional Paper no. 17.

MANKIW, G., and WEIL, D. (1989), 'The baby boom, the baby bust, and the housing market', Regional Science and Urban Economics, 19, 235–58.

MERCER O. W. (2003), Study on the Financial Integration of European Mortgage Markets, Brussels: European Mortgage Federation, October.

MOODY'S INVESTOR SERVICE (2004), '2003 review and 2004 outlook: EMEA residential mortgage-backed securities: record volumes achieved in 2003 should be matched or even exceeded in 2004', International Structured Finance, Special Report, 27 January, www.moodys.com.

NAM, S., and NAM, I. (2005), Corporate Governance in Asia: Recent Evidence from Indonesia, Republic of Korea, Thailand and Malaysia, Tokyo: Asian Development Bank Institute.

OECD (2004), 'Housing markets, wealth and the business cycle', Economic Outlook, 75 (June), Paris: Organization for Economic Cooperation and Development.

O'SULLIVAN, M. (2000), Contests for Corporate Control: Corporate Governance and Economic Performance in the United States and Germany, New York : Oxford University Press.

QUIGLEY, J. (2001), 'Real estate and the Asian crisis', Journal of Housing Economics, 10, 129–61.

SHLEIFER, A., and VISHNY, W. (1997), 'A survey of corporate governance', Journal of Finance, 52, 737–83.

TIROLE, J. (2006), The Theory of Corporate Governance, New York: Princeton University Press.

CHAPTER 2

....

FINANCE AND GROWTH

A MACROECONOMIC ASSESSMENT OF THE EVIDENCE FROM A EUROPEAN ANGLE

....

ELIAS PAPAIOANNOU

1. INTRODUCTION

....

RECENT research has provided compelling evidence that financial development exerts a significantly positive effect on economic growth. Ross Levine (2005) provides a thorough review of both the theoretical and empirical work linking the depth and breadth of capital markets to economic performance.[1] The current study aims to be complementary to Levine's extensive review. It does so by trying to place the

This chapter was written when the author was working at the Financial Research Division of the European Central Bank. I thank Xavier Freixas and Philipp Hartmann for comments and suggestions and Markus Baltzer for superb research assistantship. This paper has benefited from the input provided by the ECB team developing indicators on 'The performance of the European financial system'.

[1] See Levine 2003, 1997 for shorter reviews.

recent empirical evidence in a growth-accounting macro framework.[2] Not only does this appear quite useful in understanding how the finance–growth nexus works in a standard neoclassical model frame, but it also helps to reveal the theoretical channels on how finance contributes to economic performance. Starting from a general macro structure also helps us to discuss issues related to causality, which is of course key for both research and policy. In addition the current study assesses the evidence from a European standpoint, exploring how financial sector reforms which are an important component of the Lisbon Agenda can contribute to EU productivity growth.[3]

The survey starts by laying down a growth-accounting framework that helps to understand the main channels of financial development's effect on aggregate growth. Starting from a neoclassical production function, aggregate country-level growth is decomposed in capital deepening (investment), human capital accumulation (education), and total factor productivity (the Solow residual, which measures how effectively physical capital and labour is employed in production). The growth decomposition enables us to study the distinct effects of financial markets efficiency on the three main components of aggregate growth. This framework is also useful in understanding whether financial development speeds up convergence to steady-state growth or whether it promotes long-run growth.

Second, the survey summarizes the evidence from the cross-country empirical work. This work, which was initiated with the King and Levine (1993) study, investigates the correlation between various indicators of financial development and aggregate country-level growth rates over the past decades. The overall message of this work is that various indicators of financial development explain a significant part of the overall variation in growth rates. Recently, however, the cross-country growth regressions have been criticized, mainly because the results appear quite sensitive to small model permutations (e.g. Levine and Renelt 1992; Sala-i-Martin 1997; Sala-i-Martin, Doppelhofer, and Miller 2004; Ciccone and Jarocinski 2006). Thus, in this section, I also discuss before–after event studies that quantify the growth and investment effects of financial liberalization policies. Although these studies focus mainly (though not exclusively) on developing countries, they push forward on the causality front by quantifying the macroeconomic effects of discrete policy changes, controlling for unobserved country heterogeneity and common global trends.

In Section 3, I discuss work that takes a more micro perspective using industry-level data. Following the influential study of Rajan and Zingales (1998) cross-country industry-level studies have become popular, mainly because they assuage many of the limitations of cross-country work (such as omitted variables, reverse causation, and multicollinearity). These studies also enable a closer study of the theoretical channels on how financial development affects aggregate growth.

---

[2] Therefore the current study does not cover in detail the work that links financial modernization with risk sharing, output volatility, or international specialization. In addition the current review does not go over micro firm-level studies that assess the effect of well-developed financial markets in relaxing firms' financial constraints.

[3] Of course the current review also covers research that followed Levine's chapter (2005–7).

In Section 4, I review event studies that quantify the effects of banking deregulation and access to finance mainly in the United States, but also in some other developed countries, such as France and Italy. These studies fit in a recent trend in development economics to exploit quasi-natural (policy) experiments to move on causal inference. Besides providing more accurate estimates, this strand of the finance and growth literature is also the most relevant for the ongoing process of EU financial integration.

Section 5 summarizes.

2. THEORETICAL CHANNELS IN A GROWTH-ACCOUNTING FRAMEWORK

2.1. Growth Accounting

Following Francesco Caselli's (2005) recent study on development accounting, growth accounting asks, 'how much of the variation in income growth can be attributed to differences in (physical and human) capital accumulation, and how much due to changes in the efficiency with which capital is used.' Growth accounting provides thus a useful analytical tool to assess how various factors, such as government policies, institutions, natural resources, and in our context financial intermediation, affect the main sources of economic growth (e.g. Barro 1991; Barro and Sala-i-Martin 1995). For example, does financial development foster growth, by mitigating capital market frictions and fostering investment in education, as in Galor and Zeira's (1993) model? Or does the effect of financial development work primarily by lowering the cost of capital and thus spurring investment, as in most neoclassical theories? Or do efficient financial intermediaries spur growth through productivity, for example by channelling resources quickly to the most productive entrepreneurs, firms, and sectors?

Growth accounting starts with specifying a general country-level (neoclassical) aggregate production function (e.g. Mankiw, Romer, and Weil 1992):

$$Y_{i,t} = AK^{\alpha}(Lh)^{1-\alpha}. \tag{1}$$

This simple production function relates aggregate country (i) output Y in period (year) t to the aggregate capital stock K, the labour force L, which in the above specification is adjusted for the average human capital of workers (h), and the level of technology A (which in (1) enters in a 'Hicks-neutral' way). α and $1 - \alpha$ measure the share of capital and quality-adjusted labour in the aggregate economy (under constant returns to scale the shares sum up to one). We can express the production function in per worker terms (intensive form):

$$y = Ak^{\alpha}h^{1-\alpha}. \tag{2}$$

Differentiating (2) over time we get:

$$\dot{y}/y = \alpha\dot{k}/k + (1-\alpha)\dot{h}/h + \dot{A}/A. \tag{3}$$

Equation (3) partitions output growth per worker into three parts: the first term in the right-hand side captures capital deepening (investment), the second term human capital accumulation (education), and the third term total factor productivity, which measures how efficiently capital and labour are employed in the production.

From our standpoint two issues need to be emphasized. First, in this framework technical change is measured as a residual (the so-called Solow residual) and thus includes all factors not related to education or physical capital investment. Second, in almost all theories education and investment are endogenous factors, and thus equation (3) represents just an analytical device to decompose the sources of growth rather than a structural estimation that links growth to its deep fundamental determinants.

2.2. Placing Theory in Growth Accounting

It is useful to categorize theoretical work on how financial intermediation fosters growth into this framework.[4]

In standard neoclassical theories investment savings is the engine of growth. In these models there are no capital market frictions and thus financial intermediation is not explicitly modelled. However, these models assume that savings translate directly to investment and thus one could argue that finance affects growth primarily through capital deepening (investment).

A different class of theoretical models argues that financial development may foster growth by raising human capital accumulation. In Galor and Zeira (1993) model income inequality and credit market frictions impede growth, since not all individuals can invest in education. They argue thus that financial intermediation can spur growth (and eventually decrease inequality) by fostering human capital accumulation.

Most theories on financial intermediation and growth stress the beneficial effects of well-developed capital markets for innovation and productivity. For example Joseph Schumpeter (1911) argued that financial intermediaries promote growth by selecting entrepreneurs with the most innovative and productive projects. In the same vein, Walter Bagehot (1873) emphasized the importance of banks and capital markets during the Industrial Revolution in the United Kingdom in channelling funds in sectors with high innovation and high growth prospects.[5]

A priori financial modernization effect on productivity looks like the most relevant channel for Western European and other developed countries, which are capital

---

[4] This subsection does not intend to cover the vast theoretical literature on the impact of financial intermediation on growth. It just covers some theoretical work to illustrate how the growth-accounting framework can help move from theory to estimation.

[5] See Greenwood and Jovanovic 1990 and Acemoglu, Aghion, and Zilibotti 2006 for recent reformulations of these arguments.

abundant. In contrast the capital-deepening channel appears mostly relevant for emerging and underdeveloped economies that lack capital to finance investment projects and education.

It should be stressed, however, that not all theoretical work can fit easily in the simplified growth-accounting framework, since many models yield an effect of financial intermediaries in both productivity and (human and physical) accumulation. Take for example the important contribution of Acemoglu and Zilibotti (1997). They build an endogenous growth model, where capital is scarce, investment projects have an indivisible part (for example because of minimum size requirements or start-up costs), and agents dislike the risk model. Under these weak (and realistic) assumptions Acemoglu and Zilibotti show that financial underdevelopment will yield both slower physical capital accumulation and lower productivity, because agents will prefer investing in low-risk, low-return projects rather than undertake the most profitable opportunities.

2.3. Estimation

Building on (3) and (1), most empirical cross-country growth analyses of the effect of financial development on growth estimate variants of the following regression equation:

$$\Delta \ln y_{i,t} = \beta \ln y_{i,t-1} + \gamma \Delta \ln h_{i,t} + X'\Phi + \lambda F D_{i,t} + \varepsilon_{i,t}. \tag{4}$$

The dependent variable is per capita GDP growth rate. The set of explanatory variables usually includes:

- The initial log level of income ($\ln y_{i,t-1}$). The standard prediction of neoclassical models is that growth rates will be higher the further away a country is from its steady state. If the country is far away (poor), then the return to capital will be higher, and consequently, through enhanced capital accumulation, there is going to be higher growth. (Alternatively one could replace in the estimation equation the convergence term with physical capital accumulation $\Delta \ln K_{i,t}$ (e.g. Benhabib and Spiegel 2000).) In line with the neoclassical prediction most studies yield a significantly negative β coefficient on the convergence term, once other factors that drive growth are accounted for.
- A proxy variable of human capital accumulation, such as changes in schooling or education enrolment rates (probably adjusted for the quality of education).
- The set of explanatory variables (X') also includes other controls, such as institutional quality, geography, government policies, trade openness, human capital level, that aim to account for cross-country differences in productivity.
- The focus of the analysis is on the coefficient (λ) on a proxy measure of financial development (FD).

The literature started estimating variants of equation (4) using cross-sectional approaches, averaging growth rates, financial development proxies, and the other controls over the 1960–90 period. Since growth rates are quite volatile research wanted to first identify the long-run effects of financial development departing from short-term business cycle fluctuations. Second, the literature used panel techniques using averaged data over ten- or five-year periods. The main merit of this work is that it can account for unobserved time-invariant country effects and common global (or regional) trends. This is done by modelling the error in (4) as having a country time-invariant and a general period component, i.e. $\varepsilon_{i,t} \equiv \eta_i + \vartheta_t + \nu_{i,t}$. Third, recent studies employ dynamic panel techniques working with annual frequency data. The main benefit of these studies is that by properly modelling growth dynamics, one can estimate both the short- and the long-run effects of financial development on growth.[6]

3. CROSS-COUNTRY STUDIES

3.1. Overall Country-level Effect of Finance on Growth

Studying the long-run cross-country correlation between financial development and aggregate growth was the first step in the empirical work. (Table 2.1 summarizes the main cross-country growth studies.)

3.1.1. *Cross-sectional Evidence*

In an early contribution King and Levine (1993) employed Robert Barro's (1991) cross-country cross-sectional regression framework (equation (4)) to investigate the effect of various proxies of financial development in explaining variation in cross-country growth rates. Given (theoretical and conceptual) difficulties in measuring properly capital markets' breath and depth King and Levine employ four different measures of financial development (FD in (4)): (i) financial system's liquid liabilities as a share to GDP; (ii) commercial bank credit plus central bank's assets to GDP; (iii) credit to the private sector relative to GDP; and (iv) the ratio of claims to non-financial private sector to aggregate domestic credit. King and Levine use averaged data from seventy-seven industrial, developing, and underdeveloped countries in the period 1960–89. Their first set of results is that there is a significantly positive correlation between all four proxy measures of financial development and economic growth. This result appears robust to different controlling sets and model perturbations. Yet this correlation does not establish causality, because capital markets may increase lending and expand credit in periods of fast growth. Thus King and Levine also use initial

---

[6] Durlauf, Johnson, and Temple 2005, Temple 1999, and Dulauf and Quah 1999 provide eloquent reviews of the cross-country growth literature, addressing the main merits and disadvantages of the employed techniques. Hauk and Wacziarg 2004 use Monte Carlo simulations to compare the efficiency of the various estimation techniques.

Table 2.1. Overview of main cross-country studies of finance and growth

Study	Dep. Variable(s)	Sample	Technique	Results
King and Levine (1993)	GDP p.c. growth; physical capital growth; TFP growth.	77 countries; 1960–89.	OLS; cross-section.	Initial and contemporaneous values of various proxies of financial development are positively correlated with overall, capital, and TFP growth.
Levine and Zervos (1998)	GDP p.c. growth; investment; savings; TFP growth.	40–4 countries; 1976–93.	OLS; cross-section.	Initial values of bank credit to GDP and stock market liquidity are both significant determinants of overall, physical capital, and productivity growth.
Levine, Loayza, and Beck (2000a, 2000b)	GDP p.c. growth; physical capital growth; TFP growth; savings rate.	63–77 countries; 1960–95.	OLS and IV; cross-section.	All finance proxies (private credit, bank credit, liquid liabilities, market turnover) in both OLS and IV are positively correlated with GDP and productivity growth. The finance–investment (savings) link is less robust.
Benhabib and Spiegel (2000)	GDP p.c. growth; investment; human capital accumulation; TFP growth.	90 countries; 1965–85.	OLS and IV; cross-section; panel.	Various measures of financial intermediaries' liquidity (e.g. private and bank credit to GDP) are robustly correlated with overall and TFP growth. Bank credit is also positively correlated with human capital (schooling) accumulation.
Beck and Levine (2004)	GDP p.c. growth.	40 countries; 1976–98.	Dynamic panel.	In most models both bank and capital markets development proxies are positively correlated with overall GDP p.c. growth.

Notes: In 'IV' models the exogenous (historically determined) component of financial development is extracted by instrumenting the finance proxy with legal origin variables. Following La Porta et al. 1998, 1999 the law and finance literature has shown that in countries with either common law or German-originated or Scandinavian civil law system investors (shareholders and creditors) have superior protection and thus the financial system is more developed. 'Panel' models enable to control for unobserved time-invariant country heterogeneity (e.g. social capital; rule of law) by exploring the correlation between changes in financial development and output.

values of the financial development proxies in a *post hoc, ergo propter hoc* approach. Due to data unavailability on the financial development indicators in the early 1960s, these models were performed to a subset of fifty-seven countries. The evidence reveals that initial levels of financial development can explain a significant part of subsequent growth (around 60 per cent of the overall variation).

Using different proxy measures of financial development and working in different samples, subsequent studies have likewise produced similar results, strengthening the robustness of the finance–growth nexus in a wide cross-section of countries. Quantitatively, the long-run effect of financial development appears large. For example the estimates imply that if Belgium (which had an average private credit to GDP ratio of 25 per cent) were to reach the level of financial development of the Netherlands (with a private credit to GDP ratio of 85 per cent) annual growth would increase by 3 per cent. However recent work provides more conservative estimates of around 0.5 to 1 per cent (e.g. Favara 2003).

The next step was to follow the growth decomposition approach summarized in Section 1 and break down overall growth in investment, human capital accumulation and total factor productivity (TFP) growth. The cross-country growth decomposition studies hint that financial development fosters growth mainly by increasing TFP and to some lesser extent by fostering investment in physical and human capital (King and Levine 1993; Levine, Loayza, and Beck 2000b; Benhabib and Spiegel 2000).

Subsequent work investigates which features of the financial system are key for fostering growth. Levine and Zervos (1998) examine whether banking sector or capital market development contributes the most. They do so by augmenting otherwise prototypical growth regressions (4) with proxy measures of banking and equity markets development. The cross-section growth regressions hint that both banking sector development and stock market liquidity have independent positive effects on economic growth. These results are also related to a distinct (theoretical and empirical) literature on whether a bank-based or a market-based system is the most efficient (see Levine 2002 and Tadesse 2003 for some new insights). These results suggest that the type of the financial system is of secondary importance in the development path. These results add to other empirical work (e.g. Beck and Levine 2002) that supports the middle-ground 'financial functions view'. What is key for growth is the existence of liquid and efficient financial intermediaries, irrespective of whether there are equity markets or banks. In addition, the Levine and Zervos findings hint that equity markets and banks exert complementary services to the economy. From a European standpoint this evidence is important, since it shows that both the continental European paradigm of bank-based finance and the British system of arm's-length finance can stimulate growth.

La Porta, López-de-Silanes, and Shleifer (2002) move away from size measures of financial depth and explore the effect of a particular aspect of the financial system, state ownership of the banking sector, in economic growth. Their cross-country regressions (equation (4)) show that state ownership and control of the banking sector in the late 1960s early 1970s is associated with slower subsequent growth. The authors also decompose aggregate growth and explore the effect of state ownership in subsequent capital accumulation (and savings) and productivity growth. State ownership of banks has a small and usually insignificant effect on future investment, but a large impact on future productivity growth. This result appears very robust; quite importantly it retains significance even when the authors control for the initial size of the capital markets and other institutional quality controls. The La Porta et al. (2002) evidence is supportive to so-called political 'public choice' theories of state control, according to which state intervention to credit leads to resource misallocation. Their results contradict 'development' theories of state ownership that emphasize the positive effect that government can have in banking, for example by mitigating negative externalities, encouraging risk-taking investment, financing strategic sectors, etc.[7]

Aghion, Howitt, and Mayer-Foulkes (2005) investigate whether financial development increases steady-state growth rates (as the cross-country work suggests) or whether it speeds up convergence to the technological frontier. The authors estimate otherwise standard cross-country growth and productivity regressions (of the form of (4)), augmented however with an interaction term between initial distance to the technological frontier (the ratio of domestic GDP to the US GDP) i.e. augmenting (4) with an interaction between $FD * (y_{i,t-1}/y_{us,t-1})$. Using various techniques (OLS; IV with legal origin; and dynamic panel methods) they show that the coefficient on the finance-initial relative GDP interaction is highly negative and significant. In addition the coefficients on initial relative GDP (which aims to capture for the well-documented conditional convergence effect) and financial development are positive, although not always statistically significant. These results show that financial development is highly beneficial for converging to the technological frontier. The results imply that countries above some critical level of financial development should converge in growth rates and that in such countries finance has a positive but eventually vanishing effect on steady-state GDP.[8]

3.1.2. Caveats

It is, however, quite hard to establish causality with cross-country cross-sectional regressions, for a number of reasons:

First, it is almost impossible to account for all possible factors that may foster growth. This is because we have reliable data for a maximum of a hundred countries, while

[7] See also Sapienza 2004, Dinc 2006, and Papaioannou 2005 for further evidence supporting public choice political theories. Using detailed individual loan contracts from Italy, Sapienza 2004 shows that the lending behaviour of state-owned banks is affected by the electoral results of the party affiliated with the bank. Analogously, Dinc 2006 shows that political motivations rather than profit maximization drive the lending practices of state-owned banks in many developing countries. Papaioannou 2005 presents panel evidence that in countries where the state controls a significant part of the banking sector there is less international bank lending.

[8] Building on Schumpeterian growth models of technological innovation (see Aghion and Howitt 2006 for a review), recent work by Philippe Aghion and Peter Howitt has employed the cross-country growth regression framework to identify specific channels through which financial development influences growth. This work uncovers interesting interactions between financial development and macroeconomic factors in explaining country growth rates. This work is summarized by Philippe Aghion in another chapter and thus not covered here.

there are more than fifty variables of which one could reasonably argue that they exert an effect on growth. In addition countries that perform well tend not only to have well-developed financial systems, but also to have an educated workforce, to be politically stable, to have uncorrupted government, to score high in institutional quality indicators, etc. Multicollinearity among the regressors thus makes it very hard to isolate the effect of the various independent variables on economic growth (e.g. Mankiw 1995). It comes thus as no surprise that only a few variables emphasized as significant growth determinants have been found to be robust to alternative conditioning variables (e.g. Levine and Renelt 1992; Sala-i-Martin 1997; Sala-i-Martin, Doppelhofer, and Millar 2004). Moreover even small model permutations (for example using GDP data from different sources or using updated series) yield sizeable differences in both the statistical and economic significance of the estimates (Ciccone and Jarocinski 2007).[9]

Second, the effect of financial development may be quite heterogeneous across countries. For example Aghion, Howitt, and Mayer-Foulkes (2005) have shown that efficient financial intermediaries are more useful in countries that are far from the technological frontier. In addition one could argue that financial development may be more growth enhancing in human capital-rich countries or when the country is open to international trade. The cross-country work imposes a same slope for financial development across all countries and years. It has been long argued in the empirical growth literature that this might yield distortions in the estimates, because the effect of finance may not be homogeneous across regions and countries (see, for a discussion on the work on parameter heterogeneity in growth regressions, Durlauf, Johnson, and Temple 2005 and Durlauf and Quah 1999).

A third drawback is potential reverse causation. Financial development can be both the cause and the consequence of economic growth. Thus the significant association between financial modernization and growth may be driven by economic growth fostering bank or stock market development. Thus although using initial values of financial development is a significant step towards causality, there are still non-negligible endogeneity concerns. The employed financial development proxies, such as market capitalization, may increase in anticipation of future productivity growth.

Third, there are non-trivial data issues. The employed financial development proxies (mainly private domestic credit to GDP and market capitalization and turnover as a share of GDP) are rather coarse and not theory-driven proxies of financial intermediaries' efficiency. Ideally one would want to use indicators that follow closely the theoretical channels on how finance contributes to growth (i.e. using financial accessibility indicators). It is unclear how measurement error will affect the estimates. On the one hand if there are no systematic biases in the measurement of capital markets and banking sector size as well as the other controls such noise should make empirical researchers not detect a significant correlation. Attenuation bias, although not desirable, would imply that the estimates of these studies were conservative.

---

[9] Quite surprisingly, financial development is missing from the studies on the robust determinants of growth.

Measurement error however may yield inflated estimates on financial development proxies, if the other controls are also contaminated with error.[10]

Fourth, these studies pool all countries (industrial, emerging, and underdeveloped) in the estimation. Although this is the most efficient way to estimate the empirical model, parameter heterogeneity is a non-negligible concern. For example, employing dynamic panel techniques designed to account for parameter heterogeneity, Favara (2003) provides compelling evidence of sizeable differences in the effects of financial development on growth. To a great extent the finance–growth nexus is driven by the huge variation in economic performance and financial development between the developed and the developing world (and also among underdeveloped countries). Although many studies exclude for robustness African countries from the estimation, the finance–growth correlation turns weaker (and not seldom statistically insignificant) in the more homogeneous but much smaller group of high-income (or OECD) countries. It is often hard to say whether the statistical insignificance results from the low number of observations available for these countries or from the absence of effects by crude indicators of financial development in them.

3.1.3. *Instrumental Variables, Time Series, and Panel Studies*

Recent research has tried to address these caveats and push for the causal interpretation of the finance–growth association.

At the empirical side, the literature has employed panel techniques that enable researchers to control for time-invariant unobserved country characteristics that may be the deep determinants of both long-term growth and financial development (e.g. efficiency of the legal system or trust).[11] Fixed effect panel techniques examine the effect of increases in bank credit or market turnover on economic growth. Thus these studies are less prone to endogeneity concerns. Employing various panel techniques Levine, Loayza, and Beck (2000a, 2000b), Benhabib and Spiegel (2000), and Beck and Levine (2004), among others, show that improvements in financial liquidity are followed by higher growth.[12]

To account for parameter heterogeneity Loayza and Ranciere (2006) employ the dynamic panel pooled mean group estimator, developed by Pesaran and Smith (1995)

[10] To see this clearly assume a standard growth regression with only two regressors, finance and human capital, proxied by education. If human capital in measured with error (because human capital is not only education, but also on-the-job training, quality, etc.), while financial development is not, because the two variables are positively correlated, the coefficient on financial development will capture (part of the effect of) the mis-measured human capital proxy (see Mankiw 1995 and Krueger and Lindahl 2001 for a more elaborate discussion).

[11] Most panel studies on finance and growth have employed the GMM dynamic panel techniques developed by Arellano and Bond 1991, Blundel and Bond 1998, and Arellano and Bover 1995. See Bond, Hoeffler, and Temple 2001 for a discussion of the these methods in empirical cross-country work on growth.

[12] A problem with the dynamic panel techniques is that they are quite sensitive to even small model permutations. (See Hauk and Wacziarg 2004 for general assessment of panel techniques in the context of growth econometrics. Favara 2003 indeed shows that the evidence from the dynamic panel techniques is sensitive.)

and Pesaran, Shin, and Smith (1999). Besides general fixed effects (that control for time-invariant unobservable characteristics), this technique allows for short-run heterogeneous country effects, while it constrains the long-run effect of the regressors to be equal across the panel. The main benefit of using this technique is that it allows for financial development to have differential effects across countries. The main result of the paper is that although there exists a significantly positive long-run relationship between financial development and growth, in the short run this relationship turns negative for many countries. This finding adds to the cross-country results on a significantly positive long-run effect of financial intermediation on growth, but at the same time shows that fast-expanding credit can lead to financial crises and slower growth.[13]

Time-series studies have studied the finance–growth relationship mainly employing Granger-causality tests in a vector autoregression framework (e.g. Arestis and Demetriades 1997). This work shows that the finance–growth relationship is driven by both factors affecting each other. Thus although these studies do show that financial intermediaries' development contributes to growth, they illustrate the issue of reverse causation. From a European standpoint quite important is the work of Rousseau and Wachtel (1998), who, using data from five industrial countries (namely the USA, the UK, Canada, Norway, and Sweden) over the 1870–1929 Period, show that the finance–growth nexus is mainly driven by financial intermediation variables affecting growth.

To further address endogeneity and measurement error the literature has also searched for exogenous variation (instruments) in financial development. Building on the law and finance literature (La Porta et al. 1997, 1998, 1999), Levine et al. (2000a, 2000b) use the family of a country's legal system to extract the exogenous (historically predetermined) component of financial development on growth.[14] They, as well as subsequent instrumental variables (IV) studies, show that the finance–growth nexus retains statistical significance. The IV studies further alleviate (although do not minimize) concerns that financial liquidity may simply reflect anticipated future growth or may be the consequence of overall economic performance.[15]

To address measurement error the World Bank, the OECD, and the ECB are currently constructing detailed indicators of the efficiency of the banking system, the liquidity of capital markets, and the regulatory and legal environment for a large sample of countries. This work also builds on the work of Beck, Demirgüç-Kunt, and Levine (2000) on the construction of the Financial Sector Database. It also follows the influential work of La Porta et al. (1997, 1998, 1999) and Djankov et al. (2003, forthcoming), who have constructed cross-country indicators that measure corporate governance practices and the overall efficiency of the legal system. Employing detailed

---

[13] The main problem of this work is that the efficiency of employed dynamic panel technique depends crucially in having a long time span (to properly model the short- and the long-run effects). In addition this approach is quite sensitive to outliers and small model permutations (see Favara 2003).

[14] See Beck and Levine 2005 for a review of the law and finance literature.

[15] The main problem of these IV approaches is that legal origin may affect economic growth through other channels, for example via regulation. In this case the IV estimates, which are typically higher than the OLS coefficients, will be the upper bound of the true effect of financial development (see Acemoglu and Johnson 2005).

indicators of financial systems' functions is key for the identification of the theoretical functions of financial intermediation. For example equity market features such as venture capital (VC) and private equity investment may be more important for productivity and innovation, while bank financing may be more important for capital accumulation, especially in early stages of development. In addition specialized financing products (such as standardized student loans that are quite common in the USA) may be important for human capital accumulation.

3.2. Event Studies of the Effects of Financial Liberalization

A somewhat distinct cross-country work quantifies the growth effects of financial liberalization policies mainly in emerging economies. Peter Blair Henry (2003) and Bekaert, Harvey, and Lundblad (2003) provide brief summaries of this work. These event studies address some important limitations of the purely cross-country work (discussed above), such as omitted variables and unobserved country heterogeneity. This is because these studies compare the evolution of growth and investment in countries before and after financial sector reforms. Although these studies might not look particularly relevant in assessing the productivity and growth differences among developed countries, such as the USA, the UK, or euro area countries, they are particularly relevant for the new EU member countries that are expected to join the monetary union in the future. This work strengthens the robustness of the cross-country finance–growth correlation and most importantly pushes forward on the causality front.

Bekaert, Harvey, and Lundblad (2001, 2005) study almost all countries that removed capital account restrictions in the period 1980–2000 (including many current EMU members and other high-income countries). They show that (controlling for country fixed effects and general time trends) these policies resulted in an overall increase of the annual per capita GDP growth of approximately 0.5 to 1 per cent. The authors also perform two important checks to advocate the causal interpretation of their results. First, they show that this effect is robust to controlling for other reforms (such as privatization, trade liberalization, product market deregulation) that usually coincide with financial reforms. This gives more confidence that the estimates are not capturing other liberalization policies that are typically in the same policy agenda. Second, they control in their empirical model for future country-level growth opportunities, using the country's industrial mix. This test is also important, because countries may liberalize their financial system when growth prospects for their products are favourable.[16]

Although these studies do not decompose growth (into productivity, physical, and human capital accumulation), parallel work by Henry (2000, 2001, 2003) on twelve Latin American and East Asian countries that liberalized their financial system in

---

[16] Bekaert et al. 2001, forthcoming, also provide some (weaker) evidence that financial reforms have a larger impact when countries have an educated workforce and proper legal system enforcement of investor rights.

the 1980s suggests that this growth effect stemmed mainly from increased investment (rather than TFP growth). Specifically both the macro (Henry 2000, 2001) and the firm-level studies (Chari and Henry 2004a) show that liberalizations yield an overall fall in the cost of capital. The consensus in the academic research community seems to be that this fall was on average around 100 basis points. Yet there is a wide range of estimates from 20 to 200 basis points on stock returns around liberalization episodes. Firms with good growth prospects and firms that foreign investors can easily invest in (e.g. as they are quoted on the stock market) experience the highest stock returns and invest the most after the reforms. Using detailed firm-level data from twenty-eight (mainly developing) countries that liberalized their capital markets in the last decade Mitton (2006) finds that stocks that are open to foreign investors experience higher sales growth, greater investment, greater profitability, greater efficiency, and lower leverage. The increase in sales growth and in the proxy of labour productivity is estimated to be around 1.5 to 2.0 per cent.

The application of these figures to the EU has to be considered cautiously, as at least most old member states have conducted such liberalizations already a long time ago. Yet these studies suggest that new member states and accession countries may benefit significantly from liberalized financial systems that are integrated with world financial markets, e.g. by speeding up their convergence in income levels to the levels observed for old EU member countries.

3.3. Summary Cross-country Regression Evidence

The main result of the cross-country work is that many (though rather coarse) proxies of both banking and securities market development (such as bank credit to GDP or stock market liquidity) are positively correlated with overall per capita output growth. In spite of the general drawbacks of cross-sectional studies this result appears quite robust (see however Favara 2003 for a more critical appraisal). Instrumental variable studies and dynamic panel approaches have further strengthened the finance–growth nexus, while event studies of financial liberalization policies mainly in emerging economies have pushed ahead on the causality front.

4. INDUSTRY-LEVEL ANALYSES

The literature has recently been moving away from purely cross-country to within-country, cross-industry approaches. These studies were developed to assuage some of the limitations of the cross-country models, such as omitted variable, reverse causality, and multicollinearity (Rajan and Zingales 1998). In addition this more micro approach enables researchers to shed light on the theoretical mechanisms of how finance contributes to economic growth. They are thus becoming increasingly popular in other fields of development economics.[17] (Table 2.2 summarizes the main industry-level studies.)

4.1. Financial Development and Industry Reliance on External Finance

In a highly influential paper Rajan and Zingales (1998) proposed a cross-industry, cross-country approach that addresses many of the limitations of the purely cross-country work (discussed in Section 2). Specifically Rajan and Zingales scrutinized whether if better-developed financial intermediaries help overcome market frictions that drive a wedge between the prices of external and internal finance, then industries that are naturally heavy users of external finance should benefit disproportionately more from financial development compared to other industries. Rajan and Zingales proposed a two-step approach. First, using US financial statement data, the authors construct an industry-level measure of reliance on external finance. Second, using cross-country industry data they test whether sectors that rely more on external finance tend to grow faster. Using data for forty-one countries and thirty-six manufacturing industries in the 1980s Rajan and Zingales find strong evidence in favour of this hypothesis.

Besides being closer in theory the appealing feature of the Rajan and Zingales approach is that it controls for both country and industry fixed effects. Country fixed effects assuage critique that other than finance country-level features, such as human capital, institutional quality, and trust, are driving the results. Industry fixed effects account for differences in overall productivity across sectors.[18]

Subsequent studies confirmed the stronger positive effect of financial development for the growth of industries that depend relatively more on external finance. For example, Claessens and Laeven (2003) show that the differential effect of financial development on sectors that rely on external finance is robust to accounting for the effect of sound property rights institutions on intangible-intensive sectors. Braun (2003) shows that financial development is particularly useful for intangible-intensive and R&D-intensive sectors. Guiso et al. (2005) also show the disproportional impact that financial development exerts on the growth of industries which are more dependent on external finance in a much larger sample of sixty-five countries (that also covers the 1980–95 period). Guiso et al. also perform two simulations to quantify

[17]   For example Perotti and Volpin 2004, Fisman and Sarria-Allende 2004, Klapper, Laeven, and Rajan forthcoming, Ciccone and Papaioannou forthcoming use this method to assess the effect of product market regulation on entry. Ciccone and Papaioannou 2005 employ this approach to explore the impact of human capital on growth, while Acemoglu, Johnson, and Mitton 2005 use it to study the effect of contractual institutions on vertical integration.

[18]   Rajan and Zinagles also include in their empirical model the initial share of the industry to total manufacturing value added. This variable controls for international specialization: for example financially developed countries may specialize in capital-intensive sectors that require a lot of external finance. For studies linking financial development and the pattern of international trade, see Beck 2002, Levchenko 2004, and Manova 2006.

Table 2.2. Overview of main cross–industry, cross–country studies of finance and growth

Study	Dep. variable(s)	Sample	Results
Rajan and Zingales (1998)	Value-added growth; entry; average firm size.	42 countries; 1980–9; 36 manufact. industries.	In financially developed countries, sectors that for inherent technological needs depend more on external finance grow faster. There is also higher entry in external–finance-dependent sectors.
Guiso et al. (2004)	Value-added growth; output growth.	65 countries; 1981–90; 36 manufact industries.	In financially developed countries, sectors that for inherent technological needs depend more on external finance experience faster value-added and output growth.
Fisman and Love (2004a, 2004b)	Value-added growth; share of industry in total manufacturing.	42 countries; 1980–9; 36 manufact. industries.	In financially developed countries, sectors that have good opportunities (measured by US sales growth) grow faster. Financially developed countries specialize in sectors that for technological reasons depend more on external finance.
Ciccone and Papaioanou (2006)	Value-added growth.	67 countries; 1980–9; 28 manufact. sectors.	In financially developed countries there is a small wedge between realized and optimal (target) investment.
Beck et al. (2005)	Value-added growth.	42 countries; 1980–9 and 1980–99; 36 manufact industries.	In financially developed countries, sectors that for inherent technological reasons have a large portion of small and medium-sized enterprises grow faster.
Bekaert et al. (forthcoming)	Country-level growth.	50 countries; 1980–2000.	Industry-level global opportunities weighted by country–industry output mix predict growth. Financially integrated open to foreign investment countries exploit better global growth opportunities.
Wurgler (2000)	Investment growth.	65 countries; 1963–95; 28 manufact. industries.	In financially developed countries and in countries with a non-state-controlled banking system the elasticity of industry value-added growth to investment growth is higher.

Notes: The table reports the main cross-industry, cross-country studies that assess the effect of financial development on sectoral growth.

the potential effect of financial development in the EU. First they assess what would be the growth effect (at the industry and the country level) if the EU were to reach the level of financial development (defined as the sum of domestic credit and stock market capitalization over GDP) of the USA and/or the level of the Netherlands (the country with the highest measure of financial development in the EU). Second, acknowledging that financial development is itself promoted by well-protected investor rights and an efficient legal system, they simulate what would be the country/industry effects if institutional reforms were to improve on a similar scale. Their simulations provide three insights:

- Averaging across all countries and sectors, the overall effect on annual value-added growth if the EU were to reach the US level of financial development is 0.7 per cent for overall and 0.9 per cent for manufacturing growth.
- Countries that score lower in the measures of financial development would be the biggest gainers (growth effects exceeding one percentage point). This group includes Greece, Ireland, Portugal, Spain, Italy, Belgium, Denmark, and to a somewhat lesser extent Germany.
- Industries that depend on external finance (such as pharmaceuticals or professional equipment) would experience the highest increase in value added.

This evidence is further supported by the recent work of de Serres et al. (2006). Using data that cover OECD economies in the 1990s de Serres et al. likewise show that external finance sectors grow faster in financially developed countries. The authors also investigate exactly which features of the financial system are the most important. Their regressions show that state ownership of banks and entry barriers to banking appear to be the most significant impediments to growth and entry.

4.2. Financial Development, Capital Reallocation, and Sector Growth Opportunities

Recent work has also linked financial development with the ability of industries and countries to exploit global growth opportunities. The main hypothesis, which dates back to Walter Bagehot (1873) and Joseph Schumpeter (1911), is that efficient financial institutions speed capital reallocation to sectors that are anticipated to grow faster and thus face better investment prospects (see Rajan and Zingales 2003 for modern exposition).

Fisman and Love (2004a) employ Rajan and Zingales' (1998) cross-country, cross-industry framework to test whether financial development exerts a disproportional impact in industries that face good growth prospects. After proxying global sector growth opportunities with sales growth in the USA, Fisman and Love show that financially developed countries experience faster value-added growth in the sectors which grow faster in the USA. Using a somewhat different approach Fisman and Love (2004b) find that industry value-added growth patterns are more closely correlated for country pairs with similar levels of financial development.

Ciccone and Papaioannou (2006) build a multi-sector world equilibrium model that formalizes the Schumpeterian capital reallocation hypothesis. In response to sector-specific global technological, relative price, and demand shocks industries have to adjust their optimal investment. Countries with relatively frictionless financial markets sectors that face high demand or experience technical progress are able to attract the necessary capital. However in financially underdeveloped countries capital moves only slowly to sectors with high prospects. Using industry-level data from twenty-eight manufacturing industries in a wide cross-section of sixty-seven countries in the 1980s, Ciccone and Papaioannou (2006) show that in financially underdeveloped countries there is a wide wedge between actual and optimal-target capital investment. This suggests that finance fosters productivity by swiftly reallocating resources to sectors with good global investment prospects. Besides various other sensitivity checks, the authors also show that the economic importance of the capital reallocation hypothesis increases when they account for measurement error in future sector opportunities.

4.2.1. *Alternative Approaches Using Industry Data*

Wurgler (2000) also studies the effect of financial markets' size in allocating capital to sectors with good prospects. His analysis also proceeds in two steps. First, using manufacturing data in sixty-five non-socialist countries over the period 1963–95, he constructs country-level indicators of the responsiveness of sectoral investment to value-added growth. He does so by regressing country-by-country industry investment growth on value-added growth. Neglecting issues of endogeneity and data quality and under the assumption that current output growth is proxy for future productivity, Wurgler's idea is that investment should be more responsive to output in financially advanced countries. Second, Wurgler examines whether, conditional on various other country characteristics, countries with larger capital markets display greater investment responsiveness to value-added growth. Although this approach requires many a priori restrictive assumptions, it has become quite influential because it is quite intuitive (see also Almeida and Wolfenzon 2005). If well-developed financial systems foster aggregate productivity, then in financially advanced countries investment should be more correlated with output. The cross-country regressions show that financial development can explain a significant part of the variation in the investment–output elasticity.[19]

---

[19] Building on Wurgler's approach in ongoing work Ciccone and Papaioannou 2007b use updated data (that span the period 1963–2002) and construct country-level investment–output elasticity measures that isolate the intersectoral investment responsiveness. The authors then show that investment in expanding industries is greater in countries with larger capital markets. This continues to be the case when one focuses on increases in capital market size due to lower government bank ownership, stricter insider trading legislation, and more efficient legal systems. These results are robust to alternative estimation techniques, outliers, and additional controls. Quite interestingly from a European standpoint the strong correlation between capital market size and the intersectoral investment responsiveness is also present even in the group of high-income countries.

Bekaert et al. (forthcoming) also examine the role of financial development and market integration in enabling countries to exploit growth opportunities. Country growth opportunities are estimated by combining the country's pattern of industrial specialization with indicators of global industry growth opportunities (proxied by average price–earnings ratios across countries). Their dynamic cross-country panel regressions reveal four main results:

- First, industry global market opportunities weighted by domestic country–industry output mix predict growth in both developed and emerging countries.
- Second, the authors find that in countries that are financially 'open' (integrated) to foreign investment, firms manage to better exploit the available (global) growth opportunities.
- Third, they find some evidence (albeit weaker) that countries with more liquid financial markets gain more from positive global shocks to the industries they specialize in.
- Fourth, the authors also document that the global opportunities–growth link is particularly strong in countries that are financially integrated in the global markets (as indicated by the amount of cross-border capital flows) and have efficient legal institutions (measured by well-protected shareholder and creditor rights; fast resolution of corporate disputes in courts; sound property rights protection).

The Bekaert et al. study is particularly relevant for the ongoing process of European financial integration, both among the current EMU members, but also with regard to the new accession countries, since it emphasizes the importance of financial openness. Their results are also theoretically plausible, since even if a country does not have the most well-developed financial intermediaries, if it is open to international investment, then it will be able to attract the necessary capital to finance sectors with positive prospects.

4.3. Financial Development and Entry

Rajan and Zingales (1998) also delve deeper into the components of growth, de-composing the overall growth effect into growth in new firms (establishments) and growth in the average firm size. This is particularly interesting since most theories suggest that financial development fosters growth by relaxing mainly small and new firms' constraints (since established firms have internal cash to finance investment and also easier access to bank-and-marked-based finance). The results suggest that the differential impact of financial development for growth of external finance-dependent sectors works primarily through entry of new firms and to a lesser extent through an increase in average firm size.[20] From a European viewpoint de Serres et al.

---

[20] Since a distinct literature (e.g. Aghion et al. 2006) has shown that there exists a significant correlation between entry and productivity, these results point out that financial development has a particularly sizeable effect for productivity.

(2006) find similar evidence in a sample of twenty-five (mainly developed) OECD economies. Klapper, Laeven, and Rajan (forthcoming) also find a strong differential effect of financial development in entry in external finance-dependent sectors using a panel of twenty European (advanced and transition) countries in the late 1990s.

Beck et al. (2004) also employ a cross-country cross-industry, approach to explore the effect of financial intermediation efficiency on entry. The authors first construct an industry-level size variable that measures the industrial reliance on small firms. Sector size is defined as the ratio of firms with less than twenty, ten, or five employees in the USA in the early 1990s. Second, the authors examine whether in financially developed countries industries with a high share of small firms grow on average faster. The results confirm this hypothesis.

4.4. Summary of Industry-level Work

The cross-country, cross-industry work has strengthened the financial development–growth nexus from both a technical and a conceptual standpoint. At the empirical side these studies alleviate endogeneity and reverse causation concerns and thus make an important step on causality. At the theoretical side these studies are better suited to identify the channels of how financial markets foster aggregate growth.

These studies are particularly important for the ongoing process of European financial integration, since they show that further improving financial services can have a direct effect on productivity. Efficient financial markets help to move economic activity to the sectors that face positive global growth opportunities. In addition these studies clearly show a strong differential effect of financial modernization for the growth of small and medium-sized enterprises, which are very important in most European countries.

5. COUNTRY-SPECIFIC CASE STUDIES

Following a recent trend in developing economics, research on finance and growth has tried to use policy changes in a quasi-natural experiment framework that establishes causality. Besides the econometric benefits, the use of micro-level (industry and firm) data is quite informative in exploring how financial sector reforms affect economic performance.

5.1. US-based Evidence on Banking Deregulation

A quite important strand of the finance and growth literature quantifies the effect of banking sector reforms, notably the removal of branching restrictions in the

United States. Philip Strahan (2003) provides a brief summary of this work. Focusing in a single country gives more confidence that the finance–growth correlation is not driven by the difficulty of controlling for country characteristics, such as social capital, law, property right protection, regulation, etc. This strand of the finance and growth literature is also relevant for the ongoing European financial integration debate. Retail banking is still among the least integrated parts of the European financial system (e.g. Hartmann et al. 2003, 2006; Baele et al. 2004; ECB 2005; Cappiello et al. forthcoming). In addition, these studies investigate the growth effects of financial reforms in a developed country which is quite similar to the ones of the euro area (in terms of human capital, institutions, etc.).

In the United States between 1970 and 1994, thirty-eight states removed regulatory restrictions on branching. In addition in the period 1978 to 1992 almost all states removed restrictions on intrastate bank ownership. Table 2.3 summarizes the main studies that explore differences in the timing of implementation across US states and assess the effect on financial system performance as well as state growth, productivity, and entrepreneurship.

Jayaratne and Strahan (1996) exploit differences in the *timing* of these bank reforms to assess their impact on growth. Controlling for state and year unobserved characteristics and trends, their estimates imply that state banking deregulation was associated with a 0.6 to 1.2 per cent increase in real per capita state growth. The evidence also implies that the gains in growth emerged from enhanced productivity ('quality of banking') rather than from increased investment. The authors also show that the share of non-performing loans and write-offs dropped significantly after the reforms (approximately −0.3 per cent to −0.6 per cent). Jayaratne and Strahan (1998) show that banking reforms resulted in a fall of non-interest costs, wages, and loan losses. These efficiency gains translated into lower loan prices. Stiroh and Strahan (2003) argue that the spur in bank acquisitions (the annual acquisition rate rose by 1.6 per cent after the approval of laws allowing interstate banking) and other forms of consolidation enabled banks to seize scale economies and specialization benefits.

Black and Strahan (2002) provide further evidence that deregulation enhanced competition, which in turn fostered entrepreneurship (new firm incorporations and growth in the number of establishments). They estimate that new firm incorporations increased by 4 to 8 per cent per year after deregulation. Cetorelli and Strahan (2006) show that reforms fostered productivity growth of small and medium-sized firms.

Kroszner and Strahan (1999) show that liberalization was mainly driven by political local factors rather by efficiency consideration. Thus, these results are not prone to critique that states removed restrictions in banking when economic conditions were favourable or in anticipation of future growth.

Not only is this work particularly relevant for the ongoing banking and financial system integration that takes place in the EU, but the results also indicate that finance contributes to growth by enhancing productivity.

Table 2.3. Overview of main studies on banking system deregulation in the United States

Study	Dep. variable(s)	Results
Jayaratne and Starhan (1996, 1998)	Gross state product (GSP) growth; banking efficiency.	State banking deregulation was associated with a 0.6 to 1.2% increase in real GSP growth. The share of non-performing loans and loan write-offs dropped significantly after the reforms (−0.3% to −0.6%).
Stiroh and Strahan (2003)	Bank system competition; banking merger and acquisition activity.	State banking systems became more competitive following deregulation. Annual acquisition rate rose by 1.64% after the passage of laws allowing interstate banking (compared with a mean rate of 2.8%). Significant consolidation, especially in small banks. No significant increase in bank acquisitions following branching deregulation. Banks expand by purchasing branches of existing banks rather than by acquiring all of the branches.
Black and Strahan (2002)	Banking competition; entrepreneurship (entry).	New incorporations (entry) increased following deregulation by approx. 4–8%. The effect of bank sector consolidation on the new firm incorporation is significantly negative. The effects of branching deregulation occurred, in part, because of changes in market structure such as declines in the share of small banks and changes in local market concentration. Deregulation had a zero effect in states that already had a competitive banking sector, but in states with highly concentrated banking systems (like Alaska, Mississippi, and Oregon) the effect of deregulation was very strong.
Cetorelli and Strahan (2004)	Entrepreneurship (entry).	Bank competition (which followed bank deregulation) is particularly beneficial for entry of small and medium-sized firms. Deregulation fostered entry in sectors that for technological reasons depend more on external (and bank) finance.

Note: The table reports the summary of results on research assessing the impact of banking sector deregulation across US states.

5.2. Case-study Evidence from EU Countries

5.2.1. *France*

The growth and productivity enhancing effects of banking deregulation are also found in a recent study that quantifies the effect of French banking reforms in 1985. Using detailed firm- and industry-level data for the period 1978 to 1999 that cover all sectors of the French economy, Bertrand, Schoar, and Thesmar (forthcoming) provide a thorough before–after analysis of the effects of banking deregulation. French reforms differed from the US deregulation described before. The deregulation package in France involved four major reforms: (i) elimination of subsidized loans; (ii) elimination of the 'encadrement du credit', which imposed monthly ceilings on credit growth for each bank; (iii) unification of banking regulation in a comprehensive Banking Act; and (iv) some privatization.

The authors document that, controlling for business-cycle effects, industry-specific trends, and unobserved characteristics, the reforms had two main effects:

- A major restructuring and increased firm-level productivity (proxied by firm return on assets) mainly of bank-dependent sectors.
- Increased entry and exit in bank- and finance-dependent industries. In addition, after the reforms, worse-performing firms experienced a higher likelihood to exit the market, suggesting enhanced competition in the product markets.

5.2.2. *Italy*

The most likely causal effect of financial development on growth and productivity is further strengthened by a detailed study on the effects of firms' access to finance and growth across Italian regions. Guiso, Sapienza, and Zingales (2004) investigate the effects of differences in local financial markets across Italian regions. This study further strengthens the hypothesis that financial development is a key determinant of entrepreneurship, innovation, and productivity growth. It does so by providing compelling micro-level evidence that even within an integrated and relatively developed financial system, differences in firms' access to finance do matter.

First, using survey data on firms' access to finance and credit rationing the authors construct a regional index of financial constraints. Second, they run cross-region and cross-firm regressions analysing the effect of financial development at the regional level on various aspects of firm and regional growth. Their results can be summarized as follows:

- The likelihood for an entrepreneur to raise capital for financing a start-up is 5.6 per cent higher if he moves from the least financially developed region (Calabria) to the most financially developed one (Marche).
- Entry of new firms is much higher in financially developed regions. Quantitatively the ratio of new firms to population is 25 per cent higher in the most financially developed provinces than in the least financially developed ones.

- Local financial development fosters competition in product markets. The estimates suggest that firms operating in the most developed regions have on average a 1.3 percentage point lower mark-up compared to firms in the least financially developed provinces.
- In financially developed regions firms experience faster sales growth. The estimates imply that, conditioning on various firm and region characteristics, a firm operating in the least financially developed region grows by 5.7 per cent less than a similar firm in the most financially developed region.
- At the provincial level financial development is associated with higher growth rates. The regressions suggest that in the most financially developed region, annual per capita domestic product grows by approximately 1 per cent more than in the least financially developed one.

These results seem to be robust to a number of sensitivity checks and most importantly are not driven by north–south differences.

5.3. Summary Country-specific Studies

The case-specific evidence from the United States and the two European countries provides compelling evidence that financial development contributes to growth in industrial countries by increasing firms' efficiency, enhancing entrepreneurship, fostering competition, and thus accelerating productivity growth. Similar results are also provided by Haber's (2005) detailed analysis of the role of financial markets in the industrialization of the USA as compared to Mexico in the nineteenth century. Banerjee (2004) and Banerjee and Duflo (2005) summarize similar case-specific evidence from the developing world. These micro studies also give more confidence to the conclusion that the association between financial development and growth found in cross-country studies represents something more than a simple correlation. The quite detailed analyses of the French, Italian, and US banking reforms provide direct further evidence on the 'Schumpeterian hypothesis' that reforms leading to financial development can foster productivity growth through creative destruction.

6. CONCLUSION

This study reviews the empirical literature on the finance–growth nexus within a neoclassical growth framework, placing an emphasis on the policy implications of this work in the current European environment that has placed financial reforms high on the policy agenda.

The chapter started by laying down a neoclassical growth framework to discuss the empirical work linking financial intermediation to economic growth. Decomposing aggregate growth into investment, human capital accumulation, and total factor productivity growth appears useful to understand the theoretical channels on how financial development fosters growth. Then the chapter discusses the recent empirical research. Besides reviewing the main contributions of this work, the current study also puts a special focus on the key issue of causality. Over the past years the empirical literature has employed genuine and intuitive approaches to push on causality. For example a growing number of studies are using industry- and firm-level approaches, which address many of the general econometric shortcoming of the cross-country work. In addition employing a more micro approach sheds light onto the theoretical mechanisms of how finance fosters aggregate growth. The literature is also increasingly exploiting policy changes in a (quasi) natural experiment framework. These studies make crucial advancements on causal inference and also yield valuable insights on how finance contributes to economic performance.

The main results of the fast growing body of research on finance and growth can be summarized as follows:

1. In spite of the limitations of the cross-country growth regression framework there appears to be a relatively strong correlation between financial development and economic growth. Although this correlation appears quite robust, it is quite hard to push on causality with such a cross-country approach. Before–after event studies that assess the growth effects of financial liberalization policies reveal that such reforms are followed by higher growth. This work pushes forward on the causality front, since it accounts for country-unobservable characteristics, parallel reforms (such as privatization, trade openness), and also future country-level opportunities.

2. Cross-country, cross-industry (and even cross-time) studies reveal that financial development exerts a disproportionately positive impact on sectors that are external finance hungry, face good future opportunities, or are populated mainly by small firms. This work assuages many (though not all) of the shortcomings of the purely cross-country work and also enables the identification of the theoretical channels on how finance contributes to growth.

3. Novel event studies that assess the effects of banking deregulation in the USA or other countries provide strong evidence that such policies exert a significant effect on growth. Studying policy reforms in a before–after experiment setting or investigating the impact of local financing conditions using micro data gives confidence that the finance–growth nexus represents something more than a simple correlation.

From a growth decomposition standpoint the evidence points out that financial development fosters aggregate growth through a cost of capital fall-investment and a resource reallocation-capital efficiency TFP channel. The empirical results show that the first capital accumulation channel is mainly present in the developing world, while the productivity channel is mostly important for industrial countries.

References

ACEMOGLU, D., AGHION, P., and ZILIBOTTI, F. (2006), 'Distance to frontier, selection and economic growth', *Journal of the European Economic Association*, March, 4(1), 37–74.

____ and JOHNSON, S. (2005), 'Unbundling institutions', *Journal of Political Economy*, October, 113(5), 949–95.

____ ____ and MITTON, T. (2005), 'Determinants of vertical integration: finance, contracts, and regulation', MIT, May, mimeo.

____ and ZILIBOTTI, F. (1997), 'Was Prometheus unbound by chance? Risk, diversification and growth', *Journal of Political Economy*, August, 105(4), 709–51.

AGHION, P., and HOWITT, P. (2006), 'Appropriate growth policy: a unified framework', Schumpeter Lecture Delivered at the 20th Congress of the European Economic Association, *Journal of the European Economic Association*.

____ ____ and MAYER-FOULKES, D. (2005). 'The effect of financial development on convergence: theory and evidence', *Quarterly Journal of Economics*, February, 120(1), 173–222.

____ BLUNDELL, R., GRIFFITH, R., HOWITT, P., and PRANTL, S. (2006), 'The effects of entry on incumbent innovation and productivity', February, NBER Working Paper 12027.

ALMEIDA, H., and WOLFENZON, D. (2005), 'The effect of external finance on the equilibrium allocation of capital', *Journal of Financial Economics*, January, 75(1), 133–64.

ARELLANO, M., and BOND, S. R. (1991), 'Some tests of specification for panel data: Monte Carlo evidence and an application to employment equations', *Review of Economic Studies*, April, 58(2), 277–97.

____ and BOVER, O. (1995), 'Another look at the instrumental variable estimation of error-components models', *Journal of Econometrics*, July, 68(1), 29–51.

ARESTIS, P., and DEMETRIADES, P. (1997), 'Financial development and economic growth: assessing the evidence', *Economic Journal*, May, 107(2), 783–99.

BAELE, L., FERRANDO, A., HÖRDAHL, P., KRYLOVA, E., and MONNET, C. (2004), 'Measuring financial integration in the euro area', ECB Occasional Paper no. 14, May.

BAGEHOT, W. (1873), *A Description of the Money Market*, repr. Homewood, Ill: Irwin, 1962.

BANERJEE, A. (2004), 'Contracting constraints, credit markets, and economic development', in M. Dewatripoint, L. Hansen, and S. Turnovsky (eds.), *Advances in Economics and Econometrics: Theory and Applications: Eight World Congress of the Econometric Society*, Vol. iii, Cambridge: Cambridge University Press.

____ and DUFLO, E. (2005), 'Growth theory through the lens of development economics', in Philippe Aghion and Steve Durlauf (eds.), *The Handbook of Economic Growth*, Amsterdam: North-Holland.

BARRO, R. J. (1991), 'Economic growth in a cross section of countries', *Quarterly Journal of Economics*, May, 106(2), 407–43.

____ (1998), 'Notes on growth accounting', Cambridge, Mass.: Harvard University, December Mimeo.

____ and SALA-I-MARTIN, X. (1995), *Economic Growth*, Cambridge, Mass.: MIT Press.

BECK, T. (2002), 'Financial development and international trade: is there a link?', *Journal of International Economics*, January, 57(1), 107–31.

____ (2003), 'Financial dependence and international trade', *Review of International Economics*, 11(1), 296–316.

____ DEMIRGÜÇ-KUNT, A., and LEVINE, R. (2000), 'A new database on financial development and structure', *World Bank Economic Review*, 14, 597–605. September 2006 vesrion downloadable from:www.econ.brown.edu/fac/Ross_Levine/IndexLevine.htm.

BECK, T., and LEVINE, R. (2002), 'Industry growth and capital allocation: does having a market- or bank-based system matter?', *Journal of Financial Economics*, 64(2), 147–80.

—— —— (2004), 'Stock markets, banks, and growth: panel evidence', *Journal of Banking and Finance*, March, 28(3), 423–42.

—— —— (2005) 'Legal institutions and financial development', in Claude Menard and Mary M. Shirley (eds.), *Handbook for New Institutional Economics*, Norwell, Mass.: Kluwer Academic Publishers.

—— DEMIRGÜÇ-KUNT, A., LAEVEN, L., and LEVINE, R. (2005), 'Finance, firm size and growth', National Bureau of Economic Research (Cambridge, Mass.), Working Paper no. 10983.

BEKAERT, G., HARVEY, C. R., and LUNDBLAD, C. (2001), 'Emerging equity markets and economic development', *Journal of Development Economics*, December, 66(3), 465–504.

—— —— —— (2003), 'Equity market liberalization in emerging markets', *Federal Reserve Bank of St. Louis Review*, July–August, 85(4), 53–74.

—— —— —— (2005), 'Does financial liberalization spur growth?', *Journal of Financial Economics*, July, 7(1), 3–55.

—— —— —— and SIEGEL, S. (forthcoming), 'Global growth opportunities and market integration', *Journal of Finance*.

BENHABIB, J., and SPIEGEL, M. (2000), 'The role of financial development on growth and investment', *Journal of Economic Growth*, December, 5(4), 341–60.

BERTRAND, M., SCHOAR, A., and THESMAR, D. (forthcoming), 'Banking deregulation and industry structure: evidence from the French banking reforms of 1985', *Journal of Finance*.

BLACK, S., and STRAHAN, P. E. (2002), 'Entrepreneurship and the availability of bank credit', *Journal of Finance*, November, 67(6), 2807–33.

BLUNDEL, R., and BOND, S. (1998), 'Initial conditions and moment restrictions in dynamic panel data models', *Journal of Econometrics*, August, 87(1), 115–43.

BOND, S., HOEFFLER, A., and TEMPLE, J. R. W. (2001), 'GMM estimation of empirical growth models', Centre for Economic Policy Research (London) Discussion Paper 3048.

BRAUN, M. (2003), 'Financial contractibility and assets' hardness', UCLA, mimeo. www.anderson.ucla.edu/faculty/matias.braun/.

CAPPIELLO, L., GERARD, B., KADAREJA, A., and MANGANELLI, S. (forthcoming). 'Financial integration of new EU member states', ECB Working Papers.

CASELLI, F. (2005), 'Accounting for cross-country income differences', in Philippe Aghion and Steven Durlauf (eds.), *The Handbook of Economic Growth*, Amsterdam: North Holland.

CETORELLI, N., and STRAHAN, P. E. (2006), 'Finance as a barrier to entry: bank competition and industry structure in local U.S. markets', *Journal of Finance*, February, 61(1), 437–61.

CHARI, A., and HENRY, P. B. (2004a). 'Risk sharing and asset prices: evidence from a natural experiment', *Journal of Finance*, 59(3), 1295–324.

—— —— (2004b). 'Is the invisible hand discerning or indiscriminate? Investment and stock prices in the aftermath of capital account liberalizations', NBER Working Paper 10318, February.

CICCONE, A., and JAROCINSKI, M. (2007), 'Determinants of economic growth: will data tell?' UPF, mimeo.

—— and PAPAIOANNOU, E. (2005), 'Human capital, the structure of production and growth', Centre for Economic Policy Research (London) Discussion Paper 5354.

_____ _____ (2006), 'Adjustment to target capital, finance and growth', Centre for Economic Policy Research (London) Discussion Paper 5969.

_____ _____ (2007a), 'Red tape and delayed entry', *Journal of the European and Economic Association Papers and Proceedings*, April–May.

_____ _____ (2007b), 'Financial development and intersectoral investment: new estimates and evidence', European Central Bank, March, mimeo.

CLAESSENS, S., and LAEVEN, L. (2003), 'Financial development, property rights, and growth', *Journal of Finance*, 58(6), 2401–36.

DE SERRES, A., KOBAYAKAWA, S., SLOK, T., and VARTIA, L. (2006), 'Regulation of financial systems and economic growth', OECD Economics Department Working Paper (Paris) no. 506, August.

DINC, S. (2006), 'Politicians and banks: political influences on government-owned banks in emerging countries', *Journal of Financial Economics*, 77, 453–79.

DJANKOV, S., McLIESH C., and SHLEIFER, A. (forthcoming), 'Private credit in 129 countries', *Journal of Financial Economics*.

_____ LA PORTA, R., LÓPEZ-DE-SILANES, F., and SHLEIFER, A. (2003), 'Courts', *Quarterly Journal of Economics*, May 118(2), 453–517.

DURLAUF, S. N., JOHNSON, P. A., and TEMPLE, J. R. W. (2005), 'Growth econometrics', in Philippe Aghion and Steven Durlauf (eds.), *The Handbook of Economic Growth*, Amsterdam: North Holland.

_____ and QUAH, D. (1999), 'The new empirics of economic growth,' in John Taylor and Mike Woodford (eds.), *Handbook of Macroeconomics*, Amsterdam: North-Holland.

EUROPEAN CENTRAL BANK (2005), 'Assessing the performance of financial systems', *Monthly Bulletin*, October.

FAVARA, G. (2003), 'An empirical reassessment of the relationship between finance and growth', IMF Working Paper 03/123, June.

FISMAN, R., and LOVE, I. (2004a), 'Financial development and growth in the short and long run', National Bureau of Economic Research (Cambridge, Mass.), Working Paper no. 10236.

_____ _____ (2004b), 'Financial development and intersectoral allocation: a new approach', *Journal of Finance*, November, 54(6), 2785–805.

_____ and SARRIA-ALLENDE, V. (2004), 'Regulation of entry and the distortion of industrial organization', National Bureau of Economic Research (Cambridge, Mass.), Working Paper no. 10929, November.

GALOR, O., and ZEIRA, J. (1993), 'Income distribution and macroeconomics', *Review of Economic Studies*, January, 60(1), 35–52.

GREENWOOD, J., and JOVANOVIC, B. (1990), 'Financial development, growth and the distribution of income', *Journal of Political Economy*, October, 98(5), 1067–107.

GRONINGEN GROWTH and DEVELOPMENT CENTRE and the CONFERENCE BOARD (2005), 'Total economy database', www.ggdc.net, accessed August 2005.

GUISO, L., SAPIENZA, P., and ZINGALES, L. (2004), 'Does local financial development matter?', *Quarterly Journal of Economics*, August, 119(3), 929–69.

_____ JAPPELLI, T., PADULA, M., and PAGANO, M. (2005), 'Financial market integration and economic growth in the EU', *Economic Policy*, 19(40), 523–77.

HABER, S. H. (2005), 'Political institutions and financial development: evidence from the economic histories of Mexico and the United States', Stanford University, October, mimeo.

HABER, S. H., FERRANDO, A., FRITZER, F., HEIDER, F., LAURO, B., and LO DUCA, M. (2006), 'The performance of the european financial system', European Central Bank, September, mimeo.

HARTMANN, P., MADDALONI, A., and MANGANELLI, S. (2003), 'The euro area financial system: structure, integration and policy initiatives', Oxford Review of Economic Policy, Spring, 19 (1), 180–213.

HAUK, W. R., JR., and WACZIARG, R. (2004), 'A Monte Carlo study of growth regressions', National Bureau of Economic Research (Cambridge, Mass.), Technical Working Paper no. t0296, January.

HENRY, P. B. (2000), 'Stock market liberalization, economic reform, and emerging market equity prices', Journal of Finance, March, 55(2), 529–64.

——— (2001) 'Do stock market liberalizations cause investment booms?', Journal of Financial Economics, January, 58(1–2), 301–34.

——— (2003), 'Capital account liberalization, the cost of capital, and economic growth', American Economic Review, May, 93(2), 91–6.

JAYARATNE, J., and STRAHAN, P. E. (1996), 'The finance–growth nexus: evidence from bank branching deregulation', Quarterly Journal of Economics, August, 111(3), 639–70.

——— ——— (1998), 'Entry restrictions, industry evolution and dynamic efficiency', Journal of Law and Economics, January, 41(1), 239–74.

KING, R., and LEVINE, R. (1993), 'Finance and growth: Schumpeter might be right', Quarterly Journal of Economics, August, 153(3), 717–38.

KLAPPER, L., LAEVEN, L., and RAJAN, R. G. (forthcoming), 'Entry regulation as a barrier to entrepreneurship', Journal of Financial Economics.

KLENOW, P. J., and RODRIGUEZ-CLARE, A. (1997), 'The neoclassical revival in growth economics: has it gone too far?', in Ben Bernake and Julio Rotemberg (eds.), NBER Macroeconomics Annual, Cambridge, Mass.: MIT Press.

KROSZNER, R. S., and STRAHAN, P. E.(1999), 'What drives deregulation? Economics and politics of the relaxation of bank branching restrictions', Quarterly Journal of Economics, November, 114(4), 1437–67.

KRUEGER, A. B., and LINDAHL, M. (2001), 'Education for growth: why and for whom?', Journal of Economic Literature, December, 39(4), 1101–36.

LA PORTA, R., LÓPEZ-DE-SILANES, F., and SHLEIFER, A. (2002), 'Government ownership of banks', Journal of Finance, February, 57(1), 256–301.

——— ——— and VISHNY, R. (1997), 'Legal determinants of external finance', Journal of Finance, July, 53(1), 1131–50.

——— ——— ——— ——— (1998), 'Law and finance', Journal of Political Economy, 106(6), 1113–55.

——— ——— ——— ——— (1999), 'The quality of government', Journal of Law, Economics and Organization, 15(1), 222–79.

LEVCHENKO, A. (2004), 'Institutional quality and international trade', IMF Working Paper 04/231.

LEVINE, R. (1997), 'Finance and growth: views and agenda', Journal of Economic Literature, 35(2), 688–726.

——— (2002), 'Bank-based or Market-based financial systems: which is better?', Journal of Financial Intermediation, October, 11(4), 398–428.

——— (2003), 'More on finance and growth: more finance, more growth?', Federal Reserve Bank of St Louis Review, July—August, 85(4), 31–46.

——— (2005), 'Finance and growth: theory, evidence, and mechanisms', in Philippe Aghion and Steve Durlauf (eds.), The Handbook of Economic Growth, Amsterdam: North-Holland.

———— LOAYZA, N., and BECK, T. (2000a). 'Financial intermediation and growth: causality and causes', *Journal of Monetary Economics*, August, 46(1), 31–77.

———— ———— ———— (2000b), 'Finance and the sources of growth', *Journal of Financial Economics*, October, 58(1–2), 261–300.

———— and RENELT, D. (1992), 'A sensitivity analysis of cross-country growth regressions', *American Economic Review*, September, 82(4), 942–63.

———— and ZERVOS, S. (1998), 'Stock markets, banks, and economic growth', *American Economic Review*, June, 88(3), 559–86.

LOAYZA, N., and RANCIERE, R. (2006), 'Financial development, financial fragility and growth', *Journal of Money, Credit and Banking*, June, 38(4), 1051–76.

MANKIW, G. (1995), 'The growth of nations', *Brookings Papers on Economic Activity*, 1995(1), 275–326.

———— ROMER, D., and WEIL, D. N. (1992), 'A contribution to the empirics of economic growth', *Quarterly Journal of Economics*, May, 107(2), 407–37.

MANOVA, K. (2006), 'Credit constraints in trade: financial development and export composition', Harvard University, mimeo.

MITTON, T. (2006), 'Stock market liberalization and operating performance at the firm level', *Journal of Financial Economics*, September, 81(3), 625–47.

PAPAIOANNOU, E. (2005), 'What drives international bank flows? Politics, institutions and other determinants', ECB Working Paper no. 437, February.

PEROTTI, E., and VOLPIN, P. (2004), 'Lobbying on entry', Centre for Economic Policy Research (London), Discussion Paper no. 4519; updated version (April 2006), www1.fee.uva.nl/fm.

PESARAN, M. H., SHIN, Y., and SMITH, R. P. (1999), 'Pooled mean group estimation of dynamic heterogeneous panels', *Journal of the American Statistical Association*, 94(2), 621–34.

———— and SMITH, R. P. (1995), 'Estimation of long-run relationship from dynamic heterogeneous panels', *Journal of Econometrics*, 68(1), 79–113.

RAJAN, R. G., and ZINGALES, L. (1998), 'Financial dependence and growth', *American Economic Review*, 88(3), 559–86.

———— ———— (2003), *Saving Capitalism from the Capitalists: Unleashing the Power of Financial Markets to Create Wealth and Spread Opportunity*. New York: Crown Business.

ROUSSEAU, P. L., and WACHTEL, P. (1998), 'Financial intermediation and economic performance: historical evidence from five industrialized countries', *Journal of Money, Credit and Banking*, November, 30(3-2), 657–78.

SALA-I-MARTIN, X. (1997), 'I just ran 2 million regressions', *American Economic Review Papers and Proceeding*, May, 87 (2), 178–83.

———— DOPPELHOFER, G., and MILLER, R. I. (2004), 'Determinants of long-term growth: a Bayesian averaging of classical estimates (BACE) approach', *American Economic Review*, September, 94(4), 813–35.

SAPIENZA, P. (2004), 'The effects of government ownership on bank lending', *Journal of Financial Economics*, May, 72 (2), 357–84.

SCHUMPETER, J. A. (1911), *The Theory of Economic Development*, repr. Cambridge, Mass.: Harvard University Press, 1934.

STIROH, K. J., and STRAHAN, P. E. (2003), 'Competitive dynamics of competition: evidence from U.S. banking', *Journal of Money, Credit and Banking*, May, 35(5), 801–28.

STRAHAN, P. E. (2003), 'The real effects of US banking deregulation', *Federal Reserve Bank of St Louis Review*, July–August, 85(4), 111–28.

TADESSE, S. (2003), 'Fnancial architecture and economic performance: international evidence', *Journal of Financial Intermediation*, October, 11(4), 429–54.

TEMPLE, J. (1999), 'The new growth evidence', *Journal of Economic Literature*, March, 37(1), 112–56.

WURGLER, J. (2000), 'Financial markets and the allocation of capital', *Journal of Financial Economics*, 58(1), 187–214.

CHAPTER 3

....

INTERACTION EFFECTS IN THE RELATIONSHIP BETWEEN GROWTH AND FINANCE

....

PHILIPPE AGHION

1. INTRODUCTION

....

VARIOUS attempts have been made recently at explaining why productivity differences persist between rich and poor countries, and why some countries diverge from the world technology frontier in terms of their per capita GDP levels or growth rates, while other countries manage to catch up with the world frontier. In this chapter we explore the role of credit market imperfections in explaining cross-country growth performance and cross-country convergence and divergence, following Lucas' (1990) observation that capital does not flow from rich to poor countries even though the marginal return to capital is higher in the latter. We also analyse the interplay between credit market imperfections and macroeconomic policies.

The author is grateful to Xavier Freixas for very helpful comments, to Edmund Phelps for his advice and encouragements, and to the Center on Capitalism and Society at Columbia University and the Kauffman Foundation, for providing generous financial support to this project.

In his excellent survey article in the *Handbook of Economic Growth*, Ross Levine (2005) summarizes as follows the existing research on finance and growth: 'Taken as a whole, the bulk of existing research suggests that (1) countries with better functioning banks and markets grow faster; (2) simultaneity bias does not seem to drive these conclusions; and (3) better functioning financial systems ease the external financing constraints that impede firm and industrial expansion, suggesting that this is one mechanism through which financial development matters for growth.'

In fact, most of the existing literature on the subject has been concerned with cross-country, cross-sectional or panel regressions where growth is regressed over financial development (for example measured by the ratio of private credit to GDP) and additional controls (policy variables, education, political stability, initial income per capita, etc.). Existing empirical papers on finance and growth, which we briefly review in the next section, differ in terms of: (i) whether they look at cross-country data (like King and Levine 1993 and subsequent work by Levine and co-authors) or at cross-industry data like Rajan and Zingales (1998) or at cross-regional data like Guiso, Sapienza, and Zingales (2002) or at firm-level data like Demirgüç-Kunt and Maksimovic (1998); (ii) how financial development is measured: by the ratio of bank credit to GDP, or by indicators of stock market development, or if it is also interacted as in Rajan and Zingales (1998) with a measure of external financial dependence of the industry; (iii) whether one looks at cross-section or at panel data; and (iv) whether or not one instruments for financial development.

In the second part of the chapter we add to this literature by introducing interaction effects between financial development and technological or macroeconomic variables. In particular, following a very brief summary of Levine's survey of the main existing empirical contributions on finance and growth in Section 2, in Section 3 we look at the interaction between financial development and initial income relative to the current frontier (that is, the country's initial distance to the technological frontier), and argue that: (i) countries that are either initially close to the technological frontier or with a sufficiently high level of financial development will converge to the frontier in growth rates and in per capita GDP, whereas (ii) countries that are too far below the frontier and with a low level of financial development will diverge from it. In particular, the interaction between financial development and income generates a twin-peak distribution of income and growth rates in the long run. In Section 4, we consider the interaction between financial development and macroeconomic volatility, and argue that: (i) volatility is more detrimental to growth in less financially developed countries; (ii) a more counter-cyclical budgetary policy is more growth enhancing in countries with a lower level of financial development; and (iii) countries with lower levels of financial development are more likely to benefit from a fixed exchange rate regime, if, as we seem to observe, exchange rate risk is the main source of macroeconomic volatility. Finally, Section 5 concludes.

2. LEVINE'S EMPIRICAL SURVEY
IN A NUTSHELL

This section presents a very brief summary of Levine's (2005) survey of the empirical literature on finance and growth. We also refer the readers to his equally exhaustive theoretical survey in Section 2 of that same chapter. One reference which had to be missing in Levine's chapter[1] as it was just produced as another chapter for the same *Handbook of Economics Growth* is Banerjee and Duflo (2005). In this chapter, Banerjee and Duflo revisit a within-country level, Lucas' 'no-convergence' puzzle, namely: why is it that poorer countries or sectors where capital is scarce, and therefore the marginal productivity of capital is high, do not attract investments that would make them converge towards the frontier countries or sectors? In particular they argue that the most natural way to account for the observed cross-sectoral differences in returns and investment rates in a country like India is to introduce both credit market imperfections and increasing returns at the firm level.[2] We will come back to this at the end of this section when we talk about cross-firm regressions.

2.1. Cross-country and Cross-region

Levine (2005) attributes the first empirical analysis on finance and growth to Goldsmith (1969). Goldsmith uses cross-country data over the period 1860-1963 to regress average growth on financial development as measured by the size of the financial intermediary sector (measured by the value of its assets) over GDP, and finds a positive correlation between financial development and output growth. As well explained by Levine, this study has its limits: no controls in the regression, no instrumentation to address potential causality issues, the left-hand side variable is output growth instead of productivity growth, and the sample consists of thirty-five countries only. It is these limitations that King and Levine address in their seminal work in 1993.

King and Levine (1993) consider a broader sample of seventy-seven countries over the period 1960 to 1989. They regress average growth of per capita GDP or average growth in TFP over financial development and a number of control variables on the right-hand side of the regression equation. The controls include: initial income per capita, education measures, indices of political stability, and policy indicators. Financial development is measured in three possible ways: (i) the ratio between the liquid liabilities of the financial system—not its assets as in Goldsmith (1969)—and GDP; (ii) the ratio of commercial bank credit to bank credit plus central bank's domestic assets (this measure performs generally more poorly than the others);

---

[1] We also expand a little on Guiso, Sapienza, and Zingales 2002.
[2] One possible way of doing so might be to simply adapt the model in Section 3 below into a model of cross-sectoral convergence and divergence within a country.

(iii) the ratio of credit to private enterprises to GDP. Each of these measures is averaged over the period 1960–89. The cross-country regression shows a large and significant correlation between productivity growth and financial development measured as specified above. To make sure they capture the causal relationship from finance to growth and not the reverse, King and Levine repeat the same regression exercise but using initial 1960 values of the financial development measures instead of their average over the whole period. This regression also shows a positive and significant correlation between financial development and growth, which now suggests that 'financial development in 1960 is a good predictor of economic growth over the next 30 years'.

Subsequently, Levine and Zervos (1998) concentrate on the nature of financial sectors, and specifically the importance of stock market development and stock market 'liquidity'. In particular, Levine and Zervos consider what they call the 'turnover ratio', namely the total value of currently traded shares over the total value of listed shares, and based on a cross-country regression involving forty-two countries over the period 1976–93, they find that both the initial level of bank credit *and* the initial level of this turnover ratio in 1976 show a positive and significant correlation with average productivity growth over the period 1976–93.

One may object to the measures of financial development used by Levine and his co-authors; however this is the best that can be done while remaining at cross-country level.

A more serious objection is causality: what tells us that these positive correlations do not reflect either the fact that financial development occurs in prediction of forthcoming growth, or the fact that a third variable, call it institutional development (e.g. measured by property rights protection), causes both higher growth and higher financial development? To address this endogeneity problem, Levine (1998, 1999) and Levine Loayza, and Beck (2000) use the legal origins indicators of La Porta et al. (1998) as instruments for financial development. Thus the regression exercise now involves a first stage where financial development is regressed over dummy variables for Anglo-Saxon, French, and German legal origins (against Scandinavian legal origins) respectively, and a second-stage regression where average productivity growth is regressed over predicted financial development as derived from the first-stage regression and the same control variables as before. In particular, Levine et al. (2000) obtain a strongly positive and significant correlation between predicted financial development and average productivity growth over the period 1960–95.

Levine et al. (2000) go even further by performing panel cross-country regressions in which the period 1960–95 is subdivided in five-year subperiods, and where, for each five-year subperiod, average productivity growth over the subperiod is regressed over current and past financial development, controlling for country fixed effects. And again, they find positive and significant correlations between (current and lagged) financial development and average productivity growth during the subperiod.

Because they move from cross-country to cross-regional analysis within a country (Italy), Guiso, Sapienza, and Zingales (2002) can construct more precise measures of financial development and show that financial development as they measure it is an important determinant of cross-regional convergence. More specifically, GSZ construct their measure of regional financial development by estimating a linear probability model in which they regress the probability that individuals will be denied access to credit (they obtain information about individual access to credit from the Survey of Households Income and Wealth, which also provides information on the region to which each individual belongs) over regional dummies and a set of control variables. The coefficients on the regional dummies are the measures of regional financial development, which GSZ instrument using the regional composition of banking branches in 1936.[3]

2.2. Cross-industry

The pioneering attempt at getting at a more microeconomic level by looking at cross-industry comparisons across countries, is by Rajan and Zingales (1998). Their insight is that growth in industries that rely more heavily on external finance should benefit more from higher financial development than growth in industries that do not rely so much on external finance. The problem is to identify those industries that are more prone to rely on external finance than other industries.

Rajan and Zingales regress average growth of value added of industry k in country i over: (i) country and industry dummies; (ii) the share of industry k in total manufacturing in country i; and (iii) the interaction between financial development (measured by stock market capitalization plus domestic credit over GDP) in country i and industry k's dependence upon external finance (measured by the fraction of capital costs not financed internally in that same industry in the USA). The underlying idea is that firms are not financially constrained in the USA, so that this measure of external dependence can be thought of as being independent from financial development and to depend instead upon technological factors only. Rajan and Zingales do not include financial development independently, as this would create collinearity with the country dummies.

Using a sample of thirty-six industries in forty-two countries, Rajan and Zingales find an interaction coefficient between external dependence and their measure of financial development, which is positive and highly significant at the 1 per cent level, thereby providing strong evidence to the effect that higher financial development enhances growth in those industries that rely more heavily on external finance.

Building upon the Rajan–Zingales methodology, Beck et al. (2004) use cross-country/cross-industry data to look at the effect on productivity growth of the interaction between financial development and the average size of firms in the corresponding industry in the USA (again relying on the implicit assumption that only technological factors, not financial market frictions, determine this average size in the USA). They find that higher financial development enhances growth in those

---

[3] The year 1936 corresponds to the enactment of a law restricting subsequent entry into the banking sector.

industries that comprise a higher fraction of small firms. This result is consistent with previous work by Bernanke, Gertler, and Gilchrist (1999) suggesting that smaller firms face tighter credit constraints than large firms.

2.3. Cross-firm

Demirgüç-Kunt and Maksimovic (2001), henceforth DM, analyse the extent to which long-term debt and outside equity financing can foster firm growth. To this end, they first compute the growth rate of firms that would not have access to long-term debt or outside equity (that is, the growth rate of firms that only rely on retained earnings and short-term debt); then they calculate the fraction of firms that grow faster than the no-outside-finance rate; this they interpret as being the fraction of firms that rely on outside finance, and DM compute this fraction f_i for each country.

Then, using a sample comprising all large publicly traded manufacturing firms in each of twenty-six countries, DM regress the fraction f_i of firms that grow faster than the no-outside-finance rate, over financial development (measured either by the ratio of market capitalization to GDP, or by the turnover ratio of Levine and Zervos to capture the liquidity of the stock market, or by the ratio of bank assets to GDP to capture the size of the banking sector) and control variables. The main finding in DM is that the turnover ratio and the bank assets to GDP ratio are both positively and significantly correlated with f_i.

Another important piece of work on credit constraints at firm level is the innovative paper by Banerjee and Duflo (2004), which uses firms' investment response to an exogenous policy change affecting the amount of subsidized directed credit, to assess the importance of credit constraints faced by firms. The underlying idea is that an unconstrained firm would respond to such a policy change by simply substituting directed credit for (unsubsidized) market credit, but without changing capital investment (which in that case would only be determined by rate of return considerations). The policy change is that the limit on total capital investment for a firm to belong to the so-called priority sector eligible for subsidized credit was raised substantially in 1998 and then lowered back in 2000. Banerjee and Duflo then show that bank lending and firm revenues increased for the newly targeted firms immediately after 1998, and then decreased in the years after the 2000 policy change, thereby providing evidence to the effect that those firms were indeed credit constrained.

3. INTERACTING FINANCIAL CONSTRAINTS WITH TECHNOLOGICAL DEVELOPMENT

This section, which summarizes Aghion, Howitt, and Mayer-Foulkes (2005), henceforth AHM, investigates the interaction between financial development and initial income per capita (or equivalently the initial distance to the technological frontier, which we typically measure by the ratio of a country's average productivity to the frontier country's productivity).

3.1. The Main Idea

The theory in AHM embodies two opposite effects of technological backwardness, that is, of a country's productivity level being initially far from that of the world technology frontier: on the one hand, a far-from-frontier country makes bigger leaps with innovations that allows its sectors to catch up with the current frontier technology, and this advantage of backwardness pushes towards convergence. On the other hand, a far-from-frontier country has fewer initial resources to pledge into innovation; in the absence of perfect capital markets[4] this will limit its ability to innovate and thereby catch up with the technology frontier: this disadvantage of backwardness pushes towards divergence. In particular, tighter financial constraints will reinforce the negative effect of a low initial income per capita in lowering the innovation rate of a country and its ability to converge in growth rate or in per capita GDP towards the world technology frontier. Thus, one should expect that diverging countries will be those that: (i) are initially very far from the world frontier; and (ii) have sufficiently low levels of financial development.

3.2. What the Data Say

In fact the model in AHM delivers the following predictions:

1. the likelihood that a country will converge to the frontier growth rate increases with its level of financial development;
2. in a country that converges to the frontier growth rate, financial development has a positive but eventually diminishing effect on steady-state per capita GDP, relative to the frontier; and
3. the steady-state growth rate of a country that fails to converge to the frontier growth rate increases with its level of financial development.

AHM confront these predictions to cross-country data on financial development and growth/convergence. They test the effect of financial development on convergence by running the following cross-country growth regression:

$$g_i - g_1 = \beta_0 + \beta_f F_i + \beta_y \cdot (y_i - y_1) + \beta_{fy} \cdot F_i \cdot (y_i - y_1) + \beta_x X_i + \varepsilon_i. \qquad (1)$$

---

[4] AHM follow Bernanke and Gertler 1989 in modelling credit market imperfections as a constraint whereby firms cannot borrow more than a fixed multiple of their current cash flow. The microeconomic foundation for the credit multiplier can itself be derived from an ex post enforcement problem as in Aghion, Banerjee, and Piketty 1999, or from an ex ante moral hazard problem as in Holmström and Tirole 1998 or Tirole 2006.

where g_i denotes the average growth rate of per capita GDP in country i over the period 1960–95, F_i the country's average level of financial development, y_i the initial (1960) log of per capita GDP, X_i a set of other regressors, and ε_i a disturbance term with mean zero. Country 1 is the technology leader, which they take to be the United States.

Define $\widehat{y_i} \equiv y_i - y_1$, country i's initial relative per capita GDP. Under the assumption that $\beta_y + \beta_{fy} F_i \neq 0$ we can rewrite (1) as:

$$g_i - g_1 = \lambda_i \cdot \left(\widehat{y_i} - \widehat{y_i}^* \right)$$

where the steady-state value $\widehat{y_i}^*$ is defined by setting the RHS of (1) to zero:

$$\widehat{y_i}^* = -\frac{\beta_0 + \beta_f F_i + \beta_x X_i + \varepsilon_i}{\beta_y + \beta_{fy} F_i} \tag{2}$$

and λ_i is a country-specific convergence parameter:

$$\lambda_i = \beta_y + \beta_{fy} F_i \tag{3}$$

that depends on financial development.

A country can converge to the frontier growth rate if and only if the growth rate of its relative per capita GDP depends negatively on the initial value $\widehat{y_i}$; that is if and only if the convergence parameter λ_i is negative. Thus the likelihood of convergence will increase with financial development, as implied by the theory, if and only if:

$$\beta_{fy} < 0. \tag{4}$$

The results of running this regression using a sample of seventy-one countries are shown in Table 3.1, which indicates that the interaction coefficient β_{fy} is indeed significantly negative for a variety of different measures of financial development and a variety of different conditioning sets X. The estimation is by instrumental variables, using a country's legal origins, and its legal origins[5] interacted with the initial GDP gap $(y_i - y_1)$ as instruments for F_i and $F_i (y_i - y_1)$. The data, estimation methods, and choice of conditioning sets X are all taken directly from Levine, Loayza, and Beck (2000) who found a strongly positive and robust effect of financial intermediation on short-run growth in a regression identical to (1) but without the crucial interaction term $F_i (y_i - y_1)$ that allows convergence to depend upon the level of financial development.

AHM show that the results of Table 3.1 are surprisingly robust to different estimation techniques, to discarding outliers, and to including possible interaction effects between the initial GDP gap and other right hand side variables.

---

[5] See La Porta et al. 1998 for a detailed explanation of legal origins and their relevance as an instrument for financial development.

Table 3.1. Growth, financial development, and initial GDP gap

Estimation of equation: $g - g_1 = \beta_0 + \beta_f F + \beta_y(y - y_1) + \beta_{fy} F(y - y_1) + \beta_x X$

Financial development (F)	Private credit			Liquid liabilities			Bank assets		
Conditioning set (X)	Empty	Policy[a]	Full[b]	Empty	Policy[a]	Full[b]	Empty	Policy[a]	Full[b]
Coefficient estimates									
β_f	−0.015 (−0.93)	−0.013 (−0.68)	−0.016 (−0.78)	−0.029 (−1.04)	−0.03 (−0.99)	−0.027 (−0.90)	−0.019 (−1.07)	−0.020 (−1.03)	−0.022 (−1.12)
β_y	1.507*** (3.14)	1.193* (1.86)	1.131 (1.49)	2.648*** (3.12)	2.388** (2.39)	2.384** (2.11)	1.891*** (3.57)	1.335* (1.93)	1.365 (1.66)
β_{fy}	−0.061*** (−5.35)	−0.063*** (−5.10)	−0.063*** (−4.62)	−0.076*** (−3.68)	−0.077*** (−3.81)	−0.073*** (−3.55)	−0.081*** (−5.07)	−0.081*** (−4.85)	−0.081*** (−4.46)
Sample size	71	63	63	71	63	63	71	63	63

Notes: The dependent variable $g - g_1$ is the average growth rate of per capita real GDP relative to the USA, 1960–95. F is average financial development 1960–95 using three alternative measures: private credit is the value of credits by financial intermediaries to the private sector, divided by GDP, liquid liabilities is currency plus demand and interest-bearing liabilities of banks and non-bank financial intermediaries, divided by GDP, and bank assets is the ratio of all credits by banks to GDP. $y - y_1$ is the log of per capita GDP in 1960 relative to the United States. Estimation is by IV using L (legal origins) and $L(y - y_1)$ as instruments for F and $F(y - y_1)$. The numbers in parentheses are t-statistics. Significance at the 1%, 5%, and 10% levels is denoted by ***, **, and * respectively.

[a] The policy conditioning set included average years of schooling in 1960, government size, inflation, the black market premium and openness to trade.

[b] The full conditioning set includes the policy set plus indicators of revolutions and coups, political assassinations, and ethnic diversity.

4. Interacting Financial Development and Macroeconomic Volatility

In this section we consider the interaction between financial development and macroeconomic volatility and policy in the growth process. The common view in macroeconomics is that there should not be such an interaction as macroeconomic policy (budget deficit, taxation, money supply) is considered to affect primarily the short run whereas financial development and other structural characteristics of an economy are all that matters for its long-run growth rate.

4.1. The Main Idea

Here again, Schumpeterian growth theory provides hints as to the nature and direction of the interaction effect we are looking for. The Schumpeterian view on volatility and growth is that recessions provide a cleansing mechanism for correcting organizational inefficiencies and for encouraging firms to reorganize, innovate, or reallocate to new markets. The cleansing effect of recessions is also to eliminate those firms that are unable to reorganize or innovate. Schumpeter himself would summarize that view as follows: '[Recessions] are but temporary. They are means to reconstruct each time the economic system on a more efficient plan.' Now, if firms could always borrow enough funds to either reorganize their activities or move to new activities and markets, and the same was true for workers trying to relocate from one job to another, the best would be to recommend that governments do not intervene over the business cycle, and instead let markets operate.

However, credit market imperfections may prevent firms from innovating and reorganizing in recessions. In particular, suppose that firms can choose between short-run capital investment and long-term R&D investment (this choice amounts to a research arbitrage condition). Innovating requires that firms survive short-run liquidity shocks (R&D is a long-term investment) and that to cover liquidity costs firms can rely only on their short-run earnings plus borrowing. Suppose in addition that growth is driven by innovations, with the growth rate of knowledge (or average productivity) being proportional to the flow of innovating firms in the economy. Absent credit constraints, and provided the value of innovation is sufficiently high, volatility will not affect innovation and growth as firms can always borrow up to the net present value of their future earnings in order to cover the short-run liquidity costs. But now suppose that the borrowing capacity of firms is proportional to their current earnings (the factor of proportionality is what we refer to as the credit multiplier, with a higher multiplier reflecting a higher degree of financial development in the economy). In a recession, current earnings are reduced, and therefore so is the firms' ability to borrow in order to innovate. This, in turn implies that the lower financial development, the more the anticipation of recessions will discourage R&D

investments if those are decided before firms know the realization of the aggregate shock (since firms anticipate that with higher probability, their R&D investment will not pay out in the long run as it will not survive the liquidity shock).

Based on cross-country panel data over the period 1960–2000, Aghion et al. (2005a) show that the interaction term between financial development and volatility is indeed significantly positive. In theory, one could imagine a counteracting effect of volatility on growth, namely that higher volatility also means higher profits in booms, and therefore a possibly higher ability for firms to innovate during booms; however the regressions in AABM, Ramey and Ramey (1995), or below all suggest that this latter effect is of second order.

4.2. The Effects of Countercyclical Macropolicies on Growth

Having shown that macroeconomic volatility tends to be more harmful to growth the lower the level of financial development, a natural conjecture is that the tighter the credit constraints faced by firms, the greater the scope for appropriate government intervention in particular to reduce the costs that negative liquidity shocks impose on credit-constrained firms. That government intervention might increase aggregate efficiency in an economy subject to credit constraints and aggregate shocks has already been pointed for example by Holmström and Tirole (1998). However, this point has never been formally made in the context of a growth model, nor have its potential empirical and policy implications been explored so far. This subsection reports a first attempt[6] at filling this gap, more precisely by analysing the interplay between financial development and the growth effects of different types of cyclical macropolicies.

To the extent that, in an economy with tight credit constraints, the occurrence of a recession forces a number of firms to cut on innovative investments in order to survive idiosyncratic liquidity shocks, a natural idea is that a countercyclical budgetary may foster innovation and growth by reducing the negative consequences of a recession (or a bad aggregate shock) on firms' innovative investments. For example, the government may decide to increase the volume of its public investments, thereby fostering the demand for private firms' products. Or the government may choose to directly increase its subsidies to private enterprises, thereby increasing their liquidity holdings and thus making it easier for them to face idiosyncratic liquidity shocks without having to sacrifice R&D or other types of longer-term growth-enhancing investments. From our analysis in the previous subsection, a natural prediction is that the lower the level of financial development, that is, the tighter the credit constraints faced by firms, the more growth enhancing such countercyclical policies should be.

Current work by Aghion and Marinescu (2006) (AM) analyses the effects of (counter)cyclical budgetary policies on growth, using annual panel data on seventeen

---

[6] The material in this subsection is drawn from current work by Aghion, Barro, and Marinescu on cyclical budgetary policies and productivity growth.

OECD countries over the period 1965–2001; in particular, they restrict their analysis to a subset of 'reasonable' countries for which Easterly (2005) would predict no effect of policy! Then, AM perform a two-stage regression procedure where:

1. The first stage regressions estimate, for each year, the correlations between: (i) on the left-hand side of the first-stage equation, variables such as: government debt, primary budget deficit, government investment, government consumption, defence spending, social security spending, direct subsidies to private enterprises; (ii) on the right-hand side of the first-stage equation: (a) the current output gap (measured by the difference between the real GDP and the maximum potential GDP, that is the GDP at minimum level of non-inflationary employment for given capital stock); and (b) the current gap in government expenditures (measured by the deviation of government expenditure to its trend); and (iii) the lagged public debt to GDP ratio (which reflects the share of public spending used to meet the outstanding public debt obligations).

   Figure 3.1 below summarizes the results from the first-stage regressions with the primary budget deficit as the left-hand side variable for France and the UK. We see that, unlike in France, the primary budget deficit has become significantly more countercyclical in the UK over the past two decades.

2. The second-stage regressions estimate the annual growth rate of per capita GDP (left-hand side variable) as a function of: (i) the lagged value of the cyclicality coefficient obtained from the first-stage regression, which we denote by $lcycl$; (ii) lagged financial development, lpc, which we measure once again by the ratio of private credit to GDP; and (iii) the interaction $lcycl\_lpc$ between these two variables. Our prediction is that the coefficient on $lcycl$ should be negative (a procyclical budgetary policy is bad for growth in a country with no credit at all) whereas the interaction coefficient on $lcycl\_lpc$ should be positive (a procyclical budgetary policy is less detrimental to growth the higher the level of financial development).

The second-stage results with regard to the primary deficit show that a more procyclical primary deficit is detrimental to growth (the coefficient on $lcycl$ is negative, equal to -0.008 if we consider the whole sample of countries, and to -0.015 if we restrict the analysis to countries where the variance in the $cycl$ coefficient in a VC estimation for the first stage is non-zero.

Having shown that countercyclical budget deficits can be growth enhancing, the next step is to look at the composition of public spending. AM consider the following categories of spending: (i) public investment; (ii) defence spending, which is part of (i); (iii) direct subsidies to private enterprises; (iv) government consumption; and (v) social security. For each category, AM perform first-stage regressions of the corresponding variable on the output gap for each country, which yields the corresponding cyclicality coefficient; then in the second-stage regression, productivity growth is regressed over that coefficient, financial development, and the interaction between the two, controlling for country, or year fixed effects, or both.

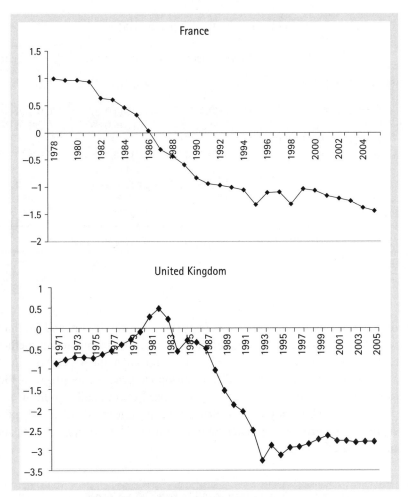

Fig. 3.1. Results from the first-stage regressions

Here we shall only show the tables for public investment and government consumption, as the difference between the two is striking. On the one hand, as shown in Table 3.2, countercyclical public investments are highly growth enhancing at low levels of financial development with highly negative and significant correlations between productivity growth and the lagged cyclicality of public investment (negative coefficients which are significant at the 5 per cent both, in the regression controlling for the linear time trend or that controlling for year fixed effects), whereas the interaction coefficients are positive and significant at the 5 per cent or 1 per cent when controlling for year fixed effects.

On the other hand, when we turn to government consumption in Table 3.3, everything becomes insignificant.

Looking at the other components of government spending, AM find: (a) that countercyclical defence spending is growth enhancing at low levels of financial development (negative significant direct coefficient with or without year fixed effect or

Table 3.2. Public investment (growth of GDP per capita)

	No year effects	Linear time trend	Year fixed effects
Lag (procyclicality of public investment)	−0.082 (0.054)	−0.077 (0.054)	−0.072 (0.035)[b]
Lag (private credit/GDP)	−0.013 (0.007)[a]	−0.015 (0.007)[b]	−0.012 (0.005)[b]
Lag (procyclicality of public investment [a]private credit/GDP)	0.071 (0.034)[b]	0.080 (0.034)[b]	0.082 (0.025)[c]
Relative GDP per capita	0.001 (0.004)	0.032 (0.013)[b]	0.038 (0.021)[a]
Year		0.001 (0.001)[b]	
Constant	0.039 (0.017)[b]	−2.441 (0.973)[b]	0.225 (0.115)[a]
Observations	453	453	453
R-squared	0.06	0.07	0.42

Notes: All regressions include country fixed effects; robust standard errors in parentheses.
[a]Significant at 10%.
[b]Significant at 5%.
[c]Significant at 1%.

linear time trends) but the interaction coefficient is never significant; and (b) that the coefficients for social security are insignificant (apart from the interaction coefficient in the regression with year fixed effects, which is significant at the 10 per cent); that the direct and interaction coefficients for direct subsidies to private enterprises are highly significant in the regression controlling for year fixed effects, still significant in the regression not controlling for year fixed effects or linear time trend, but not significant in the regression controlling for linear time trend only. All these regressions control for country fixed effects.

Table 3.3. Government consumption (growth of GDP per capita)

	No year effects	Linear time trend	Year fixed effects
Lag (procyclicality of government consumption)	−0.005 (0.028)	−0.005 (0.027)	0.007 (0.021)
Lag (private credit/GDP)	−0.006 (0.008)	−0.008 (0.008)	−0.006 (0.006)
Lag (procyclicality of government consumption [a]private credit/GDP)	−0.008 (0.032)	−0.007 (0.032)	−0.004 (0.023)
Relative GDP per capita	0.002 (0.004)	0.028 (0.013)[b]	0.028 (0.022)
Year		0.001 (0.001)[b]	
Constant	0.037 (0.017)[b]	−2.101 (1.000)[b]	0.168 (0.116)
Observations	453	453	453
R-squared	0.05	0.06	0.41

Notes: All regressions include country fixed effects; robust standard errors in parentheses.
[a]Significant at 10%.
[b]Significant at 5%.
[c]Significant at 1%.

Table 3.4. Money supply (M2/GDP) (growth of GDP per capita)

	Country fixed effects	Year fixed effects	Country and year fixed effects
Lag (procyclicality of M2/GDP)	0.001 (0.004)	−0.005 (0.003)	−0.003 (0.004)
Lag (private credit/GDP)	−0.006 (0.007)	−0.002 (0.002)	−0.008 (0.006)
Lag (procyclicality of M2/GDP ^{a}private credit/GDP)	0.001 (0.004)	−0.007 (0.002)^c	0.005 (0.003)
Relative GDP per capita	0.003 (0.005)	0.001 (0.001)	0.029 (0.019)
Constant	0.038 (0.019)^b	0.028 (0.004)^c	0.172 (0.099)^a
Observations	453	458	458
R-squared	0.06	0.37	0.41

Notes: Robust standard errors in parentheses.
^{a}Significant at 10%.
^{b}Significant at 5%.
^{c}Significant at 1%.

So far, we have concentrated on budgetary policy. But one could as well perform similar exercises with variables such as the M2/GDP ratio also used by Easterly (2005) or short-term real interest rates which are also linked to monetary policy. For the purpose of this chapter, we have looked at the former, and the second-stage regression is summarized in Table 3.4 above.

Unlike for budgetary variables, the coefficients are not very significant except in the regression where one controls for linear time trends; the regression where one controls for year fixed effects shows an interaction coefficient which is significant at the 15 per cent. Thus there is something to having a countercyclical M2/GDP ratio at lower levels of financial development, but nothing as significant as the effect of countercyclical government investment for example.

Finally, what can we say about the interplay between countercyclical budgetary policies and structural reforms such as product or labour market liberalization? Table 3.5[7] shows that the two are complementary: namely, a higher degree of product or labour market liberalization increases the positive growth impact of counter-cyclical budgetary policy. A plausible explanation for such complementarity is that government support during a recession is useful only to the extent that it helps firms maintain long-term innovative investments aimed at entering a new market or a new

---

[7] Product market liberalization is captured by the OECD index *pmin3* which, for each OECD country, corresponds to the average degree of deregulation of entry over all sectors in that country. This variable is constructed from data compiled by Giuseppe Nicoletti and Stefano Scarpetta. The dependent variable *dlnGDPcap* is just the growth rate of per capita GDP, and the *igaa* variable is the value of government fixed investment, for which annual data for all OECD countries are available from 1960 to 2005. The cyclicality calculations for *igaa* were done as in the previous tables through a time-varying coefficients estimation in first-stage regressions of government investment over the output gap for each country separately. The first column controls for country fixed effects only. The second column controls for country fixed effects and year fixed effects.

Table 3.5. Product market liberalization (growth of GDP per capita)

	Year fixed effects	Country and year fixed effects
Procyclicality of public investment	−0.048 (0.025)[a]	−0.033 (0.047)
Product market liberalization	−0.011 (0.008)	0.002 (0.019)
Procyclicality of public investment *product market liberalization	0.126 (0.057)[b]	0.134 (0.077)[a]
Constant	0.024 (0.003)[c]	0.035 (0.008)[c]
Observations	352	352
R-squared	0.33	0.39

Note: Robust standard errors in parentheses.
[a]Significant at 10%.
[b]Significant at 5%.
[c]Significant at 1%.

activity or at improving management methods. However, high entry costs or high labour mobility costs will reduce firms' ability to enter those new activities or to hire employees for the new tasks, with or without government support. This finding goes counter to a common view whereby the implementation of structural reforms would reduce the need for proactive macroeconomic policies to enhance growth.

4.3. Exchange Rate Regimes

The existing theoretical literature on exchange rates and open macroeconomics does not look at long-run growth. Based on the intuition that growth in countries with lower financial development benefits more for macroeconomic stability, and that exchange rate fluctuations represent a major component of aggregate macroeconomic volatility, Aghion et al. (2005b), henceforth ABRR, predict that in economies with a lower level of financial development, a flexible exchange rate regime will tend to generate excessive currency appreciations which in turn will make all firms (including the most performing ones) become more vulnerable to other shocks, e.g. on the liquidity needs of long-term (productivity-enhancing) investments. This, in turn, will tend to discourage innovative investments.

Thus the lower financial development, the more growth enhancing it is for a country to have a fixed exchange rate regime. On the other hand, in economies with high levels of financial development, exchange rate flexibility may enhance average growth by weeding out the less innovative firms while promoting the more innovative. This prediction turns out to be fully vindicated by the data. In particular, using a GMM panel data system estimator for eighty-three countries over a sequence of five-year subperiods between 1961 and 2000, ABRR regress the growth rate of output per worker on exchange rate flexibility and its interaction with financial development. The results are summarized in Table 3.6. We see that the direct effect of exchange rate flexibility on growth is negative and significant, while the interaction term between

Table 3.6. Growth effects of the flexibility of exchange rate regime: the role of financial development

	[2.1]	[2.2]
Degree of the exchange flexibility (Reinhart and Rogoff classification)	−0.1912 (0.3493)	−1.1352[a] (0.5794)
Financial development (private domestic credit/GDP, in logs)	0.6843[b] (0.3471)	0.1845 (0.1597)
Initial output per worker (log(Initial output per worker)	−0.1498 (0.4181)	−0.1170 (0.4473)
Flexibility [a] Financial Development		0.3029[b] (0.1459)

Notes: Dependent variable: growth rate of output per worker. Estimation: 2-step system GMM estimation with Windmeijer Small Sample Robust Correction and Time Effects (standard errors are presented below the corresponding coefficients). Period: 1961–2000. Unit of observation: non-overlapping five-year averages.
[a]Significant at 10%.
[b]Significant at 5%.

financial development and exchange rate flexibility has a positive and significant co-efficient. Thus, as predicted by ABRR, the higher the degree of financial development, the less negative the effect of exchange rate flexibility on growth.

This result may have interesting policy implications. For example, it may raise further questions for those European countries that are contemplating joining the EMU system. Given their level of financial development, should they tie their hands by adopting the euro rather than maintaining a fully flexible exchange rate regime? The above result may also call for further organizational changes within the euro zone, so that it would look more like one country with a flexible exchange rate vis-à-vis the rest of the world.

5. NEW DEVELOPMENTS

In this chapter we have shown that interacting financial development with macro-economic variables such as average productivity or output volatility in growth and finance regressions generates a rich set of new empirical predictions, e.g. on convergence and divergence, and on the growth effect of countercyclical macroeconomic policies.

One next step we are currently exploring, in joint work with Peter Howitt, is to look at finance and growth in the context of an open economy. Our focus is on the extent to which the relationship between domestic savings and growth remains significant once we allow for free capital movements across countries, and whether or not the significance of the correlation between domestic savings and growth depends upon a country's distance from the technological frontier and/or its level of financial development.

Another direction is to look further into microdata, and explore the effect of credit constraints on firms' entry and post-entry growth. This direction is explored in current work by Aghion, Fally, and Scarpetta (2006), henceforth AFS. Using cross-sectoral annual panel data covering fourteen OECD countries plus five Latin American countries[8] plus four transition economies over the period 1990–2000,[9] AFS show: (i) that credit constraints are a main source inhibiting entry and post-entry growth of firms; (ii) that credit constraints dominate labour market regulations in explaining entry of small firms, whereas labour market regulations appear to be more binding for large firms; and (iii) that credit constraints dominate labour market regulations in explaining post-entry growth of firms.

This and other extensions should generate further exciting research on finance and growth.

References

AGHION, P., and BANERJEE, A. (2005), *Volatility and Growth*, Clarendon Lectures, Oxford: Oxford University Press.

————— and PIKETTY, T. (1999), 'Dualism and macroeconomic volatility', *Quarterly Journal of Economics*, 114, 1359–97.

————— FALLY, T., and SCARPETTA, S. (2006), 'Credit constraints as a barrier to the entry and post-entry growth of firms: lessons from firm-level cross country panel data', Harvard University, mimeo.

————— HOWITT, P., and MAYER-FOULKES, D. (2005), 'The effect of financial development on convergence', *Quarterly Journal of Economics*, 120, 173–222.

————— and MARINESCU, I. (2006), 'Cyclical budgetary policy and economic growth: what do we learn from OECD panel data?', Harvard University, mimeo.

————— ANGELETOS, M., BANERJEE, A., and MANOVA, K. (2005a), 'Volatility and growth: the role of financial development', Harvard University, mimeo.

————— BACCHETTA, P., RANCIERE, R., and ROGOFF, K. (2005b), 'Productivity growth and exchange rate regime', Harvard University, mimeo.

BANERJEE, A., and DUFLO, E. (2004), 'Do firms want to borrow more? Testing credit constraints using a directed lending program', BREAD Working Paper 2003–5.

————— (2005), 'Growth theory through the lens of development economics', in P. Aghion and S. Durlauf (eds.), *Handbook of Economic Growth*, vol. iA, Amsterdam: North-Holland, 473–552.

BECK, T., DEMIRGÜÇ-KUNT, A., LAEVEN, L., and LEVINE, R. (2004), 'Finance, firm size, and growth', World Bank, mimeo.

BERNANKE, B., and GERTLER, M. (1989), 'Agency costs, net worth and business fluctuations', *American Economic Review*, 79, 14–31.

---

[8] Argentina, Mexico, Brazil, Colombia, and Chile.
[9] Latvia, Estonia, Slovenia, and Hungary.

_____ _____ and GILCHRIST, S. (1999), 'The financial accelerator in a quantitative business cycle framework', in J. Taylor and M. Woodford (eds.), *Handbook of Macroeconomics*, Amsterdam: North-Holland, 1341–93.

DEMIRGÜÇ-KUNT, A., and MAKSIMOVIC, V. (2001), 'Law, finance, and firm growth', *Journal of Finance*, 53: 2107–37.

EASTERLY, W. (2005), 'National policy and economic growth: a reappraisal', in P. Aghion and S. Durlauf (eds.), *Handbook of Economic Growth*, vol. iA, Amsterdam: North-Holland, 1015–59.

GOLDSMITH, R. (1969), *Financial Structure and Development*, New Haven: Yale University Press.

GUISO, L., SAPIENZA, P., and ZINGALES, L. (2002), 'Does local financial development matter', NBER Working Paper no. 8922.

HOLMSTRÖM, B., and TIROLE, J. (1998), 'Private and public supply of liquidity', *Journal of Political Economy*, 106, 1–40.

KING, R., and LEVINE, R. (1993), 'Finance and growth: Schumpeter might be right', *Quarterly Journal of Economics*, 108, 717–38.

LA PORTA, R., LÓPEZ-DE-SILANES, F., SHLEIFER, A., and VISHNY, R. (1998), 'Law and finance', *Journal of Political Economy*, 106, 1113–55.

LEVINE, R. (1998), 'The legal environment, banks, and long-run economic growth', *Journal of Money, Credit, and Banking*, 30, 596–613.

_____ (1999), 'Law, finance, and economic growth', *Journal of Financial Intermediation*, 8, 36–67.

_____ (2005), 'Finance and growth: theory and evidence', in P. Aghion and S. Durlauf (eds.), *Handbook of Economic Growth*, Amsterdam: North-Holland, 866–934.

_____ LOAYZA, N., and BECK, T. (2000), 'Financial intermediation and growth: causality and causes', *Journal of Monetary Economics*, 46, 31–77.

_____ and ZERVOS, S. (1998), 'Stock markets, banks, and economic growth', *American Economic Review*, 88, 537–58.

LUCAS, R. (1990), 'Why doesn't capital flow from rich to poor countries?' *American Economic Review Papers and Proceedings*, 80, 92–6.

RAJAN, R., and ZINGALES, L. (1998), 'Financial dependence and growth', *American Economic Review*, 88, 559–86.

RAMEY, G., and RAMEY, V. (1995), 'Cross-country evidence on the link between volatility and growth', *American Economic Review*, 85, 1138–51.

TIROLE, J. (2006), *The Theory of Corporate Finance*, Princeton: Princeton University Press.

CHAPTER 4

THE ROLE OF FINANCIAL MARKETS AND INNOVATION FOR PRODUCTIVITY AND GROWTH IN EUROPE

PHILIPP HARTMANN

FLORIAN HEIDER

ELIAS PAPAIOANNOU

MARCO LO DUCA

An earlier version of this chapter was prepared upon request of the Finnish Presidency as a background document for a discussion of European Union finance ministers and central bank governors at the Informal Ecofin Meeting in Helsinki on 8 and 9 September 2006. It partly draws on work and papers to which also the following persons contributed: Annalisa Ferrando, Angela Maddaloni, Simone Manganelli, and Markus Baltzer (European Central Bank), Antonio Ciccone (Universitat Pompeu Fabra), Friedrich Fritzer (Oesterreichische Nationalbank), and Bernadette Lauro (European Central Bank). We are grateful for the encouragement and the many comments we received from Lucas Papademos, Lucrezia Reichlin,

1. INTRODUCTION

THE extended period of relatively slow growth and low employment until recently in many European countries has led to increased efforts to identify policies that can be successful in improving economic performance. The reasons for the economic slowdown are manifold, and the Lisbon Agenda underlines the need for a multi-sector approach. This chapter focuses on the financial sector, potential ways to improve its functioning, and its contribution to productivity, innovation, and growth in Europe.

The focus on the financial system seems to be particularly timely, as various recent events put a question mark on the global competitiveness of European financial institutions and markets. For example, in parallel with the introduction of the euro overseas financial institutions significantly extended their market share in the underwriting of the growing market for European corporate bonds (see e.g. Santos and Tsatsaronis 2003). Recent research also suggests that US banks may have a comparative advantage in the cross-border provision of financial services whereas non-US banks find it difficult to conduct this business profitably (see e.g. Berger et al. 2000, 2004). Moreover, a major European stock exchange—Euronext—has merged with the New York Stock Exchange and another one—London Stock Exchange—is partly owned by NASDAQ. Last but not least, settling securities across European borders remains very costly compared for instance to settling them in the USA (see e.g. Schmiedel, Malkamäki, and Tarkka 2006). These developments are particularly surprising, as the introduction of the euro and further integration of European capital markets was very much expected and in many respects did strengthen the internal market for financial services and increase the competitiveness of European financial institutions and markets. The relative success of overseas operators compared to domestic European markets and institutions may be indicative of a more pressing need for further reforms that increase their international competitiveness and enhance the contribution of the single market for financial services to employment and growth in Europe.

Based on an extensive literature underlining the role of financial systems for productivity, innovation, and growth, this chapter analyses the performance of European capital markets and their contribution to the performance of European economies. In some contrast to the finance and growth literature, though, which concentrates very much on developing countries and emerging market economies, the emphasis is more on industrial countries so that stronger conclusions for the 'old' European Union member states can be drawn.

the participants of the Ecofin Meeting, Violetta Damia, Francesco Drudi, Doris Keller, Hans-Joachim Klöckers, Philippe Moutot, and many other people who cannot all be listed here. None of the persons listed, however, should be held responsible for the content of the chapter. The results presented have been derived from internal and external research. They do not necessarily reflect the position of or bind the European Central Bank.

This chapter is structured as follows. The next section outlines a conceptual framework to analyse the functioning of financial systems and their contribution to economic performance. In so doing, it also summarizes briefly the main results from the relevant economic literature on how financial development and modernization affects productivity and overall growth. Section 3 presents seventeen indicators for the performance of the euro area financial system, in particular its efficiency, as compared to similar systems. Apart from the twelve euro area countries, the chapter covers other European countries (Sweden, Switzerland, and the United Kingdom) as well as Japan and the United States.[1] The indicators span eight dimensions of a financial system that can be used to characterize its performance. Since the European Central Bank has already published a wide set of indicators for financial integration (see ECB 2005a), the emphasis here is more on indicators of financial development or modernization. Section 4 summarizes the main results of current research that investigates a specific channel by which the efficiency of a financial system contributes to productivity growth. The approach tests whether economies with more developed financial systems allocate capital faster from declining industries to those with better growth opportunities. The aim is to identify particularly those features that would accelerate this reallocation of capital in the EU-15, which already comprises relatively developed financial systems. The results of Sections 3 and 4 are indicative for the areas in which further European policy efforts may be justified. The last section summarizes the chapter and draws the main conclusions.

The results found are derived from internal research at the European Central Bank (ECB) and from external research. They do not necessarily reflect the position of the ECB, and the ECB is not committed by them. They are presented to generate discussion and to identify areas in which more work could be undertaken to further substantiate advice for policy makers. They also have to be interpreted in relation to the economic literature, to specific assumptions made by the different approaches used, and keeping in mind other caveats listed below. Some indicators used that refer to legislation and law enforcement should not be interpreted from a legal or even criminal perspective but in terms of their relevance for financial system efficiency only.

2. FINANCIAL SYSTEMS AND ECONOMIC PERFORMANCE: CONCEPTS AND LITERATURE

There is no widely accepted theory of financial systems that can be used easily to structure the practical discussion in the following sections. Against this background the present section outlines a number of key concepts for financial sector work and how they relate to each other. This discussion is inspired by standard theories, which

---

[1] Slovenia became the thirteenth member of the euro area of 1 January 2007. It is not included as all the data refer to the period before its entry.

describe the role of a financial system as allocating resources from agents who have a surplus to those who have a shortage of funds (early work in this area includes Schumpeter 1911, Goldsmith 1969, and McKinnon 1973), and by the most relevant empirical evidence.[2]

For example, firms may see profitable real investment opportunities but not have enough internal funds to finance them. Households may have more income than they wish to consume during part of their life cycle and invest it in assets that return the difference with a profit at some future time, e.g. when their regular income is much reduced due to retirement. Finally, governments may wish to increase investment spending during recessions, drawing on the savings of other sectors.[3] A financial system can then be defined as the set of markets, intermediaries, and infrastructures through which households, corporations, and governments obtain funding for their activities and invest their savings (see Hartmann, Maddaloni, and Manganelli 2003).

A simple conceptual framework that distinguishes three levels of the analysis is summarized in Figure 4.1. The first level (top of the figure) concerns 'conditioning' elements of financial systems that do not change very fast and therefore tend to be taken as given by market participants ('fundamentals'). The second level (middle of the figure) relates to the outcomes of financial systems; how well they function ('performance'). The third level (bottom of the figure) anchors the discussion in the performance of the economy as a whole, focusing on the standard economic objectives (notably growth and price stability).

The performance of a financial system has two basic dimensions, its efficiency and its stability.[4] The efficiency of a financial system can be understood as a condition in which the resources available in a financial system are allocated towards the most valuable investment opportunities at the lowest possible costs. In an efficient financial system markets are competitive, information is accessible and widely distributed, and agency conflicts are resolved through contracts enforced by legal systems. Market failures lead to inefficiency. And lack of efficiency usually impairs the contribution of finance to growth, as illustrated in Figure 4.1 by the arrow between level 2 and level 3.[5]

Certain aspects of financial systems respond to market failures and frictions thereby improving efficiency. A first very important friction is asymmetric

---

[2] Levine 2005 lists four financial system functions that support the allocation of savings to investment: the ex ante production of information about real investments and the allocation of capital, the monitoring of investments and the exertion of corporate governance after the provision of finance, the facilitation of trading, diversification, and management of risk, as well as the mobilization and pooling of savings. He also adds a fifth function of a financial system: easing the exchange of goods and services. These functions will be discussed below in terms of how financial systems help to solve certain frictions that emerge among savers and investors.

[3] Accordingly, the euro area flow of funds shows that the household sector is a net provider of funds, whereas the government and non-financial firm sectors are net receivers of funds. In line with its intermediation role in these flows the financial sector is in balance (ECB 2002).

[4] The distinction between these two concepts is based on standard economic theory, which distinguishes e.g. the efficiency and the stability of equilibria in an economic system, and on the fact that ensuring efficiency and stability requires often quite different policies.

[5] One needs, however, to keep the theory of 'second best' in mind, which states that in the presence of several market failures the removal of one does not need to improve growth and welfare (see Lipsey and Lancaster 1956).

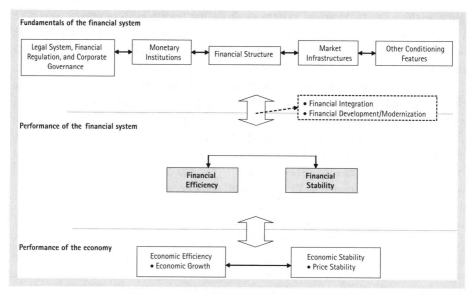

Fig. 4.1. Financial system concepts and their interrelation

information among economic agents active in the financial system. For example, financial investors mostly delegate real investment decisions to firm managers who have usually better information about them. Since the former, however, cannot perfectly monitor the latter, they demand a premium on their investment return that increases the cost of capital for firms and may therefore yield underinvestment with respect to the first best outcome (the underinvestment problem reflects adverse selection as in Stiglitz and Weiss 1981 or Myers and Majluf 1984). Well-functioning financial systems, through accounting systems, well-defined and enforced investor rights, deal with information frictions better, thus mitigating these credit constraints emerging from adverse selection. (See also the parts on transparency and information in Section 3 and Hartmann et al. 2006.) Venture capital financing and bank relationship financing are further responses of financial systems to this problem, which is particularly pronounced for small and medium firms that constitute large parts of the corporate sector and employment in European economies. For larger and more mature firms the pricing mechanism in stock markets is of great importance for reducing asymmetric information.

An important related friction is associated with different investment objectives between agents that provide and use funds. For example, firm owners may wish to maximize value, whereas managers (or unions) may have different interests (maintaining control, increasing the size of the firm, or preserving employment; see for example Jensen and Meckling 1976). Similarly, borrowing households may have different risk preferences from lending banks (who are primarily interested in loan repayment). These differences can lead either to underinvestment (moral hazard leads to lack of effort) or to overinvestment (e.g. managers enjoy private benefits of control). Good corporate governance and reliable enforcement through the legal system help financial systems to minimize such inefficiencies (see the respective parts in Section 3 and Hartmann et al. 2006).

Third, financial systems help to overcome the dispersion of capital across many investors and mismatches between the time horizons of financial investors and real investment projects (see for example Allen and Gale 1997). The dispersed supply of capital needs to be pooled through intermediaries and markets using standardized contracts, in contrast to an unrealistic network of bilateral contracts. Moreover, human capital and physical assets used in production are usually highly illiquid, whereas households will often wish to preserve flexibility in using their savings for consumption. Financial institutions and markets solve these problems to a large extent by pooling large numbers of investors and by performing maturity transformations.

Finally, there are frictions in the exchange of goods and services more generally, such as transaction costs, which can be alleviated through an efficient financial system. On the side of households' sight deposits, credit cards with overdraft possibilities and special forms of finance such as consumer credit help the general exchange process.

Distinct from financial efficiency, financial stability can be understood as a condition in which the financial system—comprising financial intermediaries, markets, and market infrastructures—is capable of withstanding shocks and the unravelling of financial imbalances, thereby mitigating the likelihood of disruptions in the financial intermediation process which are severe enough to significantly impair the allocation of savings to profitable investment opportunities. Severe forms of financial instability (financial crises) disturb the intermediation process allocating savings to real investment opportunities and therefore have usually strong negative effects on growth and welfare (see again the vertical arrow in Figure 4.1).[6] Conversely greater efficiency of a financial system will usually enhance stability, in particular in the long term.[7] In this chapter, the main emphasis is on the efficiency of financial systems and its implications for productivity, innovation, and growth. A comprehensive analysis of financial stability would require a detailed discussion in itself, which cannot be undertaken here. The ECB Financial Stability Review regularly presents a practical analysis for the EU (see ECB 2007b).

The performance of a financial system, notably its efficiency, is influenced by its fundamentals (top level in Figure 4.1) in conjunction with the processes of integration and financial development (arrow between the top and middle level). The fundamentals include (1) the legal system, financial regulation, and corporate

---

[6] Caprio and Klingebiel (1996) or Hogarth, Reis, and Saporta (2001), for example, estimated the adverse real effects of financial crisis. Some researchers argue, however, that emerging countries with occasional financial crises grow on average faster (over longer periods of time) than countries without such crises (see Ranciere, Tornell, and Westermann 2003).

[7] There can, however, also be conflicts between efficiency and stability, in particular in the short term. For example, periods of significant innovations and development in financial systems can be associated with instabilities in the transition, as not all financial actors are fully accustomed to the new techniques and risks associated with them and some actors may lose (e.g. default) and others win (see e.g. Keeley 1990). Also, excessive regulatory and public control may lead to a high level of stability but at the same time impair efficiency (see e.g. Guiso, Sapienza, and Zingales 2005b).

governance, (2) monetary institutions, (3) financial structure (balance between markets and intermediaries), (4) market infrastructures (payment, clearing, settlement, and trading systems), and (5) other conditioning features (e.g. social norms, basic freedoms, and political systems). The empirical literature strongly suggests that the quality of many of these fundamentals is of great importance for the efficiency of financial systems and their contribution to productivity and growth (see for example the survey in the chapter by Papaioannou).[8]

Explicit evidence is available particularly for legal systems, corporate governance, financial regulation, and socio-economic factors. For example, in a country with an inefficient and slow proceeding legal system, financial contracts cannot be enforced effectively and creditors have more limited rights (Djankov, McLiesh, and Shleifer 2006; Djankov et al. 2003, 2006; La Porta et al. 1998; La Porta, López-de-Silanes, and Shleifer 2006). Countries with well-defined and adequately enforced investor rights exhibit more entrepreneurship and greater product market competition. Moreover, they have more liquid private bond, venture capital and primary equity markets (see La Porta et al. 1997, 1998; La Porta, López-de-Silanes, and Shleifer 2006). There is also evidence that sound investor protection rights and a fast proceeding legal system attract foreign capital (Alfaro, Kalemli-Ozkan, and Volosovych 2005; Papaioannou 2005) and spur cross-border M&A activities (Rossi and Volpin 2004). Finally, efficient and fast proceeding legal systems foster syndicated lending (Quian and Strahan 2005) and the financing of large projects (Esty and Megginson 2003). Without good corporate governance, managers may be able to steer funds away from owners, raising the cost of capital (see for example La Porta et al. 2000).

Ill-designed financial regulations may hamper the savings investment process in a variety of ways (see Strahan 2003; Bertrand, Schoar, and Thesmar forthcoming; Guiso, Sapienza, and Zingales 2005b; and Barth, Caprio, and Levine 2006). As regards financial structure, it can be argued theoretically that financial systems with underdeveloped securities markets limit large firms' investment strategies and cross-sectional risk sharing (see Allen and Gale 1997 on the latter point). Even though market infrastructures are not a popular theme in the research literature, unsafe payment systems may hamper banks' liquidity management, and the absence of efficient settlements systems is likely to limit the growth of securities markets. Last but not least, social coherence helps agents to rely on financial contracts (see Guiso, Sapienza, and Zingales 2004, 2005a).

In regions like the European Union or the euro area, which are composed of separate countries, the process of financial integration is of particular importance. Fragmentation across countries will usually reduce the efficiency of the area-wide financial system, as it will constrain the range of financing sources and investment opportunities, limit scale economies, and leave possible liquidity advantages unexploited. The market for a given set of financial instruments and/or services

---

[8] While there is a vast empirical literature showing that these fundamentals matter for financial performance, there is little theoretical work about them. An exception is Shleifer and Wolfenzon 2002, who present an equilibrium model of corporate investment and financing decisions with different sets of legal institutions.

can be regarded as fully integrated if all potential market participants with the same relevant characteristics (1) face a single set of rules when they decide to deal with those financial instruments and/or services, (2) have equal access to the above-mentioned set of financial instruments and/or services, and (3) are treated equally when they are active in the market (see Baele et al. 2004). One implication of this definition of financial integration is the validity of the law of one price in financial markets, i.e. assets with the same risk–return characteristics should trade at the same price, irrespective of their origin or the location of trading.

The literature has provided some evidence of cases in which increased financial integration has contributed to greater productivity, growth, and economic stability, notably the case of the removal of branching restrictions in US banking, which allowed a much higher integration of markets for banking services across and within states (see Jayaratne and Strahan 1996, 1998).

A different process that is highly relevant for the performance of financial systems more generally is financial development.[9] This can be understood as a process of financial innovations and institutional and organizational improvements in the financial system that reduces asymmetric information, increases the completeness of markets and contracting possibilities, reduces transaction costs, and increases competition.[10] Theoretically, there is a strong positive link between the development and the efficiency of a financial system and its contribution to productivity and growth (see for example Greenwood and Jovanovic 1990). Allen and Gale (1997) argue that banks support intertemporal risk sharing whereas stock markets support cross-sectional risk sharing. Also many new financial instruments and institutions improve risk sharing between agents in the economy (see e.g. DeMarzo 2005). Well-functioning financial intermediaries also help to reduce transaction costs (Gurley and Shaw 1960) and minimize informational asymmetries between suppliers and users of funds (Diamond 1984).

There is a vast empirical literature that substantiates more and more the great importance of financial development for the contribution of a financial system to productivity and growth (see Levine 2005 for a general survey and the chapter by Papaioannou for a survey of the most relevant results for industrial countries). Based on a wide cross-country panel data set, King and Levine (1993) provide early econometric evidence that overall credit to the private sector matters for economic growth. Levine and Zervos (1998) add that the extent of bank lending and the development of stock markets both have independent beneficial effects on cross-country growth. Levine, Loayza, and Beck (2000), Levine, Norman, and Beck (2000), and Benhabib and Spiegel (2000) further show that the positive effect of financial intermediation on growth is due to increases in total factor productivity rather than increased investment and the accumulation of human capital. Rajan and Zingales (1998) add

---

[9] As the main interest here is in industrial countries, such as the ones of the euro area, that typically have already highly developed financial systems one may rather want to use the term financial modernization.

[10] Strictly speaking, the absence of distortionary taxes is also a requirement for financial markets to be perfect and fully developed.

that in financially developed countries (as proxied by bank credit, stock market capitalization, and the quality of accounting standards) sectors that for technological reasons depend more on external financing grow faster than in less financially developed countries. Demirgüç-Kunt and Maksimovic (1998) add evidence along similar lines using individual firm data. Further empirical work suggests that higher levels of financial development allow countries to adopt new production technologies faster (see Aghion, Howitt, and Mayer-Foulkes 2005), accelerate the reallocation of productive capital to rising industries (see Wurgler 2000; Fisman and Love 2003, 2004; Ciccone and Papaioannou 2006), and stimulate Schumpeterian 'creative destruction' through enhanced firm entry (Beck et al. 2004).

One complication with most of the finance and growth literature is that it is very much based on large cross-country studies, which do not always distinguish very well between industrial and developing countries. Also, some studies are of a more historical nature when the level of regulation was still much higher and the level of financial development much lower than in the present European context. Even though a number of studies control for the level of income and general economic development, it is therefore not clear whether all the results are directly applicable to the euro area or EU-15. Most directly applicable to the European context seem the recent studies by Strahan (2003) and Bertrand, Schoar, and Thesmar (forthcoming) on US and French banking sector deregulations. The next two sections are therefore geared particularly towards identifying aspects of financial systems whose improvements would have beneficial effects among industrial countries.

3. Measuring the Efficiency of the European Financial System

There are many indicators that could be used to assess how well a financial system performs its functions and overcomes the frictions described in Section 2. The present section builds on the empirical finance and growth literature that has already proposed a large variety of indicators to measure and quantify the functioning of financial systems and their contribution to productivity and economic growth. It presents a selection of indicators, both new ones and updates of existing ones, which seem to suggest more substantive conclusions for European countries, and discusses their implications. A much larger and more comprehensive set of indicators can be found in Hartmann et al. (2006), on which this section draws.[11]

In order to structure the analysis, the indicators are divided into eight groups, each describing an important dimension or characteristic of a financial system. The groups, which are summarized and briefly explained in Table 4.1, span the fundamental features of a financial system and the processes of financial development

---

[11] A smaller set of indicators has already been published in the ECB's *Monthly Bulletin* (see ECB 2005b).

Table 4.1. Dimensions of financial system performance covered by the indicators

1. Size of capital markets and financial structure	Financial systems with larger overall capital markets will provide easier financing for real investment. This relates to both larger securities markets and more bank credit. Systems that rely primarily on one but not the other may be less efficient. Also the liquidity of the different markets is relevant for this dimension.
2. Financial innovation and market completeness	Many financial innovations reduce capital market imperfections and make markets more complete. This opens up new possibilities to allocate capital across space, time, and risk preferences. New financial instruments and practices for example allow firms to manage certain risks by shifting them to investors who have a better ability to bear them.
3. Transparency and information	Financial systems help produce and spread information about investment opportunities, market conditions, and the behaviour of agents. The better they function, the lower should be asymmetric information between firms and outsiders and the more information should be incorporated into stock and corporate bond prices.
4. Corporate governance	There are conflicts between insiders who control a firm and outside investors who provide financing. Better governance will ensure that investors receive the full return on their investment and that there will be little deadweight cost due to opportunistic behaviour by firm insiders, with beneficial effects on the cost of capital.
5. Legal system	A key aspect of a financial system is how well it enforces contracts. As it allocates capital across time and space, contracts—either explicit or implicit—are needed to connect providers and users of funds. The legal system and how it is applied by legal institutions determine the 'distance' over which capital can be reallocated.
6. Financial regulation, supervision, and stability	Government intervention in financial systems tends to be stronger than in other economic sectors. Well-designed regulation and supervision should correct for market imperfections and enhance stability, whereas imperfect policies may have adverse effects on the performance of the financial sector.
7. Competition, openness, and financial integration	More openness of a financial system and more competition among banks and other financial intermediaries lower capital market imperfections. Pressure from competition, for example, should ensure that financial institutions operate efficiently, earn fewer rents from market power, and provide new instruments to customers.
8. Economic freedom, political and socio-economic factors	Economic freedom means the absence of constraints to economic activities, e.g. corruption, administrative burdens, or non-efficiency-related political interventions. Given the great importance of information, contract enforcement, and ease of exchange in financial transactions, there is also a significant role for social capital in the form of cooperativeness, ethics, and trust.

and integration (with the main emphasis on the former), i.e. they relate to the top two levels of the analysis shown in Figure 4.1. The following subsections are organized according to the framework displayed in Table 4.1.

The indicator approach has a number of advantages. First, it allows to start from a fairly comprehensive view of a financial system and then to select the smaller number of areas where the results signal a greater need for further attention. Second, each indicator is firmly grounded in the economic literature and many have been used previously in various (including quantitative) studies on financial systems. And third, it allows to cross-check the results of the econometric analysis in Section 4 and to examine whether European countries score high or low on indicators that are statistically significant. It is important, however, to be also aware of a number of caveats. First, despite the breadth of information from which the presented indicators are chosen, it should be noted that not all aspects of European financial systems may be fully captured. Data unavailability and non-comparability across countries for a number of markets constrain the analysis, for example with respect to relatively new markets and financial innovations. Moreover, publicly available data and the literature might not provide access to some issues that are only identified by individuals that are active in the respective market. Similarly, while formal laws and rules are easier to measure, informal rules could be as influential. Second, there is typically more information available on wholesale activities and market-based forms of financing than about retail activities and relationship-based forms of financing. Third, the quality and timeliness of available data may vary across indicators. These caveats notwithstanding there are clear benefits in discussing the efficiency of the European financial system with the help of explicit indicators and a transparent description of data compared to a discussion that would not be informed in that way.

3.1. Size of Capital Markets and Financial Structure

Several contributions to the literature have shown that the sizes of various capital markets, such as private credit or stock market capitalization, can be important indicators of financial development (see for example King and Levine 1993; Levine and Zervos 1998; and Rajan and Zingales 1998). An important aspect of this finding is that the often cited relative share of market versus bank financing ('financial structure') is not the key variable, but that both the size of securities markets and the amount of bank lending positively affect growth (see Levine 2002).

As the main focus of the chapter is on industrial countries, a broad measure of capital market size is preferable to the narrower measures typically used in the context of developing and emerging market countries. Therefore, Figure 4.2 shows the aggregate size of stock, bond, and loan markets in proportion to GDP for the sample countries. This choice is confirmed by the empirical results reported in Section 4, which suggest that the breadth of capital markets is an important summary variable

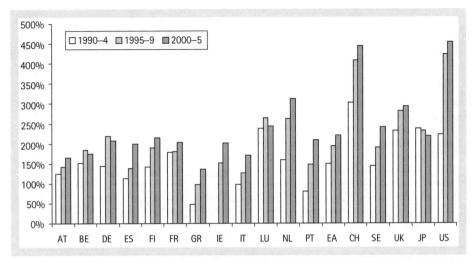

Fig. 4.2. Size of capital markets (in % of GDP)

Notes: Sum of (i) stock market capitalization, (ii) bank credit to the private sector and (iii) domestic debt securities issued by the private sector divided by GDP. Data for Luxembourg (LU) exclude debt securities. Data for Germany (DE) start in 1991. Data for Ireland (IE) start in 1995. For the US stock market capitalization is the sum of NYSE and NASDAQ markets. Euro area (EA) figures are averages of EA country data weighted by GDP

Sources: BIS, ECB, Eurostat, IMF, and World Federation of Exchanges

capturing the overall level of financial development in an economy and driving the allocation of real investment and productivity.

It turns out that Switzerland and the US have the largest capital markets relative to their own economy, followed by the United Kingdom and the Netherlands. Euro area capital markets tend to be smaller and are roughly comparable in size to Japanese capital markets. Some euro area countries with smaller financial sectors have however experienced strong growth of their capital markets over the last fifteen years (e.g. they have more than doubled in Greece and Portugal). Overall, European capital markets do not seem to be as developed as they could be.

3.2. Financial Innovation and Market Completeness

The principal role of financial innovation is to make markets more complete so that firms, households, and governments can better finance, invest, and share risk among themselves (see for example Allen and Gale 1997 or Acemoglu and Zilibotti 1997). In this subsection the focus is put on two aspects of innovation, securitization and venture capital financing.

Securitization allows transforming formerly illiquid assets into portfolios of assets that can be sold widely. The risks of the associated assets can therefore be sold to economic agents that have additional capacity to bear them. Banks for example need to retain costly economic capital as a buffer for their risky lending activities.

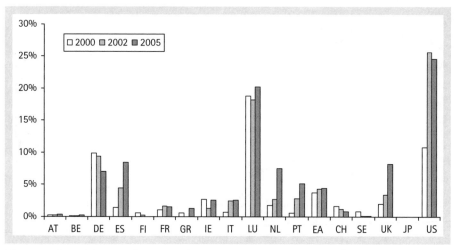

Fig. 4.3. Securitization (in % of GDP, by country of collateral)

Notes: For European countries data report the issuance placed in the Euromarket or in European domestic markets. For the US data refer to issuance placed in the US market. As there is no information about the country of collateral for the US, it is assumed that US issuances have mainly domestic collateral. Data include asset-backed securities, mortgage-backed securities and Pfandbriefe. Data for Japan (JP), and for Finland (FI) in 2005 are not available. Euro area (EA) figures are averages of EA country data weighted by GDP

Sources: European Securitisation Forum, Bond Market Association, and Eurostat

Selling off some of this risk via securitization allows them to hold less costly capital and to reinvest freed-up resources into the economy. Moreover, the prices of asset-backed or mortgage-backed securities convey additional information to the market (see for example DeMarzo 2005). Some securitizations may however be motivated by regulatory or tax arbitrage, which could entail efficiency losses. Generally, the empirical effects of European securitizations have only started to be analysed more carefully. It is therefore somewhat difficult to clearly assess here how the undoubted benefits of securitization in Europe compare to some open issues and risks.

Securitization has recently grown substantially in a number of developed financial systems. Arguably, this growth constitutes—together with the growth of credit derivatives—the most important recent structural development in modern financial systems. Figure 4.3 shows a measure of the extent of securitization of loans, mortgages, or receivables for the sample countries relative to GDP, using the location of the collateral as the geographic entity.

Due to the Pfandbriefe Germany has a relatively active securitization business and Spain, the Netherlands, Portugal, and the UK have caught up recently. But for most other EU countries covered (except Luxembourg) the tradeability of illiquid assets has not really picked up. Average euro area securitization remains a fraction of the level seen in the USA. It seems that significant further growth of asset- and mortgage-backed securities in the EU countries could help the allocation of risks and extend the financing capacity of European capital markets. More concretely, as for example the lack of integration in the European mortgage markets suggests (see e.g.

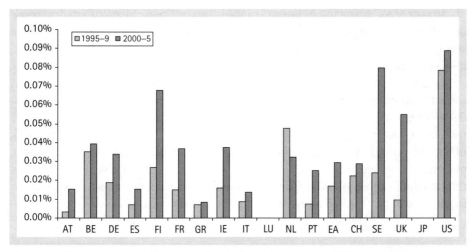

Fig. 4.4. Venture capital financing (early investment stage) (% of GDP, by country of management)

Notes: Venture capital early stage investment is defined as private equity raised for seed and start-up financing. Data reports investment by venture capital firms according to their country of residence. Data for Luxembourg (LU) and Japan (JP) are not available. Switzerland (CH) data start in 1999. Euro area (EA) figures are averages of EA country data weighted by GDP

Sources: European Private Equity and Venture Capital Association, PricewaterhouseCoopers, and Eurostat

ECB 2005a; EU Commission 2005a), the ease with which issuers can include illiquid assets from any European country, irrespective of their own location, seems to be an important determinant of further securitization. Obstacles to this may include financial regulations, consumer protection rules, or aspects of taxation. At the same time, however, many issues regarding the driving forces and effects of enhanced securitization are still unexplored in Europe. So more research seems to be needed before drawing strong policy conclusions.

Financing real investment projects is particularly difficult for start-ups and for young and small firms which need additional capital. For these firms, asymmetric information is particularly pronounced so that they have no access to public capital markets. Even bank financing may be difficult, as they usually have little collateral to offer. Modern financial systems therefore provide significant private equity and venture capital funds. The related investors maintain an equity stake in firms and monitor and advise them so as to overcome the asymmetric information problems. Active venture capital markets ensure that competition and 'creative destruction' promote the emergence of new firms and products. Figure 4.4 measures total venture capital financing (at early investment stage) as a share of GDP for the sample countries.

Despite having grown substantially over the last ten years, venture capital financing in European countries remains only a fraction of venture capital financing in the United States, except in Finland, Sweden, and the UK, which have the highest level of early-stage VC financing in Europe in more recent times.[12] Particularly low levels of early-stage VC financing are recorded for Austria, Greece, Italy, and Spain. While average euro area venture capital financing in the late 1990s was larger than in the UK, this is no longer the case.

These findings suggest that the further promotion of venture capital financing in some EU countries could give a stimulus to entrepreneurship, innovation, and productivity growth. The available evidence is however not sufficient to decide whether the lack of venture capital financing is caused by a lack of capital supplied, by a lack of liquidity in still somewhat nationally segmented venture capital markets, by a lack of demand from entrepreneurs, or by a shortage of exit options for venture capitalists through liquid equity markets. The sources of the European VC financing weaknesses would have to be explored more before drawing strong policy conclusions.

3.3. Transparency and Information

The production and dissemination of information is a crucial part of the functioning of a financial system. For example, sufficient public reporting by firms and efficient intermediaries processing such and other information alleviates the control problem between outside investors and firm insiders, with beneficial effects on the cost of capital (see for example Holmström and Tirole 1993). In this subsection the emphasis is on indicators that measure how information is processed in the stock market. The first indicator shows differences in opinion among equity analysts for the same firm and the second describes to what extent firm-specific information is priced.

Figure 4.5 exhibits differences among analysts' earnings forecasts. The more analysts disagree about the prospects of firms in a given country, the more asymmetric information there is about firms and the less efficient is a financial system's processing of information. By this measure, the USA and to some extent Ireland have more homogeneous earnings forecasts. Other European countries, in particular Germany, Italy, and Portugal as well as Japan, seem to have greater asymmetric information about their firms, although differences are not particular large in Europe recently.[13]

Figure 4.6 displays an econometric indicator estimated from stock returns that measures the degree to which firm-specific information is priced. The higher are the bars in the figure, the greater the role of market-wide factors in stock market pricing in the respective countries. The lower are the bars the more idiosyncratic firm-specific information is included in the stock market valuation of firms. A high score of this

---

[12] The results are quite similar if one considers venture capital that finances later-stage replacements and if one looks at venture capital by country of destination (see Hartmann et al. 2006). The differences from the USA are not driven by the stock market bubble of 1999–2000, as it affected most countries in a similar fashion (only Finland, Sweden, and Portugal seem to have been significantly less affected by it).

[13] The peaks of uncertainty in Finland and Sweden in the early 1990s reflect those countries' financial crises and should therefore be discounted.

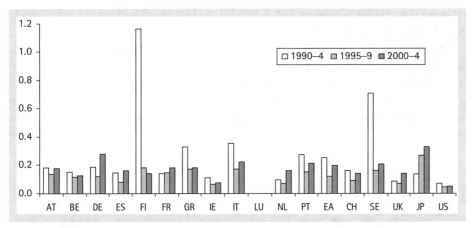

Fig. 4.5. Dispersion of analysts' forecasts (relative to the level of earnings per share forecasts)

Notes: Average standard deviation of the earnings per share (EPS) forecasts for a given year divided by the level of the EPS forecasts for that year. The average standard deviation of the EPS is an average of firm level standard deviation of EPS forecasts weighted by the market capitalization of firms and the level EPS forecast is an average of the firm level EPS forecast weighted by the market capitalization of firms. Data for Luxembourg (LU) are not available, while for the Netherlands (NL) and Portugal (PT) the data end in 2001. Euro area (EA) figures are averages of EA country data weighted by the stock market capitalization covered by analysts in each country

Sources: Thomson Financial's First Call database

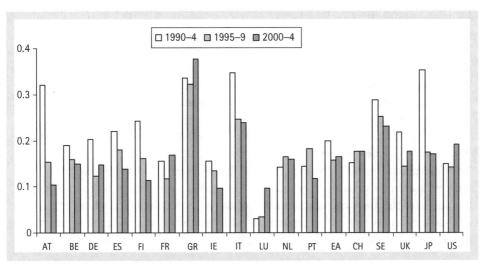

Fig. 4.6. Pricing of firm-specific information (R^2 statistics)

Notes: Country average R^2 statistics from regressing firms' stock prices on market factors, i.e. the returns on the domestic, the euro area, the US and emerging countries stock market indices. Low bars indicate that stock prices reflect more firm specific information. Euro area (EA) figures are averages of EA country R^2 statistics weighted by stock market capitalization

Sources: Datastream and own calculations

measure is found for countries with less developed financial systems (Morck, Yeung, and Yu 2000) and for firms that invest inefficiently (Durnev, Morck, and Yeung 2003).

The results suggest that the informational efficiency of stock markets in the euro area is comparable to the UK and the USA. Nevertheless, a few European countries, notably Greece, Italy, and Sweden, seem to have stock markets that incorporate less firm-specific information into stock prices. Overall, there seems to be some room for improving the information processing for listed firms in specific EU countries.[14]

3.4. Corporate Governance

Corporate governance addresses potential conflicts between investors and firm managers and among investors, e.g. large versus minority shareholders. Better governance ensures that their interests are more aligned, so that investors obtain a better return and there will be a smaller loss of efficiency due to opportunistic behaviour by managers. Two corporate governance issues are addressed in the subsection: laws protecting shareholders and the pros and cons of ownership concentration.[15]

A classic measure of corporate governance is the protection of minority shareholder rights in shareholder meetings (see La Porta et al. 1997, 1998, 2000). Since the voting rights of shareholders at company meetings have generally improved in Europe, the measure is not reported here.[16]

A related improved and more recent measure used in the literature quantifies the enforcement of shareholders' rights against expropriation by corporate insiders through self-dealing (see Djankov et al. 2006). Various forms of such self-dealing include executive perquisites to excessive compensation, transfer pricing, self-serving financial transactions such as directed equity issuance or personal loans to insiders, and outright theft of corporate assets. Several approaches to counter self-dealing are possible. One possibility is to facilitate ex ante private enforcement of good behaviour through extensive disclosure and approval procedures for transactions. Another possibility is to facilitate ex post private litigation when self-dealing is suspected.

Figure 4.7 shows that the enforcement of shareholder rights against self-dealing by corporate insiders is particularly easy in the UK, the USA, but also in Ireland. They are much weaker in Austria, Greece, Luxembourg, and the Netherlands. The euro area average score on this index of shareholder protection is about a half of the score for the USA and about a third of the score for the UK. Overall, it may be advisable to remove obstacles for minority shareholders to take efficient legal actions against self-dealing by corporate insiders in a large number of European countries.

---

[14] A similar conclusion can be reached when looking at mandatory and voluntary disclosure in annual reports of firms, where Austrian, Greek, and Portuguese firms provide less information than firms of other EU-15 countries. See the CIFAR disclosure index displayed for example in Hartmann et al. 2006.

[15] For a more extensive discussion of corporate governance, with a particular emphasis on lessons that can be learned from the US Sarbanes–Oxley Act, see the chapter by Röell.

[16] See Hartmann et al. 2006 for the most recent information. There is also some debate about the accuracy of this early measure of minority shareholder protection (see for example Spamann 2006).

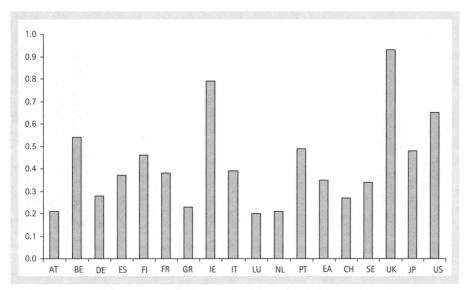

Fig. 4.7. Enforcement of shareholder rights against self-dealing (anti self-dealing index)

Notes: The index ranges from 0 to 1. Higher bars indicate better shareholder protection. The index incorporates ex-ante and ex-post private control of self-dealing transactions. Ex-ante control includes the following issues for a transaction between a corporate insider and an outside buyer: 1) Must disinterested shareholders approve the transaction? 2) Must the buyer disclose the nature of the transaction and a possible ownership of the buyer by the corporate insider?, 3) Must the corporate insider disclose the transaction and its nature? and 4) Is an independent review, e.g. by a financial expert, required?. Ex post control considers the following points: 1) Are transactions disclosed in periodic filings such as annual reports?, 2) Can a 10% shareholder sue the corporate insider for damages suffered as a result of the transaction?, 3) How easy is it to rescind the transaction, 4) How easy is it to hold the corporate insider liable for civil damages?, 5) How easy is it to hold approving corporate bodies liable for civil damages?, 6) How easy is it to access evidence about the transaction? Euro area (EA) figures are averages of EA country data weighted by stock market capitalization. Data refer to 2003

Source: Djankov et al. (2006)

The econometric results in Section 4 suggest that this would promote stock markets and improve the reallocation of capital among industries.

Related but different is a measure of the protection of creditor rights that includes for example whether secured creditors have priority for the proceeds of a firm in liquidation or whether bondholders have a say in reorganizations. It has been shown that better protection of creditor rights increases the breadth and depth of capital markets (see La Porta et al. 1997, 1998, 2000). This measure of creditor rights therefore includes rights in both reorganization and liquidation. In fact, the attempt is to make this measure as neutral as possible towards the different issue as to whether bankruptcy laws should favour early liquidations or leave ample room for reorganizations.[17]

Figure 4.8 suggests large differences across countries for creditor rights. Whereas the UK has strong creditor rights, the USA has much weaker ones and is in this respect similar to a number of European countries (including Finland, France, Greece,

---

[17] It is a matter of debate which is preferred from a social viewpoint (see Aghion, Hart, and Moore 1992). Most countries rely to some extent on both procedures.

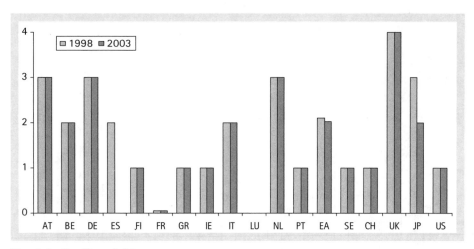

Fig. 4.8. Creditor rights

Notes: The index ranges from 0 to 4. The higher the score the higher the protection. A score of four is assigned when each of the following rights of secured lenders is defined in laws and regulations: First, there are restrictions, such as creditor consent or minimum dividends, for a debtor to file for reorganization. Second, secured creditors are able to seize their collateral after the reorganization petition is approved, i.e. there is no 'automatic stay' or 'asset freeze.' Third, secured creditors are paid first out of the proceeds of liquidating a bankrupt firm, as opposed to other creditors such as government or workers. Finally, if management does not retain administration of its property pending the resolution of the reorganization. Euro area (EA) figures are averages of EA country data weighted by GDP. Data for Luxembourg (LU) are not available.

Sources: Djankov, McLiesh, and Shleifer 2006 and World Bank

Ireland, Portugal, Sweden, and Switzerland). Other European countries, such as Austria, Germany, and the Netherlands, have however quite strong creditor rights. This raises the question whether creditor rights should not be strengthened in specific European countries. While in the short term the strengthening of creditor rights could reduce the demand for debt financing, the idea is that the benefits of a greater willingness to lend should dominate in the long term.

The relative merits of dispersed versus concentrated firm ownership structures are theoretically ambiguous. On the one hand, large outside shareholders can monitor firms and facilitate takeovers. On the other hand, large shareholders may themselves derive private benefits of control and not act in the interest of minority shareholders (see Shleifer and Vishny 1986). La Porta et al. (1999, 2000) argue that the costs of concentrated ownership dominate the benefits.[18] Figure 4.9 exhibits two measures of ownership concentration, suggesting that the countries with relatively dispersed shareholdings are Ireland, the Netherlands, Switzerland, the UK, and the USA. In most other European countries corporate ownership is much more concentrated.

The literature has found that the identity of large shareholders is relevant for good governance. In particular, institutional investors monitor firms carefully and actively intervene when needed (see for example Hartzell and Starks 2003), whereas large family shareholders (or other entrenched individuals) tend to act less favourably (see

[18] As far as banks are concerned, it is quite common, and indeed often appropriate, that small banks have controlling shareholders (see Basel Committee on Banking Supervision 2006).

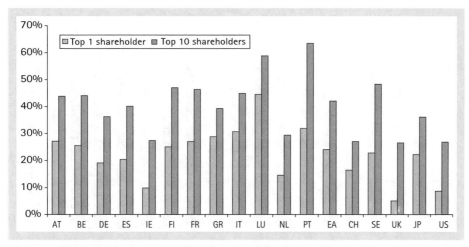

Fig. 4.9. Ownership concentration in top-10 quoted companies (fraction of shares held by the largest and by the largest 10 shareholders)

Notes: Calculated on the basis of data available for the largest shareholders in top 10 quoted companies in terms of market capitalization in each country. The comparison highlights the concentration of share capital in the hands of the largest compared to the 10 largest shareholders. Euro area (EA) figures are averages of EA country data weighted by market capitalization. Data refer to 2005

Source: Own calculations using Reuters Kobra database

for example Morck, Wolfenzon, and Yeung 2005). Therefore, Figure 4.10 reports the proportion of institutional shareholders among the largest shareholders of firms in our sample countries. Institutional shareholders play a large role in Ireland, the UK, Sweden, Switzerland, and the USA. They play a smaller role for Italian, Luxembourg, Portuguese, Spanish, or Japanese firms. In sum, it could be beneficial for the European financial system if ownership became somewhat more dispersed and included more institutional investors.

3.5. Legal System

The reliability and efficiency of legal systems are important for the performance of financial systems. The intertemporal nature of many financial contracts implies that investors relinquish control of their funds for a promise of future cash flows. The legal system enforces that such contracts are honoured. Just one example is how the legal system helps enforcing the creditor and shareholder rights discussed in the previous subsection. Research shows for example that international banks' investment decisions are sensitive to the enforcement of creditor rights (Papaioannou 2005) and stock market turnover, block premia, private credit, and market capitalization are strongly correlated with the enforcement of shareholder rights (La Porta, López-de-Silanes, and Shleifer 2006).

Figure 4.11 displays a measure of legal efficiency called 'duration of enforcement' (see Djankov et al. 2003). It indicates the speed with which financial conflicts are

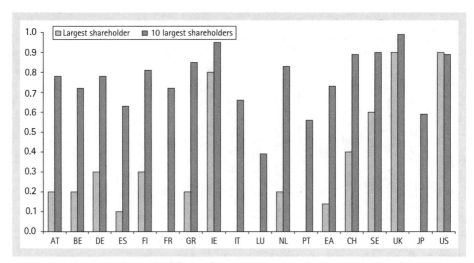

Fig. 4.10. Proportion of institutional shareholders in top–10 quoted companies (proportion of companies whose largest shareholder is an institution and proportion of institutions among largest shareholders)

Notes: Calculated on the basis of data available for the largest shareholders of the top-10 quoted companies in terms of market capitalization in each country. Institutional holdings are defined as holdings by buy-side institutions (the investing institutions such as mutual funds, pension funds, and insurance firms). An institution is an entity in the business of investment management (e.g., they employ investment professionals, have assets under management etc.). Investments may be managed on behalf of third parties or proprietary. Euro area (EA) figures are averages of EA country data weighted by market capitalization. Data refer to 2005

Source: Own calculations using Reuters Kobra database

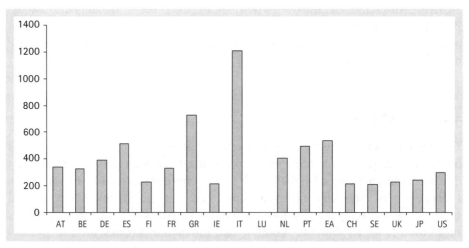

Fig. 4.11. Duration of enforcement (number of calendar days)

Notes: Total number of calendar days needed to recoup a bounced cheque, i.e. the time between the moment of issuance of judgement and the moment the creditor obtains payment of a cheque. This is the sum of: (1) duration until completion of service of process; (2) duration of trial; and (3) duration of enforcement. The survey refers to a cheque worth the equivalent in local currency of 200% of GNP per capita of the respondent country. The survey also considers administrative procedures for the collection of overdue debt. Euro area (EA) figures are averages of EA country data weighted by GDP. Data refer to 2005. Data for Luxembourg (LU) are not available

Source: World Bank

resolved in the courts, by counting the number of days it takes on average to resolve a simple financial conflict. The legal system seems to be particularly slow in Italy, where such a conflict takes nearly four years on average to resolve, and also in Greece (about two years). It is much faster in Finland, Ireland, Switzerland, and Sweden. In other words, by this indicator there is room in a small number of European countries to improve the speed with which legal systems solve financial conflicts.[19] Section 4 underlines the importance of legal efficiency with a strongly related index on legal formalism. The regressions reported there suggest that less legal formalism and faster processing of financial conflicts will foster capital market growth and the efficient reallocation of capital.

3.6. Financial Regulation, Supervision, and Stability

The financial sector is 'special' compared to other sectors due to its greater potential for instability and a strong need to protect small and relatively uninformed investors (see e.g. Dewatripont and Tirole 1993 or Goodhart et al. 1998). The regulations and supervisory practices, which are mostly motivated by financial stability considerations, could correct for market imperfections but if not well designed they could also impair financial efficiency (see for example Barth, Caprio, and Levine 2004). This subsection considers two dimensions of supervisory interventions: discretion in bank supervisory interventions ('forbearance') and proneness of deposit insurance arrangements to bank moral hazard.

The indicator in Figure 4.12 assesses the scope for supervisory forbearance by combining information about the existence of prompt corrective action provisions, possibilities to forbear prudential regulations, and reporting requirements about infractions of prudential regulations. The higher are the bars, the greater is the room for discretion ('forbearance'). There is some experience that too much forbearance may distort banks' risk-taking decisions and increase the costs of financial crises (see Kane and Yu 1995; Calomiris, Klingebiel, and Laeven 2004; and Honohan and Klingebiel 2003). The figure shows that there are significant differences across countries, with some benefiting from a lot of discretion (e.g. Germany, Sweden, the UK, and perhaps Belgium) and others not (including Finland, Spain, Japan, and the USA).

The second regulatory indicator combines information about features of bank deposit insurance schemes that could lead to moral hazard, i.e. banks could develop a tendency to rely too much on them and not adequately control risks (see Demirgüç-Kunt and Detragiache 2002). These features include, for example, whether the scheme also covers wholesale deposits and whether it is fully funded or not. Figure 4.13 shows significant differences across countries. High bars, indicating a significant risk

---

[19] Another way a legal system supports the functioning of a financial system is through the protection of property rights. As reported in Hartmann et al. 2006, the protection of these rights is quite high and it varies only to a limited extent across sample countries. A similar finding (except for a very small number of EU countries) emerges for a 'law and order' indicator that assesses the observance of the law, its strength, and impartiality.

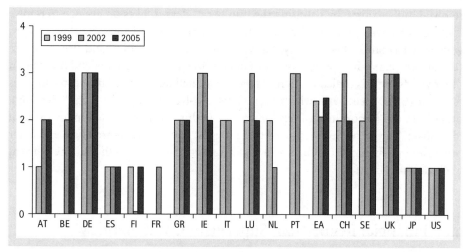

Fig. 4.12. Supervisory forbearance discretion

Notes: The index ranges from 0 to 4. The higher the index the higher the discretion. The index is the sum of the values given for the answers of the following questions. Does the law establish pre-determined levels of solvency deterioration which forces automatic actions such as intervention? No =1. Can a supervisory agency or any other government agency forbear certain prudential regulations? Yes=1. Must infraction of any prudential regulation found by a supervisor be reported? No=1. Any mandatory actions in these cases? No = 1. 2005 updates are not available for France (FR), Italy (IT), the Netherlands (NL) and Portugal (PT). 1999 data for Belgium (BE) and FR 2001 data are not available. Euro area (EA) figures are averages of EA country data weighted by total assets of the banking sector. Due to data availability 2005 information had to be weighted with 2004 assets

Sources: World Bank for 1999 and 2002, own survey for 2005

of moral hazard, are found for Finland, Germany, and Italy or even the USA. In contrast, the risk of bank moral hazard due to deposit insurance seems to be low in Switzerland.

Overall, there seems to be room for improving the incentives of banks given by European banking regulation and supervision. On the one hand, prompt corrective action provisions and reductions in discretion leading to forbearance could be considered. On the other hand, deposit insurance schemes could be clearly limited to retail deposits, more accurately priced, and provided with better funding solutions. Other bank regulations supporting market discipline are, however, in place in most sample countries (see Hartmann et al. 2006).

3.7. Competition, Openness, and Financial Integration

Competition among financial intermediaries lowers lending rates and increases the provision of credit (see for example Claessens and Laeven 2005). It also gives incentives for intermediaries to explore the provision of new financial services. Competition is fostered, inter alia, by the openness of a financial system to entry and the provision of services from abroad, which will promote financial integration. The focus

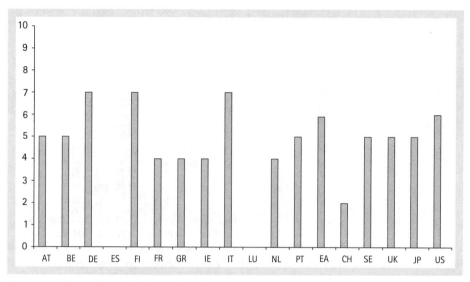

Fig. 4.13. Deposit insurance moral hazard

Notes: The index ranges from 0 to 10. The higher the index the higher the risk of moral hazard. Index values are the sums of the values assigned to the following questions: 1) coinsurance required (yes=1, no=0); 2) foreign currency deposits are covered (yes=1, no=0); 3) interbank deposits are covered (yes=1, no=0); 4) deposit insurance is funded (yes=1, no=0); 5) source of funding (the scores are: 2 if government, 1 if government and banks, 0 if banks only); 6) type of management of deposit insurance (the scores are: 3 if private, 1 if official, 2 if joint); 7) type of membership (the scores are: 1 if compulsory, 0 if voluntary). Data are not available for Spain (ES) and Luxembourg (LU). Data refer to the period 1999-2000. Euro area (EA) figures are averages of EA country data weighted by total deposits

Sources: Demirgüç-Kunt and Detragiache (2002)

in this subsection is on concentration, public ownership, and foreign penetration of banking markets.

Market concentration is one possible but admittedly imperfect measure of competition (see for example Cetarelli and Strahan 2006, as well as Demirgüç-Kunt, Laeven, and Levine 2004). The more concentrated a product-differentiated market such as a loan market is, the greater may be monopoly profits and the higher loan rates. Figure 4.14 shows the Herfindahl index based on banks' assets for sample countries. Section 4 provides some evidence that too much bank concentration may hamper the contribution of a financial system to efficient real investment in high-income countries. The issue seems important given the high level of bank concentration in a number of European countries, as shown in Figure 4.14.

One way to counter domestic bank concentration is to encourage foreign entry. Foreign entry in loan and deposit markets, e.g. through cross-border mergers and acquisitions, is pro-competitive. Figure 4.15 shows the asset market shares of foreign bank branches and subsidiaries in the sample countries. Except for Luxembourg and recently Finland and perhaps Ireland, foreign penetration is still limited, not only in Western Europe.[20] In other words, foreign bank penetration has not yet

[20] The situation is very different in Central and Eastern Europe where high foreign bank ownership is observed in many countries. The present chapter paper does not cover those countries.

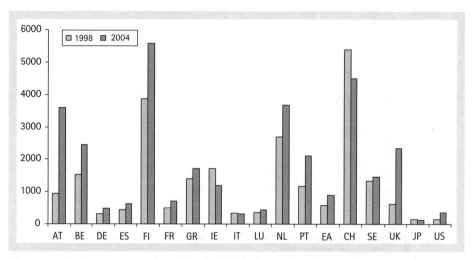

Fig. 4.14. Bank concentration (Herfindahl index computed on total assets)

Notes: The Herfindahl index has been computed by summing the squares of the market share of each bank using unconsolidated accounts in terms of total assets. The index has been rescaled in order to range from 0 to 10,000, with higher scores indicating more concentrated markets. Euro area (EA) figures are averages of EA country data weighted by total assets of the banking sector

Sources: Bankscope and own calculations

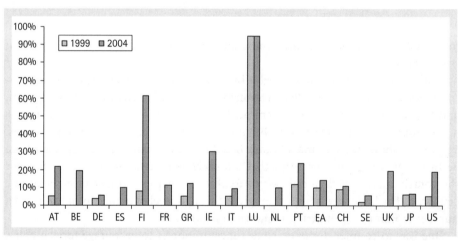

Fig. 4.15. Foreign bank penetration (assets of foreign–owned banks over total domestic assets, %)

Notes: 1999 data are unavailable for Belgium (BE), France (FR), Ireland (IE), Netherlands (NL) and UK. For Luxembourg (LU), Switzerland (CH), Japan (JP) and the US data are available only until 2002, World Bank. Euro area (EA) figures are averages of EA country data weighted by total assets of the banking sector

Sources: World Bank for 1999 and ECB for 2004

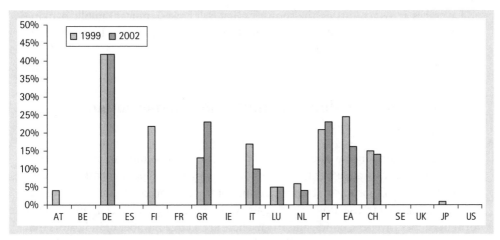

Fig. 4.16. State ownership of banks (% of total banking assets)

Notes: Data for Ireland (IE) and 2001 data for Belgium (BE), France (FR), and Sweden (SE) are unavailable. Euro area (EA) figures are averages of EA country data weighted by total assets of the banking sector

Source: World Bank

been able to limit domestic concentrations.[21] So, one way to counter the potentially adverse effects of domestic concentration, while permitting consolidation, is to allow for more foreign entry, e.g. through cross-border bank M&As. Previous work using cross-country data and the experience of bank deregulation in the USA also suggest that higher bank concentration is associated with lower growth whereas cross-state entry of banks had a number of positive effects (see Cetorelli and Gamberra 2001; Strahan 2003; Cetorelli and Strahan 2006).

One possible obstacle to foreign bank entry is public ownership and control of domestic banks. Moreover, extensive public ownership may distort competition in national banking markets, e.g. it could be associated with funding advantages. Previous research also suggests that government-owned and -controlled banks may pursue political objectives (e.g. lending to politically connected firms and entrepreneurs) at the expense of profit maximization (see for example Dinc 2005 for emerging markets or Sapienza 2004 for Italy in the 1990s) and that countries with a large share of state-owned banks have less developed financial markets (La Porta et al. 2002). The econometric analysis in Section 4 and the literature further indicate that public banking may be associated with smaller and less developed capital markets, which in turn hampers the reallocation of capital.

Figure 4.16 displays public involvement by assets in the sample countries. Only a small number of industrial countries still have significant shares of public banks.[22] Many countries have no public banks anymore. Even though the results from the literature and the econometric analysis in Section 4 refers to earlier time periods

[21] See also EU Commission 2005b for a list of current obstacles to foreign bank entry in a number of areas.

[22] The Portuguese number refers just to one large public bank.

and averages across countries, the countries that still have significant public banking may find it advisable to verify that their public bank sector functions better than the average described by those results.

3.8. Economic Freedom, Political, and Socio-economic Factors

Economic freedom means the absence of constraints to economic activities, e.g. corruption, administrative burdens, or non-efficiency-related political interventions. Given the great importance of information, contract enforcement, and ease of exchange in financial transactions, there is also a significant role for social capital in the form of cooperativeness, ethics, and trust. There are a large number of indicators that attempt to capture these aspects. This subsection presents one of them that figures prominently in the finance and growth literature, namely the control of corruption (see La Porta et al. 1997, 1998). Higher levels of corruption make it for example more difficult for private investors to enforce their rights through courts or for firms without political connections to obtain credit.

The measure in Figure 4.17 refers to the exercise of public power for private gain, for example excessive patronage, state capture by vested interest, or outright theft. As one could expect, a larger number of European countries have very good control of public power for private gain and only very few have lower control. These findings are

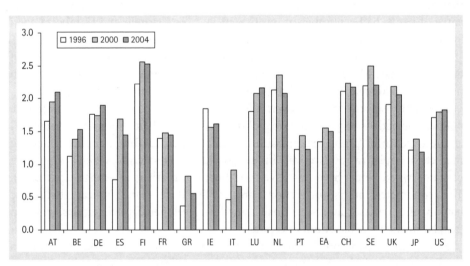

Fig. 4.17. Control of corruption

Notes: Higher values indicate better control of corruption. The index is constructed using an unobserved components methodology and uses indicators of corruption coming from a large number of different sources (see Kaufmann, Kraay, and Mastruzzi 2006, for details). The index measures the exercise of public power for private gain (e.g. nepotism, state capture or corruption). Euro area (EA) figures are averages of EA country data weighted by GDP

Source: World Bank

only mentioned in relation to the efficiency of financial systems and not in relation to legal or criminal issues.

4. FINANCIAL DEVELOPMENT, REALLOCATION OF CAPITAL, AND PRODUCTIVITY: ECONOMETRIC RESULTS

The last step is to establish a direct empirical link between the performance of the financial system and the performance of the economy (see Figure 4.1 in Section 2). Building on the large literature on financial development and economic growth (see Levine 2005), this section discusses one possible approach employing a number of the indicators of financial system efficiency presented in Section 3.[23]

The basic idea of the present approach goes back to Schumpeter (1912) and Bagehot (1873) who argued that a well-developed financial system enhances productivity by accelerating the speed of capital reallocation in the process of 'creative destruction'. The idea is that financial intermediaries help channelling resources (mainly capital) from declining industries to firms, entrepreneurs, and sectors with good growth prospects. So, financially well-developed economies converge faster to the efficient production frontier and experience higher overall productivity growth, since capital is allocated to the sectors that earn higher returns.[24]

Recent empirical research using industry data has shown that financially developed and open countries manage to exploit technological innovations better (e.g. Fisman and Love, 2003, 2004; Bekaert et al. 2006; Ciccone and Papaioannou 2006).

Wurgler (2000) develops an intuitive test for examining how financial development supports the alignment of actual with optimal industry investment. The main hypothesis is that industries with better growth prospects should experience faster investment growth in countries that benefit from a higher level of financial development. Wurgler founds this notion on the q-theory of investment (see Tobin 1969), which establishes a positive linear relationship between capital growth (at the firm and industry level) and Tobin's q (formally the market value of capital divided by its replacement cost—it is often approximated by the market-to-book ratio of the market over the book value of a firm's or industry's assets). The higher q is for a given

[23] This section is based on and summarizes the more extensive analysis presented in Ciccone and Papaioannou forthcoming.

[24] In this vein, some observers have attributed the surge in productivity growth in the USA after the mid-1990s, which was mainly concentrated in information technology and R&D-intensive sectors, to the efficiency with which US financial intermediaries channelled capital to start-up firms in software, biotech, pharmaceuticals, and telecommunications industries (see the literature reviewed in the chapter by Papaioannou).

industry the better are the growth prospects of this and industry and the more should be invested in it.[25]

The present implementation of this intuitive approach follows a sequence of estimations akin to Wurgler's (2000) two-step approach. It significantly refines, however, the economic argument and econometric specification, focuses on high-income countries, and adds more recent industry data. In a first step real investment growth is regressed on value-added growth at the industry level, controlling for time, country, industry effects, and interactions between them (to account for all possible sources of unobserved heterogeneity). Value-added growth is used to measure sector investment opportunities.[26] The idea is that expanding sectors i.e. those with high growth of value-added, should invest more to further exploit positive future growth opportunities. The first estimation yields an should invest more to further empirical elasticity investment to value added (the 'speed of intersectoral capital reallocation') derived for each country. In a second step the estimated country-specific elasticity is regressed on a variety of variables from Section 3 that measure the efficiency of financial systems and on non-financial variables that account for other influences on capital reallocation, such as income or human capital. As discussed further below, the aggregate size of capital markets turns out to be the most significant predictor of cross-country variations in the inter-sectoral speed of capital reallocation. Therefore, an instrumental variable, i.e. two-stage, regression, is added as a third step. In the first stage, various institutional and structural variables (many of which correspond e.g. to the 'fundamentals' of a financial system, as defined in Section 2) are regressed on capital market size. The predicted part of capital market size is then regressed on the speed of capital reallocation.

The three subsections below follow the sequence of these three steps of the analysis. The first subsection shows graphically the estimated speed of capital reallocation for each country. The second estimates the role of capital market size as one of the economic variables determining the speed of capital reallocation. The third subsection estimates the determinants of capital market size and assesses the importance for the reallocation of capital.

The approach chosen and the use of quantitative econometric evidence have a number of advantages. First, the reallocation of capital across industries is clearly one important mechanism though which a financial system fosters productivity, especially in industrial countries. Second, the estimation approach addresses a number

[25] Ciccone and Papaioannou 2006 establish more developed foundations for the Schumpeterian capital reallocation hypothesis by examining a multi-industry world equilibrium model where industries are subject to country-specific as well as global demand and technology shifts. These (partly anticipated) shocks drive a gap between the actual allocation of capital and the target allocation across industries, i.e. the optimal allocation that would emerge if capital were reallocated immediately to where it is most productive. Financial development is modelled as an adjustment mechanism that potentially speeds up the flow of capital from declining to rising sectors.

[26] Wurgler 2000 argues that in countries with adequate data availability value-added growth is significantly correlated with Tobin's q and other proxies of future industry opportunities (e.g. sales growth).

of technical problems, such as biases arising from omitted variables, unobserved heterogeneity, and reverse causality. Third, the use of econometric analysis makes it transparent under which assumptions the results hold. Last, the results found are fully in line with those of the more structural analysis presented by Ciccone and Papioannou (2006) using different data.

These advantages have to be set against a number of challenges and caveats. First, the reallocation channel analysed is only one among many relevant ones through which a financial system may affect productivity and economic growth (see inter alia Section 2). The literature has also highlighted for example the importance of financial intermediation in fostering investment (capital deepening), education (human capital accumulation), and the adoption of new technologies (see Levine 2005; the chapter by Papaioannou). The employed approach is silent about the existence of such other channels and whether the financial variables identified play similar or different roles in them. Second, since many of the indicators from Section 3 are used, the same caveats as listed above apply. In addition to measurement error this also relates to the unavailability of some data for the earlier and later periods of the sample. Furthermore, industry data are quite noisy and thus may not accurately reflect economic conditions across countries. However, as long as mismeasurement is not systematic, then the regresssions will yield conservative rather than inflated estimates. Third, the parts of the estimations using only the small number of high-income OECD countries may exhibit some small sample problems. Fourth, the estimations are new and have not yet been exposed to scientific peer review.

4.1. Data and Description of the Estimated Speeds of Intersectoral Capital Reallocation

The speed of capital reallocation is estimated with international data on sectoral investment (gross fixed capital formation) and production (value added) from the Industrial Statistics Database of the United Nations Industrial Development Organization (UNIDO). They cover twenty-eight manufacturing industries in sixty-five (non-socialist) economies during the period 1963–2003. The section presents results for the entire sample of countries (since this is the most efficient statistical approach), but it pays special attention to industrial countries by also (i) excluding low-income countries and (ii) considering only twenty-eight high-income countries.

Figure 4.18 plots the estimated speed of capital reallocation on the vertical axis against capital market size as a measurement of financial development for the full sample. It shows a clear positive relationship. For example, inter-sectoral capital reallocation is significantly faster in the group of industrial countries than in emerging and developing countries.

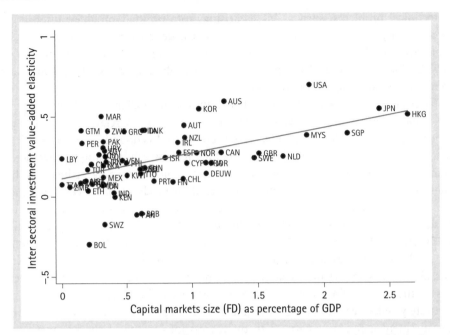

Fig. 4.18. Capital reallocation (intersectoral investment to value added elasticity) and financial development (capital market size) in the full sample

A question then is whether the positive association between financial development and capital reallocation is driven by the differences between industrial and developing countries other than the size of capital markets. Figure 4.19 shows the same information as Figure 4.18, just for the subsample of high-income countries, and again there is a positive relationship.[27] High-income countries with low levels of financial development also tend to have slower capital reallocation. Moreover, there is considerable variation i the speed of capital reallocation ranging from 0.1 (Portugal) to 0.7 (United States). This is only slightly less than the variation for the full sample, which includes developing countries. It suggests that the results obtained for the full sample of countries are not driven by differences between industrial and developing countries and that the results hold for industrial countries, too.

4.2. Role of Capital Market Size

To explore the role of financial development in determining the speed of capital reallocation more formally, Table 4.2 shows results from regressing the estimated elasticity of investment to value added on capital market size and other controls, such

---

[27] The high-income countries are twenty-two OECD countries (Australia, Austria, Belgium, Canada, Denmark, Finland, France, Germany, Greece, Ireland, Italy, Japan, the Netherlands, New Zealand, Norway, Portugal, South Korea, Spain, Sweden, United Kingdom, United States) and Barbados, Cyprus, Hong Kong, Israel, Kuwait, Malta, and Singapore.

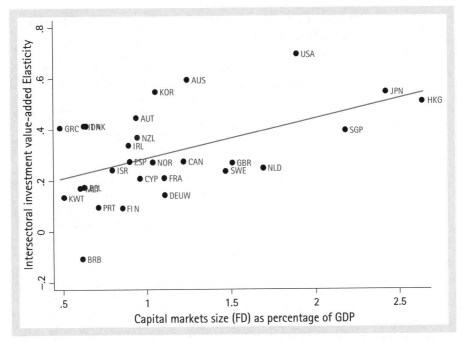

Fig. 4.19. Speed of capital reallocation and financial development in the sample of high-income countries

as income, human capital, and the overall quality of institutions. In columns (1)–(3) the effect of capital market size on the investment–value-added elasticity is estimated controlling for the overall level of economic development. In columns (4)–(6) controls for human capital and the overall efficiency of institutional structures are added.

It turns out that capital market size is a statistically and economically significant determinant of capital reallocation. Even more, it is a much stronger determinant of it than any of the other variables. This result is present in the full sample of countries (column (1)), the sample without low-income countries (column (2)), and the sample of high-income countries (column (3)). In other words, financial development fosters the reallocation of capital also in major industrial countries, such as the EU-15. Even controlling jointly for income, education, and institutional quality, capital market size remains highly significant across all samples (columns (4–6)). Moreover, no other financial variables, such as the ones discussed in Section 3, seem to be significant direct determinants of capital reallocation when added to the regression. In other words, aggregate capital market size seems to constitute a summary measure of overall financial development in both developing and industrial countries.

The economic significance of capital market size as an explanatory variable for capital reallocation can be illustrated with a simple example. Between 1980 and 1995 Austria had a capital market size of 94 per cent of GDP (roughly the mean value for

Table 4.2. Econometric results on the relationship between financial development and capital reallocation

	All countries (1)	No low income (2)	High income (3)	All countries (4)	No low income (5)	High income (6)
Capital markets size	0.236**	0.253***	0.350**	0.319***	0.318***	0.413***
stand. error	(0.082)	(0.085)	(0.112)	(0.087)	(0.088)	(0.108)
p-value	0.01	0.00	0.01	0.00	0.00	0.00
Income-real GDP per capita	0.019	0.019	0.019	0.033	0.046	0.032
stand. error	(0.015)	(0.018)	(0.072)	(0.023)	(0.036)	(0.075)
p-value	0.19	0.28	0.80	0.17	0.21	0.68
Schooling				0.013	0.014	0.031**
stand. error				(0.012)	(0.012)	(0.014)
p-value				0.30	0.26	0.04
Institutional quality				−0.066	−0.070	−0.133*
stand. error				(0.041)	(0.045)	(0.067)
p-value				0.12	0.12	0.06
Intercept	−0.049	−0.057	−0.124	−0.238	−0.362	−0.324
stand. error	(0.101)	(0.131)	(0.677)	(0.157)	(0.274)	(0.651)
p-value	0.63	0.67	0.86	0.14	0.19	0.62
Adjusted R-squared	0.256	0.249	0.255	0.300	0.300	0.393
Countries	62	54	28	59	50	28

Notes: The dependent variable is the estimated country-specific elasticity of investment to value-added. The estimation controls for country, industry, time, country-industry, industry-time, and country-year fixed effects. Capital market size is the sum of private credit by deposit money banks (and other financial institutions) and stock market capitalization as a share of GDP, averaged over the period 1980–1995 (source: World Bank Financial Structure Database; see also Beck, Demirgüç-Kunt, and Levine 1999). Income-real GDP per capita is in logs and from 1981 at constant 1995 international US dollars (source: World Bank). Schooling is average years of schooling in the population aged 25 and over in 1980 (source: Barro and Lee 2005). Institutional quality is a composite index based on three sub-indicators of government effectiveness (which proxies mostly bureaucratic efficiency and functioning), rule of law (which proxies for contract enforcement, protection of intellectual property rights, and judicial efficiency), and corruption (which proxies for corruption among public officials, effectiveness of anticorruption initiatives, and mentality regarding corruption) (source: World Bank Aggregate Governance Indicators Database; see also Kaufman, Kraay, and Mastruzzi 2006). Heteroskedasticity-adjusted standard errors are reported in parenthesis below the coefficients, p-values are reported in italics below the standard errors. ***, **, and * denote statistical significance at the 1%, 5%, and 10% level respectively.

high-income countries). According to the estimations in Table 4.2, if Austria were to enlarge its capital markets to the size of the Netherlands (169 per cent of GDP, the most financially developed country in the EU by this measure), then the intersector elasticity of investment to value added in Austria would increase by 8.6 percentage points per year. Spain would then reach the speed of capital reallocation found in New Zealand.[28]

---

[28] The regressions were also run for the smaller subsample of twenty-one (twenty-two) high-income OECD subsample (including South Korea). In spite of the small sample size, the point estimates were quite similar to the ones in Table 4.2 (although marginally insignificant). Ciccone and Papaioannou

4.3. Driving Factors of Capital Market Size

The last step of the analysis is aimed at gaining insights into which financial sector policies could promote the ability of European countries to reallocate capital faster from declining to rising industries. To this end, capital market size is first regressed on a variety of fundamental and structural financial variables and then the speed of capital reallocation is regressed on the explained part of capital market size from the first stage. If both parts yield significant results, then policies that improve these fundamental and structural features of a financial system are also likely to improve capital reallocation (via financial development).

Table 4.3 reports such two-stage regressions for four groups of variables from Section 3. Legal efficiency refers to a first-stage regression in which a measure of legal formalism is the main explanatory variable of capital market size (see Djankov et al. 2003; Acemoglu and Johnson 2006). This measure indicates to which extent a legal system has formalities that can delay even simple legal cases (it is similar to the duration index reported in Section 3). It is widely used in the finance and growth literature to describe how well a legal system supports financial transactions. The expected sign of it is negative, as more formal and slow proceeding legal systems hamper the development of capital markets. In line with previous work, countries with a slow proceeding judiciary have on average smaller capital markets. This result also holds in the group of high-income countries. Investor protection rights refer to a regression in which Djankov et al.'s (2006) self-dealing index is inserted as the main explanatory variable. As discussed in Section 3, this index describes how well good corporate governance can be enforced in a given country. More precisely, it describes how easy it is for minority shareholders to enforce rules against self-dealing transactions by majority shareholders or company directors. The expected sign of the index is positive, as less protection again self-dealing will increase the cost of capital and deter savers from investing in capital markets. The evidence in Table 4.3 shows that countries where shareholders can better enforce protection against self-dealing have larger capital markets. The third regression in Table 4.3 relates to insider trading in stock markets. The main explanatory variable in the first-stage regression is the number of years it took a country to enforce insider legislation for the first time since its introduction (see Bhattacharya and Daouk 2002). A laxer enforcement of insider trading should raise the cost of capital since investors expect to sometimes trade against better-informed insiders. The results indicate that the introduction and enforcement of insider trading has a positive effect on capital markets. The last two regression models concentrate on structural features of the banking sector. More competition among banks is expected lower the cost of lending and ease the access to credit (see for example Claessens and Laeven 2005). Measuring (imperfectly) competition using concentration, the expected sign on the size of capital markets is negative. One possible distortion of competition in banking is extensive public ownership of banks (see also La Porta et al. 2002). The expected

forthcoming provide additional sensitivity checks indicating that the positive association between capital market size and the speed of capital reallocation is quite robust.

Table 4.3. Driving factors of financial development and capital reallocation (separate two–stage estimations)

	All countries (1)	No low income (2)	High income (3)	All countries (4)	No low income (5)	High income (6)	All countries (7)	No low income (8)	High income (9)	All countries (10)	No low income (11)	High income (12)	All countries (13)	No low income (14)	High income (15)
Panel A: Second Stage Estimates															
Capital markets size	0.341*	0.347**	0.382*	0.520***	0.515***	0.419	0.415***	0.427**	0.473	0.276**	0.202**	0.284	0.476**	0.684*	1.057**
stand. error	(0.183)	(0.163)	(0.221)	(0.182)	(0.176)	(0.320)	(0.151)	(0.177)	(0.300)	(0.096)	(0.101)	(0.215)	(0.211)	(0.395)	(0.459)
p-value	0.07	0.04	0.10	0.01	0.01	0.20	0.01	0.02	0.13	0.01	0.05	0.20	0.03	0.09	0.03
Panel B: First Stage Estimates															
Legal formalism	−0.130***	−0.151***	−0.124**												
stand. error	(0.031)	(0.028)	(0.049)												
p-value	0.00	0.00	0.02												
Investor protection				0.556***	0.591***	0.386*									
stand. error				(0.159)	(0.157)	(0.192)									
p-value				0.00	0.00	0.06									
Insider trading legislation							0.025***	0.022***	0.014***						
stand. error							(0.005)	(0.005)	(0.005)						
p-value							0.00	0.00	0.00						
Gov. oxnership of banks										−0.586***	−0.600***	−0.473***			
stand. error										(0.095)	(0.099)	(0.129)			
p-value										0.00	0.00	0.00			
Bank concentration (HHI)													−0.140**	−0.095	−0.098
stand. error													(0.509)	(0.059)	(0.058)
p-value													0.01	0.11	0.1
1st stage R2	0.231	0.388	0.200	0.214	0.262	0.155	0.273	0.260	0.239	0.403	0.423	0.358	0.101	0.336	0.104
Countries	59	49	28	47	42	24	60	50	28	56	48	26	60	48	27

Notes: The table reports second–stage (in panel A) and first–stage (in panel B) estimates of two–stage least squares (2SLS) models. The dependent variable in the second stage is the country-specific elasticity of investment to value-added. The estimation controls for country, industry, time, country-industry, industry-time, and country-year fixed effects. See Table 4.2 for a definition of capital market size. Market size is instrumented in the first-stage model with (i) Investor Protection; (ii) Insider Trading Legislation; (iii) Government Ownership of Banks or; (vi) Bank Concentration. Investor Protection is the anti self-dealing index that measures the *de facto* ex-ante and ex-post private control of self-dealing transactions. The ex-ante components are the disclosure requirements in periodic filings and the ease of proving wrongdoing. The ex-post components are approval requirements of disinterested shareholders and ex-ante disclosure. The index ranges from 0 to 1, with higher values indicating better protection against insiders' self-dealing activities (i.e. higher *de facto* investor protection) (*source*: Djankov et al. 2006). Insider Trading Legislation is the number of years in 1995 that the country had established and implemented legislation against insider trading (*source*: Bhattacharya and Daouk 2002). Government Ownership of Banks is the share of the assets of the ten largest banks in a country controlled or owned by the government in 1970. The percentage of the assets owned by the government in a given bank is calculated by multiplying the share of each shareholder by the share that the government owns in that shareholder, and then summing the resulting shares (*source*: La Porta et al. 2002). Bank Concentration is the Herfindahl-Hirschman Index of the banking system, based on unconsolidated (domestic) financial statement data on all (commercial, saving investment, etc.) banks' assets. The HHI for each country is defined as the sum of squared market shares. The variable is the average in the period 1994–1996 and is expressed in logs (*source*: Bankscope). The table also reports the first-stage R-squared. Heteroskedasticity-adjusted standard errors are reported in parentheses below the coefficients. ***, **, and * denote statistical significance at the 1%, 5%, and 10% level respectively.

impact of the extent of state ownership of banks before the wave of privatization started in the 1980s on the size of capital markets is negative. Table 4.3 confirms these predictions, although the result for bank concentration is only marginally significant.

Overall the results in Table 4.3 suggest that all these factors play a role for financial development and all factors have the expected signs. Too formal and inefficient legal systems, government ownership (or other forms of public control) of banks, and bank concentration tend to limit the development of capital markets. Good enforcement of corporate governance (in particular protection against corporate self-dealing) and a solidly implemented insider trading legislation tend to foster capital market development.[29] Turning to the effect of capital market size on the speed of intersectoral capital reallocation (panel A: second-stage estimates), the estimates show that the respective components of financial development explained by the above factors are significant explanatory variables for the speed of capital reallocation in a country. When the focus is on the twenty-eight high-income countries, the results weaken somewhat but remain statistically and economically significant. In sum, the components of capital market size predicted separately by legal formalism, investor protection, government ownership of banks, and, to a lesser extent, bank concentration foster the speed with which capital is reallocated from declining to growing industries in a country. A final check is to estimate the effect of capital market size on capital reallocation using the drivers of financial development simultaneously in the first stage. The results are shown in Table 4.4. Legal formalism, insider trading legislation, and state ownership of banks are significant predictors of the size of capital markets in the different country samples. Moreover the component of financial development explained by these institutional factors is a significant correlate of the intersectoral capital reallocation.[30] All the conclusions drawn from Table 4.3 continue to hold in this specification.

5. Summary and Conclusions

The extended period of limited growth until recently in many European countries raises the issue of which policies will be most effective in improving their economic performance. This chapter argues that further financial sector reforms may be a valuable complement to ongoing efforts to reform labour and product markets. There

---

[29] Various other institutional factors and measures, such as banking system competition, foreign bank penetration, and banking supervision (see Section 3), have been tested but legal efficiency, corporate governance, and state ownership of banks appear to be most significant drivers of capital market size across all country samples.

[30] The results are similar when one replaces legal formalism with the anti-self-dealing index, due to their colinearity.

Table 4.4. Driving factors of financial development and capital reallocation (joint two-stage estimations)

Dependent variable: Intersectoral investment responsiveness	All countries (1)	No low income (2)	High income (3)	All countries (4)	No low income (5)	High income (6)
Panel A: Second Stage Estimates						
Capital markets size (FD)	0.341***	0.329**	0.367*	0.360***	0.350***	0.421**
stand. error	(0.095)	(0.110)	(0.190)	(0.088)	(0.105)	(0.162)
	0.00	0.00	0.07	0.00	0.00	0.02
Panel B: First Stage Estimates						
Gov. ownership of banks	−0.381***	−0.326***	−0.308**	−0.394***	−0.343***	−0.363**
stand. error	(0.089)	(0.099)	(0.136)	(0.084)	(0.100)	(0.138)
	0.00	0.00	0.03	0.00	0.00	0.02
Legal formalism	−0.058**	−0.079**	−0.066**	−0.084**	−0.075**	−0.0850
stand. error	(0.028)	(0.028)	(0.046)	(0.032)	(0.033)	(0.051)
	0.04	0.01	0.02	0.01	0.03	0.11
Insider trading legisl.	0.013***	0.011***	0.008**	0.013***	0.010***	0.008**
stand. error	(0.003)	(0.003)	(0.003)	(0.003)	(0.003)	(0.003)
	0.00	0.00	0.03	0.00	0.00	0.02
Legal origin	No	No	No	Yes	Yes	Yes
OID test; J-statistic	0.279	1.344	1.7220	1.2470	2.5050	2.3670
p-value	0.86	0.51	0.42	0.94	0.78	0.80
1st stage R-squared	0.606	0.616	0.475	0.655	0.646	0.536
Countries	56	48	26	54	46	26

Notes: The table reports second-stage (in panel A) and first-stage (in panel B) estimates of two-stage least squares (2SLS) models. The dependent variable in the second stage is the country-specific elasticity of investment. The estimation to value-added controls for country, industry, time, country-industry, industry-time, and country-year fixed effects. See Table 4.2 for a definition of capital market size. Capital market size is instrumented in the first-stage model with (i) Legal Formalism; (ii) Insider Trading Legislation; (iii) Government Ownership of Banks; and (iv) Legal Origin (in columns 4–6). See Table 4.3 for the definition of Legal Formalism, Insider Trading Legislation and Government Ownership of Banks. Legal Origin is a dummy variable that identifies the legal origin of the Company law or Commercial Code of each country. There are five legal families: English (Common Law), French (Civil Law), German (Civil Law), Nordic (Civil Law) and Socialist (although socialist countries are excluded from the analysis altogether) (*source*: La Porta et al. 1999).

The table also reports the first-stage R-squared and a test of overidentifying restrictions (OID), where under the null hypothesis the instruments are valid. Heteroskedasticity-adjusted standard errors are reported in parentheses below the coefficients. ***, **, and * denote statistical significance at the 1%, 5%, and 10% level respectively.

is a long-standing view in the economic literature that well-functioning financial systems allow economies to exploit the benefits of innovation in terms of productivity and growth. Moreover, measured productivity differentials between Europe and the United States seem to originate particularly from the financial sector and from sectors that are finance dependent.

Building on and summarizing the existing literature, this chapter first introduces a number of concepts that are important for financial sector analyses and policies.

It then presents a selection of indicators describing the efficiency and development of the European financial system along a variety of dimensions. Third, an attempt is made to estimate the extent to which greater financial efficiency and development might improve the allocation of productive capital in Europe. While in the recent past the research and policy debate in Europe has very much revolved around fostering financial integration, the present chapter puts the main emphasis on financial development or modernization in the sense of the finance and growth literature.

One contribution of the chapter is to present seventeen indicators describing different aspects of the efficiency of a financial system. They are selected from a large and comprehensive set of indicators that is currently assembled by ECB staff. All indicators are derived from economic theory in the context of our encompassing conceptual framework and from the empirical literature on finance and growth. They can be grouped in eight dimensions of the functioning of a financial system: (1) size of capital markets and financial structure; (2) financial innovation and market completeness; (3) transparency and information; (4) corporate governance; (5) legal system; (6) financial regulation, supervision, and stability; (7) competition, openness, and financial integration; and (8) economic freedom, political, and socio-economic factors. The present chapter displays a selection of one to two indicators for each dimension. The choice of indicators was made on the basis of the robustness of the messages they convey and whether lower outcomes for many or at least some European countries suggest relevance for policy.

To the extent that data are available, each indicator is tracked over time and across countries. Results for the twelve euro area countries are compared to other European countries (Sweden, Switzerland, and the United Kingdom) as well as to Japan and to the United States.[31] In contrast to most of the existing literature, this chapter therefore concentrates on assessing the performance of financial systems for industrial countries with relatively well-developed financial systems.

A second contribution of the chapter is to employ the indicators presented above to investigate empirically specific channels through which financial development and ultimately greater financial efficiency promote productive investment and economic growth. Specifically, the chapter presents econometric estimations of whether a more developed financial system accelerates the reallocation of capital from declining industries to industries with better growth prospects. Building on and refining previous academic research, the analysis proceeds in two steps. First, real investment growth is regressed on measures of growth prospects for twenty-eight manufacturing industries in sixty-five countries between 1963 and 2003. Expanding sectors should invest more to exploit their potential. The elasticity derived from this estimation describes the 'speed of capital reallocation' for each country. It serves as a capital efficiency (productivity) measure. Second, the estimated 'speeds of capital

---

[31]   See footnote 1.

reallocation' from the first step are regressed on the financial indicators described above and on non-financial control variables that may also influence the reallocation of capital, e.g. income or human capital. The results of such estimations are informative about the extent to which a financial system contributes to the 'process of creative destruction' in the sense of Schumpeter. In the presentation of the results special attention is given to the group of industrial countries most relevant for the euro area.

The main results of the chapter are results that are supported by all elements of the analysis presented, i.e. by (1) the empirical and theoretical results of the existing literature; (2) the implications drawn from relevant indicators; and (3) the results of the econometric analysis. For example, the literature and the own econometric analysis may suggest which financial variables drive productivity and growth in industrial countries in general. The indicators may then show for which dimensions of a financial system European capital markets or capital markets of specific European countries underperform. If all the elements point in the same direction, then it seems worthwhile to consider whether any problems in the European financial system can be addressed with policy.

Overall, the main results suggest that there is significant room for further modernizing and developing European capital markets. A first finding is that in terms of their size euro area capital markets have considerable potential for further growth. Their (relative) size is roughly comparable to Japan, but much smaller than the case for the Netherlands, the United Kingdom, Switzerland, or the United States. Moreover, the econometric estimations suggest that overall capital market size (defined as the aggregate of bank, corporate bond, and stock market financing as a share of GDP) is the main financial determinant of the speed of capital reallocation. Other economic variables or specific aspects of financial modernization play much less of a role. Hence capital market size constitutes a summary measure for gauging the overall financial development of industrial countries.

More specifically, the analysis identifies three areas where the financial market framework conditions in Europe that allow capital markets to flourish can be improved.

1. The first area concerns certain aspects of corporate governance. The literature strongly suggests that minority shareholder rights are an important aspect of well-functioning securities markets. Better governance ensures that there are fewer conflicts of interest among investors, between them and managers, that investors obtain a better return, and that there will be a smaller loss of efficiency due to opportunistic behaviour by managers. While general shareholder rights have significantly improved over time in many European countries, the anti-self-dealing index displayed in this chapter suggests that it is still quite difficult for minority shareholders to enforce protection against self-dealing by controlling shareholders or company directors in many countries. Previous literature suggests that the ease with which this protection can be enforced is associated

with various measures of financial modernization, such as higher stock market capitalization, a larger number of initial public offerings (IPOs), more developed corporate bond markets, etc. The econometric evidence presented in this chapter shows a significantly positive effect of the protection against self-dealing on the size of capital markets and therefore on the speed of capital reallocation. In conclusion, it may be advisable to remove obstacles for minority shareholders to take efficient legal actions against self-dealing by corporate insiders.

2. The second area is the efficiency of the legal system in resolving financial conflicts. The literature emphasizes the great importance of efficient legal systems for the well functioning of financial systems since the intertemporal nature of financial contracts and the large values contracted upon require a high degree of confidence in their enforcement. Slow and formalist legal systems discourage savers and investors from entering financial markets, as they face greater expropriation risk, thereby limiting the supply of capital and the liquidity of the markets. A widely used indicator of the speed with which legal systems solve financial conflicts suggests that legal efficiency could be enhanced in a small number of European countries. The econometric analysis confirms that a fast resolution of financial conflicts by a legal system has a positive effect on capital market development and thus improves the reallocation of capital in an economy.

3. The third area relates to structural features of European bank sectors. Over the last decades most banking systems in industrial countries have been liberalized extensively, but a small number of European countries still have relatively significant levels of public bank ownership. There is a substantial strand of the academic literature that detects distortionary effects of public bank ownership. For example, publicly owned or controlled banks have been found to pursue political objectives (e.g. lending to firms with politically connected managers). They may also adversely affect competition, e.g. by benefiting from funding advantages or constraining domestic and foreign entry. The econometric analysis of the present chapter and the literature further indicate that public banking may be associated with smaller and less-developed capital markets, which in turn hampers the reallocation of capital. For the countries that still have significant public banking it may therefore be advisable to verify that their public bank sector functions better than the average described by the above results.

The literature has also found adverse effects of high bank concentration on economic growth, although it was not successful in establishing a clear link between concentration and the level of competition in the bank sector. The econometric results in this chapter to some extent corroborate this finding in relation to capital market size and the reallocation of capital. The high levels of bank concentration observed at the national level in some European countries could for example be countered by more integration, such as an enhanced provision of financial services across borders. In the light of the continuing need for further financial consolidation in many European countries exposed to the consequences of globalization, also cross-border bank mergers could be helpful for avoiding that this consolidation leads to excessive concentration in geographically limited retail markets.

Moreover, the analysis also singles out European risk capital markets as an important part of the financial system to improve. For the two main areas of risk capital markets identified, however, there is not enough information available at present to derive strong conclusions for policy. While the comments below can be made, these areas would both benefit from further research.

1. An important source of economic value added and growth are start-ups and other small innovative firms. The financing of their investment projects is however particularly difficult. They have no access to public capital markets and may have difficulties obtaining private bank financing due to asymmetric information, e.g. related to the absence of a track record, high risk, and little collateral. Significant private equity and venture capital markets help to overcome these difficulties in modern financial systems. The indicators show that venture capital financing in the euro area is much lower than what is observed for example in the United States relative to the size of the two economies. This is particularly visible in early-stage financing but holds also for expansion- and replacement-stage financing. While it is clear that many new and innovative firms do not emerge with so little venture capital activity, the available evidence is not sufficient to decide whether the lack of venture capital financing is caused by a lack of capital supplied, by a lack of liquidity in still somewhat nationally segmented venture capital markets, by a lack of demand from entrepreneurs, or by a shortage of exit options for venture capitalists through liquid equity markets.

2. An important aspect of the ongoing development of financial systems in industrial countries in general is the securitization of illiquid assets. Securitization markets are, however, much larger in the United States than in Europe. A significant further growth of European securitizations could help to improve the allocation of risks and free bank capital for further lending to firms. A specific improvement that could further accelerate securitization is that issuers should be able to easily include illiquid assets from European Union countries, irrespective of their location and without being hampered by obstacles in the areas of financial regulation, consumer protection, or taxation. There are however some issues whether all securitization activities are unambiguously beneficial (some could for example be motivated by regulatory or tax arbitrage) and whether they could also pose risks to financial stability. Overall, the benefits and risks of securitization activities need to be understood better.

The chapter finds a number of other results supported by at least two but not all three elements of the analysis. These less strong conclusions are the following.

1. An important function of financial systems in general and stock markets in particular is to provide information about real investment opportunities. Various indicators suggest that there is greater uncertainty about firm prospects and a lesser pricing of idiosyncratic risk in specific European countries. It has been shown in the literature that a low pricing of idiosyncratic risk is associated with less developed financial systems and with inefficient investment by firms. So, there seems to be some room for improving the information-processing capacity of stock markets in these countries.

2. In contrast to shareholder rights, the rights of creditors in case of bankruptcy have not really improved over time. At the same time, past research shows that giving secured creditors priority for the proceeds of a firm in liquidation and allowing bondholders to have a say in reorganizations increases the breadth and depth of capital markets. This raises the question whether some European countries may benefit from enhancing those rights.

3. There is a debate whether more dispersed or more concentrated firm ownership is better for corporate performance. According to some recent research the costs of concentration appear to outweigh the benefits, but the presence of large institutional shareholders improves external monitoring. Based on the indicators of ownership concentration presented in this chapter, it would then seem beneficial for European capital markets if firm ownership became somewhat less concentrated in those instances where concentration remains high, and if the role of institutional investors in ownership was enhanced.

4. Financial regulation and supervision play a significant role in financial sectors by addressing market failures and enhancing stability. Available indicators suggest, however, that in a number of European countries some aspects of banking regulation and supervision could be improved in terms of the incentives they give to banks to take and manage risks. In particular, the moral hazard implications of deposit insurance funds could be further limited. Also deposit insurance schemes could benefit from better funding solutions and more accurate pricing.

REFERENCES

ACEMOGLU, D., and JOHNSON, S. (2006), 'Disease and development: the effect of life expectancy on economic growth', NBER Working Paper 12269.

_____ and ZILIBOTTI, F. (1997), 'Was Prometheus unbound by chance? Risk, diversification and growth', *Journal of Political Economy*, 105, 709–51.

AGHION, P., HART, O., and MOORE, J. (1992), 'The economics of bankruptcy reform', *Journal of Law, Economics and Organization*, 8, 523–46.

_____ HOWITT, P., and MAYER-FOULKES, D. (2005), 'The effect of financial development on convergence: theory and evidence', *Quarterly Journal of Economics*, 120, 173–222.

ALFARO, L., KALEMLI-OZKAN, S., and VOLOSOVYCH, V. (2005), 'Why doesn't capital flow from rich to poor countries? An empirical investigation', NBER Working Paper 11901.

ALLEN F., and GALE, D. (1997), 'Financial market, intermediaries and intertemporal smoothing', Journal of Political Economy, 105, 523–46.

BAELE, L., FERRANDO, A., HÖRDAHL, P., KRYLOVA, E., and MONNET, C. (2004), 'Measuring financial integration in the euro area', ECB Occasional Paper 14, May.

BAGEHOT, W. (1873), Lombard Street: A Description of the Money Market, Homewood, Ill.: Irwin, 1962.

BARRO, R. J., and LEE, J. W. (2001), 'International data on educational attainment: updates and implications', Oxford Economic Papers, 53, 541–63.

BARTH, J. R., CAPRIO, G., and LEVINE, R. (2004), 'Bank regulation and supervision: what works best?', Journal of Financial Intermediation, 13, 205–48.

_____ _____ _____ (2006), Rethinking Bank Regulation: Till Angels Govern, New York: Cambridge University Press.

BASEL COMMITTEE ON BANKING SUPERVISION (2006), 'Enhancing corporate governance for banking organisations', Bank for International Settlements.

BECK, T., DEMIRGÜÇ-KUNT, A., and LEVINE, R. (1999), 'A new database on financial development and structure', Policy Research Working Paper 2146, World Bank.

_____ _____ LAEVEN, L., and LEVINE, R. (2004), 'Finance, firm size and growth', NBER Working Paper 10983.

BEKAERT, G., HARVEY, C. R., LUNDBLAD, C., and SIEGEL, S. (2006), 'Global growth opportunities and market integration', Journal of Finance, forthcoming.

BENHABIB, J., and SPIEGEL, M. (2000), 'The role of financial development in growth and investment', Journal of Economic Growth, 5, 341–60.

BERGER, A. N., DEYOUNG, R., GENAY, H., and UDELL, G. F. (2000), 'Globalization of financial institutions: evidence from cross-border banking performance', Brookings-Wharton Papers on Financial Services 2000, 23–120.

_____ BUCH, C., DELONG, G., and DEYOUNG, R. (2004), 'The comparative advantage of nations at exporting financial institutions management via M&As', Journal of International Money and Finance, 23, 333–66.

BERTRAND, M., SCHOAR, A., and THESMAR, D. (forthcoming), 'Banking deregulation and industry structure: evidence from the French banking reforms of 1985', Journal of Finance, forthcoming.

BHATTACHARYA, U., and DAOUK, H. (2002), 'The world price of insider trading', Journal of Finance, 57, 75–108.

CALOMIRIS, C., KLINGEBIEL, D., and LAEVEN, L. (2004), 'A taxonomy of financial crisis resolution mechanisms: cross-country experience', in L. Laeven and P. Honohan (eds), Systemic Financial Crises: Containment and Resolution, Cambridge, Cambridge University Press.

CAPRIO, G., and KLINGEBIEL, D. (1996), 'Bank insolvencies: cross-country experience', World Bank Policy Research Working Paper 1620.

CETORELLI, N., and GAMBERRA, M. (2001), 'Banking market structure, financial dependence and growth: international evidence from industry data', Journal of Finance, 56, 617–48.

_____ and STRAHAN, P. E. (2006), 'Finance as a barrier to entry: bank competition and industry structure in local U.S. markets', Journal of Finance, forthcoming.

CICCONE, A., and PAPAIOANNOU, E. (2006), 'Adjustment to target capital, finance, and growth', Frankfurt, mimeo.

_____ _____ (forthcoming), 'Financial development and intersectoral investment: new estimates and evidence', ECB WP Series.

CLAESSENS S., and LAEVEN, L. (2005), 'Financial dependence, banking sector competition, and economic growth', *Journal of the European Economic Association*, 3, 179–207.

DEMARZO, M. (2005), 'The pooling and tranching of securities: a model of informed intermediation', *Review of Financial Studies*, 18, 1–35.

DEMIRGÜÇ-KUNT, A., and DETRAGIACHE, E. (2002), 'Does deposit insurance increase banking system stability? An empirical investigation', *Journal of Monetary Economics*, 49, 1373–406.

_____ and MAKSIMOVIC, V. (1998), 'Law, finance, and firm growth', *Journal of Finance*, 53, 2107–37.

_____ LAEVEN, L., and LEVINE, R. (2004), 'Regulation, market structure, institutions, and the cost of financial intermediation', *Journal of Money, Credit and Banking*, 36, 593–622.

DEWATRIPONT, M., and TIROLE, J. (1993), *La Réglementation prudentielle des banques*, Lausanne: Éditions Payot.

DINC, S. (2005), 'Politicians and banks: political influences on government-owned banks in emerging countries', *Journal of Financial Economics*, 77, 453–79.

DIAMOND, D. (1984), 'Financial intermediation and delegated monitoring', *Review of Economic Studies*, 51, 393–414.

DJANKOV, S., MCLIESH, C., and SHLEIFER, A. (2006), 'Private credit in 129 countries', *Journal of Financial Economics*, forthcoming.

_____ LA PORTA, R., LÓPEZ-DE-SILANES, F., and SHLEIFER, A. (2003), 'Courts: the Lex Mundi project', *Quarterly Journal of Economics*, 65, 453–517.

_____ _____ _____ _____ (2006), 'The law and economics of self-dealing', Working Paper.

DURNEV, A., MORCK, R., and YEUNG, B. (2003), 'Value enhancing capital budgeting and firm-specific stock returns variation', *Journal of Finance*, 59, 65–106.

ESTY, B. C., and MEGGINSON, W. L. (2003), 'Creditor rights, enforcement, and debt ownership structure: evidence from the global syndicated loan market," *Journal of Quantitative and Financial Analysis*, 38, 37–59.

EUROPEAN CENTRAL BANK (ECB) (2002), 'Report on financial structures', October.

_____ (2005a), 'Indicators of financial integration in the euro area', September.

_____ (2005b), 'Assessing the performance of financial systems', *Monthly Bulletin*, October.

_____ (2006), 'Financial stability review', June.

_____ (2007a), 'Financial integration in Europe', March.

EU COMMISSION (2005a), 'White paper: financial services policy 2005–2010', Brussels, December.

_____ (2005b), 'Cross-border consolidation in the EU financial sector', Commission Staff Working Document SEC (2005) 1398.

FISMAN, R., and LOVE, I. (2003), 'Trade credit, financial intermediary development, and industry growth', *Journal of Finance*, 58, 353–74.

_____ _____ (2004), 'Financial development and growth in the short and long run', NBER Working Paper 10236.

GOLDSMITH, R. (1969), *Financial Structure and Development*, New Haven: Yale University Press.

GOODHART, C., HARTMANN, P., LLEWELLYN, D., ROJAS-SUAREZ L., and WEISBROD, S. (1998), *Financial Regulation: Why, How and Where Now?*, London: Routledge.

GORTON, G., and PENNACCHI, G. (1990), 'Financial intermediaries and liquidity creation', *Journal of Finance*, 45, 49–71.

GREENWOOD, J., and JOVANOVIC, B. (1990), 'Financial development, growth, and the distribution of income', *Journal of Political Economy*, 98, 1076–107.

GUISO, L., SAPIENZA, P., and ZINGALES, L. (2004), 'The role of social capital in financial development', *American Economic Review*, 94, 526–56.

—— —— —— (2005a), 'Cultural biases in economic exchange', CEPR Discussion Paper 4837, January.

—— —— —— (2005b), 'The cost of banking regulation', Working Paper, Northwestern University, September.

GURLEY, J. G., and SHAW, E. S. (1960), *Money in a Theory of Finance*, Washington, DC: Brookings Institution.

HARTMANN, P., MADDALONI, A., and MANGANELLI, S. (2003), 'The euro area financial system: structure, integration and policy initiatives', *Oxford Review of Economic Policy*, 19, 180–213.

—— FERRANDO, A., FRITZER, F., HEIDER, F., LAURO, B., and LO DUCA, M. (2005), 'The performance of the European financial system', mimeo, European Central Bank.

HARTZELL, J. T., and STARKS, L. T. (2003), 'Institutional investors and executive compensation', *Journal of Finance*, 58, 2351–75.

HOGGARTH, G., REIS, R., and SAPORTA, V. (2001), 'Costs of banking system stability: some empirical evidence', *Financial Stability Review*, 10, 175–82.

HOLMSTRÖM, B., and TIROLE, J. (1993), 'Market liquidity and performance monitoring', *Journal of Political Economy*, 101, 678–709.

HONOHAN, P., and KLINGEBIEL, D. (2003), 'The fiscal cost implications of an accommodating approach to banking crises', *Journal of Banking and Finance*, 27, 1539–69.

JAYARATNE, J., and STRAHAN, P. E. (1996), 'The finance-growth nexus: evidence from bank branching deregulation', *Quarterly Journal of Economics*, 111, 639–70.

—— —— (1998), 'Entry restrictions, industry evolution and dynamic efficiency', *Journal of Law and Economics*, 41, 239–74.

JENSEN, M. C., and MECKLING, W. H. (1976), 'Theory of the firm: managerial behaviour, agency costs and ownership structure', *Journal of Financial Economics*, 3, 303–60.

KANE, E., and YU, M. (1995), 'Measuring the true profile of tax-payer losses in the S&L insurance mess', *Journal of Banking and Finance*, 19, 1459–77.

KAUFMANN, D., KRAAY, A., and MASTRUZZI, M. (2006), 'Governance matters V: governance indicators for 1996–2005', World Bank Institute, www.worldbank.org/wbi/governance/index.html.

KEELEY, M. (1990), 'Deposit insurance, risk and market power in banking', *American Economic Review*, 80, 1183–200.

KING, R., and LEVINE, R. (1993), 'Finance and growth: Schumpeter might be right', *Quarterly Journal of Economics*, 153, 717–38.

LA PORTA, R., LÓPEZ-DE-SILANES, F., and SHLEIFER, A. (2006), 'What works in securities laws?', *Journal of Finance*, 61, 1–32.

—— —— —— and VISHNY, R. (1997), 'Legal determinants of external finance', *Journal of Finance*, 52, 1131–50.

—— —— —— —— (1998), 'Law and finance', *Journal of Political Economy*, 106, 1113–55.

—— —— —— —— (1999), 'Corporate ownership around the world', *Journal of Finance*, 49, 471–517.

—— —— —— —— (2000), 'Investor protection and corporate governance', *Journal of Financial Economics*, 58, 3–27.

—— —— —— —— (2002), 'Government ownership of banks', *Journal of Finance*, 57, 265–302.

LEVINE, R. (2002), 'Bank-based or market-based financial systems: which is better?', *Journal of Financial Intermediation*, 11, 1–30.

——— (2005), 'Finance and growth: theory, evidence, and mechanisms', in P. Aghion and S. Durlauf (eds.), *The Handbook of Economic Growth*, Amsterdam: North Holland.

——— LOAYZA, N., and BECK, T. (2000a), 'Financial intermediation and growth: causality and causes', *Journal of Monetary Economics*, 46, 31–77.

——— ——— ——— (2000b), 'Finance and the sources of growth', *Journal of Financial Economics*, 58, 261–300.

——— and ZERVOS, S. (1998), 'Stock markets, banks, and economic growth', *American Economic Review*, 88, 559–86.

LIPSEY, R. G., and LANCASTER, K. (1956), 'The general theory of second best', *Review of Economic Studies*, 24(1), 11–32.

MCKINNON, R. I. (1973), *Money and Capital in Economic Development*, Washington, DC: Brookings Institution.

MORCK, R., WOLFENZON, D., and YEUNG, B. (2005), 'Corporate governance, economic entrenchment and growth', *Journal of Economic Literature*, 43, 657–722.

——— YEUNG, B., and YU, W. (2000), 'The information content of stock markets: why do emerging markets have synchronous stock price movements?', *Journal of Financial Economics*, 58, 215–60.

MYERS, S., and MAJLUF, N. (1984), 'Corporate financing and investment decisions when firms have information that investors do not have', *Journal of Financial Economics*, 13, 187–221.

PAPAIOANNOU, E. (2005), 'What drives international bank flows: politics, institutions and other determinants', ECB Working Paper 437, February.

QUIAN, J., and STRAHAN, P. (2005), 'How law and institutions shape financial contracts: the case of bank loans', NBER Working Paper 11052.

RAJAN, R. G., and ZINGALES, L. (1998), 'Financial dependence and growth', *American Economic Review*, 88, 559–86.

RANCIERE, R., TORNELL, A., and WESTERMANN, F. (2003), 'Crises and growth: a re-evaluation', NBER Working Paper 10073.

ROSSI, S., and VOLPIN, P. (2004), 'Cross-country determinants of mergers and acquisitions', *Journal of Financial Economics*, 74(2), 277–304.

SANTOS, J., and TSATSARONIS, K. (2003), 'The cost of barriers to entry: evidence from the market for corporate euro bond underwriting', BIS Working Paper 134.

SAPIENZA, P. (2004), 'The effects of government ownership on bank lending', *Journal of Financial Economics*, 72, 357–84.

SCHMIEDEL, H., MALKAMÄKI, M., and TARKKA, J. (2006), 'Economies of scale and technological development in securities depository and settlement systems', *Journal of Banking and Finance* (Special Issue on Frontiers in Payment and Settlement Systems), 30, 1783–806.

SCHUMPETER, J. (1912), *Theorie der wirtschaftlichen Entwicklung*, Munich: Duncker and Humblot.

SHLEIFER, A., and VISHNY, R. (1986), 'Large shareholder and corporate control', *Journal of Political Economy*, 94, 461–88.

——— and WOLFENZON, D. (2002), 'Investor protection and equity markets', *Journal of Financial Economics*, 66, 3–27.

SPAMANN, H. (2006), 'On the insignificance and/or endogeneity of La Porta et al.'s anti-director rights index under consistent coding', John M. Olin Center for Law, Economics and Business Fellow's Discussion Paper no. 67/2006.

STIGLITZ, J. E., and WEISS, A. (1981), 'Credit rationing in markets with imperfect information', *American Economic Review*, 71, 393–410.

STRAHAN, P. E. (2003), 'The real effects of US banking deregulation', *Federal Reserve Bank of St Louis Review*, 85, 111–28.

TOBIN, J. (1969), 'A general equilibrium approach to monetary theory', *Journal of Money, Credit, and Banking*, 1, 15–29.

WURGLER, J. (2000), 'Financial markets and the allocation of capital', *Journal of Financial Economics*, 58, 187–214.

CHAPTER 5

MEASURING EUROPEAN FINANCIAL INTEGRATION

LIEVEN BAELE

ANNALISA FERRANDO

PETER HÖRDAHL

ELIZAVETA KRYLOVA

CYRIL MONNET

1. INTRODUCTION

DURING the last decade, the European financial landscape has changed dramatically, and the establishment of the Economic and Monetary Union (EMU) seems to have

This chapter draws on the results of a project on 'Measuring financial integration in the euro area', conducted while Lieven Baele and Elizaveta Krylova were visiting the European Central Bank (ECB). Lieven Baele also wishes to acknowledge partial financial support from the 'Interuniversity attraction poles' programme of the Belgian Federal Science Policy Office (Contract no. P 5/21). The authors would like to thank Jesper Berg, Vitor Gaspar, Philipp Hartmann, Hans-Joachim Klöckers, Francesco Mongelli, and Francesco Papadia for providing useful comments at various stages of the project, as well as an anonymous referee for helpful suggestions. The views expressed in this chapter are those of the authors and do not necessarily reflect those of the ECB, the Eurosystem, or the Bank for International Settlements.

accelerated the pace of these changes. One important change has been the continued process of integration in European financial markets. However, some segments of the market seem to have made greater progress than others in terms of integration.

The objective of this chapter is to present a set of specific measures to assess (i) the current level of integration in different euro area financial markets and (ii) whether integration is progressing, stable, or regressing. The measures proposed here are applied to a number of key markets in the euro area, namely the money, corporate bond, government bond, credit, and equity markets. We exclusively focus on the euro area, as these countries have chosen to integrate not only economically but also monetarily by adopting the euro and a single monetary policy.

As a working definition of financial integration,[1] we use the law of one price, which states that in financially integrated markets, assets generating identical cash flows should be priced identically, irrespective of where they are transacted. We consider two broad categories of measures based upon the law of one price: price-based and news-based measures.

Price-based indicators measure discrepancies in prices or returns on assets caused by the geographic origin of the assets. If assets have sufficiently comparable characteristics, cross-market price or yield differentials over time constitute a measure of time-varying market integration that is easy to calculate and interpret. If assets have different risk characteristics, however, prices have to be made comparable first by correcting for differences in systematic risk. As a measure of the degree of integration in a particular market segment, we frequently use the cross-sectional dispersion of interest rate spreads or asset-return differentials. An increase in the degree of market integration should lead to a convergence in cross-country yields (returns), and hence a decrease in their cross-sectional dispersion.

Our second broad category of integration measures is news based. The main idea behind this indicator is that common news should become a more important driver of local asset-price fluctuations as integration increases. Suppose an asset whose price fluctuations are exclusively the result of variation in the discount factor. As market integration increases, cross-country discount rates should fully converge, and asset returns should become increasingly correlated. Empirically, we test this by relating local asset returns to those in a benchmark asset, typically a representative asset in the most liquid and integrated market. As a measure of integration, we use both the time-varying sensitivity of local asset returns to movements in the benchmark asset's price, as well as the proportion of local asset returns explained by the common factor.

In the case of euro-denominated bonds with the same maturity and cash flow structure, we expect yields to move perfectly in tandem with the yield on the benchmark asset, and local yield changes should be 100 per cent explained by yield innovations in the benchmark asset. Local news may, even in financially integrated markets, continue to drive local bond yields through its effect on the bonds' default probability. However, we expect this component to be relatively small for government bonds, especially for bonds from countries with the same credit rating.

---

[1] For a broader definition of financial integration, see, for example, Baele et al. 2004.

Unlike bonds, equity prices do not only move because of a change in the discount rate, but also because of revisions in cash flow expectations. As a result, a rising importance of common shocks in explaining local stock returns may be the result of a gradual convergence in discount rates and/or in cash flow expectations. The latter may be especially important for the euro area, as it has gone through a period of considerable economic integration. Moreover, a convergence in the discount rate is likely to be also the result of a convergence in real interest rates and inflation (expectations), and hence of the process of European monetary integration. However, previous research (see, for example, Campbell and Ammer 1993) has shown changes in stock returns to be mainly determined by changes in expected returns, and to a much lesser extent by changes in cash flow expectations. Consequently, an increase in the exposure of local equity returns to a common benchmark portfolio should be to a large extent the result of a convergence in expected returns, and hence an increasing degree of integration.

Notice that, prior to 1999, discount rates may have been different across markets because of the existence of an exchange rate risk premium, and not necessarily because of a lack of financial integration. Consequently, our indicators can be considered pure integration measures only after the introduction of the single currency in 1999. However, as during the years preceding 1999 most currencies operated within a narrow band around the European Currency Unit (ECU), we expect this component not to dominate the other discount rate components. Still, our measures before 1999 should be interpreted with care.

In addition to the price- and news-based measures, we also offer a number of quantity-based indicators. More specifically, we investigate whether the recent efforts to strengthen financial integration have induced investors to internationalize their portfolios. A reduction in the barriers to cross-border investments should induce investors to reap fully the large potential benefits from international diversification by increasingly holding non-domestic assets. Finally, at the beginning of each section, we give a brief overview of the main market events that have been instrumental to the current degree of integration in each market.

In the remainder of this chapter, we evaluate the degree and evolution of integration in, in turn, the money market, government bond market, corporate bond market, credit market, and equity market. Section 7 concludes.

2. Euro Area Money Markets

The money market is commonly defined as the market for short-term debt, where 'short-term' means a maturity of up to one year. There are various segments within the money market, and this section focuses on the unsecured and the repo market segments. Other segments of the money market are not explored, either owing to data limitations, as in the case of the commercial paper segment, or because the market is

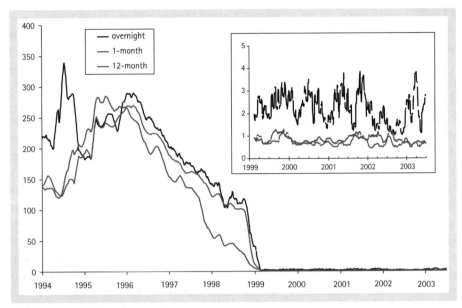

Fig. 5.1. Cross-sectional standard deviation of unsecured lending rates among euro area countries (thirty-day moving average, basis points)

Source: European Banking Federation, Global Financial Data Inc., authors' calculations

concentrated almost completely outside the euro area, as in the case of short-term interest-rate (Euribor) futures and options.[2] Some limited evidence on integration of euro area swap markets can be found in Baele et al. (2004).

2.1. The Unsecured Deposit Market Segment

The unsecured deposit market is where banks exchange short-term liquidity without any collateral as guarantee. When examining price-based measures of integration in the euro area unsecured money market, we focus on interest rate differentials between countries. The characteristics of money market instruments or transactions in individual euro area countries are similar enough for us to allow direct interest rate comparisons to be informative regarding the degree of integration. Specifically, in perfectly integrated markets, interest rates on contracts of the same type and of the same maturity should be identical across all countries.

Figure 5.1 plots the dispersion of overnight, one-month, and twelve-month lending rates in the euro area, measured as the cross-sectional standard deviation of such rates among the twelve average country rates (eleven before 2001) at each point in time. Specifically, for the period after 1998, this measure is based on average lending rates for each of the euro area countries, as reported by the banks participating in

---

[2] After an initial period during which EURIBOR futures and options were actively traded on both LIFFE in London and EUREX in Frankfurt, trading activity subsequently became almost completely concentrated on LIFFE.

the EONIA and Euribor panels.[3] The figure also includes five years of pre-EMU data (for those countries where data are available, but excluding Greece) to provide some perspective on this measure.[4] The chart shows that the cross-sectional standard deviations were of the order of several hundred basis points in the mid-1990s. The convergence process appears to have started around late 1996 or early 1997, bringing the standard deviations down considerably by late 1998. Following the introduction of the euro on 4 January 1999, the cross-sectional standard deviations collapsed to very low levels for all maturities, and have remained low ever since. Of course, the elimination of exchange rate risk and the gradual harmonization of national economic policies, rather than increased market integration, are likely to have accounted for the bulk of the drop in interest rate dispersion during the run-up to EMU. After 1998, when exchange rate risks were eliminated, this measure should be much more informative about the state of integration. As shown by the insert in Figure 5.1, the post-EMU standard deviations have remained at just a few basis points since the beginning of 1999, indicating a high degree of integration in the unsecured market segment. This result is in line with Adam et al. (2002), and with Hartmann et al. (2001), who examined the microstructure of the euro area money market using a short intra day sample based on quotations by brokers in several countries.

It may be interesting to examine whether the discrepancies between country rates that show up after 1998 in Figure 5.1 are larger than the 'normal' dispersion among banks within each member state. In an integrated market, we would not expect the cross-country dispersion to be greater than the within-country dispersion. We use the daily EONIA and Euribor panel data to try to investigate this issue. The specific measure we use is based on (i) all possible combinations of absolute lending rate differences between panel banks reported on a given day in any two different EMU countries; and (ii) all possible combinations of such absolute differences between panel banks within any given country. Calculating the ratio between the average of (i) and the average of (ii) for each day gives us our measure of integration. The ratio between these two measures of dispersion should be close to one if the market is fully integrated, since integration would imply that rates are not more dispersed across countries than within countries.[5] Figure 5.2 plots this ratio for the three maturities

---

[3] Specifically, the overnight rate for each country is the average of the overnight lending rates reported by the EONIA panel banks in the respective country, weighted by the total overnight lending amount, while the longer unsecured rates are simple averages of the indicative quotations from Euribor panel banks in each country. The data are gathered by the European Banking Federation (EBF). We thank the EBF for making these data, as well as data from the Euribor and EUREPO panels, available to us.

[4] The pre-EMU period is added for comparison reasons; it should be recognized that there is no reason why the overnight rates among individual countries should be identical prior to EMU, although increased coordination of policies would tend to result in convergence of rates.

[5] Notice that this is not a perfect measure of integration, as the data set only comprises information on the daily average lending rates/quotations of the contributing banks. This means that we cannot differentiate between domestic and cross-border transactions (for overnight rates) or quotations (for longer rates). Moreover, the EONIA/Euribor panel consists of large banks, which are likely to be more involved in cross-border transactions than smaller banks, hence possibly reducing the average rate difference between banks in our panel. In this case, our measure may tend to overstate somewhat the degree of integration in the market.

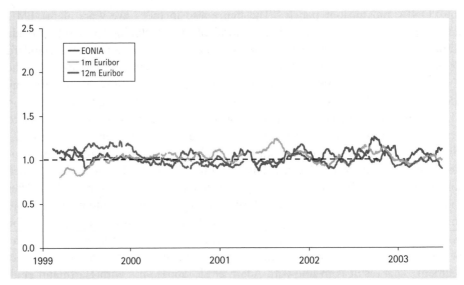

Fig. 5.2. Ratio between average cross-country unsecured interest rate deviations and average within-country deviations (thirty-day moving average)

Source: European Banking Federation, authors' calculations

considered before. As shown in the chart, the ratio has been quite close to one since the introduction of the euro, for all three maturities, consistent with a high degree of integration in the unsecured money market. Moreover, this measure suggests that the high degree of integration has been an enduring feature of this market since 1999.

2.2. The Repo Market Segment

In the repo market, financial agents exchange securities for liquidity, with a simultaneous agreement to reverse the transaction at some pre-specified future date and at a pre-set price. By contrast with developments in the unsecured money market, the euro area repo market segment has been making slower progress towards integration, despite some considerable improvement. Initially, various factors contributed to impeding the process of integration of the euro area repo market, including a lack of standardized and harmonized legal documentation in the market. Such problems have gradually been addressed—for example, with the introduction of the EUREPO index as the benchmark for secured money market transactions in the euro area.[6]

Poor data availability significantly restricts the range of possible integration indicators that can be implemented for the repo market. The introduction of the EUREPO index in early 2002 improved matters somewhat, in that it brought with

---

[6] EUREPO is the rate at which one prime bank offers funds in euro to another prime bank in exchange for EUREPO general collateral (GC). The daily EUREPO index is calculated as an average of quotations obtained from a representative panel of prime banks for each of the maturities considered. See www.eurepo.org for further details.

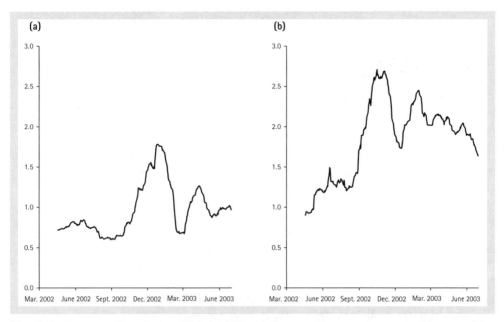

Fig. 5.3. Cross-sectional standard deviation of repo rates among euro area countries (thirty-day moving average, basis points) (a) One-month maturity (b) Twelve-month maturity

Source: European Banking Federation, authors' calculations

it the possibility of comparing repo quotations across individual euro area countries. Figure 5.3 plots the cross-sectional standard deviation of one- and twelve-month repo rates across country averages of the quotations reported by the banks participating in the EUREPO panel. The figure shows that the cross-sectional standard deviation has remained relatively low throughout this short sample period, suggesting that the degree of integration in the euro area repo market has been reasonably high during this period, albeit somewhat lower than in the unsecured market segment.

Turning to the degree of cross-country dispersion relative to the degree of within-country dispersion, the daily EUREPO quotations of the banks participating in the panel allow us to study the ratio of these two average dispersions. As shown in Figure 5.4, this measure of integration has tended to deviate from one more than in the case of the EONIA or the Euribor market segments, suggesting that the degree of integration in the repo market is lower than in these other segments. Looking at the results for the two different maturities, it seems that for the twelve month maturity, the cross-country to within-country ratio has exhibited more pronounced deviations from one than for the one-month maturity. This may reflect the fact that much of the trading in the repo market is concentrated at short maturities, and that a lack of liquidity for longer maturities may tend to hamper integration for these market segments. However, at the same time, the degree of cross-country dispersion in repo rates should not be exaggerated: the average cross-country twelve-month repo rate

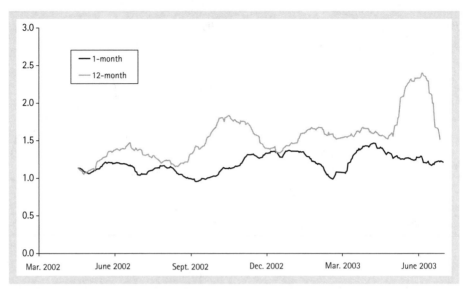

Fig. 5.4. Ratio between average cross–country EUREPO rate deviations and average within–country deviations (thirty-day moving average)

Source: European Banking Federation, authors' calculations

difference is 1.6 basis points, compared to 1.1 basis points for the average within-country difference.

3. Euro Area Government Bond Markets

Similarly to the case of the money market, the introduction of the euro and a common monetary policy has had, both directly and indirectly, a considerable impact on the euro area government bond markets. With the elimination of exchange rate risk, investors have started to focus more on credit and liquidity risk. At the same time, bond portfolios became increasingly internationally diversified, especially in the smaller euro area countries. In this more competitive environment, governments have put great effort into making their outstanding debt and new issues more attractive to international investors. First, in an effort to improve liquidity, issue sizes have become bigger and sovereign issuers, particularly small countries, have started to focus increasingly on creating benchmark issues. Second, debt managers have made issuance activity more regular and predictable by introducing pre-announced auction calendars, thereby improving market transparency. At the same time, trading of government bonds is increasingly taking place on electronic trading platforms (such as EuroMTS), and less and less over the counter (OTC). Finally, the development of a highly liquid interest rate swap and futures market has made it much easier for investors to hedge interest rate risks, thereby further contributing to the bond market's liquidity.

3.1. Price-based Measures of Government Bond Market Integration

As argued before, the law of one price should hold in financially integrated markets. Insofar as government bonds are sufficiently homogeneous across the various euro area markets, one can directly test the law of one price by comparing the yields on local government bonds with the yield that would prevail in perfectly integrated markets. As the latter is not directly available, most studies have used benchmark bond yields instead. In the ten-year segment, German bonds are considered the benchmark to which other bonds should be compared, while in the shorter to maturity segments, French bonds seem to have a slight edge over German bonds.

Notice, however, that, in practice, government bond markets may not be perfect substitutes. Most importantly, before 1999, exchange rate risk was a source of considerable yield differences, even between otherwise identical government bonds. While this component disappeared completely after 1999, yields may still differ because of differences in perceived credit and liquidity risk.[7] As a consequence, part of the yield differences may be the result of systematic risk differences rather than a lack of integration. To partly offset this problem, we only consider the most liquid bonds,[8] while in the discussion we explicitly compare government bonds with an identical credit rating.

In Table 5.1, we report the average yield spread relative to Germany for the different euro area countries over time. Whereas countries such as Austria, Belgium, France, and the Netherlands had relatively low yield spreads relative to Germany over most of the last decade, the yields in Finland, Ireland, Italy, Portugal, Spain, and, more recently, Greece have exhibited a dramatic convergence toward German levels. The dramatic decrease of interest rates in the latter countries towards the German levels mainly reflects the convergence in economic fundamentals, especially the decrease in expected inflation following the introduction of a common monetary policy. While the level of convergence is impressive, integration in euro area government bond markets is not complete, in the sense that yields of government bonds with similar, or in some cases identical, credit risk and maturity have not entirely converged. For instance, even though Austria, Finland, France, Ireland, and the Netherlands all share the Aaa credit rating with Germany, in 2002 their governments had to pay on average 16.8, 18.2, 8.4, 21.6, and 11.1 basis points more than Germany. Note, however, that relative to 2000 levels, spreads in most countries appear to have decreased further in 2001 and 2002. As argued before, differences in liquidity across markets may account

---

[7] For more information about the determinants of yield differences, see, for example, Codogno, Favero, and Missale 2003 and Favero, Paganot, and von Thadden 2004.

[8] More specifically, we use Datastream's *benchmark* bond indices.

Table 5.1. Average yield spread for ten-year government bonds relative to Germany

	Austria Aaa	Finland Aaa	France Aaa	Ireland Aaa	The Netherlands Aaa	Belgium Aa1	Spain Aa1	Italy Aa2	Portugal Aa2	Greece Aa2
1993	18.4	230.1	25.5	119.9	−16.2	70.6	369.9	467.2	468.1	1685.7
1994	16.6	217.5	35.3	122.9	0.2	88.8	313.3	365.8	361.2	1402.7
1995	28.4	194.0	68.6	160.2	4.9	63.1	442.7	535.7	462.1	1042.6
1996	11.3	88.3	11.6	115.0	−5.9	27.8	252.2	313.1	235.5	842.0
1997	3.3	76.5	−7.1	65.1	−7.3	10.1	73.9	118.0	71.8	454.4
1998	16.3	24.6	8.5	24.5	7.0	19.1	27.8	33.7	28.6	393.3
1999	20.3	22.6	11.8	21.6	14.1	26.2	24.2	25.1	31.2	190.8
2000	29.9	20.3	13.9	25.2	15.2	33.3	27.0	33.3	35.1	82.2
2001	27.4	22.8	13.3	19.3	14.9	32.0	28.8	37.5	35.8	48.9
2002	16.8	18.2	8.4	21.6	11.1	19.8	15.2	24.2	22.6	32.3

Sources: Datastream, authors' calculations. Credit ratings (end 2002) are from Moody's.

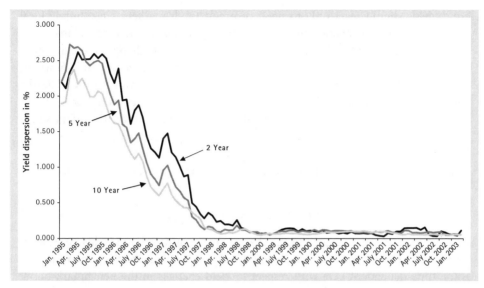

Fig. 5.5. Dispersion in government bond yield spreads for two-, five-, and ten-year maturities

Source: ECB

for a sizeable portion of the observed differences in bond yields. This suggests that further market liquidity-enhancing policy measures may considerably reduce debt-servicing costs.

A similar picture emerges from Figure 5.5, which plots the cross-sectional dispersion in yield spreads across countries for the ten-year, five-year, and two-year maturities.[9] Dispersions in monthly yields in the ten-year segment have fallen from an average of 1.98 in 1993 to 0.06 in 2002, or by more than 97 per cent. The cross-sectional dispersion for the two- and five-year maturities follows closely the pattern observed for the ten-year maturity bonds. Notice, however, that before 1998, the dispersion in ten-year government bond yield spreads was systematically lower compared to the other segments. While the degree of dispersion is comparably low for all maturities after the introduction of the single currency, no further decrease is observed after 1999.

3.2. News-based Measures of Government Bond Market Integration

While most studies of government bond market integration have focused on yields, the following set of indicators investigates the extent to which changes in local yields are driven by common rather than by local news.[10] When markets are fully integrated,

---

[9] Previous studies reported the cross-sectional dispersion in yields rather than in the spread relative to Germany. By using the yield spread, we hope partly to eliminate potential level effects, i.e. the empirical regularity that interest rate volatility tends to be positively related with the level of interest rates.

[10] A similar approach is followed by Christiansen 2003.

bond yields should react only to news common to all markets, since purely local risk factors can be diversified away by investing in bonds in different regions. Local news may affect bond yields, but only to the extent that it changes the perception market participants have about the euro area economy as a whole. This, however, presupposes that the degree of systematic risk is identical across countries. Clearly, before 1999, considerable differences in interest rate dynamics were due to time-varying exchange rate risk premia. In addition, also after the introduction of the single currency, differences in credit and liquidity risk may prevent common factors from fully explaining local bond yields.

To separate the effects of local and common news, we estimate the following regression:

$$\Delta R_{i,t} = a_{i,t} + \beta_{i,t} \Delta R_{B,t} + \varepsilon_{i,t} \tag{1}$$

where $\Delta R_{i,t}$ and $\Delta R_{B,t}$ represent the change in government bond yields for, respectively, country i and the benchmark country B, $a_{i,t}$ is a time-varying intercept, $\beta_{i,t}$ is the time-dependent beta with respect to yield changes in the benchmark bond, and $\varepsilon_{i,t}$ is a country-specific shock. Under the assumption that $a_{i,t} = 0$, equation (1) decomposes the total yield change in a component due to common news, $\beta_{i,t} \Delta R_{B,t}$, and a purely local news component, $\varepsilon_{i,t}$.

Because we are not only interested in the parameters' magnitude, but also in their dynamics over time, we use a simple moving regression technique. Specifically, we start by estimating the parameters using the first eighteen months of data. We then repeatedly move the data window one month ahead and re-estimate, until the last observation has been reached. By using this simple procedure, we obtain a time series for both $a_{i,t}$ and $\beta_{i,t}$.

As integration increases, we expect (i) the beta with respect to the benchmark asset, $\beta_{i,t}$, to converge to one, and (ii) the proportion of the variance in $\Delta R_{i,t}$ explained by the common factor, $\Delta R_{b,t}$, to increase towards one. To see why (i) should hold, recall that the estimate for $\beta_{i,t}$ is given by

$$\beta_{it} = \frac{Cov_{t-1}(\Delta R_{i,t}, \Delta R_{b,t})}{Var_{t-1}(\Delta R_{b,t})} = \rho_{i,b,t}\frac{\sigma_{i,t}}{\sigma_{b,t}} \tag{2}$$

where Cov_{t-1} and Var_{t-1} are, respectively, the conditional covariance and variance operators, $\rho_{i,b,t}$ is the conditional correlation between yield (price) changes of the local and the benchmark assets, and $\sigma_{i,t}$ and $\sigma_{b,t}$ are the conditional standard deviations of these yield (price) changes respectively. Hence, $\beta_{i,t}$ depends on both the correlation between local and benchmark yield changes, and the ratio between local and benchmark yield volatilities. When integration increases, yield changes should increasingly be driven by common factors, and the correlation should increase towards one. For the same reason, the level of local volatility should converge towards that of the benchmark asset. As a result, increasing integration implies that $\beta_{i,t}$ should converge to one.

Condition (ii) follows from the fact that, to the extent that assets are sufficiently comparable across countries, the country-specific error $\varepsilon_{i,t}$ should shrink as integration increases. We therefore use the proportion of local variance explained by the common factor as another measure of integration. Under full integration, only common news should drive local yields (under the assumption that the degree of systematic risk is identical across bonds), and the variance proportion should be close to 100 per cent. Alternatively, when yields are driven purely by local factors, this ratio will be zero. To calculate the variance ratio, first note that $\Delta R_{b,t}$ and $\varepsilon_{i,t}$ are orthogonal by construction. The total variance of local yields is then given by

$$Var(\Delta R_{i,t}) = \beta_{i,t}^2 Var(\Delta R_{b,t}) + Var(\varepsilon_{i,t}) \qquad (3)$$

and the variance ratio by

$$VR_{i,t} = \frac{\beta_{i,t}^2 Var(\Delta R_{b,t})}{Var(\Delta R_{i,t})}. \qquad (4)$$

The variance ratio $VR_{i,t}$ is positively related to the beta of local yield changes with respect to the benchmark asset, and with the relative size of volatility in the benchmark and local bond market. A variance ratio close to one is obtained when the beta goes to unity and when the volatility in local and benchmark bond yield changes are of similar magnitude.

Figure 5.6 reports the evolution of the estimated beta coefficients through time for the ten-year segment. Given its high development, we use the rates from the German ten-year government bond market as a benchmark. .Betas varied substantially across countries until around 1998, when they converged considerably. Again, Greece was an exception owing to its later membership of the monetary union. To understand better the dynamics of the betas over time, it is instructive to look at the evolution

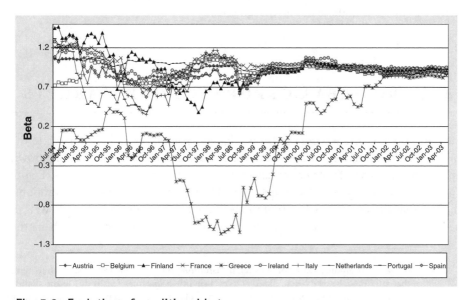

Fig. 5.6. Evolution of conditional betas

Source: Datastream, authors' calculations

of two components of the betas.[11] First, in all countries, the correlation of local yield changes with those in Germany gradually increased and reached levels close to one as of the beginning of 1999. This increase largely explains why the betas of countries that initially had relatively low betas (especially Italy, Greece, Portugal, and Spain) gradually increased to levels close to one by 1999 (January 2002 for Greece). Second, we observe that while the level of yield volatility in many countries was considerably higher than in Germany, yield volatilities have converged strongly since 1999. This suggests that local bond markets are considerably less affected by idiosyncratic local news than before (this effect, of course, also includes the elimination of exchange rate risk). This further contributes to the convergence of betas to values close to one.[12]

As a final measure, Table 5.2 reports the proportion of variance in local yield changes that is explained by changes in benchmark government-bond yields. We do not only report results for the ten-year maturity segment, but also for government bonds that are two to five years from maturity. As argued before, German bonds are the natural benchmark in the ten-year segment, whereas we choose French bonds for the two-year and five-year maturity segments.

Before 1998, common news in the ten-year segment explained less than 50 per cent of the total yield variance in Finland, Greece, Italy, Portugal, and Spain. While the variance ratios are considerably higher for the other countries, it is only in 1999 that levels close to 100 per cent are reached. From 2000 onwards, typically less than 5 per cent of yield changes remain unexplained by shocks in the benchmark bond market, suggesting a very high degree of integration in this segment of euro area bond markets.[13] While variance proportions have increased as well in the two- and five-year segments, they do not reach the same high levels as in the ten-year segment. This may, in part, reflect a lower level of liquidity, as well as the absence of well-developed derivatives markets in these maturity segments.

4. EURO AREA CORPORATE BOND MARKETS

The European corporate bond market is relatively young, certainly compared to the government bond market. However, in recent years the size of the market has grown rapidly and the market's structure has undergone some important changes. Before 1998, the market was dominated by debt issued by highly rated financial corporations, whereas thereafter industrial corporations have increasingly found their way to the corporate bond market. Moreover, there has been a dramatic growth in the

---

[11] Charts of the two components are not reported to economize on space, but are available on request.
[12] Notice that after 1999, betas have stabilized at a level slightly *below* one. This is due to the slightly higher volatility of yield changes in German ten-year government bond yields compared to other markets.
[13] The only exception is Greece, where only 54% of government bond yield changes are explained by the common factor. This is, in part, due to the fact that Greece only joined the euro area in 2002.

Table 5.2. Average proportion of local variance explained by benchmark for two-, five-, ten-year maturities (%)

	Rating end 2002	2-year maturity		5-year maturity		10-year maturity	
		1995–8	1999–2003	1995–8	1999–2003	1995–8	1999–2003
Austria	Aaa	60	83	61	92	90	98
Finland	Aaa	38	87	53	85	38	93
France	Aaa	benchmark	benchmark	82	98		
Germany	Aaa	55	88	72	96	benchmark	
Ireland	Aaa	n.a.	n.a.	58	83	77	95
The Netherlands	Aaa	59	93	72	91	95	99
Belgium	Aa1	61	84	70	94	86	98
Spain	Aa1	37	87	59	90	47	96
Italy	Aa2	23	81	46	91	32	94
Portugal	Aa2	44	63	62	85	40	96
Greece	A2	n.a.	n.a.	n.a.	70	7	54

Sources: Datastream, authors' calculations.

lower-rated A and BBB market segments since then. For an overview of the recent development in the corporate bond market, see Carnegie-Brown and King (2003) and Baele et al. (2004).

4.1. Price-based Measures of Corporate Bond Market Integration

A direct comparison of corporate bond yields across countries does not serve as a good indicator of integration, as yield differences may reflect differences in pervasive risk rather than a lack of integration. In order to make yields comparable, for each month, we estimate a cross-sectional regression relating corporate-bond yield spreads[14] to a constant, the bond's coupon, liquidity and time to maturity, and a set of dummies proxying for, respectively, rating and sector.[15] To test for integration, we investigate whether the residuals from this cross-sectional regression—the part of the yield differential not explained by our risk factors—still contain a systematic country component.

For each month, we performed the cross-sectional regression using all corporate bonds contained at that moment in the Merrill Lynch EMU corporate bond market index.[16] The estimation results are contained in Table 5.3. The values for the rating effects are nearly all statistically significant and in line with expectations. Relative to the intercept, which represents the yield on an equally weighted portfolio of all corporate bonds, highly rated bonds have a lower credit spread, as reflected by the negative coefficients for AAA, AA, and A+ rated bonds. Conversely, coefficients for bonds with lower ratings are positive, reflecting higher spreads for A, A–, and BBB-rated bonds. On average, the yield on BBB bonds is about 103 basis point higher than on AAA bonds.

The parameters related to the coupon and the time to maturity are statistically significant, but small in economic terms. The positive sign of the time to maturity effect is in line with the observed upward-sloping term structure of corporate bond spreads. The liquidity effect is statistically significant and has the expected negative sign, reflecting a lower spread for more liquid bonds. The estimates for the sector effect are small and not statistically significant, but the average size of the coefficient confirms the stylized fact that bonds of financial companies have on average lower spreads than non-financials.

---

[14] The yield spread is calculated by subtracting from each corporate bond yield the zero coupon yield on a German government bond with identical time to maturity.

[15] For a more detailed discussion of this estimation procedure, see Baele et al. 2004.

[16] This index covers the largest part of the most liquid European investment grade corporate bonds. To obtain sensible estimates for the country effects, we eliminate data from countries that do not have at least ten bonds in the index over the full period. This leaves us with six euro area countries (Austria, France, Germany, Ireland, the Netherlands, and Spain). Thus our original sample of 2,215 individual corporate bonds has shrunk to 1,256 bonds.

Table 5.3. Average parameter estimates for cross-sectional regression (with *p*-values)

Rating effect			Country effect		
AAA	−33.79	0.00	Austria	2.21	0.00
AA1	−23.09	0.00	Germany	−1.54	0.06
AA2	−21.74	0.00	Spain	3.86	0.00
AA3	−14.66	0.00	France	−7.64	0.00
A1	−2.55	0.21	Ireland	5.78	0.00
A2	17.94	0.00	The Netherlands	−0.57	0.01
A3	24.10	0.00			
BBB	69.46	0.00			
			Common effect	86.52	0.00
Sector effect			Maturity effect	1.88	0.00
Financial	−0.27	0.19	Coupon effect	4.17	0.00
Non-financial	0.31	0.38	Liquidity effect	−66.19	0.00

Given the correction for risk, we can obtain measures of corporate bond market integration by investigating whether or not risk-adjusted yield spreads have a systematic country component. In a first step, we relate the risk-adjusted spreads to a number of country dummies. Under the hypothesis of full integration, the parameters related to the country dummies should not be statistically different from zero. As a measure of overall corporate bond market integration, we calculate at each point in time the proportion of total yield spread variance explained by country effects. In a highly integrated market, this proportion should be close to zero.

As is shown in Table 5.3, in every case except Germany, the parameter related to the country dummy is statistically significant at the 5 per cent level, but the country-specific spread is relatively small in economic terms. Spanish, Irish, and Austrian corporations pay country premia of about 4, 6, and 2 basis points, respectively, while French corporations get a premium of about 8 basis points. The premium is close to zero for Germany and the Netherlands. These country premia are only slightly higher than for the government bond market and, moreover, not statistically significant for Germany.[17] Therefore, these results indicate that the corporate bond market is reasonably well integrated.

To get an understanding of the relative importance of the various factors, we calculate the proportion of cross-sectional variance explained by the various components over time.[18] On average, the factors explain about 33 per cent of the cross-sectional variance, which is of similar magnitude to that in other studies (see, for example, Varotto 2003). The bulk of the total variance explained can be attributed to the rating effect, which on average explains 25 per cent of the total variance. The common, coupon, maturity, liquidity, and sector effects explain the remaining 8 per cent.

[17] We should take into account that we constructed our spreads with respect to German government bond yield. Another approach would be to use government bond yields of each corresponding country.
[18] For detailed results, see Baele et al. 2004.

Country effects explain a very small proportion of the cross-sectional variance of corporate bond yield spreads—typically no more than 2 per cent, confirming that the degree of corporate bond market integration is reasonably high.

4.2. Quantity-based Measures of Corporate Bond Market Integration

Further information on the dynamics of bond market integration can be gained from data on international portfolio compositions of institutional investors. As the data do not permit us to investigate government and corporate bond holdings separately, we treat them jointly.

Figure 5.7 shows the proportion of assets invested in bond market funds with a European-wide investment strategy for eight euro area countries, together with an unweighted average across these countries. The chart clearly displays a general upward trend in the relative size of Europe-wide bond investment funds, including a particularly pronounced increase coinciding with the introduction of the euro. Overall, while the average market share amounted to only 17 per cent in 1998, it had increased to about 60 per cent by 2002. Over this period, the share of European-wide managed bond funds increased in all countries.

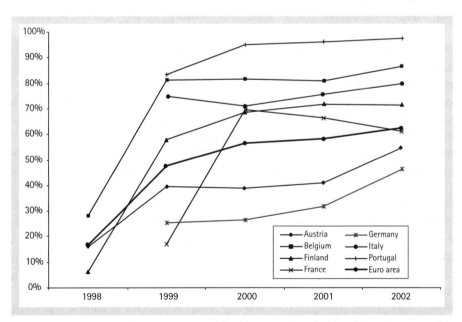

Fig. 5.7. Proportion of assets invested in bond market funds with a Europe–wide investment strategy

Source: Fédération Européenne des Fonds et Sociétés d'Investissement (FEFSI) and authors' calculations

To determine whether the increasing share of funds with a Europe-wide investment strategy is part of a general trend towards more global diversification, rather than the result of increasing European bond market integration, we compared the average share of bond funds with, respectively, European or global investment strategies. Throughout the last five years, the share of bond funds with a global bond allocation strategy has remained more or less constant at around 20 per cent, while the share of Europe-wide bond funds has increased dramatically. This indicates that the reduction in the home bias in bond portfolios was restricted to the euro area only, suggesting that bond market integration has increased to a much greater extent between the various euro area markets than between world bond markets. Hence, our results suggest that while the country home bias has largely been eliminated, it may instead have been replaced with a 'euro area home bias'.

5. EURO AREA CREDIT MARKETS

In this section we focus mainly on the retail banking market, where integration has clearly been slower than in other banking activities. Previous studies showed that the degree of integration in the retail banking system was quite limited at the beginning of the 1990s, but that it increased slightly just before the introduction of the single currency in 1999. However, in contrast to some of the other markets considered in this article, the introduction of the single currency does not seem to have represented a clear watershed.[19] There are many reasons for this. First of all, retail lending products are less exposed to international competition pressures, as proximity to customers is quite important. Asymmetric information and the existence of switching costs are additional reasons for less competitive and integrated retail banking markets.

This notwithstanding, strong efforts towards liberalization and integration were made on the regulatory side. These efforts started well before the 1990s with the introduction of the First (1977) and Second (1988) Banking Directives and continued with the publication of the Financial Services Action Plan (FSAP) in 1999. As regards retail financial services, one of the FSAP's stated strategic objectives was the creation of open and secure retail markets. In this respect, the FSAP proposed nine specific measures aimed at eliminating price differentials across the EU and enhancing consumer protection. Since then, most of those measures have been adopted. In this respect, integration in the euro area banking markets may be considered quite advanced from a legal perspective. The apparent lack of integration in this market segment suggests that there are other types of non-regulatory barriers to integration that have remained in place. In this context, we need to be able to measure market

---

[19] See, for instance, Cabral Dierick, and Vesala. 2002 and Kleimeier and Sander 2002.

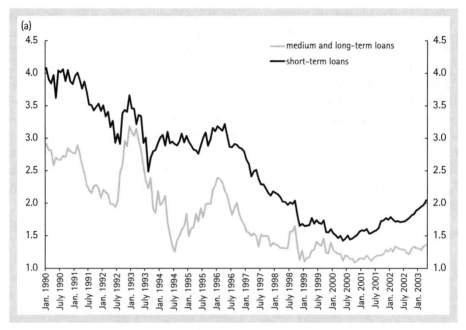

Fig. 5.8a. Cross–sectional standard deviation of interest rates on short–term and medium– and long–term loans to enterprises Part b: Cross–sectional standard deviation of interest rates on consumer and mortgage loans

Source: ECB, authors' calculations

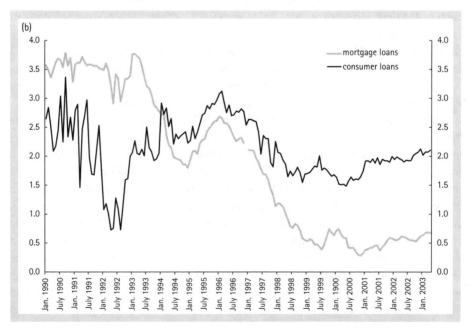

Fig. 5.8b. Cross–sectional standard deviation of interest rates on consumer and mortgage loans

Source: ECB, authors' calculations

integration accurately in order to understand better the integration process and help identify any remaining obstacles.

5.1. Price-based Measures of Banking Integration

A rather simple indicator of financial integration is based on the cross-sectional dispersion of interest rates across countries. Under the hypothesis that financial integration should make the returns of comparable but not completely homogeneous financial assets more similar, dispersion should decrease as integration across markets increases.

Figure 5.8 plots the cross-sectional standard deviation since the beginning of the 1990s, excluding Greece from the calculations. For our analysis, we report four lending rates: short-term loans, medium- and long-term loans to enterprises, and loans to households for consumer loans and mortgage loans.[20]

We distinguish between three subperiods. The first period, 1990–4, spans from the removal of short-term capital controls to the ERM crisis of 1992–3 and its aftermath. Interest rates were quite volatile during this period, as shown by the high dispersion of rates, which peaks around 1992–3. This is particularly evident for lending rates to enterprises, for which the dispersion peaked at the end of 1992 owing to high rate increases in Italy, Ireland, and Spain for short-term lending, and in Finland and Ireland for medium- and long-term lending. For lending to consumers, the high variability in the dispersion at the beginning of the 1990s is mainly due to sudden changes in Irish and Spanish rates.

The second period, 1995–8, covers a time when interest differentials were strongly affected by the so-called 'convergence trades' in the financial markets, driven by expectations of EMU. The process induced a general convergence in interest rate levels during this period. Indeed, after peaking in late 1995/early 1996, the dispersion decreased substantially until 1998.[21] Again, in the case of consumer loans the high level of dispersion is due to the persistence of high interest rates in Spain and Portugal, while rate differentials in the other euro area countries were diminishing at the same time. Similarly, Spanish rates highly influenced the dispersion of medium- and long-term term rates.

The third period, 1999 onwards, coincides with the first years of stage 3 of the EMU. With the removal of exchange rate risk within the euro area, we can expect the cross-sectional dispersion measure to be informative with respect to the degree of integration in this market segment during this period. In this last period, the dispersion seems to have decreased for medium- and long-term loans to enterprises

---

[20] The analysis is based on the ECB retail interest rate series, available from the ECB website. Since January 2003, the ECB is publishing new series based upon better-harmonized retail rates. We used the old series as it goes back much further in time. Preliminary evidence indicates, though, that our measures are very similar for the new and old series.

[21] This peak is, in part, explained by the fact that data for some countries are available only from 1995.

and for mortgage loans, while remaining at roughly the same level or even increasing in the case of short-term loans to enterprises and loans for consumer credit.

5.2. News-based Measures of Banking Integration

As for the previous markets, we also present the relative importance of common factors as an indicator of integration. The idea behind this measure is that lending rates should not only converge to the same level as integration increases, they should also react to the same news. This means that lenders belonging to the same risk category but from a different country should be offered the same rate. At the same time, news about the relative riskiness of this group of lenders should affect lenders in different countries in the same way, and purely local news will only have an effect to the extent that it contains information about the riskiness of all investors within this risk category.

Finding an appropriate benchmark for the lending market is not as straightforward as in, for example, the government bond market. To start with, we assume common news to be well reflected by yield movements of government bonds with a comparable maturity.[22] Thus, we first estimate the relationship between the change in the level of a specific bank interest rate in one country and the change in the level of the corresponding benchmark rate during four subperiods, being 1994–6, 1997–8, 1999–2000, and 2001–3. As a measure of integration, we then calculate the percentage of local lending rate changes explained by the yield changes in the benchmark asset. This proportion should increase as integration becomes more complete.

Figure 5.9 plots the average variance ratios among euro area countries that measure the part of local variance of the various bank interest rates explained by the common factors, i.e. the chosen benchmark market interest rates. Overall, the results in the chart suggest that credit market integration in the euro area has advanced significantly since the introduction of the euro only in those segments of the market related to lending to corporations. In particular, in the case of short-term loans to enterprises, the average proportion of variance explained in the years 1994–6 is on average around 9 per cent and remains unchanged in the following two years. Thereafter, the proportion explained by common factors jumps to 32 per cent on average.

For bank interest rates on medium- and long-term loans to enterprises, the average proportion of variance explained by the model is still quite low, although it has increased on average over time (to 38 per cent after 2000, up from 15 per cent in the mid-1990s). Despite the overall increase over the five years, the fact that the average variance ratio is not higher than 40 per cent can be interpreted as an indication that the level of credit market integration reached so far is not particularly high. Turning to the interest rates for loans to households, the lack of integration is even more evident.

---

[22] For interest rates on short-term loans, we choose the three-month money market rate as benchmark, while for the medium- and long-term rates, we use the two-year government bond yield. For consumer loans and loans for house purchases, we employ the yields on two- and five-year government bonds, respectively.

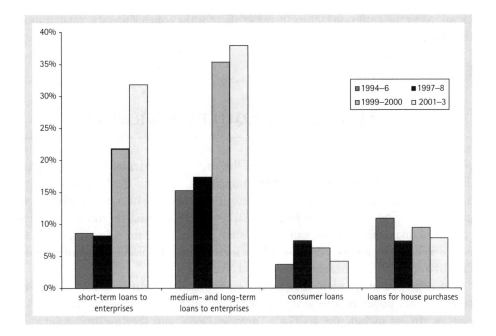

Fig. 5.9. Proportion of variance of various interest rates explained by common factors (euro area average)

Source: ECB, authors' calculations

The variance ratios are very low (around 8–10 per cent) in the case of both consumer credits and mortgage loans, and it seems that there has been no change, on average, in the proportion of variance explained by the model in the last ten years.

Notice, however, that the benchmark market rate is not the only factor determining lending rates. First, lending rates may also change because the risk premia banks charge to their lenders vary through time. More specifically, as the risk of financing projects is larger in recessions than in expansions, lending rates (in excess of the risk-free rate) will typically increase in business downturns. This effect should be more important for lending products with a longer maturity. The dynamics of local lending may also differ across countries because of a different risk structure in the pool of lenders, or because of certain specificities in the lending contract (e.g. a tendency to slightly longer/shorter maturities).

To test for the robustness of our results to time-varying risk premia and certain specificities of the local market, we added the local and euro area term spread[23] as an additional explanatory variable. The term spread is an often used indicator of the state of the business cycle. Generally, we find that while the proportion of variance

---

[23] We include both the short- and long-term term spread. We define the short- (long-) term spread as the difference between government bonds with, respectively, two (ten) years and three months (two years) to maturity.

explained by the common factors increases slightly, the conclusions stay qualitatively the same.

6. Euro Area Equity Markets

At the beginning of the 1990s, the size of the various continental European equity markets was relatively small, especially compared to those in the United Kingdom and the United States. Over the last decade, however, European equity markets have grown faster than both the UK and US markets, and have become more important sources of financing for European corporations. At the same time, investors seem to have developed an equity culture and have increased their holdings of equities, both directly and indirectly through pension and investment funds.

The degree of integration of European equity markets benefited from initiatives taken by both policy makers and market participants. Early milestones in the integration process include the UCITS[24] Directive (1985) and the Investment Services Directive (1993). Recent initiatives are contained in the Financial Services Action Plan (FSAP) and the Lamfalussy report on the regulation of European securities markets, as well as in the work of the Giovannini Group. At a market level, equity market integration was facilitated by technological progress, as well as by competition between stock exchanges to attract (non-domestic) turnover. Consolidation among exchanges has until now been limited to the relatively successful merger of the exchanges of Amsterdam, Brussels, and Paris in September 2000, which now constitute Euronext.[25] At the same time, horizontal consolidation is also taking place in the clearing and settlement infrastructure. This is hoped to bring down cross-border transaction costs as well as to facilitate further consolidation among stock exchanges (see Köppl and Monnet 2004). Despite some consolidation in the clearing and settlement infrastructure, transaction costs remain considerably larger in Europe than in the USA, and will continue to be so unless some considerable progress is made.

6.1. News-based Measures of Equity Market Integration

To what extent have initiatives to promote equity market integration affected the pricing structure of European equities? Similarly to the analysis performed for other markets, we try to answer this question by investigating whether domestic stock returns are increasingly driven by news common to all European investors rather than by purely idiosyncratic shocks. We suppose that news common to all investors is

---

[24] Undertakings for the Collective Investment in Transferable Securities.
[25] Euronext expanded further in 2001, when it acquired LIFFE, the London derivatives trading platform, and agreed to integrate also the Portuguese exchanges of Lisbon and Porto.

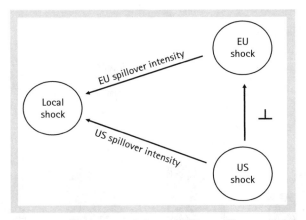

Fig. 5.10. Structure of the volatility spillover model

well reflected in the innovations in the US equity market—a proxy for world news—
and in the European equity market—a proxy for regional European news[26] (see
Figure 5.10). While all country returns share the same factors, they are allowed to
have different sensitivities, or 'betas', to common shocks. These betas measure the
intensity by which euro area and world return shocks are transmitted to local equity
markets. We interpret the part of local returns not explained by the common factors
as the return reaction to purely local news.

To allow the betas, and hence the degree of equity market integration, to vary over
time, we introduce three dummy variables that distinguish between different periods,
relative to the basis period 1973–85. Specifically, we consider the following periods: the
period following the Single European Act (1986–92); the period between the Treaty of
Maastricht and the introduction of the single currency (1992–8); and the post-euro
period (1999–2003). The specification for the betas is then given by

$$\beta_{i,t}^{eu} = \zeta_{i,0} + \zeta_{i,1} D_t^1 + \zeta_{i,2} D_t^2 + \zeta_{i,3} D_t^3$$
$$\beta_{i,t}^{us} = \Psi_{i,0} + \Psi_{i,1} D_t^1 + \Psi_{i,2} D_t^2 + \Psi_{i,3} D_t^3$$

where D_t^1, D_t^2, and D_t^3 are dummies for the three last subperiods listed above.

Figure 5.11 reports the average sensitivities of local equity market returns to common European and US shocks.[27] The average sensitivity to European shocks increased
from about 0.40 in the period 1973–85 to about 0.65 in the period 1986–91, i.e. an
increase of about 63 per cent. The intensity increased a further 17 per cent in the
period 1992–9 and an additional 10 per cent in the period directly following the introduction of the euro. In nearly all cases, period-by-period changes in shock spillover

[26] To separate global from European news, we orthogonalize European and US shocks, assuming that
part of the EU shock is explained by return innovations in the US equity market. Moreover, to avoid
spurious correlation, as a proxy for EU equity market returns, we calculate a market-weighted average of
the equity returns in all countries, except the country whose stock market is being analysed.

[27] More detailed estimates can be found in Baele 2004 and Baele et al. 2004.

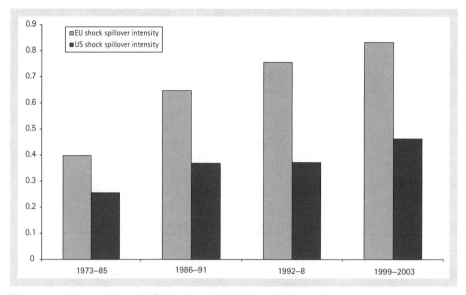

Fig. 5.11. Euro area and US shock spillover intensity

Source: Datastream and authors' calculations

intensities are highly significant. Similar, albeit more modest, increases are found for the US shock spillover intensities. The joint rise in euro area and US shock spillover intensities suggests that the degree of integration has not only increased within the euro area, but also globally among major world equity markets.

Figure 5.12 plots the proportion of local variance explained by euro area and US shocks. As for euro area shocks, the pattern is similar to that observed for the shock spillover intensities. During the period 1973–86, only about 8 per cent of local return variance was explained by common European shocks, but this proportion increased gradually to about 23 per cent in the period 1999–2003. Interestingly, while the importance of US shocks in explaining local variance was higher relative to euro area shocks in the period 1973–91, euro area shocks have become more important since 1992, reflecting the proportionally stronger increase in euro area shock spillover intensities since 1992. This suggests that regional euro area integration has proceeded more quickly than global market integration.

A question that remains is what values for the shock spillover intensities and the variance proportions are to be expected under full equity market integration. Unfortunately, a theoretical benchmark is not readily available, as stock prices are not only determined by discount rates, but also by cash flow expectations. Results for non-European markets may, however, offer some guidance. Bekaert, Harvey, and Ng. (2005) estimate a similar model as in this chapter for a large number of emerging markets. According to their table 2, the proportion of variance explained by European and US shocks amounts to 12.1 per cent for Turkey. In South America, the importance of common factors amounts to 3 per cent in Colombia, 5.7 per cent in Venezuela, but 28.5 per cent in the more developed Argentinan and Brazilian markets. Similar

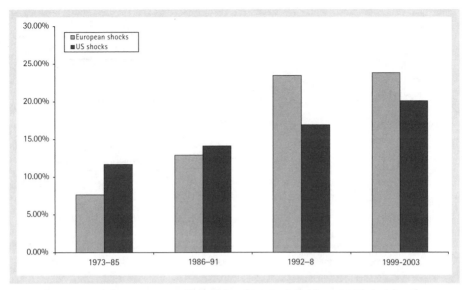

Fig. 5.12. Proportion of variance explained by European and US shocks

Source: Datastream and authors' calculations

results are found for the Asian stock markets. According to our own calculations, the importance of common European and US shocks amounts to about 30 per cent for Hungary and Poland, and about 10 per cent for the Czech Republic. The considerably higher variance proportions for the euro area markets (about 43 per cent) compared to many non-European markets suggest that the euro area equity markets are relatively highly integrated.

6.2. Quantity-based Measures of Equity Market Integration

We now investigate whether the increase in equity market integration suggested by the price-based indicators is confirmed by an increased internationalization of equity holdings. Figure 5.13 reports the share of equity funds[28] that invest domestically, European-wide, and worldwide, respectively, over the period 1995–2003. Over the period 1995–9, the share of investment funds with a purely domestic strategy has decreased from about 60 per cent to less than 35 per cent. Investment funds with a non-domestic, or global, investment strategy were the main beneficiaries, and increased from a market share of about 40 per cent in 1995 to levels close to 70 per cent after 1999.

In all euro area countries, the share increased over the period 1995–2002 and, by 2002, the share of investment funds with a non-domestic strategy surpassed 75 per cent in six of the ten countries in the sample. Looking at the average for the euro area as a whole, the investment funds' share of non-domestic equity increased from

---

[28] The data were obtained from FEFSI.

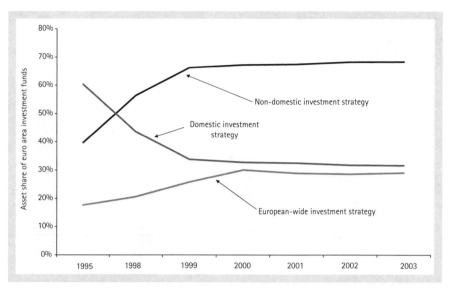

Fig. 5.13. Share of equity funds with domestic, European, and non-domestic investment strategy

Source: Fédération Européenne des Fonds et Sociétés d'Investissement (FEFSI) and authors' calculations

about 40 per cent in 1995 to close to 70 per cent in 2002. Interestingly, the share of European-wide investment funds increased only moderately, from about 18 per cent in 1995 to about 30 per cent after 1999. This suggests that—unlike in the government bond market—investors do not stop at the European borders while diversifying their equity portfolios.

7. CONCLUSION

The main objective of this chapter is to present a set of specific measures to quantify the state and evolution of financial integration in the euro area. Five key markets are considered, namely the money, corporate bond, government bond, credit, and equity markets. Building upon the law of one price, we developed two types of indicators that can be broadly categorized as price-based and news-based measures. We complemented these measures by a number of quantity-based indicators, mainly related to the evolution of the home bias.

We find that the degree of integration has increased in all markets except for the credit market. The money market is found to be the most integrated among the markets we consider. However, differences still remain between various sectors of the money market. For instance, we find that the repo market remains less integrated than the unsecured segments of the money market.

Turning to the euro area government bond market, our analysis indicates that the degree of integration in this market has been very high since the introduction of the euro. Not only have government bond yields converged swiftly in all countries, but yields have also become increasingly driven by common news, and less by purely local risk factors. However, we also find that yields on government bonds with similar, or in some cases identical, credit risk and maturity have not fully converged. Moreover, local factors continue to play a role, though a small one, in explaining yield movements in individual countries. Apart from imperfect integration, differences in perceived credit risk among bonds issued in different countries, as well as liquidity considerations, may also explain this finding to some extent.

This chapter provides the first analysis of the state of integration in the euro area's rapidly expanding corporate bond market. Using methods that disentangle country effects from other possible systematic influences, we find that the euro area corporate bond market seems reasonably well integrated. Specifically, our results show that— once corrected for pervasive risk—country of issuance has only marginal explanatory power for the cross-section of corporate bond yield spreads. We also find evidence that throughout the last five years, the share of European-wide bond funds has increased dramatically, indicating a reduction in the home bias of bond portfolios (both government and corporate bonds) in the euro area.

Our analysis of the state of integration in euro area banking markets indicates that, while this market may be considered quite advanced from a legal perspective, price differentials remain relatively high. Moreover, we find that the degree of integration varies in different segments of the banking market. In the corporate lending market, for example, our analysis indicates that the medium-/long-term segment is more integrated than the short-term segment. With respect to lending to households, mortgage loan rates seem to be more uniform across countries than in the past, while the consumer credit segment remains highly fragmented.

Finally, also for the euro area equity markets, our integration measures indicate a rising degree of integration. More specifically, we find that equity returns in the various euro area equity markets are more and more determined by common news factors and less by country-specific factors. Moreover, there is considerable evidence that the home bias in the equity holdings of institutional investors has decreased considerably over the last few years.

REFERENCES

ADAM, K., JAPPELLI, T., MENICHINI, A. M., PADULA, M., and PAGANO, M. (2002), 'Analyse, compare, and apply alternative indicators and monitoring methodologies to measure the evolution of capital market integration in Europe', Report to the European Commission.

BAELE, L. (2005), 'Volatility spillover effects in European equity markets', *Journal of Financial and Quantitative Analysis*, 40(2), June.

――― FERRANDO, A., HÖRDAHL, P., KRYLOVA, E., and MONNET, C. (2004), 'Measuring financial integration in the euro area', ECB Occasional Paper no. 14.

BEKAERT, G., HARVEY, C., and NG, A. (2005), 'Market integration and contagion', *Journal of Business*, 78(1), 39–69.

CABRAL, I., DIERICK, F., and VESALA, J. (2002), 'Banking integration in the euro Area', ECB Occasional Paper no. 6, December.

CAMPBELL, J. Y., and AMMER, J. (1993), 'What moves the stock and bond markets? A variance decomposition for long-term asset returns', *Journal of Finance*, 48, 3–37.

CARNEGIE-BROWN, B., and KING, M. (2003), 'The transformation of the European financial system', in V. Gaspar et al. (eds.), *The Transformation of the European Financial System*, Frankfurt: European Central Bank.

CHRISTIANSEN, C. (2007), 'Volatility-Spillover Effects in European Bond Markets', *European Financial Management*, 13(5).

CODOGNO, L., FAVERO, C., and MISSALE, A. (2003), 'Yield spreads on EMU government bonds', *Economic Policy*, October, 503–32.

FAVERO, C., PAGANOT, M., and VON THADDEN, E.-L. (2004), 'Valuation, liquidity and risk in government bond markets', Working Paper.

FRATZSCHER, M. (2002), 'Financial Market integration in Europe: on the effects of EMU on stock markets', *International Journal of Finance and Economics*, 7, 165–93.

HARTMANN, P., MANNA, M., and MANZANARES, A. (2001), 'The microstructure of the euro money market', *Journal of International Money and Finance*, 20, 895–948.

KLEIMEIER S., and SANDER, H. (2002), 'European financial market integration: evidence on the emergence of a single eurozone retail banking market', Meteor Research Memorandum, 02/063.

KÖPPL, T. V., and MONNET, C. (2004), 'Guess what: it's the settlements!', ECB Working Paper no. 375.

VAROTTO, S. (2003), 'Credit risk diversification: evidence from the Eurobond market', Bank of England Working Paper 199, September.

CHAPTER 6

FINANCIAL INTEGRATION AND ECONOMIC WELFARE

SEBNEM KALEMLI-OZCAN

BENT SØRENSEN

1. INTRODUCTION

ACROSS the world financial markets are becoming increasingly more integrated. Economists usually consider this a good thing while to the general public 'globalization' sometimes has a sinister ring. Being written by economists, this essay will stress the advantages of financial integration. For a more comprehensive discussion, see Obstfeld and Taylor (2004) who provide an excellent account of the many issues surrounding global capital markets. Most academic economists argue that financial integration has positive effects on growth and risk sharing for most countries although exact, or even approximate, quantification of these effects is elusive for researchers.

Financial assets allow individuals to disentangle consumption from income, which increases welfare. This process can take two forms: (1) saving and borrowing (or running down savings), which allows individuals to separate the timing of consumption from the timing of income, and (2) income insurance (diversification), which allows individuals to maintain their usual level of consumption in the face of calamities such as job loss, fire, or natural disasters or—less drastic, but maybe more relevant—misfortunes such as declining income during recessions.

At the international level, the channelling of resources from (developed) countries with high savings to (developing) countries with low savings is referred to as 'development finance' by Obstfeld and Taylor (2004). The clearest example of development finance may have been the financing of colonial infrastructure by British savers in the late nineteenth century. Development finance increases the welfare of savers, who get a higher return, and investors, who obtain physical investments faster and without temporary declines in consumption to finance investment (as was forced upon the Russians during Stalin's industrialization in the 1930s). The bulk of capital flows in recent years seems, however, to be better described as 'diversification finance' where gross flows of capital are large while net flows are small.

It is tempting to think of development finance as a reflection of individuals' desire to smooth consumption intertemporally (associated with saving and dis-saving) and diversification finance as a reflection of individuals' desire to insure against unforeseen shocks (associated with assets with state contingent returns). In reality, things are less clear-cut: individuals save for retirement and decide to diversify their life-cycle savings. Insurance contracts are, of course, explicitly state contingent but assets such as equities and, more clearly, derivatives have returns that depend on future contingencies.[1]

In Section 2, we will start by discussing the theoretical and empirical literature on the determinants of net capital flows and growth and welfare effects from better international allocation of capital. Our survey of this area is very selective relative to the large literature and the interested reader will have no trouble locating more comprehensive surveys. In Section 3, we discuss international risk sharing and the potential gains from risk sharing. Section 4 focuses on determinants of risk sharing.

2. NET CAPITAL FLOWS: FINANCIAL INTEGRATION AND THE ALLOCATION OF CAPITAL

The most powerful argument in favour of international capital mobility, voiced by Stanley Fischer, Maurice Obstfeld, Kenneth Rogoff, and Larry Summers, is that it facilitates an efficient global allocation of savings by channelling financial resources to their most productive uses, thereby increasing economic growth and welfare around the world. Other prominent academics such as Joseph Stiglitz, Dani Rodrik, and Jagdish Bhagwati are among the sceptics who argue that capital account liberalization

---

[1] Allen and Gale 1997 formulate a model where intertemporal smoothing can be defined precisely as the aggregate amount of physical assets carried over from time period to time period, but in the real world it is hard to distinguish intertemporal smoothing from pure insurance.

does not result in a more efficient allocation of worldwide capital because international capital flows are driven by animal spirits and have little connection to real economic activity. There is extensive research on both sides. We focus on the benefits of international financial integration and start by reviewing the theoretical and empirical literature.

2.1. Capital Mobility in Neoclassical Growth Models

Closed economy neoclassical growth models—such as Solow and Ramsey—highlight the importance of saving, technological progress, and population growth. One robust prediction of these models is that differences in output per worker across countries can be due to differences in saving rates and population growth. Another prediction is that countries exhibit slow convergence to their steady-state levels of output per worker due to the fact that new investment must be financed by domestic savings.

In the context of an integrated global economy these models imply that worldwide capital gets allocated in the most efficient way and that cross-country differences in rates of return to capital disappear. For the Solow model, where countries use the same technology, this implies instantaneous convergence of returns and the equalization of output per worker in all countries. In reality, there are frictions in international capital markets and thus slower convergence of returns.

Barro, Mankiw, and Sala-i-Martin (1995) investigate capital mobility in a neoclassical growth model with one particular kind of friction, moral hazard. The key idea is that creditors can seize physical capital but not human capital and, therefore, human capital cannot serve as collateral. Although the reality of these assumptions is debatable, this model has been a workhorse in the literature because it delivers more realistic speed-of-convergence rates. The inability to borrow against human capital slows down the accumulation of physical capital in an open economy and provides an explanation for the slow convergence in per capita output even across regions linked by integrated financial markets.[2] Obstfeld and Rogoff (1996) develop an alternative small open economy OLG model where borrowing is limited to be at most a fraction of current output and shows that this model also explains slow convergence.

These type of models rely on differences in cross-country capital stocks to explain cross-country income and welfare differences, as opposed to endogenous growth models that rely on differences in technology. If technological progress spreads rapidly across countries convergence would probably be much faster, regardless of capital flows. However, in reality, technological diffusion is often caused by the same factors that contribute to financial integration or technology and may even be embedded in capital flows if these take the form of foreign direct investment (FDI).

Endogenous growth models focus on endogenizing productivity and thus can offer various channels through which global integration can affect integrating countries' growth rates and welfare. The pioneering work of Romer (1986) and Lucas (1988)

---

[2] Barro and Sala-i-Martin 2004 find a convergence rate of 2% for US states and Japanese prefectures—rates similar to those found at the country level.

started the era of endogenous growth. The basic AK model underlines the importance of learning-by-doing in generating persistent growth. The open economy version of the AK model illustrates that international capital market integration can raise world output levels by channelling the world's capital to its most productive global use.

Another implication of Romer-type endogenous growth models is that when two economies integrate, their steady-state growth rate will go up since they can exploit scale economies better (Rivera-Batiz and Romer 1991). (Although it is possible for a country to have a lower level of growth after opening to trade due to adverse changes in its terms of trade as shown in Grossman and Helpman 1990.) Other dynamic stochastic general equilibrium models show that an increase in the productivity of the home country shifts world investment towards the home country, increasing growth.[3]

Young (1995) shows that the East Asian experience is fully consistent with an exogenous growth model with diminishing returns to capital. On the other hand, recent research highlights the importance of TFP as opposed to factor accumulation in explaining international differences in output per worker (Hall and Jones 1999; Klenow and Rodriguez-Clare 1997). In general, the empirical growth literature points to political and institutional factors as the main determinants of growth; however, identifying causality has always been a sticky issue.

There is an extensive empirical literature that shows international capital flows are not consistent with the predictions of the standard neoclassical model in the sense that capital is not flowing from capital-abundant countries to capital-scarce countries but just the opposite. As noted by Obstfeld and Taylor (2004), one-way net development flows from rich to poor countries have stayed at low levels since the 1970s in spite of the large increase in two-way gross diversification flows. In fact, net flows have not yet reached the levels that were attained at the start of the twentieth century. Capital may not be entering poor countries due to factors such as weak property rights as shown by Alfaro, Kalemli-Ozcan, and Volosovych (2007).[4]

Institutions can also affect the *composition* of capital flows. Wei (2000) and Wei and Wu (2002) show that countries with better public institutions and less corruption are likely to attract more FDI relative to bank loans. Albuquerque (2003) finds that countries with low investor protection receive disproportionately large flows of foreign direct investment relative to portfolio investments. He interprets this finding as the result of direct investment being harder to expropriate by host governments and he shows that a calibrated general equilibrium model with this feature can mimic some of the observed patterns. One other reason why investment in some countries is below the level predicted by neoclassical models is that price distortions and transaction costs can drive a wedge between domestic and world price of capital. On the other hand, financial and trade openness themselves seem to be two important factors in reducing the size of such distortions. We return to the discussion of barriers to capital flows in Section 4.1.

---

[3] See Obstfeld and Rogoff 1996 for further details.
[4] See also Reinhart and Rogoff 2004.

2.2. Growth and Welfare

Financial integration could lead to an increase in a country's growth rate and welfare through a number of channels. The direct channels that work via net flows are (1) allowing investment to be higher (or lower) than domestic savings (Mundell–Fleming model), (2) reducing the cost of capital via a more efficient allocation of capital (Henry 2000; Stulz 1999), (3) transferring technology (Grossman and Helpman 1991), and (4) stimulating domestic financial development (Levine 2005; Bekaert, Harvey, and Lundblad 2005). An indirect channel that can operate through either net flows or gross flows is an increase in specialization which may lead to higher growth and welfare (Kalemli-Ozcan, Sørensen, and Yosha 2003; Imbs and Wacziarg 2003; Obstfeld, 1994a; Acemoglu and Zilibotti 1997). This happens because capital market integration permits individuals to diversify their income allowing them to allocate a larger fraction of their wealth into high-yielding risky investments. Such a pattern is typically associated with higher industrial specialization.

We have learned from the last twenty years of growth research that two-thirds of the variation in cross-country output per worker is accounted for by total factor productivity (TFP) and only one-third is accounted for by capital. Does this imply that a country that opens up its capital account can raise its level of physical capital so that one-third of the gap in its income and welfare compared to rich countries will be permanently erased? The answer is no, because even in the absence of capital flows, domestic savings would eventually reach the level where the capital stock is at the steady state. The gain from immediate convergence of the capital stock is therefore transitory compared to the situation where the convergence would occur slowly from savings. There is also the additional service on foreign debt. More importantly, the optimal capital stock itself depends on TFP and TFP probably depends on institutional factors such as protection of property rights—the same factors that are important for capital flows as argued above. As shown by Blomstrom, Lipsey, and Zejan (1996) and Clark and Feenstra (2003), in a world of completely mobile capital the amount of physical capital installed in a country relative to the world average is fully explained by total factor productivity. Building on this, Kalemli-Ozcan et al. (2005) and Ekinci, Kalemli-Ozcan, and Sørensen (2007) show that capital flows between regions *within* countries such as the United States and Germany are consistent with the predictions of neoclassical models while those *between* European countries are not.

Standard estimates of production function parameters imply that although poor countries' steady-state level of capital stock is far below that of rich countries they are not that far away from their own steady state. Thus, instantaneous convergence to the steady state as a result of opening up the capital account might deliver small welfare gains. This is particularly true if the steady state reflects the same domestic distortions and institutional weaknesses that deter foreign capital inflows in the first place. Gourinchas and Jeanne (2006) calculate the welfare gains resulting from gaining access to foreign capital as a means to speed convergence. They use a Ramsey growth model for their calibration exercise and find very small welfare gains, equivalent to the welfare gain from a 1–3 per cent permanent increase in consumption, at most. One reason for this low number is that for a country that is very close to its steady state, opening up the capital account does not mean much since the cost of foreign borrowing is close to the return. Another reason is that the Ramsey model delivers very high convergence rates—about 11 per cent—which is at odds with the empirical estimates of convergence rates of about 2 per cent. The faster the convergence without integration, the smaller the gains from integrating. A final reason Gourinchas and Jeanne (2006) find small welfare gains from capital market integration lies in the high discount rate they choose (a combination of the discount rate and population growth rate). This assumption puts relatively less weight on the immediate future where the capital gap really matters. They note that increasing TFP could lead to welfare gains that are an order of magnitude higher than the gains obtained from financial integration. Thus, the main implication of their result is that it is better in terms of welfare gains to find a way to increase future TFP; for example by permanent institutional reform.

Many researchers look at the effects of financial development on growth. We refer the reader to the recent article by Levine (2005)—or the shorter summary by Aghion elsewhere in this volume—which does an excellent job of surveying this vast literature. Other researchers look at the effect of trade openness and financial openness on growth. There is little controversy regarding the effect of trade openness on growth (Sachs and Warner 1995; Frankel and Romer 1999; Rodriguez and Rodrik 2000), but this cannot be said for the potential effects of financial openness on growth. In fact, the empirical estimates of the growth effect of financial openness vary from large effects to absolutely no effects. Prasad et al. (2003) provide an excellent survey of this topic.

To summarize briefly, Bekaert, Harvey, and Lundblad (2005) find equity market liberalization leads to a 25–45 per cent increase in financial development as measured by domestic credit relative to GDP, and Henry (2000) finds that equity market liberalization leads to investment booms. Henry (2003) and Stulz (1999) also discuss the evidence on decreasing costs of capital and more efficient capital allocation following stock market liberalization. Empirical work on these issues is complicated by problems such as dating effective liberalization correctly and properly accounting for the changes in the capital stock.[5] A deeper objection to empirical work on this issue is that changes in policy towards liberalization are likely to be endogenous and reflecting the 'institutions' of the country, where 'institutions' are broadly defined to include the quality of markets, courts, government, etc. Alfaro, Kalemli-Ozcan, and Volosovych (2007) show that FDI increases the growth rate of the host countries with developed financial markets and Klein (2003) shows that financial integration leads to the biggest gain in economic performance and welfare for developing countries that have achieved a minimum level of institutional development.

---

[5] See Quinn 1997.

3. GROSS CAPITAL FLOWS: RISK SHARING TO INSULATE CONSUMPTION FROM OUTPUT SHOCKS

The idea that people trade assets in order to hedge themselves against future contingencies has been integrated in rigorous economic analysis since Arrow (1964) and Debreu (1959). Their—now standard—paradigm of complete markets allows us to think about risk allocation in the same way we think about the allocation of commodities over time or across agents. The empirical economic literature on risk sharing departs from the benchmark model of perfect markets, which in a setting of endowment economies under standard assumptions implies that consumption growth rates are equalized ('perfect risk sharing'). The assumption of endowment economies totally ignores the motivation behind development finance. In reality, net capital flows are determined by both diversification and development motives. Diversification motives are likely to matter more for the explanation of capital flows between countries at similar levels of development as argued by Obstfeld and Taylor (2004), who point out that the recent increase in gross capital flows is mainly a 'rich–rich' country story. While development finance is important for capital flows to emerging markets we ignore this issue in the present subsection. A country with large net savings abroad will, obviously, also want to diversify. However, it takes a large amount of financial investment in foreign countries to provide capital income flows of an order of magnitude large enough to help stabilize average income. Most countries do not possess such large holdings of net foreign assets. In the common situation of small net international savings, countries need to sell domestic assets to foreigners and then use the proceeds to purchase foreign assets. This is the reason why we identify diversification with gross flows. In order to achieve a significant amount of risk sharing from capital income flow from abroad the gross flows need to be at a magnitude that is three to five times the level of GDP.[6]

3.1. Measuring Risk Sharing

Macroeconomists typically focus on measuring consumption smoothing. Smoothing of consumption relative to endowment shocks can be thought of as involving two steps: the smoothing of income relative to the endowment (for countries, the overall output can be considered the endowment) and smoothing of consumption relative to income which involves transfers or borrowing and lending. Although economists generally agree that risk sharing isn't perfect, a strikingly large amount of risk is shared between individuals (Mace 1991; Nelson 1994; Cochrane 1991; Attanasio and Davis 1996; Hayashi, Altonji, and Kotlikoff 1996). However, risk is also shared on

---

[6] See Sørensen et al. 2007.

anonymous financial markets with individuals in distant locations. This in turn leads to the insurance of income and consumption of entire regions such as states or provinces (Crucini 1999; Hess and Shin 1998; Lewis 1996; Kalemli-Ozcan, Sørensen, and Yosha 2003; Mélitz and Zumer 1999). At the country level, financial integration is still too rudimentary to insure country level consumption much against aggregate shocks (Backus, Kehoe, and Kydland 1992; Sørensen and Yosha 1998) although Kalemli-Ozcan, Sørensen, and Yosha (2005) find positive income smoothing among EU countries for the most recent period and Sørensen et al. (2007) find that consumption also is less sensitive to output shocks in the broader OECD since the mid-1990s.

The financial literature typically focuses on whether investors can obtain better risk–return trade-offs from investing in international markets using return distributions estimated from actual market returns. In an early paper, Grubel (1968) points out that international diversification can improve the mean–variance trade-off compared to holding a purely domestic portfolio and Lewis (1999) shows that this is still true. This literature also concludes that countries typically hold fewer foreign assets than seems optimal.

Asdrubali, Sørensen, and Yosha (1996)—in an application to US states—combine the estimation of income and consumption smoothing in a common framework that also quantifies the role of federal net transfers in risk sharing. The role of international transfers (such as remittances or aid) in risk sharing is, however, quite modest, even within the European Monetary Union.[7]

3.2. Potential Welfare Gains from Risk Sharing

How large a welfare gain could countries obtain if they moved to a situation of perfect international risk sharing? The literature demonstrates that welfare gains from risk sharing, assuming exogenous output, can be quite substantial. Van Wincoop was the first to quantify potential welfare gains from risk sharing in a general equilibrium model. Van Wincoop (1994) finds for OECD countries that *further* consumption smoothing (i.e. moving from the actual consumption distribution to the perfect risk-sharing allocation) would improve welfare by the same amount as would a permanent increase in consumption of 3 per cent. Kalemli-Ozcan, Sørensen, and Yosha (2001) construct a closed form expression for risk sharing when the distribution of shocks is close to a random walk and consumers have constant relative risk aversion preferences.[8] They estimate potential welfare gains from risk sharing for US states and European Union countries. They find potential welfare gains for countries at the same order of magnitude as van Wincoop and similar magnitudes for US states, except that the gains can be much larger for oil states such as Wyoming and Alaska that face large shocks to the value of their output. These shocks are negatively correlated with the

---

[7]   See Balli and Sørensen 2006.

[8]   Obstfeld 1994b provides a closed form solution for the welfare gains due to a reduction in consumption variability in a partial equilibrium setting.

shocks faced by other states which gives the oil states much better access to capital income flows that smooth their income. The potential gains from risk sharing are based on a counterfactual thought experiment: moving from autarkic (rather than actual) consumption to perfect risk sharing.[9]

While agents ultimately care about smooth consumption it appears that consumption is often subject to large taste shocks (broadly defined). If a researcher is not able to identify desired movements in consumption due to taste shocks from undesired movements, he or she will mistake them for welfare-reducing volatility. We, therefore, think that a more robust way of estimating the welfare improvement from risk sharing is to calculate the potential amount of risk sharing moving from autarky to perfect risk sharing and then combine this with a measure of how much risk sharing is actually obtained rather than attempting to construct measures based directly on the volatility of consumption. It seems that much more research is needed in order to be able to give more than rough empirical estimates of welfare gains from risk sharing.

Another important issue in this literature is the fact that the magnitude of potential welfare gains depends on the persistence of output shocks. Tesar (1995) explored the sensitivity of estimates of country-level welfare gains from risk sharing and found estimates that varied from near zero, in the case where output shocks are transitory, to about 2 per cent when shocks are close to random walk. While this indicates that welfare gains are less important when shocks are transitory, it is also the case that risk sharing may be much easier to come by when shocks are transitory: Baxter and Crucini (1995), using a calibrated general equilibrium model, find that having access to a bond market is sufficient for smoothing consumption almost as well as with perfect capital markets in the face of transitory shocks, while state-contingent securities are necessary in order to achieve significant risk sharing in the face of permanent shocks. Everyday logic can explain this result: a few weeks of unemployment need not affect consumption because it can be financed by a short-term loan; however, in the case of a permanent loss of ability to work, disability insurance is needed to maintain a reasonable level of consumption. Disability insurance is, of course, just one of many real-world examples of state-contingent contracts.

3.3. Empirical Estimates of Potential Welfare Gains from Risk Sharing in the 2005 Expanded European Union

We display results from a recent application of the mentioned methods that is of particular relevance for Europe. Kalemli-Ozcan, Sørensen, and Yosha (2001) find that under simple assumptions, including logarithmic utility and independently normally distributed growth rates, the welfare gain for country i from moving from autarky to

---

[9] Kalemli-Ozcan, Sørensen, and Yosha 2001 utilize the potential welfare gain as a measure of the asymmetry of output shocks.

perfect risk sharing with a group of countries can be expressed as

$$\frac{100}{\delta} \left(\frac{1}{2} \sigma^2 + \frac{1}{2} \sigma_i^2 - \text{cov}^i \right). \tag{1}$$

Here δ is the common intertemporal subjective discount rate which we set to 0.02 and σ^2 is the variance of the growth rate of per capita real aggregate GDP (i.e. deflated by the consumer price index) of the group of countries, σ_i^2 is the variance of per capita real GDP of country i in autarky, and cov^i is the covariance of country-i GDP with aggregate GDP.[10]

The measure is calculated as the utility equivalent of a permanent increase in consumption expressed in percent. In the empirical implementation, the parameters σ^2, σ_i^2, and cov^i are estimated using regional and aggregate output data.

Demyanyk and Volosovych (2005) apply this method to evaluate the potential risk-sharing benefits that would accrue to the 2005 European Union accession countries. In Table 6.1, we display their numbers for each accession country as well as for the longer-standing members of the European Union. For large countries, such as Germany and the UK, the potential welfare gains are minor at about one-tenth of 1 per cent, while the estimated gains for the accession countries can be very large. The largest estimate is 18.5 per cent for Lithuania, which is very much a result of Lithuania's output being negatively correlated with aggregate output such that output pooling can decrease their volatility steeply. The actual welfare gain is going to be significantly smaller since perfect risk sharing is unlikely to obtain and the output composition of Lithuania is likely to change as its goods market gets integrated further with the European Union. Nonetheless, the numbers indicate that risk-sharing benefits for the accession countries of joining the European Union can be large if they obtain sufficient financial integration.

4. DETERMINANTS OF RISK SHARING

In the stylized Arrow–Debreu model, contingent contracts can be written at no cost and full risk sharing will obtain. In the real world there are costs involved in 'writing contracts' and contracts will only be written if the benefits exceeds the costs. The benefits are the gains from risk sharing just discussed while the costs of risk-sharing contracts take many forms. Obstfeld and Rogoff (1996) provide a textbook treatment and conclude that even if they are not perfect, they will still be very important in facilitating risk sharing and intertemporal trade.

With the possible exception of family connections, financial assets are traded through financial intermediaries such as banks or exchanges and the amount of risk

---

[10] Strictly speaking aggregate GDP cannot be log-normally distributed if each region's GDP is log-normally distributed but this standard approximation will not affect our results.

Table 6.1. Potential welfare gains for acceding and long-time EU countries, 1994–2001

	Pot. welfare gain G_i	Variance σ_i^2	Covariance cov^i	Correlation $corr^i$
Acceding countries				
Cyprus	1.06	4.61	0.39	0.28
Czech Republic	2.97	11.26	−0.10	−0.05
Estonia	7.80	28.22	−1.28	−0.37
Hungary	0.87	3.31	0.12	0.10
Latvia	6.97	25.81	−0.82	−0.25
Lithuania	18.55	68.95	−2.42	−0.45
Malta	0.49	3.11	0.79	0.69
Poland	1.24	7.06	1.27	0.74
Slovak Republic	3.18	12.88	0.30	0.13
Slovenia	0.96	4.64	0.62	0.44
Arithmetic mean	4.41	–	–	0.13
Weighted average	2.73	–	–	0.38
EU-15 countries				
Austria	0.06	0.95	0.56	0.88
Belgium	0.16	1.21	0.50	0.70
Denmark	0.31	1.41	0.29	0.38
Finland	1.07	5.68	0.90	0.59
France	0.17	0.96	0.35	0.55
Germany	0.08	1.16	0.64	0.91
Greece	0.53	1.33	−0.19	−0.26
Ireland	1.66	7.77	0.77	0.43
Italy	0.12	0.25	0.10	0.32
Luxembourg	2.50	12.17	1.30	0.58
The Netherlands	0.26	1.18	0.29	0.41
Portugal	0.22	1.21	0.38	0.53
Spain	0.24	1.20	0.33	0.46
Sweden	0.17	1.88	0.81	0.91
United Kingdom	0.18	0.36	0.04	0.11
Arithmetic mean	0.51	–	–	0.50
Weighted average	0.19	–	–	0.49

Notes: Column 1 shows potential welfare gains calculated based on 1994–2001 data as $10^2 \cdot \frac{1}{\delta} \left(\frac{1}{2} \sigma^2 + \frac{1}{2} \sigma_i^2 - cov^i \right)$, where $\sigma_i^2 = var(\Delta \log GDP^i)$, $cov^i = cov(\Delta \log GDP^i, \Delta \log GDP)$, σ^2 is the variance of the total EU-25 GDP growth, i.e. $\sigma^2 = var(\Delta \log GDP)$, $10^4 \cdot \sigma^2 = 0.42$, and $\delta = 0.02$. The potential welfare gain is the gain—in terms of equivalent permanent consumption increases—that a country would obtain from fully diversifying any country-specific variance in output expressed in terms of the percent permanent increase in GDP that would result in the same utility gain. Column 2 is $10^4 \cdot \sigma_i^2$, and Column 3 is $10^4 \cdot cov^i$. Column 4 is the correlation of each country's GDP growth with the total EU-25 GDP growth, i.e. $corr^i = corr(\Delta \log GDP^i, \Delta \log GDP)$. Weighted averages are population weighted.

sharing obtained is determined by the amount and type of foreign assets hold. We next turn to a discussion of factors that may limit foreign asset holdings.

4.1. Barriers to International Contracting: Moral Hazard, Asymmetric Information, and Sovereign Risk

In the developed world, financial intermediation is typically well developed within countries while cross-border intermediation has lagged behind. 'Financial integration', therefore, typically refers to the lowering of barriers (or costs) of cross-border financial intermediation. International financial intermediation poses particular problems. These can be grouped in terms of (a) higher costs associated with international assets trade, (b) lower information transparency for foreign investors, (c) limits to enforcement of international contracts, and (d) currency risk. Note that these barriers are relevant not only for gross flows but also for net flows.

The portfolio holdings of most countries exhibit 'home bias'. Home bias refers to the observation that countries hold far fewer foreign assets than predicted by standard models such as the CAPM. French and Poterba (1991) and Tesar and Werner (1995) were among the first to document such home bias. Recent studies include Ahearne, Griever, and Warnock (2004), who study US foreign equity holdings, and Sørensen et al. (2007), who study home bias in foreign bond and equity holdings for OECD countries. Buch, Driscoll, and Ostergaard (2005) show that banks' asset portfolios also seem to be biased towards the home country.

Transaction costs. Domowitz, Glen, and Madhavan (2001) find that transaction costs associated with international asset trading are important, especially for emerging markets, although Cooper and Kaplanis (1994) find that with reasonable level of risk aversion, observable costs of holding foreign equity do not explain home bias in equity holdings. Tesar and Werner (1995) find that foreign equity is being turned over at a higher rate than domestic equity which is hard to reconcile with higher trading costs of foreign equity. Warnock (2002) argues that the measurement of turnover rates may be problematic although he too finds no direct effect of transaction costs on home bias. Mann and Meade (2002) find small but statistically significant effects of (directly measured) transaction costs. Overall, it seems that transaction costs may have a small effect on home bias but cannot fully explain home bias on their own.

Informational barriers. Another class of potential explanations of home bias centre on the role of information: specifically, lack of information adding to the riskiness of foreign investment.[11] Kang and Stulz (1997) demonstrate that Japanese investors overinvest in large firms, consistent with a role for informational costs, and Ahearne, Griever, and Warnock (2004) show that patterns of US equity investments in foreign countries are consistent with informational asymmetries. Edison and Warnock (2004) find that equities that are cross-listed on a US exchange do not seem to be subject to home bias in US portfolios. Coval and Moskowitz (1999) and Huberman

---

[11]   See for example Gehrig 1993.

(2001) even suggest that informational asymmetry may explain intranational invest-ment patterns within the USA.[12]

Moral hazard and sovereign risk. The standard theory assumes there are no re-strictions on the range of financial contracts people can sign and defaulting is not an option. In the real world, moral hazard (Gertler and Rogoff 1990) and sovereign risk (Eaton and Gersovitz 1981; Bulow and Rogoff 1989) create enforcement problems and this can significantly affect international investment, and even the ability of the governments of countries that are considered unstable to smooth transitory shocks through borrowing. Within the OECD, defaults on government bonds are unlikely events, but taxes and fees can be tailored to fall disproportionally on foreign investors.

International risk sharing via multinational corporations. International diversifi-cation might be obtained indirectly through multinational corporations. Jacquillat and Solnik (1978) demonstrate that this channel is not able to provide much diver-sification for investors who attempt to lower their exposure to domestic shocks by purchasing stock of multinationals. Cai and Warnock (2004) find that taking into account such 'indirect' foreign investment via multinationals makes apparent home bias smaller. Rowland and Tesar (2004) look at returns and find weak evidence that investing in multinationals helps provide diversification, but that further gains can be obtained from holding international assets. Looking at the financial returns to investors may, however, underestimate the role of multinational corporations in in-ternational risk sharing. Budd and Slaughter (2004) and Budd, Konings, and Slaugh-ter (2005) find that risk often is shared between units of multinational firms through profit sharing or equalization of wages across units. For example, if a Canadian parent company enjoys high profits, this is typically associated with higher wages in US subsidiaries according to Budd and Slaughter (2004).

Further suggested explanations for home bias include Obstfeld and Rogoff (2000), who suggest that home bias is caused by high *costs of trading goods* internationally, and Strong and Xu (2003) who find that fund managers' *subjective expectations* are such that they are relatively more optimistic about high future returns for their home markets.

Hedging of currency risk may be another explanation for home bias: the interna-tional version of the CAPM alluded to above implicitly assumes purchasing power parity (PPP). In the absence of PPP, investors may optimally want to deviate from the aggregate world portfolio in order to hedge currency risk as detailed by Adler and Dumas (1983). However, Cooper and Kaplanis (1994) find that inflation hedging is not a likely explanation of home bias.

4.2. Evidence: Risk Sharing and Institutions

In this section, we provide simple suggestive evidence that institutions broadly de-fined are important determinants of risk sharing. We limit ourselves to income

---

[12] Portes and Rey 2005 find that informational variables, such as telephone traffic, help explain both gross and net capital flows.

insurance and we measure the amount of income insurance in, say, Germany, by one minus the coefficient in a regression of the annual growth of German gross national income (GNI) on the annual growth of German gross domestic product (GDP) where both variables are in terms of deviations from world growth. This country-by-country measure of risk sharing is quite noisy and hence considered a random variable centred around the true value.

In Figures 6.1 to 6.6, we plot the estimates of risk sharing measured for European Union countries and potential entrants on the y-axis against various indicators of institutional development on the x-axis. We use data from Volosovych (2006) in our illustration and refer the reader to Volosovych (2006) or Sørensen et al. (2007) for details on the calculation of the risk-sharing measure. We show how various country characteristics such as the output level, the distance to London, etc. correlate with the amount of income insurance obtained by showing six scatter plots. Table 6.A1 in the appendix provides a list of the countries considered.

Figure 6.1 shows that distance to the European financial centre of London is inversely related to risk sharing obtained while Figure 6.2 reveals that risk sharing obtained is positively correlated with the ICRG index of investor protection.[13] Figure 6.3 shows that richer countries obtain more risk sharing while Figure 6.4 confirms the finding of Sørensen et al. (2007) that risk sharing obtained correlates negatively with home bias, which we here measure simply as the amount of foreign portfolio equity holdings relative to GDP. Figures 6.5 and 6.6 show that high risk sharing also correlates positively with openness to trade and with the share of banks with foreign ownership—an alternative measure of financial integration. Volosovych (2006) finds similar results for a larger sample. The natural question is which of these indicators of 'good institutions' (including financial and trade openness) is the main determinant(s) of positive risk sharing. Multiple regressions would be the natural tool but we do not display the results from such regressions here because of the high correlation of the potential determinants of risk sharing. This happens because countries with good institutions in one dimension typically also have good institutions in other dimensions.[14] However, there is no doubt, as can be seen from the figures, that wealthy, financially integrated countries with good institutions obtain more risk sharing than countries with worse institutions. We expect that financial integration among developed countries will continue to gather strength, leading to non-negligible welfare gains along the dimensions described in the present survey.

---

[13] This index is from the International Country Risk Guide (ICRG) and reflects a combination of factors that affect the risk to the returns of foreign investors. It ranges from 0 to 4, where 4 indicates very low risk. The subcomponents of the index are 'Contract viability/expropriation', 'Profits repatriation', and 'Payment delays'. It is rescaled from 0 to 10 where higher score means low risk and higher protection.

[14] Volosovych 2006, using a larger sample in a multiple regression context, finds that investor protection seems to be the most important institutional variable.

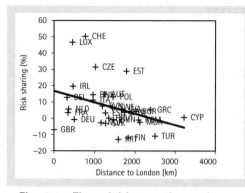

Fig. 6.1. Financial integration and distance to financial centre: 1985–2004

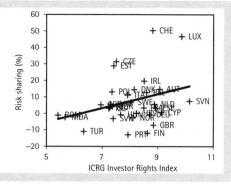

Fig. 6.2. Financial integration and investor rights: 1985–2004

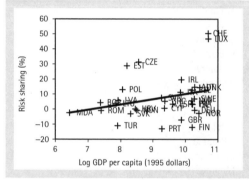

Fig. 6.3. Financial integration and output: 1985–2004

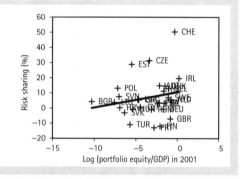

Fig. 6.4. Financial integration and home bias: 1985–2004

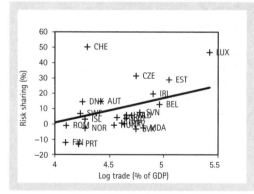

Fig. 6.5. Financial integration and openness: 1985–2004

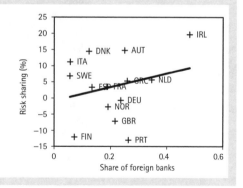

Fig. 6.6. Financial integration and foreign bank ownership (EU only): 1985–2004

APPENDIX

Table 6.A1. Country list

Codes	Names
AUT	Austria
BEL	Belgium
BGR	Bulgaria
HRV	Croatia
CYP	Cyprus
CZE	Czech Rep.
DNK	Denmark
EST	Estonia
FIN	Finland
FRA	France
DEU	Germany
GRC	Greece
HUN	Hungary
ISL	Iceland
IRL	Ireland
ITA	Italy
LVA	Latvia
LTU	Lithuania
LUX	Luxembourg
MDA	Moldova
NLD	The Netherlands
NOR	Norway
POL	Poland
PRT	Portugal
ROM	Romania
SVK	Slovak Rep.
SVN	Slovenia
ESP	Spain
SWE	Sweden
CHE	Switzerland
TUR	Turkey
GBR	UK

REFERENCES

ACEMOGLU, D., and ZILIBOTTI, F. (1997), 'Was Prometheus unbound by chance? Risk, diversification, and growth', *Journal of Political Economy*, 105, 709–51.

ADLER, M., and DUMAS, B. (1983), 'International portfolio choice and corporation finance: a synthesis', *Journal of Finance*, 38, 925–84.

AHEARNE, A. G., GRIEVER, W. L., and WARNOCK, F. E. (2004), 'Information costs and home bias: an analysis of U.S. holdings of foreign equities', *Journal of International Economics*, 62, 313–36.

ALBUQUERQUE, R. (2003), 'The composition of international capital flows: risk sharing through foreign direct investment', *Journal of International Economics*, 61, 353–83.

ALFARO, L., KALEMLI-OZCAN, S., and VOLOSOVYCH, V. (2007), 'Why doesn't capital flow from rich to poor countries? An empirical investigation', *Review of Economics and Statistics*, forthcoming.

——— CHANDA, A., KALEMLI-OZCAN, S., and SAYEK, S. (2004), 'FDI and economic growth, the role of local financial markets', *Journal of International Economics*, 64, 113–34.

ALLEN, F., and GALE, D. (1997), 'Financial markets cycles and the asset structure of foreign trade', *International Economic Review*, 36, 821–54.

ARROW, K. (1964), 'The role of securities in the optimal allocation of risk bearing', *Review of Economic Studies*, 31, 91–6.

ASDRUBALI, P., SØRENSEN, B. E., and YOSHA, O. (1996), 'Channels of interstate risk sharing: United States 1963–90', *Quarterly Journal of Economics*, 111, 1081–110.

ATTANASIO, O., and DAVIS, S. (1996), 'Relative wage movements and the distribution of consumption', *Journal of Political Economy*, 104, 1227–262.

BACKUS, D., KEHOE, P., and KYDLAND, F. (1992), 'International real business cycles', *Journal of Political Economy*, 100, 745–75.

BALLI, F., and SØRENSEN, B. E. (2006), 'The impact of the EMU on channels of risk sharing between member countries', Unpublished manuscript, University of Houston.

BARRO, R. J., MANKIW, N. G., and SALA-I-MARTIN, X. (1995), 'Capital mobility in neoclassical models of growth', *American Economic Review*, 85, 103–15.

——— and SALA-I-MARTIN, X. (1995), *Economic Growth*, Cambridge, Mass.: MIT Press.

BAXTER, M., and CRUCINI, M. J. (1995), 'Business cycles and the asset structure of foreign trade', *International Economic Review*, 36, 821–54.

BEKAERT, G., HARVEY, C. R., and LUNDBLAD, C. (2005), 'Does financial liberalization spur growth?', *Journal of Financial Economics*, 77, 3–55.

BLOMSTROM, M., LIPSEY, R. E., and ZEJAN, M. (1996), 'Is fixed investment the key to economic growth?', *Quarterly Journal of Economics*, 111, 269–76.

BUCH, C. M., DRISCOLL, J. C., and OSTERGAARD, C. (2005), 'Cross-border diversification in bank asset portfolios', ECB Working Paper 429.

BUDD, J. W., and SLAUGHTER, M. J. (2004), 'Are profits shared across borders? Evidence on international rent sharing', *Journal of Labor Economics*, 22, 525–52.

——— KONINGS, J., and SLAUGHTER, M. J. (2005), 'Wages and international rent sharing in multinational firms', *Review of Economics and Statistics*, 87, 73–84.

BULOW, J. I., and ROGOFF, K. (1989), 'Sovereign debt: is to forgive to forget?', *American Economic Review*, 79, 43–50.

CAI, F., and WARNOCK, F. E. (2004), 'International diversification at home and Abroad', Federal Reserve Board, International Finance Discussion Paper no. 793.

CLARK, G., and FEENSTRA, R. (2003), 'Technology in the great divergence', in M. D. Bordo, A. M. Taylor, and J. G. Williamson (eds.), *Globalization in Historical Perspective*, National Bureau of Economic Research Conference Report.

COCHRANE, J. (1991), 'A simple test of consumption insurance', *Journal of Political Economy*, 99, 957–76.

COOPER, I. A., and KAPLANIS, E. (1994), 'Home bias in equity portfolios: portfolios, inflation hedging, and international capital market equilibrium', *Review of Financial Studies*, 7, 45–60.

COVAL, J., and MOSKOWITZ, T. (1999), 'Home bias at home: local equity preference in domestic portfolios', *Journal of Finance*, 54, 2045–74.

CRUCINI, M. J. (1999), 'On international and national dimensions of risk sharing', *Review of Economics and Statistics*, 81, 73–84.

DEBREU, G. (1959), *Theory of Value*, New Haven: Yale University Press.

DEMYANYK, Y., and VOLOSOVYCH, V. (2005), 'Macroeconomic asymmetry in the European Union: the difference between new and old members', CEPR Working Paper no. 4847.

DOMOWITZ, I., GLEN, J., and MADHAVAN, A. (2001), 'Liquidity, volatility and equity trading costs across countries and over time', *International Finance*, 4, 221–55.

EATON, J., and GERSOVITZ, M. (1981), 'Debt with potential repudiation: theory and estimation', *Review of Economic Studies*, 48, 289–309.

EDISON, H. J., and WARNOCK, F. E. (2004), 'U.S. investors' emerging market equity portfolios: a security-level analysis', *Review of Economics and Statistics*, 86, 691–704.

EKINCI, M., KALEMLI-OZCAN, S., and SØRENSEN, B. (2007), 'Capital flows across Europe: do regions differ from countries?', unpublished manuscript, University of Houston.

FRANKEL, J. A., and ROMER, D. (1999), 'Does trade cause growth?', *American Economic Review*, 89, 379–99.

FRENCH, K. and POTERBA, J. (1991), 'Investor diversification and international equity markets', *American Economic Review: Papers and Proceedings*, 81, 222–26.

GEHRIG, T. (1993), 'An information based explanation for the domestic bias in foreign exchange and stock markets', *Scandinavian Journal of Economics*, 95, 97–109.

GERTLER, M., and ROGOFF, K. (1990), 'North–south lending and endogenous domestic capital market inefficiencies', *Journal of Monetary Economics*, 26, 245–66.

GOURINCHAS, P.-O., and JEANNE, O. (2006), 'The elusive gains from international financial integration', *Review of Economic Studies*, 73, 715–41.

GROSSMAN, G., and HELPMAN, E. (1991), *Innovation and Growth in the Global Economy*, Cambridge, Mass.: MIT Press.

GRUBEL, H. L. (1968), 'Internationally diversified portfolios: welfare gains and capital flows', *American Economic Review*, 58, 1299–314.

HALL, R. E., and JONES, C. I. (1999), 'Why do some countries produce so much more output per worker than others?', NBER Working Paper no. 6564.

HAYASHI, F., ALTONJI, J., and KOTLIKOFF, L. (1996), 'Risk sharing between and within families', *Econometrica*, 64, 261–94.

HENRY, P. B. (2000), 'Stock market liberalization, economic reform, and emerging market equity prices', *Journal of Finance*, 55, 529–64.

—— (2003), 'Capital account liberalization, the cost of capital and economic growth', *American Economic Review*, 93, 91–6.

HESS, G. D., and SHIN, K. (1998), 'Intranational business cycles in the United States', *Journal of International Economics*, 44, 289–313.

HUBERMAN, G. (2001), 'Familiarity breeds investment', *Review of Financial Studies*, 14, 659–80.

IMBS, J., and WACZIARG, R. (2003), 'Stages of diversification', *American Economic Review*, 93, 63–86.

JACQUILLAT, B., and SOLNIK, B. (1978), 'Multinationals are poor tools for diversification', *Journal of Portfolio Management*, 4, 8–12.

KALEMLI-OZCAN, S., SØRENSEN, B. E., and YOSHA, O. (2001), 'Regional integration, industrial specialization and the asymmetry of shocks across regions', *Journal of International Economics*, 55, 107–37.

—— —— —— (2003), 'Risk sharing and industrial specialization: regional and international evidence', *American Economic Review*, 93, 903–18.

———— ———— ———— (2005), 'Asymmetric shocks and risk sharing in a monetary union: up-dated evidence and policy implications for Europe', in H. Huizinga and L. Jonung (eds.), *The Internationalisation of Asset Ownership in Europe*, New York: Cambridge University Press.

———— RESHEF, A., SØRENSEN, B. E., and YOSHA, O. (2005), 'Capital flows and productivity: evidence from U.S. states', unpublished manuscript, University of Houston.

KANG, J., and STULZ, R. M. (1997), 'Why is there a home bias? An analysis of foreign portfolio equity ownership in Japan', *Journal of Financial Economics*, 46, 3–28.

KLEIN, M. W. (2003), 'Capital account openness and the varieties of growth experience', NBER Working Paper 9500.

KLENOW, P. J., and RODRIGUEZ-CLARE, A. (1997), 'The neoclassical revival in growth eco-nomics: has it gone too far?', *NBER Macroeconomics Annual*, 73–114.

LEVINE, R. (2005), 'Finance and growth: theory and evidence', in P. Aghion and S. Durlauf (eds.), *Handbook of Economic Growth*, Amsterdam: Elsevier Science.

LEWIS, K. (1996), 'What can explain the apparent lack of international consumption risk sharing?', *Journal of Political Economy*, 104, 267–97.

———— (1999), 'Trying to explain home bias in equities and consumption', *Journal of Economic Literature*, 37, 571–608.

LUCAS, R. (1988), 'On the mechanics of economic development', *Journal of Monetary Eco-nomics*, 22, 3–42.

MACE, B. (1991), 'Full insurance in the presence of aggregate uncertainty', *Journal of Political Economy*, 99, 928–56.

MANN, C., and MEADE, E. (2002), 'Home bias, transactions costs, and prospects for the euro: a more detailed analysis', unpublished manuscript, London School of Economics.

MÉLITZ, J., and ZUMER, F. (1999), 'Interregional and international risk sharing and lessons for EMU', *Carnegie-Rochester Conference Series on Public Policy*, 51, 149–88.

NELSON, J. A. (1994), 'On testing for full insurance using consumer expenditure survey data', *Journal of Political Economy*, 102, 384–94.

OBSTFELD, M. (1994), 'Are industrial-country consumption risks globally diversified?', in L. Leiderman and A. Razin (eds.), *Capital Mobility: The Impact on Consumption, Investment and Growth*, New York: Cambridge University Press.

———— (1994b), 'Risk-taking, global diversification, and growth', *American Economic Review*, 84, 1310–29.

———— and ROGOFF, K. (1996), *Foundations of International Macroeconomics*, Cambridge, Mass.: MIT Press.

———— ———— (2000), 'The six major puzzles in international macroeconomics: is there a common cause?', *NBER Macroeconomics Annual 2000*, 339–90.

———— and TAYLOR, A. M. (2004), *Global Capital Markets: Integration, Crisis, and Growth*, New York: Cambridge University Press.

PORTES, R., and REY, H. (2005), 'The determinants of cross border equity flows', *Journal of International Economics*, 65, 269–96.

PRASAD, E., ROGOFF, K., WEI, S., and KOSE, M. A. (2003), 'Effects of financial globalization on developing countries: some empirical evidence', IMF Occasional Paper.

QUINN, D. (1997), 'The correlates of change in international financial regulation', *American Political Science Review*, 91, 531–51.

REINHART, C., and ROGOFF, K. (2004), 'Serial default and the 'paradox' of rich to poor capital flows', *American Economic Review*, 94, 53–8.

RIVERA-BATIZ, P., and ROMER, P. (1991), 'Economic integration and economic growth', *Quar-terly Journal of Economics*, 106, 531–55.

RODRIGUEZ, F., and RODRIK, D. (2000), 'Trade policy and economic growth: a skeptic's guide to the cross-national evidence', *NBER Macroeconomics Annual 2000*, 261–325.

ROMER, P. (1986), 'Increasing returns and long-run growth', *Journal of Political Economy*, 94, 1002–37.

ROWLAND, P. F., and TESAR, L. (2004), 'Multinationals and the gains from international diversification', *Review of Economic Dynamics*, 7, 789–826.

SACHS, J., and WARNER, A. (1995), 'Economic reform and the process of global integration', *Brookings Papers on Economic Activity*, 1, 1–118.

SØRENSEN, B. E., and YOSHA, O. (1998), 'International risk sharing and european monetary unification', *Journal of International Economics*, 45, 211–38.

——— WU, Y., YOSHA, O., and ZHU, Y. (2007), 'Home bias and international risk sharing: twin puzzles separated at birth', *Journal of International Money and Finance*, forthcoming.

STRONG, N., and XU, X. (2003), 'Understanding the equity home bias: evidence from survey data', *Review of Economics and Statistics*, 85, 307–12.

STULZ, R. (1999), 'International portfolio flows and security markets', in M. Feldstein (ed.), *International Capital Flows*, Chicago: University of Chicago Press.

TESAR, L. (1995), 'Evaluating the gains from international risk sharing', *Carnegie-Rochester Conference Series on Public Policy*, 42, 95–143.

——— and WERNER, I. (1995), 'Home bias and high turnover', *Journal of International Money and Finance*, 14, 467–92.

WARNOCK, F. E. (2002), 'Home bias and high turnover reconsidered', *Journal of International Money and Finance*, 21, 795–805.

WEI, S. (2000), 'Local corruption and global capital flows', *Brookings Papers in Economic Activity*, 2, 303–46.

——— and WU, Y. (2002), 'Negative alchemy? corruption, composition of capital flows, and currency crises', in S. Edwards and J. A. Frankel (eds.), *Preventing Currency Crises in Emerging Markets*, Chicago: University of Chicago Press.

VAN WINCOOP, E. (1994), 'Welfare gains from international risk sharing', *Journal of Monetary Economics*, 34, 175–200.

VOLOSOVYCH, V. (2006), 'Financial market integration, risk sharing, and institutions: theory and evidence', Unpublished manuscript, University of Houston.

YOUNG, A. (1995), 'The tyranny of numbers', *Quarterly Journal of Economics*, 110, 641–80.

PART II

FINANCIAL SYSTEMS AND THE CORPORATE SECTOR

CHAPTER 7

....

CORPORATE FINANCE IN EUROPE: A SURVEY

FRANÇOIS DEGEORGE

ERNST MAUG

1. INTRODUCTION

....

THIS survey takes stock of research on corporate finance in Europe. The ambition is
to provide the reader with an overview of what we have learned about the subject,
particularly since the beginning of the 1990s. We focus on two themes when studying
corporate finance in Europe. First, the practice and institutions in Europe are heterogeneous and different from those in the United States and we demonstrate the importance of this observation. Second, we wish to draw some more general conclusions
with respect to the law and finance paradigm that has dominated recent research on
comparative institutional analysis, and the diversity of European institutions seems
to present an ideal testing ground for this approach.

The body of research on corporate finance is large and the subject has many facets,
so we selected some topics that we deem important and that provide a particular

We are grateful to Colin Mayer for helpful comments on an earlier draft of this chapter. Degeorge
acknowledges financial support by the National Centre of Competence in Research 'Financial Valuation
and Risk Management' (NCCR FINRISK). The NCCR FINRISK is a research programme supported by
the Swiss National Science Foundation. Maug thanks the Rudolph von Bennigsen-Foerder-foundation
for financial support and Thomas Diete and Karmonthip Wichmann for excellent research assistance.

European perspective. As a result, we do not include extensive discussions of theoretical developments unless they grapple with specifically European issues and we discuss research on other countries only in order to provide comparisons and to put European research in context. We refer the reader to the excellent and extensive surveys in Constantinides, Harris, and Stulz (2003) for comprehensive general surveys on topics in corporate finance we cover here. Even with this limited scope we make no pretence to be comprehensive, and we focus on articles that test hypotheses that emerge from the European context and that exploit European institutional features. We selectively include articles that mainly replicate similar research on the United States for Europe or for single European countries.

We warn the reader that 'Europe' in the sense of this survey article is not a well-defined, homogeneous geographical region, and is heterogeneous with respect to the institutions under study here. To some extent this is what makes research on Europe fascinating. For example, Rajan and Zingales (2003a) point to a north–south divide in the financial development indicators of European countries. A basic analysis of the financial indicators of La Porta et al. (1997, 1998, henceforth LLSV) suggests that their variation across legal systems within Europe is even greater than outside Europe—in spite of the fact that European countries share similar economic development histories. In order to simplify our task—and given the scarce research available to date—we omit former communist countries from our survey.

We address in turn: equity primary markets; privatizations; cross-listings; capital structure and pay-out policy; mergers and acquisitions; business groups, pyramids, and dual class shares; and valuation and the cost of capital.

2. EQUITY PRIMARY MARKETS

2.1. The Decision to Go Public

European research on equity primary equity markets has been quite active in the past decade. Several papers have exploited European institutional features, or access to confidential data, to address issues of wide relevance.

Pagano, Panetta, and Zingales (1998) tackle the issue of why firms go public. Surprisingly, this question had received fairly little academic attention. Their study uses an Italian sample of IPOs—and most importantly, a control sample of privately owned Italian companies, for which they obtained confidential data from the Bank of Italy. They find that the main factor affecting the probability of an IPO is the market/book ratio at which firms in the same industry trade. This could be due to the higher investment needs of sectors with high growth opportunities. It could also reflect an attempt by issuers to time the market. The latter explanation gains additional weight from the fact that investment and profitability decrease on average after the IPO.

Pagano et al. document that independent companies experience a reduction in cost of bank credit after the IPO (40 to 70 basis points)—even when controlling for firm characteristics and for reduction in leverage after going public (30 to 55 basis points). Moreover, after the IPO, firms borrow from a larger number of banks: the reduced cost of credit could be due to better public information associated with exchange listing or a stronger bargaining position vis-à-vis banks.

How generalizable are the conclusions from this Italian study? The typical Italian IPO is much larger and older than its US equivalent. But this is true also of other European countries (e.g. see Högholm and Rydqvist 1995 on Sweden), and Italian IPOs are not unlike mature US IPOs (for example, like reverse LBOs in the USA, Italian IPOs use the proceeds more to rebalance accounts than to finance growth). Italy certainly differs from the USA by the small size of its stock market relative to its economy. Most continental European countries share this feature, which points to a broader question: why does the stock market cater to large, mature companies in continental Europe, while the opposite is true in the USA? There are several possible, not mutually exclusive answers. One, popular ten years ago, was that appropriate stock markets were lacking in Europe. Since then, several markets specifically targeted to small, innovative firms have been launched. Their success has been mixed: the German Neuer Markt has closed, and the French Nouveau Marché has been merged.

The line of work of LLSV suggests another answer: if minority shareholder protection is low in some countries—and broadly speaking, that tends to be true in continental Europe—then external equity finance is expensive to raise. The evidence on this is mixed. LLSV (1997) find a higher frequency of IPOs in countries with high minority investor protection. But Holmen and Högfeldt (2004), using LLSV data, find that the different frequency of family-controlled firms across countries is unrelated to levels of minority investor protection. This suggests that the reluctance of European families to relinquish control of their firms in an IPO stems from other factors.

Recent work by Fama and French (2004) adds a new perspective on this debate. They document that the annual number of new issues has considerably increased in the USA since the early 1970s, due to an apparent decline in the cost of equity that allows weaker firms, and firms with more distant expected pay-offs, to issue public equity. Why this change occurred in the USA, and not in Europe, is a fascinating open question for future research. Note that the change in the USA is not necessarily for the better. If US IPOs are overpriced (Purnanandam and Swaminatham 2004; Loughran and Ritter 1995), the lower number of IPOs observed in Europe might actually be closer to the economic optimum.[1]

On the whole European IPOs are more mature firms and smaller and younger firms generally do not go public in Europe as much as they do in the United States.

---

[1] See Fama and French 2004: 268–70 for a discussion of this point.

Three explanations have been advanced for this observation, all with radically different implications: (1) Europe has weaker investor protection (implying that US practice is superior), (2) IPOs are overpriced in the USA, creating too strong an incentive to go public (implying that US practice is inferior), and (3) falling cost of capital has led to more IPOs in the USA, but not in Europe, which then raises the question whether the cost of capital is higher in Europe than in the USA.

2.2. Developments of IPO Mechanisms

In the United States, book building is the traditional method for taking companies public. A price range is set; the underwriter collects non-binding bids from investors; the final price is set; and the underwriter allocates the shares with complete discretion. Book building has attracted a fair amount of criticism in recent years. A first line of attack centred on fees. Chen and Ritter (2000) document that bankers' fees are exactly equal to 7 per cent of IPO proceeds for a surprisingly large number of deals. While the interpretation of these high fees is still controversial (see Hansen 2001) it is interesting to note that over the past decade, book building has become more widespread worldwide. As Ljungqvist, Jenkinson, and Wilhelm (2003) document, outside the USA, book building is more expensive in fees than the traditional fixed price methods. They argue that book building provides a benefit to issuers in the form of more accurate pricing: once they control for the endogeneity of the choice of IPO procedure, they find that—especially when it is combined with a US underwriter and a US investor clientele—book building can reduce underpricing significantly.

One of the salient characteristics of the book-building procedure is the discretion that underwriters and issuers enjoy in allocating shares. While this feature has recently attracted controversy in the context of IPO scandals in the United States,[2] a body of corporate finance theory suggests that the discretion enables underwriters to reward investors for revealing private information about the value of the firm taken public (e.g. Benveniste and Spindt 1989). The confidentiality of IPO share allocations makes it difficult to test directly whether underwriters indeed allocate shares to investors providing positive information, but a few European papers take a stab at this issue. Cornelli and Goldreich (2001) use a unique data set of investor bids and allocations for thirty-nine international equity issues managed by a major European investment bank. Their evidence supports the view of book building as an information extraction mechanism: the investment banker awards more shares to bidders who reveal information through limit prices than to other bidders. In another paper using a European sample of sixty-three international equity issues, Cornelli and Goldreich (2003) find that the bids that most influence the issue price are the ones that are favoured in the allocation of shares—consistent with the view that investors supply information in

---

[2] One of the controversies centred on the practice of 'spinning', i.e. allocating shares of underpriced IPOs to the executives of prospective investment banking clients.

exchange for a more favourable allocation. By contrast, Jenkinson and Jones (2004) find little evidence that more informative bids (that is, limit orders, revised bids, or bids submitted early in the book-building period) receive preferential allocation. Jenkinson, Morrison, and Wilhelm (2005) suggest that in Europe information revelation by investors may occur before the IPO prospectus is issued, rather than during the book-building period per se (for regulatory reasons this is not possible in the USA). This would also explain why very few European IPOs are eventually priced outside the initial range: unlike in US IPOs, the initial range in European IPOs already benefits from the information collected from investors.

European markets offer a useful perspective on the issue of what is the best way to offset the asymmetric information problem plaguing IPOs. For example, while IPO auctions are rarely used in the United States, they have long been used in France. Book building has also been used in France since it was introduced in the early 1990s, so that the French IPO market offers an interesting setting in which to compare the costs and benefits of book building vs. auctions. Derrien and Womack (2003) find that IPO auctions in France exhibit a smaller mean and variance of underpricing. Therefore, one of the important costs of going public, underpricing, seems to be lower for auctions compared to book building. Underwriter fees tend to be lower for auctions too. Since IPO auctions exhibit no noticeable difference in long-term performance relative to book building (Degeorge and Derrien 2001) it is hard to argue that the higher costs paid by issuers choosing book building are somewhat offset by valuation advantages. Nor are the results driven by intrinsic firm characteristics, as they are robust to controls for endogeneity in the choice of IPO procedure.

Overall then, the growing dominance of book building as the preferred IPO procedure in Europe raises a puzzle: book building entails higher fees than auctions (the main competitor to book building where more than one procedure exists); it is associated with more underpricing; and the discretionary power of the underwriter in share allocation makes the procedure prone to abuse. Yet in all countries where book building has been introduced recently, pre-existing auction mechanisms have disappeared or lost significant market share (Sherman 2004). Even if book building works well to extract information from investors, it is not obvious that well-designed auction mechanisms could not perform the same function (Biais, Bossaerts, and Rochet 2002; Biais and Faugeron-Crouzet 2002). Why then have auctions become less popular in IPOs? Degeorge, Derrien, and Womack (2005) offer an 'analyst hype' explanation for this puzzle. They hypothesize that issuers are willing to pay the higher cost of book building in exchange for increased and more favourable research coverage, and find confirming evidence. Their findings, while based on a French sample, have relevance outside Europe—in particular for the USA, where the 2004 Google IPO auction has revived the interest in IPO auctions.

While auctions have received much attention lately, they are not the only alternative to the standard book-building procedure. Derrien and Kecskés (2005) exploit a characteristic of the UK primary equity market: firms can list without issuing equity, and issue equity thereafter. Such listings are called 'introductions'. A market price for the equity is nevertheless established through transactions between current shareholders and anyone who wishes to buy shares in the firm. They argue that the existence of a market price reduces uncertainty about the firm's value, and should result in lower levels of initial returns when the firm offers shares for sale to the public. Indeed, they find that initial returns for these firms are 10 to 33 percentage points lower than for comparable IPOs. Their results are robust to endogeneity controls, suggesting that firms might be able to save on underpricing costs by considering this unusual two-stage method of going public.

While much of the IPO literature focuses on the issue of how to incorporate private information into the IPO price, Derrien and Womack (2003) document that market conditions (measured by the market return in the months before the offering) have a much greater—positive—impact on IPO underpricing for book-built offerings than for auctioned offerings. So, auctioned IPOs appear to be better at incorporating *public* information than book-built IPOs. Because it relies on semi-strong form market efficiency, the traditional asymmetric information paradigm is silent on the issue of whether some IPO procedures do better than others at incorporating public information into the IPO price. A behavioural perspective on IPO pricing provides some insight here. Derrien (2005) argues that IPO prices are influenced by investor sentiment. Overly bullish noise traders drive up the price, but the underwriter is reluctant to fully incorporate investor sentiment in the IPO price, because he worries that when investor sentiment vanishes, he will have to pay the cost of price support. In this behavioural framework IPO initial returns may be influenced by market conditions. Derrien finds support for this framework on a sample of French IPOs using the *Offre à Prix Ouvert*, a unique IPO mechanism in which a fraction of the IPO shares is reserved for individual investors.

In a similar vein, Cornelli, Goldreich, and Ljungqvist (2004) use a unique institutional feature of the European IPO market to test behavioural theories of IPO market pricing. They focus on the grey (or 'when-issued') market in European IPOs, which enables investors to speculate on the future stock prices of companies that are about to go public. The grey market starts when issuers publish the filing range, and ends when the IPO starts trading. From a behavioural perspective the grey market is interesting because it primarily attracts small investors. A high grey market price indicates small investor optimism. Cornelli et al. find that high grey market prices are a good predictor of first-day aftermarket prices, while low grey market prices are not. Moreover, IPOs with high grey market prices experience long-run price reversals. Their findings are consistent with a story in which sophisticated book-building investors sell their shares to small investors if the latter are over-optimistic, but not if they are overly pessimistic.

In the final conclusion, the demise of traditional offering methods in Europe in favour of book building still presents a puzzle that has not been resolved completely. Clearly, this is an area where European practice has converged to that of the USA and where institutional heterogeneity has been diminished during the last decade.

3. PRIVATIZATIONS

The privatization of state-owned companies has been one of the major economic transformations of the past two decades, involving many countries. Several multi-country studies of privatizations use samples that include Europe, although they often reach far wider. Megginson and Netter (2001) offer an excellent survey of empirical studies on privatization around the world. We limit ourselves to studies with a more European focus, and we emphasize work that appeared after their survey.

The large literature on privatizations falls into several categories: the determinants of privatizations; how privatizations are done; post-privatization performance; and the impact of privatizations. In Western Europe privatizations have usually been done through share issues, while voucher privatization schemes have often been used in former communist countries. Bortolotti, Fantini, and Siniscalco (2003) find that share issue privatizations are all the more common as the government is conservative and government deficit is high. They also find that governments from French civil law countries are less likely to privatize, other things being equal. Jones et al. (1999) document that governments often use share-issue privatizations for political ends. Governments typically tilt allocation patterns toward domestic investors, impose control restrictions, and underprice the shares at the offering—but probably for very different reasons from the typical IPO (possibly to pick up votes from voters in the process—see Biais and Perotti 2002).

Keloharju, Knüpfer, and Torstila (2005) analyse in detail the incentives given to retail investors. They find that many countries use bonus schemes and discounts to increase investor participation in privatizations, and that they increase investor participation much more cost-effectively than underpricing—although it is still costly (up to $248 per additional investor!). Degeorge et al. (2004) analyse the case of the France Telecom privatization in 1997. They find that inducing employees to participate was no easy task: in spite of various incentives amounting to an 80 per cent discount, one-third of the employees did not participate.

Many studies document increases in performance in privatized companies (see for example D'Souza and Megginson (1999) and the studies summarized therein). Interestingly, however, Bortolotti and Faccio (2004) find that greater government control of the firm post-privatization tends to be associated with *higher* market valuations. This puzzling finding is hard to square with accepted theories of privatizations.

Finally, a number of studies examine the impact of privatizations on stock market development. A general theme is that privatization increases stock market capitalization, trading, and participation by individual investors in the stock market (see Megginson and Netter 2001). Whether this last phenomenon will survive the bull market of the 1990s is unclear. In France for example, the France Telecom privatization brought many first-time investors to the stock market. Anecdotal evidence suggests that the subsequent crash in the France Telecom stock may have done lasting damage to individual investors' appetite.

Privatizations present a multifaceted phenomenon, and few conclusions emerge as governments pursue privatizations with different political objectives (government deficits, developing stock markets, broadening stock ownership, reducing the involvement of government in economic activity) and accordingly with different results.

4. Cross-Listings

Cross-listings of companies have attracted increasing attention by researchers and regulators in recent years. Here we use a broad definition of cross-listings, encompassing all companies where at least one class of stock is listed on an exchange in a country other than the country of incorporation. Pagano et al. (2001) document that in the years from 1986 to 1997, European companies have become more mobile and increasingly listed on foreign exchanges, with the US exchanges being the primary destination: during this time, the number of listings of companies from the EU-9 in the USA almost quadrupled from 53 to 207, while the number of cross-listings within the EU-9 increased from 267 to 309. At the same time, US companies have reduced their listings in Europe, and foreign listings from all countries in the EU-9 went down.

Researchers have followed several paradigms in order to explain why companies list abroad, what benefits this activity generates, which types of companies list, and what characteristics explain their listing choices. Of particular interest here is the increased attractiveness of the USA and the reduced attractiveness of Europe as a destination for cross-listings. The law and finance literature views cross-listings as a method to bond companies to a higher corporate governance standard by listing on an exchange that imposes tighter governance and disclosure standards (Coffee 1999).[3] Evidence in favour shows for example that managers and large shareholders of foreign companies that do not cross-list in the USA differ from those of non-US companies that do list in the USA: cross-listing firms enjoy smaller private benefits of control and their managers have fewer control rights (Doidge et al. 2005). The bonding hypothesis also seems to be supported by the fact that companies with ADR-listings in the USA attract more investment funding after the listing (Reese and Weisbach 2002). Doidge, Karolyi, and Stulz (2001) also document that US-listed firms enjoy a cross-listing premium, which is larger for firms with larger growth opportunities, and that these growth opportunities are larger for firms from countries that rank low on the LLSV investor protection scale. Nonetheless, the bonding hypothesis of cross-listings is subject to a number of reservations. With respect to US listings, the argument

---

[3] The bonding hypothesis of listing choice in a purely domestic context can be traced back at least to Gordon 1988, who argues that listing on the NYSE commits the firm to a single class share structure.

relies crucially on the notion that a cross-listing subjects the company to US securities laws. Siegel (2005) shows that this is generally not the case and foreign companies do obtain significant exemptions from SEC rules. He shows in particular that there is no evidence that minority shareholder protection is enhanced. A closely related argument pertains to disclosure standards. Here, Pagano et al. (2001) document that European firms list on exchanges where they are subject to lower accounting standards than at home, a fact that is largely driven by British companies: UK accounting standards are excellent and many UK firms list abroad. Licht (2001) goes even further and argues that Israeli companies list in the USA precisely in order to benefit from less stringent disclosure requirements and in order to avoid the 'disinfecting sunlight' imposed by domestic regulations. Licht formulates the alternative 'avoiding hypothesis' according to which firms regard higher disclosure standards as a cost, a claim that is also supported by the survey of Bancel and Mittoo (2001). In their survey of foreign listings from six European countries, they found that the primary benefits cited by managers are increased visibility and growth of the shareholder base, whereas SEC compliance and reporting requirements are viewed as a cost.

For European companies, the patterns of cross-listings seems to be better explained by other considerations. Pagano et al. (2001) show that more liquid markets with lower trading costs attract more foreign listings, which potentially also explains the attractiveness of the USA. The importance of the liquidity of deep markets may also explain why they find that many cross-listings are privatized companies that plan future sales of their shares. Within Europe, geographical and cultural proximity seems to play a significant role: 57 per cent of all European cross-listings take place within regions defined by close cultural and linguistic ties, compared to 24 per cent that would be expected if listings were distributed randomly (Pagano et al. 2001). This is supported by related findings by Portes, Rey, and Oh (2001) who investigate international cross-border equity flows and show that these flows depend negatively on geographical distance, a finding that they relate to informational frictions. Portes et al. also show that companies that list in the USA are typically fast growing high-tech companies, which possibly receive better expert attention by analysts on the US market. This argument accords well with the finding that European companies that list in the USA are significantly more likely to make acquisitions in the USA, and are more likely to use stock when paying for acquisitions, compared to their domestically listed peers (Tolmunen and Torstila 2005). By comparison, the Pagano et al. study shows that companies that cross-list within Europe are more likely to be mature companies that do not grow fast and increase their leverage after cross-listing. In an earlier study, Saudagaran (1988) found also significant relationships between cross-listings and the proportion of foreign sales, documenting that product market considerations are also relevant. The bonding hypothesis cannot explain why European exchanges have become less attractive over the last decade—investor protection and disclosure standards in Europe have, if anything, increased. It is conceivable that changes in cross-listing decisions are influenced by related changes in product markets and trade flows, but we are not aware of any study that has tested this hypothesis. Listings in the USA may have become more attractive for European companies for the same reasons that they became so for US companies (see our discussion of Fama and French 2004, above).

The overall evidence on cross-listings is somewhat mixed. Whereas some papers come out clearly in favour of the bonding hypothesis, others cast doubt on its premises and emphasize alternative reasons and mechanisms like liquidity, trading costs, and product market considerations. Moreover, most of the evidence supporting the bonding hypothesis is somewhat indirect, drawing conclusions from control rights, patterns of cross-listings, and investment funding. The challenge to future research seems to be to find more direct evidence to settle this debate.

5. Capital Structure and Pay-Out Policy

Differences in accounting rules create many challenges for an empirical study of capital structure at the European level—so much so, in fact, that to the best of our knowledge no such academic study exists. Nevertheless, Rajan and Zingales (1995) do a careful analysis of capital structure in a sample of G-7 countries, which contains four major European countries (France, Germany, Italy, and the United Kingdom). In particular, they adjust the data for differences in accounting standards. Several interesting patterns emerge. First, firms in the United Kingdom and Germany have lower leverage than in France and Italy, independent of company size. Institutional differences probably explain some of the cross-country differences. For example, creditor protection is higher in Germany and the UK than in France and Italy, and that might be the reason for the lower levels of leverage in the former two countries: firms may be less likely to lever up if they anticipate that they will be automatically liquidated in case of bankruptcy. Second, the factors affecting leverage are remarkably similar across countries. Asset tangibility is positively correlated with leverage— presumably because tangible assets can better serve as collateral. Market to book (a proxy for investment opportunities) is negatively correlated with leverage. This finding is consistent with the idea that highly levered companies are more likely to pass up profitable investment opportunities; it is also consistent with firms attempting to time the market and to issue equity when they perceive their stock price to be high. Rajan and Zingales also report a puzzling finding: size is positively correlated with leverage in all countries except Germany. While theory gives ambiguous predictions on the relation of size to leverage, why the relation in Germany should run opposite to that in other countries is not clear. The authors conclude that 'a deeper understanding of the actual determinants of the effects of institutional differences is necessary'.

Bancel and Mittoo (2004) take a stab at this issue using a survey approach. Similar to Graham and Harvey (2001) for the USA, they interview chief financial officers in sixteen European countries. Their results suggest that European and US managers use similar criteria in making their financial decisions: they find modest support for the trade-off and pecking order theories of capital structure, and almost no support for the asset substitution and free cash flow hypotheses.[4] Within Europe, there are differences both across and within legal systems as defined by La Porta et al. (1997, 1998).

Survey evidence by Bancel, Bhattacharya, and Mittoo (2005) indicates that European managers' views on pay-out policy are largely similar to those of their US peers (Brav et al. 2004). The two most important determinants of dividend policy are the stability and level of future earnings, and an aversion to cutting dividends. But as in the case of capital structure, some cross-country differences emerge, not easily explained by differences in legal systems. For example, German managers are much less concerned with cutting dividends than their peers in civil law countries. Perhaps German banks use their influence over German companies to protect their creditor claims (Amihud and Murgia 1997; Goergen, Renneboog, and Correia da Silva 2005).

Relative to the USA, repurchases have been less common in Europe. The practice has recently picked up, however, and more academic studies of European repurchases are likely to appear.[5]

Compared to other issues in corporate finance, pay-out policy and capital structure policy seem to be much more homogeneous across Europe with only a moderate influence of institutional differences, possibly with the notable exception of Germany. The factors driving capital structure and pay-outs are similar to those in the USA, and the increasing importance of repurchases provides further evidence for convergence. Interestingly, agency-based explanations like the free cash flow approach and asset substitution receive less support from survey-based evidence than asymmetric information approaches.

6. MERGERS AND ACQUISITIONS

Goergen and Renneboog (2004) study the European M&A market in the 1990s by analysing a sample of 187 large mergers and acquisitions in eighteen European countries as well as some aggregate statistics. They establish many results that are similar to those from previous studies on the M&A market in the United States. Event study

---

[4] Brounen, de Jong, and Koedijk 2004 find similar results in a survey of CFOs from the UK, the Netherlands, Germany, and France.

[5] For example, Ginglinger and Hamon 2005 exploit stringent French disclosure requirements to perform a study of actual repurchases by companies of their stock. They find that companies purchase against market trends, and that repurchases are associated with a decline in stock liquidity.

results reveal that investors owning a target company from forty trading days before an acquisition announcement until the end of the event day realize average abnormal returns of 23.1 per cent. The same number is 0.4 per cent for bidders. Cash offers are associated with larger announcement effects than acquisitions with stock or other securities. Announcements of mergers and friendly acquisitions generate similar returns over the same event window (23.4 per cent and 20.3 per cent respectively), whereas market reactions for hostile acquisitions are larger (29.2 per cent), confirming related evidence for the USA. Surprisingly, however, multiple bidder contests do not generate significantly larger returns. Also, in all cases the pre-announcement run-up over forty trading days seems to be large: across all types of announcements, the cumulated return over the (-1.0) event window is less than 40 per cent of the return over the larger (-40.0) window, potentially indicating that insider trading regulations and enforcement are not as strict in Europe as they are in the USA. Shareholders of bidding companies benefit from mergers and friendly acquisitions (abnormal returns starting forty trading days before the announcement of 4.6 per cent and 4.8 per cent respectively), but suffer losses from hostile bids by their companies $(-2.5$ per cent abnormal announcement return). There are also regional differences within Europe. Shareholders of UK targets benefit more than those from continental Europe, with the difference being statistically significant for all event windows. Results are not statistically significant for bidding firms, although acquirers of southern European targets tend to benefit less than those of German and Central European targets.

A second set of studies investigates how mergers and acquisitions in Europe affect other stakeholders, like consumers and workers. Gugler and Yurtoglu (2004) analyse the impact of mergers on employment in a sample of 646 mergers in the 1987–98 period. They find that firms in the USA have pre-merger labour productivity similar to non-merging firms, and mergers in the USA have no impact on employment. By contrast, in Europe, merging partners have labour productivity 9 per cent below their non-merging industry peers before the merger, and they increase their labour productivity by 10 per cent to the industry average through lay-offs after the merger. The authors explain this fact by differences in labour markets: mergers in Europe serve to break implicit contracts and overcome labour market rigidities, whereas no such implicit contracts need to be broken in the USA where labour markets are more flexible. Surprisingly, the effect is stronger in the UK than in continental Europe. The authors attribute this finding to the UK's comparatively less flexible labour markets.

Focarelli and Panetta (2003) analyse whether mergers harm consumers by investigating how the deposit rates of Italian banks are influenced by mergers. Controlling for a number of factors, they show that the anti-competitive effect of mergers is short-lived: while deposit rates decline in the year of the merger, they increase eventually. This supports the hypothesis that mergers create efficiency gains that are passed on to consumers in the long run.

Regulating the impact of mergers on consumers is the role of competition authorities, and within Europe this role rests with the European Commission for large mergers.[6] The role of the European Commission in this regard has caught the attention of researchers as well as politcal commentators, in particular since the Commission has recently also regulated mergers among companies not domiciled in the EU.[7] Aktas et al. (2001) point out in their analysis of the Boeing–Mc Donnell Douglas acquisition the European Commission's increasing tendency to show its strength even in non-European mergers. This is supported by an important difference in legal rules: the European Commission can block a merger, whereas the US system requires that the competition authorities obtain the consent of a judge for a ban (Aktas et al. 2001). Aktas, de Bodt, and Roll (2004a) analyse 604 merger cases investigated by the European Commission in the 1990–9 period, of which 101 involved *only* non-EU firms. The Commission proceeds in two stages, where most decisions are reached in the first stage after a maximum of one month, and only few cases are scrutinized more closely in the second stage that can take up to four months. The Aktas, de Bodt, and Roll study shows that concluding stage 1 is generally accompanied by positive stock market reactions for all companies, particularly for targets, whereas entering stage 2 is accompanied by losses for all companies concerned. Large returns on the initial announcements seem to indicate large monopoly rents and are more likely to lead to more thorough stage 2 investigations. The study also investigates which variables predict the decision of the Commission. They find that approval is positively associated with size, which the authors attribute to the better bargaining position of large companies. Also, higher announcement returns predict success, which indicates that firms bargain more successfully with the Commission if more value from the deal is at stake. In a follow-up study, Aktas, de Bodt, and Roll (2004b) analyse a sample of 290 merger cases where both parties are listed companies and demonstrate that the Commission is more likely to block mergers where European companies are harmed from increased competition, and also if the bidder is a foreign company, lending support for the claim that the Commission's policy is protectionist.

European markets for mergers and acquisitions present some rather striking differences from their US counterparts. While some are easily explained by institutional differences (difference in the protection of stakeholders other than shareholders, competition law), others (premia for hostile bids) are more surprising. Anecdotal evidence suggests that some separation of national markets and therefore institutional heterogeneity are likely to persist. We would like to see more studies that investigate how well the European market for corporate control performs relative to other regions and how it contributes to the performance of European economies. Research on mergers and acquisitions in Eastern Europe is, to the best of our knowledge, non-existent.

---

[6] The rules specify that the merging partners have to pass a size threshold. A minimum proportion of their sales must be in at least two EU countries for the Commission to be responsible, otherwise national authorities are in charge. The domicile of the firms is irrelevant for this question.

[7] In the Boeing–McDonnell Douglas case, the European Commission forced Boeing to give up some exclusivity contracts with European airlines, which implied a significant loss of value for Boeing shareholders. Other well-publicized cases included the merger of General Electric with Honeywell and the EMI/Time Warner deal.

7. BUSINESS GROUPS, PYRAMIDS, AND DUAL CLASS SHARES

Several European studies have investigated the organization of firms into business groups through pyramidal forms of ownership and cross-shareholdings. Interestingly, with the notable exception of Faccio and Lang (2002), all studies focus only on one European country. Studies in this area focus on one (and sometimes both) of two aspects. The first aspect emphasizes how holding companies and business groups act as internal capital markets that may be useful (if they reduce transaction costs) or harmful (if they lead to inefficient cross-subsidization). The second aspect focuses on the fact that pyramidal ownership and business groups can be ways to deviate from the one share/one vote principle (Nicodano 1998) and help ultimate owners and managers to extract private benefits of control. The last aspect puts these forms of ownership into the same context as dual class shares.

Buysschaert, Deloof, and Jegers (2005) show that accounting performance in Belgian business groups is significantly lower than that of similar stand-alone firms and attribute this fact to inefficient allocation of capital within groups. However, the same authors (Buysschaert, Deloof, and Jegers 2004) also provide evidence based on equity sales that Belgian business groups do not expropriate minority shareholders. Rather, share issues seem to serve the creation of more transparent group structures, suggesting that traditional structures may have become obsolete.

Cronqvist and Nilsson (2003) analyse accounting performance as well as stock market valuations of almost all Swedish firms in the 1990s and argue that Sweden uses more dual class shares, more cross-shareholdings, and more stock pyramids than most other countries. They find that the control of vote ownership by controlling minority shareholders is costly and reduces Tobin's q by 6–25 per cent. Holmen and Knopf (2004) focus on mergers in Sweden where pyramids and dual class shares create situations such that shareholders have stakes in the bidder and the target. They find evidence for distorted acquisition decisions (lower bidder returns, more diversifying acquisitions) but little direct evidence for minority shareholder expropriation (tunnelling). Boehmer (2000) analyses takeovers by bidding firms in German business groups and finds that the presence of minority owners is associated with higher bidder returns, whereas the presence of majority owners is not, suggesting that it is difficult to empirically disentangle the monitoring role of business groups and the distortion they created. The evidence therefore suggests that minority shareholders in pyramids and business groups suffer mainly from investment decisions that benefit controlling shareholders (e.g. by reducing the likelihood of a takeover, see also Bøhren and Norli 1997 for Norway), but are not subject to direct expropriation, which contrasts with the evidence for East Asia (see e.g. Bae, Kang, and Kim 2002 on Korea and Bertrand, Mehta, and Mullainathan 2002 on India) or Eastern Europe (e.g. Atanasov 2005).

Dual class shares. The large literature on dual class shares has mainly tried to measure voting premia and to identify variables that could explain them. Most studies are single-country studies, which is to some extent explained by the fact that the specific institutional details that differentiate shares with superior and inferior voting rights differ across countries. Becht, Bolton, and Röell (2003) cite altogether seventeen studies on mostly European countries that measure voting premia ranging from −6.4 per cent (Odegaard 2002 for Norway) to 82 per cent (Zingales 1994 for Italy). We do not discuss these studies here in detail (see also Rydqvist 1992 for an earlier survey on dual class shares). Nenova (2002) presents a cross-country analysis that interprets voting premia as a measure of private benefits of control in a study of 661 companies with dual class shares from the world's thirty largest stock markets. Her measure attempts to value voting blocks rather than individual voting shares. She then applies regression analysis and enters variables that control for the probability of a control contest, block-holding costs, takeover rules, and ownership concentration. Her estimates for control block premia seem to agree qualitatively with the findings on voting premia from individual country studies, although the differences for some countries are large.[8] All Scandinavian countries except Norway have premia of 1 per cent and lower, whereas Italy and France have control block premia of 28–9 per cent. Germany and the UK fall in between with control block premia of 9.5 per cent and 9.6 per cent respectively. She claims that legal indicators related to investor protection can explain about two-thirds of the cross-sectional variation in voting premia, which supports the notion that her control block premia are related to private benefits of control and investor protection. Note, however, from the figures reported above that the correlation between her control block premia and the common law/civil law divide seems to be weak at best.

Neumann (2003) advances a different hypothesis on voting premia that particularly addresses the fact that for some companies the superior voting shares trade at significant discounts to their non-voting counterparts. In his study of Danish stocks he shows that these discounts are related to liquidity variables and trading costs. It seems that superior voting stocks are more closely held, which makes them less liquid, more expensive to trade, and ultimately worth less. This might also explain the related observation that registered shares rose and bearer shares fell in value (so that prices converged) after the Swiss company Nestlé announced that it would allow foreign investors to trade in its stock (Loderer and Jacobs 1995).[9]

Business groups, pyramids, and dual class share structures all present different strategies for large shareholders to increase their control rights relative to their cash flow rights. However, their consequences are often less dramatic than expected. Overall, these deviations from the one-share/one-vote principle seem to become less prevalent, another area where practice in Europe appears to converge to that of the USA.

---

[8] Nenova 2002 finds 9.5% for Germany (compared to 26.3% in Hoffmann-Burchardi 1999), 6.3% for Norway (compared to –6.4% in Odegaard 2002), and 47.7% for Korea (compared to 10% in Chung and Kim 1999).

[9] This explanation would also be supported by Gardiol, Gibson-Asner, and Tuchschmid 1997.

8. VALUATION AND COST OF CAPITAL

There are only a few contributions that have analysed specifically European aspects of valuation and the cost of capital, although the US literature on these subjects is large. Bris, Koskinen, and Nilsson (2003) document that the introduction of the euro as a common currency has increased corporate valuations by an average of 7.4 per cent compared to those European countries (the Scandinavian countries, Switzerland, and the UK) that did not introduce it. The authors argue that this can be attributed to two channels: first, reductions in the cost of capital by increased benefits from diversification (reduction in the home bias), and, secondly, by increasing cash flows as international trade is usually larger in common currency areas. The effect is concentrated entirely in those countries that were subject to currency crises before the introduction of the euro and does not apply to those countries which managed to stay within the European Monetary System. The last finding accords well with Hail and Leuz (2004), who find that conventional risk factors and macroeconomic variables like inflation explain almost 60 per cent of the cross-sectional variation in the cost of capital in a study of forty countries (of which sixteen are European).

9. CONCLUSION

One of the major themes of this survey is the continuing heterogeneity of Europe. Apart from the LLSV categorization (common law vs. civil law), we referred to the north–south divide (Rajan and Zingales 2003a), the monetary divide (inside/outside the European monetary system), and we barely looked at the continuing differences between east and west and the (shifting) divide between countries inside and outside the EU. Repeatedly, we found that the legal approach developed by LLSV has only a limited capacity to capture the relevant differences within Europe with respect to corporate finance. However, as of now, no coherent alternative has emerged and the question of which analytic approach best captures the heterogeneity of Europe with respect to the development of equity primary markets, privatization mechanisms, the construction of business groups, and the value generated through M&A activity remains on the research agenda. While European practice seems to be different in some areas of corporate finance, we have indicated several areas where the gap to US practice appears to be narrowing overall.

Little research addresses specifically European issues in corporate finance. We can think of several reasons for this sparseness. The diversity of institutional systems and languages presents a non-trivial barrier for researchers. To the extent that European practices are less market based than in the USA, they are also less observable. More subtly perhaps, most of the stylized facts that have informed corporate finance theory are rooted in US empirical evidence. Theories relevant for the European context are less developed, and in turn, European research in corporate finance benefits from little theoretical guidance.

While the complexity and heterogeneity of Europe are real, a small number of recent studies (we cited Faccio and Lang 2002 and Goergen and Renneboog 2004, among others) use the cross-sectional variation available by looking at pan-European panels of companies. We feel that more research along these lines is needed to increase our understanding of European corporate finance.

REFERENCES

AKTAS, N., DE BODT, E., and ROLL, R. (2004a), 'European M&A regulation is protectionist', Université Catholique de Louvain and UCLA, mimeo.

——————(2004b), 'Market response to European regulation of business combinations', *Journal of Financial and Quantitative Analysis*, 39, 731–57.

————LEVASSEUR, M., and SCHMITT, A. (2001), 'The emerging role of the European Commission in merger and acquisition monitoring: the BoeingMcDonnell Douglas case', *European Financial Management*, 7, 447–80.

AMIHUD, Y., and MURGIA, M. (1997), 'Dividends, taxes, and signaling: evidence from Germany', *Journal of Finance*, 52, 397–408.

ATANASOV, V. (2005), 'How much value can blockholders tunnel? Evidence from the Bulgarian mass privatization auctions', *Journal of Financial Economics*, 76, 191–234.

BAE, K.-H., KANG, J.-K., and KIM, J.-M. (2002), 'Tunneling or value added? Evidence from mergers by Korean business groups', *Journal of Finance*, 57, 2695–740.

BAKER, H. K., NOFSINGER, J. R., and WEAVER, D. G. (2002), 'International cross-listing and visibility', *Journal of Financial and Quantitative Analysis*, 37, 495–521.

BANCEL, F., BHATTACHARYYA, N., and MITTOO, U. R. (2005), 'Cross-country determinants of payout policy: a survey of European firms', Working Paper.

——and MITTOO, U. R. (2001), 'European managerial perceptions of the net benefits of foreign stock listings', *European Financial Management*, 7, 213–36.

————(2004), 'Cross-country determinants of capital structure choice: a survey of European firms', *Financial Management*, 33, 103–32.

BECHT, M., BOLTON, P., and RÖELL, A. (2003), 'Corporate governance and control', in G. M. Constantinides, M. Harris, and R. M. Stulz (eds.), *Handbook of the Economics of Finance, iA: Corporate Finance*, Amsterdam: Elsevier North Holland.

BENVENISTE, L. M., and SPINDT, P. A. (1989), 'How investment bankers determine the offer price and allocation of new issues', *Journal of Financial Economics*, 24, 343–61.

BERTRAND, M., MEHTA, P., and MULLAINATHAN, S. (2002), 'Ferreting out tunneling: an application to Indian business groups', *Quarterly Journal of Economics*, 117, 121–48.

BIAIS, B., BOSSAERTS, P., and ROCHET, J.-C. (2002), 'An optimal IPO mechanism', *Review of Economic Studies*, 69, 117–46.

——and FAUGERON-CROUZET, A. M. (2002), 'IPO auctions: English, Dutch, ... French, and internet', *Journal of Financial Intermediation*, 11, 9–36.

——and PEROTTI, E. (2002), 'Machiavellian privatization', *American Economic Review*, 92, 240–58.

BOEHMER, E. (2000), 'Business groups, bank control, and large shareholders: an analysis of German takeovers', *Journal of Financial Intermediation*, 9, 117–48.

BØHREN, O., and NORLI, O. (1997), 'Determinants of intercorporate shareholdings', *European Finance Review*, 1, 265–87.

BORTOLOTTI, B., and FACCIO, M. (2004), 'Reluctant privatization', ECGI: Finance Working Paper no. 40.

——— FANTINI, M., and SINISCALCO, D. (2003), 'Privatisation around the world: new evidence from panel data', *Journal of Public Economics*, 88, 305–32.

BRAV, A., GRAHAM, J. R., HARVEY, C. R., and MICHAELY, R. (2004), 'Payout policy in the 21st century', NBER Working Paper.

BRENNAN, M., and SUBRAHMANYAM, A. (1996), 'Market microstructure and asset pricing: on the compensation for illiquidity in stock returns', *Journal of Financial Economics*, 41, 441–64.

BRIS, A., KOSKINEN, Y., and NILSSON, M. (2003), 'The euro is good after all: evidence from corporate valuations', CEPR Discussion Paper Series.

BROUNEN, D., DE JONG, A., and KOEDIJK, K. (2004), 'Corporate finance in Europe: confronting theory with practice', *Financial Management*, 33, 71–101.

BUYSSCHAERT, A., DELOOF, M., and JEGERS, M. (2004), 'Equity sales in Belgian corporate groups: expropriation of minority shareholders? A clinical study', *Journal of Corporate Finance*, 10, 81–103.

——— ——— ——— (2005), 'Is group affiliation profitable in developed countries? Not in Belgium', Vrije Universiteit Brussel, mimeo.

CHEN, H.-C, and RITTER, J. R. (2000), 'The seven percent solution', *Journal of Finance*, 55, 1105–31.

CHUNG, K. H., and KIM, J.-K. (1999), 'Corporate ownership and the value of a vote in an emerging market', *Journal of Corporate Finance*, 5, 35–54.

COFFEE, J. C. (1999), 'The future as history: the prospects for global convergence in corporate governance and its implications', *Northwestern University Law Review*, 93, 641–708.

CONSTANTINIDES, G. M., HARRIS, M., and STULZ, R. M. (2003), *Handbook of the Economics of Finance*, 1A: *Corporate Finance*, Amsterdam: Elsevier North Holland.

CORNELLI, F., and GOLDREICH, D. (2001), 'Bookbuilding and strategic allocation', *Journal of Finance*, 56, 2337–69.

——— ——— (2003), 'Bookbuilding: how informative is the order book?', *Journal of Finance*, 58, 1415.

——— ——— and LJUNGQVIST, A. P. (2004), 'Investor sentiment and pre-issue markets', CEPR Discussion Paper no. 4448.

CRONQVIST, H., and NILSSON, M. (2003), 'Agency costs of controlling minority shareholders', *Journal of Financial and Quantitative Analysis*, 38, 695–719.

DEGEORGE, F., and DERRIEN, F. (2001), 'Les Déterminants de la performance à long terme des introductions en bourse: le cas français', *Banque & Marchés*, November–December, 8–18.

——— ——— and WOMACK, K. L. (2005), 'Analyst hype in IPOs: explaining the popularity of book-building', *Review of Financial Studies*, forthcoming.

——— JENTER, D., MOEL, A., and TUFANO, P. (2004), 'Selling company shares to reluctant employees: France Telecom's experience', *Journal of Financial Economics*, 71, 169–202.

DERRIEN, F. (2005), 'IPO pricing in 'hot' market conditions: who leaves money on the table?', *Journal of Finance*, 60, 487–521.

——— and KECSKÉS, A. (2005), 'The initial public offerings of listed firms', Working Paper.

——— and WOMACK, K. L. (2003), 'Auctions vs. bookbuilding and the control of underpricing in hot IPO markets', *Review of Financial Studies*, 6, 31–61.

DOIDGE, C., KAROLYI, G. A., and STULZ, R. M. (2001), 'Why are foreign firms listed in the U.S. worth more?', NBER Working Paper.

————————Lins, K. V., Miller, D. P., and Stulz, R. M. (2005), 'Private benefits of control, ownership, and the cross-listing decision', NBER Working Paper.

D'Souza, J., and Megginson, W. L. (1999), 'The financial and operating performance of privatized firms during the 1990s', *Journal of Finance*, 54, 1397–438.

Encaoua, D., and Jacquemin, A. (1982), 'Organizational efficiency and monopoly power: the case of French industrial groups', *European Economic Review*, 19, 25–51.

Faccio, M., and Lang, L. H. P. (2002), 'The ultimate ownership of western European corporations', *Journal of Financial Economics*, 65, 365–95.

Fama, E. F., and French, K. R. (2004), 'New lists: fundamentals and survival rates', *Journal of Financial Economics*, 73, 229–69.

Focarelli, D., and Panetta, F. (2003), 'Are mergers beneficial to consumers? Evidence from the market for bank deposits', *American Economic Review*, 93(4), 1152–72.

Gardiol, L., Gibson-Asner, R., and Tuchschmid, N. S. (1997), 'Are liquidity and corporate control priced by shareholders? Empirical evidence from Swiss dual class shares', *Journal of Corporate Finance*, 3(Dec.), 299–323.

Ginglinger, E., and Hamon, J. (2005), 'Actual share repurchases, timing and corporate liquidity', Université Paris-Dauphiné, mimeo.

Goergen, M., and Renneboog, L. (2004), 'Shareholder wealth effects of European domestic and cross-border takeover bids', *European Financial Management*, 10, 9–45.

———— ———— and Correia da Silva, L. (2005), 'When do German firms change their dividends?', *Journal of Corporate Finance*, 11, 375–99.

Gordon, J. N. (1998), 'Ties that bond: dual class comman stock and the problem of shareholder choice', *California Law Review*, 76, 1–85.

Graham, J. R., and Harvey, C. R. (2001), 'The theory and practice of corporate finance: evidence from the field', *Journal of Financial Economics*, 60, 187–243.

Gugler, K., and Yurtoglu, B. B. (2004), 'The effects of mergers on company employment in the USA and Europe', *International Journal of Industrial Organization*, 22, 481–502.

Hail, L., and Leuz, C. (2004), 'International differences in cost of equity capital: do legal institutions and securities regulation matter?', ECGI Law Working Paper.

Hansen, R. S. (2001), 'Do investment banks compete in IPOs? The advent of the '7% plus contract'', *Journal of Financial Economics*, 59, 313–46.

Hoffman-Burchardi, U. (1999), Corporate Governance Rules and the Value of Control: A Study of German Dual-Class Shares, FMG Discussion Paper no. 315(Mar.).

Högholm, K., and Rydqvist, K. (1995), 'Going public in the 1980s: evidence from Sweden', *European Financial Management*, 1, 287–315.

Holmen, M., and Högfeldt, P. (2004), 'A law and finance analysis of initial public offerings', *Journal of Financial Intermediation*, 13, 324–58.

———— and Knopf, J. D. (2004), 'Minority shareholder protections and the private benefits of control for Swedish mergers', *Journal of Financial and Quantitative Analysis*, 39, 167–91.

Jenkinson, T., and Jones, H. (2004), 'Bids and allocations in European IPO bookbuilding', *Journal of Finance*, 59, 2309–38.

Jones, S. L., Megginson, W. L., Nash, R. C., and Netter, J. M. (1999), 'Share issue privatizations as financial means to political and economic ends', *Journal of Financial Economics*, 53, 217–53.

Keloharju, M., Knüpfer, S., and Torstila, S. (2005), 'Do retail incentives work in privatizations?', EFA 2004 Maastricht Meetings Paper.

La Porta, R., López-de-Silanes, F., Shleifer, A., and Vishny, R. (1997), 'Legal determinants of external finance', *Journal of Finance*, 52, 1131–50.

———— ———— ———— ———— (1998), 'Law and finance', *Journal of Political Economy*, 106, 1113–55.

LICHT, A. N. (2001), 'Managerial opportunism and foreign listing: some direct evidence', Working Paper.

LJUNGQVIST, A. P., JENKINSON, T., and WILHELM, W. J. (2003), 'Global integration in primary equity markets: the role of U.S. banks and U.S. investors', *Review of Financial Studies*, 16, 63–99.

LODERER, C., and JACOBS, A. (1995), 'The Nestle crash', *Journal of Financial Economics*, 37, 315–39.

LOUGHRAN, T., and RITTER, J. R. (1995), 'The new issues puzzle', *Journal of Finance*, 50, 23–51.

MEGGINSON, W. L., and NETTER, J. M. (2001), 'From state to market: a survey of empirical studies on privatization', *Journal of Economic Literature*, 39, 321–89.

MORRISON, A., JENKINSON, T., and WILHELM, W. J. (2003), 'Why are European IPOs so rarely priced outside the indicative price range?', University of Virginia, mimeo.

NENOVA, T. (2002), 'The value of corporate votes and control benefits: a cross-country analysis', *Journal of Financial Economics*, 68, 325–51.

NEUMANN, R. (2003), 'Price differentials between dual-class stocks: voting premium or liquidity discount?', *European Financial Management*, 9, 315–32.

NICODANO, G. (1998), 'Corporate groups, dual-class shares and the value of voting rights', *Journal of Banking and Finance*, 22, 1117–37.

ODEGAARD, B. A. (2002), 'Price differences between equity classes: corporate control, foreign ownership or liquidity? Evidence from Norway', Norwegian School of Managment, mimeo.

PAGANO, M., PANETTA, F., and ZINGALES, L. (1998), 'Why do companies go public? An empirical analysis', *Journal of Finance*, 53, 27–64.

——RANDL, O., RÖELL, A. A., and ZECHNER, J. (2001), 'What makes stock exchanges succeed? Evidence from cross-listing decisions', *European Economic Review*, 45, 770–82.

PORTES, R., REY, H., and OH, Y. (2001), 'Information and capital flows: the determinants of transactions in financial assets', *European Economic Review*, 45, 783–96.

PURNANANDAM, A. K., and SWAMINATHAN, B. (2004), 'Are IPOs really underpriced?', *Review of Financial Studies*, 17, 811–48.

RAJAN, R. G., and ZINGALES, L. (1995), 'What do we know about capital structure? Some evidence from international data', *Journal of Finance*, 50, 1421–60.

————(2003a), 'Banks and markets: the changing character of European finance', NBER Working Papers.

————(2003b), 'The great reversals: the politics of financial development in the twentieth century', *Journal of Financial Economics*, 69, 5–50.

REESE, W. A., and WEISBACH, M. S. (2002), 'Protection of minority shareholder interests, cross-listings in the United States, and subsequent equity offerings', *Journal of Financial Economics*, 1, 65–104.

RYDQVIST, K. (1992), 'Dual-class shares: a review', *Oxford Review of Economic Policy*, 8, 45–57.

SARKISSIAN, S., and SCHILL, M. J. (2004), 'The overseas listing decision: new evidence of proximity preference', *Review of Financial Studies*, 17, 769–809.

SAUDAGARAN, S. M. (1988), 'An empirical study of selected factors influencing the decision to list on foreign stock exchanges', *Journal of International Business Studies*, 19, 101–28.

SHERMAN, A. E. (2004), 'Global trends in IPO methods: book building vs. auctions with endogenous entry', Working Paper.

SIEGEL, J. (2005), 'Can foreign firms bond themselves effectively by renting U.S. securities laws?', *Journal of Financial Economics*, 75, 319–59.

TOLMUNEN, P., and TORSTILA, S. (2005), 'Cross-listings and M&A activity: transatlantic evidence', *Financial Management*, 34, 123–42.

WILHELM, W. J., MORRISON, A. D., and JENKINSON, T. (2003), 'Why are European IPOs so rarely priced outside the indicative price range?', Oxford Financial Research Center Working Paper.

ZINGALES, L. (1994), 'The value of the voting right: a study of the Milan Stock Exchange experience', *Review of Financial Studies*, 7, 125–48.

CHAPTER 8

THE ECONOMICS OF THE EU'S CORPORATE INSOLVENCY LAW AND THE QUEST FOR HARMONIZATION BY MARKET FORCES

OREN SUSSMAN

The European Parliament and the Council of Ministers shall endeavour to achieve the objective of free movement of capital between Member States and third countries to the greatest extent possible.

(Constitution for Europe, draft, 2003, Article III-46)

I would like to thank Julian Franks, Colin Mayer, Gabriel Moss, and Ken Okamura for helpful comments.

These objectives cannot be achieved to a sufficient degree at national level and action at Community level is therefore justified.

(Council regulation on insolvency proceedings, 1346/2000)

1. Introduction

Two propositions are often taken for granted while discussing the regulation of cross-border transactions. First, that any harmonization is for the better. For without rules that reconcile conflicting laws, international transactions lack structure and discipline. Moreover, in a world where international trade is both commendable and unstoppable, even a domestic transaction may become international at some stage, either by coincidence or as a deliberate attempt to avoid domestic regulation. As a result, international disorganization might bite into an otherwise well-functioning domestic order. The second proposition is that harmonization can only be achieved through political or bureaucratic initiative. In this chapter I examine theses propositions within the context of the 2000-EU insolvency law and find reasons—theoretical and empirical—to doubt both; indeed, my statistical analysis is consistent with the hypothesis that the legislation has actually increased the cost of cross-border insolvency. I therefore conclude the chapter suggesting an alternative approach to harmonization, which is based—to a much larger extent—on market forces rather than on political action.

Any analysis of harmonization requires some understanding of the 'spontaneous order' that prevails in its absence. Based on a study of a shipping insolvency case where jurisdiction was disputed between English and American courts, I stipulate that the basic problem with the unharmonized state is a heightened degree of legal uncertainty, resulting from the poor articulation of the rules that determine to what jurisdiction each case belongs. In such a setting each party tries to push the case to her favourite jurisdiction. Worse, there is a certain first-mover advantage in this interaction, where the first party to litigate increases the likelihood of achieving his preferred jurisdiction. That creates a phenomenon similar to a creditors' run, leading to excessive litigation and premature liquidation. It is noteworthy, however, that although such a setting is probably suboptimal, it is by no means lacking order altogether: even if the outcome follows no expressed legal doctrine, and even if the players' unilateral actions have a greater effect on the outcome than deemed desirable, we may still think of that outcome as an equilibrium in a well-defined game. The question that needs to be explored is whether the rules in this game can be changed to the benefit of the parties involved.

Putting the problem in that way one is forced to admit that harmonization may actually worsen the situation relative to the spontaneous order. It is not even clear that harmonization per se decreases the level of legal uncertainty. It is actually possible that the outcome in the spontaneous-order game is fairly predictable, while the harmonization rules are too vague, or maybe leave too much room for judicial discretion, making the final outcome even harder to predict in advance. That might actually increase the incidence of premature liquidation and the cost of bankruptcy. Looking at a court case of a Parmalat subsidiary—already adjudicated under the new EU legislation—one may conclude that this is indeed a possibility that deserves a careful consideration.

Whether legal uncertainty (and the cost of insolvency) has actually increased, and whether this has affected a substantial fraction of firms, is thus an empirical question. To answer it, I merge accounting, shareholding, and subsidiary information, provided by Amadeus, a database that covers German, Spanish, French, British, and Italian companies beyond a certain size threshold. One can then classify companies as being likely to be affected by the new legislation if there is a significant ownership by a non-domestic EU industrial shareholder, or if the company has a significant ownership of non-domestic EU subsidiaries.

There are two main findings. First, cross-border ownership is an important, though not overwhelming phenomenon. Around 6 per cent of companies have a non-domestic EU industrial shareholder, while the incidence of a non-EU shareholder is at least double that much. About 40 per cent of companies have subsidiaries, about 5–6 (on average) each, of which about 10 per cent are non-domestic EU, and about the same amount located out of the EU.[1]

Second, there is some evidence that companies with such cross-border ownership have seen an increase in their cost of borrowing during 2001–3 (when the law became effective). Since I have no direct information about the cost of borrowing, I use the level of gearing (leverage) as an indicator. Under well-established theory, companies that face increased bankruptcy costs (e.g. due to enhanced coordination problems in bankruptcy) would see their effective cost of borrowing increase and respond by decreasing their gearing. Controlling for company characteristics, including the effect of having local industrial holders or subsidiaries, industry, the business cycle, etc., I estimate the marginal, accumulated change in gearing for companies with such EU ownership. It turns out that German, Spanish, and British companies with a non-domestic EU industrial holder have significantly decreased their level of gearing by 15 per cent to 40 per cent over the 2001–3 period. Similar effects were found for non-EU industrial holders. Hardly any effect was detected for companies with non-domestic EU subsidiaries.

Hence, there is a reason to doubt whether the new legislation has achieved its goals. I thus suggest an alternative approach: that each (corporate) contract should specify a jurisdiction under which legal disputes are to be resolved. Since insolvency is just a standardized form for the default clauses of the debt contract, the settlement of a debt contract in default is subject to the same rule. I do recognize that some jurisdictions are inconsistent with others, but argue that individual firms should be

---

[1] See Scott and Smith 1986 for a similar analysis regarding the effect of the 1978 bankruptcy reform in the USA on the terms of credit.

responsible for avoiding such conflicts, by placing their contracts under jurisdictions consistent one with the other. Note that companies are likely to bear a significant extra cost of litigation in case their contracts are mutually inconsistent, and thus have an incentive to invest effort in finding a satisfactory solution to the problem. Note also that companies are allowed to choose the solution of placing all their contracts under a single jurisdiction. That may be their domestic jurisdiction, or a foreign one, so that companies can benefit from a larger set of contractual menus and enhanced legal diversity.

It is also noteworthy that the proposal above does not insist on—though it allows—putting all the assets of the company under a single insolvency jurisdiction. Thus, for example, a company that has assets in several countries may borrow from local banks and place each contract under domestic jurisdiction; in case of insolvency each contract would fall into a separate procedure. This arrangement, which seems to prevail anyway under the spontaneous order, cannot be dismissed up front on grounds of inefficiency. For if the objective of legislation is to minimize the cost of insolvency, then either (in case of a unified insolvency procedure) the creditors migrate to settle disputes where the company files, or (in case of a split jurisdiction) the company migrates to settle disputes where the banks operate. Since it is not a priori clear which arrangement is more cost efficient, it makes sense to leave the decision in the hands of market participants.

The chapter is organized as follows: Section 2 explores the state of spontaneous order, Section 3 describes the new EU legislation, Section 4 analyses the data, Section 5 provides the alternative proposal, and Section 6 concludes.

2. SPONTANEOUS ORDER

To understand harmonization one needs to grasp what happens in its absence. In the next subsection I describe this spontaneous order drawing heavily on a specific Anglo-American shipping case. I use this non-EU case because it is an extreme one: ships have no geographical characteristics and thus do not fall 'naturally' into a certain jurisdiction; also, England and the USA do not belong to any political union and thus better exemplify the state of spontaneous order.[2] I conclude this section with a brief description of the pre-harmonization diversity in European insolvency laws.

A few words ought to be said at this point regarding the conventional hard/soft taxonomy of insolvency systems, harder meaning that default is more likely to lead to liquidation. It was argued elsewhere that this is an oversimplification, since one has to distinguish between hard contracts and hard laws; see Franks and Sussman (2005). A contract may be deemed hard if it gives some creditors default-contingent liquidation

---

[2] There are many international conventions that are supposed to impose order, but they play a limited role in adjudicating the cases; see Bowtle and McGuinness 2001.

rights. A law may be deemed hard if it strictly enforces the contractual rights of the creditors—whether hard or soft. In that respect, English insolvency law is hard (though somewhat softened by recent legislation); in a sense, corporate insolvency law is just the practical wisdom accumulated along many years of contract enforcement. (That creditors in England typically hold hard contracts is then a mere description of the equilibrium outcome in the debt market.) In contrast, the American and the continental approach is to put the creditors' contractual rights—particularly the secured creditors' liquidation rights—under judicial discretion. Often, the court would assist the company's restructuring efforts by granting it 'protection' from its creditors who attempt to seize its assets. (That contracts are softened by such a 'stay' is thus an ex ante restriction on the set of permissible contracts.) In other words, English law follows a freedom of contracting policy, while American law adheres to a policy of judicial activism.

2.1. Spontaneous Order: How Does it Work in Practice?

In absence of harmonization a legal order is established 'spontaneously' by the unilateral moves of the contracting parties, the legislators, and the courts. Legislators commonly grant their courts the broadest possible powers over insolvency. Hence, Section 109(a) of the US bankruptcy code states that 'only a person that resides or has domicile, a place of business, or property in the United States ... may be debtor under this title'. The debtor need not be a US citizen (or, in the case of a company, incorporated in the USA), operate within the USA, nor should its US assets be of a significant magnitude.[3] Indeed, the case of Theresa McTague[4] created the precedent that a bank account with $194 is sufficient to satisfy the requirement of having 'property-in the United States'. The case involved a US citizen, permanently residing in Canada, who defaulted on some $17,000 credit card debt in the USA. After moving most of her money across the border, she petitioned for a chapter 7 discharge so that she could 'visit the United States in the future without fear of seizure of her automobile'. The court recognized that the $194 deposit was left behind 'for the very purpose of creating a jurisdiction here'. The trustee tried to dismiss the discharge petition on grounds that the deposit was insignificant and that the debtor behaved opportunistically. It failed, as the court was reluctant to place any restriction on its own power of adjudication. Similarly, English law allows the court to wind up a foreign company; it is sufficient that the company has assets in the UK, and that the law 'is exercisable' on at least one concerned party.[5]

---

[3] Yukos—a Russian Oil company caught in a power struggle with the Kremlin—is a famous recent case where a company with no substantial US activity managed to file for US bankruptcy; see 'Method and madness', *The Economist*, 29 December 2004.

[4] *In re Theresa McTague, Debtor*, 198 BR 428. 15 July 1996.

[5] See Bowtle and McGuinness 2001: 234–5.

To see how legal disputes are resolved in such a world, consider the case of Cenargo,[6] a shipping company 'with main office in England; the parent company and most of its subsidiaries are organized under English law'. (It is common practice in shipping to organize a business as a holding company with each vessel owned by separate subsidiary, so that every vessel is a separate debtor.) The debtors 'conduct their business primarily in England, Ireland and elsewhere in Europe and adjacent waters. None of the Cenargo debtors conduct business in the United States. No Cenargo vessels sail to the United States.'

Nevertheless, Cenargo issued in the USA some $175 million of 'high yield' debt, which was governed by US law. Although the 'indenture trustee'—Deutsche Bank—held a lien on 'at least one of Cenargo's operating subsidiaries', the high-yield notes were 'believed to be under secured'. At the same time, Cenargo had two other over-secured creditors: Lombard, a leasing company and a subsidiary of the Royal Bank of Scotland, and the Bank of Nova Scotia with £17.8 million of debt outstanding. By the autumn of 2002 Cenargo was in financial distress and aimed to swap the high-yield debt for equity. Towards this end, 'the Cenargo debtors also opened joint bank accounts in the United States, providing further support for filing under the Bankruptcy Code'.

On 14 January 2003, under pressure from the American bondholders, Cenargo filed for chapter 11. As a result of the automatic stay imposed by the filing, any action, by any creditor, to collect debt from Cenargo—within the USA or out of the country—could be deemed in contempt of the American court. Nevertheless, on 28 January 2003 Lombard 'requested the commencement of English provisional liquidation ... without requesting relief from the automatic stay in this [American] court'. Lombard also obtained an anti-suit injunction from the English court, disallowing Cenargo's directors to take 'any steps in the Chapter 11 proceedings ... without the prior consent of this [English] court. ... The directors are resident within the United Kingdom and subject to the jurisdiction of the English court. If they breach the term of the injunction, they lay themselves open to contempt proceedings before the English court.'

On 5 February 2003—after much haggling—Lombard, the American bondholders, and Cenargo all agreed to move the case to England (and also to switch the English process from liquidation to administration—a reorganization procedure), and obtained permission from the American court to do so. 'Ironically, given the amount of time and money spent on jurisdictional issues ... the Joint Administrators do not expect to depart materially from this [American] restructuring approach.' Chapter 11 proceedings were suspended on 14 February 2003.

The issue of contempt was resolved when the English court sent the American court a letter of request with assurances that Lombard's motion 'was lawful and proper under English law' and suggested that no party—either English nor American—would be held in contempt of court. The American court—though critical of Lombard's acting 'precipitously and unilaterally'—agreed 'under the peculiar

---

[6] *In re Cenargo International, Plc et al., Debtors*, 294 BR 571, 27 June 2003.

facts of these cases, that no party would be unduly penalized for violating the conflicting injunctions' of the English and the American courts.

2.2. Spontaneous Order: Analysis

On the face of it, spontaneous order does not seem to be an optimal arrangement. Yet, its social costs, and possibly some of its benefits, seem to deserve a more careful analysis. Three aspects, particularly, call attention: the heightened level of legal uncertainty, the greater diversity of legal forms, and the possibility that the assets of an insolvent company are split across several jurisdictions.

2.2.1. *Legal Uncertainty*

It is evident that there is some 'legal uncertainty' in non-harmonized cross-border insolvencies; in absence of precise rules to determine jurisdiction, each party files within the jurisdiction that suits her best. Then, complex negotiations between the parties and the courts commence, of which the final outcome is hard to predict.

It is not clear, however, that legal uncertainty per se is economically inefficient because, according to the Coase Theorem, the parties can avoid the uncertainty altogether by an out-of-court settlement. Moreover, by settling out of court the parties would save the legal expenses, which could then be distributed to their own benefit. Hence, a settlement buys the parties free (or, actually, negative premium) insurance. If the bargaining process is ex post efficient, then the parties should be able to strike such a deal with no difficulty.

Similarly, the *dilution* of payments and incentives as a result of legal uncertainty—e.g. when a hard contract is affected by the prospect of a soft adjudication—can be mitigated by adjusting the contract ex ante in order to compensate for the possible dilution later on. This mechanism works even better if an out-of-court settlement is easy to strike. Consider, for example, the case where an English debtor uses the threat of chapter 11 in order to renegotiate (ex post) a certain write-down. Moreover, the debtor foresees the write-down and decreases ex ante the effort she puts into avoiding distress. But then, the creditor also foresees the write-down and adjusts the initial repayment (upwards) so as to restore the expected return and the effort incentive to the level aimed for without the legal uncertainty. There are some theoretical examples where the dilution effect can be completely eliminated by a proper adjustment of the debt contract; see Franks and Sussman (2005). Although these results are not generic, it is still safe to conclude that the mechanism can at least mitigate the negative dilution effect.

One has to recognize, however, that these Coasian arguments have their limit. For if they held universally, all disputes would be resolved out of court and litigation would remain 'off the equilibrium path'. Several factors may explain why this does not happen, but the one that seems to be most relevant to the current analysis is that the parties seem to gain a certain advantage by moving first. The Cenargo case may serve as an illustration; the bondholders—being under-secured—probably felt that they could negotiate more favourable terms for the debt–equity swap in chapter 11. Then, Lombard appealed for a liquidation order with a sole purpose of moving the case from the USA back to England. As we have seen, Lombard—being over-secured— could afford to wait longer, and was indeed willing to switch from liquidation to administration once English jurisdiction was secured. With hindsight, it was probably a mistake on Lombard's part not to litigate pre-emptively in England, which could save it the trouble of facing contempt charges in the USA.

A possible equilibrium in such a game is a 'run for the exit' where each party litigates just in order to prevent the other from gaining the first-mover advantage. Two types of economic inefficiencies emerge. The first is premature liquidation, where a company is liquidated due to a creditors' run rather than because its time has come (note again that Lombard was actually willing to wait further). The second is an increase in the direct cost of litigation: not only that the incentive to settle out of court is weaker but the race might end with a duplication of legal proceedings (as has happened with Cenargo).

Note that though the lack of harmonization clearly results in loss of economic efficiency, some rules still emerge under spontaneous order, which impose a certain structure on the non-cooperative litigation game. Going back to the Cenargo case, the US court must have realized that since the company's secured assets were out of its own national territory, it had little power to enforce the stay. The only thing it could do was to hold Lombard in contempt, which—by Lombard's revealed action— had a limited effect. At the same time the US court must have realized that the English court would not allow an English company to breach a contract with a UK lender, particularly if the assets involved were within its reach (either in the UK or elsewhere in Europe). Although the English and the American courts put some effort in resolving their dispute, politely, the outcome also reflects the hard facts on the ground: courts will maintain jurisdiction on assets within their territory, particularly if legal rights of their own citizens may be breached.

2.2.2. *Diversity of Legal Forms*

By itself, diversity of legal forms adds no economic value. One may conceive a situation where insolvency cases are allocated into different jurisdictions—either through an explicit rule or as a result of uncoordinated interaction—in an arbitrary manner. Two conditions need to be satisfied if diversity is to make a difference. First, different jurisdictions should have some real effect on companies' value, even after all the Coasian adjustments have already been executed. Second, cases should be allocated to the jurisdiction that maximizes their value. The most natural way to achieve such an allocation is by allowing companies to choose jurisdiction ex ante.

Hence, it is fair to say that the spontaneous order does not realize its full potential in terms of enabling choice of legal form. This is because too much weight is given ex post to the physical location of the assets, which in the case of ships may be entirely coincidental. Yet, limited choice is better than no choice. Moreover, even in the current state of affairs, the parties have some effect on the choice of jurisdiction, particularly in England where the law does recognize the principle of freedom of contracting. Hence, had Cenargo indicated in the debt contract it had signed with Lombard that disputes should be adjudicated in the USA the English courts would take such an expression into consideration. Any other American connection, such as listing or creditors in the USA, would affect the court's decision as well.

It is worth mentioning here that the academic debate regarding the optimal insolvency regime—US or English type—has not converged to any consensus. In such a situation it is probably best to leave the decision to market participants. At least for international companies, the spontaneous order provides a modest amount of that choice.

2.2.3. *The Possibility of Asset Split Across Jurisdiction*

If—under spontaneous order—the physical location of assets has a great effect on the jurisdiction, then it is possible that assets of the same company would be subject to separate insolvency procedures, each in a different jurisdiction.

It is worth pointing out that such an asset split is not necessarily inefficient. Consider the case where distress is fairly independent of the incentives provided by insolvency law. In that case, the company's main objective is to minimize expected bankruptcy costs. More precisely, the question is whether—for a company that has assets both at home and abroad—placing all of them under a single jurisdiction necessarily decreases bankruptcy costs (relative to splitting jurisdiction). Note that if foreign creditors fund the foreign assets, then one of the parties would have to step out of her domestic jurisdiction. Whether it is more cost efficient for the creditors to settle where the company is domiciled or vice versa is an empirical question.

Note also that in the argument above one has to include all sorts of stakeholders—particularly workers—among the company's creditors. Suppose, for example, that a company tries to bring foreign assets under domestic jurisdiction. However, the company also has foreign workers who are employed in proximity to the assets abroad. Their contracts fall under foreign employment laws and are adjudicated by foreign courts. Possibly, resolving conflicts between foreign employment laws and domestic insolvency laws is a costly business. Hence, it might be cost effective to avoid these conflicts altogether by placing the assets under foreign insolvency law. That may also be compatible with funding the investment by foreign banks, which might have a cost advantage over domestic banks in monitoring the assets.

2.3. Diversity of Insolvency Laws within the EU

It is obviously the case that harmonization matters only when the insolvency laws differ in the way they treat the debt contract. It is thus worth discussing, briefly, the cross-EU differences in insolvency law.

Table 8.1. Comparative insolvency in Europe

	UK	Germany	France
Bankruptcy procedure			
Automatic stay	none	3 months	unlimited
Dilution of contractual rights	none	limited	significant
Firm characteristic			
Book leverage (mean)	0.61	0.87	0.65
Security over debt (mean, %)	85	60	124
Interest margins (mean, %)	2.23	2.90	2.24
Current assets over current liabilities (mean)	1.05	n.a.	1.35
Resolution of distress			
Default to recovery duration (median, years)	0.78	3.58	1.81
Piecemeal liquidation (mean, %)	43	57	62
Collateral realization (mean, %)	83	73	35
Recovery rate (mean, %)	74	76	54

Note: Comparative insolvency statistics as reported by Davydenko and Franks 2006. Their database constitutes 2,280 small firms (up to €75 million by turnover, but in excess of €100k in exposure), in distress (by Basel II definition), during the period 1995–2003 (earlier in France).

Davydenko and Franks (2006) provide an exhaustive comparative study of corporate bankruptcy in Europe (see Table 8.1). They start by ranking the laws of three major countries according to the courts' power to block creditors' contractual rights. While the UK strictly enforces the debt contract, France's 1985 Bankruptcy Code explicitly states the rescue of the company as its top objective. For that purpose, the court is empowered to place a stay of unlimited duration on the company's debt. Germany comes in between France and the UK in terms of its commitment to the enforcement of creditors' contractual rights.

The main focus, however, of Davydenko and Franks (2006) is the comparison of the actual performance of the different laws. They collect data on 2,280 small firms (turnover below €75 million) in financial distress, and follow them for a period of time until distress is resolved in either turnaround or liquidation. One of the main findings is that debtors and creditors already internalize their insolvency regime and ex ante adjust capital structure accordingly. Most significantly, French banks cover their lending by a higher collateral relative to UK banks, so as to protect themselves against the dilution of the liquidation rights by the courts (125 per cent against 85 per cent mean coverage, respectively). Another indicator that points in the same direction is the average current ratio (current assets over current liabilities), which is 1.35 in France against 1.05 in the UK. Possibly, French banks classify clients as distressed at an earlier stage, so that given the slower pace of French proceedings they would still have time to deal with the distressed company. Somewhat surprisingly, interest rate spreads and leverage do not differ significantly across countries.

Indeed, proceedings are longer in France; median length is 1.81 years against 0.78 years in the UK. At the same time, the average recovery rate on French collateral is only 35 per cent against 83 per cent in the UK. However, since French loans tend to be better covered by securities, the difference in average recovery rate on loans is smaller: 54 per cent in France against 74 per cent in the UK. Nevertheless, the French system does not seem to achieve one of its main goals, which is to decrease liquidation rates. Sixty-two per cent of distressed French companies end in piecemeal liquidation, against 43 per cent in the UK.

Hence, it seems French insolvency law offered a better deal to a debtor in default relative to England. Yet, until the 2000 harmonization law there were many gaps in the rules that determine jurisdiction. Lombardo (2001) provides the following peculiar example. English legal theory, under freedom of contracting, states that a company is governed by the law under which it is incorporated. Many continental countries adhere to the 'real seat' doctrine, by which a company is governed by the corporate law of the country where its head office is located. Hence, both English and German law rule that an English-registered company with a head office in Germany falls under their own jurisdiction. At the same time, both laws should rule that a company registered in Germany with a head office in the UK does not fall under any jurisdiction. It is unclear, however, whether courts would be impressed with such legal theory, or would rather follow the spontaneous order described above, exercising their powers over assets within their jurisdiction.

3. European Legislation

In May 2000, after many years of haggling, the EU finally came up with its own harmonization law; see Omar (2003) for a comprehensive history of the process. One of the main dilemmas facing the legislator was that of harmonization versus convergence, the former being a set of rules that determine which case falls under what jurisdiction, the latter being a single insolvency law for all EU companies. The former approach was adopted eventually. We turn next to a more detailed description of the new legislation.

3.1. Insolvency Legislation of 2000

The main points in Regulation 1346/2000 (dated 29 May 2000, entering into force on 31 May 2002) are:[7]

- Bankruptcy is governed by the 'real seat' doctrine, namely the laws of the member state 'where the debtor has the centre of his main interest', i.e. the 'place where the debtor conducts the administration of his interests on a regular basis'.

[7] See Rajak 2004 and Wessels 2004 for a juridical analysis of the new legislation.

In absence of proof to the contrary, it is presumed that this is simply the location of the company's registered office.

- Bankruptcy would not affect 'rights in rem[8] of creditors', namely rights in assets that creditors hold as a security. The law recognizes explicitly 'collections of indefinite assets as a whole which change from time to time', i.e. floating charges (see Article 5). It is explicitly recognized that contractual rights in land, a 'ship or an aircraft' are all governed by the laws of the member state where the object is located or registered. Likewise, employees' rights are subject to the laws of the member state where the employment takes place.
- Any party, including the liquidator in the primary proceedings, may initiate 'secondary insolvency proceedings' in another member state 'where the debtor has an establishment' with power over assets situated within the territory of the other member state. The secondary-proceedings court '*shall* stay the process of liquidation in whole or in part on receipt of a request from the liquidator in the main proceedings' (my emphasis). The liquidator of the secondary proceedings may ask the liquidator in the main proceedings 'to take any suitable measure to guarantee the interests of the creditors in the secondary proceedings.... [However], such a request from the liquidator may be rejected only if it is manifestly of no interest to the creditors in the main proceedings.'
- Judgments in one member state are recognized by others. However, 'any Member State may refuse to recognise insolvency proceedings in another Member State or to enforce judgement handed down in the context of such proceedings where the effect of such recognition or enforcement would be manifestly contrary to that State's public policy' (see Article 26).

3.2. The Effect of Legislation

Two characteristics of the new law deserve special attention. First, the law does not facilitate choice of legal form. Rather, the law adopts the 'real seat' doctrine, which imposes on a company the jurisdiction of its 'centre of main interest' location. I shall defer an elaborate discussion of this characteristic to Section 5 below. Second, the law is highly discretionary. Some of its key concepts are defined in general terms, leaving much room to judicial discretion on the interpretation of concepts such as 'main interest' and 'matters of public policy'. Probably, judicial discretion will be in great demand where the law is committed to conflicting principles that need to be balanced off, one against the other. Thus, for example, the law protects creditors' rights in rem, but also member states' right to exercise their own laws, particularly on matters of public policy. As argued above, a few countries empowered their courts to place a stay on the company's debts, in violation of the creditors' rights in rem, due to a public policy that tries to preserve the corporate entity. That might have increased the amount of legal uncertainty in the system.

---

[8] Namely, 'the thing itself', primarily rights in assets to secure debt repayment.

To illustrate this point, consider the case of Eurofood, a wholly owned subsidiary of the Italian food giant Parmalat (€7.5 billion turnover 2002), which went bust in 2003 amid a huge financial scandal.[9] Eurofood was incorporated in Ireland and had a registered office in Dublin's International Financial Services Centre (IFSC), a structure that had certain tax advantages. Its only business was to arrange finance to companies in the Parmalat group (e.g. in Brazil or Venezuela), and it conducted most of its business with the Dublin branch of Bank of America. There were no Irish employees. The company had four directors, two Italians—Parmalat employees based in Italy—who were the de facto managing directors of the company, and two Irish, one of whom was an employee of Bank of America. There were no allegations of wrongdoings by Eurofood.

Both Italian and Irish courts ruled that Eurofood fell under their own jurisdiction. The main argument on the Italian side was that the 'effective seat of Eurofood was in Parma in Italy where its executive directives were based and where all significant decisions were taken. . . . Parmalat SA was the real entity behind the formal arrangement of a separate entity'; moreover, it was claimed that the Italian directors participated in most board meetings by phone from Italy.

The case was appealed, eventually, to the Supreme Court of Ireland, which rejected the demand to transfer adjudication to Italy on two main grounds. First, Eurofood was incorporated in Ireland and had its registered office in Dublin. The court ignored the fact that the de facto management was done in Italy on grounds that Eurofood's corporate charter did not make any formal distinction between executive and non-executive directors. Hence, Eurofood's creditors had good reasons to organize 'their business on the basis that they were dealing with an Irish company subject to Irish law which was administered in Ireland with its centre of main interests in this jurisdiction'.

Second, Bank of America was not given sufficient notice about court hearing in Parma. The Irish court found this to be a major breach of 'fair procedure', which is 'in Irish law, a principal of *public policy* of cardinal importance. It derives both from the rules of natural justice of the common law and from constitutional guarantees of personal and individual rights' (my emphasis). As noted above, member states are not obliged to enforce decisions by the courts in other member states if they conflict with their own 'public policy'.

Hence, at least as far as the Eurofood case is concerned, the discretionary nature of the new legislation has actually contributed towards more legal uncertainty. In absence of the new legislation all the parties involved would probably assume that the case should be resolved in Ireland, and that Irish courts would exercise jurisdiction on Irish companies and their Irish creditors, as in the spontaneous order. Then came the new legislation and laid down some principles that Parmalat could use in order to bring the case back to Italy. However, no clear rules were provided, so that there were legal grounds for both transferring the case to Italy and objecting such a

---

[9] See *In the matter of Eurofoods IFSC Limited* [2005] IL Pr. 2. and IL Pr. 3 for the Irish proceedings and *Re The Insolvency of Eurofood IFSC Limited* IL Pr. 14 for the Italian proceedings.

transfer. Eventually, the process and the outcome were similar to those that would have prevailed under the spontaneous order (albeit lacking the good manners that characterized the English–American court exchange in the Cenargo case, the Irish court expressing strong opinions on the conduct of its Italian counterpart). With one important difference: that the legal uncertainty created by the new legislation encouraged litigation.

There is even some evidence in the Eurofood case that the legal uncertainty has raised the possibility of a creditors' run. It is claimed that one reason behind Bank of America's appeal for an Irish insolvency procedure was an 'expressed concern that an attempt would be made to move the centre of main interests of the company ... from Ireland to Italy'. Hence, the reason for the litigation was not insolvency per se but rather the creditor's fear that its rights would be diluted by a debtor's action to adjudicate the case in the jurisdiction of its own convenience.

Additional evidence to that effect can be found in the *Financial Times,* which reports practitioners' opinions regarding the legal environment created by the new legislation.[10] 'The jurisdictional problem arises because of ambiguity about what is meant by the phrase "centre of main interests" ... In the face of this uncertainty, there has been a tendency to give weight to the courts which first handle the matter—hence lawyers' warnings about the need to act speedily.'

4. DATA ANALYSIS

Proponents of the European legislation might highlight the case of ISA Daisytek SAS, a French subsidiary of an English company.[11] Here, the French Court of Appeal in Versailles set aside a decision by the Pontoise District Commercial Court that refused to recognize an administration order by the High Court of Justice in Leeds. The Versailles court examined the decision of the court in Leeds, was convinced that it was taken on the basis of substantive arguments for Daisytek having the centre of its interests in England, and ruled that the administration order is recognized in France 'with no further formalities'. Hence, a new insolvency order might be emerging in Europe after all, which might welfare-dominate the spontaneous order. Whether this is the case is an empirical question that should be considered on the basis of evidence.

In this section I turn attention to the data in order to address two questions. The first is, simply, how common is it European companies to operate across several jurisdictions? More specifically, what percentage of companies own subsidiaries, or have corporate owners abroad—within or out of the EU? he second question is

---

[10] The case was actually appealed to the European Court of Justice where the Advocate General recommended that Eurofood would remain under Irish law; See *Financial Times,* 28 September 2005.

[11] See [2004] I.L Pr. 6.

whether companies involved in such cross-country ownership have seen an increase in their cost of borrowing around the period when the law became effective.[12]

I have no direct information about the cost of borrowing. Instead, I address the second question by analysing the change in the level of gearing (leverage: debt over equity) across companies. It is stipulated that coordination problems within insolvency would increase the cost of bankruptcy and induce companies to decrease their gearing. The disadvantage is that gearing may be affected by factors other than the cost of bankruptcy; for example, cyclical changes in the probability of bankruptcy, unrelated to bankruptcy costs. As much as I can, I control for these factors. However, analysing the problem via changes in gearing also has the advantage of capturing costs that are not reflected in the direct cost of lending; for example bankruptcy costs that ultimately fall on the equity holders rather than on the lenders.

To perform the analysis I use the Amadeus database for Europe's 'top 250,000' companies, which contains data on both listed and unlisted companies. I limit the analysis to five countries: Germany, Spain, France, the UK, and Italy. Accounting, shareholding, and subsidiaries information is reported in three different subdatabases, which need to be merged; each company is thus identified across the three subfiles. Regarding cross-country ownership I limit myself to industrial ownership alone (ignoring ownership by pension funds, other financial institutions, foundations, and private individuals), where I expect the coordination problems discussed above to be more acute. Several criteria are used in order to identify 'substantial' ownership; these criteria, with other technical detail regarding the construction of the data set, are described in the data appendix. The final outcome is a data set with 116,445 companies, for the five countries mentioned above, covering the period 2001–3 (with 2000 as a base point).

4.1. Descriptive Statistics

Table 8.2 provides some descriptive statistics about the five countries in the data set. The data are sorted by company size, where size is measured by the number of employees, a variable with a relatively low incidence of 'non-available information' (except for the UK). Note that the German and British subsamples are less skewed towards small companies: the share of companies with less than fifty employees is 18 per cent and 15 per cent, compared with 35 per cent, 26 per cent, and 32 per cent in Spain, France, and Italy (respectively). Also noteworthy is the higher level of gearing for German and British companies, 4.4 and 4.3, compared with 2.3 and 2.1 in Spain and France (respectively) with Italy in between at 3.7. This is still valid even after controlling for size: for companies with more than 5000 employees the corresponding numbers are 3.5 and 4.6, in contrast to 1.5 and 1.8 with Italy at 3.4.

The phenomenon of cross-corporate ownership—either foreign or local—is quite common. Only about 30 per cent of companies in Germany, France, and Britain do

---

[12] For a similar study based on US data see Scott and Smith 1986.

Table 8.2. Owners and subsidiaries by size groups

N of empl.	Accounting info.				Incidence of firms reporting an industrial shareholder (if any) by location of shareholder (%)					Distribution of subsidiaries (if any) by location of subsidiaries (mean %) and N of subsidiaries				
	N of firms	Gear	Sales (m€)	Assets (m€)	None	Local	EU	Non-EU	n.a.	None	Local	EU	Non-EU	N of subs.
Germany														
n.a.	2,318	5.7	130	175	32.7	55.6	6.9	11.0	6.7	66.4	29.3	3.9	0.4	4.3
0–50	4,922	4.5	50	117	44.0	43.6	6.1	10.6	3.5	76.8	21.0	2.0	0.2	3.0
51–100	3,434	3.3	43	108	31.6	57.2	6.3	10.7	3.7	72.7	23.9	3.0	0.3	2.5
101–250	7,253	4.3	52	132	28.8	62.6	4.9	9.6	4.8	66.0	29.0	4.4	0.6	2.5
251–1,000	7,019	3.5	105	155	24.4	67.0	5.5	10.4	6.2	54.6	37.6	6.8	1.0	3.6
1001–5,000	1,757	3.4	475	551	19.7	70.8	7.9	15.0	5.5	36.4	50.8	10.6	2.3	7.8
5,001+	546	3.5	4972	7844	20.5	71.6	7.7	11.5	3.1	33.0	51.1	11.1	4.9	33.7
Total	27,249	4.4	178	520	30.4	59.7	5.8	10.6	5.0	63.3	31.0	4.9	0.8	4.8
Spain														
n.a.	1,575	4.8	41	94	43.3	49.1	5.7	7.8	1.2	65.0	30.3	2.7	2.0	3.4
0–50	6,175	2.6	19	28	50.5	40.5	4.6	9.4	1.3	60.5	35.6	2.2	1.8	3.5
51–100	3,252	1.9	28	26	42.1	46.0	6.1	12.8	1.7	50.5	41.4	4.7	3.4	3.4
101–250	3,951	1.8	33	35	38.3	48.6	6.8	16.6	1.8	46.5	43.1	5.7	4.6	4.2
251–1,000	2,320	1.7	95	88	27.6	54.0	10.5	23.8	2.6	32.8	53.3	7.8	6.1	6.7
1,001–5,000	502	1.6	387	446	17.9	61.8	10.4	32.7	3.2	18.9	62.5	9.8	8.8	12.9
5,001+	116	1.5	2853	3799	11.2	75.0	12.1	30.2	5.2	6.9	65.8	12.7	14.5	43.7
Total	17,891	2.3	64	79	41.5	46.6	6.4	14.1	1.7	50.9	41.1	4.5	3.6	5.1
France														
n.a.	2,133	4.3	43	244	38.1	48.0	8.6	13.5	2.5	60.1	33.4	4.4	2.1	4.8
0–50	5,448	2.2	39	54	40.7	46.0	6.6	13.0	0.4	65.8	29.5	3.2	1.6	4.4
51–100	3,294	2	32	30	29.7	58.6	6.2	14.5	0.3	70.0	24.8	3.7	1.5	3.0
101–250	5,157	1.6	45	39	23.2	64.8	7.2	15.9	0.7	60.2	31.4	5.7	2.8	3.4
251–1,000	3,735	1.7	108	93	18.1	69.2	9.3	19.2	0.8	47.9	38.6	9.1	4.4	5.3

(Cont.)

Table 8.2. Continued

N of empl.	Accounting info.				Incidence of firms reporting an industrial shareholder (if any) by location of shareholder (%)					Distribution of subsidiaries (if any) by location of subsidiaries (mean %) and N of subsidiaries				
	N of firms	Gear	Sales (m€)	Assets (m€)	None	Local	EU	Non-EU	n.a.	None	Local	EU	Non-EU	N of subs.
1,001–5,000	983	1.9	480	367	11.7	74.8	10.8	23.7	1.0	24.4	52.5	14.6	8.5	13.3
5,001+	233	1.8	7132	8170	15.9	67.8	14.6	21.9	3.0	7.7	54.6	20.3	17.4	73.9
Total	20,983	2.1	155	178	28.7	58.5	7.6	15.7	0.8	58.7	32.6	5.8	2.9	6.7
UK			(m€)	(m€)										
n.a.	7,741	7.4	41	414	13.8	78.4	7.3	19.3	2.0	48.4	49.2	1.9	0.5	5.5
0–50	4,850	4.8	34	68	29.4	52.5	9.1	23.2	2.6	49.5	48.8	1.1	0.5	5.2
51–100	3,633	3.2	27	47	31.6	51.3	7.5	23.1	2.6	47.8	50.3	1.6	0.3	3.9
101–250	7,297	3.1	32	36	34.4	51.5	6.9	21.7	2.9	39.1	58.7	1.8	0.4	3.9
251–1,000	7,048	3.4	73	96	31.9	54.2	7.0	22.8	3.0	31.7	65.3	2.2	0.8	5.0
1,001–5,000	2,233	4.4	278	479	23.5	59.7	8.3	29.4	4.1	16.8	78.0	3.3	1.9	9.6
5,001+	653	4.6	2180	2925	27.0	51.9	4.4	25.9	8.0	6.3	80.2	6.4	7.1	27.0
Total	33,455	4.3	112	228	27.2	59.0	7.4	22.3	2.8	40.0	57.3	2.0	0.7	5.9
Italy			(m€)	(m€)										
0–50	5,309	4.8	31	38	85.9	9.6	1.6	2.4	2.2	80.5	15.3	1.3	2.9	2.4
51–100	3,159	3.3	31	30	77.3	14.2	2.6	5.5	3.9	69.8	21.2	2.7	6.3	2.7
101–250	5,013	3.2	43	41	68.2	18.9	3.9	8.6	5.5	65.4	22.4	4.5	7.8	3.1
251–1,000	2,791	3.2	121	136	56.7	25.1	6.2	14.3	7.2	49.2	29.6	9.9	11.3	5.2
1,001–5,000	496	2.7	614	653	38.9	34.1	13.1	22.2	9.1	28.4	40.4	12.6	18.6	11.3
5,001+	99	3.4	7131	10835	41.4	43.8	14.1	10.1	7.1	28.3	37.0	15.6	19.1	25.6
Total	16,867	3.7	108	135	72.5	16.7	3.6	7.4	4.5	67.0	21.7	4.3	6.9	4.2

Notes: Size groups are determined according to the number of employees (if available). Accounting information appears on the left-hand side. All accounting variables are averages of firm averages for the years 2001–3. Data regarding the incidence of an industrial shareholder—if any—are provided in the middle section of the table. 'None' indicates no such holder. Industrial shareholders are sorted by country of registration: locally (within the home economy), abroad but within the EU and out of the EU. 'n.a.' indicates a shareholder of unknown location. (Numbers do not add up as a company may have more than one industrial shareholder.) Data regarding subsidiaries—if any—are provided on the right-hand side. 'None' indicates percentage of firms with no subsidiaries. 'Local' provides mean percentage of local subsidiaries (out the total number of subsidiaries). Similar definitions apply for 'EU' and 'non-EU'. 'N of subs' provides for the mean number of subsidiaries (of all locations) per company, conditional on having a subsidiaries. See data appendix for more information regarding sources and definitions.

not report an industrial shareholder. The numbers for Spain are somewhat higher, but that may be a small-company phenomenon. Italy is an outlier with 73 per cent of companies reporting no industrial shareholder, the effect being present across all size groups. The phenomenon of foreign holder is less common, but by no means insignificant. Between 6 and 8 per cent of companies in Germany, Spain France, and the UK report a non-domestic EU shareholder; however, only 3.6 per cent of Italian firms report such a shareholder. Interestingly, the phenomenon of non-EU industrial ownership is more common than EU ownership, the incidence of the former being about double the latter; for the UK, the ratio is three to one. (Note that the columns in the holder section of Table 8.2 do not add up to 100 per cent, for a company may report both a local and a foreign industrial owner.)

Somewhat surprisingly, subsidiaries are not such a common phenomenon. Even among companies with more than 5,000 employees, about 30 per cent of German and Italian companies do not report any subsidiaries; the numbers are lower for the other countries: 7 per cent in Spain, 8 per cent in France, and 6 per cent in the UK. Conditional on having subsidiaries, the average number of subsidiaries per company is from four in Italy to eight in Germany; the number of subsidiaries increases steeply with size. The vast majority of these subsidiaries are located locally, but the number of foreign subsidiaries is still significant for most countries. Conditional on having (non-zero number of) subsidiaries, the proportion of them located abroad but within (out of) the EU is[13] 13 per cent (2 per cent) for Germany, 9 per cent (7 per cent) in Spain, 14 per cent (7 per cent) in France, 3 per cent (1 per cent) in Britain, and 6 per cent (10 per cent) in Italy. Unlike the case of industrial holders, owning non-EU subsidiaries is less common than owning non-domestic EU subsidiaries.

Answering our first empirical question—how significant is foreign ownership among sizeable European companies—we thus conclude that the phenomenon is important, though not overwhelming. Around 6 per cent of companies have a non-domestic EU industrial shareholder, while the incidence of a non-EU shareholder is at least double that. About 40 per cent of companies have subsidiaries, about five to six (on average) each, of which about 10 per cent are non-domestic EU, and about the same amount located out of the EU.

4.2. Changes in Gearing

We run country-specific regressions where the dependent variable is either the level (Table 8.3) or the yearly differences (Table 8.4) in the logarithm of the level of gearing. The independent variables are firm characteristics such as total assets, return on assets, age, dummies for listing or industry, and information about the presence of an industrial holder or the ownership of subsidiaries—foreign or domestic. The ownership of foreign subsidiaries is captured by a dummy (rather than a continuous variable, as in Table 8.2): the variable 'EU subsidiaries' receives a value of one if the

[13] $100 \times 4.9/(100-63.3)$; see Table 8.2.

Table 8.3. The level of gearing

	Germany	Spain	France	UK	Italy
Log(assets)	0.020 (1.95)	0.123 (12.62)[b]	0.106 (15.04)[b]	0.097 (18.22)[b]	−0.028 (3.39)[b]
Return on assetst	−0.009 (8.62)[b]	−0.059 (51.16)[b]	−0.046 (56.75)[b]	−0.027 (45.04)[b]	−0.062 (61.53)[b]
Log(age)	0.079 (5.57)[b]	−0.303 (19.07)[b]	−0.044 (3.99)[b]	−0.347 (39.98)[b]	−0.020 (1.45)
Dummy: QUOTED	−0.627 (13.15)[b]	−0.024 (0.26)	0.072 (1.47)	−0.658 (15.77)[b]	−0.546 (7.80)[b]
Dummy: industrial holder	0.087 (2.44)[a]	−0.081 (3.25)[b]	−0.011 (0.54)	0.509 (26.47)[b]	−0.201 (8.18)[b]
Dummy: EU holder	−0.032 (0.55)	−0.110 (2.40)[a]	−0.109 (3.27)[b]	−0.049 (1.57)	−0.156 (3.37)
Dummy: non-EU holder	−0.200 (4.41)[b]	−0.507 (14.74)[b]	−0.434 (17.25)[b]	−0.185 (8.90)[b]	−0.338 (9.33)[b]
Dummy: holder, location unknown	−0.304 (4.85)[b]	0.134 (1.60)	0.046 (0.42)	−0.065 (1.44)	0.129 (3.08)[b]
Dummy: subsidiaries	−0.098 (2.82)[b]	−0.054 (2.16)[a]	−0.177 (8.81)[b]	−0.144 (8.35)[b]	0.007 (0.32)
Dummy: EU subsidiaries	−0.046 (0.94)	−0.005 (0.11)	−0.112 (3.38)[b]	−0.089 (1.88)	−0.040 (1.02)
Dummy: non-EU subsidiaries	−0.081 (0.98)	0.047 (0.95)	0.013 (0.30)	−0.316 (4.45)[b]	0.198 (6.37)[b]
Dummy: year 2002	−0.025 (0.78)	−0.043 (1.95)	−0.082 (4.31)[b]	−0.049 (2.73)[b]	−0.038 (2.18)[a]
Dummy: year 2003	0.011 (0.24)	−0.185 (2.98)[b]	−0.107 (4.45)[b]	−0.110 (5.42)[b]	−0.122 (1.54)
Dummies: industries	F = 22.48[b]	F = 10.50[b]	F = 9.75[b]	F = 26.23[b]	F = 17.98[b]
N	9,042	30,254	44,087	59,876	25,918
R-squared	0.07	0.12	0.08	0.09	0.15

Note: Regression results for 2001–3. Dependent variable: log (gear). The incidence of subsidiaries is indicated by dummies: 'dummy: EU subsidiaries' equals 1 if '% local subs'. (out of the total number of subsidiaries, see data appendix) is greater than 25%. Regressions' intercepts are not reported. The absolute value of t-statistics appears in parentheses. Twelve industry dummies are included, for which the joint significance is indicated by an F test.
[a] Indicates significant at 5% level.
[b] Indicate significant at 1% level.

Table 8.4. Change in gearing

	Germany	Spain	France	UK	Italy
Log(gear)$_{-1}$	−0.230 (29.89)[b]	−0.183 (50.81)[b]	−0.231 (70.84)[b]	−0.180 (69.45)[b]	−0.203 (51.55)[b]
Log(assets)$_{-1}$	−0.007 (1.05)	0.004 (0.65)	0.005 (1.21)	0.019 (5.91)[b]	−0.029 (5.80)[b]
Return on assets	−0.002 (2.11)[a]	−0.012 (15.99)[b]	−0.010 (16.50)[b]	−0.003 (8.16)[b]	−0.009 (12.71)[b]
Log(age)	0.040 (3.94)[b]	−0.075 (7.43)[b]	−0.001 (0.17)	−0.038 (6.72)[b]	−0.039 (4.41)[b]
Dummy: QUOTED	−0.029 (0.92)	0.103 (1.94)	0.107 (3.47)[b]	−0.009 (0.39)	0.125 (2.84)[b]
Dummy: industrial holder	0.028 (0.71)	0.020 (0.97)	0.025 (1.19)	0.087 (4.56)[b]	−0.047 (2.23)[a]
Interaction dummy: holder[a] 2002	0.035 (0.65)	−0.046 (1.59)	−0.058 (1.95)	0.031 (1.19)	0.018 (0.60)
Interaction dummy: holder[a] 2003	−0.041 (0.55)	−0.096 (1.06)	−0.012 (0.33)	0.003 (0.09)	−0.009 (0.08)
Dummy: EU holder	0.044 (0.66)	−0.071 (1.77)	−0.060 (1.77)	−0.001 (0.02)	−0.057 (1.36)
Interaction dummy: EU-holder[a]2002	−0.076 (0.84)	−0.049 (0.86)	0.078 (1.65)	−0.051 (1.25)	0.036 (0.61)
Interaction dummy: EU-holder[a] 2003	−0.250 (2.16)[a]	−0.144 (1.15)	0.012 (0.20)	−0.099 (1.88)	0.017 (0.11)
Dummy: non-EU holder	0.054 (1.06)	−0.089 (2.99)[b]	−0.134 (5.20)[b]	−0.028 (1.42)	−0.063 (1.98)[a]
Interaction dummy: non-EU-holder[a] 2002	−0.084 (1.22)	−0.029 (0.69)	0.006 (0.18)	−0.029 (1.06)	0.005 (0.11)
Interaction dummy: non-EU-holder[a] 2003	−0.120 (1.31)	0.044 (0.47)	0.037 (0.85)	0.002 (0.07)	−0.119 (0.82)
Dummy: holder, location unknown	−0.095 (1.37)	0.046 (0.64)	−0.003 (0.02)	−0.009 (0.20)	0.087 (2.33)[a]
Interaction dummy: unknown-holder 2002	0.109 (1.16)	−0.038 (0.37)	0.014 (0.08)	0.022 (0.35)	−0.079 (1.50)
Interaction dummy: unknown-holder[a] 2003	0.089 (0.64)	−0.004 (0.02)	−0.061 (0.30)	−0.013 (0.20)	0.070 (0.47)

(Cont.)

Table 8.4. Continued

	Germany	Spain	France	UK	Italy
Dummy: subsidiaries	0.008 (0.21)	0.030 (1.49)	−0.019 (0.97)	0.034 (2.04)[a]	−0.004 (0.19)
Interaction dummy: subsidiaries[a] 2002	−0.031 (0.63)	0.004 (0.16)	−0.033 (1.21)	−0.023 (0.99)	−0.033 (1.26)
Interaction dummy: subsidiaries[a] 2003	0.101 (1.47)	−0.072 (0.86)	0.021 (0.62)	−0.034 (1.34)	0.023 (0.20)
Dummy: EU subsidiaries	−0.020 (0.40)	−0.020 (0.51)	0.021 (0.63)	−0.009 (0.21)	0.052 (1.55)
Interaction dummy: EU subs.[a] EU2002	0.045 (0.64)	−0.012 (0.22)	−0.016 (0.34)	−0.069 (1.09)	−0.050 (1.04)
Interaction dummy: EU subs.[a] 2003	−0.062 (0.68)	0.157 (1.34)	−0.009 (0.16)	0.099 (1.36)	−0.155 (1.18)
Dummy: non-EU subsidiaries	−0.019 (0.24)	0.024 (0.57)	0.005 (0.12)	−0.148 (2.19)[a]	0.083 (3.10)[b]
Interaction dummy: non-EU-subs.[a] 2002	−0.012 (0.10)	0.066 (1.11)	0.083 (1.34)	0.147 (1.59)	−0.013 (0.35)
interaction dummy: non-EU subs.[a] 2003	0.059 (0.42)	−0.213 (1.78)	−0.020 (0.28)	−0.026 (0.27)	0.065 (0.55)
Dummies: industries	F = 1.93[a]	F = 2.39[b]	F = 1.29[b]	F = 5.09[b]	F = 2.22[b]
Dummy: year 2002	−0.173 (3.40)[b]	−0.019 (0.79)	−0.010 (0.39)	−0.020 (0.78)	−0.015 (0.99)
Dummy: year 2003	−0.220 (3.11)[b]	0.037 (0.41)	−0.067 (2.08)[a]	−0.073 (2.62)[b]	−0.054 (0.66)
Constant	1.142 (18.08)[b]	0.999 (25.39)[b]	0.917 (26.56)[b]	0.763 (26.57)[b]	1.227 (31.94)[b]
N	6,816	27,389	40,450	51,124	24,713
R-squared	0.14	0.09	0.11	0.09	0.10

Notes: Regression results for 2001–3 (and some 2000 lags). Dependent variable: log(gear)–log(gear)₋₁. The incidence of subsidiaries is indicated by dummies: 'dummy: EU subsidiaries' equals 1 if '% local subs.' (out of the total number of subsidiaries, see data Appendix) is greater than 25%. The absolute value of t-statistics appears in parentheses. Twelve industry dummies are included, for which the joint significance is indicated by an F test.
[a] Indicates significant at 5% level.
[b] Indicate significant at 1% level.

percentage of EU subsidiaries (of the total number of subsidiaries the company has) is greater than 25 per cent.

As before, we note the significant cross-country differences in the pattern of funding across Europe. Most striking is the effect of listing (the dummy 'QUOTED') on gearing (see Table 8.3). In theory, the sign of this variable is ambiguous: a listed firm may afford a higher level of gearing knowing that it has access to a liquid equity market in case of distress, or may decrease gearing once the constraint of not having access to the equity market is removed. In Germany and Britain, the second effect is clearly dominating and is highly significant, both statistically and economically, the level of gearing being 60 per cent lower among listed companies relative to unlisted ones. In Italy, the effect of listing is of the same sign, but is weaker economically and statistically. In France and Spain listing shows no significant effect on the level of gearing. The similarity in that respect between Britain and Germany is surprising given the common tendency of classifying them as two polar cases on the market-versus-institutions line of financial systems; see Alan and Gale (2000).

It is equally surprising that in spite of the structural differences, all five countries portray a very similar pattern of finance with respect to the return on assets and the lag gearing (in Table 8.4). Both effects are negative, have similar levels of statistical and economic significance, and are consistent with the trade-off theory where firms with high levels of gearing (due to 'profit shocks') revert back to a target level of gearing; see Mayer and Sussman (2006).

As for the main purpose of these regressions, Table 8.4 analyses the changes in gearing during 2001–3. The dummies for (say) non-domestic EU and non-EU industrial holders are interacted with the yearly dummies. Note that having any industrial holder—either a domestic or foreign—is included in the regression as a separate variable. Hence, the variable 'EU-holder^a of 2002' captures the marginal effect having a non-domestic EU industrial holder, relative to companies that have any industrial holder.

The sheer number of variables in the regression, and the fact that variables sometimes switch signs across years, makes the results a bit difficult to interpret. The economic significance of the results is best conveyed through the accumulated effect of foreign ownership over the three years. Since 'EU holder' captures the base level 2001 effect of EU holding, and since 'EU-holder^d 2002' captures the marginal 2002 effect relative to the base level, the total 2002 effect (of EU holding) is the sum of these two variables. It follows that the accumulated 2001–3 effect equals

$$3 \times (\text{EU holder}) + (\text{EU-holder}^a 2002) + (\text{EU-holder}^a 2003).$$

Corresponding measures for the accumulated effects of having non-EU industrial holders and for the ownership of subsidiaries (both non-domestic EU and non-EU) are calculated as well. The results, together with the relevant F tests, are presented in Table 8.5.

Evidently, German, Spanish, and British companies with a non-domestic EU industrial holder have significantly decreased their level of gearing by 15 per cent to 40 per cent during the period 2001–3 over and above industry or cyclical effects, or

Table 8.5. Accumulated 2001–2003 effect on gearing

	Germany	Spain	France	UK	Italy
EU industrial shareholder	−19% (2.06)[a]	−40% (9.33)[b]	−9% (1.61)	−15% (6.52)[b]	−11% (0.55)
Non-EU industrial shareholder	−4% (0.23)	−25% (6.13)[a]	−36% (47.67)[b]	−11% (7.63)[b]	−30% (4.11)[a]
EU subsidiaries	−8% (0.58)	9% (0.49)	4% (0.33)	0% (0)	−5% (0.13)
Non-EU subsidiaries	−1% (0.01)	−8% (0.31)	8% (0.82)	−32% (6.74)[b]	30% (5.98)[a]

Notes: The marginal effect–on gearing–of having an EU or a non-EU shareholder or a subsidiary, accumulated over the entire 2001–3 period. Calculations are based on Table 8.4 regressions. The marginal effect of having, say, an EU industrial shareholder in 2002 equals to the base 2001 effect, namely 'dummy: EU holder' *plus* the 'interaction dummy: holder 2002'. Marginal effects for 2001 and 2003 are similarly calculated and added up so as to get the accumulated effect. An F statistic to test the hypothesis that the above-calculated accumulated effect equals to zero appear in parentheses.
[a] Indicates significant at 5% level.
[b] Indicate significant at 1% level.

even above the effect of just having an industrial holder (regardless of location). In France and Italy there was an insignificant fall in gearing. No significant change in gearing was detected for companies having non-domestic EU subsidiaries. The results for having non-EU subsidiaries have conflicting signs for the UK and Italy with the other countries having insignificant signs.

As with any other empirical result, the usual reservations apply: one would hope for more and higher-quality data, more directly related to insolvency and distress, and follow the trend for a few more years before firm conclusions can be drawn. And yet, one should be concerned with the virtual absence of evidence that is consistent with a reduction in the cost of capital following the new legislation. An alternative interpretation is that the fall in gearing is associated with only a temporary increase in the level of legal uncertainty, which accompanies any legal reform. Hopefully, future judgements would establish more precise rules regarding what exactly counts as public policy or centre of interests.

5. AN ALTERNATIVE APPROACH TO HARMONIZATION

The results of the previous sections raise the concern that the new EU legislation has not achieved its goals. Admittedly, at this point the results are not—and cannot be—conclusive. Nevertheless, they do justify an effort of thinking about an alternative.

It seems that underneath the many technicalities that the new law deals with, there lies the fundamental view by which companies owe their very existence to the nation state, and should live (and die) according to rules created by politicians and bureaucrats. Even the dispersed activities of an international company must gravitate towards a certain location, revealing its 'real' identity, placing it under rules and regulations of its parent nation state. It is doubtful, however, to what extent this view of companies is useful in an increasingly globalized world (as much as it is doubtful whether this view is valid to individuals). Nowadays a company may be born in one country, expand into another, merge and acquire companies of yet another country, and so on. So when it dies, the question of its 'real' identity is logically meaningless and practically unhelpful in resolving the conflicts among the remaining stakeholders.

Rather than insisting on a national identity of a fictitious personality, it is probably more useful to think of a company as a nexus of contracts, and to recognize up front the international dispersion of contractual counterparts and assets to which these contracts are linked. Since a mechanism for enforcing the contract and settling emerging disputes is an integral part of the contract itself, it makes sense to allow every contract to determine these clauses without state interference and independently of other contracts that the company has signed, and independently of decisions such as location of head office. No exceptions should be made for insolvency, which is just a standardized form of the default clauses of the debt contract. Essentially, I suggest that harmonization of insolvency laws should pass from the nation state to the market. Obviously, that can't be done without the state recognizing the right of the company to contract freely, including the right to choose the rules under which the disputes should be resolved. The EU could have adopted a much simpler, more limited legislation to that effect, avoiding many of the difficulties that the current legislation has created.

Two possible objections to this proposal might arise; first, that some jurisdictions are inconsistent with others, and second, thus such an arrangement would weaken the state's ability to save companies in which the public has a vital interest.

Regarding the first point, it is indeed very likely that such conflicts between jurisdictions exist; it is argued, however, that such conflicts should be resolved by the company itself, and that it is in its best interest to do so properly. It was already noted above that no compelling argument exists to the effect that concentrating all assets in default under a single jurisdiction is indeed economically efficient. Moreover, it was argued that concentrating all assets under a single jurisdiction (as in the EU legislation) may actually create more costly conflicts between (say) insolvency laws that are determined by the location of the head office and the employment laws that are determined by the identity (or place of employment) of the workers. Note also that the current proposal still allows the company to place all its assets under a single jurisdiction if it wishes to do so.

The second objection is that national governments will no longer be able to rescue companies of vital public interest in those cases where foreign courts prefer the interests of foreign creditors to those of domestic stakeholders. Note, however, that this does not prevent a rescue but makes it more costly because the domestic government needs to bail out the distressed company from its foreign creditors. But this also highlight the more sinister side of schemes like chapter 11, for it allows not just to rescue distressed companies but also to dump the cost on the secured creditors, typically on the (ever politically unpopular) banks. Even if this is a desirable solution, it still faces the difficulty of imposing a certain restriction on all companies just in order to address a problem that exists with only a few (i.e. publicly vital). A better policy would be to identify ex ante those companies where externalities exist, and place the restriction on them only. That may be done by disallowing such companies to mortgage assets to any creditors, domestic or foreign. (See Franks and Sussman 2005 for a description of restrictions to that effect imposed by the British government on the corporate charters of public utilities.) In short, the power to stay insolvency proceedings on all the assets—domestic and foreign—of any company is unlikely to be the optimal solution to the problems created by financial distress.[14]

6. CONCLUSIONS

Relatively little time has elapsed since the EU's insolvency law came into effect. Hence, any judgement about its performance is bound to be 'too early'. In this chapter, I was forced to fill in gaps in the evidence with speculation and common sense. Still, I believe that the combined effect of all the arguments put together has some weight, raising the concern that the legislation has not achieved the goal of decreasing cross-border borrowing. It may be premature at this stage to actually overturn the legislation, but not premature to start thinking—at least academically—about a Plan B. The approach proposed here differs radically from the one adopted in the EU legislation, in that it delivers the task of harmonization from politicians and bureaucrats to market participants.

DATA APPENDIX

The data set used for the analysis of this paper is constructed as follows. I start with 'Amadeus financials—top 250,000 companies' (for Germany, Spain, France, the UK, and Italy). To be included in this 'top' category, firms need to satisfy at least one of the following criteria: revenue equal at least €15m, total assets equal at least €30m, number of employees equal at least 150 (for Spain, the numbers are 10, 20, and 100, respectively). I discard financial companies (SIC codes 60–3) and those whose 'legal status' is other than 'active'. In cases where the data contained both consolidated and unconsolidated accounts I used the consolidated accounts. I have used data for the years 2001–3 (and 2000 where lags are required); data for 2004

---

[14] Note also that in any case the EU legislation did not resolve this issue, for a company may have the centre of its operation firmly established in one country, and still generate significant externalities in another country.

Table 8.A1. Table of variables

Var. name	Source/description
Amadeus Financial	
Empl.	[EMPL].
Gear	[GEAR] = (loans + Non Current Liabilities)/(Shareholders Funds). Zeros excluded.
Sales	[OPRE] Operating Revenue or Turnover (in $ terms)
Assets	Total Assets [TOAS], £ for the UK, € for the rest.
Age	2004–(Year of Incorporation, [YEARINC])
Return on assets	[RTAS] = (profit before taxation)/(Total Assets)
Quoted	[QUOTED] dummy, equals 1 if firm is listed
Industry	[USCOR] SIC industry code (2 digit). The following industry dummies were defined
	dagr: agriculture (1–9)
	dmin: oil and mining (10–14)
	dctr: construction (15–17)
	dfdt: food and tobacco (20–1)
	dtxt: textile and clothing (22–3)
	dwod: wood, pulp, and paper (24–7)
	dchm: refining, rubber, and chemicals (28–30)
	dmch: metal and machinery
	dtrs: land transport (40–2)
	dshp: shipping (44)
	darl: airlines (45)
	dutl: utilities (46–9)
	dtrd: trade, wholesale, and retailing (50–9)
Amadeus shareholders–top five shareholders	
No shareholder	a dummy indicating that no industrial shareholder was identified
Local holder	a dummy indicating that the holder is domestically registered in the home country
EU holder	a dummy indicating that the holder is registered abroad but within the EU
Foreign holder	a dummy indicating that the holder is registered out of the EU
n.a. holder	a dummy indicating an industrial shareholder with unknown place of registration
Amadeus shareholders–top five shareholders	
No subsidiaries	a dummy indicating that no subsidiaries were identified
N of subs	number of subsidiaries (at least 20% stake) identified
% local subs.	(number of local subsidiaries)/(N of subs.)
% EU subs.	(number of subsidiaries registered abroad but within the EU)/(N of subs.)
% non-EU subs.	(number of subsidiaries registered out of the EU)/(N of subs.)

Notes: Data sources and definitions for all variables used in the chapter, by Amadeus subdatabases. Variable names in square brackets indicate an Amadeus variable name.

are still scarce, at present. For more detail about data extracted from Amadeus financial see Table 8.A1.

The financial data were then matched with two other databases. The first is 'Amadeus shareholders—top five shareholders'. Among these, I identify shareholders that are classified as 'Industrial Companies', ignoring shareholders such as financial institutions, foundations, families, or the public. I did not use information about the ownership stake due to the high incidence of missing data, which could result in a significant drop in sample size. It is my impression, however, that the stake is significant, 100 per cent in many cases. Industrial shareholders are then sorted by country of registration, and dummy variables are defined accordingly (see Table 8.A1). Note the incidence of companies with several industrial shareholders of different locations.

The second database is 'Amadeus subsidiaries—all subsidiaries'. I discard subsidiaries where the stake of the owner (either direct or indirect) is smaller than 20 per cent. I then track the number of subsidiaries per company, and calculate the percentage of them that is registered domestically, within the EU and out of the EU. See Table 8.A1 for more detail.

It is notable that Amadeus financial is a dynamic database, while Amadeus shareholders and Amadeus subsidiaries are static databases. I have no choice but to treat changes in ownership during 2001–4 as measurement errors.

REFERENCES

ALLEN, F., and GALE, D. (2000), *Comparing Financial Systems*, Cambridge, Mass.: MIT Press.

BOWTLE, G., and McGUINNESS, K. P. (2001), *The Law of Ship Mortgages*, London: Lloyd's Shipping Law Library.

DAVYDENKO, S., and FRANKS, J. (2006), 'Do bankruptcy codes matter? A study of defaults in France, Germany, and the UK', *Journal of Finance*, forthcoming.

FRANKS, J., and SUSSMAN, O. (2005), 'Financial innovations and corporate bankruptcy', *Journal of Financial Intermediation*, 14, 283–317.

LOMBARDO, S. (2001), 'Regulatory competition in company law in the European Community', Frankfurt am Main: European University Studies, Series 5.

MAYER, C., and SUSSMAN, O. (2006), 'The financing of investment: is it internal? Structure', Working Paper, University of Oxford.

OMAR, P. J. (2003), 'Genesis of the European initiative in insolvency law', *International Insolvency Review*, 12, 147–70.

RAJAK, H. (2004), 'The inter-relationship between main and secondary bankruptcies', paper presented in Academy of European Law and the Czech Bar Association, Prague, 4–5 November.

SCOTT, J. A., and SMITH, T. C. (1986), 'The effect of the Bankruptcy Reform Act 1978 on small business loan pricing', *Journal of Financial Economics*, 16, 119–40.

WESSELS, B. (2004), 'Realisation of the EU insolvency regulation in Germany, France and the Netherlands', *European Business Law Review*, forthcoming.

....

CHAPTER 9

TAKEOVERS

....

MIKE BURKART

FAUSTO PANUNZI

A takeover typically involves much more than the mere transfer of ownership since the acquired firm subsequently undergoes a major reorganization. Its divisions are merged with or subordinated to those of the acquiring firm, divested, or even dissolved. Furthermore, such restructuring takes hold of entire industries as takeovers occur in waves and are within each wave clustered by industries (Andrade, Mitchell, and Stafford 2001).

Whether these changes primarily create or destroy value, or redistribute wealth among different constituencies, such as employees and shareholders, is the subject of a long-standing debate. Initially, the controversy revolved around the gains from realizing economies of scale and scope on the one hand, and the cost of concentrated economic power to competitors, labour, and consumers on the other hand. In the mid-1950s, tender offers emerged as a new form of takeover in the UK and some years later also in the USA (Singh 1971). Contrary to mergers, tender offers allow bidders to bypass management by making an offer directly to target shareholders. In this form, takeovers can have a motive apart from spurring firm growth or exploiting synergies, namely rectifying managerial failure.[1]

During the takeover wave of the 1980s hostile tender offers became a regular mode of acquisition in the UK and USA. For instance, Mitchell and Mulherin (1996) report that almost a quarter of the large US corporations received a hostile bid during that time. To be certain, the majority of acquisitions during that time were friendly,

We thank Colin Mayer (the editor) for helpful comments on an earlier draft.

[1] Prior to the appearance of tender offers, controlling blocks had to be accumulated through individual trades, and proxy fights—which is to say direct voting by the firm's existing shareholders—were the principal mechanism for a hostile change of management (Hansmann 1996).

negotiated with the target management.[2] Outside the UK and USA, the incidence of takeovers during the 1980s was much lower, and hostile takeovers—in the sense of tender offers launched in the market—were extremely rare if not non-existent. The 1990s saw takeover activities rebound to unprecedented levels in the USA but with a substantially lower incidence of hostile bids (Holmström and Kaplan 2001). Europe and Asia experienced a massive surge in takeover activity, though hostile bids outside the UK remained rare until the end of the 1990s. In 1999 a significant number of hostile bids occurred in continental Europe, including some high-profile cases such as the Vodafone–Mannesmann deal.

Although hostile bids are primarily an Anglo-American phenomenon and occasional events even in these countries, they have long been at the centre of the takeover debate—at least among financial economists. This focus is in part a reflection of the media exposure, public interest, and fierce criticisms that hostile takeovers in the 1980s provoked, notably those involving very large corporations, the heavy use of leverage, and the subsequent sell-off of numerous divisions. More importantly, hostile takeovers are a mechanism to discipline managers and thereby address problems raised by the separation of ownership and control. Indeed, a functioning takeover market is the most direct way to achieve control contestability which many commentators consider an essential component of an effective governance system (Berglöf et al. 2003). In recent years, this view has also gained support among European regulators and politicians, as the discussions surrounding the European Takeover Directive show. In particular, the European Commission and its expert group sought to open up Europe for takeovers to promote restructuring.[3] According to the Commission, Europe badly needs more restructuring if it wants to accomplish the goal, set forth in the 2000 Lisbon Declaration, to become the world's most dynamic economic region.

The existing research on takeovers is vast and covers a wide range of topics. In this survey,[4] we focus on takeovers as a remedy for managerial failure and the incentive problems inherent in control transactions. Much of this literature presupposes a publicly listed target firm with dispersed ownership and with no takeover barriers, making shares and their votes freely transferable. Yet, the available evidence on ownership structures demonstrates that dispersed ownership of large firms is rare outside the United States (La Porta, López-de-Silanes, and Shleifer 1999). In Europe, dispersed ownership is the prevalent organizational form only in

[2] Even at their peak hostile bids never represented more than 30% of all US transactions (Schwert 2000). The small number of hostile takeovers underestimates, however, their impact as many friendly transactions would (might) not have been done but for the background threat of a hostile bid.

[3] After the European Parliament rejected the proposed directive in 2001, the Commission appointed a 'High Level Group of Company Law Experts' under the chairmanship of Jaap Winter to provide independent advice. The Winter Report's most radical proposal is the so-called breakthrough rule (European Commission 2002). It stipulates that a party owning a qualified majority (75%) of the equity capital can undo any statutory defences, including any differentiation of votes. Due to tremendous opposition the breakthrough rule was omitted from the directive that was finally adopted on 22 December 2003.

[4] There are several reviews of the theoretical and empirical research on takeovers, including Andrade, Mitchell, and Stafford 2001; Becht, Bolton, and Röell 2003; Bhagat, Shleifer, and Vishny 1990; Bruner 2002; Holmström and Kaplan 2001; Hirshleifer 1995; Jensen 1988; McCahery et al. 2004; Scherer 1988; and von Thadden 1990.

the United Kingdom and Ireland where more than 60 per cent of the listed firms are widely held (Faccio and Lang 2002). By contrast, continental European firms typically have a large shareholder, though there is considerable variation in the extent of ownership concentration across countries. In half of the listed non-financial firms in Austria, Belgium, Germany, and Italy a single shareholder controls more than 50 per cent of the votes. In Dutch, Spanish, and Swedish firms the median blockholder holds 43.5, 34.5, and 34.9 per cent, respectively (Barca and Becht 2001). A distinctive feature of this survey is that it also discusses in some detail how the presence of both minority and majority blocks affects the incidence and efficiency of control transfers. We note the implications for regulatory policy throughout the chapter.

This essay proceeds as follows. Section 1 introduces the concept of the market for corporate control and discusses the efficiency effects of takeovers. Section 2 examines the tender offer process, and Section 3 explores control transfers of firms whose ownership structure is not dispersed. Concluding remarks are in Section 4.

1. EFFICIENCY OF TAKEOVERS

The academic literature on the market for corporate control and the term itself originate from Manne (1965). In this market shareholders can sell, possibly against the will of the incumbent management, the control (rights) over the firm to an outsider. Given that the share price reflects (expected) firm performance, an outsider who is better able to run the firm finds it profitable to acquire control in order to subsequently employ the firm's assets more profitably. Moreover, competition among outsiders or, in the parlance of Jensen and Ruback (1983), competing management teams ensures that resources flow to their highest-value use. Efficiency is increased ex post by replacing managers who are either less competent or are not acting in the shareholders' best interest. Hence, the takeover mechanism ensures that firms which do not maximize profits do not survive, even if market forces on the product and input markets fail to eliminate them. In addition, the mere threat of a takeover raises efficiency ex ante as it disciplines managers, thereby reducing the agency costs stemming from the separation of ownership and control (Grossman and Hart 1980a; Scharfstein 1988).

This line of reasoning presupposes that takeovers are motivated by value improvements brought about either by exploiting synergies or by correcting inefficient managerial behaviour. It further assumes that the takeover market operates efficiently, notably that a firm whose current share price is less than it could be under the control of a different party is indeed acquired by that party. The question whether or not these two conditions are met, or more generally, whether the market for corporate control operates efficiently, is the subject of numerous theoretical and empirical studies. The various caveats boil down to two assertions: On the one hand, frictions in the takeover market result in too few value-improving takeovers and, on the other hand, takeovers may succeed even though they do not create value. In addition, it is argued that the existence of the takeover threat may well exacerbate the agency conflict between managers and shareholders, rather than mitigate it. In what follows, we review the debate over the efficiency of the takeover mechanism in more detail. Due to the large representation of studies on US takeovers, the discussion relies heavily on the US experience, and reported findings refer to US evidence, unless stated otherwise.

1.1. Disciplinary Takeovers

As described above, one takeover motive is to improve target firm performance by altering the strategies of the incumbent managers and possibly replacing them. Such disciplinary takeovers occur when the firms' internal governance mechanisms fail to prevent managers from pursuing their own goals.[5] This problem is particularly pertinent for cash-rich firms that enable managers to undertake unprofitable but power-enhancing investments (Jensen 1986).[6] Consequently, firms undertaking poor investments and, more generally, poorly performing firms are more likely to be the target of a (hostile) takeover bid.

These predictions are only partly supported by the available evidence. While studies on US and UK data consistently document that takeover targets are smaller than other firms, only some report that hostile takeovers tend to be directed towards poorly performing firms in troubled industries (e.g. Morck, Shleifer, and Vishny 1988). Other studies find no significant difference in pre-takeover performance between targets and non-targets, or between targets of friendly and of hostile bids (e.g. Comment and Schwert 1995; Martin and McConnell 1991; Franks and Mayer 1996). These results suggest that the selection process in the market for corporate control relies more on size than performance.

As for unprofitable investments by target firms, the evidence is also mixed. On the one hand, takeover targets are more likely to have made poor acquisitions previously, notably poor diversification acquisitions (Mitchell and Lehn 1990; Berger and Ofek 1996).[7] These findings suggest that recouping equity value lost through poor acquisitions is one source of takeover gains. In support of this interpretation, Allen et al. (1995) document that a major source of gains from spin-offs is the reversal of earlier unwise acquisitions. On the other hand, large firms in the gas and oil industry apart,

---

[5] Disciplinary takeovers are commonly associated with hostile bids, (initially) opposed by target board and management. In contrast, friendly takeovers are viewed as motivated by synergies arising from combining the firms' assets (Morck, Shleifer, and Vishny 1988). In practice, many takeovers contain elements of both friendly and hostile bids. Indeed, Schwert 2000 finds hostile and friendly takeovers to be indistinguishable in economic terms. He argues that the choice of hostile (friendly) offer is largely a reflection of the acquiring firm's negotiation strategy.

[6] According to Jensen 1988, 1993, the 1980s takeovers in the USA were caused by a failure of internal governance mechanisms to bring about the restructuring required to meet the technological and regulatory changes.

[7] Some recent studies (e.g. Campa and Kedia 2002), however, suggest that the diversification discount is due to the diversifying firms being different, rather than to diversification being value destroying.

there is no systematic evidence that takeover targets overinvest in internally developed projects or that capital expenditures change after the takeover (Servaes 1994; Healy, Palepu, and Ruback 1992; Bhagat, Shleifer, and Vishny 1990).

In summary, the empirical evidence lends only limited support to the notion that takeovers are directed at underperforming firms or at firms with a poor investment record.[8] Even if takeovers may not be an effective means to correct inefficiencies, they may nonetheless create value by, for instance, exploiting synergies.

1.2. Takeover Gains

To assess the economic consequences of takeovers, a plethora of empirical studies examines stock returns surrounding the announcement dates. These event studies document unanimously that target shareholders gain substantially from takeovers. For US takeovers, average abnormal returns for target shareholders are typically found to be in the range of 15 to 30 per cent (Andrade, Mitchell, and Stafford 2001; Bruner 2002). The findings for the UK are similar to those for the USA (McCahery et al. 2004), while target shareholder returns in continental European takeovers are lower but still substantial at around 10 per cent (Goergen and Renneboog 2004; Campa and Hernando 2004).

The evidence on acquiring firms' shareholder return is far less conclusive. Some studies report positive abnormal bidder returns (e.g. Goergen and Renneboog 2004; Schwert 1996), others document negative bidder returns (e.g. Andrade, Mitchell, and Stafford 2001), and still others find no significant effects (e.g. Stulz, Walkling, and Song 1990). Whether positive or negative, bidder returns are small, ranging from +5 to −5 per cent.[9] There is more consensus about the net shareholder wealth effect of takeovers. Most studies report that the combined average abnormal returns are positive but relatively small ranging from 1 to 3 per cent (e.g. Andrade, Mitchell, and Stafford 2001; Campa and Hernando 2004).

Overall, the studies on announcement period stock returns suggest that takeovers create gains to shareholders, but that these gains accrue (almost) entirely to target shareholders.[10] These gains are the evidence upon which Jensen (1988) among others bases the claim that takeovers create value. The inference from observed stock price

---

[8] Managerial turnover has been found to increase in target firms following the completion of the takeover, particularly if the pre-takeover performance has been poor (e.g. Martin and McConnell 1991). An inverse relation between forced CEO turnover and firm performance has also been documented for firms that are not takeover targets (see the survey by Murphy 1999). This suggests that both internal and external control mechanisms serve to monitor and discipline managers.

[9] While many studies do not distinguish between (friendly) mergers and (hostile) tender offers, those that do tend to find higher target as well as bidder returns in hostile takeovers and tender offers than in friendly acquisitions and mergers (McCahery et al. 2004). In addition, target and/or acquiring firms' announcement returns are found to vary systematically with other characteristics, such as means of payments (Travlos 1987), relatedness of bidder's and target's businesses (Comment and Jarrell 1995), book-to-market value ratios (Rau and Vermaelen 1998).

[10] One problem when interpreting stock returns is that takeover announcements also reveal information about the stand-alone value of target and bidder firms. When correcting for the revelation bias,

increases to efficiency improvements relies, however, on some stringent (implicit) conditions, in particular informationally efficient stock markets and the absence of externalities and redistribution.

The efficient market hypothesis has been challenged by long-run performance studies documenting abnormal positive and negative stock returns following different corporate events, such as equity issues, stock splits, and acquisitions. These findings suggest that investors systematically misjudge the impact of corporate events. Accordingly, short-term announcement period returns are flawed measures of shareholder wealth effects of corporate events.[11] In their review of the literature on long-run stock returns following acquisitions, Agrawal and Jaffe (2000) argue that there is evidence of abnormal underperformance in mergers but that share prices during tender offer announcements do not overestimate future gains. Compared to other studies, Mitchell and Stafford (2000) find smaller—often insignificant—abnormal returns and less variation across subsamples of acquisitions, e.g. cash financed versus stock financed. Overall, their study suggests that long-run abnormal stock returns following acquisitions are limited to small acquiring firms.

Irrespective of how accurately positive abnormal stock returns during the announcement period reflect the long-run wealth effects, documented shareholder gains are merely suggestive of efficiency improvements. Event studies cannot reveal the source of the shareholder gains. These gains may arise from the correction of mismanagement or from synergies or may stem from expropriation of target stakeholder or from transfers at the expense of the acquiring firms' shareholders.

Accounting data-based studies attempt to identify the source of gains by comparing firm performance before and after the takeover. If shareholder gains reflect true value creation, improvements in operating performance should be the counterpart of these gains. However, operating performance studies offer conflicting evidence.[12] Some studies report improvements in operating cash flows of the combined firms relative to their industry peers (e.g. Healy, Palepu, and Ruback 1992) and productivity improvement at the plant level (Lichtenberg and Siegel 1987, 1989). Other studies do not find evidence of improved performance (e.g. McGuckin and Nguyen 1995; Schoar 2002) or even document a post-takeover decline in the target's performance compared to non-acquired comparable firms (e.g. Ravenscraft and Scherer 1987).

When interpreting the different findings, it should be borne in mind that poor post-takeover performance does not necessarily imply value destruction. If industry shocks are the source of takeovers, firms consolidating via takeovers should not necessarily be expected to outperform a pre-shock benchmark (Mitchell and

---

Bhagat, Shleifer, and Vishny 2005 find larger combined abnormal returns than the returns found in earlier studies using traditional announcement period estimation methods (e.g. Bradley, Desai, and Kim 1988).

[11] This literature has itself come under attack from studies documenting the sensitivity of long-term performance estimates to modifications of either the sample or the methodology. For a discussion of these issues, see Fama 1998.

[12] An exception are leveraged buyouts (LBOs) for which the available evidence documents improvements in operating performance (Holmström and Kaplan 2001).

Mulherin 1996). Nonetheless, the lack of clear evidence in support of performance improvements is puzzling in view of the documented large (target) shareholder gains and casts some doubt on the claim that takeovers create value. Indeed, it has been contended that takeover premia reflect redistributive gains rather than efficiency improvements.

Transfers from acquiring firms are one possible explanation for low returns to their shareholders but high returns to target shareholders. Managers of acquiring firms may overestimate their ability to improve the target firm's operation and as a result pay a too high acquisition price (Roll 1986). Alternatively, takeovers can be a manifestation of the managers' ability to pursue their own interest at the expense of the shareholders. Such acquisitions serve the purpose of empire building (Marris 1963, 1964), diversification of the manager's human capital risk (Amihud and Lev 1981), or simply reflect the availability of excess cash (Jensen 1986).[13]

Empirical studies strongly suggest that managerial self-interest can trigger or even drive takeovers, and that such acquisitions generate low if not negative returns to acquiring shareholders. Previously discussed evidence in support of the notion that takeovers can be a manifestation of agency problems within the acquiring firm includes the mixed evidence on post-takeover performance, the high degree of overlap between target and bidder firms, and the target firms' poor record of past acquisitions. Other findings also indicate that managerial self-interest matters for takeovers. Bidding firms tend to have large amounts of free cash flow and relatively low leverage, and firms with more excess cash are more likely to make acquisitions with poor returns for their shareholders (Harford 1999; Lang, Stulz, and Walkling 1991; Bruner 1988). Furthermore, bidder returns are higher when managers of the acquiring firm own larger shareholdings (Healy, Palepu, and Ruback 1997; Lewellen, Loderer, and Rosenfeld 1985). Thus, managerial motives appear to be an important determinant of takeover activity. The positive combined shareholder returns reject, however, the hypothesis that target shareholders gain purely at the expense of the acquiring firm's shareholders.

In an influential paper, Shleifer and Summers (1988) expound the concern that takeovers can be a means to redistribute wealth from target stakeholders to shareholders. They argue that bidders, notably in hostile bids, renege on existing contracts, either explicit or implicit, and expropriate rents from the target stakeholders. Anticipating this breach of contract, target shareholders demand higher prices from the bidders, and thus the post-acquisition transfers show up as (part of) the takeover premia. Potential victims of such redistributions are employees, creditors, consumers, and the tax authorities.

The empirical evidence on transfers from stakeholders as the primary motivation for takeovers is not convincing. Generally neither blue-collar lay-offs nor wage cuts are found to explain more than a small fraction of the takeover premium (Brown and Medoff 1988; Kaplan 1989a; Lichtenberg and Siegel 1989; Rosett 1993). In hostile

---

[13] In Jensen's (1986) view such acquisitions are the lesser of two evils. They involve less waste than unprofitable internal projects and disgorge cash to investors if not purely made with shares (share exchange offers).

takeovers, cutbacks—disproportionately targeted at white-collar employees—are more important and account for 11 to 26 per cent of the premium on average (Bhagat, Shleifer, and Vishny 1990).[14]

Bondholders may be hurt by increased leverage in takeovers because of the higher default risk. In addition, the higher level of debt may itself induce shareholders or managers acting on their behalf to opt for riskier ventures, further increasing the likelihood of a future bankruptcy (Jensen and Meckling 1976). Studies on leverage buyouts document reductions in corporate bond prices during the announcement period but these losses are very small relative to the shareholder gains (Marais, Schipper, and Smith 1989; Warga and Welch 1993).[15]

As takeovers often involve firms in the same or closely related industries (Bhagat, Shleifer, and Vishny 1990), shareholder gains may also reflect increased extraction of consumer surplus. To test for market power, empirical studies examine the stock market reaction of rival firms in response to takeover announcements. The underlying idea is that an anti-competitive takeover raises product prices and thus benefits all firms in the industry. Using this approach, Stillman (1983) and Eckbo (1983, 1985) reject the market power hypothesis. Later studies question the reliability of the approach and find evidence of anti-competitive effects (McAfee and Williams 1988; Mullin, Mullin, and Mullin 1995). While the evidence on market power is not conclusive, transfers from consumers are most likely not an important effect of takeovers.

Takeovers can generate tax benefits through increased utilization of tax loss and tax credit carry-forwards or through higher interest deductions associated higher debt levels. The available evidence suggests that takeovers benefited from tax savings, amounting in some cases to more than a quarter of the takeover premium (Bhagat, Shleifer, and Vishny 1990). Although tax advantages are a source of takeover gains,[16] they do not seem to be a major force behind the takeover activity.

In conclusion, empirical studies find that stakeholders indeed experience wealth losses in takeovers. As major restructuring typically follows a takeover, such losses are—to some extent—inevitable but have to be accounted for when assessing the efficiency effects of takeovers. On balance, stakeholder losses explain, however, only a modest fraction of the total gains to shareholders, suggesting that efficiency improvements clearly outweigh redistribution away from stakeholders.

[14] Employees may also be harmed by reductions in pension provisions following a takeover. Empirically, pension reversions are neither a primary motivation for takeovers nor an important source of gains, accounting for about 1% of the total premia (Ippolito and James 1992; Mitchell and Mulherin 1996; Pontiff, Shleifer, and Weisbach 1990).

[15] Increased leverage may also strengthen the firm's bargaining power as the associated higher bankruptcy risk can force stakeholders, e.g. workers and suppliers, to make concessions to management and shareholders (Perotti and Spier 1993). Brown, Fee, and Thomas 2005 document that suppliers experience deteriorating stock market and operating performance when an important customer (accountable for 10% or more of the revenues) undergoes a LBO.

[16] According to Kaplan 1989b, 1991, tax savings account for most of the premium in management buyouts. These benefits are, however, significantly reduced by the rapid debt repayment.

1.3. Takeover Threat

The market for corporate control has not only a profound impact on target and acquiring firms but also on non-transacting firms. That is, the mere threat or possibility of a takeover can induce managers to alter their behaviour. Whether the resulting effects are primarily beneficial or detrimental is at least as controversial as the efficiency effects of actually completed takeovers. On the one hand, it is argued that the takeover threat deters managers from pursuing their own interests at the expense of the shareholders. For instance, the large-scale restructuring carried out by incumbent managers during the 1980s is attributed to the concurrent real takeover threat (Holmström and Kaplan 2001).

On the other hand, it is contended that the takeover threat may induce managers to distort their behaviour rather than promote profit-maximizing actions. First, incumbent managers can use anti-takeover measures, like poison pills, stock repurchases, or litigation, to fend off hostile takeovers.[17] Furthermore, if takeovers are undertaken for reasons other than reversing inefficiencies, acting in the shareholders' best interest need not be an effective protection against a takeover. In fact, the above evidence that size consistently reduces the takeover probability (and more so than good performance) implies that growth rather than efficiency is a viable defence strategy. Alternatively, managers may entrench themselves by tailoring the firm's operations more to their own abilities to become less easily replaceable, even though this course of action reduces firm value (Shleifer and Vishny 1989).

Second, the possibility of losing the job may discourage managers from investing in firm-specific human capital. More generally, if takeovers imply some form of contract renegotiation the firm's stakeholders are reluctant to undertake firm-specific investments, thereby reducing ex ante efficiencies (Shleifer and Summers 1988).

Finally, the takeover pressure may induce managers to sacrifice long-term profitability to boost short-term earnings (Stein 1988). Moreover, such short-termism may be in the shareholders' best interest. For example, suppose that the manager has superior information about the value of the firm, and that the sale of an asset is the only way to credibly convey the actual value to uninformed shareholders. Although this short-term action is costly, i.e. the sold asset is worth less outside the company, it is a best response to an imminent takeover. The loss incurred through costly signalling is more than offset by the takeover returns, as it prevents the bidder from acquiring the firm at too low a price. More generally, a takeover threat may hinder firms from pursuing profitable long-term strategies, such as investment in R&D.

To assess the impact of the takeover threat, empirical studies examine the effects that firm-specific takeover defences and anti-takeover legislation have on stock returns, firm performance, and operating decisions. The conflicting views on this topic may be summarized by two hypotheses. The entrenchment hypothesis holds that anti-takeover provisions are detrimental: they raise the cost of a takeover and hence

---

[17] By the end of the 1980s, most S&P 500 firms and a vast majority of those firms listed on the NYSE or Amex were covered by several anti-takeover devices, ranging from poison pills, supermajority amendments, to state anti-takeover laws (Danielson and Karpoff 1998).

reduce the disciplinary force of the market for corporate control. This hinders an efficient redeployment of corporate assets and allows managers to pursue their own interests to a larger extent. As a result, firms covered by defensive devices are less efficient and their value is correspondingly lower.[18] Under the shareholder interest hypothesis, defensive devices allow for more efficient contracting with the manager, thereby encouraging firm-specific human capital investment (Knoeber 1986), prevent coercive bids (Bebchuk and Hart 2001), make the manager a tougher negotiator in the takeover (Harris 1990),[19] and promote competition among bidders once the company has come into play (Shleifer and Vishny 1986a). Moreover, defensive devices protect managers (and firms) from the disruptive effects of takeovers, enabling them to focus on long-term profitable strategies.

The shareholder wealth effects of firm-specific takeover defences are examined in numerous studies, surveyed by Coates (2000) and Weston, Mitchell, and Mulherin (2003: chapter 19). Early studies (e.g. Malatesta and Walkling 1988; Ryngaert 1988) tend to find that the adoption of takeover defences is associated with small negative abnormal returns of less than 1 per cent. However, later studies (e.g. Comment and Schwert 1995; Heron and Lie 2006) report insignificant average stock price reactions but higher takeover premia. This suggests that takeover defences strengthen the target firms' bargaining position without preventing many takeovers. Overall, the evidence is mixed, ranging from small negative to non-existent abnormal stock returns, and difficult to interpret because the adoption of a takeover defence may simultaneously signal that management expects a takeover bid.[20]

Several studies attempt to determine the impact of anti-takeover statutes on stock returns. By and large, these studies find abnormal negative stock returns (e.g. Szewczyk and Tsetsekos 1992; Karpoff and Malatesta 1989; Ryngaert and Netter 1988), though some report no significant effects (e.g. Margotta, McWilliams, and McWilliams 1990; Pugh and Jahera 1990).[21] Overall, the studies appear to favour the entrenchment hypothesis, though some caution seems in place also because the different states' anti-takeover statutes vary in the extent to which they are a deterrent to would-be acquiring firms (Daines and Klausner 2001).

---

[18] In this view, the widespread use of takeover defences and the increase in anti-takeover legislation are one of the reasons both for the ending of the 1980s takeover wave and for the paucity of hostile bids during the 1990s takeover wave (Holmström and Kaplan 2001).

[19] Takeover defences can also resolve information problems to the benefit of target shareholders (Sarig and Talmor 1997) and to the benefit of both target shareholders and acquiring firms (Hirschleifer and Titman 1990).

[20] Claessens et al. 2002 and Gompers, Ishii, and Metrick 2003 among others document that firms with good corporate governance, as measured by various proxies, earn significantly higher returns and are more highly valued over a long horizon. These results suggest that anti-takeover devices, being a reflection of poor governance, have an adverse impact on firm performance. However, the results may also reflect changes in the business environment not directly related to firm governance (Becht, Bolton, and Röell 2003).

[21] Compared to firm-specific takeover defence studies, these studies avoid problems of mixed signals and selection bias. Their main difficulty is to choose, i.e. assume, the date at which the market became aware of a new anti-takeover statute and impounded the effect into the stock prices (Bertrand and Mullainathan 2003).

A smaller body of work examines the effects of firm-specific takeover defences and anti-takeover legislation on firm performance and managerial decisions. The adoption of firm-specific takeover defences is found to be associated either with no subsequent decline in firm performance (Johnson and Rao 1997) or with a subsequent improvement (Field and Karpoff 2002; Danielson and Karpoff 2006). In contrast, Bertrand and Mullainathan (2003) report that total factor productivity declines in firms after they are covered by anti-takeover laws. Moreover, anti-takeover statutes lead to fewer new investments and fewer disinvestments. This result suggests that managers, shielded from the takeover threat, do not behave like empire builders, but tend to become sluggish. Garvey and Hanka (1999) document that firms protected by anti-takeover laws substantially reduce their leverage. This suggests that legal barriers to takeovers increase financial slack.

The evidence on the argument that the takeover threat causes managers to behave myopically is scarce and divided.[22] Meulbroek et al. (1990) find a decrease in R&D expenditures following the adoption of firm-level takeover defences. Using a broader measure of R&D expenditure, Pugh, Page, and Jahera (1992) present contrary results, consistent with the notion that the takeover threat forces managers to sacrifice long-term investments.

Finally, managers of firms that adopt takeover defences (Borokhovich, Brunarski, and Parrino 1997) or are covered by anti-takeover laws (Bertrand and Mullainathan 1998) receive higher salaries. These findings are consistent with the view that takeover defences increase agency costs (entrenchment hypothesis). Wage increases following the introduction of anti-takeover statutes are not restricted to CEOs. Bertrand and Mullainathan (1999) find that anti-takeover laws raise annual wages by 1 to 2 per cent. As the associated increase in the total wage bill exceeds the negative share price reaction to these laws, the wage increase does not represent pure transfers but also leads to higher profits. This is consistent with the view that a reduced takeover risk encourages valuable firm-specific human capital investment (Shleifer and Summers 1988).

In sum, the evidence on the effects of anti-takeover devices is too inconclusive to draw general or strong conclusions. In particular, the results are not sufficiently strong to infer that anti-takeover devices necessarily harm shareholders and degrade firm performance. They seem to be associated with higher takeover premia and in some cases with benefits that exceed the loss in share value.

When debating the effects of defensive measures it is important to distinguish between the impact of defensive measures and the power to undertake them. The conflict of interests between managers and shareholders is particularly pronounced in takeovers: managerial turnover increases significantly following the completion of a takeover, and those managers who lose their jobs do not easily find another senior executive position (Martin and McConnell 1991; Agrawal and Walkling 1994). Hence,

[22] Share prices are found to react positively (negatively) to the announcement of an increase (decrease) in investment expenditures (McConnell and Muscarella 1985). This finding is inconsistent with the view that the stock market has a myopic time horizon. It is, however, also compatible with managers acting myopically (Stein 1988). If managers are reluctant to invest, the present value of those few projects that they undertake is very high, and the market should hence react positively to the announcement of such investments.

if a manager can apply defences without shareholder ratification, he may abuse this discretion. Indeed, managers seem less inclined to resist when they gain financially more from a successful bid (Cotter and Zenner 1994; Song and Walkling 1993). Consequently, shareholders need to supervise the manager's defensive actions closely, and to facilitate this task, defensive measures should be subject to shareholder ratification.

2. TENDER OFFER PROCESS

In addition to takeovers being motivated by value improvements, the tenet of an efficient market for corporate control relies on the assumption that a party who can improve the firm's market value finds it profitable to launch a takeover and succeeds in doing so. High transaction costs which are involved in takeovers particularly of large firms are one reason why the allocation of control may not be efficient. Another related reason concerns the division of takeover gains between target and acquiring firms. Indeed, if the acquiring firm appropriates too small a fraction of the surplus to cover its costs, it does not make a bid, even if the takeover were to create value. Grossman and Hart (1980b) and Bradley (1980) argue that such an unequal distribution of takeover gains is not simply a remote possibility but inherent to the tender offer process. Their argument therefore offers a rationale for why—as recounted in the previous section—nearly all the takeover gains accrue to the target shareholders. Ultimately, this implies that managers who are either inefficient or pursue self-serving actions need not be vulnerable to a takeover bid. Subsequently, we review the analysis of Grossman and Hart (1980b) as it is central to the understanding of the tender offer process and represents—to the current day—the point of reference for many issues in the takeover debate.

2.1. Free-rider Problem

Grossman and Hart (1980b) consider a firm with a completely dispersed ownership that is approached by an outside buyer, henceforth the rival. Let X_I denote the firm's stock market value under the incumbent management and X_R its market value under the rival's control. The corresponding per-share values are x_I and x_R respectively, where by assumption $x_R > x_I$.[23] That is, we restrict attention here to the commonly considered case of a value-increasing takeover.

To gain control, a rival has to win the approval of a majority of shareholders and to outbid any competing offer.[24] To focus on the target shareholders' impact on the

[23] For simplicity, we also assume that the current share price is not forward-looking, i.e. does not incorporate the possibility of a takeover, but is equal to x_I. The qualitative arguments would not change if we were to include the impact that the prospect of a takeover has on the current share price.

[24] To succeed an offer also has to overcome managerial resistance. However, as tender offers are directly addressed to shareholders, incumbent managers cannot unilaterally discard a tender offer once it is made.

tender offer outcome, we abstract for the time being from competition by another would-be acquirer and discuss it later. Hence, the rival gains control if he succeeds in inducing shareholders to tender at least 50 per cent of the shares. (All shares carry the same number of votes.) To this end, the rival makes an unrestricted tender offer with a price p for each share, conditional on getting (at least) 50 per cent of the shares. The rival does not own any shares prior to the bid and incurs a takeover cost $C > 0$. Shareholders do not coordinate their response to the offer, but decide non-cooperatively and simultaneously whether to tender their shares. Given the large (infinite) number of shareholders, each of them rightly presumes that his decision does not affect the tender offer outcome. For simplicity, firm (share) values X_I and X_R (x_I and x_R) and the takeover cost C are known to all parties.

When deciding whether or not to accept the offer, each shareholder compares the benefits and costs of tendering in case of success and failure of the takeover. If less than 50 per cent of the shares are tendered, the offer is void, and each individual shareholder's decision is immaterial. Incumbent management remains in control and the share value is x_I. If the offer succeeds, a shareholder receives the offered price p when tendering and the post-takeover share value x_R when retaining his share. Consequently, he prefers to retain his share for any price p below x_R. As all shareholders behave in the same manner, the lowest price at which the rival can succeed is $p = x_R$. At this price the rival not only makes no profit but incurs a loss due to the takeover cost C.[25]

Thus, we have replicated the seemingly paradoxical result of Grossman and Hart (1980b): A value-increasing takeover of a completely dispersed firm cannot succeed because of the small shareholders' free-riding behaviour. The success of the takeover is a public good, but each individual shareholder prefers to hold out to extract the maximum gain. As a result, the rival cannot appropriate any fraction of the value improvement and has therefore no incentives to undertake the takeover in the first place.[26] That is, there are too few takeovers.

2.2. Acquirer Gains

The theoretical literature on takeovers suggests several ways how the free-rider problem may be overcome. Common to all the different proposals is that they increase the share of the gains appropriated by the rival and consequently reduce that of the target

Nonetheless, incumbent managers can resort to various defensive tactics to influence the shareholders' perception of an offer, to solicit a competing offer, or even to deter a bid in the first place. Some of these defensive tactics and their likely effects have been discussed in the previous section.

[25] This result is independent of the value improvement $x_R - x_I$ that the rival can realize. Moreover, even if shareholders do not know the post-takeover share value x_R, they can anticipate that it must exceed the offered price because the bidder would otherwise make a loss.

[26] With a finite rather than infinite number of shareholders, each individual shareholder takes into account that his decision is with positive probability pivotal for the aggregate outcome. Hence, he is willing to tender at a price (slightly) below the post-takeover share value, leaving the bidder some profits (Bagnoli and Lipman 1988; Holmström and Nalebuff 1992). In support of this prediction, acquirers of unlisted firms earn positive abnormal announcement returns (Faccio, McConnell, and Stolin 2005; Moeller, Schlingemann, and Stulz 2004).

shareholders. Grossman and Hart (1980b) propose to allow the rival to withhold part of the proceeds from the minority shareholders. Dilution creates a wedge between the post-takeover share value to the rival and that to minority shareholders, enabling the rival to make a profit. More specifically, suppose that the rival can divert a fraction $\phi \in (0, 1)$ of the proceeds V_R generated under his control as private benefits B_R. For instance, the rival could pay minority shareholders only $(1 - \phi)$ of the dividends that he collects.[27] Consequently, investors price the share after the takeover at $x_R = (1 - \phi)v_R$, and each shareholder is willing to tender at a price $p = x_R$. Provided that the private benefits are sufficient to cover the takeover cost ($\phi V_R > C$), the rival finds it profitable to undertake the bid.[28]

The proposal of Grossman and Hart (1980b) makes the fundamental trade-off between promoting takeovers and protecting minority shareholder interests very transparent. To the extent that (target) shareholder protection amounts to granting them a substantial share of the gains, it necessarily discourages would-be acquirers. Hence, an active takeover market relies on ceding acquirers benefits that do not accrue to other shareholders on a pro rata basis. As a corollary, it follows that maximum shareholder protection need not be in the shareholders' best interest. Banning all extraction, i.e. imposing $\phi = 0$, prevents the rival from making a profit, thereby frustrating takeovers. This is also costly for the target shareholders, as they forgo the takeover premium.

A closely related point is that minority protection aimed at restricting the dilution of minority shares does not serve as a screening device (Berglöf and Burkart 2003). Better minority protection does not frustrate those bids where the acquirer is the primary recipient of the takeover gains without discouraging even more those bids where the gains are more evenly shared.

Another way to overcome the free-rider problem is to finance the takeover with debt, backed by the assets of the target firm (Mueller and Panunzi 2004). Since debt is senior to equity, leverage reduces the post-takeover share value. Thus, loading debt on the target reduces the bid price, while the acquirer receives (part of) the proceeds from the debt issue.

Yet another way to exclude target shareholders from part of the takeover gains is to grant successful acquirers a squeeze-out right, i.e. the right to compel remaining minority shareholders to sell their shares (Yarrow 1985; Amihud, Kahan, and

---

[27] Discriminatory dividends are merely an illustrative example of private benefit extraction that should not be taken literally. While the law in most countries forbids overt minority shareholder expropriation, there are various more subtle forms that are either difficult to prove in court, or even not against the letter of the law. For instance, the rival can sell at below market prices output or assets of the target firm to another firm under his control. Other forms of dilution are investment in unprofitable ventures (empire building), excessive salaries to the executive, the consumption of perks, and the appointment of friends or family members to management positions.

[28] Bid price and shareholder wealth do not depend on whether the bid is unrestricted or restricted (to 50%). In either case, the rival offers a price equal to the post-takeover minority share value, and the shareholders neither gain nor lose from tendering their shares.

Sundaram 2004).[29] When an offer conditional upon acceptance of the freeze-out fraction succeeds, the rival has the option to squeeze out the remaining minority shareholders. As a result, these shareholders realize at most a return equal to the bid price p and therefore may as well accept the offer. This holds true also for bid prices below the post-takeover share value ($p < x_R$). That is, a takeover conditioned on the squeeze-out threshold prevents shareholders from becoming minority shareholders, thereby solving the free-rider problem.

Direct dilution of minority shareholder rights, debt financing, and the squeeze-out rule all solve or mitigate the free-rider problem by reducing the post-takeover share value. Another somewhat distinct solution is the acquisition of a stake prior to the tender offer (Shleifer and Vishny 1986b; Chowdhry and Jegadeesh 1994). Suppose the rival already owns a stake in the target firm before mounting the tender offer. Even if the rival cannot dilute minority shareholder rights and has to offer the full post-takeover value ($p = v_R$), the takeover may be profitable. While the rival makes zero profit on the shares acquired in the tender offer, he captures (some of) the value improvement of his initial stake, provided the pre-takeover price of the stake is relatively low.[30] This argument shows that the possibility to (secretly) acquire shares prior to the offer is an important source of acquirers' profit. Indeed, pre-takeover holdings are found to have a positive impact on bidder gains and on the success probability of takeovers (Stulz, Walkling, and Song 1990; Choi 1991).[31]

The ease and extent to which an acquirer can accumulate an initial stake through secret open market purchases depend on the market depth and the disclosure requirement. Once an acquirer has to disclose his identity and holdings, further open market purchases become increasingly less attractive. As disclosure requirements limit the numbers of shares that an acquirer can secretly accumulate prior to a bid, they affect the division of takeover gains. Loose disclosure standards allocate a larger share of the takeover gains to the bidder, thereby promoting takeovers market. This, however, comes at the expense of those shareholders that sold their shares prior to the bid, thereby forgoing the takeover premium.

These extensions and modifications of the Grossman and Hart (1980b) model show that takeovers of widely held firms can be profitable. They do not, however, alter the basic insight that the free-rider behaviour prevents an acquirer from making a profit on those shares that he purchases in the tender offer. This holds true irrespective of the extent to which (and the ploy with which) the acquirer excludes minority

[29] The European Takeover Directive (Article 14) introduces the squeeze-out right with a threshold of 90% of the equity capital, but grants member states the discretion to apply in some circumstances a higher threshold with an upper limit of 95%.

[30] Kyle and Vila 1991 show that noise trading allows the bidder to acquire an initial stake at favourable prices so that the takeover becomes profitable. Complementing this result, Cornelli and Li 2002 demonstrate that trading by risk arbitrageurs in the post-announcement market facilitates takeovers of firms with an initially dispersed ownership.

[31] Goldman and Qian 2005 argue that while owning a larger initial stake increases the acquirer's profit if the tender offer succeeds, it also increases the loss if the offer fails. Consequently, acquirers may prefer to accumulate less than the maximum legally allowed pre-takeover stake, as documented by empirical studies (e.g. Betton and Eckbo 2000; Jennings and Mazzeo 1993).

shareholders from the takeover gains. Once the acquirer has control and extracts private benefits ϕV_R, he values the shares (not needed for having control) at $x_R = (1 - \phi)v_R$, the price that he has to offer the shareholders. The large takeover premia seem to suggest that the possibilities to expropriate target shareholders are—at least in advanced market economies—limited. Hence, the acquirers' profit prospects are small and too few value-increasing takeovers occur as posited by Grossman and Hart (1980b).

Closely related to the failure of value-increasing bids is another—diametrically opposed—inefficiency, namely the success of value-decreasing bids. To assess this possibility, we replicate the above analysis with the assumption of a value-decreasing rival ($x_R < x_I$). Anticipating failure, each shareholder is indifferent between tendering and retaining and may as well retain his shares. Hence, failure of a value-decreasing bid is an equilibrium outcome. However, anticipating success, each shareholder prefers to tender if the rival offers at least the post-takeover share value. Thus, success of a value-decreasing bid (marginally) above the post-takeover share value ($x_I > p > x_R$) is also an equilibrium outcome, even though it is against the collective interest of the shareholders. Confronted with such a bid, shareholders face a pressure-to-tender problem (Bebchuk 1988). Tendering becomes individually rational to avoid being in a less favourable minority position ($p > x_R$). As for the rival, he obviously attempts such a bid only if its success entails substantial private benefits. While success of a value-decreasing bid is an equilibrium outcome of the takeover game, its empirical relevance seems questionable in view of the consistently documented large gains to target shareholders.

As noted in the literature (e.g. Bebchuk and Hart 2001), the success of a value-decreasing bid has the same cause as the failure of a value-increasing bid: each shareholder bases his tendering decision only on a comparison between bid price p and post-takeover share value x_R, without taking the pre-takeover share value x_I into account. As a result, a shareholder retains his shares even though he prefers the bid to succeed (free-rider problem) or he tenders his shares even though he prefers the bid to fail (pressure-to-tender problem).[32]

A different limitation of the takeover mechanism is identified by Burkart, Gromb, and Panunzi (1998) who examine the implications of the post-takeover incentive problems on the part of the successful acquirer. As for the dilution of shareholder rights, the discussion so far implicitly assumed that the extraction of private benefits is efficient, that is, each dollar withheld from the shareholders yields one dollar of private benefit. By contrast, Burkart, Gromb, and Panunzi (1998) assume that such extraction is inefficient and exhibits decreasing marginal returns. As the rival owns more shares, he internalizes more of this inefficiency and therefore extracts fewer private benefits, which implies a higher post-takeover share value. Thus, private benefit extraction with a convex deadweight loss is but one way of formalizing the

---

[32] Both problems can be resolved by making target shareholder approval by a majority vote a necessary and sufficient condition for an offer to be accepted (Bebchuk and Hart 2001). The pressure-to-tender problem is also removed by a mechanism that requires approval by majority vote and (at least) a majority of shares tendered separately, such as a sell-out right with a 50% threshold (Burkart and Panunzi 2004).

alignment effect: A corporate insider with a larger equity stake is more prone to act in the (outside) shareholders' interest (Jensen and Meckling 1976).

As in Grossman and Hart (1980b), target shareholders do not tender unless the bid price matches the post-takeover minority share value. The free-rider behaviour has two consequences. First, the equilibrium supply of shares is increasing in the bid price. Since the post-takeover share value increases in the acquirer's final holding, the number of shares tendered has to increase with the price to preserve that the post-takeover share value equals the bid price. Second, the rival cannot make any profit on the tendered shares, and the private benefits constitute his only profit. As a result, the rival takes control by purchasing as few shares as necessary, i.e. 50 per cent, thereby maintaining high incentives to extract private benefits. From a social point of view, the ownership structure is not sufficiently concentrated as private benefit extraction entails a deadweight loss. However, the socially efficient ownership concentration is not feasible because the rival makes no profit if he acquires all the shares.

3. SHARE BLOCKS AND CONTROL TRANSFERS

The preceding analysis of the tender offer process presumes target firms with dispersed ownership. Yet, companies with diffuse ownership are infrequent. Outside the UK and USA, widely dispersed ownership, even among the largest corporations, is not the prevalent organizational form (e.g. Denis and McConnell 2003; Barca and Becht 2001; La Porta, López-de-Silanes, and Shleifer 1999). But even in the USA and the UK where publicly traded corporations stand out as having a more widely dispersed ownership, many listed firms have a shareholder owning 5 to 10 per cent (Gadhoum, Lang, and Young 2005; Holderness 2007).

The free-rider problem, caused by dispersed ownership, and its solution by means of a pre-bid stake may suggest that the presence of a blockholder facilitates a takeover. Instead of accumulating an initial stake through open market purchases, an acquirer can negotiate a block sale with its current owner. While the blockholder may capture some of the subsequent gains, the block trade enables the acquirer to purchase shares below their post-takeover value, making a bid more (likely to be) profitable. Moreover, if the share block is sufficiently large, the acquirer can gain (*de facto*) control through a block trade, circumventing the free-rider problem altogether.[33] However, casual observations seem to defy this conjecture. The volume of takeover activity in the UK and especially the USA has been much higher than in other countries. In fact, the low level of takeover activity in these countries is commonly attributed to the predominance of concentrated ownership structures, often enhanced with dual class

---

[33] Control over a firm does not necessarily require a majority of the shares (votes), in particular, when the remaining shares are dispersed.

shares, pyramiding, or cross-holdings.[34] Thus, while blockholders have the ability to promote a takeover by either selling or tendering their shares, they also have the power to impede or block it, and experience indicates that the latter outcome prevails.

When comparing cross-country takeover activity, it should, however, be noted that blocks may be traded without a full-scale takeover occurring. Indeed, an active market for large share blocks is documented for European countries, such as Belgium, France, Germany, and the UK (e.g. Dherment-Ferere, Köke, and Renneboog 2001; Goergen and Renneboog 2000). Moreover, block sales tend to be related to poor past performance and followed by increased management turnover (Köke 2001; Franks, Mayer, and Renneboog 2002). Subsequently, we discuss how the presence of a blockholder affects the incidence and efficiency of control transfers.

3.1. Sales of Controlling Blocks

Obviously, a blockholder's influence over the control allocation increases with the block size, or more precisely, with the number of votes. If the incumbent blockholder holds a majority of the votes—the associated fraction of shares can be (substantially) smaller due to a dual class share structure—a control transfer can only take place with his consent. As shown by Kahan (1993) and Bebchuk (1994), the incidence and efficiency of majority block transactions depend on the regulatory regime as regards the obligation to buy out minority shareholders. If the rival is not obliged to let the minority shareholders participate in the control transaction, he can simply buy the majority block at any price the incumbent blockholder is willing to sell. Consequently, a control transfer takes place when the controlling block has a higher value under the rival's than under the incumbent's control. How incumbent and rival split this surplus determines the block price. Having purchased the controlling block, the rival has always the option to buy out the minority shareholders. However, the rival cannot gain from making a voluntary tender offer because the small shareholders do not sell unless the price equals the share value under the rival's control.

Since the value of the controlling block comprises all the private benefits but only part of the firm's market (share) value, a surplus from a block trade does not imply efficiency nor does efficiency imply a surplus. In particular, when the incumbent's private benefits are relatively small compared to the rival's private benefits, a control transfer can be mutually beneficial even if the loss in share value exceeds the increase in private benefits. Conversely, when the rival's private benefits are relatively small compared to the incumbent's private benefits, incumbent and rival may not want to trade the block even though a control transfer would add value.

Under the mandatory bid rule as formulated in, for example, the European Takeover Directive (Article 5), the rival cannot purchase the controlling block without offering all small shareholders the same per-share considerations. In such a regime, a

---

[34] Takeover barriers other than concentrated ownership and takeover defences include close bank–firm relationships, codetermination and the relatively small number of listed firms. For a brief discussion see Berglöf and Burkart 2003.

control transfers takes place if, as before, it is beneficial to the rival and the incumbent, and if the rival earns a profit when having to offer small shareholders the same per-share price. These two conditions imply a total acquisition price above the total firm value under the incumbent's control, including his private benefits. Hence, the mandatory bid rule prevents inefficient control transfers. However, it also makes it more likely that an efficient control transfer is frustrated.[35] The obligation to offer all shareholders the same per-share price may increase the total acquisition price beyond the rival's willingness to pay, even though a control transfer would be efficient. Thus, the mandatory bid rule can also be to the disadvantage of the small shareholders since they may forgo share value improvements. Furthermore, the impact of the mandatory bid rule is also sensitive to changes in the (assumed) setting (Burkart and Panunzi 2004). For instance, if the private benefits of the incumbent and rival are of the same order of magnitude, it is impossible that a block trade generates a surplus but the control transfer is inefficient. Thus, the mandatory bid rule loses in this case its beneficial effect of preventing inefficient control transfers.

Empirical studies on block trades in the USA find that such trades are on average associated with abnormal share price increases. Moreover, the abnormal returns are smaller, but still positive, when no subsequent takeover occurs (Holderness 2003). This evidence suggests that improved management rather than extraction of private benefits is the primary source of gains in block trades. Studies on block trades in other countries find the share price reaction to be positive or insignificant and to vary with the identity of the buyer (e.g. Banerjee, Benoit, and Vermaelen 1997; Trojanowski 2002). Overall, the evidence does not support the claim that block trades are primarily undertaken with the purpose of looting companies at the expense of small shareholders.

If a large shareholder does not own a majority block, a would-be acquirer does not have to seek his consent to take over the firm. That is, control is contestable. Confronted with a takeover attempt, a minority blockholder can respond in different ways. He may choose to compete with the rival, negotiate a block sale, accept or reject the rival's tender offer. The possible responses are distinct, and accordingly the presence of a minority blockholder can have diverse effects on the takeover outcome, as the following discussion shows.

3.2. Bidding Competition

Obviously, a bidding contest does not only emerge in the presence of a minority blockholder but can just as likely take place between two outside parties, neither of whom owns an initial stake. Most research on bidding competition considers this latter case and abstracts from the free-rider problem. Instead, it is assumed that the target accepts the highest bid, provided it offers a premium relative to the current

[35] Both effects are diluted by less stringent versions of the mandatory bid rule. If some discrimination between the per-share price in the block trade and the subsequent tender offer is allowed, fewer efficient control transfers are frustrated and some inefficient transfers are not prevented.

market value.[36] The bidding contest which yields the winning offer is commonly modelled as an English auction. In simple versions, bidders make offers and counter-offers at no cost, each offer incrementally higher than the previous, until the bidder with the highest valuation wins at a price equal to the valuation of the second highest bidder. Thus, competition leads to an efficient control allocation. It also benefits target shareholders as bids and counter-bids drive up the price that the winner (highest valuation bidder) has to pay. Empirical evidence shows that target shareholders earn higher returns in multiple bidder contests (e.g. Bradley, Desai, and Kim 1988; Franks and Harris 1989; Stulz, Walkling, and Song 1990).

In the English auction analysis, an initial bidder should bid low until competitors arrive in which case each bidder should increase the previous bid only by a small increment. The strategies provide, however, a poor description of actual takeover contests in which initial bidders typically offer a substantial premium and each successive bid entails a sizeable increase over the last preceding bid. These patterns obtain in richer frameworks where bidders have to incur costs to revise their bids or to learn their (private) valuation of the target. In models with costly bid revision or costly investigation, large bid increases and high initial bids signal a high willingness to pay and may therefore induce other bidders to quit the contest or not to enter (e.g. Fishman 1988). Such pre-emptive bids reduce efficiency and expected target shareholder wealth because a bidder other than the highest valuation bidder can take over the target at a price below the valuation of the second highest bidder.[37] High initial offers are found to be associated with a lower likelihood of competing offers (Jennings and Mazzeo 1993).

Inefficient bidding outcomes can also be caused by the firm's security-voting structure, or more specifically, by deviations from the one share/one vote rule (Grossman and Hart 1988; Harris and Raviv 1988). When a firm has several classes of shares, bidding competition can lead to the same distortions as majority block trades. The value of control to a bidder—like the value of a majority block—comprises all the private benefits but only part of the firm's market value. Hence, the bidder with the larger private benefits may win the takeover contest instead of the bidder under whose control total firm value is highest. By contrast, the one share/one vote rule gives equal weight to private benefits and to the firm's market value in determining each bidder's willingness to pay. Accordingly, the bidder under whose control total firm value is highest is always able to outbid any competitor, ensuring an efficient control allocation. By contrast, deviation from the one share/one vote rule can benefit target shareholders because it may intensify competition, thereby allowing them to extract a larger share of the winning bidder's private benefits. However, such a surplus extraction strategy runs the risk of an inefficient control allocation in

---

[36] Effective competition among rivals by definition implies that the requirement to outbid, rather than winning shareholder approval, determines the bid price. Hence, ruling out the free-rider problem should be viewed as a simplification rather than a restrictive assumption.

[37] For an extensive discussion of multi-bidder models see Spatt 1989 and Hirshleifer 1995.

which case target shareholders are also worse off than under the one share/one vote rule.[38]

As for the role of minority blockholders in bidding contests, their stake gives them an advantage over would-be competitors as they need to acquire fewer shares to attain majority control (Dewatripont 1993; Ravid and Spiegel 1999). Moreover, a bidder with an initial stake has an incentive to bid more aggressively, in fact, to bid more than his valuation of the target firm (Burkart 1995; Singh 1998). Such overbidding aims at provoking a counter-bid, and thereby increasing the returns when losing the bidding contest. However, the bidder may actually win the contest, instead of merely improving the selling price. In this case, the takeover outcome may be inefficient and the winning bidder (with an initial stake) may make a loss. Thus, overbidding brought about by initial stakes provides an explanation why acquirers sometimes overpay that is consistent with profit-maximizing behaviour.

Initial stakes may not only distort the outcome of bidding contests, but can also prevent them. Overbidding reduces the expected gains for a potential competitor as he has to pay a higher price when winning. As a result, he may be deterred from incurring the costs to participate in the contest. Compared to the private value setting, the deterrence effect is amplified in the common value auction framework because overbidding exacerbates the winner's curse problem for the competitor, inducing him to bid more conservatively (Bulow, Huang, and Klemperer 1999). Empirical studies document that initial stakes are on average larger in single-bidder takeovers than in multi-bidder contests (Stulz, Walkling, and Song 1990; Betton and Eckbo 2000).

As bids and counter-bids drive up the tender price, takeover contests undoubtedly benefit target shareholders and on the whole also improve efficiency, notwithstanding the distortions inherent in the bidding process. By contrast, competition is undesirable from the bidders' perspective; they may come away empty-handed, have to pay a higher price to acquire the target, or—in case of minority blockholders— have to increase their holdings to defeat an attempted takeover by another bidder. Interestingly, even if a large minority blockholder is outbid by a rival and sells his block, the takeover contest may not be in his best interest (Burkart, Gromb, and Panunzi 2000). Instead of engaging the rival in a bidding contest, the blockholder can (reluctantly) hand over control in a private block trade.[39] When private benefit extraction is inefficient, the crucial difference between these two transaction modes concerns the fraction of shares that the rival ultimately owns. The block trade preserves the low ownership concentration, inducing more private benefit extraction. In contrast, the competitive pressure in the tender offer forces the rival to make a bid that leads to more shares being tendered. As a result, the rival owns a larger fraction of the shares and therefore diverts fewer private benefits. Although total firm value is

---

[38] Field and Karpoff 2002 document that over 5% of the 1,019 industrial firms that went public in the USA between 1988 to 1992 had dual class share structures. Furthermore, many firms had takeover defences in place at the time of the IPO.

[39] Jenkinson and Ljungqvist 2001 document that many seemingly friendly block transfers in Germany involve a considerable amount of hostility.

higher following a tender offer, the blockholder and the rival strictly prefer to trade the block. It allows them to appropriate a larger share of the takeover gains because the block trade bypasses the small shareholders who would otherwise free-ride. Thus, Burkart, Gromb, and Panunzi (2000) show that the choice how to transfer corporate control may itself be subject to agency problems. Consequently, the reported gains for small shareholders in block trades imply neither that firm value is maximized nor that a block trade is the best feasible outcome.

3.3. Tendering Minority Blocks

Once negotiations over the block trade have failed, say due to inefficient bargaining, the minority blockholder has the option to compete for control or to decide whether to accept the rival's (uncontested) offer. He may choose not to compete because he lacks the financial resources or managerial capabilities. Alternatively, he may be an institutional investor, such as a pension fund, that is prevented from taking over a firm. In what follows, we explore how the presence of a 'passive' minority shareholder who merely decides whether or not to tender affects the outcome of the tender offer.

Relative to the outcome with a fully dispersed ownership, the presence of a minority shareholder is immaterial if, as in Grossman and Hart (1980b), private benefits and post-takeover share value are exogenous. To succeed, the rival must attract enough shares from the small shareholders. Hence, he must offer a price equal to the post-takeover share value, which is given and independent of the rival's final shareholdings. The minority blockholder's tendering decision is irrelevant, as he is not decisive for the outcome.

The presence of a 'passive' minority blockholder only matters if the supply of tendered share increases with the bid price. As shown in Section 2.2, inefficient extraction of private benefits generates an upward-sloping supply curve. Using this framework, Burkart, Gromb, and Panunzi (2006) show that the presence of a minority shareholder can increase the bid price.[40] Since the rival must induce (some of) the small shareholders to tender, their free-riding behaviour implies that the bid price must equal the post-takeover share value. As a result, the rival's optimal strategy is to acquire as few shares as necessary. He cannot make a profit on the tendered shares and the private benefits decrease with his final holding.

The positive relationship between post-takeover share value and the rival's final holding implies that the blockholder's tendering decision interacts with those of the small shareholders. If the blockholder tenders more shares, the small shareholders tender fewer shares to restore the match between post-takeover share value and bid price.

---

[40] Models with atomistic shareholders who have different (expected) opportunity costs of tendering due to varying liquidity needs or tax rates also yield an upward-sloping supply curve (Stulz 1988; Hirshleifer and Titman 1990). In such a setting, the presence of minority blockholders can also affect the equilibrium bid price. For example, if the blockholder has the highest opportunity cost of tendering, the bid securing a 50% supply of the shares increases (Stulz 1988; Stulz, Walkling, and Song 1990).

Relative to the small shareholders, the blockholder has stronger incentives to tender his shares, given that the bid succeeds. His gains from tendering additional shares are twofold; the bid price for these shares and the value appreciation of all his remaining retaining shares, as the additional tendered shares increase the rival's final holding, leading to a higher post-takeover share value. This implies that, in equilibrium, the blockholder sells all his shares in a successful takeover.

Since the rival attempts to take over the firm with as few shares as necessary, selling all shares can make the blockholder decisive for the tender offer outcome. If the blockholder anticipates that he is decisive, he does not tender unless the bid price is above the (per-share) value of his block prior to the takeover. Hence, his presence imposes an additional condition that a successful bid must satisfy. The condition can be binding because the blockholder enjoys private benefits. In this case, the rival has to increase the bid price either until the blockholder favours the offer as he is compensated for the forgone private benefits, or until the offer attracts enough shares (50 per cent) from the small shareholders, making its success independent of the blockholder's decision. A larger minority stake and larger private benefits increase the bid premium that the rival has to offer to succeed.

From the small shareholders' perspective, such blockholder resistance comes with the benefit of a higher takeover premium but also with the cost of a reduced takeover likelihood. The empirical research on the impact of managerial and outside blockownership offers conflicting findings. For instance, Stulz, Walkling, and Song (1990) document that institutional ownership affects target firms' gains negatively, in conflict with the findings of Gaspar, Massa, and Matos (2005). Mikkelson and Partch (1989) and Song and Walkling (1993) show that targets have lower managerial ownership than non-targets, while Ambrose and Megginson (1992) find that neither managerial ownership nor institutional holdings are related to takeover likelihood.

Finally, the presence of a blockholder also constitutes a binding constraint for value-decreasing rivals. As above, the rival must increase the bid price either to win the blockholder's support or to attract enough shares from the small shareholders. The higher price may deter some value-decreasing rivals. Otherwise, it reduces or even eliminates takeover losses for target shareholders. Thus, the presence of a minority blockholder mitigates the pressure-to-tender problem.

4. CONCLUDING REMARKS

Manne (1965) argues that the market for corporate control promotes efficient utilization of corporate resources. Takeovers remove managers who either pursue their own goals or fail to make the best use of the firm's resources. In addition, the mere threat of a takeover disciplines managers and thereby mitigates agency problems in large public corporations. This view is, however, too narrow and biased, as closer examination of the takeover process in subsequent research reveals. There are impediments to an effectively operating takeover market such as the free-rider problem pointed out by Grossman and Hart (1980b). In addition, the existence of a market for corporate control can induce behaviour that is detrimental to efficiency like managerial entrenchment or underinvestment in firm-specific human capital. Thus, the overall conclusion is ambivalent: The takeover mechanism gives rise to both beneficial and adverse effects: it disciplines managers and allows a more efficient use of corporate assets, but it also exacerbates the agency problem and triggers inefficient actions. Moreover, the empirical evidence on many controversial issues is not conclusive enough to give clear answers.

On reflection, the inconclusive verdict is hardly surprising. The separation of ownership and control inevitably entails agency problems, and takeovers are a mechanism to mitigate these problems. However, takeovers, like other governance mechanisms such as boards or large active shareholders, are not free of agency problems. For instance, most takeovers are not undertaken by corporate raiders but by firms headed by professional managers (Shleifer and Vishny 1991). Hence, takeovers may also serve the purpose of empire building. That is, takeovers can be the cure of an agency problem, but also the symptom of an(other) agency problem. Similarly, the bidders' ability to divert corporate resources as private benefits helps to overcome the free-rider problem. While this promotes takeovers and enhances their disciplinary power, it also creates or exacerbates the agency problem between shareholders and the new controlling party.

Among a number of unresolved issues in the takeover literature, two stand out as the most fundamental. First, empirical studies document substantial gains to target shareholders, but the sources of these gains have not been fully identified. On the one hand, there is no systematic evidence that improvements in post-takeover operating performance can account for the target shareholder gains. On the other hand, the documented losses to stakeholders, such as employees or bondholders, only explain a modest fraction of the shareholder gains. Clearly, a better understanding of how takeovers create shareholder wealth is important and a prerequisite for a more informed assessment of their efficiency effects.

Second, theoretical work puts forward that the takeover threat gives rise to various conflicting effects, such as disciplining managers vs. sacrificing long-term profitability. As many of these benefits and costs of an (in)active takeover market are indirect and economy-wide, they are difficult to prove or refute empirically. Indeed, there is still little consensus about the effects of takeover defences on shareholder wealth, despite the large number of papers on this topic. This applies also to the broader question of the efficiency effects of takeover defences on operating decisions and firm performance, and more generally, the question of the impact that the takeover threat and variations thereof have on firm behaviour. More work addressing these challenging issues is warranted.

This essay also discusses the much smaller body of work analysing takeovers of firms whose ownership structure is not completely dispersed. When the blockholder owns a majority of the votes, control is obviously not contestable, and a control transfer only occurs with his consent. Inefficient control transfer can take place and efficient control transfer may fail to take place because the trading parties do not take into account that a control transfer has a negative or positive externality on the wealth of the minority shareholders.

If control is contestable, the presence of a minority blockholder can promote or hinder a control transfer. In case of a substantial minority block, control can be transferred either through a (hostile) tender offer or through a block trade. Both blockholder and new controlling party prefer to trade the block because it excludes the small shareholders from a larger share of the takeover gains. That is, the acquirer benefits from the presence of a blockholder as it enables him to circumvent the free-rider problem. The reverse conclusion obtains in cases where a tender offer is, for one reason or another, the only option available to an acquirer. In case of a passive blockholder who values the status quo highly, the acquirer must offer a higher price either to win the blockholder's support or to attract enough shares from the small investors so that this support is no longer needed. In case of a competing blockholder, the bidding contest is biased against the acquirer as the initial stake commits the blockholder to bid aggressively. Thus, fewer takeovers occur when ownership is partially concentrated, compared to the case of completely dispersed ownership.

These predictions are consistent with broad-brush empirical evidence. For instance, the level of takeover activity in continental European countries is lower than in the USA or UK, though there seems to exist an active market for share blocks.

Large (controlling) shareholders are an obstacle to an active market for corporate control. Accordingly, breaking up concentrated ownership structures to promote takeovers has been advocated in the (European) governance debate as a means to further restructuring and, more generally, the capacity for adaptation (e.g. European Commission 2002). However, any proposal must take into account that corporate governance systems vary from country to country. Each system consists of many interacting components, making the effectiveness of a given mechanism highly dependent on the overall system. That is, the absence of large shareholders per se neither ensures that an active takeover market evolves, nor that it performs its desired governance role. An effective takeover mechanism requires further institutions, such as strong (legal) protection of investors, transparency, disclosure, and unbiased enforcement of contracts. Furthermore, in (continental European) countries where these institutions are weaker, partial ownership and control concentration are the main mechanism to constrain managerial behaviour. Thus, the role of takeovers— or large shareholders for that matter—as a disciplining mechanism must ultimately be analysed within the overall governance system. Obtaining a better understanding of the interaction among different mechanisms and of the relative performance of different systems is the fundamental challenge that corporate governance research faces.

REFERENCES

AGRAWAL, A., and JAFFE, J. F. (2000), 'The post-merger performance puzzle', in C. Cooper and A. Gregory (eds.), *Advances in Mergers and Acquisitions*, Amsterdam: Elsevier Science, i. 7–41.

——and WALKLING, R. A. (1994), 'Executive careers and compensation surrounding takeover bids', *Journal of Finance*, 49(3), 985–1014.

ALLEN, J. W., LUMMER, S. L., MCCONNELL, J. J., and REED, D. K. (1995), 'Can takeover losses explain spin-off gains?', *Journal of Financial and Quantitative Analysis*, 30(4), 465–85.

AMBROSE, B. W., and MEGGINSON, W. L. (1992), 'The role of asset structure, ownership structure, and takeover defenses in determining acquisition likelihood', *Journal of Financial and Quantitative Analysis*, 27(4), 575–89.

AMIHUD, Y., KAHAN, M., and SUNDARAM, R. K. (2004), 'The foundations of freeze-out laws in takeovers', *Journal of Finance*, 59(3), 1325–44.

——and LEV, B. (1981), 'Risk reduction as a managerial motive for conglomerate mergers', *Bell Journal of Economics*, 12(2), 605–17.

ANDRADE, G., MITCHELL, M., and STAFFORD, E. (2001), 'New evidence and perspectives on mergers', *Journal of Economic Perspectives*, 15(2), 103–20.

BAGNOLI, M., and LIPMAN, B. L. (1988), 'Successful takeovers without exclusion', *Review of Financial Studies*, 1(1), 89–110.

BANERJEE, S., BENOIT, L., and VERMAELEN, T. (1997), 'Large shareholdings and corporate control: an analysis of stake purchases by French holding companies', *European Financial Management*, 3(1), 23–43.

BARCA, F., and BECHT, M. (eds.) (2001), *The Control of Corporate Europe*, Oxford: Oxford University Press.

BEBCHUK, L. A. (1988), 'The pressure to tender: an analysis and a proposed remedy', in J. C. Coffee, L. Lowenstein, and S. Rose-Ackerman (eds.), *Knights, Raiders, and Targets*, Oxford: Oxford University Press, 371–97.

——(1994), 'Efficient and inefficient sales of corporate control', *Quarterly Journal of Economics*, 109(4), 957–93.

——and HART, O. D. (2001), 'Takeover bids vs. proxy fights in contests for corporate control', CEPR Discussion Paper no. 3073.

BECHT, M., BOLTON, P., and RÖELL, A. (2003), 'Corporate governance and control', in G. M. Constantinides, M. Harris, and R. M. Stulz (eds.), *Handbook of the Economics of Finance*, vol. iA. Amsterdam: Elsevier Science, 1–109.

BERGER, P. G., and OFEK, E. (1996), 'Bustup takeovers of value-destroying diversified firms', *Journal of Finance*, 51(4), 1175–200.

BERGLÖF, E., and BURKART, M. (2003), 'European takeover regulation', *Economic Policy*, 36, 171–213.

——HOLMSTRÖM, B., HÖGFELDT, P., MEYERSSON-MILGROM, E., and TSON SÖDERSTRÖM, H. (2003), 'Corporate governance and structural change challenges to European corporate ownership and control', SNS Economic Policy Group Report.

BERTRAND, M., and MULLAINATHAN, S. (1998), 'Executive compensation and incentives: the impact of takeover legislation', NBER Working Paper no. 6830.

————(1999), 'Is there discretion in wage setting? A test using takeover legislation', *Rand Journal of Economics*, 30(3), 535–54.

————(2003), 'Enjoying the quiet life? Corporate governance and managerial preferences', *Journal of Political Economy*, 111(5), 1043–75.

BETTON, S., and ESPEN ECKBO, B. (2000), 'Toeholds, bid jumps, and expected payoffs in takeovers', *Review of Financial Studies*, 13(4), 841–82.

BHAGAT, S., SHLEIFER, A., and VISHNY, R. W. (1990), 'Hostile takeovers in the 1980s: the return to corporate specialization', *Brooking Papers on Economic Activity: Microeconomics*, 1–84.

—— ET AL. (2005), 'Do tender offers create value? New methods and evidence', *Journal of Financial Economics*, 76(1), 3–60.

BOROKHOVICH, K. A., BRUNARSKI, K. R., and PARRINO, R. (1997), 'CEO contracting and antitakeover amendments', *Journal of Finance*, 52(4), 1495–517.

BRADLEY, M. (1980), 'Interfirm tender offers and the market for corporate control', *Journal of Business*, 53(4), 345–76.

—— DESAI, A., and KIM, E. H. (1988), 'Synergistic gains from corporate acquisitions and their division between the shareholders of target and acquiring firms', *Journal of Financial Economics*, 21(1), 3–40.

BROWN, C., and MEDOFF, J. L. (1988), 'The impact of firm acquisition on labor', in A. J. Auerbach (ed.), *Corporate Takeovers: Causes and Consequences*, Chicago: Chicago University Press, 9–25.

BROWN, D. T., FEE, C. E., and THOMAS, S. E. (2005), 'Financial leverage and bargaining power with suppliers: evidence from leverage buyouts', University of Florida, Working Paper.

BRUNER, R. F. (1988), 'The use of excess cash and debt capacity as a motive for mergers', *Journal of Financial and Quantitative Analysis*, 23(2), 199–217.

—— (2002), 'Does M&A pay? A survey of evidence for the decision maker', *Journal of Applied Finance*, 12 (Spring/Summer), 48–68.

BULOW, J., HUANG, M., and KLEMPERER, P. (1999), 'Toeholds and takeovers', *Journal of Political Economy*, 107(3), 427–54.

BURKART, M. (1995), 'Initial shareholdings and overbidding in takeover contests', *Journal of Finance*, 50(5), 1491–515.

—— and PANUNZI, F. (2004), 'Mandatory bids, squeeze-out, sell-outs and the dynamics of the tender offer process', in G. Ferrarini, K. J. Hopt, J. Winter, and E. Wymeersch (eds.), *Modern Company and Takeover Law in Europe*, Oxford: Oxford University Press, 737–65.

—— GROMB, D., and PANUNZI, F. (1998), 'Why takeover premia protect minority shareholders', *Journal of Political Economy*, 106(1), 172–204.

—— —— —— (2000), 'Agency conflicts in public and negotiated transfers of corporate control', *Journal of Finance*, 55(2), 647–77.

—— —— —— (2006), 'Minority blocks and takeover premia', *Journal of Theoretical and Institutional Economics*, 162(1), forthcoming.

CAMPA, J. M., and HERNANDO, I. (2004), 'Shareholder value creation in European M&As', *European Financial Management*, 10(1), 47–81.

—— and KEDIA, S. (2002), 'Explaining the diversification discount', *Journal of Finance*, 57(4), 1731–62.

CHOI, D. (1991), 'Toehold acquisitions, shareholder wealth, and the market for corporate control', *Journal of Financial and Quantitative Analysis*, 26(3), 391–407.

CHOWDHRY, B., and JEGADEESH, N. (1994), 'Pre-tender offer share acquisition strategy in takeovers', *Journal of Financial and Quantitative Analysis*, 29(1), 117–29.

CLAESSENS, S., DJANKOV, S., FAN, J. P. H., and LANG, L. H. P. (2002), 'Disentangling the incentive and entrenchment effects of large shareholdings', *Journal of Finance*, 57(6), 2741–71.

COATES, J., IV (2000), 'Takeover defenses in the shadow of the pill: a critique of the scientific evidence', *Texas Law Review*, 79(2), 271–383.

COMMENT, R., and JARRELL, G. A. (1995), 'Corporate focus and stock returns', *Journal of Financial Economics*, 37(1), 67–87.

_____ and SCHWERT, G. W. (1995), 'Poison pill or placebo? evidence on the deterrence and wealth effects of modern antitakeover measures', *Journal of Financial Economics*, 39(1), 3–43.

CORNELLI, F., and LI, D. D. (2002), 'Risk arbitrage in takeovers', *Review of Financial Studies*, 15(3), 837–868.

COTTER, J. F., and ZENNER, M. (1994), 'How managerial wealth affects the tender offer process', *Journal of Financial Economics*, 35(1), 63–97.

DAINES, R., and KLAUSNER, M. (2001), 'Do IPO charters maximize firm value? Antitakeover protection in IPOs', *Journal of Law, Economics and Organization*, 17(1), 83–120.

DANIELSON, M. G., and KARPOFF, J. M. (1998), 'On the uses of corporate governance provisions', *Journal of Corporate Finance*, 4(4), 347–71.

_____ _____ (2006), 'Do pills poison operating performance?', *Journal of Corporate Finance*, 12(2), 536–59.

DENIS, D. K., and McCONNELL, J. J. (2003), 'International corporate governance', *Journal of Financial and Quantitative Analysis*, 38(1), 1–36.

DEWATRIPONT, M. (1993), 'The leading shareholder strategy, takeover contests and stock price dynamics', *European Economic Review*, 37(5), 983–1004.

DHERMENT-FERERE, I., KÖKE, J., and RENNEBOOG, L. (2001), 'Corporate monitoring by blockholders in Europe: empirical evidence of managerial disciplining in Belgium, France, Germany and the UK', Centre for European Economic Research (ZEW), Discussion Paper no. 01–24.

ECKBO, B. E. (1983), 'Horizontal mergers, collusion, and stockholder wealth', *Journal of Financial Economics*, 11(1–4), 241–73.

_____ (1985), 'Mergers and the market concentration doctrine: evidence from the capital market', *Journal of Business*, 58(3), 325–49.

EUROPEAN COMMISSION (2002), *Report by the Group of High-Level Company Law Experts on Issues Related to Takeover Bids*, Brussels: European Commission.

FACCIO, M., and LANG, L. H. P. (2002), 'The ultimate ownership of Western European companies', *Journal of Financial Economics*, 65(3), 365–95.

_____ McCONNELL, J. J., and STOLIN, D. (2005), 'Returns to acquirers of listed and unlisted targets,' *Journal of Financial and Quantitative Analysis*, forthcoming.

FAMA, E. F. (1998), 'Market efficiency, long-term returns, and behavioral finance', *Journal of Financial Economics*, 49(3), 283–306.

FIELD, L. C., and KARPOFF, J. M. (2002), 'Takeover defenses of IPO firms', *Journal of Finance*, 57(5), 1857–89.

FISHMAN, M. J. (1988), 'A theory of pre-emptive takeover bidding', *Rand Journal of Economics*, 19(1), 88–101.

FRANKS, J. R., and HARRIS, R. S. (1989), 'Shareholder wealth effects of corporate takeovers: the U.K. experience 1955–1985', *Journal of Financial Economics*, 23(2), 225–49.

_____ and MAYER, C. (1996), 'Hostile takeovers and the correction of managerial failure', *Journal of Financial Economics*, 40(1), 163–81.

_____ _____ and RENNEBOOG, L. (2002), 'Managerial disciplining and the market for (partial) corporate control in the UK', in J. A. McCahery, P. Moerland, T. Raaijmakers, and L. Renneboog (eds.), *Corporate Governance Regimes: Convergence and Diversity*, 19, Oxford: Oxford University Press, 441–56.

GADHOUM, Y., LANG, L. H. P., and YOUNG, L. (2005), 'Who controls US?', *European Financial Management*, 11(3), 339–63.

GARVEY, G. T., and HANKA, G. (1999), 'Capital structure and corporate control: the effect of antitakeover statutes on firm leverage', *Journal of Finance*, 54(2), 519–46.

GASPAR, J., MASSA, M., and MATOS, P. (2005), 'Shareholder investment horizons and the market for corporate control', *Journal of Financial Economics*, 76(1), 135–65.

GOERGEN, M., and RENNEBOOG, L. (2000), 'Insider control by large investor groups and managerial disciplining in listed belgian companies', *Managerial Finance*, 26(10), 22–41.

—— —— (2004), 'Shareholder wealth effects of European domestic and cross-border takeover bids', *European Financial Management*, 10(1), 9–45.

GOLDMAN, E., and QIAN, J. (2005), 'Optimal toeholds in takeover contests', *Journal of Financial Economics*, 77(2), 321–46.

GOMPERS, P., ISHII, J., and METRICK, A. (2003), 'Corporate governance and equity prices', *Quarterly Journal of Economics*, 118(1), 107–55.

GROSSMAN, S. J., and HART, O. D. (1980a), 'Disclosure laws and takeover bids', *Journal of Finance*, 35(2), 323–34.

—— —— (1980b), 'Takeover bids, the free-rider problem, and the theory of the corporation', *Bell Journal of Economics*, 11(1), 42–64.

—— —— (1988), 'One share–one vote and the market for corporate control', *Journal of Financial Economics*, 20, 175–202.

HANSMANN, H. (1996), *The Ownership of Enterprise*, Cambridge, Mass.: Harvard University Press.

HARFORD, J. (1999), 'Corporate cash reserves and acquisitions', *Journal of Finance*, 54(6), 1969–97.

HARRIS, E. G. (1990), 'Antitakeover measures, golden parachutes, and target shareholder wealth', *Rand Journal of Economics*, 21(4), 614–25.

HARRIS, M., and RAVIV, A. (1988), 'Corporate governance: voting rights and majority rules', *Journal of Financial Economics*, 20, 203–35.

HEALY, P. M., PALEPU, K. G., and RUBACK, R. S. (1992), 'Does corporate performance improve after mergers?' *Journal of Financial Economics*, 31(2), 135–75.

—— —— —— (1997), 'Which takeovers are profitable: strategic or financial?', *Sloan Management Review*, 38(4), 45–57.

HERON, R. A., and LIE, E. (2006), 'On the use of poison pills and defensive payouts by takeover targets', *Journal of Business*, 79(4), forthcoming.

HIRSHLEIFER, D. (1995), 'Mergers and acquisitions: strategic and informational issues', in R. A. Jarrow, V. Maksimovic, and W. T. Ziemba (eds.), *Handbook of Operations Research and Management Science*, Amsterdam: Elsevier Science, ix. 839–85.

—— and TITMAN, S. (1990), 'Share tendering strategies and the success of hostile takeover bids', *Journal of Political Economy*, 98(2), 295–324.

HOLDERNESS, C. G. (2003), 'A survey of blockholders and corporate control', *Economic Policy Review*, 9(1), 51–64.

—— (2007), 'The Myth of Diffuse Ownership in the United States', *Review of Financial Studies*, forthcoming.

HOLMSTRÖM, B., and KAPLAN, S. N. (2001), 'Corporate governance and merger activity in the United States: making sense of the 1980s and 1990s', *Journal of Economic Perspective*, 15(2), 121–44.

—— and NALEBUFF, B. (1992), 'To the raider goes the surplus? a re-examination of the free rider problem', *Journal of Economics and Management Strategies*, 1(1), 37–62.

IPPOLITO, R. A., and JAMES, W. H. (1992), 'LBOs, reversions and implicit contracts', *Journal of Finance*, 47(1), 139–67.

JENKINSON, T., and LJUNGQVIST, A. (2001), 'The role of hostile stakes in German corporate governance', *Journal of Corporate Governance*, 7(4), 397–446.

JENNINGS, R. H., and MAZZEO, M. A. (1993), 'Competing bids, target management resistance, and the structure of takeover bids', *Review of Financial Studies*, 6(4), 883–909.

JENSEN, M. C. (1986), 'Agency costs of free cash flow, corporate finance and takeovers', *American Economic Review*, 76(2), 323–9.

_____ (1988), 'Takeovers: their causes and consequences', *Journal of Economic Perspectives*, 2(1), 21–48.

_____ (1993), 'The modern industrial revolution, and the failure of internal control systems', *Journal of Finance*, 48(3), 831–80.

_____ and MECKLING, W. H. (1976), 'Theory of the firm: managerial behavior, agency costs, and ownership structure', *Journal of Financial Economics*, 3(4), 305–60.

_____ and RUBACK, R. (1983), 'The market for corporate control: the scientific evidence', *Journal of Financial Economics*, 11(1–4), 5–50.

JOHNSON, M. S., and RAO, R. P. (1997), 'The impact of antitakeover amendments on corporate financial performance', *Financial Review*, 32(3), 659–90.

KAHAN, M. (1993), 'Sales of corporate control', *Journal of Law, Economics, and Organization*, 9(2), 368–79.

KAPLAN, S. (1989a), 'The effects of management buyouts on operations and value', *Journal of Financial Economics*, 24(2), 217–54.

_____ (1989b), 'Management buyouts: evidence on taxes as source of value', *Journal of Finance*, 44(3), 611–32.

_____ (1991), 'The staying power of leveraged buyouts', *Journal of Financial Economics*, 29(2), 287–313.

KARPOFF, J. M., and MALATESTA, P. H. (1989), 'The wealth effects of second-generation state takeover legislation', *Journal of Financial Economics*, 25(2), 291–322.

KNOEBER, C. R. (1986), 'Golden parachutes, shark repellents, and hostile tender offers', *American Economic Review*, 76(1), 155–67.

KÖKE, J. (2001), 'Control transfers in corporate Germany: their frequency, causes and consequences'. Centre for European Economic Research (ZEW), Discussion Paper no. 00-67.

KYLE, A. S., and VILA, J. (1991), 'Noise trading and takeovers', *Rand Journal of Economics*, 22(1), 54–71.

LANG, L. H. P., STULZ, R. M., and WALKLING, R. A. (1991), 'A test of the free cash flow hypothesis: the case of bidder returns', *Journal of Financial Economics*, 29(2), 315–35.

LA PORTA, R., LÓPEZ-DE-SILANES, F., and SHLEIFER, A. (1999), 'Corporate ownership around the world', *Journal of Finance*, 54(2), 471–517.

LEWELLEN, W. G., LODERER, C., and ROSENFELD, A. (1985), 'Merger decisions and executive stock ownership in acquiring firms', *Journal of Accounting and Economics*, 7(1–3), 209–31.

LICHTENBERG, F. R., and SIEGEL, D. (1987), 'Productivity and changes in ownership and management of plants', *Brooking Papers on Economic Activity*, 1987(3), 643–73.

_____ _____ (1989), 'The effect of control changes on the productivity of U.S. manufacturing plants', *Journal of Applied Corporate Finance*, 2(2), 60–7.

McAFEE, R. P., and WILLIAMS, M. A. (1988), 'Can event studies detect anticompetitive mergers?', *Economic Letters*, 28(2), 199–203.

McCAHERY, J. A., RENNEBOOG, L., RITTER, P., and HALLER, S. (2004), 'The economics of the proposed European takeover directive'. in G. Ferrarini, K. J. Hopt, J. Winter, and E. Wymeersch (eds.), *Modern Company and Takeover Law in Europe*, Oxford: Oxford University Press, 575–646.

McCONNELL, J. J., and MUSCARELLA, C. J. (1985), 'Corporate capital expenditure decisions and the market value of the firm', *Journal of Financial Economics*, 14(3), 399–422.

McGUCKIN, R., and NGUYEN, S. (1995), 'On productivity and plant ownership change: new evidence from longitudinal research database', *Rand Journal of Economics*, 26(2), 257–76.

MALATESTA, P. H., and WALKLING, R. A. (1988), 'Poison pill securities: stockholder wealth, profitability, and ownership structure', *Journal of Financial Economics*, 20, 347–76.

MANNE, H. G. (1965), 'Mergers and the market for corporate control', *Journal of Political Economy*, 73, 110–20.

MARAIS, L., SCHIPPER, K., and SMITH, A. (1989), 'Wealth effects of going private for senior securities', *Journal of Financial Economics*, 23(1), 155–91.

MARGOTTA, D. G., McWILLIAMS, T. P., and McWILLIAMS, V. B. (1990), 'An analysis of the stock price effect of the 1986 Ohio takeover legislation', *Journal of Law, Economics and Organization*, 6(1), 235–51.

MARRIS, R. L. (1963), 'A model of the "managerial" enterprise', *Quarterly Journal of Economics*, 77(2), 185–209.

—— (1964), *The Economic Theory of Managerial Capitalism*, London: Macmillan.

MARTIN, K. J., and McCONNELL, J. J. (1991), 'Corporate performance, corporate takeovers, and management turnover', *Journal of Finance*, 46(2), 671–87.

MEULBROEK, L. K., MITCHELL, M. L., MULHERIN, J. H., NETTER, J. M., and POULSEN, A. B. (1990), 'Shark repellents and managerial myopia: an empirical test', *Journal of Political Economy*, 98(5, part 1), 1108–17.

MIKKELSON, W. H., and PARTCH, M. M. (1989), 'Managers voting rights and corporate control', *Journal of Financial Economics*, 25, 263–90.

MITCHELL, M. L., and LEHN, K. (1990), 'Do bad bidders become good targets?', *Journal of Political Economy*, 98(2), 372–98.

—— and MULHERIN, J. H. (1996), 'The impact of industry shocks on takeover and restructuring activity', *Journal of Financial Economics*, 41(2), 193–229.

—— and STAFFORD, E. (2000), 'Managerial decisions and long-term stock price performance', *Journal of Business*, 73(3), 287–329.

MOELLER, S. B., SCHLINGEMANN, F. P., and STULZ, R. M. (2004), 'Firm size and the gains from acquisitions', *Journal of Financial Economics*, 73(2), 201–28.

MORCK, R., SHLEIFER, A., and VISHNY, R. W. (1988), 'Characteristics of targets of hostile and friendly takeovers', in A. J. Auerbach (ed.), *Corporate Takeovers: Causes and Consequences*, Chicago: Chicago University Press, 101–29.

MUELLER, H., and PANUNZI, F. (2004), 'Tender offers and leverage', *Quarterly Journal of Economics*, 119(4), 1217–48.

MULLIN, G. L., MULLIN, J. L., and MULLIN, W. P. (1995), 'The competitive effects of mergers: stock market evidence from the U.S. Steel dissolution suit', *Rand Journal of Economics*, 26(2), 314–30.

MURPHY, K. (1999), 'Executive compensation', in O. Ashenfelter and D. Card (eds.), *Handbook of Labor Economics*, Amsterdam: Elsevier Science, iiiB. 2485–563.

PEROTTI, E., and SPIER, K. (1993), 'Capital structure as a bargaining tool', *American Economic Review*, 83(5), 1131–41.

PONTIFF, J., SHLEIFER, A., and WEISBACH, M. S. (1990), 'Reversions of excess pension assets after takeovers', *Rand Journal of Economics*, 21(4), 600–13.

PUGH, W. N., and JAHERA JR., J. S. (1990), 'State antitakeover legislation and shareholder wealth', *Journal of Financial Research*, 13(3), 221–31.

—— PAGE, D. E., and JAHERA JR., J. S. (1992), 'Antitakeover charter amendments: effects on corporate decisions', *Journal of Financial Research*, 15(1), 57–67.

RAU, R. P., and VERMAELEN, T. (1998), 'Glamour, value and the post-acquisition performance of acquiring firms', *Journal of Financial Economics*, 49(2), 223–53.

RAVENSCRAFT, D., and SCHERER, F. M. (1987), 'Life after takeover: the profitability of mergers', *Journal of Industrial Economics*, 36(2), 147–56.

RAVID, S. A. R., and SPIEGEL, M. (1999), 'Toehold strategies, takeover laws and rival bidders', *Journal of Banking and Finance*, 23(8), 1219–42.

ROLL, R. (1986), 'The hubris hypothesis on corporate takeovers', *Journal of Business*, 59(2), 176–216.

ROSETT, J. G. (1993), 'Do union wealth concessions explain takeover premiums', *Journal of Financial Economics*, 27, 263–82.

RYNGAERT, M. (1988), 'The effect of poison pill securities on shareholder wealth', *Journal of Financial Economics*, 20, 377–417.

_____ and NETTER, J. M. (1988), 'Shareholder wealth effects of the Ohio anti-takeover law', *Journal of Law, Economics and Organization*, 4(2), 373–83.

SARIG, O. H., and TALMOR, E. (1997), 'In defense of defensive measures', *Journal of Corporate Finance*, 3(3), 277–97.

SCHARFSTEIN, D. (1988), 'The disciplinary role of takeovers', *Review of Economic Studies*, 55(2), 185–99.

SCHERER, F. M. (1988), 'Corporate takeovers: the efficiency arguments', *Journal of Economic Perspectives*, 2(1), 69–82.

SCHOAR, A. (2002), 'The effect of diversification on firm productivity', *Journal of Finance*, 62(6), 2379–403.

SCHWERT, W. G. (1996), 'Markup pricing in mergers and acquisition', *Journal of Financial Economics*, 1(2), 153–92.

_____ (2000), 'Hostility in takeovers: in the eyes of the beholder?', *Journal of Finance*, 55(6), 2599–640.

SERVAES, H. (1994), 'Do takeover targets overinvest?', *Review of Financial Studies*, 7(2), 253–77.

SHLEIFER, A., and SUMMERS, L. H. (1988), 'Breach of trust in hostile takeovers', in A. J. Auerbach (ed.), *Corporate Takeovers: Causes and Consequences*, Chicago: Chicago University Press, 33–56.

_____ and VISHNY, R. W. (1986a), 'Greenmail, white knights, and shareholders' interest', *Rand Journal of Economics*, 17(3), 293–309.

_____ _____ (1986b), 'Large shareholders and corporate control', *Journal of Political Economy*, 94(3, part 1), 461–88.

_____ _____ (1989), 'Management entrenchment: the case of manager-specific investments', *Journal of Financial Economics*, 25(1), 123–39.

_____ _____ (1991), 'Takeovers in the 60s and 80s: evidence and implications', *Strategic Management Journal*, 12 (Special Issue: Fundamental Research Issues in Strategy and Economics), 51–9.

SINGH, A. (1971), *Takeovers: Their Relevance to the Stock Market and the Theory of the Firm*, Cambridge: Cambridge University Press.

SINGH, R. (1998), 'Takeover bidding with toeholds: the case of the owner's curse', *Review of Financial Studies*, 11(4), 679–704.

SONG, M. H., and WALKLING, R. A. (1993), 'The impact of managerial ownership on acquisition attempts and target shareholder wealth', *Journal of Financial and Quantitative Analysis*, 28(4), 439–57.

SPATT, C. S. (1989), 'Strategic analyses of takeover bids', in S. Bhattacharya and G. M. Constantinides (eds.), *Financial Markets and Incomplete Information, Frontiers of Modern Financial Theory*, Totowa, NJ: Rowman and Littlefield Publishers, 106–21.

STEIN, J. (1988), 'Takeover threats and managerial myopia', *Journal of Political Economy*, 96(1), 61–80.

STILLMAN, R. (1983), 'Examining antitrust policy towards horizontal mergers', *Journal of Financial Economics*, 11(1–4), 225–40.

STULZ, R. M. (1988), 'Managerial control of voting rights: financing policies and the market for corporate control', *Journal of Financial Economics*, 20, 25–64.

_____ WALKLING, R. A., and SONG, M. H. (1990), 'The distribution of target ownership and the division of gains in successful takeovers', *Journal of Finance*, 45(3), 817–33.

SZEWCZYK, S. H., and TSETSEKOS, G. P. (1992), 'State intervention in the market for corporate control: the case of Pennsylvania Senate Bill 1310', *Journal of Financial Economics*, 31(1), 3–23.

TRAVLOS, N. G. (1987), 'Corporate takeover bids, methods of payment, and bidding firms' stock return', *Journal of Finance*, 42(4), 943–63.

TROJANOWSKI, G. (2002), 'Equity block transfers in transition economies: evidence from Poland', CEPR Discussion Paper no. 3280.

VON THADDEN, E. (1990), 'On the efficiency of the market for corporate control', *Kyklos*, 43, 635–58.

WARGA, A., and WELCH, I. (1993), 'Bondholder losses in leveraged buyouts', *Review of Financial Studies*, 6(4), 959–82.

WESTON, J. F., MITCHELL, M. L., and MULHERIN, J. H. (2003), *Takeovers, Restructuring, and Corporate Governance*, 4th edn., Englewood Cliffs, NJ: Pearson Prentice Hall.

YARROW, G. K. (1985), 'Shareholder protection, compulsory acquisition and the efficiency of the takeover process', *Journal of Industrial Economics*, 34(1), 3–16.

CHAPTER 10

RECENT DEVELOPMENTS IN CORPORATE GOVERNANCE

AILSA RÖELL

THIS chapter discusses salient current developments in corporate governance, both in terms of academic research and of initiatives in policy and practice.[1] The chapter attempts to provide a transatlantic perspective by describing the regulatory and business environment in the USA and contrasting it with that in Europe. The focus is on developments in the past five years.

The corporate scandals that marked the start of the twenty-first century on both sides of the Atlantic (among the most notorious are Enron, Hollinger, and WorldCom in the USA and Parmalat, Vivendi, and Ahold in Europe), together with continuing outrage over executive pay practices, have precipitated a new attention to investor protection and ways to resolve the tension between incentivizing management and reining in managerial self-dealing.

One can distinguish a number of mechanisms by which shareholders (and, of course, other stakeholders in the firm as well) can attempt to influence and incentivize company management to take decisions that are aligned with their interests. We start in Section 1 by focusing on the role of public disclosure. Section 2 focuses on the

---

[1] The state of research regarding the market for corporate control, a central issue in corporate governance, is surveyed by Burkart and Panunzi in this volume. A complementary survey of broader corporate governance research is Becht, Bolton, and Röell 2007.

Sarbanes–Oxley Act of 2002 and its provisions regarding the increased accountability for executives, conflicts of interest for auditors, and the role of whistleblowers. Section 3 considers the board of directors and shareholder democracy, while Section 4 focuses on private securities litigation. Section 5 briefly outlines the role of hedge funds and private equity.

1. Corporate Disclosure

New Deal-era Supreme Court Justice Brandeis famously opined that sunlight is the best disinfectant. (Brandeis 1914) Experiences with the gradual tightening of disclosure requirements on a number of fronts point to the strengths and weaknesses of accelerated or more detailed disclosure as a means of preventing and redressing corporate governance failures.

1.1. Disclosure of Compensation

Recent revelations about options backdating provide a striking example of the power of prompt disclosure in preventing abuses. The surprising ability of companies to time their executives' option grants to coincide with the end of a period of abnormally low stock returns and the start of a period of unusually high returns has been documented by Yermack (1997) and others.[2] Recently, an influential paper by Heron and Lie (2007) has provided convincing statistical evidence that this phenomenon was not primarily driven by uncanny predictive skills or self-serving timing of news releases on the part of company management. Instead, the exceptionally high returns seemed concentrated in a period when option awards did not yet have to be disclosed to the SEC until the end of the fiscal year. When more timely (48-hour) disclosure of option grants was required, starting at the end of August 2002, much of the excess returns disappeared, and to the extent that they remained, they were concentrated amongst companies that were unwilling or unable to file with the SEC in time. Heron and Lie interpreted this as prima facie evidence of backdating of option awards, and the tidal wave of newspaper publicity[3] and judicial investigations that followed the public release of their research findings confirmed that this was indeed the case. The practice seems to have been widespread. By the end of November 2006, the number

[2] Options are usually awarded at the money: until very recently, options granted at or above the market price of a stock did not have to be recorded as a company expense in financial results. Accounting regulators proposed changing this rule in 1993 but backed off following opposition from Congress and Silicon Valley. Then-SEC chairman Arthur Levitt later wrote in his memoir that failing to support the accounting change was his 'biggest mistake' as chairman. The Financial Accounting Standards Board finally adopted the expensing of options, starting with fiscal years ending on or after 15 June 2005.

[3] Notably, a *Wall Street Journal* article with striking pictures of stock price dips on the exact option grant dates of six prominent companies (Forelle Bandler 2006).

of corporate officials losing their jobs in the options backdating scandal was already over sixty, and prominent figures such as Steve Jobs[4] were implicated.

It is clear that the new accelerated disclosure requirements regarding option awards much reduced the quantitative significance of the backdating problem and closed off an important backdoor means of increasing executive pay at the expense of shareholders.

But with regard to executive pay there can also be a downside to widespread disclosure. Envy is no less powerful a human failing than greed. Many observers attribute the huge increases in executive pay in the last fifteen years at least in part to a new SEC rule introduced in 1992 that required companies to make public the main elements of the pay awarded to their five highest-paid executives. Pay was then ratcheted up in an ever-increasing spiral, as managements were able to persuade their board and compensation committee that their pay should be at least as high as that of carefully selected peers in the industry: the 'Lake Wobegon effect' where every board deems its CEO to be above average and compensates him accordingly. The *Wall Street Journal* compared controlling executive pay with 'moving Jell-O' and described the impact of disclosure and tax policies as follows:

In 1992, Democratic presidential candidate Bill Clinton made executive pay a campaign issue. Washington responded.

The SEC said it would require more disclosure about compensation, particularly stock options and executive perks. The following year, after Mr. Clinton was elected, Congress decided companies could no longer take tax deductions on executive compensation of more than $1 million, unless it was related to performance.

Neither approach slowed the upward march of executive compensation. In fact, the disclosure rules allowed CEOs to see what others were getting, encouraging a competitive spiral. The tax law, meanwhile, drove up the compensation of CEOs who were making less than $1 million. Executives considered the cap a 'minimum wage for CEOs,' says Mr. Koppes, the former Calpers official. (Lublin and Thurm 2000)

In July 2006 the SEC adopted new rules that would require more detailed disclosure of elements of pay packages that were a hidden and (not coincidentally) growing part of total compensation in recent years: payment of executives' own taxes, perks such as personal use of corporate jets, detailed elements of deferred compensation, severance, and retirement plans. Other requirements are a better explanation of how pay is linked to performance; more detailed descriptions of stock option grants; a table on director compensation; and a figure summing up the total compensation paid to top executives.[5] The new compensation disclosure rules take effect with the upcoming crop of annual reports for fiscal years ending after 14 December 2006.

[4] Though the Apple Computer board's internal investigation of improper dating absolved Jobs of responsibility, this conclusion was strongly disputed by Bebchuk 2007.

[5] This summary figure is likely to be the most closely watched. In December 2006 The SEC relented somewhat, allowing option and restricted stock grants to be included in the summary compensation table when they are vested, rather than when they are granted as in the July proposal.

But it seems that public outrage at high pay awards is only occasionally successful at shaming executives into reducing their take. Disclosure in itself is not enough, and may even be counterproductive.

A mechanism that seems to be more effective is to complement disclosure with some measure of shareholder voice in the matter. In the UK, executive pay packages are subjected to shareholder voting. Even though such voting is only precatory, executives and boards are sensitive to the threat of explicit shareholder displeasure, and often take advance soundings of major investors' opinions before finalizing pay proposals. Recent work by Conyon et al. (2006) confirms earlier research that US pay is higher than UK pay,[6] though the gap is narrowing over time (from 2.2 to 1.3 times as high from 1997 to 2003, controlling for firm characteristics); the difference is attributable to CEO incentives, which are substantially higher in the USA (8.8 times the UK value in 2003, down from 14.4 times in 1997).

Academic researchers such as Bebchuk and Fried (2004) and Jensen et al. (2004), would argue that the payment gap is a symptom of systematic problems with US governance. But there are alternative hypotheses. Thomas (2003) argues that the depth of the US venture capital market, and the ready availability of financing for lucrative start-ups by talented entrepreneurs, drives up the opportunity cost of management employment at US publicly listed firms. A third story, favoured by Conyon et al. (2006), is that a large part of the pay difference can be rationalized as a risk premium required for bearing the risk associated with stock price-based incentives. This of course begs the question of why US executives need to be incentivized so much more strongly than their British counterparts; and indeed, over time European pay practices are moving in the direction of increased incentivization.

More radically, some have argued that the only way to rein in executive pay is to bring back the hostile takeover market. The argument is that over the last fifteen years state anti-takeover laws, together with the ubiquity of poison pills, have made it virtually impossible to remove incumbent management without their explicit cooperation. Effectively, a large pay-off to existing management is required to remove them from office.[7] Arguably, this veto power also drives up the pay they can negotiate whilst in office.

1.2. The Role of the Media

Meanwhile, the watchdog role of the media is a very new area of enquiry that is starting to yield tantalizing insights. Sherman (2002) and Dyck and Zingales (2003a) point out that journalists, like analysts, are under pressure to accentuate the positive

[6] Note that while continental European CEO compensation is also known to be substantially lower than that in the USA, these differences are more readily explained by the predominance of powerful controlling investors (see Becht and Mayer 2001) rather than by detailed aspects of the laws and policies relating to corporate governance.

[7] Particularly notorious 'heads-I-win, tails-you-lose' severance deals for failing executives include that of Disney's Michael Ovitz ($140 million after fourteen months' employment) and, more recently, Home Depot's Robert Nardelli ($210 million).

as a means of ensuring continued preferential access to company information sources. They measure media capture by the degree to which the presentation of material in company press releases—in particular, the emphasis on GAAP earnings versus unstandardized and possibly massaged 'Street' earnings—is mirrored in press reports. They find that, in particular, non-*WSJ* coverage and that of less well-researched firms (in terms of analyst following) is more likely to echo the company's 'spin' in stressing 'Street' earnings whenever the company's press release does so. There is an interesting cyclicality in spin. In the post-2000 downturn, even though company press releases emphasized Street earnings more, the press became more focused on GAAP; and Dyck and Zingales (2003b) also find that Harvard Business School case writers rely more on independent sources during downturns. The authors attribute the cyclicality in spin to higher demand for news during stock market boom periods: if company news sources are in relatively fixed supply, they are able to exert more pressure on journalists during booms. This line of work is plausible but still somewhat speculative; we can expect it to be a growing area of research.

The story of the role of journalists in uncovering the Enron debacle is an instructive one. Sherman (2002) describes the surprising blindness of the financial press to obvious red flags in Enron's publicly available financial reports in the period before the scandal broke. The signs of manipulation, hidden in plain sight, were pointed out by a short seller, who managed to persuade a journalist at Forbes to investigate the story and write it up. Protests and pressure from Enron's management then suppressed any follow-up work until two influential *WSJ* journalists took up the investigation. What is notable in this account is both the importance of publicity from the press in alerting investors, and the power of money—both the short seller interested in a price correction, and the management wishing to sustain the fiction of a valuable company—in influencing the flow of journalistic information. The outcome of a number of recently filed lawsuits against short sellers for alleged stock price manipulation is of considerable interest in determining how easily this particular corrective mechanism can be activated.

1.3. Disclosure of Mutual Fund Voting Records

On 31 August 2004, mutual funds started publicly disclosing their voting guidelines and voting records (going back to 1 July 2003), as required by new SEC rules adopted in January 2003[8] in the face of strong opposition from the mutual fund industry. Davis et al. (2006) argue that disclosure of fund voting has led to changes in voting patterns, in that before the vote disclosure system was in place, mutual funds virtually always backed management. They cite Vanguard as a case in point. Vanguard voted yes at 90 per cent of director elections in 2002; once it became clear that votes would be made public, it stiffened guidelines and voted a straight yes at just 29 per cent of companies a year later. Here again, it is not clear that disclosure by itself is enough

---

[8] Similar rules were subsequently adopted in Canada and France.

to persuade institutional investors to vote against management. The problem is that company management is unlikely to channel lucrative business, such as investment banking or the management of employee 401(k) plans, to financial institutions that are unsupportive shareholders, as discussed in Section 3.5 below.

2. Increased Accountability: The Sarbanes–Oxley Act

The Sarbanes–Oxley Act (SOX) is a direct response to key governance failings at companies such as Enron and WorldCom. It primarily targets the kinds of abuses in earnings manipulation and financial reporting uncovered by the Enron and World-Com failures. Its main aim is to restore confidence in company financial statements by dramatically increasing penalties for misreporting earnings performance and re-ducing conflicts of interest for two main groups of monitors of firms, auditors, and analysts. In addition, SOX provides stronger protections for whistleblowers.

2.1. Executive Accountability

The provision in SOX that has perhaps drawn the most attention is the stiff criminal penalties CEOs and CFOs face if they are now found to knowingly or willingly falsify financial statements. Post-SOX, CEOs and CFOs must personally certify public accounts and if they are later found to have falsely reported earnings they may face steep jail sentences. What is more, to the subsequent great irritation of the management community, SOX also requires CEOs to assess and attest to internal controls; for small companies, the costs involved can be a significant deterrent to going public. To limit the incentives to manipulate earnings, SOX also now requires top executives to reimburse any contingent payments they received based on past overstated earnings.[9] In addition, companies are now forbidden to extend loans to CEOs (repayable in company shares), thus banning a dubious practice that had taken extreme proportions in the case of WorldCom.[10]

2.2. Auditors

To further strengthen financial reporting SOX reduces the conflicts of interest in auditing that have arisen with the rapid growth in consulting activities by the major auditing firms. It has been argued that an important reason why Arthur Andersen had

---

[9] So far, even in cases of egregious earnings manipulation, companies have rarely been able to recover undeserved bonuses and other merit pay from those responsible. Once money has been paid out it is extremely difficult to get it back, and companies want to move on and not become mired in a costly rehash of past misdeeds by a now departed management team that could reinforce the negative image of the company in the mind of the public.

[10] Bernie Ebbers received loans from WorldCom totalling a staggering $400 million.

been so lax in monitoring Enron's accounts is that by probing the firm's accounting practices too deeply it risked losing its most valuable consulting client. The SOX legislation targets this basic conflict with several new regulations. First, the auditor of a firm is strictly limited in its consulting activities for that firm. Second, the auditing firm is now selected by an audit committee entirely composed of independent directors instead of by the CFO, a major step in ensuring that audits are credible. Third, the entire accounting profession is now regulated by a new body, the public chartered accountants oversight board (PCAOB), charged with monitoring the accounting firms. Fourth, to further reduce the risk of collusion between the auditor and firm, the lead accounting partner must rotate every five years: a compromise designed to balance the cost of transferring knowledge of the company's affairs to a new auditor against the cost of a too-cosy relationship.[11] Finally, SOX also requires greater disclosure of off-balance sheet transactions to reduce the risk of Enron-style accounting manipulation.

Coffee (2006: 89) argues that 'there is less reason to believe that gatekeepers—that is, professional agents serving shareholders but selected by the corporation—can work as well in concentrated ownership regimes as they can in dispersed ownership regimes', and observes that auditors were implicated in the fraud at Parmalat to a much greater extent than in the typical US earnings manipulation case. In effect, the auditor serves at the pleasure of the controlling shareholder. Thus SOX-style reforms are unlikely to be as effective in concentrated ownership systems.

2.3. Whistleblower Protection

Another interesting provision that is aimed at reducing the risk of financial fraud is the greater protections given by SOX to whistleblowers. Should they lose their jobs for exposing financial wrongdoing then SOX guarantees whistleblowers' reinstatement, as well as back pay and legal fees. Unfortunately, however, SOX requires that whistleblowers file a complaint with the Occupational Safety and Health Administration (OSHA), a division of the Labor Department, which has little financial or accounting expertise and so far has dismissed most cases as frivolous complaints. Inevitably the OSHA's extreme conservatism has quickly undermined the effectiveness of this important reform.[12]

2.4. Evaluation of SOX

There are many interesting aspects of this new securities law that merit a deeper discussion than we can provide here: the political battles surrounding the passage

---

[11] The reforms stopped short of implementing more radical proposals requiring rotation of the entire auditing firm after a fixed period of time, as in Italy (every nine years). Interestingly, it is the implementation of this rule that prompted Parmalat to do its accounting manipulation offshore, where it was allowed to continue to retain its old auditor. Had Italy required this rotation of auditors for all activities, including offshore ones, chances are that the Parmalat scandal would never have happened.

[12] See Solomon and Scannell 2004.

of the law; what its effects have been; whether it is an adequate response to the types of abuses that have been uncovered by the corporate scandals; and whether its benefits in terms of strengthening the quality of financial reporting outweigh the greater compliance and auditing costs. Several recent contributions provide such an in-depth analysis of the legal and economic issues, among which see Ribstein (2003), Gordon (2003), Romano (2005b), and Skeel (2005).

An empirical study of the impact of SOX on firm value by Chhaochharia and Grinstein (2005) finds that upon announcement of the new rules, firms that needed to make more changes to comply generally outperformed those that needed to make fewer changes. Thus the impact was largely positive. But there was one important exception: in the case of small firms, the effect was reversed and those needing to make more changes underperformed. Indeed, the requirement that companies document their internal controls—section 404 of SOX—is perhaps the most contentious of the SOX reforms, as the compliance costs involved loom very large for small companies.[13] The SEC has taken note of these problems and is working on rules that would lighten the burden on small companies.

The 2006 Interim Report of the Committee on Capital Markets Regulation, a group of leading academics and practitioners focusing on the competitiveness of US capital markets, singled out over-regulation as one of their leading areas of concern. Arguably the costs of complying with SOX are high enough to deter smaller companies from going public (at least in the USA: there have been quite a few recent US companies migrating to London's lightly regulated Alternative Investment Market),[14] and foreign companies from seeking a US listing, a concern shared by Ribstein (2003). It is unclear, however, whether the spectre of over-regulation is a significant factor. Other issues come to mind: the sinking dollar, fear of class action shareholder litigation, or simply the movement of new issue activity away from traditional US market users such as Israel to big new players like China and India.

3. Board Reforms and Corporate Democracy

The SEC also swung into motion and attempted to reform the proxy voting process, making shareholder voting more effective, in particular board elections (see Bebchuk

[13] The report estimates the average cost of complying with section 404 at $4.36 million in the first year.
[14] By the end of September 2006, there were thirty-six US companies listed on AIM, all but four of which arrived in 2004 and after (part of AIM's attraction over London's main market lies in the fact that it does not impose pre-emptive rights). Recent extreme underperformance of some companies listed on AIM, however, could bolster arguments that US regulation is doing its job in protecting US investors from dubious ventures.

2003a, 2003b). This proposal met with considerable resistance from the corporate sector and has been defeated. The SEC's proposed reforms on board elections have also reignited a peripheral debate among US legal scholars on the old question of the respective positions of federal regulations and state law (in particular the role of Delaware corporate law) in regulating corporate governance.[15] These issues are becoming increasingly important for Europe, where the internal market Commissioner is moving to remove the barriers that prevent European companies from shifting their registered offices to a location that offers the best tax and regulatory deal. Britain, Ireland, or Luxembourg could well become the European Delaware once the corporate mobility directive takes effect.

3.1. Reforming the Board of Directors

The corporate scandals have set off a raging debate on the role of the board of directors and its effectiveness in monitoring management.[16] Many observers have pointed out that Enron had an exemplary board by the corporate governance standards of the day, with a larger than average number of independent directors and with greater incentive compensation for directors. Nevertheless, Enron's board clearly failed to protect Enron's shareholders.

At WorldCom the failures of the board were more obvious. Interestingly, in an effort to restore trust and to signal that the new company would have impeccable corporate governance standards, the bankruptcy court commissioned a study by Richard C. Breeden—former SEC chairman—to recommend new rules for the board of directors and the compensation and audit committees. As a result, part of the bankruptcy-reorganization agreement for WorldCom has been to require the new company to emerge from chapter 11 (renamed MCI) to introduce a strengthened and more independent board as well as other corporate governance changes.

In his report, Breeden (2003) made several concrete proposals for reforming the board, which define a new benchmark for spotless corporate governance. Breeden recommends that all directors should be independent, that the chairman of the board should not be the CEO, that at least one new director be elected each year to the board, that shareholders be allowed to nominate their own candidates for election to the board (by allowing them to include their chosen candidates in the management's proxy statement), that the CEO be banned from sitting on other boards, that directors

---

[15] Roe 2005 argues that the 'federal response' (by Congress, the NYSE, and the SEC) shows that there is no regulatory competition between US states: Delaware has a monopoly and when Delaware law gets out of bounds, the federal authorities step in Romano 2005a argues that the US corporate scandals cannot be attributed to shortcomings of Delaware law.

[16] Congress was not the only US institution to pursue corporate governance reform. The New York Stock Exchange revised its listing rules and imposed de facto mandatory rules. It now requires, for example, that listed companies must have a majority of independent directors, with a tightened definition of independence. It also requires companies to have a nominating/corporate governance committee and a compensation committee composed entirely of independent directors.

of MCI be banned from sitting on more than two other company boards, that board members be required to visit company facilities and meet with the CFO and General Counsel in the absence of the CEO, etc.

Needless to say, most publicly traded companies in the USA today are far from living up to this standard. Perhaps the Breeden standard is just excessive, especially if the company already has gained the trust of its shareholders. But it is less clear whether one of Breeden's proposals initially advocated by the SEC, to allow shareholders to include their own candidates for election on the board in the management proxy statement, is excessive.

At the heart of this debate on board reform lies a fundamental unresolved economic question on the exact role of the board. Should the board of directors be seen as having only an (inevitably adversarial) monitoring role, or should directors also play their traditional advisory role? And, even if the board's role is mainly one of oversight, will the board be able to effectively play this role if it has to rely on a CEO wary of the directors' response to disclose the relevant information about the company's operations? Beyond the role of the board there is also an unresolved question as to the exact role of the CEO. Is the CEO simply an agent for shareholders whose excesses need to be reined in, or does he play a more important leadership role? If it is up to the CEO to determine and implement the overall strategy for the corporation then shouldn't one expect that even directors with the best intentions will defer to the CEO's judgement? All these questions have not received much attention prior to the corporate scandals and much more analysis and research is needed to be able to answer them conclusively and thus come to a determination of the appropriate policy towards boards.

3.2. Shareholder Access to the Proxy

On both sides of the Atlantic, recent years have seen a number of initiatives to give shareholders more voice in corporate decisions and to enable them to exert more influence on the decisions and composition of the board of directors. And even when these ambitious proposals have not made it into law, some companies have initiated action to comply voluntarily.

In the USA, in 2004 the SEC proposed new rules to allow shareholders to nominate candidates for board seats on the company's ballot. This would make it cheaper and easier to nominate a competing slate, because filing a separate ballot to undertake a full-scale proxy fight is costly. The SEC proposal was to facilitate the nomination through a two-step procedure: the first step being some event (in particular, 35 per cent of proxy votes being withheld from the company's nominees) that would force the company to open the proxy to 'major' shareholders' nominees; and the second step being a vote on candidates nominated by the shareholders. Some corporate governance scholars, in particular Bebchuk (2003a) and Bebchuk and Fried (2004), have strongly argued in favour of this reform. But the business community and other commentators generally perceive this to be a radical overly interventionist rule (see Bebchuk 2003b). Though the proposal seemed fairly timid (prominent legal scholar Mel Eisenberg unkindly described it as a 'sheep in wolf's clothing') it met with considerable resistance from the corporate sector[17] and was not adopted.

The SEC has historically sided against shareholders requesting direct proxy access on the grounds that the process for allowing shareholders to nominate directors through the proxy would be too cumbersome. But in September 2006, the US Second Circuit Court of Appeals changed the game by ruling against AIG and in favour of a shareholder (a large public employee union, AFSCME), which had asked AIG to include in the company's official election materials a proxy measure that would change the company's by-laws to allow shareholders to nominate their own slate of directors. The Second Circuit ruled that proxy access by-law proposals are non-excludable by the SEC, on the grounds that past SEC interpretations of proxy access rules were 'at odds' with each other. The SEC responded by scheduling an October hearing on proxy access, subsequently delayed to December 2006. The delay makes it possible for at least some access proposals to find their way into the proxies on director ballots in the spring 2007 annual shareholder meeting season, as the SEC is unlikely to be able to enact new rules to preclude access before then. Thus the SEC seems to be testing the waters on this matter. And in the longer run, the SEC is working to simplify the forms and facilitate internet use in the proxy process. This would also lower the costs of mounting a proxy campaign considerably and give all shareholders a greater chance to participate.

The US system of board elections is far from the most responsive to shareholder power. In the UK, shareholders already have limited ability to nominate directors, which makes companies more responsive to shareholders. The UK experience also serves to allay the concerns voiced in the USA, that direct access would open the way to special-interest directors with their own agendas. The need to garner 50 per cent of votes cast seems to take care of that, according to Financial Services Authority officials.

3.3. Majority Voting

Meanwhile, during the 2006 proxy season proponents of shareholder democracy have also forced or persuaded some companies to include in their proxy materials a 'majority rule' that would require directors standing for election to tender their resignation if they do not receive a majority of votes. This enfranchises shareholders in situations where directors run unopposed, and the only way to express opposition is to withhold a vote. Some money managers oppose this type of proposal on practical grounds: how would the majority standard 'work from a corporate law perspective if

---

[17] For example, the proposal was vigorously opposed by the Business Roundtable (which represents the views of corporate executives), mainly on the grounds that proxy access could open the door to pressure from special-interest groups such as unions and environmental activists, whose primary objective is not shareholder value maximization.

a full board wasn't elected, if there weren't sufficient directors that got a majority vote to enable the board to continue to operate?'[18] Nonetheless, by September 2005 some thirty-six companies had already adopted majority voting for directors; proposals requiring directors to win more than half of the shareholders' votes to gain a board seat appeared at over 140 companies during the 2006 proxy season; and between February and October 2006, the proportion of S&P 500 companies with some form of majority voting by-law or charter provision rose from 16 per cent to at least 36 per cent; see Allen (2006). There is some concern that the idea may unintentionally entrench directors, as 'it becomes almost impossible to elect a dissident slate with the kind of voting provisions that have been adopted at some companies'.[19]

3.4. Broker Voting

At the same time, the NYSE is considering a plan, announced with great fanfare in June 2006, to prevent brokers from voting their clients' shares (held in their 'Street name') in board elections when the stockholders themselves have not given any instructions. This practice tends to entrench board members because broker votes are almost always cast for management. However, following opposition from the Business Roundtable and the Society of Corporate Secretaries, the rule change is quietly being postponed so that it will not be in effect until the 2008 proxy season. Brokerage firms hold an estimated 80 per cent of public companies' shares and typically control about 25 per cent of the votes at annual meetings. This is a significant amount, particularly for companies that have instituted policies requiring directors who receive less than half of the votes cast in an election to tender their resignation.

Similar issues of shareholder disenfranchisement arise in countries like Germany— where banks exercise power by voting the shares they hold for their clients—or the Netherlands—where many companies have set up management-controlled foundations that hold the voting shares while the investors receive non-voting certificates.

A related issue is the borrowing of stock as a means of affecting the outcome of resolutions put to a vote at annual shareholder meetings. A study by Kerr Christoffersen et al. (2006) finds that in both the UK and the USA, there is a spike in securities lending on the record date for corporate voting (the date on which an investor needs to have possession of the stock in order to vote a resolution), suggesting that stock is borrowed solely to acquire votes. Such trading is particularly marked in poorly performing stocks and stocks with a high bid–ask spread (a sign of greater volatility and/or information asymmetry). In principle, stockholders whose stock is held in Street name could find themselves unable to vote if their stock has been lent out by their broker.[20]

---

[18] Vanguard's Glenn Booraem, as cited by Morgenson 2005.

[19] Investment banker Gary Lutin, cited by Morgenson 2006.

[20] In general, this is but one of many ways to exercise voting rights without owning an equivalent economic stake. In 2004, hedge fund Perry capital took a 9.9% position in Mylan Labs equity but hedged its entire position; its goal was to push through Mylan's takeover bid for King, thus boosting the value of

3.5. Voting by Institutional Investors

Since August 2004, a new SEC regulation requires US mutual fund companies and registered investment management companies voting on behalf of investors to divulge how they have voted on proxy issues. The SEC data on fund voting patterns have recently become available, and they have been analysed in two recent studies. Interestingly, Rothberg and Lilien (2005) have found that mutual funds almost always vote with management on operational issues and social or ethical issues, but they often vote against management on anti-takeover (34 per cent vote against) and executive compensation (59 per cent) issues. In addition, stock pickers tend to vote against management less often than index funds, and in particular less often than big fund families, which abstain or vote against management 19 per cent of the time. Davis and Kim (forthcoming) focus more specifically on conflicts of interest arising from business ties between mutual funds and their corporate clients: many mutual fund companies derive substantial revenues from their involvement in corporate benefit plans. They find no sign that proxy voting depends on whether a firm is a client or not.[21] However, in the aggregate, mutual fund families with heavy business ties are less likely to vote in favour of shareholder proposals opposed by management.

More broadly, it is no coincidence that shareholder activism by institutional investors is spearheaded by pension funds, not mutual funds, banks, or insurance companies,[22] and in particular by pension funds of public or non-profit sector employees like CalPers and TIAA-CREF (private companies' pension funds would not, in general, be encouraged to adopt a philosophy that is critical of sitting managements).

4. Private Securities Litigation

Many US market observers share the view of the Committee on Capital Markets Regulation (2006) that securities class action litigation is a costly distraction and

its separate holding in King shares. Carl Icahn, who was long in Mylan and short in King stock, sued on the grounds of stock manipulation. The SEC was supportive of Icahn's complaint and the Mylan–King transaction was shelved.

[21] A case in point: after the 2002 proxy battle over Hewlett-Packard's proposed acquisition of Compaq, dissident shareholder Walter Hewlett contended that management won Deutsche Bank Asset Management's pivotal vote by threatening that Deutsche Bank's 'future business dealings with H-P would be jeopardized' unless it voted in favour of the deal (note however that he was unable to substantiate his claim, which would amount to a breach of fiduciary duty by Deutsche Bank's money managers, in court. But on the eve of the crucial shareholder vote, Carly Fiorina, HP's CEO executive, left a— subsequently leaked—voice mail message with a senior aide, saying that they might 'have to do something extraordinary' to sway two large investors, one of whom was Deutsche Bank AM).

[22] 'A bank is not just a shareholder, but also has the firm as a client. For insurers the same applies. That distinction between roles is not easy to make. Moreover many firms have no understanding for such a distinction' (R. Maatman, lawyer for ABP, the Dutch public employees' pension fund). 'You are in a difficult position if you want to present a new contract to the management board whilst you have voted against one of their proposals the day before'(D. Brilleslijper of Dutch insurer Delta Lloyd).

even a major threat to the competitiveness of the US public capital markets. Others stress that the threat of such litigation deters malfeasance; and empirical research confirms that securities litigation is related to aggressive accounting, insider trading, and option-based remuneration (see Peng and Röell forthcoming) and references cited therein). But all would agree that private securities litigation has been at best a poorly focused and wasteful deterrent. In particular, the incentives to sue are largely determined by stock price movements which are only loosely connected to actual harm caused; lawyers' fees take up a gigantic proportion of settlements; and the burden of paying up falls on the D&O insurers and the long-suffering shareholders of the company, while payments by the individuals who perpetrated and benefited from the frauds are minimal (they do suffer longer-term career damage).

In recent years US lawmakers have attempted to restrict the scope for such suits in order to discourage frivolous and opportunistic lawsuits, most notably in the Private Securities Litigation Reform Act of 1995. PSLRA 1995, enacted over President Clinton's veto, was expressly designed to discourage frivolous securities litigation, and in particular securities class actions. Ways in which it has made such litigation more onerous are: a requirement that the lead plaintiff be the 'most adequate plaintiff',[23] procedural obstacles, the shifting of defendants' attorneys' fees to the plaintiff if the complaint lacks substantial legal or factual support, limits on attorneys' fees, full and detailed disclosure of any settlement, and reduced liability for unknowing violators (such as outside directors). In 1998 Congress curtailed jurisdiction shopping by requiring that class actions involving allegations of securities fraud be brought exclusively in federal, not state, courts. In addition, since a landmark Supreme Court decision in 1994, the liability of 'aiders and abettors', such as accountants who certify false financial statements and lawyers who advise on fraudulent schemes, has been severely curtailed. Meanwhile, the statute of limitations for Rule 10b-5 actions (the Securities Exchange Act of 1934's principal anti-fraud remedy) was tightened in 1991 to bring it into line with that of other private actions explicitly authorized in the Securities Acts of 1933 and 1934, and then lengthened again somewhat in the Sarbanes–Oxley Act of 2002.[24] Johnson et al. (2007) find that PSLRA 1995 has had some measure of success in discouraging baseless suits. But such pro-defendant reforms do generally make it harder for plaintiffs to sue successfully, thus weakening the role of private securities class action as a complement to government action in deterring securities fraud.

Until recently class action lawsuits were virtually unheard of outside the USA. Recently several European Union countries have enacted or considered legislation

[23] Discouraging the race to the courthouse and the use of 'professional plaintiffs' who make small investments in many companies and lend their names to securities lawyers, in return for a fee, whenever there are stock price swings.

[24] The limitation period is now two years (up from one year in 1991), that is, action must be brought within two years after discovery of the facts constituting the violation (or within two years after they could reasonably have been ascertained). The repose period is five years (up from three years): the action must be commenced within five years of the violation.

that would permit collective shareholder actions; among them France, Germany, Italy, the Netherlands, and Spain. The political repercussions of shareholder losses in recent scandals (over 100,000 investors held defaulted Parmalat and Cirio bonds) played a role in these developments. Investors have followed up immediately, initiating class action lawsuits such as the case against Airbus parent company EADS in the Netherlands. While class action lawsuits can be a valuable tool for investor protection, it is unlikely that their use will reach US levels. A number of features of the European legal system reduce the incentives to litigate: cases will be heard by judges, not more investor-friendly juries; requirements to lodge a claim are more stringent; contingency fees to lawyers tend to be strictly limited; and European judges may not impose punitive damages.

At the same time, the nature of shareholder litigation in the USA has shifted. Increasingly, settlements have included corporate governance reforms, designed to check future abuses, alongside recovery of funds. The reforms include removal of 'shareholder rights' plans (poison pills), stipulations regarding the presence of independent directors on the board and its key committees, separation of the roles of chairman and CEO, restrictions on stock option awards, limits on the range of services audit firms can provide, and the regular rotation of audit firms. An advantage is that such reforms through the judicial system are legally binding, while shareholder resolutions, even when passed by an overwhelming majority, are merely precatory.

One disquieting feature of the evidence concerning private securities litigation is the utterly passive role played by many institutional investors. Cox and Thomas (2005) find that in the period leading up to 2002, far from initiating legal action, the majority of financial institutions did not even bother to submit claims in settled class actions, leaving large amounts of money lying on the table and arguably neglecting their fiduciary duty to investors.

5. ACTIVISM BY HEDGE FUNDS AND PRIVATE EQUITY

In the past few years the role of private equity in capital markets, and investors' appetite for junk bonds, has increased enormously; the mega-LBO deal has returned to a prominence last experienced over fifteen years ago, when the US hostile takeover market was all but closed down by state anti-takeover legislation and the proliferation of defences such as poison pills and staggered boards. Activism by private equity funds and hedge funds can be seen as a new substitute mechanism for the removal of entrenched management. Such funds take large minority stakes in underperforming or undervalued companies, and once their holding is publicly disclosed via the

Table 10.1. Number of proxy fights and dissident success rate

Year	Number of proxy fights	Dissident success rate (%)[a]
2002	68	46
2003	75	37
2004	41	46
2005	56	55
2006	103[b]	59

[a]Measured as number of outright victories, partial victories, and settlements as a percentage of all proxy fights where a settlement has been reached.
[b]Of which five are pending.
Source: FactSet TrueCourse, Inc.

obligatory 13D filing at the SEC, similar investors pile, take minority stakes, and support the original activist investor's plan for value-enhancing changes. Such informal coordination permits the exercise of voting power without amassing a majority stake or launching a full tender offer. Moreover, US boards have become more willing to listen to minority investors' views now that Sarbanes–Oxley holds them more accountable for company performance.

A high-profile European case of hedge fund activism was the successful campaign to halt Deutsche Börse's bid for Euronext. A current case involves a bid by US and UK hedge funds owning a third of the capital of Dutch company Stork to force through divestiture of all its non-aerospace activities.[25] Meanwhile, in the USA, both the number of proxy fights and their success rate is on the rise, as shown in Table 10.1.

Interestingly, some activism plays out through the distressed debt market: such debt is now increasingly bought not just in hopes of recovery, but also as a means of obtaining control once bond covenants are breached and/or the company is forced into bankruptcy or reorganization. Indeed Altman (2006) suggests that the current distressed debt market is not unlike a gigantic Ponzi scheme. Insolvent companies are being propped up by their ability to raise new risky debt; some distressed debt hedge funds are even providing rescue equity buyouts.[26] The resulting unusually high recovery rates and low default rates are helping to sustain investors' appetite for more such distressed debt. This liquidity-driven boom in the debt market could be very fragile.

There are signs that Congress is moving to regulate the hedge fund industry,[27] but the focus seems to be more on ensuring financial stability than restraining activist investing. A modest increase in the cut-off wealth limit at which investors are judged to be sufficiently well off to invest in unregulated vehicles is planned. But a

[25] The company issued voting preference shares to its friendly foundation in response—a common Dutch takeover defence that is being challenged in court, on the grounds that this is not a hostile takeover situation but a legitimate use by existing shareholders of their statutory voting rights.

[26] For example, Plainfield Asset Management's rescue of English luxury jeweller Asprey & Garrard.

[27] A 'Hedge Fund Study Act' calling for an evaluation of the hedge fund industry and recommendations regarding disclosure was introduced in the House in late 2006.

further issue that is receiving increasing public attention is the potential disconnect between hedge funds' voting power and their underlying economic interest (see Hu and Black 2006 for a discussion of disclosure and other policy options). Funds can hedge their positions or even go short, as well as take positions in related businesses. Indeed hedge funds have no fiduciary duty toward their fellow shareholders, and there is no guarantee that hedge fund votes will support value-maximizing decisions.

A further concern with going private transactions is the potential for self-dealing by the management team in leveraged buyouts. Are they buying a stake in a broken company, fixing it by making improvements that are somehow infeasible for a public company, and then exiting at an IPO price that rewards the improvements made during its stint as a private company? Or, less laudably, are they simply identifying undervalued companies, taking them private at a bargain price, and then reselling them in an IPO at a higher price commensurate with their true underlying value?

If so, a revival of the takeover market would be a better way to reap the benefits of improved operating efficiencies. In the USA this would involve banning poison pills and repealing state anti-takeover legislation. For Europe, Goergen et al. (2005) report that takeover regulation seems to be converging on the Anglo-Saxon standard; however they argue that blockholder control is likely to remain an important feature of the landscape.

6. CONCLUSION

Recent developments in corporate governance have been fuelled by public outrage over two related phenomena: huge executive pay awards and the aftermath of a series of major corporate scandals. And currently, the pervasiveness and audacity of the self-dealing revealed in the recent US options-backdating scandal has taken aback even the most cynical of observers.

Some argue that the huge pay awarded to executives of leading companies is consistent with shareholder value maximization, as the scarcity of top talent, together with its importance for shareholder value creation in large companies, requires a superstar pay scale (Gabaix and Landier 2006). But US public opinion is generally more sympathetic to the views of Bebchuk and Fried (2004) and others, who point to failures in corporate governance.

Our survey has taken its cue from the current public debate by focusing on issues of malfeasance, self-dealing, and outsize pay. But this focus neglects some of the less eyecatching but perhaps more fundamentally important underlying issues. After all, if outsize pay is instrumental in prodding management to produce even higher efficiency gains, shareholders benefit. Causal relationships between corporate governance and firm performance are not easy to substantiate convincingly, as problems of reverse causality and unobserved interfirm heterogeneity arise. A growing body of empirical evidence is being amassed,[28] but an assessment of the causal relationship between CEO incentive pay and firm performance remains elusive.

We have reviewed related developments in public policy and market practice aimed at strengthening corporate governance and restoring trust. Public disclosure, shareholder power, private litigation, and the use of private equity are all mechanisms that may go some way to resolving the issues. But perhaps more is needed: is it time to bring back the hostile takeover market?

REFERENCES

ALLEN, C. H. (2006), *Study of Majority Voting in Director Elections*, Neal, Gerber & Eisenberg LLP.

ALTMAN, E. I. (2006), 'Are historically based default and recovery models in the high yield and distressed debt markets still relevant for investment funds in today's credit environment?', New York University Salomon Center Special Report.

BEBCHUK, L. A. (2003a), 'The case for shareholder access to the ballot', *Business Lawyer*, 59: 43–66.

——— (2003b), 'Symposium on corporate elections', Harvard Law and Economics Discussion Paper no. 448.

——— (2007), 'Inside Jobs', *Wall Street Journal*, 6 January.

——— and FRIED, J. (2004), *Pay without Performance: The Unfulfilled Promise of Executive Compensation*, Cambridge, Mass.: Harvard University Press.

BECHT, M., and MAYER, C. (2001), 'Introduction, in F. Barca and M. Becht (eds.), *The Control of Corporate Europe*. Oxford: Oxford University Press, 1–45.

——— BOLTON, P., and RÖELL, A. (2007), 'Corporate Governance and control', in A. M. Polinsky and S. Shavell (eds.), *Handbook of Law and Economics*, Amsterdam: North Holland Elsevier.

BLACK, B., JANG, H., and KIM, W. (2006), 'Does corporate governance predict firms' market values? Evidence from Korea', *Journal of Law, Economics, and Organization*, 22(2), 366–413.

BRANDEIS, L. D. (1914), *Other People's Money*, New York: Frederick A. Stokes.

BREEDEN, R. C. (2003), *Restoring Trust: Report on Corporate Governance for the Future of MCI, Inc.*

CHHAOCHHARIA, V., and GRINSTEIN, Y. (2005), 'Corporate governance and firm value: the impact of the 2002 governance rules', *Journal of finance*, forthcoming.

COFFEE, J. C. (2006), *Gatekeepers: The Professions and Corporate Governance*, Oxford: Oxford University Press.

Committee on Capital Markets Regulation (2006), *Interim Report*, Washington, DC.

CONYON, M. J., CORE, J. E., and GUAY, W. R. (2006), 'How high is US CEO pay? A comparison with UK CEO pay', SSRN.

COX, J. D., and THOMAS, R. S. (2005), 'Letting billions slip through your fingers: empirical evidence and legal implications of the failure of financial institutions to participate in securities class action settlements', *Stanford Law Review*, 58(November), 411–54.

---

[28] An interesting example is a paper by Black et al. 2006, who show that a corporate governance index, and more specifically a preponderance of outside directors, significantly improves the performance of Korean firms.

DAVIS, G. F., and KIM, E. H. (forthcoming), 'Business ties and proxy voting by mutual funds', *Journal of Financial Economics*.

DAVIS, S., LUKOMNIK, J., and PITT-WATSON, D. (2006), *The New Capitalists: How Citizen Investors are Reshaping the Corporate Agenda*, Boston: Harvard Business School Press.

DYCK, A., and ZINGALES, L. (2003a), 'The media and asset prices', mimeo.

——(2003b), 'The bubble and the media', in P. K. Cornelius and B. Kogut (eds.), *Corporate Governance and Capital Flows in a Global Economy*, New York: Oxford University Press, 83–102.

FORELLE, C., and BANDLER, J. (2006), 'The perfect payday', *Wall Street Journal*, 18–19 March.

GABAIX, X., and LANDIER, A. (2006), 'Why has CEO pay increased so much?', Working Paper, Department of Economics, MIT.

GOERGEN, M., MARTYNOVA, M., and RENNEBOOG, L. (2005), 'Corporate governance convergence: evidence from takeover regulation reforms', ECGI Working Paper Series in Law no. 33.

GORDON, J. N. (2003), 'Governance failures of the Enron board and the new information order of Sarbanes–Oxley', *University of Connecticut Law Review* (symposium issue), 35, 1125–43.

HERON, R. A., and LIE, E. (2007) 'Does backdating explain the stock price pattern around executive stock option grant?', *Journal of Financial Economics*, 83(2), 271–95.

HU, H. T. C., and BLACK, B. S. (2006), 'The new vote buying: empty voting and hidden (morphable) ownership', *Southern California Law Review*, 79, 811–908.

JENSEN, M. C., MURPHY, K. J., and WRUCK, E. G. (2004), *Remuneration: Where We've Been, How We Got to Here, What are the Problems, and How to Fix Them*, SSRN Working Paper.

JOHNSON, M. F., PRITCHARD, A. C., and NELSON, K. K. (2007), 'Do the merits matter more? The impact of the Private Securities Litigation Reform Act', *Journal of Law, Economics and Organization*, 23(30, 627–52.

KERR CHRISTOFFERSEN, S. E., GECZY, C. C., MUSTO, D. K., and REED, A. V. (2006), 'Vote Trading and Information Aggregation' (revised January 2007), AFA 2006 Boston Meetings Paper, available at http://ssrn.com/abstract=686026.

LUBLIN, JOANN. S., and THURM, S. (2006), 'Money rules: behind soaring executive pay, decades of failed restraints—instead of damping rewards, disclosure, taxes, options helped push them higher—return of golden parachutes', *Wall Street Journal*, 12 October.

MORGENSON, G. (2005), 'Who's afraid of shareholder democracy?', *New York Times*, 2 October.

——(2006), 'Finally, shareholders start acting like owners', *New York Times*, 11 June.

PENG, L., and RÖELL, A. A. (forthcoming), 'Executive pay and securities litigation', *Review of Finance*.

RIBSTEIN, L. E. (2003), 'International implications of Sarbanes–Oxley: raising the rent on U.S. law,' *Journal of Corporate Law Studies*, 3(2), 299–327.

ROE, M. (2005), 'Regulatory competition in making corporate law in the United States—and its limits', *Oxford Review of Economic Policy*, 21(2), 332–42.

ROMANO, R. (2005a), 'Is regulatory competition a problem or irrelevant for corporate governance?', *Oxford Review of Economic Policy*, 21(2), 212–31.

——(2005b), 'The Sarbanes–Oxley Act and the making of quack corporate governance', *Yale Law Journal*, 114, 1521–611.

ROTHBERG, B. G., and LILIEN, S. B. (2005), 'Mutual funds and proxy voting: new evidence on corporate governance', Steven B. Baruch College Working Paper, City University of New York.

SHERMAN, S. (2002), 'Enron: uncovering the uncovered story', *Columbia Journalism Review*, 40(6), 22–8.

SKEEL, D. (2005), *Icarus in the Boardroom*, Oxford: Oxford University Press.

SOLOMON, D., and SCANNELL, K. (2004), 'SEC is urged to enforce 'whistle-blower' provision', *Wall Street Journal*, 15 November.

THOMAS, R. S. (2003), 'Explaining the international CEO pay gap: board capture or market driven?', *Vanderbilt Law Review*, 57, 1171–267.

YERMACK, D. (1997), 'Good timing: CEO stock option awards and company news announcements', *Journal of Finance*, 52, 449–76.

CHAPTER 11

....

THE
DEVELOPMENT
AND
PERFORMANCE
OF EUROPEAN
PRIVATE EQUITY

....

TIM JENKINSON

1. INTRODUCTION

....

PRIVATE equity represents one of the most interesting and important developments in the provision of capital to companies. Definitions of private equity vary, but in this chapter we consider the entire asset class including early-stage venture capital (VC), expansion financing, and buyouts.[1] Private equity consists of equity investments in companies that are not listed on a stock exchange. Although much attention has been focused on VC, the impact of private equity on economic performance has arguably

I am grateful to Colin Mayer for comments on an earlier draft of this chapter.

[1] I will use the term buyouts to refer to all later-stage deals, including management buyouts, buyins, and public-to-private transactions.

been greatest in the buyout arena. Certainly, within Europe, the vast majority of the funds raised have been devoted to buyouts.

In this chapter we analyse the development of the European private equity sector: how it has grown, the distribution of investments, and the returns. From being a niche sector only a few years ago, the private equity sector within Europe has emerged from the shadows and is becoming increasingly the focus of attention. In part this is due to the sheer amount of capital being raised by the private equity sector. For instance, as we document later, a conservative estimate of new commitments made in 2005 to private equity funds investing in Europe is €60 billion. Buyout funds attracted around three-quarters of this sum and, given the leverage that they use in acquisitions, this implies that private equity funds could make new investments of about €150 billion based on 2005 fund raising alone.

However, it is not just the scale of investment, but the fact that within Europe an increasing number of high-profile companies have attracted the attention of private equity funds, that has excited the interest of politicians and regulators alike. For instance, in Germany a leading politician branded private equity funds 'locusts' in respect of their interest in German mid-sized companies. In somewhat more complimentary vein, *The Economist* referred to private equity funds as 'Capitalism's new kings'.[2] Not surprisingly, regulators are also starting to pay more attention to the sector, which in many European countries has enjoyed relatively low levels of regulation, and tax authorities have increasingly been looking at various details of the rules relating to private equity funds, such as thin capitalization rules and the taxation of profits.

The notoriously secretive private equity firms themselves are starting to realize that greater transparency and disclosure—over important issues such as performance, fees, and even compensation—might be in their own self-interest. Little is actually known about what private equity funds do, and how they add value.[3] Despite this, the growth of private equity has started to raise some fundamental questions about the traditional ownership and governance arrangements for public quoted companies. For instance, a recent survey[4] of European executive directors found that 70 per cent of finance directors and 80 per cent of chief executives and chairmen were interested in a job in private equity. The survey suggested a perception that stock exchange-listed companies are overly bureaucratic, and involve executives being constantly under the public microscope. Furthermore, private equity shareholders were viewed as more informed, more focused on delivering returns, and more decisive.

There are, therefore, some fundamental questions that will form an interesting research agenda for the next few years. However, the aims of this chapter are more

---

[2] *The Economist*, 27 November 2004.

[3] For instance, Henry Kravis—founder of Kohlberg Kravis Roberts, one of the first and most successful private equity firms—is recently quoted as saying, 'Although we are private organisations, better understanding of how we create value is in our enlightened self-interest', *Financial Times Fund Management*, 27 February 2006, p. 1.

[4] The survey was conducted by the *Financial Times* and involved 160 executives. It was reported in the *Financial Times* on 19 September 2005, p. 23.

modest. Little is actually known about the growth of the European private equity market, how it is distributed across countries or types of investment, and how it has performed. This chapter provides some evidence on all of these issues. But it also highlights the limitations of the available evidence and the challenges that researchers in this field face. The structure of the remainder of the chapter is as follows. In the next section we briefly explain the key structural features of private equity funds. This is necessary to understand some of the later discussion regarding activity and performance. The extent and distribution of private equity funds within Europe is discussed in Section 3. In Section 4 we review some of the evidence on performance and highlight the problems currently faced in assessing how well this asset class performs. Section 5 concludes.

2. The Structure of Private Equity Funds

The private equity sector has a number of unusual features. Most funds are structured as limited partnerships with a fixed life (typically ten years, although allowing for possible extension periods). The partnerships comprise the investors—typically pension funds, endowments, rich individuals, etc.—who are the *limited partners* (LPs) and the *general partner* (GP), which will be the private equity fund The GP and/or individuals working for the private equity fund will normally contribute some of the capital to the fund, but the great majority of the funds will be provided by the LPs. The LPs commit money to the fund but the GP only draws down the funds as and when they identify investments. There is, therefore, a lag between the commitment of capital and investment.

For the vast majority of private equity funds that are structured as limited partnerships, the funds committed are only invested once. The private equity fund will make an investment in a company and will normally aim to exit the investment within two to five years. When they do exit—whether by sale to another company, IPO, or recapitalization—the proceeds are immediately returned to investors; there is no reinvestment. Therefore, although funds have a notional ten-year life, the duration of the investment from the viewpoint of the investor is much shorter than this. Furthermore, as we shall see in Section 4, one of the key performance measures of private equity funds is the internal rate of return calculated over the period that the funds are invested. Therefore, the private equity funds only ask for the committed capital as it is required, and are keen to return the proceeds to investors as soon as possible after realization. A further important implication of this structure is that the private equity organizations have to raise fresh capital on a regular basis. Reputation for having producing good returns is a key determinant of future successful fund raising.

Although most European private equity is invested via limited partnerships, there are some idiosyncrasies. For instance, some private equity funds are publicly quoted and do not return capital to investors upon realization. Instead they pay dividends in the same way as other public companies. The leading example of such an entity is 3i, which is one of the largest private equity organizations in Europe (certainly by number of portfolio companies, if not capital under management).[5] Also in the UK there are currently over 100 *venture capital trusts* (VCTs), which are quoted investment vehicles focusing on smaller companies. Again, the development of these entities was encouraged by government, this time by the provision of generous tax relief to individual investors.

However, despite these examples of alternative structures, it remains the case that the limited partnership is the main vehicle used within Europe for private equity investing. The fee structures observed in such partnerships are fairly similar across countries. Investors pay a management fee, which is a proportion of the *committed* capital (not the actual amount that is invested at any point in time). The management fee ranges from 1 to 3 per cent p.a., with 2 per cent being quite ubiquitous. Sometimes this fee reduces during the second half of the ten-year life of the limited partnership, as by this stage most of the capital should have been invested (and many of the management costs are associated with sourcing deals) and, indeed, some capital may already have been returned. In addition to the management fee investors also pay a profit share or *carried interest*, which is typically 20 per cent of the net profits of the fund. There is little variation in this proportion across funds, although some funds charge up to 30 per cent and some as little as 10 per cent. In practice, therefore, a '2 and 20' remuneration structure is very common and similar to that observed in the other main 'alternative' asset class, namely hedge funds.

The impact of these fees on the net returns earned by limited partners is very significant. For instance, under plausible assumptions about the time profile of investments and realizations, a fund that returned a gross 25 per cent internal rate of return (IRR) might only return around 18 per cent to investors. These fees are clearly much higher than those observed on mutual funds that invest in public equity, and so expected private equity returns must consequently be significantly higher. We return in Section 4 to review the evidence as to whether this has been the case in Europe.

It is worth noting one final aspect of fund structure and incentives: given that the income of the private equity fund is a non-linear function of committed capital (management fees) and the absolute size of the profits earned by the fund (the carried interest), there is typically much more money to be earned from investing in large deals. This assumes, of course, that expected returns for both types of deal are similar. It also assumes that large investments do not incur proportionately higher costs than small deals, but this is certainly the case in practice. Indeed, smaller early-stage deals often involve much more prolonged and intensive input from the private equity fund than large later-stage buyouts. The latter can certainly be complex to execute and

---

[5] 3i was originally formed (as Investors in Industry) by the UK banks, with the encouragement of the government, to address the perceived 'equity gap' facing UK small and medium-sized companies. 3i went public in 1994 and currently has a market capitalization of around £5 billion.

involve a wide range of specialist advisers, but, in the case of successful deals, the costs of these are typically borne by the portfolio company being acquired.[6] But once acquired they may involve proportionately much less input from the private equity fund. Furthermore, as we shall discuss later, buyouts can be leveraged using debt financing which significantly increases the expected size of the carried interest, and therefore the expected income of those sharing in the carried interest. All the economic incentives, therefore, tend to pull the most skilled private equity professionals towards the larger funds, which will tend to focus on buyouts. Whether this results in higher returns earned on later-stage funds depends on the competition for such deals. We look at the European evidence on the proportion of capital devoted to private equity by stage of investment in the next section, before looking at the out-turn returns in Section 4.

3. How Significant is the European Private Equity Sector?

In this section we document the development of the private equity sector within Europe in recent years. We start by looking at the overall quantity of private equity, and the distribution between VC and buyouts. We then look briefly at who the investors are in European private equity. Since many of the later-stage deals are highly leveraged we then look at trends in the use of debt financing. An interesting recent trend has been the coincidence of much higher levels of debt alongside increasing valuation multiples for European buyouts. Finally in this section we provide some evidence on the distribution of private equity across selected European countries.

It should be noted at the outset that it is difficult to obtain primary data on the flows of money into and out of private equity funds, and, in particular, data on the returns (which we consider in the next section). Private equity funds are under no obligation to reveal such information to anyone other than their limited partners. This is a problem that applies equally in Europe and the USA. Indeed, in the USA there have been various attempts to make the investors associated with public pension funds or publicly funded universities reveal their investments and their returns.[7] However, such attempts have generally only succeeded in obtaining

---

[6] Private equity funds are particularly concerned about the transaction costs associated with deals that are not completed. In many cases they may ask advisers to work (either implicitly or explicitly) on a contingent basis, with only a proportion (if any) of the normal fees being charged in the case of deals that do not complete.

[7] The first significant attempt was by Mercury News to obtain information from the California Public Employees' Retirement System (Calpers). Information on the returns from their various private equity investments are published by Calpers on their website, but only at the fund level. The identity, and performance, of the individual portfolio companies is not revealed.

aggregate information at the fund level, rather than the full detail of the cash flows into and out of the fund that researchers would require.

There are a few academic papers with this level of detail, such as Kaplan and Schoar (2005) which analyses US private equity returns using a survey of performance and fund raising conducted by Venture Economics. A recent paper by Mayer, Schoors, and Yafeh (2005) provides some detailed information on sources of funds and investment activities for Germany and UK (along with Israel and Japan) for 1999/2000, but does provide information on performance. In this section we also make use of Venture Economics survey data as reported by the European Private Equity and Venture Capital Association (EVCA). However, since the underlying data have not been released we rely on the reported aggregate figures. To some extent the analysis of this section provides an update to that of Bottazzi and Da Rin (2002) who, as well as analysing the extent of VC financing of recently listed European companies, looked at EVCA data up to 2000. In this section we consider the funds raised across all European countries over the last decade.

3.1. How much European Private Equity?

Before presenting the evidence for Europe, it is worth noting a few important features of the data.[8] First, the EVCA data are derived from a survey of currently active PE firms investing in Europe, regardless of whether they are members of the EVCA or any national industry association. For the most recent survey 1,600 eligible PE companies were identified, of which around 73 per cent completed the questionnaire. Many PE companies would have more than one active fund, and so the latest sample includes information on approximately 2,600 European focused funds. The EVCA estimate that in terms of capital under management, the activity survey covers around 90 per cent of the market.[9] Given this relatively high response rate no adjustments are made to the totals to account for non-responders. However, figures before 2000 did make such adjustments and the EVCA suggest that 'caution should be exercised when making comparisons between pre-2000 figures and data from the last four surveys' (EVCA 2005b: 307).

Second, it is worth noting that all the figures reported in this section relate to private equity investments within Europe, irrespective of the original source of the committed capital, a significant proportion of which will come from outside Europe (mainly US investors). Furthermore, later in the section where we analyse the distribution of private equity across European countries, activity can be designated according to the location of the office raising the money, or by the location of the portfolio company into which the investment is made. In general, the UK has a disproportionate share of the headquarters (or main offices) of private equity funds

---

[8] These details are derived from chapter 20 of the EVCA (2005b), which deals with methodology and definitions.

[9] It is important to note that the investment activity survey obtains a very much higher response rate than the performance survey that we will discuss in Section 4.

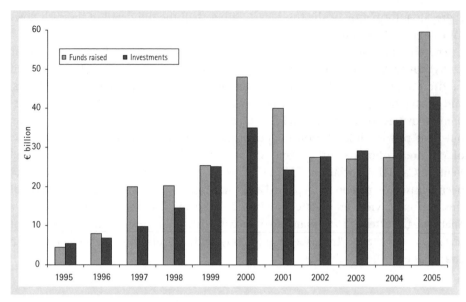

Fig. 11.1. European private equity: funds committed and invested

Note: This figure presents evidence from EVCA (2005a, 2006a) on funds committed to, and invested by, private equity funds focussed on Europe. Funds committed by investors are drawn down by the private equity fund and invested over a number of years

within Europe, and so judged by the 'office' approach will typically appear to attract a disproportionate share of the capital. However, much of this is invested in portfolio companies in other European countries, and it is important to distinguish between this 'market' approach and the office approach to reporting activity when considering activity at the national level.

Given the structure of private equity funds, there is a distinction between the amount of money that has been committed by investors, and the amount that is actually invested. Furthermore, the total size of the transactions executed by private equity funds differs significantly from the total equity invested, since in many later-stage deals significant amounts of debt are also invested. We consider debt financing later and discuss the significant developments in the European debt markets.

Starting with the aggregate size of the European market, in Figure 11.1 the amounts committed to private equity funds over the last decade are presented, along with the amounts actually invested. Funds raised by private equity funds total around €300 billion over the last decade. The difference between the funds raised and investment figures reflects the lag between the commitment of capital and its deployment, as explained above. However, in some cases—in particular for funds raised in the boom years of 2000 and 2001—it is likely that some funds will never draw down and invest all the funds that have been committed.

Alongside the flows of private equity investments, there are also substantial divestments, as the funds return the invested capital to their LPs. Netting off these flows produces an estimate of the stock of invested capital, which is interesting in its own right. However, the process of arriving at a stock figure encounters certain complexities. In particular, although private equity funds report the extent of their divestments as soon as they occur, the way unrealized investments are valued is much more difficult and funds may not be consistent in the approach adopted. We discuss this issue in more depth in Section 4. Nonetheless, the EVCA estimate that the stock of private equity investments as of end 2004 amounted to some €156 billion, having risen from €139 billion at the end of 2003.

However, these figures understate the total value of *transactions* conducted by private equity funds, as they only measure the equity component of the deals. Since buyouts typically employ significant amounts of debt, it is necessary to take this into account in estimating the total (enterprise) value of the companies controlled by private equity funds. We return to this issue later in the section.

In total, therefore, 2004 and 2005 witnessed record levels of investment in private equity within Europe. Indeed, as we shall see below, 2004 was the first year in which the level of investment in European private equity approximately equalled that of the USA. However, as well as the overall quantity, the distribution between different stages of investment is an important consideration, to which Figure 11.2 refers. The consistent finding is that—in terms of capital invested—buyouts dominate the European private equity market. This is not altogether surprising, given that buyouts are aimed at more mature companies with cash flows to support high levels of debt. Indeed, in recent years the size of private equity buyouts has been growing dramatically: for instance, in 2004 there were fifty-five European private equity deals valued at more than €1 billion. As a result, the proportion of capital allocated to buyouts has, if anything, been increasing in recent years, with the most recent estimates suggesting that nearly 80 per cent of European private equity funds is allocated to buyouts.

Of course, in terms of the number of portfolio company investments, the picture would look quite different—with the relatively small proportion of funds allocated to early-stage ventures representing a much larger proportion of the number of investments. In terms of the split between high-tech and other investments—which only really applies to the early-stage and development categories—Figure 11.2 shows that the proportion of funds allocated varies quite considerably over time. Whereas more than 20 per cent of funds was allocated to high-tech investments in 2001, this proportion has fallen by about one-half in recent years. Given that funds invested have been growing over this period, the absolute level of investment has fallen by much less than 50 per cent, but clearly much of the growth of private equity activity in recent years has been devoted to buyouts.

By way of comparison, in Figure 11.3 we present similar figures for the USA.[10] Until recently, the main difference between Europe and the USA has been the overall scale of the private equity sectors. For instance, in the boom year of 2000, total investment in US private equity was around $131 billion, compared with $41 billion in Europe.

---

[10] Note that different sources are used for the data in Figures 11.1 and 11.3 and so the estimates of total European investment for 2004 are slightly different.

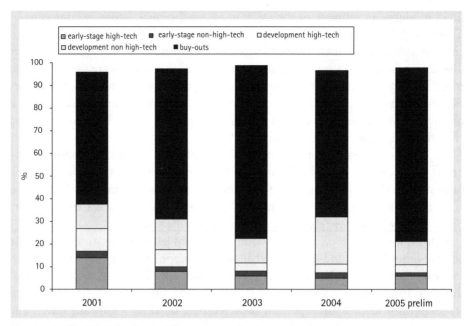

Fig. 11.2. The distribution of European private equity investments

Note: Investments by private equity funds are classified according to their stage of investment. For early stage and development stage investments, which together comprise venture capital, the figures distinguish between high-tech and non high-tech investments. Unclassified investments are not reported, but comprise the residual between the presented figures and 100%. The 2005 figures are preliminary

Source: EVCA (2006a)

However, as Figure 11.3 shows, in 2004 total private equity investments in Europe and the USA were very similar, as are the sizes of the economies. Consequently, in 2004 private equity investments in the USA totalled 0.40 per cent of GDP, only marginally exceeding the comparable proportion for Europe of 0.37 per cent. However, as we shall see below, the distribution of private equity investing across European countries is far from even, and some countries—such as the UK—achieve levels of investment of a similar magnitude relative to GDP to those observed in the USA.

Furthermore, the distribution of private equity investments is very similar in Europe and the USA, with buyouts comprising around two-thirds of total investment. As noted earlier, in terms of the number of transactions, there would be many times more early-stage investments—most of which are for relatively small amounts—than buyouts, where single equity investments can be several hundred million euros. It is also noticeable that the small proportion of capital devoted within Europe to early-stage investments is only slightly higher in the case of the USA.

It is important to note that there are cyclical swings in private equity fund raising and investment, and that the proportion of US investment in early-stage companies has been much higher in certain periods—in particular 1999 and 2000. However, the most recent figures on US early-stage investing suggest that there have only been modest increases in investment in recent years. Compared with the $3.6 billion

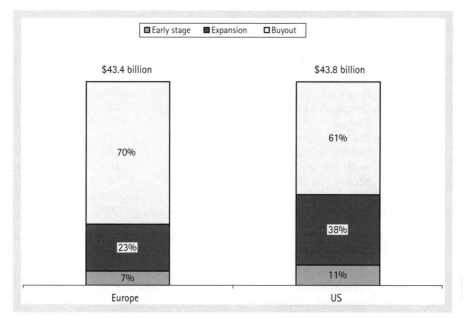

Fig. 11.3. The distribution of European and US private equity investment, 2004

Note: This figure presents total sums invested by private equity funds in 2004. The source of this is the PWC Global Private Equity Survey, 2005. The classifications used in the survey differ slightly between regions, and so we have include 'seed' capital in the early stage category and 'replacement' in the expansion category for Europe, and 'other late stage' in the expansion category for the USA

invested in US early-stage companies in 2003, the sums invested in 2004 were around $5 billion in 2004, and similar levels of investment are forecast for 2005.[11]

Given that the majority of private equity investments, in both Europe and the USA, are applied to buyouts, it is important to note that such equity investments are made alongside significant debt financing. Therefore, to assess the economic significance of the private equity sector—in terms of the total transactions executed—it is necessary to take account of the leverage of private equity investments. We do this later in Section 3.3.

3.2. Who Invests in European Private Equity?

The growth in the amount of capital committed to European private equity has been impressive, but who has provided the funds? In Table 11.1 we present the most recent evidence on the sources of funding for private equity funds operating within Europe. Note that this analysis is not limited to European *investors*—indeed, a substantial proportion of the capital committed to European private equity would have come from the USA and other regions.

[11] See the NVCA/PwC/Venture Economics survey at www.nvca.org/pdf/05Q3MTRelFinal.pdf.

Table 11.1. Investors in European private equity

Type of investor	2005	2001–4
Corporate investors	6.9%	6.2%
Private individuals	4.5%	5.9%
Govt. agencies	2.5%	7.4%
Banks	31.4%	23.5%
Pension funds	26.1%	21.2%
Insurance companies	12.6%	11.8%
Fund of funds	6.0%	13.6%
Academic institutions	0.5%	1.8%
Capital markets	1.7%	0.7%
Other	7.7%	8.0%
Total new funds raised (€m)	57,081	113,040

Note: This table presents the total new funds raised by European private equity funds, drawing on the evidence published in EVCA 2006a. Realized capital gains are excluded (they are included in the data underlying Figure 11.1).

The figures in Table 11.1 show that banks are the largest single source of capital, and in 2005 contributed nearly a third of new funds raised within Europe. The proportion of funds committed by pension funds has been growing but remains at relatively low levels given their share of investment funds. In contrast to the USA, European pension funds have historically allocated a relatively small proportion of their assets to private equity. For instance, Barros et al. (2005) report that from 1995 to 1999, around one-half of all US venture capital was derived from pension funds. Furthermore, few European endowments—such as academic institutions—have invested in private equity on anything like the scale observed in the US counterparts (see, for example, the evidence presented in Swensen 2000). Most surveys of European institutional fund managers project an increasing allocation to private equity in the future, and so the traditional importance of banks as a source of capital may well reduce over time.

These figures only relate to equity investment. However, given the importance of buyouts, it is critical to consider the role of debt financing, to which we now turn.

3.3. How Leveraged are Private Equity Investments?

Early-stage private equity investments typically do not involve the use of external debt.[12] However, in the case of buyouts the private equity firm that sponsors the

---

[12] In practice, the investments made by private equity firms in portfolio companies may often be structured as having debt components, but this is mainly for tax reasons. Control would then be exercised via the equity, or convertible equity, part of the transaction. However, recently some tax authorities have started to limit the ability of private equity funds to structure their investments in this way, by revising so-called thin capitalization rules.

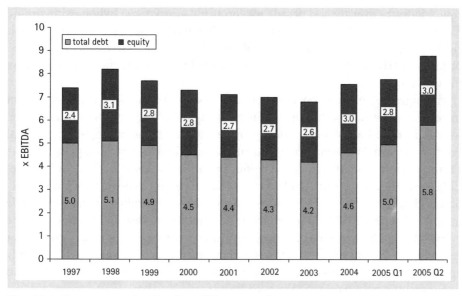

Fig. 11.4. Leverage and valuation of European buyouts

Note: This figure shows the average ratio of total debt and equity to earnings before interest, tax, depreciation and amortisation for European buyouts. This represents the financial structure that private equity sponsors employ in the companies they acquire. Total debt includes senior and subordinated debt

Source: Derived from S & P LCD European LBO Review Q2 2005

transaction will usually put together significant debt financing in order to purchase the company. Indeed, the extent of the leverage that private equity sponsors impose on the portfolio companies is, at least when viewed through the lens of the public equity markets, surprising. As can be seen in Figure 11.4 the proportion of debt in the capital structure of private equity buyouts averages around two-thirds. This is in contrast to the public equity markets where the proportion of *equity* in total capital structure is typically around two-thirds (see, for example, Rajan and Zingales 1995).

The debt employed by private equity sponsors is raised, at least in the first instance, almost entirely from the loan market. This market has developed very strongly in Europe and liquidity in recent years has been abundant. The loans are initially provided by the lead banks but are then syndicated to other banks and investors (including, increasingly, hedge funds). The size and sophistication of the European leveraged loan market now appears to be at least equivalent to that of the US market.

In terms of measuring the impact of private equity, the figures of equity raised, or invested, given in the previous section will clearly understate the significance—in terms of companies bought and controlled—significantly. Given that about two-thirds of total private equity is devoted to buyouts, and that buyouts are themselves leveraged significantly, the total value of investments made by the European private equity industry over the last decade was probably nearly €500 billion, with around €430 billion being invested in buyouts.[13] Therefore, although much attention is rightly devoted to analysing the availability of early-stage VC financing, the vast majority of private equity investments are devoted to acquiring and enhancing more mature companies.

The other notable development that can be seen in Figure 11.4 is the significant increase in the valuation multiples that are being paid for European buyouts, along with an increased willingness of debt providers to lend higher multiples of earnings. From their recent low point in 2003, valuations have risen from an average of 6.8 times earnings before interest, tax, depreciation, and amortization (EBITDA) to 8.8 times EBITDA in the second quarter of 2005.[14] At the same time, lenders have increasingly been willing to extend higher amounts of debt, relative to earnings, with a remarkable jump to 5.8 times EBITDA observed in the most recent quarter. This lending multiple is considerably higher than historical norms, and has raised some concerns about excess liquidity in the loan market. To put these levels of debt in context, UBS recently analysed the net debt to EBITDA ratio of public companies across many countries and found that the ratio averaged 1.1 in 2005.[15]

An interesting issue is the extent to which these higher valuations are related to the increased availability of debt, and whether risks are being appropriately priced in the loan market. In recent years, the weighted average spread on European leveraged loans has been remarkably stable, despite the observed increase in leverage. This is an promising area for future research.

So far we have focused at the pan-European level, but it is also interesting to analyse differences in the development of private equity across European countries. We do this in the next section.

3.4. How Is Private Equity Invested Across Europe?

In assessing the development of European private equity, it is interesting to consider the differences between countries. Using the most recent figures published by the EVCA, it can be seen in Figure 11.5 that over one-half of all the (equity) investments made during 2004 were by private equity funds managed from the UK. This reflects the fact that most of the large pan-European private equity funds are based in the UK. Across Europe, 86 per cent of investments by number, and 65 per cent by value, made during 2004 were by funds located in the same country as the portfolio company. In

---

[13] These estimates are based on the total sum invested in private equity (from Figure 11.1) of €214 billion, and assuming (a) that buyouts represent two-thirds of the total equity invested, (b) buyouts employ one-third equity in the total capital structure, and (c) all other investments by private equity firms are unleveraged.

[14] The use of EBITDA as a benchmark for both valuation and lending is ubiquitous in the private equity sector. This is usually reported on a trailing EBITDA basis—that is, the most recent reported values—rather than using prospective values, and so all the figures used in this chapter are measured on the trailing basis.

[15] As reported in the *Financial Times*, 19 September 2005, p. 20.

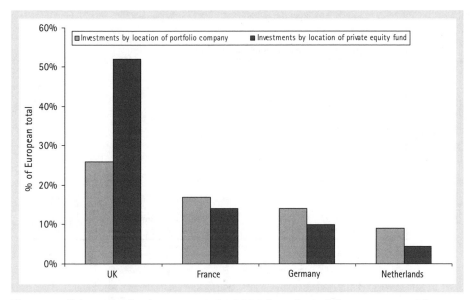

Fig. 11.5. Private equity investments in 2004 for selected European countries

Note: This figure shows the distribution of private equity investment within Europe in 2004 according to two criteria: by the location of the portfolio company receiving the investment and by the location of the private equity fund making the investment

Source: EVCA Activity Report, 2004

the main, the flow appears to be from UK-managed funds to portfolio companies in mainland Europe. Hence, the investments in portfolio companies located in the UK accounted for 26 per cent of total investment—exactly one-half of the proportion of funds managed from the UK. On the other hand, companies in France, Germany, and the Netherlands attracted investments from funds managed in other European countries. Along with the UK, companies in these four countries attracted two-thirds of European private equity investment, and accounted for four-fifths of funds managed.

Therefore, the distribution of the European private equity industry, by either measure, is relatively concentrated. The UK stands out as an outlier, although the proportion of funds being invested in France and Germany has been increasing significantly in recent years. However, if one looks at the development of the private equity sector across the rest of Europe, the amount of private equity activity falls away quickly. For instance, and again focusing on 2004 activity, Figure 11.6 shows that in most European countries the funds managed locally are extremely limited. Of course, there may be some cross-border investments, but as noted earlier, with the exception of the UK, the overwhelming majority of investments are made in portfolio companies located in the same country as the funds are managed.

Whilst some have questioned whether the current level of fund raising is sustainable, and whether the opportunities for profitable private equity investing in Europe have been exhausted, this evidence shows that many European countries are relatively

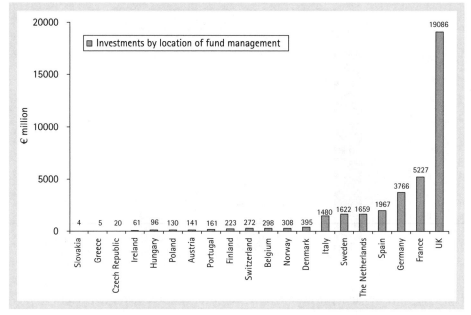

Fig. 11.6. Private equity funds managed in selected European countries, 2004

Note: This figure shows the distribution of private equity investment within Europe in 2004 according to the location of the private equity fund making the investment

Source: EVCA Activity Report, 2004

unexposed to private equity investing. This suggests that sizeable opportunities still exist, which may explain the recent spate of fund raising for enormous European funds.[16]

4. How has European Private Equity Performed?

Measuring the returns earned by private equity funds is a challenging exercise. The funds are under an obligation to report regularly to their investors, but have no obligation to report to anyone else. Surveys are conducted by various industry associations and commercial data providers, but the underlying data are seldom made available. The potential biases could be significant: for instance, the probability of reporting on the performance of a particular fund will probably decrease with the performance of the fund. Furthermore, there are various problems in measuring returns per se.

---

[16] For instance, both CVC and BC Partners have recently each raised funds totalling around €6 billion targeted at Europe, and Permira is rumoured to be seeking nearer €10 billion for its next European fund.

It is straightforward to measure returns once all the investments have been realized and the cash returned to the limited partners. However, most private equity funds have a ten-year life, and so if performance is measured before the fund has finally exited all the investments then the value of the unrealized investments—known as the *residual value*—will be measured by the fund itself. Funds can differ a great deal in the way they measure such investments, and the extent to which they attempt to 'mark to market', rather than carry investments at book value. Indeed, industry bodies have often differed in their advice to private equity funds on the appropriate way to value investments. However, within Europe there has been an initiative to agree valuation guidelines, and there now exists an agreed approach to valuation that has been endorsed by all the main national industry associations in Europe, and many outside Europe (a notable exception, at present, is the US National Venture Capital Association).[17] This should result in greater consistency across funds in measuring the intermediate returns on funds before they have fully exited their investments, although these will still, inevitably, be a mixture of cash and accounting valuations.

In the remainder of this section we first discuss the ways in which the performance of private equity funds is typically measured by investors. Then we address the data issues regarding European private equity returns.

4.1. How Is Private Equity Performance Measured?

There are two main measures that investors tend to focus on when analysing performance. The first is the internal rate of return (IRR), net of fees and carried interest, earned by the limited partners on their investment. The IRR is calculated as an annualized rate, and in the case of unrealized investments the residual values are treated as a terminal period cash flow to investors. In the early years of a fund the estimated IRR will clearly be dominated by the residual value; however, as funds mature the IRR becomes based upon actual cash flows. The relevance of the IRR to investors is that it takes careful account of the time that their capital is employed by the private equity fund, and provides a consistent measure of the rate of return they receive. However, high IRRs are not an end in themselves: the real end is higher cash returns. For this reason, in measuring the performance of private equity funds, attention is also directed towards the multiple of the original investment that is returned by the fund to investors. There are various measures of this, but probably the most widely reported is the ratio of total value to paid-in capital (or *TVPI*). The total value includes both cash flows back to investors along with residual value, and so, as noted early, is initially based mainly on estimates of residual value and becomes cash based as the fund matures. TVPI measures the size of the profits for the LPs relative to the initial investment, without regard to the time period over which the capital was employed. Although high IRRs and high TVPI tend to go together, the relationship is clearly

---

[17] See International Venture Capital and Private Equity Valuation Guidelines, available from www.privateequityvaluation.com. At the time of writing, the guidelines had been endorsed by twenty-seven regional and national industry associations.

complex. For instance, high IRRs on investments that are quickly harvested may be associated with low TVPI. Many funds will have joint targets for these two measures—such as to return a 25 per cent IRR and twice the originally invested capital.

4.2. Data on European Private Equity Returns

For Europe, probably the best information on the returns earned by private equity investments is the annual Thomson Venture Economics (TVE) survey, which is produced in association with the EVCA. The most recent version, a summary of which is reported in EVCA (2005a, 2006b), covers funds formed from 1980 to 2004, and includes returns information on 956 funds in total. This survey represents the most comprehensive source of performance data that is currently available for Europe and allows for the analysis of longer-term trends. Interestingly, the survey is sent to both the GPs and LPs, who are both asked to report the cash flows into and out of their funds, along with the valuation of unrealized assets. This allows for cross-checking of the returns, and must increase the reliability of the data.

However, there are inevitably some sample selection issues with this self-reported survey. First, although performance is reported back to 1980, the first European survey was conducted in 1996. Therefore, although respondents are asked for historical performance data, TVE caution[18] that coverage for the vintage years before 1987 is lower than average, since few GPs reported returns earned on funds that had completed their life cycle. For funds formed between 1987 and 1999 TVE estimate that the coverage in terms of the number of funds averages 51 per cent, although when weighted by capital under management this figure increases to 77 per cent. However, the coverage inevitably drops again for the most recent vintages, since for funds in the early stages of their life there are few, if any, realized investments, and so the valuations are based on accounting measures rather than cash returns. As a result, the coverage of the performance survey is considerably less comprehensive than that of the investment survey, which was discussed in the previous section. The latest version of the performance survey covers 956 funds that are either currently active or existed at some stage over the period from 1980–2004. In contrast, the most recent investment survey achieved a response rate of around 73 per cent from the 1,600 private equity companies that operate, or invest, in Europe, which between them run around 3,000 funds. In terms of capital under management the EVCA estimate that the investment survey achieves a response rate of over 90 per cent.

Second, given that funds voluntarily report their performance, to the extent that there is a bias in reporting it is likely to be an under-representation of poorly performing funds. Of course, GPs may still report on such funds, but this is unlikely to entirely eradicate the bias.

Third, as we shall see in the next section, a large proportion of the reported returns are associated with the residual values of unrealized investments, which are estimated

---

[18]   Details on the European performance survey are available in EVCA (2005b).

by the GPs. Worries about the reliability of these estimates have caused the few academic papers to have studied private equity returns to focus on funds which are largely liquidated. Even then, the results derived can differ significantly.

For instance, two studies that analyse the TVE survey of US private equity returns arrive at strikingly different conclusions. Kaplan and Schoar (2005) find that average returns (net of fees) earned by private equity investors in funds started by 1995 (this cut-off was imposed to ensure the funds were largely liquidated) are about the same as those that would have been earned on the S&P 500. In contrast, Phalippou and Zollo (2006) use an updated version of the Kaplan and Schoar data and make certain adjustments for sample selection, aggregation, and remaining unrealized investments. As a result of these adjustments the authors claim that the net returns earned by US private equity funds lagged public equity markets by as much as 3.3 per cent per annum.

No equivalent analysis has been performed using the European private equity performance survey, but this research on US returns cautions that the raw returns need to be interpreted with some caution. Nonetheless, the TVE survey of European private equity performance remains the best available measure, and in the next section we present its main findings.

4.3. Long-term Performance

There are various possible ways of measuring the average performance across the many separate funds and time periods. The most comprehensive way of looking at private equity as an asset class is simply to treat all cash flows into and out of all the funds—along with the accounting valuations of unrealized investments—as a single investment pool, and to calculate the pooled IRR and pooled TVPI. We start by looking at the returns earned by investors in European private equity firms from the early days of the industry in 1980 to the end of 2004. All the figures we analyse are net of management fees and carried interest, and therefore represent the net returns to the limited partners.

In Table 11.2 the returns are broken down by stage of investment. Starting with the early-stage funds, it is remarkable that, over the last twenty-five years, if all such investments were considered as a single European portfolio, the IRR on early-stage investments would have been only 0.2 per cent, and the funds would have barely returned the original invested capital to the LPs. It is worth stressing that these figures make no adjustment for inflation, let alone risk, and that during this period equity markets experienced considerable growth. Consequently, on average, early-stage private equity investments in Europe yielded extremely disappointing returns. This is an interesting and important finding, given that policy makers often claim there to be a lack of early-stage financing for entrepreneurial ventures within Europe. Of course, this macro view of the performance experience over the last twenty-five years tells us nothing about the causes of the disappointing returns. But there is at least a suspicion that supply of funds may not be the real

Table 11.2. European private equity returns

	# funds	IRR	Multiple of original investment... Paid out	Remaining	TVPI
Panel A: all funds					
Early stage	252	0.2%	0.40	0.60	1.00
Development	173	8.2%	0.74	0.68	1.42
Balanced	146	7.9%	0.66	0.59	1.25
All venture capital	571	6.0%	0.60	0.62	1.22
Buyout	307	12.3%	0.70	0.67	1.37
Generalist	78	8.7%	0.98	0.37	1.35
All private equity	956	9.5%	0.72	0.60	1.32
Panel B: top quartile funds					
Early stage	65	14.9%	0.93	0.64	1.57
Development	46	18.7%	1.43	0.61	2.04
Balanced	43	21.3%	1.10	0.71	1.81
All venture capital	154	18.6%	1.13	0.66	1.79
Buyout	84	28.7%	1.23	0.66	1.89
Generalist	17	12.3%	1.00	0.47	1.47
All private equity	255	23.3%	1.19	0.65	1.84

Note: This table presents internal rates of return (IRR) on an annualized pooled basis for European private equity funds over the period 1980–2004. IRRs are calculated as the return investors receive, net of fees and carried interest. The cash flows for each fund are aggregated into a pool as if they were a single European fund, and the IRR is presented on an annualized basis. The multiple of original investment paid out compares the cumulative cash distribution to investors as a proportion of the original investment. The remaining unrealized value, as estimated by the private equity fund, is also compared with the original investment. The sum of these two ratios is the ratio of total value to paid-in capital, or TVPI.

Source: EVCA 2005.

problem, as low out-turn returns are often the result of competition between rival private equity funds to invest in ventures, which pushes up valuations and reduces returns.

Returns are somewhat higher in the case of later-stage companies in need of development capital. For these investments the pooled IRR observed in Europe has been 8.2 per cent, with a TVPI or 1.42. Balanced venture capital funds—which invest in both early and expansion stages—similarly exhibit somewhat better average returns. As a result, the returns for European venture capital as a whole have been modest but positive with an IRR of 6 per cent and funds returning 22 per cent more cash than was paid into them. However, it is worth remembering that such levels of returns would mean that investors would have been better off putting their money into government securities for the last twenty-five years.

Returns improve significantly for later-stage investments: the average IRR on expansion funds is 8 per cent and is 12 per cent for buyouts. Although there is considerable time-series variation on the returns to private equity, all the evidence points to the much stronger returns earned by European funds focused on later-stage investments and buyouts. However, as noted earlier, later-stage investments are highly leveraged, and so a comparison of the relative performance—either in comparison with early-stage investments or public market benchmarks—should take this into account. The academic analyses published to date, which have had access to the precise timings of the cash flows into and out of the private equity funds, have taken account of movements in the general stock market (matched to the timing of the private equity cash flows) but have not accounted for the higher leverage observed in private equity portfolio companies than in public companies. This is very difficult without detailed information on the capital structure of the portfolio companies, and remains an interesting avenue for future research. However, the direction of bias in the results is clear—comparative returns on buyouts will tend to overstate risk-adjusted returns relative to returns on VC investments and public market comparators.

In this section we have focused on the long-term returns observed on private equity in Europe, more or less since the inception of the asset class. However, there are various reasons for also being interested in the time series of these returns. First, it is well established that realized returns are highly cyclical. In particular, vintages of funds that are invested during periods when the competition for deals is less intense, and when exit opportunities, and exit prices, are generous, tend to perform very well. Such exceptional vintages can dominate the longer-term average returns, although this will only become apparent when the time-series evidence is analysed. Second, as outlined earlier, much of the growth in the size of the private equity sector within Europe has occurred in the last few years, and so the returns on these funds are inevitably based more on the fund's own views of the residual value of their investments, rather than the out-turn cash returns received by investors. Given the typical cycle of investing and realization, funds raised before about 1996 should have been substantially liquidated by end of 2004 (the latest observation in our data set).[19] Therefore, if the focus of attention is on the realized returns it is necessary to go back into the detailed evidence for individual years. This we do in the next section.

4.4. How do European and US Private Equity Returns Compare Over Time?

Although the main focus of this chapter is on the European private equity industry, as we move towards analysing the time-series variation in returns it becomes increasingly difficult to establish benchmarks against which to judge the quite volatile returns. As noted above, to a considerable extent the returns on funds are linked to their vintage, since the market conditions experienced for investing and exiting will

---

[19] This is clearly a generalization, and depends on the nature of the fund, with buyout funds tending to exit their investments somewhat more quickly than VC funds. Some public domain evidence to support this claim can be found from the regular reports on the private equity investments of the California Public Employees Retirement Scheme (Calpers), available from their website at www.calpers.ca.gov.

be similar across funds of the same vintage. Therefore, in this section we broaden the focus of analysis somewhat and compare the performance of European funds with roughly equivalent US funds.

To do this we analyse the sample provided in the VentureXpert database. The data for Europe are essentially the same as those summarized in Table 11.2 above, and so draws on the returns reported in surveys of LPs and GPs. Equivalent surveys have been undertaken for many years in the USA, and in this section we compare the returns earned in both Europe and the USA for funds raised from 1986 to 2001. This is a somewhat truncated sample compared with that used earlier in the aggregate figures. The reasons for starting the sample in 1986 is that before this date the European sample sizes each year were extremely small (for instance, only three or fewer of the European VC funds raised between 1980 and 1983 reported their returns each year, and the European buyout sample only started in 1984 with four respondents). Such small samples are less important when measuring the long-term returns on the asset class over many years, but would render a time-series analysis largely irrelevant. Similarly, since we are more interested in out-turn returns, rather than funds' estimates of their residual value, we exclude the more recent vintages. Even the funds raised in 1999–2001 will have been reporting (at the end of 2004) returns largely based on unrealized investments. However, some of these more recent figures are interesting in that this was a boom period for fund raising, and some of these funds—especially those focused on earlier-stage investments—are likely to have suffered during the bursting of the dot-com bubble, and consequent stock market falls, in 2000/1.

We present the evidence in Figure 11.7, where we separate the buyout funds from the VC funds. For each vintage year the solid bars show the median return among the sample of funds that reported their performance. In addition, the lines show the seventy-fifth percentile of returns. Therefore, these figures show the minimum return in each vintage year that would be necessary in order to be a top quartile fund (to be clear, they do *not* show the average returns earned by firms that comprise the upper quartile). Starting with the buyout returns, it is noticeable that the cyclical patterns are indeed similar between the USA and Europe. However, it is also striking that the median and upper quartile returns have been higher in most years in Europe than the USA, and that this difference increased for funds formed in 1994–7. As mentioned above, later years are less reliable at present as funds of a more recent vintage will have a high proportion of unrealized investments. It is worth stressing that these results are based on limited samples—for instance the impressive upper quartile IRRs for 1994 vintage funds are only based on returns from thirteen European funds—but nonetheless the evidence points towards superior performance by European buyout funds compared with their US counterparts.

Turning to the lower part of the chart, similar evidence is presented for VC returns. It is important to note first the difference in the scale relative to the buyout chart—this is necessitated by the extraordinary performance of US VC funds formed in 1996. For the thirty-three US funds from the 1996 vintage that reported their results, the median IRR was 37 per cent and to be classified as upper quartile the IRR would have to exceed 96 per cent. The adjacent US vintages of 1995 and 1997 also produced impressive

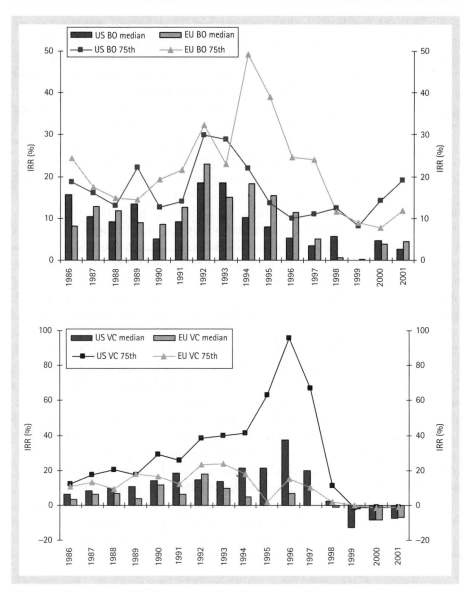

Fig. 11.7. Returns on European and US private equity funds, by vintage year

Note: In this figure 50th percentile (median) and 75th percentile IRRs are reported for European and US private equity funds, according to the year in which the fund started investing (the vintage year). The upper panel reports buyout returns and the lower panel reports venture capital returns

Source: VentureXpert, based on returns reported up until 30 June 2005

returns, especially amongst the top quartile. However, the other noticeable pattern is that in the case of venture capital the European returns have been consistently lower than those obtained by US funds, and there have not been any 'bumper' vintages to boost returns: indeed, an IRR of 20 per cent would put a European fund in the top quartile in most years.

Whilst the extraordinary performance of US VC funds formed in 1996 stands out in Figure 11.7, the experience of US VC investing may look somewhat different in a few years as the more recently formed funds mature. In particular, there was a huge influx of capital into US VC in the 1999 and 2000, and yet at the end of 2004 the median returns on such funds were −13 per cent and −8 per cent respectively. At approximately halfway through the lives of these funds this does not bode well for the final realized performance. Similar trends are also evident in the European figures.

Therefore, this brief analysis of the recent trends in performance suggests that relatively strong and consistent European performance in buyouts is matched by relatively weak performance in earlier-stage investing. Although there may be sample selection biases—which, as argued, might be expected to lead the reported figures to overstate average returns—these biases are likely to be similar between the European and US surveys. This evidence suggests various interesting questions for future research. First, is the systematically superior performance of European buyouts compared with European VC a robust result (for instance, would appropriate risk adjustment alter the pattern)? Second, what explains the noticeably inferior performance of European VC funds relative to their US counterparts? This is a surprising result given that policy makers often complain that a lack of early-stage finance is a major competitive disadvantage facing Europe. In general, when competition for deals is low, returns would be expected to be high, which would encourage additional capital. So are the low realized returns associated with more general structural features facing European early-stage companies and VC firms (such as a lack of the network benefits and externalities associated, for instance, with locations like Silicon Valley). Or is all the best talent within Europe being tempted by the more attractive economics associated with running buyout funds? Understanding the factors influencing the relatively disappointing European early-stage returns is an important future area for research. Third, given the ability of investors to choose between investing in local or overseas private equity funds, it would also be interesting to know more about the flow of funds between Europe and the USA. One might expect net outflows of capital from European investors to US-focused VC funds along with net outflows of capital from US investors to European-focused buyout funds. However, little is known about the extent or direction of such international capital flows.

5. CONCLUSIONS

In this chapter we have presented a range of evidence on the development of the European private equity industry. From a relatively small asset class only fifteen years ago, significant amounts of capital are now being allocated to European-focused funds. Indeed, it is noticeable that capital raised by European and US private equity funds was virtually identical in 2004. Most of this money is flowing into later-stage funds—in particular buyout funds—where the historical returns have been the highest. As a result, private equity funds are now involved in a very significant proportion of European corporate acquisitions and restructurings.

However, although the performance and growth of European buyout funds has been impressive, the same cannot be said of European venture capital. Although there have clearly been some excellent performers, average returns on early-stage investing have been very low, both in absolute terms, and certainly relative to appropriate benchmark returns.

Finally, it is worth noting that, in comparison with many other areas in finance, our knowledge about the performance, and certainly the factors that influence performance, of the private equity sector is very limited. This is especially true of the European private equity sector, and we have noted a number of areas where future research is required. The paucity of existing research reflects, to a large extent, the difficulty of obtaining reliable and comprehensive information about the sector. However, as increasing amounts of capital are allocated to private equity, and as private equity funds become significant investors in both early-stage and, in particular, more mature companies, the importance of such research will only increase.

REFERENCES

BARROS, P. P., BERGLOF, E., FULGHIERI, P., GUAL, J., MAYER, C., and VIVES, X. (2005), *Integration of European Banking: The Way Forward*, London: CEPR.

BOTTAZZI, L., and DA RIN, M. (2002), 'European venture capital', *Economic Policy*, April, 231–69.

EVCA (2005a), *Pan European Survey of Performance. From Inception to 31 December 2004*, annual survey conducted by Thomson Venture Economics in cooperation with the EVCA, available at www.evca.com.

—— (2005b), *European Benchmark Performance Statistics*, EVCA Statistics & Performance Working Group Paper, March.

—— (2006a), *Preliminary Activity Figures, 2005*, available at www.evca.com.

—— (2006b), *Preliminary Performance Figures, 2005*, available at www.evca.com.

KAPLAN, S. N., and SCHOAR, A. (2005), 'Private equity performance: returns, persistence and capital flows', *Journal of Finance*, 60, 1791–823.

MAYER, C., SCHOORS, K., and YAFEH, Y. (2005), 'Sources of funds and investment activities of venture capital funds: evidence from Germany, Israel, Japan and the United Kingdom', *Journal of Corporate Finance*, 11, 586–608.

PHALIPPOU, L., and ZOLLO, M. (2006), 'The performance of private equity funds', Working Paper.

RAJAN, R., and ZINGALES, L. (1995), 'What do we know about capital structure? Some evidence from international data', *Journal of Finance*, 50, 1421–60.

SWENSEN, D. (2000), *Pioneering Portfolio Management: An Unconventional Approach to Institutional Investment*, Glencoe, Ill.: Free Press.

PART III

FINANCIAL INSTITUTIONS

CHAPTER 12

TECHNOLOGY, REGULATION, AND THE GEOGRAPHICAL SCOPE OF BANKING

HANS DEGRYSE

STEVEN ONGENA

We received many valuable comments from Xavier Freixas. This chapter updates Degryse and Ongena 2004, a paper published in the *Oxford Review of Economic Policy* issue on *European Financial Integration* edited by Xavier Freixas, Philipp Hartmann, and Colin Mayer (Volume 20, No. 4). Writing that paper we received comments from an anonymous referee, Chris Allsopp (editor), Jan Bouckaert, Xavier Freixas (issue editor), Philipp Hartmann (issue editor), Colin Mayer (issue editor), John Muellbauer, David Myatt (discussant), and participants at the editorial seminar at Saïd Business School (Oxford). We also received comments from workshop participants at the University of Ghent, attendees of the 50th anniversary celebration of the Center for Economic Studies of the KU Leuven, and conference participants at the 2003 European Central Bank—Center for Financial Studies Network Meeting on 'Capital markets and financial integration' (Helsinki), where this paper was delivered as a keynote speech. Degryse received financial support from the Fund for Scientific Research–Flanders (FWO).

1. INTRODUCTION

....

SPECTACULAR advances over the last decades in information-processing and communication technology as well as continued deregulation of the financial marketplace on both sides of the Atlantic may have dramatically expanded the geographical reach of financial institutions and their clients. Bankers, consultants, and financial journalists alike now envision a future world in which consumers and businesses seek and access bank services 24/7 (i.e. 24 hours a day, 7 days a week) from any physical location on the wired part of the planet.

Yet (and notwithstanding all the hype) the daily grind of obtaining financing for most businesses still seems strikingly different from a world where 'distance is about to die'. For example, the median small US business reports in the 1998 National Survey of Small Business Finance (NSSBF) that it is located a mere 8 kilometres (5 miles) away from its lending bank (though it should be noted that this distance has been increasing steadily over the last decades). In addition, small businesses in the USA still communicate predominantly in person with their lending bank (Petersen and Rajan 2002).

European small firms are possibly located even closer to their lenders. For example in Degryse and Ongena (2005) we document how the median entrepreneur borrowing from a large Belgian bank in 1997 travelled only 2.25 kilometres (1.4 miles) to the bank branch granting the credit. This very short distance has actually increased by only 30 metres (0.02 miles) per year over the last three decades. Other work has also highlighted the lack of integration of (European) retail banking markets. Different measures of integration show that retail banking markets are not (yet) integrated in Europe (Baele et al. 2004), in contrast to for example corporate bond and equity markets that have integrated rapidly since the early 1990s.

Why is proximity to a bank branch still very important for most borrowing European small and medium-sized enterprises (SMEs)? And how does geography affect lending conditions and the structure and operation of European retail banking markets? Will technological developments and regulations shape and alter this impact? Will distance only 'die another day' in European retail banking markets?

We summarize answers given to these questions by recent banking research. Reviewing contemporary contributions naturally leads us to highlight open issues and pinpoint unanswered questions. We also provide some recommendations with respect to competition policy in banking and banking supervision towards the end of the chapter.

We start by distinguishing between *distance* and *borders*. While intimately related, these concepts are often usefully separable when assessing the geographical scope of financial markets.[1] *Distance* pertains to physical proximity that can be bridged by traditional modes of transportation, say car or train travel. In other words, by spending

---

[1] Recent empirical work on the geographical scope of banking by, for example, Berger and DeYoung 2001, Berger et al. 2003, and Buch 2004b include measures for both physical *distance* and cultural, informational, and/or regulatory *borders* in their specifications. Studies by, for example, Grinblatt and

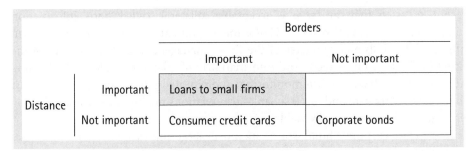

Fig. 12.1. The importance of distance and borders in European financial markets

some distance-related costs banks or their clients can overcome the distance and engage in transactions with one another. For given locations of banks and borrowers, distance per se is exogenous and bridging it (i.e. the lender visiting the borrower and/or the borrower visiting the lender) may be adequate to deal with informational problems for the lender concerning its decision about granting and pricing the loan. As a result, given location, banks play no (or a rather mechanical) role in theoretical competition models featuring only distance.

Borders, on the other hand, are not merely bridgeable by car or train travel, or even more modern technological ways of interacting. Borders result as an artefact of exogenous regulation or endogenously arise through the actions of the competing lenders. We think of borders as being tightly interrelated with informational problems that cannot be easily resolved or ameliorated by technological developments. The national borders of the countries in Europe often coincide with the cultural, informational, and/or regulatory borders that are relevant in this respect (we classify and discuss borders in Section 2).

Bank lending to small firms in Europe, we contend in this review, remains confined by both distance and borders (Figure 12.1). In contrast, large multinationals issue corporate bonds on a pan-European market anchored in London, Frankfurt, or Luxembourg. In the corporate bond market neither distance nor borders are relevant any longer. The same can probably be said about European investment/wholesale banking and interestingly enough also about venture capital markets as documented by Mayer, Schoors and Yafeh (2004) (for simplicity reasons we did not include all these markets in Figure 12.1).[2] Consumer credit cards are an interesting intermediate case. In quite a few European countries banks compete nationwide to enlist credit card users; distance plays no role anymore. However, no banks we know of yet target credit card customers across national borders.

Why do we observe this remarkable diversity in geographical scope of financial and banking markets in Europe? Part of the explanation may reside in the different informational requirements in each of these markets. Small and young businesses often lack publicly accessible accounting statements, an observable repayment track

Keloharju 2001 on the portfolio choices of Finnish investors and Portes and Rey 2004 on international capital flows also include both distance and border variables.

[2] See also Degryse, Ongena, and Penas 2006a.

record, or assets that can serve as acceptable collateral (called 'hard' information in Petersen 2002 and Stein 2002). Hence the assessment by the lending bank's loan officer of the skills and character of the firm's management and the quality of the firm's business vision (called 'soft' information) will play a key role in the lending decision. 'Handshakes', *in situ* monitoring, and repeated interaction will create trust in the borrowing firm and foster a bank–firm relationship, but may require physical proximity to be economically viable.

In contrast, corporate bond issuers are mostly large and well-known international firms that can easily be assessed by many investors and banks located across Europe on the basis of accounting statements and public track record. Hence corporate bond markets integrated rather rapidly as regulatory impediments dissolved and a common currency was introduced. Credit cards are intermediate in this regard. Consumers can be readily scored on the basis of observable characteristics such as age, income, and marital status and card balances can be pooled and securitized, making distance within each country increasingly irrelevant. However consumer characteristics, preferences, and regulatory protection still differ substantially across European countries making cross-border bank forays more complex.

What are the consequences of a geographical scope determined by both distance and borders for the conditions and structure in the retail banking markets in Europe? Previewing the main lessons we draw in this chapter, recent work suggests that:

1. Bank lending to small businesses in Europe may be characterized both by (local) spatial pricing and resilient (regional and/or national) market segmentation;
2. Because of informational asymmetries in the retail market, bank mergers and acquisitions seem the optimal route of entering another market, long before cross-border servicing or direct entry are economically feasible;
3. Current technological and regulatory developments may to a large extent remain impotent in further dismantling the various residual but mutually reinforcing frictions in the retail banking markets in Europe.

We organize the rest of the chapter as follows. Section 2 reviews the theoretical predictions and empirical findings regarding the geographical scope of banking. Section 3 discusses the impact of technology and regulation on the geographical scope while Section 4 assesses the current state of the banking sector in the Europe. Section 5 provides some policy recommendations and concludes.

2. GEOGRAPHICAL SCOPE OF BANKING

2.1. Distance versus Borders

To structure our analysis, we commence by distinguishing between *lending conditions* and *market presence* as the first dimension and between *distance* and *borders* as the

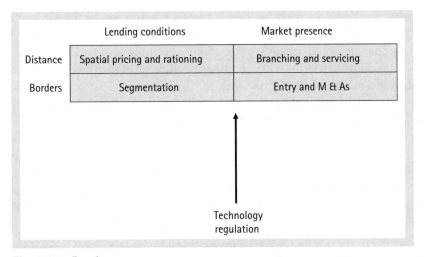

	Lending conditions	Market presence
Distance	Spatial pricing and rationing	Branching and servicing
Borders	Segmentation	Entry and M & As

Technology
regulation

Fig. 12.2. Road map

second dimension. These divisions yield a four-celled matrix as in Figure 12.2. We aim to position the relevant theoretical contributions and empirical findings in the banking literature in one of these four cells. *Lending conditions* naturally concern the offering, pricing, and rationing of loans, while *market presence* relates to the location and characteristics of bank branches.

We have already introduced our distinction between *distance* and *borders* in the introduction (Section 1). We further follow Buch (2002) in distinguishing between 'regulatory' and 'economic' borders. *Regulatory borders* may simply prohibit 'foreign' banks from engaging borrowers, setting up branches, and/or acquiring local banks. But the Riegle–Neal Act and Second European Banking Directive in effect removed most if not all such regulatory borders in the United States and Europe, respectively. Most *economic borders* however remain unaffected by these specific directives. Take the existing *exogenous economic borders* such as legal origin and system, supervisory and corporate governance practices, political framework, language or cultural differences. We will argue in more detail in Section 4 that these borders, in Europe in particular, remain in place and have been almost unaffected by either technological developments or deregulation.

Endogenous economic borders on the other hand are mainly informational and may well be affected by technological developments and deregulation. However the extent to which the endogenous economic borders are affected by these developments remains unclear. Informational borders arise because of the formation of bank–firm relationships, adverse selection, or information sharing between (a group of) banks. Take the formation of a *bank–firm relationship*. Banks learn about borrowers by privately observing repayment of earlier loans or observing borrowers' type (Sharpe 1990). It is this informational asymmetry between the 'inside' bank and other 'outside' banks which gives the inside bank a competitive edge and almost assures continued interaction, i.e. the existence of a *relationship*, between the bank and its high-quality borrowers. Inside banks make economic rents while outside banks succeed occasionally in 'poaching' mostly low-quality borrowers and at best break even (Rajan 1992; von Thadden 2004), in the absence of other frictions. Hence, relationships arise as an endogenous barrier to entry limiting the number of incumbent inside banks operating in a market (Dell'Ariccia 2001).

Banks are also faced with *adverse selection*. *De novo* or 'foreign' banks screening a particular pool of borrowers for the first time face an adverse selection problem as incumbent local banks will continue to engage the best customers (Broecker 1990; Shaffer 1998). The entrants can be expected to end up 'fishing in a pretty bad pool'. The harshness of the adverse selection problem faced by the new banks depends on, for example, the banking structure (e.g. number of incumbent banks), the correlation in outcomes of the screening processes by new and incumbent banks, and the investment in screening accurateness made by the incumbents (Gehrig 1998).

Information sharing between banks, when accessible by outside banks, may lower this endogenous barrier of pre-existing bank–firm relationships. Indeed, the information dissipated through the information-sharing network decreases the inside bank's informational advantage (Padilla and Pagano 1997), reducing the informational lock-in. Initiatives to start the cross-border sharing of information in Europe may lower the informational economic border. On the other hand information sharing also serves as a collusive device allowing banks to coordinate and be used as a strategic device to soften competition, as it introduces non-information-related switching costs (Gehrig and Stenbacka 2001; Bouckaert and Degryse 2004, 2006). If coordination can take place and remain (somewhat) exclusive, information sharing between incumbent banks constitutes another endogenous economic border outside banks need to overcome to enter a market. Alternatively, information sharing introduces other economic borders as switching costs.

2.2. Distance and Lending Conditions: Spatial Pricing

Recent theoretical papers highlight the importance of distance in explaining the availability and pricing of bank loans (the north-west cell 'Distance/lending conditions' in Figure 12.2). As suggested by a number of theories, lending conditions depend on the distance between the borrower and the lender, and the distance between the borrower and the closest competing bank. We borrow from Degryse and Ongena (2005) in our discussion of *spatial pricing* in this section and return to *spatial rationing* in Section 3. Table 12.1 summarizes the theoretical predictions regarding spatial pricing.

2.2.1. *Transportation Costs for Borrowers*

In location differentiation models (Hotelling 1929; Salop 1979), borrowers incur distance-related transportation costs in the action of visiting a bank. Banks

Table 12.1. Theoretical models linking loan rates and distance

Arguments and discussed models	Impact on the loan rate of the		
	Distance to the lender[a]	Distance to the closest competitor[a]	Number of competitors
Transportation costs (for borrower)			
Uniform pricing	No	no	negative
Discriminatory pricing	negative	positive	negative
Monitoring costs (for lender)			
Marginal cost pricing	positive	negative	negative
Discriminatory pricing	negative	positive	negative
	Distance to the relationship bank[a]	Distance to the transactional bank[a]	Number of competitors
Asymmetric information			
Dell'Ariccia (2001)	negative	no	negative
Hauswald and Marquez (2006)	negative	positive	positive/negative

Source: Degryse and Ongena 2005.
[a] For a given number of competitors.

necessarily have to price uniformly if they cannot observe borrower location,[3] or are prevented from charging different prices to different borrowers. Borrowers pay the same interest rate, but the total transportation costs incurred differ, depending on the firm's location vis-à-vis the lending bank.

However, if banks observe the borrowers' location and offer interest rates based on that information, they can engage in spatial price discrimination. Banks are often informed about the borrower's address before even granting or pricing a loan. If borrowers pay for their own transportation, as is mostly likely to be the case, a bank optimally charges a higher interest rate to those borrowers that are located closest to its bank branch (Lederer and Hurter 1986). The reasoning is that closer borrowers face higher total transportation costs when visiting competing banks (which are located further away than the lending bank), resulting in some market power for the lender over closer borrowers. Similarly, a monopolist bank optimally charges a higher loan rate to close borrowers, as these borrowers incur lower total transportation costs. We summarize these relationships in Table 12.1.

---

[3] Lenders may initially be unsure about the exact location of the borrower. For example, if the borrower is an independent salesman or software consultant and maintains multiple centres of activity, it is not clear at first for the bank where to monitor. In that case, the bank can engage in discriminatory pricing only upon becoming informed about the location and transportation costs faced by their borrowers. In Dell'Ariccia 2001, banks become informed about the location of the borrower through first-period lending. In his model, only 'relationship' banks, lending to the same firm for a second time, can engage in spatial price discrimination, while *de novo* 'transactional' banks have to resort to 'mill pricing'.

2.2.2. *Monitoring Costs for Lenders*

The cost of monitoring a borrower could also be related to physical distance. Total monitoring costs increase with borrower–lender distance, because of extra communication costs or transportation costs incurred by banks visiting the borrowers' premises. Loan rates passing through such costs increase with distance. However, distance-related monitoring costs might also allow for discriminatory pricing.

In Sussman and Zeira (1995), banks face monitoring costs known to be increasing in distance. As a result, lenders extract rents from close borrowers, because more distant competing banks take into account their own higher monitoring costs in their loan rate offers. As indicated in Table 12.1, spatial price discrimination based on bank monitoring costs again implies a negative (positive) relationship between the loan rate and the borrower–lender (borrower–closest competing bank) distance (for a given number of banks).

2.2.3. *Distance and Lender Information*

The severity of the asymmetric information problem itself may also increase with distance. Hauswald and Marquez (2006) for example develop a model in which the precision of the signal about a borrower's quality received by a bank decreases with (informational) distance. Because banks receive more precise signals about close borrowers in Hauswald and Marquez (2006), competing banks face increasing adverse selection problems when approaching borrowers closer to the most informed bank. Hence, the informed relationship bank can charge higher interest rates to closer borrowers, while the uninformed transactional banks charges higher interest rates to borrowers located further away (due to the increase in the adverse selection problem). Or to put it differently: the uninformed (transactional) lender charges a higher loan rate to remote borrowers in order to compensate for the adverse selection problem, which intensifies in the vicinity of an informed (relationship) lender. The informed lender accordingly extracts a higher loan rate from closer borrowers. *Ceteris paribus*, Hauswald and Marquez (2006) derive a negative (positive) relationship between the loan rate and the distance between the borrower and the relationship (transactional) bank. We indicate this result again in Table 12.1.

We note that the model developed by Hauswald and Marquez (2006) in effect straddles our 'Distance and borders' categorization. Their model also features 'relationship borrowers', whose current borrowing conditions may be determined by past and future borrowing. The transportation and monitoring cost models discussed so far seem mostly relevant for 'transactional borrowers', whose current borrowing conditions are unaffected by past or future borrowing. Recent work suggests both types of engagements may coexist in banking markets and the mix be optimally determined by banks and/or firms (Boot and Thakor 2000; Elsas 2005; Degryse and Ongena 2006b; Egli, Ongena, and Smith 2006).

2.2.4. *Number of Banks*

In spatial models, the number of banks in the market is typically positively related to the magnitude of the transportation cost, and inversely related to the distance between the lender and the (closest) competing banks. An increase in the number of banks (harsher competition) increases the likelihood of receiving a lower loan rate offer. A decrease in the fixed set-up costs per bank (in, for example, Sussman and Zeira 1995) increases the number of banks, decreases the distance between any two neighbouring banks, and decreases the loan rate for each bank–borrower distance combination.[4]

On the other hand, an increase in the number of banks aggravates an adverse selection problem by enabling lower-quality borrowers to obtain financing, resulting in moral hazard and credit rationing (Petersen and Rajan 1995) or a higher interest rate (Broecker 1990). In Dell'Ariccia (2001), adverse selection generates an endogenous fixed cost, constituting a barrier to entry in the industry limiting the number of competing banks even when markets become very large.

Similarly, a decrease in the fixed-cost component of the relationship-building technology in Hauswald and Marquez (2006) not only leads to an increase in the number of banks and more competition, but also results in a retrenchment towards relationship lending. The lower entry barrier then leads to sharper adverse selection problems and higher loan rates for the borrowers closest to the relationship lender, but lower loan rates for customers further away. In effect, loan rates will decrease (increase) more per unit of distance between the borrower and the relationship (transactional) bank.

2.2.5. *Distance, Borrower Information, and Experience*

Casual observation suggests that borrowers do not always frequent the closest bank, as most spatial models dictate they should. Incomplete borrower information and other bank product characteristics cause borrowers to visit more distant banks.

First, borrowers may not be fully informed about the precise location of all competing banks and the availability and conditions of the loans offered there. Grossman and Shapiro (1984) and Bester and Petrakis (1995) model such location cum informational differentiation. In Grossman and Shapiro (1984), consumers buy a product from a particular seller upon becoming informed of its location through advertising. The advertising itself is not localized. The sales price in their model exceeds the full information price, by the magnitude of the transportation cost, as informational differentiation lowers the elasticity of demand. In addition, consumers in their model, as they are unaware of all sellers, do not necessarily patronize the closest one. Bester and Petrakis (1995) model the advertising of lower price offers. In the absence of advertising, customers are only informed about 'local' prices. Producers will advertise

---

[4] An increase in the number of banks also decreases the loan rate in more general models of imperfect Cournot competition between a finite number of banks. See, for example, the rendition of the Monti 1972–Klein 1971 model in Freixas and Rochet 1997: 57–60.

lower prices to attract customers from more distant locations. Hence, more distant informed customers will be observed to receive lower prices.

Second, while borrowers often mention bank branch proximity as a major concern (Elliehausen and Wolken 1990; Binks and Ennew 1997), location is obviously just one characteristic of a bank's product that is important for its customers. Hence, borrowers may not patronize the closest bank branch when another bank's loan product exhibits other, more preferred, characteristics (Pinkse, Slade, and Brett 2002). And, once borrowers have experienced a good match and have observed the high-quality services provided by their current bank, they will switch to another bank only when offered a considerably lower price (Tirole 1988: 294).

2.2.6. *Distance and Bank Organization*

Recent theoretical models argue that a bank's organizational structure determines its agents' incentives and as a result its lending technology. Stein (2002), for example, models the organizational impact of the ease and speed at which different types of information can 'travel' within an organization. 'Hard' information (for example, accounting numbers, financial ratios, etc.) can be passed on easily within the organization while 'soft' information (for example, a character assessment or the degree of trust) is much harder to relay. Hence, if the organization employs mostly soft information, a simple and flat hierarchical structure and local decision making may be optimal (see also Takats 2004).

Degryse, Laeven, and Ongena (2006) present a stylized banking competition model ascribing a role to the own and rivals' organizational structure in determining spatial pricing. Their theoretical model predicts that when rival banks are more hierarchically organized, spatial pricing softens.

To conclude, price discrimination models imply a negative (positive) correspondence between the borrower–lender (competing bank) distance and the loan rate, caused by either transportation costs (for either the borrower or the lender) or asymmetric information. Information availability, experience, product, and bank organizational characteristics may abate the strength of the distance—loan rate relationship.

2.2.7. *Empirical Evidence on Spatial Pricing*

Petersen and Rajan (2002) are among the first to provide concrete evidence on the possible presence of spatial pricing in bank lending. They find for example that a small business located 1 mile from the lending bank *ceteris paribus* pays around 38 basis points less than a borrower located around the corner from the lending bank (see also evidence for large US firms in Bharath et al. 2006). In Degryse and Ongena (2005) we also include the distance to the closest competitors in the specifications. Please notice that the three papers include a variety of controls (and exercises to control) for firm risk to avoid picking up the spurious effects of spatial rationing on pricing.

In Degryse and Ongena (2005) we find a somewhat smaller impact of physical distance on the loan rates than Petersen and Rajan (2002), but the impact we measure is still highly statistically significant and economically relevant. The impact on the loan rate of both distance to the lender and distance to the closest competitor is actually similar in absolute magnitude, but of an appropriate opposite sign, which in itself is also evidence suggestive of spatial price discrimination. For example, for small loans loan rates decrease 7 basis points per mile to the lender and similarly increase 7 basis points per mile to the closest (quartile) competitor. We further deduce that, given current transportation costs and opportunity costs of travel, the average first-time borrower in our sample needs to visit the lender between two and three times to obtain a bank loan.

Degryse, Laeven, and Ongena (2006) further find that the organizational form of the closest competitors matters for loan pricing. In particular the presence of large rival banks implies substantially softer spatial price discrimination. Also the presence of a foreign bank in the vicinity of a borrower decreases the impact of geography on loan pricing.

On the other hand, most studies find no impact of the number of competitors on the loan rate, while the magnitude of the impact of the concentration index varies widely (see the appendix in Degryse and Ongena 2003 for details). However, it remains difficult to compare results across specifications, banking markets, periods, and HHI measures. Concentration measures are alternatively based on loans, deposits, or branches, and vary widely (across studies) in geographical span (Edelstein and Morgan 2006).

2.2.8. *Location Rents for Banks*

To conclude, spatial price discrimination as a response to either (borrower) transportation costs, (lender) monitoring costs, or asymmetric information may explain the results in both Petersen and Rajan (2002) and Degryse and Ongena (2005). Transportation cost provides the most consistent and comprehensive interpretation of all the results documented in Degryse and Ongena (2005). Inferred changes in lending technology may make an interpretation of the results in Petersen and Rajan (2002) more difficult. In Degryse and Ongena (2005) we run through a number of straightforward exercises but cannot find any trace of adverse selection increasing in the (admittedly short) distances to the uninformed lenders. In either case, our results suggest that the distance to the closest competitors is important for competitive conditions and that the actual location of the bank branches may be relevant when assessing the intensity of competition.

Our estimates in Degryse and Ongena (2005) also indicate that spatial price discrimination targeting borrowers located near the lending bank branch yields average bank rents of around 4 per cent (with a maximum of 9 per cent) of the bank's marginal cost of funding. Taken at face value, our findings substantiate an important source of rents accruing to financial intermediaries, based on location. 'Location rents' are distinct from rents derived from customer switching costs (Klemperer 1995), which are in credit markets often attributed to pervasive informational asymmetries or the endogenous economic borders discussed earlier (Sharpe 1990; Rajan 1992;

von Thadden 2004).[5] Kim, Kliger, and Vale (2003), for example, provide the first estimates of switching costs faced by bank borrowers. Their findings imply average annualized bank rents of roughly 4 per cent of the banks' marginal cost of funding. In Degryse and Ongena (2005), the increase of the loan rate during the average bank–firm relationship points to annual 'information rents' of less than 2 per cent of the bank's marginal cost of funding.

2.3. Distance and Lending Conditions: Spatial Rationing

Distance also affects the availability of credit. Remember that hierarchically organized banks favour hard information whereas decentralized banks prefer soft information. The type of information, hard or soft, that is needed and available to arrive at optimal lending decisions also translates into a correspondence between distance and credit rationing. For example lines embedded in credit cards are extended solely on the basis of a quantitative analysis of hard and easily verifiable information (for example, age, profession, address, etc. of the applicant). As a result credit cards are offered by mail and across large distances in the USA (Ausubel 1991).

A lot of small business lending on the other hand is still 'character' lending. To screen successfully, loan officers need to interact with the borrower, establish trust, and be present in the local community. The 'soft' information collected in this way is much harder to frame and to convey to others within the organization. As a result small (opaque) firms borrow from close, small banks (Petersen and Rajan 2002), while large banks mainly lend to distant, large firms employing predominantly hard information in the loan decision (Berger et al. 2005). Small firms then may be subject to credit rationing when seeking financing across larger distances. Similarly when rival banks are more hierarchically organized, the lending bank branch's own geographical reach decreases in Degryse, Laeven, and Ongena (2006).

However, from an empirical point of view, the severity of the rationing of credit affecting small firms is not entirely clear. For example, the results in Petersen and Rajan (2002) indicate that the effect is economically rather small in the USA, while preliminary findings by Carling and Lundberg (2005) seemingly indicate the absence of distance-related credit rationing in the Swedish banking sector. Alternatively, results in Degryse and Ongena (2005) suggest that transportation costs that are fixed per loan (i.e. do not vary by loan size) may explain why larger loans are obtained across larger distances (mainly by larger firms). Evidence in Degryse, Laeven, and, Ongena (2006) ties the fixed costs per loan to the organizational characteristics of the lending bank and its rivals. They find that bank branch reach is lower when the closest competitors are large, foreign, hierarchical, and technologically more advanced. Potential borrowers from these types of banks expect that fewer visits are required to obtain a loan.

---

[5] See Carletti 2006 and Degryse and Ongena 2006a for a theoretical and empirical review of the sources of bank rents, respectively.

2.4. Distance and Market Presence: Branching and Servicing

Only very few papers study the importance of distance in determining market presence, i.e. the branching and servicing within certain areas (the north-east cell 'Distance/market presence' in Figure 12.2). A recent paper by De Juan (2003) is an exception. She studies how distance between own branches influence bank branching decisions in Spain. She finds that the number of own branches in a particular (sub)market has a positive (but small) effect on the further entry decision of the bank in that market. Hence, her results suggest that branch expansion is partly affected by the proximity of other branches of the same bank.

Results by Berger and DeYoung (2001) provide a partial explanation for these findings. Berger and DeYoung (2001) document how efficiency of bank branches slips somewhat as the distance between branch and headquarters of the bank increases. Hence, in order to guarantee consistency in servicing across bank branches, banks decide to branch out methodically across certain areas rather than to build isolated outposts.

2.5. Borders and Lending Conditions: Segmentation

Next we turn to the impact of borders on lending conditions and market presence. A recent literature has started to investigate how different types of borders shape lending conditions and result in segmentation of credit markets (the south-west cell 'Borders/lending conditions' in Figure 12.2).

National borders that often coincide with many of the exogenous economic borders discussed earlier continue to play an important role across the world. But other type of borders may also result in segmented credit markets. Empirical evidence suggests that 'outside' lenders often face difficulties (or hesitate) in extending credit to mainly small local firms (Shaffer 1998; Guiso, Sapienza, and Zingales 2004). This happens in particular when for example existing relationships between incumbent banks and borrowers are strong (Bergström, Engwall, and Wallerstedt 1994) or when the local judicial enforcement of creditor rights is poor (Bianco, Jappelli, and Pagano 2003). In all these cases borders will lead to market segmentation and difficulties for cross-border outside banks to engage any local borrowers. In effect this market segmentation highlights the importance for the outside banks to strive to build an actual physical presence in the targeted market.

2.6. Borders and Market Presence

Indeed, academics and bankers alike have long recognized borders as important factors in impelling bank entry and cross-border bank mergers and acquisitions (the south-east cell 'Borders/market presence' in Figure 12.2).

2.6.1. *Bank Entry*

An older literature going back to Goldberg and Saunders (1981) and .Kindleberger (1983) asserts that banks often pursue a 'follow-the-customer' strategy when deciding upon cross-border market entry. However, recent evidence casts some doubt on this 'follow-the-customer' strategy as the only game in town. In particular banks entering the US market have not primarily a follow-the-home-country-customer motive or at least have not persevered in servicing only the home country customers. Indeed, foreign banks in the USA also apparently engage many local borrowers (Seth, Nolle, and Mohanty 1998; Stanley, Roger, and McManis 1993; Buch and Golder 2001).

However, banks encounter many difficulties (in other countries than the USA) in successfully pursuing a strategy of engaging local firms by cross-border entry through local branches. DeYoung and Nolle (1996) and Berger et al. (2000) for example document how most foreign bank affiliates are less efficient than domestic banks, the exceptions being the foreign affiliates of US banks in other countries and most foreign bank affiliates in for example Eastern Europe and South America. The latter affiliates are often financially sounder than the domestic banks (Crystal, Dages, and Goldberg 2002). Why are most foreign bank affiliates less efficient than the local crowd? A paper by Buch (2004b) documents that the inefficiencies by foreign bank affiliates are mostly due to the presence of economic borders (language, culture, etc.) and do not seem driven by physical distance.

But there is a second reason why banks shy away from following the customer, apart from the fear of getting stuck with inefficient branch outposts. Findings by Berger et al. (2003) suggest customers are not that interested in being followed! Indeed, they find that foreign affiliates of multinational companies choose host nation banks for cash management services more often than home nation or third nation banks. This result is consistent with so-called 'concierge' benefits dominating 'home cookin' benefits. This is a surprising finding given that these large multinationals might be expected to be prime targets for preferential treatment by their home nation banks. On the other hand, the opening of a foreign affiliate is a good occasion for a firm to escape a hold-up problem at 'home'. In this way, the establishment of new plants or subsidiaries in foreign countries is an opportunity to add a new (foreign) bank relationship.

Berger et al. (2003) also find that the geographical footprint of the selected bank, which they call 'bank reach', thereby distinguishing between global, regional, and local banks, is strongly associated with the nationality of the selected bank. For example, if a host nation bank is the choice of nationality, then the firm is much less likely to choose a global bank. Finally, they also find that bank nationality and bank reach both vary significantly with the legal and financial development of the host nation. For example, firms appear to be much less likely to choose a host nation bank and more likely to choose a global bank when operating in the former socialist nations of Eastern Europe.

Berger et al. (2003) conclude on the basis of this evidence that the extent of future bank globalization may be significantly limited as many corporations continue to prefer local or regional banks for at least some of their services, though, as pointed out by Dermine (2003), this conclusion is partly predicated on the continuing (and endogenous) absence of foreign direct investment and possibly more importantly cross-border mergers taking place.

2.6.2. *Frequency and Value of Cross-Border Bank Mergers and Acquisitions*

However, cross-border bank mergers and acquisitions (M&As) are still a relatively rare species in many parts of the world, though the number in the euro area has steadily increased. Hartmann, Maddaloni, and Manganelli (2003), for example, document that in 1995 61 per cent of all mergers involved institutions in the same country and only 11 per cent involved banks situated in two different countries of the euro area. By 2002 the percentage domestic deals dropped to 47 per cent, while the euro area deals remained stuck at 11 per cent. Focarelli and Pozzolo (2001) also demonstrate that cross-border bank M&As occur relative to within-border M&As less frequently than cross-border M&As in other industries, *ceteris paribus*, while Berger, Demsetz, and Strahan (1999) show that cross-border bank M&As occur less frequently than domestic bank M&As. And it is again economic borders,[6] not distance, that make cross-border bank M&As less likely (Buch and DeLong 2004).

Hence, taken together, these studies suggest that not only exogenous economic borders (that also affect other industries) but also endogenous economic borders specific to the banking industry (information asymmetries in assessing target bank portfolios) may make it hard to pull off a successful cross-border bank M&A.

Bank managers are apparently aware of the difficulties awaiting them when engaging in a cross-border M&A and seem to refrain from undertaking many. But also investors recognize the dangers. A nice recent study by Beitel, Schiereck, and Wahrenburg (2004) for example documents that the combined cumulative abnormal returns for stocks of bidder and target bank in cross-border bank M&As in Europe over the last few decades are actually zero or negative! This finding stands in stark contrast with other industries where the combined CARs of cross-border M&As are typically found to be positive. Hence investors seemingly evaluate cross-border bank M&As as destroying value. Beitel, Schiereck, and Wahrenburg's (2004) results are quite similar to findings in DeLong (2001). She reports that in the USA only the combined CARs of geographically focused bank M&As are positive, although it is not entirely clear what factors are driving this empirical finding.

---

[6] Regulatory borders explicitly prohibiting bank M&As have been removed in Europe. However, national and political interests frequently result in the mobilization of the national anti-trust or banking safety apparatus to block cross-border bank M&As (see for example Carletti, Hartmann, and Ongena 2006). We acknowledge these actions resort somewhere in the grey area between explicit prohibition of cross-border bank M&As (regulatory borders) and inherent political and cultural differences creating difficulties in making a cross-border bank M&A possible and successful (economic borders).

2.6.3. *Borders and Cross-Border Bank Mergers and Acquisitions?*

The evidence presented so far is not clear whether it is exogenous or endogenous (informational) economic borders that create most problems in making a cross-border bank M&A possible and successful. A paper by Campa and Hernando (2004) suggests exogenous borders play a role. Their study shows that the combined CARs of M&As are typically lower in industries, such as banking, that until recently were under government control or are still or were most heavily regulated. CARs of cross-border M&As in these industries are actually negative, evidence in line with Beitel, Schiereck, and Wahrenburg (2004). One possible interpretation is that the (lingering) effects of regulation make for harder economic borders.

However, while such residual regulatory and 'institutional reasons are undoubtedly important, strong economic forces may impede the unification of banking markets' (Rosengren 2003). Economic forces may explain why there has also been so little interstate merger activity in the USA, despite very homogeneous banking markets. Cost savings are often impossible in cross-border mergers. In-market mergers however allow for a reduction in redundant branch networks, underwriting activities, and/or local monitoring of credits. Anticipating such savings may allow an in-market (domestic) acquirer 'to bid more' than any other out-of-market (foreign) acquirer 'in the auction of the target assets'. More in general the promise of cost cutting and indirect labour shedding may allow domestic banks to gain an upper hand in any complex and politicized merger dance involving also foreign suitors. In addition, acquiring an in-market competitor limits the number of entry points for any out-of-market competitors and may increase the in-market acquirer's market power and monopoly profits.

Bank industry observers sometimes also note that for example bank organization and corporate governance may be an area shaped in ways that hinders merger activity. The mutual structure of dominant banks in France and Germany in particular (for example, Crédit Agricole, Landesbanken) is often passed off as a major hurdle for these banks to initiate and pursue a successful M&A (Wrighton 2003). But exogenous economic borders may also make cross-border bank M&As result in complex holding structures (Dermine 2003), i.e. cross-border consolidation in Europe functions through subsidiaries and not branches as is common in US cross-state banking. Hence, it appears as if the so-called 'single passport' of the European Second Banking Directive is not very much used. Subsidiary configurations possibly further complicate future M&A activity.

Finally, the impact of endogenous (informational) economic borders on cross-border bank M&A activity is less researched. It is possible that the domestic merger activity, we have observed until now in Europe, creating so-called 'National Champions', is partly made possible by the existence of informational borders. Outside banks seeking to acquire a local bank find it more difficult than incumbent banks to assess the value of the loan portfolio of the possible target banks. As a result of the winner's curse problem, outside banks refrain from stepping in and most M&A activity, driven by for example (revenue and cost) scale and scope considerations, occurs between domestic banks.

However, as the domestic banks increase in size, diversify,[7] and possibly partly refocus their lending towards larger firms they become easier-to-value targets. If this is indeed the case we contend that the informational asymmetries facing the outside acquiring banks may actually endogenously decrease over time as possible target banks that are shielded within the bordered area prosper, grow, and merge among themselves resulting in a further diversification of their loan portfolios. National competition policy concerns may ultimately hinder further domestic consolidation. As further local mergers may be under scrutiny of competition policy authorities, winner's curse problems may further decrease, facilitating cross-border M&As. Hence one could argue that informational borders and the accompanying winner's curse problem have a tendency to partly and endogenously self-destruct, that M&As may become the optimal route of entering a market long before cross-border servicing or direct entry are economically feasible, and that 'National Champions' will almost inevitably metamorphose into 'European Champions'.

A natural question is then how borrowers will be affected by cross-border bank M&As. It is possible that 'in the first round' small local firms serviced by domestic target banks suffer somewhat as with domestic mergers (Sapienza 2002; Bonaccorsi di Patti and Gobbi 2005). Eventually niche banks may arise taking over part of the foreclosed lending activities (Berger et al. 1998). But technological developments and regulation undoubtedly will also play a role (see for example Degryse, Ongena, and Penas 2006b). That is the topic of the next section.

3. The Impact of Technology and Regulation on the Geographical Scope of Banking

We argued so far (in Section 2) that the impact of distance on loan rates seems considerable, that the impact on credit rationing is currently unclear, and that the impact on bank branching and servicing is seemingly minor. We have also discussed how the impact of borders on both lending conditions and market presence seems substantial. We now turn to the second question broached in this chapter, which is how technology and regulations may shape the correspondence between distance and borders on the one hand and lending and market presence on the other.

---

[7] We conjecture the winner's curse in von Thadden 2004 for example would decrease in case success across multiple projects undertaken by many borrowers was uncorrelated.

3.1. Technology and Distance

Berger (2003) investigates how advances in technology, in particular in communication and information processing, substantially alter current practices in the banking sector. He argues that recent technological developments reduce 'distance-related diseconomies', in particular in four areas: (1) the monitoring and risk management of loans, (2) the offering of traditional banking services, through for example improvements in credit scoring, (3) the management of staff, and (4) the provision of new services over the internet. Hence Berger in effect argues that technological developments will change the impact of distance on both lending conditions and bank market presence. While Berger is having US experiences in mind when making these prognoses, the European banking industry is most likely to be similarly affected.

However, advances in communication technology and increased capacity for information need not imply more exchange of information at different levels. First, take information exchange *inside the banks*. Wilhelm (2001) for example argues that loan officers have limited incentives to transfer information, as they are the content originators but also the monopolists in the human capital needed to create proper credit assessments. Hence loan officers may try to tie the now commodity-like distribution (sending reports by email) to its origination. They can do so by arguing some information cannot be hardened or is too sensitive to move through the bank (or branch) organization.

In addition, loan officers may initially be uncertain about the value added by the new technologies and may therefore be unaware of its desirability. Recent work in game theory shows that both adoption and non-adoption of new technology are potential equilibria, leaving an important role for coordination in equilibrium selection. Pre-play communication or cheap talk may help to choose the Pareto-dominant equilibrium and solve the coordination problem. Myatt, Shin, and Wallace, (2002) show that adoption not only hinges on the expected value added by the new technology, but also on both the 'fundamental uncertainty'—uncertainty concerning the value added—and the 'strategic uncertainty'—uncertainty concerning the actions of others. The interaction of these two types of uncertainty determines the strategy selected by the individual players and hence the actual adoption of the new technology.

The advances in communication technology and increased capacity for information need also not imply more exchange of information *between firms and banks*. For example, Yosha (1995) and Bhattacharya and Chiesa (1995) have argued that firms choose the type and the number of financiers on the basis of concerns for confidentiality vis-à-vis product market competitors regarding proprietary information (R&D results, etc.). Similar concerns restrain firms from giving the chosen financier(s) more specific information or limit the format in which the information is transferred (for example firms prefer to provide oral presentations rather than supply full-fledged project manuals; improved communication technology has not altered this desire).

Finally, technological developments do not necessarily enhance sharing of information *between banks*. While technological progress shapes the structure of the information-sharing industry itself (as it allows for example exploiting economies of scale), the degree of information sharing or incentives to share information may remain unaffected. Concerns about free riding between banks and adverse selection and moral hazard at the firm level have long been recognized as a driver of the determination of the optimal degree of information sharing. Even dramatically lower costs of information sharing may not alter such fundamental strategic calculations (Padilla and Pagano 1997; Bouckaert and Degryse 2004). Similarly, Vercammen (1995) for example argues that it is optimal for information-sharing bureau to limit the number of years of credit history that are maintained in the database. Not for technological reasons (for example the cost of data storage) but because the incentive of the borrowers for compliance is reduced as credit histories lengthen and the value of a negative piece of information is reduced. And indeed in all European countries surveyed by Jappelli and Pagano (2003) the public credit register eventually 'forgets', though the precise memory system varies from country to country. Again, it seems unlikely that technological developments will alter these specific trade-offs.

3.2. The Impact of Technology on Spatial Pricing

Nevertheless technology may have an impact on spatial pricing of deposits and loans. For example, on-line banking spurs competition and alters the impact of distance on deposit rates (Bouckaert and Degryse 1995). Vesala (2000) for example shows that loan mark-ups were decreasing substantially in recent years in Finland, in lock step with the rapid development of internet and mobile banking in that country. On the other hand, Corvoisier and Gropp (2001) find only a small increase in contestability in European loan markets in recent years despite technological advances in many countries and despite an increase in contestability in deposit markets.

A paper by Hauswald and Marquez (2003) offers an explanation for these differential findings, providing yet another take on how technology need not lead to more exchange of information and competition. In their model better access to information by banks leads to more competition and lower loan rates, but the improved ability by banks to process information actually leads to higher loan rates and higher bank profits as banks are better able to 'carve out a niche' and generate informational rents.

3.3. The Impact of Technology on Spatial Rationing

The impact of technology on spatial rationing is equally unclear. Technological developments may increase competition from both capital markets and rival banks, as individual investors and rival banks can more cheaply obtain and process information. Increased capital market competition pushes the natural habitat of bank financing towards more opaque firms (Berger and Udell 1993; Greenbaum and Emmons

1998; Mannonen 2001). However, increased capital market competition also leads for example to changes in bank orientation away from relationship banking towards more transactional banking and more bank industry specialization (Boot and Thakor 2000).

In contrast, they argue that more interbank competition leads to more relationship lending. A bank offering a relationship loan augments a borrower's success probability. Relationship lending then allows extracting higher rents from the borrower. Fiercer interbank competition pushes banks into offering more relationship lending, as this activity permits banks to shield their rents better. Any reorientation in Boot and Thakor (2000) alters both financing habitats and informational needs of the banks and possibly affects the impact of technology on the availability of credit. Degryse and Ongena (2006b) and Elsas and Krahnen (1998) provide empirical evidence broadly supporting these hypotheses.

Controlling for firm and lender characteristics, Petersen and Rajan (2002) estimate a rather substantial increase in the (predicted) distance between lender and borrowing firms in the USA over the last decades, from around 11 miles in 1973 to around 18 miles in 1991 (their figure 3).[8] Petersen and Rajan (2002) also find that the modes of communication between lender and borrowers have become more impersonal over time. In contrast, firms in Belgium 'moved away' from their bank by only 0.02 miles per year in the period 1973 to 1997 (Degryse and Ongena 2005). Differences in technological development seem unlikely to be the only explanation for this divergent growth rate in lender–borrower distance in the USA and Europe, as the divergence started early in the 1970s and seems to have continued to this day.

3.4. The Impact of Technology on Branching and Servicing

The impact of technology on bank branching and servicing may be equally muted. Berger and DeYoung (2001) for example assert that technological developments only partially mitigate the negative effects of distance on efficiency. But then remember that the effects were relatively mild to start with. In addition, Cabral (2002) points out that the so-called 'multi-channel' route in banking has now established itself as the standard in many countries. Bank customers access bank services through ATMs, telephone, internet, and through personal contact in the bank branch itself!

Hence branch proximity continues to play a non-negligible role in determining bank choice, muting the impact technological developments may have. There is even reason to believe bankers and industry watchers for a while have underestimated the importance for customers of bank branch proximity. 'The hot news in banking:

---

[8] However Brevoort and Hannan 2006 provide evidence that this increase in distance occurred primarily at the high side of the distribution of lending distances and that if anything distance has become more of a factor for small banks and firms. On the other hand the evidence for deposit markets seems to run in the same direction as in Petersen and Rajan 2002. Heitfield and Prager 2004 for example document that the geographical scope of competition in US bank deposit markets is still smaller than statewide though not necessarily local any longer.

bricks and mortar. Customers prefer branches so banks are opening 'em like crazy,' headlined an article on 21 April 2003 in *Business Week* (Gogoi 2003) suggesting that debranching may have gone too far and that incumbent or *de novo* banks are correcting these recent mistakes. In addition, banks have incentives not to cut back on branches too much in order to keep potential entrants out of their incumbent markets.

To conclude, the impact of technological advances may be limited to abating somewhat the impact of distance on the pricing and availability of loans and market presence. There is still only limited evidence that advances in technology completely removed 'the tyranny of distance'; in particular in Europe 'distance still rules' as before.

3.5. Regulation and Borders

The impact of changes in regulation both in the USA and Europe has been substantial and profound. Nevertheless, retail loan markets in European countries remain surprisingly segmented, in contrast to wholesale capital markets in both Europe and the USA (Danthine, Giavazzi, and von Thadden 2001; Adam et al. 2002). In addition, the distance at which banks lend 'internationally' in European countries, and hence cross-border, has not at all increased over time in Europe in contrast to the USA where the distance at which banks lend internationally has steadily increased (Buch 2004a). Admittedly, one has to be careful attributing the same significance to cross-border activities in Europe and the USA.

4. STATE OF THE EUROPEAN UNION

4.1. Exogenous Economic Borders

What does this all mean for European banking? Most regulatory borders are, as already noted, removed and in principle the European banking market should be open for business for all banks chartered in the European Union and provided with the single passport of the European Second Banking Directive. In practice things are not that simple, as both exogenous and endogenous economic borders remain formidable barriers.

Take differences in legal systems and practices. Europe contains within its national boundaries all the (former) standard bearers from all major legal regimes, creating work for corporate lawyers but headaches and costs for bank management. Another example: the variation in banking supervisory practices within the European Union is as large as the variation in the World (Barth, Caprio, and Levine 2001). Needless to say, it is close to zero within the United States. Differences in corporate governance and the mutual structure of a few key banks in Europe create further barriers to integration.

And then we haven't touched yet upon the undeniably profound differences in politics, language, and culture within the European Union. Is there any other common market on earth where people from its various places and corners are for example so specialized in very different sports with assorted Olympic medals and world titles to show for it? Just think about the Norwegians in cross-country skiing, the Dutch in ice skating, and the Flemish in cyclo-crossing.[9]

4.2. Endogenous Economic Borders

Endogenous (informational) economic borders also remain quite high in Europe. As pointed out before, the impact of technology on informational borders is unclear a priori from a theoretical point of view. But Europe further faces specific problems when it comes to reducing informational asymmetries. Hardening of information for example could in principle alleviate some of the informational asymmetries. But hardening of information may also be more problematic in Europe than in the USA as it is not clear that all information that is already hardened is equally reliable across Europe. For example, La Porta et al. (1998) report a *Rating on Accounting Standards* that ranges between 36 and 83 for countries in Europe and between 24 and 76 for the rest of the world (the US score equals 71 while the average for all countries is 61). In addition a lot of local knowledge is often still needed to correctly interpret the 'hard facts', often involving translating 'hard information' into 'soft information'.

Technological developments may bring an outcome. But the introduction of new lending technology seems rather slow in most parts of Europe. Various factors such as the small distances, a lower GDP per capita, centralized decision making, a wait-and-see attitude, and lack of financing for innovation could reasonably be listed as suspects, but more research seems needed to identify the true culprits.

4.3. Distance Dies Another Day

To conclude, borders (and as a result also distance) 'may die another day' in Europe. We would argue that as most lending occurs over shorter physical distances in Europe, informational asymmetries increasing in distance might not be an important issue. Hence lending practices on the ground may be driven more by transportation technology than by changes in communication and information-processing technology.

However, information asymmetries increase dramatically when crossing a border. In this regard one could argue that the various exogenous and endogenous economic borders are mutually reinforcing and also that current technological and regulatory

[9] Riding (or running with) a road bike on a mountain bike track full of mud and puddles is called cyclo-crossing.

developments remain to a large extent impotent in dismantling these formidable barriers.

5. Policy Recommendations and Conclusions

Our review of the academic banking literature highlights that retail banking markets remain to a large extent local: pricing and availability of credit hinges on local market conditions. We pointed at a number of exogenous and endogenous market imperfections that persistently make retail banking markets 'less competitive' than in the absence of these imperfections. The most recent deregulatory steps and the recent technological developments will most likely not remove the remaining exogenous and endogenous economic borders. Retail 'relationship' banking in Europe in effect may have to remain 'optimally segregated' in the foreseeable future.

Nevertheless there are a number of caveats and matching policy recommendations, in particular in terms of strengthening competition policy that are straightforward, and that withstood the test of time in terms of having been recommended frequently (Barros et al. 2005)! That doesn't make them any less relevant.

To the extent that the rush towards building 'National Champions' was the result of a winner's curse problem, the trend may have partly run its course (Danthine, Giavazzi, and von Thadden 2001). It is therefore time that the National Champions can start naturally spilling across borders as well if and when it would be optimal for the market participants involved to so. We should note however that (1) cost savings are often impossible in cross-border mergers and (2) current cross-border mergers have produced negative combined cumulative abnormal returns. To allow cross-border M&As to occur, national supervisors need to treat domestic and cross-border merger candidacies fully equally. But again, it is not clear a priori if cross-border mergers have to and will occur even without the slightest obstacle in their way, as cost economies or revenue synergies may simply not be there.

Indeed, in a few high-profile cross-border M&A attempts that took place in Europe, national supervisors wielded their informal and/or formal mandate in the bank merger review process to derail or maim the planned cross-border bank merger. The role of banking supervisors in the merger review process is a natural and indisputable proper corollary to (1) its licensing mandate (capital requirements, 'fit and proper management', etc.); (2) its role in the bank default or restructuring process; and (3) its general engagement and responsibility for the maintenance of banking sector stability (Carletti and Hartmann 2003). However, it appears as if in a number of these recent instances national banking supervisors were mobilized or swayed by domestic political interests to block European cross-border bank mergers, fielding arguments of improper management or financial instability as only the flimsiest of excuses. Further pressure from the European executive branch and judicial system, and enhanced national competition and supervisory control independence (from domestic political pressures), should put a stop to such rather dubious practises (Carletti, Hartmann, and Ongena 2006).

In tandem with national bank supervisors, national and European competition authorities should pursue a proactive competition policy and cut large financial institutions seeking yet another domestic partner no slack. In addition, there may be a need for the foreseeable future for flexibility in allowing various organizational and corporate governance structures to coexist. The recently implemented European Company Statute should improve the situation on the ground in this regard. On the other hand, and admittedly somewhat contradictorily, questions may have to be raised about the further fostering (allowing) of mutual structures in banks. Finally, possibilities for active pan-European takeovers need ultimately to be created (not only in banking obviously), such that the best combinations of banks can be determined by market participants and not by politicians.

It is not clear the current supervisory framework is ready to handle National Champions growing into pan-European banking behemoths. It may be fruitful to consider rapidly reinforcing the existing web of bilateral Memoranda of Understanding with multilateral Memoranda agreed upon in one or more rounds of negotiation between national supervisors. Multilateral work if successful may ultimately be more efficient in achieving the supervisory objectives. In addition, serious consideration may have to be given to the creation of a European Bank Supervisor to which supervision and authority pan-European banks can choose to subject themselves. The newly established Lamfalussy Committees in Banking constitute major steps forward on all of these accounts. In any case, more research on these vital issues seems also warranted.

REFERENCES

ADAM, K., JAPPELLI, T., MENICHINI, A., PADULA, M., and PAGANO, M. (2002), *Analyse, Compare, and Apply Alternative Indicators and Monitoring Methodologies to Measure the Evolution of Capital Market Integration in the European Union*, Salerno: Centre for Studies in Economics and Finance, mimeo.

AUSUBEL, L. M. (1991), 'The failure of competition in the credit card market', *American Economic Review*, 81, 50–76.

BAELE, L., FERRANDO, A., HORDAHL, P., KRYLOVA, E., and MONNET, C. (2004), 'Measuring european financial integration', *Oxford Review of Economic Policy*, 20, 509–30.

BARROS, P. P., BERGLOF, E., FULGHIERI, P., GUAL, J., MAYER, C., and VIVES, X. (2005), *Integration of European Banks: The Way Forward*, London: Centre for Economic Policy Research.

BARTH, J. R., CAPRIO, G., and LEVINE, R. (2001), *The Regulations and Supervision of Banks Around the World: A New Database*, Washington, DC: World Bank, Mimeo.

BEITEL, P., SCHIERECK, D., and WAHRENBURG, M. (2004), 'Explaining M&A success in European banks', *European Financial Management*, 10, 109–40.

BERGER, A. N. (2003), 'The economic effects of technological progress: evidence from the banking industry', *Journal of Money, Credit, and Banking*, 35, 141–76.

———— and DEYOUNG, R. (2001), 'The effects of geographic expansion on bank efficiency', *Journal of Financial Services Research*, 19, 163–84.

———— and UDELL, G. F. (1993), 'Securitization, risk and the liquidity problem in banking', in M. Klausner and L. J. White (eds.), *Structural Change in Banking*, New York: New York University Salomon Center.

———— DEMSETZ, R., and STRAHAN, P. (1999), 'The consolidation of the financial services industry: causes, consequences, and implications for the future', *Journal of Banking and Finance*, 23, 135–94.

———— DEYOUNG, R., GENAY, H., and UDELL, G. (2000), 'Globalization of financial institutions: Evidence from cross-border banking performance', *Brookings-Wharton Papers on Financial Services*, 3, 23–120.

———— SAUNDERS, A., SCALISE, J. M., and UDELL, G. F. (1998), 'The effects of bank mergers and acquisitions on small business lending', *Journal of Financial Economics*, 50, 187–230.

———— DAI, Q., ONGENA, S., and SMITH, D. C. (2003), 'To what extent will the banking industry be globalized? A study of bank nationality and reach in 20 European nations', *Journal of Banking and Finance*, 27, 383–415.

———— MILLER, N. M., PETERSEN, M. A., RAJAN, R. G., and STEIN, J. C. (2005), 'Does function follow organizational form? Evidence from the lending practices of large and small banks', *Journal of Financial Economics*, 76, 237–69.

BERGSTRÖM, R., ENGWALL, L., and WALLERSTEDT, E. (1994), 'Organizational foundations and closures in a regulated environment: swedish commercial banks 1831–1990', *Scandinavian Journal of Management*, 10, 29–48.

BESTER, H., and PETRAKIS, E. (1995), 'Price competition and advertising in oligopoly', *European Economic Review*, 39, 1075–88.

BHARATH, S., DAHIYA, S., SAUNDERS, A., and SRINIVASAN, A. (2006), 'So what do I get? The bank's view of lending relationships', *Journal of Financial Economics*, forthcoming.

BHATTACHARYA, S., and CHIESA, G. (1995), 'Proprietary information, financial intermediation, and research incentives', *Journal of Financial Intermediation*, 4, 328–57.

BIANCO, M., JAPPELLI, T., and PAGANO, M. (2003), 'Courts and banks: effects of judicial enforcement on credit markets', *Journal of Money, Credit, and Banking*, forthcoming.

BINKS, M. R., and ENNEW, C. T. (1997), 'The relationship between U.K. banks and their small business customers', *Small Business Economics*, 9, 167–78.

BONACCORSI DI PATTI, E., and GOBBI, G. (2005), 'Winners or losers? the effects of banking consolidation on corporate borrowers', *Journal of Finance*, forthcoming.

BOOT, A. W. A., and THAKOR, A. V. (2000), 'Can relationship banking survive competition?', *Journal of Finance*, 55, 679–713.

BOUCKAERT, J., and DEGRYSE, H. (1995), 'Phonebanking', *European Economic Review*, 39, 229–44.

———— ———— (2004), 'Softening competition by inducing switching in credit markets', *Journal of Industrial Economics*, 52, 27–52.

———— ———— (2006), 'Entry and strategic information display in credit markets', *Economic Journal*, forthcoming.

BREVOORT, K. P., and HANNAN, T. H. (2006), 'Commerical lending and distance: evidence from Community Reinvestment Act data', *Journal of Money, Credit and Banking*, forthcoming.

BROECKER, T. (1990), 'Credit-worthiness tests and interbank competition', *Econometrica*, 58, 429–52.

BUCH, C. M. (2002), 'Financial market integration in the US: lessons for Europe', *Comparative Economic Studies*, 44, 46–71.

—— (2004a), 'Distance and international banking', *Review of International Economics*, forthcoming.

—— (2004b), 'Information or regulation: what is driving the international activities of commercial banks?' *Journal of Money, Credit, and Banking*, forthcoming.

—— and DELONG, G. L. (2004), 'Cross-border bank mergers: what lures the rare animal?' *Journal of Banking and Finance*, 28, 2077–102.

—— and GOLDER, S. M. (2001), 'Foreign versus domestic banks in Germany and the US: a tale of two markets?', *Journal of Multinational Financial Management*, 11, 341–61.

CABRAL, L. M. B. (2002), 'Comment on Clemons, Hitt, Gu, Thatcher, and Weber', *Journal of Financial Services Research*, 22, 91–3.

CAMPA, J. M., and HERNANDO, I. (2004), 'Shareholder value creation in European M&As', *European Financial Management*, 10, 47–81.

CARLETTI, E. (2006), 'Competition and regulation in banking', in A. W. A. Boot and A. V. Thakor (eds.), *Handbook of Corporate Finance: Financial Intermediation and Banking*, London: North Holland.

—— and HARTMANN, P. (2003), 'Competition and stability: what's special about banking?', in P. Mizen (ed.), *Monetary History, Exchange Rates and Financial Markets: Essays in Honour of Charles Goodhart*, Cheltenham: Edward Elgar.

—— —— and ONGENA STEVEN (2006), *The Economic Impact of Financial Laws: The Case of Bank Merger Control*, Tilburg University, Mimeo.

CARLING, K., and LUNDBERG, S. (2005), 'Asymmetric information and distance: an empirical assessment of geographical credit rationing', *Journal of Economics and Business*, 57, 39–59.

CORVOISIER, S., and GROPP, R. (2001), *Contestability, Technology, and Banking*, Frankfurt: European Central Bank, Mimeo.

CRYSTAL, J. S., DAGES, B. G., and GOLDBERG, L. S. (2002), 'Has foreign bank entry led to sounder banks in Latin America?', *Current Issues in Economics and Finance*, 8, 1–6.

DANTHINE, J.-P., GIAVAZZI, F., and VON THADDEN, E.-L. (2001), 'European financial markets after EMU: a first assessement', in C. Wyplosz (ed.), *EMU: Its Impact on Europe and the World*, Oxford: Oxford University Press.

DEGRYSE, H., and ONGENA, S. (2003), *Distance, Lending Relationships, and Competition*, Discussion Paper CES 02–16 (r) & CentER 03–123, Tilburg, Center for Economic Studies—KU Leuven & Center—Tilburg University.

—— —— (2004), 'The impact of technology and regulation on the geographical scope of banking', *Oxford Review of Economic Policy*, 20, 571–90.

—— —— (2005), 'Distance, lending relationships, and competition', *Journal of Finance*, 60, 231–66.

—— —— (2006a), 'Competition and regulation in the banking sector: a review of the empirical evidence on the sources of bank rents', in A. W. A. Boot and A. V. Thakor (eds.), *Handbook of Corporate Finance: Financial Intermediation and Banking*, London: North Holland.

—— —— (2006b), *The Impact of Competition on Bank Orientation and Specialization*, Tilburg University, Mimeo.

—— LAEVEN, L., and ONGENA, S. (2006), *The Impact of Organizational Structure and Lending Technology on Banking Competition*, Tilburg University, Mimeo.

—— —— ONGENA, S., and PENAS, M. F. (2006a), *Between Lisbon and London: Are Innovation and Growth Hurt by the Integration of the European Financial Sector?*, Tilburg University, Mimeo.

_____ _____ _____ (2006b), *Between Lisbon and London: Financial Sector Consolidation in the Context of the Lisbon Agenda*, Working Paper/Policy Brief 05–33, Paris, AEI—Brookings Joint Center.

DE JUAN, R. (2003), 'The independent submarkets model: an application to the Spanish retail banking market', *International Journal of Industrial Organization*, 21, 1461–87.

DELL'ARICCIA, G. (2001), 'Asymmetric information and the market structure of the banking industry', *European Economic Review*, 45, 1957–80.

DELONG, G. L. (2001), 'Stockholder gains from focusing versus diversifying mergers', *Journal of Financial Economics*, 59, 221–52.

DERMINE, J. (2003), 'European banking: past, present, and future', in V. Gaspar, P. Hartmann, and O. Sleijpen (eds.), *The Transformation of the European Financial System*, Frankfurt: ECB.

DEYOUNG, R., and NOLLE, D. E. (1996), 'Foreign-owned banks in the United States: earning market share or buying it?', *Journal of Money, Credit, and Banking*, 28, 622–36.

EDELSTEIN, P., and MORGANN, D. (2006), 'Local or state? Evidence on bank market size using branch prices', *FRBNY Economic Policy Review*, forthcoming.

EGLI, D., ONGENA, S., and SMITH, D. C. (2006), 'On the sequencing of projects, reputation building, and relationship finance', *Finance Research Letters*, forthcoming.

ELLIEHAUSEN, G. E., and WOLKEN, J. D. (1990), *Banking Markets and the Use of Financial Services by Small and Medium-Sized Businesses*, Staff Studies 160, Washington, DC, Board of Governors of the Federal Reserve System.

ELSAS, R. (2005), 'Empirical determinants of relationship lending', *Journal of Financial Intermediation*, 14, 32–57.

_____ and KRAHNEN, J. P. (1998), 'Is relationship lending special? Evidence from credit-file data in Germany', *Journal of Banking and Finance*, 22, 1283–316.

FOCARELLI, D., and POZZOLO, A. F. (2001), 'The patterns of cross-border bank mergers and shareholdings in OECD countries', *Journal of Banking and Finance*, 25, 2305–37.

FREIXAS, X., and ROCHET, J. C. (1997), *Microeconomics of Banking*, Cambridge Mass.: MIT Press.

GEHRIG, T. (1998), 'Screening, cross-border banking, and the allocation of credit', *Research in Economics*, 52, 387–407.

_____ and STENBACKA, R. (2001), *Information Sharing in Banking: A Collusive Device*, Discussion Paper 2915, London, CEPR.

GOGOI, P. (2003), 'The hot news in banking: bricks and mortar', *BusinessWeek*, 51–2.

GOLDBERG, L. G., and SAUNDERS, A. (1981), 'The determinants of foreign banking activity in the United States', *Journal of Banking and Finance*, 5, 17–32.

GREENBAUM, S. I., and EMMONS, W. R. (1998), 'Twin information revolutions and the future of financial intermediation', in Y. Amihud and G. Miller (eds.), *Bank Mergers and Acquisitions*, New York: Kluwer.

GRINBLATT, M., and KELOHARJU, M. (2001), 'How distance, language, and culture influence stockholdings and trades', *Journal of Finance*, 56, 1053–73.

GROSSMAN, G., and SHAPIRO, C. (1984), 'Informative advertising with differentiated products', *Review of Economic Studies*, 51, 63–82.

GUISO, L., SAPIENZA, P., and ZINGALES, L. (2004), 'Does local financial development matter?', *Quarterly Journal of Economics*, forthcoming.

HARTMANN, P., MADDALONI, A., and MANGANELLI, S. (2003), 'The euro-area financial system: structure, integration, and policy initiatives', *Oxford Review of Economic Policy*, 19, 180–213.

HAUSWALD, R., and MARQUEZ, R. (2003), 'Information technology and financial services competition', *Review of Financial Studies*, 16, 921–48.

HAUSWALD, R., and MARQUEZ, R. (2006), 'Competition and strategic information acquisition in credit markets', *Review of Financial Studies*, forthcoming.

HEITFIELD, E. A., and PRAGER, R. A. (2004), 'The geographic scope of retail deposit markets', *Journal of Financial Services Research*, 25, 37–55.

HOTELLING, H. (1929), 'Stability in competition', *Economic Journal*, 39, 41–5.

JAPPELLI, T., and PAGANO, M. (2003), 'Public credit information: a European perspective', in M. J. Miller (ed.), *Credit Reporting Systems and the International Economy*, Cambridge, Mass.: MIT Press.

KIM, M., KLIGER, D., and VALE, B. (2003), 'Estimating switching costs: the case of banking', *Journal of Financial Intermediation*, 12, 25–56.

KINDLEBERGER, C. P. (1983), 'International banks as leaders or followers of international business', *Journal of Banking and Finance*, 7, 583–95.

KLEIN, M. (1971), 'A theory of the banking firm', *Journal of Money, Credit, and Banking*, 3, 205–18.

KLEMPERER, P. (1995), 'Competition when consumers have switching costs: an overview with applications to industrial organization, macroeconomics, and international trade', *Review of Economic Studies*, 62, 515–39.

LA PORTA, R., LÓPEZ-DE-SILANES, F., SHLEIFER, A., and VISHNY, R. W. (1998), 'Law and finance', *Journal of Political Economy*, 106, 1113–55.

LEDERER, P., and HURTER, A. P. (1986), 'Competition of firms: discriminatory pricing and location', *Econometrica*, 54, 623–40.

MANNONEN, P. (2001), *Advancing Information Technology and Financial Intermediation*, Discussion Paper 770, Helsinki, Research Institute of the Finnish Economy.

MAYER, C., SCHOORS, K., and YAFEH Y. (2004), 'Sources of funds and investment activities of venture capital funds: evidence from Germany, Israel, Japan and the United Kingdom', *Journal of Corporate Finance*, 10, forthcoming.

MONTI, M. (1972), 'Deposit, credit, and interest rate determination under alternative bank objectives', in G. P. Szego and K. Shell (eds.), *Mathematical Methods in Investment and Finance*, Amsterdam: North-Holland.

MYATT, D. P., SHIN, H. S., and WALLACE, C. (2002), 'The assessment: games and coordination', *Oxford Review of Economic Policy*, 18, 397–417.

PADILLA, A. J., and PAGANO, M. (1997), 'Endogenous communication among lenders and entrepreneurial incentives', *Review of Financial Studies*, 10, 205–36.

PETERSEN, M. A. (2002), *Information: Hard and Soft*, Chicago: Northwestern University, Mimeo.

_____ and RAJAN, R. G. (1995), 'The effect of credit market competition on lending relationships', *Quarterly Journal of Economics*, 110, 406–43.

_____ _____ (2002), 'Does distance still matter? The information revolution in small business lending', *Journal of Finance*, 57, 2533–70.

PINKSE, J., SLADE, M. E., and BRETT, C. (2002), 'Spatial price competition: a semiparametric approach', *Econometrica*, 70, 1111–53.

PORTES, R., and REY, H. (2004), 'The determinants of cross border equity flows', *Journal of International Economics*, forthcoming.

RAJAN, R. G. (1992), 'Insiders and outsiders: the choice between informed and arm's-length debt', *Journal of Finance*, 47, 1367–400.

ROSENGREN, E. (2003), 'Comment on J. Dermine "European banking: past, present, and future"', in V. Gaspar, P. Hartmann, and O. Sleijpen (eds.), *The Transformation of the European Financial System*, Frankfurt: ECB.

SALOP, S. (1979), 'Monopolistic competition with outside goods', *Bell Journal of Economics*, 10, 141–56.

SAPIENZA, P. (2002), 'The effects of banking mergers on loan contracts', *Journal of Finance*, 329–68.

SETH, R., NOLLE, D. E., and MOHANTY, S. K. (1998), 'Do banks follow their customers abroad?', *Financial Markets, Institutions, and Instruments*, 7, 1–25.

SHAFFER, S. (1998), 'The winner's curse in banking', *Journal of Financial Intermediation*, 7, 359–92.

SHARPE, S. A. (1990), 'Asymmetric information, bank lending and implicit contracts: a stylized model of customer relationships', *Journal of Finance*, 45, 1069–87.

STANLEY, T. O., ROGER, C., and McMANIS, B. (1993), 'The effects of foreign ownership of U.S. banks on the availability of loanable funds to small businesses', *Journal of Small Business Management*, 31, 51–66.

STEIN, J. (2002), 'Information production and capital allocation: decentralized versus hierarchical firms', *Journal of Finance*, 57, 1891–922.

SUSSMAN, O., and ZEIRA, J. (1995), *Banking and Development*, Discussion Paper 1127, London, CEPR.

TAKATS, E. (2004), *Banking Consolidation and Small Business Lending*, Working Paper 407, Frankfurt, European Central Bank.

TIROLE, J. (1988), *The Theory of Industrial Organization*, Boston: MIT Press.

VERCAMMEN, J. A. (1995), 'Credit bureau policy and sustainable reputation effects in credit markets', *Economica*, 62, 461–78.

VESALA, J. (2000), *Technological Transformation and Retail Banking Competition: Implications and Measurement*, Study E20, Helsinki: Bank of Finland.

VON THADDEN, E. L. (2004), 'Asymmetric information, bank lending, and implicit contracts: the winner's curse', *Finance Research Letters*, 1, 11–23.

WILHELM, W. J. (2001), 'The internet and financial market structure', *Oxford Review of Economic Policy*, 17, 235–47.

WRIGHTON, J. (2003), 'Why unity in Europe hasn't yet extended to the banking system', in Wnghton (ed.), *Wall Street Journal Europe*, Paris.

YOSHA, O. (1995), 'Information disclosure costs and the choice of financing source', *Journal of Financial Intermediation*, 4, 3–20.

CHAPTER 13

ASSET MANAGEMENT IN EUROPE

JULIAN FRANKS

COLIN MAYER

LUIS CORREIA DA SILVA

1. INTRODUCTION

THIS chapter assesses the appropriate response of regulators to the risks of the asset management business and the way in which regulation should be framed at the European level. Different forms of investor protection give rise to different costs and benefits, including their impact on entry and competition. A key result of this study is that:

- industry structures differ markedly across countries;
- there is a close relationship between industry structures and regulation in different countries; and
- attempts to harmonize regulation across countries must be sensitive to these institutional differences.

This is reproduced with small amendments from Franks, Mayer, and Da Silva 2003.

The chapter begins by setting out the goals of regulation in Section 2, followed by a description of the institutional setting in Section 3. Section 4 describes regulatory systems in the six European countries included in this study and the USA, and evaluates alternative responses to the risks of the asset management business. In Sections 5 and 6, financial requirements and other responses are discussed. Section 7 evaluates the costs and benefits of the alternative forms of investor protection, and Section 8 concludes the chapter.

The results in this chapter refer to a survey of thirty-nine asset managers in six European countries with total assets under management of approximately €2.3 trillion domestically (or over €5 trillion globally).

2. GOALS OF REGULATION

The goal of regulation for banks is clear; it is to provide stability to the financial system and to limit the risks of systemic failures (Bernanke 1983; Bernanke and Blinder 1992). However, systemic risks are of much less significance. Unlike commercial and investment banks, and brokers and dealers, asset management firms do not, for the most part, take large positions on their own account. They invest on behalf of others. This is consistent with the results of the questionnaire, which reports that the levels of own positions are low and that financial insolvency is ranked as one of the lowest risks that asset management firms face.

One caveat to this is the rise of guaranteed products over the last decade, particularly in continental Europe. Unless they are adequately hedged or provided by a third party such as a credit institution (as in the case of France), like own positions they expose firms to risks of financial failure. Guaranteed products are growing rapidly in significance and have not been fully tested in a bear market. Serious consideration needs to be given as to how investors should be protected in the future from failures to fulfil guarantees.

In the absence of systemic risks, regulation of asset managers is closer to that of professional firms than that of banks. For example, in the legal profession, some of the principal risks are fraud against client funds and professional negligence. These are similar to the risks in the asset management industry. The literature regarding the regulation of the professions points to an important trade-off, enhancing quality by restricting entry and competition (Mayer and Neven 1991; Shaked and Sutton 1980). In exactly the same way, an important issue arises as to how regulation of asset managers can improve the quality of service (i.e. investor protection) without having an undue effect on competition in the supply of services.

Inadequate or excessive investor protection can be costly. The costs of inadequate investor protection include the following:

- uninformed investors, fearing that they might be exploited, will be reluctant to invest, or will invest in other financial centres;
- shrinkage of the asset management business. 'Good' firms will be tainted with the failure of 'bad' firms and will withdraw from the market or migrate to other centres;
- small, uninformed investors will be particularly exposed, giving rise to large welfare losses;
- political opprobrium resulting from financial losses may give rise to expensive and inappropriate regulation.

The disadvantages of over-regulation are as follows:

- higher costs for firms and investors;
- altering the costs of entry and competition;
- loss of competitiveness of financial centres, leading to a migration of firms from over-regulated to better (or less) regulated markets.

The form and amount of regulation are therefore crucial in determining the success or otherwise of financial institutions and financial centres.

3. The Institutional Setting

The most striking feature of the structure of the asset management business is its diversity. Countries at similar stages of economic development have very different asset management businesses. This manifests itself in several different forms. The size of the business varies markedly across countries. At the beginning of this decade, assets under management by pension funds in the UK comprised more than half of all pension fund assets in the seven European countries, and assets under management by insurance companies comprised just under half of all insurance companies' assets. However, the pension fund business in the USA is more than five times that of the UK, and the insurance company business is more than twice that of the UK.

One reason for these disparities is that continental Europe has traditionally had less well-developed stock markets and therefore had less need for a substantial asset management business. That may well be changing as stock markets expand, but, at present, asset management remains a more substantial component of Anglo-American financial systems than of continental European ones.

A second aspect of this diversity is that the nature of the asset management business differs appreciably across countries. While the UK dominates the European pension fund and insurance asset management business, it is a smaller player in mutual funds. Differences in the size of pension-managed funds reflect the greater emphasis on funded pension schemes in the UK than in other European countries, where state pensions, pay-as-you-go, and in-house corporate pension schemes predominate. The distinction in asset management businesses is not simply an Anglo-American versus continental European one. There are significant variations within continental Europe. For example, insurance companies are dominant in Germany, while the amount of mutual funds and insurance company funds is similar in France. Also, mutual funds are now growing rapidly in many continental European countries (for example, in France, profiled funds, issued mostly by insurance companies, are sharply rising, and are one of the main components of the flows to the mutual funds market).

One implication is that both the business that is being regulated and the type of investor differ significantly across countries. In some countries, clients of asset management firms are predominantly large institutional investors, and in others, private clients. In some countries, most investments are through pooled funds—the questionnaire reports that this is a particular feature of France and Italy—and, in others, through mandates (for example in Germany, the Netherlands, and the UK). Regulation therefore has a potentially different impact on investor protection across countries because of differences in the nature as well as the size of asset management businesses.

Third, countries differ in the ownership as well as the activities of asset management firms. In the questionnaire, 87 per cent of respondents reported that they were part of a larger group. Outside the UK and the USA, asset management firms are predominantly owned by banks and insurance companies, many of which may be classified as parts of large financial conglomerates. While this is the case in some of the largest asset management firms in the UK, there are also a large number of small independent firms, and in the USA, there are nearly six times as many asset management firms as in the UK. Concentration of ownership is therefore appreciably higher in continental Europe than in the UK and the USA. Furthermore, there are differences within continental Europe, where France has seen a rapidly increasing number of small, independent asset management firms.

The significance of this observation is that organization and ownership of firms crucially affect investors' exposure to loss. Firms that are part of large groups have more financial resources upon which to draw than independent firms, and may have more incentive than independent firms to provide protection to investors in the event of failure. If parent firms believe that either the intrinsic value of their asset management firms or the loss of their own reputations outweigh the cost of compensating investors, they will protect investors against loss. This was the case in Morgan Grenfell Asset Management where Deutsche Bank spent more than £210 million protecting investors against a loss in one of its fund management companies. The value of the earnings stream of that particular fund to Deutsche Bank was probably less than the cash injection to compensate investors. However, the impact of loss in reputation on profits in other parts of its funds management business and its non-asset management business may have exceeded the difference and justified the injection. Contrast that with the case of Barlow Clowes, a UK asset management firm that failed in the latter part of the 1980s. In that case, there was no rich parent with a reputation to bail out investors, and losses of £150 million were sustained.[1] Where asset management firms are large and part of larger groups, investor exposure to loss is appreciably reduced by the ability of one part of a group to bail out another.

However, this presumes that losses across different parts of groups are uncorrelated and insufficiently large to threaten the solvency of the entire group. In the case of the Barings Group, the failure of the bank and uncertainty about the scale of the losses prevented the company from raising sufficient funds to avoid the collapse of the entire group, including the fund management business. In this case, the company was acquired quickly and investors did not lose money; in other cases, however, the transfer might not have been effected so painlessly.

In sum, the design of regulation has to be sensitive to the fact that the size, the clients, the activities, and the ownership of asset management businesses differ appreciably across countries, and that this affects the desired pattern of regulation.

4. The Responses in Different Countries

- How have regulators responded to these very different institutional structures? Not surprisingly, the answer is that they have done so in diverse ways. There are seven main forms of regulation that are employed: financial resource requirements; conduct-of-business rules; separation of clients' assets requirements; disclosure rules; enforcement; auditing; and investor compensation schemes. Some of these differences are illustrated below in relation to France, Germany, the UK, and the USA.
- There are expenditure-based capital requirements in all three European countries. The broad rule is 25 per cent of annual expenditures for these countries, but adjustments to take into account exposure to position risk, foreign exchange risks, and separation of clients' monies, etc., are also present. Furthermore, in France, Germany, and the UK, there are initial capital requirements. In contrast, in the USA, there are no capital requirements at the federal level, but there may be at the state level.
- There are extensive conduct-of-business rules in the UK and self-regulatory (professional ethics) rules of conduct in France. Conduct-of-business rules are far fewer in the USA and include 'fair execution', which is also common in other countries.
- In France, the assets of clients and those of the asset management company must be kept strictly separate. In Germany, asset managers must keep securities at a credit institution or be regulated as credit institutions themselves. In the

---

[1] In this case, the British government ended up compensating investors.

UK, firms that hold clients' monies or assets are subject to more extensive capital requirements and conduct-of-business rules. In the USA, investment advisers that hold clients' securities are subject to more rigorous and random auditing.

- In the USA, there are extensive disclosure rules, auditing by private as well as public auditors, and enforcement through the courts.
- There have been significant calls on the compensation fund in the UK, amounting to more than £130 million over a five-year period. However, it is worth noting that asset management companies account for only a small proportion of total compensation paid. A limited compensation scheme for investment firms is in place in Germany. There are no (direct) compensation schemes in France or the USA.

In summary, France emphasizes conduct-of-business rules and custody requirements for collective investment schemes and mandates; Germany, capital requirements and separation of clients' assets; the UK, capital requirements, conduct-of-business rules, and a compensation scheme; and the USA, disclosure, auditing, and enforcement.

The various forms of regulation are complementary to the structures of asset management business in the four countries. In Germany, investors are in general institutional and asset management firms are part of large institutions. Investors are therefore for the most part relatively well informed and can be compensated in the event of failure by parent institutions wishing to preserve their own reputations. As a result, the cost of a mandatory compensation scheme is likely to be lower than in the UK, which has a higher number of small retail investors. The imposition of large capital requirements is consistent with the concentration of the German asset management business in large organizations.

In some countries, for example France, an asset management business has emerged over the last decade outside of the banking system and insurance companies, in particular in the form of mutual funds. Investor protection has therefore focused mainly on these institutions—for example, the imposition of depositary (trustee) requirements in France on the UCITS or mutual fund management business, but not on mandated portfolio management. The separation of clients' assets has, however, been imposed on UCITS as well as on individual mandates. The UK has a significant independent private client business but a relatively small mutual fund business.[2] Regulation has therefore sought to protect investments made through mandates as well as collective schemes. This has been done through a combination of capital requirements, conduct-of-business rules, incentives to employ separate custodians, and a compensation scheme.

The USA has the largest independent asset management business both in mandates and collective schemes. However, its approach to regulation is quite different from that of the UK. It does not rely on capital requirements, custody rules, or

---

[2] UK government initiatives to subsidize saving through schemes such as ISAs may be giving a large boost to sales of mutual funds.

Table 13.1. Institutional and regulatory forms of investor protection

	Institutional	Regulatory
France	High proportion of mutual funds	Conduct-of-business rules, capital requirements, and custodianship
Germany	Reputational capital of parent institution	Capital requirements and custodianship
UK	–	Capital requirements, conduct-of-business rules, compensation schemes, and custodianship
USA	–	Disclosure, auditing, and enforcement through the courts

compensation schemes; instead, it emphasizes disclosure, auditing, and enforcement. UK regulation relies heavily on public contracting—the screening and monitoring of firms according to pre-specified rules by public agencies—while the USA emphasizes private contracting—the provision of information to investors and their ability to enforce contracts through the courts. The difference in emphasis is clearly in part a consequence of a greater reliance on the judicial process—in particular, the ease with which private investors are able to litigate in the two countries.

Table 13.1 summarizes the institutional and regulatory forms of investor protection in the four countries. Investor protection should therefore be considered in the context of institutional arrangements in different countries, as well as in formal regulatory rules.

5. FINANCIAL RESOURCE REQUIREMENTS

The alternative responses described above are evaluated in this and the next section. This section begins, however, with financial resource requirements.

Capital requirements in asset management vary from substantial amounts in Germany to nothing in the USA, with the UK and France somewhere in between. What is the appropriate level of capital requirements for asset management firms?

Capital requirements are primarily considered in the context of banks. As noted in Section 1, while the main function of the regulation of banks is to promote financial stability, asset management firms are not for the most part subject to systemic risks, except potentially in regard to guaranteed products. Only eight of the thirty-nine firms that completed the questionnaire reported having capital at risk, and the levels of capital at risk averaged €47 million. This is fundamental to a consideration of the merits or otherwise of capital requirements.

In the case of asset management firms, capital provides clients with a cushion against losses sustained from operating failures of the business. Losses can be covered up to the value of the reserves of the business. The cost of providing the capital is therefore the value of the 'put option' that the capital gives investors to protect their investments from the effects of operating losses. The mean cost of capital reported by firms in the survey is 15.7 per cent, with a range from 7 per cent to 30 per cent. This large range possibly reflects variations in the values of the put options across firms.

The benefit of providing capital is that investors value this protection in terms of the price at which they are willing to transact with the asset management firm. In exactly the same way as capital of banks reduces the cost of raising deposits, so the capital of asset management firms raises the price at which clients will purchase asset management services. In determining the optimum amount of capital to employ, asset management firms will trade off the cost of the put option against the enhanced value of their business. Firms therefore voluntarily choose to hold capital for commercial reasons. The survey of asset management businesses reports that firms in general hold capital well in excess of regulatory requirements. The median ratio of capital held to requirements is 2.7 and the mean ratio is 5.7.

However, there is an important reason why the amount of capital that an institution chooses to hold might fall short of what is deemed to be 'socially desirable'— i.e. what a public agency might seek. The institution may fail to recoup all of the benefits from holding capital that investors derive. There are three factors that could cause a deviation between the optimal levels of capital that institutions privately choose to hold and what is collectively in the interest of investors and institutions as a whole.

The first is that some of the benefits from one firm's financial resources may accrue to other firms. There is, in the parlance of the economics literature, an 'externality'. The most pertinent example is the contagious failure of financial institutions—the instability of financial systems resulting from the failure of one institution spilling over to others. That is the fundamental justification for the imposition of capital requirements on banks in excess of what they might privately choose to hold. According to the literature, individually, banks do not take adequate account of the extent to which holding capital reduces the exposure of other institutions as well as their own, and some collective enforcement by a public agency is required (Santomero and Watson 1977). That is why it is of fundamental importance to appreciate that the regulation of asset management firms is not primarily concerned with systemic risks. The primary justification for the imposition of capital requirements on banks does not apply to asset management firms. However, there are other reasons why firms may not hold enough capital.

The second is that investors may not be well informed about risks to which they are exposed and therefore do not value them fully. There may be 'information asymmetries' in the parlance of the literature, leading to incorrect valuations. Regulators may therefore feel justified in imposing higher capital requirements on the grounds of the better information about investor risks that they possess.

The third is that asset managers have no interest in the value that clients attach to their services because they are intent on defrauding them. Levels of capital are not then chosen on the basis of 'fair' commercial criteria at all, and regulators may feel justified in imposing what they regard as fair levels.

While these last two justifications are superficially appealing, they both have serious pitfalls. First, they assume a considerable degree of information on the part of regulators, both in terms of the risks of businesses and more significantly in terms of how private levels of capital deviate from the optimal level. Even if they are fully informed about risks, regulators have little information about the costs of imposing capital requirements. As a result, regulators will find it difficult to set capital requirements across firms that are optimal from a social welfare perspective. Put more prosaically, they will find it increasingly difficult to justify levels of capital requirements that bite for some firms.

Second, there is often a confusion of symptoms with causes. Fraudulent firms may hold little capital, but firms that do not hold much capital are not necessarily fraudulent. Requiring potentially fraudulent firms to hold capital raises the same problems as requiring potential thieves to hold more money. Firms would be required to hold very substantial amounts in order for the capital to provide effective protection against fraud. But, then, this would create formidable barriers for new entrants. If capital requirements are set at modest levels then the entry of dishonest and incompetent firms is not avoided; if they are set at high levels then entry of the honest and competent is discouraged. If information asymmetries and fraud are the two main 'market failures' that afflict asset managers then capital requirements are very poor solutions. These failures require very different responses.

6. OTHER FORMS OF PROTECTION

The most serious failures reported in the survey of asset management firms were misdealing and breach of client guidelines. This was consistent with the frequency of failures, their impact when they occurred, and actual losses sustained by firms. In terms of reported complaints, the most significant items were IT systems failure, misdealing, and breach of client guidelines. Most losses were below €1 million, although there were occasional losses of, for example, €3 million for breach of client guidelines and €7 million for misdealing. The interviews indicated that losses from these operational failures could occasionally be as much as €20 million. The characteristics of operational risks are that they primarily relate to securities transactions and internal systems, and involve not infrequent modest losses.

Provided that investors are informed, they will be able to price these risks appropriately and will only be willing to purchase asset management services at an appropriately reduced price. However, if investors are ill informed about operational risks, they will not be properly priced. In this case, good firms will be unable to charge the premium over poor firms that they should be able to command. Information problems are therefore a primary source of market failure in asset management. The response in the USA has been to require extensive disclosure of information to investors and regulators.

In their 1989 study of the UK asset management business, Franks and Mayer record that fraud was the main threat to investors. Subsequent to their analysis, the Robert Maxwell pension case reinforced the potential exposure of investors to this risk. However, risks of fraud now appear to be appreciably lower. While there was some reference to fraud by respondents in the survey, it was by no means regarded as the primary risk. Incidence of losses was small, perceived frequency was low, and there were no reported complaints about fraud.

One of the significant changes since the 1989 study is the growth of custody. Separation of client funds and the growth of custodianship have contributed significantly to enhanced investor protection and, in particular, to the avoidance of fraud. In 1989, the use of separate custodians by investment management firms in the UK was rare. Possibly in response to the Maxwell affair or possibly as a consequence of the development of the custodian industry, non-group custodians (i.e. outside the group to which the asset manager belongs) now hold over 80 per cent of UK firms' assets under management.[3] The survey reports that the use of non-group custodians is in general lower on the Continent than in the UK. This may reflect the greater use of custodians within the same group of firms on the Continent.

As noted above, most operating losses are of modest scale. As a consequence, respondents to the questionnaire report that they are able to finance most operating losses from internal earnings. However, occasional large losses do occur. Morgan Grenfell Asset Management suffered losses amounting to more than £210 million. The case also illustrates the limitations of custodianship and trusteeship. While there was no theft of securities or monies, there were irregularities in the management of the funds that were not detected either internally or externally by the trustees. As a consequence, the regulator, IMRO, imposed fines of nearly £400,000 on the two trustees. It is unclear to what extent the trustees or custodians would have compensated investors for losses, had Deutsche Bank not injected £180 million to rescue the asset management firm. In particular, it is unclear whether investors would have been fully protected from loss by the existence of both a trustee and custodian, had Morgan Grenfell Asset Management not been part of a large group. Therefore, while custodianship and trusteeship can go a long way to mitigate the market failures of information asymmetries and fraud, they may not provide complete protection. Regulators may wish to improve custody contracts to clarify the degree of investor protection.

Further protection can come from insurance markets. In the sample, nineteen firms have indemnity insurance, fifteen employee fidelity and fraud insurance, and nine others insurance, including civil responsibility, real estate, and directors' and

---

[3] This is confirmed by a recent study (British Invisibles 2000), which reports a striking increase in custodianship in the UK, from 50% in 1997 to 71% in 1999.

officers' insurance. Firms regard insurance as particularly relevant to areas where substantial losses can occur as a consequence, for example, of fraud and failures in IT systems. However, some firms have expressed doubts about the promptness and reliability with which claims are met by insurers. Insurance markets, both private and mutual, are better developed in the USA than in Europe. This has led to greater standardization of contracts, a higher level of protection, and lower costs. The greater degree of disclosure of information and auditing of companies in the USA may have contributed to this result.

In the absence of well-functioning insurance markets, there is more emphasis on compensation funds in Europe, in particular in the UK. Over the recent past, the Investors Compensation Scheme in the UK has paid out more than €100 million. Since 1988, more than 12,000 people have received compensation and more than 700 firms have been declared in default. Of these totals, ten regulated firms were declared in default by the scheme. In the case of eight of these companies, compensation, amounting to almost £14 million, was paid to 317 investors.

Compensation schemes encourage (discourage) entry and competition where they are large (small) in relation to the regulatory burdens imposed on firms. In general they subsidize high-risk firms at the expense of low-risk firms or the taxpayer. They therefore, at least in part, make entry easier by mitigating the consequences of other forms of regulation, in particular capital requirements. However, like state aid, they distort competition between countries. The imposition of a common European compensation scheme might be thought to reduce this risk. In fact, differences in industry structures across countries mean that harmonized compensation schemes can be highly distorting. For example, a particular level of compensation will, on average, benefit the UK asset management industry, with its comparatively large number of small firms, relative to the more highly concentrated German industry.

In addition, compensation schemes encourage firms to hold too little capital. Since clients of asset management firms do not bear all the costs of the firms' failure where compensation schemes are in operation, they do not value the full benefits of capital—compensation funds create externalities. While this might be thought to justify the imposition of capital requirements, regulators cannot readily establish the extent to which compensation schemes influence firms' capital structure decisions. The relationship between required levels of capital and the scale of compensation schemes is therefore unknown, and, for the reasons mentioned above, will be dependent on the structure of a particular country's asset management business.

Instead, distortions to competition from compensation schemes can be avoided by having risk-based fee structures. Since such structures reflect firms' holdings of capital, they automatically induce firms to choose optimal capital structures. Again, the question is how can regulators determine fee structures? One approach might be to encourage private insurers to offer standard contracts equivalent to those of compensation schemes. Since systemic risks are not a substantial problem in asset management, the market failures that cause insurance contracts to fail in relation to bank deposits should not be present in asset management. The feasibility of having privately supplied standard compensation contracts is worth further investigation.

Table 13.2. Impact of responses on investor protection

Responses	Investor protection	Impact on entry/competition
Capital requirements	Poor, unless when set at very high levels	Significant entry barrier
Custody/trustees	Reduce risks of fraud and operational failures	Low if markets are competitive
Disclosure/auditing	Promote awareness of risks	Enhance competition and entry
Insurance	Protection against large losses	High for small firms
Compensation schemes	High if schemes are generous	Subsidize entry and competition

Table 13.2 summarizes the impacts of different responses on investor protection and entry/competition.

7. AN EVALUATION OF ALTERNATIVE FORMS OF INVESTOR PROTECTION

This chapter has emphasized the important interaction between institutional structure and forms of regulation. It has argued that investor protection comes both from specific institutional arrangements and from formal systems of regulation. In particular, in Section 4 of this chapter, four forms of investor protection were identified: two institutional and two regulatory in nature. The institutional forms were the reputational capital of firms that are parts of groups (of which asset management in Germany is the best example), and the protection that custodians and trustees provide in mutual funds (for example, in France). The regulatory forms were the promotion of private contracting through rules regarding information disclosure, auditing, and enforcement (as observed in the USA), and public contracting by regulatory bodies through capital requirements, conduct-of-business rules, and compensation funds (which is particularly significant in the UK). Clearly, these distinctions are highly stylized, and there are elements of all forms of institutions and regulation in all countries. However, they serve to illustrate the different institutional and regulatory responses. The key question that they raise is what is their comparative performance?

This chapter began by stating that the goals of regulation are to promote financial stability and to provide investor protection while avoiding adverse effects on competition—in particular, the entry of new firms. It has been argued that, for the most part, systemic risk is not relevant to asset management firms, but significant potential problems have been highlighted that may be created by the growth of guaranteed products offered by asset managers. The risk to asset managers associated

Table 13.3. Forms of investor protection

System	Degree of investor protection	Entry and product variety
Private contracting (USA)	Low—*caveat emptor*	High
Parent firms, mutual funds (France, Spain, and Germany)	Medium	Medium
Public contracting (UK)	Determined by compensation fund	Determined by capital requirements

with guaranteed products is mitigated to some extent in France, where guarantees are only offered by institutions external to the asset manager, such as credit institutions specially authorized by the regulator to fulfil this function. These activities are subsequently regulated. Leaving this aside, the different systems of regulation should be judged against two benchmarks: the degree to which they provide effective investor protection; and their impact on competition.

The private contracting system of the USA emphasizes the operation of markets through information disclosure and auditing. It encourages high levels of entry and competition, but relies on the legal system to enforce contracts through private as well as public litigation. It is therefore essentially a system of *caveat emptor*.

The public contracting system of the UK offers investors greater protection through a compensation scheme, but at the expense of limiting competition through the imposition of capital requirements and conduct-of-business rules. The scale of protection is therefore primarily determined by the size of the compensation scheme, and the effect on competition by the size of capital requirements and the nature of conduct-of-business rules. The results of the questionnaire confirm that the cost of capital varies greatly across firms, indicating that the costs of an extra unit of capital are potentially high for some companies.

The parent firm system of Germany places less reliance on public agencies; to that extent, it is less interventionist than the UK. However, it limits entry to firms that have access to substantial amounts of capital and are in general parts of large organizations. So long as asset management firms have deep pockets on which to draw, and can rely on the reputation of the parent firm to bail them out in the event of failure, they offer investors high degrees of protection.

Where investments occur largely through mutual funds, as in France and Spain, protection comes primarily from 'depositaires' or 'depositarios' respectively.

Where the parent firm system is not dominant, there is a greater potential for entry, but also greater possibility of contractual disagreements between asset managers and custodians and trustees. Investors may therefore be exposed to greater risks than under the parent firm system.

A summary of the forms of protection in different countries, the degree of investor protection they provide, and their effect on entry and competition is provided in Table 13.3.

8. SUMMARY

There are several implications of the results reported here.

- Attempts to harmonize regulatory rules across countries are inappropriate. Regulation and institutional arrangements are complementary. So long as the pronounced institutional differences that have been reported in this study persist, then so, too, should different forms of regulation.
- There is, in general, a trade-off between investor protection and competition. High levels of investor protection can be achieved through large compensation funds and high capital requirements, but at the expense of competition, product variety, and entry. Responses to the questionnaire suggest that the costs of higher capital requirements are large for some firms and could therefore have significant effects on competition.
- The market failures that occur in asset management are different from those that occur in banks. They arise from information asymmetries and fraud, not in general from systemic risks. They should be corrected directly by a combination of disclosure, auditing, enforcement, insurance, custody, and trustees, rather than indirectly through capital requirements.
- The development of insurance, markets, greater clarity of investor protection in custody arrangements, auditing, and enforcement through the courts are all key components of a move towards a more market-oriented system. The creation of an integrated financial market in Europe would benefit from such a development, but requires careful consideration of the way in which information, insurance, and legal structure can be strengthened.
- A move towards raising capital requirements would be counterproductive. It would discourage the necessary development of markets in information and insurance, as well as having a direct impact on competition and entry. High capital requirements may place the European asset management industry at a competitive disadvantage in relation to other countries, most notably the USA. Unless capital requirements are set at unrealistically high levels, they could also provide a false sense of security.

REFERENCES

BERNANKE, B. S. (1983), 'Non-monetary effects of the financial crisis in the propagation of the great depression'. *American Economic Review*, 73, 257–76.

——— and BLINDER, A. (1992), 'The federal funds rate and the channels of monetary transmission', *American Economic Review*, 82, 901–21.

BRITISH INVISIBLES (2000), 'Asset management', City Business Series 2000, Statistical Update.

FRANKS, J., and MAYER, C. (1989), *Risk, Regulation and Investor Protection*, Oxford: Oxford University Press.

_____ _____ and DA SILVA, L. C. (2003), *Asset Management and Investor Protection: An International Analysis*, Oxford: Oxford University Press.

MAYER, C., and NEVEN, D. (1991), 'European financial regulation: a framework for policy analysis', in A. Giovanni and C. Mayer (eds.), *European Financial Integration*, London: Centre for Economic Policy Research, 112–35.

SANTOMERO, A., and WATSON, R. (1977), 'Determining an optimal capital standard for the banking industry', *Journal of Finance*, 32, 1267–82.

SHAKED, A., and SUTTON, J. (1980), 'The self-regulating professions', *Review of Economic Studies*, 48, 217–34.

CHAPTER 14

PENSION FUNDS AND THE EVOLUTION OF FINANCIAL MARKETS IN THE EUROPEAN UNION

E. PHILIP DAVIS

1. INTRODUCTION

OWING to population ageing and the financing difficulties of public pension systems, as well as maturing of existing funded systems, there is a widespread trend in Europe towards funded pensions. Whereas funding of retirement income is most directly related to the development of pension funds, the broader growth of institutional investors such as mutual funds and life insurers may also link directly or indirectly to saving to meet income needs in retirement.

In this chapter, we show that pension fund growth in Europe is strong but unevenly distributed, whereas institutional investor growth in Europe is a more general trend. Meanwhile, extensive research suggests that ongoing and future pension fund growth will impact strongly on financial market development, notably in Eastern Europe, while in the euro zone there may be wider interactions of institutionalization and

EMU, moving structure and behaviour from a bank to a market paradigm. Finally, looking ahead, we show that some financial stability risks may arise from EU pension funds, although risks would be more severe where reform—and hence pension fund growth—are absent.

The chapter is structured as follows: in Section 2 we highlight long-term financial developments in Europe relating in particular to institutional investors while Section 3 looks in more detail at pension fund developments. Section 4 assesses the likely impact of pension funds on financial development in Europe while Section 5 considers the likely interaction of funding and EMU. Finally, Section 6 notes some financial stability risks that arise with ageing, notably if pension reform is not undertaken.

2. Long-term Financial Developments in Europe

A salient feature of European financial markets in recent years has been growth of institutional investors (pension funds, mutual funds, and life insurance companies) as a percentage of GDP (Table 14.1). Although part of the background to this has been sizeable growth in the overall financial sector (Table 14.2), there has also been a compositional shift towards intermediated claims (Table 14.3) and, within this aggregate, to institutional investors as opposed to banks (Table 14.4), leading to a long-term institutionalization of financial markets. Individuals have shifted away both from bank deposits and from direct holdings of securities into institutional investment. The large size of mutual funds and life insurance as well as pension funds are notable features of EU markets (Table 14.5). Comparing Table 14.6 to Table 14.5 shows the growth of pension funds in many EU-15 countries, and also shows that there are nascent pension funds in Eastern Europe (Table 14.6).

Table 14.1. Institutional investor claims as a proportion of GDP

	1970	1980	1990	2000	Change 1970–2000
France	0.07	0.12	0.52	1.20	1.13
Germany	0.12	0.20	0.33	0.84	0.71
Italy	0.07	0.06	0.15	0.76	0.69
United Kingdom	0.42	0.37	1.02	1.93	1.51
EU-4	0.17	0.19	0.51	1.18	1.01
EMU-3	0.09	0.13	0.33	0.93	0.84

Source: Byrne and Davis 2003; institutional investors are defined as pension funds, mutual funds, and insurance companies.

Table 14.2. Size indicator of financial development (total financial claims as a proportion of GDP)

	1970	1980	1990	2000	Change 1970–2000
France	4.4	4.8	6.9	11.4	7.0
Germany	2.9	3.6	4.7	7.9	5.0
Italy	3.4	3.9	4.3	7.1	3.7
United Kingdom	4.7	4.9	8.9	11.0	6.2
EU–4	3.9	4.2	6.5	8.9	5.0
EMU–3	3.7	4.1	6.0	8.7	5.0

Source: Byrne and Davis 2003; the indicator shows the sum of assets of the household, corporate, government, foreign, and financial sectors.

Table 14.3. Financial intermediation ratios (intermediated claims as a proportion of the total)

	1970	1980	1990	2000	Change 1970–2000
France	0.34	0.62	0.41	0.39	0.05
Germany	0.44	0.45	0.43	0.45	0.01
Italy	0.36	0.32	0.31	0.35	−0.01
United Kingdom	0.32	0.42	0.47	0.58	0.26
EU–4	0.36	0.38	0.40	0.48	0.12
EMU–3	0.37	0.40	0.40	0.46	0.09

Source: Byrne and Davis 2003; the indicator shows the ratio of claims held by banks and institutional investors to all claims as defined in Table 14.2.

Table 14.4. Bank and institutional intermediation ratios (proportion of intermediated claims held by banks and institutional investors)

		1970	1980	1990	2000	Change 1970–2000
France	Bank	0.94	0.68	0.82	0.65	−0.29
	Institutional	0.05	0.04	0.19	0.27	0.22
Germany	Bank	0.84	0.86	0.83	0.73	−0.12
	Institutional	0.10	0.12	0.17	0.23	0.14
Italy	Bank	0.98	0.98	0.95	0.64	−0.34
	Institutional	0.06	0.05	0.11	0.31	0.25
United Kingdom	Bank	0.58	0.64	0.55	0.44	−0.13
	Institutional	0.28	0.26	0.32	0.38	0.10
EU–4	Bank	0.84	0.79	0.79	0.62	−0.22
	Institutional	0.12	0.12	0.20	0.30	0.18
EMU–3	Bank	0.72	0.66	0.69	0.56	−0.15
	Institutional	0.30	0.30	0.36	0.36	0.07

Source: Byrne and Davis 2003.

Table 14.5. Relative size of EU institutional sectors, 2000

Percentage of GDP	Pension funds	Investment funds	Insurance
Belgium	6	30	42
Denmark	24	20	78
Germany	16	12	43
Greece	4	25	1
Spain	7	30	13
France	7	55	61
Ireland	51	144	45
Italy	3	39	21
Luxembourg	1	3,867	117
The Netherlands	111	25	65
Austria	12	40	24
Portugal	12	16	20
Finland	9	10	57
Sweden	57	34	90
UK	81	27	107
EU–15	27	292	52
EMU–11	20	358	42

Source: CEPS 2003.

Table 14.6. Total assets of pension funds in EU countries, 2004

	Total assets (US$ m)	As % of GDP
Belgium	14,325	4.1
Denmark	73,095	30.0
Germany	104,161	3.8
Greece	0	0.0
Spain	93,644	9.0
France (1)	123,255	7.0
Ireland	77,405	42.6
Italy	44,351	2.6
The Netherlands (1)	545,239	106.2
Austria	13,299	4.5
Portugal	18,868	11.2
Finland	84,271	45.3
Sweden	43,823	12.7
UK (1)	1,175,335	65.1
Czech Republic	3,884	3.6
Estonia	234	1.9
Hungary	6,859	6.8
Poland	17,021	7.0
Slovakia (1)	7,409	22.7
Slovenia	597	1.7

Source: OECD 2006: (1) 2003 data.

We can attribute the growth of pension funds and other institutional investors to a combination of demand- and supply-side factors (Davis and Steil 2001). It is important to stress the variety of such influences to avoid the impression that all such growth is due to ageing. Demand-side factors imply households have enhanced requirements for the types of financial functions that institutional investors are able to fulfil, while supply-side factors suggest that institutions have offered their services relatively more efficiently than banks and direct securities holdings, thus fulfilling the functions of the financial system more effectively.

In more detail, relevant advantages of institutional investors on the demand side indeed include demographic aspects (notably funding of pensions and population ageing) but also reflect growing wealth leading to a higher demand for long-term saving. Meanwhile, advantages on the supply side include the ease of diversification via institutional investors as well as the potential liquidity of claims, improved corporate control, benefits from deregulation, ability to take advantage of technological developments, and enhanced asset manager competition, as well as fiscal inducements and the difficulties of social security pensions.

3. TRENDS IN EU PENSION FUNDS

Long-term growth for European pension funds is in prospect for two main reasons. First, in many countries pension reforms are immature (i.e. lacking a long-term distribution between contributing workers and pensioners) so assets will tend to increase as maturity is reached. Second, there are the pressures for further reform of unsustainable social security pensions. The basis of this is twofold: first there is expected to be a sharp increase in the proportion of the population aged 65 and over in the EU (Table 14.7). This increase is largely a consequence of a decline in fertility to below replacement in most EU countries, although it also stems from an increase in average life expectancy and a low level of net migration. With an unchanged retirement age, such a demographic shift will naturally lead to an increase in the scope of transfers in the context of pay-as-you-go pension systems.

The problem is, however, aggravated since social security pension promises even for higher earners are extremely generous in a number of EU countries, with, for example, the net social security replacement rates (pension/earnings at retirement) being typically more than 50 per cent even for those on twice average earnings. The exceptions are the Netherlands, Ireland, and the UK—and Eastern Europe— which are also the countries where pension funding is most developed. Consequently, although some progress has been made, projections of social security pensions expenditure feature sharp and possibly unsustainable increases in such expenditure in a number of EU countries. As shown in Table 14.8, Dang, Antolin, and Oxley (2001) of the OECD demonstrate that with unchanged pension policies, the share of GDP

Table 14.7. Projections of elderly dependency ratio (persons over 65 as a proportion of 15–64-year-olds)

	2006	2020	2040
Belgium	26.8	32.8	46.9
Denmark	23.0	30.5	39.8
German	28.8	34.0	51.0
Greece	27.1	30.3	45.4
Spain	23.9	29.0	53.6
France	25.5	33.5	45.8
Ireland	15.8	20.6	35.5
Italy	30.7	38.9	65.6
Luxembourg	20.5	22.3	33.4
The Netherlands	21.0	29.8	45.3
Austria	25.1	31.5	53.0
Portugal	25.7	31.1	47.9
Finland	24.0	36.6	44.5
Sweden	26.6	34.5	41.9
UK	24.2	29.0	38.5
Czech Republic	20.2	31.7	45.5
Estonia	24.3	28.1	35.7
Hungary	22.2	29.9	40.7
Poland	18.2	26.1	38.2
Slovakia	16.6	24.1	39.2
Slovenia	22.3	31.2	49.5

Source: UN 2004.

accounted for by social security pension costs would be 10 per cent or more in 2040, in all EU member states except for Sweden, Ireland, and the UK as well as Hungary and Poland. These estimates may be a lower bound on future pension obligations, since the productivity estimates underlying the projections may be unduly high. A key issue in Europe is whether countries are willing to take sufficiently radical steps in major reform (Davis 2004b), which may be needed to avoid fiscal problems and financial instability when systems become unsustainable (Section 6). Against the background of such forthcoming population ageing, the Lisbon Agenda, and later EU pronouncements, have challenged member states to meet coming challenges in this field, with aims such as 'to carry out pension reforms to ensure adequate pensions, financial sustainability and modernity of the retirement systems in the long run'.

Beyond the general pressures outlined above, ongoing effects of EMU are likely to stimulate further pension reform and pension fund growth in the euro zone and candidates for EMU for a number of reasons (Davis 1999). Despite the weakening of the 'Stability Pact', there remain pressures to limit the fiscal deficits that may accompany unsustainable pay-as-you-go systems when population ageing takes place. Related to this are concerns of investors and rating agencies about long-term social security obligations in evaluating fiscal positions. EMU also facilitates comparison

Table 14.8. Projected pension costs

Percentage of GDP	2005	2020	2040	Memo: replacement rate[a]
Belgium	8.4	9.9	12.5	58–45
Denmark	6.7	9.0	9.6	45–43
Germany	11.4	12.6	16.6	93–37
Spain	9.2	10.1	16.1	94–63
France	12.2	15.0	15.8	67–51
Ireland	4.6	6.7	8.3	53–21
Italy	14.1	14.9	15.7	78–75
The Netherlands	5.3	7.3	10.5	76–31
Austria	9.7	11.5	13.3	70–70
Portugal	9.8	14.4	15.8	74–74
Finland	7.8	10.9	12.9	60–59
Sweden	9.4	10.7	11.3	63–50
UK	4.2	3.9	4.1	60–33
Czech Republic	8.2	10.4	13.3	n.a.
Hungary	4.7	4.8	6.0	n.a.
Poland	9.0	8.1	7.4	n.a.

[a] Public pension as a percentage of final salary for married man at equivalent annual final earnings of $20,000 and $50,000.

Source: Dang, Antolin, and Oxley 2001; Watson Wyatt 2000.

between costs of running businesses in different euro area countries, which leads corporations to put pressure on governments to avoid excessive tax burdens from social security contributions, with an implicit threat to shift production. Outside EMU, the adherence of the Eastern European countries has sharpened this threat.

Meanwhile, companies with book reserve pension obligations are seeking a reduction in book reserves to help improve their credit ratings in the growing euro area bond markets, and with banks operating under Basel II. Indeed in 2003, the rating agency Standard & Poor's controversially downgraded three German corporates— ThyssenKrupp, Deutsche Post, and Linde—after revising its rating methodology for corporate book reserves for pensions. They treated these reserves as foreign capital, i.e. debt similar to a bank loan. EMU also improves conditions for existing pension funds: they benefit, for example, from a better risk–return trade-off in pan-EMU markets than in narrow national markets, and an easing of the incidence of currency matching regulations that used to limit portfolio holdings to national assets and are now broadened to the euro zone. Furthermore there is enhanced competition among asset managers owing to the shift in focus from domestic to euro-wide investment, transparency in comparing costs, and the growth of passive management.

The impact of these trends on funding of pensions to date should not be exaggerated; as shown in Table 14.5, despite reforms in a number of countries, pension assets remain concentrated in countries such as the UK, Sweden, the Netherlands, and Denmark. Reforms that have taken place e.g. in Germany are modest owing to the small size of contributions and low take-up, and will not generate a rapid build-up of assets; elsewhere (e.g. France) little reform is on the horizon. On the other hand, as noted, the growth of life insurers and mutual funds in countries such as Germany and France may entail retirement saving as well as pension funds, either in formal systems or as precautionary saving. Looking ahead, the data in Table 14.5 also show that if countries currently dependent on pay-as-you-go developed pension fund and other institutional sectors comparable to the UK, institutional assets could grow by as much as 100 per cent of EU GDP.

As regards portfolios, reflecting deregulation and competition in asset management a long-term shift from bonds to equities is under way. Table 14.9 shows the current asset allocation of EU pension funds, which comparison with earlier data (as in Davis 1995) shows to be increasingly equity based. Indeed, ECB (2001) reports that the equity share of euro area pension funds doubled between 1995 and 1999. In our view, since funds have long-term real liabilities suited to matching with equities, this pattern is unlikely to be reversed more than temporarily by the recent bear market in shares (Davis 2003a). On the other hand, although, owing to EMU, currency matching is no longer a major constraint on cross-border investment in the euro zone, many countries retain restrictive portfolio regulations in terms of asset allocation (for example, insisting on large proportions of government bonds), which hamper performance; see Table 14.10. Countries such as the UK, the Netherlands, and Ireland are the exceptions, having the more appropriate 'prudent person rules' which allow investment flexibility and higher returns (Davis 2002a); these are also those that already have large pension fund sectors. The Pension Funds (IORP) Directive is mitigating some of these regulations' effects. Meanwhile, in many EU countries, investment is still dominated by oligopolistic domestic banks, which benefit from control of distribution, reputation, and banking relationships with clients, and which charge relatively high fees owing to a lack of competition; see Davis (2003b). A symptom of high costs is low take-up of low-cost passive asset management approaches such as portfolio indexation, which is only 5 per cent of assets in continental Europe compared to 30 per cent in the USA and 20 per cent in the UK (Fender 2003).

4. PENSION FUND GROWTH AND THE EVOLUTION OF EU FINANCIAL MARKETS

In assessing the likely impact of pension fund growth on EU financial markets, both at present and in the future, we consider it useful to summarize the main results of *global* cross-country studies of the impact of pension fund growth on capital markets and apply them to EU conditions. As background, Table 14.11 shows financial structure and development indicators for EU countries, while Table 14.12 shows the underlying structural determinants, notably the division between bank-based and market-based

Table 14.9. European pension fund asset allocation 2004

Countries	Cash	Government bonds	Corporate bonds	Loans	Equities	Real estate	Mutual funds	Other
Belgium	3.3	2.7	1.7	0.3	9.4	1.4	75.2	6.1
Denmark	0.3	24.7	29.0	7.2	19.8	2.1	16.9	0.0
Germany	2.6	2.5	26.6	28.1	32.2	3.8	0.0	4.2
Spain	4.9	20.3	36.4	0.0	17.5	0.2	7.5	13.3
Italy	5.9	34.8	0.0	n.a.	8.4	9.2	10.3	31.6
The Netherlands	2.2	25.5	13.8	5.3	44.6	5.0	0.0	3.5
Austria	1.2	71.6	n.a.	0.8	19.4	1.0	n.a.	6.1
Portugal	8.2	24.4	18.4	0.0	22.1	10.8	22.4	−6.4
Finland	0.9	50.1	0.0	8.5	30.4	9.6	0.0	0.5
Sweden	0.6	42.2	n.a.	34.0	6.2	n.a.	16.9	
UK	2.5	14.7	6.8	0.5	43.4	4.3	15.4	12.3
Czech Republic	9.6	51.9	31.1	0.0	5.5	0.3	0.3	1.3
Estonia	4.4	33.9	23.3	0.0	35.1	1.0	6.2	0.8
Hungary	1.3	74.9	2.0	n.a.	5.2	0.2	7.5	8.9
Poland	5.8	58.9	1.4	0.0	33.4	n.a.	0.0	0.5
Slovenia	13.3	46.3	32.4	n.a.	7.7	n.a.	0.3	n.a.

Source: OECD 2006; Swedish data for 2000 from EFRP 2001.

Table 14.10. Portfolio restrictions on EU and Swiss pension funds

Austria	> 35% in euro denominated bonds, >50% currency matching
Belgium	> 15% in government bonds
Denmark	> 80% currency matching
Finland	> 80% currency matching
France	> 50% EU government bonds
Germany	< 35% EU equities, <25% EU property, <6% non-EU equities, <6% non-EU bonds, <20% overall foreign assets, >70% currency matching
Hungary	Max. 30% foreign investment
Italy	< 20% liquid assets, <50% non-listed OECD securities, <5% non-OECD securities, >30% currency matching
Poland	Max. 5% foreign securities
Portugal	< 40% in foreign equity
Switzerland	< 50% real estate, <30% Swiss equities, <30% foreign loans, <25% foreign equities

Note: The table relates to the latest information available for those publications, in most cases 2002 or 2003. Note that regulations are subject to frequent change so the table may not reflect the current situation. Rules for Germany refer to insurance companies and *Pensionskassen*; new legislation has recently introduced the prudent man rule for a new type of pension fund.

Source: CEPS 2003; OECD 2004.

financial systems. Notable features include the lower size of banks and stock markets in Eastern Europe, and the variable size of stock markets in the EU-15 in line with the market–bank divide.

A first key impact of pension fund growth may be via saving. It is popularly suggested that pension reform can raise overall saving in an economy, thus promoting economic growth by permitting higher rates of investment as well as growing financial markets. This argument needs, however, to be developed carefully, because in a life-cycle model of *personal* saving and investment, households that are unconstrained will simply substitute one form of saving (e.g. pension funds) for another (such as bank deposits) with no net effect on household saving. This is particularly likely if saving via pension funds is voluntary. If saving is to be affected, there must be a market imperfection such as liquidity constraints on household borrowing that they might otherwise have undertaken to offset pension fund growth. Or alternatively, illiquidity of pension assets may mean that other household wealth may not be reduced one to one when pension assets increase, because households do not see such claims as a perfect substitute for liquid saving such as deposits. Note also that households may make inappropriate asset accumulation choices (i.e. inadequate saving) if they are poorly informed about their likely future pension (see Davis 2004a on this issue in the UK).

Reisen and Bailliu (1997), for example, used data from eleven countries over 1982–93 including both advanced countries and emerging market economies (EMEs) and found that the impact of pension reform on personal saving is indeed eight times larger for EMEs, which have more imperfect capital markets, than in advanced

Table 14.11. Financial structure within EU (as of 2000)

	Private credit to GDP	Concentration	Net interest margin	Stock market capitalization to GDP	Private bond market cap. to GDP	Public bond market cap. to GDP	Memo: pension assets/GDP
Austria	1.027	0.020	0.701	0.243	0.391	0.355	0.045
Belgium	0.728	0.013	0.828	1.341	0.376	0.948	0.041
Denmark	1.540	0.036	0.794	0.578	1.302	0.457	0.300
Finland	0.655	0.014	0.983	0.953	0.241	0.376	0.453
France	0.882	0.026	0.570	0.809	0.445	0.555	0.070
Germany	1.131	0.026	0.654	0.422	0.391	0.412	0.038
Greece	0.725	0.028	0.663	0.575	0.005	0.970	0.000
Ireland	1.234	0.009	0.520	0.544	0.222	0.214	0.426
Italy	0.851	0.024	0.295	0.423	0.480	0.859	0.026
Luxembourg	1.085	0.008	0.260	1.412	n.a.	n.a.	n.a.
The Netherlands	1.595	0.014	0.636	0.968	0.629	0.479	1.062
Portugal	1.471	0.035	0.907	0.394	0.307	0.525	0.112
Spain	1.155	0.031	0.644	0.846	0.344	0.435	0.090
Sweden	1.028	0.032	0.957	0.966	0.421	0.439	0.127
United Kingdom	1.476	0.026	0.493	1.230	0.161	0.278	0.651
EU–15	1.106	0.023	0.660	0.780	0.408	0.521	0.246
EMU–11	1.045	0.021	0.638	0.744	0.348	0.557	0.215
Czech Republic	0.307	0.021	0.629	0.227	0.069	0.504	0.036
Estonia	0.361	0.031	0.982	0.464	n.a.	n.a.	0.019
Hungary	0.437	0.054	0.595	0.229	0.047	0.432	0.068
Poland	0.274	0.036	0.434	0.224	0.000	0.336	0.070
Slovak Republic	0.304	0.028	0.738	0.088	0.000	0.272	0.227
Slovenia	0.426	0.029	0.700	0.262	n.a.	n.a.	0.017
EE–6	0.351	0.033	0.680	0.249	0.029	0.386	0.073

Note: Concentration is defined as the assets of the three largest banks as a share of assets of all commercial banks; the net interest margin is the accounting value of banks' net interest revenue as a share of their total interest bearing assets.

Source: World Bank 2006.

Table 14.12. Characteristics of EU financial systems

Country	Legal origin	Bank based	Market based	Anti-director rights
Austria	G	1	0	2
Belgium	F	1	0	0
Denmark	SC	0	1	2
Finland	SC	1	0	3
France	F	1	0	3
Germany	G	1	0	1
Greece	F	1	0	2
Hungary	G	1	0	3
Ireland	CL	1	0	4
Italy	F	1	0	1
The Netherlands	F	0	1	2
Portugal	F	1	0	3
Spain	F	1	0	4
Sweden	SC	0	1	3
Switzerland	G	0	1	2
United Kingdom	CL	0	1	5
United States	CL	0	1	5

Note: These are ongoing structural features of financial systems and do not relate to a particular year. Key: F: French origin, G: German origin, SC: Scandinavian origin, CL: Common law, B: Bank-based, M: Market-based financial systems.

Source: Impavido, Muslalem, and Tressel 2003.

countries. The impact will be increased if there is a simultaneous reduction in social security pensions, since these have been shown by many authors to reduce personal saving, given the implicit asset accumulation that they entail (Rossi and Visco 1995). Hence, pension fund growth is more likely to boost saving in the less developed Eastern European EU countries, which also tend to have compulsory systems, than in the voluntary systems of the financially liberalized EU-15.

A broader question is whether growth of pension funds raises *national* saving, given that governments need to finance their existing pension liabilities via debt or taxes. Lopez-Murphy and Musalem (2004) study fifty countries and find that national saving is boosted where pension funds are the result of a mandatory pension programme, but not when they are voluntary. Again, this suggests the benefit is limited to Eastern Europe. On the other hand Bosworth and Burtless (2003) found that OECD countries such as France and Sweden that seek to pre-fund social security obligations incur offsetting increases in government borrowing that again offset any difference in national saving.

It may be concluded that a rise in personal and a fortiori national saving is not a guaranteed outcome of a pension reform, especially in Western Europe. Despite this, a quantitative impact of development of pension funds on capital markets may still arise, as long as there are differences in behaviour between pension funds and the personal sector, and the personal sector does not 'offset' pension funds' portfolio choices.

Table 14.13. Correlations between pension assets/GDP and financial structure (fifty countries)

	Private credit by deposit money banks and other financial institutions to GDP	Concentration	Net interest margin	Stock market capitalization to GDP	Private bond market capitalization to GDP	Public bond market capitalization to GDP
EMEs	0.545	−0.007	−0.267	0.546	0.529	0.348
Advanced countries	0.504	0.121	0.000	0.727	0.287	−0.293
EU countries	0.547	0.212	−0.365	0.814	0.287	−0.185

Source: Davis 2005a.

Indeed, pension funds in most cases hold a greater proportion of equities and bonds than households (Byrne and Davis 2003). The implication is that even if saving and wealth do not increase, funding increases the supply of long-term funds to EU capital markets, with both quantity and price effects arising, as discussed further below. For example, there will be increases in the supply and reductions in the prices of equities, long-term corporate bonds, and securitized debt instruments. Such shifts should be beneficial to financial and economic development and stability, since at a basic level, long-term investment projects tend to be more profitable than short-term ones. More specifically, particularly for existing firms with small equity bases, there may be important competitive advantages to be reaped from equity issuance in terms of growth potential as well as reducing risks of financial distress in case of economic downturn notably in EMU—see Section 5. Furthermore, long-term debt finance is correlated with higher growth for manufacturing firms (Caprio and Demirgüç-Kunt 1998).

Supporting the idea of a shift to long-term assets as pension funds grow, Davis (2005a) observed a strong cross-sectional correlation between equity market capitalization and the size of the pension fund sector in fifty countries (Table 14.13); for EMEs including Eastern Europe it is 0.55 and for advanced countries 0.73, and 0.81 for the EU. EMEs show a strong correlation for corporate bonds with pension fund assets of 0.55, which is much higher than for advanced countries and the EU average (0.29). Consistent with the idea that government financing needs are the main reason for growth of government bond markets, the correlation for government bonds with pension funds is much smaller for EMEs (0.35) and negative for advanced countries and the EU.

Such simple correlations of course tell us nothing about causality, and hence a review of recent empirical work is also helpful. Catalan, Impavido, and Musalem (2000) sought to identify whether there is a Granger-causality relation between equity markets and contractual savings. They used two capital market indicators, stock market capitalization and stock market value traded across twenty-six countries, among which six are EMEs. They gave evidence that contractual saving institutions, e.g.

pension funds, Granger cause capital market development. The potential benefits of developing such contractual saving sectors are stronger for developing countries (e.g. Eastern Europe) with small markets than for developed countries (EU-15), according to their work. In terms of bond markets, in a further cross-country study, Impavido, Musalem, and Tressel (2003) found a positive relationship between contractual saving assets and bond market capitalization/GDP, with a 1 per cent increase in the former leading to 0.4 per cent rise in the latter. Consistent with Table 14.13, Hu (2005) shows in a panel error correction model that growth of pension funds stimulates private bond finance, notably in developing countries, both in the short and long run.

Turning to effects of pension fund growth on asset prices, a panel study focused on thirty-three emerging markets by Walker and Lefort (2002) found that pension funds decrease dividend yields and increase price-to-book ratio, implying a drop in the cost of equity capital. Underlying these results, pension funds may for example promote growth of primary equity markets as they are well diversified and require a smaller risk premium for taking on IPOs. Boersch-Supan and Brugiavini (2001) also argue that pension funds may enhance equity market liquidity, by generating 'thick market externalities' reducing the cost of financing further.

Concerning volatility of asset prices, in normal times pension funds, having a long time horizon, being willing to trade, having good information, and facing low transaction costs should tend to speed the adjustment of prices to fundamentals (Committee on the Global Financial System 2003). Besides reducing volatility, such market sensitivity generates an efficient allocation of funds and acts as a useful discipline on lax macroeconomic policies. Again, the liquidity that institutional activity generates may dampen volatility, as is suggested by lower average share price volatility in countries with large institutional sectors.[1] And evidence on average day-to-day asset price fluctuations shows no tendency for such volatility to increase (Davis and Steil 2001). Walker and Lefort (2002) find that pension fund growth reduces security price volatility for thirty-three emerging market economies. This result implies that the risk premium on investment should itself be lower, thus benefiting corporate investment again particularly in Eastern Europe. On the other hand results in Davis (2004b) suggest a positive link between equity price volatility and the share of equity held by pension funds and life insurance across advanced countries at a macro level. He notes that such a link in the G-7 and Anglo-Saxon countries might be due to the shift in sectoral holdings of equities rather than institutional holdings per se. But on the other hand Fender (2003) suggests that incentive structures for asset managers in advanced countries such as the EU-15 are making them less willing to undertake portfolio adjustments that could ensure market efficiency and dampen volatility.

Pension funds' activity also appear to promote more stable balance sheet structures, which may in turn offer further benefits in terms of the cost of funds as well as financial stability per se. As regards the corporate sector, looking at individual

---

[1] This is not to deny that markets may be subject to forms of excess volatility relative to fundamentals, but that the scope of average volatility does not seem to be linked to institutionalization. See also Section 6.

company data, Impavido, Musalem, and Tressel (2002b) found that in market-based economies, an increase in the proportion of shares in the contractual savings portfolio leads to a decline in firms' leverage (which reduces risk). In bank-based economies, in contrast, it is associated with an increase in firms' leverage (which raises risk) and debt maturity (which they argue reduces risk in a more than offsetting manner). Overall, they consider that firms are likely in both contexts to be more resilient to shocks and hence warrant a lower cost of capital. It can also be argued that banks may undertake less maturity transformation if pension funds supply the longest maturities, thus exposing themselves to a lesser risk of 'runs', while governments can issue long-term debt and are at a lesser risk of refinancing crises.

Apart from equity market growth, the banking industry is also positively linked to economic growth and financial development, see for example Barth, Caprio, and Nolle (2004). As noted by Impavido, Musalem, and Tressel (2002b), pension funds compete with banks for household saving and corporate financing, as well as via money markets as holders of money market instruments that compete with bank deposits. Such competition may increase the efficiency of the banking sector, benefiting the non-financial sector via lower spreads between the loan rate and the deposit rate. Consistent with this, we see in Table 14.13 that in EMEs such as Eastern Europe there is a marked negative correlation between pension fund assets and spreads of around −0.3, and the link is stronger in the EU average. Security underwriting costs may also decrease owing to economies of scale and enhanced competition, thus lowering the cost of access to capital markets. Banks may respond to the associated pressure on their profits partly by increasing their focus on non-interest income—including asset management income per se, mutual funds, and insurance—and reducing excess capacity by merger or branch closure Moreover, banks may respond to more intense competition by concentrating on their core comparative advantage—that is their superior ability to monitor firms and offer loans to borrowers where information is asymmetric such as small firms. This may entail a lower maturity; as bank liabilities are liquid, this would reduce the balance sheet mismatch of the banking sector.

Pension funds may also be complementary to banks. They may purchase long-term debt securities issued by banks, or could invest in long-term bank deposits (notably Eastern and southern Europe, Table 14.9). Banks are essential components of capital market activity per se (as providers of collateral, clearing, settlement, etc. services), and may also provide asset management and administrative services to pension funds per se. The development of contractual savings institutions may therefore increase the profitability of the banking system when regulation and supervision are effective.

Impavido, Musalem, and Tressel (2002a) test using individual bank data over 1991–2000 in thirty countries for effects of contractual saving institutions on banks and find positive effects on efficiency and stability. Consistent with Table 14.13, they find that in countries with larger institutional sectors, and allowing for standard determinants of bank performance, banks offer lower spreads and thus more efficient intermediation, while also having higher profits, which the authors suggest is due to lower credit risk. Contrary to the suggestion above, they offer longer-maturity loans when pension funds are large, suggesting that there is complementarity in long-term finance. Banks also have lower short-term liabilities on average, implying lower liquidity risks. Note that in Section 6 below we inject a note of caution to this analysis.

Overall shifts to long-term assets and reductions in their prices, as well as benefits to other sectors such as banking, may raise productive capital formation in the EU as pension funds grow, even if saving does not rise. Economically, efficient capital formation could in turn raise output and, 'endogenously', growth itself, independently of a change in saving (Holzmann 1997; Davis and Hu 2004). This adds to the economic benefit of increased labour supply and demand that should result from a pension reform that increases actuarial fairness and reduces corporate social security contributions (Disney 2004).

Besides the quantitative effects noted above, the development of pension funds is also likely to trigger qualitative developments in financial markets. These may further benefit economic growth in the EU by promoting better resource allocation. They are in general subject to positive externalities, as once instituted for or by pension funds, other investors may also benefit from them. One qualitative improvement is financial innovation, which in Eastern Europe may include equities per se, junior markets, corporate bonds, securitization, CDs, derivative markets, and indexed instruments. In the EU-15, defined benefit pension funds' need for hedging against shortfalls of assets against liabilities has led to the development of a number of recent financial innovations such as index futures. Pension fund investment in hedge funds has spurred the growth of the sector also.

Modernization of the infrastructure of securities markets as required by pension funds entails improved clearing and settlement on the one hand and more sensitive price information on the other, thus improving resource allocation. As a consequence it may help reduce the cost or increase the availability of capital market funds, and hence aid industrial development and growth per se as well as facilitating privatizations. In Eastern Europe, pension funds' influence may be seen in terms of development of the overall market infrastructure (such as trading and settlement systems), lower transactions costs, and enhancement of liquidity and transparency. In the EU-15, given their focus on liquidity and lesser emphasis on investor protection, pension funds offer benefits to wholesale equity markets as opposed to heavily regulated retail markets (Steil 1996). They are footloose in their trading, being willing to shift from domestic to efficient offshore markets (notably London), and thus make the business of trading 'contestable' rather than monopolistic. Pressure is hence put on domestic markets to reduce trading costs themselves. Pension funds also put pressure on cartels in bond issuance.

For Eastern Europe, as well as bank-dominated members of the EU-15, there are important indirect benefits in this context, as pension funds press for improvements in what Greenwald and Stiglitz (1990) call the 'architecture of allocative mechanisms', including better accounting, auditing, brokerage, and information disclosure. Modern banking and insurance supervision, new securities and corporate laws, junior equity markets, and credit rating agencies are also stimulated to develop. Pension funds bring increased specialization in the investment decision-making process which should aid the efficient allocation of resources. Here we have in mind economies of scale, which lead to development of better securities analysis and a research industry, and more generally lowering of costs and increased availability of information.

Development of equity markets and their dominance by pension funds would have implications not just for corporate finance but also for corporate governance, implying a greater degree of control by capital markets and pension funds (for a survey see Shleifer and Vishny 1997). Pension funds acting for future pensioners have scope to become important representatives of minority shareholders' interests, possibly electing independent board members as well as being able to access regulators and influence public opinion. As they are large investors, they are more likely to monitor management and exert control over non-profit-maximizing activities. They can exercise heightened control not just due to their size but also due to ability to undertake coordinated action with other institutions.

There is a growing literature on the impact of corporate governance initiatives on company performance, albeit mainly focusing on the effects on share prices per se. Positive results may be favourable to economic growth in the EU via efficiency gains. For example, Wahal (1996), in a sample of forty-three cases, found that efforts by institutional investors to promote organizational change via negotiation with management are associated with gains in share prices. Faccio and Lasfer (2000) show that the monitoring role of UK pension funds is concentrated among mature and low-performing firms and that in the long run, the firms in which pension funds have large stakes markedly improve their stock returns. On the negative side, Del Guercio and Hawkins (1999) found no evidence that activism had a significant effect on US stock returns over the three years following the relevant action.

All of these studies are based on micro evidence and hence only indirectly bear on the issue of whether pension funding of corporations affects wider financial development and growth in the EU. Davis (2002b) undertook macro work based on the share of equities held by pension funds and life insurers. Results were found which are consistent with a disciplining role of institutions in the Anglo-Saxon countries, particularly life insurers and pension funds. The signs on their share of equity in the total are consistent with the view that they exert restraint of fixed investment (which can otherwise be wasteful if there is inadequate shareholder monitoring), and lead to a boost to dividends and to total factor productivity. Furthermore, higher institutional holding is favourable to R&D (Davis 2004b).

5. PENSION FUNDS, FINANCIAL DEVELOPMENT, AND EMU

Going beyond the above, in assessing the relation between pension funding and EU market developments now and in the coming years, it is also important to consider pension fund and institutional investor growth in combination with EMU, as generating a cumulative effect together beyond that which each would have viewed alone. Davis (1999) showed that both have effects, inter alia, of increasing the role of securities markets, boosting cross-border investment, putting pressure on bank profitability, leading to increased competition among bourses to host trading activity, and helping to shift corporate governance to Anglo-Saxon modes (hostile takeovers and direct pressure on firms by institutional investors). Of course, identifying a precise EMU effect is difficult since the trends identified are under way in any case due to other factors, but many commentators acknowledge an additional EMU impact.

We illustrate the interaction by giving two examples—corporate governance and trading—in more detail. As noted, growth of institutional investors such as pension funds is predicted to lead to a shift from modes of corporate governance based on primacy of banks (as creditors and shareholders) to primacy of institutional share-holders. Increased competition among banks is weakening 'relationship banking' links and there is increased shareholder pressure on firms for adequate returns on equity in integrated EMU equity markets. Despite the pause in issuance following the bear market, in the long run firms will seek to issue more equity in EMU to finance restructuring and increase robustness as banking links weaken, which will reinforce shareholder leverage. Meanwhile, institutional trading is willing to relocate and favours markets offering liquidity for large transactions. Institutions are less concerned with investor protection than retail investors, while EMU leads to potential for concentration of trading in a smaller number of exchanges.

Drawing on experience since 1999, there is already ample evidence of intertwined pension fund and EMU effects on the structure and behaviour of EU capital markets. Concerning securities market growth, we see growth in corporate bond issuance, stimulated by institutional investor demand and the euro—and by relatively low government deficits—which are shown by Rajan and Zingales (2003) as partly attributable to EMU. Meanwhile, Baele et al. (2004) show that annual issuance of equity in the eurozone over 1998–2000 was 4 per cent of GDP compared with 2.5 per cent in Japan, the USA, and UK. There is also enhanced cross-border investment, as witnessed by the fact that domestic equity mandates for asset managers across Europe fell 60 per cent over 1999–2001, and domestic bond mandates by 92 per cent (Davis 2003b). Pension fund sectors are raising cross-border investment, particularly in the euro zone, where currency risk ceases to hold (ECB 2001). 'Sectoral investment' and indexation are becoming key strategies therein, reducing further the competitive advantage of domestic managers In 1999–2000 forty-one of top asset managers operated in five or more European countries; in 1996 it was only seventeen (Davis 2003b).

As regards banks' profits, there is a continuing squeeze on profitability of banks in many EU countries, with narrowing interest margins, linked partly to competition from institutional saving as noted above, but also cross-border competition as is facilitated by EMU, and the disintermediation of financing via bond markets (Bank of England 2003). Compared with their traditional activities focused on domestic corporate finance, universal banks such as Deutsche Bank have shifted towards an investment banking and asset management focus, and disposed of equity holdings, thus reinforcing the development of institutional investors and securities markets as well as shifting away from relationship banking. Discussion in the period up to 2005 of a 'credit crunch' in Germany highlighted the shift from relationship-based to transaction-based banking, since the traditional approach of German banks in periods of difficulty for their corporate clients would be provision rather than restriction of loan finance.

Trading activity is witnessing privatization, mergers, and prospective mergers of bourses, with growth of alternative trading systems, due to the 'footloose' nature of pension funds and other institutional investors' trading. EMU as predicted is facilitating such concentration of trading leading to mergers such as Euronext.

In terms of corporate governance, there has been a massive growth in merger activity in continental Europe since EMU (Mannesmann, Olivetti, and Soc Gen-Paribas being key examples) where pension funds are major investors. Complementing this has been a growth in the share of equity in pension funds' portfolios. There are also increased direct corporate governance pressures on continental firms (in terms of performance, shareholder rights, management structure). The foreign share of equities in some continental markets is quite high—in France foreigners held 20 per cent of equities in 2000, and in Germany 16 per cent. In this context, a strong effect on corporate governance is being exerted by US funds, whose foreign assets are over $800bn. CALPERS', the Californian public fund, in particular sets out corporate governance guidelines for international companies. Finally, book reserve funding of pensions is in decline as firms seek to shift to external funding, owing to pressure on credit ratings, and facilitated by German tax reform.

Another key aspect of EMU linked to financing behaviour of pension funds is the scope for cross-border investment to contribute to integration of national financial markets. Baele et al. (2004) show that there was a structural break in 1999 for the scope of home bias in euro area pension funds' foreign assets, which they attributed to EMU. Such equity market integration helps in turn to drive further beneficial consequences in terms of lower costs of equity capital, reflecting lower systematic risks, better risk-smoothing possibilities for households, and access by companies to a wider range of funding sources. But the authors note that equity market integration is far from complete.

6. Ageing, Pension Reform, and Financial Stability Risks

Ageing—which is most acute in Europe among OECD countries—will generate sharp changes in quantities and prices in EU financial markets As discussed in Davis (2002c, 2005b), a possible effect on financial stability can be traced for the 'general case' of ageing, for countries where pay-as-you-go remains dominant and where funding is introduced. However, these risks should not be exaggerated for the case of funding where the issue is rather for the authorities to learn to manage new kinds of risk. They remain most serious in the case where countries cling to unsustainable pay-as-you-go systems.

Looking first at the general case of ageing, it may be anticipated that EU saving will remain high in the next few years owing to the 'baby boom generation' entering peak saving age (McMorrow and Roeger 2003).[2] Then, like Japan in the 1980s and 1990s, and as already realized to some extent, the EU is facing an external surplus and loss of competitiveness with currency appreciation. In Japan this pattern generated excess liquidity and loose macroeconomic policies (with a structural surplus being mistaken for a cyclical one). In Europe, if monetary policy is inappropriate as in Japan, such a pattern could generate a financial bubble whose deflation entails financial instability. Later, as baby boomers retire, there could be a balance-of-payments deficit, with currency crises accompanying banking crises. However, more appropriate monetary policy should help circumvent these risks.

Risks in pay-as-you-go may be best traced in the extreme case of no reform. They will be attenuated to the extent that reform as outlined above takes place. One aspect is that the inevitable uncertainty about future pensions in unreformed systems will lead to heightened precautionary saving. Besides generating low economic growth, if directed to banks, this may lead to underpricing of risk in domestic credit or international interbank markets, again as in Japan. Life insurers could invest in high-yield bonds and property, and be vulnerable to credit cycles.

Turning to fiscal effects themselves, if there is tax finance when ageing occurs (i.e. a marked rise in contribution rates) there may be major economic difficulties generating credit losses and falls in asset prices, which are unlikely to be accurately anticipated. Underlying and accompanying these problems capital as well as labour could translocate from the country concerned. In the case of bond finance, (i.e. whereby governments run deficits when there is strain on pay-as-you-go systems), one may expect a sharp rise in long-term interest rates, loss of credit rating of the government, crowding out, and a recession. Hence major credit losses for lenders may arise (we note that most past fiscal crises as in Italy were with unliberalized banking systems and hence are not a sufficient prediction of likely consequences). In this context, the government's ability to recapitalize banks in difficulty would decline and ultimately there may be fiscal solvency crises, which could be contagious, 'snowball', and give rise to a temptation to monetize, or leave EMU, or a break-up of EMU driven by the solvent countries seeking to avoid spillovers. The pension issue is arguably the most intractable one facing the single currency.

Funding may present some novel risks, although they are much less serious than for pay-as-you-go and mainly require appropriate vigilance by the authorities. Indeed, a financial structure with a sizeable institutional sector should have strong stabilizing properties, including accuracy of asset pricing, liquidity, transparency, and marking

[2] McMorrow and Roeger 2003 suggest that the EU and Japan will run surpluses for some time, but expect the USA to run ongoing deficits, reflecting growth differentials and an assumption that the absorptive capacity of slow-ageing EMEs is limited. They also note that such a continued concentration of capital flows within the OECD is more likely to generate downward pressure on rates of return and a risk of bubbles.

to market ensuring early detection of solvency risk and distance from safety net reducing moral hazard. Furthermore, the corporate sector benefits from 'multiple avenues of intermediation' whereby bond markets can provide a substitute source of funds when banking crises occur (Greenspan 1999; Davis 2001). Nevertheless, some unfamiliar risks may arise in institutionalized and securitized financial systems about which regulators need to learn: One is extreme price volatility after a shift in expectations and asset allocations (such as the 1987 crash and ERM crisis of 1992). Another is a protracted collapse of market liquidity and issuance after similar portfolio shifts (as for Russia/LTCM in 1998). Both may involve a threat to EMEs, banks, and the non-financial sector, and possibly to institutions themselves given e.g. exposure to credit risk in real estate cycles.

Both pension fund growth and EMU will promote disintermediation of banks. Besides its beneficial effects on competition, disintermediation may also help to generate banking problems. The lessons of history from advanced countries suggest a need for vigilance, particularly if disintermediation coincides with deregulation and hence heightened competition within the banking sector that is not experienced in operating a competitive environment (Davis 2000). This is because disintermediation historically at times led to increased risk taking[3] via aggressive balance sheet expansion (e.g. by lending to property developers, see Davis and Zhu 2004, 2005) with risk premia which in retrospect proved to be inadequate.[4] An example was the Japanese banking crisis where banks, no longer able to compete with capital markets for top-rated firms' borrowing, sought to maintain balance sheet expansion by lending to high-risk property companies. Attention to shifts in the riskiness of banks' portfolios, focus on capital adequacy, and the issue of excess banking capacity are warranted by regulators in this context.

On the other hand, evidence that low competition (between banks and vis-à-vis pension funds) is best for financial stability is ambiguous. For example, Beck, Demirgüç-Kunt, and Levine (2003) with a dataset from seventy-nine countries give evidence that countries with higher banking concentration (itself not strongly related to pension funds, see Table 14.13) are less likely to incur banking crises. But they also acknowledge that concentration is often a poor measure of competition, and their measures of competition reduce the risk of instability. A stronger conclusion may be that of Allen and Gale (2004), who argue that the nature of the trade-off between competition and financial stability is more complicated than was conventionally perceived. For example, they use six theoretical models to identify the relationship between competition and financial stability. Some models, e.g. a contagion model, are consistent with the view of this trade-off relation, while others, e.g. a general equilibrium model, suggest the coexistence of perfect competition and financial instability to ensure optimal efficiency, thus denying the conventional view of trade-off.

---

[3] Keeley 1990, besides showing the effect of capital market competition on bank risk taking in the USA, also highlights the underlying impact of declining franchise values of banks and deposit insurance guarantees in encouraging risk taking.

[4] It may be added that rapid economic growth and at times inappropriate monetary policy also played a role in this typical late 1980s pattern.

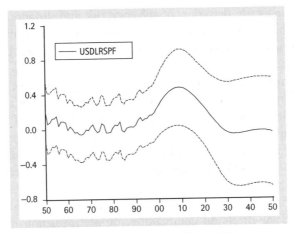

Fig. 14.1. Expected US asset prices applying
projected US demographics

Note: USDLRSPF is the logarithmic first difference of US annual share prices so 0.4 is a 40%
change. Dashed lines show 95% confidence interval

Source: Davis and Li 2003

There are also risks of asset price volatility arising from the process of asset accumulation and decumulation during ageing. Possible effects of institutional flows on equity market prices in the 1990s have already been discerned (Shiller 1999). Bubbles in debt and property as well as equities are feasible in the future. Finally there may be falls in asset prices during ageing, as shown in Figure 14.1 from Davis and Li (2003), which projects past relationships in the USA between equity prices and demographic patterns over 1950–99 into this century. After 2020 with ageing, equity prices are set to fall while bond yields rise. This may link to lower real returns on capital with a shrinking labour force; lower saving (as the peak saving cohort shrinks in the 'baby bust' generation) affecting real interest rates or risk premium; and a switch from equities to bonds.

Again, these risks should not be exaggerated, for a number of reasons, namely (1) the growing maturing and wealth of populations of emerging market economies (EMEs) such as China, India, and Brazil in the coming decades implies they could purchase shares sold in OECD countries; (2) productivity improvements as the population ages could offset declines in the return on equity owing to demand-side factors, although Davis (2005b) suggests that ageing *worsens* productivity; (3) monetary policy may be expected to respond to high real interest rates by an appropriate loosening, which will help attenuate the peaks; (4) investor demand would be likely to switch in the light of relative returns, for example to buy high-yield bonds in the later years; (5) the increase and subsequent decrease in flows may be balanced by rises and falls in equity issues, with little effect on prices and returns; and (6) since financial markets tend to be efficient and forward looking, and because demographic changes are slow moving and predictable, the market meltdown could be forestalled with rational expectations.

7. CONCLUSIONS

In conclusion, we have shown that pension fund growth in the EU is likely to lead to beneficial financial development with a wider range of instruments and a lower cost of capital. In the context of EMU pension funds growth is having a further major effect on euro area financial markets, moving them partly towards an Anglo-American system, as well as promoting integration. Upcoming financial risks linked to ageing underline the need to scale down pay-as-you-go, but be conscious of the risks to funding. It is underlined that reforms should hence focus on creating a diversified system. Political and demographic risks of pay-as-you-go may balance the market risks of funding.

REFERENCES

ALLEN, F., and GALE, D. (2004), 'Competition and financial stability', *Journal of Money, Credit and Banking*, 36, 453–80.

BAELE, L., FERRANDO, A., HOERDAHL, P., KRYLOVA, E., and MONNET, C. (2004), 'Measuring financial integration in the euro area', ECB Occasional Paper no. 14.

Bank of England (2003), 'Financial stability review, December 2003', London: Bank of England.

BARTH, J. R., CAPRIO, G., and NOLLE, D. E. (2004), 'Comparative international characteristics of banking', Working Paper WP2004–1, Washington, DC: Office of the Comptroller of the Currency.

BECK, T., DEMIRGÜÇ-KUNT, A., and LEVINE, R. (2003), 'Bank concentration and crises', Working Papers, Washington, DC: World Bank.

BOERSCH-SUPAN, A., and BRUGIAVINI, A. (2001), 'Savings, the policy debate in Europe', *Oxford Review of Economic Policy*, 17(1), 116–43.

BOSWORTH, B., and BURTLESS, G. (2003), 'Pension reform and saving', Brookings Institute, mimeo.

BYRNE, J., and DAVIS, E. P. (2003), *'Financial Structure'*, Cambridge: Cambridge University Press.

CAPRIO, G., and DEMIRGÜÇ-KUNT, A. (1998), 'The role of long term finance: theory and evidence', *World Bank Research Observer*, 13, 171–89.

CATALAN, M., IMPAVIDO, G., and MUSALEM, A. R. (2000), 'Contractual savings or stock market development: which leads?', Social Protection Discussion Paper Series no. 0020, World Bank.

CEPS (2003), 'Obstacles to pan-European asset management', Report of a Task Force, Centre for European Policy Studies, Brussels.

Committee on the Global Financial System (2003), 'Incentive structures in institutional asset management and their implications for financial markets', Reform of a CGFS Working Group, Bank for International Settlements.

DANG, T. T., ANTOLIN, P., and OXLEY, H. (2001), 'Fiscal implications of ageing: projections of age-related spending', Economics Department Working Paper no. 305, Paris: OECD.

DAVIS, E. P. (1995), *Pension Funds*, Oxford: Oxford University Press.

—— (1999), 'Institutionalisation and EMU', *International Finance*, 2, 33–61.

—— (2000), 'Financial stability in the euro area: some lessons from US financial history', LSE Financial Markets Group Special Paper no. 123.

DAVIS, E. P. (2001), 'Multiple avenues of intermediation, corporate finance and financial stability', Working Paper no. 01/115, Washington, DC: International Monetary Fund.

———(2002a), 'Prudent person rules or quantitative restrictions? The regulation of long term institutional investors' portfolios', *Journal of Pension Economics and Finance*, 1, 157–91.

———(2002b), 'Institutional investors, corporate governance, and the performance of the corporate sector', *Economic Systems*, 26, 203–29.

———(2002c), 'Ageing and financial stability', in H. Herrmann and A. Auerbach (eds.), *Ageing and Financial Markets*, Berlin: Springer Verlag–Deutsche Bundesbank.

———(2003a), 'Comparing bear markets, 1973 and 2000', *National Institute Economic Review*, 183, 78–89.

———(2003b), 'The European pension management industry', *Revue d'économie financière*, 68.

———(2004a), 'Is there a pensions crisis in the UK?', *Geneva Papers on Risk and Insurance*, 29.

———(2004b), 'Financial development, institutional investors and economic performance', in C. A. E. Goodhart (ed.), *Financial Development*, Basingstoke: Palgrave.

———(2005a), 'The role of pension funds as institutional investors in emerging markets', paper presented at the Korean Development Institute conference 'Population aging in Korea: economic impacts and policy issues', Seoul, March.

———(2005b), 'Demographic and pension-system challenges to monetary and financial stability', *Geneva Papers on Risk and Insurance*, forthcoming.

——— and HU, Y. (2004), 'Is there any link between pension fund assets and economic growth? A cross-country study', Economics and Finance Working Paper no. 04–23, Brunel University.

——— and LI, C. (2003), 'Demographics and asset prices', Brunel University Working Paper.

——— and STEIL, B. (2001), *Institutional Investors*, Cambridge, Mass.: MIT Press.

——— and ZHU, H. (2004), 'Bank lending and commercial property prices, some cross country evidence', BIS Working Paper no. 150.

——— ———(2005), 'Commercial property prices and bank performance', BIS Working Paper no. 180.

DEL GUERCIO, D., and HAWKINS, J. (1999), 'The motivation and impact of pension fund activism', *Journal of Financial Economics*, 52, 293–340.

DISNEY, R. (2004), 'Are contributions to public pension programmes a tax on employment?', *Economic Policy*, 19, 267–311.

ECB (2001), 'The euro equity markets', Study, 17 August, Frankfurt: European Central Bank.

EFRP (2001), 'European pension fund asset data', Brussels: European Federation for Retirement Provision.

FACCIO, M., and LASFER, M. A. (2000), 'Do occupational pension funds monitor companies in which they hold large stakes?', *Journal of Corporate Finance*, 6, 71–85.

FENDER, I. (2003), 'Institutional asset managers: industry trends, incentives and implications for market efficiency', *BIS Quarterly Review*, September, 75–86.

GREENSPAN, A. (1999), 'Do efficient financial markets mitigate financial crises?', speech to the Financial Markets Conference of the Federal Reserve Bank of Atlanta, 19 October.

GREENWALD, B. C., and STIGLITZ, J. E. (1990), 'Information, finance and markets, the architecture of allocative mechanisms', Working Paper no. 3652, National Bureau of Economic Research.

HARTMANN, P., MADDALONI, A., and MANGANELLI, S. (2003), 'The euro area financial system; structure, integration and policy initiatives', *Oxford Review of Economic Policy*, 19(1), 180–213.

HOLZMANN, R. (1997), 'On economic benefits and fiscal requirements of moving from unfunded to funded pensions', *European Economy Reports and Studies*, 4, 121–66.

Hu, Y. (2005), 'Pension reform, economic growth and financial development: an empirical study', Economics and Finance Working Paper no. 05-05, Brunel University.

Impavido, G., Musalem, A. R., and Tressel, T. (2002a), 'Contractual savings institutions and banks' stability and efficiency', World Bank Policy Research Working Paper 2948, January.

———— ———— ———— (2002b), 'Contractual savings, capital markets and firms' financing choices', World Bank Policy Research Working Paper 2948, January.

———— ———— ———— (2003), 'The impact of contractual savings institutions on securities markets', World Bank Policy Research Working Paper 2948, January.

Keeley, M. C. (1990), 'Deposit insurance, risk and market power in banking', American Economic Review, 80, 1138–99.

Lakonishok, J., Shleifer, A., and Vishny, R. (1991), 'Do institutional investors destabilize stock prices? Evidence on herding and feedback trading', Working Paper no. 3846, NBER.

Lopez-Murphy, P., and Musalem, A. R. (2004), 'Contractual savings and national saving', Policy Research Working Paper 3410, Washington, DC: World Bank.

McMorrow, K., and Roeger, W. (2003), 'Economic and financial market consequences of ageing populations', European Economy Economic Papers no. 182, Brussels: European Commission.

OECD (2004), 'Global pension statistics project; measuring the size of private pensions with an international perspective', OECD Financial Market Trends, 87, 229–39.

———— (2006), 'Global pension statistics project, webpage', Paris: OECD. www.oecd.org/dataoecd/56/15/36131092.xls.

Rajan, R., and Zingales, L. (2003), 'Banks and markets: the changing character of European finance', in V. Gaspar et al. (eds.), The Transformation of the European Financial System, Frankfurt: ECB.

Reisen, H., and Bailliu, J. (1997), 'Do funded pensions contribute to higher aggregate savings; a cross-country analysis, OECD Development Centre Technical Papers no. 130, Paris: OECD.

Rossi, N., and Visco, I. (1995), 'National savings and social security in Italy', Temi di Discussione del Servizio Studi, Rome: Banca d'Italia.

Shiller, R. (1999), Irrational Exuberance, Princeton: Princeton University Press.

Shleifer, A., and Vishny, R. W. (1997), 'A survey of corporate governance', Journal of Finance, 52, 737–83.

Steil, B. (ed.) (1996). The European Equity Markets, the State of the Union and an Agenda for the Millennium, London: Royal Institute of International Affairs.

United Nations (2004), Demographic database, New York: UN.

Wahal, S. (1996), 'Public pension fund activism and firm performance, Journal of Financial and Quantitative Analysis, 31, 1–23.

Walker, E., and Lefort, F. (2002), 'Pension reform and capital markets: are there any (hard) links?', Social Protection discussion paper no. 0201, January, World Bank.

Watson Wyatt (2000), 'Benefits report Europe, USA and Canada', Watson Wyatt Co.

World Bank (2006), 'A new database of financial structure and development (1960–2004)', Washington, DC: IBRD, http://siteresources.worldbank.org/INTRES/Resources/469232–1107449512766/FinStructure_60_04_final.xls.

Yermo, J. (2003), Survey of Investment Regulations of Pension Funds, Paris: OECD.

CHAPTER 15

INSURANCE AND REINSURANCE COMPANIES

RAY REES

1. INTRODUCTION

AN insurance company is an organization whose primary function is to offer contracts under which the buyer agrees to pay a fixed sum for certain, in exchange for an undertaking that compensation will be paid contingent upon occurrence of some specified, uncertain event that causes her financial loss.

It is already clear from this definition that there is a strong fiduciary element involved in an insurance contract, and this has important implications for the nature of an insurance company's activities. In particular, it implies that the insurance company will need to carry reserves to allow it to cover its obligations to meet loss claims, if the total of these should exceed the flow of premium income in any particular period.

The existence of reinsurance companies then stems in the first instance from the advantages to the primary insurer of economizing on these reserves by, in effect, buying insurance from the reinsurer. The primary insurer pays the reinsurer a premium and obtains compensation under specified circumstances, and this reduces its own need for reserves to meet its obligations.

There are in the economics literature two distinct views of the nature of an insurance company and of the role it plays in a market economy. In the following section I discuss these in some depth. Out of this discussion emerges the issue of the appropriate organizational form of an insurance company, and this will also be discussed in that section. It is impossible to discuss the activities of insurance companies with any degree of realism, without reference to the ways in which they are subject to regulation, and since the regulatory framework of insurance companies is currently under intense discussion, Section 3 surveys this topic. Turning to reinsurance companies, the most basic question is: why do they exist? It might be thought that a large, well-capitalized insurance company whose stockholders hold well-diversified portfolios would be unwilling to pay a premium to get rid of risk. An interesting issue in relation to reinsurance is that of its limits, especially in relation to natural or man-made disasters. Why does the market appear to be so limited in supplying catastrophe insurance, and what kinds of institutional changes are taking place which may go some way to expanding these limits? This is the subject of Section 4.

2. The Economic Functions of Insurance Companies

A purely descriptive view of an insurance company sees it as selling policies that offer cover against particular types of risks, investing the premium income as well as its own reserves in an asset portfolio, and processing claims, as they arise, under the terms of its contracts. Its main activities are then:

- Product design and marketing. It has to decide which types of risk will be covered and the extent and nature of loss coverage that will be offered; contracts, which define the insurance product, have to be written accordingly; and potential buyers have to be made aware of the product and the terms on which it is available.
- Risk assessment. The scale and time profile of the loss claims arising under its contracts have to be estimated, and since these are uncertain, this can only be done in terms of probability distributions or stochastic processes.
- Premium calculation. This is the pricing decision. The cost elements are the expected claims costs per contract as well as the costs of running the insurance business itself. The profit margin will reflect competitive conditions in the market being served as well as regulatory constraints (which also may influence product design).
- Determination of reserves. There will generally be a positive probability that aggregate loss claims will exceed premium income, and reserves have to be held against this eventuality. The decision on the scale of these reserves will be an important one, and it will again be influenced by regulatory conditions, as well as by the availability and cost of reinsurance.

- Asset management. The fact that premia are paid in advance of claims creates a pool of investible funds, which, together with reserves, have to be invested in an appropriate portfolio of assets. Moreover, life insurance products often bundle pure insurance with a considerable amount of (usually tax-advantaged) long-term saving, which creates a further flow of funds. Since real investment returns can never be certain, this adds a further element of risk to an insurance company's activities.
- Claims processing and settlement. Claims have to be assessed for consistency with the terms of the contract, accuracy of loss valuation, and possibility of fraud, and finally agreed payments made.

However, even though this description is already fairly abstract (it takes almost no account for example of the many types of insurance product that exist, nor of the different organizational forms of insurance companies), it does not go to the core of what economists regard as the fundamental roles that insurance companies play in an economy. These are, first, that they permit exchange of state-contingent incomes in a process of market risk allocation, and second, that they carry out a form of financial intermediation. I discuss these in turn.

2.1. Risk Allocation

A fundamental insight, which is of long standing in economics, is the idea that credit markets, such as markets for bonds or consumer loans, allow the exchange of incomes at different points in time. If I borrow, I exchange some of my future income, which is reduced by the amount of my debt repayment, for current income, the proceeds of the loan. If I lend, I exchange some of my current income for income in the future. The rate of interest is the price at which these exchanges are made, and the significance of credit markets is that they allow us to choose time profiles of expenditure (on consumption or investment) which differ from the time profile of the incomes we are endowed with.

Analogously, the role of the markets in insurance created by insurance companies is to allow us to exchange income across uncertain states of the world, and the insurance premium is the relevant price for such exchanges. For example, suppose that in the coming year I envisage two possible states of the world. In one, I am healthy and earn a particular income. In the other, I am sick, lose income, and have to pay heavy medical bills. By taking out insurance which compensates me for the loss of income and medical bills, I am effectively exchanging income in the state in which I am healthy for income in the state in which I am sick. In the first state, my income is reduced by the amount of the premium I pay, in the second, my income is increased by the amount of compensation less premium, i.e. the net compensation. In this way I am able to choose a distribution of income across states of the world—so-called state-contingent incomes—which differs from my endowed incomes. Put superficially, I am paying an insurance company to take over the risk I face. More fundamentally, I am taking income away from a state in which, at the margin, it is worth relatively less to me (because I have relatively more of it), and putting it into a state in which at the margin it is worth relatively more (because I have relatively less of it).

When one considers the large range of potential losses to which an individual is subject, one sees that in fact we face a large number of possible states of the world. The role of the various types of insurance made available by insurance companies is then to allow us to exchange income across these many possible states, and as a result make ourselves better off than if these exchange possibilities did not exist. We could define and measure the economic efficiency of insurance markets in terms of the extent to which they allow such exchanges, their 'completeness', and the prices at which they allow us to do so.

There is a further way in which the existence of insurance may create economic benefits, even though insurance in itself produces no tangible, physical output. This arises when some productive activity is associated with risk, and in the absence of insurance might not be undertaken. In fact insurance originated with maritime trading ventures, which were productive in realizing gains from trade between countries, but which required a large investment and were subject to large risks of failure due for example to shipwreck and piracy. The development of marine insurance allowed the traders more nearly to equalize the returns to their investment across the possible states of the world they faced, made them more prepared to make the investment, and therefore facilitated the growth of trade. In this sense, insurance can be thought of as a 'factor of production'.

The concept of risk sharing or, as it is more often termed, risk pooling is the central one in insurance. This is most clearly seen in the type of insurance company known as a mutual insurance company, or simply a 'mutual', in which the company is actually owned by the policy holders. In effect, a group of individuals facing a given type of risk get together and agree each to put some money into a pool, out of which compensation will be paid to whichever members of the group turn out to suffer a loss. Any surpluses, net of operating expenses and loss payments, are the property of the members of the group. If we look through the 'corporate veil', essentially the same function of risk pooling is carried out by the two other major forms of insurance company, the joint stock limited liability company, and the Lloyd's syndicate. Buyers of their insurance products are pooling their risks, putting up money via their premia and then compensating those of their number who are unlucky enough to suffer losses. The key differences are that in the joint stock company, net surpluses are the property of the shareholders (though there may be contractual arrangements or regulatory requirements under which policy holders receive a share in profits), and their liability for losses is restricted to the value of their shareholding, whereas in the Lloyd's syndicate, profits accrue to the members or 'names', who however are fully liable for losses to the extent of their total wealth. These three types of insurance company seem to be in more or less stable coexistence, which suggests that their differences may give them comparative advantages in different particular types of insurance business.

In the mutual, risk pooling takes place only among the policy holders, whereas in the other two forms, the shareholders or syndicate members, by their provision of reserves in the form of equity capital, are also sharing in the risk. This leads to the question: what is the significance of reserves to an insurance company and what determines their necessary extent? For this we need to consider the *technology* of insurance supply, which is the theory of probability. We do this in the context of the following very simple example.

Suppose there are one million individual insurance buyers. Each faces the same risk: one could lose £10,000 with probability 0.01 in any given year, or lose nothing with a probability of 0.99. The expected value of loss to each of them is therefore: $0.01 \times £10{,}000 = £100$. Assume further that these risks are independent, in the sense that the chance of occurrence of loss to any one individual is entirely independent of the chance of loss to any other.[1] Then an insurer can calculate the expected number of individuals suffering a loss within the next year as: $0.01 \times 1\,m = 10,000$. Thus the expected value of aggregate loss is: $£10,000 \times 10,000 = £100\,m$. If each individual pays an insurance premium of £100, then the insurer will have a total premium income of $£100 \times 1\,m = £100\,m$ and so will break even on average. It is a standard proposition that if each individual is risk averse,[2] she would be prepared to pay more than £100 as a premium in the insurance contract that would compensate her with £10,000 if the loss takes place. This leaves room for a loading on the premium to cover administrative costs plus profit, though let us abstract from these. Then with an insurance contract with premium £100 and full loss coverage the buyer would have the certain income of £9,900.

But this assumes that, in the event of a claim, the insurance company is in a position to honour its contract and meet all claims. Now although the expected number of claims is 10,000, this is only an average, and in fact the actual number of claims will almost certainly deviate from this. If the insurance company is lucky, the number of claims will actually be smaller and it will make an underwriting profit. On the other hand, if the number of claims turns out to be larger than 10,000, then the premium income alone will be insufficient to meet the aggregate obligations. The insurance company can only be *certain* that it will be in a position to meet all claims if it has reserves equal to the maximum possible aggregate loss, which is £10 billion. Now on the one hand, the probability of anything in the neighbourhood of 1 million. claims is extremely tiny, given the assumptions of the example, and on the other hand the costs of raising the equity capital sufficient to provide this level of reserves would be huge. Therefore the insurance company chooses a 'probability of ruin', or level of risk that total claims will exceed reserves, works out the reserve level implied by this probability, and sets its equity capital at that level. The costs of raising and

---

[1] This clearly rules out catastrophes such as earthquakes, hurricanes, disease epidemics, or terrorist attacks, where risks to the individuals are very strongly positively correlated, as well as milder forms of positive or negative correlation. In the latter case the following discussion goes through with not too much modification, while catastrophes are discussed in Section 4 below.

[2] In the sense that she would always prefer the certain sum of money X to any gamble involving sums greater and less than X, with an expected value equal to X.

remunerating this equity capital will of course be passed on to buyers in the premium (in a mutual they would have to be contributed by the members). For example, one can show that the probability of receiving more than 10,500 claims is as close to zero as even the most conservative actuary would wish (though it can still happen), and so a total reserve of £5 million, 5 per cent of premium income, would suffice. So the first gain from risk pooling is that an individual facing a loss would only have to pay slightly more than the expected value of that loss to be fully insured (up to an almost zero probability of default) against it.

A further gain from risk pooling arises as the number of insured individuals increases. It is not correct to say that the variance, or riskiness, of the *total* number of loss claims falls as this rises, it does not; it in fact increases. However, the Law of Large Numbers implies that the reserves *per individual insured* required to meet any given ruin probability fall as the size of the insured group rises, and in this sense there is an economy of scale in risk pooling.[3] In other words, the riskiness of the distribution of total losses increases less than proportionately to the number of insurance contracts.

The reserves just discussed are what are known as 'technical' or 'mathematical' reserves. They arise out of the statistical nature of the risks that are being insured. There are however other sources of risk facing the insurance company (whatever its institutional form), the two most important of which are:

- **Asset return risk.** As already mentioned, there can be no certainty concerning real investment returns, and so the possibility that the value of assets may be less than claims costs, thus causing insolvency, must be taken into account, and reserves adjusted accordingly. This of course depends on the composition of the asset portfolio and the correlation, if any, between aggregate claims costs and asset portfolio returns. Thus there can be a trade-off between the composition of the asset portfolio and its corresponding distribution of returns, on the one hand, and the level of reserves on the other.

- **Premium setting risk.**[4] In the above example we assumed that the loss probabilities facing the insured individuals were objectively known. This can be broadly true in some kinds of insurance. For example in life insurance, mortality tables give objective data on relative frequencies of death at various ages, which can be used to calculate loss probabilities and the corresponding premia. In other areas such data are not however available. Consider for example the cases where Lloyd's of London insurers write policies insuring a film star's legs. As a less frivolous example, consider the events following the attacks on the World Trade Center in New York on 11 September 2001. Insurance policies on aircraft throughout the world were suspended, as insurance companies were forced to reconsider their probability estimates of the risk of terrorist attack and calculate new premia, and it required government intervention in extending insurance

---

[3] This is not to say however that there is an economy of scale in insurance provision overall, since the average administrative costs may increase with scale, at least beyond some point.

[4] There seems to be no standard terminology in the literature for this type of risk; that used here is my own.

cover to avoid complete collapse of the air travel industry.[5] In many areas risk probabilities are at least to some extent a matter of judgement, and actuaries typically respond to this regrettable subjectivity by placing a loading on premia.

These types of risks provide further motives for holding insurance reserves. We shall return to this topic when we discuss the regulation of insurance companies in the next section. We now turn to the second interpretation of the fundamental economic role of insurance companies.

2.2. Financial Intermediation

From the point of view of theoretical finance economics, an insurance company is a levered financial intermediary with both debt and equity capital, where the debt capital takes the form of its insurance policies. Thus the company raises its debt capital by issuing insurance policies, with the premium income being the funds raised in this way. Its obligations to its debt holders are then those of meeting the loss claims under its outstanding policies. Its equity capital provides its reserves, as we have just seen. As a financial intermediary, it then transforms these financial obligations into the investments which make up its asset portfolio—purchases of stocks and bonds, mortgages, and other types of loan. Thus the insurance company shares with other financial intermediaries the role of channelling investible funds from households to corporations and government.

This view invites the comparison of insurance companies with banks, a comparison that is given added interest by the developing tendency for financial conglomerates to emerge that control both banks and insurance companies. The key difference obviously lies in the nature of their respective debt obligations, customer deposits as against insurance policies. Clearly the latter are more risky in terms of the obligations they create, in the sense that the variance of loss claims is higher than the variance of the distribution of withdrawals from bank accounts. Moreover, the distribution of the obligations created by insurance policies may have a longer and more uncertain time profile. For example, claims under property and liability insurance may take place long after the initial insurance contract has been signed, and may be affected by court decisions on liability that were not foreseen at the time of contracting.[6]

In one respect, banks may be thought to be in a less favourable position than insurance companies. Once they have been paid, premia cannot be withdrawn by the buyers of insurance, whereas banks face the possibility of bank runs following loss of confidence in their ability to meet demand for withdrawals, thus having a source of instability from which insurance companies are spared. However, given that insurance contracts are often renewed at fairly frequent intervals or can be cancelled (even at some cost to the policy holder) an insurance company could suffer from a

---

[5] This is incidentally another example of insurance as a factor of production.
[6] The impacts on insurers of court decisions on liability for health damage due to asbestos, and medical malpractice liability, are two frequently quoted examples.

loss of consumer confidence which led to a sudden sharp fall in its insurance sales, equivalent to a withdrawal of debt funding. Thus ability to meet claims plays the same role for an insurance company as ability to meet withdrawal demands does for a bank, albeit possibly with a time lag. The essential difference between the two lies in the macroeconomic consequences of a collapse of confidence. The liabilities of a bank are means of payment in the overall economy, and so a loss of confidence in banks can lead to serious consequences for economic activity as a whole, whereas loss of confidence in an insurance company is likely to be confined to that sector alone.[7]

2.3. Comparison of the Forms of Insurance Company Organization

In the economics literature, following Ronald Coase, the organizational form under which a set of economic activities is carried out is held to be determined by the minimization of transaction costs. These include not only administrative and contracting costs, but also costs arising out of the conflicting incentives that may be set up by a particular form of organization. According to this theory, if different forms of organization survive in a particular market, it must be because they serve different market segments with characteristics that match the comparative advantages of the corresponding organizational form. This approach provides a useful framework within which to consider the three main organizational forms of insurance companies: the joint stock company, the mutual, and the Lloyd's syndicate. For a fuller discussion, with also an overview of the empirical evidence, see Mayers and Smith (2000).

In the joint stock company there is a separation between policy holders, or providers of the debt capital, shareholder-owners, who provide the equity capital, and managers, who actually run the business. In a mutual, policy holders and shareholders are the same group of people, but they will typically employ managers to run the business. In a Lloyd's syndicate, the policy holders and suppliers of equity capital, who have unlimited liability, are distinct, but the latter will be involved in management, at least to a greater extent than shareholders in a joint stock company.[8]

The first dimension along which we might expect these different organizational forms to have different characterisitics is in relation to managerial discretion. In joint stock companies and mutuals, we would expect the agency problems arising out of the separation of ownership from managerial control to be greater than for the Lloyd's syndicate.[9] (though there is likely to be a concomitant gain in efficiency from

---

[7] Although again the role of insurance as a factor of production should be kept in mind. Thus the insolvency of a major company insuring building contractors could bring large parts of the construction industry to a halt, as happened in Australia quite recently.

[8] Though as in a partnership, there may well be 'names' who act as sleeping partners and take little if any direct interest in management of the syndicate.

[9] Though some court cases in the fairly recent past suggest that they are not entirely absent even in this case.

having more specialized management). These problems centre on the fact that the intrinsic interests of owner and manager diverge, and so in a world of uncertainty and asymmetric information, costs have to be incurred to align managerial decisions with owners' interests. One implication of this is that we would therefore expect managerial discretion to be lower in writing insurance in joint stock and mutual companies than in Lloyd's syndicates, suggesting an explanation of why the former would be more likely to dominate in forms of insurance where contracts can be standardized, the latter in those where underwriting involves far more subjective elements of probability judgement and risk taking.

In respect of managerial discretion, there are significant differences between the instruments available to joint stock and mutual companies for solution of the agency problems. The ownership shares in joint stock companies are tradeable on stock markets in the usual way; the ownership shares in a mutual are not. This means that joint stockholders have available capital market monitoring by stock analysts and institutional investors, and compensation packages involving instruments like stock options, to align more closely managerial and owner incentives, as well as the threat of takeover if the company underperforms. None of these is available to mutuals. This suggests that mutual managers will tend to be allowed less discretion than managers of joint stock companies, which implies a prediction about the types of insurance business in which joint stock companies may have a comparative advantage.

The second dimension along which these organizational forms differ significantly is in the relationship between policy holders and owners. In the case of mutuals there should be no incentive conflicts in this respect, while for joint stock companies and Lloyd's syndicates there are. Since insurance markets are typically competitive,[10] the core of the incentive conflict here is not so much that profit maximization may lead to high prices and output restrictions, but that solvency may be threatened by insufficient reserves or short-term opportunistic premium setting. To put this in financial terms, the equity holders have an incentive to increase debt, possibly beyond the levels that debt holders would find optimal. One can see policy holder support for regulation of insurance companies as a rational response to this incentive conflict, and I have much more to say about this in the next section.

3. REGULATION OF INSURANCE COMPANIES

In virtually every country in the world, insurance companies are at least to some extent regulated, in the sense that they are subject to specific rules and procedures over and above the standard framework of laws concerning contracts, bankruptcy, fraud, and corporate governance. In this section, I first of all map out the possible

[10]   At least potentially; but as we discuss below in the section on regulation, collusion may undermine competition in insurance markets, especially if reinforced by the regulatory framework.

dimensions along which regulatory frameworks may be constructed. Then I give two examples of countries at opposite ends of the spectrum of regulatory tightness, and comment on the implications for insurance companies in those countries. Finally I discuss recent and current developments in the approach to insurance company regulation in the European community countries.

3.1. Forms of Regulation

There are eight main areas in which a regulatory agency could seek to constrain and influence the decisions of an insurance company.

3.1.1. *Solvency*

As pointed out in the introduction, an insurance contract has a strong fiduciary element. A policy holder parts with her money in exchange for a promise of future payment under specified circumstances. A central concern of insurance regulation is therefore the solvency of the insurance company, that is, its ability to meet these claims liabilities in full as and when they arise. An insurance company is deemed insolvent when available assets are insufficient to meet outstanding claims.

The early history of insurance markets in most countries was characterized by rapid growth, premium competition, insolvencies, and a measure of fraud. Someone selling insurance makes a profit for sure if he collects the premium and absconds, while the buyer of insurance is scarcely better off if the seller turns out to be unable to meet claims because he made an erroneous or overoptimistic assessment of the loss probabilities.

Just as in the case of medical services, it was felt necessary to protect consumers from the consequences of fraud and incompetence by requiring practitioners to be licensed, and by subjecting would-be sellers to a test of their qualifications to be awarded this licence. In the case of insurance this usually takes the form of a check that the prospective insurer is a 'fit and proper person'—for example not a criminal or undischarged bankrupt—and has sufficient initial capital to meet solvency require-ments. Naturally, as also in the case of medical services, this kind of reasonable entry regulation can be used as an entry barrier to protect monopoly quasi-rents, or to pursue aims of economic policy such as protectionism.

Beyond this, insurance companies may be subject to rules which specify the rela-tionship between premium income, or some other indicator of likely claims liabilities, and the reserves available to meet them. A subject of continuing debate is the difficult problem of the appropriate design of these rules.

3.1.2. *Premium*

Normally, a non-competitive market may be subject to regulation that seeks to set *upper* limits on prices. Insurance markets, however, often are, or in the absence of regulation would be, competitive. Maximum prices in such cases therefore, if they are binding, are analogous to policies such as rent controls and can be discussed in similar terms, as in for example Jaffee and Russell (1998). More specific to insurance markets is the prevalence of *minimum* prices. Here the argument is essentially concerned with solvency. Unbridled price competition and/or incompetent or overoptimistic insurers, it is claimed, drive prices down to levels at which the future ability to meet claims is threatened. Minimum premium levels based on the regulator's calculation of expected loss levels are therefore put forward as an instrument of solvency regulation.

3.1.3. *Contract Conditions*

An insurance product is defined by the terms of the contract, in particular the risks covered and excluded, the information to be supplied by the buyer, and the way in which the characteristics of the buyer determine her risk category and therefore the nature of the cover and size of the premium. In the case of the large-scale insurance markets, contracts are standardized rather than negotiated individually between every buyer and seller. Regulation of contract conditions usually takes the form of *extreme standardization* of insurance contracts; that is, restrictions are placed on the differentiation in contract terms that insurers are allowed to offer. A further aspect of this is that insurers may not be allowed to refuse insurance to particular individuals, to reject certain risks, or to differentiate premia between different consumer classes with different risk characteristics. There may also be restrictions on the information they can require from policy holders—for example they may not be allowed to ask if the buyer has had an AIDS test or a genetic test of some sort, or to obtain the results of such a test.

3.1.4. *Profit*

Since insurance markets tend in the absence of regulation to be competitive, there is no reason in general for regulating their profits. Where, however, premium regulation is used to safeguard solvency of insurers ex ante, this often results in high profits ex post, and so regulators specify rules concerning the distribution of a proportion of profits back to policy holders, either as a direct cash rebate or, in life insurance, as an addition to the asset value of the policy. In the former case this means that the effective premium paid ex post is less than that ex ante, but by an uncertain amount, so that price is a random variable. The rebates at any one time will also differ across insurance companies, because of random differences in claims experience and asset returns, and this makes price comparisons across companies difficult. Where rebates are added to the asset value of the policy, this means that an apparently fixed interest savings instrument is in fact one with an uncertain, variable return, albeit with a given minimum.

3.1.5. *Service Quality*

Regulators' efforts in this respect tend to be minimal. There will usually be some sort of office or ombudsman, possibly financed by the insurance companies themselves rather than the regulator, which collects and processes complaints from policy holders about companies' performance, especially in respect of the promptness with which claims are settled. Aggregate statistics on these complaints may be published, but data on complaints about individual insurers are rarely made public. The complaints unit may perform an arbitrating function, but typically the policy holder's main redress must be through the legal system.

3.1.6. *Portfolio Composition*

As a further aspect of solvency regulation, constraints may be placed on the composition of an insurer's asset portfolio. Upper limits may be placed on the proportion of the portfolio that may be held in assets, such as ordinary shares, that are considered risky, and certain kinds of assets, such as financial derivatives, may be ruled out entirely. There will be further conditions to ensure a matching of assets with insurance claims liabilities, in terms for example of the currency in which they fall due (a crude way of dealing with exchange rate risk), and of the timing of the claims—the liquidity issue.

3.1.7. *Distribution*

There is not usually an attempt to regulate the basic composition of the distribution system as between independent brokers, direct selling, and use of subsidiaries and tied agents. There is evidence to suggest, however (see Finsinger and Schmid 1994), that the more tightly regulated the insurance markets, the greater the proportion of subsidiaries and tied agents. A possible explanation is that the less the variety of contract terms and more uniform the premia ex ante, the less need there is for brokers who offer a range of products. There may well be specification of maximum commission rates and selling expenses, and again this tends to be more marked where there is premium regulation, since the high profits induce more intensive selling activity.

It is instructive to compare the regulatory frameworks that were in force in, respectively, Germany and the UK up to the mid-1990s, since these lie at opposite ends of the spectrum of possible 'regulatory tightness'.

In Table 15.1 we summarize these very different regulatory regimes. To amplify this table briefly:

Germany

- **Solvency**. There were detailed and stringent requirements for solvency reserves over and above technical reserves to be held by insurers. Companies had to submit annual reports on their solvency position and the regulatory agency had

Table 15.1. Summary comparison of German and British regulation

	Germany	UK
Solvency	Detailed and stringent	Monitoring
Entry	Costly, entry deterrent	Monitoring, no entry deterrent
Contracts	Fully standardized, uniform	No regulation
Premiums	Regulated, cost-plus	No regulation
Profit	Compulsory redistribution	No regulation
Service	Complaint collection	No regulation
Portfolio	Restrictions on asset type	No regulation
Distribution	Ceiling on commissions	Disclosure regime

the right to require the insurer to adopt whatever policies it deemed necessary to correct what it regarded as an unsatisfactory position.

- **Entry.** Prospective entrants had to submit a detailed business plan specifying contract conditions, premia, expected costs and revenues, financial reserves and so on. There was a lengthy procedure of scrutiny and investigation, with frequent requests for further information. The process was regarded as costly and time consuming and seems to have worked as a deterrent to new entry.

- **Contract conditions.** In the main areas of life and property/liability insurance contract terms were fully standardized, along lines laid down by the regulator, so that in effect only one product was sold by all insurance companies. Risk categories were rather coarse and involved extensive pooling. In life insurance, there was a standard interest rate of 3 per cent as the fixed interest component of savings contracts. Companies were not allowed to refuse insurance.

- **Premia.** In life and auto insurance, as well as some other markets, there was a form of cost-plus price regulation. Premium calculation for a specific line of business was based on a standardized calculation of the expected loss, common for all insurance companies and specified by the regulatory agency. The firm could then add a loading reflecting its own costs. It was allowed a profit ex ante of 3 per cent on the final premium.

- **Profit.** The excess of the insurance company's ex post profit over 3 per cent of premium income was to be divided between policy holders and shareholders, with at least 90 per cent being paid out to policy holders. This 'surplus participation' was normally substantial and amounted in effect to a delayed, random rebate on premia paid, which, moreover, varied across companies.

- **Service quality.** The regulatory agency collected complaints concerning insurers' service and published aggregated statistics annually. It did not however publish information on individual insurers, and it is not known what action, if any, was taken in respect of insurers with high rates of complaint.

- **Portfolio composition**. There were specific restrictions on the types of assets that could be held, particularly limitations on equity holdings. This led to a high concentration of insurance company asset holding in government debt and other fixed interest assets, amounting to around 60 per cent of total assets.
- **Distribution**. There was no regulation of the form of distribution outlet. However the commissions that were paid to agents were restricted to be no more than 11 per cent of premia, and marketing expenditures in total were not allowed to exceed 30 per cent of premiums. Such restrictions of course provide evidence of high levels of selling activity.

UK

- **Solvency**. Companies were required to submit annual reports to the Department of Trade and Industry (DTI) to allow it to assess their solvency and determine whether specified solvency margins were satisfied. If so, no further action was taken. If not, the Secretary of State for Trade (head of the DTI) had quite far-reaching powers to acquire further information, require a business plan to rectify the situation, and, if need be, suspend the insurer's ability to write new business and receive new premia and place restrictions on the composition of the asset portfolio. In serious cases he was able to arrange for the insurance business to be taken over by a sound insurer.
- **Entry**. Insurers must be authorized by the relevant government department (DTI) before they can set up in business, and for this they have to submit a business plan, satisfy a capital requirement that depends on the type of business, and show that the people running the company are 'fit and proper persons'. There is no evidence to suggest that this process as such was particularly costly or acted as a barrier to entry.
- **Distribution**. This is the only respect in which the otherwise lightly regulated UK insurance markets were subject to tighter regulations than their counterparts in the rest of Europe. Under the Financial Services Act 1986, sellers of life insurance have to inform potential buyers as to whether they are recommending a particular policy out of a whole range of available products or whether they are exclusively selling the product of one company. Moreover, following the 'mis-selling scandal', in January 1995 a new 'disclosure regime' was introduced, under which the seller of an insurance contract must provide the potential buyer with information about the insurer's selling expenses, including the agent's commission. The aim clearly is to force provision of information to the buyer that will allow her to assess the incentive an apparently 'independent' agent may have in selling a particular policy. This is not necessary when the seller is an exclusive agent of a particular insurer, and so this kind of provision would not be so important in insurance markets, such as the German, where selling is mainly conducted by exclusive subsidiaries or agencies.

3.1.8. *Discussion*

The most often cited aspect of concern in relation to solvency regulation is the well-being of the policy holder, or, in the case of third-party liability insurance, the injured party. There is also a further concern, which is a version of the lemons problem. It is very difficult for an individual buyer of insurance to be able to assess the risk of insolvency of her insurance company. She would have to know the joint distribution of loss claims and the returns on its asset portfolio, now and in the future, in order to calculate the probability that claims will exceed assets. It is usually argued that a policy holder does not have this information. There is therefore intrinsic uncertainty concerning the product quality, that is, the insurer's insolvency risk. It is then held to be in the interests of all insurers that this uncertainty be kept to a minimum, otherwise the demand for insurance as a whole could be adversely affected. Since there is also a free-rider problem—it could pay any one insurer to have a high insolvency risk as long as buyers believe that it is sure to be solvent—regulation is seen as the means of ensuring that buyers' expectations of low insolvency risk are confirmed. In Germany, this was interpreted as requiring a regulatory regime that effectively ensured that no bankruptcies whatsoever took place. The question is whether the benefits of this match the costs involved.

The experience in the UK suggests that solvency regulation which allows the possibility of bankruptcy does not lead to collapse of the market under the weight of the lemons problem, for a number of reasons. Insurers have an incentive to signal their financial solidity, rating agencies exist to provide a market in evaluating solvency risks of insurers,[11] and a Guaranty Fund,[12] under which policy holders continue to have their claims met even if their insurer becomes insolvent, ensures that welfare losses due to the bankruptcy process are minimal.

If we accept, as policy makers and regulatory agencies appear to do, that some kind of solvency regulation is necessary, the question arises of whether it should be accompanied by regulation of premia, contract conditions and portfolio composition. The argument used by the German regulatory authorities was that this is also necessary in the interest of consumers to prevent ruinous price competition which then threatens solvency. This is an implausible argument. If solvency regulation is in force, this can be used to ensure that insurers have sufficient reserves to supplement premium income in meeting claims, and it is precisely the function of reserves, and not of artificially high prices, to fulfil this role. The cost-plus nature of price regulation gives no incentives for efficiency and indeed allows revenues to be absorbed

---

[11] It is noteworthy that in Germany the loosening of regulation has been accompanied by the growth of independent rating agencies.

[12] Guaranty funds are the equivalent in insurance markets to deposit insurance in banking. Typically, all insurers pay a small proportion of their premium income into a fund which then meets policy holders' claims in the event of an insolvency. As with deposit insurance, there is of course the possibility of moral hazard. Both theory and evidence lead banking economists to regard this as a serious problem. Empirically speaking, however, this does not appear to have been a problem in insurance, but this clearly is an area in which more work needs to be done.

as 'organizational slack' and 'hidden reserves', rather than being declared as profits and distributed to policy holders and shareholders.

Indeed, critics of the policies and practices of the German regulatory agency, in particular Finsinger (1983) and Eisen, Müller, and Zweifel (1993), have argued that the solvency argument was a pretext, and in fact the agency was essentially involved in running the insurance industry as a cartel. The empirical evidence from France and the UK supports the position that premium regulation cannot be said to be in the interests of consumers. A study by Finsinger, Hammond, and Tapp (1985) showed that premium rates in non-life insurance were significantly lower, and rates of return on the savings components of life insurance significantly higher in these countries than in Germany. The bankruptcy rate in France has been no higher than that in Germany (although the fact that many insurers in France were publicly owned should be taken into account here), while analysis of the causes of the bankruptcies in the UK and the USA, for example Bohn and Hall (1998), suggests that they were not due to premium competition as such, but rather to the underestimation of and inadequate provision for claims liabilities, which is a form of inefficient decision taking in the provision of insurance that is appropriately dealt with by bankruptcy.

Moreover, as we have already pointed out, policy holders need not lose coverage when their insurance company goes bankrupt. In the UK, Guaranty Funds, financed by a compulsory levy on all insurers, are used to meet claims on insolvent insurers, while portfolios of life policies are simply taken over by viable companies. It is doubtful then if the welfare losses generated by excessively high premia are compensated by benefits arising from improved solvency protection. Finally, a study by Rees and Kessner (1999), using efficiency frontier analysis, showed that the German insurance industry in the first half of the 1990s was significantly less efficient than the British, in the sense that a much higher proportion of firms in Germany had cost levels substantially above those of the most efficient firms in their sector. A function of bankruptcy in a market system is to eliminate inefficient firms, and so this is precisely the result one would expect from a regulatory system which kept firms in existence at all costs.

If premium regulation is not justified, then part of the argument for regulation of contract conditions also falls away. There are three reasons usually given for this aspect of regulation. One is that it facilitates premium regulation, since uniform prices require uniform products. The second is that it improves transparency and reduces buyers' costs, in terms of both search costs and the costs of making mistakes, since they are not faced with a 'bewildering variety' of products. Thirdly, it is often argued that on equity grounds risk categorization should be less finely differentiated than might be the case if left to the market, so that higher and lower risks are pooled and socially desirable cross-subsidization takes place.

The second of these arguments is also very weak. Although greater variety of insurance products may involve consumers in more shopping around, there is nothing peculiar to them as compared to other quite complex consumer products, such as automobiles and consumer durables, where the market is allowed to determine the degree of standardization (subject of course to constraints, such as safety regulations, which can be embodied in specific legislation).

There is more to discuss in relation to the third point. It is certainly legitimate for public policy to require that pooling of, and cross-subsidization between, certain risk classes should take place, provided this is clear, explicit, and can be publicly debated. A competitive insurance market may well generate more premium differentiation between risk classes than social policy would regard as equitable. Again, however, this is an argument for specific constraints created by explicit legislation rather than for absolute standardization of contracts.

3.2. The European Commission's Policy toward Insurance Market Regulation

In its attempt to extend the principles of the Common Market to the services sector, the European Commission (EC) had long sought to obtain agreement on a common framework for regulation of all insurance markets in the European Union (EU), but, failing to do so, in the early 1990s finally adopted a policy consisting principally of three elements.

- An insurer licensed to do business in any one EU country is able to do business in any other EU country without having to undergo a further licensing procedure.
- A common set of rules for financial reporting and for the solvency regulation of insurance companies throughout the EU (see Konrath 1996), to be administered by the regulatory authorities in each country, was introduced.
- The regulatory framework applying to the activities of an insurer is that of the country in which it is licensed—the *home* country—rather than that of a country in which it may do business—the *host* country.

In principle, any country was free to retain aspects of its regulatory system that are not directly affected by these principles, for example premium regulation, regulation of contract conditions, and so on. In practice, however, the strict regulatory regimes in countries like Germany and Italy were significantly relaxed, and, although there are still differences, there has been a substantial degree of convergence toward the looser regulatory systems of the UK and France. This is most probably the result of the competitive disadvantages insurance companies subject to tighter regulation were likely to face.

Currently at the centre of discussion is the programme Solvency II, which is proposed as a replacement for the set of principles for solvency regulation contained in Solvency I, which came into force in January 2004. Under Solvency I, insurance companies are subject to mechanical formulae relating their asset reserve requirements to their premium income, according to the type of insurance business they are in and amount of reinsurance. Failure to fulfil the reserve requirement triggers regulatory action to bring about a correction.

There is however considerable dissatisfaction with this mechanistic approach, and Solvency II is intended to replace it with an approach geared to an improved assessment of the insolvency risks of an individual insurance company before it has got into difficulties. The final set of proposals is not expected to be ready until 2008/9, but a good indication of the directions in which the discussion is tending can be gained from a paper produced by the London Working Group of the EU Insurance Supervisors Conference, known as the Sharma Report (2002).

The policy is seen as resting on three pillars. The first of these extends the approach of quantitative requirements for a company's reserves, related to the scale and nature of its liabilities. The second is more controversial, since it involves regulatory oversight of and possibly intervention in a company's internal processes and systems for risk assessment and risk management. The regulators could require a company to carry out 'stress testing' of its ability to maintain solvency against various scenarios relating to its loss claims and asset returns, or to put in place or improve its internal systems of risk analysis and control, and directly oversee its efforts in these respects. The third pillar provides for greater transparency by requiring more information, in a more standardized form, on the risks the company faces and the ways in which it is managing them. All this reflects the findings of the Sharma Report, which carried out an in-depth study of the reasons for the insolvency or 'near misses' of more than eighty insurance companies across the EU. The conclusion was that although there may have been adverse 'trigger events', such as a stock market fall or a natural disaster, that were the proximate causes of financial difficulties, the core problem in these companies was that they had inadequate systems in place to evaluate and manage the risks they actually faced, i.e. the problem is managerial failure.

A regulatory framework is usually the outcome of a process of negotiation among the interested parties involved, among whom are the companies to be regulated, the regulators, policy makers, and consumer and worker representatives. Some aspects of Solvency II, particularly its second pillar, are controversial, at least in part because of the technical difficulties involved in evaluating risk, but also because of the amount and depth of information companies will have to make available to regulators. The outside observer awaits with interest the outcome of the process.

4. REINSURANCE AND CATASTROPHES

In terms of the standard theory of capital markets, the existence of reinsurance, under which a primary insurance company insures part of its claims liabilities with a reinsurance company, could present something of a puzzle. Normally, either the reinsurer takes over a fixed proportion of the primary insurer's liabilities, or a ceiling is placed on the latter's liabilities and the reinsurer takes over all claims above this level. In capital market theory, the shareholders in a corporation hold well-diversified asset portfolios, which implies that they care only about systematic risk, the riskiness of returns to the overall market portfolio, and not about idiosyncratic risk, the variance of returns of the individual company. Therefore, they would regard reinsurance as simply reducing their shareholder value, since it is a costly way of transferring some risk associated with the underlying insurance business from the company to the reinsurer. Yet empirically we do observe joint stock insurance companies buying reinsurance.

One possible explanation is that this is an example of the agency costs of the separation of ownership from control: it may be in the interests of the managers of a company to buy reinsurance even if this reduces the net worth of the shareholders. The argument here would be that managers are unable to diversify their human capital, the returns to which are tied to the outcomes of the company they manage, and so they will be risk averse with respect to these outcomes. They will therefore be prepared to pay a risk premium to a reinsurer to reduce the riskiness of their company, even though this is not in the best interests of well-diversified shareholders.

An alternative explanation is based on the view of reinsurance not simply as a kind of risk sharing, but more importantly as a substitute for the insurance company's own equity capital. As it expands its insurance business, the primary insurance company will also have to increase its reserves. Indeed, as we saw in the previous section, this may well be mandatory under the system of regulation to which the insurance company is subject, but even if not, its own reputational concerns and the monitoring activites of rating agencies and other outside observers may have a similar effect. Perceptions of default risk lower the premia insurance buyers are prepared to pay. But raising and remunerating equity capital is costly, and there can come a point at which reducing the need for reserves by buying reinsurance may be less expensive than raising more equity capital. This kind of substitution is of course well recognized in regulatory regimes like the European, where solvency capital requirements are explicitly reduced by the purchase of reinsurance.

A third type of explanation is based on the idea that particular types of risk impose costs on a firm, and its owners, even though on the asset market they may hold fully diversified portfolios. One obvious reason for this is corporate taxation. Total tax paid is usually a convex function of profit, so a given deviation of profit above the mean increases tax liability by more than the same (in absolute value) deviation below the mean reduces it. In that case a reduction in risk reduces the expected value of the firm's tax liability. Moreover, given that managers are risk averse, and that their remuneration (for incentive reasons) depends on the profit outcome, the greater the riskiness of this, the higher the risk premium that will have to be paid to managers. Again therefore reducing risk reduces costs. Finally, where less risky profits imply a smaller likelihood of bankruptcy or financial distress, this can save the firm ex post the real costs associated with these, and this saving then has ex ante an expected value. Thus it can pay even an insurance company with well-diversified shareholders to reduce risk by buying reinsurance, among other risk management strategies.

Table 15.2. Great weather disasters, 1950–1999

Decade	Number	Econ. loss ($bn.)	Ins. loss
1950–9	13	41.2	–
1960–9	16	54.1	7.2
1970–9	29	79.4	11.5
1980–9	44	126.1	23.0
1990–9	72	425.4	98.9

Source: Munich Re., website, March 2006.

It is therefore not too difficult to explain the existence of reinsurance. A more complex question concerns its future, in a world which seems prone to increasingly costly disasters, whether in the form of natural catastrophes such as earthquakes, hurricanes, and floods, or man-made events such as terrorist attacks or major industrial accidents. The inherent nature of a catastrophe is that the risk pooling that we saw, in Section 2, to be a fundamental aspect of insurance has to be conducted on a much larger scale. Thus suppose, in the example given there, that the 1 million individuals are inhabitants of a city. Each faces a risk of loss of £10,000 with probability 0.01, but now the damage will be caused by a catastrophe. It follows that the risks are perfectly correlated: either no one suffers the loss or everyone suffers it. The insurance company would then have to have reserves of £10 billion if it is to insure the population. The advantage of the Law of Large Numbers is lost.

However, if this insurance company has access to a worldwide reinsurance market, then the reinsurance company may be able to pool this city's risks with those of a large number of other cities, and, given sufficient independence of risks, risk pooling can be restored. The problem that is developing with catastrophes, however, is that their increasing number and consequent scale of damage are becoming large relative to the aggregate reserves of the insurance and reinsurance companies worldwide, so that the question arises of whether in fact the worldwide insurance market has the reserve capacity to finance insurance of possible future catastrophes. Consider Table 15.2.

This shows the total number and damage costs of purely weather-related catastrophes in the last five decades of the past century, by decade. They are increasing in number and even more so in the value of damage caused. Reasons for this may include climactic changes and certainly the fact that increasing population and wealth levels raise the costs imposed by any given disaster. Comparison of the last two columns shows that less than one-quarter of the actual economic losses were covered by insurance. Nevertheless, particularly as these trends have continued into this first decade of the new century, the question arises of whether insurance markets can be used to cover at least part of the damage. Could a string of catastrophes of the size of Hurricane Katrina cause widespread bankruptcies of insurance and reinsurance companies?

An interesting response to this question is the development of financial instruments that effectively seek to remove the constraints presented by the restriction of the funds available for reserves to the insurance sector, by tapping into world capital markets in general, where the estimated loanable funds total around $13 trillion. If catastrophe risks can be securitized, so that they become tradeable on capital markets, then concerns about capacity levels would vanish.

An example of such securitization is the catastrophe bond (catbond). Consider again our previous example of the city with 1 million people facing a 10 per cent risk of a catastrophe that will cost £10 billion if it occurs. Suppose a reinsurance company issues £10 billion-worth of catbonds, with a duration of ten years, say. These will pay a stated rate of interest, just like any bond, and, if the catastrophe has not occurred by the time of maturity, will be repaid in full. If however the catastrophe occurs, then interest payments terminate and the bonds become worthless, with the £10 billion (which has meanwhile been invested in safe assets) then being used to cover the claims made under the insurance policies sold to the citizens. The rate of interest offered in the initial sale of the bonds will have to be so calculated that the capital market is prepared to hold them, and the difference between this and the riskless interest rate at which the sale proceeds are invested, which is a measure of the market's valuation of the riskiness of the bonds, will enter into the premium that is charged for the insurance. N. A. Doherty (2000) provides an interesting discussion of a wider set of financial instruments as well as some underlying theory.

Markets for these kinds of instruments are still quite thin, possibly because the capacity of the reinsurance industry is still regarded as sufficient to meet the demands likely to be placed on it. Nevertheless this type of financial innovation, which may change the nature of the activities of reinsurance companies in a major way, is an interesting development to watch for the future.

References

BOHN, J. G., and HALL, B. J. (1998), 'The costs of insurance company failures', in D. F. Bradford (ed.), *The Economics of Property-Casualty Insurance*, Chicago: University of Chicago Press.

DOHERTY, N. A. (2000), 'Innovation in corporate risk management: the case of catastrophe risk', in G. Dionne (ed.), *Handbook of Insurance*, Boston: Kluwer Academic Publishers.

EISEN, R., MÜLLER, W., and ZWEIFEL, P. (1993), 'Entrepreneurial insurance: a new paradigm for deregulated markets', *Geneva Papers on Risk and Insurance*, 66, 3–56.

FINSINGER, J. (1983), *Versicherungsmärkte*, Frankfurt: Campus Verlag.

_____ HAMMOND, E., and TAPP, J. (1985), *Insurance: Competition or Regulation?*, London: Institute for Fiscal Studies.

_____ and PAULY, M. (eds.) (1986), *The Economics of Insurance Regulation*, London: Macmillan.

_____ and SCHMID, F. (1994), 'Prices, distribution channels and regulatory intervention in European insurance markets', *Geneva Papers on Risk and Insurance*, 19, 22–36.

JAFFEE, D. M., and RUSSELL, T. (1994), 'The causes and consequences of rate regulation in the auto insurance industry', in D. F. Bradford (ed.), *The Economics of Property-Casualty Insurance*, Chicago: University of Chicago Press.

KONRATH N. (1996), 'Solvency of insurance undertakings and financial groups', *Geneva Papers on Risk and Insurance*, 78, 22–35.

MAYERS, D., and SMITH, C. W. (2000), 'Organizational forms within the insurance industry: theory and evidence', in G. Dionne (ed.), *Handbook of Insurance*, Boston: Kluwer Academic Publishers.

REES, R., and KESSNER, E. (1999), 'European insurance markets, regulation and efficiency', *Economic Policy*, 29, 365–97.

SHARMA, P. (2002), 'Prudential supervision of insurance undertakings,' Conference of Insurance Supervisory Services of the Member States of the European Union, available at http://ec.europa.eu/internal_market/insurance/docs/solvency/solvency2-conference-report_en.pdf.

CHAPTER 16

EUROPEAN INTEGRATION OF PAYMENTS SYSTEMS

XAVIER FREIXAS

CORNELIA HOLTHAUSEN

As they allow the transfer of property rights, payment systems play a key role in the smooth functioning of the economy. They consist of all the procedures needed for monetary transfers among economic agents, be it for retail transactions (cash, cheque, or card payments) or for large-value transactions, that is, transfers between large financial players.

In Europe, the landscape of payment systems has changed dramatically since the creation of the Economic and Monetary Union, and will continue to change. In less than ten years, the number of large-value payments systems in Europe has dropped from eighteen (in 1997) to five, two of which process the bulk of transactions. Still, while progress is spectacular in the large-value payment systems, the retail payment sector is far from being integrated and efficient.

This chapter describes developments in the European payments sector, focusing on the progress made and problems encountered in the European-wide integration of payments systems. The first section discusses some general trends in the payment system business around the world. The second section then addresses the main issues for European large-value systems. The third section deals with the increasingly important area of retail payment systems in Europe. The last section concludes.

1. The Evolution of Payments Systems

1.1. Interbank Payment Systems: A Trend Towards Safety

During the recent years there has been a clear trend in the design of payment systems. Payment systems are today faster and safer, and users are better protected against credit risk.

The main explanation for this trend is technological progress in information processing that has made viable the development of real time gross settlement (RTGS) systems. These systems are characterized by payment transfers from one bank to another on a continuous, transaction-by-transaction basis throughout the day. At the same time, deferred net settlement (DNS) systems, which accumulate payment orders and settle only multilateral net positions at a pre-specified time, have implemented new design features that reduce these systems' credit risk. Common tools for risk reduction are the use of collateral, peer monitoring of the members (with bilateral credit limits), batch settlement throughout the day, and an automatic rule of loss allocation in case of default of one of the members of the system. These tools reduce a participant's exposure to counterparty credit risk dramatically, and improve the system's overall stability. At the same time, RTGS systems have introduced liquidity-saving features such as queuing mechanism or the provision of intraday credit (against collateral or at an interest rate), which may reintroduce credit risk. As a result of these developments, most settlement systems nowadays represent in fact a mixture of the two extreme forms of payment system design.

While payment systems themselves have generally become safer, large-value payments as such may still imply risks for market participants. Especially, indirect linking to the systems via correspondent banks has important consequences, both because these bilateral agreements may limit competition, and because credit risk is reintroduced.

1.1.1. *Payment System Characteristics*

From a user perspective, the most relevant characteristics of payments systems are speed, safety, and costs.

Speed refers to the execution time of settlement. Often, the timing, i.e. same-day settlement or immediate settlement, may be crucial to the counterparties. In a pure RTGS system with intraday overdraft facilities, settlement takes place immediately, while in a pure net settlement system payments are typically settled at the end of a business day. There are many intermediary systems where settlement may occur with some delay, for instance systems with queuing or batch settlement during the day.

Safety is another important factor in the settlement process. Because settlement often takes place with some delay, banks face the risk of not receiving an expected payment. Such a settlement failure may arise, for instance, because the sending bank defaults (counterparty credit risk) or faces liquidity problems causing a settlement delay (liquidity risk), or because of a computer failure (operational risk). Many netting systems try to limit exposure to counterparty credit risk by applying safety standards such as the posting of collateral and the application of credit limits. Whenever the payment system extends unsecured intraday credit to its participants, credit risk is shifted from the receiving party to the system provider. To avoid a concentration of risk in the settlement institution, credit usually has to be collateralized, or a fee is charged so that the borrowing facility is not overused.

One of the major aspects of the safety of payment systems is the finality of payments, which refers to the legal certainty attached to any payment received. For a payment to be final it has to be irrevocably settled in central bank money. This means, in particular, that any bankruptcy occurring after the payment is received should in no way affect the credited bank. Finality is a key characteristic of a payment system in terms of systemic risk and therefore appears as one of the 'Core principles for systemically important payment systems' (BIS/CPSS 2001).

Financial intermediaries accessing a payment system face direct and indirect *costs*. Direct costs of sending payments are the fees charged by the service provider to payment system participants. Indirect costs are the opportunity cost of holding liquidity at the central bank money at below market rates. Furthermore, the potential use of collateral is costly to banks, because of fees charged for the settlement of securities, and because of the opportunity costs of using collateral. Additional costs can arise if access to a payment system is restricted, so that either the sender or the receiver of the payment has to route its transactions through a correspondent bank, or if the settlement process is not fully automated so that manual processing is needed.

Broadly speaking, as developed in a theoretical framework by Freixas and Parigi (1998), RTGS systems allow for a very speedy execution of payments at a very low risk, while netting systems with end-of-day settlement are riskier but imply lower reserves and, thus, low liquidity costs. Because safety and speed are often most relevant for larger payments, while costs are the most important characteristic for smaller ones, RTGS systems tend to attract large payments, while netting systems are preferred for smaller amounts. Indeed, the majority of developed countries have now at least these two types of payment systems: an RTGS typically used for large-value payments and a DNS for smaller amounts. The euro area is no exception with TARGET as RTGS system, and Euro 1 as netting system. Still, the share of RTGS is increasing progressively as the payment instruments evolve towards a more IT-based structure and enable real-time processing of payments. In the European Monetary Union, the remuneration of reserves makes RTGS comparatively more attractive. In RTGS systems, banks have two options to meet their liquidity needs: borrow money from the central bank or wait for incoming payments. As this second option is clearly inefficient, several authors have argued that central bank intraday credit should be free of charge (see Kobayakawa 1997; Bech and Garratt 2003).

1.1.2. *Systemic Risk and Monitoring*

Since the failure of Bankhaus Herstatt in 1974, it has become clear that payments industries have a potential for contagion and may, therefore, generate systemic effects. Because of the intertwining of claims, payment systems are, jointly with the interbank and the OTC market, a source of possible default contagion. This extent of contagion will depend upon concentration risk (as explored in Allen and Gale 2000; Freixas, Parigi, and Rochet 2000) and on the characteristics of the payment system, as developed in Freixas and Parigi (1998) and Kahn, McAndrews, and Roberds (2003). Central banks are well aware of the systemic importance of the payment systems and of the necessity to carefully oversee the payments sector, especially large-value payments systems. Even though payment systems have become much safer over the past years, as argued above, monitoring payment systems remains important in order to limit the likelihood and extent of systemic events. In Europe, ensuring the smooth functioning of payment systems is part of the mandate of the Eurosystem (see ECB 1992).[1] Ideally, the overseer of the payment system should cooperate with banking supervisors. However, when banking supervision remains national but the payment system operates internationally, national supervisors may have incentives not to disclose their information in full detail (see Holthausen and Roende 2002). As a consequence, the national regulation of payment system is suboptimal.

1.2. National Segmentation in Retail Payments

IT developments are a driving factor also behind developments in the retail payments sector. More and more retail transactions are conducted via electronic media. Of all non-cash payments in the member countries of the Group of Ten Committee on Payment and Settlement Systems (CPSS), the share of cheque payments has been shrinking substantially (31.6 per cent of all payments operations in 2003 compared to 45.1 per cent in 1999; this amounts to a value of 4.0 per cent in 2003 down from 4.7 in 1999) (see BIS/CPSS 2005: tables 13 and 14). At the same time, credit and debit card payments, credit transfers (with 94.1 per cent by far the most important in terms of value), and direct debits are gaining importance. In spite of predictions made during the 1990s that electronic money was to become an important payment medium, it has not taken off and remains marginal.

Retail payments systems are largely organized on a national basis. International payments services are often offered in-house via banks with international networks, or through correspondent banks (see BIS/CPSS 2003). Moreover, credit and recently

---

[1] Article 2 states that 'The ECB and national central banks may provide facilities, and the ECB may make regulations, to ensure efficient and sound clearing and payment systems within the Community and with other countries.'

debit cards are used to a great extent to facilitate payments abroad. The overall demand for cross-border transfers remains low and fees are very high compared to national levels. Anecdotal evidence suggests that only around 1 per cent of all retail payments in the G-10 countries are of a cross-border nature. Advances to facilitate cross-border payments and to enhance cross-border integration of retail payment systems mainly concern the euro area and are detailed in Section 3 below.

2. INTERBANK PAYMENTS IN EUROPE

Once the Maastricht Treaty paved the way for the European Economic and Monetary Union (EMU) to emerge, it was clear that the coordination of the wholesale interbank markets was necessary, as the single monetary policy required that banks could swiftly and safely make payments throughout the currency area. However, at that time, payment systems in the member states were of very diverse structure and not linked to one another.

In order not to hamper the creation of such a cross-border market for liquidity, it was decided that a system operating throughout the euro area would be appropriate. This would allow banks to settle their accounts with immediacy and finality. To this aim, it was decided that an interlinked system of national payment systems settling in real time was to be implemented under the lead of the European Central Bank (ECB). This was the origin of TARGET.[2]

From the outset, the issue was given into the hands of central banks. The possibility that the market could find a solution was discarded, both because of the short time horizon and because it was felt that such a system would be a key instrument for central banks. Indeed, such a payment system would be critical for the implementation of monetary policy, and its inherent systemic risk would require central bank monitoring.

Still, from the very beginning, it was established that entry into the market for payments was open to any payment system offering sufficient guarantees. As a consequence, other systems have developed supplying services that compete with the Eurosystem's payment system, TARGET.

2.1. Target

On 1 January 1999 TARGET was launched. It is a decentralized payment system consisting of one RTGS in each of the participating European Union (EU) member states and the ECB payment system (EPM). The national RTGS systems and the EPM

---

[2] Trans-European automated real-time gross settlement express transfer.

are interconnected by common procedures (interlinking) to allow fully automated straight-through processing (STP) of cross-border transfers throughout the European Union for interbank payments. All the individual payment systems are now connected via the interlinking system.

In addition to this technological dimension, implementing TARGET has required a second type of homogenization: the legal one. Indeed, the different countries having different bankruptcy codes, the way a payment was treated immediately before a bankruptcy could have been widely different across the different members. Consequently, the Settlement Finality Directive (European Commission 1998) imposed a number of legal requirements, so that payment orders accepted by the system were irrevocable. Hence, insolvencies have no retroactive effects (so-called 'zero hour' rule), and collateral is insulated from the effects of insolvency proceedings and can be speedily realized.

To summarize, the design of TARGET is such that each domestic RTGS maintains its specific characteristics and intramember format, while a global European link allowing intermember transfer was created. Through this link, TARGET allows credit institutions to use the same connections for both intramember state and intermember state payments, thus avoiding duplication of communication channels.

The success of TARGET has been spectacular as witnessed by a number of facts:

About 10,500 banks use TARGET to initiate payments on their own or on their customers' behalf, and 48,500, including branches and subsidiaries, are accessible through TARGET worldwide (ECB 2004b). Banks fully support EU-wide straight-through processing, using SWIFT customers' payment messages (MT103+). In addition, TARGET is used in some countries, such as Germany and Italy, to process low-value customer payments.

Regarding the time required for processing payments, 95.62 per cent of intermember state payments were processed in less than five minutes, 3.78 per cent needed between five minutes and fifteen minutes, and 0.30 per cent required between fifteen minutes and thirty minutes (ECB *Monthly Bulletin*, September 2005).

The value of payments routed through TARGET has increased steadily since its inception (see Figure 16.1). Roughly one-third of the value of all payments can be attributed to cross-border transfers (the volume of intermember transactions was 33.56 per cent in the second quarter of 2005). This share had initially been higher (39 per cent in 1999 and even 42 per cent in 2000); it has been pretty constant since then.

It should be noticed that TARGET complements other payment systems. On the one hand, it is also used by other payment systems (for instance, by Euro 1) to settle the net positions of their participants. As such, TARGET provides access to its competitors. This could, in principle, lead to an issue of access pricing. Still, as TARGET does not discriminate among banks the issue does not arise.

On the other hand, TARGET is accessible for the countries outside the euro area. In particular, the UK payment system, CHAPS, with its two components, CHAPS sterling and CHAPS euro, is directly connected to TARGET and involves a high transaction volume because of the role of London as an international financial centre.

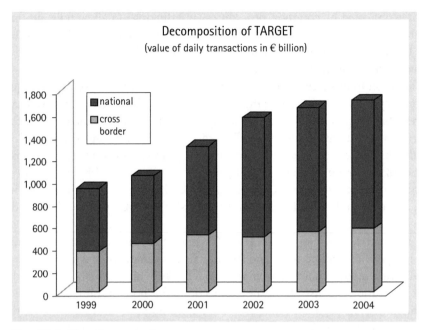

Fig. 16.1. Target payments

The correct supervision of the links with non-euro payment systems may imply monitoring the risk of liquidity shortfalls. This could occur whenever a bank that has obtained intraday credit for its operations does not repay at the end of the day. Such a situation is dealt with within the euro zone by extending the credit overnight through the marginal credit facility. Since non-euro zone banks do not have access to this facility, this leads to an additional risk that justifies the required collateral in order to obtain intraday credit.

2.2. Other Large-value Systems in Europe

Next to TARGET, a few other payment systems operate in Europe. The largest is Euro 1, run by the EBA clearing company that was set up by the EBA (European Banking Association)[3] in 1998. Currently, it has seventy participants from twenty countries and processes more than half of the number of payments that are routed through TARGET (see Table 16.1). Euro 1 operates Europe-wide and enables cross-border transfers on a multilateral netting basis. Payments are settled at the end of its business day via TARGET. The most important tool for risk mitigation is a system of bilateral and multilateral credit and debit caps. This ensures that the multilateral net amount that a participant owes to the system never exceeds a certain value. Participants can in a discretionary way adjust their bilateral limits on a daily basis.

---

[3] See www.abe.org.

Table 16.1. Payment traffic conducted via European large-value payment systems

System	Average value of daily transactions (€bn)	Average daily number of transactions	Average payment size (€)
TARGET	1,714	267,234	6,400,000
Euro 1	170	161,097	1,200,000
PNS	67	27,054	2,500,000
SEPI	1	4,285	200,000
POPS	2	2,177	900,000

Source: www.ecb.int. Figures are average numbers for 2004. SEPI was closed down in December 2004.
Notes: TARGET: Trans-European real-time gross settlement system (Eurosystem), Euro 1 (EBA); PNS (France): Paris net settlement; SEPI (Spain): Servicio español de pagos interbancarios; POPS (Finland): Pankkien On-line Pikasiirrot ja Sekit-Järjestelma.

Furthermore, a few smaller settlement systems exist in France (PNS) and Finland (POPS).[4] Both systems are of a hybrid nature, combining elements of RTGS and netting in their procedures. They process payments of much smaller aggregate values and are of little systemic importance.

Finally, cross-border transactions not conducted in euros, that is, foreign exchange transactions, have for a long time been conducted via correspondent banking: all transactions were executed via a few large international players. Because of the high risks and costs that such a structure poses on market participants, the need for a more centralized approach led to the creation of the CLS system (for continuous linked settlement). CLS has been successfully in operation since 2002 and it settles foreign exchange transactions around the world in real time with same-day finality. It settles transactions in various major currencies, including the euro (see Kahn and Roberds 2001).

2.3. Market Structure

When the Eurosystem opted for the TARGET system, it explicitly welcomed competition from the private sector for reasons of efficiency. As a result, the European market for payments is characterized by the coexistence of multilateral payment systems, through which banks have access to each other, and correspondent banking, where access to other banks is mediated by the correspondent. It is estimated that in Europe the multilateral payment systems have the largest share both in terms of value and volume with about 80 per cent of the market (Noyer 2005), while correspondent banking accounts for the remaining 20 per cent. The combined daily turnover in these large value payment systems is more than one-quarter of euro area annual GDP.

---

[4] PNS: Paris net settlement; POPS: Pankkien On-line Pikasiirrot ja Sekit-järjestelmä.

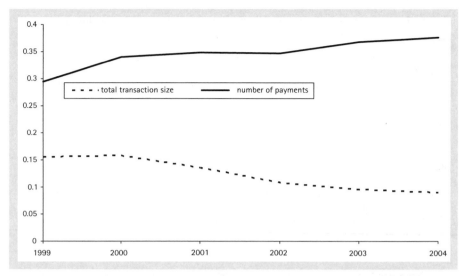

Fig. 16.2. Share of EURO 1 of combined payments made through EURO 1 and TARGET in terms of value (transaction size) and volume (number of payments)

In other words, in less than four days, the value of transactions conducted via these systems equals annual GDP.

Within the multilateral payments systems, TARGET and Euro 1 hold a dominant position in European large-value payments traffic. In 2004, TARGET accounted for 88 per cent in terms of value and 58 per cent in terms of volume (ECB 2004b) (see Figure 16.2). Euro 1 is the main alternative payment system used by European credit institutions to settle their transactions, but the difference in the value of daily processed payments is striking. Table 16.1 compares TARGET with some other interbank fund transfer systems for the year 2004.

From this table it is obvious that the average payment size in TARGET, €6.4 million, is much higher than in the other systems. It seems that banks have a preference for routing payments of high value via the RTGS system, either because of higher time criticality or because they wish to minimize credit risk exposure. From a regulatory perspective, this is a desired feature of the systems, since large payments are more likely to cause systemic events.

2.4. Future Developments

Although the present structure of large-value payment systems in Europe may be considered satisfactory, it is the result of the historical necessity to link different payment systems so as to have banks interconnected throughout the European Union, not of competitive pressure. This means that there is no guarantee that future progress in payment systems (increased speed or additional services) will be incorporated as it emerges. For this reason, on December 2004 the Governing Council of the ECB approved the introduction of a single shared platform that will be the basic structure of TARGET 2. This platform, the result of a joint initiative by Banca d'Italia, Banque de France, and Deutsche Bundesbank, is due to go live in 2008. All Eurosystem central banks will participate. Switching to a single shared platform will allow for a high level of harmonization of central bank practices. The new system will also propose a uniform price structure based on the costs of the most efficient platform, which will enhance cost efficiency.[5]

It seems reasonable to expect that the future structure of European large value payment systems might be the one of a differentiated duopoly, with TARGET 2 and Euro 1 sharing the market for large-value payments. Still, this will depend on whether the privately owned payment systems in Europe subsequently merge or close down.

3. EUROPEAN RETAIL PAYMENTS

The efficiency and level of integration of the retail payments sector has evolved quite differently from the wholesale payments industry. When in 1999 the euro replaced the former domestic currencies in eleven, now thirteen, European countries,[6] this was a major step forward in terms of integration. However, in the years following the establishment of the European Monetary Union, not much progress was made regarding the integration of non-cash payment instruments. The discrepancy in prices between domestic and cross-border transactions is still very large, and acceptance of domestic means of payment in other countries is limited.

It should be emphasized that the European Monetary Union has a particularly diverse structure regarding retail payment instruments. Some countries have a tradition of using cheques, chip cards, or direct debits while these are seldom used in others. Domestic payment systems are, naturally, well tailored to these specificities.

The different structures give rise to high transaction costs to foreign customers. First of all, domestic means of payment (in particular debit cards and electronic money) are often not accepted for payment in other countries. Second, cross-border payments are cumbersome and expensive, as generally no straight through processing is possible. Therefore, high efficiency gains are to be expected from a harmonization of payment products and standards.

For several years, however, not much progress was made concerning the integration process. One main reason is the network nature of payments systems, which requires a high degree of coordination among the parties involved. Switching to a

---

[5] Danmarks Nationalbank has also confirmed its participation. The Bank of England and Sveriges Riskbank will not be members of the Single Shared Platform.

[6] At present, these are Belgium, Germany, Greece, Spain, France, Ireland, Italy, Luxembourg, the Netherlands, Austria, Portugal, Slovenia, and Finland.

European open entry network would imply an infrastructure investment that may not be matched by higher fees in the future. It is not surprising, therefore, that the European banks were dragging their feet, as they lack incentives to pay for the switching costs.

Additionally, the high concentration of cross-border retail payments in the hands of a few market players enabled them to set very high prices and to reap substantial profits from processing cross-border payments. Probably, this also hampered their willingness to push for further integration which, in turn, would imply more competition.

The specific nature of customer–banking relations is an additional factor leading to a lack of competition in the retail payments sector: in other types of markets customers would switch from one provider to another that gives better service for the same price. In the retail banking market, this is not the case, as customers pay for a whole array of services, from current accounts to overdraft facilities, which are difficult to compare across banks and of which, usually, the European payments are only a small fraction.

At present, the precise way in which cross-border retail transactions are settled varies widely across countries and types of institutions. Some payments (at present roughly 200,000 per day) are routed via the STEP 2 system provided by the European Banking Association EBA. STEP 2 is a pan-European ACH (automated clearing house) for processing bulk payments throughout the EU operating in a centralized way. Other payments are made on a bilateral basis between local clearing houses. Additionally, some types of credit institutions (typically savings banks or post banks) have in-house systems that are linked across borders. Finally, banks operating on an international basis sometimes process cross-border payments in house. Because of this diversity, it is very difficult to characterize the typical way of processing a payment, and unfortunately, precise figures on the importance of each type of transaction are not available.

The main initiatives for further changes come from three different sides. First, the European Commission issued a regulation on the pricing of cross-border payments, in order to implement a European Union-wide single payment area (SPA). Second, the banking sector organized itself in the European Payments Council (EPC) with the aim of creating a single euro payments area (SEPA). Finally, the Eurosystem has an interest to speed up the integration process and is supporting the EPC in the creation of a single euro payments area.

3.1. The Initiative of the European Commission

Since the cost of cross-border transactions remained high, the European Commission was increasingly concerned that the benefits of having a single currency were, apart from cash payments, not visible to consumers. In 2001, it issued a regulation requiring fees for euro transactions to be the same across borders as within the member country

(Regulation 2560/2001). This regulation now applies to cash withdrawals, bank cards, and credit transfers.

The application of this regulation is somewhat problematic in several respects. First of all, domestic fees still vary substantially across Europe, so some countries' banks were hit harder by the regulation than others. Also, price regulations often do not give the right incentives for cost cutting and innovation. For instance, banks can side-step the regulation by changing the type of contract they offer to their customers with current accounts. Finally, the elevated fees for cross-border transactions do in some part reflect the higher costs faced by banks when processing these transactions. Not only is automated (straight-through) processing often simply not yet possible, but also banks themselves need to rely on correspondent banks or banking networks to conduct such payments and consequently depend on their correspondents' price setting. One further example for high costs in the cross-border business is credit card fraud risk. This risk is much higher for cross-country credit card transactions. It is therefore quite consistent that cross-country transactions bear somewhat higher fees, even if not necessarily of the present magnitude.

3.2. Banking Sector Initiatives

Central banks of Europe were heavily involved in the reform and integration of large-value payment systems. This was (and continues to be) different in the retail payments area, where the banking sector itself was responsible for integration and further development of payment instruments, while regulatory bodies adopted an arm's-length monitoring and advisory position. As mentioned, retail payment integration requires a high degree of cross-border coordination among banks. This is especially so because cross-border payments are usually conducted through correspondent banks, which reap substantial profits in the current segmented system. These are unlikely to have an interest in a change of the framework, which would imply pressures on margins.

After realizing that competition was not going to force an efficient pan-European integrated payment system to emerge, the creation of a structured body was deemed necessary by the banking community. This was done by calling into life the European Payments Council (EPC). The EPC's objective is the creation of a single euro payments area (SEPA) for the euro area with an integrated retail payments infrastructure that enabled consumers to make payments as effectively as they now do in their national markets. Its vision of a euro area-wide 'domestic' payments area was laid down in a White Paper (EPC 2002).[7]

One objective of the EPC is the establishment of a pan-European automated clearing house (PEACH) network.[8] Quite possibly, to become a sensible alternative

---

[7] SEPA is not to be confused with SPA, the initiative of the European Commission, which aims at supporting a single payments area throughout the European Union.

[8] An Automated Clearinghouse (ACH) is an electronic funds transfer system processing credit and debit transfers.

for banks to switch to, the proposed PEACH service provider should provide a full array of integrated services including direct debit. As of now, a first PEACH exists. However, little traffic has migrated to the European network, both because it has a maximum limit of €12,500, and also because it has strong information requirements and imposes a three-day execution time.

A second objective was the creation of a pan-European standard to be used for cross-border credit transfers. Such a system, Credeuro, is already in use for those transfers for which Regulation 2560/2001 applies. It is planned to expand the services provided to apply to all euro credit transfers and to implement a minimum standard for all such cross-border operations.

Furthermore, the establishment of a pan-European direct debit scheme was already endorsed by the EPC. At present, the EPC commits to delivering European-wide schemes for electronic credit transfer and direct debits by 2008.

Another successful initiative from the banking sector was the implementation of the IBAN (international bank account number) and BIC (bank identifier code) standards. The application of these standards greatly facilitates the processing of cross-border payments, as it enables straight-through processing of payments and thus reduces the costs and time needed for the execution of cross-border transactions. These codes were developed by the European Committee for Banking Standards (ECBS), a body formed by the major credit sector associations and closely cooperating with the EPC.

Will the EPC achieve its ambitious objectives? In view of the costs that the transition to a truly integrated system would pose for the banking sector, doubts remain whether the banking community will really embark on a complete integration. Still, the banking community is strongly urged by the central banks in Europe to proceed with the process.

3.3. The Eurosystem's Role

The EPC coordinates its actions with the Eurosystem. The Eurosystem (consisting of the European Central Bank and the national central banks of the countries that have adopted the euro) has an interest in the development of a pan-European payments infrastructure. It sees its role as helping the industry to find swift and effective solutions.

In particular, the Eurosystem emphasizes the necessity of developing standards, such as the bank identifier code IBAN, and their Europe-wide implementation. A further objective should be standards that enable full straight-through processing for credit transfers. The Eurosystem welcomes the choice to implement a system of PEACHes (see ECB 2004a). Concerning credit transfers, it would like Credeuro to become the common standard for retail cross-border transfers and stresses the need for enabling same-day settlement via a complementary system (Prieuro).

Generally, in the retail payments sector, the Eurosystem is much less active than it is in large-value payments. This is mainly because retail payments are considered as being less important for financial stability.

4. CONCLUSION

The various types of payments systems in Europe differ widely in the degree of cross-border integration. On the one hand, interbank payments can be made throughout Europe at low cost, in a secure way, and at high speed thanks to TARGET and other, smaller payment systems. As a result, the euro area has a deep and liquid money market. On the other hand, the market for retail payments is far from being integrated. However, also on the retail side progress has been made. Even though at present it is still unclear which of the different models for cross-border retail flows will emerge as the most prominent one, the process of integration is expected to continue in the coming years.

REFERENCES

ALLEN, F., and GALE, D. (2000), 'Financial contagion', *Journal of Political Economy*, 108, 1–33.

BANK FOR INTERNATIONAL SETTLEMENTS, COMMITTEE ON PAYMENT AND SETTLEMENT SYSTEMS (2001), 'Core principles for systemically important payment systems', CPSS Publication no. 43.

———(2003), 'Policy issues for central banks in retail payments', CPSS Publications no. 52, March.

———(2004), 'Survey of developments in electronic money and internet and mobile payments', March CPSS Publications no. 62, March 1.

———(2005), 'Statistics on payment and settlement systems in selected countries—Figures for 2003—Preliminary version', CPSS Publications no. 66, March.

BECH, M., and GARRATT, R. (2003), 'The intraday liquidity management game', *Journal of Economic Theory*, 109(2), 198–219.

EUROPEAN CENTRAL BANK (1992), 'Protocol on the statue of the European System of Central Banks and of the European Central Bank', www.ecb.int/ecb/legal/pdf/en_statute_2.pdf.

———(2004a), 'Towards a single euro payment area: Third progress report', December.

———(2004b), 'TARGET annual report 2004'.

EUROPEAN COMMISSION (1998), 'Directive 98/26/EC' (Settlement Finality Directive), http://europa.eu.int/comm/internal_market/financial-markets/settlement/index_en. htm#links.

EUROPEAN PAYMENTS COUNCIL (2002), 'Euroland: our single payments area', White Paper, May.

———(2005), 'annual report 2004', April.

FREIXAS, X., and PARIGI, B. (1998), 'Contagion and efficiency in gross and net interbank payment systems', *Journal of Financial Intermediation*, 7, 3–31.

FREIXAS, X., and PARIGI, B. and ROCHET, J. C. (2000), 'Systemic risk, interbank relations and liquidity provision by the central bank', *Journal of Money, Credit and Banking*, 32, 611–38, Part 2.

HOLTHAUSEN, C., and ROENDE, T. (2002), 'Regulating access to international large-value payment systems', *Review of Financial Studies*, 15(5), 1561–86.

KAHN, C., McANDREWS, J., and ROBERDS, W. (2003), 'Settlement risk under gross and net settlement', *Journal of Money, Credit, and Banking*, 35(4), 591–608.

——— and ROBERDS, W. (2001), 'The CLS bank: a solution to the risks of international payments settlement?', Carnegie-Rochester Conference Series on Public Policy.

KOBAYAKAWA, S. (1997), 'The comparative analysis of settlement systems', CEPR Discussion Paper no. 1667.

MILLAR, S., and SAPORTA, V. (2005), 'Background paper on the Bank of England conference on the future of payments, May 19–20 2005'.

NOYER, C. (2005), 'The contribution of payment infrastructures to the European financial integration and the establishment of the SEPA', speech given on the occasion of the 20th anniversary of the EBA Association.

PART IV

FINANCIAL MARKETS

CHAPTER 17

···

THE EURO MONEY MARKETS

···

PHILIPP HARTMANN

NATACHA VALLA

1. INTRODUCTION

···

MONEY markets are an important part of modern financial systems. Paradoxically, this is not well reflected in the economic literature in that in particular equity markets but also bond markets usually receive much greater attention. The most important function of money markets is to allocate liquidity in the economy. Efficient and stable money markets allow economic agents to elastically meet payment and short-term financing needs and profitably invest short-term revenues, even in times of great uncertainty and associated large liquidity shocks. Their importance for economic policy is underlined, inter alia, by the presence of central banks. Central bank monetary policy sets the short-term interest rate of an economy in the money markets and manages aggregate liquidity. Money markets play therefore an important role in macroeconomic stabilization, in particular in the stability of the financial system, in risk sharing, and in maintaining price stability.

The functioning of European money markets is particularly interesting and important, as Economic and Monetary Union (EMU) has led to the unification of formerly separate money markets by (at the time of writing) twelve sovereign states.[1]

We are grateful to Xavier Freixas for extensive comments and to B. Saes-Escorbiac for excellent research assistance. All errors are however our own. Any views expressed reflect only those of the authors and should not be regarded as official views of the Banque de France, the ECB, or the Eurosystem.

[1] A thirteenth state, Slovenia, joined in January 2007.

As the unification formally started with stage 3 of EMU in January 1999, the euro area money markets are still much less well understood than those of many other industrial countries in which a single currency has often prevailed for centuries. This chapter presents a comprehensive study of the euro money markets since their start in 1999, illustrating their importance and explaining their functioning. It marries micro- and macroeconomic perspectives, covering market developments and policy issues on the basis of the relevant academic literature as well as the latest and best available data.

The chapter is divided into five sections. The second section discusses in greater depth the scope and economic functions of money markets, also referring to their different segments, the agents acting in them, and the most prevalent forms of trading. Section 3 gives an in-depth description of European money markets, based on the latest data, in order to derive the most important stylized facts about them. It reports the relative sizes of the different euro money market segments, their liquidity, interest rate levels, and volatility as well as various spreads (e.g. between deposit and repo rates). The fourth section discusses a number of policy issues, including the predictability of monetary policy decisions with money market rates, the design of central bank operational frameworks, the role of payment, clearing, and settlement systems, the integration and development of money market segments, the effects of banking consolidation, as well as money market stability and the role of the lender of last resort. The last section briefly summarizes the most salient results and main policy issues.

2. SCOPE, ECONOMIC FUNCTIONS, AND COMPONENTS OF MONEY MARKETS

The money market is not one but a collection of markets. This collection forms a system so tightly integrated that it is however tempting to describe it as a single entity. Stigum (1990) generally defines the money market as 'a wholesale market for low-risk, highly liquid, short term debt instruments'. By money markets, we shall refer to the system of markets for highly liquid instruments, characterized by a relatively safe principal, and with maturities ranging from one day to one year. Together with stock and bond markets, we regard them as an important part of (the) capital market(s).

In what follows in this section we are going to characterize money markets as defined above in conceptual terms. While taking a European perspective, using examples from the euro area, much of this section will also apply to other developed money markets, such as those of the United States or Japan. We start with a discussion of their role in the overall economy. We then review their main components in terms of instruments, participants, and trading practices.

2.1. Economic Functions

The European money markets, and money markets in general, fulfil important economic functions. They solve cash flow mismatches that economic agents experience among themselves, and at the aggregate level they contribute to channelling funds from savers to borrowers. We discuss these two different but related functions in turn.

Economic agents (firms, households, public entities) often deal with positive and negative flows of funds that almost never match, but which can be 'bridged' with short-term financing and investments. Important flows of funds are channelled between net savers and net borrowers via money markets for such purposes. Moreover, the uncertain nature of flows often implies additional short-term funding and investment needs that cannot be fully planned in advance. On the supply side, money markets offer 'warehouse' opportunities to financial institutions and firms seeking to park liquidity for a short period of time; thereby reducing the opportunity cost of holding cash. On the demand side, money markets are a quickly available, low-cost, short-term source of funds for financial institutions, firms, and governments. In light of these payment imbalances and uncertainties money markets enable economic agents to flexibly reallocate their funds and thereby efficiently share liquidity risks.

In Europe the following stylized patterns of macroeconomic financial flows emerge among economic sectors. As a whole, the non-financial corporations sector runs a large deficit of funds. It turns out that a large chunk of the funds received to cover this deficit comes from the sale of debt (including money market) instruments (ECB 2005c). By contrast, the balance sheet of the household sector suggests that unlike firms, consumers are net savers. In Europe, the savings rate of households remains historically high in comparison to other economic areas. Finally, the public sector (federal and local governments) generally exhibits a negative net savings rate, resulting in a structural financing need.

The flow of funds from net savers to net borrowers can take various forms and may involve direct (through markets) or indirect channels (through intermediaries). In Europe, despite the growth of corporate bonds since the introduction of the euro, most of households' surplus of funds is channelled to the business sector via loans and equity investments. Overall in Europe, the asset and liability structure of the main economic sectors shows the importance of financial intermediation in the reallocation of funds (e.g. banks still receive considerable quantities of demand and time deposits, which they use to make loans). In addition, direct and indirect finance may take place through money markets. The cost of financing and liquidity traded in money markets for example via short-term fixed income securities will therefore affect economic activity. The role of money markets in this *broad* sense is actually captured by the theory of corporate finance and theories of household portfolio choice.

Taking a *narrower* perspective, the inner core of money markets is the interbank market. In fact, a large share of money market activity serves the purpose of reallocating liquidity across financial institutions. Financial intermediaries in need of cash trade liquidity with banks that have more liquidity than they can profitably manage.

Table 17.1. Money market instruments in banks' balance sheets and liquidity profile

Assets		Liabilities	
Cash and balances at the central bank*		Deposits/savings certificates	⎫
Liquid assets*	2,100	Customers accounts	⎬ 7,500
Short-term* and other securities	⎫	Deposits by banks*	⎭
Equity shares	700	Collateralized borrowing*	⎫
Illiquid assets	⎭	Interbank market borrowing*	⎬ 3,000
Loans and advances to banks*	9,300	Debt securities in issue* (CDs, CP, MTN)	⎭
Loans and advances to customers	⎭	Capital and reserves	1,200
Other assets	6,400	Forex swaps*	
		Other liabilities	6,800
		Off-balance sheet	
		Committed credit lines*	
		Derivatives*	
Total assets	18,500	Total liabilities	18,500

Notes: Asterisks denote the balance sheet items that directly involve money market trades. Orders of magnitude are given on the right-hand side in €bn of outstanding amounts on the basis of banking data published by the ECB (January 2006). Balance sheet items are only an indicative subset of the consolidated balance sheet of euro area MFIs and do not follow standard balance sheet reporting categories.

Source: Figures rounded from the Eurosystem's balance sheet (ECB 2006).

This happens at high frequency and in large amounts. In this narrower sense, the theoretical foundations of money markets as a mutual insurance mechanism among banks against idiosyncratic liquidity shocks have been laid down by Bhattacharya and Gale (1987) and Bhattacharya and Fulghieri (1994). As shown by Freixas and Holthausen (2005), credit rationing can lead to a tiered insurance structure in this market. For example, when information about smaller foreign banks is more difficult to obtain than for domestic or larger foreign banks, then smaller banks may only be able to trade at the domestic level whereas the large and well-rated banks can exploit an international interbank market, such as the euro interbank deposit market.

As illustrated in Table 17.1, the functioning of money markets can be seen on both sides of a bank's balance sheet. On the asset side, credit institutions retain liquid assets and short-term securities, and they interact with the central bank for the fulfilment of reserve requirements. On the liability side, credit institutions engage in collateralized and interbank borrowing, foreign exchange swap trades, and issue short-term debt securities. In addition, money market participants are also involved in off-balance sheet activities, such as committed credit lines and derivatives.

2.2. Components

We choose to distinguish three components of money markets: (i) financial instruments and market segments; (ii) market participants; and (iii) trading mechanisms and systems. Money market instruments and segments are manifold. The inner core of the money market, the interbank market, traditionally refers to unsecured (deposits and other interbank liabilities) and secured (repurchase agreements (repos) and similar collateralized short-term loans) instruments and derivatives. In the first interbank market layer, there is a range of unsecured deposit market segments including the main maturities: overnight, spot- and tomorrow-next one and two weeks, one, two, three, and six months, and one year.[2] The secured repo markets (trading repurchase agreements secured by specific securities) also range from overnight to one year. The second layer of the money market consists of a variety of segments for money market derivatives. These include short-term (up to one year) forward rate agreements that are usually traded over the counter and exchange-traded futures, interest rate swaps (from overnight to one year), foreign currency swaps, and options. Finally, money market segments in the broader sense include a variety of short-term debt securities, such as Treasury bills and other short-term government securities, commercial paper, bank certificates of deposits, and certificates issued by non-bank entities (e.g. corporations, local government, mortgage institutions, and finance companies).

In general, money market instruments can be regarded as serving to minimize the opportunity cost of holding money balances. They are quickly and cheaply convertible into cash while bearing limited risk due to their short maturities. Unsecured cash transactions are used by banks to manage liquidity shocks associated with the fulfilment of reserve requirements and with fluctuations in customers' cash flows. Secured transactions are essentially used by dealers to manage liquidity and possibly exploit opportunities associated with expected interest rate changes. For a borrowing bank, the choice between a deposit and a repo contract of the same maturity depends largely on the premium—taking the form of an interest rate spread—it has to pay to enter an unsecured transaction relative to the costs it would incur to mobilize the collateral that would be necessary to back up a secured transaction. For a given desired maturity, a financial institution with scarce collateral will opt for a deposit contract, provided that the premium it has to pay is not too high. Repos are also used by the central bank for its regular monetary policy operations.

Money market derivatives are used to manage risks or even take speculative positions, saving economic or even regulatory capital. Forex swaps, for instance, are used to transform the currency denomination of assets and liabilities so as to trade in or out of a specific currency risk. Similarly, interest rate swap and forward contracts can be used to hedge against changes in interest rates, e.g. originating from monetary policy decisions. They can also be used to take speculative positions, e.g. to bet on a certain change in interest rates. For example, in the euro money market overnight interest rate swaps (OIS) seem to be the primary trading instrument to hedge against

---

[2] 'Tomorrow (or tom) next' refers to transactions whereby actual delivery of an asset on the same day is avoided by closing a position at a day's closing price and reopening it at the next opening price so as to push the settlement date forward to the next trading day. These types of transactions are often repeated over time until a bank wishes to ultimately close a position and settle the asset.

or speculate on interest rate movements.[3] Finally, short-term securities serve several purposes. Certificates of deposits usually certify time deposits and are used by banks as a short-term source of financing. Commercial paper is typically an unsecured promissory instrument issued by firms.[4] Commercial paper can be issued for various reasons—by banks to finance new loans, or by non-financial corporations as a short-term source of funding.

A second component of the money markets relates to the institutions participating in it. A very important money market participant is the central bank. Here, it carries out its open market operations, injects or withdraws liquidity from the banking sector, and thereby implements the short-term interest rate reflecting its monetary policy stance.[5] Money market rates therefore constitute the 'starting point' of the transmission of monetary policy. They determine to a very large extent the structure of short-term interest rates (including e.g. the short end of the government yield curve) and the cost of borrowing for issuers of commercial paper. The structure of short-term interest rates constitutes one important element of the cost of corporate financing in the economy and a key determinant of retail interest rates, i.e. the interest rates charged by banks on loans or credit lines extended to their customers. The operations of the central bank in the money market are further described in Section 4 and, particularly, in a separate chapter on monetary policy implementation.

While the central bank 'creates' and ultimately supplies liquidity, trading in the 'secondary' money market is conducted by other economic entities. The most significant share is interbank trading described before as the core of the money market, including both domestic and foreign banks. Some large banks play the role of market makers (or dealers) by offering quotes and being willing to trade on a permanent basis. Outside the interbank market, also other financial institutions, such as money market funds, insurance companies, pension funds, or large non-financial corporations, play an important role. Governments are particularly important as borrowers in the primary short-term securities segment of the money markets. *De facto*, euro money markets are dominated by a number of large banks operating over more than one money market segment. These big players are involved in multiple separate but related areas ranging from traditional banking to money market dealing or even clearing for non-bank dealers.

The third money market component consists of trading mechanisms and systems. Most segments of euro money markets are over-the-counter markets. An important market segment that is exchange traded is the interest rate futures market. The important three-month Euribor contract is traded on Euronext.liffe (London International Financial Futures and Options Exchange).

[3] An OIS is a fixed-for-floating interest rate swap where the floating rate leg corresponds to an index of daily interbank rates, the EONIA in our case.
[4] Commercial paper can, however, be backed up by bank credit lines.
[5] During 2005 and 2006 the ECB tended to allot around €300bn in each of its weekly main refinancing operations. In its monthly longer-term refinancing operations it tended to allot €30–40bn (See table 1.3 in the statistical annex of the ECB *Monthly Bulletin*.)

A small survey conducted by Hartmann, Manna, and Manzanares (2001) among money market dealers showed that in the euro interbank markets, basically all the main mechanisms of trading are present; direct bilateral trading through electronic market communication facilities (such as Reuters) or over the phone, voice brokering, and electronic trading systems. The relative use of these trading mechanisms varies according to the market participant concerned and also according to the country. For example, Italy is so far the only country with a fully-fledged electronic trading system, e-MID (electronic market for organized interbank deposits), where the matching of counterparties inserting prices and quantities is automatic. This system is dominant in the Italian segment of the euro interbank deposit market, but in the early days of EMU it did not play a significant role in cross-border money market trading in the euro area. But through an increasing number of non-Italian member banks international transactions in this system have increased in the last few years (ECB 2005a). As market microstructure literature suggests, small and medium-sized banks find the higher trade transparency of electronic systems like e-MID more attractive than large players, whose block trades may become more costly with a high degree of transparency.

According to Hartmann, Manna, and Manzanares (2001), voice brokering plays a particularly large role in Spain and for cross-border interbank market trading in the euro area. Direct dealing is more pronounced in France, Germany, and the Netherlands. From Section 4.4 it will however become clear that the heterogeneous trading mechanisms, which originate from the diverse national money markets before the start of EMU, do not seem to constitute obstacles to euro money market integration.

As the ECB money market study suggests, the relative importance of trading mechanisms also vary significantly across money market instruments (ECB 2005a: chart 32). Direct dealing is most pronounced in unsecured, interest rate swap, cross-currency swap, and short-term securities transactions. Voice brokering has its largest role in forwards and overnight interest rate swaps. Electronic trading systems are strongest with regard to repos, where a number of platforms are leading (BrokerTec, Eurex Repo, and EuroMTS), and perhaps for FX swaps.

3. STYLIZED FACTS ABOUT EURO MONEY MARKETS

After having characterized money markets from a European perspective in more conceptual terms, this section presents a detailed empirical description of the euro money markets since the start of stage 3 of EMU. We first characterize the relative sizes of the different market segments. We then have a look at the liquidity in a few main segments. Third, we discuss volatility patterns in euro money markets and, fourth, we have a brief look at risk premia as reflected in interest rate spreads.

Table 17.2. Average growth rates of the turnovers in the main money market segments between 2000 and 2004

	Unsecured lending	Unsecured borrowing	Secured lending	Secured borrowing	Interest rate swaps (OIS)	FX swaps	Short-term securities
Overnight	6.0	−1.0	9.7	15.5			
Up to 1 month[a]	6.8	6.1	22.7	32.7	23.2	9.4	24.9
1 month to 3 months	−20.8	−16.7	27.9	10.9	6.1	30.8	56.4
3 months to 1 year	−9.4	−2.6	57.2	51.2	23.5	27.4	35.1

[a]Tom/next to one month, excluding overnight transactions for unsecured and secured transactions.

Source: ECB, own calculations (%).

3.1. Market Size and Structure

In order to show the most and least dynamic euro money market segments, turnover data are shown since the year 2000.[6] Facts are presented in two parts. The first part reviews what we described in Section 2 as the inner core of the money market, the interbank market, covering the cash market (unsecured deposits, secured repos, and foreign exchange swaps) and the market for interest rate swaps. The second part describes the evolution of outright short-term securities.

As suggested by Table 17.2 (and Figure 17.9 in Section 4.5), market activity has overall significantly expanded since the start of EMU. There are, however, marked differences in growth rates across segments and maturity buckets. Between 2000 and 2004, total turnover in the secured market rose by a yearly average of around 28 per cent.[7] The repo market is now overall estimated to be larger than the unsecured market (ECB 2005a). Foreign exchange and interest rate swap markets also grew at a sustained pace of annual rates of about 22 per cent and 17 per cent on average (across all maturities). The fastest growth has been seen in the outright issuance of euro-denominated short-term securities, with an average annual growth rate of about 39 per cent, apparently led by issuance in the banking sector. But one has to keep in mind that this segment started from very low levels, and still remains a minor part of the euro area money market, even after this substantial growth. Also swap markets started from a lower level than deposit or repo markets, which puts their growth into perspective. In what follows, we show in some detail that even within market segments turnover developments can be significantly different, depending on the maturity considered.

[6] To derive the main stylized facts, we make extensive use of data that have been collected by the ECB together with National Central Banks of the Eurosystem for its Money Market Studies covering the years 2000 to 2004 (see e.g. ECB 2005a). These data are collected from a sample of credit institutions, which has grown over time. This is why they focus on yearly growth rates, where the size of each market segment in 2000 is normalized to 100. The number of reporting banks also varies from one segment to the other, but there does not seem to be panel attrition within each segment over time.

[7] These numbers are rough approximations, as they are equally weighted averages of the figures in Table 17.2 and therefore do not take the differences in activity in the different maturities into account.

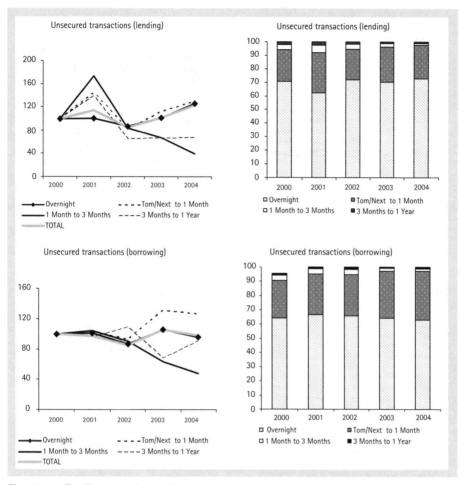

Fig. 17.1. Trading activity and maturity structure in unsecured markets

Source: ECB, own calculations

While the unsecured market has been clearly the largest money market segment at the start of EMU (see Section 4.5, Figure 17.9), it has not developed as dynamically as other segments. Whereas tom/next to one-month interbank deposits somewhat gained over the first five years of EMU longer-running deposits lost some market share, with the overall size of the unsecured segment remaining roughly unchanged (see Figure 17.1). Most plausibly, market participants focused at the start on the least complex interbank deposit trading, but over time developed more their repo and some derivatives activities, which then also limited the scope for further deposit market development. Another noteworthy feature of unsecured deposits visible in Figure 17.1 is their extreme concentration at very short maturities, in particular overnight (*c.*70 per cent of lending and 60 per cent of borrowing in this segment). Apart from the high degree of flexibility this maturity offers, this feature certainly also reflects efforts by market participants to limit credit risk exposure. Moreover, a

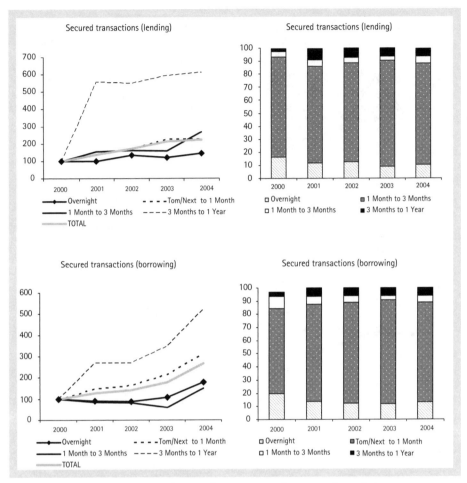

Fig. 17.2. Trading activity and maturity structure in secured markets

Source: ECB, own calculations

relevant aspect in the strong preference for very short deposits is that repo collateral is usually not settled spot.

Activity in the secured interbank market has continuously expanded, with very marked dynamics in longer-running repos (three months to one year; see Figure 17.2). The strong repo market growth has probably been spurred by the (late) introduction of benchmark indexes and some progress in integrating this market segment (see Sections 4.4 and 4.5). Market turnover remains dominated by contract maturities of one to three months. This fact and the pronounced growth of repos up to one year illustrates the greater need to control credit risk for longer-running interbank transactions.

Immediately after the introduction of the euro, cross-currency trading across the legacy currencies disappeared, implying a deceleration in forex swap activity (see e.g. Santillan, Bayle, and Thygesen 2000). Figure 17.3 shows, however, that swap activity

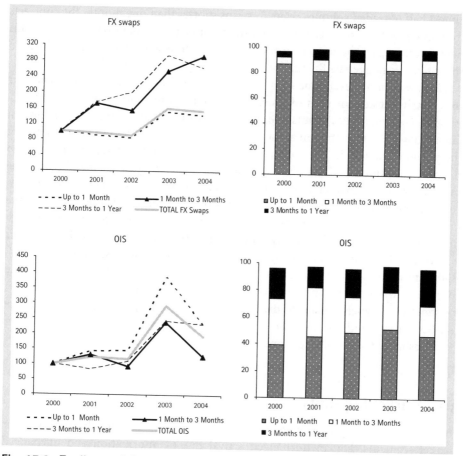

Fig. 17.3. Trading activity and maturity structure in swap markets

Source: ECB, own calculations

with currencies outside the euro area grew soon after the start of EMU. The segment is dominated by shorter maturities up to one month, which account for more than 80 per cent of trades, but longer maturities developed more dynamically.

Markets for interest rate swaps existed already in euro legacy currencies, in particular in the Deutsch mark and in the French franc. The market for interest rate swaps in euros started in significant size at the beginning of EMU. In 2003, when expectations of short-term interest rate changes emerged, enhanced interest rate hedging (and speculation) gave it a significant boost, which was only partly corrected in the calmer year 2004 (see Figure 17.3, which shows the data for OIS). Interestingly, also the still remaining fragmentation of European government securities markets (see Baele et al. in this volume) helped the interest rate swap market to grow. It induced traders to position themselves more in the swap market for speculative or hedging purposes against interest rate movements than would otherwise be the case (Remolana and Wooldridge 2002). An interesting feature of the interest rate swap market is the more evenly distributed maturity structure compared to other market segments. While almost half of traded volumes relate to swaps shorter than one month, the contracts from one month to one year are still a significant share of the overall market. This may reflect in part the longer-term character of monetary policy compared e.g. to short-term exchange rate fluctuations.

We now turn to developments in the market for short-term securities. The year 1999 clearly marked the start of a steady development in short-term debt securities issuance (see Figure 17.4). Outstanding amounts rose from around €560 billion in January 1999 to c. €980 billion at the end of 2005—a much faster growth than during the previous decade. In particular, issuance in the banking sector (monetary and financial institutions, MFIs) grew at a fast pace, implying that banks became the main actors in this market, both in terms of outstanding amounts and net issuance. In 2004, the volume of outright transactions of short-term securities issued by the banking sector was about six times that of 2000. The issuance of short-term debt instruments is traditionally heavily influenced by the public sector (which, together with banks, represented in 2005 more than 80 per cent of total outstanding amounts). Both banks and governments have contributed to the steep rise in gross issuance since 1999, as shown in the second panel of Figure 17.4. Overall, however, the euro market for short-term paper remains underdeveloped, fragmented, and domestic in nature (see Sections 4.4 and 4.5), even though nowadays activity in euro commercial paper (ECP) issuance is also gaining momentum.

3.2. Market Liquidity

In this Section we approximate market liquidity with bid–ask spreads in a few major market segments. For an unchanged arrival rate of information and unchanged volatility, decreasing spreads tend to indicate an improvement in market liquidity. We cover interbank deposit and EONIA swap markets.[8]

The left panel of Figure 17.5 shows quoted bid–ask spreads in the unsecured cash market segment. For all maturities spreads narrowed during 1999 and early 2000 from about 10 to 2–6 basis points.[9] After the higher risk period 2001 to 2003, spreads have again stabilized in the 2 to 6 basis points range.

Compared to the unsecured market, bid–ask spreads in the EONIA swap markets were already tight in 1999. While data at the start of our sample may be somewhat unreliable (note the large swings in 1999 and 2000), spreads tended to follow a downward trend thereafter, from about 1.5 basis points to 0.5 basis points (except for one-week swaps). The ECB money market report shows a similar decline between 2002 and 2005 from 2 to 1 basis point for the one-month EONIA swaps traded in e-MID

---

[8] Given the prevailing modalities of trading in the secured repo market since 1999, the available series for the repo interest rate did not allow to draw a reliable representative picture of bid–offer spreads in this market.

[9] The improvement in unsecured deposit market liquidity after 1999 is also documented in Ciampolini and Rohde 2000. For detailed information about bid–ask spreads in the overnight deposit market during five months at the end of 1999 and early 2000, see Hartmann, Manna, and Manzanares 2001: tables 6 to 15.

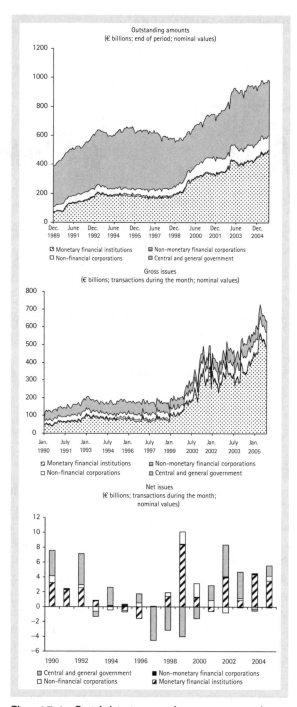

Fig. 17.4. Outright transactions, gross and net issuance of short-term debt securities issued by euro area residents

Note: Debt securities included are euro area securities other than shares. Debt securities are negotiable and may be traded on secondary markets. They do not grant the holder any ownership rights in the issuing unit. Money market paper and private placements are in principle included in the debt securities statistics. It is estimated to cover approximately 95% of total issues by euro area residents

Source: ECB Short Term Securities Statistics

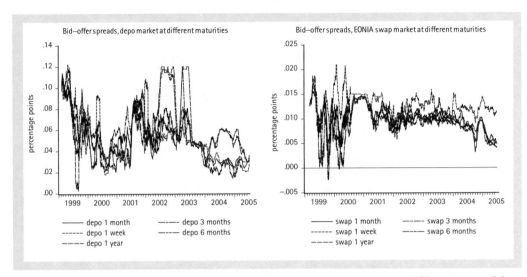

Fig. 17.5. Bid–offer spreads in the deposit and EONIA swap markets at different maturities

Source: Bloomberg, daily data

(ECB 2005a: box 3). These are extremely narrow spreads, indicative of a highly liquid market.

3.3. Market Interest Rates and Volatility

Developments in European money market interest rates are largely determined by movements in ECB policy rates (and by market expectations about their future development) and by the operational instruments for the implementation of monetary policy. To implement its monetary policy, the ECB makes use of open market operations, standing facilities, and minimum reserve requirements. Open market operations play an important role for the steering of interest rates, managing the liquidity situation in the money market so as to keep short-term rates at the level that defines the current stance of monetary policy. Standing facilities are intended to satisfy temporary liquidity needs and should, under normal circumstances, provide a ceiling (marginal lending facility) and a floor (deposit facility) for the overnight market interest rate. Finally, minimum reserves are meant to stabilize money market interest rates and create (enlarge) the structural liquidity deficit of the banking sector.[10] The Eurosystem has therefore a key influence on euro money market interest rates.[11]

---

[10] For a general description of the workings of reserve requirements, see e.g. Bindseil 2004. Details regarding reserve requirements in the Eurosystem can be found in ECB 2006.
[11] A detailed discussion of the Eurosystem's operational procedures for the implementation of monetary policy is presented in the chapter by Nyborg and Bindseil in this volume.

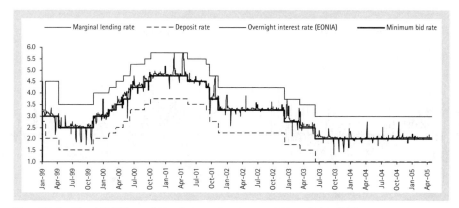

Fig. 17.6. The EONIA and the interest rate corridor of the ECB

Source: ECB

The effects of the monetary policy stance and instruments on the overnight money market are clearly visible in Figure 17.6, which shows the EONIA, together with the key ECB policy rates (the minimum bid rate in its open market operations and the rates of the two standing facilities). The EONIA follows quite closely the policy rate and basically never leaves the corridor defined by the deposit and marginal lending rate, reflecting the absence of arbitrage opportunities under normal circumstances in efficient and liquid markets. Regular spikes in the EONIA coincide with the ends of reserve maintenance periods.[12]

Evidence suggests that volatility has overall decreased since 1999 and tends to be very low at the end of the sample. This can be seen from the fluctuations in Figure 17.7, where negative and positive departures from zero depict increases in interest rate volatility. Following the methodology proposed in Durré and Nardelli (2006) volatility is defined here as the log-difference of daily interest rate levels (sixty-day moving average).[13] In all market segments, those departures have been minimal since 2003, that is to say since the start of the very long period of flat policy rates in the euro area. It can therefore not be excluded that changes in the monetary policy stance—phases of official interest rate changes—coincide with a higher level of market volatility (see the minimum bid rate depicted in Figure 17.7).

A comparison of average yearly volatilities (Table 17.3) suggests that the overnight unsecured interest rate has been significantly more volatile than one-week market segments. The general decrease in volatility over time is also reflected by a generalized decline in (and to some extent some convergence of) yearly volatilities.

---

[12] Upward spikes are the consequence of shortages and downward spikes of excesses of liquidity. It has been well known for a long time that monetary policy operational frameworks are a main factor influencing the behaviour of money market rates. Hartmann, Manna, and Manzanares 2001 have documented this with intraday data for euro area interbank deposits. Prati, Bartolini, and Bertola 2003 document that this is valid for the main industrial countries.

[13] In comparison with other volatility indicators, this realized volatility measure is adopted by Durré and Nardelli 2006 to avoid strong assumptions on the actual price process or on the link between options and their underlying assets, as e.g. the case with implied volatility measures.

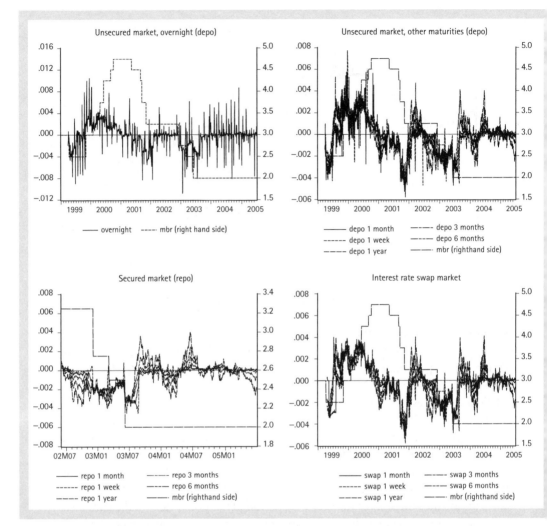

Fig. 17.7. Interest rate volatility in the main euro money market segments

Note: 'mbr' refers to the minimum bid rate of the weekly Eurosystem liquidity tenders, which is the main monetary policy rat
Volatility is defined as a 60-day moving average of log differences between daily rates as in Durré and Nardelli (2006). Series
the repo interest rate are available from 2002 on
Source: Bloomberg, own computatio

Hartmann, Manna, and Manzanares (2001) find with intraday data that overnight rate volatility increases immediately after the Thursday monetary policy decisions of the ECB's governing council, as one would expect after the arrival of information to the market. Moreover, post-auction liquidity reallocation after open market operations is also associated with slightly higher volatility than normal.[14]

---

[14] Another literature on the forward transmission of persistent volatility shocks along the term structure of money market interest rates yields mixed results. Cassola and Morana 2003 find evidence supportive of forward transmission, whereas Durré and Nardelli 2006 do not detect signs of volatility

Table 17.3. Average volatility in the main euro money market segments

	1999	2000	2001	2002	2003	2004	2005
Overnight	0.0853	0.0462	0.0578	0.0512	0.0735	0.0831	0.0848
Deposit (1 week)	0.0367	0.0295	0.0211	0.0256	0.0147	0.0079	0.0062
Repo (1 week)				0.0120	0.0144	0.0064	0.0031
EONIA swap (1 week)	0.0149	0.0120	0.0164	0.0133	0.0141	0.0101	0.0038
EONIA swap (2 weeks)	0.0105	0.0080	0.0114	0.0082	0.0093	0.0064	0.0023

Note: Standard deviation of the log-difference of daily interest rate levels, year by year. Series for the repo interest rate are available from 2002 only.

Source: Bloomberg, own computations.

3.4. Money Market Premia and Interest Rate Spreads

As discussed in Section 4 below, the general level of money market interest rates is driven by ECB policy rates, more or less tightly depending on the market segments and on the maturities. However, beyond the general level of money market rates systematic price differentials, or 'spreads', can be observed between interest rates of different instruments with comparable maturities.

While the dynamics of interest rates across different maturities has triggered a vast literature, little is known about the behaviour of same maturity money market rates. In the primary market, monetary policy operations determine the price of collateralized credit-risk or liquidity-risk free liquidity. However, the collateral accepted in the Eurosystem's open market operations has a quality that is lower than market repo agreements based on 'general collateral' (see Section 4.4. below). In principle, one may therefore expect market rates with similar maturity to be higher than the ECB main refinancing rate. In practice, this is generally the case, although the reverse can at times be observed as well. Ewerhart, Cassola, and Valla (2006) explain the occurrence of such negative spreads with respect to the main policy rate with bid shading by submitting banks, which typically occurs when banks' marginal valuation of liquidity is declining.

In the secondary market, the secured (repo) interest rate is often taken to be the closest proxy for the risk-free rate. Its liquidity risk premium is typically low, as collateral can normally be liquidated at very low cost in case of creditor default. As a result, spreads between the deposit rate, which contains risk (and possibly liquidity) premia, and the repo rate should be expected to be positive.[15] Also the spread between deposit and EONIA swap rates should be positive, as the swap rates reflect the risk premia priced in the expected overnight deposit rates (for which EONIA is a reference rate).

While spreads with the expected signs have typically been observed since 1999, occasional departures from positive values have called for further explanations. First, it

transmission from overnight rates across the yield curve. Jardet and Le Fol 2007 describe asymmetries in the responses of the conditional EONIA rate volatility to monetary policy shocks.

[15] A potential factor reducing the repo spread may be linked to cross-country settlement difficulties, which may adversely affect repo market liquidity.

may be the case that market strategies to exploit arbitrage opportunities and manage risk exposures affect cross-sectional spreads in a non-trivial way. For example, it may be profitable for a dealer to find the liquidity needed to finance a bond purchase in the repo market, and hedge against the interest rate risk in the interest rate swap market, thereby linking the repo, swap, and unsecured market segments together in a trilateral way. Alternatively, sufficiently large banks may sporadically find it profitable to corner the market by building up a futures position in the OIS market, and subsequently trading in the spot market, thereby taking advantage of the impact of price changes in the cash market on swap returns (Ewerhart et al. 2007).

4. POLICY ISSUES FOR EURO MONEY MARKETS

There are a large number of policy issues related to money markets. In the present section we address seven of them which appeared particularly important to us. We first review what money market rates teach us about the predictability of ECB monetary policy. Second, we briefly touch on the operational procedures for the implementation of monetary policy. Third, we examine the payment and settlement systems that support the functioning of money markets. The fourth subsection looks at the degree of integration in the different euro money market segments and the fifth subsection at the overall development of the euro money market. Subsection 6 examines the effects that the ongoing banking consolidation trend may have on the functioning of euro money markets. Last, we look at the behaviour of central banks in money markets during crises and review lender-of-last-resort arrangements in Europe.

4.1. Predictability of Monetary Policy

For simple arbitrage reasons short-term money market rates tend to be closely aligned with the policy rates of central banks. If a money market contract extends beyond the date of the next monetary policy decision, then the interest rate agreed in such a contract reflects also the expectations of the market about the forthcoming decision. A variety of researchers have used different money market rates to assess to which extent actual monetary policy decisions deviated from the ones expected in the market and sometimes also draw conclusions about the transparency and effectiveness of central bank communication.

This literature started in the United States, where Cook and Hahn (1989) found that Treasury bond and bill rates reacted to Federal Open Market Committee decisions changing the fed funds target rate. If such monetary policy moves had been fully anticipated, then longer rates should not react to them. Krueger and Kuttner (1996) use fed funds futures to separate anticipated and unanticipated fed funds target rate changes in the United States. Building on this methodology, Kuttner (2001) finds that unexpected target rate changes have an economically large and highly significant effect on US Treasury bills and bonds but, in most cases, not expected target rate changes. A related study by Poole and Rasche (2000) comes to very similar conclusions, although the difference between anticipated and unanticipated monetary policy changes is perhaps even clearer. Another result of this US literature is that the Fed has become more predictable for markets over time.

The predictability of ECB monetary policy decisions has been a matter of debate in the early years of EMU. In contrast to some market speak, basically all studies published in scholarly refereed journals indicate a rather high predictability of ECB policy, even relatively shortly after it started the common monetary policy in January 1999. Hartmann, Manna, and Manzanares (2001: subsection 4.2) measure that the euro overnight market rate moves on average by only 4.6 basis points in the minutes following the Thursday 1.45 p.m. release on monetary policy decisions. This change is a proxy for the expectations error in the market and turns out to be relatively small in comparison to the typical 25 or 50 basis points step size of monetary policy decisions during the sample period November 1999 to March 2000. Bernoth and von Hagen (2004) first show that the three-month Euribor futures market was informationally efficient between December 1998 and September 2003. Second, they detect that ECB monetary policy announcements are not reducing the prediction error in Euribor futures for spot rates. Both results support the hypothesis that the ECB is relatively predictable, and Bernoth and von Hagen even find that this situation has improved over time, as one would expect. Finally, a recent study of the euro area compared to thirteen other countries confirms the above results also relative to other central banks (Wilhelmsen and Zaghini 2005). In particular, the ECB does seem to be at least as predictable as the Federal Reserve or the Bank of England. Most monetary policy surprises that nevertheless occurred in the euro area seem to have taken place prior to the autumn of 2001. Generally, monetary surprises are typically associated with changes in the target rate level, whereas unchanged rates are usually better anticipated by the market.

4.2. Central Bank Operations and Monetary Regulation

The money market is different from many other financial markets in that the supply side is dominated by a large public authority, the central bank. In order to implement their monetary policy, which nowadays usually means that they keep a short-term interest rate at a certain level or within a well-specified range, central banks in industrial countries actively manage the liquidity situation in the money market for very short maturities (see e.g. Board of Governors 2005; ECB 2004). They do this, for example, with the help of open market operations, standing facilities, or reserve requirements. In this regard, the ECB and the Eurosystem are not different from other central banks, such as the Federal Reserve, the Bank of England, or the Bank of Japan (see e.g. Borio 1997, 2001, as well as Bindseil 2004).

These central bank operations, facilities, and regulations exert very important influences on how the money market functions. Early theoretical contributions in this field include Poole (1968) Ho and Saunders (1985), and Spindt and Hoffmeister (1988). Their importance for the behaviour of US money market rates has been shown e.g. by Campbell (1987) and Hamilton (1996). Hartmann, Manna, and Manzanares (2001) provided the first empirical analysis of how Eurosystem policies influence the euro money market, taking a very broad perspective across operations, facilities, and regulations. Prati, Bartolini, and Bertola (2003) compare the effects of a few regulations across G-7 countries and confirm that different approaches lead to different patterns in short-term interest rates across countries. As a full chapter is dedicated to the rationale behind and the effects of monetary policy implementation, we do not review this literature here but refer the reader to the chapter by Bindseil and Nyborg on 'Monetary policy implementation' in this book.

4.3. Cross-border Market Infrastructure

An efficient cross-border infrastructure for clearing and settling payments and securities is an important building block of a successful monetary union. In particular, efficient cross-border large-value payment systems are a precondition for the effective implementation of the single monetary policy. The smooth flow of large-value payments across an area composed of different countries is important to allow efficient arbitrage to ensure a single short-term interest rate as the reflection of the current monetary policy stance in the whole area. Efficient cross-border infrastructures for clearing and settling securities are also important as liquidity provision by the central bank is basically always collateralized and eligible collateral should therefore flow smoothly across different member countries. Finally, cross-border market infrastructures provide significant support for the integration and development of money markets in general.

In the euro area, the payment system TARGET (Trans-European automated real-time gross settlement express transfer system) was created at the start of EMU to interconnect the fifteen national real-time gross settlement (RTGS) systems and the ECB payment mechanism. Alongside TARGET the European Banking Association introduced the net settlement system Euro 1.[16] Although TARGET was immediately successful, it soon became clear that further improvements were possible. The harmonization of national real time gross settlement systems (RTGS) that had initially taken place was overall limited, although sufficient to ensure a uniform monetary policy implementation as well as a level playing field for credit institutions. By the

---

[16] To date, some 10,400 banks use TARGET to execute payments, and more than 52,750 banks are accessible through it worldwide. In 2006, around 326,196 payments with a value of €2.1 trillion per business day were transferred through TARGET (ECB 2005d).

time of publication of the present volume a much more harmonized 'new generation' of TARGET denoted as TARGET 2, will be operating.[17]

Overall, the gradual development of integrated payment systems takes place at a time when euro money markets are developing further. 'Adaptability' therefore seems to be a requirement, in particular in light of the expected enlargement of the euro area and Eurosystem. For a detailed discussion of European payment systems and their evolution, see the chapter by Xavier Freixas and Cornelia Holthausen in this volume.

Cross-border clearing and settlement are important for both the implementation of monetary policy and the development and integration of the money markets. As regards the former, the Eurosystem has implemented the correspondent central banking model (CCBM) in order to promote the equal treatment of counterparties. The CCBM—which enables counterparties to obtain credit from their 'home central bank' using collateral transferred to another national central bank—was meant to ensure that all assets eligible for use either in monetary policy operations or to obtain intraday liquidity were available to all its counterparties, regardless of the location in the euro area of the assets or the counterparty.[18] As regards the latter, money market integration and development, in particular the repo and short-term securities market segments, deserve attention.

Clearing and settlement systems were rather fragmented when the euro was introduced. Market participants soon voiced a need for standardizing systems and harmonizing the tax and legal treatment of transactions (Giovannini Group 1999). A number of private sector initiatives (such as the 'Standards for securities clearing, and settlement in the European Union' (CESR and ECB 2004) emerged to promote the integration, efficiency, and safety of the European securities infrastructure. For example, the two international central securities depositories, Clearstream and Euroclear (which settle a large part of international securities transactions), have introduced an Automated Daytime Bridge between each other. Moreover, in 2005 Eurex Repo introduced Euro General Collateral Pooling, which combines international electronic repo trading with an automated collateral allocation process, clearing and settlement. In early 2007, the ECB, in cooperation with central securities depositories and other market participants, had designed a blueprint to explore the possibility of setting up a common technical service to execute securities settlement instructions for the euro area, called TARGET 2—Securities (T2S). T2S would provide delivery versus payment for securities against central bank money. The ECB has also been active in setting standards and promoting an integrated regulatory and oversight framework,

---

[17] Originally, TARGET payments that took place across borders were transferred via the national real-time gross settlement systems (RTGS) and exchanged on a bilateral basis between national central banks. TARGET 2 provides markets with a fully integrated platform (the 'single shared platform'), extensively harmonized services, and improved cost efficiency. It also enhances the adaptability of the system to new euro area entrants, TARGET 2 'went live' in November 2007 and the entries of current euro area countries and EU member countries wishing to join it are expected to be completed during the first half of 2008.

[18] However, the CCBM is seen as a medium-term solution that will continue to operate until adequate market solutions become available. The system of 'links between securities and settlement systems' was subsequently adopted as an alternative way to settle collateral across borders.

relying—unlike other central banks—on market-driven solutions operated by the private sector. For an extensive discussion of securities clearing and settlement arrangements and their evolution in Europe, see the chapter by Giovannini, Berrigan, and Russo in this volume.

4.4. Money Market Integration

Financial integration—including that of money markets—is an important issue for European Union policy under the Lisbon Agenda.[19] In a fully integrated money market, i.e. one where there are no frictions or institutional/legal differences that fragment markets, the interest rates charged on the same instruments should be identical, irrespective of location.[20] The peculiarity of money markets in this regard is their close relationship to monetary integration. The introduction of a common currency and a single monetary policy, as well as the related large-value payment systems (see Section 4.3 above), gave a decisive impetus to money market integration, e.g. as a common monetary policy implies the implementation of a single short-term policy rate.

As the integration of the secured and unsecured money market segments is already discussed in the chapter on 'Measuring European financial integration' by Baele et al., we do not add further price-based indicators here and only briefly summarize their level of integration. Soon after the introduction of the euro, the unsecured interbank market was already extremely well integrated and continued to integrate thereafter. For example, the cross-country standard deviation for the overnight lending rates stood at around 3 basis points in 1999 and around 1 basis point in 2005 (ECB 2005b).[21] Therefore, the integration of the unsecured deposit market comes close to 'perfection'.

The integration of the secured (repo) market, although progressing, is still more limited than in the unsecured segment. The main remaining obstacles to integration relate to the mobilization of collateral when entering a repo transaction. Differences in legal systems, high costs of cross-border securities settlement, and the lack of substitutability even between debt securities with identical credit ratings lead to interest rate differentials and lower cross-border trading than for unsecured transactions. Wedges between repo rates in different euro area countries tend to be more

---

[19] The Lisbon Agenda was originally set in March 2000 by the EU heads of states and governments to foster economic reforms that would create 'growth and jobs' by far-reaching reforms at the European and national levels.

[20] See Baele et al. 2004 and ECB 2005b for the presentation of a broader definition of financial integration and how it relates to the law of one price used here.

[21] Cross-country variation in unsecured lending rates vanished also at longer maturities. Euribor lending rates for the one-month and for the twelve-month maturities remained within a 0.4 and 1.2 basis point range after the introduction of the euro and did not exceed 0.8 basis points in the last few years.

Given the nature of a monetary union it is debatable whether the convergence period before EMU should be interpreted as financial integration or not. For completeness we mention that the cross-country standard deviation of overnight rates amounted to more than 130 basis points in early 1998 and to 100 and 50 basis for one-month and twelve-month rates, respectively.

pronounced at longer maturities, such as twelve months.[22] The limited cross-border use of collateral is another sign that there is room for further integration. For example in 2004, half of the collateral for borrowing transactions originated from the same country as the borrower. The increasing pressure to open more opportunities for secured cross-border financing and sharing of liquidity risk has led to market initiatives making euro-denominated 'general collateral' ('GC') more substitutable across borders. One example for this is the recent introduction of 'Euro GC Pooling', an instrument introduced on the existing Eurex repo platform. It offers to domestic and international banks a fully integrated and automated solution for trading, clearing, and settling general collateral repos for several thousand Eurosystem-eligible securities.

The least integrated money market segment remains short-term securities. The European markets for commercial paper and certificates of deposit continue to be segmented along national borders.[23] While a small number of countries possess developed national short-term paper markets (see Section 4.5), access to them by agents from other European countries remains very constrained. This is likely to constitute a significant handicap for short-term firm financing.

Market-led actions have been launched to support the emergence of a pan-European short-term paper market. The Short-Term European Paper (STEP) initiative, led by ACI—the Financial Markets Association—is one of the most notable ones (ACI-STEP Task Force 2002). STEP has been set up to ease the convergence of standards and to foster the integration of the fragmented European short-term paper markets. It specifically aims to promote the harmonization of the standards and practices prevailing in the European short-term securities markets through market players' voluntary compliance with the standards set out in the STEP 'Market Convention' in areas such as information disclosure, documentation, settlement, and the provision of data for the production of STEP statistics. After initial discussions in 2001 and a public consultation in 2002, the STEP Market Convention was finalized and the first STEP-labelled issuance programme launched in the spring of 2006. A STEP label acknowledges the adoption of the STEP standards for the first two years after its launch. The STEP labelling is performed by the STEP Secretariat, created and managed by the European Banking Federation with the support of the Eurosystem. STEP statistics on yields and volumes are to be produced and published on an ongoing basis so as to foster integration and reduce issuers' costs through greater market transparency.

In sum, many euro money markets—in particular the unsecured interbank segments—have attained a high degree of integration following the introduction of the euro. These markets may therefore not require as much policy attention as other financial markets. However, integration issues remain with respect to repo and in

---

[22] According to ECB indicators (ECB 2005b), while the cross-country standard deviation of one-month EUREPO rates was typically below one basis point in 2005, that for twelve-month EUREPO rates is of an order of magnitude around 1.5–2.5 basis points.

[23] This fact holds, even though unpublished data about cross-border short-term securities holdings suggest that some reductions in home bias can be observed within the euro area.

particular with short-term securities markets, where market and policy initiatives to foster integration would have the largest benefits. Financial integration can also play a role in promoting financial modernization and market development, but the two concepts are economically different. Financial integration is not necessarily related to financial development and vice versa. This is why we treat money market development in the next subsection.

4.5. Money Market Development

Besides the geographic integration of markets, the general modernization and development of financial systems is also an important area. Financial development in general relates to the ability of agents active in financial systems to innovate and introduce organizational improvements that complete markets, reduce asymmetric information, resolve agency conflicts, and reduce transaction costs, etc. In the present subsection we concentrate particularly on the availability of a large enough set of liquid money market instruments, which contribute to risk sharing in the economy. As illustrated above, a wide range of instruments is available in the euro money markets. However, the various segments differ substantially in their liquidity and level of development, as briefly reviewed below.

There is no doubt that the unsecured euro deposit market is a highly liquid and fully developed market, a fact that held practically from day 1 of EMU. It started as the largest euro money market segment (see Figure 17.5, in which total money market turnover in the second quarter of 2000 is normalized to 100), and has been characterized by active domestic and cross-border trading ever since. One factor in this was the early introduction of high-quality benchmark interest rates. From early on, the EONIA (Euro OverNight Index Average) and the Euribor (Euro Interbank Offered Rate) have established themselves as the benchmarks in the unsecured euro money market.[24] As indicated by quoted bid–ask spreads (see Section 3.2) the liquidity of this market is good and, if anything, has improved over time.

While the repo market had a somewhat slower start, it has grown a lot over the last years, becoming now even the overall largest segment according to Figure 17.5. One reason for the fact that the euro repo market was less developed at the start of EMU is related to the fact that it took a longer time for widely accepted benchmarks to emerge. The EUREPO index was not introduced before March 2002. The transactions involved in a repo contract, in particular collateral handling, make this market more sensitive to problems in cross-border integration and multiple legal regimes (see e.g.

---

[24] The EONIA is an effective daily overnight rate computed as a volume-weighted average of all overnight unsecured lending transactions by the forty-nine largest players in the euro interbank market. The Euribors are the rates at which euro interbank term deposits are offered by one prime bank to another prime bank (from one week to one year maturity). In contrast to the EONIA, they are unweighted and only based on quoted rates. The benchmarks are sponsored by the European Banking Federation and by the Financial Markets Association (ACI).

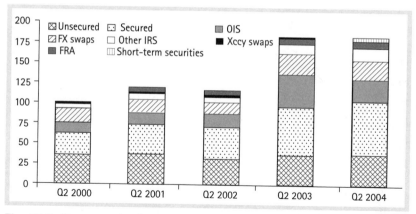

Fig. 17.8. Turnovers in the main euro money market segments

Note: FRA=forward rate agreements, FX=foreign exchange, IRS=interest rate swaps, OIS=overnight interest rate swaps, Xccy=cross currency. Q2 2000 turnovers are normalized to 100

Source: ECB Money Market Study (2005a)

Section 4.4). As these problems are addressed over time, the market can be expected to develop further.[25]

A crucial feature of a developed money market is the availability of a range of liquid derivatives markets relating to short-term interest rates. An important innovation with the introduction of the euro was the overnight interest rate (or EONIA) swap market (OIS), in which fixed and variable rate (indexed to EONIA) cash flows can be swapped for a wide range of maturities. This market segment, in which agents can optimize their interest rate exposure in response to changing expectations about e.g. monetary policy, has grown significantly over time (as have other interest rate swaps) and its high liquidity is also illustrated by bid–ask spreads that are now often narrower than one basis point (see ECB 2005a: box 3, and Figure 17.5 above). The rapid development of the EONIA swap market led to the creation of a benchmark in June 2005, the EONIA-swap index (sponsored by the Euribor-ACI). It can be expected to further promote the development of the interest rate swap market, leading to new product developments, serving as a benchmark tool for other derivatives, and being used as a controlling and valuation tool (ECB 2005a). Another active and growing derivative segment of the euro money market is foreign exchange swaps (see Figure 17.8).

The least developed areas of euro money markets remain the markets for short-term securities. As Figure 17.8 shows, they are still minimal compared to other money market segments (although they grew quite significantly from a very low basis over time). The total outstanding stock of euro-denominated short-term securities in 2004 (about €800bn) was way below the stock of US short-term securities as far back as the early 1990s (see e.g. Cook and La Roche 1993: chapters 4, 7, and 9). Another sign that there is further room for development is the dominance of banks and sovereigns. In

---

[25] The growth of tri-party repos in the secured money market segment as another innovation is described in ECB 2005a: 2.3.4.

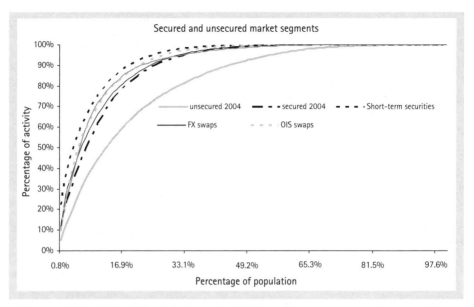

Fig. 17.9. Concentration of activity in different euro money market segments, 2004

Source: Lorenz curves based on ECB data

a fully developed short-term paper market one would expect more active non-bank activity. The dominant role of banks may signal that industrial firms receive loans which the banks (and not the firms) fund with debt securities issuance.

This situation prevails even though already prior to 1999 a small number of euro area countries had active markets for short-term paper. France, Germany, and Spain dominated issuance activity in Europe. Even today, the largest national market for commercial paper remains the market for *billets de trésorerie* in France, a subset of the market for negotiable debt instruments.[26] According to Doran (2006), the depth and liquidity of the French market is largely the result of its flexible regulations, its high levels of security and transparency, the efficient delivery-versus-payment systems that settle commercial paper, and its openness to non-resident issuers and investors. Nevertheless, at the European level issuers and investors in the European short-term paper markets remain confronted with markets characterized by limited size, depth, and liquidity as well as limited diversification opportunities.

4.6. Banking Consolidation and Competition

Since at least the 1990s an extensive trend of banking consolidation can be observed in industrial countries (Berger, Demsetz, and Strahan 1999). An important issue is how the associated reduction in the number of banks affects the functioning of

---

[26] These *titres de créances négociables* (TCN) were instituted in 1985. TCN are negotiable debt securities representing a fixed-term debt issued at the initiative of the issuer and traded on a regulated market or over the counter. TCNs include certificates of deposit (CDs) and commercial paper (CP).

money markets, most of which are basically interbank markets. The G-10 'Report on consolidation in the financial sector' (Group of Ten 2001: 20) for instance states that 'by internalising what had previously been interbank transactions, consolidation could reduce the liquidity of the market for central bank reserves, making it less efficient at reallocating balances across institutions and increasing market volatility'. But most central banks responded to a questionnaire prepared for the G-10 report that the effects of consolidation on money markets had been small so far and they did not expect this to fundamentally change in the future. This contrasts for example with the experience of Switzerland where consolidation basically led the money market to be dominated by two large players. The Swiss National Bank solved this problem by granting foreign banks easier access to its domestic money market, thereby implicitly increasing the number of trading banks.[27]

Theoretical research by Carletti, Hartmann, and Spagnolo (2003) suggests that the interbank market may be affected by bank mergers in a number of ways. First, changes in loan market competition modify the size of banks' balance sheets, which affect the distribution of liquidity shocks. For example, mergers among large banks will usually make the banking system more asymmetric, i.e. increase the dispersion between large and small banks, which amplifies the extent of aggregate liquidity fluctuations. Second, mergers create internal money markets, which allow for more precise estimates of liquidity needs and change reserve holdings. In less efficient money markets (defined here as markets in which the costs of refinancing are high) reserves decrease, worsening the liquidity situation in the money market, whereas in more efficient money markets (with low refinancing costs) reserves increase, improving money market liquidity. Depending on the direction and relative importance of the asymmetry and reserve effects, the central bank has to inject more or less liquidity to stabilize money market interest rates. In a relatively efficient market, such as the euro money market, the model would predict that fewer large mergers and more competition are likely to lead to improved money market liquidity and fewer substantial central bank interventions in the money market, whereas more mergers and less competition would lead to the opposite effect. It may, however, be that the degree of consolidation has to go much further in order to lead to any significant adverse liquidity effects in the euro money market.

Figure 17.5 illustrates the market structures in the main segments of the euro money market. The Lorenz curve for the unsecured segment suggests that consolidation has not yet led to severe concentration in interbank deposit trading. The 5 (10) per cent largest reporting banks account for 24 per cent (40 per cent) of trading volume. The repo market, however, is already more concentrated. The most concentrated segments are the interest rate swap market (other than OIS) and the forward market, in which the top 5 (10) per cent reporting banks account for 62 per cent (82 per cent) and 60 per cent (77 per cent) of turnover, respectively. In sum, it is advisable for the European Central Bank to follow how further banking consolidation affects the liquidity of the euro money market.

---

[27] Other small European countries face similar problems already today, e.g. Denmark or Sweden.

4.7. Financial Stability and the Lender of Last Resort

At least since Bagehot (1873) the great importance of the money market and the central bank for financial stability has been recognized. Accordingly, part of the financial stability literature looks at sources of instability emerging through the money market and policy interventions to ensure stability. This raises the issue how money market stability is ensured in the euro area.

4.7.1. *Interbank Contagion Risk*

A recent theoretical literature has explained bank contagion phenomena through peer monitoring in the money market (Rochet and Tirole 1996), liquidation of interbank deposits in response to unexpected deposit withdrawals (Allen and Gale 2000), liquidation of interbank deposits in response to fears of insufficient reserves (Freixas, Parigi, and Rochet 2000), or adverse selection in interbank lending when information about the solvency of borrowers is imperfect (Flannery 1996).

Many empirical papers attempted to test for bank contagion but few of them can strictly isolate the role of the money market and interbank lending (see the survey by De Bandt and Hartmann 2002). Kaufman (1994) reports the exposures of other banks to Continental Illinois, when it failed in mid-1984. The fact that sixty-five financial institutions had uninsured exposures beyond their capital to Continental Illinois illustrates the potential risks. The relatively limited actual losses of this specific failing bank, however, implied that none of these sixty-five institutions would have been insolvent in the end.

A number of papers have recently tried to assess the risk of interbank contagion further, by simulating failures and contagion from actual interbank exposures. (Such data are mostly confidential, only accessible for a few central bank researchers, and often incomplete.) Some of them find relatively limited contagion effects (see e.g. Furfine 2003 for the United States; Elsinger, Lehar, and Summer 2002 for Austria). Others find more substantial contagion risk (see e.g. Upper and Worms 2004 for Germany; Degryse and Nguyen 2004 for Belgium; Lelyveld and Liedorp 2004 for the Netherlands; Mistrulli 2005 for Italy). These studies have all been conducted for money market data of individual countries. An interesting finding of the papers on the euro area countries Belgium and Netherlands is that interbank contagion risk from abroad seems to be substantial or increasing over time. In contrast, the Italian banking system seems still to be less exposed to foreign banks through the money market.

4.7.2. *Risk Management, Supervision, and the Lender of Last Resort*

Overall, theory and empirical evidence suggest that potential instabilities in the money market and their propagation to the financial system cannot be excluded. The primary responsibility for preventing any sources of instability lies with the risk management functions of the banks that are active in the money market. Next, regulation and supervision have the burden of making sure that failures of banks' internal risk management approaches and controls do not lead to instability. In cases where none of these ex ante elements is successful, central banks are in a unique position to stabilize the money market through their liquidity management operations (see also Section 4.2 above). This role of central banks is often described as the lender of last resort (LLR). When and how should the LLR intervene? The literature on central banks' role as a lender of last resort has recently been surveyed e.g. by Freixas et al. (1999).

The 'classical' doctrine on the lender of last resort contends that central banks should only lend to solvent banks against good collateral. Credit should be extended to all illiquid banks at a penalty rate, and the readiness to lend without limits should be credibly announced to the market (Thornton 1802; Bagehot 1873). Historical evidence on the use of LLR interventions to mitigate banking crises is reviewed in Bordo (1990). Overall, it turns out that these principles have not been systematically followed. In particular, empirical evidence suggests that insolvent banks are often bailed out, and that failing banks are more often rescued than liquidated (Goodhart and Schoenmaker 1995; Hoffman and Santomero 1998).

The classical approach has been questioned on two grounds. First, it might be desirable, under some circumstances, to extend LLR loans to insolvent institutions. Practice has shown that it is often difficult to distinguish ex ante—i.e. when a decision on an emergency intervention is needed—between liquidity and solvency issues. This 'grey area' between temporary liquidity distress and more structural solvency problems in financial institutions under strain implies that it might sometimes be necessary to grant central bank funding to institutions that may turn out ex post to be insolvent (Goodhart 1985). Second, if central banks bear some responsibility for the stability of the financial system, it may be desirable not to exclude the possibility to rescue insolvent banks on financial stability grounds (Solow 1982).

While the 'grey area' between liquidity and solvency could lead to the extension of LLR facilities to potentially insolvent banks, central banks have to strike a balance between the risks of contagion and the moral hazard that such interventions induce. Ways to mitigate LLR-induced moral hazard have been suggested in the literature. In theory, banks above a certain size could be systematically rescued while smaller institutions would be only randomly bailed out (Goodhart and Huang 1999). Or, interventions could be made conditional on the amount of uninsured debt issued by the respective bank(s) (Freixas 1999). Acharya and Yorulmazer (2006) argue that the inefficient liquidation of assets in the presence of large or contagious bank failures may justify bail-outs. Liquidity assistance to surviving banks could however reach similar results. It should be kept in mind, though, that solvency issues go much beyond the realm of money markets and central banks. When it comes to bail-outs of insolvent banks then the role of fiscal authorities becomes much more important.

Fundamental critiques of emergency liquidity assistance to individual financial institutions (ELA) have put forward the ability of modern interbank markets to reallocate liquidity efficiently within the banking system when needed. As a result, interventions in favour of individual banks are unnecessary in a market context where *aggregate* liquidity imbalances can be corrected by the central bank through liquidity injections in the open market ('lending to the market'). Concentrating on the federal funds market, Goodfriend and King (1988) consider that the market spontaneously delivers the 'desired allocation of bank reserves within the banking system at the rate decided upon by the central bank'. In the same vein, Schwartz (1992) regards the market as an informationally efficient mechanism where insolvent institutions are not funded. However, liquidity reallocation solely through market mechanisms might fail to channel liquidity to banks that need it. For example, potential lenders or other market participants may refrain from providing liquidity for strategic reasons (Rochet and Vives 2004; Flannery 1996). In addition, the malfunctioning of large-value payment systems in a crisis may not allow interbank lending to reach the banks in need of liquidity (Freixas, Parigi, and Rochet 2000). Some recent empirical literature argues, however, that US banks seem to have been successful in reallocating liquidity during periods of stress (see e.g. Strahan, Gatev, and Schuermann 2004).

4.7.3. *LLR in the Euro Area*

It is sometimes claimed that the euro area arrangements for liquidity assistance are not clear. This is not too surprising, given that the 'advertising' of ELA provisions implies the risk of moral hazard. For maintaining market confidence, it is sufficient to make clear that there is a certain capability and willingness to act if really necessary (one of the 'Bagehot principles'). However, it is common practice by basically all major central banks around the world, including the US Federal Reserve, not to disclose the conditions and practicalities of ELA arrangements. What is known for the euro area is that the main responsibility for any ELA operations to individual institutions is at the national level, where all costs and risks have to be borne. This feature links naturally to the national nature of financial supervision and the absence of a significant centralized European budget.[28] Appropriate provisions yet are in place to ensure an adequate exchange of information within the Eurosystem and the ESCB about the nature of a problem that emerges and about the liquidity impact of any national ELA operations.

Liquidity operations to the money market as a whole ('lending to the market') are, however, the prerogative of the ECB, which implements the single monetary policy. For example, regular (or occasional) monetary policy operations serve the purpose of rebalancing quantities in the interbank money market. Gradual enough liquidity strains are therefore automatically reflected in revisions to the forecasts of autonomous liquidity factors that serve as a basis for determining the size of the ECB's liquidity injections in the money market (see the chapter by Bindseil and Nyborg in this volume). Besides this, financial institutions may always access the Eurosystem's marginal lending facility if for some reason their liquidity needs turn out to exceed what had been forecast. The facility is designed as a 'back-up' source of liquidity for

---

[28] Freixas 2003 and Goodhart and Schoenmaker 2006 discuss problems of the fiscal resolution of banking crises in a cross-country context.

solvent banks in need of overnight liquidity and able to mobilize adequate collateral, even though the main purpose of it (together with the marginal lending facility) is to stabilize short-term interest rates within a 'corridor'.

5. CONCLUSIONS

This chapter provides a wide overview of the structure and working of the new money markets created by EMU. It first recalls the scope and main functions of money markets and illustrates their importance for the well-functioning of financial systems. Two functions are identified, the solving of cash flow mismatches between agents at the individual level and contributions to the allocation of savings to real investment opportunities at the aggregate level. The main financial instruments and segments, market participants, and trading mechanisms and systems are described.

Stylized facts about euro money markets are presented next. Since the start of EMU, rates of expansion have been spectacular. It is not unusual to observe yearly growth rates in the order of 20–30 per cent in some market segments. The largest market segment by now is the repo market, followed by the unsecured deposit, interest rate swap, and foreign exchange swap markets. Liquidity as measured by bid–ask spreads tends to be high in the euro interbank money markets and has further improved over time. Money market rates tend to follow closely ECB monetary policy. Volatility is higher around key dates, such as the ends of reserve maintenance periods, monetary policy decisions, and open market operations. Spreads between interest rates in primary and secondary market segments with similar maturities tend to be in line with underlying risk premia, except for some special periods.

The chapter then discusses the main policy issues for euro money markets around six topics. The first is the predictability of monetary policy, which is typically evaluated with money market rates. In contrast to occasional market and press reports, scholarly research suggests a high degree of predictability of the interest rate decisions by the ECB. Second, central bank operations are presented as a key part of the institutional framework conditioning money market outcomes (liquidity management and trading strategies and ultimately quantities and prices). Efficient central bank operational procedures will be conducive to the well-functioning of money markets. Third, efficient payment and settlement systems are important ingredients for a single monetary policy and an integrated money market. The discussion sketches recent improvements in these systems and how they help to make some progress with integration.

Fourth, it is argued that the current degrees of money market integration and development still display marked divergences across market segments. Whereas the unsecured deposit and most derivative markets are highly integrated, some obstacles to the full integration of repo markets remain. Nevertheless, repo, interest rate swap, and foreign exchange swap markets have developed significantly over the last years, but both the integration and the development of the short-term securities markets leave much to be desired. The discussion summarizes in particular market-driven efforts to improve the integration and development of the markets for short-term paper, which clearly deserve more attention in the future. Fifth, the ongoing process of banking consolidation and its effects on the structure of the banking sector can have first-order consequences for the euro money markets, e.g. through the size of banks' balance sheets, the distribution of liquidity shocks, and reserve holdings. More specifically, participation in a few of derivatives segments is already highly concentrated in the euro money markets.

The sixth and last policy area addressed is money market stability and the role of the lender of last resort. The chapter underlines the great importance of money markets for financial stability, illustrates the capacity of central banks to contribute to money market stability, and sketches policy responsibilities in the euro area in times of crisis. Market-wide liquidity problems will have to be addressed in the implementation of monetary policy, whereas emergency liquidity assistance to individual institutions is largely aligned with national responsibilities for financial regulation, supervision, and public budgets.

References

ACHARYA, V., and YORULMAZER, T. (2006), 'Cash-in-the-market pricing and optimal resolution of bank failures', EFA 2006 Zurich Meetings, June: http://ssrn.com/abstract=685505.

ACI-STEP Task Force (2002), *The Short Term Paper Market in Europe: Recommendation for the Development of a Pan-European Market*, 2 September.

ALLEN, F., and GALE, D. (2000), 'Financial contagion', *Journal of Political Economy*, 108, 1–33.

BAELE, L., FERRANDO, A., HÖRDAHL, P., KRYLOVA, E., and MONNET, C. (2004), 'Measuring financial integration in the euro area', ECB Occasional Paper 14.

BAGEHOT, W. (1873), *Lombard Street: A Description of the Money Market*, 3rd edn., London: Henry S. King & Co.

BERGER, A., DEMSETZ, R., and STRAHAN, P. (1999), 'The consolidation of the financial services industry: causes, consequences, and implications for the future', *Journal of Banking and Finance*, 23, 135–94.

BERNOTH, K., and VON HAGEN, J. (2004), 'The Euribor futures market: efficiency and the impact of ECB policy announcements', *International Finance*, 7, 1–24.

BHATTACHARYA, S., and FULGHIERI, P. (1994), 'Uncertain liquidity and interbank contracting', *Economics Letters*, 44, 287–94.

_____ and GALE, D. (1987), 'Preference shocks, liquidity, and central bank policy', in W. Barnett and K. Singleton (eds.), *New Approaches to Monetary Economics*, Cambridge: Cambridge University Press.

BINDSEIL, U. (2004), *Monetary Policy Implementation: Theory, Past and Present*, Oxford: Oxford University Press.

Board of Governors of the Federal Reserve System (2005), *The Federal Reserve System: Functions and Purpose*, 9th edn., Washington, DC.

BORDO, M. (1990), 'The lender of last resort: alternative views and historical experience', *Federal Reserve Bank of Richmond Economic Review*, January–February.

BORIO, C. (1997), 'Monetary policy operating procedures in industrial countries', *BIS Conference Papers*, 3, 286–368.

—— (2001), 'A hundred ways to skin a cat: comparing monetary policy operating procedures in the United States, Japan and the euro area', BIS Paper 9.

CAMPBELL, J. (1987), 'Money announcements, the demand for bank reserves, and the behaviour of the federal funds rate within the statement week', *Journal of Money, Credit, and Banking*, 19, 56–67.

CARLETTI, E., HARTMANN, P., and SPAGNOLO, G. (2003), 'Bank mergers, competition and liquidity', ECB Working Paper 292 (forthcoming in *Journal of Money, Credit, and Banking*).

CASSOLA, N., and MORANA, C. (2003), 'Volatility of interest rates in the euro area: evidence from high frequency data', ECB Working Paper 235.

CESR and ECB (2004), 'Standards for securities clearing and settlement in the European Union', September.

CIAMPOLINI, M., and ROHDE, B. (2000), 'Money market integration: a market perspective', paper presented at the ECB conference on 'The operational framework of the Eurosystem and financial markets', Frankfurt, 5–6 May.

COOK, T., and HAHN, T. (1989), 'The effect of changes in the federal funds rate target on market interest rates in the 1970s', *Journal of Monetary Economics*, 24, 331–51.

—— and LA ROCHE, R. (1993), *Instruments of the Money Market*, Richmond, Va.: Federal Reserve Bank of Richmond.

DE BANDT, O., and HARTMANN, P. (2002), 'Systemic risk in banking: a survey', in C. Goodhart and G. Illing (eds.), *Financial Crises, Contagion and the Lender of Last Resort: A Reader*, Oxford: Oxford University Press.

DECKER, D., and VALLA, N. (2006), 'The Eurosystem's open market operations', in L. Bartolotti (ed.), *Inflation, Fiscal Policy and Central Banks*, Hauppage, NY: Nova Science Publishers.

DEGRYSE, H., and NGUYEN, G. (2004), 'Interbank exposures: an empirical examination of systemic risk in the Belgian banking system', paper presented at the Symposium of the ECB-CFS research network on 'Capital markets and financial integration in Europe', European Central Bank, Frankfurt am Main, 10–11 May.

DORAN, D. (2006), 'Financial integration and the market for short-term paper', Banque de France *Quarterly Bulletin*, 2, 88–104.

DURRÉ, A., and NARDELLI, S. (2006), 'Volatility in the euro area money market: effects from the monetary policy operational framework', European Central Bank, mimeo.

ELSINGER, H., LEHAR, A., and SUMMER, M. (2002), 'Risk assessment for banking systems', Oesterreichische Nationalbank Working Paper 79 (forthcoming in *Financial Management*).

European Central Bank (2004), *The Monetary Policy of the ECB*, 2nd edn., Frankfurt.

—— (2005a), *Euro Money Market Study*, Frankfurt.

—— (2005b), *Indicators of Financial Integration in the Euro Area*, Frankfurt.

—— (2005c), *Financial Stability Review*, Frankfurt.

—— (2005d), *Target Annual Report*, Frankfurt.

—— (2005e), *Monthly Bulletin*, Frankfurt.

—— (2006), *The Implementation of Monetary Policy in the Euro Area*, Frankfurt.

EWERHART, C., CASSOLA, N., and VALLA, N. (2006), 'Declining valuations and equilibrium bidding in Central Bank refinancing operations', ECB Working Paper 668.

—— —— EJERSKOV, S., and VALLA, N. (2007), 'Manipulation in money markets', *International Journal of Central Banking*, 3(1), 113–48.

FLANNERY, M. (1996), 'Financial crises, payment system problems, and discount window lending', *Journal of Money, Credit, and Banking*, 28, 804–24.

FREIXAS, X. (1999), 'Optimal bail-out policy, conditionality and constructive ambiguity', Financial Market Group Discussion Paper, London School of Economics 237.

——(2003), 'Crisis management in Europe', in J. Kremers, D. Schoenmaker, and P. Wierts (eds.), *Financial Supervision in Europe*, Cheltenham: Edward Elgar.

——and HOLTHAUSEN, C. (2005), 'Interbank market integration under asymmetric information', *Review of Financial Studies*, 18, 459–90.

——PARIGI, B., and ROCHET, J.-C. (2000), 'Systemic risk, interbank relations and liquidity provision by the central bank', *Journal of Money, Credit, and Banking*, 32, 611–40.

——GIANNINI, C., HOGGARTH, G., and SOUSSA, F. (1999), 'Lender of last resort: a review of the literature', *Bank of England Financial Stability Review*, 7, 151–67.

FURFINE, C. (2003), 'Interbank exposures: quantifying the risk of contagion', *Journal of Money, Credit, and Banking*, 35, 111–28.

Giovannini Group (1999), *EU Repo Markets: Opportunities for Change*, Brussels, October.

GOODFRIEND, M., and KING, R. G. (1988), 'Financial deregulation, monetary policy and central banking', Federal Reserve Bank of Richmond, *Economic Review*, May–June, 3–22.

GOODHART, C. (1985), 'Bank suspension of convertibility', *Journal of Monetary Economics*, 15, 177–93.

——and HUANG, H. (1999), 'A model of the lender of last resort', IMF Working Paper 99/39.

——and SCHOENMAKER, D. (1995), 'Should the functions of monetary policy and banking supervision be separated?', *Oxford Economic Papers*, 47, 539–60.

————(2006), 'Burden sharing in a banking crisis in Europe', LSE Financial Markets Group Special Paper 164, March.

GROUP OF TEN (2001), *Report on Consolidation in the Financial Sector*, January.

HAMILTON, J. (1996), 'The daily market for federal funds', *Journal of Political Economy*, 104, 26–56.

HARTMANN, P., MANNA, M., and MANZANARES, A. (2001), 'The microstructure of the euro money market', *Journal of International Money and Finance*, 20, 895–948.

HO, T., and SAUNDERS, A. (1985), 'A micro model of the federal funds market', *Journal of Finance*, 40, 977–90.

HOFFMAN, P., and SANTOMERO, A. (1998), 'Problem bank resolution: evaluating the options', Wharton School Working Paper 98-05-B.

JARDET, C., and LE FOL, G. (2007), 'Understanding the euro money market interest rate dynamics and volatility responses to monetary policy shocks and to recent changes in the operational framework', Note d'études et de recherche *Banque de France*.

KAUFMAN, G. (1991), 'Lender of last resort: a contemporary perspective', *Journal of Financial Services Research*, October, 95–110.

——(1994), 'Bank contagion: a review of the theory and evidence', *Journal of Financial Services Research*, 7, 123–50.

KRUEGER, J., and KUTTNER, K. (1996), 'The fed funds rate as a predictor of Federal Reserve policy', *Journal of Futures Markets*, 16, 865–79.

KUTTNER, K. (2001), 'Monetary policy surprises and interest rates: evidence from the fed funds futures market', *Journal of Monetary Economics*, 47, 523–44.

LELYVELD, I. VAN, and LIEDORP, F. (2004), 'Interbank contagion in the Dutch banking sector', De Nederlandsche Bank Working Paper 5, July.

MISTRULLI, P. (2005), 'Interbank lending patterns and financial contagion', Banca d'Italia, May, mimeo.

POOLE, W. (1968). 'Commercial bank reserve management in a stochastic model: implications for monetary policy', *Journal of Finance*, 23, 769–91.

——and RASCHE, R. (2000), 'Perfecting the market's knowledge of monetary policy', *Journal of Financial Services Research*, 18, 255–98.

PRATI, A., BARTOLINI, L., and BERTOLA, G. (2003), 'The overnight interbank market: evidence from the G-7 and the euro zone', *Journal of Banking and Finance*, 27, 2045–83.

REMOLANA, E., and WOOLDRIDGE, P. (2002), 'The euro interest rate swap market', *BIS Quarterly Review*, March.

ROCHET, J.-C., and TIROLE, J. (1996), 'Interbank lending and systemic risk', *Journal of Money, Credit, and Banking*, 28, 733–65.

——and VIVES, X. (2004), 'Coordination failures and the lender of last resort: was Bagehot right after all?', *Journal of the European Economic Association*, 2, 1116–47.

SANTILLÁN, J., BAYLE, M., and THYGESEN, C. (2000), 'The impact of the euro on money and bond markets', ECB Occasional Paper 1, July.

SCHWARTZ, A. (1992), 'The misuse of the Fed's discount window', *Federal Reserve Bank of St Louis Review*, September–October, 74, 58–69.

SOLOW, R. (1982), 'On the lender of last resort', in C. Kindleberger and J. Laffargue (eds.), *Financial Crises: Theory, History and Policy*, Cambridge: Cambridge University Press.

SPINDT, P., and HOFFMEISTER, J. (1988), 'The micromechanics of the federal funds market: implications for day-of-the-week effects in funds rate variability', *Journal of Financial and Quantitative Analysis*, 23, 401–16.

STIGUM, M. (1990), *The Money Market*, Homewood, Ill.: Dow Jones-Irwin.

STRAHAN, P., GATEV, E., and SCHUERMANN, T. (2004), 'How do banks manage liquidity risk? Evidence from equity and deposit markets in the fall of 1998', NBER Working Paper, 10982.

THORNTON, H. (1802). *An Enquiry into the Nature and Effects of the Paper Credit of Great Britain*, ed. F. A. Hayek, Fairfield: Augustus M. Kelley.

UPPER, C., and WORMS, A. (2004). 'Estimating bilateral exposures in the German interbank market: is there a danger of contagion?', *European Economic Review*, 48, 827–49.

WILHELMSEN, B.-R., and ZAGHINI, A. (2005), 'Monetary policy predictability in the euro area: an international comparison', ECB Working Paper 504.

CHAPTER 18

THE EUROPEAN BOND MARKETS UNDER EMU

MARCO PAGANO

ERNST-LUDWIG VON THADDEN

1. INTRODUCTION

THE European Monetary Union (EMU) has probably been the single most important policy-induced innovation in the international financial system since the collapse of the Bretton Woods system. It has opened the possibility for the creation of a new, fully integrated continental financial market, of the same scale as that of the United States. By eliminating exchange rate risk, EMU has eliminated a key obstacle to financial integration. Before EMU, otherwise identical financial claims issued in different euro-area currencies were imperfect substitutes and traded at different prices. EMU has eliminated this source of market segmentation.

While a single currency is a necessary condition for the emergence of pan-European capital markets, it is not a sufficient one. Other frictions may still stand in the way of full integration: even after the removal of exchange rate risk, persistent

We thank Giorgio Basevi, Carlo Favero, Gianluca Garbi, Tullio Jappelli, and two anonymous referees for very helpful comments and suggestions, and Philipp Hartmann, Philippe Rakotovao, and Paolo Volpin for supplying data. Hugo Villacres provided valuable research assistance. Both authors are members of the MTS Scientific Committee. The views expressed in this chapter do not necessarily reflect those of MTS or its Scientific Committee.

differences in tax treatment, standard contractual clauses and business conventions, issuance policy, security trading systems, settlement systems, availability of information, and judicial enforcement may still segment financial markets along national borders.

In the European bond market, however, monetary unification triggered a sequence of policy actions and private sector responses that swept aside most of the other obstacles to integration. This was facilitated by the intrinsically standardized nature of bonds and by the limited number of issuers in the sovereign bond market. The issuers coincided with the policy makers who had promoted EMU, and were determined to gain in terms of reduced funding cost from a broader and more liquid market.

While the push towards integration arose in the public bond market, it had a powerful spillover effect on the private bond market, where it generated a dramatic growth in issuance, secondary market trading, and competition among underwriters. In this chapter, we describe the emergence of an integrated market for public as well as private euro area bonds, highlighting both the impressive changes that have already occurred and the reasons why these bonds are still imperfect substitutes.[1]

We start by illustrating, in Section 2, the chain reaction of policy actions and private sector responses that reshaped the institutional framework of the sovereign bond market, leading to more homogeneous issuance and trading arrangements, and show how their effects spilled over into the market for private sector bonds. In Section 3, we document how these changes fostered convergence in government bond yields in the transition to EMU. In Section 4, we highlight that, in spite of all these achievements, euro-area bonds are still imperfect substitutes, and investigate the reasons and implications of the remaining yield differentials and of their changes over time. Section 5 concludes by summarizing and taking a look at possible future developments in this market.

2. EMERGENCE OF INTEGRATED BOND MARKETS IN EUROPE

While the introduction of the euro sparked off bond market integration, its effects were magnified by its concomitance with a worldwide expansion in private bond issuance, which outweighed the stagnant public debt issuance of the 1990s. Indeed, it is private sector issuance that has nurtured the growth of the euro area bond market in the wake of EMU, and transformed the euro into a leading currency of

---

[1] Danthine, Giavazzi, and von Thadden 2001, Galati and Tsatsaronis 2001, and Hartmann, Maddaloni, and Manganelli 2003 provide broader overviews, including other sectors of the financial market.

denomination for international bond issues. It seems appropriate, therefore, to start our account by setting European developments in their global context. Our next step is to document how the introduction of the euro changed both the behaviour of euro area issuers and that of investors. It prodded the former to compete in the supply of more homogeneous securities to a much larger potential market, and the latter to shift their portfolio selection away from home issuers. At the same time, it opened up great opportunities to trading platforms with pan-European capabilities, and to intermediaries willing to compete for underwriting business on a pan-European basis. As we shall see, the response of markets and intermediaries to this challenge contributed to the integration of the market, by compounding the responses of issuers and investors.

2.1. The European Market in Global Perspective

Before EMU, European bond markets were largely domestic and significantly smaller than their US counterparts. Table 18.1 gives an overview of the size of international bond markets in 1998; in that year, the value of total bonds outstanding in the euro area was still 56 per cent of the value in the USA. This size differential existed for both the private and the public bond market. However, the euro area public and private bond markets taken together already accounted for 25 per cent of the world total, and were significantly bigger than their Japanese counterparts.

Segmentation along national boundaries was a major feature of bond markets in Europe. At the start of the 1990s, almost all public debt was still issued domestically, while for private sector issues the ratio of domestic to international debt securities in Europe was about 4:1. Except for a few public or semi-public benchmark bonds, such as the ten-year Bund or the German Pfandbriefe, secondary market activity in Europe also remained largely domestic until the late 1990s.

All this changed drastically in the late 1990s. There was sustained growth in issuance of bonds worldwide, and Europe shared in this growth of the market

Table 18.1. Size of international bond markets in 1998

	Total bonds outstanding[a]	Of which: government bonds
USA	11, 656.45	7, 031.77
Euro zone	6, 526.42	3, 577.49
Japan	3, 958.94	2, 824.40
Rest of the world	4, 369.43	2, 229.01
World total	26, 511.24	15, 662.67

[a] By country of origin of issuer, in $bn, end of third quarter 1998.
Source: Bank for International Settlements (BIS), own calculations.

especially with much increased corporate bond issuance and international debt issuance. Table 18.2 shows that global net debt issues increased by 65 per cent between 1994 and 1999, and Figure 18.1(a) indicates that this was mostly driven by the growth in bond issuance by the private sector. This growth occurred on both sides of the Atlantic, though with slightly different timing.

In the United States, the economic boom of the mid-1990s was accompanied by a strong expansion of private sector debt issues, with volumes rising from $280 billion in 1994 to $1,061 billion in 1998, as shown by Figure 18.1(b). Yet, in the aftermath of the Long Term Capital Management and Russian debt crises, private sector issues in the USA declined sharply in 1999 and 2000, before issuing activity picked up again.

In the euro area, the private sector debt expansion was more modest than in the United States in the mid-1990s: it rose from $124 billion to $273 billion between 1994 and 1998. But, after the introduction of the euro, private issuance more than doubled to $657 billion in 1999, as illustrated by Figure 18.1(c). Despite the subsequent reduction, euro area private sector issuance later remained much higher than in the first part of the decade. That the 1999 boom is associated with the euro is underscored also by the different pattern of private bond issuance observed for European countries outside the euro area (Figure 18.1(d)), where the growth occurred gradually since 1994, as in the USA.

In Japan, private sector issues were almost flat in the 1990s, owing to the prolonged recession. In contrast, public debt issuance increased drastically after 1998. This pattern is the opposite to that observed in the USA and Europe, where net government borrowing decreased for most of the period. The spike of public debt issues in the USA in 1998–9 was exclusively due to strong issuing activity by local governments and the housing finance agencies.

Hence, global bond issuance expanded dramatically in the 1990s, in three different areas: first, US private sector issues in the mid-1990s; second, euro area private sector issues after the introduction of the euro; and third, Japanese public borrowing after 1998. As of 2004, all these three features seemed to be persistent: between 1999 and 2003, average private bond issuance in the USA was about $900 billion, up from $280 billion in 1994; that in the euro area was about $550 billion, more than four times the 1994 level; and Japanese government borrowing averaged roughly $450 billion, up from an average of $250 billion in 1994–8.

The strong expansion of the euro area bond market is reflected in an increase in the importance of the euro as international issuing currency. Table 18.2 shows no increase in the relative importance of the euro (or its precursor currencies) with respect to the dollar, but these numbers aggregate domestic and international debt issues. Unfortunately, the empirical classification of bond issues in these categories is controversial. According to the international statistics of the BIS, the euro overtook the US dollar in 1999 as the most heavily used currency for international debt issues, and has traded the lead in this category with the dollar since then. International issues, according to the BIS, include all issues except the domestic currency bonds issued by residents and targeted to domestic investors. However, Detken and Hartmann (2000) have rightly pointed out that these numbers understate the international use of the

Table 18.2. Global net issuance of debt securities

Currency	1994	1995	1996	1997	1998	1999	2000	2001	2002
US dollar	664.3	796.9	1,125.4	1,255.5	1,726.4	1,511.9	1,053.5	1,302.1	1,443.6
Euro						876.4	626.3	562.9	714.0
Euro area currencies	425.3	366.3	528.7	326.9	435.3				
Yen	336.7	434.6	458.7	237.9	185.8	496.1	450.6	570.6	280.6
Other currencies	578.3	544.1	392.6	362.4	438.9	470.7	375.9	450.6	494.3
Total	2,004.6	2,141.9	2,505.4	2,182.7	2,786.4	3,355.1	2,506.3	2,886.2	2,932.5

Source: BIS, own calculations.

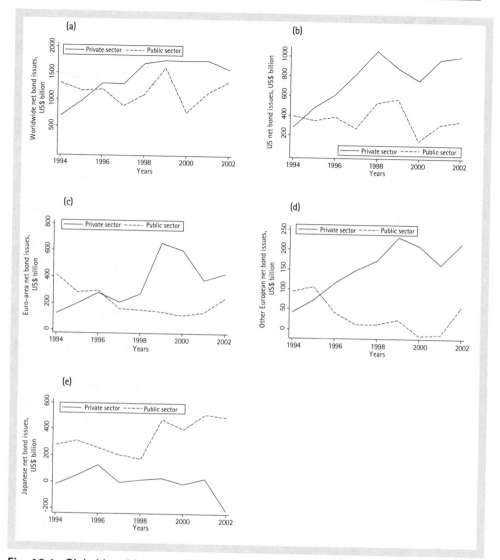

Fig. 18.1. Global bond issuance: (a) Total net bond issues, worldwide; (b) Total net bond issues, USA; (c) Total net bond issues, Euro area; (d) Total net bond issues, rest of Europe; (e) Total net bond issues, Japan

Note: Net issues in US$ billions. Private sector comprises financial institutions and non-financial corporations, public sector comprises central governments, local governments, public sector firms, and international organizations

Source: BIS, own calculations

dollar, because of the global importance of the US market. They present data on announced debt issues that take this bias into account and find that the dollar has remained the most important international issuing currency, although the euro has doubled its share in international debt issues between 1994 and 2003.[2]

[2] We are grateful to Philipp Hartmann for sharing his updated data with us.

2.2. The Supply Side

2.2.1. *Public Issues*

The fiscal discipline stemming from the Maastricht Treaty criteria has restrained the total volume of sovereign bonds issued in the euro area. As shown in Figure 18.1(c), total public sector debt issues in the euro area fell from $414 billion in 1994 to $111 billion in 2000. Recently this process has been partially reversed, but despite the *de facto* scrapping of the Stability and Growth Pact in 2003, its remnants can still be expected to curb the expansion of public debt in the foreseeable future.

Yet, despite this overall restraint on the size of the public debt market, the introduction of the euro has deeply changed the way in which public debt is issued in Europe. In fact, the changes in issuing policy by sovereign issuers went far beyond a simple currency conversion.

In 1995, EU governments decided that, as of January 1999, all new fungible public debt by EMU member states should be issued in euros. This was a direct consequence of the introduction of the euro and in itself would have already created relatively large euro markets for long-term public debt. Yet, governments were undecided at the time whether to redenominate their outstanding debt into euros with the inception of EMU. Redenomination would not only have added large volumes to the long end of the yield curve, but also created euro markets for shorter maturities. This potentially beneficial effect needed to be balanced against the costs and technical difficulties of such a switch. The French and the Belgian governments opted very early in favour of redenomination, whereas the German government for a long time seemed to be undecided. However, mostly for fear of a loss of competitiveness of the Frankfurt bond market, the German 'Euro Introduction Law' of June 1998 stipulated the full conversion of existing German fungible federal debt by 1 January 1999.[3] In the wake of these decisions, all other EMU countries followed suit soon afterwards.[4]

The debate about debt conversion was driven by the concern about the benchmark status of national debt. As in the private debt market, benchmark status confers substantial benefits on the country that enjoys it, but a large market size is obviously a key requirement for this status. Therefore, the 'race to the benchmark yield curve' was probably the most important factor in the decisions of governments to redenominate their outstanding public debt.

The competition behind the race for benchmark status was complemented by important cooperative elements in the development of the European public bond market. In fact, once the debt conversion decision was made, governments decided to go one step further and homogenize bond conventions. Shortly after the introduction of the euro, all member countries switched the day count of their outstanding and new issues to a common standard, and most of them switched to using the operating days of the TARGET settlement system as official business days for the service of

---

[3] Except for some short-term obligations, which comprise less than 3% of the fungible federal debt.
[4] With some minor exceptions such as Austria, which redenominated only the most liquid portion of its tradeable debt (34%).

their public debt. Many private bond issuers adopted similar reconventioning plans.[5] These changes made public bonds more easily comparable and substitutable. While not logical consequences of the introduction of the euro, they show that unification in one area brought about by the euro—the redenomination of bonds—entailed a further element of unification—the reconventioning.

Subsequently, euro area governments took several even further-reaching decisions concerning the harmonization of issuing practices, the coordination of issuing dates, the optimal choice of issuing formats, and similar matters.[6] Although more progress is still possible on these fronts, issuing practices, in particular of smaller euro countries, have changed considerably since the 1990s. Pre-announced auction calendars have become standard; reopenings and clusterings of issues in different parts of the maturity spectrum have become widely used tools of public management. In general, issue sizes have increased, with Treasuries buying back old illiquid and/or short-dated bonds and exchanging them for new issues and concentrating new issues in fewer benchmark securities. Some smaller issuers introduced syndicated procedures instead of auctions to attract more investors. Moreover, the competition between national Treasuries pushed them to innovate the menu of bonds offered: Spain and France have issued constant-maturity bonds; France, followed by other issuers, has introduced inflation-indexed bonds. Initially, these were indexed to national price indices, but more recently some issues have been indexed to a European price index.

Interestingly, the euro has reached out even into the non-euro area. For example, the Bank of England has been issuing euro-denominated Treasury bills since 1999. This broadening of the euro-denominated public debt market has partly compensated for the reduction in issuing volumes in most of the euro area countries until the early 2000s.

2.2.2. *Private Sector Issues*

As documented by Figure 18.1(c), the private bond market in Europe experienced a major change in 1999, when issuing volumes more than doubled from $273 billion to $657 billion. While the 1998 issuing volume in the euro area was less than 26 per cent of that in the USA, the 1999 volume was more than 74 per cent of the US level. Part of this surge probably reflects exceptional and transient factors. First, the financial crisis of late 1998 resulted in catch-up issuing activity in early 1999 (which, however, was equally relevant for the USA and Europe). Second, the desire to set benchmarks with euro issues pushed issuers to go to the market earlier and in more concentrated volumes than they might have chosen otherwise. But Figures 18.1(b) and 18.1(c) show that a significant part of this change was longer-lived.

The relatively small corporate bond market in Europe until the late 1990s is mirrored by the correspondingly greater importance of bank lending. While in the USA bank loans play a negligible role in the financing of large companies and face strong

---

[5] For details, see Bank of England 1998. By 'reconventioning' we mean changing the terms of legacy transactions to bring them into line with the new harmonized euro conventions.

[6] For a discussion, see Favero, Missale, and Piga 1999.

Table 18.3. Bank debt of non-financial firms

	All non-financial firms, 1993	239 largest manufacturing firms, 1996
Benelux	83.2	48.1
France	80.2	44.3
Germany	85.1	63.2
Italy	94.6	73.9
Spain	77.3	—
United Kingdom	49.4	34.1
United States	32.4	9.4
Japan	—	56.4

Note: Numbers are shares of bank debt in total debt.

Source: Danthine, Giavazzi, and von Thadden 2001.

competition from the bond market even for medium-sized companies, they have been traditionally the dominant source of debt financing for almost all European companies, even the largest ones, as shown by Table 18.3.

This feature of European corporate finance began to erode in the second half of the 1990s. It is difficult to tell whether the change towards a stronger reliance on bonds has been driven mainly by firms or by the banks themselves. Part of the explanation is certainly the increasing reluctance of European banks to provide traditional loans, which inflate the asset side of balance sheets and thus depress key earnings ratios and require higher regulatory capital. But the introduction of the euro has clearly also been a crucial event for the other side of the market: companies have seen the opportunity of accessing a larger pool of investors and diversifying their liabilities, so as to provide some competition to their bank financiers and decrease their vulnerability to credit crunches.

As in the public sector, bond issuance policy in the private sector changed fundamentally in Europe in the late 1990s. For example, the size of the largest issues increased substantially. While in 1998 there were just three bond issues in euro legacy currencies above the equivalent of €1 billion, the three issues by Tecnost, the financing vehicle for Olivetti's takeover of Telecom Italia, in June and July 1999 alone raised €15.65 billion. Although these issues were widely perceived as exceptional, issue sizes in general in Europe have increased significantly since 1999, with issues above €1 billion becoming more and more frequent.

Furthermore, the quality range of bond issues expanded significantly. In particular, the average credit rating of issuing companies has fallen significantly since EMU. While European bond markets used to be dominated by AAA and AA issues, almost 50 per cent of all corporate bonds issued in 1999 had a single A credit rating. Further down the spectrum, even the first signs of a European junk bond market exist, although this segment is still underdeveloped.

Interestingly, Rajan and Zingales (2003) show that the boom of the corporate bond market after the introduction of the euro was indeed stronger in the euro area than outside. They conduct a simple panel data analysis for a sample of European

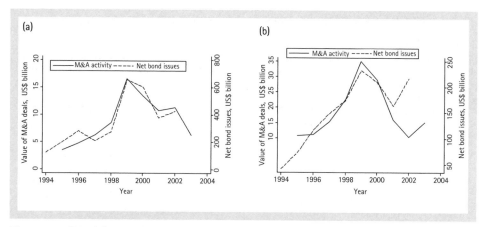

Fig. 18.2. Bond issuance and M & A activity in Europe: (a) Private net bond issues and value of M&A deals, Euro-area; (b) Private net bond issues and value of M&A deals, other European countries

Note: M & A activity is the total value of all M & A deals whose value is reported in the SDC Platinum database (US$ billion). Net bond issues are private sector issues (US $ billion)

Source: Thomson Financial Securities Data and BIS, respectively

countries since 1990 and find that net private debt issues became significantly larger for countries that adopted the euro. This suggests that the introduction of the euro had a causal impact on the development of the corporate bond market in Europe.

Much of this supply-side development is undoubtedly due to the boom of some industries, such as telecommunications, which were liberalized and deregulated in the late 1990s in many Western European countries. The resulting restructuring and consolidation fuelled a wave of mergers and acquisitions (M&A) that were largely financed by bonds. After the collapse of the equity market in 2000 and the worsening of the commercial paper market in the early 2000s, the bond market gained particular importance as a source of long-term funding. Figure 18.2(a) and 18.2(b) shows that debt issuance was closely correlated with M&A activity both in the euro area and in other European countries (chiefly the UK, which accounts for most M&A activity in the second group). The correlation is actually greater in the euro area (94.3 per cent) than in other European countries (66.3 per cent), but the total value of M&A deals is much larger in the second group of countries.

Finally, Table 18.4 shows that the lion's share of private sector international debt securities in Europe continues to be issued by financial institutions.[7] This feature was weakened in 1998–2001, when the share of non-financial corporate issues began exceeding 20 per cent, but was reasserted in 2002–3 when it declined to traditional levels of 10 per cent and lower. However, the current breakdown is not dissimilar to that in the USA.

[7] The breakdown of domestic private issues is not available for the whole 1994–2003 interval. However, from available data European non-financial corporations appear more active domestically than internationally, which contradicts the finding in Table 18.4.

Table 18.4. Issuance of private sector international debt securities by area and type of issuer

Area/issuer	1994	1995	1996	1997	1998	1999	2000	2001	2002	2003
United States										
Financial institutions	19.3	32.9	84.0	98.1	138.5	182.8	230.4	191.8	302.2	246.6
Corporate issuers	18.9	24.4	32.0	64.7	61.6	155.6	47.3	72.4	28.6	27.8
Euro area										
Financial institutions	68.6	87.5	154.0	147.2	163.8	356.5	430.3	325.2	385.6	591.4
Corporate issuers	7.2	8.1	4.4	17.1	32	120.5	96.1	82.7	10.6	56.8

Note: Net issues in US$ billion.

Source: BIS, own calculations.

2.3. The Demand Side

At the same time as the supply of euro area bonds increased and issuance policies converged, geographical diversification increased strongly in euro area bond portfolios on the demand side.

This change was felt most dramatically with private issues. While until 1998 bond distribution in the euro zone for all but the very few largest firms was almost exclusively domestic, the larger bond issues were already in 1999 sold on a truly European scale that surprised even most market participants. A typical example was the €1 billion issue of Alcatel, the French telecom firm, in February 1999, 28 per cent of which was placed with Italian and more than 20 per cent with German investors. Alcatel's surprised Chief Finance Officer remarked, after the issue, 'that a French corporate can sell its bonds primarily to Italy is something new'. A similar example was the 1999 issue by Principal Life, a US insurer, where the head of the syndicate at Crédit Suisse First Boston for the European issue noted that 'we sold 30 per cent of this deal in France. In the past we might have sold 3 per cent there.'[8]

A similar evolution happened in the public bond market. According to European Central Bank (ECB) data quoted by Blanco (2001: table 3), the share of euro area government securities held by non-residents increased steadily from 16 per cent in 1991 to 26.8 per cent in 1998 and up to 33.5 per cent in 2000. As shown by Adam et al. (2002), much of this increase is due to institutional investors. Their study looks at the share of assets managed by money and bond funds that pursued a Europe-wide investment strategy between 1997 and 2001, based on data provided by the Fédération Européenne des Fonds et Sociétés d'Investissement (FEFSI).[9] The figures given by Adam *et al.* (2002) have been recalculated and updated to 2003 by Baele et al. (2004). Both studies indicate that the adoption of the euro is associated with a large increase in the asset share of internationally investing bond funds in Austria, Finland, France,

---

[8] See *Euromoney*, August and September 1999.

[9] However, the FEFSI classification of funds according to their investment strategy (domestic, European, or global) and type (money market, bond, or equity) seems not entirely consistent across countries, being based on national schemes.

Table 18.5. International diversification of bond portfolios in the euro area

Country	Share of assets invested in bond market funds with Europe-wide investment strategy, % in 2003	International investor base as fraction of total investor base, % in 2004
Austria	55	90–9
Belgium	88	48.4
Finland	61	62
France	60	37
Germany	52	–
Greece	–	55
Ireland	–	75
Italy	81	42
The Netherlands	–	81
Portugal	98	80
Spain	0	37
Average	62	61.2

Sources: The numbers in column 1 are from Baele et al. 2004: 53; those in column 2 are from MTS Group 2004: 13.

and Germany, with most of the change occurring at the time of the introduction of the euro. The euro area unweighted average of the share of assets invested in bond funds with a Europe-wide strategy rose from 17 per cent in 1998 to 60 per cent in 2002 (Baele et al. 2004: chart 21).

Incidentally, a similar shift occurred also in the investment policies of pension funds and life insurance companies, since EMU relaxed a number of regulatory restrictions on the currency matching of assets and liabilities, such as a 20 per cent ceiling on the permissible mismatch in their denomination and other restrictions on the purchase of foreign assets.

Table 18.5 (column 1) shows that by 2003 more than half of the assets of bond funds were invested with an Europe-wide strategy in each euro area country except Spain (the latter being likely due to misclassification of Spanish funds in the FEFSI database). The countries where bond funds are more diversified are Belgium, Italy, and Portugal. The greater appetite for diversification by investors based in these countries may reflect their greater concern with the solvency risk of their respective home issuers: Belgium, Italy, and Portugal have the lowest-rated debt among those for which these data are available.[10]

Interestingly, this shift in portfolio allocation strategy is limited to the euro area, in two senses. First, it is peculiar to bond funds based in the euro area: in Denmark, Sweden, and the UK the share of bond funds with a European-wide investment strategy remained low and rather stable between 1998 and 2001 (Adam et al. 2002). Second,

---

[10] These figures are a lower bound on the diversification attainable by individual investors since, even if all funds in a given country completely specialize in domestic investments, individual investors can diversify internationally by holding a mix of funds offered by foreign intermediaries, if they have access to the investment products of other countries.

euro area funds did not extend their diversification strategy also to bonds issued outside the euro area itself: the share of bond funds with a global bond investment strategy actually declined from 30 per cent in 1998 to 20 per cent in 1999 and stood roughly constant at that level until 2003. Apparently, euro area investors now view the euro area bond market as their home market, so that the traditional home bias 'may have been replaced with a "euro area home bias"' (Baele et al. 2004: 54).

Rather than asking how diversified euro area bond portfolios are, one can look at the weight of foreign investors in each of the euro area bond markets. The latter is only to a certain extent related to the former. For example, the investors from a given country can have diversified portfolios and still absorb most of the domestically issued bonds. Moreover, foreign investors include also those based outside the euro area.

But it turns out that along this dimension, too, the euro area bond market has become highly integrated. Euro area public debt bought by international investors is currently 61.2 per cent of the total (unweighted average, excluding Germany), according to data collected by national Treasuries and reported by MTS Group (2004). As shown in column 2 of Table 18.5, the investor base is more international in euro area countries with a smaller absolute amount of outstanding debt, such as Austria, Finland, Ireland, the Netherlands, and Portugal, possibly because foreign institutional investors loom larger in these small markets.

2.4. The Response of Intermediaries

While euro area governments laid the institutional framework for an integrated bond market, financial intermediaries supported this integration by providing increasingly homogeneous secondary trading facilities and by competing on the primary market for government debt and corporate issues. This response by financial intermediaries was obviously triggered by the considerable business opportunities stemming from a pan-European bond market, but in turn it reinforced the process of integration, by feeding back into the behaviour of other market participants. For instance, trading platforms set homogeneous and more demanding requirements on issuers' policies and on dealers' market-making activity, and at the same time allowed investors to access an increasingly large menu of bonds with standardized trading procedures.[11] Similarly, investment banks' more aggressive competition for underwriting business reduced and homogenized the fees they charged to corporate customers, increasing companies' inducement to issue bonds even in the low-grade segment.

2.4.1. *Public Debt Trading Platforms*

The emergence of pan-European trading platforms has been an important force in the process of integrating the secondary market for European government bonds. The

---

[11] While the contribution of electronic trading platforms to euro area bond market activity appears to be substantial, we are not aware of any formal econometric analysis that attempts to quantify such a contribution.

most important among them are MTS in the cash market, and Eurex in the futures market.

MTS is a quote-driven, electronic trading platform that emerged from a public institution created in 1988 by the Italian Treasury and the Bank of Italy in collaboration with Italian primary dealers, to improve the liquidity of the Italian government bond market. The success of its trading model led to its privatization in 1997 and to the expansion in 1999 into the Netherlands, Belgium, and France, establishing similar trading platforms—a first set of domestic MTS markets.

Currently, MTS is the parent company that partially owns subsidiaries in all the euro area countries and in Denmark,[12] and trades government bonds in several Eastern European countries through its division 'New EuroMTS' (since November 2003). MTS S.p.A. is owned by financial intermediaries: 55 per cent of its capital belongs to non-Italian banks, and 45 per cent to Italian ones.

The breakthrough in MTS's business model was the creation of EuroMTS, a pan-European inter-dealer platform that offered trading facilities for the largest and most liquid European government bonds and subsequently became the standard setter for European benchmark bonds—that is, the newly issued bonds at the five- and ten-year maturities. The key to the success of this trading platform is to be found not only in its technical capabilities but also in MTS's ability to bring together issuers and dealers and to commit them to a few simple rules so as to foster secondary market liquidity— a mutual commitment that MTS labels a 'liquidity pact'. Dealers commit to quote continuously two-way firm prices with a maximum spread, and issuers commit to an issue listing size at least equal to €5 billion for benchmark bonds and to a random allocation of bonds among bond dealers for quoting obligations. Moreover, MTS volumes contribute to the total trading volume that Treasuries require of all dealers for admission to the primary market. In this way, the MTS-sponsored 'liquidity pact' has promoted the homogenization of the euro area sovereign bond market around minimum standards of size and liquidity.[13] For its part, MTS guarantees high pre-trade transparency, feeding real-time price and quantity data to final investors via twenty data distributors, and thereby encouraging competition in quotation setting.

Table 18.6 illustrates the impressive liquidity of the ten year and five-year benchmark bonds traded on EuroMTS. The bid–ask spread statistics in the table are based on daily data for 2002 and 2003 and refer to the best bid and ask prices quoted at 11 a.m. during all business days across all the cash markets. The data show that the average bid–ask spreads are tiny, ranging between 2 basis points in the most liquid market (Italy) to almost 5 in the least liquid (Finland). Interestingly, the German cash market is not the most liquid one, even in the ten-year maturity bucket for which the

---

[12] MTS created subsidiaries or divisions in the Netherlands in September 1999, Belgium in May 2000, France and Portugal in July 2000, Finland in April 2002, Spain in May 2002, Ireland in June 2002, Austria in June 2003, and Denmark, Greece, and Germany in November 2003 (but has traded German bonds since April 2001 through a division of EuroMTS).

[13] More recent innovations by EuroMTS include a real-time index of European government bonds (since 2003), the vertical integration into clearing and settlement, and the expansion into the corporate bond market through its BondVision subsidiary. At the time of writing, it is too early to evaluate these developments.

Table 18.6. Liquidity of the EuroMTS market

Country	10-year benchmark bonds, daily bid–ask spread data, 2002–3			5-year benchmark bonds, daily bid–ask spread data, 2002–3		
	Average	Minimum	Maximum	Average	Minimum	Maximum
Austria	4.6	2.8	9.8	4.1	2.8	6.5
Belgium	3.5	2.4	6.6	2.7	2.0	3.6
Finland	4.9	2.8	8.4	4.1	2.8	6.2
France	2.9	1.6	5.0	2.5	1.8	3.4
Germany	3.2	2.0	7.0	3.2	1.8	5.0
Italy	2.5	1.2	15.0	2.1	1.0	3.7
The Netherlands	3.5	2.6	5.6	3.7	2.4	5.0
Portugal	4.3	2.7	8.4	3.2	2.2	4.6
Spain	3.5	2.0	6.4	2.9	1.6	4.6
Average	3.66	2.23	8.02	3.17	2.04	4.73

Note: The bid–ask spread is measured in basis points and computed as the difference between the best bid and ask prices (divided by the mid-quotation) quoted at 11 a.m. during all business days in EuroMTS cash markets.

Source: MTS Group.

Bund is considered the benchmark. This is because most of the trading for ten-year German bonds occurs on the futures market, which is more liquid and far deeper than the corresponding cash one. Table 18.6 also shows that the bid–ask spread does vary over time: for instance, for Italy it ranges between a minimum of 1.2 and a maximum of 15 basis points. As we shall see, the time variation of liquidity is important in the empirical analysis of yield differentials.

Liquidity is lower for issues that are no longer benchmark bonds. These are traded in the domestic MTS markets, where the liquidity and size requirements established on EuroMTS for benchmark bonds are not enforced. However, the benchmark requirements tend to extend automatically also to these bonds, as older issues are gradually replaced with new ones, which formerly were benchmark issues.

While the market discipline imposed by the 'liquidity pact' on dealers creates obvious benefits to all market participants, the discipline is not perfect and the 'pact', like most other multilateral arrangements, is prone to moral hazard. The problem is that individual market participants can benefit from the liquidity provided by everybody else even at the expense of others, in which case the discipline can become a liability for the complying market makers. This indeed happened on 2 August 2004, when Citigroup flooded MTS (and other trading platforms) with sales of almost €12 billion across more than 200 bonds within seconds, pushing down prices by about 15 cents. As banks tried to hedge on the Bund future market, the future price dropped 47 cents. At that point, Citigroup bought back €4 billion of bonds at lower prices on the MTS trading system.[14] The price drop was quickly reversed, and Citigroup earned an

---

[14] This account is based on a number of news reports in August 2004 and MTS sources.

estimated €15 million at the expense of other market makers.[15] In effect, Citigroup was able to earn this sum because it had a fleeting informational advantage over the rest of the market: the information about its own future trading strategy, which is price relevant because of the sheer size of the orders that it can place. Normally, when they suspect that they may be receiving orders from an informed trader, market makers protect themselves by widening their quotes or refusing to trade. But the MTS market makers were committed to quoting firm prices for large amounts and keeping tight spreads, and this allowed Citigroup to trade such a large amount before they could react.

Besides exposing the market's vulnerability to manipulation by large traders, this episode may be a deliberate attempt to break the 'liquidity pact' by a large market maker. That Citigroup shows little concern for the liquidity of MTS may partly stem from its inherent conflict of interest vis-à-vis this trading platform—a situation common to several other large market players. It is at the same time a market participant and dealer in all eleven MTS sovereign bond markets, a shareholder of MTS, and a potential competitor of the trading platform owing to its in-house trading capabilities and its participation in competing platforms. This episode indicates that, for all their benefits to issuers, the implicit rules that guarantee the impressive liquidity of MTS are not unchallenged.[16] Accordingly, it has raised concerns by government officials that disruptions to market liquidity may increase the cost of issuing debt, and prompted investigations by security regulators for the possible breach of trading rules.

While MTS is by far the largest trading platform in the euro area cash market (especially in the Italian market), it has a low profile in the German bond market, where trading concentrates in the derivatives market, especially in the futures market managed by Eurex. The volume of trade on Eurex increased almost tenfold between 1996 and mid-2001, from €172.4 billion to €1,639.1 billion (see Blanco 2001: table 4).[17] In the process it killed off Bund futures trading on London's LIFFE. Also futures trading in French, Italian, and Spanish bonds dwindled into disappearance by 2001.

The trading activity in the futures based on German bonds is so large that the open interest of the Bund futures contracts often exceeds the stock of deliverable bonds. This occasionally generates 'squeezes', which are situations where few market participants buy a large fraction of the deliverable bonds before the maturity of the future contract. If successful, they profit at the expense of the holders of short positions in the futures contract, who must borrow deliverable bonds and lend money at below-market rates in the repo market. Squeezes generate sudden increases in

---

[15] Citigroup's profit could have been even larger if a few dealers had not eventually stopped trading as the US bank kept buying back bonds at lower prices, as reported by Munter and van Duyn 2004.

[16] It should be noticed that the formal rules of MTS do not prescribe spreads as tight as those actually quoted: the actual spreads are five times tighter than the required ones. But issuers informally require banks to quote the tightest possible spreads, and this induces them to take such positions with so little reward and, as this episode highlighted, so much risk.

[17] Between 1999 and 2003, the number of contracts for Bund, Bobl, and Schatz traded yearly on EUREX increased by 126.6%; by comparison, over the same interval, the value of yearly trading volume on the MTS cash platform increased by 46.7% (data kindly provided by Philippe Rakotovao).

the price of bonds, which spill over to the corresponding cash and repo markets. The problem is amplified by the relative lack of depth of the German cash market, coupled with the fact that other euro area bonds are still less than perfect substitutes of German Bunds, as we shall see in Section 3.

2.4.2. *Corporate Bond Underwriters*

The successful integration of secondary government bond markets in the euro zone is not paralleled in the corporate bond market, which is more fragmented. Most of this fragmentation is due to the fragmentation of clearing and settlement systems in Europe. Although the problem has been well known since the late 1990s (see, for example, Padoa-Schioppa 1999), progress has been slow. Securities settlement in the euro area is still dominated by national players, whose number had only come down from twenty-three to fourteen by 2003 (compared to two in the USA), and hampered by national rules that restrict cross-border activities of settlement houses.[18]

Yet, as highlighted in Section 2.2, the true explosion of bond issuance associated with EMU occurred in the corporate bond market, not in the sovereign bond segment. An important reason for this success was the corporate bond underwriters' response to EMU. As the barriers that segmented the European market for corporate bond underwriting began to erode, investment banks started to benefit from the scale economies in the provision of underwriting services and from the lower entry barriers in the industry. Santos and Tsatsaronis (2002) show that, as a result, underwriting fees in the euro-denominated market converged rapidly with the corresponding fees in the dollar-denominated segment of the industry. They show that, while total underwriter proceeds quadrupled between 1998 and 1999 (and remained around the new level until 2001), the average gross fees in the euro-denominated segment of the bond market halved in the year the euro was introduced, dropping from 1.7 per cent in 1998 to 0.8 per cent in 1999, and remained at the average level of 0.6 per cent in the 1999–2001 period—exactly the same figure as in the US-denominated segment (Santos and Tsatsaronis 2002: table 5). By multivariate regression analysis of a sample of 3,110 bonds, they highlight the key role of EMU in the reduction of fees.

Melnik and Nissim (2004) confirm the convergence of underwriting characteristics (extent of underpricing, underwriter compensation, bond maturity, syndicate size) in the euro area and the USA after EMU, but point out that the reduction of fees alone does not mean that EMU has reduced underwriter compensation. In a careful analysis of the pricing of Eurobond issues around 1999, they show that the strong reduction in underwriter fees after 1998 was almost fully compensated for by an increase in the underwriter spread (i.e. the difference between the price charged to the public and the price guaranteed to the issuer). Thus total underwriter compensation remained largely stable with the introduction of EMU. The real impact of EMU, according to

---

[18] The report by the Giovannini Group (2003) provides an assessment of the situation and proposes various policy reactions.

Melnik and Nissim (2004), was the almost complete elimination of the significant bond underpricing that had prevailed until 1998.

At the same time, the degree of concentration in the industry dropped, especially as a result of the entry of US investment banks into this market: the Herfindhal index more than halved, from 971.2 in 1998 to 400 in 1999, and the share of the top five banks dropped from 57.1 to 33.4 per cent (Santos and Tsatsaronis 2002). The increased competition was felt particularly in the smaller currency segments, where before EMU the share of the top five bookrunners was higher than 75 per cent. Interestingly, borrowers appear to have switched away from their home currency underwriters for their euro-denominated issues, compared to those in legacy currencies (59.5 per cent versus 80.5 per cent before EMU). Essentially, European corporate issuers moved away from their home bankers, generally towards the larger US investment houses.

3. Convergence of Yields in the Transition to EMU

The combined effect of EMU, concomitant institutional changes, and private sector responses illustrated so far translated into a dramatic convergence of the yields on public debt of the same maturity on the eve of monetary unification. This is illustrated in Figure 18.3 with reference to the ten-year benchmark bonds (but qualitatively similar pictures are obtained for other maturities).

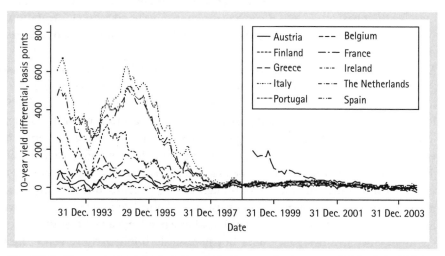

Fig. 18.3. Ten-year benchmark bond yield spreads, January 1993–July 2004

Note: Yield differentials are computed as the difference relative to the yield on German
ten-year benchmark bonds, based on monthly data (end-of-month observations)

Source: Datastream

The figure shows end-of-month yield spreads for euro area benchmark government bonds relative to Germany from January 1993 to July 2004. The convergence of the spreads toward zero is dramatic. Considering all initial EMU participants (and thus excluding Greece), the mean yield spread over the German yield fell from 218 basis points in 1995 to 111 in 1996, 39 in 1997, 19 in 1998, and 20 in 1999. It rebounded slightly in 2000–1, before resuming its downward trend.

Most of the action in these years derives from the convergence of the non-core EMU participants: Finland, Ireland, Italy, Portugal, and Spain, and later Greece, which joined the euro area at the beginning of 2001. The bonds issued by Austria, Belgium, France, and the Netherlands already featured low spreads relative to German bonds since 1996. This is because, before EMU, the probability of depreciation relative to the Deutschmark was considerable in the first set of countries, but not in the second. Indeed, for the non-core EU countries the drop of the ten-year yield spreads is overwhelmingly due to the elimination of this possibility, as shown by Blanco (2001). He measures this risk factor by the spread between the ten-year swap rate of the currency and the German swap rate, and finds that the foreign exchange factor accounts for 41 of the 46 basis points of the 1996–8 yield differential for Finland, 37 out of 45 for Ireland, 132 out of 154 for Italy, and 96 out of 115 for Spain. In contrast, it accounts for a negligible fraction of the differentials for Austria, Belgium, France, and the Netherlands.

The convergence associated with the transition to the euro is confirmed also by formal indicators proposed by Adam et al. (2002) using panel data techniques. The idea behind these indicators is that markets are integrated if price differentials are not *persistent*, i.e. if price discrepancies are rapidly eliminated by arbitrage, and if price *dispersion* for these products is small or absent. Applied to bond yields, β-convergence measures whether they converge to the same steady-state value, by regressing their changes on their past levels, and σ-convergence measures bond market integration at a point in time, by assessing whether the cross-sectional dispersion of yields decreases over time.

Adam et al. (2002) measure β-convergence of bond yields on data from January 1995 to September 2001 for euro area countries (plus Denmark). They regress the changes in bond yield spreads relative to Germany on their past levels (allowing for different coefficients in the pre- and post-EMU regimes), controlling for fixed country effects and lagged interest rate changes. The coefficients of the lagged interest rate level—if negative—measure the speed of convergence before and after the transition to the single currency. The estimated coefficients are respectively -0.041 and -0.079, both significantly different from zero, though not significantly different from each other. So β-convergence appears to be consistent with the data for the whole interval.

However, measuring σ-convergence can be of independent value to assess financial integration, since β-convergence does not necessarily imply σ-convergence: mean reversion does not require the cross-sectional variance to decrease, and it could even be associated with σ-divergence.[19] Adam et al. (2002) report that in the ten-year

---

[19] See Quah 1993 for further details on this issue.

government bond market the standard deviation of yield differentials relative to the German yield in 1999 declined to one-quarter of its 1995 value. They also regress the cross-sectional standard deviation on a broken linear time trend, the break point being January 1999. In the regression for euro area countries only, the estimated coefficients of the two time trends indicate that σ-convergence took place until the launch of the euro, but not afterwards: only the coefficient that applies to the pre-EMU interval is negative and statistically different from zero. This evidence adds an important element relative to that on β-convergence: the convergence in the euro area government bond market occurred before 1999, not later. This already points to the persistence of residual segmentation under EMU—consistent with the evidence that will be reviewed in the next section.

Baele et al. (2004) propose yet another method of measuring the changing degree of bond market integration, based on the idea that in an integrated market local yields changes are driven by common rather than local shocks. To measure the relative role of these shocks, they estimate a regression of the changes in each country's ten-year government bond yield on a constant and the change in the German yield. They estimate the regression over a moving window of eighteen months, so as to obtain a time series of constant and slope estimates for each country, and find that the slope coefficients start to converge towards one after 1998. So local bond markets have become less affected by idiosyncratic local news. Accordingly, the fraction of the total variance in local yield changes explained by changes in the German yield increased from less than 50 per cent to over 97 per cent between 1997 and 2002 in Finland, Greece, Italy, Portugal, and Spain.

The same authors also analyse the degree of integration of the corporate bond market under EMU. They wish to estimate whether corporate yields embody country effects, after controlling for all the other measurable characteristics associated with the time profile of the bond's cash flow, with the likelihood of default, and with liquidity. To this purpose, they collect the yields of 1,256 corporate bonds from Austria, France, Germany, Ireland, the Netherlands, and Spain for the EMU period, and estimate cross-sectional regressions of yield differentials (relative to an equally weighted corporate bond portfolio) on a constant and a set of bond characteristics: coupon, liquidity, time to maturity, rating, sector, and country. The estimation produces a time series of coefficients for each explanatory variable. Among these, the country dummies' coefficients may be seen as a measure of the respective country-specific risk factors. For all countries except Germany, these country coefficients are significantly different from zero at the 5 per cent level, but are extremely small: 4, 6, and 2 basis points for Spanish, Irish, and Austrian bonds, −8 basis points for French ones, and close to zero for German and Dutch bonds. They typically account for no more of 2 per cent of the cross-sectional variance of yield differentials. This suggests that the corporate bond market has also achieved a remarkable degree of integration.[20]

---

[20] An interesting attempt to estimate the determinants of yield spreads of individual corporate issues in the euro zone is Driessen 2002, who uses a three-factor model for corporate bonds of various rating classes and distinguishes between global factors, rating-class-specific factors, and issuer-specific factors.

This study of the corporate bond market is a useful reminder that bond market integration does not require complete convergence of bond yields. Even in an integrated market, differentials may persist to the extent that they are a reflection of the various bonds' different risk, maturity, or cash flow characteristics, rather than stemming from trading costs, taxes, clearing and settlement costs, or other institutional barriers to trade. Due to their highly standardized nature and low idiosyncratic risk, government bonds are well suited to an assessment of such differentials. This is the objective of the following section.

4. Bond Yield Differentials Under EMU

Despite the dramatic convergence documented in the previous section, yield differentials have not disappeared completely under EMU, so that euro-area sovereign bonds are still not perfect substitutes. This can be seen in Figure 18.4, which is based on the same data as Figure 18.3 except for the time interval, which includes only the EMU period, and for the omission of Greece, whose yield differential would dwarf all the others. Table 18.7 reports descriptive statistics by country and by year based on the same data. Taken together, Figure 18.4 and Table 18.7 show four important facts.

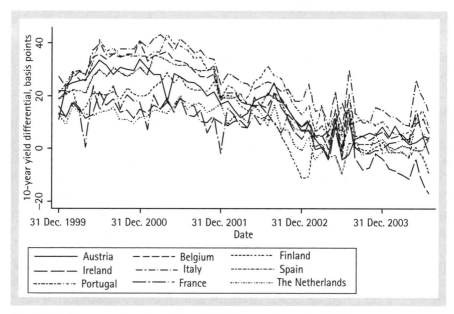

Fig. 18.4. Ten–year benchmark bond yield spreads under EMU

Note: Yield differentials are computed as the difference relative to the yield on German ten-year benchmark bonds, based on monthly data (end-of-month observations)

Source: Datastream

Table 18.7. Ten-year benchmark bond yield differentials under EMU (descriptive statistics by country and by year)

	Average	Standard deviation	Minimum	Maximum
Time-series statistics by country				
Austria	16.2	11.1	−4.1	33.8
Belgium	19.8	12.3	−0.6	40.9
Finland	11.9	11.0	−11.1	28.8
France	10.5	6.8	−1.9	23.9
Ireland	7.7	10.0	−17.1	21.4
Italy	26.0	10.6	6.5	43.1
The Netherlands	9.4	6.7	−4.4	20.4
Portugal	22.7	12.0	−1.0	43.3
Spain	16.2	12.9	−9.5	35.2
Cross-country statistics by year				
1999	20.0	7.0	6.7	29.4
2000	24.4	8.3	11.5	34.9
2001	26.8	9.0	11.0	37.8
2002	15.3	6.0	5.3	25.2
2003	5.3	6.1	−4.9	16.5
2004 (January–July)	3.0	7.0	−10.3	14.5

Note: Yield differentials are computed as the difference relative to the yield on German ten-year benchmark bonds. The statistics are based on monthly data (end-of-month obser-vations). The standard deviation, minimum, and maximum by year shown in the lower panel of the table are the yearly averages of the respective monthly cross-sectional statistics.

Source: Datastream.

First, yield differentials vary considerably *across countries*, from 8 basis points for Irish debt to 26 basis points for Italian debt. This raises the question of what explains these cross-country differences.

Second, for each given country the yield differential varies considerably *over time*. Therefore, yield spreads are a source of additional risk that must be taken into account and priced by investors and traders. This is especially important for traders who go long in the cash market on higher-yield bonds while hedging their interest rate exposure by shorting the very liquid German Bund on the future market: these positions are risky, since they are exposed to yield spread risk. In fact, there are traded derivatives, such as spread options, that explicitly refer to observed yield spreads.

Third, the yield spreads have a clear tendency to comove. This is evident from Figure 18.4, but it is formally confirmed by the statistical evidence reported in Codogno, Favero, and Missale (2003), and Geyer, Kossmeler, and Pichler (2004). This comovement implies that yield spread risk cannot be fully hedged by holding a diversified portfolio of euro area bonds, and raises the question of what generates such comovement. As we shall see later in this section, the empirical studies just quoted have made considerable progress in this direction.

Finally, in the figure there is a distinct trend reduction in yield differentials relative to the Bund. One may be tempted to conclude that convergence has continued also after the inception of EMU, so that euro area yield differentials will soon be a thing of the past. This would be a mistake, however. The *level* of most yield differentials features a trend decline because the yield on the Bund has been rising relative to most other euro area public debt, possibly in connection with the deteriorating position of the German budget. But in absolute value the yield differentials are not declining or disappearing. To see that, it is sufficient to consider that their cross-sectional *dispersion* has remained rather stable around a value of 7 in the period 1999–2004, as shown by the lower panel of Table 18.7. Also, the difference between the maximum and the minimum has not changed much (about 25 basis points) over this time period, even while both the minimum and the maximum declined gradually.

Therefore, since yield differentials cannot be yet written off in the euro area government bond market, we now analyse the determinants behind their variation across countries and over time, and review the available evidence.

4.1. Possible Determinants

The reasons why yield spreads may continue to be non-zero under EMU fall into two groups: (fundamental) risk factors and residual market frictions.

As already noticed in our discussion of the corporate bond market, yield spreads owing to risk differences are not inconsistent with market integration. They may arise from either (i) intrinsic differences in country-specific default risk (due, for instance, to different debt–GDP ratios of different countries) or (ii) different sensitivities of the bonds' future pay-offs to common shocks. As an example of the latter, consider the scenario in which EMU eventually collapses and euro area countries revert to national currencies. In such a scenario, the convergence process analysed in the previous section would most likely operate in reverse, with countries such as Italy, Greece, Portugal, and Finland experiencing large increases in yield differentials owing to the resurgence of their currency risk. In this scenario, the holders of these bonds would suffer larger losses than those of other sovereign bonds. Ex ante, a revision of the estimated probability of a future EMU collapse (a common shock) has greater effects for the prices of these euro area bonds, which should therefore be considered as riskier.

The other possible explanation for the persistence of euro area yield differentials—market frictions—is instead synonymous with segmentation. Frictions include (i) trading costs, arising from bid–ask spreads, brokerage commissions, or transaction fees; (ii) clearing and settlement fees; and (iii) taxes. From the perspective of market participants, some trading costs (such as the cost of market presence, clearing and settlement fees, and taxes) are exogenous, while other trading costs (such as search costs and bid–ask spreads) are endogenous in the sense that they result from strategic responses by market participants to the structure of the market and the information available. Practitioners generally refer to all these factors related to the ease and cost of trading under the common label of 'liquidity', and, in fact, often argue that the residual euro area yield differentials are due to differential liquidity.

Interestingly, illiquidity can itself generate a particular type of risk—liquidity risk. One may have to liquidate an asset at an unexpected time of need or buy at an unexpected time of affluence. Risk-neutral investors would value a euro of transaction costs identically in all contingencies. Instead, a risk-averse investor would value it differently in different states of the world, since his or her marginal utility of wealth differs across different states of nature. In this sense, transaction costs not only have a welfare cost for investors in terms of their income effect (as they reduce lifetime resources), but also because of their risk-bearing implications. If the size of the transaction cost can vary, this creates a further source of risk.

In addition, fundamental risk and liquidity may interact with each other in nontrivial manners, which are potentially quite important for empirical work, as we shall see in Section 4.2 Favero, Pagano, and von Thadden (2004) make this point in the context of a general equilibrium model where idiosyncratic liquidity shocks may force investors to sell their bonds before maturity. They show that the interaction between liquidity and fundamental risk has different effects on yields depending on whether one refers to *current* or to *future* liquidity.

If a bond has high *current* transaction costs, this *softens* the negative price impact of an increase in fundamental risk. Here the intuition is similar to the logic of trading distortions resulting from taxation in public economics. Suppose that, on an asset, the buyer and seller must pay a proportional transaction tax. Then the larger the transaction tax, the lower the after-tax price faced by either one. If the asset becomes riskier, the effect on the price will be smaller the larger the tax, since the initial after-tax price is correspondingly lower. The tax effectively reduces the variance of the price arising from news about the future.

The opposite is the case if a bond is expected to have a high *future* transaction cost, that is, when the bond may have to be liquidated. In this case, illiquidity tends to *amplify* the price effect of an increase in risk. To understand why, consider that an asset with risky fundamentals is one whose future cash flow is likely to be low in 'bad times'. If such an asset is also relatively illiquid, the investor who sells it in 'bad times' not only is likely to get a low price because of poor fundamentals, but will also pay a high transaction cost. So liquidity risk exacerbates the effects of fundamental risk. By the same token, future liquidity may compensate for fundamental risk: when the price of risk increases—for instance because of an increase in aggregate fundamental risk—investors may prefer a more liquid bond, even if it is more sensitive to fundamental risk.

All this suggests that, to identify at the empirical level the factors that explain euro area yield spreads, one has not only to account for differences in fundamental risk, and for differences in liquidity, but also for their interactions.

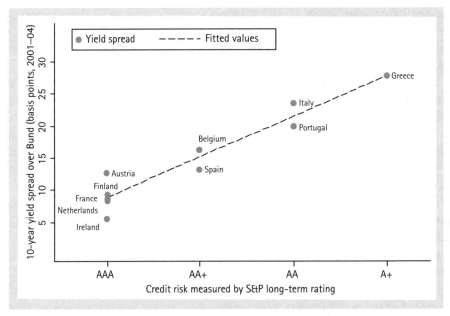

Fig. 18.5. Ten-year average yield differentials and credit risk

Note: Yield differentials are averages of the difference relative to the yield on German
ten-year benchmark bonds, based on monthly data from January 2001 to July 2004

Source: Yields are from Datastream, S&P long-term ratings are from MTS Group 2004: p. 11

4.2. The Evidence

Figure 18.5 shows that fundamental risk clearly plays a role in euro area yield spreads.
It plots average ten-year bond yield differentials relative to the German yield against
the respective Standard & Poor's (S&P) long-term ratings, which presumably are a
summary measure of credit risk. The points are clearly scattered along a regression
line with positive slope, with Greece, Italy, and Portugal at the top of the range,
Spain and Portugal in the middle, and Austria, Finland, France, Ireland, and the
Netherlands, all with AAA rating, closely clustered in a range from 5.5 to 12.7 basis
points.

Despite the paucity of the data points, this suggests that credit risk can, indeed,
explain a considerable portion of cross-country differences in yields. This already is
striking, as a sovereign default of any of these countries within ten years seems far-
fetched, given their economic history since the Second World War.[21] But ratings may
also reflect the different currency risk of these bonds in the event of a collapse of the
EMU and a reintroduction of national currencies.

---

[21] The relevance of sovereign default risk is further supported by credit default swap (CDS) data,
available for most EMU countries since 2001. As documented by Codogno, Favero, and Missale 2003
for 2002, CDSs were priced between close to zero basis points (for France) to more than 12 basis points
(for Italy) relative to Germany, suggesting that markets perceived and priced the possibility of a default
for at least some euro zone countries (this evidence should not be overstated, as the market for CDSs is
fairly thin and market prices, therefore, are noisy).

Even though they are closely correlated with the cross-country variation in yield spreads, ratings explain very little of their variation over time, which creates 'yield spread risk'. Explaining this time variation is quite challenging, mainly because its two possible determinants—liquidity and fundamental risk—are detectable on very different time scales. Liquidity is best captured in relatively high-frequency data, where a precise measurement of transaction costs is possible. Fundamental risk determined by macroeconomic variables, instead, is better measured at lower frequencies, or by evaluating the impact of macroeconomic news over a long time horizon.[22] Existing studies place themselves at different points in this difficult trade-off to identify the two potential determinants of yield spreads.

Geyer, Kossmeier, and Pichler (2004) estimate a multi-issuer state-space version of the Cox–Ingersoll–Ross (1985) model of the evolution of bond yield spreads (over Germany) for four EMU countries (Austria, Belgium, Italy, and Spain). They work with weekly yield spreads for the full maturity spectrum of two to ten years from January 1999 to May 2002. Their approach allows the factors driving the process of yield spreads to be left unspecified and the number and type of relevant factors to be identified. Their main findings are that (i) one single ('global') factor explains a large part of the movement of all four processes; (ii) idiosyncratic country factors have almost no explanatory power; and (iii) the variation in the single global factor can to a limited extent be explained by EMU corporate bond risk (as measured by the spread of EMU corporate bonds over the Bund yield), but by nothing else (in particular not by measures of liquidity), and thus remains largely mysterious.[23]

The most striking finding by Geyer, Kossmeier, and Pichler (2004) is the virtual absence of country-specific yield-spread risk. In fact, when they estimate a version of their model restricted to one common factor and one country-specific factor for each country, the four country-specific factors still have an average correlation of 0.76, almost as high as the correlation among common factors in individual country models. Therefore, they focus on a model with two common factors for all issuers and no country-specific factors. In this estimation, all country-specific factor weights are highly significant and standard errors of residuals small. They conclude that 'there is no ... issuer specific structure in EMU government bond spreads' and that 'country-specific variation in spreads is best modeled by country-specific Gaussian errors' (p. 188).

Therefore, it is no surprise that these authors find no role for their liquidity variables, which are typically related to local market features and frictions. Their measurement of liquidity variables is, however, not very satisfactory, as they do not use data on bid–ask spreads, which are commonly considered to be the best measures of liquidity,[24] but rather indirect measures of liquidity, such as the yield differential between on-the-run and off-the-run bonds and the issue size.

---

[22] For such analyses using US data see Balduzzi, Elton, and Green 2001 and Green 2004.

[23] The same applies to the result by Collin-Dufresne, Goldstein, and Martin 2001, who analyse US corporate bond spreads.

[24] See, for example, Fleming 2001.

The studies by Codogno, Favero, and Missale (2003) and Favero, Pagano, and von Thadden (2004) address this problem, by using richer data to measure liquidity, including data on bid–ask spreads in the EMU government bond market. Furthermore, these studies are more explicit in the search for relevant risk factors, by including specific international and domestic factors in their regressions.

Using monthly data, Codogno, Favero, and Missale (2003) proxy the country-specific risk factor by national debt to GDP ratios (noting that other variables do not add explanatory power) and international risk factors by US bond yield spreads.[25] Similarly to Geyer, Kossmeier, and Pichler (2004), they find that the domestic risk factor is irrelevant, except for the cases of Austria, Italy, and Spain. Interestingly, for the last two countries the ratio of debt to GDP is insignificant as a single variable, but significant when interacted with one of the US risk factors. This non-linearity points to a possible interaction between international market conditions and domestic fundamental risk. In particular, it suggests that, at least for Italy and Spain, international investors take domestic risk into account when reacting to changing world market risk (as proxied by US market conditions).

In a second approach, Codogno, Favero, and Missale (2003) combine the daily data on US bond prices with daily data on bid–ask spreads and market activity for European government bonds in 2002. With daily data, of course, macroeconomic variables move too slowly to allow estimation of the impact of the domestic risk factor, and thus are not included. In this estimation, the international factor is statistically significantly different from zero for all countries except for Finland, France, and Ireland, while liquidity (as measured by the trading volume on EuroMTS) plays a statistically significant and correctly signed role for France, Greece, the Netherlands, and Spain. When compared to the first set of results in the same paper, the fact that international risk remains significant for several countries, once liquidity is controlled for, may imply that 'differences in default risk are the main propagation mechanism' (p. 524). But, as the authors admit, this conclusion is not very strong. In particular, most countries in the sample display very similar debt to GDP ratios, with only Belgium and Italy clearly above, and Ireland clearly below the median. Hence, it seems difficult to attribute observed market segmentation directly to these national differences.

Favero, Pagano, and von Thadden (2004) analyse the possible causes and consequences of liquidity in more detail. In particular, they point out that transaction costs should affect yield differentials in two ways: directly with a positive sign (as investors require higher returns to compensate them for transaction costs), and indirectly through the interaction of liquidity with fundamental risk. The sign of the coefficient of this interaction term depends on whether the liquidity variable reflects current or future trading costs, as explained in Section 4.1 above. Depending on which component is more prominent, the impact of changing international (common) risk factors

---

[25] More precisely, the two variables considered are (i) the spread between fixed interest rates on US swaps and US government bond yields and (ii) the spread between the yields on US AAA corporate bonds and government bonds (all for ten years). The variables proxy the risk of the banking and the corporate sectors, respectively.

may be different. The main insight of the theory for the econometric specification is that liquidity effects should enter both linearly and via their interaction with the risk factor.

The empirical analysis by Favero, Pagano, and von Thadden (2004) uses two years of daily transactions data from EuroMTS and bid–ask spreads carefully synchronized with return data. First, they confirm the previous two studies' finding that the international risk factor is highly significant for all countries.[26] Second, they find a greater role for liquidity variables, provided they are interacted with risk variables in the specification, as suggested by their model. Focusing for brevity on their results for the ten-year maturity, the coefficient of the bid–ask spread is positive for all countries except Finland, but significantly different from zero only for Austria, Belgium, the Netherlands, and Portugal. So, as predicted by the theory, for these four countries a higher bid–ask spread is associated with a higher yield spread. Importantly, in all four cases, the positive effect of the bid–ask spread on yield differentials is paired with a significantly negative coefficient of the interaction term between the liquidity measure and the international risk factor. This illustrates the importance of non-linearities in the effect of liquidity indicators on yield differentials. In fact, the coefficient of the liquidity differential is significant only when this interaction term is included.

In conclusion, despite their considerable differences in the methodology and data used, all three studies agree on the finding that yield differentials under EMU are driven mainly by a common risk (default) factor, related to the spread of corporate debt over government debt. They also agree on the conclusion that liquidity differences have at best a minor direct role in the time series behaviour of yield spreads, and—according to the last of the three studies—an indirect role, in that they modify the impact of the risk factor on yield spreads.

An open question remains about why the common international risk factor is best measured by the differential between corporate and public bond yields in Europe and in the USA: Does this capture events in the USA that have a direct impact on European bond markets? Or is there a common latent variable that makes European and US data comove? And if there is such a common factor, is its impact on European spreads mainly a direct one or is it mediated by liquidity or macroeconomic variables?

A possible approach towards answering the first two questions is to study the dynamic linkages between the time series of bond returns explicitly. This is done by Skintzi and Refenes (2004) who estimate an extended GARCH model of European and US weekly bond returns and (time-varying) volatilities.[27] They find stronger evidence for spillovers between the volatilities of the return series than for the returns themselves. In particular, they find return spillovers from a euro area index into the series of four out of eight EMU countries (Belgium, France, the Netherlands, and

[26] In this study, the international risk factor is measured as the spread between the fixed interest rates on US swaps and the yield on US government bonds of the same maturity.

[27] The EMU countries in their study are Austria, Belgium, France, Germany, Ireland, Italy, the Netherlands, and Spain; the European non-EMU countries Denmark, Norway, Sweden, and the UK. They rely on the national Datastream Benchmark Bond Indices (total returns) with five years, average maturity for the period 1 February 1991 to 31 December 2002.

Spain), and volatility spillovers for six out of the eight countries (Austria, Belgium, France, Germany, Italy, and Spain). These spillovers have intensified after the start of EMU. For the four European non-EMU countries in the sample, they find no spillovers for returns, but volatility spillovers into the series for Denmark, Sweden, and the UK.

Concerning the impact of the US series (modelled as an exogenous factor), Skintzi and Refenes (2004) find an impact on returns within EMU only for Austria, Belgium, and Spain (and the three Scandinavian countries), but a clear impact on the volatilities of all eight EMU countries. The first of these two results is surprising in the light of the findings discussed earlier in this section, and the second suggests that further studies should pay more attention to volatilities, and not only returns.

5. Conclusions

The years since monetary unification have witnessed the emergence of an integrated euro area bond market. Issuers and investors alike have come to regard the euro area bond market as a single one. Primary and secondary bond markets have become increasingly integrated on a pan-European scale. Issuance of corporate bonds has taken off on an unprecedented scale in continental Europe. In the process, both investors and issuers have reaped the considerable benefits afforded by greater competition in the underwriting of private bonds and in the auctioning of public ones, and by the greater breadth and liquidity of secondary markets.

These benefits have been particularly valuable for euro area governments, many of whom must service a large stock of public debt: for them, even shaving a few basis points off the cost of debt servicing makes a considerable difference in terms of reduced taxes to be raised in the future. But the benefits have been no less important for European companies, which have acquired cheaper access to a market that can disenfranchise them from banks for the provision of debt finance. The effect on company financing and the attendant effects on credit markets are likely to be the most pervasive legacy of European bond market integration.

Bond yields have converged dramatically in the transition to EMU. The persistence of small and variable yield differentials for sovereign debt under EMU indicates that euro area bonds are still not perfect substitutes. However, to a large extent this is not the reflection of persistent market segmentation but of small differentials in fundamental risk—either in default risk or in vulnerability to the risk of eventual EMU collapse. Liquidity differences appear to play at most a minor direct role, but a more significant role through their interaction with changes in fundamental risk.

The challenges and opportunities still lying ahead are numerous. First, there is a striking unbalance between futures and cash markets. Euro area futures refer almost entirely to German bonds, while the cash market for German bonds is far less developed, which periodically determines squeezes and inefficient price volatility.

In contrast, other large cash markets, such as the Italian one, are very liquid but lack a corresponding future market.

Second, the impressive liquidity of the cash markets is due to market makers' collective commitment to quote bid and ask prices for very large amounts at very tight spreads; but this commitment is vulnerable to free riding and manipulation by large financial institutions, as the August 2004 Citigroup episode demonstrates. It is still unclear whether such opportunistic behaviour is a serious threat to the persistence of the current liquidity levels.

Third, the possibility of joint bond issuance by euro area countries has been repeatedly considered because of its ability to exploit fully the liquidity benefits of a completely unified market. However, issuers have so far discarded it because it would generate an implicit debt guarantee by some countries in favour of others, with potentially serious incentive effects on fiscal discipline. The challenge here is to design a scheme capable of reaping the liquidity benefits of joint issuance, while minimizing its adverse effects. For instance, joint issuance could be allowed only to EU countries that respect certain standards of fiscal discipline and/or could be limited to short-maturity bonds.

Another challenge is to overcome the persistent fragmentation of clearing and settlement systems in the euro area bond market, which prevents a full integration of the market for private sector bonds.

Last, but not least, the euro area bond market will expand further as new EU member countries gradually join EMU. In fact, in anticipation of this outcome, their bonds are already being actively traded on the same platforms that cater to the bonds of existing EMU members.

REFERENCES

ADAM, K., JAPPELLI, T., MENICHINI, A., PADULA, M., and PAGANO, M. (2002), 'Analyse, compare, and apply alternative indicators and monitoring methodologies to measure the evolution of capital market integration in the European Union', Report to the European Commission, http://europa.eu.int/comm/internal_market/en/update/economicreform.

BAELE, L., FERRANDO, A., HÖRDHAL, P., KRYLOVA, E., and MONNET, C. (2004), 'Measuring financial integration in the euro area', ECB Occasional Paper Series no. 14, April.

BALDUZZI, P., ELTON, E. J., and GREEN, T. C. (2001), 'Economic news and bond prices: evidence from the US Treasury market', *Journal of Financial and Quantitative Analysis*, 36, 532–43.

Bank of England (1998), *Practical Issues Arising from the Introduction of the Euro*, various issues.

BLANCO, R. (2001), 'The euro-area government securities market: recent developments and implications for market functioning', Banco de España—Servicio de Estudios Working Paper 0120.

CODOGNO, L., FAVERO, C., and MISSALE, A. (2003), 'EMU and government bond spreads', *Economic Policy*, 18(37), 503–32.

COLLIN-DUFRESNE, P., GOLDSTEIN R. S., and MARTIN, S. J. (2001), 'The determinants of credit spreads', *Journal of Finance*, 56(6), 2177–207.

Cox, J. C., Ingersoll, J. E., and Ross, S. A. (1985), 'A theory of the term structure of interest rates', *Econometrica*, 53(2), 385–407.

Danthine, J.-P., Giavazzi, F., and von Thadden, E.-L. (2001), 'The effect of EMU on financial markets: a first assessment', in C. Wyplosz (ed.), *The Impact of EMU on Europe and the Developing Countries*, Oxford: Oxford University Press.

Detken, C., and Hartmann, P. (2000), 'The euro and international capital markets', Working Paper, European Central Bank.

Driessen, J. (2002), 'Is default risk priced in corporate bonds?', Discussion Paper, University of Amsterdam.

Favero, C., Missale, A., and Piga, G. (1999), 'EMU and public debt management: one money one debt?', CEPR Policy Paper no. 3, December.

_____ Pagano, M., and von Thadden, E.-L. (2004), 'Valuation, liquidity and risk in government bond markets', May, mimeo.

Fleming, M. (2001), 'Measuring Treasury market liquidity', Discussion Paper, Federal Reserve Bank of New York.

Galati, G., and Tsatsaronis, K. (2001), 'The impact of the euro on Europe's financial markets', BIS Working Paper 100, Basel.

Geyer, A., Kossmeier, S., and Pichler, S. (2004), 'Measuring systematic risk in EMU government yield spreads', *Review of Finance*, 8(2), 171–97.

Giovannini Group (2003), *Second Report on EU Clearing and Settlement Arrangements*, Brussels: European Commission, April.

Green, T. C. (2004), 'Economic news and the impact of trading on bond prices', *Journal of Finance*, forthcoming.

Hartmann, P., Maddaloni, A., and Manganelli, S. (2003), 'The euro-area financial system: structure, integration, and policy initiatives', *Oxford Review of Economic Policy*, 19(1), 180–213.

Melnik, A., and Nissim, D. (2004), 'Issue costs in the underwriter market: effects of monetary integration', University of Haifa, mimeo.

MTS Group (2004), *The European Government Bond Market: A Single Market with Unique Segments*, London, March.

Munter, P., and van Duyn, A. (2004), 'The world's largest bank is thought to have netted €15m through rapid-fire selling and buying last month', *Financial Times*, 10 September.

Padoa-Schioppa, T. (1999), 'PSSS in EMU', speech, European Central Bank.

Quah, D. (1993), 'Galton's fallacy and tests of the convergence hypothesis', *Scandinavian Journal of Economics*, 95(4), 427–43.

Rajan, R., and Zingales, L. (2003), 'Banks and markets: The changing character of European finance', in V. Gaspar, P. Hartmann, and O. Sleijpen (eds.), *The Transformation of the European Financial System*, Frankfurt: European Central Bank.

Santos, J., and Tsatsaronis, K. (2002), 'The cost of barriers to entry: evidence from the market for corporate euro bond underwriting', Federal Reserve Bank of New York and IMF, mimeo.

Skintzi, V., and Refenes, A. (2004), 'Volatility spillovers and dynamic correlation in European bond markets', Athens University of Economics and Business, mimeo.

CHAPTER 19

EQUITY RETURNS AND INTEGRATION

IS EUROPE CHANGING?

KPATE ADJAOUTÉ

JEAN-PIERRE DANTHINE

1. INTRODUCTION

How significant is the mark left by the all-important process of economic and financial integration, including the advent of the euro, on equity markets? From the viewpoint of equity investors, can one assert that the promises of European integration are materializing? Our strategy to shed light on these questions is to analyse sequentially the effects of economic and financial integration on the *fundamentals* being priced in European financial markets (Section 2) and on the characteristics of the *pricing mechanism* (Section 3), before turning to the observations that can be made on equity returns themselves (Section 4). Section 5 summarizes the answers we provide to these questions.

This chapter was preceded by and builds on Adjaouté and Danthine 2001, 2003, 2004, as well as Adjaouté et al. 2000 and Adjaouté, Danthine, and Isakov 2005. Thanks are due to Sergei Sontchik for research assistance. Danthine's research is carried out within the National Center of Competence in Research 'Financial valuation and risk management'. The National Centers of Competence in Research are managed by the Swiss National Science Foundation on behalf of the federal authorities.

2. FUNDAMENTALS

Can we trace the impact of the process of economic and financial integration in Europe on the fundamentals being priced in European equity markets? Currency unification is synonymous with full convergence of monetary policies and, in the euro area, with some degree of harmonization of fiscal policies as well. It has often been argued that the currency component in equity returns is rather minor and that the equity-pricing mechanism should be little affected by the euro. The resulting changes in the underlying (macro and micro) fundamentals could, nevertheless, have a significant impact on equity markets, and this is what this section attempts to assess. With that goal in mind, we follow traditional factor asset-pricing models in viewing equity returns as being affected by a series of factors identified with the specific characteristics of the companies being priced, the industries to which they belong, and their country of origin.

At the *company level*, we note the growing trend toward multinational companies. Although this trend may be unrelated to European Monetary Union (EMU) and the single market, it is, in any case, relevant for the identification of the factors determining equity returns. In particular, one may expect that country-specific shocks will have a decreasing importance for returns, to the extent that a larger fraction of the national markets is represented by multinational companies. In the same vein, a trend toward multi-industry firms, i.e. conglomerates, would also be relevant as it would tend to blur the lines of identification of industrial sectors as specific segments of the market capitalization. At this level, fashion comes and goes, however, and after a much criticized tendency for managers to spread their wings across industries, the current mood is to encourage firm managers to stick to their trade and to be 'focused'. Finally, growing international trade, especially to the extent that it concerns intermediate goods, *de facto* renders the operation and performance of a company with a given location and affiliated to a given industry more dependent on economic events originating in other countries and other industrial sectors. This set of issues bears on the task of Standard Industry Classification providers, as highlighted in Morgan Stanley Capital International (MSCI)–Standard & Poor's joint GICS (Global Industry Classification Standard) publications. The classification of companies into given sectors proves increasingly difficult, with many business segments contributing to the turnover or the operating income, the criteria used to typify companies. Assigning a country to a company has become equally tricky, with the country of origin or the country where the company is actually headquartered often having very little to do with the geographical areas that effectively influence the business of the company.

The euro and the single market do not seem to have a specific impact on the development of industrial sectors themselves. The growing importance of services and, above all, the recent extraordinary evolution of the IT and telecommunications sectors are worth mentioning, however, as the latter, in particular, may bias the measure of the importance of the industry factor in determining equity prices and returns.

Much more is to be said of the *macro environment*, precisely because the underlying context of economic and financial integration, in particular the EMU and the single market, is likely to have a profound impact on economic structures and, of course, on macroeconomic policies.

The impact of economic development and regional integration on economic structures has been the subject of a rich literature. Most arguments support the view that the lowering of barriers to trade goods and financial assets tends to promote more specialization of national industrial structures. The first such arguments are those building on Ricardian trade theory: decreases in impediments to international trade make it possible for countries to stick to their comparative advantages. The new economic geography has emphasized the existence of pecuniary externalities associated with agglomeration as a source of geographical specialization. Monopolistic competitors tend to cluster to take advantage of these externalities, a theory for which Krugman (1991) finds support in the comparison of employment patterns in the USA (which is more specialized) and in Europe (which is less). There may be counteracting forces: a strategic objective toward diversification—so as to produce a more stable economic structure—and a taste for diversity, principally. The latter may suggest that a higher level of economic development could be associated with less specialization. At given levels of development, however, even these considerations imply that more economic integration, to the extent that it means the lowering of trading costs, and more financial integration, because it provides other means for diversification, should be associated with more specialization.

The diversification argument for financial integration goes as follows. Under full financial segmentation, local investors have no choice but to finance local firms and, conversely, firms depend on local investors for their financing. Limited diversification possibilities for investors mean that they will require a high compensation for holding participations in risky, undiversified firms. The cost of capital of the latter will be high. This implies that firms have an incentive to diversify on their own if they can, especially if they can do it by expanding abroad—for example, through the build-up of conglomerates or association with multinationals. This is the case even if, from a larger perspective, these attempts at diversifying at the firm level are inefficient. Similarly, within a country, one may observe the existence of productive activities which may be relatively inefficient, or for which the country may not have a comparative advantage, simply because they increase the local diversification possibilities and as a result benefit from a lower cost of capital. By contrast in an integrated financial market, there is no financial premium to industrial sectoral or geographical diversification and better specialization is affordable. Financial integration thus has the potential of changing the mix of investment projects being financed and may open the way to a higher degree of industry specialization across countries. What is the evidence? Imbs and Wacziarg (2003) show empirically that industrial concentration follows a U-shaped pattern as a function of the level of economic development: after an initial development phase where agriculture takes the lion's share of resources, countries start to diversify, with labour being spread more equally across various industrial sectors. But at a later stage of development they begin to specialize again. The turning point occurs relatively late in the development process and is estimated at per capita GDP of approximately $10,000. They interpret their findings as resulting from the interplay of productivity increases and decreasing transport costs. The latter clearly constitute a force of concentration. In a Ricardian model, an increase in a country's productivity relative to the rest of the world translates into an increasing range of goods being produced domestically. The observed stages of diversification then depend on which force dominates at any given point in a country's growth path.

These effects on industry structures may, however, be offset by the convergence of macroeconomic policies that is a hallmark of EMU. With a single monetary policy, closely aligned interest rates, and fiscal policies subject to a common discipline, the macroeconomic influences on company profits and euro-wide discount factors are clearly converging. Policies and structures are thus exerting conflicting influences on the fundamentals of equities. But structural changes are expected to be slow. More-over, there may be a ratchet effect from earlier decisions regarding localization and diversification. With fixed costs, slowly changing incentives may not lead to a reversal of previous decisions. By contrast, the effects of the coordination of macroeconomic policies are more immediate and the changes provoked by the euro are in some cases dramatic. The convergence of yields of public bonds, documented by Adjaouté and Danthine (2003) and elsewhere, is a case in point. All in all, one could thus rationalize that euro-area business cycles are becoming more as well as less synchronized. But our prior is that the effects of policy will dominate, and this is, indeed, what we find.[1]

Figure 19.1 reports the pairwise correlations of GDP growth rates across the euro area, while Figure 19.2 displays the time series of the cross-sectional dispersion of the same GDP growth rates. GDP figures are collected from Datastream on a quarterly basis for each of the EMU member countries, from the first quarter of 1986 to the first quarter of 2004. The highly changing nature of the relationships we are focusing on and the limited size of the post-euro sample of observations motivate us to complete the traditional measures of correlations with measures of dispersions. Cross-sectional dispersions are meant to be the cross-sectional counterpart to correlations and to pro-vide the same underlying information. If returns or growth rates are highly correlated, we expect that more often than not they will move together on the upside or on the downside. If they do, the instantaneous cross-sectional variance of these returns or growth rates will be low. Conversely, lower correlations mean that returns/growth rates often diverge, a fact translating into a high level of dispersion. Dispersions and correlations are thus inversely related. While correlations require a minimum

---

[1] Note that, somewhat ironically, if common policies make country specificities within the euro area less prominent, they also decrease the diversification benefits brought about by financial integration. In other words, as financial integration makes diversification within the euro area increasingly easy, economic integration makes diversification inside the euro area increasingly less relevant. In that sense, there is some redundancy in economic and financial integration!

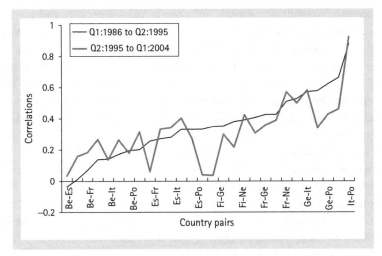

Fig. 19.1. Country pair correlations (GDP growth rate): before and during convergence

Source: GDP data from Datastream

sample length to be estimated with some precision, no such requirement is needed for dispersions, although the measure will be more imprecise if the number of returns or growth rates entering in the variance measure is too small. Cross-sectional dispersions were first used in the context of equity returns by Solnik and Roulet (2000). As the dispersions are very noisy, we typically smooth them with Hodrick–Prescott (HP) filters to get a better idea of the underlying trends.

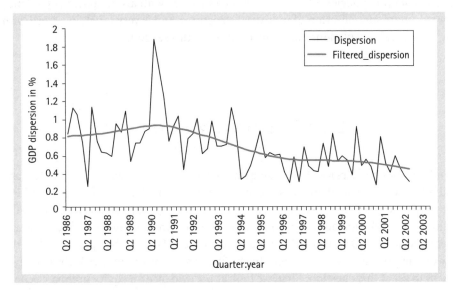

Fig. 19.2. Quarterly GDP growth rate dispersions

Source: GDP data from Datastream

In Figure 19.1, we split our sample into two equal subperiods and compare the pairwise correlations in the first with those obtained in the second. Figure 19.1 does not reveal a clear aggregate pattern of increasing or decreasing correlations. If anything, those country pairs for which correlations were low during the first part of the sample turned out to be higher in the second part, and conversely. There are a few exceptions, for example Belgium/Italy and Belgium/Portugal with low correlations remaining low, and the pairs Netherlands/Portugal, Germany/Netherlands, with high correlations getting even higher. This instability in pairwise correlations has its counterpart in the sizeable volatility of the dispersions displayed in Figure 19.2. Here, however, a clear trend is identifiable, a trend that begins around 1991 and that persists all the way to the end of our sample. The average level of dispersion was 0.86 for the period from 1986 to 1994 and 0.51 only for the period from 1995 to 2004. There thus appears to be a remarkable evolution towards more synchronization in the business cycles (broadly defined, that is, in terms of non-detrended data, as appropriate, given the focus of our enquiry) of the euro area countries.

Our results are in line with, and update, those obtained elsewhere in the literature with a variety of methodologies. See, among others, Agresti and Mojon (2001), Dueker and Wesche (1999), and Ormerod and Mounfield (2002). Imbs (1999) also concludes that euro area business cycles have moved closer together and that they are now more alike than in the immediate post-war period. His analysis is of interest (despite the absence of post-euro data) because it is centred on the estimation of Solow residuals and thus permits a finer diagnosis. He concludes, in particular, that supply shocks are no more synchronized between European countries than elsewhere, and that the observed evolution is due to demand factors. This strongly suggests that the higher synchronicity of business cycles indeed results from increasingly common macroeconomic policies. It is, thus, not incompatible with a simultaneous tendency towards more specialization of industrial structures, and is very much in accord with the theoretical speculations entertained earlier in this section.

3. THE PRICING MECHANISM

Fundamentals being priced have changed; what about the pricing mechanism? Financial integration can be defined as the law of one price applying to financial markets. Although there is a consensus that early measures of capital market integration—the lifting of capital controls and restriction of the free financial flows—were essential, there is also a broad agreement that full integration is far from being achieved. Is the law of one price increasingly applicable to financial assets in Europe? We pursue two tracks to get at this question. First, we look at the evidence on equity premia. Second, we report on a more direct attempt at measuring the evolution of the stochastic discount factors (implicitly) used by European investors.

If European markets are becoming more integrated, we expect that equity risk is increasingly priced in the same way across the various European markets. Of course, the equity risk premium is an ex ante context and it is difficult to uncover from historical data. We use the standard approach consisting of measuring ex post excess returns, implicitly assuming (despite obvious data limitation with the post-euro experience) that on average the ex ante premia were confirmed.

First, let us come back to our earlier argument that financial integration renders industrial diversification obsolete because it improves the diversification opportunities available more cheaply with financial instruments. The consequence of this argument is that, indeed, the equity premium, or equivalently the cost of capital, should be lower, *ceteris paribus*. In the case of full segmentation, local investors hold undiversified portfolios (from the viewpoint of the global economy). Their reference market portfolio is limited to national firms. The appropriate measure of risk for the local country portfolio is its standard deviation. Everything else being the same, one expects that the risk premium will be high as a result of investors holding (internationally) undiversified positions. In a single financial market, by contrast, investors hold internationally diversified portfolios. The proper measure of risk for the local country portfolio is not its standard deviation, but its beta with respect to the world portfolio. There is, thus, less undiversifiable risk to be remunerated. There is, therefore, a presumption that the risk premium should be lower.

To make this concrete, let us follow Stulz (1999) and assume a simple situation where all individuals display constant relative risk aversion. The price per unit of risk is constant and identical in initially segmented markets or in the whole integrated area. Let us denote it by P. The reasoning above effectively states that, under segmentation, the risk premium on a given security i will be $\sigma_i^2 P$, where σ_i^2 is the variance and σ_i is the standard deviation of the returns on asset i. The same asset in an integrated market will yield a risk premium of $\beta_i P = \rho_i \sigma_i \sigma_m P$, where β_i is the beta of asset i, a function of its covariance with the market portfolio which can also be written in terms of the correlation coefficient between the market portfolio and the return on asset i, ρ_i. From this little exercise one obtains that, if the following condition is satisfied,

$$[\sigma_i / \sigma_m] > \rho_i$$

and thus, in particular, if $\sigma_i > \sigma_m$, then the risk premium in an integrated market will necessarily be smaller than in segmented markets. If this condition holds in Europe, financial integration should go hand in hand with a decrease in the cost of capital.

Of course the world is a bit more complex than the one sketched above. Degrees of risk aversion may vary from one country to the next, as well as from one period to the following (e.g. a popular assumption of habit formation implies that the rate of risk aversion fluctuates with the growth rate of consumption). As a result, under market segmentation, the price of risk may vary across countries. It will be a function of the local capital market's conditions: relative abundance of savings, relative risk appetite. With integration, the price of risk should converge. It is not impossible that the single post-integration risk premium is in fact higher for some markets. This is the case if, before integration, a given country was characterized by a relative

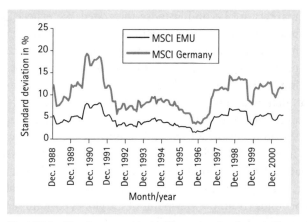

Fig. 19.3. Twelve-month trailing standard deviation

Source: Adjaouté and Danthine 2003

abundance of savings, a stronger than average tolerance to risk, and/or a scarcity of risky investments to be financed. This cannot hold on average, however. For most market participants, one expects that the risk premium will be lower and more stable after integration. Moreover, integration results in the premium being increasingly impacted by common factors, including those affecting the common price of risk. One should thus expect an increasing correlation between the national equity premia as well.

What is the evidence? Figure 19.3 plots the twelve-month trailing standard deviation of the German equity index (MSCI indices) against the standard deviation of the MSCI EMU index. Similar results are provided in Adjaouté and Danthine (2003) for the other euro area countries. These results are unambiguous. The EMU-wide systematic risk, as measured by the standard deviation of the MSCI EMU index, is always smaller than the corresponding measure for the national markets. The latter would be relevant in the case of full segmentation. Thus, at this first level of observation, the message is clear: an important condition for financial integration to result in a decreasing equity premium is satisfied.

Fully in line with this message, Hardouvelis, Malliaropulos, and Priestley (2001) report that, within EU sectors, the cost of equity capital has fallen by between 0.5 and 3 per cent in the 1990s and that there is evidence of convergence in the cost of capital for similar sectors across countries (stocks in the same sector tend to have the same cost across countries). Convergence across different sectors appears to be slower, however.

Going one step further, Figure 19.4 displays the HP filtered equity excess returns for the EMU countries. Specifically, we have computed the excess returns as the monthly total return on national equity indices over the one-month euro currency return for the corresponding country. Two observations stand out. First, there is a clear convergence in excess returns up to the mid-1990s, a little-known fact that we find striking and fully in line with what we expect from the first unambiguous measures

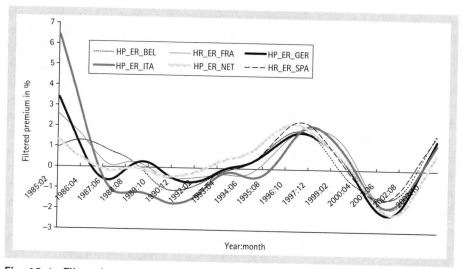

Fig. 19.4. Filtered equity premia for EMU countries

Source: Datastream

promoting financial integration. At this level of observation, the evidence for the second part of the 1990s is less spectacular. The severe market conditions of the end of the 1990s, where expected equity premia have certainly not been confirmed, and the recovery of the later years are dominating the observations.

We then proceed to measure the dispersion of equity excess returns. The HP filtered series is presented in Figure 19.5. We find this graph particularly remarkable. It of course confirms the decrease in the dispersion observed in the previous figure for the end of the 1980s. But it also suggests that, after reaching a plateau in the

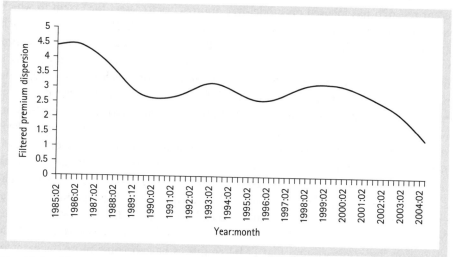

Fig. 19.5. Filtered dispersion of equity premia

Source: Datastream

1990s, the decrease in the equity premia dispersion (increase in the correlation) has continued to lower levels in the beginning of the new century. The convergence of excess returns is thus being pursued with a dispersion level falling lower than the 2.5 per cent mark for the first time since the beginning of our sample (1985) in 2002, and reaching the 1.3 per cent mark in July 2004. We need to be cautious in interpreting this result. For one thing, ex post excess returns may be a poor measure of the equity premium—a problem that is especially acute when they fall into negative territory, as they have between 2000 and 2002. Moreover, measured excess returns are quite volatile and a longer observation period would be necessary to rule out special circumstances. Finally, the evidence on dispersion may be partly the mechanical consequence of the observation of the previous section: the fundamentals underlying the priced assets are getting increasingly similar; even if the pricing mechanism was unchanged, one should expect some convergence in the equity premia to occur. Yet, the strong congruence between this observation and the prediction made on the consequences of financial integration for equity premia encourages us to take seriously this additional evidence of a further increase in financial integration in Europe.

A converging assessment on the integration of European equity markets is obtained in Baele et al. (Chapter 5). These authors conclude, in particular, that the euro area domestic stock returns are increasingly driven by news common to all European investors and that the local return variance is increasingly explained by common European shocks. They interpret this finding as suggesting that euro area integration of equity markets has proceeded more quickly than global equity market integration.

The evidence on equity premia does not distinguish pricing issues from the evolution of fundamentals (nor does the analysis of Baele et al.). To go beyond and confirm the lessons of the preceding exercise, one would need formally to test some asset-pricing model. Given the limitations of parametric asset-pricing frameworks, recent research has focused on model-free approaches to assess the extent to which stochastic discount factors have indeed converged in the EMU context. One such attempt is by Sontchik (2004), who uses an integration measure initially developed by Chen and Knez (1995). Chen and Knez's measure of integration is essentially a distance measure between two stochastic discount factors, each pricing a separate market. The smaller the distance, the more integrated the two markets are: under full integration, the same discount factor would price the two markets. The integration measure can be viewed as representing the maximum pricing error one could make if countries or industries are (wrongly) treated as fully integrated at the European level. In essence, defining any set of assets to be priced by no arbitrage as a market, Sontchik (2004) finds that integration has *decreased* since the introduction of the euro; that is, the pairwise distance between the stochastic discount factors pricing individual national markets has increased, rather than decreased, in the last few years. This finding is surprising and highly counter-intuitive: it is hard to conceive that financial integration has regressed and that EMU countries have become more 'segmented' after the convergence process. Our interpretation is that, at the pure pricing level, the effects of financial integration are not detectable yet, possibly because of the fragility of the statistical methods available, or because the large magnitude of the cyclical circumstances of the last few years makes it hard statistically to identify pure pricing changes. It is conceivable as well that these effects are an order of magnitude smaller than those recorded in fundamentals.

4. RETURNS

In this section we concentrate on equity returns themselves. In the final analysis, can we say that something has been changed at the level of ex post equity returns as a result of economic and financial integration in Europe? One of our goals is to interpret the evidence in the light of the considerations made on fundamentals and pricing in the two preceding sections.

4.1. The HR Approach: Country versus Sectors

As our starting point, consider the possibility that equity returns are impacted by several (orthogonally defined) factors: sectors, countries, and global (euro area/ world).[2] The most celebrated version of this hypothesis was initiated by Heston and Rouwenhorst (1994, HR from now on), in which the return generating process was described as

$$R_{it} = \alpha_t + \gamma_{kt} + \delta_{jt} + \varepsilon_{it},$$

where α_t is the global component, γ_{kt} is the country factor, δ_{jt} is the industry factor, and ε_{it} is the idiosyncratic return. This framework has been used in a large number of papers to investigate the issue of the relative importance of country and industry factors. In a first step, the dummy variable model is estimated, and in a second stage the relative influence of both factors is evaluated by comparing either the relative variances, or the mean average deviations (MAD) of country/industry effects. This approach is relevant here because recent research has documented changes in the relative contributions of the various factors that may be associated with the process of economic and financial integration at work in Europe.

Indeed, until recently, the literature was nearly unanimous in finding that country factors dominated industry factors. This finding was robust across different data sets. Sample papers in this vein include Beckers, Connor, and Cures (1996), Griffin and Karolyi (1998), and Rouwenhorst (1999). Rouwenhorst (1999), for instance, analyses the returns of all 952 European stocks included in the MSCI indices of twelve European countries. His data set ends in August 1998. With an eye on the potential

---

[2] Kuo and Satchell 2001 and Hamelink, Harasty, and Hillion 2001 assume that returns are impacted by yet another factor, namely style.

impact of economic and monetary integration on the results of the variance decomposition, he concludes that the superiority of country effects has been effective at least since 1982 and that it has continued during the 1993–8 period 'despite the convergence of interest rates and the harmonization of fiscal and monetary policies following the Maastricht Treaty'.

The unanimity, however, appears to have broken down recently. Using more recent data sets, various studies have detected an increase in the industry effects. Arnold (2001) prolongs the study of Rouwenhorst (1999), using data up to 1999, and finds that, in the year following the introduction of the euro, industry factors have dominated country factors. Baca, Garbe, and Weiss (2000) find that both industry and country effects have converged, while Cavaglia, Brightman, and Aked (2000) also document that industry factors have weighed more heavily than country factors since 1997. Isakov and Sonney (2004), on the other hand, confirm the dominance of country effects for the period 1997–2000 with a sample including twenty developed countries, but they detect a shift in the last part of their sample. As shown in Figure 19.6, allowing for time variations in the decomposition, Isakov and Sonney confirm that industry factors are growing in importance and that they have explained a larger fraction of the variance of returns after March 2000. Alternative lines of research include Galati and Tsatsaronis (2001), who look at the companies in the FTSE Eurotop 300. They find that industry factors became more important than country factors for the first time a few months prior to the formal arrival of the euro. Contrary to most other researchers, however, they also find that the superiority of the country

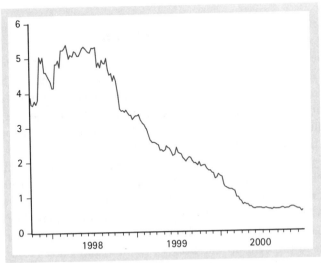

Fig. 19.6. Evolution over time of the relative country/ industry influences

Note: This graph represents the evolution of the ratio of the varience of the country effects to the industry effects. Variences have been estimated over thirty–six-week intervals
Source: Isakov and Sonney 2004

factors was insignificant after the beginning of 1996 and even as early as 1992. A possible reconciliation with Rouwenhorst (1999) arises from observing that Galati and Tatsaronis concentrate their analysis on very large capitalizations. As anticipated in our discussion on fundamentals, such stocks have been found to be less sensitive to country factors than smaller cap stocks; see, for example, Isakov and Sonney (2004).

At this stage, one may wonder whether the growing importance of sectors relative to countries is specific to the euro area, thus being plausibly associated with greater economic and financial integration, and whether it is likely to be permanent. Alternatively, one may speculate that it could be a more universal phenomenon and/or that the recent stock market bubble could have played a role in this observation.

Brooks and Del Negro (2002a) provide interesting evidence in these regards. First, they observe that the correlation of the US equity market with other developed equity markets has moved from a low level of 0.4 in the 1980s to almost 0.9 in the late 1990s. They argue that this may be due to a decline in home bias, so that the marginal investor in the German stocks is not necessarily German and, as a result, country-specific investor sentiment now plays a minor role. Alternatively, the general rise in comovement of equity markets may be the manifestation of firms becoming more diversified internationally, and therefore increasingly exposed to the global business cycle, causing stock markets to move together more. Finally, there is the possibility that the rise in comovement of stock markets is a temporary phenomenon associated with the recent stock market boom and bust.

Brooks and Del Negro use a sample of companies representing three geographic regions, in MSCI's terminology: the Americas, Far East, and Europe. They estimate the standard dummy variables HR model and use MADs of country and sector factors to assess the relative importance of each shock. The empirical evidence for the whole sample seems to suggest that industry factors have outgrown country factors in the late 1990s, in conformity with what we reported for the euro area. However, when US stocks and companies in the telecommunications, media, biotechnology, and information technology (TMBT) sectors are excluded from the sample, the evidence of industry factors dominating country factors disappears. The absence of evidence beyond TMBT sectors and the USA is interpreted by the authors as an indication that the recent dominance of industry effects over country effects is a *temporary* phenomenon associated with the stock market bubble. At the regional level, however, they report that the European evidence is *not* affected by the removal of TMBT sectors. Isakov and Sonney (2004) provide a converging assessment. Even when TMBT sectors are excluded from the sample, the recent superiority of sectors holds true in Europe.

To summarize, in general the estimation of the relative importance of countries and sectors is sensitive to the inclusion or exclusion of specific countries (the USA in particular) or sectors (TMBT). The fact that the evidence is more robust in the case of the euro area supports the hypothesis that something more fundamental is at work in that region.

Are these observations in accord with our understanding of the evidence on fundamentals and pricing? Let us start with pricing. As mentioned before, financial integration implies the convergence toward a single pricing kernel or discount factor. This pricing convergence affects both country and sector portfolios. Full segmentation would mean that a basket of French stocks is priced by French investors in a way that is largely disconnected from the way a basket of German stocks is priced by German investors. It also means that the German stocks in a particular industry basket would be priced via a pricing kernel that could differ and evolve differently through time from the pricing mechanism of the French stocks belonging to the same industry. The convergence of risk-free rates and of risk premia expected under financial integration implies that, *ceteris paribus, both* country and sectoral baskets of stocks will have a tendency to be priced closer together. But, of course, our discussion in the previous sections indicates that the *ceteris paribus* does not apply. If the pricing component of equity returns converges, the objects being priced also change, potentially introducing increasing divergence in returns. Thus, in particular, if a country industrial structure becomes more specialized, the fundamentals of country indices are getting more dissimilar and returns on country indices are subject to two conflicting influences that could entail more synchronized as well as less synchronized returns. If, on the contrary, national economic structures are getting more alike, and/or if, as we have observed, the influence of increasingly common policies is the dominating factor, then indeed, both components of the pricing of country indices would display a tendency toward increasing correlation. Our reasoning thus suggests that the waning of the country factors may, indeed, be the expected consequence of economic and financial integration in Europe.

As far as sector returns are concerned, the pricing effect of financial integration should, in principle, dominate the much less clear changes in fundamentals. Financial integration should then translate into portfolios of stocks representing an industry across the geographical area being priced closer together. But short samples are a specific problem here: a specific history of sectoral shocks, leading, for instance, to a temporarily diverging performance (namely the IT sector in recent times) may pollute our appreciation of the correlation between industry indices. Over the medium run, it is difficult to make a link between increasing financial integration and diverging sectoral returns. Note that the short sample problem also plagues the appreciation of the correlation between country returns if countries do not correspond to well-diversified portfolios of sectors. Isakov and Sonney (2004) suggest this is not the case, however.

4.2. Country versus Sectors: An Alternative View

A troubling element in the preceding discussion resides in the conflicting results reported with the HR approach. The latter appear to be very sensitive to the data used, the definition of sectors, and the period of analysis. Table 4 in Isakov and Sonney (2004), for example, shows that the ratio of the fraction of return variances explained by countries and industries varies across studies in a ratio of 2 to 11.5! This lack of robustness may be due to several deficiencies in the HR methodology. The first problem associated with this approach is that it imposes the restriction that a firm belongs to one country and one industry only and that it is not sensitive to other countries/industries. This assumption is highly disputable in the face of the trend toward multinational firms and the reality that many firms have outputs or inputs connected with multiple industries. If the restricted HR model were true, the covariance of stock returns would show non-zero terms only for stocks in the same sector or belonging to the same country. This is far from being the case. This is illustrated in Adjaouté and Danthine (2003) with the correlation matrix corresponding to a higher level of sector disaggregation. With 77 country sectors identified within EMU (the unit being a sector in a country), the correlation matrix includes 2,926 (77*76/2) independent correlations, out of which 2,369 should be zero under the HR hypotheses. In reality, only 41 (68) of these correlations are less than 0.1 in the first (second) period covered by our sample!

A second problem associated with the HR approach is that it assumes that all stocks from the same country/industry have the same sensitivity to the country/industry factors. There are reasons to believe, however, that the exposure to a country factor may vary across firms in the same country, as some are more international than others. Brooks and Del Negro (2002b) test this hypothesis and unambiguously reject the constraints that the coefficients to own country factors are all unity.

These defects justify complementing the HR analysis with a more versatile test of the relative importance of countries versus global sectors. Figure 19.7 displays the Hodrick–Prescott filtered cross-sectional dispersions of country and global sector returns. The time series of raw country return and global sector return dispersions are highly time varying while also following some cycles. The cyclical pattern appears clearly if one filters the series to extract their slowly moving components, as is apparent in Figure 19.7. This analysis is revealing. Both country and sector

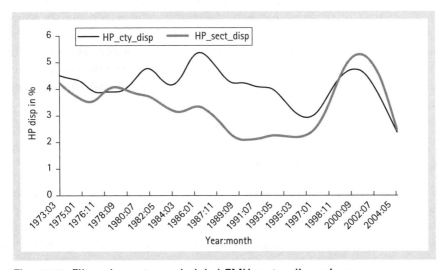

Fig. 19.7. Filtered country and global EMU sector dispersions

Source: Datastream

dispersions displayed a downward trend until the autumn of 1996, an evolution that Adjaouté and Danthine (2001) credit to the widespread view that correlations among country indices were increasing in Europe owing to European integration and that, indeed, diversification opportunities were being hampered. But these dispersions have trended upward since reaching their most recent peaks around the end of 2000. By then the dispersion levels were at an all-time high for sectors and had almost matched their highest point of the mid-1980s for country indices. The movement towards lower dispersion resumed around mid-2001 and the country return dispersion series has reached its lowest level ever, while the sector dispersion series is approaching its lowest, at the end of our sample. The overall trend for country dispersion is clearly downwards; the difference between the two series has narrowed; and the sector dispersion rose above the country dispersion around mid-1999. The two series are, however, barely distinguishable at the end of the sample.

A number of conclusions follow. First, based on the cross-sectional dispersion of countries and sectors, the superiority of a country-based asset allocation was clear for most of the period (in conformity with Rouwenhorst 1999). That is, as the country returns were more dispersed than the sector ones, diversification along country lines delivered higher gains. Second, the reversal taking place in early to mid-1999 confirms the reversal of the variance inequality uncovered by various authors in the HR context.[3] Third, the overall tendency is consistent with the finding that the euro area business cycles have become more synchronized, so that the orthogonal portions of the euro area country factors are showing increasingly smaller variances. Yet, it is not true that, as often expressed, the post-euro period has been unfavourable for diversification within the euro area as the strong pick-up in both country and sector dispersions from 1996 to 1999 attests. Finally, the variability of the relationships and the fact that reversals have occurred in the past (this was the case from around 1977 to 1979) and that the current superiority of sectors may be petering out are sources of questioning. First, these facts suggest that methods, such as the HR approach, relying on time averaging over relatively long periods are vulnerable to the dating of the sample split and have a hard time identifying and dating the breaks. Second, caution should be exercised before definitively linking the latest reversal to permanent structural changes.

4.3. Other Evidence on Returns

The discussion on returns has so far been held entirely in terms of correlation/covariance matrices abstracting from the other side of the asset allocation equation— that is, from the vector of expected returns. The reason for this omission is straightforward. While there is some degree of stability in return correlations, permitting

---

[3] The exact dating of the reversal is likely to depend on the specific filtering or data-smoothing method.

us, with caution, to approximate expected relationships with historical correlations, the same is definitely not true for expected returns. In an attempt to provide a more complete account of the observed evolutions of equity returns, Adjaouté and Danthine (2003) nevertheless conduct mean–variance optimizations on country and sector portfolios. They consider two subsamples, the first starting in May 1987 and ending in December 1994, the second starting in January 1995 and ending in August 2002, and they allow for short selling. Focusing first on country portfolios, they find that the first-period performance of both the minimum variance and the tangent portfolios is better compared to the later period. On the other hand, when optimization is performed on the basis of sector portfolios, the performance of the minimum variance portfolio has improved during the euro period, although the opposite is true for the tangent portfolio. Most interestingly, the Sharpe ratio of the optimal portfolios composed on the basis of sector indices is always superior to the Sharpe ratio of the optimal portfolios constructed from country indices. Proceeding with utmost caution, Adjaouté and Danthine thus conclude that if one takes on board the message from average returns, there is a distinct possibility that, for a much longer period, portfolio weights implicit in sector indices have been more conducive to portfolio performance than the portfolio weights implicit in country indices.

Recent work by Ehling and Ramos (2004) and Gerard, Hillion, and de Roon (2002) helps qualify this last statement, however. The first of these authors also propose a full mean–variance efficiency test, inspired by the work of Basak, Jagannathan, and Sun (2002). When they look at the 1991–2003 period, they find that unconstrained geographic and industry diversifications are statistically equivalent, although the signs of their tests indicate that the industry efficient frontier lies outside the country efficient frontier as found by Adjaouté and Danthine. They show, however, that, once short-selling restrictions are introduced, the industry efficient frontier shrinks dramatically and lies well inside the country efficient frontier. Gerard, Hillion, and de Roon (2002) also find that industry portfolios are more strongly affected by short sales constraints than country portfolios, although, in the absence of short sales restrictions, country and industry diversifications appear as redundant strategies.

Both Adjaouté and Danthine (2003, 2004) and Ehling and Ramos (2004) also consider the possibility of performing mean–variance optimization at a lower level of data aggregation. This is because, while the factor analysis has a tendency to rationalize asset allocation strategies in terms of country or industry indices, it is not clear that one can understand either strategy relative to the alternative of proceeding to a full optimization across both countries and sectors. To illustrate, why limit oneself to ten country indices or ten global sector indices when one could equally well use the full 10 × 10 matrix of what can be labelled 'country sector' indices? The results may be illustrated in terms of the dispersion measures reported in Figure 19.8 and depicting the time evolution of the country sector dispersion along with the dispersions of country and sector returns. The lower part of the figure with the

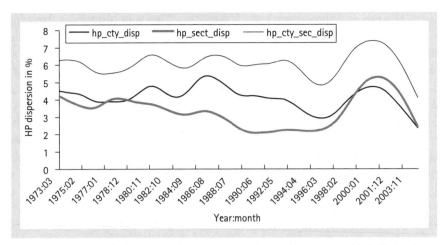

Fig. 19.8. Filtered country, global sector, and country sector EMU dispersions

Source: Datastream

two crossing lines representing the country and global sector dispersions replicates Figure 19.7. The country sector dispersion is always above these two lines and this is the striking message of this analysis. At the lower level of aggregation, the dispersion line consistently moves by a wide margin above the two others for the entire sample, i.e. 1973–2004; correlations are lower and the benefits of diversification are higher. This result, although not surprising, represents a puzzle to the extent that European asset managers appear to be torn between selecting an asset allocation model based on countries or on industries (see Adjaouté and Danthine 2003 for an elaboration) while they could significantly improve the efficiency of their portfolios by following a more disaggregated approach, diversifying simultaneously across countries and sectors. The result is not surprising in the sense that standard portfolio analysis cannot justify imposing restrictions on portfolio weights such as those in force when one is limited to either country indices or sector indices as the building blocks of asset allocation. This is confirmed by the portfolio optimization exercises of Adjaouté and Danthine (2003) and is consistent with Ehling and Ramos's (2004) finding that a structure with a lower level of aggregation, such as country–industry pairs, clearly outperforms both industry and geographic diversifications, with or without short selling constraints. Beyond these observations, it is interesting to note that the variability of the country sector dispersion appears to have increased recently, with both the peak of late 2000 and the current trough being unprecedented events. Unfortunately, they are both too recent for us to be able to draw any usable inference. Note, as well, that the slight downward trend in the country sector dispersion observed in the 1990s is consistent with the long-run effect of financial integration—convergence in pricing—and with the recorded evolution of the macro fundamentals—more synchronous business cycles.

5. CONCLUSIONS

The process of financial and economic integration in Europe is manifest through significant changes in the fundamentals underlying equity markets. Of these, the most important is the increased synchronization of macroeconomic activities across the euro area, an evolution that is certainly due to the increased coordination of policies, but may mask a diverging evolution in industrial structures. The internationalization of corporate ownership, of the scope of corporate activities, and the increasing reliance on intra-European trade (in intermediate goods, in particular) are also relevant to the extent that they tend to blur the national and sectoral lines typically used to segment the European equity markets.

The evolution in pricing may be deemed less spectacular. It is not negligible, however. We note, in particular, that the decrease in the cost of capital and the convergence in equity premia that are legitimately associated with financial integration appear to be materializing in Europe, although pure pricing changes are more difficult to identify statistically.

Against this background, the observations made on returns are harder to sort out. A considerable literature has focused on identifying the respective roles of country and industry factors on returns. This is understandable to the extent that the identified changes in fundamentals rationalize a diminishing role for geography and thus a relative increase in the force of industry diversification. Moreover, important changes in the organization of the industry—from an organizational focus on countries to one that is geared toward industries—would seem to add credibility to this change. Using cross-sectional dispersions as a tool to be more precise as to the timing of changes and their persistence, we are led to exercise great caution, however. Yes, there appears to be a long-run trend towards a decrease in the dispersion of returns—that is, an increase in their correlation—for country portfolios (equity portfolios composed on the basis of country indices), but the period 1996–1999 was one where these correlations were unusually low and thus geographical diversification was unusually effective. Yes, there seems to be a long-run evolution consistent with a narrowing of the superiority of country factors and even a reversal taking place in early to mid-1999. But the latest (2004) observations suggest this reversal was short-lived and they support the view that, on the basis of covariances only, a distinction between the two approaches is not warranted. Moreover, standard investment restrictions, such as short selling limits, appear to bite harder on the diversification potential of industry portfolios than is the case for country portfolios. The alleged superiority of sectoral diversification, justifying the reorganization of the industry, is thus hard to confirm. In the end, the main message emerging from the study of European equity returns may be the following: one cannot exclude that we are witnessing long-run upward trends in correlations of both country and sector returns. The existence of these trends is in accord with the evolution of fundamentals we have highlighted and with what we understand to be the consequences of integration on pricing. Confronted with this reality, the benefits to be gained from finding diversification opportunities at a more disaggregated level (at the level of country sectors) are higher than ever.

REFERENCES

ADJAOUTÉ, K., and DANTHINE, J.-P. (2001), 'EMU and portfolio diversification opportunities', FAME Research Paper no. 31.

――――― (2003), 'European financial integration and equity returns: a theory-based assessment', in V. Gaspar, P. Hartmann, and O. Sleijpen (eds.), *The Transformation of the European Financial System*, Frankfurt, European Central Bank.

――――― (2004), 'Portfolio diversification: alive and well in Euroland', *Applied Financial Economics*, 14, 1225–31.

――――― and ISAKOV, D. (2005), 'Portfolio Diversification in Europe', in H. Huizinga and L. Jonung (eds.), *The Internationalisation of Asset Ownership in Europe*, Cambridge, Cambridge: University Press, 140–72.

――― BOTTAZZI, L., DANTHINE, J.-P., FISCHER, A., HAMAUI, R., PORTES, R., and WICKENS, M. (2000), 'EMU and portfolio adjustment', CEPR Policy Paper no. 5.

AGRESTI, A. M., and MOJON, B. (2001), 'Some stylized facts on the euro area business cycle', ECB Working Paper no. 95.

ARNOLD, I. (2001), 'Country and industry effects in Euroland's equity markets', in J. Choi and J. Wrase (eds.), *European Monetary Union and Capital Markets*, Amsterdam, Elsevier, ii. 137–55.

BACA, S. P., GARBE, B. L., and WEISS, R. A. (2000), 'The rise of sector effects in major equity markets', *Financial Analysts Journal*, 56(October), 34–40.

BAELE, L., FERRANDO, A., HÖRDHAL, P., KRYLOVA, E., and MONNET, C. (2004), 'Measuring European financial integration', *Oxford Review of Economic Policy*, 20(4), 509–30.

BASAK, G., JAGANNATHAN, R., and SUN, G. (2002), 'A Direct Test for the Mean–variance Efficiency of a Portfolio', *Journal of Economic Dynamics and Control*, 26, 1195–215.

BECKERS, S., CONNOR, G., and CURDS, R. (1996), 'National versus global influences on equity returns', *Financial Analysts Journal*, 52, 31–9.

BROOKS, R., and DEL NEGRO, M. (2002a), 'The rise in comovement across national stock markets: market integration or global bubble', IMF Working Paper, September.

――― (2002b), 'International diversification strategies', IMF Working Paper, November.

CAVAGLIA, S., BRIGHTMAN, C., and AKED, M. (2000), 'The increasing importance of industry factors', *Financial Analysts Journal*, 56, 41–54.

CHEN, Z., and KNEZ, P. J. (1995), 'Measurement of market integration and arbitrage', *Review of Financial Studies*, 8(2), 287–325.

DUEKER, M., and WESCHE, K. (1999), 'European business cycles: new indices and analysis of their synchronicity', Federal Reserve Bank of St Louis, Working Paper 1999–019B.

EHLING, P., and RAMOS, S. B. (2004), 'Geographic vs industry diversification: constraints matter', FAME Research Paper no. 113.

GALATI, G., and TSATSARONIS, K. (2001), 'The impact of the euro on europe's financial markets', BIS Monetary and Economic Department, Working Paper no. 100.

GERARD, B., HILLION, P., and DE ROON, F. (2002), 'International portfolio diversification: industry, country and currency effects revisited', Working Paper.

GRIFFIN, J. M., and KAROLYI, A. G. (1998), 'Another look at the role of the industrial structure of markets for international diversification strategies', *Journal of Financial Economics*, 50, 351–73.

HAMELINK, F., HARASTY, H., and HILLION, P. (2001), 'Country sector or style: what matters most when constructing global equity portfolios', FAME Research Paper no. 35.

HARDOUVELIS, G., MALLIAROPULOS, D., and PRIESTLEY, R. (2001), 'The impact of globalization on the equity cost of capital', Banque de France, Working Paper.

HESTON, S., and ROUWENHORST, K. (1994), 'Does industrial structure explain the benefits of industrial diversification?', *Journal of Financial Economics*, 36(1), 3–27.

IMBS, J. (1999), 'Technology, growth and the business cycle', *Journal of Monetary Economics*, 44, 65–80.

—— and WACZIARG, R. (2003), 'Stages of diversification', *American Economic Review*, 93(1), 63–86.

ISAKOV, D., and SONNEY, F. (2004), 'Are practitioners right? On the relative importance of industrial factors in international stock returns', *Swiss Journal of Economics and Statistics*, 140(3), 293–9.

KRUGMAN, P. (1991), *Geography and Trade*, Cambridge, Mass.: MIT Press.

KUO, W., and SATCHELL, S. E. (2001), 'Global equity styles and industry effects: the preeminence of value relative to size', *Journal of International Financial Markets, Institutions and Money*, 11, 1–28.

ORMEROD, P., and MOUNFIELD, C. (2002), 'The convergence of European business cycles 1978–2000', *Physica A*, 307, 494–504.

ROUWENHORST, K.G. (1999), 'European equity markets and the EMU', *Financial Analysts Journal*, 57–64.

SOLNIK, B., and ROULET, J. (2000), 'Dispersion as cross-sectional correlation', *Financial Analysts Journal*, January–February, 54–61.

SONTCHIK, S. (2004), 'Financial integration of european equity markets', HEC University of Lausanne and FAME, mimeo.

STULZ, R. (1999), 'Globalization of equity markets and the cost of capital', *Journal of Applied Corporate Finance*, Fall, 8–25.

CHAPTER 20

....

POST-TRADING SERVICES AND EUROPEAN SECURITIES MARKETS

....

ALBERTO GIOVANNINI

JOHN BERRIGAN

DANIELA RUSSO

1. INTRODUCTION

....

TEXTBOOK financial analysis typically assumes that a securities transaction begins and ends with the trade between buyer and seller: in fact this could not be further from reality. The trade is just the beginning of a chain of actions designed to safely transfer ownership of the security from the seller to the buyer in return for payment. This chain of actions involves an inevitable degree of operational complexity, mainly due to the large volume of transactions to be processed simultaneously, the need for a proper sequencing of the various actions, and the participation of agents other

The views expressed in this chapter do not necessarily represent those of the authors' respective affiliations.

than the buyer and seller of the security. Needless to say, this operational complexity has increased over time in function of the growing size of securities markets and the globalization of capital flows. The provision of post-trading services is now a highly sophisticated industry, as reflected in the availability of a wide range of ancillary services (e.g. the extension of credit, securities lending facilities, netting) and the extended use of information technology in an increasingly dematerialized environment.

It is the predominantly operational nature of post-trading activities which has condemned this aspect of securities market functioning to virtual obscurity in standard financial market analysis. The role of post-trading in the market is variously described as 'subterranean' or 'plumbing', and analytical interest in the field has been confined to a small coterie of true connoisseurs. The paradox is that this traditionally ignored dimension of securities market functioning is, in fact, the very essence of the market, because it constitutes the basic process of exchange between buyers and sellers of securities.[1] It is impossible to conceive of an efficiently functioning securities market without the availability of correspondingly efficient post-trading services. Not surprisingly, therefore, interest in post-trading services has broadened in the context of recent efforts to promote financial integration in the EU. Indeed, it is increasingly recognized that the prospect of an efficiently integrated market for securities now hinges crucially on the future of the post-trading industry.

While post-trading involves a number of functions apart from clearing and settlement, the term clearing and settlement has been used as a portmanteau for the whole post-trading landscape.[2]

Within the EU, the clearing and settlement industry is highly segmented because national systems have evolved over time to reflect the specific preferences and culture within their respective financial systems.[3] Improvements in the interoperability of the many clearing and settlement systems within the EU have been proposed (typically in a more global context) by several eminent bodies since the late 1970s, including the G-30, the International Organization of Securities Commissions, and the Bank for International Settlements.

Despite the authority of these bodies and the high quality of their work, efforts at reform have met with only limited success. Several explanations have been offered for this unsatisfactory outcome, notably the rather broad and voluntary nature of recommendations made to the industry and public authorities. Perhaps their main

---

[1] In this context, it is apparent that the term 'stock exchange' has become an anachronism in the sense that modern exchanges now consist only of trading platforms, with the actual exchange taking place elsewhere in the market infrastructure.

[2] In simplified terms, the functionalities of clearing and settlement involve a number of steps as follows: (a) confirmation of the terms of the trade as agreed between the buyer and seller, which can be achieved either directly or indirectly; (b) clearing, by which credits and debits of buyers and sellers are netted and their settlement positions (or obligations) are established, and which is a service normally provided by a clearing house, a central counterparty, or a central securities depository; and (c) settlement of the securities transaction which is normally achieved when delivery (requiring the transfer of the securities from the seller to the buyer) and payment (requiring the transfer of funds from the buyer to the seller) have been finalized; securities' transfer is typically provided by a central securities depository.

[3] See also Section 2.

handicap, however, has been the absence of a proper context in which to galvanize the support of the various stakeholders in the reform process. This context has now been provided by the intensified political commitment to the process of EU financial integration.

The purpose of this chapter is to describe the issues surrounding the reform of clearing and settlement in Europe. This reform has a number of features that make it a kind of canonical case:

- it is essentially a liberalization, aimed at eliminating barriers to trade;
- it is taking place on a market that is currently functioning, but that will profoundly change as a result of the reform itself;
- it aims at modifying not only laws, but also standards and conventions in the marketplace, thus it involves a multiplicity of different actors, who need to be coordinated;
- because it is wide ranging, and will conceivably have wide-ranging implications, it is expected to induce profound changes in the organization of financial markets more generally; and
- while it is essentially technical in nature—as it deals with probably the deepest function of the financial system—it excites feelings of national pride, often influenced by those private interests that are to be negatively affected by a larger and freer European market.

In this chapter, unless otherwise specified, we refer to clearing and settlement of cash equities. However, our remarks will qualitatively carry to other instruments, such as bonds and derivatives.

The next section, Section 2, describes the current European clearing and settlement industry. Section 3 provides a chronology of reform initiatives by European authorities designed to enhance the efficiency of the industry. Section 4 discusses clearing and settlement reform in the broader context of the financial system reform in the EU. Liberalizations of the financial system all have the peculiarity of dealing with an industry that gains its very vitality from change and evolution, and seeks to deliver services to its clients at ever decreasing costs: this process originates from the fact that the financial industry is an information industry, and information technology has been experiencing, at least since the Second World War, huge technical progress. We try to determine whether the reform of clearing and settlement, like the broader process of financial integration, conflicts with either national objectives, individual rights, or democratic principles. Section 5 describes the logic and structure of the reform strategy adopted by the European Commission, to which both the private sector and national authorities are contributing, discusses the reasons why it has been chosen over top-down and more invasive initiatives, as well as the main challenges to the reform. Section 6 summarizes the arguments offered in this chapter and contains a few concluding observations.

2. The EU Clearing and Settlement Industry

The European clearing and settlement industry is characterized by the presence of national monopolies in almost all countries, be it by law or by prescriptions contained in the trading and clearing membership rule books.[4] This situation reflects considerations of heritage and economic efficiency. On the one hand, the specific structure of national clearing and settlement provision is a function of historical evolution in the broader national financial system, as driven by a country's economic system, cultural, technical requirements, and the prevailing legal environment. On the other hand, it is also a function of an economic rationale, which has favoured monopoly provision of clearing and settlement as the means to maximize scale economies and minimize high fixed investment costs. In many EU countries, however, monopoly public sector providers have been subsequently privatized, leaving the newly privatized entities with governance structures that do not adequately take account of the nature of their business and in particular of their status as providers of basic functions in the financial system.

In this environment of segmented national monopolies, the EU clearing and settlement industry exists as an inefficient patchwork of different systems with a limited capacity for interlinkage among themselves. Segmentation in the clearing and settlement industry was not a significant problem so long as exchange rate risk was the dominant factor in determining patterns of investment within the EU. However, the adoption of the euro has eliminated exchange rate risk on the bulk of EU financial flows and stimulated investor demand for cross-border securities trading. In these new circumstances, the problem of segmentation in clearing and settlement has been brought into sharp relief. In addition to segmentation in the market, issues of oversight, supervision, and regulation in the field of clearing and settlement are addressed differently across the EU. CSDs (Central Securities Depositories) are regulated independently in all of the member states and, despite the achievement of a degree of harmonization in some fields following implementation of EU directives (e.g. custody risk), differences persist in the scope of national laws and regulations, the degree of cooperation among regulatory authorities, and the enforcement powers of the various regulators. The situation becomes even more complex insofar as some CSDs are allowed to engage in banking activities. In most of the member states, CSDs are legally prohibited from extending credit, but CSDs may have a banking licence and, therefore, conduct settlement-related credit business in Austria, Belgium, Germany, and Luxembourg.[5] In other member states, CSDs are allowed to provide

---

[4] This observation is based on a study of London Economics (2005) for the Competition Commission of the European Commission examining the scope of choice regarding clearing and settlement service providers.

[5] In the cases where banking regulations apply to CSDs, the regulatory framework is identical. In practice, however, there are still differences which are partly driven by regulation and partly by the market.

settlement-related credit, but only subject to specified conditions. For instance, in Italy credit can be extended on the basis of adequate guarantees, while in Portugal full collateralization is required.

In contrast to the segmentation of the EU clearing and settlement industry among national CSDs, the so-called ICSDs have emerged as pan-European providers of clearing and settlement, notably in bond markets. Euroclear and Clearstream International[6] were established in the 1960s to supply a post-trading infrastructure for eurobonds, the offshore bonds invented by European and American banks mostly for European investors which were traded over the counter. Since then, the scope of the ICSDs' activities has expanded to sovereign bonds and these entities have recently been merging with national CSDs to further extend their activities to the field of equities. ICSDs are not the only actors involved in cross-border clearing and settlement. Domestic[7] as well as global custodians, enabling communication between foreign banks and domestic CSD's, act as gateways to their domestic infrastructures and therefore are major players in facilitating cross-border securities transactions.[8]

Figures 20.1 and 20.2 provide some basic statistics on the size of the European market for settlement. Figure 20.1 reports the value of securities deposited in securities settlement systems in Europe, the euro area, and the United States. Figure 20.2 reports the number of instructions handled by securities settlement systems in Europe, the euro area, and the United States. Both figures show that if the European market is taken as a whole, it is roughly the same size as the US market. Yet, the degree of consolidation is much more limited in Europe. Figure 20.3 shows the number of securities settlement systems and the number of securities central counterparties in the euro area and the USA. Despite a decrease in the number of service providers between 1999 and 2004 (that is, since the creation of the single currency), the degree of consolidation in the euro area is much more limited than in the United States. Tables 20.1 to 20.4 contain more detail on national CSDs and CCPs, and their activities.

Figure 20.4 shows more detail on the structure of trading and post-trading services in cash equities. Two facts are immediately evident from this figure. The first is the extent of fragmentation among the different links of the value chain: trading, clearing, and settlement. The second is the variable geometry of the industry, where different kinds of aggregation coexist: vertical 'silos' like those in Germany, Greece, Italy, and Spain, and horizontally integrated structures, like LCH Clearnet, the

---

For example, the Austrian CSD is allowed to grant credit only in relation to certain activities and the credit is fully collateralized by the Austrian government. Also, liquidity management has been imposed as part of the oversight activities of the relevant authorities. Finally it is worth mentioning that the two ICSDs voluntarily limit their banking services to activities related to settlement or asset management as a part of their risk management procedures.

[6] Formerly CEDEL.   [7] Also described as agent banks.

[8] Indeed, global custodians can also act as common depositories for the safekeeping of Eurobonds on behalf of the two ICSDs.

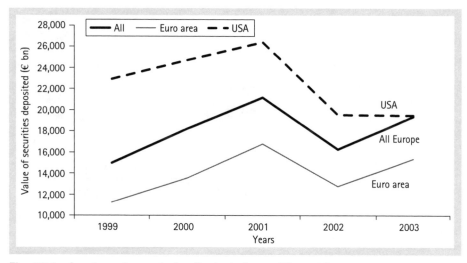

Fig. 20.1. Assets under custody of selected securities settlement systems

Source: European Central Bank

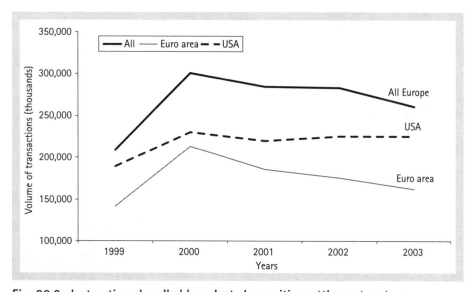

Fig. 20.2. Instructions handled by selected securities settlement systems

Source: European Central Bank

Euroclear Group, and the Euronext 'federation'. Finally, Figure 20.5 compares costs of transactions. While US and EU domestic transactions are roughly comparable in cost terms, a transaction between two residents of different EU member states is many times more expensive than the corresponding domestic transaction.

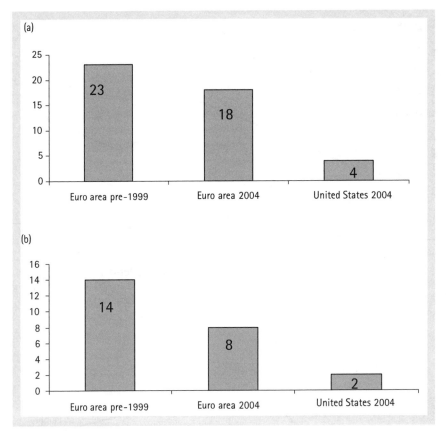

Fig. 20.3. (a) Securities settlement systems (b) Securities central counterparties

Source: European Central Bank

Over time, the respective roles of the various players, national CSDs, ICSDs, and custodians have become increasingly blurred, and substantially overlapped, making it difficult to clearly identify the incentives faced by each actor in the integration and consolidation process. In general, their incentives to achieve an enhanced integration may be limited by three sets of factors. First, some providers will have invested heavily in infrastructure that could become rapidly obsolete in a fully integrated environment. Second, some providers gain from the existing web of complexities in international securities clearing and settlement, whose services would not be required if these complexities were eliminated. Finally, some providers may want to control the rate at which the market integrates and simplifies, in order to maximize their profitability in the transition, as well as possibly internalizing the public good of market size and risk pooling. An additional complication is that, as is normally the case, these objectives conflict with those of competitors. Hence the reform arena becomes the place where conflicting interests of competitors are played out. Issues

Table 20.1. CSDs in the euro area, 1999–2004

Country	January 1999	October 2004
Austria	OeKB	OeKB
Belgium	NBB–SSS	NBB–SSS
	CIK	Euroclear Bank
	Euroclear	
Finland	APK	APK
France	Sicovam	Euroclear France (former Sicovam)
Germany	Deutsche Börse Clearing (DBC)	Clearstream Frankfurt (former DBC)
Greece	BOGS	BOGS
	CSD SA	CSD SA
Ireland	CBISSO	NTMA
	NTMA	
Italy	Monte Titoli	Monte Titoli
	CAT	
Luxembourg	Cedel	Clearstream Luxembourg (former Cedel)
The Netherlands	Necigef	Euroclear Netherlands (former Necigef)
Portugal	Interbolsa	Interbolsa
	SITEME	SITEME
Spain	CADE	Iberclear
	SCLV	SCL Bilbao
	Espaclear	SCL Barcelona
	SCL Bilbao	SCL Valencia
	SCL Barcelona	
	SCL Valencia	

Note: Greece joined the euro area on 1 January 2001.

relating to conflicting incentives in the process of integration will be described in more detail in Section 5.

3. CHRONOLOGY OF REFORM INITIATIVES

Since 1999, the introduction of the euro and the progressive implementation of a common EU regulatory framework in the form of the Financial Services Action Plan (FSAP) have stimulated demand for cross-border securities trading. As a result, long-standing problems with interoperability between national clearing and settlement systems have come to the fore and the need for a more integrated industry has appeared as a major item on the EU policy agenda. Indeed, over time it became apparent that efficient clearing and settlement were integral parts (in fact, a logical pre condition) of the financial markets reform organized under the FSAP. In this context,

Table 20.2. CCPs in the euro area, 1999–2004

Country	January 1999	October 2004
Austria	Vienna Stock Exchange (derivatives)	Vienna Stock Exchange (derivatives)
Belgium	BELFOX (derivatives)	None
Finland	HEX (derivatives)	OMX (derivatives)
France	Bourse de Paris (SBF) (equities and options); Matif (derivatives; subsidy of SBF) Clearnet (repos, gov. bonds; subsidy of Matif)	LCH.Clearnet SA (deriv., repos, securities, also for markets in BE, NL, PT and for MTS markets)
Germany	Eurex Clearing (derivatives)	Eurex Clearing (derivatives, repos, securities)
Greece	ADECH (derivatives)	ADECH (derivatives)
Ireland	None	None
Italy	CC&G (derivatives)	CC&G (derivatives, securities, also for MTS Italy)
Luxembourg	None	None
The Netherlands	Effectenclearing (securities); EOCC (derivatives)	None
Portugal	BVLP (derivatives)	None
Spain	MEFF Renta Fija (deriv. on debt instr.) MEFF Renta Variable (deriv. on equities)	MEFF Renta Fija (repos, gov. bonds, deriv. on debt instr.) MEFF Renta Variable (derivatives on equities)

Note: Greece joined the euro area on 1 January 2001.

two reports by the Giovannini Group[9] have sought to distil the main policy issues arising in the integration of the EU clearing and settlement industry and to devise a clear strategy for addressing these issues.

- The first report,[10] which was published in November 2001, analysed the extent of fragmentation in the industry. Noting that one of the main sources of complexity in clearing and settlement is the need to use intermediaries between buyer and seller, the analysis demonstrated that the number of intermediaries increases dramatically in the context of cross-border[11] securities transactions. The involvement of additional intermediaries reflects the need to overcome national differences in the myriad of clearing and settlement systems operating across the

[9] The Giovannini Group is a committee of private sector experts, under the chairmanship of Alberto Giovannini, which advises the European Commission on matters relating to the evolution of EU capital markets.

[10] Giovannini Group 2001.

[11] Technically, it is more correct to refer to cross-system securities transactions in this context as it is perfectly feasible to process a cross-border transaction on the same terms as a domestic transaction within a given clearing and settlement system. However, for convenience, the term cross-border is retained through the remainder of this chapter.

Table 20.3. Activity of CSDs in the euro area, 2003

Country	Name of institution	Value of assets under custody ($€b_n$)	Volume of transactions settled (thousands)
Austria	OeKB	399	784
Belgium	NBB-SSS	293	175
	CIK	128	353
	Euroclear Bank	2,047	22,000
Finland	APK	1,204	4,613
France	Euroclear France	3,511	27,812
Germany	Clearstream Frankfurt	4,938	45,592
Greece[b]	BOGS	36	384
	CSD SA		11,433
Ireland	NTMA	85	1.5
Italy	Monte Titoli	1,643	1,749
Luxembourg	Clearstream Luxembourg	2,603[a]	12,540
The Netherlands	Euroclear Netherlands	705	3,854
Portugal	Interbolsa	111	1,822
	SITEME	6	0.3
Spain	CADE[c]	518	11,346
	SCLV[c]	95	17,668
	SCL Bilbao, Barcelona, Valencia	36	180

[a]Figure from 2001.
[b]Greece joined the euro area on 1 January 2001.
[c]The CSD Iberclear was launched on 1 April 2003, as a result of the merger between CADE and SCLV.

EU—adding significantly to the cost and to the risk in cross-border securities trading. The report concluded by identifying the main sources of segmentation among national systems, which need to be addressed so as to deliver a truly integrated EU clearing and settlement industry. These fifteen so-called 'Giovannini barriers' relate to market practice/regulation, legal certainty, and taxation, and responsibility for their removal is shared between the public and private sectors (see Table 20.5).

- The second report,[12] which was published in April 2003, returned to the fifteen barriers and laid out a clear strategy and aggressive timetable for their removal (see Figure 20.6, which also highlights the distribution of tasks between markets and authorities). The strategy reflected several considerations, including the need to prioritize among barriers and the need to properly sequence their removal insofar as they may be interrelated. A further consideration in designing the strategy was the importance of identifying clearly the specific action(s) required to remove each barrier and allocating responsibility for these action(s) to the appropriate private sector or public sector agent(s). Recognizing that the prospect of an integrated clearing and settlement industry would trigger

[12] Giovannini Group 2003.

Table 20.4. Activity of CCPs in the euro area, 2003

Country	Name of institution	Value of trades cleared (€b_n)	Volume of transactions cleared (thousands)
Austria	Vienna Stock Exchange (derivatives)	n.a.	n.a.
Belgium	None	n.a.p.	n.a.p.
Finland	HEX (derivatives)	n.a.	n.a.
France	LCH.Clearnet SA (deriv., repos, securities, also for markets in BE, NL, PT and for MTS markets)	968	97,000
Germany	Eurex Clearing (derivatives, repos, securities)[a]	1,282	53,000
Greece[b]	ADECH (derivatives)	15	6,727
Ireland	None	n.a.p	n.a.p
Italy	CC&G (derivatives)	1,199	41,440
Luxembourg	None	n.a.p	n.a.p
The Netherlands	None	n.a.p	n.a.p
Portugal	None	n.a.p	n.a.p
Spain	MEFF Renta Fija (deriv. on debt instr.)[c] MEFF Renta Variable (deriv. on equities)	n.a.	n.a.

[a] Eurex Clearing (Equities) started business in March 2003. Figure for 2003 is partly estimated.
[b] Greece joined the euro area on 1 January 2001.
[c] MEFFCLEAR, a CCP for public debt securities, was launched on 18 September 2003.

structural adjustments, the report also explored the implications of consolidation for cost efficiency, competition, investor protection, and financial stability. Finally the report called for continuous interaction between the private and public sector in the process of removing the barriers.

These two reports draw heavily on the earlier work of other bodies and so have provided a consistent analytical basis for the formulation of the Commission's policy in the field of clearing and settlement.

In formulating this policy, the Commission has enjoyed the continuous support of the European Central Bank, reflecting the importance which the Eurosystem assigns to an efficiently functioning post-trading infrastructure in discharging its responsibilities for the conduct of monetary policy and safeguarding financial stability. The post-trading infrastructure can be regarded as providing essential 'highways for collateral' in monetary policy operations.[13] Almost all of the eligible collateral for monetary policy operations in the euro area flows through securities settlement systems, leaving the conduct of day-to-day monetary policy highly dependent on smoothly functioning post-trading services. Problems in the delivery of post-trading services could block some of these highways for collateral, leaving the Eurosystem

[13] The ESCB Statute (Art. 18) requires that all credit from the Eurosystem be adequately collateralized.

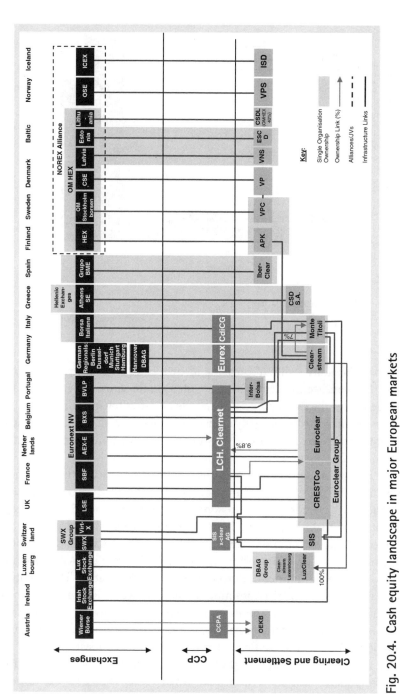

Fig. 20.4. Cash equity landscape in major European markets

Source: Merril Lynch; Euroclear; Accenure; company information

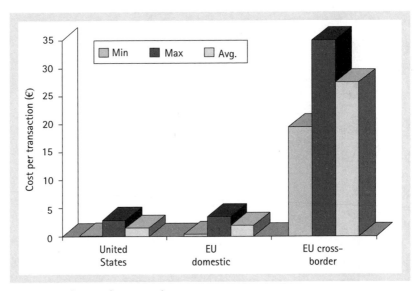

Fig. 20.5. Costs of transactions

Source: European Central Bank

unable to manage liquidity (without breaking its own rules on collateral) and complicating efforts to consistently deliver a single interest rate across the euro area as a whole. More generally, the ECB appreciates that the post-trading infrastructure plays a crucial role in maintaining the integrity of financial markets, with the risk that choke points in the infrastructure could seriously disrupt market functioning and ultimately pose a risk to financial system stability.

In 1999, the European Central Bank published 'Standards for securities settlement systems to be used in Eurosystem credit operation' (the so-called 'User Standards'). The User Standards have contributed to some harmonization of CSD features in the field of intraday finality, operating hours, and risk management. An initiative to establish more complete common standards at the European level has been under way since October 2001 via a joint working group of the ESCB (European System of Central Banks) and the Committee of European Securities Regulators. The intention has been to adapt the earlier CPSS (Committee on Payments and Settlement Systems, a committee of the Group of ten countries, run within the Bank for International Settlements—BIS)–IOSCO (International Organization of Securities Commissions) recommendations on securities settlement systems to the European context.[14] In October 2004, this initiative resulted in the release of a report of nineteen standards. The proposed standards will come into force when some open issues have been

---

[14] See BIS and IOSCO 2001.

Table 20.5. Summary table of actions, actors, and deadlines for removing the barriers to an integrated EU clearing and settlement environment

Barrier	Necessary action	Responsible	Deadline
Barrier 7	Operating hours and settlement deadlines should be harmonized.	ECSDA should take the lead in this initiative, in close cooperation with ESCB–CESR.	Within 2 years
Barrier 1	National differences in the information technology and interfaces used by clearing and settlement providers should be eliminated via an EU-wide protocol.	Protocol should be defined by SWIFT and, once defined, should be immediately adopted by the Eurosystem in respect of its operations.	Within 2 years
Barrier 4	Intraday settlement finality in all links between settlement systems within the EU should be guaranteed.	ECSDA should coordinate necessary measures. These measures should be drawn up in close consultation with ESCB–CESR.	Within 2 years and 3 months
Barrier 6	Settlement periods for all systems within the EU should be harmonized on $t + 2$.	No responsible entity identified. The task would be to draw up a blueprint toward this objective.	Within 2 years and 3 months
Barrier 3	National rules relating to corporate actions, beneficial ownership, and custody should be harmonized.	Local agent banks, via ECSA, and ECSDA should coordinate private sector proposals. National governments should coordinate their response via the relevant EU Council.	Within 2 years and 3 months
Barrier 8	National differences in securities issuance practice should be eliminated.	IPMA and ANNA should draw up proposals to this end.	Within 2 years and 3 months
Barrier 11		National governments should coordinate their actions via the relevant EU Council.	Within 2 years and 3 months
Barrier 12	Any provisions requiring that taxes on securities transactions be collected via local systems should be removed to ensure a level playing field between domestic and foreign investors.	National governments should coordinate their actions via the relevant EU Council.	Within 2 years and 3 months

Barriers 13, 14, 15	The EU Collateral Directive will remove much of the legal uncertainty relating to netting and the uneven application of conflict of laws. Member states should ensure the adoption of this directive by the scheduled date of end 2003. While this should be enough to allow the lifting of the restrictions on location of securities and securities settlement, there would remain a longer-term need for modernization of substantive law about investment securities. Only a common EU framework of laws applying to securities can address this need.	A European Securities Law Reform project should be agreed upon by national governments, be mandated to draft the target reform, and be given the resources to fulfil the mandate	Within 3 years
Barriers 2, 9	National restrictions on the location of clearing and settlement and on the location of securities should be removed, as an essential precondition for a market-led integration of the EU clearing and settlement environment.	National governments should adopt the relevant elements on the location of clearing and settlement in the new Investment Services Directive as proposed by the Commission. National governments should then coordinate to remove restrictions on location of securities.	Within 3 years
Barrier 5	Practical impediments to remote access to national clearing and settlement systems should be removed in order to ensure a level playing field.	National governments should draw up a set of conditions upon which remote access can be guaranteed across the EU. These conditions should be drawn up in conformity with the requirements of ESCB/CESR.	Within 3 years
Barrier 10	Restrictions on the activity of primary dealers and market makers should be removed.	National governments should coordinate their actions via the relevant EU Council.	Within 3 years

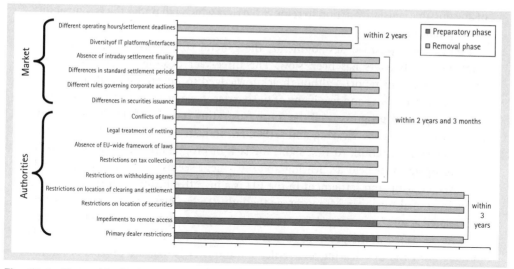

Fig. 20.6. Timetable for removal of the fifteen barriers

Source: Giovannini Group

resolved, although they could be modified in the context of any legislative action by the EU.

Several important steps in the formulation of an EU policy on clearing and settlement have been taken since the publication of the second Giovannini Group report in 2003. The Commission has established the broad contours of its approach to the question of integration on the basis of a broad public consultation.[15] In this context, a standing group of industry experts and EU officials, CESAME,[16] has been established to monitor efforts to eliminate the fifteen barriers and to provide technical input to the Commission's thinking on the possible need for legislative action. In addition, CESAME provides the important service of gathering and disseminating information on the process of reform to parties not directly involved in its meetings, mainly through a dedicated website. Two additional groups have been established to focus more specifically on legal barriers and fiscal compliance barriers: the Legal Certainty Group and FISCO—the Fiscal Compliance Group. Like CESAME, these two groups gather and publicly disseminate information about their work on dedicated web-sites.[17]

These groups have met at regular intervals since mid-2004 and have taken the first concrete steps to remove many of the barriers, particularly those in the areas of information technology interfaces and market practices. For its part, the Commission has begun the now mandatory task of performing an in-depth impact assessment ahead

[15] European Commission 2004.
[16] Clearing and Settlement Advisory and Monitoring Expert Group; see References section for relevant web links.
[17] See References section.

of any possible legislative action to remove barriers which fall under the responsibility of the public sector.

Despite these positive developments, the general consensus is that progress in removing the barriers has been slow. The three-year deadline established in the second Giovannini report—although acknowledged to be aggressive at the time—is rapidly approaching and few if any of the barriers have been conclusively removed. This slow pace of progress is all the more frustrating in light of the crucial importance of reforming the clearing and settlement industry for the broader agenda of EU financial integration. At first sight, the lack of progress in removing barriers in such an operational field as clearing and settlement seems difficult to understand. However, clearing and settlement in the EU is a lucrative business worth billions of euros in annual turnover. Moreover, as the industry has evolved, a complex web of interrelated actors has emerged, whose interest may or may not be served by integration. As described in the previous section, the central tenet of the current approach to integrating the EU clearing and settlement industry is that the process of reform should not 'go against the grain' of the market in the sense of being imposed from the top. Within this strategy, the role of the public sector is twofold—(1) to remove those barriers under its own responsibility and (2) to assist in coordinating the removal of those barriers under private sector responsibility. This twin-role is reflected in the Commission's ongoing work in assessing the need for EU legislation to eliminate regulatory restrictions on access to clearing and settlement and in the establishment of the CESAME. The possibility of more direct public sector intervention—so as to deliver a US-type solution—is attractive, but it has not been envisaged because it would not address the underlying sources of market fragmentation created by the fifteen Giovannini barriers. Issues related to the Commission's special reform strategy are discussed in the following two sections.

4. The Strategic Underpinnings of Clearing and Settlement Reform

The financial system has attracted the attention of EU policy makers as a leading candidate for wide-ranging reform, amid increasing awareness of its potential as an engine of economic growth. The introduction of the euro prompted a step-change in the pace of financial integration in the EU by eliminating exchange rate risk on the bulk of financial flows. Implementation of the FSAP should result in further integration. The impact of these developments is to reduce the segmentation of the financial system across member states, thereby stimulating competition and, at the same time, fostering consolidation of those financial functions that are characterized by significant scale economies.

Financial integration is a natural and very appropriate strategic priority in the EU. The financial system plays an essential role in channelling resources to most productive uses over both space and time. An integrated EU financial system also offers the prospect of positive and widely spread economic spillovers via intensified competition, the opportunity to exploit economies of scale, and increased liquidity. While these spillovers cannot be estimated precisely, it is clear that all aspects of economic activity benefit from a larger and more complete set of appropriate financial services. Moreover, the benefits of financial system reform come at much lower social cost than reforms and liberalizations in other sectors of the economy, because their high skill levels and correspondingly high earning power make workers in the financial industry unusually mobile. Indeed, the very nature of the financial system is of a continuously changing and adapting organism, so that those who work in the system are relatively familiar with and more adaptable to change.

The national characteristics of a financial system stem from two main sources: Regulation and historical evolution. Regulation is a fundamental feature of the financial system. As financial services are information intensive, they give rise to a wide variety of moral hazard and adverse selection problems, which are dealt with by a complex web of regulations. Clearly, such regulations stem from the law of the land and have a country-specific nature. National characteristics also reflect the historical evolution of the financial system. With the possible exception of the United Kingdom, EU financial systems have been characterized, until quite recently, by significant state involvement. Indeed, state ownership has been a common feature in many member states. This degree of state involvement has left different national imprints on the financial cultures in the member states. Finally, it is an inevitable by-product of history that financial systems that work in isolation from each other may develop mores and conventions that are at least partly inconsistent.

A process aimed at integrating member states' financial systems has the unavoidable effect of diluting those factors which promote distinctive national characteristics. In the first place, integration requires adoption of common standards, common conventions, and consistent regulations. Only under a broad set of common rules will integration be feasible. It is also a consequence of integration, and the related phenomenon of consolidation, that cross-border transactions and cross-ownership of financial businesses will become relatively more important than in the case of isolated or non-integrated financial markets. The fundamental challenge, shared with much of the rest of the EU project, relates to the appropriate management of the integration process. How deep can it be and in what areas? What changes in institutions are needed to make it work, and what issues of accountability, democracy, and protection of individual rights and freedoms are raised by it? Sometimes these questions are difficult to identify precisely and/or technically difficult to answer. As a result, the debate on integration is often prey to nationalistic rhetoric, which is routinely adopted by those involved in the defence of private interests.

Recent events have provided an interesting set of issues raised by the eventuality of cross-border consolidation of parts of the member state financial systems. National authorities have sometimes resisted cross-border consolidation on the grounds that foreign influence will imply the adoption of less reliable rules and regulations than the domestic ones. In other instances, the reactions have brought up more strategic (and vaguer) issues, related to a presumed intangible public good of nationality in financial intermediaries, supposedly delivering stronger commitment to local community than internationally owned intermediaries. Unfortunately, the flip-side of local commitment is conflicts of interest, leading to non-economic decisions in the allocation of financial services like credit, with often disastrous consequences.

In the case of the EU clearing and settlement industry, we need to ask the same questions as in the case of the broader financial integration process.

- *First, is there any justifiable reason for the integration of the industry to be limited?* Clearing and settlement are such basic functions that there is no prima facie reason why their integration should be less than complete. Integration of the EU clearing and settlement industry means that the certainty and protection of domestic securities transactions is assured in cross-border securities transactions. Increasing the degree of certainty and protection of cross-border transactions will not require any reduction in the certainty and protection of domestic transactions. It can be argued that integration will trigger a consequent consolidation in the clearing and settlement industry, which—if taken to its limits-could result in monopoly provision of these services. While it is clear that such an outcome would be inconsistent with objectives for enhanced competition, it is equally clear that consolidation among providers of clearing and settlement services is perhaps the only way to exploit economies of scale and risk pooling to the maximum. In this context, the experience of individual countries (in Europe and elsewhere) overwhelmingly suggests a desire to consolidate their national clearing and settlement industries. Hence, the desirability—or not—of a consolidated clearing and settlement industry at the EU level hinges crucially on whether the benefits from scale economies and risk pooling will be public goods or will be kept internal to the providers. Of course, the second outcome must be avoided, but this can be achieved in a number of different ways (see third bullet point, below).
- *Second, are the institutional changes needed to make integration of the industry feasible, and is there a possible conflict with other objectives in EU or national policy making?* In answering this question, we must recall that by integrating the EU clearing and settlement industry, we specifically mean removal of barriers that make the provision of these services across borders unduly expensive and create operational risk. As these barriers are due to inconsistent technical standards, inconsistent conventions, and inconsistent regulations and laws, they will be removed by substituting new and common technical standards, conventions, and laws. Two sets of issues arise in this respect. One relates to actual changes in national laws and regulations, e.g. laws defining securities ownership, which differ from country to country. Modifying laws that define ownership would be a deep intervention in national legal systems, but would be justified by the need to adapt rules to the reality of a modern securities market. This sort of adaptation is exclusively dictated by technological issues, the most important of

which are the lack of materiality of securities and the sheer volume of securities transactions that has to be processed every day. The fact that all changes will be made consistent through the EU reform process is not in any way a top-down standardization to be imposed by European bureaucrats and with no particular economic justification. It is rather a device to achieve two objectives at the same time—the adaptation of national legal systems to the reality of securities transactions and the elimination of inconsistencies across national legal systems, which is one of the most important barriers to cross-border securities transactions. Other regulations impinging on clearing and settlement relate to restrictions on the location of securities, on the location of clearing and settlement activities, and impediments to remote access. Such restrictions were justified in the past as a means to make laws easily enforceable by making securities easily reachable by authorities, and by the perceived efficiency of pooling securities within a single depository. However, national jurisdiction over securities held outside the country of issuance is no longer consistent with treaty provisions on the free movement of capital, apart from specified exceptions. As for the use of a single depository, the market can be expected to drive such a process if the perceived benefits are sufficiently significant so that a possible coordination problem is not of particular concern.

Another example of achieving consistency between the integration process and national objectives arises in the area of fiscal compliance. For the purpose of administering withholding taxes, countries use mechanisms such as a requirement that withholding agents be local residents or that the taxes on securities transactions be collected via local systems. Such requirements again represent barriers to cross-border transactions. These barriers can be eliminated through provisions allowing all financial intermediaries established within the EU to offer withholding agent services in all of the member states so as to ensure a level playing field between local and foreign intermediaries. Once again, the elimination of barriers, if properly implemented, does not raise any inconsistency with local regulations or the ability of national authorities to perform their functions.

- *Third, are there any issues of protection of individual rights raised by integration of the industry?* In this case, the question of individual rights protection can only be interpreted in a broad sense. However, integration should actually improve on the status quo, by providing an effectively competitive environment for providers of clearing and settlement services. Even in the likely case of EU-wide consolidation, EU and national laws provide a full set of safeguards against the abuse of dominant positions in the marketplace. In addition, there is ongoing discussion about the appropriateness of coupling ex post competition rules with ex ante mechanisms, such as appropriate governance structures. These would in principle provide additional safeguards.
- *Lastly, are there any issues of accountability or democratic deficit raised by the integration of the industry either in the process or in the final outcome?* In this respect, it can be observed that the integration process has been expressly designed to achieve the maximum amount of input by all actors involved. The greatest risk of a democratic deficit is—as always—that providers will have greater influence on

the reform process than users. This risk is very well known and present in every democracy (Ohlson 1965). The European Commission is keenly aware of this, and has responded by investing significantly in know-how and analysis, so as to become an independent producer of ideas and suggestions in the project. On the final outcome, even in the case of maximum consolidation to single central counterparty and a single security depository, the risk of a democratic deficit would be practically non-existent. The simple reason is that those two entities will be passive actors in the marketplace, providing basic, utility-like services. As such, they will not be in a position to take discretionary actions or initiatives affecting the welfare of EU citizens, but will only passively effect trades decided elsewhere, and ensure the integrity of the trading system.

The conclusion of this analysis is that the removal of barriers to cross-border clearing and settlement in the EU does not conflict in any relevant way with the needs of member states to enforce their national rules effectively, or with the need to maintain an adequate degree of democratic accountability in Europe-wide institutions, or with safeguards to individual rights. Much of the resistance that will be encountered, therefore, will just be the expression of the desire of special interests to maintain the status quo, which by its sheer complexity is a source of profitability. These issues are discussed in greater detail in the next section.

5. A NOVEL APPROACH TO THE PROCESS OF REFORM, AND ITS CHALLENGES

In discussions on the integration and consolidation of the EU clearing and settlement industry, the experience of the United States is often cited. In the USA, before the creation of the National Securities Clearing Corporation (NSCC) and the Depository Trust Company (DTC), the New York Stock Exchange, the American Stock Exchange, and the NASD all had their clearing corporations. These were merged into the NSCC. Later on regional exchanges eliminated their clearing organizations, and their functions were assumed by NSCC. In other words, post-trading infrastructure was creating by dismantling vertically integrated structures. In 1999, the US authorities created the Depository Trust & Clearing Corporation (DTCC) as a holding company, consolidating NSCC and DTC. This consolidation was due to a concern that NSCC and DTC would start to overlap in the functions they provided, thus creating conflict and unnecessary complexity.[18]

Of course, these top-down initiatives occurred in a highly integrated (albeit geographically dispersed) market, subject to a common legal and regulatory framework (despite a number of state-specific regulations). Thus, the provision of clearing and

---

[18] See Cross-Border Subcommittee of the Securities Industry Association 2005.

settlement has been consolidated to the maximum and is neatly separated from the marketplaces served. The US precedent is very informative for the process of reform in Europe. While there are important legal and regulatory differences, it would appear natural to create such basic service providers by mimicking the initiatives taken by US authorities—under the admittedly very important assumption that legal and regulatory differences among EU member states can be removed by the ordinary process of reform.

Another interesting precedent in this kind of reform is the process on monetary integration in the context of EMU. The management of monetary union and the creation of the ECB/Eurosystem were a process whose outlines were largely conceived from the top,[19] beginning with a high-level working group composed of central bankers—and headed by Jacques Delors—that offered an argument for monetary union and a vision of how to construct it (i.e. through gradual convergence of macroeconomic performances and monetary policies). This vision was subsequently made a legal reality by an intergovernmental conference, which produced the draft Maastricht Treaty. Finally, the legal provisions were made operational by the Council based on a Green Paper presented by the Commission. The institution responsible for the conduct of the single monetary policy in the euro area and ensuring the smooth functioning of the euro payment system is the ECB/Eurosystem. There are some notable similarities between the creation of an institution that manages monetary policy, the issuance of currency, and the functioning of payments among a group of countries, and the creation of an institution that manages payments in securities and cash around securities transactions. These similarities are due to the nature of these various functions: they all constitute the infrastructure of a financial system. Thus, it is important that whatever structure emerges for the provision of clearing and settlement in an integrated EU economy, it ensures the maximum safety and efficiency in the daily processing of transactions.

As safety and efficiency are public goods, it could be argued that the supply of such public goods should be managed by governments. Yet, we believe that some features of clearing and settlement provision in Europe make it undesirable to implement a top-down solution like the one that started the process of creating the ECB. One reason is that individual national CSDs and CCPs are not in almost all cases public entities, in contrast to the central banks that converged into the European System of Central Banks. Another reason is that a top-down solution amid the wide diversity of clearing and settlement providers and regulatory frameworks in which they operate seems much less feasible than in the case of the ECB. However, the foremost reason not to jump into a top-down creation of single providers of clearing and settlement services following the DTCC model or the ECB process is that such an infrastructure would still be required to navigate through the Giovannini barriers and so could not hope to match the efficiency of its US equivalent.

---

[19] This observation of course does not in any way imply that the process was less than democratic: the final legal product, the Maastricht Treaty, had to go through a ratification procedure that, though different from member state to member state, required sometimes special parliamentary majorities and sometimes national referenda.

These observations have led the Commission to embark on a reform process that has a character of novelty and at the same time is grounded on solid logical arguments. For the purpose of describing the reform process it is best to distinguish between two logical elements—framework and architecture. The framework for an integrated EU clearing and settlement industry comprises a common set of technical standards, conventions, regulations, and laws. The architecture within an integrated industry is the number of suppliers, the activities performed by suppliers and their degree of specialization, and the size of suppliers relative to the market.

A key decision by the Commission has been to concentrate reform efforts on the creation of a common framework and is justified for two reasons. First and foremost, a common framework is necessary for effective functioning of integrated clearing and settlement services, independently of the architecture of such services. Indeed, any degree of cross-border consolidation in the industry would not work properly without the proper framework. Second, as already indicated, a directed solution would be particularly unwieldy given the sheer number and variety of institutions involved.

Starting from this very basic premiss, the reform process designed by the Commission is a coordination effort. The basic logical structure is the list of barriers from the Giovannini Reports. The elimination of each barrier requires a reform or set of reforms of certain standards, conventions, rules, regulations, or laws. Standards and conventions are created and can be modified by private market participants or service providers; rules, regulations, and laws can be modified by governments.

From the fifteen barriers stems a rather large to-do list involving a complex set of interconnected actions by a diverse set of actors. In practice, this to-do list is a matrix containing the sequenced actions and the corresponding principal actors. Progress in the to-do list is periodically assessed by the Commission and all the participants in the reform process, and inputs are provided both in periodic meetings and through access to the Commission. A consistent effort is made at gathering and circulating information to all interested parties, to authorities, and to users. Information gathering and dissemination are an integral part of the reform process.

A special feature of this strategy is that it is inherently dynamic. In other words, since there is no ex ante commitment to any specific final architecture, it allows the maximum degree of adaptability. In particular, the work so far undertaken does not rule out acceleration in the integration and consolidation process that may be the result of either private or public initiatives. What is important to stress is that the strategy of laying out the framework for the efficient provision of clearing and settlement will under all circumstances be the necessary condition to ultimately deliver a truly integrated market.

The logic behind the non-invasive approach by the public sector is that the removal of the Giovannini barriers will create an integrated clearing and settlement environment, in which the incentive to consolidate, to exploit scale economies in an industry characterized by extremely low marginal costs, will play to the full. The outcome of this consolidation would be many fewer providers of clearing and settlement services than exist today. To the extent that the strategy to remove the barriers is credible to market participants and service providers are forward-looking agents, consolidation efforts are likely to commence well before the barrier-free clearing and settlement environment has been put in place. In fact, there has already been ample evidence of consolidation in recent years. Whether this consolidation process is allowed to reduce the industry to a very few providers or even a single provider is an open question and will depend on the implications for competition and financial stability. Analysis of such aspects is, however, beyond the scope of this chapter, although they were touched upon in the second report of the Giovannini Group.

The Commission's approach to the process of integration in the clearing and settlement industry has been widely welcomed. However, despite the broad support for the reform strategy, one cannot simply assume that the slow pace of progress in integration so far has nothing to do with the Commission's light-handed approach to public intervention. So, it is useful to ask what the prospects are for a market-led solution with the current constellation of interests in the EU clearing and settlement industry and whether a somewhat heavier hand by the public sector will inevitably be required to bring about a satisfactory outcome. In this context, we would typically expect to find two opposing forces at play in determining the pace of progress in integration—both led by profit motives.

On one side would be those who would support the status quo of a segmented industry. Among these would be providers with sufficient geographical reach to effectively internalize the costs and risks associated with barriers to cross-border clearing and settlement and exploiting the available (but not full) scale economies. In effect, these providers offer users the opportunity to bypass the existing barriers and share the benefits of any associated efficiency gains between the users and themselves. This situation can be categorized as one of constrained optimization, in which users certainly benefit but not to the same extent as in a truly integrated environment. Those in favour of the status quo would also include smaller-scale domestically oriented providers, lacking geographical reach across the EU. Market segmentation is seen by these providers as offering a degree of protection from those larger players who could exploit the scale economies offered by an integrated market to eliminate their smaller competitors.[20]

On the other side would be those expecting to increase profits in an integrated clearing and settlement environment by exploiting scale economies to ride the average cost curve down at the appropriate profit maximization rate. In such circumstances, a significant consolidation would also be expected, so that the lower unit revenue delivered in a competitive environment would be compensated not only by a growing market but by a substantial rise in market share. Such a strategy would rely on the fact that clearing and settlement displays many of the features of a network industry, so that larger players—not only offering lower prices but also a wider pool of potential counterparties and securities—would enjoy a decisive advantage over smaller competitors. For these providers, consistency over time in the implementation of

---

[20] As we argue in the next section, seeking protection in higher costs of cross-border trading is very likely to be a self-defeating strategy in the long run.

the integration strategy is of paramount importance because investment costs in preparing for integration must be incurred up front with the risk of heavy losses if the strategy fails to deliver.

In such a clear-cut confrontation between the opposing forces of conservatism and reform, the appropriate course of action for the public authorities would be determined by the likely gains to the users. Given the strong case for integration, to the advantage of both market users and the economy as a whole, there would be an undeniable role for the public sector to intervene and drive the reform process to completion. In reality, however, the situation is more complicated. Few voices have spoken against integration of the EU clearing and settlement industry, presumably in light of the self-evident benefits. Instead, the main source of controversy has been the nature of the integration to be achieved. Two main issues dominate this controversy: the appropriate role of clearing and settlement in the functioning of a modern securities market; and the appropriate infrastructure for providing these services in an integrated market.

On the appropriate role of clearing and settlement in the securities market, one view is that these services are essential services and so should be available to all market participants on equal terms. Proponents of this view argue in favour of strict separation in the provision of these so-called core services and any other market services so as to avoid that the bundling of essential services and banking facilities may lead to an abuse of monopoly power that will result in the obligation for investors to use the banking facilities provided by the CSD. The opposing view is that, in a modern securities market, the clearing and settlement functionalities cannot be reasonably separated from the range of other value-added services that have been developed to enhance efficiency in the process. According to this view, splitting the various services will result in a loss of efficiency, implying higher costs and a reduction in the speed of processing transactions. Thus, it is argued that a complete segregation of these functions would ultimately reduce the benefit to users and be counter to the objectives of integration.

On the appropriate infrastructure for delivering clearing and settlement services in an integrated market, views are even more diverse. One view focuses on the entire value chain of securities transactions and argues that vertical integration of trading and post-trading functionalities is desirable to allow the investors to exploit the benefits (i.e. economies of scope) deriving from vertical integration. The counterview is that a clear separation between trading and post-trading activities is essential to avoid the potential for abuse of monopoly power when a stock exchange is majority or exclusive owner of the post-trading infrastructure.[21] It has been suggested that such a governance structure would allow the stock exchange to require investors to use its in-house clearing and settlement system for exchange-traded securities, while denying access to these in-house clearing and settlement services to potentially competing trading platforms. However, proponents of this 'horizontal' view of integration in clearing and settlement differ on the degree of consolidation which should accompany the integration process. For some, consolidation to a single provider is the only

---

[21] See, for example, Koeppl and Monnet 2004.

solution, given current technology, which will allow the benefits of integration to be maximized. Others favour a lesser degree of consolidation, which would result in a network of providers in competition with each other, as necessary to maintain pressure for cost control and innovation.

Private sector agents cannot resolve these conflicting views. Resolving them is the challenge for public sector authorities. In particular, authorities will need to understand clearly what model of integration best serves the public interest and in so doing disentangle the often valid theoretical arguments put forward by both sides from considerations of vested interest. The guiding principle must be to ensure that the integration process is as efficient as possible, but that any associated consolidation of the industry could not result in an abuse of dominant position. Not only must these conflicts be resolved by the authorities, but they must be resolved soon so as to provide necessary clarity to private sector agents about the environment in which the various participants will operate post-reform. In the absence of such clarity, the integration risks becoming bogged down for some time to come. Thus, it is greater clarity on the objectives and accepted models of integration that is required from the public sector authorities and not a more heavy-handed intervention in the market.

The solution to these conflicts exists, and is consistent with the general principles of open markets and generalized access that have inspired the reform project all along. The implication of the principles of open markets and generalized access is that an open architecture for all the the segments in the clearing and settlement value line has to be available to all users as a default option. That is, users have to have the option of purchasing the services of individual segments of the value line separately. Of course, this does not prevent suppliers from bundling some of these segments, if they think bundling will result in more convenience from the viewpoint of users. The decision as to the merits of a bundled option versus an unbundled option has to be based on price and convenience. Suppliers should not be allowed to force bundling through distorted pricing of individual segments (while this is not a problem with a fully competitive system, it may arise in cases where some services are offered in a regime of quasi monopoly).

The ongoing controversy about access to and separation of services in clearing and settlement could be more easily resolved by addressing a very fundamental flaw in current market practice—the absence of transparent and standardized pricing structures. The fundamental importance of clearing and settlement to the functioning of financial markets and the enormous volume transactions effected means that these services should be treated as standard and not tailor made. The lack of standardization and transparency in fee structures, which characterizes the EU clearing and settlement industry currently,[22] is unacceptable and can be traced to two main factors on the supply and demand side of the market respectively. On the supply side, providers of high-volume services can obtain large revenue impacts from small differences in prices. On the demand side, the incentive to enforce a discipline of transparency is

---

[22] This phenomenon is documented in the first Giovannini Report, where an attempt at measuring differential costs of cross-border clearing and settlement, because of the lack of any comparability of prices, had to resort to estimating unit revenues from profit and loss accounts.

limited by the fact that the largest portion of clearing and settlement fees is paid by asset managers, and charged to the mutual funds they manage. Therefore these costs are passed on to final investors.

In the effort to establish standardization and transparency in fee structures, a natural starting point is ESCB-CESR (Committee of European Securities Regulators) standard no. 17, which would require every CSD to 'provide market participants with sufficient information for them to identify and accurately evaluate the risks and costs associated with clearing and settlement'. Providing information on prices/fees, services offered, key statistics, and balance sheet data can promote competition between services providers and lower costs and improve levels of service. Transparency would apply not only to basic clearing and settlement services but also the so-called value-added services so that each service and option would be priced separately to provide a proper basis for users to select the services which they wish to use.

6. Concluding Remarks

Post-trading services represent the most basic function of securities markets, almost to the point of defining the scope and reach of the markets themselves. Securities markets in Europe are fragmented by high costs (observable and hidden) of cross-border securities clearing and settlement. These costs result from a complex web of barriers that originate, essentially, from the fact that national financial markets in Europe have been largely isolated from each other until very recently. There is a universal perception that a free, integrated securities market will be one fundamental building block to a more dynamic, productive society throughout Europe.

Maintaining the status quo does not seem to be a particularly attractive option, because the status quo appears to be the cause of a process of partial involution of financial intermediation. Since all investors can and want to diversify their portfolios across the whole of the EU, they request services from intermediaries that allow broad diversification. However, only those intermediaries that are large enough to be able to cover the significant fixed costs necessary to grant access to all different markets can provide such access at acceptable cost. Fragmentation of securities markets infrastructure has the perverse effect of driving out the smaller, local intermediaries to the advantage of larger, multinational players.

The main objective of the reform of clearing and settlement in Europe is to lower the cost of market access, to all users and investors, thereby fostering the development of a large and liquid financial system, able to attract capital from the rest of the world, and to effectively channel capital out of unproductive sectors and into the most dynamic sectors in the EU economy.

In this chapter we have described the strategy aimed at reforming clearing and settlement in Europe, and the challenges that this strategy has to meet. We have described the reasons why a bold, government-led, invasive solution to the problem of integrating clearing and settlement has been set aside, in favour of a coordinated, dynamic strategy that involves commitments from both private market participants and government authorities. This reform path is more complex than the alternative and probably slower, but it is needed to ensure that many of the barriers that currently make cross-border transactions expensive are tackled effectively.

The most important result of the process of reform achieved so far is the degree of awareness and agreement on the problems to be addressed. There is also widely shared agreement on the general principles that need to be upheld to ensure consistency of the reform with its objectives. One may be confident that maintaining this consistency will be the mechanism that will permit the resolution of the current conflicts among different private interests on the role and content of legislative actions by government authorities.

REFERENCES

Note: the website of CESAME contains and updates the stock of information on the EU reform process in the area of clearing and settlement:
www.europa.eu.int/comm/internal_market/financial-markets/clearing/cesame_en.htm;
for the Legal Certainty group, see:
www.europa.eu.int/comm/internal_market/financial-markets/clearing/certainty_en.htm;
for the fiscal compliance group, see:
www.europa.eu.int/comm/internal_market/financial-markets/clearing/compliance_en.htm.

BIS AND IOSCO (2001), *Recommendations for Securities Settlement Systems: A Report of the Committee on Payment and Settlement Systems and the Technical Committee of the International Organization of Securities Commissions*, November.

CROSS-BORDER SUBCOMMITTEE OF THE SECURITIES INDUSTRY ASSOCIATION (2005), *Background Note on the Organization in the US Market for Clearing and Settlement*, May.

EUROPEAN CENTRAL BANK AND COMMITTEE OF EUROPEAN SECURITIES REGULATORS (2003), *Standards for Securities Clearing And Settlement Systems in the European Union*, August, European Central Bank.

EUROPEAN COMMISSION (2002), *Clearing and Settlement in the European Union: Main Policy Issues and Future Challenges*, Communication from the European Commission to the Council and Parliament.

_____ (2004), *Clearing and Settlement in the European Union: The Way Forward*, Communication from the European Commission to the Council and Parliament.

GIOVANNINI GROUP (2001), *Report on Cross-Border Clearing And Settlement Arrangements in the European Union*, Commission of the European Communities.

_____ (2003), *Second Report on EU Clearing and Settlement*.

KOEPPL, T. V., AND MONNET, C. (2004), *Guess What: It's the Settlements!*, European Central Bank no. 335, July.

LONDON ECONOMICS (2005), *Securities Trading, Clearing, Central Counterparties and Settlement in EU 25: An Overview of Current Arrangements*, Report Commissioned by the Competition Directorate General of the European Commission.

OHLSON, M. (1965), *The Logic of Collective Action*, Cambridge, Mass.: Harvard University Press.

CHAPTER 21

....

DERIVATIVES MARKETS

....

RONALD W. ANDERSON

KENNETH MCKAY

1. INTRODUCTION

....

In this chapter we survey the development in derivatives markets over the last twenty years. In 1985 the American derivatives markets were visibly riding the crest of a wave of innovation that had started some ten years earlier with the introduction of exchange-traded financial derivatives such as stock options, foreign exchange futures, interest futures, and stock index futures. In Europe exchange-traded derivatives were largely limited to the long-standing London markets in metals and soft commodities and the newly opened London International Financial Futures Exchange (LIFFE) that had been modelled on the big Chicago markets. It is true that European players were already deeply involved in the development of the swap contracts which grew out of the Eurodollar market.[1] However, at that time in Europe derivatives knowledge and experience were confined to a rather limited set of specialists.

Since the mid-1980s derivatives markets have developed dramatically worldwide, and we will see that Europe has played a very big part in that development. We have taken a European perspective in writing this chapter, but in doing so, we shed light on some of the key drivers of derivatives market growth worldwide. Some of the questions we address are:

We thank the British Bankers Association for making available to us its Credit Derivatives Survey.

[1] The first significant Eurodollar interest rate swaps were written in 1981 (Stigum 1990: 929).

- What has been the experience in European derivatives markets in the last twenty years in relation to the USA and the global derivatives markets?
- What have been the major new markets that have developed over this period and what new markets appear to be emerging?
- What have been the major innovations in organization and operation of derivatives trading during that period?
- Who are the users of derivatives and to what extent have derivatives become integrated in securities markets generally?
- What are the main public policy issues related to derivatives trading?

The scope of our study is fixed by our answers to two questions: what are derivatives? And what are markets? Like many simple questions they do not give rise to simple, definitive answers. We take a pragmatic line on these issues. By derivatives we have in mind forwards, futures, options, and kindred products. With respect to markets we include both organized exchanges and over-the-counter markets (OTC). The inclusion of OTC markets complicates our task because by their nature there are no simple limits to where the markets operate. However, given the enormous growth of OTC derivatives in recent times, any discussion of derivatives that omitted them would give a very misleading impression. As a practical matter we focus on those OTC derivatives for which public information is available. This involves the relatively more standardized segments of the market where there are well-established norms for documentation and clearing which make them more readily comparable to exchange-based markets.

The remainder of the chapter is organized as follows. In Section 2 we trace the growth of the major categories of derivatives in the last twenty years and document the fact that the growth of OTC markets has been particularly strong. Section 3 is devoted to describing major product innovations. We highlight particularly developments in equity, energy, and credit derivatives. Section 4 covers developments in the way derivatives markets operate. It describes the rise of electronic trading platforms and the effects these have had on competition among exchanges. In Section 5 we look at the issue of how derivatives are being used and by whom. Some major regulatory changes are described in Section 6, and Section 7 concludes. It should be noted that we do not provide an introduction to the principles of derivatives pricing or the basic trading operations of hedging, speculation, and arbitrage. The interested reader who is unfamiliar with these subjects is referred to standard textbooks.[2]

2. THE GROWTH OF DERIVATIVES MARKETS

Futures and options exchanges have long published information about volume of trading and open interest (i.e. contracts outstanding). The BIS has consolidated this

[2] A standard reference is Hull 2000.

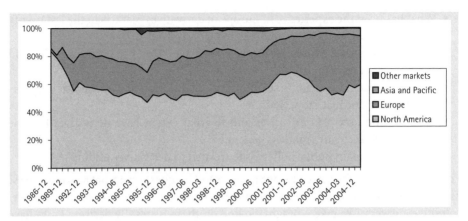

Fig. 21.1. Exchange traded financial derivatives (% of total open interest expressed in US$)

Source: BIS.

information worldwide for financial futures including foreign exchange, interest rate derivatives, and equity-related derivatives from 1986 until the end of 2004, thus giving us a perspective on the evolution of financial derivatives trading worldwide.

Open interest on futures and options exchanges worldwide went from US$614 billion at the end of 1986 to US$46,621 billion at the end of 2004, representing a growth rate of 27 per cent annually (BIS 2005: Statistical Annex, table 23). Part of the story behind this very strong growth of financial derivatives has been the emergence of financial derivatives trading in Europe. In Figure 21.1 we graph evolution of the shares of financial derivatives open interest in four major regions. We see that European financial derivatives were negligibly small in world derivatives trading which was split between North America (84 per cent) and Asia (14 per cent). In 2004, the North American share had fallen to about 59 per cent with Europe accounting for about 35 per cent.

At 48 per cent growth per year European financial derivatives have grown much more strongly than the overall world market trend. From Figure 21.1 we can see that some of that growth occurred between 1986 and 1991, a period that coincided with Big Bang in London and the completion of reforms of the public finances and monetary markets in Western Europe. However, the deepening of exchange-traded financial derivatives markets in Europe continued throughout the 1990s.

The BIS data concentrate on financial derivatives. It might be thought that by omitting derivatives based on commodities such as metals or agricultural products we may be neglecting important developments in derivatives trading. In fact, since their emergence in the 1970s financial derivatives have dominated the trading on derivatives exchanges. This is reflected in Figure 21.2 which gives the evolution of open interest on futures exchanges for commodities and financials separately. Thus following the development of financial derivatives gives a good indicator of the factors driving the bulk of derivatives business. However, there have been interesting developments outside the areas of the now standard interest rate, foreign exchange, and equity index

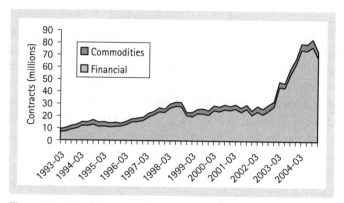

Fig. 21.2. Worldwide futures open interest

Source: Source BIS.

products. We discuss these below. A second fact that emerges from Figure 21.2 is that there has been an upsurge in derivatives trading in 2003–4.

So far we have confined this discussion to exchange-traded derivatives. In fact, since the introduction of interest rate and currency swap contracts, OTC derivatives trading has been an important part of the worldwide derivatives picture. During the 1980s the International Swap Dealers Association (ISDA) began to survey its members on their activities in swaps and other OTC interest rate and currency derivatives. More recently, the Bank of International Settlements (BIS) has compiled OTC derivatives data from reports from large banks in G-10 countries covering activity in foreign exchange, interest rate contracts based on a single currency, equity index products, and bank-traded commodity derivatives (notably gold). Combining these two data sources we present in Figure 21.3 the values outstanding of OTC and exchange-traded financial derivatives since 1987.

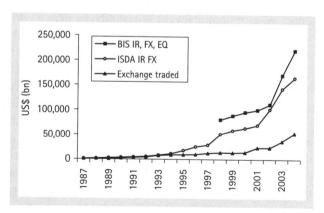

Fig. 21.3. Financial derivatives outstanding (US$bn)

Note: Open interest of exchange-traded financial futures and options at year end except 2004 which is reported for June. Notional amounts outstanding of OTC financial derivatives

Source: BIS, ISDA

We see that amounts outstanding of ISDA-reported OTC derivatives and exchange-traded derivatives were comparable in 1987 (US$865 bn versus US$865 bn). Since then the growth of OTC has strongly outpaced that of exchange-traded financial derivatives (35 per cent annually versus 27 per cent annually) so that by mid-2004 ISDA reported interest rate and FX derivatives outstanding of US$164 trillion versus US$53 trillion of open interest on financial futures and options exchanges. We see that since the mid-1990s financial derivatives as reported by the BIS tell much the same story, except that the total level of derivatives reported by BIS is greater, reflecting their more comprehensive reporting base and their inclusion of equity derivatives. The net result is that the OTC market appears to dominate the exchange-based market for financial derivatives—in June 2004 there were US$220 trillion OTC financial derivatives reported versus open interest in exchange traded of US$53 trillion.

In making this comparison we need to raise a note of caution in interpreting reports on amounts outstanding of OTC derivatives. This is best seen in comparing similar transactions, one executed on an exchange and another executed on the OTC market. Suppose a treasurer wishing to hedge a rate of interest on three-month funds that will be available in nine months time buys a Euribor contract on the Euronext.liffe market with contract maturity in nine months. This transaction by itself will increase open interest by one contract or a nominal €1 million. If one month later the same treasurer comes to believe strongly that interest rates will rise, he may choose to lift his hedge and will sell one contract of Euribor on Euronext.liffe. This will liquidate his position and reduce open interest by one contract (€1 million). Suppose instead the treasurer did something comparable on the OTC market. Initially, he would shop around for the best deal on a Forward Rate Agreement (FRA) with loan initiating in nine months' time choosing to execute the FRA with the bank offering the highest rate. This is registered as an increase in OTC derivatives outstanding of €1 million. A month later after revising his expectations he would seek to sell an FRA with the same maturity date as his initial contract (now eight months hence). After shopping for the lowest rate, he signs a sold FRA contract with a different bank. He now holds *two* FRA contracts, one bought and one sold. This gives him a neutral position on interest rates. However, OTC contracts outstanding are now €2 million (rather than 0 as in the case of the futures market transaction). And he faces counterparty risk with two banks. From this hypothetical example we see that in the process of closing out or otherwise dynamically trading a financial exposure using OTC derivatives a large notional position can be established which may represent a much smaller net exposure to the risk underlying the contracts. This fact is particularly applicable to long-dated OTC derivatives (e.g. ten-year interest rate swap contracts) where there is an increased chance that the exposure may be revised in light of major changes in market circumstances or business circumstances of the contracting party.

Another way of looking at the development of the OTC derivatives market is in relation to the underlying financial risk. Focusing on interest rate risk, in 1987 according to the BIS the total developed country debt outstanding was US$795 billion whereas total interest rate swaps and options reported by ISDA were US$682 billion, representing derivatives to underlying ratio of 86 per cent. By 1997, the last year for which ISDA reported detail on interest rate swaps and options, developed country debt stood at US$2556 billion; whereas interest rate swaps and options were reported as US$27,211 billion, that is, about 10 to 1. More recently, however, there are indications that the expansion of OTC interest rate derivatives relative to the underlying market has levelled off. According to the BIS survey in 1998 the ratio of OTC interest rate derivatives to developed country debt was about 15 to 1. In mid-2004, this ratio was still 15 to 1 (BIS 2005: Statistical Annex, tables 11 and 19; ISDA Market Survey 2004).

Finally, it should be noted that the development of OTC derivatives is a worldwide phenomenon and that Europe is very much a leader. According to the BIS survey on turnover in OTC derivatives, the market shares of total world turnover (in US$) in 2004 were 42.6 per cent for the UK, followed by the USA (23.5 per cent), France (10.2 per cent), Germany (3 per cent), Italy (2.7 per cent) and Japan (2.6 per cent). Furthermore, the leading position of the UK has increased over time as reflected in the fact that in 1995 its share of world turnover was 27.4 per cent (ahead of the US with 19.6 per cent).

The institutional change that lies behind the numbers we have presented on the growth of derivatives markets is that interest rate derivatives trading has become a highly developed adjunct to the normal functioning of fixed income markets. Issuers, investors, underwriters, and other participants routinely will use interest rate swaps, caps, collars, and similar derivatives to shape their exposures to the underlying interest rate movements. The maturity of this market is such that practitioners refer to these products as 'plain vanilla' contracts, implying a high degree of standardization with, as a consequence, greater competitive pressure squeezing margins of OTC derivatives market makers. A similar maturing process had occurred in foreign exchange markets where the interbank forward market had become fully integrated with the underlying market for spot foreign exchange.

In order to expand and to find more profitable trades, the derivatives markets have needed to innovate into new areas. In the next section we will highlight some of the major innovations in derivatives markets in recent years.

3. MAJOR PRODUCT INNOVATIONS

The development of the financial derivatives market was perhaps the major financial innovation of the 1970s. The enormous growth of financial derivatives since that time has brought with it a steady stream of new products which were innovative, at least to some degree. The US Commodity Futures Trading Commission (CFTC) has the mandate to approve exchange-traded derivatives in the USA; accordingly, CFTC approvals give some measure of the pace of innovation of derivative products. There were 174 new products approved or pending approval by the CFTC during the period 1998 to 2003 (CFTC n.d.). Many of these new products were relatively straightforward modifications of existing contracts, e.g. futures on new currency pairs. Others have been genuinely quite innovative involving substantially new risks that are traded and often requiring new pricing techniques. Outside the USA innovations in exchange-traded derivatives are harder to document, and in the world of OTC derivatives information is patchier still. In what follows we summarize our search through the literature, highlighting the most important areas of development where 'important' is judged by our impression of the scale of impact the innovations have had among practitioners. In particular, we focus on three areas: equity, credit, and energy. We recognize that in so doing we may be omitting some innovations that reflect considerable imagination and pose interesting analytical puzzles that may still be unsolved.

3.1. Equity

Equity derivatives in our understanding go back to the 1970s introductions of single-name equity options traded on the Chicago Board Options Exchange and of futures on broad indices of US stocks, most importantly on the S&P 500 index. Subsequently, in the 1980s similar products have been introduced in many other geographic areas. Also during the 1980s the cash market began to modify its trading practices to accommodate trading of portfolios of stocks, so-called 'basket trades', thus facilitating continuous arbitrage between derivatives and underlying equity markets.

More recently in the 1990s the equity derivatives market has deepened considerably with innovations in exchange-traded and OTC markets. In our view some of the most significant are:

- Futures on many more indices. This has allowed more targeted strategies, e.g. hedging a specific portfolio of shares.
- Equity-indexed structured products. The popularity of 'portfolio insurance' in the 1980s demonstrated the appeal to investors of creating a floor for portfolio values while allowing the investor to benefit from equity price increases. After the failure in the October 1987 stock crash of strategies based on high-frequency dynamic trading, the name 'portfolio insurance' is rarely still heard. However, investment funds which promise similar attributes to these strategies are still extremely attractive to investors. Since the late 1990s a number of fund managers have had considerable success with 'structured products' which give capital guarantees plus a degree of equity market participation. Some of these products are implemented through a combination of bond plus stock index derivatives (futures and options) component with no direct equity market participation.
- Equity swaps. This involves the periodic (e.g. monthly) payment of the total return on a stock (or stock index) and receipt of a floating rate of interest (e.g. LIBOR). For the investor paying the equity return, it allows a hedge of an existing equity position without giving up ownership of the share, thus maintaining voting rights and avoiding possibly adverse tax consequences. For the investor

receiving equity return, it creates equity exposure without actually taking own-ership of shares.

- Single stock equity futures. These exchange-traded contracts began trading in the USA in 2002. They allow equity market participation without actually taking possession of the shares, and are somewhat substitutable with equity swaps. These contracts can offer greater leverage to investors as compared to buying on margin and also facilitate short selling of shares which can be difficult or costly in cash equity markets.
- Flex options for stocks on exchanges which allow the purchasers to determine strike price, maturity, and other features much as they would be able to do with OTC stock options.
- Long-dated options. Long-term Equity Participation Securities (LEAPs) on the CBOE extended maturities to three years on American-style equity options.
- Options on managed funds (e.g. options on Vanguard VIPERS traded on the American stock exchange).
- Volatility swaps and futures. Since the late 1990s OTC volatility swaps have been traded in which a (periodic or single) return is paid that is the difference between a fixed volatility rate and the *realized* volatility within the period. More recently, futures on indices of *implied* volatility have been introduced on Eurex and the CBOE. Potential users of these contracts include options market makers who may often find that they are largely hedged against the direction of equity price movements ('delta neutral') but are exposed to changes in volatility.

It will be noticed from the above list that in many cases similar products are available both OTC and on exchanges. In fact, these OTC and exchanges compete with one another but they also complement each other. For example, a retail investor may find it convenient to buy a structured equity product rather than actively manage a futures position or buy options. However, the fund manager may well hedge his exposures using exchange traded options and futures.

3.2. Credit

One of the most important developments in derivatives markets in the last ten years has been the emergence of credit derivatives as a major tool for shaping credit risk ex-posures. Unlike other derivatives innovations, this is an area where exchange-traded products have had very little impact. Instead, credit derivatives have emerged out of the techniques that banks have developed to structure commercial and industrial loans. As a pure OTC phenomenon, it is hard to fix a date to the birth of credit derivatives. However, in the second half of the 1990s a credit derivatives market was recognizable as reflected in the fact that in 1997 the US Federal Reserve Board began to include credit derivatives in its Call Reports (FRB 2003: 490). A major step toward the development of a liquid market in credit derivatives was the adoption of standard

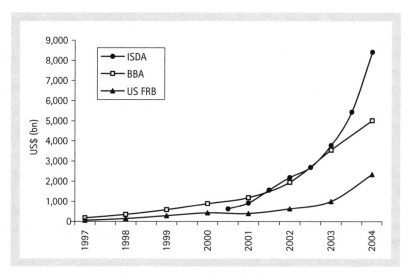

Fig. 21.4. Credit derivatives outstanding (US$bn)

Source: ISDA Market Survey, US Federal Reserve Board Call Reports, and British Bankers Association Credit
Derivatives Surveys

contract forms following ISDA guidance, initially in 1999 and subsequently revised
several times (Rule 2001: 135).

Figure 21.4 records the growth of the credit derivatives markets since 1997. In addition to the US data from the Federal Reserve Board, periodic surveys have been conducted by the British Bankers Association covering major banks internationally. More
recently, ISDA began to track the credit derivatives market. The picture from all three
data sources is one of extremely fast growth (60 per cent annually based on BBA data
and 70 per cent annually based on FRB data). This market has come from a relatively
minor adjunct to credit markets to become a central part of those markets used both
as a pricing reference and as a tool for investment and hedging. A number of factors
suggest that the high-growth phase of the market is still far from being exhausted.
There are still a relatively small number of major players in the market.[3] Furthermore,
despite the rapid increase in the number of names covered by credit derivatives, there
are still many large issuers of debt for which credit derivatives do not trade.

The essence of a credit derivative is a contract in which a credit protection seller
promises a payment to a credit protection buyer contingent upon the occurrence
of a credit event. The various types of derivatives differ according to the terms and
conditions that govern the promised payment. The critical feature of credit derivatives is the definition of 'credit event'. In practice a number of definitions have been
used including formal bankruptcy, default according to a variety of criteria, and,
more recently, penetration of pre-set barriers by listed equity prices. In early stages
of the market, significant problems emerged from the ambiguity of some contractual

---

[3] In the third quarter of 2003 in the USA ten banks represented 97 per cent of the credit protection
sold (FRB 2003: 490).

Table 21.1. Fraction of credit derivatives outstanding by type (%)

BBA survey	Single name CDS	Portfolio CLOs	Credit-linked notes	Total return swaps	Basket products	Asset swaps	Other
2001	45	22	8	7	6	7	5
2003	51	27	6	4	4	4	5

Source: BBA Credit Derivatives Survey, 2003–4.

terms. For example, it was not clear whether protection sold on debt issued by a firm continued to apply once the issuer was transformed through merger or corporate restructuring.[4] This gave rise to a number of lawsuits over disputed claims. Revisions of the ISDA standard documentation for credit derivatives has eliminated many of the major sources of ambiguity that troubled earlier trades.

Table 21.1 indicates the relative market shares (of notional principal protected) for the major types of credit derivatives as reported in the British Bankers Association surveys. The most popular type of credit derivative is the single-name credit default swap (CDS). In this contract upon the occurrence of a pre-specified credit event (e.g. default) the protection seller promises to buy at par from the protection seller a specified bond issued by name covered by the contract. Thus when WorldCom defaulted in June 2002 purchasers of WorldCom CDSs were able to deliver WorldCom paper worth about 10 per cent of par in return for full payment by the CDS sellers, a net economic gain of 90 per cent of the face value of the bond.[5] Prior to the credit event the protection buyer pays the protection seller a premium that reflects the participant's assessment of the probability of default (PD) and the expected loss given default (LGD). Other types of single-name credit derivatives include credit-linked notes, total return swaps, and asset swaps.[6]

In contrast with single-named CDSs a variety of credit products are based on a portfolio of credit-sensitive instruments. These products differs depending upon whether they are backed by bonds and other marketable securities or a portfolio of illiquid loans. They may be issued by a bank directly or they may involve the creation of a special purpose vehicle. The underlying portfolio may be static or it may be actively managed. Synthetic CLOs involve little or no capital but rather are backed by exposures taken in CDSs or other credit derivatives. The common feature of all of these vehicles is that they typically create a hierarchy among the creditors. The riskiest (most junior) category is the first-lost tranche which is the first to lose its claim in the case some of the portfolio is defaulted upon. Next more senior is the mezzanine tranche which incurs losses once the first-loss tranche is exhausted. Several more senior tranches may intervene in similar fashion until the most senior tranche is met. Through this technique of tranching, a collection of debt obligations

---

[4] See the discussion of the National Power demerger contained in Rule 2001: 135.

[5] Based on recovery rates reported in *Credit Magazine* 2005.

[6] For a introduction to the principles of pricing CDSs and other credit derivatives see Duffie and Singleton 2003.

Table 21.2. Participation in credit derivatives markets (by value, % of total at the end of 2003)

	Protection sellers	Protection buyers
Banks	38	51
Securities houses	16	16
Hedge funds	15	16
Corporates	2	3
Mono-line/reinsurers	17	5
Insurers' companies	3	2
Mutual funds	4	3
Pension funds	4	3
Gov/ agencies	1	1

Source: BBA Credit.

all bearing the same investment grade rating (e.g. BBB) may be transformed into a series of new obligations with credit quality varying from the highly speculative grade first-loss tranche to an almost risk-free grade of super-senior obligations.[7]

The success of credit derivatives is that they have attracted the participation of a wide group of institutions which use the products for hedging, investment (yield enhancement), and arbitrage. Table 21.2 gives an indication of the participation of various categories of participants. As might be expected banks are major buyers of credit protection. These tools allow them to reduce risks that may be concentrated in loan book positions to major clients. Credit derivatives allow the banks to keep on their books the loans granted thus maintaining a close client relationship while at the same time shifting some of the associated credit risks to other participants. It will be noticed that banks are as well major sellers of credit protection, reflecting their strategy of trying to leverage their expertise to make markets in these derivatives as well as financing some of their credit protection purchases by writing credit protection for names where the bank has relatively little exposure otherwise. After banks, the most important sellers of credit protection are insurance companies, in particular reinsurers and mono-line insurers.[8] Other active participants include securities houses and hedge funds for whom credit risk tends to be rather uncorrelated with their other risk exposures to major market factors such as equity prices and interest rates.

3.3. Energy

The third area where derivative product innovation has been notable in recent years is in the area of energy. While the number of new products that have been introduced is quite large, many have been unsuccessful. As a consequence, the sector has still not fulfilled the promise for development that many have been predicting. Indeed, the

---

[7] For further discussion see Duffie and Singleton 2003 and Rule 2001.

[8] Mono-line insurers are specialized insurance institutions which provide credit guarantees used in a variety of securitized financial structures.

study of some of the setbacks in energy derivatives reveals a number of fundamental issues that are specific to energy products and which are not yet fully understood.

The first energy derivatives covered petroleum products and emerged after the fundamental restructuring of the world petroleum market in the 1970s. The major factors that gave the impetus to these developments were the emergence of OPEC, the opening of North Sea oil production, and the break-up of the dominance of the big, vertically integrated oil companies. In this context, a genuine spot market emerged with a wide variety of new participants. Upon this base, the development of forward contracting for Brent and other grades of crude was a natural next step. At roughly, the same time, energy products began trading on derivatives exchanges with crude oil, heating oil, and gasoline futures on the New York Mercantile Exchange (NYMEX) and gas oil and Brent crude on the International Petroleum Exchange (IPE).[9] Since then derivatives for the petroleum complex have become an integral part of the marketplace and are regularly used by major participants.

Based on the success of petroleum derivatives, there has been substantial interest in developing derivatives trading for other energy sources, in particular, natural gas and electrical power. The experience of these two sectors illustrates some of the important conditions in the underlying physical market that may favour or impede the development of derivatives trading. In the case of natural gas, a spot market emerged only after a significant deregulation of the sector in the 1980s. Natural gas futures were introduced on NYMEX in 1990 and proved to be a success. In Europe IPE natural gas futures are traded;[10] however, market development has been slowed by the continued prevalence of long-term contracting between large, vertically integrated producers. In particular, Western Europe depends heavily upon Russian gas supplied by the state monopoly Gazprom under long-term contracts with periodically negotiated prices.

The development of derivatives markets for electrical power has been particularly eventful. Interest in derivatives for electrical power started with the deregulation and privatization of the industry beginning with Britain in 1989 and shortly followed by the Nordic countries[11] and later imposed on the rest of Europe with the EU Single Market Electricity Directive in 1996 (ABS Energy Report 2005). In the United States the Energy Policy Act of 1992 promoted greater competition with the Federal Energy Regulatory Commission (FERC) implementing plans for wholesale competition in 1996 (ABS Energy Report 2005: 189). This was motivated by the view that there was a potential for a competitive market in power generation once all participants would be given equal access to the power grid. In principle, greater efficiency could be gained through the workings of a competitive spot market for power. Once prices were free to fluctuate as a function of changes in supply and demand, derivatives trading was viewed as a natural solution to managing the associated price risks.

[9] Brent benchmark crude futures contracts began trading on the International Petroleum Exchange in 1988 (Intercontinental Exchange 2005). The IPE began trading gas oil futures in 1980.

[10] The IPE natural gas contract based on UK delivery has been actively traded since 1997. In 2001 the IPE was acquired by the International Commodity Exchange (ICE) which operates an electronic platform for trading futures, options, and OTC contracts for a variety of energy products.

[11] The UK's electricity market was 30 per cent open by 1990 and fully open by 1998, Norway's market was completely opened by 1995, Finland by 1997, Sweden by 1998.

Table 21.3. Spot price volatility (% per year)

Electricity (California-Oregon Border, peak-load)	Natural gas	Light sweet crude	S&P 500 Stock Index	Coffee	Soybeans
309	78	38	15	37	23

Source: EIA 2002.

The key feature of this deregulation was to separate the activities of power transmission and power generation.[12] While deregulation at the federal level in the USA was aimed at creating wider marketplaces, this has not always been facilitated by state regulators who were typically more concerned with regular supply and stable prices for consumers within their jurisdiction. The result has been a complicated patchwork of regional power markets that do not conform to a single design which are linked by limited (and often saturated) capacity of transmission across regions. In this context spot trading of electricity among wholesale market participants has grown up. Spot prices have proved to be extremely volatile when compared to a variety of markets for which derivatives are actively traded, as can be seen in Table 21.3.

It is not surprising then that a number of participants attempted to manage these risks by engaging in trading forward contracts and other OTC derivatives. While no systematic data on trading of OTC energy derivatives are available, it was clear that the market was very active by the late 1990s and was growing very rapidly in early 2000. Furthermore, futures and options for electrical power at a variety of locations had been introduced by NYMEX and the CBOT. This pattern of rapid development was brought to an abrupt halt by the end of 2000 when trading dried up amid signs of distress in the energy markets, most notably in the California market which experienced extreme price fluctuations and shortages. The creditworthiness of major players was a serious concern. These fears were confirmed as justified in December 2001 with the bankruptcy of the Enron, the largest player of all. In February 2002 NYMEX delisted all its electricity futures for lack of trading interest.

In the aftermath of the disruptions of power trading in 2000 and 2001, there were a number of analyses which focused on a variety of obstacles to using derivatives in the electrical power markets.[13] First, physical characteristics of electricity are very different from other commodities for which derivatives are successfully traded. In particular, the fact that it is delivered virtually instantaneously and is not practically storable means that the basic mechanism of intertemporal arbitrage employed in most derivatives markets does not apply to electrical power. This combined with inelastic short-term demand creates the extreme volatility of spot prices. Next, the

---

[12] The key steps toward power deregulation in the USA at the national level were the Public Utilities Regulatory Policy Act of 1978 and the Energy Policy Act of 1992 which created wholesale generators that were exempted from regulation and an obligation of regulated utilities to transmit power from a variety of qualified producers. See ISDA 2003.

[13] See EIA 2002; ISDA 2003.

transmission of power is governed by physical laws which create a high degree of interdependence among participants connected on the same grid. Thus even if agent A is willing to supply power demanded by agent B, his incremental power production may flow through the grid to other actors. This adds to the complexity of predicting effective supply and demand at any particular location. These physical characteristics are further complicated by the fact that many of the main actors in the industry remain highly vertically integrated, implying that spot trading in any region may be confined to the residual of power flows not covered by the major players. Finally, regulations remain differentiated across regions and are subject to change. All these features combine to make for a highly complex marketplace which is prone to becoming segmented on a temporary basis.

Derivative contracts have been used to manage these risks. Several major exchanges provide a 'spot' market for physical delivery in the near future and a 'financial' market with contract maturities ranging between several days to years which are usually cash settled. However, the trading of power derivatives on exchanges is still in its infancy. To put volumes in perspective, European power consumption in 2004 was 2,911TWh ($199.2 bn) (Datamonitor 2005). The European Energy Exchange in 2005 traded 517TWh in its financial market and 85.7TWh in its spot market (EEX 2006). Nord Pool traded 590TWh in its financial market and 167TWh in its spot market. Its OTC clearing service cleared 1207TWh (Nord Pool 2006).

The exchange-traded futures and options only make up a small part of the energy-trading markets with most of the energy trading occurring on a bilateral basis in the OTC markets. An FSA survey found that 1 per cent of UK power volume was conducted on an exchange with negligible exchange volumes for continental European power. These markets allow for the trading of the plain vanilla forwards, futures, swaps, and options as well as more exotic, tailor contracts including:

- Spark Spread Options. A cross-commodity derivative used to hedge the price difference between electricity prices and the fuel used to generate it.
- Callable and Putable Forwards. The callable forward allows the supplier of energy to interrupt supply if demand (prices) spike. Similarly the putable forward allows the holder to cancel delivery.
- Swing Options. A swing option gives the holder the right to specify the amount of power to be delivered at each exercise period (hence the 'swing' in the volume) subject to restrictions on the minimum and maximum amount at each interval and in total.

An FSA survey found that the forward physical markets dominate the financial markets in the UK with financial contracts representing only 3 per cent of UK power volumes. In continental European power financial contracts comprised 18 per cent of volumes. This suggests that with the immaturity of global energy markets, the infrastructural obstacles which fragment markets, and difficulties in pricing many of these exotic contracts, the market for energy derivatives is still at a relatively early stage of development.

The lack of an integrated spot market has meant that it has been difficult for exchanges to establish a single, liquid benchmark for trading and which would allow trading to other regions with stable bases (i.e. differences between spot markets and a given reference futures). Instead there has been a strong preference for tailoring contracts to specific needs through OTC trading. This implied that the market could thrive only if the participants were viewed as mutually creditworthy. The perception of creditworthiness is very fragile and can disappear very quickly as the cases of Enron and, more recently, Refco have demonstrated. The other consequence of market segmentation is that the sector seems to be prone to manipulations such as market corners (intentional withdrawal of supply to benefit from price increases on existing long forward positions) and other abuses of short-term monopoly power.[14] Both the fragility of creditworthiness and the potential for market manipulations were aggravated in the case of the electrical power sector by the lack of transparency of OTC transactions. This was most evident when the activities of Enron were scrutinized following its collapse. It appears that opaque OTC derivatives trades may have been used to effectively disguise a high level of leverage which if recognized generally would have led counterparties to downgrade Enron's credit quality.

In large part because of the experience of electrical power derivatives, there have been important developments in derivatives market regulation in the USA which may have deep and long-lasting effects on the future of derivatives trading for electrical power and for derivatives markets generally.[15] In particular, the Commodity Futures Modernization Act of 2000 cleared the legal status of a large variety of OTC transactions as being exempt from the many regulatory requirements applied to traditional exchanges that are open to a wide variety of participants. Furthermore, it paved the way for these OTC transactions to be cleared by clearing houses in much the same manner as exchange-based trades. In the aftermath of the Enron collapse OTC clearing has proved to be a popular means of dealing with counterparty risk in the energy sector. This attractiveness may well mean that it could be adapted to trading for other products as well. An important by-product of OTC clearing is that once they are cleared as exchange-based trades OTC trades fall under the regulatory oversight of the CFTC in matters of market manipulations. This has led to the CFTC pursuing fifty separate cases of false trade reporting or market manipulations in the energy sector.

It remains to be seen whether these changes of market structure suffice to address the difficulties posed by the particularities of the electrical power markets. The complexity of the power market itself has led some participants to turn their attention to dimensions of energy markets which while uncertain may be less volatile than power spot prices. One of these has been the trading emissions quotas that are allocated to power generators by regulation. This has proved quite successful with $4 billion of sulphur dioxide futures being traded in 2001. The other area that has received strong interest is weather derivatives, such as indices as number of heating days at a particular location, which correlate quite well with measures of energy usage.

---

[14] See Anderson 1992 and Kyle 1984.
[15] These have recently been summarized by the chairman of the Commodity Futures Trading Commission (Jeffrey 2005).

4. Organization of Derivatives Markets

Until fairly recently, there has been a clear difference in the trading of derivatives on exchanges as compared to trading in over-the-counter (OTC) markets. Exchange-traded futures and options were contracts with standardized delivery or settlement terms with price negotiated by openoutcry in a centralized physical marketplace ('the pit'). The trades negotiated on the exchange were publicly reported and were cleared in a clearing house associated with the exchange with the clearing house being party to all trades. Therefore, if, for example, the seller defaults, the clearing house still will be obliged to honour the trade by delivering to the buyer according to the agreed terms. The solvency of the clearing house was protected by marking all positions to market daily through a system of margins. The exchanges were typically not-for-profit membership organizations with the purchase of a membership giving the right to carry out trades on the floor of the exchange. As a result decision making at exchanges was often dominated by the community of floor traders.

In contrast, the OTC market involved bilateral trades where all contract terms such as delivery quality, quantity, location, and date as well as price were negotiable. Trades were arranged by telephone or other means of communication between principals, known to each and willing to assume the associated credit risk. Generally, transaction prices were not reported publicly.

Thus exchange-based and OTC derivatives were very different types of contracts carrying with them distinct sets of advantages and disadvantages. Exchange-based contracts tended to be more liquid and tended to minimize counterparty risks. However, since they involved standardized contracts they posed problems of basis risk, and marking to market means that hedging with derivatives may pose problems of arranging for short-term financing. OTC contracts tended to be less liquid both because they are not standardized and because trades are tied to specific counterparties. Furthermore, they tend to be fragile markets in the sense that trading can become difficult if credit risks are perceived to be high. On the other hand they avoid problems of basis risk and short-term financing of mark-to-market positions.

In recent years this traditional pattern has been altered considerably, and the distinction between OTC and exchange-traded derivatives is becoming much less clear. In part, this is a reflection of competitive developments, and in part it is a reflection of changing technology.

4.1. Developments in OTC Trading

Some of the major complications of OTC trading included the trade confirmation process and issues surrounding creditworthiness of counterparties. To overcome these issues the International Swap Dealers Association (ISDA) was formed in 1984 to provide a standardized set of documentation and OTC market practices. The ISDA

Master Agreement provides a standard contract for the ongoing relationship between counterparties with a schedule detailing unique terms (ISDA 2002). The standardization provided by ISDA documentation has helped to make it easier for more participants to access the OTC markets. It further makes the trade process simpler by providing the details of the ongoing OTC relationship and allowing for only the terms of an individual trade to be reported on a short confirmation document.[16]

It seems likely that better documentation standards have encouraged the OTC markets to converge to conventional terms that aid in creating more liquidity. For example, suppose agent A enters into a forward contract to sell agent B a commodity according to the market's conventional terms regarding quality and delivery conditions and for a date and price mutually agreed upon. Suppose later agent A wishes to unwind his exposure, perhaps because he expects the price to rise. To do so he enters into a forward contract to purchase the commodity from agent C again using the market's conventional terms, for the same date as the previous contract and at a price agreeable to C. In this way A will have eliminated price-level risk. Furthermore, since the delivery terms were identical for the two contracts, he has eliminated basis risk as well. If agents know that it is possible to eliminate both price-level and basis risk through subsequent trading, they will be more willing to enter into the initial OTC contracts in the first place, and market liquidity will be promoted. Notice, however, that unlike in exchange-based contracts where the clearing house is a party to every trade, in the example we see that in dynamic trading of OTC contracts counterparty risks are not eliminated. As a result, credit risk emerges as one of the most important risks associated with OTC derivatives. As the case of electrical power derivatives demonstrated, the increase in perceived risk in credit exposures can give rise to a market collapse.

Not surprisingly then, ISDA has also been active in trying to overcome the counterparty risk problems of OTC trading by developing standards for credit support. In part, this has occurred through the development of 'close-out netting'—the process where, in the event of bankruptcy of one of the counterparties, inflows and outflows of multiple contracts between the two counterparties are netted against each other to prevent the solvent party from making a payment and not receiving his cash flow from the defaulted party. More recently, ISDA has been active in developing standards for collateralizing relationships. Finally, as we discussed in relation to the power market above, increasingly OTC trades are being cleared through clearing houses in much the same manner as exchange-based contracts.

As was seen in Section 2, these developments have helped OTC derivative markets to increase in size rapidly in recent years both in absolute terms and in relation to exchange-traded derivatives. With the better documentation framework, the real benefit of the OTC—namely customization—has further driven volumes and innovations in derivatives. Another advantage of OTC is that it may be possible to execute greater size through an individual negotiation than by attempting to trade on standardized markets for maturities where trading is thin (or non-existent).

---

[16] In addition, ISDA has worked closely with governments to ensure that their documentation will be upheld under the country's legislation. See ISDA 1996.

The rapid growth in OTC markets has not been without its share of problems. We have already discussed the collapse of the electrical power derivatives markets in 2001–2. More generally, while better documentation was created to help reduce operational risks, dealers have reported a backlog in uncompleted master agreements with as much as 5–20 per cent of counterparties or more (BIS 1998). Furthermore, unconfirmed trades have been a problem. Automation of OTC derivatives confirmations had grown to the point that in 2004 reportedly one-fifth of plain vanilla swaps and one-third of credit derivatives were being confirmed on an automated basis. However, the growth of the credit derivatives market was so great in 2005 that the US Federal Reserve System actively voiced its concerns with the growing backlog of uncleared trades (MacKenzie 2005).

4.2. Developments in Exchange Trading

4.2.1. *Transition to Electronic Trading*

The last twenty years, the time span we have dealt with in this survey, roughly coincides with the IT revolution. It is not surprising then that one of the major themes in the derivatives world during this time has been the adoption of electronic trading technologies. In general, the new marketplaces that have developed since the 1980s, including most of those in continental Europe, have been early adopters of electronic trading. In contrast, exchanges that were established prior to 1985, especially the US exchanges, have been slow to abandon older technologies such as open-outcry floor trading.

In Europe, the trading of financial derivatives took off in 1982 with the opening of the London International Futures Exchange (LIFFE). LIFFE was modelled very much along the lines of the US markets and adopted open-outcry floor trading. The continental financial derivatives markets entered somewhat later. While some, for example MATIF, adopted open-outcry floor trading as the transaction technology, others, such as the Spanish financial derivatives market, made an early commitment to electronic trading.[17] The exchange that really drove the charge was Deutsche Terminboerse (DTB). Founded in 1991, DTB adopted electronic trading at its outset. It introduced trading of futures on the Bund (German government bond) in direct competition with a contract already trading on LIFFE. By 1998 the DTB had wrestled the Bund contract away from LIFFE which was still floor based. The DTB (merging with SOFFEX to become Eurex) grew to overtake the CBOT as the largest derivatives exchange in 1999 (Eurex 1999).

The success of the DTB was the catalyst which forced other exchanges to rethink their commitment to floor trading. The French MATIF completed the first transition from floor to electronic trading in only a short time during 1998. Also in 1998 LIFFE began its move to electronic trading with the development of the Liffe Connect

---

[17] The Spanish financial derivatives market MEFF was established in 1989 and trades futures and options on Spanish government bonds and stock indices.

platform. The American exchanges had been experimenting with a variety of electronic platforms to run alongside open outcry since the late 1980s. This transition accelerated in the late 1990s. In 2005 70 per cent of the volume on the CME was executed electronically (CME 2006). At the CBOT electronic trading accounted for 65 per cent of total volume in 2005 (CBOT 2006).

The advantages of electronic trading over floor-based exchanges may include factors such as transparency of the order-matching process, speed of execution, audit trails, scalability, and anonymity (Tsang 1999). All these factors affect the total costs of trading. Generally it appears that the direct costs of electronic trading are much lower than on traditional exchanges; the development of a new trading floor is estimated to be two to forty times the development cost of an electronic system which has far lower operating costs (Domowitz 2001: 4). While this allows for lower direct costs, such as fees and commissions (as well as the competitive effect on direct costs at other exchanges), it is much more difficult to measure the difference in the total costs of trading between the floor-based and electronic exchange. Domowitz and Steil (1999) review a number of studies on the differences between implicit trading costs for pairs of automated and traditional stock and derivative markets with overall results favouring the electronic markets. In the DTB/LIFFE fight over the Bund, studies have found that bid–ask spreads were at least as tight on the DTB. In general, Domowitz and Steil find that bid–ask spreads are 'approximately the same across automated and traditional venues' and '[m]arket depth is generally found to be greater in the automated market.'

Table 21.4 summarizes the volume and types of contracts traded on the largest derivatives exchanges worldwide for 2004 according to data collected by the World Federation of Exchanges (with volume in terms of numbers of derivatives contracts). It shows that Eurex continues to lead the CME by about 25 per cent. The next largest exchange is Euronext created at the millennium through the merger of LIFFE with continental European derivatives exchanges. This shows that the formerly dominant Chicago derivatives markets have been more than equalled by their European rivals which have emerged only in the course of the 1990s.

A word is in order on the Korea Exchange which appears as the largest derivative exchange by numbers of contracts traded. This reflects the fact that over 97 per cent of the contracts traded were in the KOSPI 200 options and a further 2 per cent in KOSPI 200 futures which both have small contract sizes aimed to appeal to retail investors. The Korea Exchange is an all-electronic exchange.

The growth of the two big European exchanges has been very much a story of the success of electronic trading, and their success has been instrumental in forcing the North American exchanges to accelerate their adoption of electronic trading. However the decision whether to move to electronic trading is still not clear to all. While electronic exchanges may cut on transaction costs by disintermediating unnecessary brokers, there are still many functions which an electronic market cannot perform. For instance, electronic markets provide a simple trading algorithm which is typically anonymous and order driven. However, the human interaction which takes place on a trading floor can provide a much more sophisticated and valuable

Table 21.4. Largest derivative exchanges (by number of contracts traded in 2004)

Exchanges	Region	Contracts traded	(2004)	Stock options	Stock futures	Stock index options	Stock index futures	ST interest rate options	ST interest rate futures	LT interest rate options	LT interest rate futures	Currency options	Currency futures	Commodity options	Commodity futures	Floor-based trading
Korea Exchange	Asia Pacific	2,586,570,860	29.8%	✓		✓	✓		✓		✓		✓			
Eurex	Europe	1,065,639,010	12.3%	✓		✓	✓		✓	✓	✓		✓			
Chicago Mercantile Exchange (CME)	North America	805,341,861	9.3%		✓	✓	✓	✓	✓			✓	✓	✓	✓	F
Euronext	Europe	790,385,210	9.1%	✓	✓	✓	✓	✓	✓	✓	✓	✓	✓	✓	✓	
Chicago Board of Trade (CBOT)	North America	599,994,385	6.9%			✓	✓	✓	✓	✓	✓			✓	✓	F
Chicago Board Options Exchange (CBOE)	North America	361,087,394	4.2%	✓		✓	✓			✓						F
International Securities Exchange (ISE)	North America	360,769,161	4.2%	✓												
São Paulo SE	South America	235,349,478	2.7%	✓		✓	✓						✓			
MexDer	North America	204,170,751	2.4%				✓		✓		✓		✓			
American SE	North America	202,692,231	2.3%	✓		✓	✓									
BM&F	South America	178,851,381	2.1%				✓	✓	✓				✓	✓	✓	F
New York Mercantile Exchange (NYMEX)	North America	163,157,807	1.9%											✓	✓	F
Philadelphia SE	North America	133,404,843	1.5%	✓		✓	✓					✓	✓			F
Pacific SE	North America	103,262,458	1.2%	✓		✓										F
Buenos Aires SE	South America	94,827,742	1.1%	✓		✓	✓					✓	✓			F
OMX Stockholm SE	Europe	94,690,499	1.1%	✓		✓	✓				✓		✓			F

Source: World Federation of Exchanges.

negotiating service. The non-anonymity of the floor provides better information on the quality of order flow. It also allows for negotiation beyond the strict rules of a trading screen such as better volume/size information and the ability of brokers to find customers when certain opportunities arise who may be willing to trade but not currently in the market. One exchange which is betting on this is NYMEX which restored open-outcry market to its London trading branch in late 2005. In addition, electronic markets have their share of problems such as service outages from attack/manipulation and trading mistakes which, when they happen, are much bigger in scale and harder to fix.

Trading platforms are another area within the development of electronic markets where Europe has been a leader. Europe's early foray into electronic trading required it to develop the first platforms. The success of these platforms was not matched by a similar success with the US platforms. With high development costs many exchanges now buy in sophisticated platforms from a number of providers including Liffe Connect, OM's Click, and the Eurex platform (e.g. the ISE, USA's first fully electronic exchange in May 2000, uses OM's Click platform).[18]

4.2.2. *Ownership/Governance Structure*

We have already noted that there is a strong tradition of commodity derivatives exchanges being organized as member-owned cooperatives. This tradition was particularly strong in the USA where major decision-making positions were typically filled by powerful 'locals', i.e. floor traders who trade for their own account as well as execute client trades. These traders are naturally concerned that the market be organized in a manner that enhances the total profits that they derive from trading. Some observers complain that this structure prevents exchanges from adapting to competitive threats or from pursing opportunities that might benefit customers for fear that membership prices may suffer.

The traditional approach to organizing derivatives exchanges was called into question when LIFFE lost its position in the Bund contract in 1997–8 to the electronic start-up DTB. It was argued at the time that the mutual structure had been an impediment to LIFFE adopting electronic trading and that the Bund contract was lost as a consequence. Accordingly, in 1999 LIFFE undertook to reorganize itself as a corporation where shareholder rights were split from trading membership. This corporate structure gave the exchange a single, clear objective—maximization of profits. LIFFE's demutualization sparked off a wave of other exchanges following suit. The ownership status of the major derivatives exchanges is summarized in Table 21.5.

While many exchanges have begun or have completed the process of 'demutualization', some still have not completely separated the trading right from the shareholding right. Such a case where the two components are required to be kept together is still

---

[18] Liffe Connect is used by the CBOT, the Kansas City Board of Trade, Minneapolis Grain Exchange, Winnipeg Commodity Exchange, and Tokyo International Financial Futures Exchange. The OM platform is also used by Borsa Italiana's Italian Derivatives Market (Idem) and the Australian Stock Exchange.

Table 21.5. Ownership status of derivatives exchanges

Exchange	Demutualization	Listed
LIFFE	1999	Yes (acquired by Euronext)
Eurex	2000	No
NYMEX	2000	No
Euronext	2000	2001
CME	2000	2002
ISE	2002	2005
PHLX	2004	No
CBOT	2005	2005
CBOE	Transition	No
AMEX	No	No

a member-owned and -operated exchange. True demutualization occurs when the rights of owners and users are completely split, usually following an IPO.

Thus recent experience suggests that the case in favour of organizing derivatives markets as for-profits business is clear. Conceptually, however, the case is less clear-cut. Hart and Moore (1996) provide a framework to compare for-profits markets with member cooperatives. They show that both structures can be inefficient. Outside ownership becomes relatively more efficient where variation of the membership interests becomes more polarized and where the exchange faces more competition.

This debate is important for at least two reasons. First, exchanges are entrusted with responsibility for self-regulation including monitoring of trading practices and dispute resolution. Under the cooperative structure here is a conflict of interest between the end-user's want of a fair market and the member's interests. It may be that shareholders' interests would be more closely aligned with those of the public.

Second, exchanges need to evolve to meet that competition. It is probably the case that members at exchanges which still have open-outcry floors have displayed the most resistance to a change in their ownership structure and have been the slowest to adopt electronic trading. Demutualization may provide the decision-making ability and ability to raise capital for growth required in the more competitive exchange environment.

5. USERS OF DERIVATIVES

In our description of the growth of derivatives markets over the last twenty years we have documented the fact that derivatives trading has become thoroughly integrated in markets for foreign exchange, equity, government debt, and, increasingly, credit. This is manifested by the presence on derivatives markets of the major financial service firms including investment banks, fund managers, and commercial banks. The same is true of the Treasury arms of governments, central banks, and governmental agencies.

In contrast with banking and fund management, insurers have been relatively more reluctant users of derivatives. Cummins, Philips, and Smith (2001) report that in a 1992 sample of North American insurers 11 per cent of life insurers and 7 per cent of property-casualty insurers participated in derivatives markets. They report that larger insurers and mutual insurers (as compared to unaffiliated companies) were relatively more likely to use derivatives. However, there are a number of signs that the worlds of insurance and derivatives are getting closer. This tendency was noted by Warren Buffett (no lover of derivatives) who wrote about General Re's (the major reinsurer) involvement in derivatives as follows, 'the reinsurance and derivatives business are similar: like Hell, both are easy to enter and almost impossible to exit' (Berkshire Hathaway 2002). One point of contact has been the catastrophe risk where large reinsurers have been active in organizing issues of catastrophe bonds and other catastrophe-contingent claims. This is an area where the derivatives exchanges have attempted to innovate as well (e.g. CBOT's catastrophe-linked futures and options contracts) but with limited success until now. As we have seen above, insurance companies and reinsurers are major players in the credit derivatives markets, in particular as suppliers of credit protection. Table 21.6 presents total derivatives usage based on a survey of large insurers and reinsurers.

From these data we see that the heaviest derivatives use is interest rates and equity derivatives and is for hedging purposes. This is consistent with the fact that derivatives usage is relatively heavier for life companies, as these companies tend to have a significant mismatch between assets and liabilities that can be managed with these kinds of derivatives. The use of credit derivatives appears to be for return enhancement, as insurers appear to be predominantly providers of credit protection.

Until fairly recently it has been difficult to determine how widely derivatives have been used by non-financial firms. This has changed following changes in accounting rules requiring firms to provide information on derivatives usage. Accordingly, academics have begun to explore these data to determine to what extent companies use derivatives and for what purpose. In particular, there have been some attempts

Table 21.6. Derivatives positions held by insurers and reinsurers (US$m)

Type of contract	Held for hedging		Held for non-hedging		Total	
	Notional amount	Fair value	Notional amount	Fair value	Notional amount	Fair value
Interest rate	118,896	999	8,998	128	127,894	1,127
Equity	13,331	828	946	22	14,277	850
Foreign currency	2,186	82	2,385	−69	4,571	13
Credit derivatives	84	3	44,947	−48	45,031	−45
Other	40	1	1901	−25	1941	−24

Source: IAIS Global Reinsurance Market Report 2004.

at testing some of the qualitative arguments for why risk management by firms may increase firm value. These include reducing financial distress costs (Mayers and Smith 1982), taxes (Smith and Stulz 1985), and costs of external finance (Froot, Scharfstein, and Stein 1993). Following changes in FASB rules on derivatives reporting Mian (1996) studied the annual reports for 1992 of a sample of 3,022 US firms. Of this sample 543 firms (18 per cent) reported they used derivatives for hedging, and a further 228 firms (8 per cent) reported they used derivatives without indicating they were specifically used for hedging. Mian finds weak support for the idea that derivatives are used to reduce tax costs. Interestingly, the data do not support the idea that firms with greater growth options are more likely to use derivatives.

Other studies have explored managerial motives for derivatives use including those, such as managerial risk aversion, which may conflict with firm value maximization. In a study of a detailed data set on forty-eight North American gold-mining firms between 1991 and 1993 Tufano (1996) finds little evidence that firms use derivatives for the value-maximizing motives indicated above. Instead, he documents a systematic tendency for firms where managers hold options to not hedge (i.e. retain more gold price risk). In contrast, firms where managers hold stock tend to hedge. This is consistent with the view that because managers are risk averse when their compensation depends linearly upon firm performance they will use risk management to reduce the firm's idiosyncratic risk. However, when they are compensated with call options, a convex claim on firm performance, they will abstain from tools which reduce idiosyncratic risk. In a clinical study of foreign exchange hedging in a single firm Brown (2001) finds that hedging may be used to align managerial incentives with firm objectives.

Bartram, Brown, and Fehle (2004) is probably the most comprehensive study to date of the uses of derivatives by non-financial firms. Their data cover 7,263 firms from forty-eight countries including the USA based on financial reports for either 2000 or 2001. In contrast with most previous studies they find that derivatives were widely used, with 60 per cent of firms reporting some use of derivatives of which 45 per cent use foreign exchange derivatives, 33 per cent use interest rate derivatives, and 10 per cent use commodity derivatives. The higher level of derivatives found in this study may indicate that derivatives use has been growing over time; although it could be a reflection of increasingly stringent reporting standards or the fact that the data set covers mostly large firms. They found derivatives use was positively related to firm leverage, and interpret the finding as indicating firms' desiring to minimize costs of financial distress. Interestingly they found that the degree of development of local derivatives markets was positively associated with derivatives use.

6. REGULATORY ISSUES

In most markets derivatives trading is governed by existing contract and securities laws, and public regulation, as opposed to self-regulation by exchanges or professional bodies, is subsumed under general securities regulation. The most important exception to this general pattern is the United States where derivatives trading was traditionally dominated by commodity markets and where there has existed a strong body of regulations specifically aimed at derivatives trading.

The legislative foundation of US derivatives regulation is the Commodity Exchange Act of 1936. This Act reflected the view based on the experience notably of grain trading that commodity futures markets were susceptible to manipulation through restrictions of deliverable supply, often giving rise to abusive price distortions. This produced a system which monitors markets through reports on futures market open interest classifying large position as having either a speculative or hedging purpose. The CEA was modified significantly in 1974 by legislation creating the Commodity Futures Trading Commission which was endowed with 'exclusive jurisdiction' to regulate commodity futures. One of the basic regulatory requirements was that all futures transactions were required to be executed on recognized exchanges, thus promoting transparency and helping the CFTC to obtain a comprehensive view of positions on the market. This requirement clearly intended to facilitate the CFTC in pursuing its purpose of preventing manipulations. The development of exchange-traded financial derivatives in the 1970s created a problem for financial regulation in the USA. These involved futures contracts which were generally regulated by the CFTC being written for securities such as stocks which were regulated by the Securities Exchange Commission (SEC). This gave rise to a well-documented 'turf war' between these two US regulators.[19] The result over time has been a series of accommodations which left futures trading largely under the jurisdiction of the CFTC and option trading under the SEC.

The resolution of frictions between the SEC and the CFTC did not however resolve the rather ambiguous status of OTC derivatives which were growing strongly through the 1980s and 1990s. For many of these instruments it was not clear which set of regulations, if any, would apply. For example, do interest rate swaps, which are commonly hedged by holding portfolios of Eurodollar futures, fall under the jurisdiction of the CFTC, the SEC, neither, or both? The CFTC's presumption of exclusive jurisdiction over derivatives was thrown into doubt by the case of forward foreign exchange contracts which had long been traded on a very deep international, inter-bank market. As other OTC markets were developing internationally among major financial institutions, the CFTC was forced to accept other exceptions to the precept of exclusive jurisdiction. The basic criteria that was adopted for a derivative to qualify as an regulatory exception were: (a) the contract was not standardized, (b) they were traded by specialist institutions rather than the general public, and (c) there was no 'mutualization of credit risk', i.e. these were contracts where participating parties were knowingly assuming the credit risks involved (Pirrong 2002). These principles did not really remove the ambiguous status of OTC contract. For example, we have seen that efforts to establish clear documentation standards were contributing to a greater degree of standarization than was previously associated with OTC

---

[19] See a compendium of articles from the period, Peck 1985.

contracts. Furthermore, the exceptions were established very much on a case-by-case basis leaving the status of any new market that might come along Considerably in doubt.

With the continued growth of OTC derivatives in the 1990s, fuelled by the development of electronic trading technologies, there was growing pressure to come to some general resolution of the status of OTC derivatives. The result was the Commodity Futures Modernization Act of 2000. This has changed derivatives regulation in the USA in the following ways: (a) OTC derivatives were deemed to fall outside the jurisdiction of the CFTC, (b) futures exchanges *and their associated clearing houses* were regulated by the CFTC, and (c) OTC derivatives transactions could under certain circumstances be cleared by regulated clearing houses. As we have seen, the last two features have combined in the case of energy trading to mean that the CFTC has authority to monitor OTC energy transactions to the extent that such transactions have passed through clearing houses. This means that potentially OTC markets may be subject to monitoring and possibly remedies for market manipulations.

As has been already noted in Europe and other non-US markets, derivatives regulation has tended to be treated as a subcategory of general securities regulation. Accordingly in most non-US markets there is nothing comparable to large trader reports or the range of judicial remedies to alleged manipulations which have long existed in the USA.[20] Instead, national regulation has concentrated on the authorization of institutions for taking customer business, suitability of persons working in the field, prudential standards such as capital requirements, and, in some cases, market transparency. To the extent that there is any concern for market manipulations it tends to fall under prohibitions against insider trading. Furthermore, attempts to create transparent markets have generally not gone so far as to establish monopoly of trading on a single centralized marketplace. This tolerance probably has been a key factor in facilitating the growth of OTC derivatives outside the USA. In contrast, the USA, despite its very highly developed derivatives exchanges, has over time tended to lose its dominant position as the OTC markets have grown in importance.

Probably the greatest regulatory challenge for derivatives trading in Europe was the fact that trading was potentially regulated by a large number of national regulators whose rules and enforcement practices differed. This obviously stood as an impediment to the development of deep international markets. The major breakthrough since 1985 has been the efforts at the European level to integrate banking and securities markets, notably through the 1989 Second Banking Coordination Directive and the 1993 Investment Services Directive which is to be superseded by the Markets in Financial Instruments Directive (MiFID). These maintained the authority of national regulators but established important limits to their effective control because financial firms were granted a single 'passport' which allowed them to operate throughout the EU subject to the regulations of their home country. This creates a tendency toward a single standard in those dimensions of regulation in which regulatory competition is most effective.

---

[20] This point was made relative to UK and US regulations in Anderson 1986.

7. CONCLUSION

We have documented the strong development of derivatives markets over the last twenty years. Building on the development of financial derivatives in the USA during the 1970s, derivatives markets have expanded worldwide to the point where they are thoroughly integrated into the operations of debt and equity capital markets.

One notable feature of this growth has been the strong relative development of European derivatives markets as reflected in the fact that two of the five largest derivatives exchanges globally are European and that London is the largest centre of OTC derivatives trading in the world. This strong European growth has been driven by the reform of European debt and equity markets, capital flow liberalization within Europe, market integration, and the introduction of the euro. However, a key additional factor favouring European derivatives growth has been the development of electronic trading which allowed European exchanges to leapfrog their North American rivals.

Another feature of this experience has been the fact that the growth of OTC derivatives markets has outstripped that of derivatives exchanges. This also has been facilitated by the IT revolution. However, part of the development of OTC derivatives markets can be attributed to the efforts of the major players in global financial markets to establish common standards for documentation and trading practices. These factors are nowhere clearer than in the rapid rise of credit derivatives trading which has been almost entirely an OTC phenomenon.

REFERENCES

ABS ENERGY REPORT (2005), 'Electricity deregulation report global Ed 4 2005', October.
ANDERSON, R.W. (1986), 'Regulation of futures trading in the United States and the United Kingdom', Oxford Review of Economic Policy, 2(4), 41–57.
—— (1992), 'Cornering the market', in: P. Newman et al. (eds.), The New Palgrave Dictionary of Money and Finance, Basingstoke: Macmillan.
BANK FOR INTERNATIONAL SETTLEMENTS (BIS) (1998), 'OTC derivatives: settlement procedures and counterparty risk management', www.bis.org/publ/cpss27.pdf.
—— (2005), Quarterly Review, March.
BARTRAM, S., BROWN, G., and FEHLE, F. (2004), 'International evidence on financial derivatives usage', Working Paper, University of North Carolina.
BERKSHIRE HATHAWAY (2002), Annual Report.
BROWN, G. (2001), 'Managing foreign exchange risk with derivatives', Journal of Financial Economics, 20, 401–49.
CHICAGO BOARD OF TRADE (CBOT) (2006), CBOT 2005 Volume Surpasses 674 Million Contracts and Marks Fourth Consecutive Year of Growth, press release, 3 January, www.cbot.com/cbot/pub/cont_detail/0,3206,1236+35861,00.html.
CHICAGO MERCANTILE EXCHANGE (CME) (2006), CME Posts Sixth Consecutive Record Year as Total Volume Soars to More than 1 Billion Contracts; Exchange Average Daily Volume Approaches 4.2 Million Contracts, up 34 Percent Compared with 2004, press release, 3 January, htt://investor.cme.com/ReleaseDetail.cfm?ReleaseID=182951.

COMMODITY FUTURE TRADING COMMISSION (CFTC) (2000), *Congress Passes Commodity Futures Modernization Act*, press release, 15 December, www.cftc.gov/opa/press00/opa4479-00. htm.

____ (CFTC) (n.d.), *Contracts Approved by the CFTC Submitted by Designated Contract Markets (since 1998)*, www.cftc.gov/dea/deacontract_approved_list.htm.

CREDIT MAGAZINE (2005), 'Severity of default is key', May, *www.creditmag.com/public/ showPage.html?page=133193*.

CUMMINS, J. D., PHILLIPS, R. D., and SMITH, S. D. (2001), 'Derivatives and corporate risk management: participation and volume decisions in the insurance industry', *Journal of Risk and Insurance*, 68, 51–91.

DATAMONITOR (2005), 'Electricity in europe: industry profile', August.

DOMOWITZ, I. (2001), 'Liquidity, transaction costs, and reintermediation in electronic markets', www.ny.frb.org/newsevents/events/research/2001/Domowitz.pdf.

____ and STEIL, B. (1999), 'Automation, trading costs, and the structure of the securities industry', http://fmg.lse.ac.uk/upload_file/29_domowitz.pdf.

DUFFIE, D., and SINGLETON, K. (2003), *Credit Risk*, Princeton: Princeton University Press.

ENERGY INFORMATION ADMINISTRATION (EIA) (2002), *Derivatives and Risk Management in the Petroleum, Natural Gas, and Electrical Power Industries*, Washington, DC, www.eia. doe.gov/oiaf/servicerpt/derivative/.

EUREX, COMPANY INFO/MILESTONES (1999), www.eurexchange.com/about/company_info/ milestones.html+&hl=en; www.eurexchange.com/about/business_areas/milestones_1996_ en.html; www.eurexchange.com/about/press/press_49_en.htm.

EUROPEAN ENERGY EXCHANGE (EEX) (2006), press release, 12 January, www.eex.de/publications/press_center/index_e.asp#20060112.

FEDERAL RESERVE BOARD (2003), 'Recent developments in business lending by commercial banks', *Federal Reserve Bulletin*, December.

FROOT, K., SCHARFSTEIN, D., and STEIN, J. (1993), 'Risk management: coordinating corporate investment and financing policies', *Journal of Finance*, 48 1629–58.

HART, O., and MOORE, J. (1996), 'The governance of exchanges: members' cooperatives versus outside ownership', *Oxford Review of Economic Policy*, 12, 53–69.

HULL, J. (2000), *Options, Futures, and Other Derivatives*, 4th edn., Harlow: Pearson.

INTERCONTINENTAL EXCHANGE (2005), *IPE Brent Crude Futures Contract*, www.theice.com/ publicdocs/IPE_Brent_Crude_futures_contract_specification.pdf.

INTERNATIONAL SWAPS and DERIVATIVES ASSOCIATION (ISDA) (1996), 'Financial transactions in insolvency: reducing legal risk through legislative reform'.

____ (2002), 'An introduction to the documentation of OTC derivatives: "Ten Themes"'. www. isda.org/educat/pdf/ten-themes.pdf.

____ (2003), 'Restoring confidence in US energy trading markets', www.isda.org/ press/pdf/isdaenergywhitepaper.pdf

____ (2004, 2005), 'ISDA Market Survey', www.isda.org/statistics/historical.html.

JEFFREY, R. (2005), 'Market integrity: a shared mission', speech to ISDA, 6 December.

KYLE, A. (1984), 'A theory of futures market manipulations', in R. W. Anderson (ed.), *The Industrial Organization of Futures Markets*, Lexington, KY.: Lexington Books.

MACKENZIE, M. (2005), 'Credit-derivatives deadline looms', *Wall Street Journal*, 13 December.

MAYERS, D., and SMITH, C. W. (1982), 'On the corporate demand for insurance', *Journal of Business*, 55, 281–96.

MIAN, S. L. (1996), 'Evidence on corporate hedging policy', *Journal of Financial and Quantitative Analysis*, 31, 419–39.

NORD POOL (2006), *Further Volume Growth for Nord Pool in 2005*, press release, issued 5 January 2006, www.nordpool.com/information/press_releases/2006-001.html.

PECK, A. (ed.) (1985), *Futures Markets: Regulatory Issues*, Washington, DC: American Enterprise Institute.

PIRRONG, C. (2002), 'A growing market', *Regulation* (Cato Institute), www.cato.org/pubs/regulation/regv25n2/v25n2–6.pdf.

RULE, D. (2001), 'The credit derivatives market: its development and possible implications for financial stability', *Financial Stability Review*, Bank of England (June).

SMITH, C. W., and STULZ, R. (1985), 'Determinants of firms' hedging policies', *Journal of Financial and Quantitative Analysis*, 20, 391–405.

STIGUM, M. (1990), *The Money Market*, 3rd edn., New York: McGraw Hill.

TSANG, R. (1999), 'Open outcry and electronic trading in futures exchanges', *Royal Bank of Canada Review*, Spring.

TUFANO, P. (1996), 'Who manages risk: an empirical examination of risk management practices in the gold mining industry', *Journal of Finance*, 51, 1097–137.

STRUCTURED FINANCE

MACIEJ FIRLA-CUCHRA

1. INTRODUCTION

STRUCTURED finance is one of the leading growth areas in capital markets, encompassing different business segments from classic securitizations of mortgages to repackagings and synthetic portfolios of credit derivatives. According to Alan Greenspan (1998), former chairman of Federal Reserve, securitization is one of the major financial innovations to have occurred over recent decades. The rapid expansion in both depth and breadth of structured finance markets has resulted in a remarkable assortment of financial products. As a result of this diversity, no single generic structure can be identified which would adequately describe all types of structured finance. Still, a few, general characteristics largely shared across different types of transactions can be outlined.

The key concept behind all structured finance products is the conversion of idiosyncratic assets, real or synthetically created, into tradeable financial securities, underlying the term 'securitization'. Common structuring characteristics among securitizations typically include the process of selecting and pooling groups of assets, the subsequent separation of these assets from the rest of the originator's business, and their transfer to a stand-alone legal vehicle, with the purpose of issuing financial securities, either directly backed by these assets or contractually linked to their risk profile (hence the term 'asset-backed securities').

The expansion of credit derivatives in recent years has resulted in the rapid growth of the market for credit risk and in a division between 'synthetic' and 'true sale' transactions among securitizations.[1] On one hand, in the long-established, mainstream securitizations referred to as 'true sale', the *actual* transfer of securitized assets represents a key part of the transaction.[2] On the other hand, synthetic deals typically involve either derivatives of existing assets, or financial contracts on purpose-defined external signals (credit events). Moreover, in transactions referred to as 'funded', secondary assets are posted as collateral against the contractual obligations, whereas in transactions referred to as 'unfunded' no collateral is posted against the liabilities of the sellers of protection.

Recently, issuance of synthetic securitizations has concentrated among collateralized debt obligations (repackaged pools of loans) where they are estimated to constitute between 50 and 90 per cent of the total volume. In other asset classes, such as mortgage-backed securities and other asset-backed securities, synthetic securitizations represent less than 5–15 per cent of the total issuance.[3] Synthetic securitizations are generally expected to expand further into other asset classes, similarly to the earlier development of the 'true sale' transactions that have grown to include a wide selection of assets: from third-party liabilities to entire stand-alone businesses.

From the corporate finance theory perspective, securitizations can be seen as approximations of 'complete' contracts in the spirit of the incomplete contract theory, in contrast to standard financing contracts, which are often described as inherently 'incomplete' (Hart 1988). This is because in most securitizations the use of securitized assets is not open to managerial discretion, but governed by a detailed legal contract, signed up front, and based on extensive information disclosure about securitized assets.[4] This contract, specifying in detail how the securitized assets can be utilized and how the cash flows originating from those assets should be allocated (also known as the 'cash waterfall'), is implemented by independent, external agents (payments, custody, etc.) and by the trustee. The trustee is the legal owner of the assets, who acts within the scope of his duties to secure the rights of the beneficial owners, i.e. creditors. A schematic representation of a generic securitization structure is shown in Figure 22.1.

The role of the trustee is that of a watchdog rather than a decision maker, who also aims to overcome the coordination problem among multiple creditors. Hence, in reality, there is little scope for an agency problem between creditors and the trustee. From this perspective, therefore, securitizations might be seen as very

---

[1] This chapter is largely devoted to traditional securitizations and does not explicitly discuss the credit derivatives market beyond some examples from collateralized debt obligations and synthetic securitizations.

[2] For an introduction to the legal background on structured finance see Schwarcz 2003; see e.g. Deacon 2004 for the market perspective.

[3] There is no industry-wide standard for measuring CDO issuance; estimates are available from leading arrangers and vary significantly depending on the source.

[4] There exist some exceptions to this general rule such as e.g. managed loan portfolios among CDO issues.

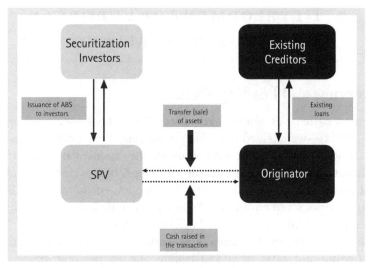

Fig. 22.1. Generic securitization structure

attractive to creditors, if the nature of the assets permits the use of the securitization technology.

Following on the market development of securitizations, professional as well as academic literature has emerged to describe this phenomenon and to explore new horizons for further financial innovation. In general, this literature has largely concentrated on the description of the securitization process, with its many nuances, as well as on the practical, legal, and market-specific considerations. It has also accounted for the securitization markets' development over time. At the same time, professional research in security design as a part of structured finance has largely concentrated on the issue of pricing of asset-backed securities and on the development of continuous- and discrete-time pricing models necessary to value correctly various structures of increasing complexity.

The academic literature on securitizations has explored the rationale for 'pooling' and 'tranching' of securities—two fundamental parts of the structuring process— and their potential to create value in the presence of asymmetric information and market incompleteness.[5] Less attention has been paid to the rationale behind securitizations from the originator's perspective. In this context, potential tax and liquidity benefits, as well as opportunities for regulatory arbitrage, have been pointed at as the key drivers in earlier research. More recent studies have explored the question about the rationale behind structured finance in greater depth and explored issues such as the effects of securitizations on originators, their access to funding, and their relationships with creditors more generally.[6]

---

[5] See for example DeMarzo 2005.
[6] For a review of different theories see for example Iacobucci and Winter 2005.

2. DEVELOPMENT OF EUROPEAN
SECURITIZATION MARKETS

2.1. Overview and Leading Trends

The first, most basic types of asset-backed securities (ABSs)—the mortgage-backed securities (MBSs)—were issued over thirty years ago in the United States, but it is over the last twenty years that we have witnessed the exponential growth of ABSs in the United States and, over the last decade, in Europe. In 1999, the total outstanding volume of the so-called 'agency securities' in the USA, encompassing MBSs issued by government-sponsored entities (GSEs) such as Fannie Mae and Freddie Mac, as well as non-agency MBSs, has surpassed that of the US Treasury securities. By 2005, a considerable gap had opened between these markets with the combined outstanding volume of MBSs and ABSs of US$7.4 trillion—i.e. 80 per cent greater than the Treasuries and over 50 per cent greater than corporate bonds.[7] This prompted some market participants to view the agency MBSs as a potential key benchmark for fixed income securities alongside or even in lieu of the US Treasuries.[8]

European securitization markets have developed much later than the US market with first MBSs issued in the UK in 1987 (Davidson et al. 2003). Nevertheless, subsequent development has been characterized by rapid growth, especially between 1998 and 2003, featuring 50 per cent average annual growth rate over this period. European markets have been growing faster than the US markets, reaching €250 billion in 2004 and US$290 billion over the twelve months until July 2005, according to one estimate.[9] By the third quarter of 2006, total European securitization issuance had reached the estimated record high of €283 billion with the expected total for the year to reach €350–400 billion, as shown in Figure 22.2.

To put this recent growth in perspective, it is worth noting that the total amount of asset-backed securities issued in the first quarter of 2005 in Europe was close to that for the entire year 2000. Still, the combined volume of the outstanding European MBSs and ABSs represents just 16 per cent of the US ABS market alone (excluding all agency securities) and under 4 per cent of the combined MBSs and ABSs volume. This supports the conclusion that European securitization markets can be seen as relatively underdeveloped vis-à-vis the USA.[10]

The growth trend in European structured finance slowed down or even reversed in 2004 with the estimates of the annual growth in the total issuance ranging from

---

[7] In terms of the corporate debt alone, by the end of the first quarter of 2005, ABSs (excluding MBSs) represented just fewer than 40% of the corporate bond market in the USA according to the Bond Markets Association.

[8] Market observers have pointed at GSEs' own use of the term 'benchmark' with respect to some of their securities.

[9] Total issuance over twelve months until 22 July 2005 according to JP Morgan Global Structured Finance Research.

[10] See Cuchra and Jenkinson 2005.

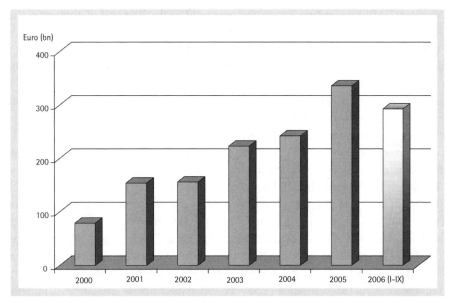

Fig. 22.2. European securitization issuance, January 2000–September 2006

Source: See footnote 11

12 to −2 per cent, according to different sources.[11] However, European securitization markets managed to revert back to their double digit growth in 2005 and 2006. For example, the total volume in the third quarter of 2006 was nearly three times greater than in the third quarter of 2005.[12] In contrast, issuance of MBSs in the USA increased by 40 per cent in the second quarter of 2005 after a peak in 2003 and a 40 per cent drop in 2004 (Bond Market Association 2005).

In the long term, European issuance might be expected to increase again given the size of the balance sheets of some European banks and corporates. However, repeated and consistent use of securitizations as one of the mainstream funding mechanisms, akin to that in the USA, is probably necessary for substantial future development. In this context, both the European Commission and the European Investment Bank have undertaken some steps to investigate the possibility of stimulating growth of securitization markets. While it is difficult to estimate how long it might take European markets to reach the US volume of issuance, Cuchra and Jenkinson (2005) estimate the current gap at thirteen years on the basis of the nature of structuring in securitization issues.[13]

However, to underline the European market's significant growth potential as well as its somewhat erratic development, the issuance of commercial mortgage-backed

---

[11] Sources: European Securitization Forum: www.europeansecuritization.com; Commerzbank Corporates & Markets 2005. Differences between sources are likely to be due to different classification methods of some secured loan transactions.

[12] FT after McGraw Hill.   [13] See Cuchra and Jenkinson 2005.

securities (CMBS) in Europe has grown sevenfold in the first half of 2005 versus the first half of 2004 according to Moody's, a rating agency.[14]

This highlights the nature of European markets' expansion, where in contrast to recent trends in the USA, MBSs have been growing relatively faster than ABSs since 2000. For example, in the second quarter of 2003, ABSs grew by 3 per cent and MBS by 31 per cent vis-à-vis the second quarter of 2002 and by the end of 2004, MBS issuance was approximately twice as large as ABS issuance—a significant change from a lag of circa 20 per cent in 2001. This might be taken as an indication of the European market slowly converging towards the American template of MBS dominance, even though with a fundamentally different underlying product structures.

These patterns of growth could be seen as typical of a relatively young and potentially slightly unstable, but already firmly established industry, which has moved beyond the initial stage of development. The fact that European securitization markets have been characterized by a high degree of adaptation and a broad selection of different asset classes, which have not been seen in the USA before, has produced many avenues for future growth. Also, with the increasing number of investors becoming familiar with structured finance products and reductions in fees, new originators might be willing to take advantage of the growing demand for asset-backed securities as the market matures.

Nevertheless, it should also be noted that despite reportedly sharp falls in spreads, there has been no dramatic increase in the volume of ABS transactions. Somewhat counter-intuitively perhaps, this might be linked to the increased use of securitizations for funding new growth in addition to refinancing of existing debts. According to a recent survey of first-time European securitization issuers by Pricewaterhouse-Coopers, the primary objective of securitizations for corporates is simply better access to funding (Asset Securitization Report 2005).

In this context, there might be a correlation between ABS growth and the restrictions on corporate access to the unsecured bond markets. According to this view, the earlier growth of ABSs has been indicative of firms seeking alternative forms of funding to temporarily less accessible, traditional funding sources in fixed income. As investors became more cautious, securitizations have offered attractive, more secured alternatives to simple, unsecured debt products. However, when available, corporations would still prefer unsecured credit.

These observations lead towards the conclusion that there might exist a negative correlation between structured finance issuance and the overall economic climate. However, there is little explicit evidence from empirical studies to confirm this hypothesis. Moreover, the fact that European markets seem to be suffering from relative volatility in demand and supply over time might be attributed to other factors. For example, it could be at least partly driven by the fact that European ABS issues have not been dominated by repeated offerings from the same group of consistent issuers as in the case of the USA. Instead, European issues are often highly idiosyncratic with a lower average number of tranches per issue than in the USA.

---

[14]   Ibid.

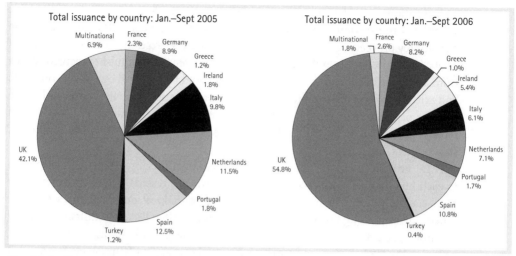

Fig. 22.3. European securitization issuance by country

2.2. National Markets and Legal Jurisdictions

European securitization issuance is rather unevenly distributed geographically with approximately half of the entire market concentrated in the UK in terms of both the origin of assets as well as that of investors. Beyond the UK, countries such as Spain, the Netherlands, Italy, and Germany stand out as other critical areas for asset origination. In terms of collateral, they represented approximately 12, 11, 10, and 9 per cent of the total volume in the first three-quarters of 2006, respectively (source: European Securitization Forum). Figure 22.3 presents the comparison of the total securitization issuance by country of collateral for the first three quarters of 2006 and the analogous period in 2005.

Since the five leading countries together represent over 90 per cent of the entire market, there remains a substantial scope for growth in other jurisdictions. However, important legal, structural, and tax differences exist between the UK and the leading followers, and other jurisdictions.[15] These differences are not limited to the unique development of the legal notion of a 'trust' and the associated separation of the concepts of beneficial and legal ownerships present in the English legal tradition, which are important for the operation of an SPV.[16] They also include other key areas such as, for example, the laws as well as the legal practice determining the 'true sale' and the 'true control' status—one area that has proved to be open to judicial interpretation on both sides of the Atlantic.

In broad terms, the 'true sale' concept refers to the ex post recognition of the legal separation of securitized assets from the parent's balance sheet, primarily in the case of a credit event or default. The concept of 'true control' mainly applies to corporate

---

[15] See for example Deacon 2004.
[16] In other jurisdictions alternative mechanisms have been set up to imitate the trust structure.

securitizations and refers to creditors' ability to operate assets following a credit event. Whether a transaction is recognized as 'true sale' is critical to the conduct of the bankruptcy proceedings and recognition of the legal separation of different groups of assets. Similarly, applicability of 'true control' provisions distinguishes securitizations from a standard debt contract where a default could be followed by the stay on assets and existing management ability to conduct reorganization, effectively preventing any transfer of control. In some jurisdictions, control might be transferred to a special receiver appointed by the court where the receiver represents the interests of different stakeholders, including creditors.

Legal provisions concerning securitized creditors differ by market and according to each jurisdiction's own securitization laws (where present). These laws often have not been fully tested in practice. At the same time, local deal structures typically reflect corresponding jurisdictions' special features, often linked to different levels of creditors' protection and creditors' ability to exercise control over assets.[17] Therefore, unlike in the USA, European securitization markets can be often seen as fragmented in legal as well as regulatory terms.

This is in contrast to the more universal investors' realm, which has resulted in a degree of structural coordination across jurisdictions as exhibited by, for instance, listings where regulatory requirements have led to the development of the Luxembourg Exchange as the default listing place. There is also some concern that the legal and regulatory differences might have formed an effective barrier to the application of the securitization technology in some European markets because of the high set-up costs of first transactions in the absence of legal precedents.

3. LEADING CHARACTERISTICS OF EUROPEAN SECURITIZATIONS

3.1. Asset and Originator Characteristics

Greater diversity of European assets is not only caused by cross-country differences, but also by the wider range of originators and continuing push for new, innovative structures aimed at exploiting specific market niches in imperfectly integrated and relatively idiosyncratic European corporate markets. In contrast with the USA, structured finance in Europe has been particularly innovative in the areas of synthetic securitizations and in the corporate sector, despite the fact that, in line with the USA experience, corporate securitizations have represented a relatively small part of the total pool of securitized assets. In this respect, Europe, and the UK in particular, have

---

[17] See for example La Porta et al. 1996.

produced entirely new, innovative types of securitizations such as whole business or inventory securitizations, or securitizations of future flows.

Growth of synthetic transactions in Europe has been stimulated by the European banking sector keen to optimize their credit exposure. In particular, synthetic transactions have proved attractive for European banks keen to manage their large loan portfolios, which have not been securitized. The banks have used this tool to reallocate risks by trading credit exposure among themselves in order to arrive at the optimal allocation of risk. Although banks have generally dominated synthetic securitizations, some evidence also points at the conclusion that the banks have been transferring their credit risk outside the banking sector, to the insurance industry in particular.

More broadly, European securitizations have been characterized by a lower number of deals per originator and, related to that, less common occurrence of very frequent, off-the-shelf securitizations by the same originators that characterize the USA market. While the latter has been dominated by a number of consistent issuers, European companies' approach to structured finance, although with some notable exceptions, has been much more sporadic. In many cases, therefore, European financial institutions have approached securitizations in a relatively more exploratory manner than their USA peers. On one hand, this could be seen as a barrier to the development of an efficient, standardized securitization market. On the other hand, it can be associated with greater innovation and more flexible adaptation of basic structures for a variety of different funding purposes. This can also be linked to a wider range of potential rationales for the use of securitizations in the first place.

A particularly striking feature of the European market in that respect is significant differentiation between similar companies in their approach to securitizations. For example, even in relatively developed securitization markets, such as the UK or France, leading banks of similar size operating in the same jurisdiction might take fundamentally different approaches to securitizations varying from non-participation to the complete embrace of the technology in a way largely similar to their USA peers. While these distinctions might indicate significant potential that awaits European securitization issuance in the future, it might also point at the lack of a single, overarching rationale behind existing transactions.

Overall, European structured finance markets differ from their USA counterparts not only because of their greater asset diversity, but also due to their lower level of structural standardization, lower degree of tranching, and a different role of the public sector—namely that of an active issuer. While these differences do not undermine the simple fact that the securitization technology and its *modus operandi* are fundamentally the same on both sides of the Atlantic, any analysis of the European structured finance markets must account for these differences.

Since it would be difficult in this short review to provide the full account of all different asset classes being securitized in Europe, we discuss further just three market segments that have been particularly characteristic of European securitizations. These segments include the largest asset class—the mortgage-backed securities, corporate securitizations—with its many structural variations unique to Europe, and the recent growth of synthetic securitizations.

3.2. European Mortgage-backed Securities

In the absence of GSE-equivalent institutions on either the continent- or the country-wide level, the European market for securities backed by pools of mortgages has developed effectively from the bottom up largely from the activity of the financial sector without any government intervention. This 'organic' type of growth might be responsible for the lack of the most basic 'pass-through' securities, which have initiated the USA securitization market. As a result, agency securities that dominate the USA market have been absent from the European conception of securitizations, replaced instead by more structured issues to which investors were exposed from the start. In that respect, Europe has been characterized not only by the lack of government coordination in creating the secondary market for residential housing loans, but also by the lack of strict standardization of issues or of the underlying collateral.

Overall, MBSs represented over 50 per cent of European securitization issuance with the total volume reaching €150.6 billion in the first nine months of 2006, up by 70 per cent from 2005.[18] Approximately 50 per cent of that total was backed by prime residential mortgage-backed securities (prime RMBSs), followed by sub-prime RMBSs—a market akin to home equity loans in the USA. The non-conforming (non-standard) issues typically represent between 10 and 16 per cent of the RMBS volume. Originators' realm in European MBSs has been traditionally dominated by a few leading issuers, including Royal Bank of Scotland, Northern Rock, and Abbey National in the UK, joined by BNP Paribas, ABN Amro, and Banco Santander from the Continent.[19]

In comparison with the USA, European MBS markets can still be seen as relatively underdeveloped. For example, the total outstanding agency MBS issuance in the USA was USA$3.5 trillion at the beginning of 2005, which represented an increase of over USA$1 trillion over the last four years, excluding circa USA$500 billion of outstanding securities backed by home equity loans and manufactured housing credits. At the same time in Europe, RMBS represent just 4 per cent of the total outstanding residential market loans—almost ten times less than in the USA. European RMBS volumes were also highly differentiated by country, ranging from 3.6 per cent for the UK, through 7–8 per cent for Spain and the Netherlands, to 10 per cent for Ireland, whereas residential debt to GDP in Europe has been historically highest

---

[18] European Securitization Forum Data Report, Autumn 2006.
[19] Based on the database of European securitization transactions compiled by JP Morgan International Securitization Research Desk, London, and the listings of structured finance transactions from *Structured Finance International*, www.ew-sfi.com.

in the Netherlands (almost 100 per cent), Denmark (*c*.90 per cent), and the UK (*c*.70 per cent).[20]

In parallel to structured RMBSs, alternative forms of mortgage-related products have emerged in several countries outside the UK, such as the so-called 'Pfandbriefe' bonds in Germany or Switzerland. Still, the UK market has dominated pan-European issuance with over 50 per cent of the total volume. In contrast to the USA, the UK RMBS market continues to be dominated by floating rate issues. In fact, even the UK 'fixed rate' issues often remain fixed only for a specific period of time, considerably shorter than maturity—typically two to five years. This reflects the key characteristics of UK mortgages. Moreover, a significant share of all UK mortgages remains non-amortizing with the interest-only securitizations still representing as much as 50 per cent of all originations (Hayre 2001; Fabozzi and Choudhry 2004). UK RMBS markets have also been characterized by their 'true sale' nature with no synthetic RMBS structures issued in the UK in contrast to e.g. France or Germany.

The UK market is generally expected to continue to represent the majority of the European total with the share of non-conforming loans, already above the USA level, likely to rise further. There is also some expectation of a rise in the number of conduits set up by banks with portfolios of different loans repackaged as bonds. It is thought that there are now about a dozen conduits in Europe, compared with as many as seventy in the USA.

Moreover, pre-payment rates on RMBSs in the UK have been historically more stable than in the USA, even though the housing turnover has remained at a similar level. Although the pre-payment differential has now persisted for a couple of decades, there are signs that it might be diminishing, albeit slowly. In the UK, the actual pre-payment rates have been historically at approximately 8 per cent CPR and rarely exceeded 11–13 per cent levels.[21] Nevertheless, this might change as markets become more competitive with a rising number of alternative financing options offered to borrowers.

The UK sub-prime RMBS have also exhibited very low loss rates, decreasing since 2001 to *c*.0.2 per cent by the year-end of 2004. In comparison, in the USA, where the average recovery rate has been approximately 60 per cent for RMBS, the average annual default rate has been 0.4 per cent and the historic loss rate 0.2 per cent. European RMBS issues have also exhibited rather stable ratings—a factor contributing to low spreads. According to Fitch, 99.6 per cent of single A-rated European RMBS issues had the same or higher rating when compared with a year before. The analogous figures for BBB-rated and B-rated issues were at 99.4 per cent and at 100 per cent, respectively.[22]

---

[20] Sources: European Securitization Forum, www.europeansecuritization.com; Commerzbank Corporates & Markets 2005; KfW Bankengruppe, Market Data 2004 (European ABS Markets).

[21] Ibid. and Fitch Ratings Research: www.fitchratings.com.

[22] Fitch Ratings Research: www.fitchratings.com.

3.3. Synthetic Securitizations

Synthetic securitizations rely on an Effective risk transfer rather than an explicit asset transfer as in the case of 'true sale' securitizations. In that respect, they more closely resemble what can be described as 'collateralized insurance policies' rather than off-balance sheet financing or sales of assets.

In a generic *synthetic* transaction, the originator buys protection for a portfolio of assets, against its exposure to a specific, carefully defined, credit event, by entering into a contract with creditors via a special purpose vehicle (SPV). If the credit event occurs, the SPV is obliged by the contract to compensate the originator (protection buyer) for its losses according to the terms of the transaction. In a synthetic securitization the assets never actually leave the originator's balance sheet, but investors synthetically 'buy' them by agreeing to assume their risk in exchange for an interest premium linked to the level risk.

The SPV issues credit securities, which are placed in the market with a selected group of protection sellers, and invests the proceeds from the issue in liquid assets to serve as collateral against the SPV's contingent liability to the originator. At maturity or at another contractual date, the SPV pays back the principal to investors by selling the remaining collateral reduced by the amount of the collateral previously used to service any claims from the originator or protection buyer. Payments from the originator supplemented by returns from the collateral investment are used to service synthetic securities.

According to one estimate, the total synthetic issuance was circa USA\$600 billion in 2004, but a large part of that represented the notional volume of all forms of credit derivatives, which have experienced a remarkable level of growth in recent years. Synthetic CDO issuance itself has been growing steadily year on year in Europe and reached the all-time record of over €200 billion globally in 2005.[23] In practice, the division between securitization and credit derivatives markets is hard to define explicitly, and the former has represented a key growth area in the financial markets over the last few years, but the analysis of the credit derivatives market is beyond the scope of this short review.

At the same time, an important part of this market has been represented by the so-called 'bespoke' issues, which are privately arranged between banks and/or other counterparties and are not always publicly disclosed, so that the market volume estimates have proved highly differentiated in the past. Pure synthetic, 'funded' securitizations represented just 6 per cent of the total securitization issuance in 2004 in Europe (7 per cent decline versus 2003) and synthetic 'unfunded' securities represented 11 per cent of the total issuance (53 per cent decline versus 2003) (Commerzbank Corporates & Markets 2005).

According to Fitch, total synthetic CDO issuance in Europe in 2004 reached almost €20 billion (Skorecki 2004). Approximately 40 per cent of that total probably has been the CDO^2 issues—portfolios of credit derivatives on credit derivatives

---

[23]   Tett 2005, quoted JP Morgan estimates.

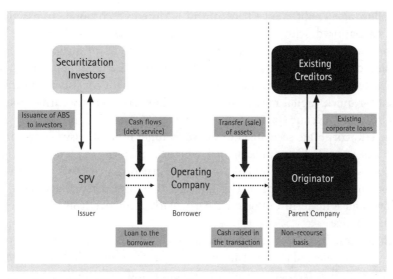

Fig. 22.4. Simplified example of a generic corporate securitization structure

portfolios, which allowed for higher gearing, and hence greater risk exposure, but also offered considerably higher spreads.

3.4. Corporate Securitizations

Despite being much smaller than either RMBS or CDO in terms of the total issuance, corporate securitizations have grown in Europe to become one of the most innovative and interesting areas of structured finance. This segment can be defined to include project finance, equity securitizations, monetizations, as well as whole business securitizations, where the latter can be seen as hybrid structures encompassing features of both: corporate loans and traditional securitizations.

The basic principles behind corporate deals are essentially the same as in the case of loan securitizations by financial institutions and consist of the separation of assets from the rest of the business, information disclosure, and the issuance of asset-backed securities backed by securitized assets. However, since the collateral often involves productive assets other than simple receivables, the contractual relationship between the originator and ring-fenced assets is often more complex than in the case of, for example, packages of loans. For example, an operating company is often created, which is separated from the originator and ring fenced. This company borrows funds from the SPV, which is the issuer of securitized notes, as shown in Figure 22.4.

The relationship between the originator and the ring-fenced assets often requires not only the 'true sale' status, but also creditors' ability to continue to operate the assets following a credit event ('true control'). Moreover, corporate transactions are far less standardised, while featuring a more diverse asset range than in the case of MBSs or consumer loans. In fact, the assets can be stocks or business inventories, properties, or even main productive assets, alongside the most popular types such as receivables or leases. A separate category in this segment consists of 'future flows', favoured for quick capital release by leveraged buyouts, where securities issued are backed by future revenue streams rather than tangible, stand-alone assets.

In the UK, corporate securitizations have featured multiple issues from the same industry, the water industry in particular, where the majority of players have adopted highly leveraged structures. Similarly, other infrastructure assets such as marine ports or airports have been securitized. This indicates that infrastructure assets with stable cash flows and long-term outlook are particularly attractive from the structure finance perspective.

Much interest has also been generated by corporate securitizations of popular brands such as Formula One, Lanson Champagne, Canary Wharf, or Madame Tussaud's, as well as transactions involving unique industries and/or assets, such as diamonds, funeral houses, hospitals, or ports. Some of these transactions have been termed 'whole-business securitizations' (WBS) because they involve ring-fencing of entire companies, akin to project finance, rather than just a selected group of assets.[24]

In contrast to standard debt contracts, in corporate securitizations the originator effectively surrenders control over securitized assets to creditors according to a detailed legal contract creating value by reducing agency costs, removing opaqueness which might lead to a pricing discount, and reducing variability of returns, while increasing leverage. Therefore, the corporate securitizations could be seen as a remedy and answer to potential agency problems with regards to perquisites, the misuse of free cash flows, or the investment in non-core, risky or NPV-negative projects by managers, which investors would not be willing to implement themselves.[25]

The corporate securitization contracts specify management of some critical aspects of the business through an exhaustive list of business and financial covenants monitored by external agents with the help of extensive information disclosure imposed on the originator of assets. For example, the rules might limit acquisitions and disposals, specify the details of the routes and/or the maintenance programme of securitized aeroplanes or trains, or define the champagne production process, In the sense of the incomplete contract theory, therefore, they represent close approximations to what could be called 'complete contracts', as described earlier, and limit creditors' exposure to business and managerial risks.

---

[24] Insolvency ring-fencing structure of the whole business securitizations in the UK is dependent on the ability of the holder of a floating charge to appoint an administrative receiver in order to block the appointment of an administrator and moratorium proceedings and the ability of that receiver to run the business (Deacon 2004).

[25] See Cuchra 2004.

3.5. Pricing of Securitization Transactions

Structured credit spreads have been gradually decreasing in Europe over the last few years, accelerating further down in 2004, but exhibiting greater volatility while growing slightly in 2005. This has reduced the gap between corporate and asset-backed paper, although the spreads on unsecured loans have also decreased. For example, European AAA-rated prime RMBS have fallen by more than 50 per cent since 2003 for AAA-rated issues. In contrast, the corporate credit spreads have gone down by less than 20 per cent over the same period.[26]

There is much reported interaction between corporate and structured finance spreads, CDOs in particular, with some evidence of mutual reinforcement of their respective trends. On one hand, explosion in European CDO markets has added liquidity and increased spanning in corporate securities, hence bringing corporate spreads down, as expected. On the other hand, falling corporate spreads have been said to exercise further downward pressure on the asset-backed market. At the same time, growing participation of synthetic issues in the overall product mix is generally associated with significant increases in volatility.

Arbitrage might be seen as the crucial driver behind investment banks' involvement in synthetic securitizations with promises of large returns, given possible levels of effective leverage awaiting sophisticated arbitrageurs. Since synthetic markets are still seen as relatively idiosyncratic and non-transparent, opportunity for arbitrage is not surprising. However, risks involved are underscored by heavy losses sustained by some funds and investment banks active in this market.

Although arrangers and market specialists have been improving their pricing models, these are still perceived as potentially inadequate given the multiplicity of related risks. As a result, segments such as synthetic portfolios of credit derivatives are seen as still relatively opaque.

One problem has been to account correctly for portfolios' correlation risk. Another problem is that many synthetic products have not been tested in practice for their structural robustness and counterparty or contractual risks. Hence, potential consequences of a systemic shock or a sharp, coordinated rise in credit events remain largely unclear. One relatively mild stress test came in May 2005 following unexpected downgrades of Ford and GM, resulting in small-scale market turmoil. Another one occurred recently following a series of defaults on sub-prime mortgages in the USA. This might be one reason why, despite significant falls, option-adjusted spreads remained above levels predicted by historical or modelled default rates. Another might be the so-called 'complexity premium', as investors and issuers alike struggle to keep up with the pace of financial innovation in the area. Nevertheless, these considerations do not seem to have affected the returns negatively in the medium to long term.

Actual prices in securitization transactions have also been investigated in the academic literature. For example, Boudoukh et al. (1997) concentrate exclusively on

---

[26]   The Bond Market Association, www.bondmarkets.com.

pricing of the GSE-sponsored, mortgage-backed securities in a multifactor interest rate environment motivated by the implicit, default-free nature of such agency MBS issues. Similarly, Goodman and Ho (2002) model the spread of mortgage-backed securities over USA Treasuries. In one of the more recent studies, Ammer and Clinton (2004) investigate the impact of changes in credit ratings on the price of ABS issues using a Merrill Lynch data set of USA securities from 1996 to 2003.

4. Seeking the Rationale Behind Securitizations

Given the great multiplicity of structures and applications, it is clear that securitizations might be driven by a plethora of rationales in addition to funding, which distinguish them from standard debt contracts. There has been some confusion as to what exactly drives securitization, whom it benefits, and why. This is partly due to complexity of transactions and the discussion being dominated by arrangers' marketing effort. For example, it is rarely explained why higher leverage characteristic of those transactions is associated with added value. This is particularly important given relatively high transaction costs and alternative funding opportunities.

In this section, we review some of the key rationales for structured finance, as suggested in the literature. In order to better link the specific solutions present in the securitization technology to different purposes they are designed to serve, we divide our analysis into two sets of issues. The first group concerns securitized assets' portfolio *design* as well as the structuring process of creating the asset-backed securities, also known as *pooling* and *tranching*. These themes have been primarily addressed by the security design literature and they include issues such as market incompleteness, market segmentation, liquidity, and asymmetric information among investors.

The second group concerns institutional and contractual features of securitization, as explained by the corporate finance theory. Here, different analyses have concentrated on the rational for ring-fencing the assets and their separation from the rest of the firm based on the non-recourse design of contracts governing securitized assets and cash flows, rules of managerial discretion, and availability of funding in the presence of various externalities.

4.1. Market Incompleteness, Segmentation, and Inelastic Demands

According to Greenspan (1998): 'securitization is, without a doubt, the major tool used by large banks to engage in arbitrage.' If structuring leading to securitizations is driven by arbitrage opportunities reflected in profitable activity by sophisticated arbitrageurs, this must be due to market incompleteness characterised by missing securities and missing markets, existing markets' segmentation, or persisting barriers to arbitrage such as informational asymmetries.

For example, under 'market incompleteness' structuring and tranching becomes a process by which new securities, not available before, are created where previously absent. From a spanning point of view, there must be incentives in such an environment to set up markets for securities for which there are no close substitutes. This implies that sophisticated structuring might be optimal from the perspective of the assets' seller in segmented or illiquid markets. Both professional and theoretical literature suggests that this primarily concerns markets targeted by junior tranches since the market for AAA-rated securities is usually assumed to be large and efficient.

Early academic studies of market incompleteness include Duffie and Rahi (1995), who combine spanning with the problems of asymmetric information among investors as well as their mutual interactions. This is appealing because these rationales are likely to coexist and reinforce each other. Among the most recent contributions to the incompleteness literature, Gaur, Seshadri, and Subrahmanyam (2003) model a market where all assets cannot be uniquely priced: attainable claims have unique prices, but prices of unattainable claims can only be bounded. In this set up, holders of unique assets can take advantage of markets' incompleteness by focusing on claims that augment market spanning. The authors show that the value of a new asset can be enhanced by 'stripping away' the maximal attainable portfolio—the senior, near-riskless tranche—for which market prices are readily available, and selling the rest (the junior tranches) at the arbitrage-free prices. These models partly explain what has been termed the 'clientele effects' of tailoring securities to investors' specific idiosyncratic needs.

Evidence from other markets and from the professional literature on structuring suggests that market segmentation might justify tranching and structuring if each market segment has limited capacity and limited arbitrage opportunities exist. This would imply that an arranger, when trying to place a larger, 'composite' issue with its idiosyncratic characteristics, might face a downward-sloping demand curve in contravention of effective arbitrage outlined by Scholes (1972). Downward-sloping demand curves are well documented in other financial markets. In effect, the market segmentation problem is related to market incompleteness insofar as the latter highlights the potential premium that might be obtained by moving a part of a large issue into a new market segment, but differs in terms of its rationale.

In the segmentation context, structuring could be value-creating by tapping greater demand in several market segments at the same time, while avoiding the problem of limited capacity in any specific segment as in the case of a composite security. This 'market segmentation hypothesis' implies that splitting larger issues into several carefully structured tranches should be particularly important for large issues, junior classes, and in difficult market conditions. Hence, first, by dividing the issue the arranger would enlarge the investors' base and avoid a detrimental effect of quantity on price. Second, structuring might offer funding opportunities where there is credit rationing.

4.2. Remedies to Informational Asymmetries

Although markets often see securitizations as effectively driven by market incompleteness and segmentation, a majority of security design literature has focused on asymmetric information. Among the more influential asymmetric information models is Boot and Thakor's (1993) noisy rational expectations model. The authors aim to explain issuers selling multiple, stratified financial claims that partition cash flows from a pool of securitized assets into tranches differentiated by their information sensitivity. Here, investors are assumed to differ in their ability to screen the collateral. The authors claim that such 'informational leveraging up' implies that an informed trader can be compensated for his information acquisition cost with a smaller divergence between the 'true value' and the equilibrium price when the information-sensitive tranche is separated from the composite security. Riddiough (1997) proposed a related model, where tranching is optimal because, by splitting assets into info-invariant and info-sensitive tranches, the capital-constrained issuer reduces liquidation costs from the lemons problem. Highly info-sensitive assets need to be tranched to avoid these costs.

Another example of this literature is a series of papers by DeMarzo (2001, 2005), who considers the problem of a financial intermediary selling assets in the presence of asymmetric information and encounters a lemons problem. The lemons problem results in illiquidity or a downward-sloping demand. The model is driven by the assumption that an informed intermediary, with some private information, can acquire assets with some common residual risk from informed and uninformed investors. DeMarzo describes an 'information destruction effect' of pooling based on the premise that an informed intermediary will not prefer to sell a single, pass-through security, but individual securities. At the same time, uninformed originators will prefer to sell pooled assets to avoid adverse selection by informed intermediaries. However, pooling and tranching might be optimal for an informed investor due to the 'risk diversification effect', which allows an informed investor to create a riskless tranche. This combination is optimal when private information is common to all assets, but information risks are idiosyncratic or asset specific; it is shown to allow for the creation of a riskless tranche, the ultimate goal with no asymmetric information.

One consideration with respect to information asymmetry models is that some ex ante information asymmetries might be eliminated by the rating process. However, since at least some junior tranches are typically unrated, the credit-rating agencies might actually exaggerate the information asymmetry between junior and senior tranches. Complexity of securitizations means technology might often exaggerate informational asymmetry overall. As an alternative, Allen and Gale (1991) focus on short sale restrictions, which might result in situations where two portfolios of securities paying the same total amount may sell for different prices—the difference becomes the source of value in securitizations akin to market incompleteness. Authors assert that issuers do not attempt to identify unspanned risks and cater directly to the implied needs for insurance, but they merely issue the package of securities fetching the highest announced market value net of issuing costs: 'One is breaking the point into pieces and selling the pieces to the clientele that values it most. It is this ability to increase the value of the firm that provides the incentive to innovate and allows the cost of innovation to be covered' (Allen and Gale 1991).

4.3. Limiting Managerial Discretion, Enhancing Control over Cash Flows, and Disclosure

Several theoretical models attempt to explain the application of securitization technology by looking at the relationship of securitized assets to the originator, their governance structure, and the relationship between creditors and managers. Among the most recent studies are those that have focused on securitization as a solution to the agency problem (divergent interests of managers and stakeholders—creditors and owners), as suggested by Cuchra (2004).

Cuchra (2004a) shows that financial contracts based on the degree of assets' separation (ring-fencing) and limits on managerial discretion (via contracts governing assets and cash flows waterfall administered by trustees instead of managers) can remedy agency costs of free cash flows. These costs, which cannot be addressed by the standard debt contracts, make securitizations optimal for low-return, NPV-positive assets that might not otherwise be financed. According to Cuchra (2004a), securitizations are optimal in this framework, providing that costs of eliminating active management and severing cross-subsidization linkages between different parts of the firm are not too high. Implicitly, in this framework issuers obtain more financing (higher leverage at the same or lower cost) by giving creditors control over cash flows, limiting opaqueness, and tying up managers' hands.

There is also some debate regarding the rationale behind securitizations among legal scholars. For example, the analysis by LoPucki (1996) suggests that securitizations act as 'judgement-proofing' devices, ultimately designed to 'kill liability' vis-à-vis e.g. tort claimants and involuntary creditors. In economic terms, this could be translated as a method for asset expropriation away from creditors. Stulz and Johnson (1985), among others, suggest that expropriation might be the rationale behind securitizations in cases where managers invest proceeds in NPV-negative projects.

More generally, Lang, Poulsen, and Stulz (1995) argue that sales of assets might allow managers to engage in non-value-maximizing projects. Various scholars have also suggested that securitizations might be designed to reduce the costs of bankruptcy.

This point has been made early by e.g. Frost (1997). More recently, this argument has been explored further by Skarabot (2001) and Gorton (2005).

Another possible rationale for securitizations suggested by Iacobucci and Winter (2005) is the avoidance of the lemons discount with the help of external financing based on full information disclosure ensured by the SPV structure as well as the 'signalling benefit'. The latter is essentially based on the same argument as the above under the assumption that high-quality firms are more willing to disclose information about their assets and securitized assets are representative of the firm as a whole. Essentially, managers engage in reducing asymmetry of information where it is possible and beneficial to them: i.e. for high-quality assets, which can be made fully transparent (such as receivables).

Finally, Calomiris and Mason (2004) as well as Ambrose et al. (2003), among others, discuss securitizations as means of regulatory arbitrage, especially with respect to capital requirements for banks. These theories explain how banks might benefit more from securitizations than other financial intermediaries might due to minimum capital requirements. This behaviour has been well observed in practice, although Basel II (the second of the Basel Accords) might reduce incentives behind such use of technology.

Securitizations have also been linked to Myers' (1977) underinvestment problem insofar as firms in a weak financial position or facing the debt overhang problem might engage in securitizations to raise financing for new projects, which could not otherwise be funded. Berkovitch and Kim (1990), Stultz and Johnson (1985), as well as James (1988), all show that any secured debt can be used to address the underinvestment problem. These theories imply that highly indebted firms could benefit from securitization, providing investors are confident that new projects will be NPV positive.

5. CONCLUSIONS

Securitizations are now at the frontier of contemporary finance and their better understanding and further development can be seen as one of the most critical determinants of future innovation and value creation by the financial industry worldwide. This is particularly clear from the increasing sophistication of securitization contracts and the continuously widening range of assets being securitized. Areas that require particular attention globally include improvements in pricing models to facilitate new product development and to eliminate opaqueness, particularly in synthetics, assessments of costs and benefits of securitizations from the issuer's perspective, and continuous investors' engagement. In the European context, elimination of legal and regulatory risks would greatly benefit securitizations, reducing transaction costs, improving efficiency, and encouraging standardization.

References

ALLEN, F., and GALE, D. (1988), 'Optimal security design', *Review of Financial Studies*, 1(3), Autumn 229–63.

_____ _____ (1991), 'Arbitrage, short sales, and financial innovation', *Econometrica*, 59(4), 1041–68.

AMBROSE, B., LaCOUR-LITTLE, M., and SANDERS, A. (2003), 'Does regulatory capital arbitrage or asymmetric information drive securitization?', working paper.

AMMER, J., and CLINTON, N. (2004), 'Good news is no news the impact of credit rating changes on the pricing of asset-backed securities', International Finance Discussion Papers 809, New York: Federal Reserve Board.

ASSET SECURITIZATION REPORT (2005), *Thomson Media*, 20 June.

BERKOVITCH, E., and KIM, H. (1990), 'Financial contracting and leverage induced over- and under-investment incentives, *Journal of Finance*, 45, Papers and Proceedings, Forty-Ninth Annual Meeting, American Finance Association, Atlanta, Ga., 28–30 December, 1989 (July 1990), 765–94.

BOND MARKET ASSOCIATION (2005), *Research Quarterly*, May, www.bondmarkets.com.

BOOT, A., and THAKOR, A. (1993), 'Security design', *Journal of Finance*, 48, 1349–78.

BOUDOUKH, J., RICHARDSON, M., STANTON, R., and WHITELAW, R. (1997), 'Pricing mortgage-backed securities in a multifactor interest rate environment: a multivariate density estimation approach', *Review of Financial Studies*, 10(2), 405–46.

CALOMIRIS, C., and MASON, J. (2004), 'Credit card securitization and regulatory arbitrage', *Journal of Financial Services Research*, 26, 5–28.

COMMERZBANK CORPORATES & MARKETS (2005), 'Structured finance (pan European)', *Facts & Figures 2004: The Way It Was*, 11 February.

CUCHRA, M. F. (2004a), 'Financial contracting at the boundary of a firm', mimeo.

_____ (2004b), 'Explaining launch spreads on structured bonds', Oxford University Department of Economics Series, Ref. 230.

_____ and JENKINSON, T. (2005), 'Why are securitization issues tranched?', EFA 2005 Moscow Meetings Paper.

DAVIDSON, A., SANDERS, A. WOLFF, L., and CHING, A. (2003), *Securitization: Structuring and Investment Analysis*, New York: John Wiley & Sons, Inc.

DEACON, J. (2004), *Global Securitization and CDOs*, New York: John Wiley & Sons, Ltd.

DEMARZO, P. (2001), 'The pooling and tranching of securities: a model of informed intermediation', working paper.

_____ (2005), 'The pooling and tranching of securities: a model of informed intermediation', *Review of Financial Studies*, 18, 1–36.

DUFFIE, D., and RAHI, R. (1995), 'Financial innovation and security design', *Journal of Economic Theory*, 65, 1–42.

FABOZZI, F. (ed.) (2001), *The Handbook of Mortgage-Backed Securities*, New York: McGraw-Hill Education.

_____ and CHOUDHRY, M. (eds.) (2004), *The Handbook of European Structured Finance Products*, New York: John Wiley & Sons, Inc.

FROST, C. W. (1997), 'Asset securitization and corporate risk allocation', *Tulane Law Review*, 72, 72–152.

GAUR, V., SESHADRI, S., and SUBRAHMANYAM, M. (2003), 'Market incompleteness and super value additivity: implications for securitization', EFA 2004 Meetings Paper no. 2714.

GOODMAN, L., and Ho, J. (1997), 'Modelling the mortgage-treasury spread', *Journal of Fixed Income*, Euromoney.

Gorton, G., and Souleles, N. (2005), 'Special purpose vehicles and securitization', working paper.

Greenspan, A. (1998), 'The role of capital in optimal banking supervision and regulation', *Federal Reserve Bank of New York Policy Review*, 4, 163–8.

Hart, O. (1988), 'Incomplete contracts and the theory of the firm', *Journal of Law, Economics and Organisation*, 4(1), 119–39.

Hayre, L. (ed.) (2001), *Salomon Smith Barney Guide to Mortgage-Backed and Asset-Backed Securities*, New York: John Wiley & Sons, Inc.

Higgins, E., and Mason, J. (2004), 'What is the value of recourse to asset-backed securities? A clinical study of credit card banks', *Journal of Banking and Finance*, 28, 875–99.

Hu, J. and Cantor, R. (2003), 'Structured finance rating transactions 1983–2002: comparisons with corporate ratings and across sectors', Moody's Investors Service, New York.

Iacobucci, E., and Winter, R. (2005), 'Asset securitization and asymmetric information', *Journal of Legal Studies*, 34, 161–206.

James, C. (1988), 'Loan sales and standby letters of credit', *Journal of Monetary Economics*, 22, 395–422.

La Porta, R., López-de-Silanes, Shleifer, A., and Vishny, R. (1996), 'Law and finance', National Bureau of Economic Research Working Paper 5661.

Lang, L., Poulsen, A., and Stulz, R. (1995), 'Asset sales, firm performance, and the agency costs of managerial discretion', *Journal of Financial Economics*, 37, 3–37.

LoPucki, L. M. (1996), 'The death of liability', *Yale Law Journal*, 106.

Myers, S. (1977), 'Determinants of corporate borrowing', *Journal of Financial Economics*, 5, 147–75.

Oldfield, G. (2000), 'Making markets for structured mortgage derivatives', *Journal of Financial Economics*, 57, 445–71.

Riddiough, T. (1997), 'Optimal design and governance of asset-backed securities', *Journal of Financial Intermediation*, 6, 121–52.

Scholes, M. S. (1972), 'The market for securities: substitution versus price pressure and the effects of information on share prices', *Journal of Business*, 45, 179–211.

Schwarcz, S. (1993), 'The alchemy of asset securitization', *Stanford Journal of Law, Business and Finance*, 1, 133–54.

——— (2003), *Structured Finance*, 3rd edn., New York: Practicing Law Institute.

Skarabot, J. (2001), 'Asset securitization and optimal asset structure of the firm', mimeo.

Skorecki, A. (2004), 'CDO2 meets search for yield', *Financial Times*, 20 December.

Stulz, R. M., and Johnson, H. (1985), 'An analysis of secured debt', *Journal of Financial Economics*, 14, 501–21.

Tett, G. (2005), 'Global CDO issuance sees sharp upturn', *Financial Times*, 4 August.

Thomas, H. (2001), 'Effects of asset securitization on seller claimants', *Journal of Financial Intermediation*, 10, 306–30.

CHAPTER 23

LOCATION OF AND COMPETITION BETWEEN FINANCIAL CENTRES

THOMAS P. GEHRIG

1. INTRODUCTION

BY removing traditional borders and impediments to competition, the process of financial integration tends to open up possibilities of restructuring within the global financial system. Hence, integration triggers restructuring activities within industries, across traditional industry border lines, and especially also across national borders. This immediately opens up the question about the new geographical structure of financial activity in the integrated economic area. Will geography become irrelevant as regulatory and political frictions are eliminated, or will financial activity be increasingly concentrated on a few ever more dominating financial centres? Where will those centres be located and who ultimately exerts political control over these (remaining) financial centres? Will they be able to exert market power, and how will they be

Without implicating them I am grateful for discussions with and comments from Thierry Foucault, Philipp Hartmann, Hans-Helmut Kotz, and Adrian Tschoegl. Mareille Drechsler provided able research assistance.

disciplined by competition from other centres? Will they coordinate their activities by friendly cooperation agreements, or will they effectively bid for dominant market positions? How do institutional frameworks affect the ability of national financial centres to compete? These issues are politically charged because they affect control over investment activities and growth opportunities. Moreover, they have immediate consequences for financial sector employment.[1]

Of course, any answer has to explain the nature of a financial centre. What is a financial centre, and will financial centres be viable in an integrated market? To the extent that market integration generates economic conditions closer to an ideal textbook-like economic world, the question arises of why financial activity will cluster at all. Indeed, in a frictionless world the location of financial activity is a matter of irrelevance. The 'death of geography' (O'Brien 1992) can be viewed as the final stage of a process converging towards such a frictionless benchmark. The mere existence of financial centres and the viability of the dominant centres, however, seem to prove the contrary: geography (still) matters. The existence of financial centres is evidence for the relevance of frictions in real-world markets.

Thus, for example, Kindleberger (1974) clearly associates financial centres as geographical agglomerations of banks, financial intermediaries, and security dealers when he defines financial centres in terms of the functions they perform:

financial centres are needed not only to balance through time the savings and investments of individual entrepreneurs and to transfer financial capital from savers to investors, but also to effect payments and to transfer savings between places. Banking and financial centres perform a medium of exchange function and an inter-spatial store-of-value function ... [T]he specialized functions of international payments and foreign lending or borrowing are typically best performed at one central place that is also (in most instances) the specialized centre for domestic interregional payments ... Banks, brokers, security dealers, and the like establish branches in such centres.

(Kindleberger 1974: 6, 57)

Implicitly, Kindleberger rules out virtual centres based on computer networks performing similar functions. Hence, in his mind, and in most of the recent literature, financial centres are viewed 'as geographical locations with agglomerations of branches or subsidiaries of banks and other financial intermediaries' (Gehrig 2000).

Based on Kindleberger one might expect that the proximity to central banks would be an important factor for the development of financial sectors.[2] Thus, the creation of the European Central Bank should have been a major stimulus for the development of Frankfurt as a financial centre. However, as we will see below, the relative role of Frankfurt as an international financial centre has diminished since the 1990s. On the other hand, the role of Hong Kong and Shanghai has increased since the 1990s despite

---

[1] Tschoegl 1989 reports that financial centres tend to benefit disproportionately in terms of employment and tax revenues.

[2] In fact, also banking payment services are increasingly outsourced to cost-efficient locations or countries.

the fact that neither financial centre hosts a central bank. This observation is in line with Gehrig's (2000) classification of financial activities, who argues that 'trade in informationally sensitive securities is likely to be geographically concentrated at those locations where information about those securities is aggregated and communicated' and that 'trade in standardized securities is more likely to be footloose, reacting more sensitively to (regulatory) cost differentials' (p. 417). Since payment activities are typically not informationally complex, the proximity of central banks per se is not necessarily an agglomerative force, or a prerequisite for financial centres. According to Gehrig (2000), in (truly) integrated markets, geography matters mainly for information-sensitive activities, such as trading of securities and bank lending. These are the activities that tend to cluster in financial centres as opposed to the footloose activities of trading standard products.

This chapter is organized as follows. Section 2 sketches the most pertinent recent developments in banking centres and securities markets. Section 3 discusses the most relevant centripetal and centrifugal forces that affect the structure of financial centres. Section 4 discusses the regulatory framework and the role of accounting standards in particular. Competition between financial centres is discussed in Section 5. Section 6 concludes with comments from a European perspective.

2. THE CHANGING STRUCTURE OF INTERNATIONAL FINANCIAL CENTRES

There is widespread consensus about the existence of a hierarchy of financial centres. For example, Reed (1981) explicitly ranks eighty financial centres into five groups according to their economic importance for banking and financial services. In his study in 1980 London appeared as the top centre ahead of New York and Tokyo who were jointly grouped in level two. Amsterdam, Chicago, Frankfurt, Hamburg, Hong Kong, Paris, San Francisco, and Zurich were associated with level three, while another thirty centres were associated with level 4 and the remaining thirty-nine centres with level 5. Clearly, today one would expect that the Asian centres of Beijing, Kuala Lumpur, Shanghai, Seoul, Taipeh, and Singapore should move to higher-category centres as well.[3]

Currently, during the period of globalization, the process of restructuring among the top financial centres attracts primary attention. The current focus on competition between financial centres also reflects the interest in how financial integration affects the domestic financial systems as a whole. A major concern is the viability of domestic financial centres in a global financial system. Prior to globalization the focus of research was directed on regional or domestic development of financial centres,

---

[3] For example, Zhao 2003 documents the tremendous growth of the Chinese financial centres.

placing more attention on the role of lower-level financial centres. At that time interest focused on the hierarchical structure between financial centres on a regional level and the viability of regional centres (e.g. Reed, 1981; Smith 1991; Gehrke and Rasch 1993). In contrast, nowadays much of the discussion on competition between financial centres concentrates on the strategies of the dominant national centres, which tend to be higher level centres.

Reed (1981) finds the group rankings of financial centres are strongly correlated with the number of bank branches. We will therefore start with tracing the evolution of branching patterns of the largest multinational banks, before we discuss recent developments on securities markets. We will be particularly interested in the developments of the European centres.

2.1. Bank Branching

In a series of papers Choi, Ischoegl, and Yu (1986) and Choi, Park, and Tschoegl 1996, 2002) analyse the intertemporal branching pattern of the 300 largest multinational banks for the years 1970, 1980, 1990, and 2000. They document the banks' location choices for the following fourteen high-level financial centres: London, New York City, Tokyo, Amsterdam, Brussels, Frankfurt–Hamburg, Hong Kong, Los-Angeles–San Francisco, Panama City, Paris, Rome–Milan, Singapore, Toronto–Montreal, and Zurich–Geneva.

Summarizing their work, Table 23.1 provides a matrix (x_{ij}) with x_{ij} denoting the number of banks headquartered in centre i that maintain branches in centre j. When $x_{ij} > 0$ a one-way link exists from centre i to centre j reflecting some form of influence from centre i on centre j. When additionally $x_{ji} > 0$ a two-way link exists between centres i and j suggesting mutual flows of influence. The sum $x_{.j} = \sum_i x_{ij}$ measures the attractiveness of centre j in terms of number of branches established in j. The links can be used to measure the degree of interconnectedness among the centres.

Interestingly, Table 23.1 reveals a steady build-up of an international presence of banks in virtually all fourteen international centres 1970–90. However, the 1990s witness consolidation among the banks in the sample and a reduction in the size of their average branching networks. Even the absolute number of foreign bank branches or subsidiaries started to decline in the 1990s, not only in the dominant centres of London, New York, and Tokyo. The European centres are affected more by the (relative) decline in banking presence than the emerging Asian centres, especially since emerging centres such as Beijing, Kuala Lumpur, Seoul, Shanghai, and Taipeh are not covered in their analysis. In fact, and probably most surprisingly, the attractiveness of Frankfurt is declining despite the fact that the European Central Bank started operations in Frankfurt during that period. After starting with thirteen international branches in 1970, Frankfurt moved to fifty-four international branches in 1980 and 1990 before falling back to thirty in 2000. In relative positions Frankfurt thus moved from rank 11 in 1970 to 6 in 1980 and 6 in 1990 before falling back to 7 in 2000.

Table 23.1. Head offices of major banks and their representations in other centres, 1970, 1980, 1990, and 2000

	LO	NY	TO	HK	SI	FH	PA	ZG	MR	LS	TM	BR	AM	PN	Sum
							To								
From:															
LO	14	9	4	1	1	4	8	1	2	2	0	2	7	0	55
	8	8	8	7	4	5	6	3	2	4	4	4	3	1	67
	9	4	5	4	3	2	5	4	2	1	3	3	3	0	48
	7	4	4	4	3	3	2	3	2	1	2	2	3	2	42
NY	10	13	8	6	3	7	8	3	5	0	1	4	5	2	75
	9	9	8	8	9	8	8	5	7	7	4	4	3	4	94
	8	8	8	8	8	7	6	8	7	0	6	3	3	2	82
	2	4	3	3	3	3	3	2	3	2	2	3	2	1	36
TO	8	8	17	2	2	2	2	1	1	6	1	1	1	0	52
	14	15	23	8	11	10	7	4	1	11	6	3	2	2	117
	17	18	20	14	14	13	10	6	7	13	9	7	3	5	158
	9	12	14	9	10	2	1	5	1	3	3	3	2	1	75
HK	1	1	1	1	1	1	1	0	0	1	0	0	0	0	8
	1	1	1	1	1	1	1	1	0	1	1	0	1	0	11
	1	1	1	1	1	1	0	0	0	0	0	0	0	1	7
	2	1	0	4	1	0	0	0	0	1	0	0	0	0	9
SI	0	0	0	1	1	0	0	0	0	0	0	0	0	0	2
	1	1	1	1	1	0	0	0	0	0	0	0	0	0	5
	3	3	3	3	3	0	0	0	0	3	0	0	0	0	18
	3	1	4	5	5	0	0	0	0	3	0	1	0	0	22
FH	3	2	1	0	1	12	1	0	0	0	0	0	0	0	20
	3	6	4	5	3	12	2	0	1	1	2	1	0	1	42
	8	6	5	5	5	12	3	5	2	5	3	2	2	0	63
	5	3	3	5	3	9	3	6	3	3	2	3	2	1	51
PA	5	3	3	1	1	3	7	1	4	1	0	3	4	1	37
	11	13	9	9	6	8	14	2	8	4	2	3	5	3	97
	8	8	7	7	7	5	12	6	8	4	4	5	2	3	86
	4	5	4	4	5	5	7	4	4	3	3	4	3	2	57
ZG	1	1	1	1	1	0	1	3	0	1	1	0	1	0	12
	3	3	3	3	2	0	2	5	0	3	2	0	1	0	27
	2	3	3	3	2	0	1	4	1	2	2	0	1	1	25
	2	2	2	3	3	2	3	5	2	2	2	0	1	1	30
MR	4	5	0	0	1	5	4	2	12	1	1	3	0	0	38
	7	7	5	3	4	6	4	0	10	4	3	4	0	0	57
	7	7	4	7	3	7	5	2	11	4	3	4	2	0	66
	4	4	2	2	3	3	2	0	5	2	0	3	1	0	31
LS	5	4	5	5	1	2	1	1	1	8	0	2	1	1	37
	4	4	4	4	4	4	3	1	2	4	2	1	1	1	39
	3	2	3	3	3	2	2	2	1	4	1	1	1	1	29
	1	1	0	0	0	0	0	0	0	2	0	0	0	0	4
TM	5	5	4	4	0	2	2	1	1	4	7	2	1	0	38
	5	5	5	5	4	4	4	1	2	5	5	1	1	2	49

(*Cont.*)

Table 23.1. (Continued)

	LO	NY	TO	HK	SI	FH	PA	ZG	MR	LS	TM	BR	AM	PN	Sum
From:															
	7	6	6	5	6	4	4	3	2	4	7	0	1	1	56
	6	6	4	5	6	0	1	2	1	3	6	0	0	1	41
BR	0	1	0	0	0	1	0	0	0	0	0	3	0	0	5
	3	3	3	2	3	1	1	2	2	0	0	7	0	0	27
	4	4	3	3	1	0	1	2	2	1	0	6	0	0	27
	2	4	1	2	3	1	3	2	3	1	0	4	4	0	30
AM	2	2	1	2	0	0	0	0	0	1	0	0	3	0	11
	2	3	2	2	2	0	0	0	1	2	0	1	4	1	20
	2	2	2	2	2	1	2	2	2	1	1	2	2	1	24
	2	2	2	2	2	2	2	2	2	1	2	2	3	1	27
PN	0	0	0	0	0	0	0	0	0	0	0	0	0	1	1
	0	1	0	0	0	0	0	0	0	0	0	0	0	1	2
	0	1	0	0	0	0	0	0	0	0	0	0	0	1	2
	0	1	0	0	0	0	0	0	0	0	0	0	0	1	2
Sum	58	54	35	39	45	13	24	25	13	23	20	5	26	11	391
	72	80	52	59	76	54	58	46	24	21	29	16	36	31	654
	79	73	70	65	58	54	51	46	45	42	39	33	20	16	691
	49	50	43	48	47	30	27	31	26	27	22	25	21	11	457
Rank	1	2	5	4	3	11	8	7	11	9	10	14	6	13	
	3	1	7	4	2	6	5	8	12	13	11	14	9	10	
	1	2	3	4	5	6	7	8	9	10	11	12	13	14	
	2	1	5	3	4	7	8	6	10	8	12	11	13	14	

Source: Choi, Park, and Tschoegl 2002.

Possibly this decline in terms of relative attractiveness also mirrors a decline of the relative importance of European capital markets. Comparing the number of branches in 2000 relative to the number of branches in 1990, Frankfurt with a ratio of 56 per cent (see Table 23.1) compares well with Paris at 53 per cent and Milan at 51 per cent. London with 62 per cent, but also Tokyo with 61 per cent, perform only marginally better.

While the decline of the absolute international banking presence is particularly strong in the case of Frankfurt, this observation holds true for all fourteen centres analysed in the sample. Also New York moved from 54 (1970) to 80 (1980), 73 (1990), and 50 (2000) international branches, while London attracted 58 in 1970, 72 in 1980, 79 in 1990 and 49 in 2000. With ranks 3 and 4 Hong Kong and Singapore improved in relative attractiveness while Tokyo lost its number 3 rank in 1990, to move down to number 5 in 2000. Interestingly, Zurich–Geneva moved up from rank 8 in 1990 to rank 6 in 2000 ahead of Frankfurt–Hamburg. This seems to suggest that the institutional framework may be more important for the relative attractiveness of financial centres than central bank proximity.

Table 23.2. The ranking and centrality of the fourteen centres

Centres	1970		1980		1990		2000	
	Rank	Cent.	Rank	Cent.	Rank	Cent.	Rank	Cent.
New York	2	.85	1	1.00	2	1.00	1	1.00
London	1	.77	3	.92	1	.92	2	.92
Hong Kong	8	.69	5	.92	4	.92	3	.92
Singapore	11	.54	6	.92	5	.92	4	.85
Tokyo	3	.69	2	.92	3	.92	5	.85
Zurich/Geneva	11	.54	12	.62	8	.77	6	.62
Frankfurt/Hamburg	4	.69	4	.69	6	.69	7	.62
Paris	3	.69	7	.77	7	.77	8	.69
Los Angeles/San Francisco	7	.69	8	.77	10	.77	8	.92
Milan/Rome	6	.54	9	.69	9	.77	10	.69
Brussels	10	.54	11	.69	12	.62	11	.62
Toronto/Montreal	13	.31	10	.69	11	.69	12	.54
Amsterdam	9	.54	13	.62	13	.69	13	.62
Panama	14	.23	14	.62	14	.62	14	.62

Notes: Rank = sum of columns in Table 23.1; Centrality = proportion of banks from other centres present in the given centre.
Source: Choi, Park, and Tschoegl 2002.

Also in terms of centrality (Table 23.2) Frankfurt lost from rank 4 in 1970 (index value 0.69) to rank 6 in 1990 and rank 7 in 2000 (index value 0.62).[4] In terms of the centrality measure London maintains a value of 0.92 since 1980, which keeps it among the top three centres. Hong Kong and Singapore moved up to values of 0.92 already in the 1990s. Interestingly, the Los Angeles–San Francisco centre has moved up steadily from a degree of interconnectedness of 0.69 in 1970 to 0.92 in 2000, suggesting that California has developed into an independent economic zone in its own right. All the centres discussed above seem to be more attractive for branching activities to banks domiciled in any of the other centres than Frankfurt.

While the degree of interconnectedness (Table 23.3) increased substantially in the 1970s and slightly in the 1980s, the 1990s witnessed a slight decline. Choi, Park, and Tschoegl (2002) hypothesize that the surviving largest banks domiciled in the largest financial centres may have increased their international presence, while smaller banks typically domiciled in smaller centres have rationalized their international presence and withdrawn from remote centres.

Overall these results suggest that New York and London clearly maintained their dominant positions among multinational banks. However, the Asian financial centres as well as California seem to have moved up to second tier while the continental

---

[4] Centrality is measured as the proportion of the remaining thirteen financial centres to which links are established. A measure of 1 suggests that banks domiciled in any of the remaining centres maintain links to the given centre.

Table 23.3. Measures of the degree of interconnectedness of the centres

	Number of presences			Percentage of links		
	Main diagonal	Off-diagonal	Density	One-way	Two-way	Actual to potential
1970	102	187	1.1	78	59	60
1980	105	444	2.5	91	64	77
1990	100	491	2.9	93	65	79
2000	76	381	3.0	93	54	74

Note: The density is the ratio of the number of off-diagonal presences to the product of 168 (the number of off-diagonal cells) and the number of banks (i.e. the sum of the main diagonal). It can range from 0 to 1.

Source: Choi, Park, and Tschoegl 2002.

European centres have fallen down to the third tier in terms of international banking attractiveness.

2.2. Securities Markets

The Big Bang of the London stock market in 1986 marks the beginning of a period of intense competition between European stock exchanges and subsequent restructuring of European stock trading (see Grilli 1989; Blattner 1992). Until then, competition between stock exchanges was largely a domestic issue. After the Big Bang many of the national stock trading systems became consolidated in one single exchange in attempts to reduce domestic fragmentation of trading and to meet international competition. The process of restructuring European stock trading has still not come to an end as the repeated attempts to take over the London Stock Exchange by the Deutsche Börse and Euronext, which itself is the result of a merger of the Amsterdam, Brussels, and Paris stock exchanges, clearly demonstrate.

The London Big Bang has initially reformed both the trading system and the listing procedure. Notably, London started trading stocks listed at other national exchanges without request or permission, essentially free riding on the foreign standard setting and standard control. This aggressive move considerably intensified competition in Europe, triggering a wave of competitive responses by continental exchanges, such as Paris, Frankfurt, Milan, Madrid, and Zurich. By now, with the notable exception of London, most European exchanges have changed from specialist or market-making systems to electronic auction systems for standard trades.[5] At the same time we witness a process of demutualization of European exchanges, rendering the concerned exchanges more profit oriented.

On a global level, competition between exchanges has largely employed listings as a strategic variable. Cross-listings became an active way for US exchanges to compete

---

[5] Large orders are typically traded in some variant of a market-making system. Hence, Pagano classifies continental European exchanges as hybrid systems.

Table 23.4. Stock listings at NYSE

	US companies	Non-US companies	Percentage non-US/total
2004	2,289	458	16.7
2003	2,283	467	17.0
2002	2,310	473	17.0
2001	2,336	462	16.5
2000	2,428	434	15.1
1999	2,619	406	13.4
1998	2,722	392	12.6
1997	2,691	356	11.7
1996	2,603	304	10.5
1995	2,429	246	9.2
1990	1,678	96	5.4
1980	1,532	38	2.4
1970	1,318	33	2.4
1960	1,119	24	2.1

Source: NYSE-online factbook 2005.

with their European counterparts. For example, the NYSE almost doubled its number of foreign listings from 246 in 1995 to the peak number of 473 in 2002 (Table 23.4). Thereafter, in pursuit of the internet bubble, there has been a slight decline in international cross-listings.

General listings fees have become a main source of revenues for the NYSE. In 2004 listing fee income of $320.9 million more than doubled trading revenues of $153.6 million. Also the rival exchange NASDAQ earns significant income from listings. Listing fees at NASDAQ turned out to be $167.3 million 2003, which is about two-thirds of trading revenues, while average daily trading volumes of NYSE and NASDAQ are almost split equally in the last fifteen years (Table 23.5). It seems that competitive pressure eliminates NYSE rents in trading, leaving listing fees as the main instrument to exploit any remaining local market power. In the case of NASDAQ trading is more profitable, but listings on the other hand only earn about 50 per cent of the NYSE listings revenues. The lower listing income of NASDAQ can be explained in part by the fact that the NYSE is the primary board with the tightest listing standards. Hence, eligible companies tend to prefer a NYSE listing and pay a higher price.

Pagano et al. (2002) document that in the period 1991–7, European companies have largely acquired a US cross-listing, while US companies have reduced their European listings, as they did with listings in Tokyo. This finding might be a mirror image of the declining attractiveness of European financial centres to international banks.

Despite the fact that listings seem to be the crucial strategic instruments, it turns out that trading revenues of domestic exchanges are largely concentrated on trading domestic securities (Table 23.6). Only the London Stock Exchange is an exception,

Table 23.5. NYSE and NASDAQ trading volumes

	Av. daily volume NYSE (shares_mil.)	Av. daily volume NASDAQ (shares_mil.)
2005	**1,582**	1,415
2004	1,457	1,259
2003	1,398	1,449
2002	1,441	1,722
2001	1,240	**1,874**
2000	1,042	1,757
1999	809	1,076
1998	674	802
1997	527	648
1996	412	544
1995	346	401
1994	291	295
1993	265	263
1992	202	191
1990	157	132

Source: NYSE-online factbook 2005.

earning larger revenues from trading foreign stocks (53 per cent in 2002) than domestic stocks. For all other exchanges in 2002 the contribution of trading in foreign stocks is less than 10 per cent of overall trading revenues. Moreover, while more than 20 per cent of the listed stocks are foreign at the NYSE only 7 per cent of trading revenues

Table 23.6. Values of shares traded and company listings in 2002

	Total value of trading (%)		Number of listed companies	
	Domestic	Foreign	Domestic	Foreign
Euronext	98%	1%	1,114	n.a.
Frankfurt	92%	8%	715	219
Hong Kong	100%	0%	968	10
Milan	91%	9%	288	7
London	47%	53%	1,890	382
NASDAQ	96%	3%	3,268	381
NYSE	91%	7%	1,894	472
Madrid	99%	1%	2,986	29
Tokyo	99%	0%	2,119	34
Zurich	97%	2%	258	140

Note: Data for 2002. Remaining percentages are investment funds.
Source: World Federation of Exchanges (Ramos and von Thadden 2004).

Table 23.7. Relative revenues from listing fees in 2004

	Listing fees	Trading revenues	Information	Total
Deutsche Börse (€m)	13.1	562.4	247.1	1,449.6
Euronext (€m)	43.3	514.4	87.3	896
LSE (£m)	38.5	94.1	101	250
NASDAQ ($m)	205.8	334.5		540.4
NYSE ($m)	320.9	153.6	167.6	1076.0

Note: The largest position of the Deutsche Börse is revenues from Clearstream (€578.8m). Likewise the NYSE earns significant data-processing fees ($220.7m).
Sources: Annual Reports 2004.

can be derived from trading foreign stocks. These numbers suggest that turnover in foreign stocks is disproportionately low and that stocks are mainly traded in their domestic markets.

Therefore, it may not be surprising that Deutsche Börse and Euronext earn considerably larger total revenues than the London Stock Exchange.[6] Domestic exchanges may benefit from (considerable) market power based on domestic bias (Gehrig 1993; Gehrig, Stahl, and Vives 1994; Brennan and Cao 1997; Hau 2001). Moreover, in addition to local market power they also enjoy technological advantages relative to their competitors such as superior settlement and clearing technologies, from which they earn significant revenues.

Finally, and in contrast to their US competitors, listing fees are not an important source of revenues for the European exchanges. They comprise only about 14 per cent of total revenues at the London Stock Exchange, 5 per cent at Euronext, and 1 per cent in Frankfurt (Table 23.7).[7]

By way of summarizing, also on securities markets European financial centres are losing attractiveness in relative terms. However, it does not seem that continental European exchanges are materially hurt since their losses of trading revenues still seem rather limited. Hence, their competitive responses tend to be sluggish, unlike their responses to the Big Bang. Moreover, as European financial centres tend to consolidate, we witness the build-up of a new structure of global financial centres in Asia.

But why has the performance of European financial centres weakened during the process of financial integration? Given that the vision underlying the Treaty of Rome was a strengthening of European markets, why do we seem to observe so much evidence to the contrary?

---

[6] For example, Andersen 2005 reports that for the years 1998–2001 Deutsche Börse and Euronext each earn total revenues that are more than twice total LSE revenues.

[7] Especially listing fees for foreign companies are negligible. After the Big Bang in 1986 London started listing foreign securities at zero fee, without any listing request of the companies concerned.

3. THE ECONOMICS OF FINANCIAL CENTRES

Before discussing the European perspectives and policy relevance, let us try and understand the underlying economic mechanisms. Why does geography play a role in financial markets? Why do we observe financial centres at all, and why and where do they matter?

3.1. The Frictionless Benchmark of Perfect Capital Markets

Clearly, in the frictionless world of traditional finance textbooks, the location of financial activity is irrelevant. A simplistic view towards integration might therefore predict that successful integration will ultimately render geography irrelevant. The dissolution of lower-order financial centres in the western hemisphere accords well with this view.

On the other hand, even in integrated economic areas, such as the USA we do observe a certain amount of fragmentation. We observe the increasing relevance of the California banking cluster and a vertical structure of security exchanges with several minor regional centres and two leading exchanges in New York. We do observe costly cross-listings also of US companies outside the USA. In fact, we do observe a spike in cross-listings in precisely that very period in which the US and the European markets started to integrate very closely, in the 1990s (Pagano, Röell and Zechner 2002). The mere presence of financial clusters is clear evidence of the relevance of frictions beyond political borders.

In order to understand the formation of financial centres it is useful to separate centripetal from centrifugal forces in financial activity. The classification of effects allows a detailed analysis of the likely effects of financial integration on the new emerging structure of financial centres.

3.2. Centripetal Forces in International Financial Markets

Clearly, economies of scale and externalities in trading are strong centripetal forces. For example, they explain why the payment mechanism is highly concentrated, but also why trading volume of a given security tends to concentrate on a single stock exchange.[8] The increased liquidity reduces trading costs and tends to reduce price volatility. Pagano (1989) has shown that 'thick markets' tend to increase liquidity, because the presence of many traders increases the chances of other traders finding trading partners with opposing trading needs. Hence, it is the thick market externality that enhances liquidity, stabilizes transaction prices, and, thus, fosters agglomeration of trading in a single exchange. To the extent that informational spillovers are relevant

---

[8] See Gehrig 2000 for more empirical details of the information system and stock trading.

in trading, they are another centripetal force supporting agglomeration of trading in a single marketplace. Finally, search per se is a strong centripetal force (Stigler 1961).

3.3. Centrifugal Forces in International Financial Markets

Apart from regulatory intervention and politically motivated transaction costs, market access costs, competition, and localized information are the major centrifugal forces in financial services (Gehrig 2000). The localization of information is recognized as a primary source of domestic bias, and hence fragmentation, in security markets (e.g. Gehrig 1993; Brennan and Cao 1997; Kang and Stulz, 1997; Coval and Moskowitz 1999) as well as a primary centrifugal force in banking markets (e.g. Gehrig 1998a; Dell'Arriccia, Friedman, and Marquez 1999; Degryse and Ongena 2005).

In particular it is the interaction of localized information with the other frictions that generates geographical fragmentation. As is well known, the combination of market access costs and competition tends to generate fragmented structures, since firms tend to relax competition and build up local market power by locating as far as possible from their rivals.[9] But also with market access costs and informational asymmetries fragmentation may occur, when market participants do not enter all available markets. In this case it may happen that investors knowledgeable about country A stocks coordinate on country A's stock market and investors knowledgeable about country B stocks coordinate on country B's stock market (Gehrig, Stahl, and Vives 1994). The extra diversification benefit from investing in the foreign market can easily be overcompensated by market access costs and adverse selection costs, which are incurred because of the informational disadvantages. Moreover, to the extent that increasingly common factors are driving the returns of both markets, the extra diversification benefit of 'global' investments is reduced. While a unified stock market might even Pareto-dominate the fragmented structure, the evolution of historically grown local markets does not necessarily converge to the unified structure as long as the frictions exist (and interact). Historical 'coordination failure' therefore may persist. Given the extent of home bias in international financial markets (e.g. Gehrig 1993; Brennan and Cao 1997; Kang and Stulz 1997), and even in regional markets within the US (Coval and Moskowitz 1999), the theoretical example given above contains considerable empirical appeal.

3.4. The Geography of International Financial Activity

The interaction of agglomerative (centripetal) and deglomerative (centrifugal) forces is quite useful for the analysis of the geography of financial activity. So why is it that currency trading and payments are such footloose activities, while stock trading

[9] See Gehrig 1998b for application of such a framework to analyse competing markets or stock exchanges.

or banking activities seem to be concentrated on certain geographical locations? Since market access costs for trading are similar for currencies and company stocks, the major structural difference among them is their informational content. While currency is a rather standardized commodity and return information is largely public, the valuation of company stocks is more complex and may require substantial amounts of private information, even in access to the published and publicly available accounts. Venture capital funds even specialize in valuing innovative ideas, screening, and supporting them with management advice before selling these ventures to the market. Similarly, banks specialize in the generation of local information (e.g. Gehrig 1996; Hauswald and Marquez 2005).

Highlighting the role of information is not denying that other economic factors may play crucial roles as well in affecting the location of financial activity. Clearly, regulation such as trade or investment restrictions may directly impede the workings of basic economic forces. Moreover, prospects of economic growth, the distribution of wealth, and legal institutions can easily impact on the location of economic activity as well. *Ceteris paribus*, however, we conjecture that footloose activities would react more sensitively to regulatory or legal arbitrage opportunities. Moreover, it would seem more difficult to raise tax revenues from footloose activities solely by taxation (Gehrig 1998b).

The empirical evidence seems to suggest that financial activity is particularly concentrated for simple financial activities or securities such as payment systems and currency trading (Gehrig 2000). These are precisely the activities that are the most footloose. The offshore Eurocurrency centres such as the Cayman Islands and the Bahamas are the centres for trading informationally rather simple products.[10] The agglomeration of trading in the offshore centres reflects a particularly favourable regulatory environment and the *raison d'être* of those offshore activities is primarily the avoidance of regulation in the home markets. In contrast, the offshore centres are not known for trading of more complex securities like stocks, despite potential regulatory advantages. Those securities are still mainly traded in the financial centre of the home market according to the location of the company headquarter (e.g. Grammig, Melvin, and Schlag, 2005; Foerster and Karolyi 1998).

Accordingly, it may be fair to refer to financial centres as the geographical centres of information aggregation for a given region. The region may be viewed as the informational hinterland, while the (geographical) centre attracts all the expertise to produce and analyse the information relevant for companies located in the hinterland. Thus, the centre economizes on economies of scale and thick market externalities in trading as well as informational spillovers, and still remains attractive for (regional) market participants. The strength and size of a financial centre largely depends on its overall

---

[10] Ito, Lyons, and Melvin 1998 and Lyons 2001 find evidence of information trading also in FX markets. Clearly, our classification does not deny the importance of semi-fundamental information such as information about trading needs of large players or the potential value of informational leakages about central bank interventions. However, the return structure of the underlying securities is much simpler than that of an international stock company. A set of risk factors of such an international company includes international sales and purchases valued at exchange rates determined in the FX market.

attractiveness to market participants, the size of the underlying frictions, and the political and regulatory framework.

Importantly, reductions in communication costs need not necessarily render the informational role of financial centres obsolete. To the contrary, Gehrig (2000) argues that the role and dominance of financial centres are likely to be stimulated by technological advances. Reductions in communication costs and advances in computing abilities help to intensify the demand for informationally complex securities and tend to strengthen centripetal forces. The fate of financial centres, however, is largely tied to their role in the process of information production. Hence it is critically affected by the regulatory and political framework of the informational hinterland, such as (national) accounting rules and transparency requirements.

4. Cross-listings, Accounting Standards, and the Informational Role of Financial Markets

How important is the role of financial centres in information production? After all cross-listings are a mechanism that forces financial centres into intensive competition for trading revenues. Moreover, the information generated by a listing in markets with high listing standards is readily available also in other markets with lower standards. In fact, as we have argued earlier, SEAQ-International started competing with the European exchanges by trading their stocks without the permission of those exchanges in 1987, free riding on their listing standards. Moreover, is there an additional role of accounting standards on information aggregation in financial centres?

4.1. Systematic Patterns in Cross-listings

Interestingly, Pagano, Röell, and Zechner (2002) observe systematic patterns in the cross-listing behaviour of European companies during the 1990s. In particular, technological companies with high-growth options tend to seek a New York listing at NYSE or NASDAQ, while companies with relatively concentrated ownership structures seem to exhibit a preference for a cross-listing in London. In aggregate these authors document a delisting of US companies in Europe. This is a surprising finding, since in addition to the regular transaction fees a cross-listing in New York also requires a reporting requirement according to the US-GAAP.[11] This reporting requirement again imposes major transactional costs on the listing companies since

---

[11] Note that the temporary increase in cross-listings as a response to increased market integration is strong evidence about the relevance of market frictions even in relatively integrated markets.

it requires a duplication of accounts and reduced flexibility. While there are various benefits of cross-listings (see Pagano, Röell, and Zechner 2002 for an extended discussion of the various motives for cross-listing), it seems a major rationale is the certification aspect. Along this line, Doidge, Karolyi, and Stulz (2004) find pervasive evidence in favour of the information hypothesis. They argue that higher US accounting standards create value for cross-listings firms, reaching up to 37 per cent of firm value, controlling for firm and country characteristics. Essentially, the cross-listing can be viewed as a bonding mechanism against opportunistic behaviour that is more costly to hide under US-GAAP. In the same vein Ammer et al. (2004) find that cross-listings significantly reduce bid–ask spreads in secondary trading. This evidence suggests that cross-listings reduce the aggregate impact of informed trading.

4.2. An Informational Role of Accounting Systems

In a more general sense, the whole legal infrastructure matters in reducing the cost of equity capital. Lambert, Leuz, and Verrecchia (2005) and Hail and Leuz (2005) document that more extensive disclosure, stronger securities regulation, and stricter enforcement significantly reduce cost of capital, and, thus, enhance the attractiveness of the underlying financial systems.

Since US cross-listings are very costly, the very phenomenon of European companies seeking a cross-listing in the USA is clear evidence of inefficiencies in European financial stock markets. Moreover, European companies do not seem to value the lower funding costs of US markets equally. According to Pagano, (2002) primarily innovative companies with high growth potentials are willing to incur those bonding costs. It is precisely those companies with relatively large growth options that tend to value more the reductions in financing costs relative to the private benefits of control.

Baruch, Karolyi, and Lemmon (2003) provide evidence that cross-listings are also related to underlying common factors of the cross-listing firms and the markets where cross-listings occur. For example, firms are more likely to be cross-listed in the USA when return correlations are higher with a US index. This finding seems to suggest that cross-listings are also a mechanism to access US expertise in valuing foreign securities. Especially innovative high-tech firms seem to be interested in accessing the US expertise in their segments. For example, Blass and Yafeh (1999) document a strong preference of high-tech companies from Israel in the US market. In this vein Foucault and Gehrig (2007) argue that cross-listings are a useful mechanism to access specific industry expertise in fragmented markets. This mechanism is particularly useful when markets are segmented. In such markets, the strategic allocation of shares across markets can be used to reward informed investors for their informational investments, and thus stimulate the generation and production of market information. Foucault and Gehrig show that the strategic allocation of stocks across markets affects the cross-listing premium. This result provides an explanation for the empirical observation of King and Segal (2005), according to which the strategic cross-listing decision is especially valuable for investment decisions of companies with high growth opportunities. Indeed, and also in line with the fundamental working hypothesis of Foucault and Gehrig (2007) and Chen, Goldstein, and Jiang (2005) document a high degree of correlation between stock prices and real investments for the USA Hence, stock prices are informative about underlying investment opportunities. In such a setting entrepreneurs can benefit from market information by strategically allocating stocks across markets and investor groups. This strategy adds value when the informational gains exceed the costs of decreased liquidity caused by market fragmentation.

4.3. Recent Developments in European Financial Markets

Fortunately, for European companies there is also some good news. Based on a small sample of cross-listed European firms that voluntarily reported according to IAS, Ammer, Clifton, and Nini (2005) find that bid–ask spreads under IAS reporting are roughly comparable to firms reporting under US-GAAP. Hence, these authors conjecture that mandatory reporting according to IAS from 2005 onwards will reduce the informational benefit, and hence the attractiveness, of a US cross-listing for many European companies. This may be good news also for companies that so far have shied away from a cross-listing, since it implies that the informational value of their accounts will be higher after 2005, reducing their cost of capital at little additional cost. Possibly, the international attractiveness of European stock markets will increase after mandatory IAS reporting.

It may be worth noting that the bursting of the internet bubble effectively destroyed any private initiatives to enhance listing standards and the informational listing values in Europe. Prior to the internet bubble, the so-called 'new markets' tried to increase listing standards for their innovative high-tech segments by requiring accounts according to IAS or US-GAAP.[12] However, as the bubble burst, enforcement of these standards and widespread fraud became a major problem.[13] In consequence, those innovative market segments were abandoned in 2003 after the bubble ended.

Overall, the regulatory framework and the legal infrastructure appear to have developed into prime determinants of the attractiveness of financial centres for international investors. Moreover, the European experience suggests that decentralized regulation may not work as effectively in global markets as centralized statutory regulation in the USA.[14]

---

[12] Leuz 2003 finds that investors of the German 'Neuer Markt' seem to value IAS and US-GAAP on equal terms.

[13] Needless to say enforcement of standards has also become a major problem in the USA as the Enron and WorldCom cases illustrate.

[14] Clearly, the timing of the beginning of the operations of the new markets in Europe at the beginning of the internet bubble was rather unfortunate. However, arguably the bubble only accelerated the underlying design problems.

5. COMPETING FINANCIAL CENTRES

When analysing competing financial centres, it is useful to separate two levels of competition. Typically, there is internal competition within the centre among its members; but there is also external competition with other centres and their members. For example, by competing aggressively, market makers steal business from rival market makers in a given securities exchange. Moreover, indirectly they also contribute to lower average trading costs, whereby they enhance the exchange's global attractiveness. This improvement in attractiveness might attract further companies for a listing at that exchange, which again generates new (future) trading revenues to the benefit of all market makers. Hence, competitive pressure and low prices generate positive externalities, since they enhance the overall attractiveness of the exchange. Low transaction prices are a common good in financial exchanges.

Accordingly, it is useful to view competition between financial centres as a strategic game with two groups of players, the (potentially) interested public, and private firms trading in their own interest (Gehrig 1998b). The role of the public player consists of designing the national legal framework including accounting standards and transaction taxes, affecting market entry, and ensuring compliance with the legal framework. The private players maximize their self-interest, while the public player internalizes the competitive externalities and enhances the public interests of an exchange. Since we view financial centres and particularly stock exchanges as the centres of information aggregation, informational spillovers and other information-related externalities are highly relevant.

As our discussion in Section 3 reveals, the regulatory framework and the official accounting standards do significantly affect the ability to attract listings and to earn listing revenues. The relative weakness of the (continental) European stock exchanges in generating listing revenues seems to mirror both relatively high trading costs, as indicated by relatively high trading revenues (see Table 23.7), too much accounting diversity (Choi and Levich 1996), and comparatively weak regulatory oversight. European markets cannot yet rely on a strong regulatory authority equivalent to the SEC in ensuring the pursuit of national interests. The US exchanges, on the other hand, are characterized by intensive internal competition and correspondingly low trading revenues, yet high volume of trading and considerable market power in the listing market. Thus US financial centres can offer low cost of funding even for rather small companies. Consequently, they seem better suited for financing small innovative ventures than their European counterparts.

As the European example of the new high-tech markets also shows, relying on self-regulation by the members of a financial centre may not allow to reap the full benefits of coordination. A delegated (public) regulator may have stronger enforcement incentives then committees composed of members.

Another interesting question is how mandatory IAS accounting will affect the ability of European exchanges to keep European markets segmented and profitable for trading after 2005. The answer will depend on the extent, to which IAS contributes to homogenize the various informational regions within Europe. Clearly, those 'informational hinterlands' are not identical with nations, but they are likely to be tied to regions with similar economic, legal, and cultural traditions.

Currently we witness lively merger activities in various contiguous regions in Europe. Euronext was created from a merger of initially three national exchanges, Amsterdam, Brussels, and Paris. OMX is a strategic alliance between the national securities markets of Denmark, Sweden, Finland, and the new Baltic exchanges, and NOREX additionally includes Norway and Iceland. Deutsche Börse and the Swiss Exchange cooperate in futures and derivatives trading, and there has been repeated interest in a merger between Deutsche Börse and LSE. It seems that these developments accord well with the informational hypothesis. Moreover, in most countries stock trading has converged to a single (national) market. Currently, only Germany, the USA, Canada, and Japan seem to maintain fragmented systems with several viable regional exchanges. The other national exchanges are most often the result of previous mergers or takeovers.

How will this vivid process of consolidation ultimately affect trading costs? While consolidation can be viewed as a competitive response to increasing homogeneity within a given informational economic region, it does not necessarily imply higher trading costs. In fact, the US experience seems to suggest the opposite. For example, Arnold et al. (1999) document that consolidation in the USA meant strictly declining transaction costs. This decline is possible because of the realization of larger economies of scale and reduced adverse selection costs.

Moreover, complementarities in trading will also lead to strategic reductions in bid–ask prices in dealership markets. Gehrig and Jackson (1998) show that the strategic properties of securities, 'substitutes in trade' versus 'complements in trade', not only depend on the asset correlations but also on the nature of the trading event. For example, the strategic properties can be completely reversed in basket trading versus portfolio rebalancing. To the extent that institutional investors seem to increasingly dominate global equity markets the role of basket trading increasingly affects pricing and merger incentives suggesting lower bid–ask spreads when securities are positively correlated.[15] This finding is largely in line with the empirical record of the various mergers in US history (Arnold et al. 1999).[16]

Finally, the Gehrig and Jackson (1998) argument even applies to mergers with electronic exchanges, such as the recently agreed NYSE–Archipelago deal or the pending NASDAQ–Instinet merger deals.[17] Again, when trading of securities in those trading systems is largely of a complementary nature, overall transaction costs should decline in response to the merger. For example, exchange-listed funds only available on Archipelago could be such complementary securities. But ultimately this property is an empirical issue. It should be said that the Gehrig–Jackson analysis does not apply

---

[15] This argument is particularly true when securities returns of stock exchanges are proxied by a market index. With positive index correlation basket trading generates trading complementarities.

[16] For extensions of this argument to markets with adverse selection see Strobl 2003.

[17] See section 7 of Gehrig and Jackson 1998.

to trades of the same securities in either system. For those reduced fragmentation should definitely lower adverse selection costs and, thus, also trading costs.

6. A EUROPEAN PERSPECTIVE

European financial integration has also opened up financial markets to competition. So in the last two years we witnessed intense takeover fights for the London Stock Exchange. So far the attempts of the Swedish Exchange, Deutsche Börse, Euronext, and even NASDAQ and Macquarie from New Zealand have not been successful. However, it seems clear that both the structure of European financial centres, and also the structure of global financial centres, is changing. Thus, and given the relatively dim prospects for economic growth, it seems fair to predict even further concentration of securities trading to ever fewer trading places in Europe. Unlike Asia with vigorously growing economies, in Europe the entry of new trading places does not seem an imminent prospect.

This process of competition between securities exchanges started with the Big Bang in 1986. This process has meanwhile proceeded to significantly lower transaction costs in Europe at large. Moreover, this process is unlikely to have come to an end yet, so that further reductions in trading costs are feasible. Competition has also generated innovation and product differentiation. For example, by introducing an entry standard, the Deutsche Börse has explicitly generated an exit platform for (German) venture capitalists, which ceased to exist after the end of the IT bubble. Finally, competition has become fierce also on the quality dimensions such as settlements and trading platforms, apart from listings.

As far as listings are concerned introducing common accounting standards such as IAS is likely to reduce incentives for European cross-listing even more. The various exchanges will tend to differentiate according to informational hinterlands in their listing strategies. By concentrating on different informational segments the dominant regional platforms build up local market power.

Of course, ultimately the success of the competitive strategies of individual exchanges and financial centres largely also depends on the political and regulatory environment (Gehrig 1998b). The extent to which European financial centres will be able to contribute to financing innovative activities will largely depend on the ability of the various regions to generate marketable innovations. Economic success in some (informational) hinterland can easily translate into the success of that hinterland's financial centres. So regional innovation policies should directly impact the prospects of regional financial centres.

But social policies are also important, such as reforms of pension systems, for example. The role of information, and informational hinterlands, is particularly important in countries with large funds available for (relatively) unrestricted investments. In countries based on (complete) pay-as-you-go pension systems, much smaller pension savings will be available for investment, relative to countries with completely funded systems. Obviously, the informational role of financial centres plays more prominently in the latter type of countries. In addition, in countries with completely funded pension systems secondary markets would tend to be more liquid, placing the corresponding financial centres at an extra competitive advantage.

Finally, regulation and taxes will affect the performance, and location, of financial centres. Even when pension systems are funded, investments of pension funds often (still) are restricted, e.g. with regional or branch limitations, or according to risk classes. It has often been argued that the Employment Retirement Income Security Act (ERISA) of 1979, with the abolition of major investment restrictions for pension funds, was instrumental for the take-off of the venture capital industry, and, hence, for the success of the California cluster as a financial centre. To the extent that similar investment liberalizations are taking place in Europe, they will certainly directly affect competition among European financial centres.

By way of summarizing: while it seems evident that further concentration of financial activity in fewer financial centres may still be possible, the European con-solidation process tends to reach its natural limits, defined by the fragmentation of the underlying informational hinterlands. As the current battle for the takeover of the London Stock Exchange and, thus, for primacy among the European financial centres documents, the emerging structure still remains unclear. Ultimately, it is likely to depend on growth prospects, as well as on the availability of savings and investment capital. Needless to say regulation and taxation will play a crucial role as well.

References

AMMER, J., CLIFTON, N., and NINI, G. (2005), 'Accounting standards and information: infer-ences from cross-listed financial firms,' International Finance Discussion Paper 843, Federal Reserve Board.

——— HOLLAND, S., SMITH, D., and WARNOCK, F. (2004), 'Look at me now: the role of cross-listings in attracting U.S. shareholders', International Finance Discussion Paper 815, Federal Reserve Board.

ANDERSEN, A. (2005), 'Essays on stock exchange competition and pricing', doctoral disserta-tion, University of Helsinki.

ARNOLD, T., HERSCH, P., MULHERIN, J., and NETTER, J. (1999), 'Merging markets', Journal of Finance, 54(3), 1083–107.

BARUCH, S., KAROLYI, A., and LEMMON, M. (2003), Multi-Market Trading and Liquidity: Theory and Evidence, Ohio State University, mimeo.

BENOS, E., and WEISBACH, M. (2004), 'Private benefits and cross-listings in the United States', NBER Working Paper 10224.

BESSEMBINDER, H., and KAUFMANN, H. (1997), 'A cross-exchange comparison of execution costs and information flow for NYSE-listed stocks', Journal of Financial Economics, forth-coming.

BLASS, A., and YAFEH, Y. (1999), Vagabond Shoes Longing to Stray: Why Foreign Firms List in the United States, Hebrew University of Jerusalem, mimeo.

BLATTNER, N. (1992), 'Competitiveness in banking: selected recent contributions and research priorities', in N., Blattner, H. Genberg, and A. Swoboda (eds.), *Competitiveness in Banking* Heidelberg: Physica-Verlag.

BRENNAN M., and CAO, H. H. (1997), 'International portfolio investment flows', *Journal of Finance*, 52(5), 1851–80.

CHEN, Q., GOLDSTEIN, R., and JIANG, W. (2005), *Price Informativeness and Investment Sensitivity to Stock Prices*, Duke, Wharton, Columbia, mimeo.

CHOI, F. and LEVICH, R. (1996), 'Accounting diversity', in B. Steil (ed.), *The European Equity Market*, London Z. Royal Institute of International Affairs, 259–312.

——— PARK, D., and TSCHOEGL, A. E. (1996), 'Banks and the world's major banking centers', 1990', *Weltwirtschaftliches Archiv*, 132, 774–93.

——— ——— ——— (2002), *Banks and the World's Major Banking Centers*, 2000, Wharton School, mimeo.

——— TSCHOEGL, A. E., and YU, C.-M. (1986), 'Banks and the world's major financial centers', 1970–1980, *Weltwirtschaftliches Archiv*, 122, 48–64.

COCHRANE, J., SHAPIRO, J., and TOBIN, J. (1995), 'Foreign equities and US investors: breaking down the barriers separating demand and supply', NYSE Working Paper.

COOPER, I. and KAPLANIS, E. (1994), 'What explains the home bias in portfolio investment?', *Review of Financial Studies*, 7(1), 45–60.

COVAL, J., and MOSKOWITZ, T. (1999), 'Home bias at home: local equity preference in domestic portfolios', *Journal of Finance*, 54, 45–74.

DEGRYSE, H., and ONGENA, S. (2005), 'Distance, lending relationships, and competition', *Journal of Finance*, 60(1), 231–66.

DELL' ARRICCIA, G., FRIEDMAN, E., and MARQUEZ, R. (1999), 'Adverse selection as a barrier to entry in the banking industry', *RAND Journal of Economics*, 30, 515–34.

DOIDGE, C., KAROLYI, G. A., and STULZ, R. (2004), 'Why are firms listed in the U. S. worth more?', *Journal of Financial Economics*, 71, 205–38.

ECONOMIDES, N., and SIOW, A. (1988), 'The division of markets is limited by the extent of liquidity (spatial competition with externalities)', *American Economic Review*, 78(1), 108–21.

EUROPEAN COMMISSION (2005), *The Economic Costs of Non-Lisbon: A Survey of the Literature on the Economic Impact of Lisbon-Type Reforms*, European Economy, Directorate General for Economic and Financial Affairs, March.

FOERSTER, S., and KAROLYI, A. (1998), 'Multimarket trading and liquidity: a transactions data analysis of Canada-U.S. interlistings', *Journal of International Financial Markets, Institutions and Money*, 8(3–4), 393–412.

FOUCAULT, T., and PARLOUR, C. (2005), 'Competition for listings', *RAND Journal*, forthcoming.

——— and GEHRIG, T. (2007), 'Stock price informativeness, cross-listings, and investment decisions', *Journal of Financial Economics*, forthcoming.

GEHRIG, T. (1993), 'An information based explanation of the domestic bias in international equity investment', *Scandinavian Journal of Economics*, 95(1), 97–109.

——— (1996), 'Market structure, monitoring, and capital adequacy regulation', *Swiss Journal of Economics and Statistics*, 132(4/2), 685–702.

——— (1998a), 'Screening, cross-border banking, and the allocation of credit', *Research in economics*, 52, 387–407.

——— (1998b), 'Competing markets', *European Economic Review*, 42, 277–310.

——— (2000), 'Cities and the geography of financial centers', in J. Thisse and Huriot, J. M. (eds.), *The Economics of Cities*, Cambridge: Cambridge University Press, 415–45.

——— (2003), 'Corporate governance: fine tuning the condition for innovation and job growth in a global economy', *Journal of Institutional and Theoretical Economics*, 159, 656–65.

_____ and JACKSON, M. (1998), 'Bid–ask spreads with indirect competition among specialists', *Journal of Financial Markets*, 1(1), 89–119.

_____ STAHL, K., and VIVES, X. (1994), 'Competing exchanges', in *The Location of Economic Activity*, Vigo: CEPR Conference Volume, 549–81.

GEHRKE, W., and RASCH, S. (1993), 'Europas Wertpapierbörsen im Umbruch', *ZEW Wirtschaftsanalysen*, 306–36.

GOLDBERG, L., and GROSSE, R. (1994), 'Location choice of foreign banks in the United States', *Journal of Economics and Business*, 46, 367–79.

GRAMMIG, J., MELVIN, M., and SCHLAG, C. (2005), 'Internationally cross-listed stock prices during overlapping trading hours: price discovery and exchange rate effects', *Journal of Empirical Finance*, 12(1), 139–64.

GRILLI, V. (1989), 'Financial markets', *Economic Policy*, 388–413.

HAIL, L., and LEUZ, C. (2005), 'International differences in the cost of equity capital: do legal institutions and securities regulation matter?', *Journal of Accounting Research*, forthcoming.

HAU, H. (2001), 'Location matters: an examination of trading profits', *Journal of Finance*, 56(5), 1959–83.

HAUSWALD, R., and MARQUEZ, R. (2005), 'Competition and strategic information acquisition in credit markets', *Review of Financial Studies*, forthcoming.

HELLWIG, M. (1980), 'On the aggregation of information in competitive markets', *Journal of Economic Theory*, 22, 477–98.

HUDDART, S., HUGHES, J., and BRUNNERMEIER, M. (1998), 'Disclosure requirements and stock exchange listing choice', *Journal of Accounting and Economics*, 26, 237–69.

ITO, T., LYONS, R. K., and MELVIN, M. (1998), 'Is there private information in the FX-market? The Tokyo experiment', *Journal of Finance*, 80, 1111–30.

JEGER, M. HAEGLER, U., and THEISS, R. (1992), 'On the attractiveness on financial centers', in N. Blattner, H. Genberg, and A. Swoboda (eds.), *Competitiveness in Banking*, Heidelberg: Physica–Verlag.

JOHNSON, H. G. (1974), 'Panama as a regional financial center', *Economic Development and Cultural Change*, 261–86.

KANG, J.-K., and STULZ, R. (1997), 'Why is there a home bias? An analysis of foreign portfolio equity ownership in Japan', *Journal of Financial Economics*, 46, 3–28.

KIM, S. (1990), 'Labour heterogeneity, wage bargaining, and agglomeration economics', *Journal of Urban Economics*, 28, 160–77.

KINDLEBERGER, C. P. (1974), *The Formation of Financial Centers: A Study of Comparative Economic History*, Princeton: Princeton University Press.

KING, M., and SEGAL, D. (2005), *The Longer Horizon Importance of U.S. Investors and Trading for Cross-Listed Firms*, Toronto, mimeo.

LAMBERT, R., LEUZ, C., and VERRECCHIA, R. (2005), 'Accounting information, disclosure, and the cost of capital', Working Paper, Wharton School of Economics, University of Pennsylvania.

LEUZ, C. (2003), 'IAS versus US GAAP: information asymmetry based evidence from Germany's new market', *Journal of Accounting Research*, 38, 91–124.

LEWIS, K. (1999), 'Trying to explain home bias in equities and consumption', *Journal of Economic Literature*, 37(2), 571–608.

LYONS, R. K. (2001), *The Microstructure Approach to Exchange Rates*, Cambridge, Mass.: MIT-Press.

McANDREWS, J., and STEFANADIS, C. (2002), 'The consolidation of European stock exchanges', *Current Issues in Economics and Finance*, 8(6), 1–6.

NYSE FACT BOOK (n.d.), www.nysedata.com/factbook.

O'BRIEN, R. (1992), *Global Financial Integration: The End of Geography*, London: Royal Institute of International Affairs, Chatham House.

PAGANO, M. (1989), 'Trading volume and asset liquidity', *Quarterly Journal of Economics*, 104(2), 255–74.

_____ and RÖELL, A. (1990), 'Trading systems in european stock exchanges: current performance and policy options, *Economic Policy* 10, 63–115.

_____ _____ and ZECHNER, J. (2002), 'The geography of equity listings: why do companies list abroad?', *Journal of Finance*, 57(6), 2651–94.

PARK, Y. S. and ESSAYYAD, M. (1989), *International Banking and Financial Centers*, Boston: Kluwer Academic.

PORTEUS, D. (1996), *The Geography of Finance*, Aldershot: Aoebory.

RAMOS, S., and VON THADDEN, E. L. (2004), *Stock Exchange Competition in a Simple Model of Capital Market Equilibrium*, HEC, Lausanne, mimeo.

REED, H. C. (1980), 'The ascent of Tokyo as an international financial center', *Journal of International Business Studies*, 11(3), 19–35.

_____ (1981), *The Preeminence of International Financial Centers*, New York: Praeger.

SHUCKLA, R. and VAN INWEGEN, G. (1995), 'Do locals perform better than foreigners?', *Journal of Economics and Business*, 47, 241–54.

SMITH, C. (1991), 'Globalization of financial markets', in A. Meltzer and C. Plosser (eds.), *Carnegie Rochester Series on Public Policy*, Amsterdam: North-Holland, 19–33.

STIGLER, G. (1961), 'The economics of information', *Journal of Political Economy*, 49, 213–25.

STROBL, G. (2003), *On the Optimal Allocation of New Security Listings to Specialists*, Wharton, October, mimeo.

TESAR, L., and WERNER, I. (1996), 'Home bias and high turnover', *Journal of International Money and Finance*, forthcoming.

TSCHOEGL, A. E. (1989), 'The benefits and costs of hosting financial centers', in Y. S. Park, and M. Essayyad (eds.), *International Banking and Financial Centers*, Boston: Kluwer Academic, 49–66.

_____ (2000), 'International banking centers, geography, and foreign banks', *Financial Markets, Instruments and Institutions*, 9(1), 1–32.

ZHAO, S. X. B. (2003), 'Spatial restructuring of financial centers in mainland China and Hong Kong: A geography of finance perspective, *Urban Affairs Review*, 38, 535–71.

PART V

FINANCIAL REGULATION AND MACROECONOMIC POLICY

CHAPTER 24

EU SECURITIES MARKETS REGULATION

PROBLEMS, POLICIES, AND PROCESSES

BERNHARD SPEYER

It is widely understood that financial market integration brings substantial welfare gains. Nonetheless, even in the mid-1990s and despite decades of integration policy, Europe's financial markets were still fragmented (and, despite considerable progress, continue to be so until today). This market fragmentation became even more glaring in the light of the run-up to European Monetary Union; in that context, market fragmentation also gave cause for concern: segmented financial markets would not only prevent potential efficiency gains from the introduction of the single currency actually materializing, they might also impede the smooth functioning of monetary union by negatively affecting the monetary transmission mechanism and the intertemporal and interregional transfer within the single currency area. Responding to this deficiency, European policy makers, in 1998, devised the EU's Financial Services Action

The author expresses his personal opinion which is not necessarily representative for that of Deutsche Bank AG or Deutsche Bank Research.

Plan (FSAP), which launched a comprehensive legislative programme designed to truly integrate Europe's financial markets. Soon, however, it became apparent that it was not only the content of European financial market regulation that was deficient, but also the process by which these rules were created and the way in which they were implemented in member states. This has led to a fundamental redesign of the structure for securities market regulation in the EU in the shape of the so-called Lamfalussy process.

After presenting the rationale of EU securities market integration in Section 1, this chapter presents an overview of the FSAP and the main securities markets-related legislative acts. Section 3 presents the genesis and structure of the Lamfalussy process. Section 4 gives a tentative assessment of the FSAP, whereas Section 5 analyses the benefits and deficiencies of the Lamfalussy process including a discussion of possible alternatives to it. The chapter closes with an outlook on securities market regulation in the 2005–10 period covered by the respective EU Commission's White Paper (Section 6) and a conclusion.

1. THE RATIONALE OF EU SECURITIES MARKET INTEGRATION

EU securities market integration is a logical part of the overall EU integration project. If anything, it is surprising that almost fifty years after the signing of the Treaty of Rome, securities market integration has not been completed. Quite to the contrary, securities markets in particular and financial markets more generally were amongst those markets where the level of integration still lagged behind seriously even in the mid-1990s and in some segments continues to do so until today. There are a number of reasons for this. First, there is a strong interlinkage of securities market regulation with other areas of law, such as contract law and accounting rules. This makes market opening less easy than in goods markets.[1] Second, even in those areas where a common EU legislative framework existed, this was either incomplete, outdated, allowed the continuous protection of national markets—often under the guise of protecting the 'national good'—or was applied inconsistently (Committee of Wise Men 2001: 13–15; Kern 2002: 7–8). Third, another reason has been the fact that full financial market integration requires full capital account liberalization, which was only achieved in the entire EU in the early 1990s. Finally, the fragmentation of the EU into various monetary areas prevented securities market integration. Against the backdrop of the latter it is perhaps not surprising that the start of European

---

[1] Incidentally, the integration of services markets generally lags behind that of goods markets, of course.

Monetary Union (EMU) gave renewed impetus to the project of EU securities market integration.

In economic terms, the full integration of EU securities markets promises substantial benefits not only for the EU financial services industry, but, more importantly, for the users of financial services. Market integration is conducive to higher market efficiency. This manifests itself on the one hand in lower financing costs for firms. With more integrated markets, issuers have access to a wider investor base. This makes possible larger issuing volumes, which in turn enhance market liquidity in any given title, reducing the liquidity premium and, hence, lowering financing costs. Larger issues also allow issuers to realize economies of scale by spreading the largely fixed costs of issuing securities (prospectuses, legal fees, ratings, etc.) over a larger issuance volume. Integrated markets also give issuers access to a wider choice of intermediaries, which, through more intensive competition, lowers fees and encourages product innovation (OECD 2003: 103).

On the other hand, higher market efficiency manifests itself in higher risk-adjusted yields for savers by means of more diversified portfolios, inter alia by a reduction of home bias. Like issuers, investors gain access to a broader range of intermediaries and consequently benefit from higher competition amongst those intermediaries in the form of lower fees and a broader product range. In addition, assuming that market integration leads to a reconfiguration of the market infrastructure (exchanges, clearing, and settlement systems), issuers, investors, as well as intermediaries may also benefit—in the form of lower transaction costs and higher liquidity—from efficiency gains there. Consolidation of trading platforms would eliminate the need for dual listings and would allow intermediaries to eliminate redundant investments in different systems. For intermediaries—EU securities firms and asset managers—market integration entails greater competitive pressures, which are already being felt in the shape of lower margins (Cabral, Dierick, and Vesala 2002: 21). However, for the successful firms this is being compensated by access to a wider client base and higher volumes as well as by the possibility of reaping economies of scale. Importantly, only with an integrated European market will European securities firms ever be able to compete against their global (i.e. US) competitors, who, on the back of a large and sophisticated home market, are strong competitors not only in the USA, but increasingly in Europe, too.

While issuers, investors, and intermediaries are the direct beneficiaries of more integrated markets, the benefits of securities market integration extend beyond them to the economy at large. More efficient capital markets lead to a more efficient resource allocation, which in turn increases the rates of return on overall investment and, ultimately, the economy's growth rate. Similarly, it allows savers to increase the return on their investments, which is, of course, of particular importance in Europe in light of the underfunding of public pensions schemes. Securities markets integration assumes a particularly important role in this respect against the background of the gradual shift of the (continental) European financial systems from predominantly bank-based to more capital markets-based systems. While the alleged dichotomy between those two systems is usually exaggerated, it no doubt holds true that a convergence between both systems takes place in Europe (Hartmann, Maddaloni, and Manganelli 2003: 12 f.). EU firms are more willing to tap financial markets directly—in the form of corporate bond issues, equity, private equity, venture capital, and securitization of receivables. Similarly, the traditional on-balance sheet intermediation is giving way to active balance sheet management by banks, whereby risks from lending activity are being passed on to capital markets by means of securitizations, loan trading, and derivatives. All of this, of course, mirrors recent research showing that more sophisticated and more efficient financial markets correspond to higher growth rates (Levine 2003; OECD 2001). Against this background it is not surprising that the objective to fully integrate the EU's securities markets explicitly became part of the EU's Lisbon Agenda for higher growth and competitiveness.

However, these benefits will only materialize in a truly integrated market where investors and issuers are free to source their services from any supplier across the EU, where intermediaries have full and unimpeded access to clients in all member states, where issuers can sell their securities to investors in the entire EU on the basis of a single documentation, and where the market infrastructure is integrated to an extent that allows cross-border transactions to be made as cost efficiently as domestic transactions.

While, thus, the economic rationale for integrated markets is strong, it is not immediately apparent why this should require (new) EU securities markets regulation, rather than a simple liberalization that would give EU-based market participants—securities firms, issuers, and investors—more access to counterparties in other member states. The answer is fourfold. First, securities market regulation has been vital to create the solid legal basis for market integration. Securities being confidence goods, there must be legal certainty about the nature and definition of any single product and the respective rights and obligations of debtors/issuers and investors. Since securities markets are so tied to legal systems, it is not enough for market integration to remove national obstacles; rather, these have to be replaced with a common legal framework applicable in the entire new, integrated market space. Second, as there is an inherent danger of market inefficiency in securities markets due to information asymmetries, regulation is necessary to preserve market integrity in the integrated market, too. Investors should enjoy the same high level of protection irrespective of whether they source from domestic or foreign suppliers. Third, apart from market integrity, maintaining market stability is a concern for authorities. As market integration entails that shocks originating in one country are more easily transmitted to another jurisdiction, the structure of securities market supervision must be reconfigured so as to ensure that financial stability is guaranteed in the wider market, too. Fourth, since resulting from the above the securities industry is a tightly regulated one, level playing field issues are important for suppliers, which leads to calls for a harmonization of at least core rules (see also below).

2. THE FINANCIAL SERVICES
ACTION PLAN (FSAP)

The creation of an integrated EU securities market required both an update of existing regulations and, in some fields, the formulation of new rules. To enhance the political visibility, the planned measures were bundled into a legislative package, the Financial Services Action Plan (FSAP) (European Commission 1999; Kern 2002 gives a concise overview). FSAP encompassed forty-three legislative measures aimed at the creation of an adequate framework for a single European market in financial services that would satisfy three overarching objectives: a single wholesale market, an open and secure retail market, and adequate prudential rules and supervision. In principle, FSAP builds on the tested integration method that combines a harmonization of core standards, home country control, an EU passport for financial services providers, and mutual recognition. FSAP was scheduled to be completed by 2005; the European Council subsequently brought forward the deadline for securities market related measures to end 2003.

For securities markets, the most important elements of the FSAP were the Transparency Directive, the Prospective Directive, the Market Abuse Directive, the IAS Regulation, and the successor to the Investment Services Directive (initially dubbed 'ISD II' and later re-christened 'Market in Financial Instruments Directive, MiFID). To some extent it proved unfortunate that the MiFID was left until late in the process, as it constitutes something akin to the 'basic law' of EU securities markets, setting fundamentals that could have been referenced by other directives.

Box 24.1. The Key Securities Markets Measures of the FSAP

Transparency Obligation Directive (TOD): The TOD aims at enhancing investor protection and the attractiveness of Europe's capital markets by introducing minimum transparency requirements for information which must be provided by companies whose securities are traded on a regulated market. All securities issuers are obliged to provide annual financial reports within four months after the end of the financial year; those issuing shares have to provide, in addition, meaningful half-yearly reports. Issuers that do not publish quarterly reports must provide quarterly management statements.

Prospectus Directive (PD): The PD replaces the previous directives on the public offer of securities and admission to trading. The aim is to ensure adequate and equivalent disclosure standards in all member states. The directive also restates a European passport for issuers in order to lower the cost of raising capital on an EU-wide basis. While the predecessor to the PD, in principle, already established a passport regime, in practice, mutual recognition of prospectuses did not take place. In order to differentiate between the different needs for protection of wholesale and retail investors, the PD exempts offers addressed exclusively to qualified investors, or securities whose denomination per unit amounts to at least €50,000, from the obligation to publish a prospectus. Bond issuers issuing securities with a per-unit amount of at least €1,000 are given freedom of choice as regards the competent authority

> **Box 24.1. continued**
>
> for approval; clearly, an unrestricted freedom of choice would be desirable. The directive also defines the liabilities of all parties involved.
>
> *Market Abuse Directive (MAD)*: The MAD updates and replaces the 1989 Insider Trading Directive and aims at closer cooperation and more intensive exchange of information between competent national authorities on market abuse concerning securities admitted to at least one regulated market in the EU. The Directive stipulates that each member state must appoint a single supervisory agency to combat market abuse.
>
> *IAS regulation*: The regulation aims at improving the comparability of financial accounts of companies with securities listed on EU regulated markets. Notwithstanding some transition periods, all of these companies must prepare their consolidated accounts according to International Accounting Standards (IAS) or, as they are meanwhile called: International Financial Reporting Standards (IFRS), by 1 January, 2005 (for a broader discussion cf. D'Arcy 2004: 3–10).
>
> *Markets in Financial Instruments Directive (MiFID)*: MiFID updates the 1993 Investment Services Directive (ISD) and gives investment firms a single passport allowing them to operate EU-wide on the basis of an authorization of their home member state. While, in principle, the passport regime had already been established in the ISD, in reality member states had undermined it by effectively keeping away foreign firms by using the general good clause. MiFID defines the rights of investors when sourcing the services of EU investment firms and stipulates the obligations of investment firms when executing transactions on exchanges, other trading systems, or internal systems. As regards the latter, the issue of pre-trade transparency, i.e. the obligation of internalizers to disclose prices at which they are willing to trade, was a contentious issue, which was solved with a compromise whose usefulness remains to be seen.
>
> *Source*: This draws, inter alia, on Gerster et al. 2004.

While FSAP was, by and large, completed on time on the EU level, transposition into member states' laws, where necessary, and national implementation are behind schedule in a considerable number of member states.[2] In other words, in the area of securities market legislation—as in other areas of EU legislation—too many member states fail in the basic tasks of transposition, of coherent implementation, and effective application of internal market legislation.

3. THE LAMFALUSSY PROCESS

3.1. The Rationale

As the realization of FSAP progressed, it became apparent that the problems ran deeper than a lack of adequate rules. As a result, in July 2000, the Ecofin Council

---

[2] The state of play is regularly updated by the European Commission, DG Internal Market, and available at: http://europa.eu.int/comm/internal_market/finances/actionplan/index_en.htm#transposition.

appointed a Committee of Wise Men chaired by Alexandre Lamfalussy (the 'Lamfalussy Group'). In doing so, the Ecofin was motivated by the understanding that growth and competitiveness of European securities markets were being hampered by the then existing regulatory and legislative framework. Therefore, the Lamfalussy Group was given the mandate to identify administrative, regulatory, and other types of obstacles which impede trans-border securities transactions and to make suggestions as to how to remedy these shortcomings. The Group's mandate was explicitly limited to securities markets only; issues concerning prudential supervision were also excluded.

After six months' work, which included an extensive consultation of various stakeholders, the Lamfalussy Group delivered their Final Report (Committee of Wise Men 2001). In a nutshell, the report concluded that Europe's securities markets basically suffered from two major weaknesses. First, there were gaps in the existing legislation and, more importantly, the legislative process as such was far too cumbersome, unwieldy, and produced ambiguous results. Second, EU legislation governing financial markets was implemented in an inconsistent way by EU member states. Concepts, structures, and competencies not only differed, but still drifted apart; outright protectionism of national markets occurred not too infrequently.

Reforms were therefore needed both on the EU and the national level. As an answer to the above-mentioned deficiencies, the Wise Men Committee proposed a new framework for the regulation of European securities markets. It consisted of a four-level approach, which came to be known as the 'Lamfalussy process'. Levels 1 and 2 of the process are mainly concerned with making the legislative process more flexible, whereas improving the consistency of the implementation and execution of EU securities legislation is the main concern of levels 3 and 4.

On the EU level, it was, above all, the legislative process which needed to be tackled. Considering the fast pace of change in financial markets, the regulatory system was seen as too slow, too rigid, and ill adapted to the needs of modern financial markets. It was therefore proposed to split financial market legislation into framework legislation (level 1), which stipulates the basis political objectives of any regulatory action and is subject to conventional co-decision by EU legislators, and technical provisions, which can be changed by means of executive orders by the EU Commission under the so-called comitology procedure (level 2).

The Wise Men's proposals for the redesign of the legislative process (levels 1 and 2) actually mirror a more general notion in global financial market regulation. The creation of hard law and rigid institutions are increasingly seen as inappropriate in light of the fast pace of evolution of financial markets. Financial markets are marked by a high degree of innovativeness. Institutional structures of financial markets, the kind of instruments preferred by actors on financial markets, as well as the structure and volume of international capital flows can and do change quickly reflecting changes in the preference of investors, debtors, and traders. Without a corresponding regulatory regime, market opportunities for EU financial services providers will be lost to competitors from nimbler jurisdictions. Similarly, such changes simultaneously alter the scope, nature, and distribution of risks within the financial system—which will trigger regulatory and supervisory action, if and to the extent that authorities regard the new risk structure as undesirable. Consequently, a flexible regulatory framework is needed to maintain the competitiveness of the financial services industry and to keep rules and supervisory structures in line with the actual risk situation.

Action on the EU level, so say the Wise Men, would have to be supplemented by action on the national level, though. Any attempt to speed up processes at EU level must fail, if national authorities are unwilling or unable to implement rules agreed upon on the EU level or if their day-to-day supervisory action results—intentionally or unintentionally—in an inconsistent implementation of EU rules. Hence, levels 3 and 4 called for greater cooperation of national supervisors as well as more rigid enforcement of EU securities markets law by the EU Commission.

3.2. The New Structure

Speed, professionalism, consistency, and transparency are the guiding principles of Lamfalussy process. The structure, as it stands now, is set out in Figure 24.1.

3.2.1. *Level 1*

Level 1 describes the first part of the legislative process. Based on its right of initiative, the EU Commission makes proposals for legislative acts concerning financial markets. The proposed level 1 measures are to concentrate on the core political principles (essential elements) of the issue at hand. In other words, level 1 legislation should be limited to defining the broad framework principles whereas implementing powers and technical details are delegated to level 2. The Commission's proposals are to be based on the results of an open, transparent, and systematic public discourse with all stakeholders. The Commission's proposals would then be discussed, adjusted, and agreed upon under normal EU legislative procedures, i.e. by co-decision of Council and European Parliament (EP).[3] Importantly, when passing level 1 legislation, the two co-legislators decide on which issues and to what extent implementing measures are delegated to level 2.

3.2.2. *Level 2*

Level 2 concerns technical implementing measures. Based on the respective provisions in level 1 framework legislation, these are issued by the EU Commission proposal. When drafting these measures the EU Commission is advised by a network of

---

[3] The Lamfalussy Group suggested that the so-called fast track procedure, which allows an early adoption of an Act after the first reading in the EP, should be used as often as possible, so as to speed up the legislative process. However, as it turned out, all stakeholders are wary of using the fast track procedure as it leads to informal, behind-the-scenes negotiations between the co-legislators which make the legislative process less transparent. Hence, it is widely agreed amongst all stakeholders that fast track should only be used when the issue at hand is uncontroversial, when there is broad interinstitutional agreement, and when the matter concerned requires a speedy reaction by lawmakers.

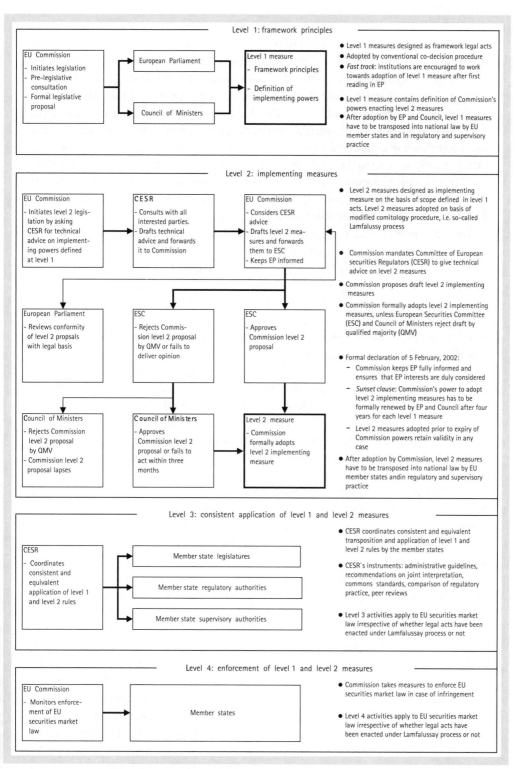

Fig. 24.1. The Lamfalussy process in practice

Source: Deutsche Bank Research

EU national supervisors organized in the newly established Committee of European Securities Regulators (CESR).[4] The Commission's level 2 measures can be rejected by the European Securities Committee (ESC)—a forum of high-ranking representatives of the EU member states, chaired by the responsible EU Commissioner. The fact that member states, in the shape of the ESC only have negative powers (they can only reject Commission proposals with qualified majority; in other words, the Commission does not need the active approval of its proposals by the ESC in order for them to take effect), nearly prevented the establishment of the Lamfalussy process. It was only after the Commission committed itself 'to avoid going against predominant views which might emerge within the Council, as to the appropriateness of such measures' that Council consented to the establishment of the Lamfalussy process.

This, however, led to demands by the European Parliament that it be granted similar powers. Underlying this demand is an issue that exists quite irrespective of the Lamfalussy process, namely the general issue of Parliament's rights in the comitology process. As an equally empowered co-legislator, the European Parliament demands that it is put on an equal footing with the Council in the comitology process, and therefore also in the Lamfalussy process. Parliament fears that the delegation of level 2 implementing measures may, if interpreted too generously, dilute or even render valueless the Parliament's right of co-decision.

Against this background, the European Parliament only consented to the establishment of the Lamfalussy process when the EU Commission, in a solemn declaration by then Commission President Romano Prodi, promised several mechanisms to safeguard Parliament's interests. These included active information of Parliament, making available all documents, a commitment to take concerns voiced by Parliament into account to the atmost and accepting that Parliament may attach sunset clauses to level 2 powers delegated to the Commission. Thus, comitology powers of the Commission under financial market legislation would expire, unless renewed by Council and Parliament. The European Parliament certainly takes a very keen interest in the issues under discussion and members of the responsible parliamentary committee (ECON) have developed considerable expertise in the legislative matters under discussion.

Apart from the commitments undertaken by the Commission in the solemn declaration of February 2001, the European Parliament's original agreement to the Lamfalussy process was also conditioned on the introduction of a call-back right for Parliament for level 2 legislation. The draft revised treaty (the 'Constitution') would have provided the European Parliament with such a call-back right under Articles I-36 and I-37. However, following the uncertainty about the future of the draft Constitutional Treaty, the EU institutions agreed, in July 2006, on a reform of the comitology procedure in the context of the Lamfalussy process. While this compromise, called the 'regulatory procedure with scrutiny', does not give the European Parliament the powers envisaged under the Constitutional Treaty, it does grant the Parliament more

---

[4] CESR actually builds on the previous informal cooperation of EU securities regulators, as organized in the Forum of European Securities Commissions (FESCO).

information rights and the power to veto any level 2 measure by absolute majority. Future financial services legislation will no longer include sunset clauses.

3.2.3. *Level 3*

On level 3, CESR works in a different capacity. Rather than advising as on level 2, regulators in their level 3 capacity form a network of national authorities with the aim of ensuring that EU legislation is implemented and applied in a consistent way in all member states. In order to do so, CESR has meanwhile developed a raft of instruments, including joint interpretations, guidelines, and common standards as well as peer reviews.

3.2.4. *Level 4*

Level 4 concerns strengthening the enforcement of Community rules. Fundamentally, level 4 reminds member states of their legal obligation to adhere to the rules agreed upon at the EU level. The Commission is encouraged to forcefully exercise its role as the guardian of the European treaties and to reproach member states that do not live up to their obligations. The private sector is encouraged to complain whenever business opportunities are denied or costs of business are increased due to a breach of the treaties by one or more member states.

As the Lamfalussy process was widely regarded as a success by all stakeholders, the framework was extended to banking, occupational pensions and insurance in 2004. The resulting committee structure is shown in Figure 24.2.

	Securities (including UCITS)	Banking	Insurance and occupational pensions
Level 2	European Securities Committee (ESC)	European Banking Committee (EBC)	European Insurance and Occupational Pensions Committee (EIOPC)
	Chair: Commission	Chair: Commission	Chair: Commission
	Location: Brussels	Location: Brussels	Location: Brussels
Level 3	Committee of European Securities Regulators (CESR)	Committee of European Banking Supervisors (CEBS)	Committee of European Insurance and Occupational Pensions Supervisors (CEIOPS)
	Chair: Eddy Wymeersch	Chair: Danièle Nouy	Chair: Thomas Steffen
	Location: Paris	Location: London	Location: Frankfurt

Fig. 24.2. Committee structure

3.3. Inclusion of Stakeholders in the Lamfalussy Process

An important, novel feature of the Lamfalussy process is the systematic inclusion of the private sector. The full participation of market participants in the deliberations of the Committee of Wise Men had already been essential for a fuller understanding of the deficiencies and had positively influenced the resulting proposals. While the recognition of this fact did not translate into a formal representation of market participants in the Lamfalussy process,[5] it has nonetheless embedded a practice of intensive consultation of all stakeholders on all levels of the process—so much so, actually, that there is already talk of 'consultation fatigue'! In particular, the level 3 committees, such as CESR (2001), have adopted codes on consultation practices which are exemplary.

Again, developments on the European level as regards the consultation of stakeholders mirror a wider trend in global financial rule making. More specifically, the greater involvement of non-state actors in the genesis of financial markets rules has been a supply-push as well as a demand-pull process. Supply-push can easily be explained by the fact that financial regulation is 'deeper integration' *par excellence*. 'Deeper integration' denotes forms of international integration that include rule making on 'behind the border' issues—in contrast to conventional forms of integration that deal with so-called border measures only, i.e. the reduction or removal of tariffs and quotas. Financial regulation particularly represents the notion of 'deeper integration', not least due to the strong connection to other areas of regulation, such as company law, taxation, and accounting.[6] (Incidentally, it is no surprise that these areas are regularly identified by industry representatives as major obstacles to financial market integration in the EU. Similarly, a recent report by the European Commission (2005a) on obstacles to cross-border consolidation in the EU financial industry identified issues such as taxation and consumer protection laws as the major obstacles. This highlights that a full integration of EU financial markets requires action beyond the area of financial regulation in a narrow sense.)

Hence, firms are keen to bring about regulatory structures that will ensure a level playing field. This goes back to the above-mentioned notion that regulation determines the international competitiveness of financial institutions. In addition, supply-push was triggered by the fact that the coexistence of different regulatory regimes causes substantial costs for internationally active institutions, as they have to run multiple reporting systems, have to satisfy parallel demands from several regulators/supervisors, and are faced with duplicative reporting duties. These burdens have, over time, become ever heavier, as financial institutions have centralized core functions such as compliance departments and risk management. As a consequence, the

---

[5] This has to do, inter alia, with the practical difficulties of ensuring the consultation of a representative sample of market participants and the conceptual problem of asking the regulated to formally advise on what should be imposed upon them in terms of regulation.

[6] As Robert Gilpin rightly observed: 'Liberal economists conceive of societies as black boxes connected by exchange rates; as long as exchange rates are correct, what goes on inside the black box is regarded as not very important. With the increasing integration of national economies, however, what states do inside the black box to affect economic relations has become much more important' (Gilpin 1987: 393).

gap between industry practice and the fragmented structure of financial regulation and supervision has become ever greater and, hence, more costly for firms (European Financial Services Roundtable 2005: 17 f.).

As regards demand-pull, regulators worldwide increasingly recognize that the advancement of financial product design and risk management technology is driven forward by the industry. Consequently, the state-of-the-art expertise is to be found in the industry which makes it inevitable that regulators draw on that expertise when devising or adjusting the regulatory framework. Secondly, asking the financial industry to participate in the drafting of financial regulation binds in the industry and thereby enhances the probability that the rules will be adhered to. Given the fact that regulation will inevitably always be limited to defining broad rules rather than constitute a micro-management of firms' behaviour, ways must be found to ensure a buy-in into the rules—and binding in those that will be regulated by them is an important way of enhancing the chances for that to happen. Finally, greater involvement of the financial industry in devising the regulatory framework can also be traced back to the fact that, in many EU member states (chiefly in the UK), there is a long tradition of consulting the financial industry on upcoming regulation as well as on making use of self-regulation—and these member states wanted to see these traditions applied on the EU level, too.

Apart from consultation on individual regulatory proposals, the Lamfalussy framework also features a monitoring mechanism for the Lamfalussy process as such. Again, this goes back to a proposal by the Wise Men Group, which advocated that the four-level approach be monitored continuously, so as to ensure that it delivered the objectives intended and did not become ossified. To ensure the full participation of all the European institutions, a monitoring group was set up consisting of six members nominated (two each) by Council, European Parliament, and the Commission. The Interinstitutional Monitoring Group (IIMG), as it became known, was constituted in July 2002 and was mandated to observe the implementation of the Lamfalussy process and to identify possible inherent bottlenecks. It issued three reports on the Lamfalussy process.[7] When the Lamfalussy process was extended to banking and insurance markets, the IIMG was reconstituted in July 2005 with new members and an extended mandate covering all three market segments.

4. An Assessment of the FSAP Results

While it is obviously too early for a comprehensive assessment of the FSAP, a general satisfaction can be deduced from stakeholders' answers to the recent consultation on the FSAP process by the Commission. Nonetheless, there are a number of concerns

---

[7] These, together with the comments by various stakeholders received thereon, are available at: http://europa.eu.int/comm/internal_market/securities/monitoring/index_en.htm.

that are already discernible and that EU policy makers must be (and indeed mostly are) aware of with an eye to future regulatory action.

First, it is also widely agreed that the FSAP produced various inconsistencies between legislative acts. Moreover, as FSAP was only one in a series of other regulatory initiatives affecting European financial institutions over recent years, an extensive set of rules and regulations resulted, which inhibits market innovation and unnecessarily raises the costs of financial services. Against this background, the possibility of consolidating the EU's securities market regulations into a single Act, i.e. an EU Securities Markets' Code, should be assessed thoroughly, as it could grant substantial benefits to investors and financial services providers.

Second, FSAP suffered from the lack of a set of overarching principles to which all regulatory acts and actions should be subject. Such principles would help to ensure the horizontal consistency of individual regulatory measures and would provide an anchor for both authorities and market participants when evaluating solutions to new regulatory issues. Such a set of principles would, for instance, include a commitment to make pan-European efficiency and international competitiveness the yardstick of all EU regulatory action. It was, again, the Wise Men Group (2001: 22) that called upon the institutions to jointly commit to such a set of overarching principles, and while the idea has been taken up by some private sector players (e.g. Inititiative Finanzstandort Deutschland 2004), the EU institutions have so far not responded to the call.

Third, rigorous evidence-based policy making was not consciously and systematically applied when preparing FSAP legislation. Rigorous use of evidence-based policy making will help to improve the quality of legislation and will help to avoid unintended side effects of financial rule-making such as damaging the competitiveness of EU financial services providers or causing excessive regulatory burdens. Against this background there now seems to be a wide consensus to base further legislative and regulatory action upon strict impact assessments; for instance, the European Commission's (2005b: 5) White Paper on Financial Services Policy 2005–10 states that a regulatory impact assessment (RIA) is a useful tool to enhance the quality of the political decision-making process and that it can contribute to a more targeted approach to the legislative process. Similarly, the 2003 Inter-Institutional Agreement on 'Better Law-Making' between Council, the EP, and the Commission also sets out useful and important principles, including emphasis on reasons for not legislating, for the use of co- and self-regulation and committing the institutions to simplifying, or even repealing legislation. However, it must be born in mind that RIA is no panacea, not the least because it suffers from methodological weaknesses. Against this background, the most important contribution of RIA may lie in the process of identifying benefits and costs of a piece of legislation rather than in the RIA's concrete (numerical) results. While RIA can help to make the political decision-making process more objective, it cannot act as a substitute for a diligent political judgement. Importantly, RIA has to be conducted at a very early stage of the legislative process. In addition, for major policy proposals, impact assessments should also be updated on a continuous basis during the legislative process, i.e. legislative proposals with high impacts on industry competitiveness are to be accompanied by consecutive impact assessments.

Fourth, the FSAP was originally designed as a predominantly intra-European project which paid little attention to the external dimension and developments on the global level. This is astonishing inasmuch as it is widely understood that financial services providers operate in a truly global business environment and that, hence, new EU regulation most always be framed with an eye to enhancing, or at least maintaining, the international competitiveness of the European financial services sector. Achieving a consensus on financial rules for the EU can never be an aim in itself; rather the results of this consensus must equip EU financial services providers with a platform on the basis of which they are able to compete globally. The intra-European focus may have contributed to the unwelcome fact that several major regulatory projects, each originating on a different level (national, EU, global), cumulated at the same time in an uncoordinated way—although, in fairness, it must be noted that some of these were reactions to unforeseen events (e.g. 9/11; the corporate scandals—Enron, WorldCom et al.—that led to the passage of the Sarbanes–Oxley Act). It is probably also true that in some cases independent EU action was useful in order to strengthen the EU's position in the international arena—the IAS regulation is a case in point.

The lack of an international dimension has meanwhile been recognized and EU authorities on various levels have recently initiated (in some cases: intensified) a regulatory dialogue with key EU commercial partners, especially the USA, Japan, and China. Similarly, Canada, Switzerland, and India are important partners and the dialogue has been extended to them, too. This will help to enhance the European influence on the global scene, to ensure the global competitiveness of European financial markets and financial services providers and to avoid that EU financial institutions are being subjected to extraterritorial effects of other nations' financial rule making. It is important to point out that the success of these regulatory dialogues ultimately has one important precondition on the part of the EU: the EU must ensure that regulatory measures are applied and enforced consistently, reliably, and in high quality in all twenty-seven member states. Only if the quality of regulation and supervision can be guaranteed for all market segments and across the entire EU can regulatory equivalence be established as a guiding principle in the EU's regulatory dialogue with other countries.

5. AN ASSESSMENT OF THE LAMFALUSSY PROCESS

5.1. Does it Work?

In the eyes of most stakeholders, the Lamfalussy process has proved to be an important mechanism to foster supervisory convergence across the EU as well as a valuable step to enhance the flexibility and pace of the legislative process.[8] In addition, the new architecture of 'level 3' committees—CESR, the Committee of European Banking Supervisors (CEBS), and the Committee of European Insurance and Occupational Pension Supervisors (CEIOPS)—laid the foundation to develop an unprecedented amount of cooperation between national supervisors.

Having said this, to date, it is too early to pass a definite judgement on the Lamfalussy process as only few pieces of legislation have been passed under the framework[9] and no experience of amending level 2 legislation in response to market changes has yet been gained—the latter being, as was said above, the true test for the Lamfalussy process. In addition, level 4 remains largely untested in practice and, for obvious reasons, hardly any experience with the Lamfalussy framework has yet been accumulated in banking and insurance.

Notwithstanding the overall positive assessment of the process, there still exists room for practical improvement. As a matter of principle, when evaluating the process it is crucial to carefully distinguish between content-related drawbacks of individual directives that were adopted under the Lamfalussy framework and shortcomings inherent to the Lamfalussy process itself. Five seem to be particularly relevant as regards the latter.

First, in marked contrast to the core objective of the Lamfalussy process, there is a trend to incorporate excessive details in level 1 legislation. This is partly due to a lack of trust amongst the institutions; partly due to uncertainty—reflecting a lack of experience—on the side of market participants about the policies that will be followed by the institutions responsible for level 2 and level 3 measures. In order to make full use of the potential of the Lamfalussy process, institutions and level 3 committees would therefore need to fully adhere to the assigned boundaries and functions of each layer of the Lamfalussy framework.

Second, while consultation has improved considerably, the consultation procedure has various shortcomings: notably timetables for consultation are too tight, implying the risk of lowering the quality of consultations and excluding some (smaller) market participants by disproportionally burdening their resources. It is obvious that tight timetables as well as a high burden on industry's resources in general partly resulted from the high pace of FSAP legislation. In general, the consultation process could probably be improved by extending consultation periods to a minimum period of three months and by providing consultees with regular meaningful feedback on their input. The latter may also prevent a tendency by industry representatives to keep pressing the same points again and again.

A further issue, which the IIMG and other observers as well as parties to the process have been concerned about as regards consultation, is that while the intermediaries are active participants in the consultation process, the end-users of financial services—consumers and investors, but also issuers—are under-represented. The

---

[8] It needs pointing out that, at least in the eyes of the members of the Lamfalussy Group, making the EU's legislative process more flexible was always considered more important than making it quicker.

[9] These are the Transparency Obligation Directive, the Prospective Directive, the Market Abuse Directive, and the Markets in Financial Instruments Directive.

IIMG has reverted to this theme repeatedly in its reports (IIMG 2003: 29; IIMG 2004: 24/5). Consumer representatives argue that a lack of resources, expertise, and language skills is responsible for this; and while this certainly plays a role, prioritization might be an issue here, too.

Third, as the IIMG's third report noted (IIMG 2004: 29), the rising use of the 'soft law' approach has its limits and the multiplication of non-binding rules at level 3 may lead to a grey area where legal certainty is absent and political accountability is unclear. While market participants fully back the enhanced supervisory cooperation at level 3, the accountability problems of level 3 committees *de facto* setting legally binding rules without possessing a legal and institutional mandate to do so need to be clarified. In its 'Himalaya report', CESR (2004) indicated that it is aware of the issue and hinted at the possibility that, over time, the level 3 committees may need to be established on a firmer legal footing.

Fourth, the Lamfalussy process can ultimately only work if regulators work together in the spirit of corporation and mutual trust, and if they are organizing their cooperation (especially at level 3) in a way which allows to develop common approaches where necessary. While it is recognized that level 3 committees cannot issue official guidelines on level 3 before the implementation dateline of legislation on previous levels is reached, market participants should be provided with informal guidance on implementation questions well before such date. Furthermore, for some of the level 3 rules passed so far, it was not clear why certain issues have been chosen for level 3 harmonization, whilst others have not. Finally, it should also be ensured that CESR maintains permanent working groups of regulators in which questions related to the implementation of directives can be discussed on an ongoing basis.

Fifth, the monitoring of national implementation by the Commission at level 4 constitutes an essential part of the Lamfalussy process. In practical terms, this not only requires that the Commission allocates sufficient staff to such monitoring function; the monitoring can also only work effectively if it commences already during the implementing phase of the respective directive, when comments can easily be taken up by the participants in the legislative process on a national level. For the directives based on the Lamfalussy process for which the implementation date has passed, or will come shortly, not much activity of the Commission in this field has become visible, although there are cases of national implementing rules for which the compliance with the respective directive seems more than questionable.

Whereas the first two aspects are probably transitory and expected to gradually dissolve over time, the third aspect constitutes an inherent drawback of the Lamfalussy process which is not easily amendable.

5.2. The Future of the Lamfalussy Process

The establishment of the level 3 committees (CESR, CEBS, CEIOPS) has intensified and will no doubt further improve the cooperation of supervisory authorities as well as the consistency of implementation in the EU. Conserving the status quo and complementing it with further mechanisms for improved cooperation and co-ordination would appear to have an advantage in that it is politically feasible and can be implemented without major (legal and operational) prerequisites. However, conserving the status quo is, at best, a practical stop-gap measure, but not a long-term option, as the current supervisory structure is deficient on several scores:

- As indicated above, the status of the level 3 committees is in a legal grey area (cf. also Section 5.3). The more active the level 3 committees are (often with the best of intentions), the greater the danger that they engage in activities that are not covered by their mandate.
- The level 3 committees work by consensus. This may not necessarily be the most productive way when they operate in their level 2 advisory function, as a con-sensus on the least common denominator not only obscures existing differences of opinion, but, by doing so, withholds from the Commission what might be valuable information about alternative approaches.
- Multiple reporting requirements and multiple approval processes lead to un-necessary costs for financial service providers. Efforts aimed at streamlining reporting requirements often get stuck halfway. CEBS's proposals for common prudential and financial reporting standards (COREP and FINREP) are cases in point: While the suggested reporting package was reduced substantially as compared to the last draft version, the proposed framework still represents 'maximum' harmonization. i.e. a mere agglomeration of all possible regulatory requirements with a national discretion of the regulator to pick; thus, they do not provide any harmonization effort.
- Similarly, the cooperation of national authorities in the level 3 committees has done little to eliminate inconsistent implementation of EU regulation in differ-ent member states as well as diverging levels of expertise and different super-visory philosophies, all of which continue to distort competition and maintain market fragmentation.
- Within the intergovernmental approach it is well-nigh impossible to find arrangements that simultaneously do justice to industry's desire for a fully consolidated supervision by only one supervisory authority within the EU and the responsibility (and hence understandable desire) of national authorities to safeguard the stability of their respective national financial systems; this holds true a fortiori for those jurisdictions where operations by foreign-owned entities represent a large part of financial activity.
- Due to their intergovernmental nature, the level 3 committees are unable to solve conflicts between national supervisors; efforts to solve this issue by means of some kind of mediation mechanism will be circumscribed by the limits of the soft-law approach.

At the heart of all these issues is the fact that the Lamfalussy structure tries to square the circle of, on the one hand, devising a regulatory structure that is efficient and effective for an integrated European financial market, and, on the other hand, respecting the interests and responsibilities of national supervisors. Theoretically, the two are not necessarily mutually incompatible, but in practice, they often seem to be. Unsurprisingly, this keeps the discussion of possible alternatives to the Lamfalussy structure alive.

Within the financial industry, there is, to name but one, considerable support for strengthening the power of home supervisors, e.g. under the so-called 'lead supervisor concept'. This concept has, inter alia, been analysed and is supported by the European Financial Services Roundtable (EFR 2005). Likewise, individual rules in several FSAP directives point to more progressive solutions. Thus, the Capital Requirements Directive, in Article 129, develops the concept of a 'consolidated supervisor', and the Prospectus Directive provides the possibility for the competent home authority to voluntarily transfer the approval of a prospectus to another CESR member.

More systematically, CESR, the most advanced of the three level 3 committees, discussed various options for the future structure of securities markets regulation in its 2004 consultation paper on 'Which supervisory tools for the EU securities markets?', better known as the 'Himalaya report' (CESR 2004: 19/20). In it, CESR conjectures that the traditional model of supervisory cooperation and the existing allocation of home–host responsibilities were an adequate response to a structure in which a financial institution's activities abroad constituted a small part of the overall business volume. This response may, however, be inadequate for institutions that have major business activities in many countries—which, of course, is the reality for a growing number of financial institutions across Europe. Hence, CESR discusses the appropriateness of various tools and institutional arrangements with a view to ensuring that these correspond to the evolving nature of EU financial markets. It is also suggested that CESR should specify the role of securities regulators in the management of an identified crisis (section II c i) and should identify the priorities in case of shocks.

The Himalaya paper also points out that all EU securities regulators should have the same competences within their respective jurisdictions. This is, indeed, a precondition for supervisory cooperation and soft law to work effectively. The idea of a cooperative network of securities supervisors and the instrument of peer review, as constituted by CESR, will only work satisfactorily if the participating national authorities enjoy equal powers. Similarly, the mutual recognition of regulatory decisions, let alone the delegation of regulatory powers to another member state's authority, is only conceivable if all national authorities possess equivalent competences. In addition, national supervisors should not only have the same competences, but also the same capacity to act. This requires that all national supervisors be equipped with adequate financial and human resources—adequate to fulfil their role within their respective jurisdiction, but also adequate to conduct meaningful consultation processes on the national level as well as to fully and actively participate in EU-level (CESR) activities.

The Himalaya paper also introduced the idea of a mediation mechanism to resolve instances where supervisors differ in their interpretation of a particular norm. For these cases, a mediation mechanism amongst CESR members would be a useful mechanism that avoids the lengthy process of taking issues into a formal procedure under the leadership of the Commission and, ultimately, to be decided by the ECJ.

Meanwhile, a mediation mechanism has been established by CESR. However, while such a mechanism, is no doubt will useful, it lead CESR further into a legal grey area, as the mediation mechanism needs to be reconcilable with national administrative and judicial procedures, with democratic accountability, and must not compromise the Commission's enforcements procedures—something that will be difficult to achieve within the existing legal framework.

All in all, it is probably safe to assume that the debate on the suitability of the Lamfalussy structure will continue—which is, in fact, appropriate, as the regulatory and supervisory regime must evolve with the EU's financial market structure.

5.3. The Issue of Democratic Accountability

The debate about the nature, responsibility, and role of level 3 committees reflects, as it were, a birth defect of the Lamfalussy process. The work of the Wise Men Group was guided by the prerogative to find a pragmatic solution to the deficiency of EU securities market regulation that could be implemented within the confines of the existing Treaty on the European Union. This prerogative reflected the common understanding that a treaty change (aiming for instances at new, pan-European institutions) would take too long to come about and would, in any case, be unlikely to emerge given strong resistance to the idea in many member states. Against this background, any newly created institutional structure was bound to end up in an uneasy constitutional area where strictly intergovernmental and pan-European structures overlap—as, indeed, happened in the case of the level 3 committees.

In a way, the debate about the democratic legitimacy and accountability of the level 3 committees is a good sign, as it is testament to their being successful and effective. If these fora did not achieve anything, nobody would care to criticize them. Yet, this very success makes it all the more important to seriously consider whether the charge of a lack of democratic legitimacy and accountability is justified or not. Obviously, the level 3 committees have an indirect democratic legitimacy. They represent democratically elected governments. Governments represented in the level 3 committees have the right to instruct their representatives to grant or withhold their consent to any agreement reached within the committees.

More broadly, governments and parliaments can and must define the scope of activities when they define the committee's mandate. This is a key control tool for parliaments and government. A control tool no less important is transparency and the imposition of reporting requirements on technical committees. In this vein, the Lamfalussy process has not only, as mentioned above, created an unprecedented amount of consultation based on codified procedures, but the level 3 committees are also committed to reporting to both Council and Parliament, on a regular basis, by means of testimonies, annual reports, and a proactive forwarding of documents. Their decision to draft and publish annual work programmes falls into the same category. Of course, transparency by itself does not bestow legitimacy and is no substitute for formal accountability to parliaments—but, like the control of mandates and action, it helps to alleviate concerns about *de facto* rule-setting powers.

The discussion on the democratic legitimacy and accountability of international institutions and networks will, no doubt, intensify over time. This is not surprising: the discussion reflects not only concerns about democratic deficits of these institutions; it also, if not more, reflects a more fundamental uneasiness about the erosion of the autonomy of the nation state as well as about the need for individuals, firms, and interest groups to find new channels to influence policy making in a transnational setting. Seen optimistically, international fora such as regulators' international networks are an answer to this uneasiness: by pooling sovereignty, democracies regain influence over developments beyond the control of the individual nation state—in this sense they are the solution, not the problem for modern democracies! (Zürn 2005: 141).

6. Outlook: Securities Market Regulation in the White Paper

In December 2005, the EU Commission (2005b) presented a White Paper on Financial Services Policy 2005–10 which outlines the Commission's agenda for financial market regulation in the coming years. The White Paper draws on the recommendations by four expert groups, which delivered their final reports in 2004, and the responses to the Commission's Green Paper of May 2005. In general, securities markets regulations plays a less prominent role in the White Paper than they did in FSAP; however, this merely reflects the substantial progress made in this area in the course of FSAP implementation and the relatively greater need for regulatory action in the fields of retail financial services and asset management, where market integration lags behind that in (wholesale) securities markets.

Nonetheless, for securities markets, too, the White Paper identifies a number of areas where action needs to be taken. Apart from the further development of the EU's supervisory structure, which is rightly defined as a key area of activity, the most important is the conclusion of the work on clearing and settlement structures in the EU. While clearing and settlement structures within the member states are very efficient, cross-border clearing and settlement infrastructures are far more costly, which discourages cross-border securities transactions. The work of the Giovannini Group[10] has identified various technical, legal, and fiscal factors as the reasons for these high costs and work is under way to address these. Additionally, joint technical standards and measures for effective competition between providers need to be established. On

---

[10] These are available at: www.europa.eu.int/comm/internal_market/financial-markets/clearing/index_de.htm#giovannini. Cf. also Hartmann, Maddaloni, and Manganelli 2003: 39–41.

the basis of an impact assessment the Commission will decide whether legislative action needs to be taken and, if so, how substantial this needs to be.

The second key area is the EUR 5tr EU investment fund industry. A revision of the so-called UCITS[11] Directive is already under discussion and must aim at making Europe's investment fund industry more efficient. Currently, EU investment funds are, on average, only a fifth the size of US investment funds—testament to the continuing fragmentation of Europe's UCITS markets and the resulting inability of European investment firms to exploit economies of scale in fund management. The crucial issues are an unimpeded distribution of funds across the entire EU on the basis of a single passport, cross-border fund pooling and mergers, and the ability to concentrate different parts of the investment fund value chain—production, management, administration—in different locations across the EU according to the respective comparative advantages.

Thirdly, thought is being given to the possibility of consolidating EU's securities market regulations into a single act, i.e. an EU Securities Markets' Code. As discussed in Section 4, this could bring substantial benefits to investors and financial services providers.

Finally, the international dimension of securities markets regulation will play a greater role in the coming years, with the project of a transatlantic securities market integration playing a particularly prominent role given that it would build on an already intensive interlinkage of the two financial markets on both sides of the Atlantic and given that it promises substantial efficiency gains (Steil 2002: 29 f.)

7. CONCLUSION

Securities market integration harbours the potential for substantial welfare gains for investors, issuers, and intermediaries. More integrated and, hence, more efficient markets are also conducive to higher growth. The FSAP, notwithstanding various shortcomings, has been a catalyst to the integration of the EU's securities markets. Its effectiveness has been further enhanced by the establishment of the Lamfalussy process which has not only made EU financial market legislation more flexible, but— which may be more important in the long term—created the framework for a pan-European approach to EU securities market regulation and supervision. While the specific institutional form this will take remains the subject of considerable debate, the intensive collaboration of EU financial regulators in European networks and fora will in any case be supportive of further integration efforts. Nevertheless, it needs to be recalled that processes such as the Lamfalussy process can only do so much. The successful realization of an integrated financial market in the EU will require a strong political will on the part of all three European institutions—and, not the least, the

---

[11] UCITS = undertakings for collective investment in transferable securities.

initiative by financial institutions and their clients to make use of the new market opportunities.

REFERENCES

CABRAL, I., DIERICK F., and VESALA, J. (2002), 'Banking integration in the euro area', ECB Occasional Paper Series, no. 6, Frankfurt.

COMMITTEE OF EUROPEAN SECURITIES REGULATORS (CESR) (2001), *Public Statement of Consultation Practices*, CESR/01-007c, Paris.

—— (2004), *Which Supervisory Tools for the EU Securities Markets?* ('Himalaya report'), CESR/04-333f, Paris.

COMMITTEE OF WISE MEN ('LAMFALUSSY GROUP') (2001), *Final Report on the Regulation of European Securities Markets*, Brussels.

D'ARCY, A. (2004), 'Current developments in European and German financial reporting', *EU Monitor*, 19, Financial Market Special, Deutsche Bank Research, Frankfurt.

DIECKMANN, R. (2005), 'Post-FSAP agenda: window of opportunity to complete financial market integration', *EU Monitor*, 24, Financial Market Special, Deutsche Bank Research, Frankfurt.

EUROPEAN COMMISSION (1999), *Financial Services: Implementing the Framework for Financial Markets: Action Plan*; Communication of the Commission, COM(1999)232, Brussels.

—— (2005a), *Cross-Border Consolidation in the EU Financial Sector*, Commission Staff Working Document, SEC (2005) 1398, Brussels.

—— (2005b), *White Paper Financial Services Policy 2005–2010*, Brussels, available at: http://europa.eu.int/comm/internal_market/finances/docs/white_paper/white_paper_en.pdf.

EUROPEAN FINANCIAL SERVICES ROUNDTABLE (EFR) (2005), *On the Lead Supervisor Model and the Future of Financial Supervision in the EU*, Brussels.

GERSTER, C., et al. (2004), *European Banking and Financial Services Law*, The Hague: Kluwer.

GILPIN, R. (1987), *The Political Economy of International Relations*, Princeton: Princeton University Press.

HARTMANN, P., MADDALONI, A., and MANGANELLI, S. (2003), 'The euro area financial system: structure, integration policy initiatives', ECB Working Paper 230, Frankfurt.

INITIATIVE FINANZSTANDORT DEUTSCHLAND (2004), *The Future of European Financial Market Integration*, Berlin.

INTER-INSTITUTIONAL MONITORING GROUP (IIMG) (2003), *Second Interim Report Monitoring the Lamfalussy Process*, Brussels.

—— (2004), *Third Report Monitoring the Lamfalussy Process*, Brussels.

KERN, S. (2002), 'EU on the bumpy road to a single market in financial services', *Frankfurt Voice*, EU Financial Market Special, Deutsche Bank Research, Frankfurt.

LEVINE, R. (2003), 'More on finance and growth: more finance, more growth?', *Federal Reserve Bank of St Louis Review*, 85(4), 31–46.

OECD (2001), 'Contributions of financial systems to growth in OECD countries', Economics Department Working Paper no. 280, Paris.

—— (2003), 'European banking and stock market integration', *Financial Market Trends*, 84, 99–117.

STEIL, B. (2002), *Building a Transatlantic Securities Market*, Zurich: ISDA.

ZÜRN, M. (2005), 'Global governance', in G. F. Schuppert (ed.), *Governance-Forschung*, Baden-Baden: Nomos, 121–46.

....

CHAPTER 25

THE SUPERVISION OF AN INTEGRATING EUROPEAN BANKING SECTOR

THEORY, PRACTICE, AND CHALLENGES

KOSTAS TSATSARONIS

The single market objective for financial services in Europe dates back to the earliest days of the European Economic Community. Given the dominant position of banks in the European financial landscape, the objective has always effectively implied the closer integration of national banking markets. Nevertheless, progress along in this dimension, and in particular in retail deposit and loan markets, has been slower compared to other industries. This more limited success can be partly attributed to the nature of the banking business as a service industry. Distance and cultural factors, including language, play an important role in shaping client/provider relationships.

I would like to thank, without implication, Philipp Hartmann, Xavier Freixas, and Fabio Recine for helpful comments. The views expressed herein are those of the author and do not necessarily reflect those of the BIS.

Banking is also one of the most regulated industries, and there is a two-way interaction between the degree of cross-border integration of the banking business and the degree of compatibility of national prudential frameworks. This chapter focuses on these interactions in the European context.

There is no agreement as to what constitutes the optimal architecture for the prudential framework of the financial sector. The ideal framework would strike a balance between the twin goals of promoting a competitive environment, which encourages innovation and rewards efficiency at the level of individual institutions, and of minimizing the costs from instability for the system as a whole. While the two objectives are often mutually reinforcing, in the sense that greater confidence in the resilience of the financial system fosters activity, they can also be conflicting if competitive market forces give rise to incentives for excessive risk taking. Similarly, the management of financial distress constrained by the modalities of equal treatment of market players can be ineffective in containing the spreading of financial strain. Different countries have adopted different models of prudential architecture that partly reflect the historical development of their respective financial sector.

In the international context the question is further complicated by the additional requirement that international arrangements accommodate national sovereignty. Arguably, the challenges of the achieving the triple objective of maintaining financial system stability, supervision at the national level, and fostering a high degree of integration of the financial sector are similar to achieving the 'impossible trinity' in international finance.[1]

This chapter focuses on the three components of the prudential framework for the banking sector: regulation, supervision, and crisis management. It discusses the modalities implied by a financial sector that is tightly interconnected across borders for a prudential architecture which is necessarily designed around national sovereign rights. This is a subset of the issues that relate to the overall objective of achieving financial stability. Issues related to the stability and efficiency of financial infrastructure as well as the interactions between financial stability and macroeconomic stability are covered elsewhere in this volume.[2]

The chapter proceeds from the abstract to the specific and from the positive to the normative. It is structured in four sections. The first section gives a brief overview of the main messages from a recent theoretical literature on the structure of supervision in the context of internationally active banks. The following sections focus more squarely on the European context. The second section presents the current state of affairs in terms of the cross-border integration of banking services as well as the organization of bank supervision at the national and the European levels. The third section takes a forward look outlining the different views as to the likely directions in which the prudential framework could evolve. The final section gives a summary of

---

[1] The 'impossible trinity' is typically presented as the incompatibility of full international capital mobility, an independent monetary policy, and a fixed exchange rate regime in the context of the Mundell–Fleming model.

[2] See P. Aghion's contribution on macroeconomic stability, financial development, and growth.

the themes discussed and the main policy challenges posed by the evolving profile of European banking.

1. MESSAGES FROM APPLIED THEORY

A budding applied theoretical literature studies the organization of banking supervision when banks are engaged in cross-border business. Employing highly stylized models, these studies offer several insights with regard to the structure of incentives that shape the behaviour of regulators and banks. This section aims to summarize the main messages that emerge from this literature, which are relevant beyond the specific European circumstances. These messages can be usefully classified into three groups: the identification of externalities, the analysis of incentives shaping the behaviour of supervisors, and the incentives affecting the behaviour of supervised banks. These are discussed in turn below.

The externalities that arise in the context of decision making by home and host supervisors are due to the fact that neither of the two has a 'global' perspective on the economic costs associated with a bank failure.[3] This is illustrated clearly in the model of Dell'Ariccia and Marquez (2006) where banks raise deposits domestically and lend to both the domestic and foreign market while being subject to home country prudential oversight. The prudential authority uses ex ante capital requirements to maximize the weighted sum of domestic banks' global profits and probability of survival. Higher capital requirements may increase the stability of domestic banks but reduce their global competitiveness. The externality arises from the fact that home authorities will tend to underweigh the costs to the host economy from a possible bank failure while they do account for the full benefits of domestic banks' enhanced profitability from their international operations. The same type of externality arises in the models of Acharya (2003), Freixas (2003), and Sinn (2001).[4]

A separate strand of the literature focuses on a different type of externalities which are commonly, albeit not always consistently, labelled as *contagion* and take different forms. One form is banking panics that can emerge in the wake of few isolated bank failures if there are asymmetries in the information that bank liability holders receive (Chen 1999). Another form is contagion through interbank exposures in the presence of market incompleteness that can lead to situations when solvent banks may be forced to liquidate their holdings leading to suboptimal economic outcomes (Allen and Gale 2000; Freixas, Parigi, and Rochet 2000). In contrast to the externalities in

---

[3] Home country is understood to be the country where the bank is headquartered, while the host country is another country where the bank has business activities. In certain theoretical models this labelling is in essence arbitrary while in others home country is where the bank conducts the majority of its business and where its profits accrue.

[4] The 'undersupply' of regulatory intensity and bias towards forbearance is also identified in Kahn and Santos 2004.

policy decision making, there is nothing inherently international in the nature of those mechanisms. They can arise equally well in a purely domestic setting. Clearly they become more relevant as cross-border banking integration deepens (see below), highlighting the challenges to the design of the potential policy intervention.

The second group of messages from the literature relates to how externalities distort the calibration of policy tools and, in the absence of coordination between supervisory authorities, can lead to suboptimal outcomes. Typically the asymmetry in the perception of the economic costs of distress biases the home supervisor towards greater laxity, or a higher effective degree of risk tolerance vis-à-vis bank failures. From a 'global' perspective, the outcome of the competition between the two prudential authorities is suboptimal regulatory standards, namely, the tolerance of a higher likelihood of financial distress (either in the form of higher ex ante probability of failure, or lower incidence of bail-outs) in order to enhance the franchise value (current profits) of domestic banks. This is the case in Acharya (2003), Dell'Ariccia and Marquez (2006), Freixas (2003), and Sinn (2001), but also in Holthausen and Rønde (2004), who study a related problem involving the exchange of information between home and host authorities (see below). Kahn and Santos (2004) also identify an 'undersupply' of regulatory scrutiny and bias towards forbearance in their analysis.

The specific set of policy instruments available is not an important factor in shaping supervisory behaviour. Freixas (2003) focuses on the use of an ex post decision of whether to bail out a failing bank. Acharya (2003) empowers the regulator with two ex ante policy instruments: capital requirements and a stochastic closure policy (forbearance). While the former can be coordinated internationally, the authorities' readiness to close or bail out a failed bank could differ across countries. A higher minimum capital requirement allows the regulator to opt for higher forbearance, which in turn lowers the private choice of (economic) capital by the bank. The externalities that lead to this 'competition in laxity' intensify as the differences in regulatory objectives grow, either because of differences in regulatory attitudes towards forbearance or differences in the franchise value of their respective banking systems.

The distortion is primarily due to regulatory capture (i.e. the identification of the regulator with the interests of the regulated banks) as illustrated by a comparison of the papers mentioned above with that of Dalen and Olsen (2003). In their set-up there is no regulatory capture and the prudential authority is empowered with three instruments: the amount of risk-free assets that the bank should hold, the deposit insurance premium, and the level of overall asset quality. Although strategic considerations affect the calibration of individual policy instruments, giving rise for example to lower effective minimum capital requirements, they do not affect their *combined* effect on the stability of banks as measured by the probability of failure.

Coordination between supervisors in the sense of adopting a common set of standards across borders is a way of overcoming the shortcomings of regulatory competition. The feasibility of such an outcome depends critically on the similarity of the regulatory preferences and the number of countries involved. In the set-up of Dell'Ariccia and Marquez (2006), when regulators' preferences are identical, coordination results in higher capital requirements compared to the competitive equilibrium, and it also represents a preferred choice for the two authorities who will voluntarily surrender independence.[5] When preferences of regulators differ, voluntary coordination (if feasible) results in prudential requirements that are at least as conservative as those imposed by the more conservative authority. However, the greater the divergence in the two authorities' preferences, the more difficult it is to coordinate.[6] In addition, this difficulty increases if regulatory unification is considered among a larger number of countries. Even with identical supervisory preferences, unification within a large group might not be feasible because the flexibility of being an 'out' country becomes more valuable than the benefits of joining the group as the number of countries increases.

Holthausen and Rønde (2004) analyse the cooperation between home and host authorities from the different perspective of information exchange.[7] The single policy tool in their set-up is the decision to close a bank that is deemed to be too 'risky' in order to avoid the systemic costs from a disorderly failure. The externality from the asymmetric distribution of the bank's business across the two economies leads to different degrees of effective risk tolerance (therefore, also readiness to exercise closure) for each supervisor. They find that strategic considerations will affect the precision of the information transmitted from the host to the home supervisor, and will lead to suboptimal closure decisions. The problem is more pronounced the greater the asymmetry in the perspective of the two supervisors.

The third set of results in the literature relates to how the regulatory architecture and policy stance interact with the business structure of the supervised institutions. This is a two-way interaction. On the one hand, the application of regulatory tools may be influenced by organizational choices of banks. On the other hand, banks may engage in regulatory arbitrage by allocating their resources across different jurisdictions and by optimizing their internal corporate structure in ways that minimize their regulatory burden.

Calzolari and Lóránth (2004) build on a set-up borrowed from the industrial organization literature to compare the supervisory treatment of multinational banks which may select to organize their international operations in the form of branches or subsidiaries. Subsidiaries fall under the authority of the host supervisor while branches remain under the oversight of the home authority. In their model the supervisor is also the deposit insurer and concerned primarily with minimizing the costs of bank distress, both in the ex ante sense (the cost of intervention to avoid failure) and in the ex post sense (the costs of repaying depositors). They find that the home regulator has stronger incentives than the host regulator to intervene early when a bank has a subsidiary structure because resources from the foreign operations

---

[5] By contrast, in the set-up of Harr and Rønde 2006 opportunistic behaviour between several regulators of a cross-border bank leads to higher capital requirements because the cost of capital is shared across the units of the bank in different countries.

[6] In the set-up of Acharya 2003 the costs from a 'race to the bottom' in terms of the instrument over which regulators maintain discretion (forbearance) can outstrip any benefits from coordination in the other instrument (required capital). In Repullo 2001 the takeover of a foreign bank will lead to a welfare improvement since it will reduce the excessive toughness of the home supervisor.

[7] The suboptimal exchange of information is also discussed but not explicitly modelled in Freixas 2003.

of the bank reduce the cost of intervention. In addition, when a bank is organized through branches, its home units are subject to more lenient supervision than when it is organized through subsidiaries, since the cost of repaying foreign depositors is higher in the former case. Overall, the incentive of regulators to monitor banks is higher under a branch structure than under a subsidiary structure, although host supervisors should monitor very intensively foreign subsidiaries in their jurisdiction. In Dalen and Olsen (2003) the effect of the international banks' choice of corporate structure on the calibration of policy tools is ambiguous and depends on the economic environment as well as the interlinkages between the institutions.

The response of banks to the regulatory arrangements is studied in a number of papers. Holthausen and Rønde (2004) find that the bank will allocate strategically its business across jurisdictions in order to reduce the likelihood of closure. Interestingly, this may involve shifting more business towards the country with the more conservative supervisor in order to increase the costs to that economy in the event of closure and, hence, encourage forbearance. Calzolari and Lóránth (2004) find that when the bank headquarters' operation is financially riskier, the bank will opt for a branch structure to ensure greater regulatory leniency. In the model of Morrison and Lóránth (2003) capital requirements counterbalance the moral hazard of deposit insurance. A subsidiary organization, which takes fuller advantage of the existence deposit insurance, would be preferred by banks if capital requirements are not sensitive to the overall risk of the multinational institution. Freixas, Lóránth, and Morrison (2005) also study the interaction between regulation and diversification in the context of financial conglomerates, and conclude that it leads to a preference for subsidiary structures.

In Harr and Rønde (2005) branch structures are less vulnerable in normal times as banks can reallocate excess capital across the organization more efficiently. In periods of stress, however, risk is likely to spill over from one branch to another because the incentive to gamble for resurrection intensifies. In the absence of adverse selection, optimal regulation would tend to favour branch organization. If bank risk types are not observable, optimal regulation would induce riskier banks to self-select into a subsidiary structure.

2. THE CURRENT STATE OF AFFAIRS

The prudential architecture in Europe is based on a set of national structures overlaid by a superstructure of area-wide arrangements. The design of national prudential structures reflects country-specific factors but is also increasingly influenced by international trends. The Europe-wide superstructure reflects the harmonization and coordination efforts within the context of the European single market and the EMU. The degree to which the overall prudential architecture achieves the twin goals of financial stability and competitive efficiency in the context of an integrating banking market depends critically on how the two elements interact with each other as well as with banking sector developments. A detailed analysis of the degree of integration of banking services in Europe is beyond the scope of this chapter, which will only sketch some salient features of the European banking landscape in order to place in context the discussion about prudential architecture.[8]

The vast majority of European banks are small and not systemically critical. They tend to operate within specific geographic regions and to have relatively simple corporate and balance sheet structures (Padoa-Schioppa 2004). These institutions do not represent an important challenge to the supervisory framework either at the national or European levels. More challenges arise in conjunction with the activities of a smaller, but growing, number of institutions with important business activity outside their home market. These institutions are much larger and have more complex operations than the average bank. Their international operations take the form of the provision of (primarily wholesale) banking services across borders and/or of direct presence abroad through branches or subsidiaries. In recent years, the cumulative impact of the euro and the accession of new countries into the EU have boosted the significance of these institutions.[9]

As cross-border banking activity intensifies, situations arise where the relative significance of a bank for the home and host economies might be quite different. For example, the domestic country operations of a medium-sized bank in a large economy with a developed banking sector might be relatively less important to the home system than this bank's subsidiary operations might be for a smaller economy with a less developed banking market. Similarly, the tendency of banks from smaller countries to be relatively more active abroad raises the possibility that a problem in the international operations of a bank might overstretch the home country's prudential resources.

Another source of interdependence relates to the strengthening of commonalities in the drivers of risk across institutions, in line with the intensification of cross-border banking activity. Schoenmaker and Oosterloo (2005) highlight the increasing scope of contagion due to cross-border exposures of banks in the euro area. Similarly, Hartmann, Straetmans, and de Vries (2005), using measures from extreme value statistical analysis, observe that the gradual process of banking integration has been associated with somewhat closer comovement of equity market valuations for European banks over the 1990s. They also find that the introduction of the euro led to an increase in the importance of the systematic risk component in European bank equities but, despite having brought about a closer the integration of interbank markets, did not lead to further increases in spillover risk. Gropp and Moerman (2004) and Gropp, Lo Duca, and Vesala (2006) use different statistical measures of comovement

---

[8] Cabral, Dierick, and Vesala 2002 provide a good overview of banking market integration in Europe paying attention to the differences in speed between various market segments. See also Baele et al. 2004 and Manna 2004.

[9] For further analysis see the contribution of Degryse and Ongena in this volume; CGFS 2004; Schoenmaker and Oosterloo 2005; and Baudino et al. 2004.

Table 25.1. The organizational structure of financial supervision

European arrangements	National arrangements		
	1. Sectoral	2. Cross-sector functional	3. Cross-sector integrated
A. Decentralized with cooperation	Cooperation in sectoral committees	Cooperation in functional committees	Cooperation between national FSAs
B. Decentralized with coordination	Coordination between national sectoral supervisors	Coordination between national functional supervisors	Coordination between national FSAs
C. Centralized	Separate European sectoral supervisory agencies	European prudential supervisor and European SEC	European FSA

Source: Kremers, Schoenmaker, and Wierts 2003.

of bank share prices and (equity market-derived) measures of default risk to find similar increase in the systematic risk of large European banks as well as an increase in spillover risk in the sector.

European banks tend to favour subsidiary structures when expanding into other European countries despite the theoretical benefits of a consolidated corporate structure based on branch networks. Dermine (2006) points out that inefficiencies of the regulatory environment in the form of tax disincentives and higher costs of deposit insurance are an important factor explaining this apparent puzzle.[10] Although from legal and regulatory perspectives the distinction between branches and subsidiaries is quite important, from a business perspective it becomes increasingly less relevant. Current trends in business organization tend to blur the operational distinction between the two organizational forms, at least with respect to the ability of the foreign operation to function on a stand-alone basis. More specifically, the desire to fully leverage advances in technology leads banks to consolidate certain activities such as back-office operations and IT infrastructures. Greater centralization of such functions increases the dependency of subsidiaries on parent company resources. Similarly, consolidated risk management might weaken the strategic decision-making ability of subsidiaries, whereas enterprise-wide liquidity management will arguably reduce the effectiveness of subsidiaries' ring-fencing (Srejber 2006).

Against this background, the rest of the section will focus on the prudential structures at the national and Europe-wide levels. To this end, it is helpful to use a two-dimensional organizational framework proposed by Kremers, Schoenmaker, and Wierts (2003) and outlined in Table 25. 1. Columns 1–3 correspond to different types

---

[10] He suggests that motives related to the management of internal and external informational frictions, the ability to ring-fence risks, and the ease at which a potential divestment could take place are also contributing factors.

of arrangements at the national level: Sectoral, Cross-sector functional, and Cross-sector integrated supervisory structures. Rows A–C correspond to the European arrangements: Decentralized with cooperation, Decentralized with coordination, and Centralized. The cells describe the nature of overall arrangements that combine different types of national and area-wide types. It is also helpful to distinguish more clearly between various elements of the prudential framework: regulation (the setting of rules and standards), supervision (the policing of bank activities in normal times), and crisis management (the response to financial distress at the institution and system levels).

2.1. National Prudential Structures

The architecture of banking supervision differs substantially across European countries reflecting the legacy of historical institutional designs and the structure of national financial systems. Table 25.2 provides a general overview of the national regulatory and supervisory arrangements.

In a number of countries the supervision of the financial sector is organized across sectoral lines and in the majority of these cases the supervision of banks is entrusted to the central bank. Many European countries, however, have opted for integrated financial sector supervision following the example of Norway in the mid-1980s.[11] This trend has intensified over the past ten years and is more pronounced among the new EU members. In almost all cases the reorganization brought about the creation of an independent supervisory agency and a reduction in the supervisory responsibilities of the central bank. Four countries have adopted some type of a functional architecture with bank supervision assigned to the central bank (Italy, Portugal, and the Netherlands) or to an agency that is closely associated with the central bank (France).

A reduction in the central bank's involvement in bank supervision, however, does not necessarily suggest a diminished role for the central bank in other aspects of the prudential framework. Central banks remain very much involved in the drawing up of regulations and their role is quite influencial. They are also parties to formal protocols of cooperation among prudential authorities, which include agreements for the exchange of information, participation in standing committees that share assessments on the condition of banks, and (in some cases) the right to conduct (or participate in) on-site inspections. Another area of intense central bank involvement is the analysis of overall financial stability. A number of central banks have an explicit mandate to foster financial stability in their jurisdiction. They discharge this responsibility by producing assessments of the health and performance of the financial system and by overseeing the operation of the payments and settlements infrastructure. Their analysis and assessment is often published in the form of a regular specialized report.[12]

---

[11] For more detailed description of the recent changes in the national supervisory arrangements see ECB 2003, 2006.

[12] For a discussion of the role of financial stability reports see Oosterloo 2006.

Table 25.2. Arrangements for the supervision of banks in European countries

	Supervisory model[a]	Number of agencies involved	Role of central bank		
			Regulation[b]	Supervision[c]	Macro financial stability[d]
Austria	I, SA	1	F, 1	I, R	X
Belgium	I, SA	1	I, 2	MoU, C, R	X
Finland[e]	S, BS	2	I, 3	MoU, A, R	X
France[e]	O, CB	4	F, 3	X	
Germany	I, SA	1	F, 2	I, R	
Greece	S, CB	3	F, 3	—	X
Italy	S+O, CB	4	F, 3	—	
Ireland[e]	I, SA	1	F, 3	X	
Luxembourg	S, BS	2			
The Netherlands	O, CB	2	F, 3	—	X
Portugal	S+O, CB	3		—	X
Spain	S, CB	3	F, 3	—	
Czech Republic	I, CB	1	F, 3	—	
Cyprus	S, CB	4	F, 3	—	
Denmark	I, SA	1	I, 1	MoU, C, R	X
Estonia	I, SA	1	F, 3	MoU	X
Hungary	I, SA	1	I, 2	MoU, C, A, R	X
Latvia	I, SA	1	I, 2	A	X
Lithuania	S, CB	3	F, 3	MoU	
Malta	I, SA	1	I, 2	MoU, C	X
Poland	I, SA	1	F, 2		
Slovenia	S, CB	3	F, 3	—	
Slovakia	I, CB	1	F, 3	—, R	X
Sweden	I, SA	1	I, 3	MoU, A, R	X
United Kingdom	I, SA	1	I, 1	MoU, R	X
Norway	I, SA	1	I, 3	R	X
Switzerland	I, SA	2	I, 2	R	X

[a]Supervisory model: refers to the principle guiding the supervisory architecture (I: integrated model; S: sectoral model; O: model by objectives) and the agency responsible for bank supervision (SA: single integrated agency; CB: central bank; BS: specialized banking supervisory agency). France, Italy, and Portugal have implemented a mixture of the 'sectoral' and 'by objectives' model.

[b]Involvement of central bank in design of bank regulations (F: formal; I: informal), and level of influence (1: low; 2: medium; 3: high).

[c]Broader role of central bank in bank supervision including formal mechanisms for cooperation and information sharing (P: primary supervisor; MoU: memorandum of understanding; C: committees for cooperation; A: cooperation agreement; X: other formal arrangement; I: participation in inspections; R: CB has the right to access information from supervisor).

[d]Does the central bank have an explicit macro-financial stability mandate?

[e]In Finland, France, and Ireland the supervisory authority is a self-contained agency within (the legal personality of) the central bank.

Sources: ECB 2006; Dierick 2004; national sources.

The diversity of national prudential arrangements across Europe is also evident in terms of the structures put in place to deal with crisis situations. The EU directive on deposit guarantee schemes (1994/19/EC) has partly harmonized arrangements by making them mandatory in all member states and setting a uniform *minimum* coverage of €20,000 per depositor. National schemes, however, may opt to offer higher protection levels and the directive contains no provisions on several other aspects of the arrangements, including administration and funding where national differences can be substantial (left-hand side columns of Table 25.3). The same degree of diversity exists in the rules that govern the closure of troubled banks. A variety of agencies is involved (including in many cases the ministry of finance) and in certain cases the ultimate decision is a joint one. In some situations, the body that has the ultimate responsibility is not necessarily the one that is also in charge of supervision. Similarly, other policy tools that can be used in dealing with problem banks such as takeover and securities legislation, or reorganization and winding-up procedures, differ across countries. These differences can affect materially the effectiveness of private market solutions and may give considerable discretion to national authorities in dealing with troubled institutions. Finally, the lack of uniformity in the rights attached to shareholders and in the powers of boards of directors and shareholders creates a further barrier to cross-country expansion.

An area where there is almost perfect uniformity is the provision of emergency liquidity assistance (ELA). In practically all countries the decision of whether or not to provide emergency financing to a distressed bank rests exclusively with the central bank.

In summary, the national component of prudential arrangements is quite diverse across Europe. In terms of the scheme of Kremers, Schoenmaker, and Wierts (2003) the different elements of the prudential framework occupy all three columns, although most countries are either in the first or the third column.

2.2. Europe-wide Supervisory and Regulatory Structures

Recognizing the inherent difficulties in fully harmonizing all national standards and prudential arrangements, the European Union adopted an approach founded on two basic principles. The first is the principle of mutual recognition of national regulatory competencies, subject to minimum essential harmonization of frameworks. The second is the assignment of control to the 'home country' competent authority. This latter principle was first adopted in the Second Banking Coordination Directive and has since been an integral part of the major legislative initiatives to promote the single financial market. Host country supervisors are expected to provide all necessary information to the home country authorities. Conduct of business and consumer protection rules are typically the responsibility of the host country where the services are actually provided. However, in more recent legislation there is a discernible shift

Table 25.3. Deposit insurance and crisis management arrangements

	Deposit insurance schemes[a]				ELA decision [b]	Closure[c]	
	Coverage per depositor	Co-insurance?	Funding	Administration		Ultimate decision	Consulted
Austria	20,000		Ex post	Private	Alone	SA	
Belgium	20,000		Ex ante	Joint	Alone	MF	SA
Finland	25,000		Ex ante	Private	Alone	SA	SA, CB, MF
France	70,000		Ex ante	Private	Alone	CB, SA	CB, SA
Germany	20,000	Y	Ex ante	Private	Alone	SA	SA, DI
Greece	20,000		Ex ante	Joint	Alone	CB	
Italy	103,291		Ex post	Private	Alone	MF	CB, SA
Ireland	20,000	Y	Ex ante	Public			
Luxembourg	20,000		Ex post	Private			
The Netherlands	40,000		Ex post	Joint	Alone	CB, SA	CB
Portugal	25,000		Ex ante	Public	Alone	CB	
Spain	20,000		Ex ante	Joint	Alone	MF	CB
Czech Republic	25,000	Y	Ex ante	*Private*	Alone	CB	MF
Cyprus	20,000	Y	Ex ante				
Denmark	40,212		Ex ante	Public	Alone	SA	SA, MTS
Estonia	1,278		Ex ante	Joint	Alone	SA	CB
Hungary	23,728	Y	Ex ante		Alone	SA	
Latvia	15,000		Ex ante		CB, MF		
Lithuania	13,323	Y	Ex ante		Alone	CB	
Malta	20,000	Y	Ex ante			SA	CB
Poland	20,350	Y	Ex ante + ex post		Alone	SA	SA
Slovenia	21,294		Ex post			CB, MF	
Slovakia	20,000	Y	Ex ante		Alone	SA	
Sweden	26,628		Ex post	Public	Alone	SA	CB,SA,DI,MF
United Kingdom	46,257	Y	Ex post	Public	Alone, other	SA	CB,SA,MF
Norway	240,000		Ex ante	Private	Alone	MF	CB,SA,DI,MF
Switzerland	18,650		Ex post	Private	Alone	SA	

[a]Characteristics of deposit insurance arrangements: maximum coverage per depositor/bank (converted in euros); existence of co-insurance (deductible); type of funding; type of administration (public sector, private sector, or joint arrangement).

[b]Does the central bank decide on the extension of ELA alone or in collaboration with others?

[c]Arrangements that apply to closure of troubled institutions: which authority is responsible for the ultimate decision on closure? Which other authorities should be consulted before the decision? (CB: central bank; MF: ministry of finance; SA: supervisory agency; DI: deposit insurance agency).

Sources: Barth, Nolle, and Rice 1997 as quoted in Prati and Schinasi 1999; IADI Survey of deposit insurance (www.iadi.org); Demirgüç-Kunt and Sobaci 2001.

of the balance of even these responsibilities towards the home authorities.[13] In other words, the European arrangements put more weight on rows A and B of Table 25.1.

The weaknesses in the original prudential set-up across the EU were brought to the fore by the impact from the introduction of the single currency on the financial system. These weaknesses with respect to arrangements for financial stability were also highlighted by two official reports drafted by groups chaired by Henk Brouwer (European Commission 2000, 2001). The reports suggested a number of

---

[13] Examples of this shift include the E-Commerce Directive (2000/31/EC) and the Markets in Financial Institution Directive (2004/39/EC).

enhancements aiming at improving the practical functioning of those arrangements, in particular as regards the exchange of information, the convergence of supervisory practices, and crisis management.

The rules framework for the EU as a whole was enhanced with the completion of the five-year Financial Services Action Plan (FSAP) that introduced or updated a number of important directives.[14] These include the directive on the reorganization and winding-up of credit institutions (2001/24/EC); the E-Commerce Directive (2000/31/EC); the amendments to the directive governing the capital framework for banks and investment banks; and, the Financial Conglomerates Directive (FCD, 2002/87/EC). More recently, the transposition to EU law of the new Basel II framework was achieved in the form of the Capital Requirements Directive (CRD, 2006/49/EC).

FCD and CRD represent important enhancements in the framework of cooperation across national supervisors of individual cross-border banks by upgrading the responsibilities of the home supervisor. FCD envisages a coordinating role for the home supervisor with responsibilities in the collection and dissemination of information to the college of supervisory authorities for a particular conglomerate without prejudice to the powers of host supervisors. CRD goes a step further in charging the 'consolidating supervisor' with the assessment of compliance with the directive on a consolidated basis and, in certain cases, by making its decisions binding for the host authorities (Dierick et al. 2005).

At a more 'macro' level the coordination of prudential efforts across the area is conducted mainly through a hierarchy of committees within the EU, complemented by structures within the ESCB. The role of those arrangements is to develop and implement common standards and rules for banks across the EU, as well as to achieve a coordination of the implementation of these rules across jurisdictions. In addition, arrangements are put in place for the coordinated response in the event of a crisis.

The framework for the cooperation and coordination between national regulatory authorities within the EU was redrawn in 2003 along the lines of the proposals offered by the Lamfalussy Group of 'Wise-Men'. In order to achieve a more streamlined decision and rule-making process, while maintaining sufficient political control and accountability, the framework comprises a four-level structure.[15] *Level 1* includes the usual legislative bodies in the EU (i.e. the European Parliament, the European Commission, and the Ecofin council of finance ministers) which have the exclusive power to set high-level rules and principles. The European Banking Committee (EBC), a *level 2* committee, also has rule-making powers but these are limited to mainly technical rules within the framework principles set by level 1 organs. The role of EBC is to assist the Commission in the adoption of technical measures in accordance

---

[14] For further discussion on the FSAP measures see ECB 2004.

[15] The discussion on the Lamfalussy approach as it applies to banking supervision draws on ECB 2004 and Lannoo 2005. The framework is defined in Committee Structure Directive (2005/1/EC).

with the comitology framework.[16] It is composed of high-level representatives from the member states, chaired by a representative of the Commission, and includes the ECB as an observer. Another level 2 organ is the European Financial Conglomerates Committee (FCC), which was established in 2002 and focuses on issues that relate to complex financial institutions with units that cross sectoral lines.

The role of *level 3* supervisory committees is to provide technical advice at the Commission's request and to enhance regulatory and supervisory convergence by focusing on the consistent implementation of EU legislation and technical rules across member countries. The Committee of European Banking Supervisors (CEBS) is composed of high-level officials from the competent national supervisory authorities and, without voting rights, representatives from the central banks (including from the ECB and those central banks not involved in banking supervision). In addition to achieving greater convergence in regulatory practices the role of CEBS also aims at achieving the more effective supervision of banks with significant cross-border activities. CEBS may produce guidelines for regulations to be adopted at the national level, issue interpretative recommendations, and set standards of best practice. For instance, it is the committee responsible for developing the common principles for the implementation of pillar 2 of the Basel II framework. Its decisions are not legally binding but it may be able to exercise moral suasion through the conduct of peer reviews of national practices. Finally, *level 4* refers to the application of the supervisory framework at the national level and on the enforcement of EU rules by the Commission.

The principal strengths of the Lamfalussy framework are the increased regular interaction between national authorities, which promotes a greater degree of harmonization of regulation and supervisory practices, and the improvement in the transparency of the overall process. In addition, by avoiding the complete harmonization of all aspects of the prudential framework, it allows a degree of healthy competition among national supervisory authorities.[17] According to Lannoo (2005), the framework has also some drawbacks. One is the ambiguous delineation between principles (level 1) and technical implementing measures (level 2), a distinction that is often ad hoc and, arguably, subjective. The layering of committees tends to complicate the regulatory process and be resource intensive while, at the same time, increasing the powers of the Commission.

The coordinating superstructure in the EU assigns a somewhat more restricted role to central banks and the ECB as compared to the typical case in national arrangements. Unlike a number of the euro area NCBs the ECB has no direct supervisory responsibilities. The Maastricht Treaty defines price stability as the priority objective

---

[16] Comitology refers to the delegation of technical rule-making powers by the level 1 organs to committees of experts that are not elected bodies and as such are not directly accountable to the EU citizenry.

[17] The May 2006 Ecofin decision to further enhance existing supervisory instruments (such as a common culture providing non-binding meditation among supervisors, delegation of tasks/responsibilities, streamlining the exchange of information on cross-border business of banks, etc.) is consistent with this overall strategic direction.

for the Eurosystem, entrusts it with the responsibility for the stability of the payments system, but assigns to it a subordinate role with respect to financial supervision (Articles 105(2) and (5)).[18] Article 105(6) of the treaty leaves open the possibility for supervisory responsibilities to be assigned to the ESCB at a later point, but it precludes 'insurance undertakings'. The ECB has an advisory role in the rule-setting framework, as mentioned above, and it participates along with EU central banks in level 3 committees.[19]

The ECB Governing Council established the Banking Supervision Committee (BSC) as the forum for addressing the issues raised by the introduction of the single currency, thus 'giving content to the provision of Article 105(5)', and as a means for fostering cooperation between supervisors beyond the Eurosystem (ECB 2000). BSC brings together the authorities responsible for financial stability and the oversight of payment systems with national banking supervisors. Its analytical efforts focus on delivering an area-wide perspective on the stability of the financial system that complements national views as well as formulating a common stance towards the policy challenges presented by an integrating banking system. A considerable part of these efforts is characterized as providing a macro-prudential assessment on the structural developments and the overall performance of the financial system.[20]

In the field of crisis management the ELA function allows fairly decentralized decision making. Neither the Maastricht Treaty nor the Statute of the ESCB gives the ECB an explicit mandate for providing emergency liquidity support directly to individual financial institutions. The treaty can be read as implicitly charging national central banks with this task as the 'competent national authorities'. Subsequent agreements have clarified that the Eurosystem retains responsibility for managing overall liquidity conditions through monetary operations. This distinction is facilitated by specific technical characteristics of the operating arrangements in the Eurosystem.[21] First, there is a well-defined dividing line between ELA and monetary operations as a result of the existence of standing facilities available on demand and a pre-specified set of acceptable collateral. ELA begins where normal operations stop. An ample supply of collateral and wide access to the standing facilities mean that the available cushion before ELA is technically activated is larger than elsewhere. Second, the fact that operating objectives for monetary policy are set in terms of short-term interest rates provides national central banks with some freedom to accommodate (within limits) the demand for reserves during a crisis episode without modifying the overall stance

---

[18] Article 105(5) of the Treaty of the European Union stipulates that 'the ESCB shall contribute to the smooth conduct of policies pursued by the competent authorities relating to the prudential supervision of credit institutions and the stability of the financial system'. For a fuller discussion of the treaty provisions see also Prati and Schinasi 1999.

[19] Article 25(1) of the ESCB Statutes also supports this advisory role of the Eurosystem.

[20] The GdC is another committee with a similar mandate but includes participants from the wider EEA area. For more details see Moss 2005.

[21] For a detailed discussion of the Eurosystem's monetary operating procedures see the chapter by Bindseil and Nyborg in this volume.

of policy. Mechanisms for the timely exchange of information with the Governing Council of the ECB ensure that the consequences of national actions for monetary policy implementation can be duly taken into account.[22]

EU legislation and rules outline the contours of national policy discretion in some areas. National discretion in scrutinizing bank takeovers as part of their responsibility for safeguarding financial stability is limited by the EU rules on the free movement of capital. The harmonization of procedures and rules for the reorganization and winding up of banks is not very far advanced. Policies dealing with troubled banks remain the competency of national authorities and are subject to national rules. However, the use of public funds in a bank rescue is governed by the EU rules on state aid.[23] For multinational credit institutions the 'home country' principle applies.

Given the emphasis that the EU framework places on decentralized solutions, the effective cooperation of the relevant authorities in all jurisdictions where a bank operates is of key importance. In addition to the multilateral forums mentioned above, which bring together supervisors and central bankers across the EU, a network of bilateral agreements for cooperation and exchange of information has been drawn to this effect (see Enria and Vesala 2003). These are Memoranda of Understanding (MoU) that detail the mutual obligations of various authorities in terms of the regular provision of information about the activities of a bank in their jurisdiction, the communication of assessments of its performance, and the management of episodes of distress.

There are different levels of disclosure regarding MoUs. Some are fully public; for others agreement on their text, but not necessarily their detailed arrangements, has been publicized out of concern that this might create perverse incentives among banks. A network of bilateral MoUs has been drawn between prudential authorities that oversee individual institutions with substantial cross-border business. Other MoUs cover many authorities across several countries. An example of such a multilateral MoU sets high-level principles of cooperation in crisis situations. It was agreed to by EU banking supervisors and central banks in 2003 and was further extended to cover the ministries of finance in 2005.[24] The MoU put forward principles for the sharing of information and assessments at the national and cross-border basis, as well as arrangements for the development of contingency plans. Multilateral MoUs laying the ground for supervisory cooperation are also drawn among the Nordic countries, stimulated by the substantial cross-border activities of banks in the region (Moss 2005).

---

[22] The chapter by Hartmann and Valla in this volume provides further discussion of ELA arrangements in the euro area.

[23] While acknowledging the special nature of the banking sector, the European Commission is of the opinion that Community law clearly sets a criterion of 'equal competitive conditions', hence subjecting state financial support to the Commission's scrutiny.

[24] These MoUs are not public documents. Press announcements by the ECB give a general overview of what is covered. In 2004 the list of signatories to the 2003 MoU was enlarged to include the authorities from the newly acceded countries to the EU.

3. LOOKING FORWARD

The normative issues surrounding the prudential architecture in Europe are actively debated by various observers from academia, policy, and the banking industry. Differing views have been expressed on the most appropriate regulatory blueprint for an integrated European banking market as well as on the likely influence of prudential arrangements in shaping the process of integration. It is not easy to do full justice to the nuances of these discussions in the space available. This section will present only the main arguments.

Participants in this debate approach the relevant issues from somewhat different perspectives. Policymakers tend to take a more pragmatic approach emphasizing the utilitarian aspects of current prudential arrangements. These have been designed with the intention of bringing about a necessary degree of harmonization while minimizing the required changes to existing national structures. This approach starts from the recognition that current structures meet the requirements of day-to-day supervision of the majority of European institutions and examines extensions to those structures that would accommodate the more complex supervisory challenges posed by larger, cross-border banks and the management of crisis situations. By contrast, alternative proposals in the academic literature often start from the efficiency of crisis management in the presence of cross-border banks and work backwards towards the implications for the supervision of these institutions. As a result, many proposals represent more radical departures from current structures. Bankers, in particular those with important cross-border operations, tend to focus primarily on the efficiency of their interactions with supervisors and are less concerned with crisis resolution. They tend to favour streamlined structures that reduce the number of supervisory authorities to which they need to report. The current arrangements do reflect to a large extent the perspective of the first group, so the rest of this section focuses on the latter two perspectives.

A common observation regarding the crisis management arrangements in Europe is that by assigning the primary role to the home supervisor, they give rise to situations where the incentives of those involved may not necessarily be conducive to the most efficient resolution. In particular, as highlighted in the theoretical literature surveyed above, conflicts of interest may lead to inefficient use of the resources available to deal with institutions in distress. The issues relate primarily to the allocation of responsibilities and the exchange of information among the relevant authorities. Conceivably, in certain situations this might result in incentives not fully in line with the stability needs of the area as a whole. Cases in point are those of institutions that are systemically relevant only outside their home market or that, in effect, have more than one 'home' market in view of the geographical scope of their operations and, perhaps, ownership structure. In the absence of appropriate burden-sharing mechanisms, such situations could complicate the timely elaboration of a policy response and might even lead to a certain bias towards inaction (see discussion in Vives 2001; Goodhart and Schoenmaker 2006; Srejber and Noréus 2005).

There are multiple models proposed for the European supervisory architecture mixing to various degrees centralized and decentralized decision-making arrangements.[25] The list below sketches the three main alternatives although a number of variations on these themes have also been suggested.

The first type of proposal assigns the role of a lead supervisor for a cross-border bank to the home supervisor. This is a proposal championed by the European Financial Services Roundtable, an industry body representing many large European banks.[26] The proposal assigns to the home supervisor a leadership role among the other authorities in the college of supervisors for the specific institution. The role extends beyond the assessment of vulnerability to comprise decisions regarding the use of prudential tools. In the case of a crisis, the leadership role includes the coordination of the effort and the interactions with the relevant central banks.

Another proposal gives the home supervisor an enhanced leadership role accompanied by a European mandate. Under this proposal, articulated by Schoenmaker and Oosterloo (2006), the European body of supervisors delegates all authority for decision making to the home supervisor. There is no specific function for the college of supervisors, not even as a consultative body. The organization of the ELA function would mirror the organization of supervision, with the home central bank being the responsible authority.[27]

Finally the most radical departure from the current arrangements envisages a centralization of the supervisory functions in one pan-European agency for all banks with cross-border activities. A possibility could resemble the tiered situation to that in the USA where the main supervisor is determined by the nature of the institution's charter. Parallel centralization would apply to the ELA function with the ECB being the most obvious candidate for the role. Clearly, this proposal would involve substantial redrafting of European legislation both at the national and EU levels, including amendments to the Maastricht Treaty.[28]

Some commentators have focused more specifically on the management of ELA and the arrangements for dealing with the fiscal costs of a cross-country bank failure (or a systemic crisis). Schinasi and Teixeira (2006) discuss the modalities of different arrangements and caution against disentangling this discussion from the discussion on the overall prudential architecture. In particular, they suggest that a more centralized crisis management framework will also imply the need for more centralized supervision during normal times. Goodhart and Schoenmaker (2006) highlight the political nature of the arrangements for burden sharing and the existence of free-rider situations in the case of countries that benefit from financial stability but do

---

[25] For a general discussion of the relative merits of centralized and decentralized prudential arrangements see Vives 2001; Schoenmaker 2005.

[26] See for example European Financial Services Roundtable 2006 and other publications in www.fsr.be.

[27] This provision would require changes in the mandate of the ESCB.

[28] Sveriges Riksbank Governor S. Ingves put Forward a proposal that blends elements of the second and third types outlined here. It envisages a pan-European Organization for Financial Supervision for cross-country institutions (like the third proposal) albeit with powers concentrated mostly on informational gathering and risk assessment but shared responsibility over formal supervision (Ingves 2006).

not contribute to the direct costs of ensuring it. They argue in favour of a formal ex ante agreement on specific burden sharing among countries that are directly affected by a bank failure on the basis of a pre-specified key.

There are a number of pros and cons about these proposals. They blend to varying degrees the flexibility of reliance on national structures on the one hand, with the efficiency and levelling of the playing field offered by centralized decision making on the other. Compared to current arrangements, they tend to lean towards more cooperation and centralization, namely towards rows B and C of Table 25.1. Clearly, the political hurdles are taller the further the proposals depart from current arrangements. Moreover, their longer-term merits depend critically on the degree of integration of the banking system. Having said that, it is difficult to assess the extent to which decentralization and national differences impinge on competitive conditions.[29]

4. Concluding Remarks

It is difficult to foresee how the framework for safeguarding financial stability will evolve. The scenarios discussed above are predicated on a greater degree of banking integration than has been achieved within Europe so far, although current industry trends are consistent with this direction. Conversely, it is frequently argued that a streamlining of the prudential framework would act as a further catalyst to the integration process. Much will also depend on how the current arrangements perform when put to the test and on developments in the broader political environment. Arguably, as the long-term objective of a truly integrated market comes within closer reach, the balance is likely to shift towards further centralization or harmonization. The precise modalities and timing of this shift are very hard to predict.

In any case, there is little doubt that greater financial integration puts a premium on mechanisms for the exchange of information between relevant authorities. Access to accurate and timely information is necessary both for the early detection of vulnerabilities, thereby permitting preventive action, as well as for assessing the extent and intensity of strains once they arise. The establishment of the Eurosystem has provided an opportunity for streamlining and strengthening existing mechanisms. There is, however, scope for improving the practical functioning of current arrangements, especially with regard to communication and cooperation between supervisory authorities of different sectors at an international level together with central banks, and the convergence of supervisory practices.

---

[29] For the interactions between competition and stability in the context of banking see Carletti and Hartmann 2003.

REFERENCES

ACHARYA, V. (2003), 'Is the international convergence of capital adequacy regulation desirable?', *Journal of Finance*, 58(6), December, 2745–81.

ALLEN, F., and GALE, D. (2000), 'Financial contagion', *Journal of Political Economy*, 108(1), 1–33.

BAELE, L., FERRANDO, A., HÖRDAHL, P., KRYLOVA, E., and MONNET, C. (2004), 'Measuring financial integration in the euro-area', ECB Occasional Paper no. 14, April.

BARTH, J. R., NOLLE, D. E., and RICE, T. N. (1997), 'Commercial banking structure, regulation and performance: an international comparison', Economics Working Paper 97–6, Office of the Comptroller of the Currency, US Treasury Department, Washington, DC, March.

BAUDINO, P., CAVIGLIA, G., DORRUCCI, E., and PINEAU G. (2004), 'Financial FDI to the EU accession countries', European Central Bank contribution to CGFS Paper on 'Foreign direct investment in the financial sector of emerging market economies', CGFS Publications no. 22 (www.bis.org/publ/cgfs22.htm), March.

CABRAL, I., DIERICK, F., and VESALA, J. (2002), 'Banking integration in the euro area', ECB Occasional Papers no. 6, December.

CALZOLARI, G., and LÓRÁNTH, G. (2004), 'Regulation of multinational banks: a theoretical inquiry', *Centre for Economic Policy Research*, Discussion Paper no. 4232.

CARLETTI, E., and HARTMANN, P. (2003), 'Competition and stability: what's special about banking?', in P Mizen (ed.), *Monetary History, Exchange Rates and Financial Markets: Essays in Honour of Charles Goodhart*, vol. ii, Cheltenham: Edward Elgar, 202–29.

CGFS (2004), 'Foreign direct investment in the financial sector of emerging market economies', Committee for the Global Financial System, publication no. 22, March, available at www.bis. org.

CHEN, Y. (1999), 'Banking panics: the role of the first-come, first-served rule and information externalities', *Journal of Political Economy*, 107(5), 946–68.

DALEN, D. M., and OLSEN, T. E. (2003), 'Regulatory competition and multinational banking', CESifo Working Paper 971, June.

DELL'ARICCIA, G., and MARQUEZ, R. (2006), 'Competition among regulators and credit market integration', *Journal of Financial Economics*, 79(2), 401–30.

DEMIRGÜÇ-KUNT, A., and SOBACI, T. (2001), 'Deposit insurance around the world', *World Bank Economic Review*, 15(3), 481–90.

DERMINE, J. (2006), 'European banking integration: don't put the cart before the horse', *Financial Markets, Institutions and Instruments*, 15(2), May, 57–106.

DIERICK, F. (2004), 'The supervision of mixed financial services groups in Europe', ECB Occasional Paper Series no. 20, August.

—— PIRES, F., SCHEICHER, M., and SPITZER, K. G. (2005), 'The new Basel capital framework and its implementation in the European Union', ECB Occasional Paper no. 42, December.

DUISENBERG, W. (1999), introductory statement delivered on the occasion of the presentation of the ECB's Annual Report 1998 to the European Parliament, Strasbourg, 26 October.

ECB (2000), 'EMU and banking supervision', *ECB Monthly Bulletin*, April.

—— (2003), 'Developments in national supervisory structures', www.ecb.int, June.

—— (2004), 'Developments in the EU framework for financial regulation, supervision and stability', *ECB Monthly Bulletin*, November.

—— (2005), 'Banking structures in the new member states', Report by the ECSB Banking Supervision Committee, www.ecb.int, January.

—— (2006), 'Recent developments in supervisory structures in EU and acceding countries', October, www.ecb.int.

ENRIA, A., and VESALA, J. (2003), 'Externalities in supervision: the European case', in J. J. M. Kremers, D. Schoenmaker, and P. J. Wierts (eds.), *Financial Supervision in Europe*, Cheltenham: Edward Elgar, 60–89.

EUROPEAN COMMISSION (2000), 'Report on financial stability', prepared by the ad hoc working group of the Economic and Financial Committee, Economic Paper, no. 143, May (first Brouwer report).

——(2001), 'Report on financial crisis management', July (second Brouwer report).

EUROPEAN FINANCIAL SERVICES ROUNDTABLE (2006), 'Need for improvement in EU cross-border financial (prudential) supervision', letter addressed to the President of the Commission, 14 July (www.efr.be).

FAVERO, C., FREIXAS, X., PERSSON, T., and WYPLOSZ, C. (2000), *One Money, Many Countries: Monitoring the European Central Bank*, London: CEPR.

FREIXAS, X. (2003), 'Crisis management in Europe', in J. J. M. Kremers, D. Shoenmaker, and P. J. Wierts (eds.), *Financial Supervision in Europe*, Cheltenham: Edward Edgar, 102–19.

——LÓRÁNTH, G., and MORRISON, A. (2005), 'Regulating financial conglomerates', OFRC Working Paper.

——PARIGI, B., and ROCHET, J.-C. (2000), 'Systemic risk, interbank relations and liquidity provision by the central bank', *Journal of Money, Credit, and Banking*, 32(3/2), 611–38.

GOODHART, C. A. E. (ed.) (2000), *Which Lender of Last Resort for Europe?*, London: Central Banking Publications.

——(2003), 'The political economy of financial harmonisation in Europe', in J. J. M. Kremers, D. Shoenmaker, and P. J. Wierts (eds.), *Financial Supervision in Europe*, Cheltenham: Edward Elgar, 129–38.

——and SCHOENMAKER, D. (1995), 'Should the functions of monetary policy and banking supervision be separated?', *Oxford Economic Papers*, 47, 539–60.

————(2006), 'Burden sharing in banking crises in Europe', LSE Financial Markets Group, Special Paper no. 164, March.

——HARTMANN, P., LLEWELLYN, D., ROJAS-SUÁREZ, L., and WEISBROD, S. (1998), *Financial Regulation: Why, How and Where Now?*, London: Routledge.

GROPP, R., and MOERMAN, G. (2004), 'Measurement of contagion in banks' equity prices', in I. Hasan and J. Tarkka (eds.), *Banking, Development and Structural Change*, Special Issue of the *Journal of International Money and Finance*, 23(3), 405–59.

——Lo DUCA, M., and VESALA, J. (2006), 'Cross-border bank contagion in Europe', ECB Working Paper no. 662, July.

HARR, T., and RØNDE, T. (2006), 'Regulation of banking groups', Working Paper 2006/1, France Research Unit, Institute of Economics, University of Copenhagen.

HARTMANN, P., STRAETMANS, S., and DE VRIES, C. (2005), 'Banking system stability: a cross-Atlantic perspective', NBER Working Paper no. 11698, October.

HOLTHAUSEN, C., and RØNDE, T. (2004), 'Co-operation in international banking supervision', ECB Working Paper, no. 316, March.

INGVES, S. (2006), 'Cross-border banking regulation—a way forward: the European case', speech delivered at the conference on 'International financial instability: cross-border banking and national regulation', Federal Reserve Bank of Chicago, Chicago, 16 October.

KAHN, C., and SANTOS, J. A. C. (2004), 'Allocating the lender of last resort and supervision in the euro area', in V. Alexander, J. Melitz, and G. M. von Furstenberg (eds.), *Monetary Unions and Hard Pegs: Effects on Trade, Financial Development and Stability*, New York: Oxford University Press.

KREMERS, J. J. M., SCHOENMAKER, D., and WIERTS, P. J. (2003), 'Financial supervision in Europe: an overview', in J. J. M. Kremers, D. Schoenmaker, and P. J. Wierts (eds.), *Financial Supervision in Europe*, Cheltenham: Edward Elgar, 1–14.

LANNOO, K. (2005), 'The transformation of financial regulation and supervision in the EU', in D. Masciantaro (ed.) *Handbook of Central Banking and Financial Authorities in Europe*, Cheltenham: Edward Elgar, 485–513.

——— and LEVIN, M. (2004), 'Securities market regulation in the EU: the relation between the Community and Member States', research study prepared for the wise persons' committee, Ministry of Finance, Canada, November 2003 (also a CEPS research report).

MANNA, M. (2004), 'Developing statistical indicators of the integration of the euro area banking system', ECB Working Paper no. 300, January.

MASCIANTARO, D. (ed.) (2005), '*Handbook of Central Banking and Financial Authorities in Europe*', Cheltenham: Edward Elgar.

MORRISON, A. D., and LÓRÁNTH, G. (2003), 'Deposit insurance, capital regulations, and financial contagion in multinational banks', OFRC Working Paper, forthcoming in *Journal of Business Finance and Accounting*.

MOSS, N. (2005), 'The international network of financial authorities', in D. Masciantaro (ed.), *Handbook of Central Banking and Financial Authorities in Europe*, Cheltenham: Edward Elgar, 373–97.

OOSTERLOO, S. (2006), 'Review of country financial stability reports', paper presented in the conference. 'International financial instability: cross-border banking and regulation', Federal Reserve Bank of Chicago, 5–6 October.

——— and SCHOENMAKER, D. (2004), 'A lead supervisor model for Europe', *Financial Regulator*, 9(3), 34–42.

PADOA-SCHIOPPA, T. (2004), 'How to deal with emerging pan-European financial institutions?', speech delivered at the conference on supervisory convergence organized by the Dutch Ministry of Finance, The Hague, November (www.ecb.int).

PRATI, A., and SCHINASI, G. J. (1999), 'Financial stability in European economic and monetary union', Princeton Studies in International Finance, no. 86, August.

REPULLO, R. (2001), 'A model of takeovers of foreign banks', *Spanish Economic Review*, 3, 1–21.

ROSE, A. (1996), 'Explaining exchange rate volatility: an empirical analysis of "The Holy Trinity" of monetary independence, fixed exchange rates, and capital mobility', *Journal of International Money and Finance*, 15, 925–45.

SCHINASI, G. J., and TEIXEIRA, P. G. (2006), 'The lender of last resort in the European single financial market', IMF Working Paper WP/06/127, May.

SCHOENMAKER, D. (2005), 'Central banks and financial authorities in Europe: what prospects?', in D. Masciantaro (ed.), *Handbook of Central Banking and Financial Authorities in Europe*, Cheltenham: Edward Elgar, 398–456.

——— and OOSTERLOO, S. (2005), 'Financial supervision in an integrating Europe: measuring cross-border externalities', *International Finance*, 8, 1–27.

——— ——— (2006), 'Financial supervision in Europe: do we need a new architecture?', *Cahier Comte Boël*, 12, European League for Economic Co-operation, Brussels.

SINN, H.-W. (2001), 'Risk taking, limited liability and the competition of bank regulators', NBER Working Paper no. 8669, December.

SREJBER, E. (2006), 'Are we ready to deal with a cross-border banking crisis in Europe?', speech delivered at the seminar on 'Financial institutions' value management in the integrated market in light of the Lisbon strategy, Gdarisk, 12 May. (www.riksbank.se).

——— and NORÉUS, M. (2005), 'The future relationship between financial stability and supervision in the EU', *Sveriges Riksbank Economic Review*, 4, December.

VIVES, X. (2001), 'Restructuring financial regulation in the European monetary union', *Journal of Financial Services Research*, 19, 57–82.

CHAPTER 26

....

BANK REGULATION AND MACROECONOMIC FLUCTUATIONS

....

CHARLES GOODHART

BORIS HOFMANN

MIGUEL SEGOVIANO

1. INTRODUCTION

....

MACROECONOMIC cycles have been changing in recent decades, since the end of the Bretton Woods system, and now involve more asset price volatility (so-called boom–bust cycles) and financial fragility. In the face of more frequent banking crises, regulators have moved to reinforce individual bank capital adequacy ratios, for example through the Basel I and II Accords. But bank regulation is inherently procyclical; it bites in downturns, but fails to restrain in booms. The more 'sophisticated' and 'risk sensitive' the regulation, the greater the scope for procyclicality to become a problem, particularly in view of the changing nature of macroeconomic cycles. The

The views expressed in this chapter do not necessarily reflect the views of the Deutsche Bundesbank. Our thanks are due to the participants at the seminar at the Saïd Business School, Oxford, on 1 July 2004, and especially to Chris Allsopp and Colin Mayer, our main discussants, and to an anonymous referee for helpful suggestions.

main purpose of this chapter is to explore this nexus, and the policy problems thereby generated.

With price stability (inflation targets) being the primary responsibility of the monetary authorities, the instrument of short-term interest rates is, correctly and properly, allocated to this task. So, a central bank has hardly any usable instruments for countering financial volatility on its own. This problem is enhanced in a large and diverse currency region, such as the euro zone. Asset price movements can differ sharply between regions; think of the varying experiences of housing price inflation of Ireland and Spain on the one hand, and Germany and Austria on the other. Large capital flows into, and possibly out of, the relatively small accession states can provide yet another problem. Within a wide currency union, there is little that the European Central Bank (ECB) can do.

We start this chapter, in the following section, 2.1, by recording the particular nature of the post-Second World War business cycle. In the decades immediately following the Second World War, 1945–71, demand was kept high, and one means of limiting the inflationary consequences of that was by keeping the banking system under tight credit controls. So there were virtually no banking crises, and, consequently, bank regulation was light.

After the stagflation of the 1970s, and particularly after the then Federal Reserve Board's chairman Paul Volcker's monetary policy shift in October 1979, the monetary authorities gradually learnt how to use a market-oriented monetary policy to maintain price stability. On the other hand, liberalization of banking sectors since the early/mid-1970s had increased the scope for risk taking and leverage, and thus the procyclicality of the financial system. This combination of stable consumer prices and liberalized banking sectors was accompanied by a reversion of the business cycle, in some respects, to the kind of pattern seen, for example, in the decades up till 1913, when again consumer prices remained stable. In this new pattern real shocks often tended to generate fluctuations in asset prices, which frequently led to asset price and lending booms and busts, in which latter case banks would often become fragile and fail.

In this context there was a need to strengthen financial regulation, not only nationally but also internationally, given the extent of global competition in financial intermediation. This is described in Section 2.2, where we particularly focus on the key role of the Basel Committee on Banking Supervision in enabling a coordinated international response to a global problem.

Nevertheless, the Basel approach has several weaknesses. The first is that regulation is inherently procyclical. Banks are weaker in recessions and when asset prices decline. The more that regulation is based on *current* assessed riskiness and current *market* valuations, the more procyclical the regulatory system will become. The second is that supervision is, almost necessarily, focused on the individual financial institution. But actions and procedures that may appear obvious and straightforward at the individual level may be damaging, especially if regulation reinforces herd activity, at the aggregate systemic level. So in our next section, 2.3, we consider not only the likely extent of procyclicality, but also steps that might be taken to mitigate it.

Section 2 approaches this subject at a fairly high level of generality. So we have chosen to support this overview with three more focused empirical exercises. In the first of these, Section 3.1, we analyse the procyclical effects of financial liberalization. We show how the relationship between liberalization and a subsequent asset price boom–bust has been a common phenomenon, common to Western as well as Asian countries, in developed as well as developing countries, and that financial liberalization appears to have strengthened the financial accelerator mechanism by increasing the sensitivity of bank lending to property price fluctuations.

In our main analysis, in Section 2, we suggest that an increase in required bank capital during downturns may exacerbate the recession. We seek to support that hypothesis, in Section 3.2, by looking (again) at the experience in the USA of the 'credit crunch' in the recession of 1990/1, when required bank capital adequacy ratios were being hoisted in the aftermath of the first Basel Accord in 1988.

Finally, in Section 3.3, we try to do a counterfactual simulation to see how banking capital adequacy requirements would have changed over recent history for a 'typical' bank in three countries, Mexico, Norway, and the United States, using three different regulatory approaches. These were:

(i)   the Basel II standardized approach;
(ii) the Basel II Foundation IRB (internal ratings-based) approach; and
(iii) an improved credit risk method (ICRM).

What we show is that the introduction of the Basel II IRB approach may well considerably accentuate the procyclicality of the regulatory system.

The last section, Section 4, summarizes the main findings and concludes.

2. GENERAL CONSIDERATIONS

2.1. The Changing Nature of Cycles and the Role of Asset Prices

The characteristics of trade cycles, of crises, and of financial regulation have all been changing over time. Eichengreen and Bordo (2003) and Bordo et al. (2001) divide up the 120 years since 1880 into four main periods, 1880–1913, 1919–39, 1945–71, and 1973–97. It is the third period that stands out as unique in several respects. First, inflation not only continued, but accelerated; this had never happened before then during peacetime. Second, in the developed world, output and productivity growth were much higher than previously, or (with a few exceptions) subsequently, and unemployment low and stable. Third, there were no banking crises (see Eichengreen and Bordo 2003: table 3.5, reproduced here as Table 26.1; the same data are shown

Table 26.1. Crisis frequency

Year	Banking crises	Currency crises	Twin crises	All crises
1880–1913	2.30	1.23	1.38	4.90
1919–39	4.84	4.30	4.03	13.17
1945–71	0.00	6.85	0.19	7.04
1973–97 (21 countries)	2.03	5.18	2.48	9.68
1973–97 (56 countries)	2.29	7.48	2.38	12.15

Source: Eichengreen and Bordo 2003, Table 3.5.

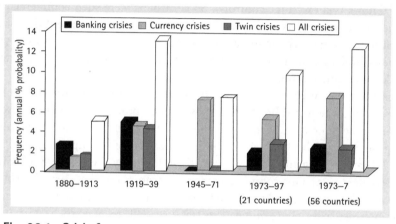

Fig. 26.1. Crisis frequency

Source: Bordo et al. 2001, Figure 1, p. 56

diagrammatically in Figure 26.1, taken from Bordo et al. 2001: figure 1, p. 56), and, no doubt largely in consequence, bank supervision and regulation remained generally light.[1] In most countries, at least until the end of this period (1945–71), bank lending to the private sector was not only directly constrained by credit controls in aggregate, but also directed towards the preferred sectors of exporting and manufacturing companies.

Demand was generally kept high enough, primarily through expansionary fiscal policies, to keep unemployment below its 'natural' rate, so that inflation tended to accelerate from peak to peak. The monetary authorities would then raise interest rates to check inflation, and also the balance-of-payments/currency crises that attended the comparatively more inflationary countries. It was said that every boom in the USA during these decades was killed off by the Federal Reserve System. Thereafter, during the stop intervals of the go–stop cycles of the time, interest rates would be lowered out of a wish to hold down the cost of public sector indebtedness and to encourage private sector investment. The increases in interest rates, sharp though

---

[1] For an account of the changing structure of bank regulation in the UK, see Goodhart 2004.

they sometimes were, caused relatively little financial fragility since the banks' assets were primarily short-dated government securities and loans to large (and generally safe) private sector (manufacturing) companies.

The economically disastrous decade of the 1970s, with stagflation, brought about a reconstruction of the policy mix. In particular, there was a maintained shift away from direct, central (government) controls towards market mechanisms. There was a similar shift from using fiscal policy, primarily to target a desired level of unemployment, to using monetary policy, primarily to target a (low and stable) level of inflation.

The banking system, owing to its central role in the economy, had been a focus for such prior controls, controls on interest rates, on credit allocation, on international financial flows (via exchange controls). So controlled were such commercial banks that they were seen as akin to public utilities, not commercial entities—boring, uninnovative, but safe. The main task of bank managers/loan officers was to say 'no' to requests for loans from prospective borrowers in less favoured sectors. Risk analysis and risk management atrophied in such circumstances.

It has, therefore, not been surprising that one facet of the liberalization of banking systems around the world has been a subsequent lending boom and a subsequent bust. As we document in Section 3.1, this has occurred in country after country, starting perhaps in the UK, where the liberalization of 'Competition and Credit Control' (Bank of England 1971) was shortly followed by the Fringe Bank Crisis in 1973/4 (see Reid 1982). One common aggravating feature was that part of the business of the controlled commercial banks had, prior to the liberalization, often been taken by new intermediaries whose *raison d'être* was essentially to avoid such controls (with, or without, the blessing of the authorities). Once liberalized, there was a grab for market share by the commercial banks to recover previously lost business and by the non-bank intermediaries to hold on to it. Stir in the lack of experience with risk management, and the shift of the largest and safest borrowers to the capital markets, and the result was a danger of a boom–bust cycle. As noted in Section 3.1, this became the experience in Scandinavia in the early 1990s, Japan in the 1990s, and much of East Asia in 1997/8; much the same syndrome may await India and China when they eventually liberalize.

This experience, though general, was not, however, universal. Several major European countries, notably Germany, avoided any such experience. In the German case this may be attributed to its banking system being re-established, after the Second World War, on a relatively liberalized basis from the outset.[2] Even so, the dangers of enhanced financial instability in the immediate aftermath of liberalization indicate

---

[2] Kaminsky and Schmukler 2003 provide a comprehensive chronology of financial liberalization for a large sample of industrialized and developing countries. Their chronology shows that the German banking sector was liberalized much earlier than the banking sectors in other industrialized countries. Ceilings on interest rates were abolished in 1967. In most other countries the removal of interest rate ceilings occurred in the 1970s or even the 1980s. The liberalization index constructed by Abiad and Mody 2003, which also takes into account other dimensions of financial liberalization, indicates that the German financial system could be characterized as already fully liberalized in the early 1970s.

the need for ensuring that financial supervision and risk management skills are improved at the same time.

Liberalization of banking systems has been one of the most potent progenitors of boom–bust cycles, but it has not been the only factor. Once the large companies, to whom the banks had primarily lent in the Eichengreen–Bordo third period (1945–71), had migrated to capital markets, banks increasingly began to lend to small and medium-sized enterprises (SMEs) and to persons. Such smaller-size borrowers were, in general, somewhat riskier, and the costs of acquiring information on a large number of idiosyncratic small borrowers were greater. So, banks placed increasing weight on collateral as a basis for lending. But this gave rise to the likelihood of enhanced dynamic instability, in the guise of the financial accelerator mechanism—see, for example, Bernanke, Gertler, and Gilchrist (1999) and Clarida, Gali, and Gertler (1999)—or the cyclical mechanism of Kiyotaki and Moore (1997).

Essentially, an upturn may be triggered by some good shock, for example to productivity or trade; profits increase, asset values rise; lending increases because collateral becomes more easily available; enhanced lending raises investment, profits, and asset values. This goes on until the rise in the capital stock becomes so large that profit margins crumble. Then, of course, everything goes into reverse. An interesting feature of such booms is that they are often characterized by stable real unit labour costs (held down by productivity gains), stable prices (often held down by currency appreciation, partly owing to capital inflows), and seemingly prudent, or even robust, fiscal policies (with rising tax revenues and declining social expenditures)—a markedly different profile from the earlier period.

Besides greater lending to SMEs, banks also increasingly muscled in on the business of mortgage lending to households, territory which had previously been confined to specialized (and often cartelized) mortgage lenders. Again, a similar nexus between some favourable initial shock leading to higher housing prices, providing a stronger collateral basis for bank lending, with such lending tending to cause yet higher housing prices, and so on, could be discerned on numerous occasions in a variety of countries, though more so in Anglo-Saxon countries, where home ownership is prized, rather than in continental Europe, especially where accommodation is more commonly rented.

In Section 3.1 we present some formal evidence supporting the hypothesis that financial liberalization has increased the procyclicality of financial systems. We first show that financial liberalizations were generally followed by boom–bust cycles in economic activity, bank lending, and asset prices. Based on rolling regressions, we also demonstrate that liberalizations of banking sectors were associated with an increased sensitivity of bank lending to property price movements, which implies a strengthening of the effect of business-cycle fluctuations on bank credit.

Such characteristics have, of course, led to the debate on whether the monetary authorities could, and should, observe and then react to deviations of asset prices from some longer-term fundamental value, i.e. asset price bubbles; see in particular the debate between Cecchetti et al. (2000) and Bernanke and Gertler (1999); see also Gertler et al. (1998). This debate continues in the aftermath of the dot-com equity bubble and bust, but it is not the remit, or purpose, of this chapter to discuss macro-monetary policies. Rather, it is our objective to discuss how policies with respect to financial regulation and supervision interact with the cycle.

2.2. Interaction between Regulation and the Trade Cycle

These changing characteristics of the trade cycle, notably liberalized financial markets combined with sharp asset price fluctuations, have resulted in a crop of banking crises, and twin banking/currency crises. Looking again at Table 26.1, the frequency of such crises reverted to the previous norm in 1880–1913, though still below that exhibited during the Great Depression in the inter-war years.

The liberalization of financial markets was meant to, and did, enhance competition. Competition led to lower profit margins. A combination of factors led to the assumption of greater risk in loan books, e.g. the migration of larger (and safer) borrowers to capital markets, initial (i.e. post-liberalization) inexperience with risk management, the desire to break into new and unfamiliar markets, and a wish to maintain the return on equity (ROE) despite declining margins for safer business. Riskier business led to a rise in non-performing loans (NPLs) and subsequent write-offs. Declining profit margins and higher NPLs, plus a desire to maintain ROEs, led to a trend decline in capital ratios. The decline in capital ratios implied worsening financial fragility.

As this was happening, in the 1970s, the institutions with particular responsibility for maintaining the systemic strength of the banking system were the central banks in the major developed countries. They had not, in practice, had much experience of such a role since the middle of the 1930s, but earlier historical developments had left them with that responsibility. As banking crises began to occur in the early 1970s, e.g. Franklin National (1973), Herstatt (1973/4), Fringe Bank Crisis (1973/4), many of the key central bankers became nervous.

Moreover, the growing development of international financial markets, the huge growth of international capital flows (following the removal of exchange controls), and the interpenetration of national financial markets at the wholesale level (and occasionally at the retail level also) by banks and investment houses with an international reach meant that no single country, even the USA, could maintain higher standards of financial probity unilaterally. The problem was that, absent exchange controls, financial intermediation could just move offshore.

This led to one of the more remarkable institutional developments of our age, the Basel Committee on Banking Supervision (BCBS) (initially called the Blunden and then the Cooke Committee, with these being the officials from the Bank of England who were its first two chairmen). This Committee was established by the conclave of the Central Bank Governors of the G-10 meeting under the auspices of the Bank for International Settlements (BIS). It had no formal or legal status, no governmental support (either international or national). Its pronouncements (Accords) were the softest of soft law. Yet there were sanctions to encourage adherence. The central banks of the countries with the main international financial markets were the leading members of the BCBS. If a country refused to abide by the Accords of the BCBS, the banks of that country could have their branches, and/or subsidiaries, banned from operating in the main financial centres.

As multinational trade flourished and international capital flows multiplied, so the leading banks and investment houses set up subsidiaries and branches in many countries. There was an urgent need to systematize and rationalize international procedures for banking supervision and, above all, to ensure that there was one lead regulator who could oversee the consolidated accounts of the bank as a whole (a need evidenced, for example, by the Banco Ambrosiano collapse in 1981). The BCBS did much excellent work on this front. But its main concern was to halt and, indeed, to reverse the trend decline in capital ratios. It achieved that objective with the introduction of the Accord on Capital Adequacy Requirements in 1988, now generally known as Basel I.[3] This was a great success for the BCBS, which by now really deserves a proper full-scale historical assessment (not attempted here).

Basel I required internationally active banks to hold capital equal to 8 per cent of their risk-weighted assets, where loans to the private non-bank sector were given a uniform risk weight of 100 per cent. Since the risk insensitivity of Basel I gave banks an incentive to move high-quality assets off the balance sheet and also did not reward the use of credit risk mitigation techniques (see Secretariat of the Basel Committee on Banking Supervision 2001: 12), it was increasingly criticized. One of the main aims of the recently approved new capital accord, Basel II, was thus to increase significantly the risk sensitivity of capital requirements. This was achieved by substantially spreading the range of risk weights and making them dependent on the external or internal ratings of the borrower.

While the introduction of capital adequacy requirements under the Basel Accord was deservedly hailed as a great achievement, nevertheless it had a number of weaknesses. It is upon these that we now mainly focus.

First, the decision was made to try to relate banks' capital requirements to the relative riskiness of the assets. That is an understandable, some might say even an obvious, decision. But the measurement of risk is horribly complex (finance academics spend a lifetime on the subject). If the authorities try to lay down risk ratings, they run into a nasty dilemma. On the one hand, they can try to keep their risk measures simple and broad-brush, as in Basel I; but that will mean that such risk measurements will be inaccurate, and hence subject to gaming, arbitrage, and avoidance, with unfortunate side effects, as indeed happened with Basel I. On the other hand, they can try to make their risk measurements as close to state-of-the-art

---

[3] Secretariat of the Basel Committee on Banking Supervision (2001) states on p. 11: 'the major impetus for the 1988 Basel Capital Accord was the concern of the Governors of the G10 central banks that the capital of the world's major banks had become dangerously low after persistent erosion through competition.'

analysis as possible. Since risk measurement is complex, the resulting requirements will similarly become dense and difficult, the more so since analytical logic often has to compromise with national idiosyncrasies. Moreover, the state of the art is evolving over time—we would hope that it is improving—so that what may be correct today will become inaccurate tomorrow, and hence, perhaps, over time as subject to gaming, arbitrage, and avoidance as simpler rules.

Moreover, the more detailed the rules, the more they will tend to require those subject to them, i.e. the banks, to respond in exactly the same way to common shocks. That will enhance herd-like behaviour, one-way markets, which many observers already have seen as a danger, even before Basel II. In response to this, the BCBS can rightly state that the internal ratings-based (IRB) component of Basel II has been an instrument to induce the banks to improve their own individual modelling of (credit) risk. On this view, Basel II is but a temporary phase (or step) in an evolving process whereby individual banks develop their own effective proprietary (credit) risk-metric models, preferably with continuing differences and innovation. Then, as has been happening with supervision of the trading/investment book, the supervisors could focus on oversight of bank models, and not try to specify such models themselves.

One continuing concern, however, is that the modelling needs of bankers differ from those of supervisors. Supervisors are mostly focused on what would happen under extreme adverse events, in the far one-sided tails of probability distributions, whereas bankers need to be concerned about the full distribution of outcomes. Whereas value at risk (VaR) models do a good job most of the time, with their assumption of log normal distributions, and so are suitable for bankers, extreme events occur more often than in a normal distribution (fat tails, kurtosis), and so the bankers' model was not, as it happened, of much use to supervisors.

The second weakness is that the supervision, the analysis, and the modelling focus primarily on the individual banking institution, not on the system as a whole. These two weaknesses are interrelated in the sense that the realization that supervisors could not rely on bankers' own VaR models led to a new generation of stress tests, or scenario simulations, in which individual banks were asked to assess the effect on their own profitability, and capital adequacy, of the onset of certain extreme shocks. But there was no possibility whatsoever, in this attempt to estimate the effect of a macro shock on each individual micro institution, of examining dynamic interactions between banks (e.g. if bank A was forced to withdraw funds from the interbank market, what effect would this have on bank B?) or between bank reactions and the wider economy (e.g. if banks cut back on making new loans in the face of an adverse economic shock, would it impart a serious further downwards impulse on the economy?). In short, the macro/micro stress tests go only part way to an assessment (and measurement) of systemic fragility.

Of course, the robustness of the system as a whole is related to the strength of the individual members. Given the myriad interconnections between banks, if the individual banks are in poor condition, then the banking system as a whole is also likely to be fragile, and vice versa. Even so, it is perfectly possible to envisage circumstances where liquidity, or solvency, problems in one bank could have a cascade effect on other banks, perhaps via some combination of fund withdrawals and asset price declines that could—possibly quite rapidly—bring initially healthy banks into serious difficulties. It is not possible to analyse and estimate such systemic weaknesses using present techniques.

Some steps have been taken to analyse the systemic implications of one of the most obvious sources of interconnection, i.e. the interbank market. Here there have been various empirical studies (e.g. Elsinger, Lehar, and Summer 2002; Wells 2002; Furfine 2003; Upper and Worms 2004), and the initial results have been quite reassuring. So long as pro rata payments on their interbank debts can be made quite quickly by failing banks and/or concern about other banks' position with the failing bank does not trigger secondary (reputational) withdrawals of funds from them, then the first-round, direct effect of interbank linkages, via the interbank market, can almost always be comfortably absorbed.

This analysis underlines one of the problems about trying to analyse financial fragility. Developments in the financial system depend critically on the state of confidence. Given that we are dealing with the aftermath of assumed extreme shocks, which by definition occur very rarely, it is almost impossible to give any quantification about the potential likelihood of such secondary (reputational) effects (though one might be able, at least in theory, to simulate them).

Be that as it may, with two colleagues at the Bank of England, one of us is trying to model the systemic effects of extreme shocks; for example Goodhart, Sunirand, and Tsomocos (2003). But that is somewhat separate from the main focus of this chapter, and we do not pursue it further here.

A common problem in this field is that regulations that are entirely sensible when applied to the individual institution can have unwanted, and often unintended, macro, aggregate effects. This is particularly so when the individual institutions are all simultaneously affected by a common factor—notably the trade cycle, as we discuss in the following subsection. But whenever a common factor affects a large proportion of the intermediaries at the same time, some unfortunate results may occur.

A good example of this occurred in the case of the UK life insurance (LI) companies in 2002. In this case the downturn in the equity market, following the dot-com bubble and bust, put pressure on the LI companies' solvency ratios, whereby they have to demonstrate that they can meet their obligations to stakeholders even should (equity) markets continue to decline (by another 25 per cent). The standard way to be sure of meeting such commitments is to match (hedge) the liabilities with assets of the same duration, and with a similar, fixed payment stream. So, the downturn in the equity market, interacting with the prudential requirements for solvency, forced the LI companies into selling equity onto a falling market, while buying long-dated (government) bonds on a rising market, thereby exacerbating both market trends. Moreover, their predicament was obvious to others, who could attempt to benefit by front-running speculation.

2.3. The Procyclicality of Regulation

The main common factor to affect banks, and most other financial intermediaries, is the trade cycle (i.e. generalized fluctuations in the economy). Regulation is inherently procyclical. Borrower and bank profits rise during booms; new capital is easier to raise; asset prices are higher. Per contra, in a downturn, non-performing loans, failures, and write-offs increase. Prudential regulations bite harder during periods of economic weakness because the individual banks are, indeed, more fragile. So, the more accurately the value, and relative riskiness, of each bank is measured at any point of time, the greater will be the procyclicality of the prudential regime. Thus Basel II will be more procyclical than Basel I; fair-value accounting methods more than historic cost; point-in-time ratings more than those averaged through the cycle; and advanced IRB assessments more than foundation IRB (especially so since loss given default (LGD) is to be treated as constant over time in the foundation method, whereas almost all empirical studies have found LGD to be strongly cyclical, perhaps as much as, or more so than, the procyclicality of default (PD) (e.g. Altman 2002; Altman et al. 2002; Acharya, Bharath, and Srinivasan 2003).

This proposition, that the greater the accuracy of current valuation, the greater the resulting procyclicality of prudential regulation, is generally accepted. A much more problematic question is what the practical, empirical scale of this relationship may be, and how important the resulting macroeconomic consequentials may have been. We examine these issues in two studies in the empirical section of this chapter. In Section 3.2 we reconsider whether, and how far, the requirement for additional capital, in order to satisfy the newly imposed capital adequacy requirement (CAR) of Basel I, exacerbated the recession of 1991/2—especially in the USA, where most of the empirical studies were carried out.

The second exercise, which we undertake in Section 3.3, is to simulate the comparative effect of Basel II, relative to Basel I, on CARs over the course of the cycle. For this purpose we use a data set from Mexico that was available to one of the authors (M. Segoviano). We also use data sets from Norway and the USA, and comment on some other empirical exercises in the literature.

This procyclicality of prudential regulation tends to exacerbate the trade cycle itself. We have already mentioned the example of the solvency regulations on LI companies enhancing the boom–bust experience on the London Stock Exchange. By the same token, if banks, in aggregate, are subject to binding prudential constraints on their lending in downturns (which constraints are relaxed during booms), the amplitude of the cycle is likely[4] to be greater.

Of course, if the scale of this problem of procyclicality is small, then we need not worry so much. But the empirical exercises in Section 3.3, though as always

---

[4] A counter-argument is that, should the binding prudential regulations during downturns succeed in reducing the number and scale of bank failures, then the probability of systemic collapses during the recession will have been lessened. Likewise, the greater sophistication of risk measurement methods may encourage private sector bank managers to curb their own risks in a voluntary manner.

inconclusive, suggest that the scale could be large. That raises the question of how best to respond.

One approach is to use some kind of averaging of the data over the cycle—to use historic cost accounting, or constant PDs (as in Basel I), or constant LGDs (as in the Foundation approach), or through-the-cycle ratings. But this goes against the grain of trying to obtain the best, and most accurate, valuations in order to guide efficient market pricing, investor information, and capital allocation.

A second possible response is to try to use fiscal, rather than monetary, measures to mitigate such procyclicality. Capital gains taxes may limit the volatility of post-tax returns. Insofar as various taxes can be adjusted according to the condition of asset markets, they could be used by the authorities to mitigate procyclicality. But this depends not only on the authorities having somehow better information on 'fundamental' asset prices, but may also introduce other distortions which usually have adverse effects.

A third, and perhaps more promising, approach is to adjust the prudential para-meters (to be applied to the most accurately estimated valuations), contracyclically over the cycle (Gordy and Howells, 2004). This possibility, however, depends quite largely on there being an identifiable cycle, which can be expected to revert back to some (estimated) normal, mean level.

Assume, for example, that there is a recognized tendency for there to be mean reversion towards some (calculable) price/earnings (P/E) ratio in the equity market. Then the solvency ratio calculations that are prescribed should require that the per-centage fall that the LI should be able to withstand should be an increasing function of the current level of the P/E in the equity market. Similarly, loan-to-valuation ratios in mortgage and property markets should, in principle, be functions of the deviation of housing/property prices from their equilibrium level.

An obvious problem in this respect, both for the economy as a whole and for the key asset markets, is that mean reversion is an extremely weak and unreliable force (think of foreign exchange markets) and that the ability to observe a long-run fundamental equilibrium is equivalently weak and doubtful. There is always a possibility that 'there really is a New Economy'. Although this latter is most often a (and in some cases a self-seeking) delusion, trends, e.g. in productivity, do change. Estimates of output gaps, and of equilibrium asset prices, will always be extremely unreliable. Nevertheless, there is a case that it would be better to tie prudential parameters to such unreliable estimates than to hold them constant over the cycle, which must have adverse effects on procyclicality. Thus it would be possible to require some contracyclical variation in minimum CARs, raising these during booms and allowing them to fall back again during recessions.

Many might welcome this idea in principle, but argue that, since the estimate of the deviation from the norm is inevitably somewhat subjective, this should properly come under pillar 2 of Basel II, as an optional, discretionary add-on for national supervisors, rather than as part of any agreed rule book. And some supervisors may already be attempting to follow this course. There is some force in this argument, but it runs up against the problem that different national authorities will respond in different ways, so that international banks will vocally complain if their national authorities impose unilaterally higher CARs on them during expansions. Note also that minimum CARs will be required by formal regulation, e.g. EU directives, under pillar 1, so that national supervision will not (at least not officially) be allowed to combine higher ratios during expansions with ratios *below* the pillar 1 requirement in recessions. So a drawback of Basel II is that any national supervisor trying to build some contracyclical effects into their own approach will simultaneously expose their own banks to higher over-time average CARs. There will be a clash between the desire for greater stability and the desire to allow their own banks to maintain international competitiveness.

Nevertheless, the main problem with this approach lies in the weakness of mean reversion and the difficulty of observing deviations from fundamentals. Once events have safely become past history, enabling the commentator to draw trend lines, historical cycles come to appear immediately obvious. If, however, one allows for changing trends, and other breaks in the time series (and these have happened before now), then the estimates of current deviations (from 'fundamental' norms) become a matter of hot, and difficult, argument. Perhaps the strongest argument for Alan Greenspan *not* raising interest rates to constrain the dot-com bubble was that this would have been extremely difficult to justify to the US Congress and the American people, the more so since there were many siren voices, and gullible investors (see Brennan 2004) who did not see the run-up in equity values as an unsustainable bubble. If it is too difficult for those in charge of monetary policy to assess deviations from fundamental equilibrium,[5] why should financial regulators and supervisors be better endowed with economic insight?

A somewhat simpler alternative than relating regulatory parameters to deviations from the norm is to relate them to rates of change, relative to past average rates of change. These latter are easily calculated (though the length of the window over which the average is to be calculated is both somewhat arbitrary and can, at times, be substantively important). The rate of growth of bank lending to the private sector has, in the past, been a good predictor of financial crises, i.e. it is unusually high before crises. Again, bubbles in asset prices tend to be characterized by accelerating prices as the peak and resulting crisis/collapse is reached. If solvency requirements, loan-to-value requirements, etc., were related to prior rates of change, it should help to avoid procyclicality.

All this discussion, however, is reminiscent of the long-past discussion on ways to stabilize the macro trade cycle via derivative or integral stabilization, etc. Much of that, however, got washed away in the general attack on fine-tuning, and the belief that demand management is better focused on long-term rules, such as achieving an inflation target and sticking to a set of 'golden' fiscal rules.

---

[5] A counter-argument is that monetary policy makers already aim to assess deviations from long-run equilibrium in the guise of the output gap, so should they not be willing to assess similar deviations from equilibrium elsewhere in the economy, e.g. in the housing market? Against this it can be replied that the aggregate economy is generally more stable, and more predictable, than individual asset markets, such as housing, equities, or foreign exchange.

By the same token, one can ask whether it is the purpose of regulatory policy to concern itself with the amplitude of cyclical swings. Perhaps not, but then it is surely the purpose of regulatory policy to avoid systemic crises, rather than to prevent all individual failures. At present, the focus of financial regulation and supervision is on the individual institution, not on the system as a whole. Through the indirect effects of procyclicality, it is at least possible that the current, and prospective, methods of individual institutional supervision could have damaging implications for the system as a whole.

3. Empirical Analysis

3.1. Financial Liberalization, Credit Cycles, and the Changing Role of Asset Prices

Since the early/mid-1970s there have been extensive efforts to liberalize banking systems in both developed and developing economies.[6] The trend towards financial liberalization was motivated by theoretical and empirical findings that higher financial development leads to higher economic growth and that financial liberalization was, in turn, a precondition for financial development. Theoretically, by easing financial constraints and improving the efficiency of the banking system, banking sector liberalization stirs higher and more efficient investment in both physical and human capital and thus spurs faster long-run growth.[7] Empirically, this hypothesis appears to be supported by the data (see e.g. Leahy et al. 2001).

In recent years, however, the perception of financial liberalization has become more critical, owing to the recurrence of violent boom–bust cycles in credit creation, economic activity, and asset markets in the wake of financial liberalization. These boom–bust cycles often ended in outright systemic crisis of the banking sector. A central finding of the large and growing literature on the causes of banking crises is that financial liberalization significantly increases the probability of a banking crisis. Various studies (Demirgüç-Kunt and Detragiache 1998; Kaminsky and Reinhart 1999) have shown that indicators of financial liberalization help to explain the occurrence of banking crises in large samples of developing and developed countries.

Tornell, Westermann, and Martinez (2004), amongst others, argue that the occurrence of occasional crises does not overturn the general result that financial liberalization is beneficial for long-run growth. They show that in a sample of developing countries the fastest growing countries are also those that experienced boom–bust cycles. They also present a theoretical model where financial liberalization leads to

---

[6] For a chronology of financial liberalization in developed and developing markets, see Kaminsky and Schmukler 2003.

[7] See Levine 1997 for a survey of the relationship between financial development and growth.

both higher long-run growth and higher financial fragility. However, there are also noteworthy counter-examples to this conclusion. Japan, for example, certainly grew at a slower pace after the boom–bust cycle which followed the liberalization of the mid-1980s than before. Thus, even if financial liberalization generally remains beneficial for growth also after controlling for the damaging effects of financial fragility, the potential occurrence of boom–bust cycles in the wake of financial liberalization remains a concern.

Rather surprisingly, only few studies have tried to derive stylized facts for the development of key macroeconomic and financial variables in the wake of financial liberalization.[8] Anecdotal evidence, e.g. Drees and Pazarbasioglu (1998) for the Nordic countries and Collyns and Senhadji (2002) for the East Asian countries, suggests that financial liberalization is followed by boom–bust cycles in bank lending, economic activity, and asset prices, especially real estate. In order to assess whether this finding also holds on a broader basis of financial liberalization episodes we looked at the development of real GDP, bank lending, property prices, and share prices in the wake of financial liberalization for a sample of sixteen OECD countries, Australia, Belgium, Denmark, Finland, France, Ireland, Italy, Japan, Korea, New Zealand, Norway, Spain, Sweden, Switzerland, the UK, and the USA.[9]

Figure 26.2 shows the unweighted country average (solid line) of the development of real GDP growth, the change in real bank lending, the change in real property prices, and the change in real share prices (four-quarter growth rates) in the ten years following financial liberalization, together with upper and lower quartiles (dotted lines). The figures reveal that, on average, financial liberalization is followed by a boom–bust cycle in economic activity, bank lending, and asset prices. Real GDP growth starts to rise immediately after liberalization and peaks after about three years. Then real growth gradually declines and falls below its initial value after about five years. Real lending growth starts to rise about five quarters after the date of liberalization and peaks after about three years. Subsequently, the growth rate of real lending declines and falls below its initial value after about seven years. Property prices start to rise one year following liberalization. The increase in property prices peaks after about three years and then gradually declines. After about six years, property prices

[8] Reinhart and Tokatlidis 2001 derive stylized facts for the long-run effects of liberalization for a large sample of developed and developing countries. They analyse the development of key macroeconomic variables, national account aggregates, monetary and credit aggregates, and interest rates before and after dates of financial liberalization in order to assess whether the pre- and post-liberalization mean of each indicator is significantly different. Kaminsky and Schmukler 2003 focus on the effects of financial liberalization on the volatility of stock prices. They find that liberalization leads to more pronounced boom–bust cycles in the short run, but more stable stock markets in the long run.

[9] Financial liberalization dates for the post-Bretton Woods period were identified based on information provided in Drees and Pazarbasioglu 1998, Glick and Hutchison 1999, Abiad and Mody 2003, and Kaminsky and Schmukler 2003. The dates of liberalization for the individual countries are 1985 for Australia, 1986 for Belgium, 1981 for Denmark, 1986 for Finland, 1985 for France, 1981 for Italy, 1985 for Japan, 1988 for Korea, 1985 for New Zealand, 1981 for Norway, 1983 for Spain, 1983 for Sweden, 1989 for Switzerland, 1981 for the UK, and 1982 for the USA. Note that the date taken for the UK from this literature differs from that specified earlier in Section 2.1, which was 1971. This indicates both that liberalization can proceed through several waves (so there may be several valid dates for a single country) and that such dating inevitably involves some, potentially fallible, subjective judgement.

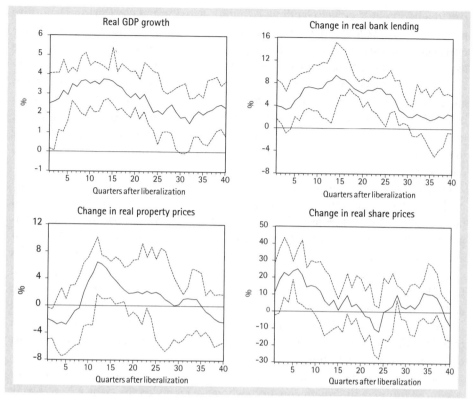

Fig. 26.2. Post–liberalization cycles

Note: Solid lines are sample averages, dotted lines are upper and lower quartiles

start to fall. Real share prices appear to be rising at a brisk pace already at the time of liberalization. After liberalization, the increase in share prices further accelerates and peaks after about six quarters. About five years after liberalization, share prices are falling. Thus, the sample averages appear to support the notion that episodes of financial liberalization are followed by pronounced boom–bust cycles.

The upper and lower quartiles, which are also displayed in Figure 26.2, also reveal, however, that there is substantial variation in the movements of the variables across countries. A look at the individual country-level data, which we do not discuss here for the sake of brevity,[10] suggests that all countries experienced a cycle after financial liberalization, but that there is substantial variation in the timing of the occurrence of the cycle. This may, however, partly be due to unavoidable imprecision in the exact dating of liberalization episodes.

Why do boom–bust cycles evolve in the wake of financial liberalization? Financial liberalization relaxes the borrowing constraints faced by the private sector and, there-fore, has similar effects to a positive, permanent productivity shock to the economy. In models with credit-constrained borrowers,[11] a positive productivity shock gives

---

[10] Individual country-level data are available from the authors upon request.
[11] The basic references of this literature are Bernanke and Gertler 1989 and Kiyotaki and Moore 1997.

rise to a boom–bust cycle in lending, economic activity, and asset prices. A positive productivity shock leads to an increase in the value of collateralizable assets. As the borrowing capacity of entrepreneurs depends on the value of their collateralizable assets, this gives rise to higher lending, which in turn further fuels economic activity and asset prices, which again increases borrowing capacity, and so on. Eventually, all variables converge back to their steady-state levels and the boom turns into a bust. The result is a credit cycle à la Kiyotaki and Moore (1997). Thus, from the perspective of models with credit constraints, the evolution of a boom–bust cycle in the wake of financial liberalization is fully consistent with theoretical models with credit constraints and a financial accelerator.

Financial liberalization is, in fact, even likely to be associated with a strengthening of the financial accelerator mechanism and thus to give rise to more pronounced boom–bust cycles. As the liberalization of banking systems has usually been accompanied by liberalizations of capital and stock markets, it became easier for the largest and safest borrowers of banks to raise funds on the capital and stock markets.[12] As a consequence, banks tried to make good the lost business by beginning to lend to SMEs and persons. These smaller borrowers were, in general, somewhat riskier, and the costs of monitoring these small borrowers were higher, so that banks placed increasing weight on collateral as a basis for lending. As a result, changes in the value of collateralizable assets, predominantly property, are likely to have a stronger impact on lending after liberalization.

In order to test this hypothesis empirically, we performed rolling regressions for a reduced form credit growth equation, where we regressed the change in real bank lending (Δc) on its own lag, the lagged change in real property prices (Δp), the lagged change in real GDP (Δy), and the lagged change in the ex post short-term real interest rate (Δr):

$$\Delta c_t = \beta_1 \Delta c_{t-1} + \beta_2 \Delta p_{t-1} + \beta_3 \Delta y_{t-1} + \beta_4 \Delta r_{t-1} + \varepsilon_t \tag{1}$$

Equation (1) was estimated by OLS for a sample of OECD countries over a rolling window of fifteen years with quarterly data. In order to have a first coefficient estimate for a sample period covering mainly the pre-liberalization period, availability of all explanatory variables back to the early 1970s was required. This data requirement reduced the sample of countries for this exercise to ten: Australia, France, Italy, Japan, New Zealand, Norway, Sweden, Switzerland, the UK, and the USA. The estimated rolling property price coefficients are displayed in Figure 26.3 in a 5 per cent confidence band. The graphs appear to support the hypothesis of an increasing effect of property prices on bank lending. Except for Australia and New Zealand, there is for all countries a clear and significant increase in the rolling property price coefficient over the 1990s. A comparison of the first and the last rolling coefficient estimates makes a clear case. The first property price coefficient estimate of the rolling regression, which corresponds to the sample period covering the pre-liberalization period from

---

[12] See Kaminsky and Schmukler 2003 for a cross-country chronology of banking sector and stock market liberalizations.

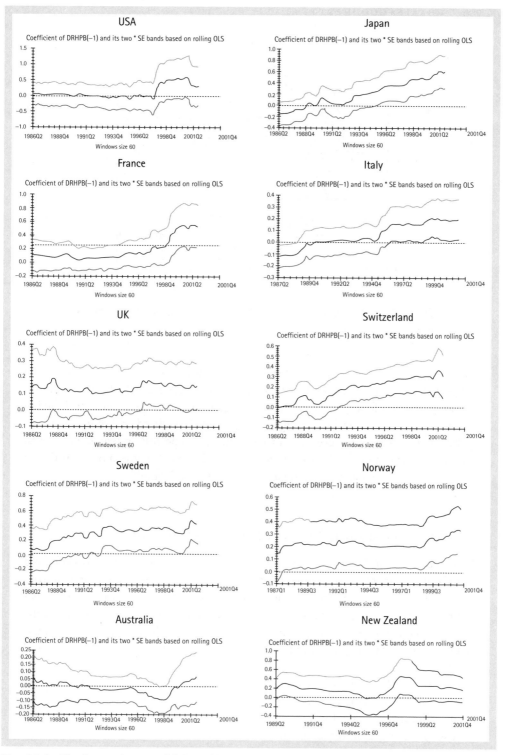

Fig. 26.3. The increasing sensitivity of bank lending to property prices

Note: The graphs report rolling OLS estimates of the property price coefficient in equation (1) over a window of 15 years

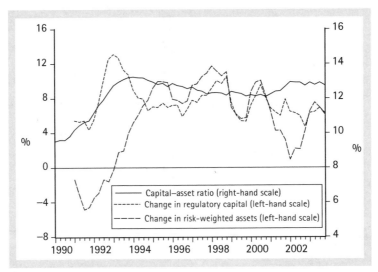

Fig. 26.4. The capital–asset ratio and its components of US commercial banks

Source: FDIC

the early 1970s to the mid-1980s, is insignificant in all countries. In stark contrast, the last property price coefficient estimate of the rolling regression, which corresponds to the sample period first quarter 1987 to fourth quarter 2001, where domestic banking sectors in all countries under investigation were fully liberalized, is significant at least at the 5 per cent level in seven out of ten countries. The rolling regression results, therefore, clearly support the view that bank lending has become more sensitive to property price movements in the wake of financial liberalization.

3.2. Macroeconomic Effects of the Basel Accord

As intended by the BCBS, the introduction of the 1988 Basel Accord was followed by a significant increase in average risk-weighted capital ratios in the G-10 countries (see Basel Committee on Banking Supervision 1999). What was not intended was that in many countries, including the USA, the introduction of the new CARs in the early 1990s coincided with a recession. The introduction of the 1988 Basel Accord may, therefore, provide a case in point of the potential macroeconomic effect of procyclical CARs.

Risk-weighted capital ratios can increase by increasing regulatory capital (the numerator) or by reducing risk-weighted assets (the denominator). Figure 26.4 shows the development of regulatory capital, risk-weighted assets, and the CAR in the USA since 1990.[13] The graphs reveal that the marked increase of the CAR from 9.5 per cent

---

[13] The data were taken from the BIS database. Unfortunately, there was no longer time series available for the USA. For other countries, time-series data for risk-adjusted capital ratios and risk-weighted assets, if at all available, do not go back further than the late 1990s.

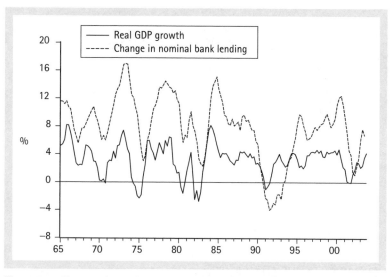

Fig. 26.5. Economic activity and credit creation in the US

to above 13 per cent between 1990 and 1993 was brought about by both an increase in regulatory capital and a decrease in risk-weighted assets. This implies that the increase of the CAR *may* have caused a reduction in the supply of credit to the economy, which is, in the literature, referred to as a 'credit crunch'. It is often argued that the adverse credit supply effects of the Basel Accord may have exacerbated the 1990/1 recession. A convincing proof of this hypothesis is still missing, mainly due to the problem with identifying and separating credit demand and credit supply movements.

Movements in real activity influence credit demand and movements in credit supply may influence real activity, which gives rise to a simultaneity problem, which has not yet been resolved convincingly. Figure 26.5 shows the development of real GDP growth and nominal lending growth in the USA since 1965. The graph reveals that economic activity and credit creation are closely correlated over the cycles, which may be reasonably explained by the effect of economic activity on credit demand. The three recessions of 1974/5, 1980/2, and 1990/1 were all accompanied by slowdowns in credit creation. However, the 1990/1 recession was the only case where credit growth turned negative. The downturn in bank lending was therefore stronger than would have been expected from prior experience. This is often taken as evidence that additional adverse supply effects were at work at that time.

Various empirical studies have investigated this question by looking at the significance of credit supply determinants in credit growth regressions (see, for example, Berger and Udell 1994). An alternative strategy, followed, for example, by Walsh and Wilcox (1995), is to take independent movements in the prime lending rate as an indication of changes of credit supply conditions. The prime lending rate (which was never a market-determined rate) used to be considered the rate at which banks lend to their best corporate customers. In practice, however, the best corporate customers borrow at rates below prime, and the prime lending rate is more a benchmark rate

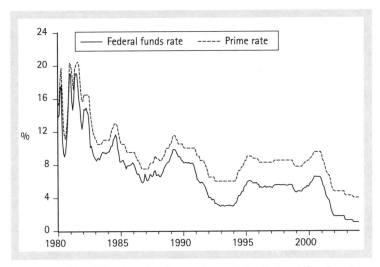

Fig. 26.6. The US prime lending rate and the federal funds rate

used to price loans for smaller firms and for less creditworthy large firms. In the long run, lending rates are set as mark-up over the bank's marginal cost of funds, which is, in the case of the prime rate, given by the federal funds rate. The mark-up of lending rates over the bank's marginal cost of funds is a function of the additional costs a bank incurs when extending a loan, such as the cost of doing a credit evaluation and, in particular, the cost of raising the capital to meet the capital requirement for the loan. This implies that, given that capital requirements have been tightened by the Basel Accord, the spread of the prime rate over the federal funds rate would be expected to rise, which would be an indication of an adverse supply effect on the credit market. Figure 26.6 shows the development of the prime lending rate and the federal funds rate since 1980. The graph suggests that the spread of the prime rate over the federal funds rate did, in fact, widen around 1990/1.

The hypothesis of a significantly widening spread of the prime rate over the federal funds rate can be tested more formally based on unit-root tests. Perron (1989) has shown that the presence of one-time breaks in the trend or mean of a time series gives rise to non-rejection of the unit-root hypothesis when not accounted for in the standard unit-root test. Perron has proposed a consistent testing strategy against breaking trend and means, both for the case of known break points (Perron 1989, 1990) and for the more general case of unknown break points, where the dates of shifts in the mean or the trend are endogenously determined in the testing procedure (Perron 1997).

Table 26.2 shows the results of a standard augmented Dickey–Fuller (ADF) unit-root test (Dickey and Fuller 1981), once allowing for a constant and a trend in the prime rate spread and once allowing only for a constant, and the ADF-type unit-root test allowing for a shift in the mean of the spread at an unknown date, to

Table 26.2. Unit-root tests for the spread of the prime rate over the federal funds rate

ADF test (constant and trend)	ADF test (constant and no trend) Perron	test (breaking constant)
−2.65	−1.99	−5.03

Notes: The 5% critical values are −3.43 for the ADF test with a constant and a trend, −2.87 for the ADF test with a constant but without trend, and −4.80 for the Perron test for the innovational outlier model. The endogenously determined break date in the Perron test is September 1990.

be determined endogenously by a sequential testing procedure, proposed by Perron (1997). The tests were performed for the spread of the prime lending rate over the federal funds rate, using monthly data over the period 1980–2003 taken from the IMF International Financial Statistics. The lag order of the lagged dynamic terms was chosen based on sequential lag reduction tests starting with a maximum lag order of twelve, which suggested retaining the maximum number of twelve lags. In both cases, the null of a unit root cannot be rejected. This finding would imply that there is no long-run relationship between the prime rate and the federal funds rate. An alternative interpretation, which would be suggested by Figure 26.5, is that there was a shift in the mean of the spread around the time of the introduction of the Basel Accord, and that the non-rejection of the unit-root hypothesis merely reflects the failure to take this shift into account in the testing procedure.

In order to assess which interpretation is right, we apply Perron's (1997) unit-root test with a break in the mean at an unknown date.[14] The lag order of the lagged dynamic terms was again chosen based on sequential lag reduction tests starting with a maximum lag order of 12, which suggested retaining ten lags. The break date was endogenously determined by calculating the unit-root test statistic for all possible break dates and then choosing the date that minimizes the unit-root test statistic. The regression results suggest that the mean spread is significantly higher after September 1990. The unit-root test statistic, which is reported in Table 26.2, is given by −5.03, which compares with a 5 per cent critical value of −4.80. Thus, the Perron unit-root test with unknown break point suggests that the spread of the prime rate over the federal funds rate is stationary around a constant mean which breaks in September 1990 and that the mean spread appears to be higher after the break. These results give some indication of potentially lasting supply effects of the introduction of the Basel Accord on the US credit market.

[14] Perron terms this model, where only a break in the mean is allowed for, the 'innovational outlier model'. In the second model he proposes, the 'additive outlier model', both the mean and the trend are allowed to break.

3.3. Basel and Procyclicality

Under the new Basel Accord (Basel II), two different approaches can be used to measure the riskiness and thus the risk weights of assets, the standardized approach, and the IRB approach. The standardized approach is based on external ratings of the credit risk of borrowers, while the IRB approach is based on the banks' internal ratings of their borrowers.

Our procedure here is to try to reconstruct a typical bank portfolio for a country and then, holding the presumed loan book unchanged over time (i.e. replacing failed loans with loans of a similar quality), to examine how the loan ratings would have shifted, and hence how the capital adequacy requirements for the banks would have varied over time under different credit risk measurement approaches; for other similar exercises, see Kashyap and Stein (2004) and Gordy and Howells (2004). To do this we use Moody's data on US corporate bonds, included on Moody's Investors Service, Credit Risk Calculator. We can only do this exercise for those countries for which Moody's data on credit ratings have a long enough time series. Unfortunately, this rules out most large European countries, since adequate Moody's data only go back to 1998 for the UK, 2001 for Germany, 2002 for France, 2003 for Italy, and 2002 for Spain. In the event, we used data provided by the Mexican Financial Regulatory Agency and the Norwegian Central Bank on Corporate Loans. The Mexican data incorporate information between 1995 and 2000 and the Norwegian data incorporate information between 1988 and 2001.

This sounds easier to do than it actually is, and a detailed exposition of this exercise has been done separately (Goodhart and Segoviano 2004) in a Financial Markets Group Discussion Paper. Among the problems are how to reconstruct a 'typical' bank portfolio; whether, and how, to deal with the problem of failing loans dropping out of the portfolio; and what account to take of the fact that Basel II is a regime change that may make banks alter their 'typical' behaviour. Very briefly, we reconstructed a typical bank portfolio as follows. We assumed that each portfolio consisted of 1,000 loans, each one with equal exposure. From each specific country data source, we obtained the *through time* proportion of assets (bonds for the USA or corporate loans for Mexico and Norway) that were classified under each of the reported ratings for a given country. With this information we constructed the *benchmark portfolio* that we used to compute capital requirements at each point in time.

By assuming that the initial bank loan book remains unchanged throughout, this is equivalent to assuming that failed loans are replaced by loans of similar initial quality. This is what Kashyap and Stein (2004) did, and seems natural. Gordy and Howells (2004) argue, however, that banks will aim for a higher-quality portfolio during recessions, and thus will replace failing loans with credits of higher than initial quality. At the macro level it is hard, in most countries, to see where the supply of such higher-quality loans would come from during recessions; in discussion of this point, at a BIS Conference in May 2004, Michael Gordy noted that, in the USA, high-quality companies tended to shift their borrowing from capital markets, for example the commercial paper market, to banks during recessions. In any case, since risk spreads widen during recessions, any extra benefit would be slight. So we feel relatively comfortable about this assumption.

The results of this exercise for the three countries examined are stark. We compared the implied capital requirements for our 'typical' bank under three regulatory regimes: first, the standardized approach in Basel II (which is close to that applied in Basel I); second, the Foundations IRB approach (i.e. assuming a constant LGD, since we have no good time series in any country for average LGD); and third, an ICRM. This last uses a Merton approach to model credit quality changes and an indirect approach to model correlations among the individual credits in the overall portfolio. The construction of an ICRM is, however, quite complex, and interested readers should consult our companion paper, Goodhart and Segoviano (2004).

In a nutshell, this latter approach entails deriving the distribution of the possible values that the portfolio of financial assets held by the bank can take. The potential different values that a portfolio could take—and their respective probabilities—are recorded in the so-called profit and loss distribution of the portfolio (P&L). For risk management purposes, the VaR, from which economic capital for a bank is defined, is obtained from this distribution. If a bank holds a portfolio of assets, we can then attempt to quantify how the diversification of its assets will affect the value of its portfolio. So, when computing the P&L, the geographical location and industrial activity of the assets held in a portfolio are taken into account. When implementing this approach, we assumed that the benchmark portfolios had loans that were evenly distributed across geographical regions and industrial activities within their respective countries. We then programmed an algorithm that simulated 10,000 different 'quality scenarios' that might affect these portfolios, and so produce a migration of loans between credit quality bands. Each quality scenario shows a change in the market value of the assets, and therefore the difference between the initial and final credit quality. Once the credit portfolio quality scenarios were simulated, we computed the losses/gains that come from the difference between initial and final credit qualities. The losses/gains obtained from the simulation process were used to build a histogram, which summarizes the loss distribution of the credit portfolio. From this distribution a VaR is defined from which we can obtain the amount of unexpected losses from the portfolio. The unexpected losses divided by the total amount of the portfolio represent the percentage that, with a given probability (for example, the 99.9 percentile), could be lost in an extreme event.

Anyhow, we have simulated the time paths of CARs under each of our three approaches, standardized, IRB Foundation (IRB F), and ICRM, for our various countries, and the results are set out in Tables 26.3–26.5, and Figures 26.7–26.9.

The important result to observe is the much greater variance of the simulated outcomes for the IRB than for the standardized or ICRM approaches. During periods of strong growth, high profits, and low NPLs (USA in the mid-1990s and Norway in 1997), the IRB has a lower CAR than the standardized approach in all our developed countries; whereas in recessions (e.g. USA in 1990/1, Mexico in mid-1995/6, and Norway in 1994/5), the CAR is markedly higher for the IRB than in the other two

Table 26.3. CARs for the USA

Period	Standardized	IRB F	ICRM
1982	9.597967	8.591044	8.070189
1983	8.933900	7.185306	6.802057
1984	8.933900	7.624870	7.032411
1985	9.133900	8.024912	7.262765
1986	9.463390	9.989917	8.736384
1987	9.463930	9.824500	8.545390
1988	9.463930	8.659141	6.990717
1989	9.563390	10.804149	6.488127
1990	9.563390	11.677029	7.601025
1991	9.986339	11.434979	7.541649
1992	9.687739	8.064210	6.470195
1993	9.287739	6.468979	4.665018
1994	8.901877	5.395182	3.783256
1995	8.507394	5.561594	4.087216
1996	8.246774	5.646111	4.316443
1997	8.294313	5.940010	4.837646
1998	8.312774	6.508256	5.831926
1999	8.403155	7.810893	6.704727
2000	8.410316	8.126805	7.163834
2001	8.531238	8.245881	7.242604
2002	8.312375	8.180511	6.779526
2003	8.107739	6.603000	6.258685
Average	8.959430	8.016694	6.509627
Variance	0.339964	3.392352	1.945790

Table 26.4. CARs for Norway

Period	Standardized	IRB F	ICRM
1989	9.991635	8.311481	7.580115
1990	10.265155	9.275921	8.127573
1991	10.465155	9.781705	8.675031
1992	10.367155	9.929912	9.034373
1993	10.265155	9.523779	9.186305
1994	10.940239	13.235447	9.821542
1995	11.320031	14.066170	11.082487
1996	10.669155	12.141937	9.722593
1997	10.265155	8.857323	7.317353
1998	10.265155	9.001267	7.422621
1999	10.265155	9.218641	7.527889
2000	10.265430	9.486551	7.930505
2001	10.360916	9.648655	8.333122
2002	10.461360	9.764866	8.343509
Average	10.440489	10.160261	8.578930
Variance	0.113401	2.941614	1.190491

Table 26.5. CARs for Mexico

Period	Standardized	IRB F	ICRM
Mar.-1995	8.765096	13.864230	10.462123
June-1995	9.221855	16.650790	12.285877
Sept.-1995	9.299730	17.103009	12.714591
Dec.-1995	9.493498	18.151470	12.820000
Mar.-1996	9.251044	17.067542	12.589874
June-1996	9.494958	18.448561	13.248221
Sept.-1996	9.557249	19.415843	14.891864
Dec.-1996	10.303734	24.230942	17.645355
Mar.-1997	9.430354	19.088714	15.153354
June-1997	9.273425	17.500911	13.895955
Sept.-1997	9.396601	18.254201	14.344051
Dec.-1997	8.928781	15.194116	14.796451
Mar.-1998	8.813186	14.397932	13.673818
June-1998	8.851211	14.428160	12.256023
Sept.-1998	9.058278	15.545394	11.622476
Dec.-1998	9.040916	15.456234	11.797630
Mar.-1999	9.052107	15.519282	12.003802
June-1999	8.981783	15.296608	12.251375
Sept.-1999	9.135013	15.979265	12.725803
Dec.-1999	8.968905	15.345409	12.100842
Average	9.215886	16.846931	13.163974
Variance	0.122662	5.644965	2.588205

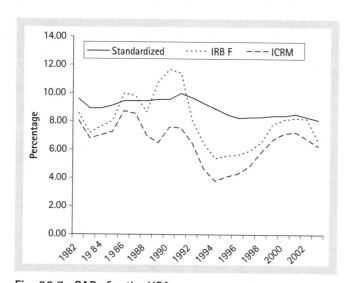

Fig. 26.7. CARs for the USA

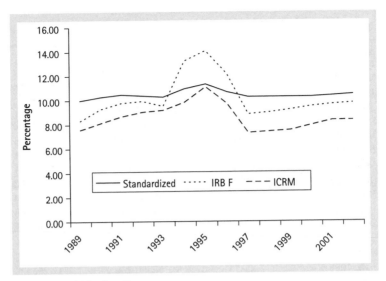

Fig. 26.8. CARs for Norway

approaches. In Mexico, an emerging market economy (EME), the average quality of loan is lower throughout than in developed countries, so the IRB gives a higher CAR in all years; but, as in developed countries, the variance of the CAR (up in recessions as in 1995/6, and lower during the better years) is greater for the IRB than in the other two approaches.

It follows that the percentage change in the required CAR under the IRB as a country moves from boom to recession (up) and back to boom again (down) will be much more extreme under the IRB than under the other two approaches. This is shown in Table 26.6.

The implication of this is that procyclicality may well still be a serious problem with Basel II, even after the smoothing of the risk curves that were introduced between Consultative Papers 2 and 3 produced by the Basel Committee to mitigate this problem. However, there will be other potentially offsetting factors. Banks normally

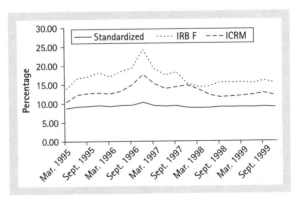

Fig. 26.9. CARs for Mexico

Table 26.6. Maximum percentage change in CARs

	Upwards				Downwards			
	1 Period	Date	2 consecutive periods	Dates	1 Period	Date	2 consecutive periods	Dates
(a) IRB								
USA	0.25	1989	0.33	1989/90	−0.29	1992	−0.49	1992/3
Norway	0.39	1994	0.45	1994/5	−0.27	1997	−0.41	1996/7
Mexico	0.25	Dec. 1996	0.30	Sept./Dec. 1996	−0.21	Mar. 1997	−0.30	Mar./June 1997
(b) ICRM								
USA	0.21	1998	0.33	1998/9	−0.28	1993	−0.47	1993/4
Norway	0.13	1995	0.20	1994/5	−0.25	1997	−0.37	1996/8
Mexico	0.18	Dec. 1996	0.30	Sept./Dec. 1996	−0.14	Mar. 1997	−0.22	Mar./June 1997
(c) Stand								
USA	0.04	June 2005	0.06	1985/6	−0.07	1983	−0.09	1994/5
Norway	0.07	June 2005	0.10	1994/5	−0.06	1997	−0.10	1996/7
Mexico	0.08	Dec. 1996	0.08	Sept./Dec. 1996	−0.08	Mar. 1997	−0.10	Mar./June 1997

keep buffers above the required minimum CARs, both for their protection against sanctions, should the minimum be infringed, and to satisfy ratings agencies, and these buffers are likely to be raised during booms when IRB CARs may fall to extremely low levels. Note, however, that we have used Moody's data for the USA from 1982 to 2003, for Norway from 1988 to 2001, and for Mexico from 1995 to 2000, which are already supposed to be averaged over the cycle, whereas most commercial banks are, so we are told by several of them, likely to use point-in-time ratings, which could worsen procyclicality yet further.

4. Conclusions

Over the last two decades, macroeconomic cycles were frequently associated with boom–bust cycles in bank lending and asset prices, often followed by financial instability. The liberalization of banking sectors since the early/mid-1970s has increased the scope for risk taking and leverage and thus the procyclicality of the financial system. As we show in this chapter, this was reflected in the frequent occurrence of boom–bust cycles in bank lending and asset price and a strengthening of the financial accelerator mechanism by increasing the sensitivity of bank lending to property price fluctuations.

In the face of more frequent financial cycles, regulators have moved to reinforce individual bank capital adequacy ratios, for example through the Basel I and II Accords, in order to mitigate the risk of systemic instability. But bank regulation is itself inherently procyclical; it bites in downturns, but fails to restrain in booms. The more 'sophisticated' and 'risk sensitive' the regulation, the greater the scope for procyclicality to become a problem, particularly in view of the changing nature of macroeconomic cycles. The simulation exercise performed in this chapter suggests that the new Basel II Accord, which deliberately aimed at significantly increasing the risk sensitivity of capital requirements, may in fact considerably accentuate the procyclicality of the regulatory system. Since the experience of the past, especially the experience of the USA in the recession of 1990/1, which we also discuss in this chapter, suggests that a required hoisting of capital ratios in downturns may be brought about by cutting back lending rather than raising capital, the new capital accord may, therefore, lead to an amplification of business-cycle fluctuations, especially in downturns.

Basel II will be a regime change, and one of the purposes of this is to make bankers more conscious of risk assessment and risk management. It has already succeeded in this. One hope is that it will induce bankers to be more prudent during booms, despite declines in CARs. An implication of a move from the standardized to an IRB approach is that the individual bank making this transition will be encouraged to shift its portfolio to higher-quality, higher-rated credits, because it then benefits from a lower CAR. This is good of itself, but the higher the quality of the credit, the steeper is the risk curve (relating quality to required risk ratio); so the procyclicality is likely to be enhanced, even if average quality improves.

When a regime change is introduced, no one in truth can predict its ramifications—certainly not us. Nevertheless, these simulations suggest that procyclicality *could* remain a serious concern. It is even possible that, with the advent of a serious downturn, if one were to occur, the impact of abiding by the IRB would be too severe for the authorities in some countries to countenance. Perhaps like the Stability and Growth Pact it would only be observed in the breach when it began to bite hard. Possibly an even greater worry might be that the adoption of Basel II, while not being so adverse as to force reconsideration, might yet exacerbate future capital fluctuations.

Certainly there remains a tension between relating CARs more closely to underlying risks in individual banks, and in trying for macroeconomic purposes to encourage contracyclical variations in bank lending in aggregate. How to square this circle must, however, be a subject for future research.

References

ABIAD, A., and MODY, A. (2003), 'Financial reform: what shapes it? What shakes it?', IMF Working Paper no. 03/70.

ACHARYA, V. V., BHARATH, S. T., and SRINIVASAN, A. (2003), 'Understanding the recovery rates on defaulted securities', London Business School, Paper in Progress, 23 November draft.

ALTMAN, E. (2002), 'Altman report on defaulted bonds and bank loans', Salomon Smith Barney, United States Corporate Bond Research High Yield.

—— BRADY, B., RESTI, A., and SIRONI, A. (2002), 'The link between default and recovery rates: implications for credit risk models and procyclicality', Working Paper, New York University.

BANK OF ENGLAND (1971), *Competition and Credit Control*, London: Bank of England, May.

BASEL COMMITTEE ON BANKING SUPERVISION (1988), 'International convergence of capital measurement and capital standards', Basel, July.

—— (1999), 'Capital requirements and bank behaviour: the impact of the Basel Accord', Basel Committee on Banking Supervision Working Paper no. 1.

BERGER, A., and UDELL, G. (1994), 'Did risk-based capital allocate bank credit and cause a "credit Crunch" in the United States?', *Journal of Money, Credit and Banking*, 26, 585–628.

BERNANKE, B., and GERTLER, M. (1989), 'Agency costs, collateral and business fluctuations', *American Economic Review*, 79, 14–31.

—— —— (1999), 'Monetary policy and asset price volatility', in *New Challenges for Monetary Policy*, Proceedings of the Jackson Hole Conference, 26–8 August, published by the Federal Reserve Bank of Kansas City, reproduced in *Economic Review*, Fourth Quarter, 17–51.

—— —— and GILCHRIST, S. (1999), 'The financial accelerator in a quantitative business cycle framework', in J. B. Taylor and M. Woodford (eds.), *Handbook of Macroeconomics*, vol. iC Amsterdon: Nort Holland, 1341–93.

BORDO, M., EICHENGREEN, B., KLINGEBIEL, D., and MARTINEZ-PERIA, M. S. (2001), 'Is the crisis problem growing more severe?', *Economic Policy*, 32, 51–82.

BRENNAN, M. J. (2004), 'How did it happen?', *Economic Notes*, 33(1), 3–22.

CECCHETTI, S., GENBERG, H., LIPSKY, J., and WADHWANI, S. (2000), 'Asset prices and central bank policy', *Geneva Reports on the World Economy 2*.

CLARIDA, R., GALI, J., and GERTLER, M. (1999), 'The science of monetary policy: a new Keynesian perspective', *Journal of Economic Literature*, 37(4), 1661–707.

COLLYNS, C., and SENHADJI, A. (2002), 'Lending booms, real estate bubbles and the Asian crisis', IMF Working Paper 02/20.

DEMIRGÜÇ-KUNT, A., and DETRAGIACHE, E. (1998), 'Financial liberalization and financial fragility', IMF Working Paper no. 98/83.

DICKEY, D., and FULLER, W. (1981), 'Likelihood ratio statistics for autoregressive time series with a unit root', *Econometrica*, 60, 423–33.

DREES, B., and PAZARBASIOGLU, C. (1998), 'The Nordic banking crises: pitfalls in financial liberalization?', IMF Occasional Paper no. 161.

EICHENGREEN, B., and BORDO, M. (2003), 'Crises now and then: what lessons from the last era of financial globalisation', in P. Mizen (ed.), *Monetary History, Exchange Rates and Financial Markets; Essays in Honour of Charles Goodhart*, vol. ii, Cheltenham: Edward Elgar, 52–91.

ELSINGER, H., LEHAR, A., and SUMMER, M. (2002), 'Risk assessment of banking systems', Oesterreichische Nationalbank, August, mimeo.

FURFINE, C. (2003), 'Interbank exposures: quantifying the risk of contagion', *Journal of Money, Credit and Banking*, 35, 111–28.

GERTLER, M., GOODFRIEND, M., ISSING, O., and SPAVENTA, L. (1998), *Asset Prices and Monetary Policy: Four Views*, London, Centre for Economic Policy Research (CEPR) and Bank for International Settlements (BIS).

GLICK, R., and HUTCHISON, M. (1999), 'Banking and currency crises: how common are the twins?', Federal Reserve Bank of San Francisco Pacific Basin Working Paper no. PB 99-07.

GOODHART, C. A. E. (2004), 'The Bank of England, 1970–2000', in R. Michie (ed.), *The British Government and the City of London in the Twentieth Century*, Cambridge: Cambridge University Press, 340–71.

GOODHART, C. A. E., and SEGOVIANO, M. (2004), 'Basel and procyclicality', London School of Economics, Financial Markets Group, Discussion Paper, forthcoming.

____SUNIRAND, P., and TSOMOCOS, D. P. (2003), 'A model to analyse financial fragility', Oxford Financial Research Centre Working Paper no. 2003fe13.

GORDY, M. B., and HOWELLS, B. (2004), 'Procyclicality in Basel II: can we treat the disease without killing the patient?', Board of Governors of the Federal Reserve System, Paper in Progress, 12 May draft.

KAMINSKY, G., and REINHART, C. (1999), 'The twin crisis: the causes of banking and balance-of-payments problems', *American Economic Review*, 89, 473–500.

____SCHMUKLER, S. (2003), 'Short-run pain, long-run gain: the effects of financial liberalization', NBER Working Paper 9787.

KASHYAP, A. K., and STEIN, C. (2004), 'Cyclical implications of the Basel-II capital standard', *Federal Reserve Bank of Chicago Economic Perspectives*, First Quarter, 18–31.

KIYOTAKI, N., and MOORE, J. (1997), 'Credit cycles', *Journal of Political Economy*, 105, 211–48.

LEAHY, M., SCHICH, S., WEHINGER, G., PELGRIN, F., and THORGEIRSSON, T. (2001), 'Contributions of financial systems to growth in OECD countries', OECD Economics Department Working Paper no. 280.

LEVINE, R. (1997), 'Financial development and economic growth: views and agendas', *Journal of Economic Literature*, 35, 688–726.

PERRON, P. (1989), 'The great crash, the oil price shock and the unit root hypothesis', *Econometrica*, 57, 1361–401.

____(1990), 'Testing for a unit root in a time series regression with a changing mean', *Journal of Business and Economic Statistics*, 8, 153–62.

____(1997), 'Further evidence from breaking trend functions in macroeconomic variables', *Journal of Econometrics*, 80, 355–85.

REID, M. (1982), *The Secondary Banking Crisis, 1973–75: Its Causes and Course*, London: Macmillan.

REINHART, C., and TOKATLIDIS, I. (2001), 'Before and after financial liberalization', University of Maryland, mimeo.

SECRETARIAT OF THE BASEL COMMITTEE ON BANKING SUPERVISION (2001), 'The new Basel capital accord: an explanatory note', Basel: BIS.

TORNELL, A., WESTERMANN, F., and MARTINEZ, L. (2004), 'The positive link between financial liberalization, growth and crises', NBER Working Paper no. 10293.

UPPER, C., and WORMS, A. (2004), 'Estimating bilateral exposures in the German interbank market: is there a danger of contagion?', *European Economic Review*, 48, 827–49.

WALSH, C., and WILCOX, J. (1995), 'Bank credit and economic activity', in J. Peek and E. Rosengreen (eds.), *Is Bank Lending Important for the Transmission of Monetary Policy?*, Federal Reserve Bank of Boston Conference Series no. 39.

WELLS, S. (2002), 'UK interbank exposures: systemic risk implications', *Financial Stability Review*, Bank of England, December, 175–82.

CHAPTER 27

....

FINANCIAL STRUCTURE AND MONETARY TRANSMISSION IN THE EMU

....

BORIS HOFMANN
ANDREAS WORMS

1. INTRODUCTION

....

Monetary policy is transmitted to output and prices via various, interrelated transmission channels (for an overview, see Worms 2004 or Mishkin 1996). Those channels
which are deemed to be the most important are the interest rate channel, the exchange
rate channel, the wealth or asset price channel, and the credit channel. The interest
rate channel refers to the direct effects of policy measures on investment and consumption decisions via changes of the cost of capital and the intertemporal discount
rate. The exchange rate channel captures the effects of a monetary policy-induced
change in the exchange rate on domestic output and prices via international trade
flows and import prices. The asset price channel summarizes the effects of monetary

This chapter expresses the authors' personal opinions and does not necessarily reflect the views of the
institutions to which they are affiliated.

policy-induced changes of real and financial wealth on spending decisions of firms and households. And finally, the credit channel is based on the existence of financial market imperfections and refers to the effects of monetary policy on spending by altering the supply of funds.

The overall strength and speed of monetary policy transmission as well as the relative strength of the various transmission channels depends amongst other things on the structural features of the economy, such as the monetary policy regime, the fiscal policy regime, the degree of trade openness, the sectoral structure of the economy, the flexibility of labour and goods markets, and of course the financial structure. In the broadest sense, the term 'financial structure' refers to the structural characteristics of a country's or a region's financial system. More specifically, such key features of the financial structure which are relevant for monetary transmission are e.g. the relative importance of direct finance (capital markets) and indirect finance (via financial intermediaries), the maturity structure of credit contracts, or the degree of competition between different financial market segments and within these segments, e.g. within the banking sector.

Knowledge of the structure and functioning of the financial system is therefore important for a better assessment and understanding of the transmission process of monetary policy. This is of particular relevance in the context of EMU. On the one hand, differences in financial structure across the euro area countries may be a cause of possible cross-country differences in monetary transmission; see e.g. Dornbusch, Favero, and Giavazzi (1999), Cecchetti (1999), and Mihov (2001). On the other hand, it is often held that EMU itself will foster securitization, disintermediation, and competition in euro area financial systems and as a result fundamentally change the financial structure of the euro area countries which, in turn, may substantially change the transmission process of monetary policy.

In this vein, this chapter aims at giving a short review of the role of financial structure for the transmission of monetary policy, sketching both the main theoretical underpinnings as well as the empirical evidence with a focus on the euro area. The role of financial structure for the interest rate channel, the asset price channel, and the credit channel is discussed in Sections 2, 3, and 4 respectively[1] with a special view to potential changes in euro area financial structure since the start of EMU and its potential implications for monetary transmission. Section 5 concludes.

2. THE DIRECT INTEREST RATE CHANNEL

The interest rate channel of monetary transmission refers to the direct effects of a policy-induced change in money market rates on capital market and bank retail rates

---

[1] We do not address the exchange rate channel as it appears not to be so much affected by the structural features of the euro area financial systems. However, in emerging markets the extent of foreign currency denomination of the liabilities of banks and firms and households may be considered as an additional feature of financial structure that matters for the exchange rate channel of monetary policy.

which in turn affect investment and consumption decisions of firms and households. The first stage of this transmission channel comprises the direct effects of a policy-induced change in short-term money market rates on longer-term capital market rates. According to the rational expectations hypothesis of the term structure (RE-HTS), long-term interest rates depend on the actual short-term interest rate, which is under control of the central bank, and on the expected path of future short-term interest rates up to the maturity of the respective long-term rate, that is, the expected future path of monetary policy; see for example Bekaert and Hodrick (2001). The longer the maturity of a long-term interest rate the more important is this expectation component relative to the current level of the short-term interest rate. This implies that the response of longer-term market rates to a change in policy rates will generally decline with the maturity of the longer-term rate, a notion which is supported by the empirical evidence.[2]

The figures reported by Allen et al. (this volume) on the size of financial markets (Figure 1.2) and the portfolio allocation of households (Figure 1.3a) in the major industrialized countries show that banks play a key role in the euro area financial system. Bank loans account for the bulk of all forms of private sector finance in the euro area and euro area households hold also the largest part of their assets in the banking sector (in the form of currency and deposits). This dominant role of banks in the euro area countries' financial systems implies that the pass-through of market rates to retail rates, i.e. to loan and deposit rates set by financial institutions, forms an important link in the direct interest rate transmission chain.

2.1. Determinants of the Speed of Interest Rate Pass-through

In standard models of the banking sector,[3] retail rates are set as a mark-up over the marginal (opportunity) cost of funds. Bank retail rates, therefore, should be tied to the market rate that most appropriately reflects the banks' maturity matching marginal opportunity costs for extending a loan or accepting a deposit. If banks exercise some market power[4] and if there are costs associated with adjusting retail rates, the decision of a bank to adjust its loan/deposit rate to a change in the corresponding capital market rate depends positively on the interest elasticity of the loan demand/deposit supply curve faced by an individual bank (see Hannan and Berger 1991). These elasticities are in turn positive functions of the degree of competition in the loan and the deposit market.

An indicator for the degree of competition in the banking sector commonly used in the industrial organization-orientated literature on interest rate pass-through is the degree of concentration in the markets in which banks operate; see for example Hannan and Berger (1991) and Neumark and Sharpe (1992). With an average share

---

[2] See e.g. Nautz and Wolters 1999 for Germany and the USA and DeBondt 2002 for the euro area.
[3] For a comprehensive exposition of these models see Freixas and Rochet 1997.
[4] The empirical evidence suggests that European banking sectors are characterized by monopolistic competition. See e.g. Davis and de Brandt 1999 and Bikker and Groeneveld 2000.

of 53 per cent in 2003 of the five largest banks in total bank assets—a commonly used concentration indicator[5]—the euro area countries are, on average, characterized by a relatively high degree of concentration.[6] However, at the individual country level there is substantial disparity. While the German and the Italian banking sectors are characterized by a comparatively low degree of concentration and, especially in Germany, also by a relatively large number of small banks, the banking sectors in many of the smaller euro area countries are more concentrated.[7] As documented in ECB (2004), concentration in euro area banking sectors has generally increased over the EMU period:[8] This is commonly explained by the increased pressure to reduce excess capacity in a more integrated and competitive euro area banking market, which has reinforced the consolidation process in euro area banking sectors; see ECB (2004, 2005a). Interpreted in this way, this development does not necessarily imply a decline in the intensity of competition.[9]

Another indicator of the degree of competition in the banking sector is the importance of state-owned banks in the banking system. As their behaviour is often characterized as being less market oriented (see e.g. La Porta, López-de-Silanes, and Shleifer 2000 and Cecchetti and Krause 2001), a high proportion of public banks in the banking sector may reduce the overall intensity of competition.[10] Government ownership of banks has significantly declined in most euro area countries since the mid-1980s. For instance, in Italy the share of total assets held by banks that are controlled by the state went down from 68 per cent in 1992 to 9 per cent in 2004. In a similar way, three waves of privatization (1986/7, 1993/4 and 1997–9) have led to an almost complete withdrawal of the state from the banking sector in France. In 2003 the share of assets of state-owned banks in total banking sector assets accounted for a mere 1.4 per cent. In Spain, state influence has traditionally been weak compared to the other large euro area countries. Since 1998 there is only one

---

[5] An alternative indicator is the Herfindahl index, which is the sum of the squared individual market shares. For the euro area and its member countries, both concentration indicators yield qualitatively very similar results (see ECB 2004: tables 6 and 7).

[6] For comparison, in the UK the share of the top five banks is 33% (ECB 2004: table 6) and for the USA it is 38% (Jones and Critchfield 2005: table A.1).

[7] For instance, in Belgium, the Netherlands, and Finland the share of the top five banks in total bank assets was above 80% in 2003 (ECB 2004: table 6).

[8] See tables 6 and 7 in ECB 2004.

[9] From a theoretical point of view, the effect of banking sector concentration on retail rate rigidity is ambiguous. While the intensity of competition should generally increase with the number of suppliers in the market, concentrated markets may as well behave like competitive markets if the market participants face the permanent threat of new competitors, domestic or foreign, entering the market, i.e. if they operate in a contestable market (Baumol, Panzar, and Willig 1982). Also, the presence of a large number of small, locally active financial institutions in the market may not indicate stronger competition but rather the existence of relationship banking. This would imply a low willingness or a low ability of customers to switch to other banks, and thus a low elasticity of loan demand/deposit supply. Moreover, higher concentration in the banking sector may result from more efficient banks growing faster than or taking over less efficient banks. Thus, more concentrated markets could potentially be characterized by higher efficiency, which could also be reflected in lower adjustment costs and a higher incentive to adjust retail rates (Berger and Hannan 1989).

[10] It should be noted, however, that the share of state-owned banks may not be a perfect proxy for overall state influence in the banking system in case there are strong ownership interdependencies.

state-owned credit institution which accounted for 1.5 per cent of total assets of credit institutions in 2004. The degree of state ownership in Germany has been fairly stable over the years without any major waves of privatization. In 2004 state-owned banks accounted for 44 per cent of total banking sector assets. However, also in Germany the influence of the state on the banking sector is declining, as reflected by the abolition of the state guarantee ('Staatsgarantie') for Sparkassen and Landesbanken as of July 2005.

Many euro area banking sectors are also characterized by long-lasting relationships between banks and loan customers, commonly referred to as relationship lending; see Ehrmann et al. (2003a). Relationship lending implies a low willingness or a low ability of customers to switch to other banks, and thus a low elasticity of loan demand. It may also imply that banks, in return, shield their customers from interest rate risk by smoothing lending rates (and the access to loans) over the interest rate cycle. Relationship lending may therefore cause retail rate sluggishness. The importance of relationship lending varies widely across the euro area countries and may therefore give rise to asymmetric interest rate pass-through. Increased competition and consolidation in the euro area banking sector is likely to also affect the availability of relationship lending; see Issing (2003).

In general, the intensity of competition in European banking markets is perceived to have increased in recent years. On the one hand, increased cross-border presence and growing cross-border banking activity of foreign banks, especially from other euro area countries in the wake of the integration of euro area banking sectors,[11] is likely to have increased competition in euro area banking sectors (see ECB 2004, 2005a), but probably only slightly so.[12] On the other hand, and perhaps more importantly, competition is also likely to have increased because direct finance in the form of corporate debt security issuance has gained importance especially for larger non-financial corporations, reducing their dependence on bank loans and thus increasing competitive pressure for banks' loan business.[13] Also, the traditional deposit-taking activities of euro area banks have been challenged by the increased importance of other financial instruments and other financial institutions (OFIs). These trends are documented in Figure 27.1, which shows that by the end of 2005 the outstanding amount of debt securities issued by non-financial corporations and the total assets managed by investment funds have more than doubled since 1998.

Besides the degree of competition in the banking markets, the pass-through of market to retail rates depends also on the contractually agreed adjustability of deposit and loan rates, i.e. the share of short-term and floating rate long-term loans and

---

[11] For an assessment of the integration of the euro area retail banking market see Baele et al. (this volume).

[12] In 2003, the share of foreign banks' subsidiaries and branches assets in total euro area banking sector assets was about 14%, only slightly up from about 12% in 1998 (ECB 2004: tables 8, 21, 23, 25, 27). On the other hand, the share of cross-border loans in total euro area bank loans is below 5% in 2003 and barely increased since 1998 (ECB 2004: chart 6).

[13] This development is also likely to have benefited from the integration of euro area corporate bond markets, as documented in Bale et al. (this volume).

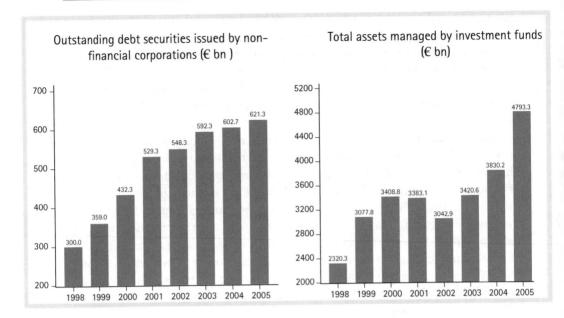

Fig. 27.1. Corporate bond markets and investment funds in the euro area

Source: ECB

deposits in total loans and deposits. The availability of information on the adjusta-bility of retail rates has significantly improved with the launch of the ECB's new harmonized Monetary and Financial Institutions (MFIs) interest rate statistics (MIR) at the beginning of 2003, which compiles harmonized statistics on interest rates applied by MFIs to euro-denominated loans and deposits. A major improvement of the MIR is that it provides a breakdown of interest rates charged on new loans by different periods of initial rate fixation.[14] Table 27.1 reports the share of new loans with floating rates or an initial rate fixation of up to one year in total new loans in the euro area and its four largest member countries at the end of 2004. The figures suggest that at the end of 2004 a substantially higher proportion of new loan contracts were short term or long term at adjustable rates in Italy and in Spain than in Germany and in France. In Italy and in Spain, about 90 per cent of total loans to households and firms are either short term or have a floating rate, compared to only about 60 per cent in France and in Germany. The figures also reveal that interest rate adjustability is generally higher for loans to firms than for loans to households. In Germany and in France the share of adjustable rate loans to households is respectively 36 per cent and 28 per cent compared to a share of respectively 72 per cent and 75 per cent for loans to firms. In Italy and in Spain interest rate adjustability is also higher for loans to firms, but less significantly so.

The available information on interest rate adjustability before the launch of the new MIR is extremely limited, so that it is difficult to assess the development

---

[14] For a detailed exposition of the other features of the MIR see ECB 2005b.

Table 27.1. Share of short-term or variable rate long-term loans in total loans

	Loans to households		Loans to enterprises		Total loans	
	1993	2004	1993	2004	1993	2004
Euro area	–	56	–	85	–	77
Germany	36	36	40	72	39	59
France	13	28	66	75	44	58
Italy	69	78	76	91	73	89
Spain	–	84	–	92	64	90

Sources: ECB; Borio 1995; own calculations.

of interest rate adjustability over time. Table 27.1 reports figures on the share of short-term or adjustable rate loans for 1993 taken from Borio (1995), which are based on central banks' responses to questionnaires on financial structure. A comparison of the figures suggests that the use of adjustable rate loans appears to have increased in all four countries. This would imply that the typical interest rate pass-through has become faster since the early 1990s. It should be noted however, that the data reported in Borio (1995) were compiled differently compared to the MIR data and refer to outstanding amounts rather than new business. For these reasons, any comparison of the 2004 MIR figures and the 1993 figure from Borio (1995) should be taken with caution.

2.2. Econometric Evidence on the Interest Rate Pass-through

There is a large empirical literature investigating the responsiveness of bank retail rates in the euro area for the pre-EMU sample period. Due to the lack of fully comparable interest rate data for the euro area countries, these studies focus on cross-country estimation and comparison of interest rate pass-through and do not try to relate the uncovered patterns of pass-through to financial structure or the past monetary policy regime.[15] De Bondt (2005: table 1) provides a survey of the available studies and compares the results. A common finding is that there appears to be significant short-term sluggishness in euro area retail rates. However, with respect to the pattern of cross-country differences the findings do vary widely, depending on the sample period and the applied methodology.

The considerations of the previous subsections suggest that due to an increased intensity of competition and a higher share of short-term and floating rate agreements, the average pass-through of official rates to bank retail rates may have increased in

---

[15] The exceptions are Cottarelli and Kourelis 1994 and Mojon 2000 who relate differences in interest rate pass-through to differences in financial structure and the monetary policy regime.

recent years.[16] Some studies have taken up this point. Angeloni and Ehrmann (2003) investigate whether pass-through to loan and deposit rates has become faster and more similar across the euro area countries since the start of EMU by investigating the impact and maximum effect of a money market rate shock on loan and deposit rates in bivariate VARs. They find evidence for a faster pass-through in all countries except in the case of Germany. Quicker adjustment of retail rates over the EMU period compared to the pre-EMU period is also found by De Bondt (2005), who analyses pass-through of capital market rates to bank retail rates of comparable maturity at the aggregate euro area level. By considering capital market and retail rates of comparable maturity rather than forcing retail rates to depend exclusively on short-term money market rates, a more accurate approximation of banks' marginal opportunity costs is achieved and potential distortions from yield curve effects are avoided. This point is also taken into consideration by Hofmann (2006), who analyses the pass-through of money market rates to the rates charged for short-term and for long-term loans to non-financial corporations. He uses error correction models for the four largest euro area countries Germany, France, Italy, and Spain estimated over the pre- and post-1999 period. In order to take into account adjustability of long-term loan rates, they are modelled as a function of both long-term capital market rates and short-term money market rates. A simulation of the pass-through of a 100 basis points increase of money market rates maintained for two years, with long-term bond yields assumed to be governed by the REHTS, suggests that since 1999 pass-through has become significantly faster in Italy, Spain, and especially France, but not in Germany. This result is in line with Angeloni and Ehrmann (2003). It is also compatible with the above discussion of the factors that determine interest rate pass-through: the German banking system is characterized by a comparatively strong government influence, there are close bank–customer relationships, and loan contracts seem to have a comparatively long maturity.

3. THE ASSET PRICE CHANNEL

Asset prices reflect, in the absence of bubbles, the discounted value of the expected future net income stream associated with this asset. Monetary policy can influence asset prices directly by affecting the discount rate and indirectly by affecting the expected future income stream itself. Household consumption depends on the lifetime resources which basically consist of lifetime income and net wealth. Since net wealth is a function of asset prices, asset price fluctuations affect consumption spending.[17]

---

[16] Bagliano, Dalmazzo, and Marini 2000 argue based on a theoretical model that the shift to EMU will give rise increased collusion among banks, which may partly countervail the effect of increased competition.

[17] The life-cycle model of household consumption was originally developed by Ando and Modigliani 1963. A formal exposition of the life-cycle model can be found in Deaton 1992 and Muellbauer 1994.

Table 27.2. Composition of household wealth as percentage of total financial wealth in 2003

	Currency and deposits	Securities other than shares	Shares and other equity	Mutual fund shares	Insurance and pension funds
Germany	37.0	11.7	10.4	12.2	28.7
France	32.1	1.8	27.1	9.8	29.8
Italy	27.3	22.2	22.8	12.4	15.2
Spain	42.1	3.2	27.2	12.9	14.5
USA	15.8	6.3	36.0	12.0	29.8

Source: Eurostat Financial Accounts, Federal Reserve Flow of Funds Accounts, own calculations.

This effect of monetary policy on consumption via household wealth is referred to as the wealth effect of monetary policy transmission.

The strength of the wealth effect depends on the composition of household wealth, as some asset prices react more strongly to monetary policy measures than others, e.g. because of differences in taxation, return, risk, collateral, and liquidity. The composition of household wealth is in turn determined by various structural factors, such as the cultural background, the structure of the pension systems, and the structure of the financial system. Accordingly, cross-country differences in the strength of the wealth effect may arise if these factors differ across countries.

As has already been discussed in the previous section, the euro area financial system is characterized by a dominant role of banks. This is reflected in the composition of household financial wealth. Table 27.2 reports the share of the different components of financial wealth as a percentage of total financial wealth in 2003 for the four largest euro area countries—and also for the USA for comparison. The figures show that bank assets, i.e. currency and deposits, account for the largest part of financial wealth in the euro area countries. In the USA, where banks play a much less important role in the financial system, bank assets are only the third largest component. Here, the most important component of financial wealth is shares and other equity, which account for 36 per cent of total financial wealth. Due to the sluggish adjustment of bank deposit rates to policy rates found in the empirical literature on retail rate pass-through discussed above and due to the rather high interest rate sensitivity of equity prices, this may, *ceteris paribus*, give rise to a lower wealth effect in the euro area compared to the USA. This notion is supported by the empirical evidence, which tends to find a larger effect of changes in equity wealth on consumption for the USA than for the euro area countries (see Altissimo et al. 2005 for an overview).

The figures reveal that there are also significant disparities in the composition of financial household wealth within the euro area. In France, Italy, and Spain a substantially larger share of financial wealth is held in equity than in Germany, which may give rise to an asymmetric equity wealth channel of monetary transmission in the euro area.[18] It is also noteworthy that Italian households, and to a lesser extent

[18] This presumption is, however, not supported by the empirical evidence (Altissimo et al. 2005).

also German households, hold a relatively large share of their financial wealth in securities. A change in bond prices in the wake of a change in monetary policy stance will therefore have a larger effect on household wealth in Italy and Germany than in France and Spain.

The structural changes in the euro area financial system described in the previous section will also affect the portfolio allocation of households. The increasing importance of security and equity markets in private sector financing and the growing importance of investment funds should, all else equal, also be reflected in a higher share of non-bank assets in household financial wealth. Altissimo et al. (2005) show that the percentage of euro area households with direct equity holdings slightly increased in the late 1990s.[19] However, financial accounts data show that the share of shares and other equity in total financial wealth has actually decreased since the start of EMU, owing to the stock market crash in 2000/1, which has reduced the value of equity and mutual fund assets and has probably increased the demand for 'safe' bank assets.

The second major component of household wealth besides financial wealth is property. In theory, house prices should reflect the discounted stream of future rents associated with the property, so that monetary policy may affect house prices via the same channels as it may affect asset prices in general. However, what matters for the effect of house prices on consumption is not only the size of the property wealth of a country, but also its distribution. If an increase in house prices is related to an increase in current or future (expected) rents, it will not only have a positive wealth effect on landlords and owner-occupiers, but it will also have a negative income effect on tenants who have to pay higher rents (see ECB 2003 for a more detailed discussion). So, the overall effect on aggregate non-housing consumption is not clear a priori, since higher house prices simply cause a redistribution of resources between tenants and prospective new buyers on one side and homeowners on the other. In principle, the lower the share of tenants, that is, the higher the share of landlords and owner-occupiers, the more likely it is that the wealth effect caused by a change in house prices dominates the income effect.

A couple of more recent studies have argued that the ability of households to borrow against rising property prices and, as a result, the strength of the nexus between house prices and the macroeconomy depends on the structural characteristics of the mortgage market; see Maclennan, Muellbauer, and Stephens (2000), ECB (2003), OECD (2004), Tsatsaronis and Zhu (2004). Household borrowing against real estate collateral is usually restricted by a wealth constraint, a loan-to-value ratio (LTV) restricting the loan from exceeding a certain proportion of the value of the house, and/or an income constraint restricting mortgage interest payments from exceeding a certain proportion of the borrower's income; see Aoki, Proudman, and Vlieghe (2004) for a formal model incorporating these features. These constraints reflect the amount of funds households can raise against the value of their property or income. Thus, the higher typical LTVs or the income constraints of mortgage rate

---

[19] Tables 3.3 and 3.4 in Altissimo et al. 2005 report the percentage of households with direct equity holdings in Germany, France, Italy, the UK, and the USA for different income and age groups.

payments, the stronger should in principle be the effect of monetary policy via house price changes on consumption. Furthermore, by determining the general availability of mortgage finance, these constraints may also affect homeownership. Based on microeconomic data for fourteen OECD countries, Chiuri and Japelli (2003) show that LTVs and owner occupancy rates are negatively correlated, especially for young households. This implies that LTVs may affect the strength of the housing wealth channel not just directly—as already mentioned—but also indirectly by affecting a country's owner-occupancy rate.

Besides typical LTVs, the possibilities of homeowners accessing an increase in housing wealth in order to be able to finance non-housing consumption, i.e. the availability of housing equity withdrawal (HEW) products, plays a crucial role for the strength of the housing wealth channel. In principle, the aggregate household sector can withdraw housing equity (a) by increasing or refinancing the mortgage loan—which would not require a transaction in the housing market—or (b) through a transaction in the secondary property market whereby the buyer can obtain a larger loan due to the higher house value. Whether these alternatives are possible and how intensively they are used depends on the structure of the mortgage markets and on the respective legal regulations. If the only possibility for a house owner to access a rise in the house value for higher consumption is (b), that is to first sell the house, then the overall effect of increasing house prices on consumption should be smaller than in the case where also opportunity (a) is available.

Various recent studies have documented the differences in national mortgage finance systems (see e.g. Maclennan, Muellbauer, and Stephens 2000; ECB 2003; OECD 2004), which are also discussed in Allen et al. (this volume). These studies suggest that, on average, LTVs in euro area mortgage markets are somewhat lower than e.g. in the USA and the UK, and HEW products are less readily available. Moreover, owner-occupation rates are also lower on average. On the whole, this would imply that changes in house prices should have a weaker effect on consumption in the euro area than in the USA or the UK.[20] Also, the mortgage systems vary widely across euro area member countries, which may give rise to differences in the strength of the housing wealth effect and thus to asymmetric monetary transmission via this channel. In order to assess the role of structural differences in mortgage markets, OECD (2004) condenses the information on structural features of mortgage markets originally provided by Mercer Oliver Wyman (2003) into a single index of mortgage market completeness, which depends, amongst other factors, positively on the availability of HEW-related products. The OECD study finds that cross-country differences in the response of consumption to changes in house prices and in HEW are strongly positively correlated with this index, that is, the response of consumption tends to be stronger in more complete mortgage markets. Evidence reported in Ludwig and Sløk

---

[20] The evidence is mixed, however. The results in Ludwig and Sløk 2004, which are also discussed in Altissimo et al. 2005, suggest that house price movements have a stronger effect on consumption in the euro area countries than in the USA and the UK, while the evidence reported in OECD 2004 suggests exactly the opposite.

(2004) also suggests that the effect of house prices on consumption may rise with the homeownership rate.

An assessment of changes in mortgage and housing markets since the start of EMU is not possible as the development of their key institutional features is difficult to monitor and assess in a continuous way. Maclennan, Muellbauer, and Stephens (2000) argue that while EMU is likely to trigger more transparency in mortgage pricing and may have also increased cross-border competition, these developments will have only limited effects on mortgage markets as significant institutional and legal barriers hindering convergence of euro area mortgage and housing markets still remain. As a result, possible asymmetries in monetary transmission arising from institutional asymmetries in mortgage and housing markets may persist also in EMU.

The asset price channel of monetary transmission also operates via investment activity. A change in equity prices influences firm investment via Tobin's q (Tobin 1969), which is defined as the market value of capital relative to the replacement cost of capital. If q rises because of an increase in equity prices firms which are listed on the stock market can buy more capital for the equity they issue. This makes it more attractive for firms to acquire new capital and so increases investment demand. With a growing number of publicly listed companies, this channel may have gained importance over the last years, see Hartmann, Maddaloni, and Manganelli (2003). However, the overall international evidence on the effects of equity prices on investment is rather limited (see Altissimo et al. 2005 and the references therein).

A change in house prices also affects the value of housing relative to construction costs, which can be seen as the Tobin q for residential investment. New housing construction becomes profitable when house prices rise above construction costs. Residential investment is therefore a positive function of house prices. Construction costs are composed of building costs and the cost of land, neither of which are directly observable. As a consequence, the Tobin q for housing investment is, like the Tobin q for business investment, also not observable. Partly because of this, only a few studies have attempted to assess the effect of property price movements on construction activity (see Girouard and Blöndahl 2001 for evidence for some OECD countries). In any case, the share of residential investment in GDP of OECD countries is generally rather small, so that the effect via this channel is likely to be of limited importance.

4. THE CREDIT CHANNEL

Loan agreements are typically characterized by the fact that the borrower has more relevant information about the use of the funds than the lender (asymmetric information). Therefore, the lender seeks for arrangements which enable him to extract at least some of this information, e.g. by having access to the borrower's balance sheets and his internal calculations or by giving the borrower an incentive to reveal this information himself. Moreover, the lender typically cannot completely control the borrower's activities once the funds have been transferred so that the borrower may act against the lender's interests (moral hazard). The lender therefore seeks for contractual arrangements which give the borrower an incentive not to act in such a way. Such a contractual arrangement is for instance the provision of collateral.

However, all these arrangements can only help to alleviate the problems caused by asymmetric information and moral hazard—they cannot completely offset them. As a consequence, borrowers have to pay an 'external finance premium' above the (opportunity) costs of internal finance to compensate the lender for the risks stemming from asymmetric information and moral hazard. If monetary policy affects this external finance premium, it does not only affect the demand for funds—as is the case e.g. with the transmission channels discussed so far—but also the supply of funds. This is important for a number of reasons: Monetary policy may have amplifying distributional effects since those banks and non-banks which are more prone to asymmetric information and moral hazard are also more affected by monetary policy. Moreover, the level of interest rates alone may be a poor indicator of the stance of monetary policy because not just the price but also the availability of funds becomes crucial. And finally, the monetary transmission process depends on the structure of the financial system. This implies that e.g. differences in the financial systems across the EMU member countries may potentially cause differences in monetary transmission across these countries. It may also imply that changes of the financial system over time can fundamentally change the transmission process.

According to the 'credit channel' theory, monetary policy affects the supply of funds because it affects the devices which were originally designed to reduce the problems caused by asymmetric information and moral hazard and therefore also affects the external finance premium. Here, the 'balance sheet channel'—one of the two sub-channels of the 'credit channel'—stresses the effects of monetary policy on borrowers' balance sheets. If balance sheet information—such as the availability of collateralizable assets—is important for being selected as a borrower by the lender, then a fall in asset prices caused by monetary policy may increase the external finance premium that has to be paid by borrowers and therefore restricts their access to new finance (Bernanke and Gertler 1989). Moreover, a monetary policy-induced increase in the interest rate level tends to raise interest payments on outstanding debt, lowering borrowers' net cash flow. This reduces their ability to internally finance expenditures—and since the external finance premium has increased, the respective borrowers cannot (completely) substitute internal for external finance. Both the lowered ability to finance expenditures internally and the reduced access to new external funds lower aggregate demand. Since this effect will be stronger for borrowers with more pronounced information and moral hazard problems, monetary policy is likely to affect those more than others.

While the 'balance sheet channel' refers to all kinds of possible lenders, the 'bank lending channel'—the second sub-channel of the 'credit channel'—works exclusively through banks, more specifically through bank loan supply. A monetary policy-induced reduction of the amount of secured deposits leads to a reduction in loan supply if banks are not able to fully offset this reduction by increasing (non-secured) liabilities and/or by reducing assets other than loans to non-banks (Bernanke and Blinder 1988). However, since financial markets are imperfect, banks with information and moral hazard problems may not be able to fully isolate their loan supply from such a drain of secured deposits. One reason for this may be that banks— like any other borrower with a non-zero probability of insolvency—have to pay an external finance premium for non-secured liabilities since their depositors will ask for a compensation for bearing the risk that the bank may become insolvent. Since this premium is higher for banks with more serious information and moral hazard problems, one would expect monetary policy to have amplifying distributional effects across banks.

Credit channel effects are difficult to detect empirically because in reduced-form macro models they are observationally equivalent to the effects caused by other transmission channels (see e.g. Cecchetti 1995). Take for example the interest rate channel: a monetary policy-induced increase in the level of interest rates renders some investment expenditures unattractive, reducing the demand for bank loans, thereby weakening aggregate activity. Ex post, restrictive monetary policy therefore comes with reduced lending—as is the case with the credit channel. However, in case of the interest rate channel this reduction in lending is caused by a reduced demand for bank loans while in case of the credit channel it is caused by a reduced bank loan supply. Hence, an empirical analysis of the credit channel has to identify loan supply effects of monetary policy. Since loan supply and demand are not directly observable, this is accomplished indirectly by testing implications of the credit channel based on indicators for the degree to which banks and non-banks (especially firms) suffer from information and moral hazard problems, such as size, leverage, or financial health. The idea is that, if informational frictions and moral hazard problems do play a role, then this would imply that smaller or financially less healthy banks and firms face stricter funding constraints and will be more strongly affected by monetary conditions than their bigger and healthier competitors. This is a testable hypothesis.

The bulk of the empirical credit channel literature focuses on the USA,[21] but over recent years there have also been a large and growing number of studies on the relevance of credit channel effects for the euro area. Cecchetti (1999) and Mihov (2001) relate cross-country differences in monetary transmission to country-wide indicators of the predicted strength of credit channel effects, which they construct based on qualitative information on the importance of banks in the financial system and their size and health. For a sample of industrialized countries, which also includes most euro area countries, they find that cross-country differences in the strength of monetary transmission can be related to differences in the predicted strength of the bank lending channel.

Peersman and Smets (2005) analyse the effect of monetary policy shocks on output in eleven industries of seven euro area countries allowing for asymmetric

---

[21] Basic references are Kashyap and Stein 1995, 2000; Christiano, Eichenbaum, and Evans 1996; as well as Gertler and Gilchrist 1994.

Table 27.3. Main results from MTN estimations with bank micro data

	Bank characteristics		Comments
	Size	Liquidity	
Austria	No	No	Loan supply responds in recessions
Finland	No	No	Government guarantees increase lending
France	No	Yes	—
Germany	No	Yes	Interbank deposits crucial
Greece	Yes	Yes	Model specification differs from other countries
Italy	No	Yes	Strong evidence of deposit shifts
The Netherlands	Yes	Yes	Strong effects for unsecured lending
Portugal	No	No	Model specification differs from other countries
Spain	No	No	No effect, even after tax reform squeezing deposits

Source: Papers published in Angeloni, Kashyap, and Mojon 2003: Kaufmann (Austria), Topi and Vilmunen (Finland), Loupias et al. (France), Worms (Germany), Brissimis et al. (Greece), Gambacorta (Italy), De Haan (the Netherlands), Farinha and Marques (Portugal), Hernando and Martínez-Pagés (Spain).

transmission over the business cycle.[22] In the second step of their analysis they relate the estimated effects of monetary policy to indicators of the production and financial structure of the different industries. They find that differences in the overall policy effects can mainly be explained by the durability of the goods produced in the sector, which they interpret as evidence for the conventional interest rate channel. On the other hand, they find that differences in the degree of business cycle asymmetry of policy effects are related to differences in financial structure, which they see as being consistent with the existence of a financial accelerator mechanism.

The relevance of the credit channel of monetary transmission has also been analysed in depth in the context of the Eurosystem 'Monetary Transmission Network'[23] (MTN) based on disaggregated data for individual banks and firms. Table 27.3 summarizes the main results of the MTN findings on the relevance of the bank lending channel. The table reports whether the reaction of bank lending to monetary policy measures was found to depend on specific characteristics of the banks, such as banks' size or the degree of liquidity of banks' assets. It turns out that size— the preferred indicator for the degree of informational problems in the respective empirical literature—is not important in most of the member countries, especially the four largest ones, which points to a comparatively weak bank lending channel in the euro area as a whole.

Several features of the euro area banking structure may help to explain this finding (see Chatelain et al. 2003a). First, the perceived risk of investing in a small bank in the euro area may have been lower than for instance in the USA due to a higher government involvement and fewer bank failures (Ehrmann et al. 2003a). Second, in

[22] Dedola and Lippi 2005 conduct a similar study coming to similar conclusions for the industries of five OECD countries.

[23] The results of the Eurosystem 'Monetary Transmission Network' are published in Angeloni, Kashyap, and Mojon 2003.

several countries, banks do not stand alone in the interbank market but are organized in networks, which access the interbank market through some large head institutions (for the case of Germany, see Upper and Worms 2004 and Ehrmann and Worms 2004). Hence, what seems to be important for the access to funds for a bank under such circumstances is not so much the actual size of this bank but the membership in such a network.

While size is not a very important bank characteristic in this respect, bank liquidity seems to be much more relevant (see Table 27.3): The more liquid a bank's assets are, the less it reduces lending in response to a restrictive monetary policy measure. This is in line with the hypothesis that banks can draw on their liquid assets to shield their loans to some extent from monetary policy-induced squeezes in deposits. In Germany, for example, banks seem to draw especially on their short-term interbank assets in reaction to a restrictive monetary policy measure in order to be able to maintain their loan portfolio (Ehrmann and Worms 2004). This may be rationalized by the so-called house bank principle according to which banks and firms establish long-term relationships from which they both can profit; see e.g. Harhoff and Körting (1998). This principle may—among other dimensions—contain an implicit insurance for the borrower against a reduction in loan supply which would otherwise be caused by a restrictive monetary policy (see Worms 2003).

In order to assess the relevance of the balance sheet channel as part of the credit channel, the MTN also analysed firm micro data. In a first step, it was tested whether firms' investment depends on their user costs of capital and their liquidity (i.e. their cash flow). Due to the fact that the interest rate level is an important part of the user cost variable, a significant dependence of firm investment on this variable would indicate the relevance of the interest rate channel. Instead, cash flow should influence firm investment only if financial markets are imperfect, which is a precondition for the existence of the credit channel. In general, the studies point to the significance of both the user cost and the liquidity variables. However, the user cost effect seems to be quantitatively much more important.

Table 27.4 summarizes the main findings of the MTN from the analysis of the relevance of firm characteristics for the strength of the effects of monetary policy on firm investment. The table reveals that no single firm characteristic was found to be consistently relevant across euro area countries. In particular, differences in size do not seem to be able to explain differences in the strength of monetary transmission across firms (see Chatelain et al. 2003a, 2003b). On the whole, the most relevant characteristic appears to be the insufficient ability to provide collateral or poor financial health, which is in line with the existence of a balance sheet channel. However, quantitatively these effects do not appear to be very strong.

The evidence regarding the importance of the credit channel in the euro area is therefore mixed, despite the dominant role of banks in the euro area financial systems. This finding can be attributed to a widespread propensity of banks to operate in networks and close, long-term relationships between borrowers and lenders, which may mitigate potential loan supply effects arising from informational frictions in the credit market. It should be kept in mind, however, that the evidence discussed in

Table 27.4. Main results from MTN estimations with firm micro data

	Results: relevant firm characteristics	
	Highest user cost sensitivity	Highest liquidity sensitivity
Austria	–	Firms with no close relationship to a house bank
Belgium	Capital-intensive industries	Small services, manufacturing
France	–	Equipment manufacturing, firms with bad credit rating
Germany	–	Firms with bad credit rating
Italy	Small firms, firms with high share of intangible assets	Small firms, firms with high share of intangible assets
Luxembourg	Young firms	Young firms

Source: Papers published in Angeloni, Kashyap, and Mojon 2003: Valderrama (Austria), Butzen et al. (Belgium), Chatelain and Tiomo (France), v. Kalckreuth (Germany), Gaiotti and Generale (Italy), Lunnemann and Matha (Luxembourg).

this section is entirely based on observations from the pre-EMU era. Obviously, the increased integration and market orientation of euro area financial systems pointed out in the previous sections will also have a bearing on the credit channel of monetary policy. The growing importance of corporate bond markets improves the funding opportunities of non-financial corporations and reduces their dependence on bank loans. This should, in principle, mitigate funding constraints in general and also the strength of the bank lending channel.

Another remarkable development that matters in this context is the improved funding opportunities of banks in the wake of the dynamic development of securitization markets in the euro area in recent years. Via securitization, financial institutions can transform their illiquid assets, such as loans, into tradeable securities. The ability to securitize loans opens additional funding sources for financial institutions so that they are less likely to be constrained in their funding ability when monetary policy is tightened. As a result, the bank lending channel of monetary policy is likely to lose importance with the further development of securitization markets.[24]

On the whole, these developments point to a further weakening of any potential credit channel of monetary transmission in the euro area. However, it is also often conjectured that the close borrower–lender relationships, which have been brought forward above as one potential explanation for the surprisingly weak evidence of the existence of a credit channel in the euro area, could become less important in the future if the financial system becomes more market oriented (see e.g. Elsas and Krahnen 2004). This might partly offset the direct effects of improved funding opportunities described before, so that the overall effect of an increased market orientation of euro area financial systems on the relevance of the credit channel remains unclear.

---

[24] Estrella 2002 finds that the weakening of the effects of monetary policy on economic activity in the USA can be related to rising securitization since the 1960s.

5. CONCLUDING REMARKS

This chapter gives a short review of the role of financial structure for the transmission of monetary policy. This topic is of particular importance in the context of EMU, as, on the one hand, differences in financial structure across the euro area countries may be a cause of possible cross-country differences in monetary transmission, and, on the other hand, ongoing structural changes in the euro area financial systems, possibly reinforced by EMU, may fundamentally change the financial structure and, as a result, the transmission process of monetary policy.

Financial integration of the euro area will further advance and thereby reinforce the trend towards more market orientation and competition in financial and banking markets observed in the first years of EMU. This suggests that the efficiency of monetary policy in the euro area should further improve. The increased importance of non-bank finance and investment opportunities implies that the transmission via capital market interest rates is likely to become more important, but also that the link between policy rates and lending rates will further be strengthened due to increased competitive pressures on banks. This should increase the efficiency of the link between the policy rate and the broad range of interest rates which are relevant for saving and investment decisions. As we have discussed, there exists in fact some early empirical evidence suggesting that the pass-through of policy rates to euro area bank lending rates has accelerated since the start of EMU. Furthermore, the credit channel of monetary transmission, for which evidence has already been weak, might lose importance with the broadening and deepening of capital markets and the thus improved funding opportunities for firms and banks via corporate bond and securitization markets. This will reduce the role of inefficient credit market distortions in the monetary transmission process.

The increasing integration and market orientation of the euro area financial systems should also contribute to a more similar transmission of monetary policy in the euro area countries and thus mitigate the potential problem of asymmetric effects of the common monetary policy in the EMU. However, as there are still significant institutional and legal barriers hindering convergence of euro area mortgage and housing markets, possible asymmetries in monetary transmission arising from institutional asymmetries in mortgage and housing markets may persist also in the EMU.

REFERENCES

ALTISSIMO, F., GEORGIOU, E., SASTRE, T., VALDERRAMA, M. T., STERNE, G., STOCKER, M., WETH, M., WHELAN, K., and WILLMAN, A. (2005), 'Wealth and asset price effects on economic activity', ECB Occasional Paper 29.

ANDO, A., and MODIGLIANI, F. (1963), 'The "life cycle" hypothesis of saving: aggregate implications and tests', *American Economic Review*, 53, 55–84.

ANGELONI, I., and EHRMANN, M. (2003), 'Monetary transmission in the euro area: early evidence', *Economic Policy*, 37, 469–501.

—— KASHYAP, A., and MOJON, B. (eds.) (2003), *Monetary Policy Transmission in the Euro Area*, Cambridge: Cambridge University Press.

AOKI, K., PROUDMAN, J., and VLIEGHE, G. (2004), 'House prices, consumption, and monetary policy: a financial accelerator approach', *Journal of Financial Intermediation*, 13, 414–35.

BAGLIANO, F., DALMAZZO, A., and MARINI, G. (2000), 'Bank competition and ECB's monetary policy', *Journal of Banking and Finance*, 24, 967–83.

BAUMOL, W., PANZAR, R., and WILLIG, R. (1982), *Contestable Markets and the Theory of Industry Structure*, San Diego: Harcourt, Brace, Jovanovich.

BEKAERT, G., and HODRICK, R. J. (2001), 'Expectation hypotheses tests', *Journal of Finance*, 56(4), 1357–94.

BERGER, A., and HANNAN, T. (1989), 'The price–concentration relationship in banking', *Review of Economics and Statistics*, 71, 291–9.

BERNANKE, B. S., and BLINDER, A. S. (1988), 'Credit, money, and aggregate demand', *American Economic Review*, 78(2), 435–9.

—— GERTLER, M. (1989), 'Agency costs, net worth, and business fluctuations', *American Economic Review*, 79(1), 14–31.

BIKKER, J. A., and GROENEVELD, J. M. (2000), 'Competition and concentration in the EU banking industry', *Kredit und Kapital*, 33, 62–98.

BORIO, C. (1995), *Credit Characteristics and the Monetary Policy Transmission Mechanism in Fourteen Industrial Countries: Facts, Conjectures and Some Econometric Evidence*, BIS Working Paper 24.

CECCHETTI, S. (1995), 'Distinguishing theories of the monetary transmission mechanism', *Federal Reserve Bank of St Louis Review*, May/June, 83–100.

—— (1999), *Legal Structure, Financial Structure and the Monetary Policy Transmission Mechanism*, NBER Working Paper 7151.

—— and Krause, S. (2001), *Financial Structure, Macroeconomic Stability and Monetary Policy*, NBER Working Paper 8354.

CHATELAIN, J.-B., EHRMANN, M., GENERALE, A., MARTÍNEZ-PAGES, J., VERMEULEN, P., and WORMS, A. (2003a), 'Monetary policy transmission in the euro area: evidence from micro data on banks and firms', *Journal of the European Economic Association*, 1 (April–May), 731–42.

—— GENERALE, A., HERNANDO, I., VON KALCKREUTH, U., and VERMEULEN, P. (2003b), 'New findings in firm investment and monetary transmission in the euro area', in M. Artis and C. Allsopp (eds.), 'EMU, four years on', *Oxford Review of Economic Policy*, 19(1), Spring, 73–83.

CHIURI, M., and JAPELLI, T. (2003), 'Financial market imperfections and home ownership: a comparative study', *European Economic Review*, 47, 857–75.

CHRISTIANO, L., EICHENBAUM, M., and EVANS, C. (1996), 'The effects of monetary policy shocks: evidence from the flow of funds', *Review of Economics and Statistics*, 78, 16–34.

CORVOISIER, S., and GROPP, R. (2002), 'Bank concentration and retail interest rates', *Journal of Banking and Finance*, 26, 2155–89.

COTTARELLI, C., and KOURELIS, A. (1994), 'Financial structure, bank lending rates and the transmission of monetary policy', *IMF Staff Papers*, 41, 587–623.

DAVIS, E., and DE BRANDT, O. (1999), *A Cross-Country Comparison of Market Structure in European Banking*, ECB Working Paper 7.

DE BONDT, G. (2005), 'Interest rate pass-through: empirical results for the euro area', *German Economic Review*, 6, 37–78.

DEATON, A. (1992), *Understanding Consumption*, Oxford: Oxford University Press.

DEDOLA, L., and LIPPI, F. (2005), 'The monetary transmission mechanism: evidence from the industries of five OECD countries', *European Economic Review*, 49, 1543–70.

DORNBUSCH, R., FAVERO, C., and GIAVAZZI, F. (1998), 'The immediate challenges for the European Central Bank', *Economic Policy*, 26, 17–64.

ECB (2003), 'Structural factors in the EU housing market', March.

——— (2004), 'Report on EU banking structure', November.

——— (2005a), 'Consolidation and diversification in the euro area banking sector', *ECB Monthly Bulletin*, May, 79–88.

——— (2005b), 'The use of harmonised MFI interest rate statistics', *ECB Monthly Bulletin*, July, 85–92.

EHRMANN, M., and WORMS, A. (2004), 'Bank networks and monetary policy transmission', *Journal of the European Economic Association*, 2(6), December, 1148–71.

——— GAMBACORTA, L., MARTÍNEZ-PAGES, J., SEVESTRE, P., and WORMS, A. (2003a), 'Financial systems and the role of banks in monetary transmission in the euro area', in I. Angeloni, A. Kashyap, and B. Mojon (eds.), *Monetary Policy Transmission in the Euro Area*, Cambridge: Cambridge University Press.

——— ——— ——— ——— ——— (2003b), 'The effects of monetary policy in the euro area', *Oxford Review of Economic Policy*, 19(1), 58–72.

ELSAS, R., and KRAHNEN, J. P. (1998), 'Is relationship-lending special? Evidence from credit-file data in Germany', *Journal of Banking and Finance*, 22, 1283–316.

——— ——— (2004), 'Universal banks and relationships with firms', in J. P. Krahnen and R. H. Schmidt (eds.), *The German Financial System*, Oxford: Oxford University Press.

ESTRELLA, A. (2002), 'Securitization and the efficacy of monetary policy', *Federal Reserve Bank of New York Economic Policy Review*, May, 243–55.

FREIXAS, X., and ROCHET, J. (1997), *Microeconomics of Banking*, Cambridge, Mass.: MIT Press.

GERTLER, M., and GILCHRIST, S. (1994), 'Monetary policy, business cycles, and the behavior of small manufacturing firms', *Quarterly Journal of Economics*, 109, 309–40.

GIROUARD, N., and BLÖNDAHL, S. (2001), 'House prices and economic activity', OECD Working Paper no. 279.

HANNAN, T., and BERGER, A. (1991), 'The rigidity of prices: evidence from the banking industry', *American Economic Review*, 81, 938–45.

HARHOFF, D., and KÖRTING, T. (1998), 'Lending relationships in Germany: empirical evidence from survey data', *Journal of Banking and Finance*, 22, 1317–53.

HARTMANN, P., MADDALONI, A., and MANGANELLI, S. (2003), *The Euro Area Financial System: Structure, Integration and Policy Initiatives*, ECB Working Paper no. 230.

HOFMANN, B. (2006), 'EMU and the transmission of monetary policy: evidence from business lending rates', *Empirica*, 4, 206–29.

ISSING, O. (2003), 'Relationship lending in the euro area', in V. Gaspar, P. Hartmann, and O. Sleijpen (eds.), *The Transformation of the European Financial System*, Conference Proceedings of the Second ECB Central Banking Conference.

JONES, K. D., and CRITCHFIELD, T. S. (2005), *Consolidation in the U.S. Banking Industry: Is the Long, Strange Trip About to End?*, Working Paper, Federal Deposit Insurance Corporation.

KASHYAP, A. K., and STEIN, J. C. (1995), 'The impact of monetary policy on bank balance sheets', *Carnegie-Rochester Conference Series on Public Policy*, 42, 151–95.

——— ——— (1997), 'The role of banks in monetary policy: a survey with implications for the European Monetary Union', *Federal Reserve Bank of Chicago Economic Perspectives*, 42(September–October), 2–18.

——— ——— (2000), 'What do a million observations on banks say about the transmission of monetary policy?', *American Economic Review*, 90(3), June, 407–28.

La-Porta, R., López-de-Silanes, F., and Shleifer, A. (2000), 'Government ownership of banks', *Journal of Finance*, 57, 265–301.

Ludwig, A., and Sløk, T. (2004), 'The relationship between stock prices, house prices and consumption in OECD countries', *Topics in Macroeconomics*, 4, 1114.

Maclennan, D., Muellbauer, J., and Stephens, M. (2000), 'Asymmetries in housing and financial market institutions and EMU', in T. Jenkinson (ed.), *Readings in Macroeconomics*, Oxford: Oxford University Press.

Mercer O. W. (2003), *Study on the Financial Integration of European Mortgage Markets*, European Mortgage Federation, Brussels, October.

Mihov, I. (2001), 'Monetary policy implementation and transmission in the European Monetary Union', *Economic Policy*, 33, 371–406.

Mishkin, F. (1996), *The Channels of Monetary Transmission: Lessons for Monetary Policy*, NBER Working Paper 5464.

Mojon, B. (2000), *Financial Structure and the Interest Rate Channel of the ECB Monetary Policy*, ECB Working Paper 40.

Muellbauer, J. (1994), 'The assessment: consumer expenditure, *Oxford Review of Economic Policy*, 10, 1–41.

Nautz, D., and Wolters, J. (1999), 'The response of long-term interest rates to news about monetary policy actions: empirical evidence for the U.S. and Germany', *Weltwirtschaftliches Archiv*, 135, 397–412.

Neumark, D., and Sharpe, S. (1992), 'Market structure and the nature of price rigidity: evidence from the market for consumer deposits', *Quarterly Journal of Economics*, 107, 657–80.

OECD (2004), 'Housing markets, wealth and the business cycle', *OECD Economic Outlook*, 75, 127–47.

Peersman, G., and Smets, F. (2005), 'The industry effects of monetary policy in the euro area, *Economic Journal*, 115, 319–42.

Tobin, J. (1969), 'A general equilibrium approach to monetary theory', *Journal of Money, Credit and Banking*, 1, 15–29.

Tsatsaronis, K., and Zhu, H. (2004), 'What drives housing price dynamics: cross-country evidence', *BIS Quarterly Review*, March, 65–78.

Upper, C., and Worms, A. (2004), 'Estimating bilateral exposures in the German interbank market: is there a danger of contagion?', *European Economic Review*, 48(4), August, 827–49.

Worms, A. (2003), 'Interbank relationships and the credit channel in Germany', *Empirica*, 30(2), 179–98.

——— (2004), 'Monetary policy transmission and the financial system in Germany', in J. P. Krahnen and R. H. Schmidt (eds.), *The German Financial System*, Oxford: Oxford University Press.

CHAPTER 28

MONETARY POLICY IMPLEMENTATION

ULRICH BINDSEIL

KJELL G. NYBORG

1. INTRODUCTION

MONETARY policy implementation is one of the most significant areas of interaction between central banking and financial markets. Historically, how this interaction takes place has been viewed as having an important impact on the ultimate objective of monetary policy, for example price stability or stimulating economic growth. In this chapter, we survey different approaches to monetary policy implementation. We cover briefly some of the historical trends, but give particular attention to the practice that is now (again) very common worldwide; namely, targeting short-term interest rates. We discuss various ways this can be done and the implications for financial markets. We emphasize different European approaches, while also providing comparisons with the Fed.

There are three main elements to monetary policy implementation:

- The first element is the *operational target*, which is an economic variable, for example the overnight interbank interest rate that the central bank aims to

We are indebted to a number of persons at central banks who helped us complete the survey tables on current operating procedures, namely Johan Arvidsson, Roger Clews, Spence Hilton, Thomas Jordan, Lars Risbjerg, Yulia Snizhkova, Flemming Würtz, Siri Valseth. We also wish to thank Philip Hartmann for useful suggestions. Of course, responsibility for any remaining errors remains exclusively with the authors. The views presented in this chapter are the views of the authors, and not those of the European Central Bank.

control on a day-by-day basis through its monetary policy instruments. The target level is decided upon by the central bank's monetary policy decision-making committee. The announced target level provides guidance to the central bank's implementation officers and also serves to communicate the stance of monetary policy to the public.

- The second element is the operational framework for controlling the target. This specifies the monetary policy instruments and how they are to be used. These instruments typically consist of standing facilities, open market operations, and reserve requirements.[1] Additional elements of the operational framework are, for example, the list of counterparties eligible for central bank repos and the list of eligible collateral in these.

- The third element is the day-to-day use of open market operations within this framework, also called *central bank liquidity management*. An important aspect of liquidity management is forecasting the so-called autonomous liquidity factors, e.g. banknotes in circulation and government deposits with the central bank, and mapping them, together with other relevant information, into open market operations volumes in a way that is consistent with the operational target level. The required precision of liquidity management, and thus the quality of autonomous factor forecasts and the frequency of open market operations, depends on the operational framework of monetary policy implementation.

As an example, consider briefly the case of the European Central Bank (ECB), whose operational target is the overnight interest rate. Rather than announcing a specific target rate, the ECB announces the minimum bid rate at which it conducts its weekly reverse open market operations. The ECB ensures that overnight market rates are close to this minimum bid rate by acting on the demand and supply conditions of the deposits of banks with the Eurosystem.[2] To do this, the ECB has at its disposal three main instruments: (i) weekly open market operations with one-week maturity through which the bulk of funds is provided to the market (in 2004 on average €250 billion); (ii) two standing facilities with overnight maturity, namely a borrowing facility at which banks can always borrow funds against collateral, and a deposit facility at which banks can always deposit excess funds; both facilities are offered by the ECB at a *penalty rate* of 100 basis points relative to the target rate, and average daily recourse to the facilities is thus rather low (in 2004 each below €0.5 billion); and (iii) Reserve requirements of on average €140 billion in 2004 which impose a structural element on the demand for reserves. By using these instruments, and by devoting resources to forecasting autonomous factors, the ECB typically achieves a high degree of control of short-term interest rates. For example, in 2004 the ECB's implicit target rate, the minimum bid rate in its weekly repo operations, was constantly 2.00 per cent,

---

[1] The term 'instrument' has also been used to designate operational and intermediate targets; see e.g. Poole 1970.

[2] The ECB and the NCBs participating to the euro collectively constitute the Eurosystem. The ECB is responsible for setting the policy rates and for the decisions relating to the conduct of monetary policy operations, but national central banks (NCBs) participating in the euro are involved as well, as banks have their accounts with the NCBs and also submit bids for repo auctions with NCBs, not with the ECB.

while the average overnight rate (EONIA) was 2.05 per cent. The standard deviation of the difference between the overnight rate and the minimum bid rate was 9 basis points, while the standard deviation of first differences in the overnight rate was 10 basis points.

There are many other ways to implement monetary policy, including controlling short-term rates, as noted by Borio (2001):[3]

Just as there are a hundred ways to skin a cat, so there are a hundred ways to implement monetary policy. These may differ considerably in terms of the interest rates that are the focus of policy, the range of instruments employed, the frequency of operations, the spectrum of counterparties and other technical elements. Such differences reflect a mixture of purely historical factors and different views regarding the fine balance between the pros and cons of the various choices. At the end of the day, however, the proof of the pudding is in the eating. The 'eating' here is the central bank's ability to convey its policy signals with the desired degree of clarity and its ability to influence short-term rates with the desired degree of accuracy.

Borio suggests that from a monetary policy perspective, it is doubtful that the implementation details are very important as long as the signalling and the short-term rate objectives are achieved. But these are relatively straightforward to meet. Signalling can take the form of publicly announcing the target level. Controlling short-term rates can be done for instance by pegging the market rate to a standing facility rate.

However, monetary policy implementation arguably has ramifications and implications beyond the pure monetary policy perspective, for example on financial markets. As shown by Hamilton (1996) and Perez-Quiros and Rodriguez-Mendizábal (2006), the volatility of short-term rates is influenced by how monetary policy is implemented. Given the ease with which short-term rates can be controlled, one may wonder why central banks often choose frameworks that admit volatility in short-term rates. In this chapter, we discuss how the choice of the operational framework may also affect other aspects of financial markets, such as the liquidity of interbank credit markets and the market for collateral. If we accept the view that short-term rates are the appropriate operational target, we would argue that optimal monetary policy implementation may be less an issue of the efficient transmission of monetary policy and more an issue of financial market efficiency.

The rest of the chapter is organized as follows. Section 2 discusses the concept of the operational target of monetary policy and provides an overview of the historical debate and today's central bank practice in this regard. Section 3 discusses the three main instruments of monetary policy implementation in the context of the central bank balance sheet. Section 4 relates balance sheet quantities to short-term interbank rates and explains how the central bank can control rates. Section 5 discusses how alternative approaches to monetary policy implementation affect financial markets. Section 6 discusses different methods for conducting open market operations. Section 7 concludes.

---

[3] For a comprehensive technical survey of monetary policy implementation techniques of industrialized countries see Borio 1997. For a survey of implementation issues in countries with less developed markets see IMF 2004.

2. THE OPERATIONAL TARGET
OF MONETARY POLICY

Today, most central banks use short-term rates as their operational target. But this has not always been so. In this section, we discuss the rationale behind targeting short-term rates. We also put the view that short-term rates are the appropriate operational target in a historical context by discussing the emergence after the first World War and eventual abandonment of the alternative policy of targeting the monetary base.

2.1. The Short-term Interest Rate

Prior to 1914, monetary policy meant first of all controlling short-term interest rates, mainly via the use of standing facilities (see in particular the surveys of the Bank of England's monetary policy implementation in the nineteenth century as provided by Bagehot 1873 and King 1936, or, for Germany, Reichsbank 1900). The theoretical foundations of this approach may be traced back to Thornton (1802) and Wicksell (1898). Wicksell (1936: 102) established the concept of the 'natural rate' of interest, which he described as follows:

There is a certain rate of interest on loans which is neutral in respect to commodity prices, and tends neither to raise nor to lower them. This is necessarily the same as the rate of interest which would be determined by supply and demand if no use were made of money and all lending were effected in the form of real capital goods. It comes to much the same thing to describe it as the current value of the natural rate of interest on capital.

That under stable prices, the rate of interest on money has to correspond to the real rate of interest, which can be thought to be independent of the 'monetary sphere' of the economy, is implied by simple arbitrage logic. Today, 'neo-Wicksellians,' e.g. Woodford (2003), again incorporate this insight as a key building block in their macroeconomic models.

But why focus on the overnight interest rate, and not on a longer-term rate, for example the one-, three-, or twelve-month rates? It could be argued that the latter rates are more relevant for monetary policy transmission, as they are the basis of more important decisions. So why not target them directly?

The main problem with targeting longer-term rates is the irregularities this may lead to in shorter-term rates. Consider as an example the case of a central bank that targets the ninety-day rate. Assume for simplicity that the central bank is predictable in its changes of interest rate targets, and that it achieves market rates at its target level with a high degree of precision. Concretely, assume that on day τ, the central bank is expected to reduce its ninety-day target rate from 5 per cent to 4 per cent. What does this imply for the overnight rate around day τ, if the expectations hypothesis of the term structure of interest rate holds? The ninety-day horizon on $\tau - 1$ and on

τ overlap by eighty-nine days. The expectations hypothesis, in its simplified linear form, tells us that

$$i_{90,t} = \frac{\sum_{j=0}^{89} i_{1,t+j}}{90},$$

where $i_{90,t}$ and $i_{1,t+j}$ are the ninety-day and overnight interest rates on day t and t+j, respectively. Thus, the difference in the ninety-day rate between $\tau - 1$ and τ has to be translated in terms of overnight rates exclusively into the overnight rates on day $\tau - 1$ and $\tau + 89$, such that $(i_{1,\tau-1} - i_{1,\tau+89}) = 90(i_{90,\tau-1} - i_{90,\tau})$. Assuming that $i_{1,\tau+89} = 4\%$, this implies $i_{1,\tau-1} = 94$ per cent. This extreme upward spike is, in a sense, anomalous, particularly since the overall level of rates is being lowered. This volatility in the overnight rate is arguably undesirable, for example because of the importance of the overnight market. It is at this maturity that most un-expected short-term liquidity fluctuations are corrected. The average daily volume of interbank overnight lending of fifty-two panel banks in the euro area is around €40 billion.

In contrast, if a predictable central bank targets an overnight rate of 5 per cent until $\tau - 1$, and then moves its target on τ to 4 per cent, the ninety-day rate will simply have moved on $\tau - 89$ from 5 per cent to approximately 4.99 per cent and will decrease by approximately 1 basis point per day until the change occurs. Therefore, the adaptation of longer-term rates takes place in the smoothest possible way if the overnight rate is changed in a predictable way. If the central bank would like to see an earlier decline in the ninety-day rate, it simply needs to cut its overnight rate earlier (which under the assumption of predictability, triggers a correspondingly earlier start of the decline of the ninety-day rate).

While it is today again generally accepted by central bankers and academics that monetary policy implementation means controlling short-term interest rates, from around 1920 to the mid-1980s, 'reserve position doctrine' (Meigs 1962) was the domi-nating view on monetary policy implementation, particularly in the USA. According to this doctrine, a central bank should, via open market operation, steer some reserve concept, which would impact via the money multiplier on monetary aggregates and the ultimate goals of monetary policy. Although this view is now out of fashion, many monetary policy textbooks still devote substantial attention to concepts, such as the money multiplier and the monetary base, which make sense primarily in a reserve position doctrine framework.

2.2. Interest Rate Targeting in Europe and the USA

While there is a high degree of consensus today regarding the targeting of short-term rates, there is substantial variation with respect to how this is done. This also means that the volatility of short-term rates varies substantially across currency areas. Table 28.1 sets out some of these differences across several central banks in Europe as

Table 28.1. Specification of operational targets and technique of changing level of target variable for selected central banks

	(1) Type of operational target and description('implicit' = through operations rate; 'explicit' = explicit reference to targeted market rate)	(2) Vol. of daily changes of ONR in bp (2004)	(3) Normal frequency of reconsideration	(4) Number of changes of target rate (2000–4)	(5) % of which are changes in direction (total number)	(6) Min/max change in basis points
Euro area	Implicit—minimum bid rate in weekly repos	10	Once a month	13	8% (1)	25/50
UK	Implicit—rate of fixed rate repo operations	22	Once a month	16	13% (2)	25/50
Sweden	Implicit—rate of weekly fixed rate repo operations	19	Eight times a year	13	23% (3)	25/50
Denmark	Implicit—'discount rate' which is he main policy rate, without direct relation to market rates; 'lending rate' fixed tender rate around which overnight rates fluctuate (at currently 15 bp above discount rate)	10	Once a month	13	8% (1)	25/50
Norway	Implicit—deposit rate	16	Every six weeks	16	13% (2)	25/100
Switzer-land	Explicit—target range for the three-month LIBOR for Swiss francs. This target range extends over one percentage point. Normally, the SNB keeps the rate in the middle of the target range.	1.3[a]	Quarterly	12	17% (2)	25/75
Belarus	The refinancing rate is an administrative rate which is largely adopted by the financial sector as a reference rate. Policies for steering the overnight rate to this are under development.	—	Once a month	44	7% (3)	100/2500
Russia	The main target is the appreciation of real exchange rate of ruble—set annually. Shorter-term targets are not disclosed to public	—	—	—	—	—
USA	Explicit—overnight interest rate (federal funds rate)	5	8 weeks	21	10% (2)	25/50

[a] In the case of Switzerland, the target rate is the three-month LIBOR, and not the overnight rate.

well as the USA. The selected central banks represent the former Western Europe—
the ECB/Eurosystem, the Bank of England, the Swiss National Bank, and the three
Scandinavian central banks—as well as those of the USA, Russia, and Belarus. This
sample will be used throughout this article.[4]

2.2.1. *Definition and Explicitness of Target Rate*

Although all the central banks in our sample target a short-term rate, typically
the overnight rate, they vary with the degree of explicitness with which they do
so. In the first column in Table 28.1, we denote central banks that specify the target explicitly by 'explicit' and central banks that are less explicit, for instance by
specifying only the rate at which they operate in the money market, 'implicit'. Announcing a rate at which to operate in the money market is also a commitment to
provide central bank funds to maintain market rates close to the operations rate,
since otherwise some arbitrage condition would be violated and markets would
be in disorder. In all cases, changes in the target level are announced right after
the meetings of the decision-making committee. This improves transparency relative to the old technique of letting the market guess the target level from the
central bank's operations. It also sharpens the focus of the markets on the target
level.

2.2.2. *Precision of Control of the Overnight Interest Rate*

The second column in Table 28.1 presents the volatility of the overnight rates in our
sample of currency areas in the period 2000–4.[5] Among the Western currency areas,
the UK is the highest, with a volatility of 44 basis points (bp) per day. The USA is
lowest in terms of overnight rate volatility (with 4 bps), while the Swiss National Bank
(SNB) reaches an even lower level for its target rate, the three month LIBOR (1.3 bp;
the SNB is the only central bank in our sample that targets a maturity of interbank
rates above one day). Ayuso, Haldane, and Restoy (1997) have shown that central
banks implement monetary policy such that short-term interest rate deviations from
the target rates tend to be non-persistent, and therefore do not normally imply
volatility of medium- and long-term rates. It would therefore be wrong to conclude
from the overnight volatility figures that monetary policy transmission in the UK is
less precise than in the USA.

---

[4] The monetary policy implementation techniques of these central banks are described for instance
in the following documents. Danmark: Danmark's Nationalbank 2003a, 2003b; ECB: European Central
Bank 2004a, 2005; Norway: Kran and Ovre 2001; Sweden: Otz 2005; Switzerland: Jordan and Kugler 2004;
Jordan 2005; UK: Bank of England 2002, 2004; Clews 2005; US: Meulendyke 1998, Federal Reserve Bank of
New York 2005. Also Websites of central bank tend to provide some up-to-date information on monetary
policy implementation techniques.
[5] This is measured as the standard deviation of first differences.

2.2.3. *Frequency of Potential Changes of the Interest Rate Target and Size of Changes*

The third column in Table 28.3 shows the frequency with which the different central banks' decision-making bodies meet, for the purpose of assessing the target level. For example, the ECB's Governing Council currently meets only once a month for this purpose (until 2000, it met every fortnight). The Fed's FOMC meets every eighth week. The other central banks in our sample are within this range.

The frequency of meetings does not appear to be very correlated with the number of actual changes: while the Fed changed rates twenty-one times since 2000 which is the record amongst western hemisphere central banks, the ECB changed its rates only thirteen times (see column 4). The frequency of actual changes could be related to the size of changes to the target level. However, there is not much variation across central banks here. These changes are mostly 25 bp or 50 bp (column 6). No central bank did a smaller rate change, while three implemented higher ones, namely Switzerland (75 bp), Norway (100 bp), and Belarus (2,500 bp).

2.2.4. *Gradual or Exhaustive Changes of the Interest Rate Target Level*

On this issue, the Bank of England and the Fed appear to present two very different approaches. Goodhart (2000) suggests that the target adjustments of the Bank of England would be such as to generate a martingale in the target rates:[6] 'When I was a member of the MPC I thought I was trying, at each forecast round, to set the level of interest rates, on each occasion, so that without the need for future rate changes, prospective (forecast) inflation would on average equal the target at the policy horizon.' Under such an approach, it should, after each change, be equally likely that target rates go up or down with the next change, regardless of the direction of the current change. The Fed in contrast has for a long time followed a gradual approach in adjusting target rates to changing economic conditions, creating auto-correlation of changes of target rates (see e.g. Rudebusch 2002). Since 1999, the Fed also has been hinting explicitly in its announcements of decisions on the direction and speed of future changes. Interpreting these verbal hints has become an important element of Fed watching. Despite the rhetoric, we see in column 5 that the Bank of England and the Fed typically change target rates in a gradual way; only 13 per cent and 10 per cent, respectively, of rate changes represent a change in direction.

Column 5 of Table 28.1 indicates that in the period 2000–4, the central banks with the most gradualist approach have been the US Fed (twenty-one changes with two changes of direction) and the ECB and Denmark (both thirteen changes with only one change of direction), while Sweden having done least changes with most changes in direction (three) seems to be the one taking the most exhaustive steps.

---

[6] The latter question is not to be confounded with the one of whether the actual overnight rate follows a martingale within the reserve maintenance period.

Table 28.2. The central bank balance sheet

	Assets	Liabilities
Autonomous factors	Foreign reserves Investment assets	Banknotes in circulation Government deposits Capital and reserves
Monetary policy operations	Reverse open market operations[a] Outright holdings of securities[a] Borrowing facility	Deposit facility
		Reserves of banks (including those to fulfil required reserves)

[a] It is assumed that open market operations supply, rather than remove, liquidity, as is the case in the euro area and the USA. Whether open market operations supply or remove liquidity depends on the size of autonomous factors and reserve requirements. In our sample, the central banks of Norway, Denmark, Belarus, and Russia have to absorb liquidity through open market operations, mainly due to their large foreign reserves position.

3. THE CENTRAL BANK BALANCE SHEET AND THE THREE MAIN INSTRUMENTS OF MONETARY POLICY IMPLEMENTATION

The central bank balance sheet is the starting point for understanding monetary policy implementation. The items in the central bank balance sheet fall into three distinct categories; autonomous factors, monetary policy operations, and reserves of banks, as illustrated in Table 28.2.

3.1. Autonomous Liquidity Factors

Autonomous factors are items which are not controlled by the monetary policy function of the central bank, such as banknotes in circulation, foreign exchange reserves, government current accounts, holdings of securities for investment purposes, and possibly others. Transactions affecting these items normally include a leg in the domestic currency and therefore affect the reserves of banks with the central bank. For central banks like the ECB that supply funds through open market operations, it is therefore important to forecast the autonomous factors accurately. Failure to do so may lead the short-term rate to deviate from its target. The weekly frequency of operations in the euro area means that autonomous factor forecasts over a one-week horizon are particularly important.

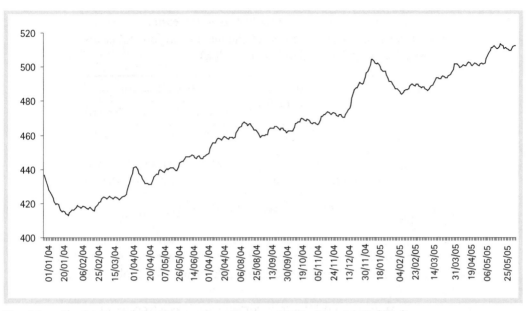

Fig. 28.1. Banknotes of the Eurosystem, January 2004–May 2005 (€bn)

Source: European Central Bank

Consider as one example of an autonomous factor banknotes in circulation, which is typically one of the largest if not the largest single item in the central bank balance sheet. The amount of euro banknotes, displayed in Figure 28.1, exhibits weekly, monthly, and seasonal patterns. These patterns reflect regularities such as withdrawing of cash before the weekend, the payment of salaries, the summer holiday season, and Christmas shopping. The forecasting model for banknotes applied by the European Central Bank in its day-to-day forecasting is discussed in more detail in Cabrero et al. (2002).

The Eurosystem produces separate forecasts for all the main autonomous factors. Table 28.3 provides, for the second semester of 2002, the accumulated volatility of the main autonomous factors as well as the forecasting errors over three different time horizons. As a fraction of volatility, forecast errors are the smallest for the most volatile series, banknotes and government deposits. This reflects the larger amount of resources devoted to the forecasting of these two key autonomous factors.

3.2. Open Market Operations

Open market operations are monetary policy operations conducted at the initiative of the central bank in order to affect the level of reserves of banks with the central bank, and thereby achieve the operational target of monetary policy. They may consist of reverse operations (i.e. repos or reverse repos) or outright purchases or sales of securities. Today, day-to-day monetary policy implementation is done almost exclusively through repos, while outright holdings of securities are used by some central banks

Table 28.3. Autonomous liquidity factors in the euro area, second half of 2002, standard deviations of changes and of forecast errors at three different forecasting horizons (€bn)

Horizon	Absolute size[a] (end 2002)	Forecast horizon		
		One day	Five days	Ten days
Banknotes	377	1.1/0.2	4.1/1.4	7.8/2.8
Government deposits	50	4.5/0.4	10.0/2.0	12.0/3.4
Net foreign assets	380	0.4/0.1	0.8/0.4	11.4/0.9
Domestic financial assets	120	0.4/0.2	0.8/0.6	1.3/1.0

[a] Note that the length of the Eurosystem balance sheet at end 2002 was €832 billion.
Source: ECB

as a means of structural liquidity supply. Section 5 will elaborate in more detail on the choice between repos and outright operations for the structural supply of liquidity to the market.

Both Keynes (1930/1971) and Milton Friedman (1982), as advocates of the reserve position doctrine, argued that open market operations, which they conceived to be outright operations in securities, would be the supreme instrument of monetary policy implementation, if not the only one really needed. Today, with the dominance of reverse operations, the distinction between open market operations and standing facilities has become more blurred, and the idea to operate without standing facilities is no longer considered. Section 6 looks at the details of repo operations using fixed rate tenders and auctions, especially in the context of the ECB.

Table 28.4 surveys current practice of repo operations for our sample of central banks. The standard frequency of the main refinancing operations in Europe is one to two weeks. The maturity of these operations tends to be one week (columns 1 and 2). In terms of tender procedure, the fixed rate tender seems to dominate in Europe with the exception of the euro are a (column 3). Like the ECB, the Fed also uses variable rate tenders (discriminatory auctions). Most central banks conduct more than one type of reverse operations (column 4), and the number of outstanding operations at any moment in time is mostly in the order of 2 to 4 (column 5).

3.3. Standing Facilities

Standing facilities are, in contrast to open market operations, monetary policy operations conducted *at the initiative of the commercial banks*, under the conditions specified by the central banks. Historically, they were only liquidity providing and were either a discount or a lombard (advance) facility. In a discount, the counterparty sells short-term paper to the central bank, but receives only a part of the nominal value of the asset, since the nominal value of the paper is 'discounted'

Table 28.4. Use of reverse open market operations by selected central banks

	(1) Frequency of reverse operations	(2) Maturity of main operation	(3) Tender procedure	(4) Other open market operations	(5) Average number of operations outstanding
Euro area	weekly	One week	Variable rate tender with minimum bid rate	Longer-term refinancing operations: monthly variable rate tenders with pre-announced volume and three months maturity; Fine tuning overnight operations: n in 2004	4
UK (new[a])	Weekly	One week	Fixed rate	Overnight operation on last day of the reserve maintenance period	
Sweden	Weekly	One week	Fixed rate tender	Daily fine-tuning operations	2
Denmark	Two weekly operations in parallel: one liquidity absorbing, one providing	Two weeks	Fixed rate tender with full allotment (at lending rate)	–	4
Norway	No standard frequency	Varying, up to 10 days	Variable rate tender	Collection of fixed-term deposits (rarely)	Few, sometimes none
Switz.	Daily	Mainly one week (also overnight, two weeks)	Fixed rate tender (rationing if demand > supply)	Fine-tuning operations, etc.	5
Belarus	Weekly	Varying (up to one month)	Variable rate tender with max. or min. bid rates	Issuance of central bank debt instruments to absorb liquidity	n.a.
Russia	Overnight repo; 3-month repo; 1- or 2-week repo	Twice a day; once a month; once a week	Variable rate tender with minimum bid rate	Issuance of central bank's bonds, deposit auctions, and reverse repo at various maturities (to absorb liquidity)	n.a.
USA	Almost daily	Overnight (192 in 2004) and two weeks	Variable rate	Other maturities up to 28 days	Around 3

[a] The Bank of England changed its monetary policy implementation technique in 2006 (see Bank of England 2004, 2007). This and the following tables refer to the new framework.

at the prevailing discount rate. The maturity of a discount hence depends on the maturity of the discounted paper. In a lombard loan, the counterparty in contrast obtains collateralized credit of a standardized maturity, today usually overnight. We will refer to a liquidity providing standing facilities as a 'borrowing facility', taking the perspective of the central bank's counterparty.[7] Practically all borrowing facilities today are lombard facilities. More recently, some central banks, e.g. the ECB, have introduced a liquidity absorbing facility ('deposit facility'). The deposit facility enables counterparties to place their end-of-day surplus liquidity with the central bank on a remunerated account.

The rates of the standing facilities are often fixed by the central bank at a 'penalty level', i.e. such that the use of the facilities is normally not attractive relative to market rates. The interest rates on the two facilities then form the ceiling and the floor of a corridor within which short-term money market rates move. Such a corridor system is applied by the Bank of England, the ECB, and the central banks of Canada, Australia, and New Zealand among others. A symmetric corridor has the important advantage, relative to an asymmetric approach à la Fed, in that it creates a general symmetry of the liquidity management problems of the central banks and the commercial banks. This symmetry allows for instance to ignore higher-order moments of autonomous factor shocks (Bindseil 2004).[8]

Systems in which standing facilities are not set at penalty levels were standard until the first half of the twentieth century, and are still applied in some cases today. Section 5 discusses some advantages and disadvantages of different approaches.

3.4. Reserves of Banks with the Central Bank and Reserve Requirements

This is arguably the most important single item on the balance, since reserves represent the good for which the short-term market interest rate is the price. Most central banks today impose reserve requirements, including the Fed and the ECB. Banks that do not fulfil reserve requirements face penalties; in the case of the ECB, it is equal to the borrowing facility rate plus 250 basis points.

The justification for imposing reserve requirements has evolved considerably (see for instance Goodfriend and Hargraves 1983 or Bindseil 2004: chapter 6). Today, there is consensus that the main purpose of reserve requirements lies in facilitating the control of short-term interest rates. This stabilizing effect works in two ways. First, if reserve requirements are set above the demand for working balances, which fluctuate from day to day, they stabilize the demand for reserves. Second, if reserve requirements are to be held only on average over a reserve maintenance period, they provide a buffer against transitory autonomous factor shocks. For instance the ECB can only achieve a high degree of interest rate stability with a weekly frequency of open market operations because of a combination of relatively high reserve requirements and the fact that these have to be maintained only on average over the one-month reserve maintenance period. This being said, reserve requirements are

---

[7] The ECB calls its liquidity providing facility the *marginal lending facility*. The Fed calls its facility the discount facility, although it is strictly speaking a lombard facility.

[8] A study on how standing facilities may be misused by banks to manipulate the money market is Ewerhart et al. 2007.

not strictly necessary to control very precisely short-term interest rates. Control can also be achieved through daily open market operations or standing facilities to which recourse is systematic and the rate of which is at the level of the operational target (as under the Norwegian and Reichsbank approaches, as they will be called in Section 5).

While in the 1990s, many authors predicted the disappearance of reserve requirements, recent years have witnessed some innovations which have raised their popularity, in particular with banks. These innovations go in the direction of taking away the taxation character of reserves. The ECB was, after de Nederlandsche Bank, the second to introduce reserve requirements remunerated at market rates (in 1999). The Fed has added to its reserve requirement a voluntary ('contractual') component. This voluntary component is remunerated at market rates, and can be chosen by the banks (within certain limits) before the start of the maintenance period. At end 2004, the total requirements (including the voluntary component) stood at US$20 billion (Federal Reserve Bank of New York 2005). The Bank of England, which has long been a strong opponent of traditional reserve requirements, is currently in the process of introducing voluntary reserves with averaging. Under its new scheme, 'banks will choose a target level of positive balances (voluntary reserves) that they will be required to hold with the Bank on average over a maintenance period lasting from one MPC meeting to the next. Reserve holdings will be remunerated at the Bank's repo rate (with ceilings on the amount each scheme-member bank can hold)' (Bank of England 2004). Table 28.6. provides a survey of features of reserve requirements in those countries of our sample that have some kind of reserve requirement system.

3.5. The Demand and Supply for Reserves

The balance sheet identity (assets=liabilities) allows us to present one balance sheet item as a residual, for example the net recourse to the standing facilities. Letting B and D denote recourse to the borrowing and deposit facilities, respectively, we have, over the course of the reserve maintenance period, if we assume that there are no excess reserves:

$$\textit{net use of standing facilities (B-D)} = -\textit{open market operations (M)}$$
$$+ \textit{required reserves (RR)}$$
$$+ \textit{net autonomous factors (A)}.$$

We see that there is a net use of the standing facilities whenever open market operations do not equal reserve requirements plus autonomous factors. We say that the banking sector is long (short) reserves in aggregate if, $M - A - RR > 0\,(M - A - RR < 0)$. In a system that penalizes users of the standing facilities, as is the case in the euro area, an efficient interbank market implies that standing facilities are used only when the banking sector is strictly long or short reserves over the monthly reserve maintenance period. In this case, short-term rates at the end of the

Table 28.5. Use of standing facilities for selected central banks

	(1) Borrowing facility	(2) Deposit facility	(3) At penalty level?	(4) Width of the corridor set by standing facilities
Euro area	Yes	Yes	Yes	+/−100 basis points around the target level for short-term rates
UK (new)	Yes	Yes	Yes	Rates on standing facilities will be the MPC's repo rate +/−25 basis points on the final day of the maintenance period, and wider on all other days
Sweden	Yes	Yes	Yes	+/−75 basis points
Denmark	none	Remuner. of current accounts at discount rate—but only up to ceiling	Light penalty level (only 15 basis points)	If one considers Danmarks Nationalbank's full allotment fixed rate open market operations as standing facilities, one could stipulate a corridor of 15 basis points. However, open market operations are only weekly, so there is no effective upper bound to the overnight rate.
Norway	Yes	Yes	Borrowing facility yes, deposit facility no	200 basis points. Note: access to the deposit facility is automatic in the sense that any deposits on the sight accounts of banks with the central banks are remunerated at the deposit facility rate.
Switzerl.	Yes	No	Yes	Borrowing facility is 200 basis points above the overnight rate (the call money rate)
Belarus	Yes	Yes	Mostly	Mid-2005: 15%, asymmetric around policy rate. Deposit facility = 3%, refinancing rate = 13%, and lending facility = 18%.
Russia	Yes (collat. borrowing at 7 days and overnight)	Yes	Yes	Mid-2005: overnight borrowing rate at 13%; overnight deposit rate at 0.5%; 1% for one-week deposits. Market rates fluctuate in between.
USA	Yes	No	Yes	Borrowing facility 100 basis points above the target level for short-term rates

Table 28.6. Main features of reserve requirement systems: missing central banks are those without any reserve requirement system

	(1) Reserve base categories; reserve ratio	(2) Size of reserve requirements	(3) Remuneration	(4) Averaging period	(5) Level available for averaging
Euro area	2% of deposits and debt securities with maturity up to two years	€ 140 billion	At rates of Eurosystem's main refinancing operations.	Approximately one month. Exact time depends on meetings of ECB Governing Council	Equivalent to reserve requirements
UK (new)	Banks choose themselves their reserve requirements up to a certain maximum	Targets for reserve balances may total £ 25 billion (Clews 2005: 215)	Remunerated at BoE repo rate	Between MPC meetings, i.e. one month	Equivalent to level chosen by banks
Switz.	2.5% of liabilities with a maturity of 90 days; 2.5% of 20% of liabilities in the form of savings deposits	CHF 7.5 billion	None	One month, from the 20th to the 19th of the following month	Around CHF 5 billion[a]
Belarus	5% of all deposits from household denominated in BYR; 10% of all deposit from firms denominated in BYR; 10% of all FX deposits	BYR 465 billion (about US$ 200 million)	None	One month, starting on 15th calendar day and ending on 14th calendar day.	20% of reserve requirements on liabilities denominated in BYR.
Russia	2% for liabilities to non-residents and 3.5% for all the others	135 billion rubles (about US$ 4,5 billion)	None	1 month	20% of total
USA	Different marginal levels, max. 10% of transactions deposits	After deduction of vault cash US$ 10 billion	None (but at market rates for 'clearing balance requirements')	Two weeks starting on a Thursday	Around US$ 20 billion (of which €10 billion is clearing balance requirement)

[a] In Switzerland, banks are allowed to use vault cash to fulfil their reserve requirements. This reduces the need to hold reserves in the form of deposits with the central bank. Currently, vault cash held by banks amounts to 4.5 billion CHF.

maintenance period are determined by whether or not the banking sector is short or long reserves. If it is long, short-term rates are determined by the deposit facility. If it is short, rates are determined by the borrowing facility. Because the autonomous factors are stochastic, this means that short-term rates at the end of the maintenance period will also be stochastic. Rates prior to the end of the maintenance period will then be given by the relative likelihood of the banking sector being long or short reserves at the end of the period. In the next section, we discuss a model that captures this idea and show how standing facilities and open market operations can be used to steer short term rates.

4. A Basic Model of Short-term Interest Rate Control and the 'Liquidity Effect'

Models of the relationship between available reserves and interest rates and how this relationship is to be used by the central bank start with Poole (1968). In Section 4.1, we will provide a simple microeconomic model following the specification of Woodford (2001). In Section 4.2, the even simpler aggregate model will be presented which is also suitable for modelling reserve maintenance periods with more than one day.

4.1. The One Day 'Individual Shocks' Model of Woodford (2001)

In this model, banks must end each day with non-negative reserve positions. That is, negative positions must be made up by using the borrowing facility. A bank with positive holdings can use the deposit facility. Within the day, the timeline is as follows: first, the central bank conducts an open market operation which determines the amount of reserves available in the system. It is assumed that the central bank is perfect in forecasting aggregate autonomous factors, and that aggregate liquidity conditions are precisely known to the market. Second, a fully efficient interbank market session takes place in which the overnight interest rate is determined. Finally, end of day clearance takes place, in which banks are subject to individual surprise cash flows, such that they may be pushed into having to use either the borrowing or the deposit facility offered by the central bank.

Let s_j be the reserves bank j chooses to hold (through dealing in the interbank market) at the beginning of the day. The bank is subsequently subject to a shock in its holdings of ε_j, taking its end of day holdings to r_j. The shocks are independently distributed across banks with $E[\varepsilon_j|s_j] = 0$, $Var[\varepsilon_j|s_j] = \sigma_j^2$. For each j, ε_j/σ_j has cumulative density function F, with a mean of zero, variance of 1, and $F(0) = 0.5$. Let i, i_B, and i_D denote the market rate, the rate of the borrowing facility, and the rate of the deposit facility, respectively. A risk-neutral bank will choose s_j to minimize expected costs C of refinancing, i.e. it will minimize

$$C(s_j) = is_j - i_B E_j[\min(s_j + \varepsilon_j, 0)] - i_D E_j[\max(s_j + \varepsilon_j, 0)] \tag{1}$$

The first-order condition is

$$(i_D - i)(1 - F(-s_j/\sigma_j)) + (i_B - i)F(-s_j/\sigma_j) = 0 \tag{2}$$

This implies desired overnight balances of

$$s_j = -\sigma_j F^{-1}\left(\frac{i - i_D}{i_B - i_D}\right). \tag{3}$$

The market clearing overnight rate is the one that ensures that demand and supply of reserves match. Thus, we must have

$$\sum_j s_j = R \tag{4}$$

where R is the aggregate reserves of banks with the central bank set at the beginning of the day. Substitution of (3) into (4) yields the solution:

$$i = i_D + F\left(\frac{-R}{\sum_j \sigma_j}\right)(i_B - i_D). \tag{5}$$

Thus by choosing R, for example through open market operations at the beginning of the day, the central bank can achieve any market interest rate within the corridor set by the two standing facilities. If $R = 0$, the market rate would be in the middle of the corridor (since $F(0) = 1/2$). This would correspond to, for instance, the case of the ECB and the central banks of Australia, New Zealand, and Canada. If R is very large, then banks will tend to load off excess liquidity with probability close to one through the deposit facility at day end, and the market price for overnight money should thus be close to i_D. If instead R has a large negative value, banks will be forced into the borrowing facility with high likelihood, and the interbank market will clear at a rate close to i_B.

Incorporating a positive level or (daily) reserve requirements into this model is straightforward: just replace R by R-RR (RR being reserve requirements) in equation (5).

4.2. A Model with Aggregate Shocks and Averaging

In this model, the relationship between aggregate reserves and the interbank interest rate is not driven by liquidity shocks at the level of individual banks, but by an aggregate shock on autonomous factors. The central bank has an unbiased forecast $E(A)$, with $A = E(A) + \varepsilon g$ Let F be the cumulative distribution function of εg We first assume that there is no averaging and that required reserves each day are zero. At the beginning of the day, the central bank conducts an open market operation of M. Along the same lines as in the previous model, we have

$$i = i_D + F\left(-(M - E(A))\right)(i_B - i_D) \tag{6}$$

This can also be written:

$$
\begin{aligned}
i &= i_D\left[1 - F\left(-(M - E(A))\right)\right] + i_B F\left(-(M - E(A))\right) \\
&= i_D\left[P(\text{'long'})\right] + i_B[P(\text{'short'})].
\end{aligned}
\tag{7}
$$

In words, the overnight rate is a weighted average of the two standing facility rates, the weights being equal to the respective probabilities that the market is on aggregate 'long' or 'short' of funds at the end of the day. If $M = E(A)$ and $F(0) = 0.5$, the interbank rate will be in the middle of the corridor.

We now introduce reserve requirements and averaging. As recourse to standing facilities at the end of the reserve maintenance period is then a matter of average reserves over the maintenance period being above or below required reserves, one simply needs to reinterpret all quantities as averages over this period. Thus let $\overline{M}, \overline{A}$ be the averages over the reserve maintenance period of daily outstanding open market operations and autonomous factors, respectively. Thus, on any day t of the reserve maintenance period, we can write:

$$i_t = i_D + (i_B - i_D)F_{t,\overline{M}-\overline{A}}(RR(t)) \tag{8}$$

where $F_{t,(\overline{M}-\overline{A})}$ is the conditional cumulative distribution function of $\overline{M} - \overline{A}$ as perceived by banks at the time of the money market session of day t, and $RR(t)$ is the remaining average reserve requirement to be fulfilled from day t to the end of the reserve maintenance period for the banking sector as a whole. Note that now both $\overline{M}$ and $\overline{A}$ are random variables, since the open market operations after day t but before the end of the reserve maintenance period are not yet known.

Consider as an illustration the following example from Bindseil (2004). First assume a three-day reserve maintenance period with an open market operation (with three days maturity) only on the first day, as displayed in Figure 28.2: For the sake of simplicity of notation, assume that $i_B = 1; i_D = 0$. For the same reason, also assume that reserve requirements are zero, but that there are no limits to averaging. Banks can thus overdraft their account with the central bank, but have to fulfil zero reserve requirements on average over the three-day period. Denote the random aggregate autonomous factors on each of the three-day by $\tilde{\eta}_1, \tilde{\eta}_2, \tilde{\eta}_3$, with realizations written without the tilde. Suppose these are iid $N(0, \sigma_\eta)$. Assume that the central bank operates a neutral liquidity policy so that M is zero as well. Then the market interest

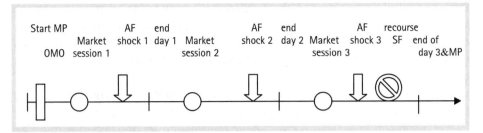

Fig. 28.2. A three-day maintenance period with one open market operation

rate on day 1 is

$$i_1 = P\left(-(\tilde{\eta}_1 + \tilde{\eta}_2 + \tilde{\eta}_3))/3 < 0\right) = \Phi\left(0\Big/\sqrt{\sigma_\eta^2/3}\right) = 1/2 \qquad (9)$$

where $\Phi()$ is the standard normal cumulative distribution function. The market rate on day 1 will always be in the middle of the corridor as liquidity conditions are neutral. This changes on day 2, as market players observe the realization of autonomous factors on day 1 (for instance the ECB publishes its relevant previous day's balance sheet figures at 9:30 a.m.). The market interest rate on day 2 will thus be

$$i_2 = P\left(-(\eta_1 + \tilde{\eta}_2 + \tilde{\eta}_3))/3 < 0\right) = \Phi\left(\eta_1\Big/\sqrt{\sigma_\eta^2/2}\right). \qquad (10)$$

The interest rate on day 3 will be:

$$i_3 = P\left(-(\eta_1 + \eta_2 + \tilde{\eta}_3))/3 < 0\right) = \Phi\left((\eta_1 + \eta_2)\Big/\sqrt{\sigma_\eta^2}\right). \qquad (11)$$

The variance of the overnight rate increases day by day in the course of this reserve maintenance period, well in line with empirical evidence.

Consider now the case in which the central bank conducts one operation with one-day maturity on each day of the maintenance period, before the respective market session. Assume the allotment policy $M_1 = 0$; $M_2 = \eta_1$, $M_3 = \eta_2$, i.e. the central bank neutralizes the autonomous factor shocks. It is easy to verify that this open market operation strategy allows a perfect stabilization of interest rates within the reserve maintenance period, since in each market session, expectations with regard to the liquidity conditions prevailing at the end of the reserve maintenance period tend to be balanced.

The same result could also be achieved for the policy $M_1 = 0$; $M_2 = 0$, $M_3 = \eta_1 + \eta_2$, as long as the market is aware that this is what the central bank does. In this case, the market trusts that the central bank delays the correction of the first day's autonomous factor shock. If the market is not aware of the central bank's neutral policy, the market will have biased expectations after observing the shock on day 1, leading to an interbank rate that deviates from $1/2$ on date 2. This example illustrates two key points. First, there may be open market policies that are distinct in terms of the distribution of liquidity supply across the reserve maintenance period, but that are equivalent in terms of the implied interest rate path, if they lead to the same accumulated liquidity supply. Second, it is important that the market has a clear picture of the central bank's strategy of liquidity supply across different open market operations within the reserve maintenance period in order that the volatilities of interbank rates are minimized.

It can be easily verified in these examples that, as implied by an unlimited averaging facility, the martingale property of short-term interest rates holds, i.e. $i_1 = E(i_2 | I_1) = E(i_3 | I_1)$ and $i_2 = E(i_3 | I_2)$, where I_t is the information set of banks at date t. The intuition behind the martingale property is as follows. Assume for instance that $i_1 > E(i_2 | I_1)$. This would mean that any risk-neutral bank should lower its total refinancing costs in the reserve maintenance period by lending on day 1 and by borrowing in the interbank market on day 2. On day 1, it would under-fulfill its reserve requirement, but it would rebalance it on the next day. As all banks would attempt to do this, however, all banks would try to lend in the interbank market at the high rate of day 1 and all banks would try to borrow at the low rate on day 2. This however cannot be an equilibrium.

4.3. Empirical Studies

The empirical literature on overnight interest rates has spotted various more or less important deviations from the martingale hypothesis, and tried to find explanation for them. Ho and Saunders (1985) focus on the possible risk aversion of banks. Campbell (1987) assumes that liquidity benefits of reserves vary across the days of the reserve maintenance period, for instance due to differing payment system activity. Transaction costs are introduced by e.g. Kopecky and Tucker (1993), Hamilton (1996), Clouse and Dow (1999), and Bartolini, Bertola, and Prati (2001). Limits to interbank trading have been mentioned by Spindt and Hoffmeister (1988) and Hamilton (1996). Effects of payment systems are analysed by Furfine (2000). Window dressing by banks is studied by Allen and Saunders (1992) for the USA, and Bindseil, Weller and, Würtz, (2002). Bartolini, Bertola, and Prati (2002) focus on volatility effects of operating procedures, confirming the increased end-of-day volatility also suggested in the simple model above. Gaspar, Perez-Quiros, and Rodriguez-Mendizábal (2004) show that the end-of-day no-overdraft constraint alone is sufficient for a breakdown of the martingale hypothesis and a tendency of short-term rates to increase in the course of the reserve maintenance period. Further empirical models of short term interest rates in the euro area are Hartmann, Manna, and Manzanares (2001), Angelini (2002), and Würtz (2003). Other estimates of the liquidity effect are Hayashi (2001) for Japan and Thornton (2001) for the USA.

The empirical evidence seems to confirm that a variety of factors beyond liquidity conditions and standing facility rates impact on actual overnight rates. However, the simple models developed in this section provide a good understanding of how monetary policy implementation works and how the short-term rate can be controlled.

Table 28.7. Central bank assets under four different implementation approaches (€bn; liability €100 billion in banknotes)

	'Reichsbank'	'Norwegian'	'US Fed'	'Eurosystem'
Net recourse to borrowing facility	100	10	0*	0
Repo operations	0	0	10	100
Outright holdings of securities	0	90	90	0

a Under the US Fed approach, there would actually be a very small expected net recourse to the borrowing facility.

5. IMPLICATIONS OF MONETARY POLICY IMPLEMENTATION FOR FINANCIAL MARKETS

There are many ways for a central bank to steer short-term rates and to provide liquidity. These place different requirements on the central and commercial banks with respect to forecasting and managing liquidity conditions, dealing in securities, and managing collateral, and therefore have different implications for financial markets. In this section, we discuss some of these issues in the context of a simple example which focuses on standing facilities and open market operations.

We consider four different implementation techniques, as illustrated in Table 28.7. The techniques differ in their emphasis on standing facilities, the use of repo operations, or outright holdings of securities. Each of the four approaches is named after a central bank with a similar actual monetary policy implementation technique. For simplicity, in our example we ignore reserve requirements and assume that central bank liabilities consist of €100 billion of banknotes.

(a) The Reichsbank approach. All central bank funds are provided through recourse to a borrowing facility, the rate of which is set at the level of the target rate. The structural recourse to the borrowing facility pegs the short term market rates (see Reichsbank 1900, 1925). This approach was practised by the German Reichsbank from 1876 until at least 1914. While we assume that the borrowing facility is collateral based, the Reichsbank's actual borrowing facility was a genuine discount facility in which eligible short-term paper was sold to the Reichsbank at the initiative of counterparties.

(b) The Norwegian approach. Under this approach, banks always need to take recourse to one standing facility, in our case to the borrowing facility (in contrast to the actual recourse to some kind of deposit facility in Norway, Indonesia, China, etc.). Deterministic recourse to the borrowing facility pegs the short-term interbank rate. However, in contrast to the Reichsbank approach, the recourse to the standing facility only covers a smaller part of the central bank assets, the rest of assets being outright holdings. Therefore the central bank has more freedom to determine the composition of its assets.

(c) The US Fed approach. Recourse to the borrowing facility is stochastic, and the short-term interest rate target is set below the borrowing facility rate (in practice,

Table 28.8. Two key dimensions of choices for designing a monetary policy implementation approach

	Technique to control short-term interest rates	
	Systematic recourse to SF[a]	Combination of OMOs[b] and stochastic recourse to SFs
Structural liquidity provision Collateral based	Reichsbank	Eurosystem
Outright holdings based	Norway	US Fed

[a] SF = Standing facilities.
[b] OMO = Open market operations.

the difference is 100 bp). There is no deposit facility. Most of the funds are provided through outright purchases. The Fed holds Treasury securities in proportion with their market capitalization, implying a portfolio duration of around five years. Fine tuning of liquidity is done via repos.

(d) *The ECB approach.* Net recourse to the borrowing facility is stochastic. There is both a borrowing and a deposit facility, which are 100 bp above and below the target rate, respectively. Both the structural liquidity supply and day-to-day liquidity management take place through repos against a wide range of eligible collateral.

Table 28.8 summarizes these four techniques with respect to how they provide liquidity—through outright holdings or collateralized loans, or repos—and how they control short-term rates—through standing facilities or open market operations. Below, we discuss the impact of these choices on financial markets.

5.1. Efficiency of Liquidity Management for Banks and for the Central Bank

For a commercial bank, liquidity management is costly in that it requires forecasting its liquidity in- and outflows and trading in the money market. This might require analysts, traders, back-office staff, management, etc. These costs do not feature in the models in Section 4, but can be important in practice. Banks face a trade-off between investing resources into analysis and trading on the one side, and the costs of suboptimal end-of-day liquidity positions on the other side. From this perspective, it is desirable to have an operational framework that minimizes the costs of liquidity management.

For the central bank similar cost issues arise. Forecasting the autonomous liquidity factors and conducting operations require staff for analysis, trading, and settlement. In contrast, recourse to standing facilities would appear to involve fewer costs for the central bank as it is undertaken by the counterparties. One could view the central bank as facing a potential trade-off between the precision of interest rate control, on the one hand, and administrative costs, including forecasting autonomous factors, on the other.

For the liquidity management of the central bank, approaches based on the systematic use of standing facilities (the two approaches on the left-hand side of Table 28.8) appear more efficient. The Reichsbank approach in particular would seem to minimize costs as it requires minimal efforts on behalf of the central bank to forecast liquidity developments. The story seems to be similar for commercial banks.

Costs of liquidity management might also be different in collateral versus outright holding-based frameworks (the vertical dimension in Table 28.8). Collateral-based operations (operated as standing facilities or repo auctions) with a wide range of counterparties facilitate channelling liquidity directly to the counterparties in need of it. With outright operations-based approaches, the liquidity has to be redistributed by the banking system itself, which would increase transaction costs. On the other hand, regularly turning over a substantial amount of the stock of liquidity might involve costs that would be avoided under the outright operations-based approach.

5.2. Market Neutrality in Terms of Relative Prices of Financial Assets

Choices with regard to the monetary policy implementation technique should avoid having distorting effects on the relative prices of financial assets. This mainly refers to the vertical dimension in Table 28.8, i.e. outright versus collateral-based approaches.

Due to the scale of central bank assets, outright purchase or sale operations can potentially influence relative asset prices. For instance, the Fed currently holds around US$700 billion, all in government securities. If the Fed decided to exchange some of its holdings to agency- or mortgage-backed securities, for example, this might well drive down the spreads of these securities relative to government securities. Since the central bank probably cannot hold the full 'market portfolio', any outright portfolio will to some extent impact market prices and will thus require difficult choices by the central bank.

It is often said that one of the main advantages of reverse collateral-based operations is that they do not distort securities prices, because the underlying assets' ownership is not affected. This appears plausible, particularly if the list of eligible collateral is wide and haircuts are set fairly. But it is possible that there is a premium on securities that are eligible as collateral, since use in central bank operations as collateral is for many banks one of the reasons to hold securities. If a security is made ineligible, then some banks may want to replace it with eligible ones, which may put pressure on prices.

In Section 5.5 we will identify some cases where eligibility of collateral seems to have influenced issuance and even legislative activities in the euro area. There is currently a debate in the euro area in the context of the high deficits or debt ratios of some euro area governments, such as those of Greece, Italy, and Portugal. According to some critics, for example J. Fels of Morgan Stanley (*Financial Times*, 1 April 2005) and Buiter and Sibert (2005), the ECB, by accepting government bonds from these countries on similar terms as government bonds of euro area countries with a better fiscal position, would narrow down spreads between these different government debt instruments and reduce incentives for governments to improve their fiscal situation.[9]

In conclusion, a market-neutral operational framework for monetary policy implementation may be hard to achieve. Collateral-based systems arguably retain the advantage that they spare the central bank the need to decide which assets to purchase.

5.3. Market Neutrality with Regard to the Yield Curve

Another dimension of market neutrality is the effect on the yield curve. Here, a collateral-based system appears to ensure market neutrality to a higher extent than an outright holdings-based system, since the ownership of assets, and therefore returns and risks, remains with the banks. This is particularly so when the central bank does not restrict the maturity of instruments submitted by banks as collateral, while it obviously would have to choose when buying assets outright.

Leaving longer-term rates to be set in the market is arguably the efficient thing to do. However, many central banks have tried at some time in their history to directly influence longer-term interest rates through monetary policy implementation. But, as summarized in Bindseil (2004: section 5.3), the results have been disappointing. Nevertheless, considerations of direct yield curve control re-emerged recently not only in deflationary Japan, but also in the USA after the stock market downturn in 2000. According to some observers, the Fed tried to 'talk down' longer-term interest rates by suggesting that there was deflation risk in the USA as well. In a speech delivered in November 2002, Governor Ben Bernanke even suggested the active use of open market operations for that purpose, and explained that he would 'personally prefer the Fed to begin announcing explicit ceilings for yields on longer-maturity

---

[9] The treatment of different government bonds by the Eurosystem is actually not the same insofar as the Eurosystem applies daily marking to market, such that a higher credit risk perceived by market participants and reflected in prices implies that a higher nominal amount of collateral needs to be provided. As a solution to the problem they perceive, Buiter and Sibert (2005: 25–8) suggest inter alia that the Eurosystem should issue sufficient debt to establish a new risk-free benchmark against which the credit risk in all public instruments would be priced. However, the (one-year) probability of default of an AAA-rated government issuer (like the German government, which currently provides the euro benchmark yield curve) is generally considered to be below 1 basis point (such a default has never occurred in history). In addition, the German government at present has an outstanding debt of around €800 billion (approximately the length of the current Eurosystem balance sheet), which implies an exceptional liquidity. To match this liquidity would probably require similar issuance volumes by the Eurosystem. Buiter and Sibert propose to balance the debt issuance through 'outright purchases of other eligible debt instruments', meaning that the Eurosystem would eventually hold significantly more credit risk than presently (where its balance sheet is much shorter and mainly based on collateralized operations), and would most likely distort financial market prices significantly more than now.

treasury debt (say bonds maturing within the next two years). The Fed could enforce these interest-rate ceilings by committing to make unlimited purchases of securities up to two years from maturity at prices consistent with the targeted yields.' However, no such concrete measures have been taken by the Fed.

5.4. Contribute to Liquid and Resilient Money Markets

The central bank is normally the largest and most important player in the money market. It therefore also sets standards which eventually influence the conventions and practice of money and collateral markets. This can have influence on the liquidity of the markets and their resilience to financial shocks. A liquid and resilient money market would be one in which (i) banks have active trading relation with each other, such as to know and trust each other to a relatively high degree; and (ii) ample collateral is available in the system (and efficient methods of collateral settlement), such that even in case that no relationship of mutual knowledge and trust is there to build upon, banks will be able to exchange funds.

5.4.1. *Technique of Liquidity Supply and Interbank Money Market Activity*

It has sometimes been argued that parts of the interbank market trading volumes are of a speculative nature, and would thus vanish if rate volatility moved close to zero. However, in the euro area or US markets for overnight funds, there is little volatility except towards the very end of the reserve maintenance period. Nevertheless, trading volumes do not tend to increase towards the end of the reserve maintenance period. This is consistent with the view that interbank activity is primarily driven by liquidity management. Hartmann and Valla (2007) provide a more detailed discussion of these issues, and of money markets in general.

Central bankers often argue that with a deterministic aggregate recourse to one standing facility, and, accordingly, overnight rates always at or very close to the relevant standing facility rate, banks would have fewer incentives to try to trade funds in the interbank market. Can one quantify this impact on the size of the overnight market? Take a very simplistic example with ten banks, half of them being short by €5 million and five long €4 million, such that a total recourse of €5 million to the borrowing facility will have to occur. Under the *ECB's symmetric corridor* approach and daily operations, the central bank would target through its open market operations a zero recourse, and would thus add €5 million to the system. If this liquidity ends up equally with the banks which were previously short, then five are short by €4 million and five are long by €4 million. In the absence of forecast errors and efficient markets, recourse to standing facilities will be zero and the interbank lending volume will be €20 million. Now assume that under the *Norwegian approach*, the initial situation is the intended one, i.e. a net recourse to the borrowing facility of €5 million is what the central bank aims at to peg the market rate at the level of the borrowing facility rate.

The trades needed to minimize refinancing costs to the banking system are now again lending of €20 million from the surplus banks to the deficit banks (the rate traded should be marginally below the borrowing facility rate—if collateral is not scarce or credit risk is not an issue). Thus, the interbank lending volume would be identical to the symmetric corridor approach. In other words, the interbank overnight market would not collapse, and it would not even shrink, at least not in this example.

What about moving further from the Norwegian to the Reichsbank approach, in which recourse to the borrowing facility would be much higher? Under the Reichsbank approach, we would find the banks in our example in completely different situations. For example, we could have five banks being short by €14 million and five short by €5 million. Each bank has 9 million less, reflecting that the €90 million which were provided under the Norwegian approach through open market operations have to be covered under the Reichsbank approach through recourse to the borrowing facility. Now, all interbank money market activity will be replaced by recourse to the borrowing facility, whereby some banks will borrow €14 million and the others €5 million. Thus, we see that how monetary policy is implemented will impact on interbank activity. A small or non-existent interbank market could be achieved by adopting the Reichsbank approach. An active interbank market could be achieved through either of the other approaches listed in Table 28.8.

5.4.2. *Impact on Debt Issuance and Collateral Standards*

To the extent that the specification of monetary policy implementation techniques, including in particular the choice of securities for outright holdings and the list of eligible collateral, is not entirely market neutral (see Section 5.3), it will have some impact on issuance activity and therefore at least indirectly also on the securities available in the interbank market for repos. Consider the following examples taken from the collateral-based case of the ECB.

1. Covered bonds like Pfandbriefe can be defined as full recourse debt instruments secured (covered) by collateral pools, namely mortgage assets and/or claims against public sector entities. They constitute 'on balance sheet securitization' (ECB 2004b) and are typically AAA rated (Association of German Mortgage Banks 2004). While being originally a German specificity, covered bonds were, from the start of the euro in 1999 on, made eligible all over the euro area as collateral for Eurosystem monetary policy operations. This also contributed to increase their attractiveness sufficiently to have banking systems and legislators work hard on quickly establishing conventions and laws supporting Pfandbriefe all over Europe. So-called Jumbo-Pfandbriefe (which are Pfandbriefe with an issuance volume of at least €1 billion) are also used to a growing extent in interbank repo markets. At the end of 2003, a total of 1 trillion of covered bonds was outstanding in the euro area.
2. Asset-backed securities (ABSs). Since 1999, ABSs were also eligible collateral for Eurosystem operations. The amount of outstanding ABSs has developed

exceptionally in Europe since then, with issue volumes reaching €268 billion in 2003 (of which 80 per cent are AAA rated—see ECB 2004b).[10] While other factors (Basel II, technological advancements) have certainly also played a major role, anecdotal evidence suggests that eligibility for Eurosystem operations gave a further push to the growth of the market. Even if ABSs are normally not used in interbank repo operations, the securitization they imply means an increased liquidity per se, as something that could not be traded beforehand (all sorts of non-standardized claims) is made easily tradeable, somehow standardized, and credit rated. This could contribute to the liquidity and resilience of financial markets.

3. Loans of banks to corporates. The ECB decided in 2004 that loans of banks to corporates would become eligible collateral euro area-wide (they were eligible only in four countries beforehand). This might to some extent reduce incentives for banks to create Pfandbriefe-style assets or ABSs with loans they will then be able to submit directly to the Eurosystem. The standards of credit assessment for loans submitted to the Eurosystem as collateral may gain some recognition in the market and help to make the market for loans more liquid.

5.5. Optimal Duration of Central Bank Assets, Risk Allocation, and the Central Bank's Risk–Return Preferences

In a collateral-based system, the central bank is constrained to hold assets with limited duration, and it also takes little credit and spread risk (credit risk materializes only in case that both the counterparty and the collateral issuer default simultaneously; spread risk is addressed through haircuts). In other words, a collateral-based system is one in which the central bank overall takes very few risks. As far as non-diversifiable risks are concerned, this implies that it leaves correspondingly more risks in the hands of the market.

Can one say anything about the optimal duration of central bank assets? One might argue that if the economy as a whole tends to have longer-term refinancing needs, then the central bank should also aim at providing longer-term financing to avoid the need of a costly duration transformation by banks. On the other side one could argue that banks want to be flexible in their financing behaviour, and thus like to have short-term liabilities towards the central bank, at least if they know that they can always refinance again at the central bank when the current refinancing matures. From the central bank's perspective, one could also view the duration decision as being a mere investment problem: how much interest rate risk does the central bank want to take into its balance sheet, and what expected return does it want? Not being

---

[10] According to ECB 2004b: 'Off-balance sheet term securitization did not take off in Europe until the late 1990s. It has seen impressive growth rates since then and has now become an established asset class in the European fixed income markets.'

threatened by liquidity problems, and having a long-term horizon as an investor, it would seem that the central bank should not be overly risk averse in the short run, and should probably not hold less interest rate risk in its balance sheet than the average investor, and thus end up with a portfolio duration not below around five years (a few of the underlying issues are discussed in Bindseil, Manzanares, and Weller 2004). If a central bank concludes that it wants to hold assets with a duration of this order of magnitude, be it for investment or more comprehensive social considerations, it will be forced to hold a part of its assets in outright form, i.e. it cannot do so under a pure collateral-based approach.

With regard to the extent a central bank should take credit or spread risk in its balance sheet, one could argue that taking these risks always requires careful analysis, and that the central bank can never be a competitive player in this field and should therefore leave such risk taking to others. The opposite argument would be that any investor should take credit risk as part of a CAPM type of diversification, and that with limited analysis, important diversification benefits can be achieved. In practice, many central banks have chosen to not incur any non-necessary credit and spread risk in their monetary policy operations, but to define a part of their assets (be they domestic or foreign) as investment assets, where they go for partial diversification into such risk.

It is difficult to draw a clear conclusions on the desirability of a higher duration of central bank assets and of the benefits from diversification into credit and spread risk. In any case, the outright approach is more flexible in this respect than the collateral-based approach, as the latter constrains risks and related return perspectives. If one believes that the central bank should get into these risks, then a pure collateral-based approach would not be optimal.

6. OPEN MARKET OPERATION MECHANISMS

We have seen that open market operations can be classified by whether they inject or remove liquidity and whether they do so through repos or outright purchases. In this section, we will focus on the mechanisms themselves, taking the type of open market operation as given. There are two broad types of mechanisms that are commonly used, namely, fixed rate tenders and variable rate tenders. Both types have been used by the ECB. These different mechanisms can have different impacts on allocations across banks in the operations and therefore on the money markets. We will focus on the case that the operation injects liquidity through a reverse repo, as is the case for the ECB.

6.1. Fixed Rate Tenders (FRT)

In a fixed rate tender, the central bank fixes the interest rate of the operation and invites eligible financial institutions to submit bids specifying how much they wish to transact at the announced rate. The most common allocation rule is the pro rata rule, where bidders receive a pro-rated share of the total amount the central bank wishes to provide. If this amount is larger than the aggregate demand in the tender, bidders receive their demand in full. An alternative is the 100 per cent rule, where bidders receive their demands in full.

Fixed rate tenders with the pro rata rule were used, for example, by the Bundesbank during the 1980s and 1990s and the Eurosystem from January 1999 to June 2000. The Bank of England also uses fixed rate tenders. The 100 per cent allotment variant was applied, for instance, by the Bundesbank in the 1950s and by the Bank of Finland in the years preceding 1999.

6.2. Variable Rate Tenders (VRT)

In variable rate tenders, the rates at which operations take place are determined by auction. Here, the bids of the counterparties are interest rate–quantity pairs, specifying the marginal quantity that the bidder demands at the specified interest rate. These bids can be organized into an aggregate demand curve. The rate where aggregate demand equals the quantity the central bank wishes to inject is referred to as the stop-out, or marginal, rate. There are two main types of auctions; uniform and discriminatory. In both types, bids above the stop-out rate are allocated in full; while bids at the stop-out rate are pro-rated. In uniform auctions, all bidders pay the stop-out rate; while in discriminatory auctions, they pay the rate of their accepted bids.

As with fixed rate tenders, the central bank may pre-announce the quantity it wishes to transact or it may decide upon this after observing bids. Since the end of June 2000, the ECB has used discriminatory auctions for all but some fine-tuning operations. There is little supply uncertainty in the ECB's operations. The ECB has a liquidity neutral policy and announces the liquidity neutral amount shortly before its main weekly operations. For its monthly longer-term operations, the ECB pre-announces the exact amount it will inject (15, 20, or 25 billion euros). When the size of the operation is non-discretionary, as in the euro area, the stop-out rate is determined by the bids submitted by the counterparties and therefore does not serve a role in signalling information from the central bank to the markets.

The choice of mechanism affects at least two important issues: (i) the rate counterparties must pay for central bank funds; and (ii) the allocation of central bank funds in the tender and therefore the activity and possibly the transaction rates in the interbank markets.

Variable rate tenders are sometimes viewed as having two main advantages relative to fixed rate tenders. (i) Variable rate tenders allow banks to express their relative preferences for central bank funds through the bid price, thus possibly aiding a more efficient allocation. (ii) Variable rate tenders solve the problem of overbidding (see below) which can occur with fixed rate tenders.

Fixed rate tenders are sometimes viewed as advantageous to variable rate tenders because: (i) fixed rate tenders send a stronger signal regarding the central bank's monetary policy stance. The idea is that there is an implicit commitment to steer the corresponding short-term market rates to levels around the tender rate. (ii) Bidding in fixed rate tenders is simpler than in variable rate tenders and therefore does not put less sophisticated bidders (e.g. smaller banks) at a disadvantage.

6.3. Empirical Comparison of Fixed Rate and Variable Rate Tenders

In this subsection, we will discuss the ECB's experience with fixed rate and variable rate tenders. The ECB used fixed rate tenders for its main refinancing operations from its inception in January 1999 to 20 June 2000. Starting with the operation on 27 June 2000, the ECB has used discriminatory auctions. The reason for the switch has mainly to do with the so-called overbidding problem that arose with the fixed rate tenders; that is, banks demanded substantially more than the liquidity neutral amount that the ECB aimed to inject and that banks needed to fulfil reserve requirements. For example, in the tender held on 30 May 2000, banks received only 0.87 per cent of their demand. This translates into a bid-to-cover of approximately 115, relative to the realized tender size.[11]

Very large and highly variable bid-to-cover ratios are considered to be a problem for two reasons. First, high bid-to-cover ratios mean that banks that have relatively small amounts of collateral might need to demand more in the tender than they have collateral for. If bidding turns out to be weak, such banks could find themselves short of collateral. Thus, banks with relatively little collateral might be at a disadvantage in the tender. This was viewed as a problem particularly because collateral was said to be unequally distributed across the euro area, with some countries being collateral rich and others being collateral poor. Second, highly variable bid-to-cover ratios make tender allotments less predictable and therefore liquidity management more difficult. Discriminatory auctions were viewed as being able to solve the overbidding problem since banks now could increase the likelihood of awards simply by bidding higher on the interest rate dimension.

Table 28.9 provides some summary statistics under the fixed rate and variable rate regimes.

We see in Table 28.9 that bid-to-cover ratios indeed fall dramatically with the introduction of discriminatory auctions. Under the fixed rate tender regime the average bid-to-cover ratio is 26.22, while under the discriminatory auction regime it is 2.06. Bid-to-cover ratios are also much less variable, their standard deviation fall from 25.47 under fixed rate tenders to 2.17 under discriminatory auctions.

---

[11] Overbidding is studied by Nautz and Oechsler 2003 and Bindseil 2005. See also Ayuso and Repullo 2003; Välimäki 2003; Ewerhart, Cassola, and Valla 2005.

Table 28.9. Comparison of fixed rate and variable rate tenders held by the ECB, January 1999–June 2001

	Minimum bid rate (%)	Bid-to-cover	Swap rate (%)	Swap spread (%)	Volatility of swap rate (bp)	Premium (rel to min) bid rate (bp)	Discount (rel to swap rate) (bp)
Panel a: fixed rate tenders. #Obs = 76							
Mean	2.95	26.22	3.05	9.20	4.62	0.00	9.20
St. error	0.05	2.92	0.06	1.20	0.17	0.00	1.20
St. dev	0.46	25.47	0.51	10.47	1.46	0.00	10.47
Minimum	2.50	1.00	2.51	−11.25	0.84	0.00	−11.25
Maximum	4.25	114.94	4.34	41.25	10.62	0.00	41.25
Panel b: discriminatory auctions (variable rate tender). # Obs = 53							
Mean	4.60	2.06	4.68	8.19	4.29	6.52	1.67
St. error	0.03	0.30	0.02	1.23	0.17	1.05	0.35
St. dev	0.20	2.17	0.18	8.85	1.22	7.55	2.51
Minimum	4.25	1.00	4.31	−5.50	1.18	0.15	−5.65
Maximum	4.75	16.66	4.93	48.25	8.54	45.95	6.76

Notes: Swap spread is the swap rate less the minimum bid rate. Premium is the average rate paid less the minimum bid rate. Discount is the swap rate less the average rate paid. Volatility of swap rate is calculated from the modified GARCH(1,1) model in Nyborg, Bindseil, and Strebulaev (2002). All variables are sampled on the tender days (swap rates are taken fifteen minutes before the tender), with the exception of the volatility which is sampled the day before (which gives the conditional volatility for the tender day). Bid-to-cover is calculated with respect to the realized tender size.

The table uses the two-week EONIA swap rate to benchmark the auction. This is the rate of the fixed leg for a two-week swap, where the floating leg pays the realized overnight rate (the EONIA). The ECB's operations during the sample period are for two-week money. As an alternative to borrowing in the tender, a bank could borrow overnight over two weeks and hedge by entering an EONIA swap, paying the fixed leg. This would mean the bank would obtain the necessary liquidity at the swap rate. Thus the swap rate can be viewed as the appropriate benchmark for the tenders. The swap rate is also more liquid than other two-week interbank rates.

The swap spread is the swap rate less the tender rate (in the fixed rate tenders) or the minimum bid rate (in the discriminatory auctions). This variable is the key to the overbidding phenomenon.

We see from Table 28.9 that the swap spread averages to 9.20 basis points under the FRT period. Thus, banks could obtain funding at on average 9.20 bp cheaper in the tenders than in the interbank market, as we see in the *discount* column. The reason is that the interbank (swap) rate reflects expectations that future tender rates will rise. The tenders therefore provide an easy way for collateral rich banks to make money.

The swap spread does not decline much under the discriminatory auction regime; it averages to 8.19 bp. But the auctions do not provide the same opportunity to make money as the fixed rate tenders. We see that the discount averages to only 1.67 bp, which is well within the typical bid–ask spread of around 3 bp. In the auctions, the huge discounts (or profits to bidders) are competed away. Banks still participate because they need the good on offer, namely central bank funds, in order to satisfy reserve requirements. We can see from the fact that the swap spread and the volatility of the swap spread is more or less the same under the FRT and VRT periods, that the reason for the reduced bid-to-cover ratios and discounts are the change of the mechanism, and not changes in other market conditions.

The experience of the ECB also suggests that allocations in the tenders across banks can be very different under fixed rate and variable rate tenders. In particular, in fixed rate tenders, collateral-rich banks would appear to have an advantage. This could potentially be a problem in that it could make squeezing more likely. Squeezing could in theory occur in the money markets since banks have to fulfil reserve requirements. What a bank does not obtain in the tender, it must obtain in the secondary market. An unbalanced tender allocation increases the likelihood of short squeezing since it becomes more likely that some banks may have market power. Thus the type of mechanism used in the operation can affect the orderliness of the secondary money markets.[12]

Besides overbidding, another problem that can arise is underbidding, whereby banks demand less in aggregate than the liquidity neutral amount; i.e. less than what they need to fulfil reserve requirements. Typically, underbidding occurs when banks expect that within the reserve maintenance period, the minimum bid (or fixed tender) rate will be reduced by the central bank, such as to allow for lower total refinancing costs by 'backloading' the reserve fulfilment. Underbidding is costly for banks because it means they must use the ECB's borrowing facility (marginal lending facility) to make up the shortfall, which comes at a penalty of 100 bp relative to the minimum bid rate in the tender. Underbidding also disrupts the planned implementation of monetary policy. If all tenders were consistently underbid, overnight rates would move up to the borrowing facility. If this were expected to be persistent, the whole yield curve also would shift up.

Underbidding has occurred in several instances. In Table 28.9, a bid-to-cover of 1 means that the quantity allotted to bidders (realized auction size) equals the total demand by bidders. These auctions were underbid relative to the liquidity neutral amount. The reason underbidding happens is that rates are expected to fall. Moreover, in most underbidding cases, the swap rate the morning of the tender is below the minimum bid rate (or tender rate), making the tenders an unattractive source of liquidity. However, after an underbid tender, interbank rates tend to increase, as banks need to go to the borrowing facility.

The ECB has solved the underbidding problem not by changing the mechanism,[13] but by matching reserve maintenance periods with meetings of its Governing Council. In particular, there is now only one Governing Council meeting at which interest

---

[12] Nyborg and Strebulaev 2001, 2004 discuss short squeezing in fixed rate tenders and auctions, respectively.

[13] Linzert, Nautz, and Bindseil 2007 provide evidence of the smooth working of pure variable rate tenders in the ECB's longer-term refinancing operations.

rates can be changed during a reserve maintenance period, and interest rate changes become effective exactly at the beginning of the period. This means that bidders cannot expect to obtain cheaper funding later in the period. Thus they have no reason to abstain from obtaining funds in the auctions.

7. CONCLUDING REMARKS

This chapter has provided an overview of monetary policy implementation. We have discussed the three elements of implementation, namely, the operational target, the framework, and liquidity management. The operational target in most economies today is a short-term rate. We have discussed a variety of ways the rate can be controlled, drawing on specific examples from Europe as well as the USA, and discussed how monetary policy implementation can distort asset prices through the type of collateral that can be used in transactions with the central bank. Finally, we touched on how the type of mechanism that a central bank uses for its open market operations can affect the allocation of central bank funds across banks and thus the money markets.

REFERENCES

ALLEN, L., and SAUNDERS, A. (1992), 'Bank window dressing: theory and evidence', *Journal of Banking and Finance*, 16, 585–623.

ANGELINI, P. (2002), *Liquidity and Announcement Effects in the Euro Area*, Banca d'Italia Discussion Paper no. 451.

ASSOCIATION OF GERMAN MORTGAGE BANKS (2004), *The Pfandbrief: Europe's biggest Bond Market. 2004: Facts and Figure*, Berlin.

AYUSO, J., HALDANE, A. G., and RESTOY, F. (1997), 'Volatility transmission along the money market yield curve', *Weltwirtschaftliches Archiv*, 133, 56–75.

—— and REPULLO, R. (2003), 'A model of the open market operations of the European Central Bank', *Economic Journal*, 113, 883–902.

BAGEHOT, W. (1873), *Lombard Street*, in *The Collected Works of Walter Bagehot*, London: The Economist.

BANK OF ENGLAND (2002), *The Bank of England's Operations in the Sterling Money Markets*, London: Bank of England.

—— (2004), *Reform of the Bank of England's Operations in the Sterling Money Markets*, London: Bank of England (press release, 22 July).

—— (2007), *The Framework for the Bank of England's Operations in the Sterling Money Markets*, London: Bank of England, February.

BARTOLINI, L., BERTOLA, G., and PRATI, A. (2001), 'Banks' reserve management, transaction costs, and the timing of Federal reserve interventions', *Journal of Banking and Finance*, 25, 1287–317.

BARTOLINI, L., BERTOLA, G., and PRATI, A. (2002), 'Day-to-day implementation of monetary policy and the volatility of the federal funds rate', *Journal of Money, Credit and Banking*, 34, 137–59.

BINDSEIL, U. (2004), *Monetary Policy Implementatio: Theory, Past, Present*, Oxford: Oxford University Press.

——(2005), 'Over- and underbidding in central bank open market operations conducted as fixed rate tender', *German Economic Review*, 6, 95–130.

——MANZANARES, A., and WELLER, B. (2004), *The Role of Central Bank Capital Revisited*, ECB Working Paper No. 392.

——WELLER, B., and WÜRTZ, F. (2003), 'Central bank and commercial banks' liquidity management: what is the relationship?,' *Economic Notes*, 32, 37–66.

BIS (1980), *The Monetary Base Approach to Monetary Control*, Basel: Bank of International Settlements.

BORIO, C. E. V. (1997), *Monetary Policy Operating Procedures in Industrial Countries*, BIS conference papers, Basel: BIS, iii. 286–368.

——(2001), *A Hundred Ways to Skin a cat: Comparing Monetary Policy Operating Procedures in the United States, Japan and the Euro area*, BIS Paper no. 9, Basel.

BUITER, W., and SIEBERT, A. (2005), *How the Euro System's Treatment of Collateral in its Open Market Operations Weakens Fiscal Discipline in the Euro Zone (and What to Do about it)*, CEPR Discussion Paper no. 5387.

CABRERO, A., CAMBA-MENDEZ, G., HIRSCH, A., and NIETO, F. (2002), *Modelling the Daily Banknotes in Circulation in the Context of the Liquidity Management of the European Central Bank*, ECB Working Paper Series, no. 142.

CAMPBELL, J. Y. (1987), 'Monetary announcements, the demand for bank reserves, and the behaviour of the federal funds rate within the statement week', *Journal of Money, Credit and Banking*, 19, 56–67.

CLEWS, R. (2005), 'Implementing monetary policy: reforms to the Bank of England's operations in the money market', *Quarterly Bulletin, Bank of England*, Summer, 211–20.

CLOUSE, J. A., and DOW, J. P. (1999), 'Fixed costs and the behaviour of the federal funds rate', *Journal of Banking and Finance*, 23, 1015–29.

Denmark Nationalbank (2003a), 'Use of monetary policy instruments', *Monetary Review*, First Quarter, 21–32.

——(2003b), *Monetary Policy in Denmark*, Copenhagen.

EUROPEAN CENTRAL BANK (2004a), *The Monetary Policy of the ECB*, Frankfurt am Main.

——(2004b), *The Euro Bond Market Study*, Frankfurt a. Main.

——(2005), *The Implementation of Monetary Policy in the Euro Area: General Documentation on Eurosystem Monetary Policy Instruments and Procedures*, Frankfurt am Main.

EWERHART, C., CASSOLA, N., and VALLA, N. (2005), 'Equilibrium and inefficiency in fixed rate tenders', ECB Working Paper no. 554, Frankfurt am Main.

————EJERSKOV, S., and VALLA, N. (2007), 'Manipulation in money markets', *International Journal of Central Banking*, 3, 113–48.

FEDERAL RESERVE BANK OF NEW YORK (2005), 'Domestic open market operations during 2004', memo.

FRIEDMAN, M. (1982), 'Monetary policy: theory and practice', *Journal of Money, Credit and Banking*, 14, 98–118.

——and SCHWARTZ, A. (1963), *A Monetary History of the United States, 1867–1960*, Princeton: Princeton University Press.

FURFINE, C. H. (2000), 'Interbank payments and the daily federal funds rate', *Journal of Monetary Economics*, 46, 535–53.

GASPAR, V., PEREZ-QUIROS, G., and RODRIGUEZ-MENDIZÁBAL, H. (2004), *Interest Rate Determination in the Interbank Money Market*, ECB Working Paper no. 351, Frankfurt am Main.

GOODFRIEND, M. (2003), review of Allan Meltzer's *A History of the Federal Reserve*, i: *1913–1951*, Federal Reserve Bank of Minneapolis, *The Region*, December.

_____ and HARGRAVES, M. (1983). 'A historical assessment of the rationales and functions of reserve Requirements', reprinted in M. Goodfriend, *Monetary Policy in Practice*, Richmond: Federal Reserve Bank of Richmond, 1987.

GOODHART, C. A. E. (2000), *The Inflation Forecast*, Working Paper, London School of Economics.

_____ (2001), 'The endogeneity of money', in P. Arestis, M. Desai, and S. Dow (eds.), *Money, Macroeconomics and Keynes*, Oxford: Routledge.

_____ (2004), 'The Bank of England, 1970–2000', in R. Michie, and P. Williamson (eds.), *The British Government and the City of London in the Twentieth Century*, New York: Cambridge University Press.

HAMILTON, J. D. (1996), 'The daily market for federal funds', *Journal of Political Economy*, 104, 26–56.

HARTMANN, P., MANNA, M., and MANZANARES, A. (2001), 'The microstructure of the euro money market, *Journal of International Money and Finance*, 20, 895–948.

_____ and VALLA, N. (2007), 'The euro money market', in X. Freixas, P. Hartmann, and C. Mayer (eds.), *Financial Markets and Institutions: A European Perspective*, Oxford: Oxford University Press.

HAYASHI, F. (2001), 'Identifying a liquidity effect in the Japanese interbank market', *International Economic Review*, 42, 287–315.

HO, T. S. Y., and SAUNDERS, A. (1985), 'A micro model of the federal funds market', *Journal of Finance*, 40, 977–88.

INTERNATIONAL MONETARY FUND (2004), *Monetary Policy Implementation at Different Stages of Market Development*, paper prepared by the staff of the Monetary and Financial Systems Department, 26 October.

JORDAN, T. J. (2005), ' Umsetzung der Geldpolitik in der Schweiz', *Schweizer Volkswirtschaft*, 4, 50–4.

_____ and KUGLER, P. (2004), 'Implementing Swiss monetary policy: steering the 3M-Libor with repo transactions', paper presented at the CFS workshop 'Implementing monetary policy' in Frankfurt am Main, 25 November.

KEYNES, J. M. (1930/1971), *A Treatise on Money*, ii: *The Applied Theory of Money*, in The Collected Works of John Maynard Keynes, vol. vi, London: Macmillan/Cambridge University Press.

KING, W. T. C. (1936), *History of the London Discount Market*, London: Frank Cass.

KOPECKY, K. J., and TUCKER, A. L. (1993), 'Interest rate smoothness and the non-settling-day behaviour of banks', *Journal of Economics and Business*, 45, 297–314.

KRAN, L.-P., and OVRE, G. (2001), 'Norges Bank's system for managing interest rates', *Economic Bulletin*, Q2/01, 65–70.

LINZERT, T., NAUTZ, D., and BINDSEIL, U. (2007), 'The longer term refinancing operations of the ECB', *Journal of Banking and Finance*, 31, 1521–43.

MEIGS, J. A. (1962), *Free Reserves and the Money Supply*, Chicago: University of Chicago Press.

MELTZER, A. H. (2003), *A History of the Federal Reserve*, i: *1913–1951*, Chicago: University of Chicago Press.

MEULENDYKE, A.-M. (1998). *US Monetary Policy and Financial Markets*, New York: Federal Reserve Bank of New York.

NAUTZ, D., and OECHSLER, J. (2003), 'The repo auctions of the European Central Bank and the vanishing quota puzzle', *Scandinavian Journal of Economics*, 105, 207–20.

NYBORG K., BINDSEIL, U., and STREBULAEV, I. (2002), *Bidder Behaviour and Performance in Repo Auctions: The Case of the Euro System*, ECB Working Paper no. 157, Frankfurt am Main.

_____ and STREBULAEV, I. (2001), 'Collateral and short squeezing of liquidity in fixed rate tenders', *Journal of International Money and Finance*, 20, 769–92.

_____ _____ (2004), 'Multiple unit auctions and short squeezes', *Review of Financial Studies*, 17, 545–80.

OTZ, A. (2005), 'The Riksbank's management of interest rates: monetary policy in practice', *Sveriges Riksbank Economic Review*, 2, 54–64.

PEREZ-QUIROS, G., and RODRIGUEZ-MENDIZÁBAL, H. (2006), 'The market for funds in Europe: what has changed with the EMU?', *Journal of Money, Credit and Banking*, 38, 91–118.

POOLE, W. (1968), 'Commercial bank reserve management in a stochastic model: implications for monetary policy', *Journal of Finance*, 23, 769–91.

_____ (1970), 'Optimal choice of monetary policy instruments in a simple stochastic macro model', *Quarterly Journal of Economics*, 84, 197–216.

Reichsbank (1900), *The Reichsbank 1876–1900*, translationed. National Monetary Commission, Washington, DC: Government Printing Office, 1910.

_____ (1925), Die Reichsbank 1900–1924, Berlin: Reichsdruckerei.

RUDEBUSCH, G. D. (2002), 'Term structure evidence on interest rate smoothing and monetary policy inertia', *Journal of Monetary Economics*, 49(6), 1161–1187.

SPINDT, P. A., AND HOFFMEISTER, J. R. (1988), 'The micromechanics of the federal funds market: Implications for day-of-the-week effects in funds rate volatility', *Journal of Financial and Quantitative Analysis*, 23, 401–16.

STRONGIN, S. (1995), 'The identification of monetary policy disturbance': explaining the liquidity puzzle', *Journal of Monetary Economics*, 35, 463–97.

THORNTON, D. L. (2001), 'Identifying the liquidity effect at the daily frequency', *Federal Reserve Bank of St Louis Review*, 83, 59–78.

VÄLIMÄKI, T. (2003), 'Central bank tenders: three essays on money market liquidity auctions', Ph.D. thesis, Suomen Pankki.

WICKSELL, K. (1936), *Interest and Prices: A Study of the Causes Regulating the Value of Money*, London: Macmillan. Translation of *Geldzins und Güterpreise, eine Studie über den Tauschwert des Geldes bestimmende Ursachen*, Jena: Gustav Fischer, 1898.

WOODFORD, M. (2001), 'Monetary policy in the information economy', paper prepared for the Symposium on Economic Policy for the Information Economy, Federal Reserve Bank of Kansas City, Jackson Hole, Wyoming, 30 August – 1 September.

_____ (2003), *Interest and Prices: Foundations of a Theory of Monetary Policy*, Princeton: Princeton University Press.

WÜRTZ, F. R. (2003), *A Comprehensive Model of the Euro Overnight Rate*, ECB Working Paper no. 207, Frankfurt am Main.

General Index

Abbey National 606
Abiad, A 694 n2, 704 n9
ABN Amro 606
accountability, and Lamfalussy process 664–5
accounting systems:
   and cross-listings 633–5
   and financial centre competition 636–7, 638
Acemoglu, D 71 n5, 72, 79 n15, 82 n17, 129, 151, 199
Acharya, V 481, 670, 671, 672 n6, 700
Adam, K 170, 365, 498, 499, 506
Adjaouté, K 522, 526, 533, 534, 535, 536
Adler, M 207
Aghion, P 71 n5, 76, 77, 86 n20, 104, 105 n4,
     109, 114, 116, 126, 135 n17
Agrawal, A 270, 275
Agresti, A M 524
Ahearne, A G 206
Ahold 298
Aked, M 530
Aktas, N 229
Alan, F 259
Albuquerque, R 198
Alcatel 498
Alfaro, L 124, 198, 200
Allen, C H 309
Allen, F 35, 54, 62, 63, 123, 124, 125, 129, 196 n1,
     409, 439, 480, 614–15, 670
Allen, J W 268
Allen, L 762
Almeida, H 85
Alternative Investment Market (AIM) (UK) 305
Altissimo, F 729, 730, 732
Altman, E I 313, 700
Altonji, J 201
Amadeus database 240, 252
Ambrose, B W 287
Amihud, Y 227, 271, 278
Ammer, J 167, 612, 634, 635
Amsterdam:
   as financial centre 621
   and multinational bank branches 622
   and securities market 626, 637
Andersen, A 629 n6
Anderson, R W 582 n14, 593 n20
Ando, A 729 n17
Andrade, G 265, 266 n4, 269
Angelini, P 762

Angeloni, I 728, 735 n22
Antolin, P 393, 395
Aoki, K 730
Arcelor 10
Arellano, M 78 n11
Arestis, P 79
Arnold, I 530
Arnold, T 637
Arrow, K 201
Arthur Andersen 303–4
Asia:
   and corporate governance 54, 57–9
     reform of 61–2
     weak enforcement 62
   and financial crises 57
   and financial structure 34
   and housing market 44
   and institutional investors 38–40
     central banks 41–2, 65
     mutual funds 38–9
     pension funds 39–40
   and mortgage market 53
asset management 13, 374
   and cross-national differences 13
   and fraud 383
   and guaranteed products 375, 385–6
   and investor protection 374
   and operational risks 382
   and regulation of 13, 375–6
     capital requirements 380–2, 387
     compensation funds 384
     costs of inadequate 375–6
     costs of over-regulation 376
     custody/trustees 383
     differing national impact 377
     distorting effect of harmonization 384
     diverse national forms of 378–80
     effectiveness of different forms of 386
     goals of 375–6, 385
     impact on competition 387
     inappropriateness of harmonization 387
     information disclosure 382–3
     insurance 383–4
   and structure of 376–8
     Anglo-American industry 376
     cross-country variations 376–7
     diversity of 376–7